D0947986

CORRECTIONS: A CRITICAL APPROACH
3RD EDITION

Corrections: A Critical Approach (3rd edition) confronts mass imprisonment in the United States, a nation boasting the highest incarceration rates in the world. This statistic is all the more troubling considering that its correctional population is overrepresented by the poor, African Americans, and Latinos.

Not only throwing crucial light on matters involving race and social class, this book also identifies and examines the key social forces shaping penal practice in the US – politics, economics, morality, and technology. By attending closely to historical and theoretical development, the narrative takes into account both instrumental (goal-oriented) as well as expressive (cultural) explanations to sharpen our understanding of punishment and the growing reliance on incarceration.

Covering five main areas of inquiry – penal context, penal populations, penal violence, penal process, and penal state – this book is essential reading for both undergraduate and graduate students interested in undertaking a critical analysis of penology.

Michael Welch is Professor in the Criminal Justice Program at Rutgers University (USA). His research interests include punishment, human rights, and social control, and his articles have appeared in journals such as *Punishment and Society, Social Justice,* and *Critical Criminology*. He has also authored numerous books, including *Crimes of Power and States of Impunity: The U.S. Response to Terror* (Rutgers University Press, 2009), *Ironies of Imprisonment* (Sage, 2005), and *Punishment in America* (Sage, 1999).

CORRECTIONS

A Critical Approach
3rd edition

Michael Welch

Routledge
Taylor & Francis Group

LONDON AND NEW YORK

First published 2011
by Routledge
2 Park Square, Milton Park, Abingdon, Oxon, OX14 4RN

Simultaneously published in the USA and Canada
by Routledge
711 Third Avenue, 8th Floor, New York, NY 10017

Routledge is an imprint of the Taylor & Francis Group, an informa business

Typeset in Adobe Garamond by GCS, Leighton Buzzard

British Library Cataloguing in Publication Data
A catalogue record for this book is a available from the British Library

Library of Congress Cataloging in Publication Data
Welch, Michael, Ph.D.

Corrections: a critical approach/by Michael Welch. – 3rd ed.

p. cm.

Includes bibliographical references and index.

1. Corrections–United States. 2. Crime–United States. 3. Prisons–United
States. 4. Prisoners–United States. I. Title.

HV9471.W459 2011

365'.973–dc22

2010028611

ISBN: 978-0-415-78208-1 (hbk)
ISBN: 978-0-415-78209-8 (pbk)
ISBN: 978-0-203-83335-3 (ebk)

To my parents

Diane J. Welch

and

Edmund F. Welch

with gratitude

CONTENTS

PART II PENAL POPULATIONS

PART IV: PENAL PROCESS

11 Jails and Detention   365

12 Prisoners' Rights   399

PART V PENAL STATE

14 Working in Prison 479

15 The Corrections Industry 505

LIST OF FIGURES

LIST OF TABLES

TABLE OF CASES

LIST OF ABBREVIATIONS

ACA	American Correctional Association
ACLU	American Civil Liberties Union
ADDD	Association pour la Défense des Droits des Détenus
AEDPA	Antiterrorism and Effective Death Penalty Act 1996
AFDC	Aid to Families with Dependent Children
AIDS	Acquired Immunodeficiency Syndrome
AIM	American Indian Movement
BIA	Bureau of Indian Affairs
BJS	Bureau of Justice Statistics
BOP	Bureau of Prisons
BT	building tender
CAP	Comité d'Action des Prisonniers
CASA	Court Appointed Special Advocates/ Center on Addiction and Substance Abuse
CCA	Corrections Corporation of America
CCC	Civilian Conservation Corps
CCPOA	California Correctional Peace Officers Association
CDC	Centers for Disease Control
CO	correctional officer
COINTELPRO	Counter Intelligence Program
CONS	Church of the New Song
DHS	Department of Homeland Security
DIAC	Department of Immigration and Citizenship (Australia)
DOC	Department of Corrections
DOE	Department of Energy
DUI	driving under the influence
DWB	'driving while black or brown'
DWI	driving while intoxicated
DYS	Department of Youth Services
EM	electronic monitoring
ERF	Extreme Reaction Force
FAMM	Families Against Mandatory Minimums
FBI	Federal Bureau of Investigation

FCI	federal correctional institution
FDA	Food and Drug Administration
GAO	General Accounting Office
GED	General Equivalency Diploma
GGI	Guided Group Interaction
GIP	Groupe d'Information sur les Prisons
GP	Gauche Proletarienne
HIV	Human Immunodeficiency Virus
ICE	Immigration and Customs Enforcement
IDC	Immigration Detention Center
INS	Immigration and Naturalization Service
IRS	Internal Revenue Service
ISP	intensive supervision program
IV	intravenous
JHL	jailhouse lawyer
JJDPA	Juvenile Justice and Delinquency Prevention Act 2002
LEAA	Law Enforcement Assistance Administration
LIFG	Libyan Islamic Fighting Group
MCA	Military Commissions Act 2006
MCC	Metropolitan Correctional Center
MS	Mara Salvartucha (Guatemalan gang)
NAACP	National Association for the Advancement of Colored People
NCJFCJ	National Council of Juvenile and Family Court Judges
NGO	non-governmental organization
NIJ	National Institute of Justice
OJJDP	Office of Juvenile Justice and Delinquency Prevention
PC	protective custody
PINS	person in need of supervision
PLRA	Prison Litigation Reform Act 1996
PMS	premenstrual syndrome
PREA	Prison Rape Elimination Act 2003
PRL	Patronado de Recluidas y Liberadas (Argentina)
PSI	pre-sentence investigation
PUC	person under control
REIT	Real Estate Investment Trust
RICO	Racketeer Influenced Corrupt Organization Act 1970
ROR	released on own recognizance
RUS	released under supervision
S&L	Savings and Loan
SORT	Special Operations Support Team
SRS	Sex Reassignment Surgery
STG	security threat group
TB	tuberculosis
TDC	Texas Department of Corrections
UNODC	United Nations Office on Drugs and Crime
VIS	victim impact statement

VORP	victim-offender reconciliation program
WAR	White Aryan Resistance
WIC	women, infants, and children
WRA	War Relocation Authority
ZOG	Zionist Occupation Government

ACKNOWLEDGEMENTS

Over the years, my critical approach to penology has benefitted from having the opportunity to conduct research and lecture at several universities around the world. For their collegiality and intellectual inspiration, I wish to acknowledge the following: Stan Cohen, Conor Gearty, and Tim Newburn at the London School of Economics; Dario Melossi at the Facoltà di Giurisprudenza, Università Degli Studi di Bologna (Italy); Maximo Sozzo at the Facultad de Ciencias Jurídicas y Sociales, Universidad Nacional del Litoral (Santa Fe, Argentina); Catherine Josset at the Institut Memoires de l'Edition Contemporaine (IMEC), Centre Michel Foucault, Abbaye d'Ardenne (Caen, France); Claire Guttinger at Service des Foucault Archives, Collège de France (Paris); and Pat O'Malley and Murray Lee at the Institute of Criminology, Faculty of Law, University of Sydney (Australia).

Back in the USA, I would like to recognize my colleagues at Rutgers University, namely: Allan Horwitz, Lennox Hinds, Anne Piehl, Paul Hirschfield, Lisa Miller, Pat Carr, Lee Jussim, Laurie Krivo, Doug Husak, Bob Szejner, Mark Desire, and (the late) Al Roberts. Also in the Criminal Justice Program, I very much appreciate years of tireless support from Betty McCoy-Carter and Sarah Laboy-Almodovar. Kind assistance from staff at the University's libraries should not go unnoticed. My Rutgers colleagues at the New Brunswick campus and I also appreciate the return of Todd Clear, who has taken over as Dean of the School of Criminal Justice at Rutgers, Newark.

For providing valuable feedback on the original and revised editions, I wish to thank Jeanne Flavin, Barbara Owen, Mary K. Stohr, Peter M. Carlson, Bruce Bikle, Rudolph Alexander, Gerald A. Ciuba, Ben Crouch, Edith Flynn, Joseph E Jacoby, David B. Kalinich, Richard Lawrence, Karen Nordone-Lemons, Thomas R. Phelps, Walter Roger, and Donald B. Walker, as well as the many students who also suggested improvements for the book.

The third edition would not have been possible without the amazing work of my research assistant Raquel Catrocho. Undoubtedly, Raquel made the book better organized and all the more presentable.

At Willan Publishing, I appreciate the artful direction from Brian Willan and Jules Willan, as well as Peter Williams, who provided expert copyediting.

Y por último, abrazos a mi 'otra mitad', Melissa Macuare – Chévere!

Michael Welch, Criminal Justice Program
Rutgers University
New Brunswick, New Jersey, USA, www.professormichaelwelch.com

PHOTO ACKNOWLEDGEMENTS

The publishers would like to thank the following for permission to reprint their material:

Figure 1.1
San Quentin. A view of California's San Quentin Prison guard lookout tower.
© iStockphoto.com
Stock photo | File #: 7531919

Figure 1.2
Pink boxer shorts.
Maricopa County Detention Officer Rene Ansley holds up one of the pink boxer style underwear male inmates wear inside Sheriff Joe Arpaio's tent city jail in Phoenix, Arizona May 3, 2010. The inmates also have matching pink socks. This area of the tent city houses misdemeanor offenders.
AFP Photo/Paul J. Richards
Photo credit © Paul J. Richards/AFP/Getty Images
Editorial image #: 98823354.

Figure 1.3
Prisoner.
© iStockphoto.com
Stock photo | File #: 1511480

Figure 2.1
Castle window. Indoor shot of a trellised historic window at Wertheim Castle in Southern Germany where light is falling.
© iStockphoto.com
Stock photo | File #: 10611365

Figure 2.2
Galley Slavery (see title: Ships rations)
10 January 1863: The French artillerymen distribute biscuits amongst the galley-slaves in Veracruz, during the war between France and Mexico. In the picture above, cherubs decorate a montage of Parisian landmarks. *Le Monde Illustré – Expedition Du Mexique* – pub. 1963. An engraving by C. Maurand from a sketch by M. Brunet.
Photo by Hulton Archive/Getty Images

Figure 2.3
Postcard of an American panopticon: 'Interior view of cell house, new Illinois State Penitentiary at Stateville, near Joliet, Ill.'
Source: Scanned from the Postcard Collection of Alex Wellerstein and reprinted with permission. Copyright expired.
http://www.hks.harvard.edu/sdn/sdnimages/

Figure 3.1
An old-fashioned prison.
© iStockphoto.com
Stock photo | File #: 12624143

Figure 3.2
Ankle shackles. Harsh stark reality of slavery implied by simple monotone composition of ankle shackles worn by slaves in the early 1800s.
© iStockphoto.com
Stock photo | File #: 10840163

Figure 3.3
Aerial view of Alcatraz Prison.
Creative image #: 78052688
© Comstock Images/Getty

Figure 4.1
Foucault.
Date created: 1 January 1960
Editorial image #: 52015405
Paris, France – January 1: French philosopher Michel Foucault shown in an undated and unlocated file photo. (*Archives*) Photo non datée du philosophe français, Michel Foucault.
Photo credit © STF/AFP/Getty Images

Figure 4.2
Head in a jar
Caption: A couple viewing the head of Italian criminologist Cesare Lombroso (1835–1909) preserved in a jar of formalin, at an exhibition in Bologna, 1978.
Photo by Romano Cagnoni/Hulton Archive/Getty Images
Date created: 1 January 1978
Editorial image #: 74844837

Figure 4.3
Abbie Hoffman Flag Show
Caption: 9 November 1970: American activist Abbie Hoffman (1936–1989), cofounder of the Yippie movement, speaks to a crowd while wearing a shirt made from a US flag during an American flag-themed art show at the Hudson Memorial Church, New York City. Hoffman was charged with desecration of the flag for wearing the shirt.
Photo by Tyrone Dukes/New York Times Co./Getty Images
Date created: 9 November 1970
Editorial image #: 3241269

Figure 5.1
Inmate. Muscular man in trouble shot in old prison setting.
© iStockphoto.com
Stock photo | File #: 13219114

Figure 5.2
Inmates perform pop icon Michael Jackson.
Caption: Inmates perform pop icon Michael Jackson's dance routine during a press preview at Cebu City provincial jail on March 4, 2010. Dressed in tangerine jump suits, the roughly 1,500 convicted murderers, rapists and other inmates perform a series of Michael Jackson-inspired dances that have helped boost their morale while also making them Internet sensations.
AFP Photo/Ted Aljibe
Photo credit Ted Aljibe/AFP/Getty Images
Date created: 4 March 2010
Editorial image #: 97742800

Figure 5.3
French prison.
Caption: View of the courtyard and buildings in the prison of Ensisheim, eastern France, on December 12, 2009 during a visit of a French official.
AFP Photo Johanna Leguerre
Photo credit Johanna Leguerre/AFP/Getty Images
Date created: 12 December 2009
Editorial image #: 94984145

Figure 6.1
Chained leg. A lock and chain around a female with bare feet.
Chained Leg – B&W
Stock photo | File #: 1357242

Figure 6.2
Christmas.
Title: Feminine prison celebrates Christmas.
Caption: Mexico City, Mexico – December 17, 2009: Paola Durante poses for a photograph during a Christmas celebration with prisoners at the Feminine Prison of Santa Marta Acatitla.
Photo by Juan Villa/Jam Media/LatinContent/Getty Images
Date created: 17 December 2009
Editorial image #: 94733241

Figure 6.3
Bolivia.
Title: Inmates in Parmasola's prison.
Caption: Inmates in Parmasola's prison, in Santa Cruz, Bolivia on November 27, 2009. In Parmasola there are some 1,500 prisoners, men and women, who coexist together in the jail's district. Children can remain with their parents until they are six years old.
AFP Photo/Desirée Martin
Photo credit should read Desirée Martin/AFP/Getty Images
Date created: 27 November 2009
Editorial image #: 93466431

Figure 7.1
Troubled teen. Troubled teen boy in close-up behind fence.
© iStockphoto.com
Stock photo | File #: 11317583

Figure 7.2
Moscow.
Title: Daily life inside a Moscow juvenile criminal institute
Caption: Young criminals work at Iksha labor colony for juvenile offenders in Moscow, Russian Federation, February 2, 2007. Russian deputy prosecutor general Sergey Fridinsky noted the previous year that criminality among juvenile offenders had grown by 10% over the last three years. Furthermore, according to reports, major offences among juvenile delinquents had also grown.
Photo by Oleg Nikishin/Epsilon/Getty Images
Date created: 2 February 2007
Editorial image #: 73349829

Figure 7.3
Rwanda.
Title: Youth prisoners accused of the genocide in Rwanda work in field in youth prison in Gitagata, Rwanda.
Caption: Youth prisoners accused of the genocide in Rwanda in 1994 work in a field in Gitagata, Rwanda on April 20, 1995. About one million people were killed in about one hundred days, making it one of the worst genocides in modern history.
Photo © Per-Anders Pettersson/Contributor/Getty
Date created: 4 November 2005
Editorial image #: 200253471-001

Figure 8.1
Prison hands. An African American male with hands hanging out prison bars.
© iStockphoto.com
Stock photo | File #: 11434582

Figure 8.2
Texas prison.
Title: Prisoners walk to work in Texas prison.
Caption: An unidentified Texas department of corrections officer watches over prisoners working outside the prison at Ellis Unit in Huntsville, Texas USA on April 17, 1997. Texas has about 450 prisoners on death row. The state leads all records in executing people around the US. The prisoners are executed by lethal injection.
Photo © Per-Anders Pettersson /Contributor/Getty
Date created: 4 November 2005
Editorial image #: 200253345-001

Figure 8.3
Leonard Peltier.
Title: Leonard Peltier.
Caption: Former AIM activist Leonard Peltier, a Chippewa-Lakota Indian serving a life sentence for the murder of two FBI agents he maintains he didn't commit, writing letter as he sits on his bunk next to sink and toilet in his cell at Leavenworth Penitentiary, KS.
Photo by Taro Yamasaki/Time Life Pictures/Getty Images

Date created: 1 April 1992
Editorial image #: 50611184

Figure 9.1

Armed guards.
Title: Armed prison officials.
Caption: Armed prison officials guard the maximum security prison, Fraijanes II 36 km west of Guatemala City, where inmates rioted April 23, 2010. Two guards of the prison system were held hostage by prisoners demanding better care. In the detention center are held Mexican cartel members of 'Los Zetas' gang and the Mara 18. AFP photo Johan Ordonez
Photo credit Johan Ordonez/AFP/Getty Images
Date created: 23 April 2010
Editorial image #: 98641805

Figure 9.2

Chino.
Title: Governor Schwarzenegger tours prison where riot took place.
Caption: The aftermath of a prison riot inside the California Institution for Men prison in Chino, California August 19, 2009. After touring the prison where a riot took place on August 8, California Governor Arnold Schwarzenegger said that the prison system is collapsing and needs to be reformed.
Photo by Michal Czerwonka/Getty Images
Date created: 18 August 2009
Editorial image #: 89881919

Figure 9.3

Guatamala.
Title: The National Civil Police and the prison guards of Pavoncito
Caption: Fraijanes, Guatemala: The National Civil Police and the prison guards of Pavoncito regain control of the maximum security prison, in the department of Fraijanes, 40 km east of Guatemala City, on March 27, 2007. At least 5 inmates were injured during the riot between members of the gang Mara Salvartucha (MS), who were transferred from the El Infierno prison after riots there, and the 'Paisas' – common prisoners who are not involved in gangs. The members of MS were first transferred from the El Boqueron prison to El Infierno, a day after the murder of four policemen apparently involved in the assassination of three Salvadoran lawmakers and their driver on February 19.
AFP Photo/Orlando Sierra
Photo credit Orlando Sierra/AFP/Getty Images
Date created: 27 March 2007
Editorial image #: 73719874

Figure 10.1

Guillotine.
Title: To go with AFP story 'Le "taureau de feu"'.
Caption: A picture from the Criminal Museum in Rome dated 12 January 2006 shows a guillotine used by the Papal State. After 1798 the Roman Republic was proclaimed to be under Napoleonic rule and Pius VI was deported to France. The French introduced the guillotine in the former Papal State. The first condemned prisoner to be put to death with the new instrument was Tommaso Tintori, beheaded on 28 February 1810. The executioner used the guillotine at least six times from 1810 to 1813.
AFP Photo/Alberto Pizzoli
Photo credit Alberto Pizzoli/AFP/Getty Images
Date created: 12 January 2006
Editorial image #: 56592113

Figure 10.2
Gary Gilmore.
Title: Gilmore.
Caption: 17 January 1977: Gary Gilmore executed in Utah State Prison for the murder of two students, the first person to be executed in the United States for over ten years.
Photo by Keystone/Getty Images
Date created: 17 January 1977
Editorial image #: 3295882

Figure 10.3
Electric chair.
Title: 'Old Sparky,' the decommissioned electric chair.
Caption: 'Old Sparky,' the decommissioned electric chair in which 361 prisoners were executed between 1924 and 1964, pictured 5 November 2007 at the Texas Prison Museum in Huntsville, Texas. From the chaplain who shares the condemned prisoner's final hours to the guard who attaches the needles and the prison director who orders the fatal injection: the relentless march of Texas executions is taking a heavy toll.
Photo credit Fanny Carrier/AFP/Getty Images
Date created: 5 November 2007
Editorial image #: 97202037

Figure 11.1
Rikers Island.
Title: Aerial view of Rikers Island.
Caption: United States – February 13: Aerial view of Rikers Island.
Photo by Todd Maisel/NY Daily News Archive via Getty Images
Date created: 13 February 2002
Editorial image #: 97211808

Figure 11.2
Immigration detention.
Title: Detainees wait to be processed inside Homeland Security's Willacy Detention Center.
Caption: Detainees wait to be processed inside Homeland Security's Willacy Detention Center, a facility with 10 giant tents that can house up to 2,000 detained illegal immigrants, 10 May 2007, in Raymondville, Texas. The US$65 million facility was constructed as part of the Secure Border Initative the previous July and is now where many of the former 'catch and release' illegals are detained for processing.
AFP Photo/Paul J. Richards
Photo credit Paul J. Richards/AFP/Getty Images
Date created: 10 May 2007
Editorial image #: 74126357

Figure 11.3
Maricopa County jail.
Title: An inmate inside Maricopa County Sheriff Joe Arpaio's tent city jail.
Caption: An inmate inside Maricopa County Sheriff Joe Arpaio's tent city jail walks away from the bulletin board area (L) of the communal air conditioned area inside the complex, May 3, 2010, in Phoenix, Arizona. This area of the tent city houses misdemeanor offenders.
AFP Photo/Paul J. Richards
Photo credit Paul J. Richards/AFP/Getty Images)
Date created: 3 May 2010
Editorial image #: 98823334

Figure 12.1
Three strikes.
Title: Joe Davis [Misc.]; Kimber Reynolds [Misc.]; Mike Reynolds
Caption: Three Strikes law crusader Mike Reynolds, the angry dad of murder victim Kimber Reynolds, going through bundles of mail and petitions on his desk while working to pass law to jail repeat offenders to prevent them from committing more crimes (Three Strikes and You're Out), at home.
Photo by John Storey/Time Life Pictures/Getty Images
Date created: 13 January 1994
Editorial image #: 50437215

Figure 12.2
Chain gang.
Title: Female chain gang.
Caption: Female jail inmates are chained together as they bury cadavers at Maricopa County's paupers' graveyard in Phoenix, Arizona, May 17, 2000. Maricopa County Sheriff Joe Arpaio began the first female chain gang. With a reputation of being the nation's toughest law enforcement officer, Sheriff Arpaio said he does not believe in discrimination. As a result, the women in Arpaio's jail are treated exactly like the men.
Photo by Joe Raedle/Liaison
Date created: 17 May 2000
Editorial image #: 2535520

Figure 12.3
Angela Davis.
Title: Black Panther.
Caption: October 1970: Assistant professor of philosophy at the University of California Angela Davis is arrested in New York for her membership of the Black Panther Party.
Photo by Keystone/Getty Images
Date created: 01 Oct 1970
Editorial image #: 2628240

Figure 13.1
Phone calls upon release.
Title: Newly released prisoners make phone calls.
Caption: Newly released prisoners make phone calls as they walk out of Tripoli's Abu Slim prison on October 15, 2009. Libya freed 45 members of the Al-Qaeda-linked Libyan Islamic Fighting Group (LIFG), which first came to wider knowledge in 1995 as it launched an armed campaign against Kadhafi's regime.
AFP Photo/Mahmud Turkia
Photo credit Mahmud Turkia/AFP/Getty Images
Date created: 15 October 2009
Editorial image #: 91910240

Figure 13.2
Parole Board.
Title: Parole Board.
Caption: The first meeting of the Parole Board set up under the Criminal Justice Act 1967 to advise the Home Secretary on the release of prisoners on license, 7 November 1967. Amongst those meeting at the Home Office are (left to right) chairman Lord Hunt, the Honourable Sir Arthur James (1916–1976, Judge of the High Court of Justice, Queen's Bench Division), criminology lecturer Roy King and the Honourable Mr Justice Roskill (1911–1996). In the background is Bill Pearce, then Chief Probation Officer for Inner London.

Photo by Wesley/Keystone/Getty Images
Date created: 7 November 1967
Editorial image #: 85837008

Figure 13.3
Paris Hilton.
Title: Paris Hilton appears in court – May 4, 2007.
Caption: Paris Hilton leaves court after being sentenced to 45 days in jail for violating probation.
Photo by Jean Baptiste Lacroix/WireImage
Date created: 4 May 2007
Editorial image #: 82986578
http://www.gettyimages.com.au/detail/82986578/WireImage

Figure 14.1
Old prison jail cells. Jail cells with the doors closed at a histororic Idaho prison.
© iStockphoto.com
Stock photo | File #: 11528523

Figure 14.2
Guard.
Title: Overcrowded prison.
Caption: Tracy, CA – September 4: Sgt D. Turner watches inmates as they walk down the long hallway on their way out to the recreation yard. Do to the jail overcrowding the inmates get only 4 hours of recreation a week at the Deuel Vocational Institution near Tracy, California.
Photo by Tony Avelar/The Christian Science Monitor/Getty Images
Date created: 4 September 2009
Editorial image #: 90443560

Figure 14.3
Inmate working.
Title: A prisoner works in a workshop.
Caption: A prisoner works in a workshop in the San Sebastian Prison in San Jose, on August 27, 2009. The prison, which houses 653 prisoners, including 150 foreigners, has installed workshops for computing, carpentry, crafts, literacy, to complement high school or college careers, for many Costa Rican prisoners who are preparing for a life of freedom and above all, to help endure captivity.
AFP Photo/Yuri Cortez
Photo credit Yuri Cortez/AFP/Getty Images
Date created: 27 August 2009
Editorial image #: 90172615

Figure 15.1
Corrections Corp.
Title: Corrections Corp. shows crime pays as states turn jails private.
Caption: Signage outside the La Palma Correctional Center in Eloy, Arizona, on May 11, 2010. La Palma, which houses about 2,900 convicts from California, is one of 65 facilities operated by Corrections Corp. of America, the largest private-prison operator in the US.
Photographer: Joshua Lott/Bloomberg via Getty Images
Date created: 11 May 2010
Editorial image #: 99033763

Figure 15.2
Private prison ship.
Title: Prison ships may ease overcrowding in jails.
Caption: A general view of HMP Weare on October 24 2006 in Portland, near Weymouth, England. The floating prison, now closed, was the only one in the UK when it opened in 1997. The then Home Secretary John Reid called on private companies to open and run similar type vessels to alleviate the overcrowding crisis in UK prisons.
Photo by Matt Cardy/Getty Images
Date created: 24 October 2006
Editorial image #: 72258804

Figure 15.3
Convict labor.
Title: Inmates work in a prison of Chongqing.
Caption: Inmates work in a sewing workshop at a prison on March 7, 2008 in Chongqing Municipality, China. There are nearly 5,000 inmates in the prison. China is working to improve education in prisons and help prisoners return to society as law-abiding citizens, with measures to better protect the legitimate rights and interests of inmates.
Photo by China Photos/Stringer/Getty Images
Date created: 7 March 2008
Editorial image #: 80154634

Figure 16.1
Mexico.
Title: Mexican drug war fuels violence in Juarez.
Caption: Medical personnel inspect a bullet-riddled body on March 23, 2010 in Juarez, Mexico. Secretary of State Hillary Rodham Clinton, Defense Secretary Robert Gates, and Homeland Security Secretary Janet Napolitano all visited Mexico that day for discussions centered on Mexico's endemic drug-related violence. The border city of Juarez, Mexico has been racked by violent drug-related crime recently and has quickly become one of the most dangerous cities in the world in which to live. As drug cartels have been fighting over ever-lucrative drug corridors along the United States border, the murder rate in Juarez has risen to 173 slayings for every 100,000 residents. President Felipe Calderon's strategy of sending 7,000 troops to Juarez has not mitigated the situation. Out of a population of 1.3 million, 2,600 people died in drug-related violence last year and 500 so far this year, including two Americans recently who worked for the US Consulate and were killed as they returned from a child's party.
Photo by Spencer Platt/Getty Images
Date created: 23 March 2010
Editorial image #: 97989154

Figure 16.2
Brazil.
Title: Rio's police occupy Morro do Borel slum.
Caption: A man is arrested as Rio's police occupy Morro do Borel slum to install a peacemaker police unit to help in the control of drug traffic on April 28, 2010 in Rio de Janeiro, Brazil.
Photo by Guilherme Pinto/Globo via Getty Images
Date created: 28 April 2010
Editorial image #: 98727099

Figure 16.3
Mentally ill inmate.
Title: A mentally ill inmate remains at Tacumbu.

Caption: A mentally ill inmate remains at Tacumbu jail in Asuncion, April 16, 2010. Tacumbu is one of the most overpopulated prisons of the world, which was built originally for 800 inmates and now houses 3,147, of which only 701 have been sentenced.
AFP Photo/Norberto Duarte
Photo credit Norberto Duarte/AFP/Getty Images
Date created: 16 April 2010
Editorial image #: 98516472

Figure 17.1
Guantanamo Bay.
Title: Guantanamo prison remains open over a year after Obama vowed to close it.
Caption: Detainees jog inside a recreation yard at Camp 6 in the Guantanamo Bay detention center in Guantanamo Bay, Cuba on March 30, 2010. US President Barack Obama pledged to close the prison by early 2010 but has struggled to transfer, try or release the remaining detainees from the facility, located on the US Naval Base.
Photo by John Moore/Getty Images
Date created: 30 March 2010
Editorial image #: 98167982

Figure 17.2
Abu Ghraib.
Caption: Visitor passes by a 285.5 kg patinated bronze sculpture by British artist Marc Quinn entitled 'Mirage' and inspired by a picture taken at Abu Ghraib prison during the preview day of Art Basel, the world's premier modern and contemporary art fair which took place from June 10 to 14, 2009, in Basel. The international art show featured 290 leading art galleries from all continents. 20th and 21st-century art works by over 2,500 artists are on display. More than 60,000 art collectors, art dealers, artists, curators and art lovers were expected to attend the annual meeting place of the art community.
AFP Photo/ Fabrice Coffrini
Photo credit Fabrice Coffrini/AFP/Getty Images
Date created: 9 June 2009
Editorial image #: 88369970

Figure 17.3
Waterboarding.
Title: Anti-war activists demonstrate waterboarding.
Caption: Anti-war activists demonstrate waterboarding torture during a demo on October 5, 2009 in front of the White House in Washington, DC. The demonstrators are calling for an end to the war in Iraq.
AFP Photo/Mandel Ngan
Photo credit Mandel Ngan/AFP/Getty Images
Date created: 5 October 2009
Editorial image #: 91460733

Every effort has been made to trace and contact copyright holders. The publishers would be pleased to hear from any copyright holders not acknowledged here so that this section may be amended at the earliest opportunity.

ABOUT THE AUTHOR

Michael Welch is a Professor in the Criminal Justice Program at Rutgers University, New Brunswick, New Jersey (USA). His research interests include punishment, human rights, and social control, and his articles have appeared in such journals as *Theoretical Criminology*, *Punishment and Society*, *Justice Quarterly*, *Journal of Research in Crime and Delinquency*, *The Prison Journal*, *Social Justice*, and *Critical Criminology*. Welch is author of *Crimes of Power and States of Impunity: The U.S. Response to Terror* (2009, Rutgers University Press), *Scapegoats of September 11th: Hate Crimes and State Crimes in the War on Terror* (2006, Rutgers University Press), *Ironies of Imprisonment* (2005, Sage), *Detained: Immigration Laws and the Expanding I.N.S. Jail Complex* (2002, Temple University Press), *Flag Burning: Moral Panic and the Criminalization of Protest* (2000, de Gruyter), and *Punishment in America* (1999, Sage). He has lectured and delivered papers throughout the United States as well as in Canada, England, Scotland, the Netherlands, France, Germany, Italy, Spain, Poland, Finland, Thailand, Argentina, Venezuela and Australia. He has served as a Visiting Fellow at the Centre for the Study of Human Rights at the London School of Economics, as well as a Visiting Professor in the Facoltà di Giurisprudenza, Università Degli Studi di Bologna (Italy) and Facultad de Ciencias Jurídicas y Sociales of the Universidad Nacional del Litoral (Santa Fe, Argentina). More recently, he was a Visiting Professor in the Faculty Law at the University of Sydney (Australia). He invites you to visit his website at [www.professormichaelwelch.com].

PREFACE

In the United States, and around the globe, the term *corrections* conjures up sharp images of the back end of the criminal justice system, leaving some people to envision such imposing institutions as Attica and San Quentin as well as an expanding arsenal of supermax prisons. For those people, increased prison construction symbolizes not only retribution but also 'no-nonsense' measures aimed at protecting the public from the dangers of crime. For other observers *corrections* brings to mind not the institutions but rather the offenders themselves, particularly those in need of rehabilitation from such ills as drug addiction.

Over the course of American history, the punitive and treatment perspectives on corrections have enjoyed considerable popularity. Presently, the punitive aspect of prisons is the cornerstone of American crime-control policy, especially in view of the escalating wars on crime, drugs, and now terror. However, since crime remains a significant social problem despite massive investments in the criminal justice system, there is growing dissatisfaction with current policies and practices. Many scholars seriously question whether the emphasis on incarceration is capable of solving the nation's crime problem; indeed, some critics suggest that efforts to do so merely make matters worse.

Mounting frustration with failures of the penal apparatus calls for a close and critical look at punishment. The objective of *Corrections: A Critical Approach* (3rd edn) is to provide such an examination. In sum, it confronts mass imprisonment particularly in the United States, a nation boasting the highest incarceration rate in the world. America's race to incarcerate is all the more troubling considering that its correctional population is overrepresented by the poor, African Americans, and Latinos.

While throwing crucial light on matters involving race and social class, the book reaches beyond description as it strives to illuminate key social forces shaping penal practice, including politics, economics, morality, and technology. By carefully attending to historical and theoretical developments, the narrative takes into account both instrumental (goal-oriented) as well as expressive (cultural) explanations since together they advance a critical understanding of punishment and the growing reliance on corrections.

SPECIAL FEATURES

This book offers several features that are intended to enhance the pedagogical value of the chapters.

- *Chapter-opening features.* Each chapter begins with a chapter outline and learning objectives. Both the outline, which lists the main headings in the chapter, and the questions, which focus on the objectives of the chapter, provide a preview of the topics to be discussed.
- *Vignettes.* Vignettes, case examples, and box inserts provide in-depth looks at pressing issues in corrections. Many of these features discuss cutting-edge and controversial topics. Tables and figures, which appear in many chapters, help clarify important points.
- *End-of-chapter features.* Each chapter closes with a summary, review questions, and recommended readings. The summary provides a review of the topics discussed. The discussion questions encourage further critical examination of the issues covered in the chapter. The recommended readings, many of which are classic works in penology, can be used as sources of additional information on a particular topic or issue.

ADDED FEATURES FOR THE THIRD EDITION

This revised third edition offers readers several added features that promise to benefit the experience of reading the book. While a critical approach delves into the significance of race, ethnicity, gender, and social class, there is supplemental focus on the role of the media in shaping popular perceptions of crime and punishment. The chapters also engage readers by introducing three types of boxed inserts designed to stimulate critical thought and lively discussion, namely Comparative Corrections, Working in Corrections, and Cultural Penology.

- *Comparative Corrections.* So that one can appreciate the global practice of punishment, a series of boxes titled Comparative Corrections is included in each chapter. Many of these excerpts address growing concerns over human rights abuses that occur in the name of retribution, security, and public safety.
- *Working in Corrections.* In an effort to illustrate the practical implications of a critical approach, most chapters contain a *Working in Corrections* box that discusses job and career-related issues. By doing so, the discussion sheds light on the sociological – and anthropological – dimensions of working inside the penal apparatus.
- *Cultural Penology.* Allowing for greater reflection on penology, each chapter offers a box labeled Cultural Penology, encompassing an array of cutting-edge topics as they intersect with culture. Whereas the sociology of punishment tends to be overly focused on the instrumental facets of punishment with respect to goals and objectives, cultural penology prompts us to consider the enduring expressive elements of the penal imagination.

The revised edition offers up-to-date coverage of crucial challenges facing the field of corrections. Seventeen chapters fall into five areas of inquiry: *Penal Context* (e.g. history, theory), *Penal Populations* (e.g. women, juveniles, and minorities), *Penal Violence* (e.g. riots, capital punishment), *Penal Process* (e.g. detention, prisoner rights, alternatives), and *Penal State* (e.g. the corrections industry, wars on drugs and terror). The subject matter promises to stimulate careful analysis of punishment. Additionally, the text takes aim at the problem of innumeracy by inserting sections titled *Critical Analysis of Data* in which readers are invited to respond to basic questions about tables and figures containing quantitative information. *Corrections: A Critical Approach* (3rd edn) is ideal for undergraduate and graduate students interested in grasping a sophisticated analysis of penology.

PART 1   PENAL CONTEXT

CHAPTER 1

Introducing a Critical Approach

Today's problems are the result of yesterday's solutions (John F. Kennedy)

LEARNING OBJECTIVES

After studying this chapter, you should be able to answer the following questions:

1 What is the overall impact of greater reliance (and spending) on corrections?
2 What is meant by the term penal populism?
3 How does the new penology depart from a traditional approach to corrections?
4 What are the racial implications contained in the new punitiveness?
5 What is the significance of culture within a critical examination of punishment?

As the nation's worst serial killer on record, John Wayne Gacy was put to death by lethal injection after being convicted of the sex-related killings of 33 young men and boys. Prosecutors told the jury that the victims had been lured to Gacy's home for sex, killed, and buried beneath the house. Eight of them were never identified: their remains were placed under gravestones that said only, 'We Are Remembered.' Gacy received more mail – and methodically answered it – than any other inmate at the prison. Callers of his 900 phone line paid $23.88 to listen to the full 12 minutes of his recorded denial of the crimes. 'For his last meal, Gacy, who in the mid-60s managed three Kentucky Fried Chicken restaurants in Iowa, asked for fried chicken, fried shrimp, french fries, and fresh strawberries' (Kifner, 1994: A19).

CORRECTIONS: A CRITICAL APPROACH

As a mother of four children – all under the age of eight – Tonya Drake struggled daily to provide for her family. 'So when Drake, 30, was handed a $100 dollar bill by a man she barely knew and was told she could keep the change if she posted a package for him, she readily agreed ... Drake received $47.70 of it. But unknown to Drake, the package contained 232 grams of crack cocaine' (Smolowe, 1994: 55). Drake did not have a history of drug use, nor did she have a prior criminal record. Nevertheless, under federal mandatory minimum sentencing laws for drug violations, Drake was sentenced to a ten-year prison term. Even the judge, Richard Gadbois Jr, acknowledged that her sentence was absurd.

As a bored teenager in a conservative Colorado town, Christian Martensen quit a minimum-wage job, packed some tie-dyed clothes, and followed the Grateful Dead band around America. He led a carefree, vagabond life for a couple of years, but then his van broke down and he needed money to keep moving. When a fellow Deadhead, as the fans are known, offered him $400 to find someone who would sell LSD, he accepted. Later, he stared out the window of a narrow cell at the Federal Correctional Institution in Tucson, Arizona. The man he thought was a Deadhead was an undercover agent. Martensen was sentenced to ten years under the mandatory minimum prison term imposed by Congress in 1986. Due to toughened parole requirements, he would serve most of that time. Institutional rules do not allow Martensen to keep Grateful Dead tapes in prison (Johnson, 1993: A16).

INTRODUCTION

In a culture consumed by stories of graphic violence, Gacy emerged as a celebrity – albeit an infamous one. Still, his case is hardly representative of the more than one million offenders currently in prison; rather, most lawbreakers resemble Tonya Drake and Christian Martensen – non-violent offenders convicted of drug violations. As this book stresses throughout, incarceration on a mass scale has clear socioeconomic and racial patterns. Consider the prosecution of Drake, a low-income African-American sent to federal prison at the annual cost of $25,000 a year at taxpayers' expense. Her imprisonment left behind four young children, 320 miles away. Drake's attorney wondered: 'How are you going to teach her a lesson by sending her to prison for 10 years?' adding 'what danger is she to society?' (Smolowe, 1994: 55). While minorities are increasingly overrepresented in prison, whites – especially, low-income ones – also have met the punitive side of criminal justice. Much like Drake, Martensen, who had no previous record, was sentenced to spend a decade behind bars – a penalty that is more severe than those typically imposed on rapists. Baffled by the harsh sentence, his lawyer said: 'Martensen made a mistake and needed a wake-up call. He didn't need to have his life ruined' (Johnson, 1993: A16).

Critics characterize mandatory minimum sentences, such as those applied to Drake and Martensen, as tragic since they tend to devastate the lives of many. 'None of these people are choirboys, and all deserve to be punished. But for how long, and who should decide [the judges or legislators]?' asks Julie Stewart, the president of Families Against Mandatory Minimums. Even the former director of the Federal Bureau of Prisons, Norm Carlson, agrees: 'Prison space is scarce, and you've got to use it judiciously ... For nonviolent offenders there are often better alternatives than prison.'

Despite those voices of dissent, there are others who adamantly defend the prevailing trend of harsh sentences. 'You can't get convicted of a drug law unless you knew what you were doing,' says Paul McNulty, a spokesman for First Freedom Coalition, a Washington organization founded by former Attorney General William P. Barr who promotes strict drug laws. 'After everything this country has been through with drug trafficking, it's very hard for people to look at these supposedly sympathetic cases and say, "Gee, we feel sorry for you"' (Johnson, 1994: A16). Such support for tougher sentencing is not uncommon. Over the past few decades, a heightened punitiveness has become more mainstream, particularly among political leaders who pander to what the public perceives to be growing social disorder (Clear, 2010, 2009, 1994; Garland, 2001; Harcourt, 2001; Pratt *et al.*, 2005).

Taking a critical approach, this chapter – as well as the entire book – aims to decipher an expanding reliance on imprisonment. While the emergence of a new punitiveness has fueled the race to incarcerate, there are a host of other social, political, and economic forces shaping America's penal landscape. This introductory presentation, to be sure, merely sketches out a few of the preliminary concerns facing the study of corrections: penal populism, the new penology, the new punitiveness, and the perpetual failure of prisons. The chapter also sets a cultural tone, bringing into relief forms of expressive punishment as they reside in the popular imagination. So as to examine the enormous impact that mass incarceration has on society at large, we open with a critical look at the price of prisons.

THE PRICE OF PRISONS

The United States increasingly has become a society of prisons. Both federal and state correctional systems are remarkable due to their vast size, scope, and continued growth. Altogether America's prisons held more than 1,610,446 convicts in 2008, producing the world's highest incarceration rate (952 per 100,000 US residents). That figure has continued to climb since 2001 when the rate had reached 896. Moreover, imprisonment rates are even more pronounced for black males (3,161) and Hispanic males (1,200) compared to their white counterparts (487). Still, those numbers do not include those in jail or under other forms of correctional supervision such as probation and parole. Especially for blacks, the huge increase in the incarceration rate is the result of drug convictions (Sabol *et al.*, 2009; see Gottschalk, 2006; 'Comparative Corrections: Prison Populations Around the Globe' below).

> Between 1987 and 2007 the prison population nearly tripled, from 585,000 to almost 1.6 million. Much of that increase occurred in states – many with falling crime rates – that had adopted overly harsh punishment policies,

such as the 'three strikes and you're out' rule and drug laws requiring that nonviolent drug offenders be locked away.

The United States, which has less than 5 percent of the world's population, has about one-quarter of its prisoners. But the relentless rise in the nation's prison population has suddenly slowed as many states discover that it is simply too expensive to overincarcerate.

(*New York Times*, 2008: EV1)

Figure 1.1 San Quentin: a view of California's San Quentin Prison guard lookout tower.

Source: © iStockphoto.com

Without question, tough-on-crime measures that boost prison populations have proven costly. State spending from general funds on corrections increased from $10.6 billion in 1987 to more than $44 billion in 2007, a 127 percent increase in inflation-adjusted dollars. By comparison, adjusted spending on higher education increased only 21 percent during the same period (*New York Times*, 2008: EV1).

The California prison system is among the most closely watched, especially as it contends with mounting costs, overcrowding, and the highest recidivism rate in the country (70 percent). Although the drumbeat to incarcerate more felons has yet to fully subside, fiscal reality coupled with a court-ordered reduction in the prison population is giving pause to political leaders. Approximately 11 percent of the budget (or $8 billion) goes to the penal system, well ahead of expenditures like higher education. Each prisoner costs, on average, $47,000 per year. Initiatives to reduce overcrowding include proposals to remove from prisons convicts who pose little or no risk outside the prison walls and those who need regular supervision. That move could save $100 million. Faced with 167,000, prisoners California authorities have vowed to reduce that population by 6,500 – more than the entire state prison population in Nebraska, New

Mexico, Utah, or West Virginia. Initiatives for early release could be accelerated by having prisoners complete drug and education programs. Curiously, the fiscal crisis has prompted a renewed interest in rehabilitation since, among other things, it offers clear financial benefits (Archibold, 2010; see Auerhahn, 2003; Gilmore, 2007).

Of course, there are those who say that higher incarceration rates produce lower crime rates. Proponents of tough-on-crime initiatives believe that a booming prison population is a small price to pay for public safety; furthermore, they contend that locking up lawbreakers for minor offenses keeps them from committing more serious offenses. Certainly, the incarceration of more than a million felons has prevented some crimes from being committed; however, critics question the ethics and wisdom of mass imprisonment. Criminologist Michael Tonry points out that 'you could choose another two million Americans at random and lock them up, and that would reduce the number of crimes too' (Irwin *et al.*, 2000: 139). Criminologists find that jurisdictions with high prison growth do not always experience comparable drops in crime. Between 1992 and 1997, New York State's prison population grew from 61,736 to 70,026, while its violent crime rate fell by 38.6 percent and its murder rate by 54.5 percent. By comparison, California's prison population increased by 30 percent, or 270 inmates per week, compared to New York State's 30 inmates per week. California's crime control dividends were less impressive: violent crime dropped by 23 percent and its murder rate fell by 28 percent (Irwin *et al.*, 2000; see Barker, 2006). Nationwide crime rates have fallen steadily since 1991 and incarceration rates have risen every year, more than doubling since 1991 and increasing by more than five times since 1973 (Tonry, 2009, 2004; see Blumstein and Wallman, 2006; Lynch, 2007; Zimring, 2007).

Simply put, a greater reliance – and spending – on incarceration does not necessarily translate into lower crime. Michael Jacobson (2005), professor and former corrections and probation commissioner for New York City, concurs: 'You can't assume that because you spend more money that you are going to drive down crime. That is a simplistic assumption' (Butterfield, 2002a: A14, 2002b; Langan and Levin, 2002; Walker, 2001). Likewise, Jeremy Travis, former director of the National Institute of Justice, the research arm of the Justice Department, suggests that it would be fiscally wiser to allocate crime

COMPARATIVE CORRECTIONS

Prison Populations Around the Globe

As an added feature to this book, critical attention is turned to correctional practices around the globe. Here we take a brief introductory look at the enormity of penal systems and their incarceration rates. More than 9.8 million people are held in penal institutions throughout the world, mostly as pre-trial detainees (remand prisoners) or as sentenced prisoners. Nearly half of those in are in the United States (2.29 million), Russia (0.89 million) or

China (1.57 million sentenced prisoners). In China, another 850,000 are held in 'administrative detention;' if those detainees were included, the overall Chinese total stands over 2.4 million, pushing the world total over 10.65 million (Walmsley, 2008).

According to the *World Prison Population List*, the United States has the highest imprisonment rate in the world, 756 (per 100,000 of the national population) followed by Russia (629), Rwanda (604), St Kitts & Nevis (588), Cuba (c.531), US Virgin Islands (512), British Virgin Islands (488), Palau (478), Belarus (468), Belize (455), Bahamas (422), Georgia (415), American Samoa (410), Grenada (408), and Anguilla (401). Internationally, prison populations are growing. More than 70 percent of the countries included the 2008 *World Prison Population List* report increases from the previous year (in 64 percent of countries in Africa, 83 percent in the Americas, 76 percent in Asia, 68 percent in Europe and 60 percent in Oceania) (Walmsley, 2008). As we shall see in forthcoming chapters, it is important to go beyond a numerical count of correctional populations as we strive to understand the rationales for a greater reliance on incarceration (see Simon and De Wall, 2009; Tonry, 2001).

control dollars to investments in the local community where crime is taking place. Specifically, money might be more effectively spent on job training, education, and family services in poor neighborhoods with high crime rates rather than 'exporting those funds to prisons, courts and police officers outside the community,' according to Travis (Butterfield, 2002a: A14; see Cook, 2009; Useem and Piehl, 2008).

It is important to realize that eventually most prisoners return to the community, where they are forced to pick up life. After years behind bars ex-cons must face the debilitating effects of prison, and with few opportunities to survive in the free world, many resort to crime and a host of self-destructive behaviors including alcohol and drug abuse (see Hirschfield and Piquero, 2010). Thus mass incarceration as a tactic in crime control is riddled with hardships and contradictions. 'America has rushed headlong into the use of imprisonment as its primary crime-fighting tool. In doing so, small fries have been locked up at far higher rates than have big fish, at enormous social and economic costs, and with little benefit to show for it' (Irwin *et al.*, 2000: 141). Robert Gangi, executive director of the Correctional Association of New York, agrees: 'Building more prisons to address crime is like building more graveyards to address a fatal disease' (Smolowe, 1994: 55; see Blomberg and Cohen, 2003).

PENAL POPULISM

In his timely book *Penal Populism*, John Pratt delivers a robust interpretation of the prison boom occurring not only in the US but in other Western countries as well. Further pointing out that the increased reliance on imprisonment occurs independently of dropping crime rates, Pratt looks to other forces contributing to what is aptly described as penal populism, the trend toward 'democratizing' punishment. The belief that citizens can develop better solutions for crime control than state bureaucrats is fueled by a political culture that panders to popular discourse embodied in grass-roots social movements and media outlets, including tabloid journalism and talk-back radio (see de Koster *et al.*, 2008).

Indeed, the sphere of punishment continues to make contact with a wider political phenomenon known as populism, a form of politics aimed to appeal to people who feel that their views and interests have been left out of the debate over governance. Penal populism narrows those cries for greater security as 'mad as hell' citizens demand harsh penalties for criminals perceived as being habitual and particularly menacing. Correspondingly, public referendums such as California's three-strikes initiative serve as expressions of punishment, advocating a new rationality that 'prison works.' From that juncture, Pratt explores the underlying causes of penal populism, notably a declining trust in politicians and the political process. Those conditions give rise to cynical politicians willing and able to capitalize on the thirst for punishment continuously echoed in crime news. With an expanding mass communications that produce a 24-hour news cycle, there is no shortage of stories depicting a 'dangerous' world in which we live (Best, 1999; Glassner, 1999; Lee, 2007).

Compounding matters, criminal justice bureaucrats and liberal judges are characterized as naive and simply 'don't get it.' Moreover, standard crime statistics (which actually demonstrate drops in criminal offenses) get tossed out and replaced with emotional obsessions over high-profile (child) victims who become memorialized and sloganized. As penal populism appears to be a growing phenomenon in countries around the world, Pratt insists it is not inevitable. In Scandinavia, for example, punitive campaigns have yet to reach a

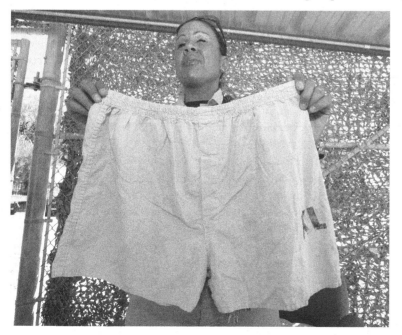

Figure 1.2 Pink boxer shorts. Maricopa County Detention Officer Rene Ansley holds up a pair of the pink boxer-style underwear male inmates wear inside Sheriff Joe Arpaio's tent city jail in Phoenix, Arizona, May 3, 2010. The inmates also have matching pink socks. This area of the tent city houses misdemeanor offenders.
Source: © Paul J. Richards/ AFP/Getty Images.

critical mass due to forms of resistance that place checks against penal populism and the race to incarcerate (Pratt, 2008).

Current research on penal populism greatly improves our understanding of how public frustration over insecurity is channeled into matters of criminal justice (see Carr, 2010; Wacquant, 2009; Whitman, 2003). In *Governing Through Crime*, Jonathan Simon points to recent political developments that have dismantled traditional approaches to crime control. Over the course of several decades, Simon observes, a pervasive commitment to fighting crime has significantly transformed American society. But rather than providing greater security, new forms of governance have stoked fear of crime which in turn generates a demand for tough-on-crime initiatives. The crackdown on crime embodied in mass incarceration tends to pull the US from its welfarist foundation in dealing with social inequality toward what Simon calls a 'penal state', inviting more – not less – government. Moreover, governance is directed by autocratic executives who have succeeded in sidelining both legislatures and judiciaries on important issues facing criminal justice. It is important to realize that governing through crime is not the same as actually governing – or even solving – such problems. The distinction rests in the manner by which the state expresses its power and its particular ambition to manage the population within its territory; along the way, government officials offer scant acknowledgement to the underlying sources of crime and related social problems.

THE NEW PENOLOGY

A critical approach to corrections considers the significance of a phenomenon identified as *the new penology*. In developing that concept, Malcolm Feeley and Jonathan Simon (1992) present an alternative view of the correctional apparatus, pointing to a new set of terms, concepts, and strategies that has begun to replace traditional penology. Whereas penology originally stemmed from criminal law and criminology and their emphasis on punishing and correcting individual offenders, the new penology adopts an actuarial approach, in which specialists assess the risks of specific criminal subpopulations (e.g. drug offenders) and recommend strategies to control those particular groups. The main objective of the new penology is to improve social-control measures for high-risk and dangerous groups, thereby establishing a greater reliance on containment and imprisonment (see Harcourt, 2007a, 2007b).

To most citizens, the proposed goals and strategies of the new penologists do not appear to be particularly troubling; indeed, to them such approaches to public safety seem to make good sense. However, scholars express unease since the new penology represents a strikingly different course for the future of corrections. An immediate area of concern is that the new penology does not set out to respond to either the individual offender or the adverse societal conditions that serve as the root of causes of crime. 'It does not speak of impaired persons in need of treatment or of morally irresponsible persons who need to be held accountable for their actions' (Feeley and Simon, 1992: 452). Rather, the new penology concentrates on maximizing social control – using prediction tables and population projections to streamline the criminal justice system.

Because the new penology takes an actuarial approach, it emphasizes efficiency, management, and control over individual justice and correction. Simply put, that new course for corrections recycles offenders from one form of custodial management to another without attempting to impose justice or reintegrate them into society (Feeley and Simon, 1992; see Gordon, 1991). Moreover, the new penology is riddled with contradictions: among them, its actuarial approach aims to improve public safety without necessarily reducing crime. According to Feeley and Simon:

> The new penology is neither about punishing nor about rehabilitating individuals. It is about identifying and managing unruly groups. It is concerned with the rationality not of individual behavior or even community organization, but of managerial process. Its goal is not to eliminate crime but to make it more tolerable through systemic coordination.
>
> (1992: 455)

With respect to drug control policy, the new penology is particularly problematic. Because treatment and rehabilitation are significantly downplayed, substance abuse takes on a different meaning. In the new penology, illegal drug use is not viewed as an individual problem that can be remedied; rather, it is interpreted as a factor used to classify the offender into a risk group. 'The widespread evidence of drug use in the offending population leads not to new theories of crime causation but to more efficient ways of identifying those at highest risk of offending' (Feeley and Simon, 1992: 462).

The new penology also offers troubling implications for the underclass, the segment of society, typically black and Hispanic, that is permanently marginalized economically and otherwise removed from America's mainstream. Since members of the underclass as a whole are unemployed, poorly educated, and possess few work skills, they are generally characterized as a threat to society. According to the new penology, that so-called dangerous, high-risk group must be controlled and managed by the criminal justice system. As previously noted, for decades there has emerged a sharp trend toward incarcerating impoverished and minority offenders. As that pattern continues, the actuarial basis of the new penology becomes more evident insofar as social control overrides individualized justice. 'This, in turn, can push corrections even further toward a self-understanding based on the imperative of herding a specific population that cannot be disaggregated and transformed but only maintained – a kind of waste management function' (Feeley and Simon, 1992; 469–70; see Welch, 1999b, 1994).

THE NEW PUNITIVENESS

For decades, mass imprisonment has been driven not only by initiatives aimed at getting tough on crime but even more narrowly by getting tough on prisoners. That form of renewed punitiveness has prompted scholars to examine public support for severe sanctions (Clear, 1994; Currie, 1998; Garland, 2001). 'But beyond the harsh policies behind this mass incarceration, there has ostensibly been a qualitative transformation in the way Americans talk, think about, and seek to manage criminal behavior' (Unnever and Cullen, 2010a: 100). That way of talking and thinking is central to one's worldview, or sensibility. While many Americans favor such liberal programs as rehabilitation, especially for youthful offenders, there is evidence of a wider shift toward conservative calls for retribution (Cullen *et al.*, 2000). Still, many observers wonder whether tougher sanctions are initiated primarily by politicians, the public, or a combination of both. According to Tonry, 'American politicians adopted unduly harsh policies and the public let them do it' (Tonry, 2004: 101; see Matthews, 2005; Pratt, 2006; Useem and Piehl, 2008).

Cutting short an otherwise lengthy treatise on the new punitiveness, it is important to consider some of the key elements that make up the growing reservoir of punitive sentiment, most notably hostility toward racial and ethnic minorities. Whereas African-Americans (and Latinos) have achieved greater civil liberties and assurances of due process over several decades, there remain forms of racism that promote punitive worldviews. As we shall see in upcoming chapters, criminologists have shed critical light onto the ways by which crime – and punishment – is racialized (Ogletree, 2002; Peterson *et al.*, 2006; Unnever, 2008).

Figure 1.3 Prisoner.
© iStockphoto.com

The racialization of crime is most prominent when scholars consider the 'picture in the head' held by members of the public when they think about crime – that is, the image that people have of the typical street-crime offender. Since the 1980s (perhaps starting even earlier with the 'riots' of the 1960s), scholars argue that a sizeable proportion of the American public perceives the crime problem through a racial lens that results in an association of crime with African-Americans, especially Black men.

(Unnever and Cullen, 2010a: 106)

From that analytical perspective, harsh sentences are interpreted as being a response to 'racially tinged perceptions of threat' and such sanctions represent 'a means to control or subordinate black people, or they may offer a way to vent anti-black sentiments' (Soss *et al.*, 2003: 401).

Keeping focus on the United States, Tonry (2009) considers several social forces shaping American punitiveness, namely: political paranoia, Protestant fundamentalism (and intolerance), and a politicization of criminal justice. While each of those phenomena contributes to a unique form of American punitiveness, Tonry elaborates on the significance of race relations, especially given that the overrepresentation of blacks in the prison population has increased substantially since the 1980s. 'Racial disparities in American prisons are as bad as they have ever been, and nearly all the laws and policies that created them remain in effect ... Once the politics got rolling, American constitutional arrangements presented few impediments, and insensitivity to the interests of black Americans made their formidable human costs both tolerable and ignorable' (Tonry, 2009: 389, 1995; see King and Maruna, 2009; Miller, 2008).

Evidence of the racialization of crime – and punishment – contained in the new punitiveness is not confined to the United States. Researchers have recently discovered similar patterns of racial and ethnic intolerance in other nations, including Canada, France, Great Britain, Denmark, Spain, Germany, and Austria (Unnever and Cullen, 2010b). Therefore, a racial punitiveness 'may be a cultural universal in societies with conflicted race relations' (Unnever and Cullen, 2010a: 107).

Taking a decidedly radical approach to the new punitiveness, Beckett and Sasson (2000) step further into realm of the political economy, especially as it intersects with culture. While also acknowledging that increased imprisonment is not simply the consequence of higher crime rates, Beckett and Sasson tap into the work of Antonio Gramsci, a neo-Marxian political theorist. By doing so, they set out to advance the concept of hegemony, the ideological foundation for social domination by the ruling class. While Eastern (Soviet) states relied on coercion to ensure compliance by its citizens, Western (capitalist) societies depend on different forms of social control. Refraining from force, Western nations turn to cultural mechanisms – hegemony – to secure cooperation and consent (Anderson, 1977). Hegemony is facilitated by highly developed mass media that allow the ruling class to exert its influence over civil society as well as government. As political actors move forward with controversial measures of social control, they launch a media campaign (owned and operated by elites) in an effort to persuade citizens that new policies are necessary to deal with a particular social problem (Gramsci, 2008; see Femia, 1981; Herman and Chomsky, 2002; Newburn and Jones, 2007).

Taking cues from Gramsci, Beckett and Sasson argue that the adoption of punitive anti-crime measures is best understood as a core component of a ruling-class hegemonic strategy. In sharpening their critical interpretation, they observe:

> Political representatives of the capitalist class responded to the upheavals of the 1960s and 1970s by attempting to secure hegemony around a vision of government that divests the state of responsibility of social welfare but emphasizes its obligation to provide 'security' against foreign and domestic threats. To mobilize support for this form of governance, these political actors argued that welfare worsened poverty and crime and they portrayed the poor as dangerous and undeserving. Policies that cut welfare payments and caseloads and that lead to the expansion of the penal system reflect the success of this hegemonic strategy.
>
> (2000: 62; see De Giorgi, 2006)

Departing from a Durkheimian perspective that explains the new punitiveness in terms of popular reaction to crime, Beckett and Sasson infuse Gramscian analysis to contend that mass incarceration is initiated by the leadership of the capitalist class and its political representatives. By use of such cultural mechanisms as the media, elites depict the poor and racial minorities as being particularly prone to crime and therefore requiring greater forms of social control. The wars on crime and drugs are aimed to win the consent of (white) citizens who perceive the state as acting appropriately rather than unjustly. Televised images of graphic violence coupled with highly coded racial rhetoric (e.g. drug kingpins, gang-bangers, welfare queens, crack whores) tap into the emotional reaction to crime. In the end, the hegemonic project moves to steer public anger toward punitive measures, creating the illusion that the implementation of harsher sanctions is somehow the product of democratic policy-making (see Lacey, 2008; Melossi, 1993; O'Malley, 1999; Sasson, 1995).

PERPETUATING FAILED PRISONS

Much like other critical thinkers, Jeffrey Reiman credits the criminal justice system with a particularly dubious achievement: that is, the degree to which it has reinforced the notion that the majority of crime is committed by members of the underclass who therefore deserve harsh punishment. In his book *The Rich Get Richer and the Poor Get Prison*, he writes about how popular criminal stereotypes significantly influence the way the penal apparatus operates, especially with respect to race and socioeconomics. Reiman observes that an enormous prison population overrepresented by impoverished minorities points to a society that has failed to come to grips with social, economic, and racial inequality.

That breakdown in democratic society is compounded by the failure of the correctional system that seems to make matters worse, evident in high rates of recidivism. According to Reiman, that failure is not a mere accident; rather, it is built into the logic of American crime control policy. To advance his argument, Reiman presents a curious task: 'Imagine that instead of designing a correctional system to reduce and prevent crime, we had to design one that would maintain and encourage the existence of a stable and visible "class" of criminals. What would it look like?' (2001: 3). The vision of a failed penal apparatus includes five basic features.

First, laws would exist that target victimless crimes such as gambling, prostitution, and drug use. Such statutes would make many individuals 'criminals' for what they believe is normal behavior, particularly for adults capable of making their own decisions. Furthermore, such laws would contribute to *secondary* crime – for example, theft committed by drug addicts in need of supporting their habits.

Second, police, prosecutors, and judges would be granted broad discretion in deciding who was to be arrested, convicted, and sent to prison. While behind bars, prisoners would discover others convicted of similar crimes but sentenced to serve less time. Therefore those in prison would experience their incarceration as arbitrary and unjust, perhaps leading to a bitter and antisocial view of the world.

Third, inmates would be subjected to a prison experience that is not only painful, but demeaning as well. Characteristic of the life behind bars would be harsh conditions of confinement alongside acts of violence perpetrated by other convicts as well as the custodial staff, furthering their perception that their punishment is excessive and unfair.

Fourth, prisoners would not be trained in any marketable skill, nor would they receive assistance from the prison officials in securing employment after release. Upon re-entering society and in search of a work, ex-cons would face discrimination by employers due to the stigma of having served a prison term. While enduring the harsh reality of chronic unemployment, some ex-cons would resort to illegal means for financial survival, such as peddling drugs.

Fifth, ex-cons would forever be treated differently from 'decent' citizens. They would lose the right to vote and other aspects of their freedom would he curtailed as well. Former prisoners would be subject to routine harassment by police and probation officers, and often considered to be 'usual suspects' of other crimes in the community. What Reiman and his students discovered is that when 'asked to design a system that would maintain and encourage the existence of a stable and visible "class of criminals," we "constructed" the American criminal justice system' (2001: 3)! In sum, Reiman maintains, the American criminal justice system fails to deal adequately with crime precisely because the system is *designed* to fail (see Boonin, 2008; Lippke, 2007; Reiman, 2009).

While Reiman's approach is both timely and novel, for years intellectuals have wondered about the persistence of failed prisons, most noticeably in the context of social theory. After delivering his sweeping critique of the prison and its intricate methods of discipline, Michel Foucault (1977, 1991a) was left with the realization that the entire penal project is a miserable failure; nonetheless, it continues to survive both as a model as well as a mechanism for dispensing punishment. The (failed) prison persists, according to Foucault, due in large part because it serves broader political purposes having to do with the distribution of power and domination over certain individuals and groups. Foucault is not alone with that perspective; throughout contemporary history, reformers and penologists have cited the major flaws of prison. The prison has not been abandoned because its advocates believe that there are strong merits in good penitentiary practice and such strategies for crime control ought to be reasserted (see Bentham, 1995; Rothman, 1971, 1980). But Foucault (1977: 271, 1988) argues further that the prison endures due to its immersion in a wider disciplinary apparatus inseparable from modern society. Similar to the more recent analysis of Reiman, Foucault argued that the failure of prison produces a form of social control aimed at the 'delinquent' (or 'dangerous') class. The persistent threat of a criminal class is met with public calls for coercive measures, a demand the state is willing to fulfill. In the end, there remains a continued investment in the maintenance of an ever-expanding criminal justice system (see Loader, 2009; Melossi, 2008).

As influential as Foucault has become in shaping penological debate, some scholars take exception to some of his conclusions. David Garland offers a full critique of Foucault's interpretation of the failure of the prison, noting: 'The prison may thus be retained for all sorts of reasons – punitiveness, economy, or plain lack of any functional alternatives – which have little do with any latent success as effective control or political strategy' (1990: 164–6). Garland reminds us that the use of prisons in modern society is more than purely instrumental, even if failure is considered to be the goal (see Bauman, 2000; Chantraine, 2008; Harcourt, 2001). As we shall explore in the next passage, imprisonment and other penal sanctions also express deeper cultural imperatives.

PRISONS, PUNISHMENT, AND CULTURE

Over the past decade, the study of crime has taken a cultural turn, producing a specialty known as cultural criminology (Ferrell *et al.*, 2004; Hayward and Young, 2004). Similarly, the field of penology also has drawn closer to culture as it contours punishment in general and the use of prisons in particular. In *The Culture of Punishment: Prison, Society, and Spectacle*, Michelle Brown sets out to capture what might be understood as punishment in everyday life, exploring the meaning of such activities as watching movies about prisons and touring correctional facilities. She observes: 'Many American citizens access punishment through cultural practices removed from formal institutions like prisons in a manner which, although largely unacknowledged, massively extends throughout our social foundations' (2009: 4). That dispersion of punishment certainly echoes Foucault and his description of a carceral continuum (or archipelago) as it reaches out from the prison into the social body. Nevertheless, Brown's treatment of that form of cultural embeddedness is more layered and nuanced as she attends to the sheer ubiquity of the spectacle in late modern society.

Furthering her analysis, Brown elaborates on 'prison theory' and the 'work of punishment' by throwing critical light onto the practice of penal spectatorship whereby bystanders look, stare, gape, gawk, and gaze at other people's pain. Brown insightfully finds parallels with Jonathan Simon's (2007) commentary on state-building capacities that promote crime control while paradoxically eroding democratic institutions, in part due to a growing populism geared at revenge. So as to deepen her cultural approach to penological theory, Brown pays tribute to not only Foucault but also Durkheim and Goffman, thereby encouraging us to appreciate macrosociological phenomena as they run in tandem with micro (individual) level experience. For instance, in examining a form of penal spectatorship known as 'prison tourism,' Brown decodes the emotional attraction of visiting correctional institutions. Indeed, she reminds us that the desire to know is very much part of the individual as well as the social psyche since touring prisons has the potential to be not only a 'horrific' personal experience but a collective one as well (see Welch and Macuare, forthcoming).

In reading recent works on punishment and culture, especially alongside the contributions of Foucault, we are sometimes left wondering which theoretical construct is being advanced: the notion of a 'society of spectacle' or rather a 'society of surveillance.' Recall Foucault's enduring remark that 'our society is one not of spectacle, but of surveillance' (1977: 217). As Boyle and Haggerty (2009) point out, that passage in *Discipline and Punish* was an uncited but unmistakable swipe at Guy Debord and his book *Society of Spectacle*, one that thereby stages a duel between two theories of modern power. Debord proposed that society was transformed into a monolithic spectacle manifested as a totalizing media event designed to feed consumption. Rejecting that formulation, Foucault advanced his paradigm for disciplinary power as it eclipsed the spectacle of the scaffold. So which interpretation is correct? Is it possible that both perspectives accurately convey the nature of power channeled through punishment? The answer probably is yes. Foucault's strict demarcation between 'society of spectacle' and 'society of surveillance' is overstated since the two coexist as twin features of modernity. In their examination of 'spectacular security' and mega-events (e.g. the Olympic Games), Boyle and Haggerty persuasively argue that the spectacle operates in concert with discipline and surveillance (see Alford, 2000). With that idea in mind, it is important to draw critical attention to the mass audience for which punishment is scripted, thereby enhancing visualization (e.g. television programs, movies) and experience (e.g. prison tours) that in turn reinforces the power of the state as it dispenses pain and suffering (see 'Cultural Penology: Escape from New York', below).

Recent interest in punishment and culture has prompted scholars to reconsider Foucault's central role in penological theory. A critique by Philip Smith (2008) does just that, contending that 'cultural sociology of punishment' benefits from a reworking of Durkheim's writings much more so than what has become standard Foucauldian interpretation. Smith returns to Durkheim's (1958) late work on socio-religious concepts (e.g. the sacred, the pure, pollution, taboo) to illuminate the expressive and communicative dimensions of penal rituals. In particular, he brings to the forefront the iconic cultural status of the guillotine, the panopticon, the electric chair, and the supermax prison, all of which are surrounded by myth and legend. Moreover, those penal inventions have become commodified for public consumption as they move into zones for entertainment, including movies and tours of prisons. Smith wants scholars to appreciate the potential for a new Durkheimian approach that draws awareness to the mysteriously dark and dreadful fascination of punishment as it serves to rid society of evil and impure lawbreakers. Smith's book is decidedly polemical, proposing that 'power and control' (Foucault) explanations should be replaced by 'culture and meaning' (Durkheim).

Critics of Smith's work, however, wonder why those different perspectives are described as being mutually exclusive. Certainly, one can locate in the penal apparatus activities that are highly routinized according to rational systems of thought embodied, for instance, in the new penology (Feeley and Simon, 1992). Those emerging bureaucracies that organize punishment do not operate in a cultural vacuum; rather they tend to gain even greater authority in response to penal populism and governance through crime (Pratt, 2007; Simon, 2007). As Garland writes, Smith's '"assault" on Foucault has really been more of a sparring match, a kind of exercise or theoretical work-out, intended to showcase the strengths of Smith's frame rather than knock out the contending alternative' (2009: 265). In the end, Smith seems to concur, proposing a 'reconciliation' synthesis in which the new Durkheimian perspective interplays with Foucauldian analysis. Garland comments further: 'Smith is no doubt correct to insist that penal practice is an ongoing effort to control meaning. But it is also, and at same time, a massive machine for the control of bodies and behavior and our analytical frameworks should aim to embrace both of these dimensions rather than privilege one at the expense of the other' (2009: 266).

The recent cultural turn in penology indeed marks an important – and lively – development as we strive to understand the depth of punishment and the rise in mass incarceration. As cultural penology sharpens its capacity to interpret the significance of punishment in modern society, one is reminded to distinguish between an analytical dimension of social relations ('the cultural') and a collective entity ('a culture') (Garland, 2006; Sewell, 2005, 1999). In the first concept, *the cultural* is depicted as a causal force shaping punishment, drawing on a wider array of influences: ideas, symbols, values and meanings. Together, those sentiments play a role in determining the image of punishment, such as public hangings; or conversely abolishing the spectacle as it becomes seen as uncivilized (Gatrell, 1994). *A culture*, the second concept, refers not to different aspects of the whole but a complete entity. Culture therefore signifies a larger universe of meaning, for instance an American culture that is assumed to embody a unique form of social life and way of doing things. Along those lines of reasoning it is generally accepted that punishment is embedded in the cultural aspects of the national environment that creates it (Melossi, 2001; Savelsberg, 2002). As a word of scholarly caution, Garland (2006) points out that there are drawbacks in separating the 'cultural' from its 'culture'; as a useful corrective, he suggests that cultural analysis integrate both perspectives.

CULTURAL PENOLOGY

Escape from New York

The 1981 movie titled *Escape from New York* starring Kurt Russell depicted the future of incarceration. The film is set in 1997, and the once great city of New York has become the one maximum-security prison for the entire country. The plan to convert the island of Manhattan into a penitentiary occurred earlier, in 1988, when the crime rate nationwide allegedly increased 400 percent. That crime wave forced government officials to rethink the traditional penitentiary. As a result, the New York Maximum-Security Penitentiary – Manhattan Island – had become the ultimate futuristic prison. A 50-foot containment wall has been constructed around the island, and all bridges and waterways have been mined with explosives. The United States Police Force is encamped like an army outside the containment wall. Liberty Island and the Statue of Liberty function as the control stations from which surveillance helicopters patrol the harbor. Officers manning choppers have orders to shoot escaping convicts. There are no guards inside the penitentiary, only prisoners and the world they create. There is only one rule: Once you go in, you don't come out. Convicts sentenced to Manhattan Island, however, are given a choice: either enter the penitentiary for life or be terminated and cremated at the control center.

Kurt Russell plays the role of Snake Plissken, who sports an unshaven face, an eye patch, and a leather jacket – making him look much like a futuristic buccaneer. Although a war hero, Plissken has been sentenced to life for robbing the Federal Reserve depository. As he enters the underworld of Manhattan Island penitentiary, he learns of the harsh reality of survival. Prisoners live in subway tunnels and sewers and rely on heightened vigilance to fend off predatory attacks from street gangs, punk rockers, and crazies, who battle violently over turf. Although *Escape from New York* is an engaging science-fiction exercise, it does address some real issues concerning incarceration. In no uncertain terms, the movie depicts a 'lock 'em up and throw away the key' sentiment that resonates in the public conversation over crime. Similarly, it reflects a major trend in penal policy, namely the construction of super maximum-security penitentiaries designed to contain what the authorities claim to be an increase in more dangerous felons.

CONCLUSION

The critical approach mapped out in this book by no means neglects the importance of culture; nonetheless, it does attempt to bring into relief the significance of power firmly embedded in punishment and the use of prisons. In the forthcoming chapters, the critical perspective will continue to unfold according to key historical, philosophical, and theoretical developments, especially as they inform us of the prevailing rationales (why) and practices (how) of the penal project. By examining both the 'why' and 'how' of punishment we are better able to discern what might be called *penal discourse*. Rather than merely attending to passages of spoken and written statements, a more conceptual use of the term discourse refers to how language structures knowledge and organizes the ways in which things are done (Carrabine, 2004; Foucault, 1972).

Although it is debatable as to exactly how many different discourses exist in penology, there is some agreement that six serve to capture a broad range of rationales and practices. Three of those penal discourses pertain to the *ends* of incarceration (rehabilitation, normalization, and control) and the remaining three to the *means* (bureaucracy, professionalism, and authoritarianism) (Adler and Longhurst, 1994; Carrabine, 2000). It is important to realize that those particular discourses are not fixed but rather dynamic, subject to being continually challenged and revised within corrections as well as society at large. In the chapters ahead we shall remain mindful of penal discourse while maintaining an ongoing dialogue over what prisons are *for*, in a macrosociological sense, and what the prison experience is *like*, in a microsociological one. Together, those fundamental concerns keep us attuned to both the instrumental (Foucault) as well as the expressive (Durkheim) elements of punishment (see Bosworth and Carrabine, 2001).

SUMMARY

This chapter introduces a critical approach to corrections by questioning the expanding use of imprisonment. Indeed, mass incarceration is not only costly but also fails to significantly contribute to public safety given that a huge proportion of offenders sentenced to prison are convicted of non-violent crimes. Moreover, it is generally unfair – even unjust – to put nonviolent offenders behind bars when they could be punished by alternative sanctions. A critical approach also remains focused on racial and socioeconomic biases evident in a correctional population that is disproportionately poor, African-American, and Latino. By attending to penal populism, the new penology, the new punitiveness, and the reproduction of failed prisons, the discussion sets the stage for upcoming chapters as they delve into such controversies as institutional violence, the death penalty, and the stepped-up wars on crime, drugs, and terror.

REVIEW QUESTIONS

1 Why is it essential to distinguish between typical and celebrity offenders?
2 What are the costs of prisons, financially and otherwise?
3 What is the overlap between penal populism and 'governing through crime'?
4 How does the new penology shift away from a traditional approach to corrections?
5 What are the fundamental differences between Foucauldian analysis and a neo-Durkheimian perspective on punishment?

RECOMMENDED READINGS

Brown, M. (2009) *The Culture of Punishment: Prison, Society and Spectacle*. New York: New York University Press.

Clear, T. (2009) *Imprisoning Communities: How Mass Incarceration Makes Disadvantaged Neighborhoods Worse*. New York: Oxford University Press.

Melossi, D. (2008) *Controlling Crime, Controlling Society: Thinking about Crime in Europe and America*. Cambridge, UK: Polity Press.

Pratt, J. (2007) *Penal Populism*. London: Routledge.

Simon, J. (2007) *Governing Through Crime: How the War on Crime Transformed American Democracy and Created a Culture of Fear*. New York: Oxford University Press.

Welch, M. (2005) *Ironies of Imprisonment*. Thousand Oaks, CA: Sage.

CHAPTER 2

A Social History of Punishment and Prisons

Those who do not remember the past, are condemned to repeat it. (George Santayana)

LEARNING OBJECTIVES

After studying this chapter, you should be able to answer the following questions:

1 What were the early developments in punishment and corrections?
2 What were the popular forms of punishment in ancient Greece, ancient Rome, the Middle Ages, the sixteenth and seventeenth centuries, and the Enlightenment?
3 How did politics, economics, religion, and technology shape punishment throughout history?
4 How did Cesare Beccaria, Jeremy Bentham, and John Howard contribute to penal reform?

On 2 March 1757 Damiens the regicide was condemned to 'make the *amende honorable* before the main door of the Church of Paris,' where he was able to be 'taken and conveyed in a cart, wearing nothing but a shirt, holding a torch of burning wax weighing two pounds'; then, 'in the said cart, to the palace de Greve, where, on a scaffold that will be erected there, the flesh will be torn from his breasts, arms, thighs and calves with red-hot pincers, his right hand, holding the knife with which he committed the said parricide, burnt with sulphur, and, on those places where the flesh will be torn away, poured molten lead, boiling oil, burning resin, wax and sulphur melted together and then his body drawn and quartered by four horses and his limbs and body consumed by fire, reduced to ashes and his ashes thrown to the winds.'

(*Pièces Originales*, 1757: 372–4)

'Finally, he was quartered,' recounts the *Gazette d'Amsterdam* of 1 April 1757. 'This last operation was very long, because the horses used were not accustomed to drawing; consequently, instead of four, six were needed; and when that did not suffice, they were forced, in order to cut off the wretch's thighs, to sever the sinews and hack the joints.'

(Foucault, 1977: 3)

INTRODUCTION

Exploring the social evolution of punishment enhances our understanding of contemporary corrections. Because punishment – in many forms, not just imprisonment – has remained an integral part of the social order throughout time, much of contemporary corrections cannot be understood apart from its history. This chapter traces the history of punishment and corrections from the emergence of formal and legal punishment, through ancient Greece and Rome, the Middle Ages, the sixteenth and seventeenth centuries, and the Enlightenment. This chapter also describes with considerable detail various forms of punishment and corrections in their historical contexts. However, because of the importance of surpassing mere description, the primary emphasis is on the analysis of penalties and prisons, especially in light of the social forces that shape them – politics, economics, religion, and technology.

Historically, political structures have determined how different social classes are treated by the criminal justice system. Economics also has played a vital role in punishment and corrections, as evidenced by the practices of monetary fines and confiscation of property, as well as the economic tendency to exploit cheap labor (through penal slavery, indentured servitude, prison industries, etc.). Religion, as a social force, has also had considerable impact on the rationale and justification for punishment and corrections, particularly in light of the belief that offenders ought to be morally reformed or corrected. Finally, technology has remained an important social influence. Throughout history, various methods of punishment have emerged from the application of science – the guillotine, the electric chair, and sundry other torture devices. Although these social forces may seem to be distinct, they overlap considerably. Correctional programs emphasizing *both* work and prayer, for instance, demonstrate the interplay between religious and economic forces. Similarly, technology commonly merges with political forces, producing mechanisms designed to exert power and control over citizens through state-of-the-art surveillance technology.

EMERGENCE OF FORMAL AND LEGAL PUNISHMENT

Exploring the various social forces that shape punishment and corrections requires understanding the ideas, rationales, and circumstances from which those forces derive. Punishment is as old as civilization itself. From the time people began living together as a society, there existed some form of social control intended

Figure 2.1 Castle window – indoor shot of a trellised historic window at Wertheim Castle in Southern Germany where light is falling.

© iStockphoto.com

to curb undesirable conduct. The rationale behind such control, or punishment, reveals the prevailing social forces.

Doctrines about the desirability and objectives of punishment have been closely related to theories of crime and criminal responsibility. In primitive times with their theory of diabolical possession, the conventional notion of punishment was either to exorcise the devil or to exile or execute the wrongdoer. In part, this was to protect the community against further outrages by the dangerous offender, but the major purpose was to *placate the gods*.

In the next stage of the doctrine of punishment more stress was laid upon *social revenge*. Crime was now considered the willful act of a free moral agent. Society, outraged at this act of voluntary perversity, indignantly retaliated. Many forms of crime were later identified with sin and were believed to offer a challenge to God and orthodox religion.

(Barnes and Teeters, 1946: 391)

Our historical discussion of punishment begins at the point when legal codes were first established. The development of language and writing skills led to the formalization of legal codes, which subsequently served as the official guidelines of society. The Code of Hammurabi, most popularly known by the phrase 'an eye for an eye, and a tooth for a tooth,' was among the first written legal codes, dating back to 1750 BC in Babylon. The basis for punishment, according to the Code of Hammurabi, was the concept *lex talionis*, meaning 'the law of retaliation,' which refers to vengeance. In most cases, the penalties were harsh, usually in the form of whipping, mutilation, and forced labor. Moreover, the injured parties themselves sometimes carried out the punishment. Hence, from

beginnings of punishment

code of Hammurabi

beheading

the beginning, the rationale for legally sanctioned punishment was retribution, or getting even. The principle of *lex talionis* remained popular throughout early civilization. It is found in the ancient Sumerian codes *Manama Dharma Astra* of India, the *Hermes Trismegitus* of Egypt, as well as the Mosaic Code.

Beheading, as a form of retribution, is traced to pre-Christian times and symbolizes the individual urge to avenge a crime. However, the precise rationale underlying beheading is subject to debate. One theory suggests that beheading was a sacrificial act to placate the gods, whereas other explanations suggest that beheading was an *apotropaic act*, that is, one that served to ward off evil. Furthermore, under some circumstances, beheading was considered an honorable death.

> Both the sword and the axe are significant sacred symbols. The axe and hammer especially were used by the Greek gods, and the sword was the symbol of valor in battle at a time when fighting was the most important social occupation that a young Greek or Roman could engage in. Thus to die in battle, usually by the sword or axe, was a most honorable death: in fact, the best way to go. The use of the tool of beheading is thus explained, as is the consistently high social status of those beheaded, since these people were the champions of battle and war throughout the ages.
>
> (Newman, 1978: 32–3)

Collective punishment

Although vengeance stems primarily from an individual urge to avenge a crime, it is also rooted in a strong social pressure to fulfill a tradition. When those individual and societal forces merge, a brutal type of retribution is formed – collective punishment, such as lynching, the firing squad, and the Halifax gibbet: an ancient contraption similar to the guillotine that was operated by citizens. An interesting feature of collective punishment is that it permits individuals to participate in the execution while avoiding direct responsibility for the death.

Among the oldest forms of collective punishment is stoning to death, a form of retribution in which members of the community enthusiastically contribute to the execution. The stone itself, like the sword and axe, had sacred meaning since it was probably humankind's first weapon. Moreover, in early societies, meteoric stones were believed to be sent to Earth from the gods (Newman, 1978). Some scholars have suggested that stoning also had a sacrificial function; others have noted that stoning had a cleansing effect on the community. The Greeks, for instance, preferred stoning offenders because it removed criminal 'pollution' from their society (Strom, 1942).

The fundamental notion of *lex talionis* stood as the principle behind various forms of retribution. That law of revenge served as the legal rationale for mutilation whereby the penalty set out to duplicate the injury inflicted. Accordingly, the blinding of a victim was punishable by blinding the perpetrator. Compounding matters, there was a preventive rationale for the practice of mutilation. While cutting off the hand of a thief certainly imposed a type of stigma (i.e. mark of social disgrace), it also was intended to prevent the offender from stealing again. Likewise, spies had their eyes gouged out, perjurers had their tongues torn out, and in ancient Assyria and Egypt, rapists were punished by castration (Barnes and Teeters, 1946: 408).

Throughout history, various forms of corporal punishment, torture, and execution were combined – as was the case with Damiens (described at the beginning of the chapter). In his book *The Lords of the Scaffold*, Geoffrey Abbott presents a brutal display of punishment taking place in 1746 in London:

> After he had hung six minutes, he was cut down and, having life in him, as he lay on the block to be quartered, the executioner gave him several blows to the breast, which not having the effect designed, he immediately cut his throat; after which he took off his head, then ripped him open and took out his bowels and heart and threw them in a fire which consumed them. Then he slashed his four quarters and put them with the head into a coffin, and they were carried to the new gaol at Southwark, and on 2 August the head was put on Temple Bar and his body and limbs suffered to be buried.
>
> (Abbott, 1991: 51–2)

COMPARATIVE CORRECTIONS

Controversy Over Amputation in Saudi Arabia

The 1987 United Nations Convention Against Torture prohibits various forms of corporal punishment, including torture and the amputation of limbs. That international treaty has 129 signatory countries that have agreed to report periodically on the measures they have taken to comply with the Convention's requirements. In 2002, diplomats from Saudi Arabia clashed with the United Nations Committee Against Torture over whether the amputation of limbs and flogging violate the international treaty. The UN committee ordered the Saudis to cease such forms of corporal punishment but Saudi delegates angrily defied the order, arguing that the committee had no jurisdiction over Shariah, the Islamic legal code derived from the Koran. Sharia law allows amputations for theft, and floggings for certain sexual offenses and drinking alcohol. Although those forms of punishment are banned by the committee mandate, other provisions of Sharia do not apply to the international treaty, such as executing murderers, drug dealers, and rapists. Taking exception to the UN committee, Turki alMadi, a Saudi diplomat, said: 'This law has existed for 1,400 years. And the committee wants to change it. I am sorry, you cannot' (Olson, 2002: A5). On behalf of the committee, Peter Thomas Burns, a Canadian law professor, stated: 'The committee itself had no doubt that flogging in almost any case constitutes torture. And amputation of limbs, in every case, would constitute torture under our definitions' (Olson, 2002: A5). Still, Saudi Arabia maintains that floggings, amputations, and other corporal punishments are not torture. A Saudi delegate reasoned: 'You can't say cutting off a hand is so severe. It harms only the criminal who harms society. Sharia protects society, not the criminal' (Olson, 2002: A5).

ANCIENT GREECE

[handwritten: reformation beginning]

Greek philosophers, reacting against the rationale of retribution as a basis of punishment, proposed instead that the offender be reformed. Plato believed that following imprisonment, the offender should emerge 'a better man, or failing that, less of a wretch,' thus affirming the notion of reform (Johnson, 1987: 3, 1984). In many ways the rationale of reform was considered rather progressive. However, due to what critics would call a 'class bias' in punishment, it was not considered progressive enough. In ancient Greece, offenders who were citizens of the Greek city-states would customarily face only monetary fines. Slaves who were convicted of crimes, on the other hand, were severely punished – often by whipping.

Other notable punishments passed on to ancient Greeks from earlier days included stoning, burning alive, strangling, banishing, branding, and penal slavery. Crucifying, gibbeting (exposing to public scorn), and garroting (strangling with an iron collar), however, originated in ancient Greece, along with breaking on the wheel. The wheel not only is a symbol of the sun in both Greek and Roman mythology, but along with the circle was believed to ward off evil. Hence, breaking on the wheel, like most other ancient punishments, possessed sacred meaning. Sometimes the execution took place without a wheel. 'The culprit was laid out on a flat board, or sometimes a crosspiece, and pegged to it with irons. The executioner then systematically broke all the major bones of the wretched criminal with sharp blows from an iron bar' (Newman, 1978: 37).

Class bias, with different punishments employed for different classes of people, was evident in the use of poisoning, which emerged as an elitist form of capital punishment. Socrates remains one of the most famous figures to be executed in that manner. Banishment (or ostracism), usually for a period of ten years, also was considered an elitist type of punishment. It is interesting to note that the decision to banish an offender derived from a vote of the citizens (Wines, 1971 [1895]). In some ways, banishment served as a symbolic death since the offender was out of sight and out of mind. Imprisonment was used by the ancient Greeks only to detain those awaiting trial or execution and to confine those who failed to pay their fines (Sellin, 1976).

ANCIENT ROME

[handwritten: incarceration as punishment]

Unlike the ancient Greeks, the ancient Romans used imprisonment for purposes beyond detention – incarceration itself was intended to punish lawbreakers. Yet the structures used for incarceration were essentially makeshift: heavy cages, basements of public buildings, and stone quarries. Although such structures were not originally intended for the purpose of imprisonment, the security they offered made them suitable for close confinement (Mattick, 1974; Johnston, 1973).

One of the most notable structures was the Mamertime prison, established about 64 BC by Ancus Maritus. Located under the Cloaca Maxima, the Mamertime prison was a primitive sewer of Rome best known for its vast system of dungeons (Johnston, 1973; American Correctional Association (ACA), 1983; Peck, 1922). Prisoners were confined to cages within dark and stench-ridden sewers. By using the sewer as a makeshift prison, Romans symbolically equated human waste, contamination, and infection with crime and deviance. 'It is as if the Fathers of Rome saw the threats of public health posed by human waste and by human deviance as equivalent, and opted to expel both from the sight and consciousness of the Roman citizenry' (Johnson, 1987: 7). To be discussed in Chapter 3, the rise of the penitentiary in America was inspired by similar environmental theories of crime, assuming that some features of social life were morally corrupting (Rothman, 1971). Because of the 'out of sight, out of mind' quality of imprisonment, it is often viewed as another version of banishment.

Economic and labor motifs of punishment also were evident in Roman times. Forced labor on public works is among the more readily documented practices; other economically driven punishments included the payment of fines and the forfeiture of property and possessions. Slaves, viewed as property as well as sources of forced labor, suffered various forms of punishment. A primary purpose of punishing slaves was to discipline them. Whipping, mutilation, branding, and confinement to stocks and furcas (V-shaped yokes designed to be worn around the neck, forcing the arms to remain stretched out) were common penal practices (Newman, 1978). Furthermore, some slaves were confined to ergastulums, primitive types of prisons designed to discipline offenders by subjecting them to hard labor while being chained to workbenches (Sellin, 1976).

Occasionally, citizens were punished by being formally pronounced slaves, thereby losing their liberty and being forced to spend their lives in penal servitude. Because such punishment was regarded as 'civil death,' the offenders' property was confiscated and their wives declared widows, eligible to remarry (Sutherland et al., 1992). Disobedient or cowardly soldiers were publicly humiliated, whipped, demoted, and fined. For severe infractions, soldiers were subject to stoning and beheading. 'In the case of mass conduct, such as may occur in battle, decimation was used: i.e., every tenth man was executed. There was one occasion, however, when 370 deserters from Hannibal were recaptured. They were all flogged and thrown from the Tarpenian Rock, the usual punishment for traitors' (Newman, 1978; 70). Like the ancient Greeks before them, ancient Romans relied on numerous forms of torture and execution – breaking on the wheel, burying alive, drowning, burning, as well as branding criminals on their foreheads (Barnes and Teeters, 1946; Newman, 1978).

The most notable documents of legal punishment during this period were the Bergundian Code and the Justinian Code. The Bergundian Code (c. AD 500) categorized types of punishment according to social class (e.g. nobles, middle classes, and lower classes). The Justinian Code, written by Emperor Justinian I

Justinian code → punishment fit the crime

of Rome in AD 529, evolved from the Law of the Twelve Tables, the earliest code of Roman Law, which had been in existence for a thousand years. The Justinian Code formalized punishment with an unusual degree of precision and uniformity insofar as crimes were listed beside their assigned penalty. In many ways, the Justinian Code reflected an attempt to make the punishment fit the crime. But it was not without its administrative headaches; because of the ambitious and lengthy inventory of crimes, enforcement was difficult. Even after the fall of the Roman Empire (AD 476), remnants of the Justinian Code continued to serve as a foundation for most of the legal codes that developed later in the Western world.

THE MIDDLE AGES

The Middle Ages refers to the period of Western European history beginning with the fall of the Roman Empire in the fifth century and ending with the emergence of the Renaissance in the fifteenth century. With the dissolution of the Roman Empire, commerce declined and the social order consequently underwent serious problems. During that era, the Roman Catholic Church prevailed as a dominant social force exerting influence over all the major institutions. Similarly, feudalism emerged as the prevailing political economy whereby service was exchanged for land, protection, and justice. The social arrangement was hierarchical. At the top of the hierarchy was the Holy Roman Emperor: below him were kings and princes, then warriors and knights, with peasants occupying the bottom strata of the vast social structure.

Control from the church

Crime, punishment, and the Church

The first several centuries of the Middle Ages – the fifth through the eleventh – are known as the Dark Ages. This era was characterized by excessive and brutal measures of social control imposed mainly by the Church. As a result of the prevailing religious forces, certain acts were criminalized, most notably heresy and witchcraft. Some sexual offenses were regarded as unnatural acts, including homosexuality and bestiality.

Under the rule of Charlemagne (c.742–814), church officials set out to 'prohibit all superstitious observances and remnants of paganism' (Newman, 1978: 80). During that era, bishops were granted authority to act as secular judges, allowing them to rule on secular matters. That development was consistent with the early religious theme of punishment since it targeted the 'sinful' nature of some crimes. Consequently, offenders had to pay their debt both to God and to society, thereby blurring the boundaries between church law and state law.

Due to the significant role of the Church in structuring and maintaining the social order, enormous emphasis was placed on monitoring religious beliefs. In its efforts to stamp out heresy, the Church replaced trials with ordeals, in which

[handwritten margin note: Ordinals = "God decided"]

guilt or innocence was determined by the suspect's ability to avoid injury while engaging in dangerous and painful tests of faith.

> Medieval punishments included trials of fire, water, the rod, and the stake. In the trial of cold water, the accused had to jump into a lake that had been blessed with offerings. He was considered guilty if he floated and innocent if he sank, in which case he would be pulled out by ropes. Servants were commonly subjected to the trial of boiling water, in which the accused was forced to grab something from the bottom of a pan of water on fire. He was found innocent if his arm came out unharmed, something that occurred very rarely.
>
> (Lombroso, 2006b: 180)

The rationale underlying ordeals was divine intervention – meaning that if the accused were truly innocent, God would intervene to prove their innocence. Needless to say, those who were subjected to these tests of faith were rarely found innocent of their charges, producing high rates of conviction (Ives, 1970 [1914]; Newman, 1978).

Confronting the threat of heresy became a central theme of formal social control, and the Holy Inquisition was established as an official law enforcement campaign in 1231. In a widespread effort to combat heresy, the Inquisition set out to save the souls of the accused. Those who refused to repent or confess were punished by having their land confiscated or by being fined, imprisoned, condemned to wear crosses, tortured, or burned alive. The Inquisition continued for several centuries throughout Europe (and Latin America) during which time thousands of people accused of heresy were brutally tortured and executed (Lea, 1969 [1887]).

[handwritten margin note: Monastaries as prisons]

That religious movement was not without its political agendas. In 1542, for instance, the Inquisition was used in Italy to counter the Protestant movement. The execution of Joan of Arc probably best illustrates the religious and political elements of social control. After being accused of heresy and witchcraft, Joan of Arc was burned at the stake in 1431. Yet her religious offenses were complicated by her political activism. Joan of Arc claimed to have had visions from God to lead French citizens away from the British occupation. Incidentally, her conviction of heresy was overturned in 1456, and she was canonized in 1920.

Other overlapping themes of crime and sin also shaped the practice of imprisonment. Early versions of prisons reflected a concern for order and discipline, thereby facilitating the task of reform by way of penance. Incarceration took place in makeshift arrangements, at times even inside monasteries. Conveniently, the monastery itself served as a model of future institutions in which criminals were isolated from the secular world so that they might privately repent and reflect (ACA, 1983). To be clear, the term *penitentiary* derives from the Latin words meaning 'penitence' and 'repentance,' yet also shares the same root with the words *punishment*, *pain*, and *revenge* (Norris, 1985).

Feudalism and social control

Feudalism eventually became the prevailing social, economic, and political system in which obedience and service stood as its primary cornerstones. Between the eighth and thirteenth centuries in Europe, feudalism emerged as a strict aristocratic, militaristic, and theological social order. Such a hierarchy, however, depended greatly on a high degree of societal legitimacy. That is, those in power went to great lengths to appear morally justified to be at the top of the hierarchy, especially in the eyes of the subordinate. In more complex terms, the legitimacy afforded to feudalism rested on the theological notion that the power structure was divinely ordained. In other words, feudal society was arranged according to the will of God, and of course it was in the best interest of those in power to perpetuate that belief.

It has been proposed that the objective of punishment is to protect society, an idea that became known as the 'social defense' thesis. With greater conceptual refinement, however, perhaps punishment should be viewed instead as a means of protecting a particular form of society (Michalowski, 1985). In the case of feudalism, punishment was often designed and implemented with the explicit purpose of maintaining the social order. Furthermore, forms of punishment contained in a particular social order are shaped by economic forces. Therefore punishment is aimed at preserving not only the social order but the economic order as well. As Michalowski postulates:

> The nature of the basic productive activities of a given society will determine the forms of punishment appropriate to that society. During the feudal era the basic productive activity was agricultural in nature, and the relations of production were such that serfs – the basic laboring class – were tied to a form of involuntary servitude by the feudal bond.
>
> (1985: 225)

The structure of punishment under feudalism, Michalowski asserts, was patterned by economic forces in several ways. First, the population distribution in agrarian society was widely scattered, which meant that there could be no high concentration of offenders. Hence, the use of penal institutions that would centralize the criminal population would be inconsistent with the decentralized nature of the agricultural society. Second, the laboring class was already attached to the land – indeed, their work was a form of involuntary servitude. Therefore punishment by way of forced labor, such as slavery, indenture, or imprisonment would be redundant. Compounding matters, the authorities 'would place the offender in a situation generally not much worse than that he or she was in prior to the crime both with respect to the conditions of life and the exploitation of his or her labor power' (Michalowski, 1985: 225). Eventually, fines and corporal punishment emerged as the primary methods of punishment because execution and banishment would result in the loss of the labor the offender had to offer (Rusche and Kirchheimer, 1968 [1939]; see O'Malley, 2009).

Early imprisonment and makeshift prisons

During the Middle Ages, incarceration practices resembled those of ancient Rome, insofar as makeshift structures were used for confinement. Due to their secure features, fortresses, castles, abutments of bridges, town gates, cellars of municipal buildings, and even private dwellings were convenient places to hold prisoners. Dungeons became synonymous with harsh imprisonment, but chambers specifically designed to house prisoners within castles did not appear until after the twelfth century. Eventually, castles were used almost exclusively as prisons and jails. That development had much to do with the advent of gunpowder, thereby altering military strategies. Consequently, the need for fortified dwellings became obsolete (Johnston, 1973). Throughout history, and even today, makeshift arrangements remain an important method of expanding jail and prison capacities given their availability and convenience (Welch, 1991c).

Galley slavery

As discussed throughout, economic forces have shaped the course of punishment throughout history. Still, as governments became more sophisticated, they recognized the significant value of labor that offenders had to offer. In fact, Thomas More proclaimed that 'it is unwise to execute offenders because their labor is more profitable than their death' (Rusche and Kirchheimer, 1968 [1939]). In light of that realization, galley slavery emerged as a routine method of punishment explicitly designed to exploit physical labor in the form of oarsmen for vessels. Although galley slavery existed in ancient Greece and Rome, it was not institutionalized as a penal practice until 1348: then it flourished during periods of global expansion, imperialism, and colonization, enduring to the year 1803. Given their enormous size, each vessel required hundreds of galley slaves. Toward the end of the fifteenth century, naval wars in the Mediterranean prompted military powers to recruit oarsmen from among prisoners. The large vessels needed as many as 350 galley slaves while smaller ships used 180. At the height of his authority, Don Juan d'Austria commanded some 5,600 galley slaves (Rusche and Kirchheimer, 1968 [1939]).

As the need for oarsmen multiplied, criminal justice officials widened their net by sentencing not only serious offenders but also thieves, beggars, and vagabonds to galley slavery. Although convict labor was greatly valued by private contractors, the slaves' ability to propel the vessels was drastically impaired by mistreatment. Before being confined to the galley, criminals were forced to march across the countryside. Whatever strength they had following the journey was further debilitated by being chained to an oar, confined in proximity to their own excrement, and infected with diseases caused by the vermin-infested conditions of the ships. The following passage captures the lives of galley slaves:

> The prisoners reached the sea-port on foot, traversing a large part of France in scanty clothing and chained by the neck in large gangs. Once drafted on

Figure 2.2   Galley slavery, January 10, 1863. The French artillerymen distribute biscuits among the galley slaves in Veracruz during the war between France and Mexico. In the picture above, cherubs decorate a montage of Parisian landmarks. (From *Le Monde Illustré – Expédition du Mexique*, published 1963, from an engraving by C. Maurand of a sketch by M Brunet.)

Photo by Hulton Archive/ Getty Images.

board ship and posted to his bench, he remained there always unless taken to the hospital or the grave. Six slaves, chained to the same beach, tugged at each oar, which was some fifty feet in length: they were compelled to keep time with the others before or behind, or they would have been knocked senseless by the return stroke. They rowed naked to the waist, partly to save clothing, still more to offer their backs to the thongs of the *souscomites* or quarter-master who flogged freely, and backed up every order with each stroke. When not rowing they sat at their benches at night, and slept where they sat. In all naval engagements of those days the oars were shot at first, hence the galley-slaves suffered first and most, and were often decimated while the garrison and crew escaped untouched.

(Marteilhes, 1894: 164–5; reprinted in Barnes and Teeters, 1948: 437)

Galley slavery was often a life sentence. Often while the ships were at port during the winter, many galley slaves were branded (for the purposes of identification and stigma) and forced to labor in workhouses, known as bagnes, located in the dockyards (Newman, 1978).

The practice of galley slavery diminished during the eighteenth century. Among the reasons for its decline were technological forces, such as advanced sailing methods that rendered galley servitude obsolete. With a surplus of galley slaves, many prisoners were later assigned to work in mines while others were transported to work in colonial lands. "What is significant in the development of the galley as a method of punishment is the fact that economic considerations alone were involved, not penal. The introduction and regulation of galley servitude were determined solely by the desire to obtain necessary labor on the cheapest possible basis" (Rusche and Kirchheimer. 1968 [1939]: 55).

THE SIXTEENTH AND SEVENTEENTH CENTURIES

Although the 1500s are characterized as a period when earlier forms of penal sanctions remained routine (e.g. execution, corporal punishment), other innovations appeared to reflect a reconceptualization of punishment. The sixteenth and seventeenth centuries mark a pivotal point in the history of punishment as workhouses and houses of correction emerged along with the practice of transportation and the use of hulks as prison 'warehouses' (see Spierenburg, 1984),

Workhouses and houses of correction

The breakdown of feudalism led to the development of early mercantile capitalism as the primary mode of production, thereby causing changes to the prevailing forms of punishment. During the transition from an agrarian economy to one that combined agriculture with guild-based production of mercantile goods, there was a shift of population from rural areas into villages, towns, and eventually cities (Michalowski, 1985). Soon serfs and laborers were stripped of their land and forced to live as scavengers. As they drifted into urban areas, they were met with hostility by well-to-do townspeople. Soon perceptions of a growing 'social disorder' became the source of alarm, prompting the state to take action against a rising underclass (see Chapter 4 on radicalism).

In London, King Henry VIII dealt with the underclass and the growing number of unemployed vagabonds by way of corporal punishment and penal slavery. Those measures of social control, however, could not keep pace with economic forces that contributed heavily to the massive influx of the homeless and jobless into urban centers. Soon workhouses or houses of correction emerged as part of the enclosure movement: that is, the practice of confining offenders and undesirables to institutions featuring punishment, work, and religious instruction. In 1556, the Bridewell was converted from an old royal palace (known as Saint Bridget's Well) to an institution in which the poor as well as the lewd and idle were confined with rogues, vagabonds, prostitutes, and an array of less serious offenders (Sutherland *et al.*, 1992). Under strict discipline, they were assigned such tasks as spinning wool, baking, and making furniture, clothing, shoes and even tennis balls for members of the elite class. Foreshadowing the contemporary form of privatization in corrections, the Bridewell was operated by businessmen under a contractual agreement with local government (Van der Slice, 1936–7; Rusche and Kirchheimer, 1968 [1939]).

Operating under the assumption that pauperism was rooted in basic laziness, those institutions relied on a rehabilitative rationale. Workhouses were aimed at instilling a work ethic and the habits of industry as well as providing skill training for their inmates. Nevertheless, prison reformers criticized officials for exploiting slave labor to produce marketable goods cheaply for private profit (Dobash, 1983). As is the case with many correctional innovations, it is sometimes difficult to distinguish genuine humanitarianism from the calculating motives of profit (Johnston, 2009).

As a unique form of social control, the workhouse movement can be interpreted as 'social sanitation' designed to sweep the undesirables from the streets and place them in institutions away from public view (Welch, 1994). In England, workhouses seemed to be so effective that in 1576 Parliament instructed all British counties to construct a workhouse according to the vision of the Bridewell (Sellin, 1976). Soon Holland built its version of workhouses in 1596, and many other nations in Europe followed suit because they, too, were responding to failing economic conditions.

The fact that the interiors of the workhouses were out of public view, compounded with public apathy concerning them, led to the proliferation of horrible conditions. Disease, violence, and sexual assaults were common in the workhouses because the segregation of men from women, the young from the old, and the sick from the healthy was not always enforced. Another feature of the workhouses was a fee system by which food, blankets, and candles were made available only to those inmates who could purchase them from the keeper. During that period, criminals convicted of serious offenses were still being publicly whipped, transported, or executed. Thus those confined to the workhouses were primarily prostitutes, vagabonds, and those with no visible means of support (see Morris and Rothman, 1995).

Transportation: banishment for profit

In an attempt to rid itself of a growing underclass and ease overcrowding in prisons and gaols (jails), England began transporting rogues, vagabonds, and sturdy beggars to colonial lands in 1598. In those distant colonies (i.e. Australia and America), penal slaves would serve lengthy sentences in forced labor. A century later, the use of transportation expanded considerably: the Transportation Act of 1718 stated that the purpose of transportation was to deter criminals as well as to supply the colonies with labor (Shaw, 1966).

Eventually, transportation applied to more than thieves and vagabonds; it also served as a convenient method of deporting political undesirables and religious dissidents. The popularity of transportation spread throughout Europe. Russia made use of Siberia; Spain deported prisoners to Hispaniola, Portugal exiled convicts to North Africa, Brazil and Cape Verde; Italy herded inmates to Sicily; Denmark relied on Greenland as a penal colony; Holland shipped convicts to the Dutch East Indies.

England transported thousands of criminals to work in the American colonies. Following the American Revolution, between the years 1786 and 1867, approximately 134,000 prisoners were sent to Australia (Sutherland *et al.*, 1992). The transportation of prisoners remained popular for centuries, even until recent times. For instance, the infamous Devil's Island in French Guiana (as depicted in the novel and movie *Papillon*) was used by French authorities until 1953. Over the years, approximately 68,000 of the 70,000 prisoners on Devil's Island died before completing their sentence (Tappan, 1960).

Transportation should be viewed as a complex form of punishment. Beyond its obvious economic underpinnings, transportation boasted a form of banishment as well as the ritual of public humiliation. In London, men and women alike were placed in heavy chains and drawn in open carts through the local crowds, who jeered and terrorized them (Johnson, 1988). In Russia, over 850,000 convicts were exiled to Siberia between 1807 and 1899, and were forced to march between 4,700 and 6,700 miles while being chained together. The journey often lasted two to three years, contributing to high death rates (Sellin, 1976).

Although transportation was used for crime-control purposes by exporting hardened criminals, it also represented a form of social sanitation serving to rid urban centers of vagrants and other undesirables. Its success in England was affirmed when, in 1787, offenders sentenced to three or more years of imprisonment were eligible for transportation, and the penalty for an unauthorized return was execution. An estimated 2,000 prisoners annually (and a quarter of a million overall) arrived in America until the beginning of the Revolutionary War. At that time, England terminated transportation to the colonies, not wanting banished felons to be recruited as soldiers against their former homeland (Rusche and Kirchheimer, 1968 [1939]; Barnes and Teeters, 1946).

Transportation was essentially privatized through contracts, under which felons became the property of the ships' captains. Perhaps due to that contractual arrangement, convicts were subjected to horrible conditions aboard these vessels (known as 'floating hells'), and many died en route to the penal colony. Felons who survived the voyage were subsequently sold at a high price to American colonists, and they usually became indentured servants. Upon completion of their term, lasting from seven to 14 years, the banished felons were allowed to remain in the colony as free citizens. In some cases, indentured servants were awarded land by their owners (Barnes, 1968 [1939]).

As a result of the prevailing economic forces, transportation flourished as a method of securing slave labor for developing colonies. Changing economic forces later contributed to its demise. As immigrants migrated to the colonies, they campaigned for the abolition of penal slavery and transportation in order to secure higher wages for themselves (Rusche and Kirchheimer, 1968 [1939]).

Hulks: prison warehouses on the waterfront

Among the motivating forces behind transportation was the need to ease prison and jail crowding, and after the American Revolution (when transportation to America was terminated), England again faced that problem. For a short period, one solution was to transform prisoners into soldiers to be sent to fight in West Africa. That plan, however, was abandoned because the convicts did not make good soldiers. In due course, England returned to a penal practice that was popular in the late fifteenth century. That is, old, unseaworthy vessels were converted into floating prisons. In the late 1400s, abandoned galley-powered vessels, which were replaced by sail ships, were used for imprisonment. By the late 1700s, officials relied on broken-down transportation ships, known as hulks, to house prisoners. Also, referred to as 'hell holds' or 'floating hells,' hulks were moored at river banks and harbors while serving as penal warehouses for men, women, and children who were subjected to disease-infested conditions without adequate food and sanitation. Prisoners were routinely flogged and forced to engage in degrading labor. At one time, the English hulk system consisted of eleven ships holding 3,552 prisoners (Barnes and Teeters, 1946).

During the Revolutionary War, American prisoners of war were held in hulks anchored in New York harbor. An estimated 12,000 prisoners of war died on those ships, their bodies simply thrown overboard, eventually drifting to the Brooklyn shore (Welch, 1991c). In the 1800s, California relied on hulks to house prisoners, and as recently as the 1970s, Louisiana, Maryland, Massachusetts, New York, and Washington considered the conversion of decommissioned warships into makeshift correctional facilities (ACA, 1983). Perhaps the most interesting replication of the hulks, though, existed recently in New York City. Between 1988 and 1993, the city housed jail inmates on the *Bibby Venture* and the *Bibby Resolution* – floating jail barges that previously served as English military barracks during the Falkland Islands War in Argentina in 1982 (Welch, 1991c).

As was the case with other makeshift innovations initially designed to serve as temporary solutions to overcrowding, the English hulks remained correctional fixtures until 1858. In fact, the last hulk remained in operation until 1875, when transportation to Australia ceased (Barnes and Teeters, 1946).

CULTURAL PENOLOGY

Franz Schmidt: Famous Executioner

Perhaps the most renowned of Germany's executioners was Franz Schmidt, who bestrode Nuremberg's scaffold from 1573 to 1617. No record of his early life has survived but it is known that his father was executioner of the German town of Bamberg. Franz was his assistant there from 1573 to 1578 and when thoroughly proficient he moved to Nuremberg, where he became chief executioner. Franz's skills with the various tools of his trade were due in no small part to his interest in anatomy, knowledge of which he put to further use in the dissection of some of his victims. Hospitals were always in need of specimens for medical research and it was the hangman's duty in most countries to supply them (Abbott, 1991).

Not that he was inhumane; on the contrary, in 1580 he used his influence to have the penalty of drowning, which was inflicted on women guilty of infanticide, changed to the more merciful one of hanging or beheading. As in England, Germany's public executioners were feared and loathed by the populace – and this included their assistants – but despite society's rejection Franz performed his duties with impersonal efficiency and dedication. Unlike many of his calling he never drank strong liquor, and such had been his upbringing that his ability to write encouraged him to keep a detailed diary of his official activities, annotated accordingly where the felon had finally confessed his misdeeds. A contemporary picture portrays Schmidt as a tall well-built man, full bearded, in jerkin and knee-length hose. He could afford to dress well, for the pay was good. He received a fixed salary, with an extra fee per execution, and half that sum for each felon tortured. He and his assistant were also loaned to neighboring authorities whenever they lacked an executioner of their own, and a higher rate was then paid. The team even received some compensation in the event of a last-minute reprieve being granted to the condemned person (Abbott, 1991; Morris and Rothman, 1998).

Nor did Franz have any rent to pay, for he occupied an official residence provided by the city council, a tower house on the stone bridge that straddled Nuremberg's River Peginitz. Like their English counterparts, German executioners did a good trade in providing the superstitious with severed portions of their victims' corpses for use as revered relics, medicines, or lucky charms. In those days a macabre belief existed among the criminal fraternity of Europe that the severed hand of a hanged man, if prepared in accordance with the ancient recipes, possessed special powers (see Newman, 1978).

A German executioner's duties did not start on the scaffold, of course, but in the cells beneath the courtroom. There the executioner and his assistant would endeavor to coax a confession from the accused, utilizing the several instruments of torture provided by the authorities. If the thumbscrews didn't persuade, the 'ladder' might, stretching the bound victim to an agonizing degree. There was the 'fass,' a spiked cradle in which the victim was tied and rocked violently, hands bound behind him, or the 'gauntlets' whereby the accused, hands bound behind him, was hoisted aloft by the wrists, weights then being attached to his ankles.

As Franz entered in his diary in 1576: 'Hans Payhel, who committed three murders; two years ago I cut off his ears and flogged him; today I beheaded him at Focheim' (Abbott, 1991: 73). Schmidt served honorably during his 44 years in office and executed no fewer than 360 felons, at least 42 being women. His busiest year was 1580, when he performed 20 executions: 2 murderers who had to be broken on the wheel, 2 other murderers and 9 thieves hanged. All of which Franz performed with his usual expertise. Many such criminals received their due deserts at the hands of Franz Schmidt – floggings, brandings, amputation of fingers and ears – until finally, in 1617 he decided to retire and become a 'respectable' person again. He lived quietly in Nuremberg for a further 17 years until his death in 1634. The old executioner was given an honorable funeral, the burial service being attended by many of the city dignitaries as a mark of respect for his services to the community (Abbott, 1991; see Foucault 1977).

THE ENLIGHTENMENT AND ITS ENDURING IMPACT ON CORRECTIONS

The Enlightenment, or the Age of Reason, flourished during the mid-eighteenth century in Europe. At that time, great changes in social and scientific thought took place. Reason became a prevailing method of analyzing social life and the world around it. One source of inspiration for the Enlightenment was Isaac Newton's *Principia* (1687), which encouraged intellectuals to investigate social and scientific phenomena methodically and objectively. Another inspiration was John Locke's *Essay Concerning Human Understanding* and his *Second Treatise on Government* (both published in 1690). In those works, reason, complemented by humanitarianism and secularism, was applied to political theory and philosophy. That intellectual current made its mark on France, England, and America, where ideas of constitutionalism and limited political power quickly transformed those nations into independent republican governments (Johnson, 1988).

The Enlightenment was not without controversy. Among its major themes was the rejection of a school of thought dominated by institutional Christianity. That challenge to theological dominance gave rise to secular reasoning, in which social and scientific inquiries were no longer filtered through a religious perspective. Consequently, there was an enormous backlash from the Church. Montesquieu (in *Spirit of the Laws*, 1748) confronted religion and the historical role of the Church in the political arrangement of society. Drawing on the notion of utility, Montesquieu offered this question: What benefit does religion offer society? In the spirit of the Enlightenment, he maintained that 'Earthly institutions and societies were no longer to be judged by religious standards; rather, religion was to be measured by the new moral standard of utilitarianism: what good it did for mankind' (Johnson, 1988: 116–17). Montesquieu's critique of religion was considered subtle. Even so, he was confined to the Bastille in 1726; later his release stipulated that he leave France. In contrast to Montesquieu, Voltaire unswervingly attacked the Church in his writings, and he too was imprisoned. Similarly, Diderot, a French philosopher, was incarcerated for publishing his *Lettre sur les Aveugles* ('Letter on the Blind') – a scathing criticism of orthodox religion.

As the role of religion became less significant in social and scientific thought, ideas of crime and punishment were also transformed. Crime and punishment could now be conceptualized in a secular context, forcibly moving the concept of sin into the periphery of criminological debate. Accordingly, the focus of crime shifted away from a theological perspective and toward the consequences that crime had on other individuals and society. In response to that new focus of crime, punishment took a utilitarian approach. First and foremost was the idea of deterrence. The goal of punishment was to discourage individuals from engaging in crime, and it was assumed that this goal could be achieved by ensuring the certainty and swiftness of punishment. In sum, the Enlightenment thinkers contributed to the field of criminal justice by criticizing capricious sentencing and inhumane punishment, and by advocating the improvement of prison conditions.

Cesare Beccaria and penal reform

Among those strongly influenced by the notions of Montesquieu and Voltaire was the Marquis de Beccaria (1738–94), an Italian economist who published his *Essay on Crimes and Punishments* in 1766. The classic essay was originally published anonymously because he too feared persecution from the Church. Although Beccaria did avoid the Church's persecution, the essay was quickly condemned by the Church because of his disapproval of torture, a common method of punishment employed by the Church during the Inquisition (Maestro, 1973).

In his work, Beccaria borrowed heavily from the utilitarian perspective that served to formalize a theory of deterrence. He proposed that if laws (and penalties) were clearly written and fully understood, crime would subsequently decline. Beccaria further advanced the idea that the *certainty* and *swiftness* of punishment, not its *severity*, would prove to be the crux of deterrence. The social utility of punishment would be the deterrence of crime, but in doing so, it also would strengthen the bonds of society.

Beccaria was critical of arbitrary and unnecessarily harsh punishment. He believed that any penalty that was not intended to discourage crime or protect society was unjust and would interfere with the goal of deterrence. In fact, Beccaria opposed the death penalty on the grounds that it was excessive and that the protection of society could be achieved through banishment. He also opposed transportation of less serious offenders, because he felt that their punishment might go unobserved, thereby undermining the value of deterrence.

Beccaria considered any excessive punishment meted out by the state as tyrannical.

In crusading for changes in the legal codes that would support his theory of utility and deterrence, Beccaria challenged the abuse of political power within the criminal justice system. Specifically, he attacked those magistrates who arbitrarily sentenced offenders, and he recommended that penalties be graduated to fit the severity of the crime.

Beccaria's utilitarian ideas on crime, punishment, and criminal law became known as the classical school of criminology. His major proposals for law reform, which remain an important contribution today, are briefly listed (Beccaria, 1981 [1764]):

1   The criminal law should be clear, so that all could know and understand it.
2   Torture to obtain confessions should be abolished.
3   Judges should be impartial, and the sovereign who makes the laws should determine guilt or innocence.
4   The accused should be allotted the time and resources necessary for their defense.
5   The death penalty should be abolished.
6   Secret accusations and royal warrants for the imprisonment of people without trial should be done away with.
7   Punishment should be quick, certain, and commensurate with the crime.
8   The true measure of crime should be the harm done to the rights and liberties of individuals in society, rather than vague standards of moral virtue.

Although Beccaria advocated specific reforms for the criminal justice system, the foundation of his school of thought was more conceptual in nature. At the heart of the classical school of criminology was the concept of free will. In brief, deterrence could be achieved if prompt and certain punishments were given to those who chose to commit crime. Operating from a highly rationalistic framework, Beccaria was criticized for assuming that all criminals would react in similar ways to the same penalty. His oversight of individual differences and the diversity in the motives of crime remain a limitation of his theory (Johnson, 1988).

Moreover, recent re-examinations of Beccaria's contributions have surfaced. Newman and Marongui (1990) assert that, for years, scholars have blindly worshipped Beccaria. Returning to Beccaria's work and its impact on liberal penology, Newman and Marongui argue that his contributions are vastly overrated. 'Many of the reforms that occurred during the eighteenth century can as easily be ascribed to social and political conditions as to Beccaria's work' (Newman and Marongui, 1990: 325). Furthermore, Newman and Marongui note that, by comparison, the contributions of Voltaire and Jeremy Bentham were more profound than Beccaria's writings. In contrast to the ritual adoration of Beccaria common among criminologists, Newman and Marongui contend that it was Bentham who advanced Beccaria's utilitarian notions and bolstered the classical school of criminology (see Chapter 4).

John Howard and institutional reform

Throughout history, the sheriff has functioned as the chief law enforcement official of a county as well as the top administrator of the jail. The term *sheriff* emerged in England, where each county or shire was assigned a political appointee, the reeve. The sheriff (or shire-reeve) collected taxes, kept the peace, and managed the county jail. John Howard (1726–90) remains one of the most famous sheriffs in history because of his lasting contributions to jail reform. Over the past few centuries, John Howard and institutional reform have become synonymous. Howard's European-wide reputation as a prison reformer began following his appointment as the sheriff of Bedfordshire in England in 1773. Perhaps Howard's interest in penology can be traced to his own capture and detention by pirates during a trip to Portugal in 1755 (Barnes and Teeters, 1946; Wines, 1895).

During his tenure as sheriff, Howard was appalled by the horrific conditions in jails and in the hulks, which led to his crusade to reform jails throughout England and Europe. Among his first achievements was abolishing the fee system in which prisoners were forced to pay jailers for their keep. Under this system, those without the necessary funds to pay their keeper were forced to remain in jail, even after being tried and acquitted. In solving this problem, Howard proposed that fees be eliminated and jailers be paid a salary. His book *State of Prisons* (1777), the product of hundreds of jail and prison inspections throughout England and Europe, exposed and systematically recorded the brutal conditions of imprisonment. However, during those inspections, Howard did witness some penal practices that were quite progressive and humanitarian, namely those in use at the Hospice of San Michele and the Maison de Force.

Howard's contributions were not limited to publishing his ideas. He drafted the Penitentiary Act, which was passed by the British Parliament in 1779. This act of legislation was built around four principles:

1 Elimination of fees.
2 Regular inspection of prisons and jails.
3 Provision of sanitary and healthful facilities.
4 Emphasis on the reformation of inmates.

Howard's institutional reform also included an element of religion. He thought that reformation could be achieved by assigning each inmate his or her own cell in which to sleep, thus creating an atmosphere of solitude and silence which would be favorable to reflection and repentance. Howard assumed that crime was associated with idleness and unemployment, and criminal tendencies could therefore be exacerbated in prison if mischief and rebellion went unchecked. Therefore Howard's reforms combined discipline and Christian charity with a humanitarian philosophy. But discipline remained an important component of his plan, which incorporated religious teaching, daily routine, and productive labor (Howard, 1929 [1777]).

Other specific reforms included the removal of the mentally ill from prisons and the separation or release of women and children. The gaol at Wymondham in Norfolk, England, in 1785, was among the first to incorporate Howard's recommendations. Howard died of jail fever (typhus) in 1790 while inspecting a prison in Russia: still, his legacy lives on (Barnes and Teeters, 1946). In his name, John Howard Societies in England and the United States continue to monitor prison and jail conditions today.

Jeremy Bentham, Utilitarianism, and the panopticon

The contributions of Jeremy Bentham (1748–1832) are an important part of any discussion of the secular theme of crime and punishment and its impact on the classical school. In his major work, *An Introduction to the Principles of Morals and Legislation* (1789), Bentham elaborated on the concept of free will to further his utilitarian theory of hedonistic calculus, also known as the pleasure/pain principle. The central assumption in his theory was that human beings are motivated by pleasure while consciously avoiding pain. In advancing the deterrence model, Bentham proposed that penalties should sufficiently outweigh the gain that the offender would achieve in committing the crime. That framework was heavily psychological in nature because it assumed that crime could be deterred by addressing the rationality of those who commit such acts. The rational component of crime advanced the notion that if an individual chooses to act criminally, then he or she should embrace the responsibility for the act, and accept the punitive consequences (Bentham, 1995).

Bentham also was active in extending the reform of English criminal law. He supported the legal reform that called for graduated punishments that would fit the severity of the crime. One of his most notable contributions, however, was a product of his keen interest in architecture. He designed the panopticon, which became known as the 'ultimate penitentiary.' In the 1770s, the panopticon (from the Greek, meaning 'everything' and 'a place of sight') was proposed as a solution to the English correctional crisis during which horrific prison conditions and the hulks became major concerns for reformers. Bentham's inspiration to design the panopticon is traced primarily to English prison reformer John Howard.

The blueprints of the panopticon (also known as the 'inspection house') outlined its physical structure, which featured a column in the center of the floor plan to serve as an indoor guard tower. Several tiers of cells were arranged in a circular format that faced the guard tower. The design provided the guards with a complete and continuous view of the inmates confined to their individual cells (Bentham, 1995). One of the most detailed analyses of the panopticon was generated by French philosopher Michel Foucault. In his *Discipline and Punish: The Birth of the Prison* (1977), Foucault examines the subtleties of social control that he asserts distinguished the panopticon from other penal institutions. Foucault argues that the panopticon illustrated how geometry can complement economics in an effort to enhance social control. The circular design of the institution would make the inmate population more visible, and thus lead

Figure 2.3 Postcard of an American panopticon: 'Interior view of cell house, new Illinois State Penitentiary at Stateville, near Joliet, Ill.'

Source. Scanned from the postcard collection of Alex Wellerstein and reprinted with permission. Copyright expired. See http://www.hks.harvard.edu/sdn/sdnimages/.

to a decrease in the guard-inmate ratio, making supervision more efficient. Conceivably, only a few guards would be needed to maintain supervision over the entire prison population (see Alford, 2000; Lyon, 1991; Mathiesen, 1997).

Foucault contends that the key to inmate control is constant inspection, which represents power in two ways: it becomes both visible and unverifiable. 'Visible: the inmate will constantly have before his eyes the tall outline of the central tower from which he is spied upon. Unverifiable: the inmate must never know whether he is being looked at any one moment: but he must be sure that he may always be so' (1977: 201; 1996). Due to the central location of the guard tower, inmates could not always be sure whether or not they indeed were the objects of observation. Therefore Foucault notes that the target of social control is not so much the inmate's body, but the inmate's mind, in that constant surveillance creates a permanent presence in the mind (similar to the effects of surveillance cameras today). 'Hence, the major effect of the Panopticon: to induce in the inmate a state of conscious and permanent visibility that assures the automatic functioning of power' (1977: 201). Perhaps Aldous Huxley's insight best captures the essence of the panopticon when he called it the 'totalitarian housing project' (Johnston, 1873: 20).

Although the plans to construct a panopticon received serious consideration by some members of Parliament, it never won complete approval in England. However, similar circular prisons were built in Holland, Spain, and the Isle of Pines off Cuba. In America, the design of the panopticon was modified, as evidenced by the architecture of the Virginia Penitentiary, the Western Penitentiary (in Pittsburgh), and later, the Stateville Correctional Center (in Joliet, Illinois) (1919).

Inventing make-work devices

As prisons in England became overcrowded, institutional jobs became scarce. Consequently, wardens had to find ways to keep other inmates busy, so many of them were assigned meaningless and repetitive tasks resembling work only in form or ritual. Emerging technological forces led to such innovative devices as the crank and the treadmill. Those devices served as methods of punishment that were monotonous, irksome, and dull, as well as degrading.

The crank, commonly referred to as a reform engine, resembled the starting device of early automobiles and was attached to a wall and a mechanical counter. The punishment involved forcing inmates to turn the crank, with a resistance of 4 to 11 pounds, as many as 1,800 revolutions per hour and 14,400 revolutions per day. The treadmill (also known as the treadwheel, or wind-grinding machine) was invented by eminent engineer Sir William Cubbit in 1818. The treadmill featured a short staircase of 24 steps. As the prisoner walked up the stairs, the steps collapsed in a manner that impeded progress (a task similar to trying to walk up a down escalator). In a given day, an inmate might climb anywhere from 7,200 to 14,000 feet (by comparison, it is estimated that a stiff mountain climb consists of 3,000 to 5,000 feet). The following describes the drudgery of the treadmill:

> The weariness of the employment results from two causes. First, the want of a firm footing for the feet – a want painfully experienced in walking through a deep soft snow; and secondly, the strength that is expended to keep the body from sinking with the step – which is equal to that required to lift a man's own weight, say 140 pounds ... No wonder that prisoners maim themselves or feign sickness (at the rate of 4,000 instances in a twelve-month) to escape such a brutal use of their bodies.
>
> (*Journal of Prison Discipline and Philanthropy*, 1857: 40, reprinted in Barnes and Teeters, 1946: 691)

The shot drill was another type of strenuous and degrading chore. The convict was forced to carry heavy cannonballs from one pile to another and back again. The repetitive and monotonous punishment kept the prisoner active because the task could never be completed. The introduction of such methods of punishment is subject to many interpretations, but it is clear that those exercises were designed to be boring and void of the satisfaction of accomplishing a task or manufacturing a product. According to Foucault (1973), those punishments mark a divorce of labor from utility and profit, meaning that the exercises took on a pure significance as punishment. That shift in the attitude toward punishment makes it apparent that the ideals of genuine rehabilitation were being replaced with the notions of retribution (Sellin, 1976)

Hospice of San Michele and Maison de Force

Two European institutions that helped shape the humanitarian philosophy in punishment and corrections were the Hospice of San Michele and the Maison de Force. Those institutions are remembered as notable contributions to the development of corrections because they systematically applied the concepts of reformation and rehabilitation. The Hospice of San Michele (Hospital of Saint Michael) opened in Rome in 1703 under the direction of Pope Clement XI. The hospice was commonly thought to be a training school for juvenile delinquents, housing about 60 boys, but it also opened its doors to orphans, as well as over 500 aged and infirm men and women (Sellin, 1926).

Among its contributions to the reformatory movement, the hospice advanced the use of individual prison cells as an alternative to large dormitories. In the course of separating inmates, individual cells provided a solitary space conducive to solitude, silence, religious meditation, and repentance: all of which were each considered necessary conditions for personal reform. Although they slept in their own cells at night, inmates worked together in silence during the day, producing items for the Vatican State. Hence reform meant combining labor with the development of the spiritual well-being of the prisoner. In the Hospice of San Michele, the monastic features of the design were joined with the mission of workhouses (Johnston, 1973). The driving force behind the program of the hospice was regarded as humanitarian in nature because it emphasized reform, not necessarily punishment. Today, after undergoing considerable changes, the hospice remains a reformatory for delinquent boys.

The Maison de Force (the Stronghouse) was founded in Ghent, Belgium, by Jean Jacques Philippe Vilain in 1773. Similar to the hospice, the Maison incorporated religion with silent work as a means of reform. Inmates were confined to private cells at night and involved in congregate work during the day. Consistent with the humanitarian approach was the provision of separate quarters for men, women, children, felons, misdemeanants, and vagrants. The Maison marked an early attempt by a large-scale penal institution to use architecture to enhance the treatment philosophy. 'The plan was in the form of a giant octagon formed by eight trapezoid-shaped units, each completely self-contained to allow for the separation of various classes of prisoners' (Johnston, 1973: 13). The combination of work with religious training and of architecture with institutional management continued in the emergence of American penitentiaries (see Chapter 3).

CONCLUSION

Looking at the social history of punishment provides clear reference points that improve our understanding of corrections. Taking a historical approach to corrections also provides evidence that the linear direction of history should not be equated with progress. Many advances and reforms in corrections were offset by a return to earlier and more barbaric forms of punishment. An important finding in the historical analysis of punishment is that the formulation and distribution of penalties developed in earlier times were vital components in the structure and maintenance of the social order. Although punishment has been used in the name of protecting society, it also has been viewed as protecting a particular arrangement of society (Michalowski, 1985).

The emergence of the prison as a form of punishment and rehabilitation took place gradually and not without the influence of such social forces as politics, economics, religion, and technology. The evolution of imprisonment can be interpreted in two interrelated ways: incarceration can be civilized as well as civilizing. As imprisonment becomes less brutal and more humane, it becomes more civilized. Furthermore, if imprisonment can achieve the purposes of both rehabilitation and reform, in the final analysis, it can also be regarded as civilizing (Johnson, 1987: Johnston, 2009).

SUMMARY

Within a critical approach to corrections, a history of punishment can be understood according to the overlapping social forces that shaped it: politics, economics, religion, and technology. From that perspective, the chapter explores punishment from the time when formal and legal penalties were established, through ancient Greece, ancient Rome, the Middle Ages, the sixteenth and seventeenth centuries, and the Enlightenment. In early European history, several themes emerged, shedding additional light on the rationale for punishment. Especially in cases involving executions, criminals were viewed as purveyors of evil clearly illustrating the overlap between religion, crime, and punishment. Indeed, the death penalty was a means to ward off evil in the community, particularly when certain *apotropaic* rituals were carried out, such as the breaking of bones, the sacred use of the wheel and the magic circle, burning bodies, drawing and quartering, drowning, beheading, and hanging (Newman, 1978).

Another form of *apotropaic* ritual is found in collective punishments, such as stoning to death. As citizens vent their anger toward the offender, a cleansing effect is believed to occur as they rid the community of evil (Newman, 1978). The chapter also explains how, in light of the prevailing religious forces, the Church and institutional religion continued to shape punishment. Finally, punishment is presented in the context of economics (penal slavery and fines), politics (the class bias and such elitist methods of execution as banishment and poisoning), and technology (various devices for torture and execution).

REVIEW QUESTIONS

1   What were some of the brutal methods of punishment that emerged throughout European history, and what was the rationale for them?
2   What role did institutional religion have in shaping punishment?
3   Explain the emergence of galley slavery and transportation. Which social force contributed most to their use?
4   What does the career of Franz Schmidt reveal about the social status of executioners in sixteenth- and early seventeenth-century Germany?
5   What is the historical relationship between urban poverty and the use of houses of correction?

RECOMMENDED READINGS

Abbott, G. (1991) *Lords of the Scaffold: A History of the Executioner*. New York: St. Martin's Press.

Foucault, M. (1977) *Discipline and Punish: The Birth of the Prison*. New York: Vintage.

Morris, N. and Rothman, D. J. (eds) (1998) *The Oxford History of the Prison: The Practice of Punishment in Western Society*. New York: Oxford University Press.

Newman, G. (1978). *The Punishment Response*. New York: Lippincott.

Rusche, G. and Kirchheimer, O. (1968 [1939]) *Punishment and Social Structure*. New York: Russell & Russell.

Sellin, T. (1976) *Slavery and the Penal System*. New York: Elsevier.

CHAPTER 3

America's Penal Past

Is it surprising that prisons resemble factories, schools, barracks, hospitals which all resemble prisons? (Michel Foucault)

LEARNING OBJECTIVES

After studying this chapter, you should be able to answer the following questions:

1 How was crime conceptualized during colonial America, and what were the common forms of punishment?
2 How was crime reconceptualized during the Jacksonian era, and how did the changed interpretation shape the nature of imprisonment?
3 How were prisons in colonial times different from those in the Jacksonian era?
4 What impact did the reformatory era have on the development of corrections?
5 What is the significance of culture within a critical examination of punishment?

Attracted by the noise of fearful screams in Mr. Ferraby's own yard, he went up, and saw a slave girl stretched out on the ground on her face, her hands and feet tied fast to stakes, her master standing over her, beating her with a leather trace from a harness, every blow of which raised the flesh if it did not gash it, and now and then kicking her in the face with his heavy boots when she screamed too loud. When he had become exhausted by this benevolent exertion, our 'patriarch' sent for sealing-wax and a lighted lamp, and dropped the blazing wax into the gashes; after which, finally, his arm being rested apparently, he switched the whip out again … And the offense of the girl was burning the waffles for her master's breakfast.

(Scott, 1938: 76)

INTRODUCTION

Whereas Chapter 2 explores the social history of punishment in early societies through the Enlightenment, here we expand our understanding of the evolution of penal practices by focusing on America's correctional experience. This chapter discusses in depth the emergence of American punishment in the context of the key social forces: politics, economics, religion, and technology. A distinct advantage of taking a historical approach to US corrections is that one can witness the rise of a new republic alongside its penal practices. The sequence of events begins with colonial America, continuing through the era of the new republic, Jacksonian America, and the reformatory era. Developments in early twentieth-century corrections also are discussed, concluding with some critical observations on the modern use of imprisonment.

COLONIAL AMERICA

As a British colony, America enforced legal codes established by the Duke of York in 1676. An added element of social control during this era was the attempt to enforce strict Puritanical codes. In general, those codes reflected the religious view that criminals were sinners giving in to demonic temptations (see Chapter 4).

Methods of punishment

As did the English, American colonists relied primarily on corporal punishments that not only were harsh, but because of their public display were also humiliating. Capital punishment often included hanging, breaking on the rack, and burning at the stake. Sanctions for minor offenses involved various methods of corporal punishment, such as flogging, branding, and subjecting offenders to the brank, the ducking stool, and the stocks and pillories. For those who were not respected property owners, banishment to the wilderness was common (Newman, 1978).

Flogging

Flogging is one of the oldest forms of corporal punishment. Historically, it has been used to instill discipline within the family, the military, and schools. Slaves and prisoners were commonly subjected to beatings by whips, birch rods, straps, and rubber hoses. Even more excruciating pain could be inflicted by whipping an offender with the cat-o'-nine tails, which featured knots of rawhide attached to a handle. Still more painful was the Russian knout, in which hooks interwoven with the rawhide would tear the flesh on contact (Barnes and Teeters, 1946; see Welch 2009b on torture).

Figure 3.1   An old-fashioned prison.
© iStockphoto.com

Flogging endured for centuries. The last two states to use whippings were Maryland and Delaware. Until 1952, wife-beaters in Maryland were subjected to whippings, and in Delaware, numerous crimes were punishable by flogging. Although the last flogging took place in 1952, the practice was not formally abolished in Delaware until 1972 (Sutherland *et al.*, 1992). Especially in cases involving youths, whipping remains a popular method of discipline. Currently, 27 states permit corporal punishment in schools. Supporters of paddling argue that it is the right of each school district to decide whether to allow corporal punishment, and the US Supreme Court has not interfered with its practice. The case of Michael Fay, who was caned in Singapore in 1994 for vandalism, renewed support for corporal punishment among many Americans because it is believed to promote discipline and serve as a deterrent (see 'Comparative Corrections: Caning of Michael Fay' below).

Branding

Branding is a form of punishment involving intentionally scarring the offender, usually on the hand, cheek, or forehead. In East Jersey between 1668 and 1675, thieves were branded with a *T* on the hand, and an *R* on the forehead for a second offense. In colonial Maryland, those convicted of blasphemy were branded with a *B* on the forehead, and *S.L.* was branded to the cheek of offenders found guilty of seditious libel. Several colonies branded drunkards with a *D*. Although women were rarely branded, they were forced to wear identifying letters on their clothing. The classic example is the scarlet letter *A* worn by an adulteress, which served to publicly degrade the offender (Barnes and Teeters, 1946). Branding is quite painful – serving as both retribution and deterrent. Since branding leaves lasting scars, it also is a type of stigma: that is, a mark of social disgrace. Early prisons tattooed inmates, which not only identified them as convicts but degraded them as well (Wines, 1895). Not to be overlooked is the economic motif in branding, since prisoners were literally registered as property (or wards) of the state – much as livestock are branded to indicate ownership.

The brank

The brank, or the dame's bridle, imported from England, was designed to punish those engaging in community gossip. In colonial America, an individual's reputation was considered his or her social passport to a prosperous life. Any attempt to destroy a person's name was punishable by public humiliation. In colonial times, women, more so than men, were likely to be punished for idle talk. Such punishment was administered by use of the brank – a birdcage-like device fastened to the offender's head. The brank featured an intricate design in which a small gate was closed over the mouth. Additionally, an iron spike was positioned at the person's throat that made speaking or even moving the tongue a painful undertaking. The use of the brank declined in early America, though a similar device was implemented in eighteenth-century Providence schools. Called a 'whisper stick,' that wooden contraption was used to punish students for talking or swearing (Earle, 1792).

The ducking stool

Gossips and village scolds were punished by the ducking stool. The accused was strapped either to a chair or to the end of a wooden plank (similar to a seesaw) and submerged in a river or pond. The purpose of the ducking stool was to create a momentary drowning sensation, and in doing so, to remind the gossip to 'keep your mouth shut.' Like other punishments involving water, the ducking stool also has a religious basis, perhaps even a symbolic cleansing effect. The ducking stool was last used in 1811 in Georgia (Barnes and Teeters, 1946; see Welch, 2009a: Ch. 16 on modern-day waterboarding).

The stocks and pillories

The stocks and pillories were wooden frames in which lawbreakers were forced into compromising postures, either sitting (stocks) or standing (pillories) for public display. Because the structures were commonly placed in the center of town, the culprit was subject to ridicule and humiliation by townspeople who often threw rotten vegetables, eggs, and sometimes stones. In some cases, offenders' ears were nailed to the pillory; upon completing their sentences, they would either have to tear themselves away or lose their ears to the knife. The pillory endured in America until 1905, when it was last used in Delaware.

COMPARATIVE CORRECTIONS

Caning of Michael Fay

The case of Michael Fay, an American teenager sentenced in Singapore to six lashes of a brine-soaked rattan cane for crimes of spray-painting and petty vandalism, reveals more about US attitudes than about Singapore justice. For years, the island-state has been a model of authoritarian rule, where the possession of marijuana can be a capital crime and possession of chewing gum and failure to flush a public toilet are punishable by a heavy fine. There are also obstacles for civil rights and liberties: one-party rule, repression of dissent, curbs on freedoms of the press and assembly, restrictions on labor organizing, detentions without charge or trial, and brutal methods of police interrogation near unto torture. The government bars Amnesty International and other human rights organizations from operating on the island.

In an episode that drew worldwide attention, Michael Fay's parents mounted a campaign for a reprieve to suspend their son's sentence of caning: no mere whipping but a brutally painful punishment administered by a martial-arts master. Such caning often produces trauma and lasting scars. An Ohio Congressman joined the campaign, and President Clinton voiced disapproval of the sentence. But Fay found little support from his fellow Americans, who usually like to think of themselves as humane and compassionate. Mail pouring into the office of Ohio Representative Tony Hall demanded not clemency but the lash. Similarly, the newspaper in Fay's hometown of Dayton reported sentiment running strongly in favor of caning, and polls suggested wide support for the pain option.

'Something seems to have snapped recently in the American political psyche, that screening device that used to suppress the public expression of mean-spirited attitudes' (Nation, 1994: 544). Critics continued to write about the significance of the Fay case. Perhaps their thoughts were always there – the yearning for the death penalty, the hunger for revenge against the 'criminal element,' the anger of insubordination – but they were kept in check in the interests of a more civil society. The example set by successive American administrations in brutalizing mutinous or 'unproductive' peoples abroad and at home cannot have helped create an era of good feeling. Nor can this country offer credible or effective criticism of practices in places such as Singapore, whose economy is intricately connected to American interests and whose regime has been supported since its inception by US policy. 'With old restraints having failed – not only in this country but in what used to be thought of as the civilized world – the fiends are suddenly on the loose, and they mock the meaning of civilization itself' (Nation, 1994: 544).

William Penn and the Great Law

In 1681, William Penn (1644–1718) settled in a colonial land that would bear his name – that is Pennsylvania. In reaction to the pervasive use of harsh and humiliating punishments, Penn set out to reform penal sanctions. In particular, he brought to America a legal code, known as the Great Law, which he had drafted with fellow Quakers in England. Enacted in 1682, the Great Law restricted the death penalty to homicide. It also replaced corporal punishments with imprisonment, hard labor in houses of correction, and fines. Additionally, the Great Law further advanced the secularization of law by eliminating religious crimes. Penn combined humanitarian reform and rehabilitation with existing notions of deterrence. His code included the following recommendations (ACA, 1983):

1 All prisoners were to be eligible for bail.
2 Those wrongfully imprisoned could recover double damages.
3 Prisons were to provide free food and lodgings.
4 The lands and goods of felons were to be liable for double restitution to injured parties.
5 All counties were to provide houses of detention to replace the pillory, stocks, and the like.

The Great Law remained in effect until 1718. The day after Penn's death, the statute was replaced by the English Anglican Code (the sanguinary laws), reinstating the use of harsh penalties, such as execution, mutilation, branding, and other corporal punishments. The Anglican Code also expanded the number of offenses considered capital crimes, including treason, murder, burglary, rape, sodomy, buggery, malicious maiming, manslaughter by stabbing, and arson. Furthermore, witchcraft by conjuration (the practice of magic involving the Devil) was added to the list of capital crimes, suggesting once again that the religious element of crime is a persistent social force (see Chapter 4). Although humanitarian sentiments were temporarily interrupted by the sanguinary laws, the ideals of Penn – along with those of Howard, Bentham, Beccaria, Voltaire, and Montesquieu – would make a lasting impression on American corrections.

Analyzing punishment in colonial America

In his highly acclaimed book *The Discovery of the Asylum: Social Order and Disorder in the New Republic* (1971), David Rothman contends that crime was *not* defined as a critical social problem by colonial Americans. 'They devoted very little energy to devising and enacting programs to reform offenders and had no expectations of eradicating crime. Nor did they systematically attempt to isolate the deviant or the dependent' (Rothman, 1971: 3). Rather, they accepted crime as a part of society. Explaining their disinclination to blame society or to cite a societal breakdown as being responsible for crime was their religious notion equating crime with sin. Therefore the use of harsh corporal and capital punishments persisted as the typical responses to crime. Ironically, deterrence failed to emerge as a primary objective of punishment. 'Their Christian sense of crime as sin, their belief that men were born to corruption, lowered their expectations and made deviant behavior a predictable and inevitable component of society' (Rothman, 1971: 17). Colonists took a simplistic view of the causes of crime and regarded errors by the parents, especially the failure to adequately train their children socially and religiously, as being a primary cause (see Johnston, 2009; Welch, 1996a; Walker, 1998).

Although jails were rather prevalent in colonial America, they were used primarily to detain those awaiting trial or sentencing as well as those unable to pay contracted debts. Most towns either had a separate institution or designated a section within the courthouse building for detention. Such jails served the purpose of facilitating the penal process but were not used as the instrument of punishment itself. Due to that particular orientation to crime, jails were not expected to provide reform or rehabilitation, especially when expulsion (banishment) remained the preferred and most effective method of dealing with recidivism and threats to public safety (Rothman, 1971: 52–3; Morris and Rothman, 1995).

PRISONS IN THE NATION'S EARLY YEARS

Although it would be decades before large-scale prisons were constructed, two institutions stood as notable exceptions among mainstream penal practices, namely the Newgate Prison in Simsbury, Connecticut, and the Walnut Street Jail in Philadelphia.

Newgate Prison, Connecticut: subterranean incarceration and political imprisonment

In 1773 an abandoned copper mine in Simsbury, Connecticut was converted into Newgate Prison, becoming the earliest prison (until 1827). The underground prison served as a makeshift institution resembling the sulfur pits of ancient Rome more than the county jails of its time. The prison consisted of three parallel excavated caverns about 800 feet long and approximately 25 feet below the surface, and one pool of fresh water. The administration buildings were built over the mineshafts (ACA, 1983; Barnes and Teeters, 1946; Durham, 1989).

A year following the prison's inception, prisoners rioted in reaction to the horrific conditions, which included violence, orgies, and severe overcrowding. It was common to have 32 inmates sleep together in a room 21 feet long, 10 feet wide, and less than 7 feet high. Iron fetters were attached to the ankles of prisoners confined to forced labor. Newgate held those convicted of violent offenses as well as non-violent crimes (i.e. burglary, robbery, counterfeiting, forgery, and horse theft). During that period, a first offense could be punishable by ten years, with a life sentence for a second offense. Compounding matters,

Newgate officials did not segregate men, women, children, or the infirm (ACA, 1983).

Newgate has become the subject of further sociohistorical research. Durham (1989, 1990) noted that when Newgate opened, it operated as a colonial prison even though incarceration in the American colonies was an unusual and infrequent method of punishment. As mentioned previously, corporal punishments and fines remained the most popular penalties, in part because they were inexpensive to administer and required little manpower. Consideration of the prevailing forms of punishments popular at that time leads to speculation as to why the colony of Connecticut ambitiously set out to construct a prison.

Durham (1989) identifies several social forces that help answer that question. Before the construction of Newgate, religion dominated the definition of crime. Lawbreakers were viewed as sinners, and therefore cruel corporal punishments were commonplace. However, by the 1770s, a more secular view of criminality emerged in the colonies, and soon incarceration replaced corporal punishments such as execution, disfigurement, and branding. Durham points out that the use of imprisonment was also driven by economic forces as a result of which prisoners were put to work. State officials assumed that the operational costs for Newgate could be offset by copper-mining revenue. Furthermore, those economic imperatives were complemented by promoting discipline and a sense of work ethic that in turn would reduce criminality. In sum: 'The shift in views regarding both the causes of crime and the appropriateness and effectiveness of traditional remedies, the long-standing interest in controlling idleness, and the desire to avoid saddling the colony with unmanageable economic burdens all contributed to the opening of Newgate' (Durham, 1989: 96).

Given the architectural features of Newgate, authorities held confidence in its security; in fact, when it opened, only one guard was assigned to manage the entire facility. However, the view that a subterranean prison was naturally secure proved to be false. There were frequent escapes during the first few years while other security problems were further compounded by the prison's lack of financial success. Even though Newgate failed to produce a profit, economic interests in general did not die easily. Newgate abandoned the practice of mining only to adopt other profit-oriented tasks: coopering (barrel making), shoemaking, wagon-making, stone-cutting, and blacksmithing. Like earlier pursuits, those efforts also failed to be profitable (Durham, 1989).

The establishment of Newgate as a prison should also be viewed in the context of the political forces that shaped its existence. During and briefly following the American Revolution, political fractionization separated the patriots from the loyalists who remained sympathetic to the British Crown. With national independence still in its infancy, loyalists were considered a political threat. Newgate thus became part of a larger social control apparatus used as 'a tool for the suppression of such deviance' (Durham, 1990: 293). Loyalists, who in fact were political prisoners, were confined with common felons and prisoners of war. The Revolution and the postwar period took their toll on Newgate as an institution and it was closed temporarily between 1782 and 1790. In the 1820s, the new state prison in Wethersfield replaced Newgate which had become too expensive to operate.

The Walnut Street Jail: penal reform and the quest for state power

Despite the vast historical record available on Newgate, the Walnut Street Jail in Philadelphia endures as a much more popular institution among penologists and historians. Perhaps one reason for that prevailing view is that Newgate is understood as an institution geared more toward retribution while the Walnut Street Jail is credited with introducing more humanitarian ideals. Nonetheless, before the Walnut Street Jail had become a famous humanitarian project, it too was plagued by horrific conditions. The following passage depicts the Walnut Street Jail at the end of the Revolutionary War:

> It is represented as a scene of promiscuous and unrestricted intercourse and universal riot and debauchery. There was no labor, no separation of those accused, but yet untried, nor even of those confined for debt only, from convicts sentenced for the foulest crimes; not separation of color, age or sex, by day or by night; the prisoners lying promiscuously on the floor, most of them without anything like bed or bedding. As soon as the sexes were replaced in different wings, which was the first reform made in the prison, of thirty or forty women then confined there, all but four or five immediately left it; it having been a common practice, it is said, for women to cause themselves to be arrested for fictitious debts, that they might share in the orgies of the place. Intoxicating liquors abounded, and indeed were freely sold at a bar kept by one of the officers of the prison. Intercourse between the convicts and persons without was hardly restricted. Prisoners tried and acquitted were still detained till they should pay jail fees to the keeper; and the custom of garnish was established and unquestioned: that is, the custom of stripping every newcomer of his outer clothing, to be sold for liquor, unless redeemed by the payment of sum of money to be applied to the same object. It need hardly be added that there was no attempt to give any kind of instruction, and no religious service whatsoever.
>
> (Gray, 1973 [1847]: 15–16)

Pennsylvania Quakers set out to reform those harsh conditions and in 1790 the renovated Walnut Street Jail opened. Unlike the workhouses, the Walnut Street Jail was used exclusively for convicted felons. Its emphasis on discipline, inspired by Dr Benjamin Rush, formed the basis of what would later become the Pennsylvania system (Barnes and Teeters, 1946). Rush, a prominent physician and signer of the Declaration of Independence, advocated the use of individual cells for dangerous prisoners and apartments for others. He believed that gardens in prisons could be the source of both food and exercise. Rush also endorsed the manufacturing of products by prisoners to be sold on the open market, thereby defraying the cost of prison operation (ACA, 1983). In brief, Rush's theory of incarceration involved crime control and societal protection together with prisoner reform. The Walnut Street Jail also was recognized for abolishing the fee system and for providing adequate food, clothing, bedding, and medical attention to prisoners. Additionally, the segregation of men and women inmates was enforced.

The penal system contained in the Walnut Street Jail did not originally feature work because it was believed that prisoners could be reformed better if they refrained from all activities except religious meditation. But as inmates suffered the adverse emotional and psychological consequences of solitary confinement, piecework and handicrafts were introduced, and eventually silent congregate work was established. Silence was enforced because it was believed to reduce 'criminal contamination' among prisoners. Indeed, the entire punishment experience was deliberately monastic – emphasizing work, discipline, obedience, silence, and isolation. 'Imprisonment was meant to involve a complete and austere system of moral quarantine. The prisoner served time in a manner reminiscent of the monk of antiquity, the heretic of the early Middle Ages, the citizen of the medieval plaguetown' (Johnson, 1987: 24–5).

Taking into account key political forces sharpens a critical understanding of the Walnut Street Jail. In the early years of national independence, there were efforts to restructure and centralize the power of the state. Takagi (1980) asserts that those political imperatives were more influential in the development of the Walnut Street Jail than were the humanitarian principles of the penal reformists. Early prison reform is commonly traced to the first prison society, known as the Philadelphia Society for Assisting Distressed Prisoners, founded in 1776. The project was inspired by the work of Richard Wistar, who was a member of the Society of Friends. That organization was believed to be the parent organization of the Philadelphia Society for Alleviating the Miseries of the Public Prisons (also known as the Philadelphia Prison Society and hereafter referred to as the Society), credited for introducing penal reform in the Walnut Street Jail. Takagi (1980) points to some misleading assumptions equating the Society with the Society of Friends: in particular, the view that Quaker ideals were the driving force behind early penal reform. Although the influences of William Penn and the Quakers on penal reform in the 1780s cannot be easily dismissed, it is important to note that when the Walnut Street Jail opened, Episcopalians governed the Society.

Whereas the Quakers were concerned with promoting penal reform, the Society was more interested in the establishment of the Walnut Street Jail as a state prison so that political power would be centralized. In short, centralized state power had economic implications: 'The demand for a strong centralized government was to guarantee the development of a new economic order on the one hand, and on the other, to solve the problem of law and order' (Takagi, 1980: 51). Transforming the Walnut Street Jail from a county jail, not unlike other county jails, to a state prison involved a coherent political vision that would monopolize penal powers. Humanitarian principles were later added to the proposal to persuade recalcitrant legislators. The advantages of being a state prison translated into the power to exact revenue, the power to appoint officials with special privileges, and the right to use force (Takagi, 1980: 54). The Walnut Street Jail eventually experienced typical institutional problems. It soon became overcrowded and by 1816 prison discipline had deteriorated, giving way to violence and riots. In 1835, the Walnut Street Jail was closed, but its contributions to the development of early penal institutions in America and Europe are clearly evident.

Newgate Prison, New York City

Another institution contributing to the development of penal reform was Newgate Prison of New York City, established in 1797 in what is now known as Greenwich Village. It succeeded in establishing prison industries that paid operating expenses for its first five years. The warden, Thomas Eddy, who was born in Philadelphia and influenced by the Society of Friends, turned his attention to adequate diets and daily menu changes, as well as developing the first prison hospital and pharmacy. Warden Eddy also hired the first full-time physician and pharmacist. It is interesting to note that Eddy and his family lived inside the prison so as to serve as positive role models for inmates as well as staff (ACA, 1983). Although Newgate initially was viewed as a progressive institution, eventually it too deteriorated – suffering from overcrowding, idleness, petty graft, and promiscuous pardons (Barnes and Teeters, 1946; McLennan, 2008)

THE JACKSONIAN ERA

Reconceptualizing crime as a social problem

The course of American corrections took a new path in the early 1830s during the administration of President Andrew Jackson, commonly referred to as the Jacksonian era. During that period, crime, poverty, and insanity were drastically reconceptualized as critical social problems. Consequently, penitentiaries, almshouses, and insane asylums quickly emerged as monolithic institutions designed to handle criminals, the impoverished, and the mentally ill.

Institutionalization as the primary means of coping with growing social problems emerged years after the American Revolution. Following the war, the United States struggled with its newborn nationhood. That strain contributed to perceptions and anxieties about social disorder and economic instability. Societal changes, such as a huge population boom leading to dense urban centers and geographic mobility, were coupled with revised intellectual notions about the causes of such social problems as crime, poverty, and mental illness. Those new ideas generated a revision of the methods of social control. As a result, institutions were created to minimize threats to the social order. In contrast to colonial America where institutions were used only as a *last* resort, the practice of incarceration during the Jacksonian era was ambitious, relying on institutions as places of *first* resort (Rothman, 1971). That innovative and radical direction in punishment has had a lasting effect on corrections, even today (see Hirsch, 1992; Staples, 1990; Welch, 1996a).

During the Jacksonian era, fear that crime would endanger the social order prompted Americans to look further into the causes of crime.

Citizens found cause for deep despair and yet incredible optimism. The safety and security of their social order seemed to them in far greater danger than [that of] their fathers, yet they hoped to eradicate crime from the new world. The old structure was crumbling, but perhaps they could draw the blueprints for building a far better one.

(Rothman, 1971: 62)

Soon the background of the convict seemed more relevant to an understanding of crime than the structure of the legal codes. During the 1830s, Jacksonians departed from their colonial past with respect to emerging theories of crimes. In holding a strict individualistic (internal) approach to crime, colonists simply viewed lawbreaking in religious terms. By contrast, Jacksonians looked to more social (external) influences and their effect on individual corruption and criminality. Thus it was posited that crime (and deviance) was symptomatic of a failing social order, and two aspects of social life were under close scrutiny – the family and the community. Since the corrupting forces were believed to exist within society, measures to deal with criminality had to be carefully reconceptualized. Soon there was a movement to reduce the external sources of wrongdoing, such as shutting down taverns and houses of prostitution. However, those measures by themselves were considered insufficient.

> Another alternative then became not only feasible but essential: to construct a special setting for the deviant. Remove him from the family and community and place him in an artificially created and therefore corruption-free environment. Here he could learn all the vital lessons that others had ignored, while protected from the temptations of vice. A model and small-scale society could solve the immediate problem and point the way to broader reform.
>
> (Rothman, 1971: 71)

Jacksonians believed that the purpose of imprisonment was not necessarily to protect society from the offender, but rather to protect the offender from the corrupting forces of society. During the Jacksonian era, further developments in criminological theory were unfolding. The external – or societal – approach to criminology was taking form as a new environmental perspective that stood in sharp contrast to the free-will orientation of the classical criminologists (see Chapter 4).

The Pennsylvania and Auburn systems of prison discipline

The Jacksonians formulated theories of crime and planned their interventions almost simultaneously. Two notable correctional developments during that era were the Pennsylvania and Auburn systems of prison discipline. There, enforcing silence for prisoners was believed to prevent criminal contamination while requiring penitence served to promote religious reform. Although silence and penitence would remain the cornerstones of a new generation of penal practice, the Pennsylvania and Auburn systems pursued key advances in criminological theory by turning attention to external sources of criminality. Penitentiaries during the Jacksonian era, with an emphasis on architecture, internal arrangement, and daily routine, reflected the American interpretation of what a well-ordered society should look like. In more ways than one, the penitentiary itself would also serve as a model for the entire society as the nation moved toward greater social stability (Rothman, 1971; see McLennan, 2008).

The Pennsylvania system: solitude and separate confinement

Emphasis on morality and religion guiding individual reform was evident in the Pennsylvania system. Prisoners were originally subjected to complete isolation without labor. It was widely believed that maximizing the time for repentance would contribute to the efficiency of reform. Western Penitentiary, built in 1826 in Pittsburgh, adopted the principle of total separation of prisoners who were to remain idle for the duration of their sentences. Western Penitentiary, consisting of 190 cells (each approximately 7 feet by 9 feet), was an unsuccessful imitation of Bentham's panopticon (see Chapter 2) (Barnes, 1968 [1927]; Lewis, 1967 [1922]). Among the many institutional problems facing Western was the high cost of maintenance, prompting prison authorities to adopt inmate labor to defray expenses. In 1829, prisoners were assigned work. However, they had to complete those tasks inside their cells that were simply too dark and too small. As an improvement, those cells were replaced by larger ones that benefitted from natural light (Barnes, 1968 [1927]).

With Western Penitentiary as a model, Eastern Penitentiary was constructed in Philadelphia in 1829. Designed by John Haviland, Eastern Penitentiary consisted of seven cell blocks radiating from the hublike center, a rotunda with an observatory tower, and an alarm bell. Although the essence of a 'separate' system was maintained, in that inmates were kept in solitary confinement, each cell (measuring 8 feet by 15 feet) was accessible to a small, individual, uncovered yard where prisoners exercised twice a day (Barnes and Teeters, 1946; Wines, 1895).

The regimen was influenced by Quaker penology. Religious and moral instruction, provided by members of the Prison Society, became an important feature at Eastern. Moreover, because the penitentiary emphasized social isolation, members of the Prison Society were the only visitors allowed. By design, the thick walls of the institution prevented communication between convicts who were blindfolded when being transferred in and out of the prison (Barnes, 1968 [1927]; Lewis, 1967 [1922]).

As was the case in Western Penitentiary, Eastern became burdened by the costs of maintenance, and soon labor was introduced to offset expenses. Prisoners were assigned individual handicrafts such as shoemaking and weaving to be completed inside their cells. Once again religious and economic forces intersected in the form of solitary confinement with forced labor. That regime at Eastern, however, remained largely symbolic since the work of prisoners did not yield profits. Nevertheless tasks of work ritualistically persisted because they appeared to uphold the ideals of reform and punishment (Barnes, 1968 [1927]; Johnston, 2009).

The Auburn system: congregate but silent

Due to the lack of productivity and profit, few institutions were willing to emulate the Pennsylvania system of complete solitary confinement. Forging an alternative to the Pennsylvania system was the New York State Prison at Auburn that implemented a 'congregate but silent' system in 1819. Under the Auburn plan, prisoners worked, ate, and prayed together in silence during the day, and were confined to their solitary cells at night. Auburn also offered a unique contribution to correctional architecture by introducing the tier system, in which the cells (measuring 3½ feet by 7 feet) were situated on different levels of the penitentiary, thereby housing inmates according to offense category (Lewis, 1967 [1922]).

Whereas prison life under the Pennsylvania system was intended to be a monastic experience, the Auburn regime introduced a quasi-military style of inmate management. Routine was reinforced by a strict schedule of activities, and even prisoner movement was regulated by lockstep marching. In addition to enforcing silence, Auburn also relied on uniforms and corporal punishment. Prisoners wore striped uniforms that were used as an early form of classification; different colors distinguished first-time from repeat offenders. Corporal punishment, such as whipping, was used to enforce silence and discipline. Auburn's first keeper, Elam Lynds, was a staunch believer in corporal punishment, viewing all prisoners as cowards who needed their spirit broken before they could be reformed.

As a result of the congregate work regimen, increased productivity became the hallmark of the Auburn system. Soon that regime emerged as the model for numerous other penitentiaries. To witness that innovative correctional experiment, American and European intellectuals visited Auburn: most notably Alexis de Tocqueville and Gustave Auguste de Beaumont (see Beaumont and Tocqueville, 1964 [1833]). In contrast to colonial-style incarceration that was essentially ad hoc and makeshift, Jacksonian institutionalization offered a utopian vision toward solving social problems. The penitentiary was proudly embraced as a unique American enterprise, becoming a fascinating object of international attention (Klein, 1920; Rothman, 1971). The Reverend Louis Dwight, secretary of the Boston Prison Discipline Society, praised the Auburn system:

At Auburn, we have a more beautiful example, still, of what may be done by proper discipline, in a Prison well constructed ... The whole establishment from the gate to the sewer, is a specimen of neatness. The unremitted industry, the entire subordination and subdued feeling of the convicts, has probably no parallel among an equal number of criminals. In their solitary cells they spend the night, with no other book than the Bible, and at sunrise they proceed in military order, under the eye of the turnkeys, in solid columns, with the lock march, to their workplaces; thence, in the same order, at the hour of breakfast, to the common hall, where they partake of their wholesome and frugal meal in silence. Not even a whisper is heard through the whole apartment.

The convicts are seated in single file, at narrow tables, with their backs towards the centre, so that there can be no interchange of signs. If one has more food than he wants, he raises his left hand; and if another has less, he raises his right hand; and the waiter changes it. When they have done eating, at the ringing of a little bell, of the softest sound, they rise from the table, from the solid columns, and return under the eye of their turnkeys to the workshops ... At the close of the day, a little before sunset, the work is all laid aside at once, and the convicts return in military order to the solitary cells; where they partake of the frugal meal, which they are permitted to take from the kitchen, where it is furnished for them, as they returned from the shops. After supper they can, if they choose, read the scriptures undisturbed, and then reflect in silence on the errors of their lives. They must not disturb their fellows by even a whisper ... The men attend to their business from the rising to the setting sun, and spend the night in solitude.

(Dwight, 1826: 36–7; also see Powers, 1826, and Hall, 1829)

Although there was considerable debate between proponents of the Pennsylvania system and those favoring the Auburn system, especially over the issue of how much confinement should be solitary, the lasting contribution to corrections of both systems was evident in their uncritical acceptance of incarceration. During the Jacksonian era, few questioned imprisonment as it emerged as a prevailing solution to crime, deviance, and social disorder (Foucault, 1979; Rothman, 1971).

Elam Lynds: warden of Auburn and Sing Sing

Elam Lynds (1784-1855) became a famed warden during the days of Auburn when the prison was in its early phases of instituting the system of congregate labor by day and separation by night. The regime enforced silence at all times, even prohibiting eye contact among prisoners. Along with his deputy and architect, John Cray, and the encouragement of Gershom Powers of the Board of Inspectors, Lynds further advanced the Auburn system by incorporating lockstep marching but, as mentioned previously, he also inflicted upon prisoners a steady routine of brutality (Barnes and Teeters, 1946: 521; McKelvey, 1977 [1936]).

Lynds served as an officer in the War of 1812 and brought his style of discipline from the military to the prison. He was a fierce disciplinarian and a firm believer in the lash – even the breaking of silence earned inmates a whipping. In a perverse sense of logic, Lynds 'regarded flogging as the most effective and the most humane of all punishments, since it did no injury to the prisoner's health and in no wise impaired his physical strength' (Barnes and Teeters, 1946: 522). Inflicting punishment without reducing the physical strength of the convict was an important consideration for Lynds, who valued prisoners for their labor. Lynds's cruelty had no boundaries: he believed that prisoners deserved floggings – even those who were insane. Relying on a rawhide whip, and at times a cat-o'-nine-tails, Lynds set out to break the spirit of inmates so that they would develop good work habits and embrace a more religious attitude. On one occasion, he is reported to have subjected a stripped inmate to 500 blows (Barnes and Teeters, 1946; Wilson, 1931; Wines, 1895).

In 1835, New York state passed legislation to construct a new prison at Mount Pleasant (Sing Sing) to displace the Newgate Prison in Greenwich Village. Lynds convinced state officials that he could build the new institution by using convict labor from Auburn. Using more than 100 inmates, Lynds supervised them with an iron hand and strictly enforced silence. After three years of cutting and placing stone, a monolithic penitentiary with the capacity to hold more than 500 prisoners was opened (Lawes, 1935). As warden of Sing Sing, Lynds had earned an international reputation for constructing the 'greatest and newest prison in the United States without an enclosing wall, and wholly by the labor of desperate convicts' (Hall, 1829: 113). Soon, state legislators reacted against Lynds's pernicious style of discipline at Sing Sing, and charges were brought against him primarily for his cruelty, despotism, and fierce style of management. Even though many legislators believed the charges were true, Lynds was eventually exonerated (Hall, 1829).

It was suggested that since the state had approved Auburn's harsh discipline, it required the strict authority of Lynds. Moreover, many legislators were reluctant to terminate Lynds because the state was benefiting from inmate labor. During his reign at Sing Sing, Lynds's convict labor produced blocks of stone used for several government buildings, courthouses, and other prisons. The lesson was clear: if managed properly, prisons can be a valuable economic resource (see Chapter 15).

Due in large part to its institutional brutality, the prison at Sing Sing gained enormous notoriety. In response, citizens of the village of Sing Sing in 1906 convinced legislators to change the name of the prison to Ossining on the grounds that the community had been unfairly stigmatized. As a curious note, the name Sing Sing derives from the Indian *ossine ossine*, meaning 'stone upon stone' (Barnes and Teeters, 1946).

The utopian vision and social experiment of the American penitentiary began to crumble by the 1850s. Institutional problems, such as overcrowding, mismanagement, and lack of sufficient funds to maintain prisons, were compounded by the impact of the Civil War and its economic repercussions. Although the penitentiary system enjoyed much optimism during the Jacksonian era, it never adequately achieved its goal of reforming criminals. Prison officials found the rule of silence difficult to enforce, and disciplinary punishments became more brutal and excessive. Eventually, few traces of the rehabilitation philosophy remained, and soon the custodial philosophy dominated the approach to institutionalization. By the 1870s, the American penitentiary had become just another 'warehouse' for convicts and recidivists hopelessly serving long sentences with few prospects for survival in the free world (see McLennan, 2008)

THE REFORMATORY ERA (1870–1910)

The American Prison Congress of 1870

In view of declining conditions in penitentiaries nationwide, a renewed interest in redeveloping the nature of incarceration emerged. In 1870, the reformatory era had been formally initiated at the first American Prison Congress in Cincinnati, Ohio, featuring 130 delegates from 24 states, Canada, and South America. Enoch Wines, chief organizer of the meeting, brought together the world's penal experts to plan the ideal prison system. Among the 'new reformists' in attendance were Gaylord B. Hubbell (warden at Sing Sing), Sir Walton Crofton (creator of the Irish System), Franklin Sanborn (an early advocate of parole), Richard Vaux (a supporter of separate confinement), and Zebulon Brockway (organizer of the Detroit House of Correction and later the administrator of the famous Elmira Reformatory). In approving a proposed 37-paragraph Declaration of Principles, the American Prison Congress delineated its positions on crime and prison reform.

In sum, the spirit of the declarations reflects the aim of re-establishing social harmony and promoting respect for the law. Through the development of a system of rewards for good conduct, the 'prisoner's destiny, during his incarceration should be placed, measurably, in his own hands' (ACA, 1970: 8). The proposals overall were revolutionary and well ahead of their time. Even by today's standards, the members of this assembly exhibited keen insight into the problems affecting corrections. Renewed optimism for penal reform focused on rehabilitating the prisoner; however, that goal would be accomplished by reforming the prison. To replace the failing penitentiary, a new correctional institution was born – the reformatory.

The Elmira Reformatory: correction and coercion

In reaction to the growing pessimism surrounding the penitentiary, participants at the 1870 American Prison Congress applied the ideas and practices of Sir Walter Crofton and Alexander Maconochie in an effort to design an 'ideal prison system.' That renewed vision of the prison quickly began to take form, and in July 1876, in the midst of the American centennial, the Elmira Reformatory (New York) was opened. Zebulon Brockway, a key participant at the Cincinnati conference, served as its first superintendent.

The mission at Elmira was to reform young (16- to 30-year-old) first-time offenders; incidentally, hardened criminals were still being sentenced to state penitentiaries. However, at Elmira remnants of the penitentiary persisted. In structure, the interior cell blocks and congregate workshops were modeled after Auburn. The program emphasized vocational training (e.g. printing, tailoring, and plumbing) and, due in large part to its famed academic instruction, the reformatory earned its nickname of 'the college on the hill.' Classification allowed for greater individualized treatment, and progress through graded stages was contingent upon the inmates' conduct and success in those programs. Ultimately, the young offenders would be reformed, paroled, and returned to the community.

Brockway, a born-again Christian, proclaimed: 'This institution, based upon the indeterminate sentence and the marking system, constitutes an ideal reformatory prison, [exemplifying] the possibility ... of a successful reformative treatment for criminals.' For Brockway, Elmira stood as a 'great industrial and educational establishment,' where the inmate would 'work out his own salvation' (Rothman, 1980: 34-5). The reformatory at Elmira also used contract industries to expand productivity and increase profits, though the institution was not expected to be self-supporting because the administration argued that labor was primarily a form of training (ACA, 1983). Brockway reasoned that inmates should be prepared – socially, morally, academically, and vocationally – for their return to society. In meeting the objectives of such an ambitious program, Elmira stressed religious training and a quasi-military regimen (Smith, 1988).

The quasi-military regimen could be witnessed at the surface of inmate control. Prisoners wore uniforms and marched in lockstep in elaborate displays of military protocol, similar to that of correctional boot camps. Moreover, when prison industries were discontinued in 1888, military drill was further emphasized to offset idleness and reinforce conformity (McKelvey, 1977 [1936]). Discipline and obedience remained important goals at Elmira, often achieved through both a religious and a military regimen. But when those methods of control failed, Brockway and his staff resorted to corporal punishment, a form of brutality previously condemned by Brockway (Pisciotta, 1983). It was reported that approximately 30 percent of the inmates were beaten twice a week by the strap: a 22-inch whip first soaked in water. The Brockway administration also relied on other punishments common in penitentiaries, including solitary confinement and the use of shackles (Rothman, 1980: 36). In sharp contrast to the genuine ideals of rehabilitation, reform was reinforced by instilling a sense of fear in the prisoners.

The Elmira Reformatory remained dedicated to the notion that institutionalization was still the answer to crime and delinquency, and that prisons should remain at the center of the criminal justice system: 'Elmira proved that prisons, if properly designed, could fulfill their original promise' (Rothman, 1980: 35). In defense of incarceration, advocates of the reformatory blamed mismanagement, not the institution itself, for any weakness in the program. 'The ideal of an institution that cured was practical and realizable – if reality fell short, then the problem rested with one or another administrator' (Rothman, 1980: 36).

Like other so-called successful institutions, Elmira became the model reformatory for other state correctional systems. Between 1876 and 1913, 18 states constructed reformatories resembling Elmira. By the turn of the century, many of these reformatories regressed to a more punitive regimen. As a result of inadequate staffing and the reemergence of retribution, the ideals of the reformatory were abandoned. Nevertheless, as is the case with many correctional trends, important innovations (e.g. indeterminate sentences, parole, educational and vocational programs) would eventually reemerge, inspiring further advances in the evolution of corrections (see McLennan, 2008).

Northern versus Southern corrections: different forms of prison labor

A fuller understanding of America's penal past benefits from examining significant regional differences. Between 1870 and 1900, the vast majority of prison construction took place in the North and the Midwest. In the dark aftermath of the Civil War, the South endured long-term economic hardship along with a devastated penitentiary system. Without adequate institutions to hold prisoners (mostly former slaves), as well as the need for convict labor to reconstruct the economy, many Southern prison systems adopted an extensive leasing system. Private contractors paid state governments for the use of inmates, forcing them to work on plantations, levees, and railroad construction.

Leasing systems were similar to the contract arrangements adopted by most Northern prisons. However, under the leasing system in the South, the inmate worked outside the institution. In a sense, the leasing system involved the hiring of the convict himself, whereas the contract system was based solely on the purchase of hourly labor. Inside Northern factory-style prisons, the inmate remained incarcerated while manufacturing such goods as shoes, nails, and other items to be sold on the open market. Despite those differences, prisoners working under either system were harshly treated, and corporal punishment was used routinely to keep them in line.

Critical economic forces and the growing recognition of the value of convict labor led Northern and Southern prisons toward the same goals – productivity and profit – even though the two systems relied on somewhat different forms of inmate labor. Due to the South's reliance on agriculture, the penal farm was born. During the same period in the North, the prison mode of production was modeled after the factory, contributing to the rise of the industrial prison (Barnes and Teeters, 1946; Melossi and Pavarini, 1981; Rusche and Kirchheimer, 1968 [1939]).

Figure 3.2 Ankle shackles: the harsh stark reality of slavery implied by a simple monotone composition of ankle shackles worn by slaves in the early 1800s.

© iStockphoto.com

TWENTIETH-CENTURY CORRECTIONS

The industrial prison: production and profits

By the beginning of the twentieth century, and for decades to follow, the idea of integrating work into the correctional system gradually evolved into industry. As the nation returned to a punitive philosophy during the late 1800s, compounded by an influx of immigrants (who, along with minorities, have traditionally been overly represented in prisons), prison populations soared. But with overcrowding, there was also a surplus of labor that could be useful in manufacturing goods for public, military, and state consumption. Although productivity and profits were central to the industrial prison, such an institution could also claim to offer rehabilitation by featuring job and skill training, promoting discipline, and instilling a work ethic.

Many industrial prisons boasted substantial profits, inspiring other penal systems to design their institutions so as to maximize the use of convict labor. The following business schemes emerged as the dominant prison industrial systems (Barnes and Teeters, 1946):

- *The contract system.* Private businesses established industries within the prison by providing raw materials and contracting the labor of inmates.
- *The leasing system.* Inmates were leased to private businesspeople in the community who remained responsible for transportation to the worksite, supervision, and discipline. Those prisoners were generally leased to work in agriculture, mining, etc.
- *The piece-price system.* Similar to the work regimen in the Walnut Street Jail, private businesses provided raw materials and prisoners manufactured the goods. The institution was paid according to the number of pieces produced.
- *The public account system.* Under that system, the state, not private business, provided the raw materials for goods manufactured by inmates.
- *State use system.* Such goods as furniture, clothing, food, and license plates were manufactured by inmates but distributed only to other state agencies.
- *Public works and ways system.* Under supervision, inmates worked outside the prison by constructing, repairing, and maintaining public roads, highways, buildings, etc. The system dates back to ancient Rome, where prisoners and slaves built public roads and buildings; nowadays, many Southern states still use such a system to defray maintenance costs.

Whereas the industrial prison advanced by selling goods on the open market, its decline was attributed to the resistance of organized labor. Unions lobbied government officials, denouncing industrial prisons for engaging in unfair competition by using convict labor instead of hiring wage-earning workers. Although such criticism had been long-standing, dating back to the 1830s, organized labor soon became a powerful political force and was instrumental in passing state and federal legislation. During the Depression, 33 states passed laws that directly altered prison industries by prohibiting the sale of their products on the open market. At the federal level, the Hawes-Cooper Act of 1929 and the Ashurst-Sumners Act of 1935 placed restrictions on the interstate transportation of prison products. In 1940, an amendment to the Ashurst-Sumners Act fully prohibited the interstate shipment of prison products. Eventually goods from the industrial prisons were completely kept off the open market and functioned only within a closed-market system consisting of government agencies and nonprofit organizations.

In view of those developments, industrial prisons were reduced to small-scale furniture and license plate shops, and soon prisoner inactivity and violence forced prison officials to take a different path toward corrections. What emerged in the 1930s, 1940s, and 1950s was a modern prison, more or less resembling what is seen in corrections today.

The modern prison: progress and problems

When the industrial prison became another casualty in correctional innovation, large penal institutions stood as shells without substance. Maximum-security prisons, known as Big Houses, mirrored penitentiaries of the past more than the prisons of the near future. Offering few programs, Big Houses became 'warehouses' where convicts remained idle and were often brutalized. In the 1930s, however, there was another push to advance penology and modernize corrections (Irwin, 1980; Rothman, 1980). Probation and parole gradually gained recognition as useful correctional innovations, and prisons were transformed into correctional institutions in accordance with the rehabilitative model.

Unlike previous rehabilitative and reform programs, modern prison programs in the 1930s began applying the strict medical concepts contained in positivist criminology. By emulating science, positivist criminologists proposed that experts be employed to diagnose and treat inmates. Advocates of rehabilitation were inspired by the views of the progressives, recommending a case-by-case approach that assumed each criminal possessed a unique set of problems. Responding to technological forces, rehabilitation took a truly medical approach. That medicalization of penology led to the expansion of state-of-the-art prison treatment programs. Therapeutic staff, including psychiatrists, psychologists, and clinical social workers, focused attention on the life history of each prisoner (Foucault, 1979; Rothman, 1980; see Chapter 4).

The emergence of the rehabilitation model should be understood in its proper social context in light of key political and social forces. The increase of federal prisoners during that time can be traced to two legislative events. First, the passing of the Harrison Act in 1914 led to the incarceration of those convicted of narcotic-related offenses. Second, the Volstead Act of 1919 produced large number of criminals involved in illegal alcohol enterprises during Prohibition (Hershberger, 1979). Both forms of legislation contributed to vast networks of organized crime, featuring infamous gangsters such as Al Capone, 'Pretty Boy' Floyd, and 'Machine Gun' Kelly (Keve, 1991; Roberts, 1994). While organized crime figures were not prime targets for rehabilitation, the expanding Federal Bureau of Prisons earned considerable government funding. Up to the

1930s, there were few federal prisons, but growing concern over the increasing federal inmate population prompted the government to begin constructing numerous correctional institutions emphasizing rehabilitation rather than mere punishment. The medical turn in rehabilitation was bolstered by the view that convicts sentenced in the federal system were good candidates for innovative programs because they were generally non-violent and were better educated than state prisoners. Although state prisons operated with limited financial support, they nevertheless attempted to replicate the federal system's advancement of classification and treatment.

By the late 1960s and early 1970s, the rehabilitation model had run its course. For many complicated reasons to be discussed in Chapter 4, rehabilitation became less relevant to the contemporary prison that was grappling with such institutional problems as overcrowding, violence, riots, inadequate funding, and inmate litigation. Indeed, several crosscurrents contributed to the demise of rehabilitation. First, some critics harshly evaluated the rehabilitation model, concluding 'nothing works.' Second, other opponents of the penal apparatus condemned the use of imprisonment, calling for a moratorium on prison construction and the improvement of conditions in existing institutions. Third, there was a demand to reintegrate offenders, drawing on the practical dimensions of community-based corrections. Fourth, conservative politicians lobbied for tough-on-crime and tough-on-prisoners campaigns. Finally, there were proposals for the prison system to adopt a new penal philosophy known as 'humane control.' That is, incarceration would remain at the center of crime control but officials would abandon notions of rehabilitation; still, prison managers would strive to establish a nonthreatening environment while preserving prisoners' constitutional rights.

As we shall continue to explore in greater detail, the modern prison has been subject to dramatic changes. Conservative law-and-order perspectives dominate the correctional landscape; nevertheless, there is growing public support for rehabilitation, especially in the realm of drug control (Chapters 4 and 16). Due in large part to their tremendous growth, prison systems have the daunting task of dealing with an increasingly diverse population, including women (Chapter 6), juveniles (Chapter 7), minorities (Chapter 8), and undocumented immigrants (Chapter 11). Likewise, correctional agencies also have to accommodate those they employ in its prisons, jails, and community-based alternatives (Chapter 13). Such enormous expansion of corrections has also caught the attention of private interests contained in the correctional-industrial complex that view convicts as a source of revenue, raising once again ethical questions over whether inmates should serve as raw materials for producing profits (Chapter 15).

CONCLUSION

Concluding this examination of the history of corrections, both in Europe (see Chapter 2) and in America, is a brief survey of the various critical interpretations of punishment. The review presents the major theoretical perspectives and summarizes their main points and contributions.

CULTURAL PENOLOGY

Alcatraz: The Rock

Alcatraz, an island in San Francisco harbor, remains one of the great symbols of American corrections. Indeed, its presence in the bay cannot go unnoticed; it is recognizable from all angles of the metropolitan area. Even though it has not operated as a prison since the early 1960s, its penological significance persists as a reminder of American law and order.

In 1775, Spanish explorer Juan Manuel de Ayala dubbed the island 'La Isla de los Alcatraces' – the island of the pelicans. In 1853, shortly after California was granted statehood, the United States Army constructed a fort on Alcatraz. Eight years later, the military post was converted into a military prison, holding Confederate sympathizers and Union soldiers for discipline. During the Indian Wars of the 1870s, American Indians were imprisoned at Alcatraz, and at the turn of the century, military prisoners from the Spanish-American War were detained there.

In 1933, the newly created Federal Bureau of Prisons took charge of Alcatraz, transforming the prison into a maximum-security penitentiary. Alcatraz housed America's most notorious criminals and gangsters – Al 'Scarface' Capone, George 'Machine Gun' Kelly, Alvin 'Creepy' Karpis, and Robert 'The Birdman of Alcatraz' Stroud. The inmate population averaged 264, and there was one guard for every five men.

In the summer of 1962, a famous escape from Alcatraz gripped the nation. Frank Lee Morris and brothers John and Clarence Anglin chipped through deteriorated concrete walls in the cells, making their way to the shore, where they boarded homemade flotation devices. The three men have never been heard from again. Federal prison officials believe that the prisoners drowned, though some speculate that Morris and the Anglins safely escaped.

A year later, in 1963, the penitentiary closed because it became increasingly expensive to operate, but the story of Alcatraz continued. In 1969, a group of Native Americans, citing an 1868 treaty, claimed and occupied the island. For the next two years, the group set out to establish a cultural, spiritual, and educational center for Native Americans. Although the immediate goal of establishing a cultural center failed, the group succeeded in bringing attention to the plight of Native Americans. Today, Alcatraz is part of the Golden Gate National Recreation Area administered by the National Park Service. As many as 750,000 tourists visit the historic prison each year (see Brown, 2009; Strange and Kempa, 2003).

Figure 3.3 Aerial view of Alcatraz Prison.

© Comstock Images/Getty

Critical interpretations of the history of corrections

Considerable debate remains over the interpretation of historical analyses of corrections. In properly situating various views on penology, Durham (1989) sorts them into four major explanatory perspectives. Although much overlap exists between the perspectives of Rothman (1971), Foucault (1977), Ignatieff (1978), and the economic-determinist position, each of those historical analyses reaches a different conclusion over the emergence of corrections (see also McLennan, 2008).

Rothman: social disorder and penal discipline

As mentioned in the discussion of the Jacksonian era, Rothman noted that, unlike their colonial forebears, Jacksonians reconceptualized crime, poverty, and insanity as critical social problems. Moreover, those ills were viewed as a growing social disorder that threatened the stability of the new republic. In response, penitentiaries along with almshouses and insane asylums emerged as the frontline solution to society's problems. Among the criticisms of Rothman's perspective is that his analysis neglected the importance of economic variables, such as unemployment and the rise of industrial and financial organizations during this era (Adamson, 1984; Durham, 1989; Welch, 1996a).

Foucault: the extension of state power

In his *Discipline and Punish*, Foucault presents a theory of the birth of the prison, focusing on sovereign power and the emergence of state governance. Under the French monarchy, the king exercised corporal punishment to reinforce his sovereign power over his subjects. However, as the public spectacle of corporal punishment, especially in the form of executions, became viewed as excessively brutal, citizens began to question the legitimacy of the king's power. Soon lawbreakers gained sympathy as public attention turned the problem of tyranny. So as to avert growing discontent aimed at the monarchy, the prison emerged as an attempt to take punishment from public view. In doing so, imprisonment was mystified in the sense that citizens envisioned the horrors taking place behind closed doors.

Those developments marked a major shift in the trajectory of punishment. Whereas corporal pain was directed at the body, imprisonment by way of continuous surveillance was aimed at the mind. Prisoners were therefore viewed as objects rather than subjects. The ultimate goal of penal discipline was to render prisoners docile, obedient, and productive for an emerging state governance and its industrial economy. Upon release, it was assumed that ex-convicts would have internalized the gaze of the authorities, becoming their own self-monitors toward a law-abiding life.

Foucault's work has been subject to varied criticism. Scholars point out several empirical inadequacies while also drawing attention to Foucault's unsystematic and anecdotal review of history (Adamson, 1984; Megill, 1979; Stone, 1983). Others expressed concern over Foucault's difficult conceptualization of power (Dreyfus and Rabinow, 1982; Giddens, 1982; Hoy, 1979). Despite such critiques, *Discipline and Punish* stands as an enduring contribution to the study of prisons and punishment in contemporary society; indeed, that work continues to inspire interesting reworkings of Foucault's original ideas (see Alford, 2000; Garland, 1990; Welch, 2010a, 2009b).

Ignatieff: industrialization and social disorder

A common theme in the works of Ignatieff, Foucault, and Rothman is looking beyond the basic notion that penal reform resulted from humanitarian social movements (Durham, 1989). In Ignatieff's analysis (1978), declining social solidarity and growing social disorder were examined in the light of the Industrial Revolution. By studying the adverse effects of industrialization, Ignatieff focused on unemployment, vagrancy, crime, public disturbances, and urban riots. In that context, the penitentiary played a key role in the transformation of class relations between workers and industrialists through its unique style of isolation, punishment, and correction for members of the lower classes.

Economic determinism and the origins of the prison

In his attempt to neatly classify the explanatory perspectives, Durham places the following penologists into a category known as economic determinism: Adamson

(1984), Melossi and Pavarini (1981), and Rusche and Kirchheimer (1986 [1939]). At the risk of oversimplifying the contributions of each of those penologists, it should be understood that they all place economic cycles at the center of their analyses. Correspondingly, they argue that patterns of punishment (e.g. use of incarceration) remain consistent with particular economic moments. For example, convicted criminals are more likely to be imprisoned during economic cycles when labor is abundantly available than in periods when labor is scarce. In sum, those penologists trace the birth of the prison and its many innovations to the prevailing economic conditions of a particular historical period (also see Hirsch, 1992; Garland, 1990; Staples, 1990).

A discussion of theoretical perspectives can best be summed up by Adamson's acknowledgment that 'no single theory accounts for the complex historical process whereby imprisonment has become the dominant form of punishment in western societies' (1984: 435). Although each interpretative framework cannot escape its own limitations, those explanatory perspectives offer unique contributions to a critical understanding of the historical development of corrections.

SUMMARY

This chapter explores America's penal past by examining the major developments under colonialism, Jacksonianism, the reformatory movement, and the twentieth century. In each of those time frames, considerable attention is paid to the social forces shaping punishment and corrections. During colonial times, for instance, notions of crime were shaped by religious views of lawbreaking, thereby reinforcing a reliance on corporal punishment. Whereas religious attitudes continued to shape the nature of incarceration during the Jacksonian era, the emergence of an environmental theory of crime led to a greater refinement of institutionalization. As prison populations grew, economic imperatives led prison officials to take full advantage of inmate labor, eventually leading to the establishment of the Southern plantation prison and its Northern industrial counterpart. Almost from its inception, imprisonment was intended to be a humane alternative to corporal punishment; still, beatings and mistreatment persisted as a means of instilling discipline. In sum, the early American prison experience has had an enormous impact on present-day corrections. Perhaps the most lasting effect on corrections today is the acceptance of institutionalization as a prevailing response to crime.

REVIEW QUESTIONS

1 Why did colonial Americans rely on corporal punishment more than imprisonment? Which social forces were responsible for such reliance on corporal punishment?
2 Why did institutionalization emerge in early America?
3 How did the Auburn system of confinement differ from the Pennsylvania system?

4 At the American Prison Congress (1870), a declaration of principles was adopted. How do those recommendations apply to corrections today?
5 How did the use of prison labor shape Northern and Southern prisons?
6 Summarize the main points in each of the critical interpretations of the history of corrections (as discussed in the conclusion).

RECOMMENDED READINGS

Garland, D. (1990) *Punishment and Modern Society: A Study in Social Theory.* Chicago: University of Chicago Press.

McLennan, R. (2008) *The Crisis of Imprisonment: Protest, Politics, and the Making of the American Penal State, 1776–1941.* Cambridge: Cambridge University Press.

Rothman, D. J. (1990) *The Discovery of the Asylum: Social Order and Disorder in the New Republic.* Boston: Little, Brown; reprinted in 1990 with a new introduction.

Staples, W. G. (1990) *Castles of Our Consciousness: Social Control and the American State, 1800–1985.* New Brunswick, NJ: Rutgers University Press.

CHAPTER 4

Theoretical penology

Nothing is more useful than a good theory.
(Kurt Lewin)

LEARNING OBJECTIVES

After studying this chapter, you should be able to answer the following questions:

1 What are the primary assumptions of classical criminology?
2 How does classicism influence present-day deterrence research?
3 What are the 'scientific' origins of positivist criminology?
4 What are the main issues in the rehabilitation debate and how does the public generally view correctional treatment today?
5 What are the major assumptions of radicalism and how do they inform a critique of prisons?

The movie *A Clockwork Orange* graphically depicts the fictional case of a juvenile delinquent named Alex. The rebellious teen boasts a violent criminal history, including assault, robbery, and rape. Upon his conviction for murder, Alex is sentenced to a correctional facility where he is selected for a bizarre rehabilitation experiment. He is medicated then forced to view violent films, leaving him nauseated even at the thought of aggression. Following the experiment, Alex is believed to have been 'cured' of his violent propensities. Critics, however, charge that the medical model succeeded in rehabilitating Alex at the expense of suppressing his free will. Indeed, the prison chaplain is outraged, arguing that Alex avoids violence simply because it makes him physically ill, not because he chooses to be law-abiding.

INTRODUCTION

Among the most pressing questions about criminal justice are the purposes and goals of corrections, for example why are certain offenders incarcerated while others are not? Are prisons primarily intended to punish, deter, or rehabilitate? If none of those aims can be achieved, then would society be better served by locking up offenders, thereby preventing them from committing other crimes?

As straightforward as those questions seem, they rarely draw simple answers. A case in point: how should the criminal justice system deal with Slacker Sam – a 22-year-old unemployed alcoholic and heroin addict with a seventh-grade education who has been convicted of burglarizing a video store for the second time? Should his incarceration serve as punishment and deterrence? Should rehabilitation become the focus of his sentence (e.g. alcohol and drug treatment, remedial education, vocational training)? Should he be punished as well as rehabilitated? Or, perhaps along with rehabilitation, should the state develop

Figure 4.1 French philosopher Michel Foucault.

© STF/AFP/Getty Images.

strategies that would reduce the number of future Slacker Sams? That is, should fundamental social changes be instituted, including broad economic reform geared at reducing inequality? This chapter explores those vexing questions by consulting three major frameworks for theoretical penology, namely classicism, positivism, and radicalism. Rather than pursue the easy answers, herein we attempt to examine in depth the complexities of crime, punishment, and society.

CLASSICISM: BEYOND RELIGION, TOWARD REASON

Historically, the road to classicism was paved by a desire to go beyond religious conceptions of criminality that framed crime as a product of evil. That ancient understanding of lawbreaking advocated corporal punishment so as to 'beat the devil out' of the criminal – literally and figuratively. In medieval times, most notably during the Inquisition, the Catholic Church embarked further on a brutal campaign to use torture as a means of securing confessions to heresy and other religious violations. Similarly, European monarchies relied on torture and execution to maintain their authority over their subjects. By contrast, the Enlightenment period (or Age of Reason), beginning in the mid-eighteenth century, stood as a challenge to the excesses of religious and royal power by promoting secularism and democratic values in the processing of criminal defendants.

The turn to a more humane system of justice was also driven by sociolegal theorists interested in understanding why certain persons resorted to crime. Rather than being compelled to commit crime by demonic forces, Enlightenment thinkers proposed that lawbreakers were acting on their own rational choice, or free will. Those 'metaphysics of crime' would eventually eclipse the age-old religious views of wrongdoing, leading to a more principled framework for criminal justice, sentencing, and punishment. Two of early classicism's most prominent figures were Cesare Beccaria and Jeremy Bentham: as we shall see, both of them advocated improvements for criminal justice drawn from their pioneering theoretical work (see Newburn, 2007).

Beccaria and deterrence

The insights of Italian scholar Cesare Beccaria (1738–94) continue to influence contemporary criminologists due to their capacity to incorporate deep philosophical as well as practical orientations to criminal justice reform. His *Essay on Crimes and Punishments* published in 1764 harshly condemned the use of torture, the death penalty, and other arbitrary penalties. Initially the essay was released anonymously because Beccaria feared persecution from state (and Church) authorities; it was banned in some nations but quickly gained an international reputation upon being translated into English and French, earning high praise from Voltaire, the great Enlightenment thinker. Today the work stands as one of the most significant commentaries on criminal justice in Western civilization (Wolfgang, 1996).

As a mathematician and economist, Beccaria forged new ways of understanding crime that would lead to formulating a more effective response to lawbreaking. At the core of his criminological theory is free will from which individuals enter crime through their own rational choice. To deter such transgressions, Beccaria proposed that sufficient penalties be registered so as to discourage criminal actions. His deterrence theory called for preventing crime by way of three basic tenets: certainty, swiftness, and severity. Under ideal circumstances, crime can be curbed by imposing a certain and swift penalty but only severe enough to act as a deterrent. In lieu of corporal punishment and execution, Beccaria advocated prison sentences drawn according to lengths of time, depending on the seriousness of the offense. The individualization of sentencing became a mark of a progressive and modern form of distributing justice that would urge the courts to exercise judicial restraint.

> The end of punishment, therefore, is no other than to prevent the criminal from doing further injury to society, and to prevent others from committing the like offense. Such punishments, therefore, and such a mode of inflicting them, ought to make the strongest and most lasting impression in the mind of others, with the least torment to the body of the criminal.
>
> (Beccaria, 1981[1764]: 43)

In addition to his contributions to an emerging theory of deterrence, Beccaria offered recommendations for the processing of criminal defendants. By doing so, he stated that law is to be clearly written so as to identify which acts are prohibited along with their precise sanctions. The law should restrict the individual as little as possible and guarantee the rights of the accused at all phases of criminal justice. Penalties should be proportionate to the crime committed and without prejudice. Finally, Beccaria issued an enduring proposal for jurisprudence and criminological theory: 'It is better to prevent crimes than to punish them' (1981 [1764]: 93; see Cullen and Agnew, 2006; Vold *et al.*, 2002). In the next passage, we see how Beccaria's pursuit of deterrence theory influenced the next major figure in classical thought, namely Jeremy Bentham.

Bentham and a theory of fictions

British philosopher Jeremy Bentham (1748–1832) gravitated to the ideas of Enlightenment thinkers in producing his own book *The Principles of Morals and Legislation* in 1781. Much like Beccaria, Bentham embraced notions of free will, but in developing a framework for deterrence, he delved into utilitarianism: a school of social thought that understood humans to be motivated by their own self-interest. From there, he introduced the pleasure-pain principle from which individuals are assumed to rationally plan their behavior by calculating the amount of expected gain subtracted by the degree of pain. Obviously, the pleasure-pain principle – or hedonistic calculus – lends itself to criminology since it proposes that an increase in penalties can deter the decision to commit crime (see Geis, 1960).

Bentham's commitment to an emerging social psychology of crime control via the pleasure-pain principle is demonstrated further in his theory of fictions whereby nonexistent entities have the capacity to influence behavior. Bentham's theory of fictions expands on his conceptualization of the panopticon insofar as a circular prison design enhances the power of the guard stationed in the central inspection tower (see Foucault, 1977, Ch. 2). Recall that convicts in the panopticon are rarely certain whether they themselves are the objects of observation; consequently, they err on the safe side by internalizing the gaze, thereby becoming their own monitor. Although Bentham advocated the use of imprisonment – most notably in the panopticon – he had misgivings about the infliction of suffering and opted in favor of instilling fear in lieu of physical pain. Indeed, it is through a theory of fictions that Bentham recommended penalties that bark louder than they bite, promoting a sense of deterrence not only for the individual lawbreaker but for others as well. A theory of fictions was intended to set an example by way of a spectacle for all to witness and learn of the grave consequences of engaging in crime (Bentham, 1995; Ogden, 1932).

> Wherein exactly does this dimension of spectacle in punishment lie? What is it that is staged in punishment? Bentham's main concern here is in achieving the greatest apparent suffering with the least real suffering, that is, achieving the greatest effect of the punishment on others with the least inflicted pain.
>
> (Bozovic, 1995: 5)

Bentham was inspired by the dramatic impact that live theatre has on its audience. Curiously, he proposed that committees charged with formulating penal law enlist a manager of a theatre who would know how to attain the greatest effect from the staging of punishment. Bentham's reluctance to inflict corporal pain coupled with a theory of fictions surfaces again in what might be called a 'house of horrors' that feigns punishment.

> For example, a building could be constructed resembling the panopticon from the outside; occasional screams, not of prisoners, but of people hired specifically for that purpose, could be heard from within. While the others would think that the offenders were being punished for their deeds, in truth, nobody at all would really be suffering punishment. A 'good of the second order' could then be produced without requiring any 'evil of the first order.'
>
> (Bozovic, 1995a: 7)

Critics of Bentham's theory of fictions argue that the use of illusion in creating feigned punishment is counter-productive since it fosters disrespect for truth. The most effective way to deter crime, according to Harrison (1985), is to use real penalties. Apart from such criticism, Benthamite theory persists in the contemporary support for deterrence strategies that also favors restraint in criminal sentencing. Indeed, many jurisdictions retain severe punishments on the books that are rarely assigned to individual offenders: it is believed that such harsh penalties remain part of the penal code so as to send a message to others (e.g. the death penalty; see Chapter 10).

Deterrence research and the econometric approach

The classical thinkers who dominated criminological thought for a century were later surpassed in popularity by the positivists in the late 1800s (to be discussed later). Then, in the late 1960s, there was a return to the original tenets of the classical school, most notably those pertaining to deterrence. Empirical methods (research based on precise observation and measurement) were employed to examine the effects that punishment might have on reducing crime rates. Because the original pleasure-pain principle proposed the rational and calculative nature of individuals, it is not surprising that economists also joined the study of deterrence.

Traditionally, economists have studied processes of economic decision-making, such as the purchasing of goods (cars, clothing, etc.) by attending to costs, expenses, risks, benefits, and gains. Similarly, economists applied the notion of calculation, formulating a theory of how offenders decide to engage in property crimes such as theft (Becker, 1968; Sullivan, 1973). In brief, it is hypothesized that offenders are likely to commit theft when the gains, rewards, or benefits outweigh the costs or expenses (e.g. the risks of being detected, apprehended, convicted, and punished). From a utilitarian standpoint, crime such as theft offers criminals a source for financial benefit as well as personal satisfaction and enhanced self-esteem derived from 'beating the system.'

The econometric approach added empirical weight to the contemporary version of classical thought and deterrence theory. Moreover, econometrics bolstered the conservative ideology of corrections, asserting the state has the rightful authority to deter criminal behavior by imposing a high cost for committing crime. In turn, penalties would be publicly announced with the purpose of instilling a fear of punishment among persons contemplating similar crimes.

Whereas early classical theorists advocated restraint on the part of prosecutors, judges, and the courts, conservative commentators currently misrepresent the work of Beccaria and Bentham by arguing that the criminal justice system is weak and consequently soft on criminals. Contradicting the principles espoused by classicism, many contemporary tough-on-crime policies attempt to strip criminal defendants of their constitutional right to due process. Overriding those concerns, conservative crime-control initiatives have gained popularity due in part to the appeal of econometric analyses of crime, rational choice, and deterrence (Akers, 1990; Cornish and Clarke, 2006; Farrington and Langan, 1992). Critics, however, argue that drops in crime rates have not been the result of deterrence but rather demographic trends (e.g. declining numbers of young people) (Steffensmeier and Harer, 1991).

Although deterrence research is intuitively appealing, detractors insist that its assumptions involve more ideology than theory. Walker (2001) refers to tough-on-crime proposals based on deterrence research as a crime-control theology, asserting that deterrence is widely accepted as an article of faith rather than being supported by empirical facts. Walker further contends that deterrence strategies remain popular among political conservatives because it stems from the deeply held belief that certain forms of punishment can discourage certain types of crime. Likewise, Gibbs (1975) suggests that deterrence exists more as a doctrine than a theory because it has become so policy-driven that any self-correcting feedback from its research has been ignored. Moreover, instead of generating additional research, deterrence enthusiasts rely on vague assumptions dating back to Beccaria and Bentham.

Deterrence models fail to account for the fact that offenders commit crimes for diverse reasons. Clearly, many of the motives for property crimes serve to alleviate the hardship of poverty while other offenses such as vandalism, graffiti, auto theft, and shoplifting are driven by emotional thrill, excitement, and adventure. Moreover, violent crimes (e.g. serious assaults and homicide) are impulsive rather than rationally planned (Katz, 1988). Therefore, deterrence strategies are less effective in discouraging those crimes that are not rationally calculated (see Newburn, 2007).

Similarly, research on the use of prisons contained in tough-on-crime campaigns also demonstrates that incarceration fails to deter repeat offenses. In their 2002 report, Langan and Levin of the Bureau of Justice Statistics revealed that 67 percent of prisoners released from state prisons in 1994 committed at least one serious new offense within three years, a 5 percent increase over those released in 1983. Many criminologists acknowledge that putting large numbers of offenders behind bars might reduce crime due to an overall incapacitation effect. However, there is greater debate over whether longer sentences produce a deterrent effect for those released from prison. 'The new report, some experts say, suggests that the answer is no' (Butterfield, 2002b: A11). According to Professor Joan Petersilia, 'The main thing this report shows is that our experiment with building lots more prisons as a deterrent to crime has not worked' (Butterfield, 2002b: A11). Petersilia also adds that a likely reason for the increase in recidivism is that governments, in an effort to reduce costs and appear tough on crime, have slashed rehabilitation programs such as drug treatment, vocational education, and classes to prepare convicts for life in the free world. Jeremy Travis, former director of the National Institute of Justice, agrees: 'Often inmates are released having received very little or no job training, drug treatment or education in how to be a better parent. Many are unable to find jobs and are barred by law from living in public housing projects so they quickly return to crime' (Butterfield, 2002b: A11; see also Lewin, 2001). The conversation on contemporary classicism and deterrence is far from over. Many critics of deterrence theory concede that they might be persuaded by studies that convincingly demonstrate a deterrent effect; still, further research is very much needed (see Nagin, 1998).

Social consensus and social conflict

Contemporary classicism also enjoys popularity among mainstream citizens. Indeed, its widespread support appears to reflect a growing consensus over imprisonment (Pratt, 2007). Such penal populism stems in part from the popular belief that the use of prisons serves to protects all citizens from crime. Conservative commentators aptly point out that crime tears apart society in numerous ways: deaths, physical injuries, financial losses, property damage, fear, and social disorganization. Perhaps paradoxically, it is argued by some sociologists that crime also brings society together (Durkheim, 1958 [1895]; Erikson, 1966; Greenberg, 1999). Community bonds, for instance, are formed as local residents share a common moral outrage against crime, thereby reinforcing notions of good versus bad. In the end, law-abiding citizens are reassured of their moral forthrightness, which in turn clarifies the boundaries between right and wrong. Consensus theory is embraced by some politicians seeking to exploit popular fears and anxieties over crime. Consider the rhetoric of those who describe criminals as super-predators, often pointing to certain murderers as examples of the embodiment of evil, such as Ted Bundy, Jeffrey Dahmer, John Wayne Gacy, Henry Lee Lucas, Charles Manson, and 'Son of Sam' (Bennett and DiIulio, 1996; Glassner, 1999).

It is important to clarify, however, that it is actually punishment more than crime that serves as a unifying force. Indeed, punishments have the potential to be activated under unusual circumstances when crime is absent and those who are targeted are innocent. The aforementioned serial killers notwithstanding, key incidents in American history reveal that many campaigns to root out evil and punish wrongdoers were driven by a collective hysteria – or moral panic. Consider for example, the witch-hunts in Salem, Massachusetts, McCarthyism in the 1950s, and the search for terrorists following the attacks of September 11, 2001. Despite evidence that such punitive campaigns simply fail to protect society, the process of scapegoating unpopular people still delivers psychic relief for those seeking emotional security (Cohen, 1972; Goode and Ben-Yehuda, 1994; Welch, 1996a, 1996b).

Sociologically, consensus theory points to common values that are presumed to exist in society. Although high degrees of solidarity are sometimes found in smaller societies, consensus declines as populations grow and become more complex. To be clear, social groups in a complex society are more often in conflict rather than in harmony. Recognizing such discord, conflict theorists argue that society is rarely united by common values; instead, people are divided by political and economic struggles over power and scarce resources (e.g. jobs, education, health care, and housing). Whereas consensus theorists assume that legal codes are written by the majority to protect the majority, conflict theorists insist that law is an instrument of control used by the powerful at the expense of the powerless (Chambliss, 1999; Quinney, 1980; Turk, 1979, 1976; Vold, 1958; see the section below on radicalism).

American historians have shown that laws against vice are the product of politically powerful groups that have succeeded in legislating personal moral beliefs. Prohibition stands as a classic example of how the elite influences legislation and crime control. In his classic examination of the campaign to ban alcohol, Gusfield (1963) revealed that a small but very powerful segment of society (i.e. rural and Protestant) was responsible for the passing of the Volstead Act, thereby forcing all citizens to abandon their legal right to consume alcohol. Today victimless crimes such as drug use, prostitution, and homosexual acts (as well as heterosexual sodomy between married couples) reflect that notion of power-oriented legislation (Lesieur and Welch, 2000). Moreover, the enforcement of such laws – especially drug control – is disproportionately aimed at the poor and minorities, thereby producing a prison population that is marked by huge socioeconomic and racial disparities. When returning to those matters in the section on radicalism below, we shall discuss further how conflict criminologists challenge the lopsided distribution of power that distorts the administration of justice.

CULTURAL PENOLOGY

Ted Bundy as Folk Devil

The case of serial murderer Ted Bundy – a modern-day folk devil – illuminates the strong emotional reaction that many people have toward violent offenders. Bundy, who died in the electric chair in 1989, began his killing spree in 1973. Before it was over in 1978, he may have killed as many as 50 young women in Utah, Washington, Idaho, Colorado, and Florida. Under his handsome and debonair exterior, Bundy was believed to hide evil and dangerousness – as is the case of many folk devils.

An illustration of the unifying forces present at Bundy's execution were the 200 people gathered outside the fence at the penitentiary several hours before it was to take place. The mood of the crowd was far from somber. Rather, the gathering took form as a tailgate party – featuring coolers full of beer, sandwiches, snacks, fireworks, and sparklers. The enthusiasts had come to the edge of the penitentiary to celebrate their idea of justice, waving signs displaying macabre humor. Several banners proudly proclaimed enthusiasm for Bundy's execution – 'Thank God It's Fryday,' 'Roast in Peace,' 'This Buzz Is for You,' 'Burn Bundy Burn.' Even older spectators joined in a morbid song (to the tune of 'On Top of Old Smoky') dedicated to the execution of Bundy:

He bludgeoned the poor girls,
All over the head.
Now we're all ecstatic
Ted Bundy is dead.

Quickly, jokes about Bundy's execution spread coast to coast: 'Do you know what Ted Bundy's last meal was?' 'Toast and a little bit of juice.' Certainly, the crowd at Bundy's execution shared many of the same characteristics of the festive public executions during the Middle Ages.

(*Sources: Newsweek*, 1989: 66; *Time*, 1989: 24.)

Just deserts: a return to retribution

The history of American corrections reads like a long list of ineffective policies and initiatives proposed by 'tough-on-crime' conservatives as well as by progressive liberals. Flaws have been found to such strategies as deterrence, incapacitation, and rehabilitation (to be discussed in the next main section). Regardless of the causes for failed interventions, politicians as well as the public in the 1970s soon began to conclude that little could be done to control crime. Within that context, many policy-makers advocated a return to the age-old practice of retribution by simply giving offenders their just deserts.

As the nation gravitated toward the political right during the 1980s, even traditional liberals became more conservative, especially with respect to criminal justice and the use of imprisonment, further paving the way for the just-deserts model. A key advocate for the resurgence of retribution was David Fogel (1979), who like Beccaria proposed fair and proportionate punishment for offenders. Moreover, incarceration should be humane rather than excessively harsh, even upholding prisoners' legal rights. Since retribution is the objective of the just-deserts model, the strategy is to establish uniformity among sentences by clarifying exactly which penalty is assigned to each corresponding crime.

A major limitation of the just-deserts model is that it does not attempt to reduce criminality; rather, it seems to offer only a pay-as-you-go type of sanction. Therefore as a modification it has been suggested that just-deserts be combined with other strategies, such as deterrence and rehabilitation (von Hirsch, 1976, 1993). Nonetheless, with an emphasis on retribution the just-deserts perspective remains vulnerable to repressive and punitive penal practices that undermine the actual delivery of justice. From a theoretical standpoint, other critics contend that the assumptions surrounding retribution tend to disregard societal conditions that contribute to crime while over-rationalizing criminal acts (see Hudson, 2003). As discussed in the following section, those concerns lend themselves to a more general critique of classicism.

A critique of classicism

Furthering a critique of contemporary classicism, we turn to two other areas of concern, namely its model of inquiry and its set of policies. Continuing the tradition of Beccaria and Bentham, classicism today also focuses on the notion of free will as the source of crime. In doing so, classicism takes a narrow approach by deliberately ignoring external sources of crime, such as poverty, racial discrimination, and so forth. What critics find demeaning about contemporary classicism coupled with tough-on-crime initiatives is its ridicule of criminologists who actually do study adverse societal conditions as they relate to crime. Curiously, longtime FBI director J. Edgar Hoover referred to academic researchers who concentrate on the external sources of crime as 'cream puff criminologists.'

In his popular book *Thinking About Crime* (1975), Wilson takes the stance that searching for root causes of crime is a wasteful activity that only interferes with government action. Such an approach to classicism departs from the traditional ideals of Beccaria and Bentham because it is essentially atheoretical, anti-intellectual, and counterproductive since it leads to deeply flawed crime-control policies. Elliott Currie, a chief critic of contemporary classicism, summarizes the prevailing approach to crime-control: 'Crime is caused by inadequate "control," … we have a great deal of crime because we have insufficient curbs on the appetites or impulses that naturally impel individuals toward criminal activity' (1985: 23). Although such a statement is not altogether false, Currie goes on to comment that the formulation of policy on the basis of sweeping generalization is simply unhelpful. What Wilson and many other conservative commentators lack is a well-articulated theory of crime to be integrated with sound policy and practice.

Expanding his critique, Currie (1998) points out that the United States for several decades has continued to lead the world in incarceration. Contrary to conservative rhetoric, American society is not soft on crime and does not hesitate to punish, especially by imprisonment. Currie reminds us that 'it is possible to be sentenced to a year behind bars for stealing six dollars' worth of meat from a supermarket, but we are still the most dangerous society in the developed world' (1985: 12). The crucial question remains: 'Are Americans any better off because of conservative criminal justice policies?' Most Americans do not feel safer today – in fact, fear is increasing faster than crime itself. Moreover, in view of the enormous criminal justice expenditures, the question persists: 'Are such costs worth it?' Government spending on criminal justice is given greater scrutiny during hard economic times. As a result, many citizens are frustrated that government spends less on education, health care, unemployment benefits, and housing because legislators allocate increasingly greater sums of money to criminal justice.

Indeed, amid budget crunching in the wake of the recent recession, it is becoming more difficult for lawmakers to justify spending between $35,000 and $50,000 per year to incarcerate a non-violent first-time offender. According to Currie, it is painfully apparent that the prevailing approach to crime control has failed to live up to its promises. Conservatives are now left with the annoying question of why such an enormous investment in punishment has produced so little impact on crime. Still, popular anger and frustration over crime continue to be exploited by politicians who in turn produce more sanctions for crime (Pratt, 2007; Welch, 2005a).

Certainly there is a need for an effective criminal justice system. However, over the past few decades, the formal response to crime has remained largely one-dimensional: locking up lawbreakers. Not only has the prison warehousing strategy proved to be vastly expensive, but it has also forced politicians onto a correctional treadmill that cannot keep pace with the increasing volume of offenders sentenced to prison. Critics of tough-on-crime initiatives challenge the claim that crime can be reduced by tossing record numbers of felons into prison. What is needed are more innovative and sensible approaches to crime control that address the social problems of poverty, unemployment, and substance abuse, along with a more pervasive level of inequality (Jacobson, 2005: Lynch, 2007; Useem and Piehl, 2008).

POSITIVISM: BEYOND REASON, TOWARD SCIENCE

As noted earlier, the classical school of criminology emerged as a reaction to social thought dominated by the Church. In turn, positivism stood as a challenge to classicism and the metaphysics of crime that dwelled on notions of free will and deterrence. Still, much like their classicist counterparts, positivists were very much influenced by the Enlightenment because it promoted a secular view of the world; for them, perhaps the most significant development was the use of scientific methods in exploring social phenomena, especially crime. As we shall see in this section, a key difference distinguishing classicism from positivism is the basic model of inquiry. Whereas classicism locates the cause of crime in the free will of the lawbreaker, positivism examines various other factors contributing to criminal behavior (e.g. mental illness or adverse societal conditions). In support of their respective approaches toward analysis, classicists tend to rely on reason whereas positivists remain committed to science.

Lombroso and criminal anthropology

In reaction to the philosophical orientation of the classical school, a new generation of criminologists in Europe became increasingly frustrated by the lack of scientific inquiry into the various causes of crime. Compounding matters, an emerging notion concerning crime asserted that criminal behavior is determined less by free will and more by personal characteristics (e.g. biological and psychological defects) as they interact with adverse social conditions (e.g. dysfunctional family, poverty).

While natural scientists were making profound discoveries in astronomy, physics, chemistry, biology, and physiology, criminologists were setting out to make equally important findings about the causes of crime. In their attempt to emulate the 'hard' scientists, criminologists adopted similar methods of investigation. Most notable were the scientific procedures involving objective observations alongside mathematical and statistical analyses. The application of those tools in the search for the causes of crime became known as positivism: 'an approach to science driven by the careful collection of facts' (Gibson and Rafter, 2006: 407; see Becker and Wetzell, 2007).

Positivist criminology involves the scientific study not merely of crime but more specifically that of criminals themselves. That emerging field became known as criminal anthropology. Leading that intellectual current was Cesare

Figure 4.2 Head in a jar: a couple viewing the head of Italian criminologist Cesare Lombroso (1835–1909) preserved in a jar of formalin, at an exhibition in Bologna, 1978.

Photo by Romano Cagnoni/Hulton Archive/Getty Images.

Lombroso (1835–1909), popularly anointed as the father of the positivist school. Lombroso was an Italian psychiatrist and professor of legal medicine at the University of Turin. In 1876, he published his major work, *Criminal Man* (see 2006), which among many things proposed that some criminals were not as highly evolved as normal persons. Lombroso, who viewed 'born criminals' as biological throwbacks, was greatly influenced by the natural sciences, especially Darwin's writings on evolution.

Keeping his focus on the body of the criminal, Lombroso initially explored basic physical traits that were assumed to be determinants of criminality. His expanding typology reflected a biological framework that went beyond 'born criminals' who resembled primitive peoples, animals, and even plants, to encompass 'insane criminals' (ranging from imbeciles to the demented), and 'criminaloids' (who did not possess outward pathological characteristics, but still engaged in criminal behavior). In the decades to follow, Lombroso became regarded as a controversial figure as contemporary criminologists embraced more progressive sensibilities toward women and people of color. More recently, however, Lombroso's work has been given another round of reflection, as Mary Gibson and Nicole Hahn Rafter write in their newly translated edition of *Criminal Man*:

> We began our project with disdain for what we understood as the simplemindedness of Lombroso's theory of atavism [a throwback to an earlier evolutionary stage in which humans were more savage] and with a fear his biological determinism was prejudicial to women, blacks, and other social groups that he deemed inferior. Many of his conclusions seemed silly, and his project a particularly frightful example of bad science. But our views

have changed, based on our careful reading of his criminological oeuvre, our investigation of his place in Italian history, and our research on the evolution of criminology in other countries. Lombroso now appears to have been a curious, engaged, and energetic polymath for natural science, medicine, psychiatry, and law. That he was careless and often wrong about the conclusions that he drew from the disparate data provided by these fields does not detract from the significance of his enterprise.

(Gibson and Rafter, 2006: 1–2)

By the end of his career, Lombroso had reached beyond a biological framework, synthesizing various social factors that also explained criminal behavior (e.g. sex and marriage customs, criminal laws, the structure of government) (Lombroso, 2006a; see Barnes and Teeters, 1946; Vold *et al.*, 1998). Those shifts in Lombroso's research brought him closer to other positivists who had previously studied the social statistics of crime. For example, Adolph Quetelet (1796–1874) tracked French crime rates using a multivariate method identifying age, sex, and climatic conditions (showing that annual crime rates remained relatively constant), and A. M. Guerry (1802–66), who examined social variables in his investigation of comparative crime rates in different locales. While the macro level of positivism remains a signficant area of social research, Lombrosian criminology continues to be known for its micro analysis of the criminal body. Still, as we shall discuss next, Lombroso's disciples – Enrico Ferri and Raffaele Garofalo – were keen to link the criminal body to the political body of society.

Ferri and Garofalo: positivism, politics and penal power

Enrico Ferri (1856–1928) emerged as one of Lombroso's most famous students. In the tradition of positivism, his work accomplished two tasks. First, Ferri forcefully debated the concept of free will, emphasizing the position that human behavior was determined by external factors (e.g. social, political, and economic forces). Second, he used state-of-the-art quantitative analysis to advance comparative studies of French and Italian crime rates.

In addition to his productive academic life, Ferri was greatly involved in politics and was an active socialist writer. Soon after Mussolini and his fascist supporters gained power in Italy, Ferri's life as a researcher and as a political activist merged. Ferri discovered parallels between his research and the political beliefs of fascism, in particular the role of a strong central government that dogmatically determines what types of people commit crime and how the state should intervene (Jenkins, 1982; Sellin, 1973).

Critics point out that a scientific-based school of criminology, such as positivism, is vulnerable to exploitation by totalitarian regimes (see Jenkins, 1982; Lynch *et al.*, 2000). For instance, under fascism, political leaders often gain legitimacy from scientists who offer recommendations for the control of unpopular and threatening populations, especially criminals. Mindful that 'knowledge is power,' fascists drew additional support from positivists due to their capacity to present scientific and technological insights into the causes of social threat. Consider for instance, the Holocaust in which the Nazis (German fascists) targeted those who did not fit the Aryan, white-supremacist model (e.g. Jews, Catholics, communists, socialists, homosexuals). Consequently, extermination programs (also known as the 'final solution,' the 'evacuation' and 'special treatment') of Jews and other unpopular groups were meticulously planned and carried out by the Nazis with the assistance of members of the scientific and medical communities (Cohen, 1985; Lifton, 1988; Plant, 1986).

Raffaele Garofalo, another pioneer in scientific criminology, also forged positivism with fascist politics. As author, magistrate, and positivist theorist, Garofalo also boasted influences from Darwin, expounding on notions of adaptation as well as the elimination of those who do not fit into society. His proposed methods of elimination included death, partial elimination (long-term or life imprisonment), and enforced reparation (Garofalo, 1914). Given the scientific prestige of Darwinian terms such as adaptation and elimination, Garofalo's proposals for criminal justice fitted neatly into Mussolini's fascist plan of social control (Vold and Bernard, 1986). The positivist approach to criminology extends state power to those who claim expertise in defining and identifying criminals, especially those deemed dangerous. Indeed, Lombroso (2006a) and many positivists to follow advocated criminal anthropology as a form of 'social defense' whereby the state could guard itself against certain persons who intend to harm society (see Becker and Wetzell, 2007; Rodriguez, 2006; Salvatore, 2007). As we shall see in the following sections, the 'social defense' thesis persists in other contemporary proposals for the use of corrections, namely incapacitation.

Incapacitation and selective incapacitation

Contemporary crime-control proposals stemming from positivism also include strategies known as incapacitation and more narrowly selective incapacitation. Incapacitation is based on the principle of crime prevention since offenders are physically prevented from committing crimes while incarcerated – or incapacitated – thereby protecting society. The term gross incapacitation has been used to describe the strategy of mass incarceration: that is, locking up large volumes of lawbreakers. However, since prison space is both expensive and relatively scarce, a more refined approach to incapacitation requires a careful selection of those offenders who are likely to commit future crimes. That procedure, known as selective incapacitation, focuses primarily on a group of hardened offenders (or career criminals) who have a lengthy history of crime. Due to selective incapacitation's reliance on multivariate methods of analysis, it is more positivistic than gross incapacitation because it strives toward a scientifically informed method of prediction.

Advocates of selective incapacitation assert that a majority of street crime (e.g. robbery, burglary, theft, assault) is committed by a small proportion of the offender population. In terms of policy, selective incapacitation proposes that a substantial percentage of crime can be reduced if high-rate offenders are imprisoned. At the same time, that policy advises the criminal justice system to use valuable prison space more wisely. 'Getting more bang for their buck' has recently become a pragmatic slogan for criminal justice officials, especially since the expensive prison-building bonanza of the past few decades has had little to do with drops in crime (see Lynch, 2007; Useem and Piehl, 2008). In response to problems created by mass incarceration, selective incapacitation claims to reduce crime without increasing the prison population. That goal is achieved by locking up the most active career criminals for longer periods of time.

Although an early study boasted that selective incapacitation could reduce crime by 80 percent (Shinnar and Shinnar, 1975), later research, such as Peter Greenwood's (1982) project, offered more modest reductions in crime. In his study, Greenwood proposed that robbery could be reduced by 20 percent without increasing the prison population. By creating an index consisting of seven characteristics, Greenwood assigned offenders a score that would identify them as being low-rate, medium-rate, or high-rate offenders. Understandably, high-rate offenders would be given longer sentences than those in the low-rate or medium-rate groups.

As promising as selective incapacitation seemed, it was confounded by several problems. First, Greenwood's study implicitly assumes that the length of criminal career is longer than the sentence imposed. In fact, the career of a criminal is relatively short (lasting five to ten years). Therefore a portion of the longer sentence would not contribute to the reduction of crime because the offender would have already ended his or her career. A second problem is that Greenwood based his analysis on the crime for which the offender was convicted. This strategy assumes that criminals are specialists, but research indicates that most criminals are generalists who engage in a variety of offenses (Visher, 2000; Walker, 2001).

Other issues further complicate the viability of selective incapacitation as an ethical mechanism of crime control: namely, fairness, offender characteristics, and accuracy of predictions. Critics charge that by attempting to predict future conduct, selective incapacitation unfairly imposes longer sentences on some offenders and shorter sentences on other offenders for precisely the same crime. This sentencing procedure appears unjust because some offenders are being punished for crimes they have not committed, or may never commit, thus violating the principle of equal or comparable punishment. However, selective incapacitation proponents argue that a judge is always presented with a range from which a sentence can be imposed, and one of the criteria for formulating a sentence is the judge's intuitive prediction of future crimes. Moreover, predicting dangerousness has traditionally been a function of paroling authorities (Visher, 2000).

Another problematic issue involves offender characteristics, such as the offender's past history – in particular, juvenile delinquency. Critics point out that including juvenile delinquency records as a criterion prejudices the prediction formula. In fact, many states prohibit the use of juvenile records against adult defendants to prevent the prosecution from prejudicing the accused. A similar issue is Greenwood's uses of unemployment as a prediction criterion, which critics argue discriminates on the basis of social class. Moreover, since social class overlaps considerably with racial and ethnic groups, the use of unemployment also fosters discrimination against African Americans and Hispanics (Visher, 2000; Welch, 2005a).

The attention that Greenwood pays to unemployment does shed additional light on the importance that economic forces have on crime, as well as imprisonment. Selective incapacitation theorists convincingly demonstrate that unemployment is a major factor in the overall pattern of crime. Critics argue, however, that rather than penalizing the offender for not having a job, it might make more sense to prevent crime by expanding employment opportunities (see Lynch, 2007; Lynch *et al.*, 2000). (That ambitious proposal and the relationship between crime and employment are discussed later in the section on radicalism.)

Ethical considerations also affect the accuracy of predictions. The fact is that all prediction-based programs are fallible; the range of errors includes both false positives and false negatives. The term *false positive* refers those offenders who are predicted to commit future crimes, but do not; as a result, the prison holds offenders believed to be high-rate but who are actually low-rate. Conversely, the term *false negative* refers to those offenders who are predicted not to commit crime but do. The problem in that case is that the court assigns a shorter sentence to offenders believed to be low-rate when actually they are high-rate offenders. Undermining the goal of selective incapacitation, after serving shorter sentences, these high-rate offenders return to the community – perhaps resuming their criminal career. Both types of errors undermine the intended purposes of selective incapacitation (Auerhahn, 1999; Zimring and Hawkins, 1995).

Selective incapacitation and prediction-based strategies, however, remain biased insofar as they focus exclusively on street crime rather than political and corporate offenses. Since white-collar offenders also inflict harm on society in terms of physical injuries and financial costs, policies such as selective incapacitation divert attention away from other serious lawbreakers (Michalowski and Kramer, 2006b).

Rehabilitation, treatment, and the medical model

Although penitentiaries during the Jacksonian era failed miserably to reform offenders, prison supporters in the reformatory era renewed the optimism of rehabilitation in the 1870s. In addition to the many structural alterations that prisons underwent were changes in prison programs. Soon prison officials once again embraced the ideals of rehabilitation by offering educational and vocational training. At Elmira Reformatory, for instance, classification was used to guide individualized treatment (see Chapter 3).

During the reformatory era, rehabilitation was not viewed in explicit medical terms. By the turn of the century, however, medical technology was rapidly improving, and it did not take long for corrections officials to take note of medical breakthroughs. In an effort to rehabilitate offenders, officials incorporated advances in medicine into correctional treatment. Taking a genuine medical approach to corrections, prison officials began reorganizing programs and introducing therapeutic staff: psychiatrists, psychologists, and clinical social workers. Obviously, the role of the therapeutic staff was to facilitate the process of rehabilitation by transforming the offender into a pro-social and law-abiding citizen. The newly created Federal Bureau of Prisons furthered efforts to integrate the medical model into corrections in the 1930s. Also during that period, classification became more refined and the medical model provided a state-of-the-art clinical orientation by developing diagnostic and treatment methods (Bosworth, 2010).

For decades now, the terms treatment and rehabilitation have been used to refer to a variety of programs which range from educational and vocational training to individual therapy and substance-abuse counseling. According to the National Academy of Science, rehabilitation is defined as 'any planned intervention that reduces an offender's further criminal activity' (Sechrest et al., 1979). In that sense, the focus of rehabilitation remains on the psychological causes of crime, excluding deterrence strategies. Although the terms treatment and rehabilitation may have slightly different meanings within the positivist tradition, in this section they are used interchangeably.

Medicalization of crime and deviance

The emergence of the medical model has provided authorities with another source of technology aimed at dealing with such social problems as crime and deviance. Whereas the moral model suggests that crime and deviance are caused by the person's immorality or 'weak will,' the medical model asserts that such behavior is linked to biological, physiological, or psychological defects. That particular approach to crime often encompasses the medicalization of deviance – the use of medical terms and concepts to provide alternative definitions of crime (Conrad and Schneider, 1992). Among the advantages of the medical model over the criminalization approach is that it promotes tolerance and compassion for such problems as drug and alcohol addictions (Lesieur and Welch, 2000). From that standpoint, a drug addict or alcoholic is viewed less as 'weak-willed' and more as suffering from a disease, thereby paving the way for medical intervention that promises to treat rather than punish. 'Medical controls are, by their very nature, more flexible and efficient than judicial controls because they can be easily adjusted to the needs of the individual patient and can be applied without formal proceedings' (Lesieur and Welch, 1995: 205).

The darker side of the medical approach, however, ought not be overlooked since the medicalization process also promotes labeling from badness to sickness, thereby obscuring issues of individual responsibility. Although it is assumed that the medical model is more humane than the criminal justice model, the medical approach may lead to treatment that might be harsher than conventional punishment, such as psychosurgery, electroshock therapy, surgical and chemical castration, as well as implanted birth control (e.g. Norplant, a contraceptive device surgically inserted into female offenders). The medicalization approach to rehabilitating offenders, undoubtedly, involves numerous ethical concerns. Critics of rehabilitation in corrections point to extreme and unusual cases to argue that when treatment goes unchecked, the medical model might go awry. Under such circumstances, the offender is not rehabilitated but, perhaps worse, is harmed or injured (Welch, 2005a).

The fusion of the medical model into corrections has also produced other unusual consequences. Consider the case of Alvin Ford, who was convicted of killing a Florida policeman then sentenced to death. While on death row, Ford began exhibiting extreme symptoms of paranoid schizophrenia. Due to concerns over the execution of an emotionally disturbed prisoner, Ford was removed from death row and placed in a psychiatric unit. A distressing question continued to follow the authorities: Was Ford undergoing treatment so that he might regain his mental health only to be returned to death row? The answer appeared to be yes. Eventually, Ford was transferred to death row after a federal district judge ruled that the prisoner had regained his sanity. Ford's attorneys appealed the judge's decision and were waiting for a ruling when Ford died of natural causes. In the Ford case, the medical model provided an avenue for rehabilitation that was not intended to return the offender to the community but simply to facilitate the process of capital punishment (Miller and Radelet, 1993; Paternoster, 1991).

An equally unusual incident was reported by lawyer Alvin Bronstein of the American Civil Liberties Union's (ACLU's) National Prison Project:

> One of his clients required triple-bypass heart surgery but refused treatment. Officials allegedly urged the prisoner to undergo surgery so he could be alive for his execution, at one point asking Bronstein to argue their case with his reluctant client. Bronstein declined. The prisoner subsequently died of a heart attack.
>
> (Johnson, 1998: 49)

The purpose of introducing these highly unusual cases is to illustrate the technological forces inherent in the medical model when such interventions are extended to the criminal justice system. Although such cases are atypical and infrequent, they offer an opportunity to rethink and re-evaluate some basic ethical and philosophical questions regarding unusual methods of science, medicine, and treatment (Welch, 1999a).

Sex offenders: questionable treatment, castration, and punishment

The medical model in corrections continues to draw criticism for its general lack of effectiveness in treating sex offenders. As a result, recent legislation requires that communities be notified when a paroled sex offender moves into their neighborhoods. Critics of those laws in Washington State and in New Jersey (where the law became known as Megan's law) argue that enforcement is problematic. Moreover, there are concerns that such laws impinge on the civil rights of the parolee and that community notification might incite vigilante violence (see Moore, 2009a).

In New Jersey, Megan's law, which was passed in 1994, was proposed after Jesse Timmendequas was convicted of strangling and raping Megan Kanka, a 7-year-old who lived across the street. The murder stirred up controversy concerning the state correctional system's program for treating sex offenders. Civil suits have been filed against state corrections officials for providing inadequate therapy for the 700 prisoners at the Adult Diagnostic and Treatment Center in Avenel, the state's prison for sex offenders (Mansnerus, 2002). Chairman of the psychological review board at Avenel, Dr Nathaniel Pallone – who was also professor of psychology and criminal justice at Rutgers University – reported that 'Megan's death illustrates that unrehabilitated sex offenders are routinely being released into communities with no mandatory therapy or supervision' (Bonapace, 1994: 13). Pallone adds that most sex offenders can be rehabilitated but not cured, and a small percentage will never respond to treatment. In view of this assertion, Pallone argues that post-prison supervision and counseling are more effective than notification laws. Similar issues have been raised in proposals to castrate convicted rapists. Steven Allen Butler pleaded guilty to the repeated rape of a 13-year-old girl. Butler suggested that he would rather undergo surgical castration than serve a 35-year sentence. The judge, who initially approved the sentence, later reversed his decision allowing Butler to avoid prison by choosing surgery instead.

With such a policy, the central question remains: Should sex offenders be allowed to opt for surgery to avoid a prison sentence? Those advocating such a proposal are generally misled about the biological underpinnings of rape. Castration lowers the level of testosterone, which theoretically reduces, but does not eliminate, the person's sex drive. More importantly, since rape is motivated by anger, such proposals appear to be self-defeating for two reasons. First, whereas castration is understood to biochemically lower a male's level of aggression, it still does not address the role of anger in the commission of those crimes. In some cases, castration may actually fuel the aggression of the rapist. Second, introducing surgery in lieu of incarceration keeps rapists in the community, thereby jeopardizing public safety. The lesson to be learned here is to remain skeptical of strategies designed to locate solely the biological causes of violence while neglecting deeper psychological problems (see Meisenkothen, 1999; Wilson, 2002).

The rehabilitation debate

The debate over rehabilitation generally occurs on two fronts. First, there is discussion over theoretical issues – most importantly, the assumptions and propositions behind rehabilitation. Second, there remains considerable controversy over program-oriented matters surrounding the ways in which rehabilitation is designed, implemented, and evaluated.

Theoretical issues

Correctional experts who support rehabilitation programs operate on two basic assumptions. First, the offender's behavior is related to a particular personal defect stemming from one's psychological makeup or from an adverse environment, or a combination of both. Second, the offender can actually be transformed into a pro-social, law-abiding person. Rehabilitation programs have been critiqued from an array of perspectives, including those challenging the very assumptions upon which treatment is based. Classicists are skeptical of the notion that an offender's criminality stems from adverse social conditions or psychological defects (or a combination of both). Moreover, they question sweeping generalizations about poverty being a cause of crime since the majority of impoverished people are actually law-abiding citizens (Wilson, 1975).

Critics also attack another assumption that proposes that the offender can be transformed into a pro-social and law-abiding person, raising further questions about the effectiveness of the medical model. Consider that prisoners in many ways resemble involuntary patients in psychiatric facilities who are incarcerated against their will; moreover, conventional wisdom suggests that forcing a convict to become pro-social is problematic. An old riddle among clinical psychologists illuminates the issue: 'How many therapists does it take to change a light bulb?' 'One – but the light bulb must be willing to change.'

Even in cases where the offender is willing and able to be rehabilitated, questions remain about the long-term effectiveness of such treatment. Such questions are especially valid as we acknowledge that ex-offenders (e.g. convicted drug peddlers with histories of addiction) eventually return to the community. Typically, those inner-city neighborhoods are characterized by high unemployment, high rates of street crime and violence, and high concentrations of illegal drug activity. Critics argue that the enduring effectiveness of rehabilitation is strained unless comparable changes are also made within the community, such as genuine economic opportunities (Currie, 1998; Reiman, 2001; Walker, 2001). Even so, from a basic logistical standpoint, it is certainly easier to try to correct offenders than it is to improve societal conditions.

'What works?' vs. 'nothing works'

Since the 1960s, critics of correctional rehabilitation have turned to a body of research that reveals the limitations of treatment programs. The evaluation study that delivered the hardest blow to rehabilitation was authored by Lipton *et al.* (1975). In a widely cited spin-off article, Martinson (1974: 25) concluded: 'With few and isolated exceptions, the rehabilitative efforts that have been reported so far have had no appreciable effect on rehabilitation' (1974). Martinson entitled his article 'What Works? Questions and Answers About Prison Reform' but it quickly became known as the 'Nothing-Works' report.

Contrary to popular opinion, Lipton *et al.* (1975) did not make the sweeping claim that 'nothing works.' In fact, they cited positive outcomes in 48 percent of the programs evaluated. In the early 1970s, there had been growing disillusionment surrounding rehabilitation, and for several years policy-makers were 'waiting for the other shoe to drop.' The publication of Martinson's article was that 'other shoe,' and the fact that it became known as the nothing-works report was testimony that the chapter on liberal-oriented rehabilitation was officially coming to a close. Just as retributionists criticized rehabilitation within prisons, many progressive reformers also voiced their dissatisfaction with correctional programs. Among other things, they pointed to the criminal justice system as the problem since the heavy criminalization approach to such problems as drug addiction made matters worse, insisting therefore that the effectiveness of rehabilitation was irrelevant. Moreover, radical commentators also launched resounding attacks, proposing that rehabilitation strategies – especially court-imposed treatment – constitute another form of social control by a specialized class of experts who assume the authority to determine the fate of those caught in the criminal justice machine (see Foucault, 1977; Lynch *et al.*, 2000; Welch, 2005).

> Seen in this light, rehabilitation was not merely a laudable goal that scientific research had failed thus far to achieve, but something more insidious – an ideology that explained crime in highly individualistic terms and legitimated the expansion of administrative powers used in practice to discriminate against disadvantaged groups and to achieve covert organizational goals (such as alleviating court backlogs and repressing political opposition).
>
> (Greenberg and Humphries, 1980: 369)

Without entirely dismissing warnings contained in the social control thesis, rehabilitation advocates point out that the demise of such programs was brought about by a political turn toward retribution aimed at undermining a progressive agenda. Cullen and Gendreau write: 'The rejection of rehabilitation has less to do with a careful reading of empirical literature and more to do with changes in the social fabric that triggered a corresponding shift in thinking about corrections' (1989: 24).

A principal method of measuring the effectiveness of rehabilitation programs was to examine the program evaluation reports. If assessment specialists found that the program was not effective, their conclusion was often uncritically accepted without further investigation. As advocates of rehabilitation programs aptly demonstrate, in many cases, the evaluation research, not the program itself, was flawed. Indeed, buried deep in Martinson's (1974) article was his exposure of the regrettable fact that many researchers had failed to follow rigorous scientific procedures while evaluating these programs. A closer look at the evaluation research of correctional rehabilitation could result in any one of three possible outcomes: (1) the possibility that the program is indeed ineffective; (2) the possibility that the program as designed is effective, but the manner by which it is administered is faulty (e.g. unqualified or incompetent staff); (3) the possibility that the evaluation methods are so flawed that they cannot accurately determine whether the problem is located in an ineffective program or ineffective administration. Should that be the case, two types of errors might occur: either concluding that the program is effective when it is not, or concluding that the program is ineffective when it is not.

In the years leading up to the 'nothing-works' controversy, social scientists focused on the research of previously published evaluation studies. Overall, most of the evaluation studies re-examined suffered from shoddy methodology, thereby raising questions about the findings and conclusions over correctional programs (see Logan, 1972; Wright and Dixon, 1977). Perhaps even more relevant to the debate are the merits of rehabilitation revealed in other evaluation studies, in particular those that provide substantial support for the effectiveness of correctional treatment (Cullen and Gendreau, 2000; Cullen *et al.*, 2001; Cullen and Applegate, 1997; Gendreau *et al.*, 1996).

Eventually, even Martinson (1979) recanted some of his earlier conclusions. Moreover, his conversion was based largely on the realization that traditional research designs were too rigid to measure accurately the effectiveness of rehabilitation programs. Martinson later wrote that some programs were indeed beneficial and some treatment programs did have an appreciable effect on recidivism. 'It is ironic, but instructive, that whereas Martinson's 1974 nothing works article is among the most cited of criminological writings, his revisionist 1979 essay earned scant attention' (Cullen and Gendreau, 1989: 26). Once again, it is helpful to view these developments in the context of important social changes unfolding in the 1970s. The United States was struggling to reassemble a strong central government after the turbulent 1960s, and one strategy of achieving that political goal was to mount a visible tough-on-crime campaign. The tough-on-crime ideology asserted that those who favored rehabilitation were 'bleeding heart' liberals who were 'soft' on crime (Simon, 2007).

The implications of that ideological shift are evident. Evaluation reports shape public opinion as well as public policy, and the two often go hand in hand. Therefore, in view of what transpired in the wake of the Martinson report (1974), the argument could be made that rehabilitation was unintentionally sabotaged by evaluation researchers (including many academics) who relied on poor or faulty methodological procedures. In addition to issues surrounding weak evaluation, proponents insist that rehabilitation programs were further sabotaged (intentionally or unintentionally) because they were never fully implemented, lacking the long-term commitment crucial for a successful overhaul of the system. Again, those developments occurred in a shifting political context favoring retribution over rehabilitation.

A case in point is the famous critique presented by retributionist Ernest van den Haag who begged the question: 'What is the likely effect of rehabilitation on the crime rate?' In answering his own question, van den Haag relied on a set of principles and equations borrowed from econometric deterrent theorists to support his contention that, 'since rehabilitation can affect criminals only after their first conviction, even total rehabilitation could reduce neither the rate of first offenses nor the overall crime rate to the extent to which it depends on first offenses' (1982: 1023). Although van den Haag recommended that the criminal justice system assert its emphasis on punishment to deter future crimes, his criticism of rehabilitation does lend itself to some valuable insight. That is, with respect to first-time offenders, he notes that rehabilitation comes too late. To a certain extent, many criminologists agree with him. But the answer does not rest in deterrence and the increased use of punishments. Perhaps a more effective approach is to prevent such crimes by improving societal conditions (e.g. improving employment opportunities) and responding to the offender's personal problems (e.g. substance dependency and substandard education).

COMPARATIVE CORRECTIONS

Retribution, Rehabilitation and the Saudi War on Drugs

In Chapter 2, it was mentioned that in Saudi Arabia, under Sharia (the Islamic legal code), drug offenses are punishable by execution. Beheadings have been administered in public squares and journalists have published the grim details. In 2000, 35 convicted drug traffickers were executed, in most cases after swift, secret trials absent of attorneys and juries. Still, amid the ancient forms of retribution, there is a small but growing awareness that drug, alcohol, and nicotine dependence ought to be treated as an illness, especially since the majority of the general population (65 percent) is under the age of 25. With bans on movie theaters, concert halls, and discos, there are few venues for entertainment. Experts are worried that young people are turning to drugs and alcohol for escape, especially considering the nation's affluence coupled with large numbers of unemployed youth (Sciolino, 2002).

In a nation of 21 million, there are only four drug treatment centers, offering group therapy, physical therapy (including massages), and more high-tech interventions such as biofeedback. Despite the modern approach to drug treatment, traditional reform persists in the form of religious observances. During detoxification, each patient is kept in a private room with a prayer rug and copy of the Koran. In adherence to Muslim customs prayer is observed five times a day. Al Amal, the name of which means hope, is a facility that serves more than 200 male Saudis. There are no drug treatment centers for women because the prevailing perception is that women do not suffer from drug and alcohol dependency. Critics, however, contend that women do struggle with addiction, especially those confined to the home and who may self-medicate to cope with depression (Sciolino, 2002).

It is important to stress that rehabilitation for drug and alcohol abuse is not the norm in Saudi Arabia; indeed, retribution is the dominant response. Correspondingly, patients undergoing treatment do so behind a thick wall of family secrecy because drug dependency is tremendously stigmatizing. For those unfortunate enough not to have access to treatment, there remain opportunities to feed one's addiction. Much like the United States and other nations, drug peddlers can be found on the streets of impoverished neighborhoods. Qarantina, a slum in Jiddah, has a reputation for poverty and drug use. Decades ago, that ghetto was named Qarantina because it was an area where pilgrims with contagious diseases were quarantined before being allowing to travel on the annual hajj to Mecca. Places like Qarantina make it difficult for ex-addicts to stay clean. According to one recovering addict, 'It's not that drugs are that prevalent in Saudi Arabia, but if you know where to look for them, you can find anything you want' (Sciolino, 2002: A2; see Chapter 16 on the war on drugs).

Paradox of programs: net-widening, labeling and beyond

As rehabilitation forged into new correctional territories, some of its own advocates expressed concerns that the emergence of more programs was unwittingly causing more problems. The paradox that more programs lead to more problems is especially evident in non-violent drug offenses and juvenile delinquency since the more interventions available to the courts, the greater the likelihood an arrested person would be pulled into the orbit of the criminal justice system. That net-widening effect is witnessed in the growing numbers of persons placed under correctional supervision, particularly in cases that do not merit formal intervention. The creation of additional intervention strategies perpetuates several ongoing problems. First, increased processing jams an already overloaded system with more cases. Moreover, formally processing persons for minor offenses imposes an undue strain on the system's scarce resources (court dockets, space in correctional facilities, probation officers, etc.) (Lynch, 2007; Useem and Piehl, 2008).

A second problem relates to those persons – namely, youths – who are processed further into the system. Most of them will likely experience a level of degradation that will deeply affect their personal identity, self-concept, and self-esteem. That humiliating process is commonly known as labeling whereby stigmatized persons are viewed and treated as being 'different' by those considered 'normal.' Especially in cases involving teenagers still struggling to establish their own identity, the labeling ceremony can be so potent that the accused eventually internalizes the stigma, proceeding toward a self-fulfilling prophecy that enhances one's chances of failure. Labeling also tends to be targeted disproportionately at minorities and those of lower income who do not have the resources to defend themselves against well-financed arrest campaigns. Developments such as these add to legitimate concerns of institutional racism and classism (see Becker, 1963; Goffman, 1963; Schur, 1971).

Finally, the paradox of correctional programs extends to the practical limitations of patching up offenders who have gone astray without seriously examining the underlying social and economic problems that greatly affect people of color and the poor (Currie, 1998). Many progressive-minded criminologists worry that the genuinely humane foundation for rehabilitation is ignored when programs merely set out to equip offenders with better coping and survival skills and then dump them back into their troubled environment. Even early positivists, especially

Lombroso (2006a), expressed reservations about the long-term effectiveness of individual-based treatments unless they were coupled with sustained social and economic reforms (see Gibson, 2007; Salvatore, 2007).

With respect to strategies of rehabilitation and reform, it has been more expedient for the government to target individuals than confront unjust social conditions. Lessons from early American history appear to confirm that approach to penology. Rothman (1990) reminds us that in the 1820s, Jacksonians resorted to building large-scale prison systems in part because their efforts to reform society had failed (i.e. closing brothels and taverns). As we shall discuss in the next section, understanding the continued correctional treadmill of building more prisons and locking up more lawbreakers for longer stretches of time prompts us to consider broader social and economic issues. By doing so, it is still important not to lose sight of individuals who are likely to benefit from the various programs designed to address such problems as poor education, addictions, etc.

RADICALISM: BEYOND THE INDIVIDUAL, TOWARD SOCIETY

As discussed previously, both classicism and positivism are subject to significant criticism – albeit for different concerns over the individual within society. In proposing that offenders freely and willfully engage in crime, classicism is faulted for neglecting the social context of lawbreaking. While positivism tends to take into account environmental factors as they affect criminal behavior, there are limitations for rehabilitation, particularly if that simply means providing the disadvantaged with the necessary skills to survive under adverse societal conditions. By focusing solely on fixing the individual so as to adapt to a harsh environment plagued with poverty, high unemployment, violence, and substance abuse, positivism, much like classicism, fails to grasp the socioeconomic forces driving street crime.

As an alternative perspective on crime, criminal justice, and corrections, radicalism sets out to understand in greater depth the social context whereby the individual is situated. By advocating sweeping social reforms that simultaneously reduce crime and promote social justice, the radical approach places less emphasis on the individual offender than does classicism and turns greater attention to society than does positivism. Radical criminologists view the prevailing pattern of lawbreaking – and punishment – as stemming from structured inequality, especially along lines of political, economic, and racial disparities in American society. While not opposing correctional programs that provide substance abuse treatment along with educational and vocational training, radicals insist that any long-term effectiveness depends on broad social reforms that alleviate poverty and other social problems that disproportionately affect residents in low-income communities (e.g. substance abuse, drug peddling, and related forms of violence).

Origins of radical criminology

Radical criminology – known also as critical criminology – has its origin in the social and economic writings of Karl Marx (1906, 1976). Among the central themes of his work, Marx examined capitalism and the complex relations between two basic classes of people, namely the workers (proletariat) and the capitalists (bourgeoisie) who employ them. Due to the dynamics of capitalism that determine the unequal class structure, a great proportion of industrial profits are hoarded by capitalists who, as a benefit of their growing wealth, enjoy luxurious lifestyles at the expense of workers whose low wages force them to live more frugally and with less financial security. Even after devoting decades to their jobs, most workers – still today – just barely survive economically, clinging desperately to pensions, social security, and public assistance. Making matters worse, those entitlements also continue to undergo cuts in government spending.

Still, radicals are not solely concerned about the exploitation of workers by their employers; they also worry about the plight of a huge segment of society that has never gained from the capitalist structure: that is, the underclass. Members of the underclass, or what Marx coined the lumpenproletariat, typically go their entire lives without any genuine economic opportunity. Faced with rampant unemployment and few prospects for work, the lucky ones settle for the lowest paid jobs while others resort to street crime (e.g. theft, selling drugs) (Chambliss and Seidman, 1982; Spitzer, 1975; Quinney, 1980).

Clearly, the capitalist structure produces not only a class-based society of workers and capitalists but also one drawn along lines of race and ethnicity since the underclass in the United States is disproportionately African-American and Latino. Given the overwhelming presence of poor people and racial minorities funneled into the criminal justice system, radical criminologists prompt us to consider once again the significance of socioeconomics and matters of race and ethnicity as they shape the course of punishment (Welch, 1999a, 1998a).

Before delving into the complexities of race, class, and incarceration, it is important to explore some critical thoughts on culture germane to capitalist society and crime. The roots of radical criminology located in Marxist sociology takes us only so far since, perhaps surprisingly, Marx wrote very little about crime. Therefore a radical approach to crime benefits from the pioneering work of other intellectuals who themselves were influenced by Marx's analyses. Enter Willem Bonger, a Dutch criminologist, who published his *Criminality and Economic Conditions* in 1916. Bonger proposed that the capitalist economic system promotes an 'ego-istic' culture that values unbridled individualism and materialism (see van Bemmelen, 1960). However, the pursuit of greed is regulated by the structures of capitalism along class lines. Capitalists enjoy an array of legal opportunities to proliferate their wealth, including the exploitation of labor; indeed, paying workers wages so low that they struggle to make ends meet is viewed by capitalists as simply good business. At the same time, greed on the part of those from the working class – and especially the underclass – is not only discouraged but also subject to formal penalties. Within that cultural and economic context, the criminal justice system emerges as a social institution that criminalizes the greed of the poor while not interfering with the avarice of the rich. Moreover, the means of committing crime vary according to social class. The poor who engage in crime rely on easily detectable tactics, such as theft of property and more recently the selling of drugs in public spaces. By contrast, wealthy criminals go about their activities behind closed doors, committing crimes that are easier to conceal from detection, including embezzlement, fraud, price-fixing, insider trading, etc.

Bonger, much like contemporary radicals, did not romanticize crimes of the poor as noble forms of rebellion against an unjust system of economics. Rather, he reasoned that offenses committed by members of the working class and underclass are nearly as harmful and predatory as those perpetrated by the capitalist. Moreover, it is difficult to argue that crimes emanating from the working and underclass are somehow 'revolutionary' acts since their victims themselves belong to the lower-income bracket. Indeed, those persons are harmed at two levels of victimization: first, by the exploitative nature of capitalist employment (i.e. low wages), and second by street crimes (e.g. burglary and robbery). Bonger concluded that the majority of crime is rooted in inequality that triggers antisocial acts among the rich as well as the poor. As a remedy, Bonger proposed socialist reforms aimed at tackling the problems created by the structure and culture of capitalism, in particular classism, economic disparities, and predatory individualism. Envisioning a society that promotes a general concern for the wellbeing of all citizens, Bonger believed that such a society would have less crime and therefore less need for punishment.

Although Bonger's radical approach to crime remained popular among European criminologists during the early part of the century, it did not take the stage in American criminology until the turbulent 1960s: a time marked by enormous social unrest fueled by struggles over civil rights and the war in Vietnam. Those issues brought to the forefront the criticism of capitalist society at home and its imperialist expansion abroad. In pursuit of social and economic justice, radicals also took aim at the racial and classist dimensions of the criminal justice system that cracked down on street criminals while ignoring harms carried out by white-collar offenders, corporations, and war profiteers (see Beckett, 1999; Blomberg and Cohen 2003; De Giorgi, 2006).

Current critical criminology

Since the 1960s, radical criminology has benefitted from an array of critical interpretations of crime and punishment, including those more narrowly described as Marxist, socialist, anarchist, conflict, peace-making, feminist, and postmodern (Pepinsky, 1978, 1991; Schwartz and Friedrichs, 1994; Tift and Sullivan, 1980; Wonders, 1999). Still, 'contrary to some views, critical criminology is not a utopian perspective but an invitation to struggle; it is a call to recast definitions of social offense more broadly than do traditional criminologies, which rarely challenge unnecessary forms of social domination' (Thomas and O'Maolchatha,

Figure 4.3   November 9, 1970: American activist Abbie Hoffman (1936–89), cofounder of the Yippie movement, speaking to a crowd while wearing a shirt made from a US flag during an American flag-themed art show at the Hudson Memorial Church, New York City. Hoffman was charged with desecration of the flag for wearing the shirt.

Photo by Tyrone Dukes/New York Times Co./ Getty Images.

1989: 148; also see Ross, 1998). Radical – or critical – criminology is not so much a theory, but a perspective based on social critique. According to Thomas and O'Maolchatha (1989: 147):

> Social critique, by definition, is radical. Derived from the Greek Krites ('judge'), the Latin term criticus implies an evaluative judgment of meaning and method in research, policy and human activity. Critical thinking implies freedom by recognizing that social existence, including our knowledge of this existence, was not simply imposed on us by powerful and mysterious forces. This recognition leads to the possibility of transcending our immediate social or ideational conditions. The act of critique implies that we can change our subjective interpretations and our objective conditions by thinking about and then acting on the world.

For the purposes of drawing a clearer picture of radical criminology – more commonly known as critical criminology – this section does not dwell on the distinctions among those overlapping versions of critique. Rather, it introduces some of the basic assumptions of radicalism, especially as they depart from the classical and positive criminologies (Lynch and Michalowski, 2006; Arrigo, 1999).

Theoretical assumptions of critical criminology

Whereas radicals debate among themselves the finer points of critical theory and analysis, there is some consensus on the following assumptions:

1 Conflict, domination, and repression are characteristic elements of a capitalist society.
2 The majority of crime in capitalist societies is a result of the inherent contradictions of capitalist social organization.
3 Laws and the criminal justice system generally protect the interests of the powerful to the disadvantage of the powerless.
4 Criminal justice makes sense only in the larger context of social justice.
    (Maguire, 1988: 134; see Lanier and Henry, 1998; Vold *et al.*, 2002)

As previously discussed, the first assumption points to the nature of conflict embedded in capitalist society whereby powerful groups dominate and exploit those with less clout. The next assumption brings to light the inherent contradictions of the capitalist society that manifest in several ways. For instance, the overarching objective of capitalism is to generate profit, and for the most part it accomplishes the task quite well. However, in doing so capitalism also generates poverty. It is often said that it takes a lot of poor people to make one person rich. By its very structure, the capitalist system is not designed to distribute wealth evenly among all people, even though workers directly contribute to the proliferation of profits (Glyn, 1990). Indeed, in a capitalist society, wealth remains highly concentrated among the few, who as a result of their fortunes wield enormous political power. Consequently, the economy and the nation's wealth become polarized, meaning that the rich get richer, and the poor as well as the middle class become poorer (Downes, 2001; Kilborn and Clemetson, 2002).

Another contradiction of the capitalist system is that unemployment is as necessary as employment itself. Whereas the employment of workers is required to manufacture goods and provide services, the presence of unemployment serves to keep wages low, thereby adding stability to the economic system (Glyn, 1990). If all citizens were to have jobs, for example, then probably everyone would demand a raise in wages. Perhaps more threatening to the capitalist class and its system of economic exploitation, workers might collectively engage in mass strikes. Those job actions would bring production and services to a halt until the bargaining parties agreed on increased wages, improved working conditions, enhanced benefits, etc.

The issue of unemployment in the context of social and economic justice deserves a bit more discussion. The capitalist system is based on structural unemployment since there are more people seeking work than there are jobs. In

Marxian terms, the unemployed are referred to as the surplus labor pool (or the surplus population, the reserve army of workers). The presence of the surplus labor pool is functional insofar as the unemployed symbolize the consequences of not complying with the demands of employers. Take for, instance, a person working at the minimum wage in a fast-food restaurant. By the first paycheck, the worker realizes how difficult it is to survive financially on those low wages. That's when reality sets in. At the minimum wage ($7.25 at the federal level) and working 40 hours per week, 52 weeks a year (no vacation), that person earns $15,080 per year (before taxes) (United States Department of Labor, 2009). Compare those earnings with the federal poverty levels formulated on the basis of income and number of persons per household reported in Table 4.1.

The scenario continues. With worries over financial survival in the face of the rising cost of living compounded by soaring rents and food prices, the worker approaches the boss and requests an increase in pay beyond the minimum wage. Not surprisingly, even after years of service, the worker is denied a raise. Adding to the insult of being refused a reasonable hike in wages, the boss reminds the worker that he or she is replaceable by one of the many local residents who would gratefully embrace the job – even at the minimum wage. Now the worker is left with the uneasy option to remain working there at the minimum wage or quit and join the ranks of the unemployed. In this illustration, not only does the presence of the surplus labor pool keep wages low but also the risk of joblessness is used as a viable threat, keeping workers compliant while pressuring them to work even at low wages. To make ends meet, such workers hold several jobs, spending virtually their entire days (and weekends) working at one job then commuting to the next (Ehrenreich, 2001).

A third contradiction in a capitalist society is the tendency to treat products and services as commodities and means of exchange to generate profit rather than using those products and services for their original purpose. As Glyn

Table 4.1 The 2009 poverty guidelines for the 48 contiguous states and the District of Columbia

Persons in family	Poverty guideline ($)
1	10,830
2	14,570
3	18,310
4	22,050
5	25,790
6	29,530
7	33,270
8	37,010

For families with more than 8 persons, add $3,740 for each additional person.

Source: Federal Register (2009).

explains: 'Capitalist production is guided by profit, not social need, or to put it more abstractly, by exchange value rather than use value' (1990: 108). For example, investors purchase homes not for the sole purpose of providing shelter for those who need it, but to profit from their investment. That said, houses and apartments remain vacant until prospective tenants are willing to fulfill the investor's profit expectation – that is, pay the landlord a certain amount of rent. For the past several decades, there has emerged a myth that there is a housing shortage, whereas in reality there is a shortage of affordable housing. Similar observations extend to the lack of accessible health care and adequate education. Such commodification has also entered the criminal justice system in the form of building prisons to house a growing number of non-violent offenders. The problem of profiteering from crime and punishment mirrors the military-industrial complex, thereby opening avenues for private corrections companies to rig government contracts that rip off taxpayers (Welch, 2003e).

Prison as economic engine

For decades, prisons themselves have become appreciated for their economic benefits and big business opportunities not only for private companies but government as well. Indeed, local, state, and federal governments continue to allocate increasingly more funds to prisons and the larger correctional systems (Selman and Leighton, 2010). For instance, county governments across the nation go to great lengths to have state prisons built within their communities since elected officials identify those institutions as a good source for local jobs at attractive salaries (beginning at $45,000 a year). In Weed, California, for instance, supporters of the proposal to construct a prison in their town held rallies and barbecues to raise money for a public relations firm that would make their case to state officials. 'A sign in a bakery window reads, "A Depressed Economy Needs Corrections"' (*New York Times*, 1994e: 28). The enthusiasm for supporting prisons sharply contrasts to the not-in-my-backyard sentiment that has faded along with better economic times (Welch and Turner, 2007–8).

Similarly in other economically depressed counties, such as those in upstate New York where the timber industry has drastically declined, political leaders battle against competing counties to be selected as the site of the next state prison. As the town supervisor of Chesterfield, New York, Roger E. Poland points out: 'A business comes in and a year or two it can't support itself and bang – it's gone.' A prison 'is something you know is going to be here for a long time.' Poland, however, understands that a prison will not simply be handed to his community, and is acutely aware of the competition from other counties experiencing similar economic hardship. In Chesterfield, where the unemployment rate stood at 15 percent, 269 residents signed the petition favoring a prison while only 19 cast votes against it. The residents of those counties generally favor such proposals because a prison is viewed as 'clean industry,' unlike nuclear plants or other manufacturers that pollute the environment. According to James Dawson, supervisor of Brasher, New York: 'Prisons are environmentally sound. They have no smokestacks, no noise, no pollution. It's like a college campus with a fence around it' (*New York Times*, 1989c: B1, B2).

Many other state governments have stimulated a similar form of competition among their counties in which the economic 'prize' is having a prison built near the community. In Illinois, such a bidding was promoted as a 'sweepstakes.' As then Governor James Thompson stated: 'Every once in a while a tiny town in a small county ought to win one,' while the mayor of one of the selected towns called the prison a 'godsend' (Egler, 1986: 2; see Maguire, 1988: 148). More than a century ago, when Washington State was still a territory, the government 'gave the citizens of this city [Walla Walla] a choice between a new college and a prison. They chose the prison because they didn't like the kind of people attracted to a college' (*New York Times*, 1990: A1, A32).

Whereas critical criminologists insist that enormous expenditures on corrections are a waste because such spending has had little effect on the crime problem, politicians favor the expansion of the prison systems (Jacobson, 2005; Lynch, 2007) Nowadays, it is believed that the incarceration industry provides some communities with an economic engine that will shore up financial setbacks; however, as discussed further in Chapter 15, campaigns for greater prison construction are driven by wishful thinking and false hopes.

Unemployment, imprisonment and social control

Since economic forces remain a central focus of the radical perspective, it is important to delineate further the link between unemployment and imprisonment. As mentioned previously, among the contradictions of capitalism is that a certain degree of unemployment remains a necessary condition of the economic structure: what mainstream economists call 'ideal unemployment' (estimated at 5 percent) (Glyn, 1990). Still, the macro level of captitalism produces microsociological consequences insofar as unemployment serves to marginalize individuals in capitalist society. In the absence of legitimate means to survive financially, jobless persons depend on the government for various forms of welfare payments, drawing the ire of mainstream citizens who blame the unemployed for 'draining' tax dollars. Simply put, to be unemployed in a capitalist society often means being the target for public hostility, becoming a modern-day pillory whereby the jobless are debased and humiliated.

Those concerns are increasingly apparent amid the recession that began unfolding worldwide in 2008. Due to diminishing prospects for employment, many jobless persons eventually give up looking for work and no longer apply for unemployment benefits. While that trend is to be found recently among so-called 'middle-class' professionals, the recession has a harsher impact on those at the bottom of the economic ladder. As a response to growing joblessness among the urban poor, governments tend to unleash greater maneuvers in crime control, including aggressive policing and the use of jail and prison (Michalowski and Carlson, 1997). Such enforcement campaigns, known as social sanitation, are tailored to deal with urban poor minorities who resort to crimes not regarded as serious offenses (e.g. drug possession) (Irwin, 1985; Welch, 1994). Again, there is nothing new about these developments since historically policing and penal systems are closely patterned by economic conditions (Downes, 2001; Rusche and Kirchheimer, 1968 [1939]; Rusche, 1982 [1933]; see Chapter 2).

To reiterate, it is the structure of economic production under capitalism that contributes to poverty since employment is not extended to all persons seeking it. In more theoretical terms, Lynch and Michalowski (2006) remind us that imprisonment is then used by the state to offset problems endemic to capitalist production – problems which generate a large mass of unemployed persons who have to be managed by the crime-control apparatus. There is not much exclusively radical or Marxist about studying imprisonment as it relates to joblessness. Unlike some conservative commentators, however, who blame unemployment on the jobless themselves, critical criminologists view unemployment as part of the normal operation of capitalism.

> As capitalism ages, technological advancements render certain forms of labor obsolete. As higher profits are sought in production, labor-saving technology is employed which frees individuals from the workforce, thus swelling the size of the surplus population. Under these circumstances, economic growth creates unemployment, and unemployment increases both crime and imprisonment.
>
> (Lynch *et al.*, 2000: 208)

For decades, radical criminologists have drawn links between economic conditions under capitalism and the use of crime-control initiatives. In a classic study of unemployment and imprisonment rates, Greenberg (1977) found a strong association between increases in prison admissions and rises in unemployment. Greenberg reports that: 'Judges are less willing to grant probation to offenders when they are unemployed' (1977: 650). Similarly, Jankovic (1982) revealed that for the lower-income bracket, unemployment was more of a reliable predictor of incarceration than were actual crime rates (see Box and Hale, 1982; Welch, 1996c; Wilkins, 1991; Yeager, 1979). That finding firmly suggests that for the lower-income group, crime rates could actually decrease while prison population increases, as long as unemployment was also on the rise. Again, that finding supports the argument of many radical criminologists that the penal apparatus serves to manage the underclass, or what Marx called the lumpenproletariat. Other studies confirm the relationship among economic forces, unemployment, and the reliance on prisons as a measure of coercive social control (Arvanites and Asher, 1998; Dunaway *et al.*, 2000; Lynch *et al.*, 1999; White, 1999).

While Chiricos and Bales similarly report 'a significant, strong, and independent impact of unemployment on pretrial and post-sentencing incarceration,' they further note the significance of race as it relates to both unemployment and punishment (1991: 701). They found that the greatest likelihood of incarceration is for unemployed black defendants, particularly those who are young males or charged with violent or public order crimes. Sharpening their analysis, Chiricos and Bales discovered that when compared with employed whites convicted of drug crimes, employed African-Americans were 5.9 times more likely to be incarcerated (Chiricos and Bales, 1991; also see Welch, 1995d). In sum, as we strive to understand further the connection between the structure of capitalist society and the penal system with respect to social class, it is also imperative to keep attention on matters of race and ethnicity (see Chapter 8).

Implications for social change and sound policy

Critical criminology had been viewed by some of its detractors as a mere set of theoretical propositions too vague and abstract for practical use and pragmatic policy (Hirst, 1975; Klockars, 1979). Against such sweeping generalizations, radicals adamantly defend their proposals for social change and sound criminal justice policy (Lynch and Michalowski, 2006; Taylor *et al.*, 1973; Welch, 2005a). Outlining the applied dimension of the critical perspective, Maguire (1988) addresses a nagging complaint even shared by some more ideological radicals that any social change short of transforming capitalism into socialism is simply a 'band-aid' approach that fails to establish enduring shifts toward economic justice.

That all-or-nothing commitment to social change tends to silence radicals who call for a wider political dialogue on criminal justice policies and practices. While it is unlikely that the United States will be converted into a bona fide socialist state anytime soon, mainstream Americans do favor social programs dating back to the 1940s when President Franklin Delano Roosevelt's 'New Deal' instituted broad reforms aimed at reducing economic inequality (e.g. unemployment benefits, social security healthcare programs, financial aid for college students).

Since the 1980s, the swing toward political conservatism has undermined much of the genuine thrust of the 'New Deal' while fueling more tough-on-crime initiatives that have consumed enormous amounts of tax dollars as well as produced the largest prison population in the world. Radicals along with progressive liberals lament the demise of social programs contained in the welfare state along with the rise of what scholars identify as the prison state (Simon, 2007; Useem and Piehl, 2008; Wacquant, 2009). In refusing to give into the penal populism whereby mainstream citizens endorse the prevailing crime-control agenda, critics demand greater fiscal accountability that forces elected leaders to operate with more transparency. By doing so, costly expenditures are subject to closer public scrutiny, thereby shedding light on the various forms of cronyism that feed into the prison-industrial complex (Jacobson, 2005; Pratt, 2007). During harsh economic times such as the most recent recession, taxpayers share heightened concern – and anger – over how government dollars are being spent (e.g. the huge bailout of US banks in 2009). With respect to meaningful social change, the present circumstances have the potential to play out in favor of radical proposals to cut wasteful spending, for instance on prisons, and redirect funding to community programs, education, health care, and affordable housing – all of which uphold the basic principles of social and economic justice (Arrigo, 1999; Currie, 1998).

With greater focus on criminal justice policy, critical criminologists confront the class and individualistic biases of the prevailing apparatus of punishment. A key assertion of radicalism, as noted previously, is that the criminal justice system is geared more to control offenses committed by members of the working class and underclass (e.g. property crimes, drug violations) than those of the middle and upper classes (e.g. price-fixing, insider trading) whose crimes are subject to more regulatory inspection (e.g. the Internal Revenue Service, the Security and Exchange Commission).

Such classism in traditional criminal justice is compounded by an individualistic bias insofar as penal strategies disproportionately target the individual offender: whether it be a drug peddler or a Wall Street fraudster. A chief limitation of the individualistic bias in criminal investigation, prosecution, and sentencing is that authorities tend to neglect significant wrongdoing by powerful groups, corporations, and government itself; indeed, many such crimes are actually framed as legitimate forms of business (e.g. war profiteering) (Michalowski and Kramer, 2006; Ruggiero and Welch, 2009). Together, class and individualistic biases deflect further attention away from societal conditions that invite street crime (e.g. poverty and drug peddling) as well as from basic capitalist arrangements that give rise to state and corporate crime (e.g., the pursuit of profit and violence by private military firms) (Welch, 2009a). Breaking through those biases, radicals concentrate less on punishing individuals and organizations, whether drug peddlers or corporations, and focus more on confronting the structural dimensions of capitalism that contribute to crimes across the spectrum. Simply put, punishment only takes us so far; attempts to truly reduce crime require a restructuring of the political economy that fosters democratic governance (e.g. greater regulation and oversight over finance, government spending, and outsourcing).

Having said all that, the issue of punishment remains an important consideration in dispensing justice. Critical criminologists, even more so than their liberal counterparts, are inaccurately portrayed as being 'soft' on crime. Contrary to the popular view, radicals hold very strong views against crime and violence whether such acts are committed by individuals or by the state (e.g. the death penalty). While criticism is commonly directed at misguided policies that fuel more prison construction that puts more offenders behind bars for longer periods of time, many critical criminologists voice support for meaningful measures of dealing with violent criminals. Paul Takagi, for instance, replies:

> While I intellectually understand and comprehend the offender that engages in gratuitous violence, I think, given our current state of knowledge, I see no alternative but to impose a long prison sentence. Not the 50 to 100 years that is sometimes imposed in these cases, but perhaps until age 30 or 35 or whatever the age is when they begin to slow down.
>
> (Maguire, 1988: 144)

David Friedrichs (1996) generally agrees, and proposes that imprisonment be extended to violent corporate offenders, including those who in the course of business undercut safety regulations that result in employee deaths and injuries, or manufacture unsafe products that kill and maim consumers (e.g. unsafe automobiles) (see Aulette and Michalowski, 2006; Matthews, 2006; Mullins, 2006). In sharpening a proactive stance toward tackling corporate violence, Friedrichs suggests that corporations identify in advance which executives are responsible and liable for company decisions that eventually lead to deaths and injuries. Too often, key decision-makers in corporations – and government – hide behind an organizational mask to avoid individual prosecution. Such a proactive tactic emulates what is commonly understood in military law as command responsibility under which commanding officers are held accountable for ordering soldiers to commit war crimes (e.g. abuse of detainees, torture) (Sands, 2008; Welch, 2009a).

Policy recommendations offered by Takagi and Friedrichs break from the strict demarcation of positivism, classicism and radicalism in criminological thought. By advocating lengthy sentences for violent offenders, Takagi appears to lend support for the practice of incapacitation commonly found among positivists. Hinting at classicism, Friedrichs seems to favor not only deterrence but also principles of personal responsibility in dealing with corporate actors.

Although some critical criminologists advocate a reworking of positivist and classicist penal strategies in the short term in dealing with individual and collective forms of violence, the primary thrust of radicalism moves toward social and economic justice (Welch, 1998a). Scholarly contributions from radicalism should not be overlooked since critical criminology has had a noticeable influence on both contemporary positivism and classicism. Economic, political, and historical considerations that generally were associated with radicalism have emerged as significant elements of mainstream criminology, prompting scholars to appreciate a more fluid crossover of criminological concepts. Moreover, in the realm of policy-making, alliances among radicals and progressive liberals alongside activists and human rights advocates are becoming increasingly important to campaigns designed to offset the dominance of tough-on-crime initiatives.

Alliance of radicals and progressive liberals

For decades, there has been considerable discussion about forging an alliance between radicals and progressive liberals given that there remains considerable consensus that the conservative agenda in criminal justice has made matters worse. Zero-tolerance penalties for drug use, mandatory minimum sentences, and mass incarceration, just to name a few examples, continue to polarize the class and racial divide in American society (Beckett, 1999). Whereas some critical criminologists are reluctant to participate in short-term social reforms that do not ultimately lead to enduring social change, others enthusiastically favor joining forces with progressive liberals in efforts to beat back conservative policies that have resulted in greater repression of less powerful people, namely the impoverished and racial and ethnic minorities.

Some years ago, radicals Lynch and Groves wrote: 'Thus, the problem radicals face is to promote meaningful social changes here and now while rallying support for their future reform efforts' (1989b: 3–4). Some fundamental reforms endorsed by critical as well as liberal criminologists include: raising bail funds for indigent defendants, aiding political prisoners, and abolishing the death penalty (Greenberg, 1981; Platt, 1982; Reiman, 2001; see Chapter 12). Similarly, Tony Platt (1985) encouraged critical criminologists to join progressive liberals to combat the rise of the conservative Right and its agenda for a law-and-order society. Platt noted that such a social movement has unfolded not only in the United States but also in England and Australia where the Right has succeeded in passing more tough-on-crime legislation. Many scholars and intellectuals have blamed the Left (radicals and progressive liberals alike) for allowing the conservative Right to dominate criminal justice debate, policy, and practice. By failing to advance progressive proposals for dealing with crime, promoting justice, and reducing social inequality, conservatives have easily swayed mainstream citizens to accept the dogmatic notion that the poor and people of color are a burden for American society: consequently, they deserve more discipline, punishment, and exclusion (see Gross 1982; Reiman, 2001; Simon, 1993).

Such an alliance goes beyond specific policy issues and moves toward advancing social theory. For some critical criminologists, having theoretical and practical alignments with liberalism is certainly beneficial. 'First, this broadens the appeal of radical theory – as it appears to mainstream the radical perspective – and makes it more acceptable to liberal policy officials. Additionally, it debunks the stereotypical view of radicals as having an unswerving commitment to revolution and nothing less than revolution' (Lynch and Groves, 1989b: 4).

CONCLUSION

At the outset of this chapter, we introduced the case of Slacker Sam, a 22-year-old unemployed drug addict and alcoholic with a seventh-grade education, convicted of burglarizing a video store for a second time. Although hypothetical, the case of Slacker Sam is certainly not atypical. Indeed, Slacker Sam is largely representative of the type of cases flooding the criminal justice system. Taking into consideration each of the characteristics of Slacker Sam, we are left with the nagging question: What should the criminal justice system do with those kinds of offenders? Each major theoretical perspective seems to offer a different answer. From the standpoint of classicism stem proposals for deterrence along with restraint on the part of the courts so as to impose only a sufficient degree of punishment that serves to discourage criminal acts. In line with more contemporary classicism, Slacker Sam would be subject to 'just deserts' that matches retribution to the severity of the offense. Still, classicists would not venture far into the realm of treatment since it reaches beyond the traditional role of the courts.

Enter the positivists who claim that Slacker Sam is a good candidate for treatment administered by well-trained experts who understand how to deal with an array of individual problems that contribute to criminal behavior. Despite undergoing intense criticism by 'tough-on-crime' politicians and their like-minded policy-makers, rehabilitation contains an enduring ideal (Cullen and Gilbert, 1982; Cullen *et al.*, 2000). Programs devoted to substance abuse counseling, education, and job training, appeal to citizens across the political spectrum. Such interventions speak to a genuine sense of humane reform while also offering lawbreakers an opportunity for redemption – a deeply engrained value in American society.

Apart from its role in rehabilitation, positivism as a 'science' maintains a steady influence in criminology; still, the legacy of Lombroso today has taken on three important distinctions.

- One lies in the fact that, whereas criminal anthropologists often spoke in terms of a nature-nurture dichotomy, theorists today speak of gene-environment interactions, holding that heredity seldom works independently of a context.
- A second major difference concerns determinism: whereas Lombroso claimed that born criminals are biologically bound to commit crime, criminologists today are likely to speak in terms of probabilities, risk factors, and antisocial predispositions.
- A third outstanding difference lies in the type of causational factors studied by biological theorists in the past and today: whereas Lombroso focused on atavism, degeneration, epilepsy, and moral insanity, theorists today study such factors as the evolution of antisocial personality traits, behavioral genetics, hormonal imbalances, and neuro-cognitive deficits.

(Gibson and Rafter, 2006: 31; see Rafter, 1997;
Walsh and Beaver, 2008; Wright *et al.*, 2008)

With renewed interest in biological criminology alongside predictive models used to assess risk factors, contemporary positivism seems to move further away from Lombroso's call for greater attention to societal conditions, especially poverty. Enter once again radicalism that generally supports rehabilitation but shifts a greater focus on the economic structures that perpetuate inequality. Much like progressive liberals, critical criminologists staunchly oppose the prevailing 'tough-on-crime' initiatives. In response to an array of social problems created by capitalism, radicals criticize the state for instituting more penal strategies rather than progressive measures that have the potential to reduce poverty, crime, and punishment.

SUMMARY

Overall, the chapter delineates major assumptions of classicism, positivism, and radicalism. At the center of the classical perspective is the notion of free will, paving the way for strategies designed to deter crime while embracing personal responsibility. In more contemporary terms, classicism has taken on a more punitive stance in the form of 'just-deserts' retribution and even more so with tough-on-crime initiatives. The positivist approach to crime generally dismisses the concept of free will and prefers to develop scientific methods for understanding criminal behavior. While taking into account both personal defects and environmental influences, positivists hold that treatment is the proper remedy for crime. Finally, radicalism offers a broader social and economic framework for interpreting crime and the government's response to it. In recognizing that inequality is structured by the capitalist system, critical criminologists take issue with the state for its reliance on a repressive penal apparatus that targets the impoverished and minorities. Criminal justice initiatives, therefore, need to be reformulated along the lines of social as well as economic justice, bringing together radicals and progressive liberals as they confront the prevailing tough-on-crime agenda.

REVIEW QUESTIONS

1 How are correctional practices shaped by the major perspectives?
2 How might correctional practices be improved, according to each perspective?
3 What are the main strengths and weaknesses of each perspective?
4 How do the three perspectives differ? How do they overlap?

RECOMMENDED READINGS

Cullen, F. T. and Applegate, B. (1997) *Offender Rehabilitation: Effective Correctional Intervention*. Aldershot, England: Ashgate/Dartmouth.

Currie, E. (1998) *Crime and Punishment in America*. New York: Henry Holt.

Lombroso, C. (2006) *Criminal Man*, trans. M. Gibson and N. H. Rafter. Durham, NC: Duke University Press.

Lynch, M. and Michalowski, R. (2006) *The New Primer in Radical Criminology* (4th edn). Monsey, NY: Criminal Justice Press.

Ross, J. I. (1998) *Cutting the Edge: Current Perspectives in Radical and Critical Criminology*. Westport, CT: Praeger.

PART II   PENAL POPULATIONS

CHAPTER 5

The Social World of Prisoners

To be in prison so long, it's difficult to remember exactly what you did to get there. So long your fantasies of the free world are no longer easily distinguishable from what you 'know' the free world is really like. (Jack Henry Abbott)

LEARNING OBJECTIVES

After studying this chapter, you should be able to answer the following questions:

1 What are the scale and scope of American corrections, and in what ways is the incarceration enterprise growing?
2 How are prisoners classified?
3 What are the dominant features of the social world of convicts?
4 What are the unique aspects of the prisoner subculture?
5 What is the significance of contraband and the underground economy in prisons?

Anthony 'Tony Ducks' Carrollo was the boss of the New York-based Lucchese crime family, a real-life Mafia godfather, and no one at the Hot House [Leavenworth penitentiary] bothered him. Not that anyone had reason to. He was a perfect gentleman. In prison, a Mafioso did his time as quietly as possible because it improved his chances for parole. There was only one time anyone could remember that a Mafia member got into trouble, and that had happened at the penitentiary in Lewisburg, Pennsylvania, where Mafia members are frequently housed because of its proximity to New York City. A guard for some reason began harassing a wiseguy. Every day the guard searched the inmate's cell, went through his mail, and frisked him as he walked the compound, until the wiseguy had simply had enough. One day a visitor from outside the prison came to see the wiseguy. The guard saw the visitor slip something into the wiseguy's hand. 'What you got there?' the guard demanded. Without protest, the wiseguy opened his fingers, revealing a photograph of the guard's six-year-old daughter playing at her elementary school. 'See how easy it can be?' the Mafioso asked.

(Earley, 1992: 91–2)

INTRODUCTION

The social world of imprisonment consists of both organizational and subcultural components. The organizational aspects are social arrangements that are formally structured, for instance prisoners being classified into distinct categories. On the other hand, the subcultural features are informally structured according to inmate subcultures existing below the surface of formal organization. Both of those components of institutional corrections determine what it is like to work as well as live in prison.

This chapter examines three major levels of correctional analysis – the macro, meso, and micro. A macro level of analysis is the widest approach to corrections, taking into account economic, political, religious, and technological forces. A meso level of analysis conforms to a mid-range focus, concentrating on correctional systems, organizations, and institutions. Finally, a micro analysis is restricted to the experiential features of imprisonment, understanding prisoners as individuals, groups, and subcultures.

SCALE AND SCOPE OF AMERICAN CORRECTIONS

As discussed in Chapter 1, the United States increasingly has become a society of captives. Indeed, state and federal correctional systems along with local jails are remarkable due to their vast size, scope, and continued growth. To reiterate some of the most significant figures, the following points are drawn from the 2008 census for prisoners.

- By year end 2008, state and federal prisons and local jails held more than 2,304,115 inmates, an increase of 0.3 percent from year end 2007. That ratio is 1 in every 133 US residents.
- Narrowing the scope to federal and state correctional systems (not local jails), those authorities held over 1,610,446 prisoners. That ratio is 1 in every 198 US residents.
- State correctional authorities held more than 1,409,166 prisoners, an increase of 10,539 state prisoners for 2008.
- Federal correctional authorities held more than 201,280 prisoners, up 1,662 federal prisoners from 2007.
- While the numbers of state and federal prisoners reached all-time year end highs in 2008, the respective growth rates for each slowed to 0.8 percent. Growth of the prison population since 2000 (1.8 percent per year on average) was less than a third of the average annual rate during the 1990s (6.5 percent per year on average).
- The incarceration rate – the number of inmates held in custody of state or federal prisons or in local jails per 100,000 US residents – reached 754 inmates: not much difference from the 756 inmates the previous year.
- Twenty-nine states and the federal prison system reported a combined increase of 21,920 prisoners.
- Pennsylvania (up 4,178 prisoners) and Florida (up 4,169) had the largest increases, followed by Arizona (1,843), the federal prison system (1,662), and North Carolina (1,512).
- Altogether, those five jurisdictions accounted for 61 percent of the growth among jurisdictions holding more prisoners. Pennsylvania also recorded the fastest rate of growth (up 9.1 percent) for 2008.

(*Source*: Sabol *et al.*, 2009).

Figure 5.1 Inmate: muscular man in trouble shot in old prison setting.

© iStockphoto.com

In line with a critical approach to corrections, it is important to recognize that contrary to popular belief, most prisoners are not serving time for serious crimes. Since 1978, much of the growth in America's prisons is accounted for by non-violent offenders, and in 1998 that total reached one million (Irwin *et al.*, 2000; see Austin and Irwin 2001; BJS, 2002a; Chapter 16 this volume). As described in Chapter 4, there are key socioeconomic forces contributing to the prison build-up, given that the vast proportion of prisoners are poor as well as being a racial or ethnic minority. Those developments suggest that mass incarceration serves as a mechanism for social control (see Chapter 8). In particular, many criminologists argue that the rising prison population marks a governmental response to public anxiety over perceived lawlessness, poor people, and racial minorities (Arvanites and Asher, 1998; Beckett and Western, 2001; Greenberg, 1999). Those fears commonly manifest in the view of an emerging 'dangerous class' that poses a threat to the nation's social and economic order (Garland, 2001: Irwin and Austin, 1998).

Fueling increases in the prison population is the expanding roster of laws and penalties, including capital punishment (see Chapter 10), mandatory minimum drug sentences (see Chapter 16), and various other tough-on-crime legislation such as Three Strikes You're Out (Zimring *et al.*, 2001; see Chapter 12). In 1994, Congress enacted the Violent Crime Control and Law Enforcement Act, a law that has a tremendous effect on the government's commitment to imprisonment. That legislation provided federal funds to states for the construction of prisons. In order to qualify for those subsidies, states must adopt 'truth in sentencing' laws stipulating that prisoners serve at least 85 percent of their sentences. Consequently, state prison populations quickly escalated due to more and more convicts being incarcerated for longer periods of time (Chambliss, 1999; Greenberg and West, 2001; McManimon 2000). In Chapter 15, we shall examine the effects that those tough-on-crime laws have had on the booming corrections industry, in which prisoners – who are disproportionately poor, black, and Latino – serve as raw materials in the production of private and governmental revenue.

Types of correctional systems

Prisons have the responsibility of incarcerating felons, those convicted of offenses punishable by sentences of more than one or two years (depending on the state). Felons are assigned to one of two types of prison systems: the federal or the state system. In addition to the more than one thousand federal and state prisons, nationwide there are also more than three thousand local (city or county) jails holding pretrial detainees and convicted misdemeanants, as well as convicted felons awaiting transfer to prison.

The federal prison system is operated by the Federal Bureau of Prisons (BOP), created by Congress in 1930 and administered by the US Department of Justice (Roberts, 1994). Federal inmates are those convicted of federal offenses, such as kidnapping, bank robbery, and tax evasion, as well as various violent crimes and drug violations. Currently, the federal prison system consists of more than 100 correctional facilities (see Bosworth, 2002)

The federal prison system includes maximum-security penitentiaries at Leavenworth, Kansas; Atlanta, Georgia; Lewisburg, Pennsylvania; Lompoc, California; and Terre Haute, Indiana. In addition to scores of medium-, low-, and minimum-security federal correctional institutions (FCIs), the BOP has established numerous federal camps, which are minimum-security units situated on the grounds of higher-security facilities. In addition to constructing new institutions, the federal prison system continues to search for available correctional space. In 1993, historic army base Fort Dix (New Jersey) was converted into a low-security correctional facility. The following year, Fort Dix housed 3,600 inmates – becoming the most populated institution in the federal prison system. Approximately 90 percent of the offenders assigned to Fort Dix are narcotics violators, especially drug couriers, or 'mules' (Katz, 1993).

Once sentences are imposed by a federal judge, the United States Marshals Service has the responsibility of transporting prisoners to their assigned correctional facility. In each of the five regions of the Federal Bureau of Prisons is a regional designator, who selects the appropriate institution for each federal inmate. Among the factors determining designation are nature and severity of offense, criminal history, history of violence, security risk, age, and medical and program needs (Cullen and Sundt, 2000; Keve, 1991; Simonsen, 1996).

State prisons are operated by state officials, usually under the direction of a state commissioner of corrections (or secretary of corrections) who is appointed by the governor. It is the duty of the commissioner to select the wardens or superintendents who oversee the daily operations of their assigned prisons; all other prison administrators and staff members report to their respective warden. State inmates are those convicted of criminal statutes enforced by that particular state, and penalties differ from state to state for similar offenses. Like the federal prison system, each state correctional system offers a range of institutional security: maximum, medium, and minimum. Currently, the state prison system with the most inmates is California followed by Texas and Florida.

State prison systems operate according to either a centralized or a decentralized structure. The centralized structure is highly unified and autonomous, and is managed by a central state government authority. Conversely, a decentralized state prison system is a wider organization that includes federal and local agencies. The centralized structure emphasizes central accountability, which enhances efficiency in the allocation of resources and adds uniformity to correctional practices. However, centralized systems are criticized for their vulnerability to the problems facing large bureaucracies. A benefit of the decentralized structure is its ability to meet the needs of the inmate population in a given locale. Its drawbacks, however, include the possible duplication of services and competition for resources.

Although most jails are county or local facilities, a few are operated by the Federal Bureau of Prisons. Those federal jails, known as metropolitan correctional centers (MCCs), are located in Chicago, Los Angeles, Miami, New York City, and San Diego. The inmates held at MCCs are being prosecuted for federal offenses, or are sentenced felons awaiting transfer to their designated prisons. Another type of correctional institution is the multi-jurisdictional, or regional, jail. Inmate population growth has placed additional financial burdens on county correctional institutions. Consequently, several counties have begun sharing resources to finance the operation of a regional jail, thereby serving the detention needs of bordering counties. Whereas multi-county jails can reduce costs of construction and operations, they often increase the cost of inmate transportation and place additional hardships on the prisoners' families and attorneys.

The military administers its own criminal justice and correctional system, consisting of more than 60 military confinement facilities. Military prisons (or stockades) are unique types of institutions because they do not necessarily operate according to geographic boundaries. Rather, jurisdictions are created by the US armed forces. Each branch of the military manages one or several military prisons for military personnel who are awaiting court-martial proceedings or have been sentenced to incarceration (Beck and Harrison, 2001).

Super maximum security prisons

Among the more controversial developments in federal and state prisons is the increased reliance on super maximum (or supermax, maxi-maxi) prisons. Whereas correctional administrators have long relied on the use of solitary confinement, known as 'the hole,' to remove violent and recalcitrant inmates from the general population, the notion of constructing facilities devoted solely to controlling such prisoners has gained popularity. The modern idea of a supermax security prison is traced to the opening of Alcatraz Island in 1933. There, the nation's most notorious criminals and gangsters were housed under exceedingly tight conditions (see Chapter 3).

When the Federal Bureau of Prisons (BOP) closed Alcatraz in 1963, federal corrections officials already had plans to operate a new, state-of-the-art, supermax security penitentiary at Marion, Illinois (Richards, 2008). Based on a series of behavior modification techniques, Marion placed prisoners under close restriction, allowing them to increase their privileges through good conduct. Beginning in the early 1970s, the BOP began sending more and more of the system's most difficult prisoners to Marion, resulting in greater tension, hostility, and major disruption. Eventually, Marion became synonymous with violence. In 1983, after a rash of assaults by prisoners against prisoners and against staff (including two homicides), the institution was placed under total lockdown. For years, prisoners were confined to their cells for 23 hours per day, and extra precautions were instituted in moving and transporting inmates (e.g. handcuffs, leg irons, digital rectal searches). In evaluating the sources of violence at Marion, experts discovered key flaws in the design of the facility, such as open cell fronts that left staff vulnerable to assault (Austin and Irwin, 2001; McShane, 1996).

In years to follow, federal and state systems carefully planned the next generation of supermax security prisons, especially from the perspective of design and architecture that would contribute further to controlling dangerous and high-risk inmates. As noted, in 1994 the BOP opened a super maximum security penitentiary in Florence, Colorado, holding 400 inmates. Currently, all but a handful of states now operate some form of super maximum prison or unit within a prison (Mears, 2008; Mears and Reisig, 2006). Still, the push for higher prison security is most pronounced in California, where the department of corrections has constructed four new supermax security prisons with a total capacity of 12,000. These prisons were designed according to the 'pod' model, in which prisoners are housed in small self-contained units surrounded by heavily armed officers. The Pelican Bay super maximum security penitentiary, located in Northern California, is recognized as one of the most tightly controlled institutions in the nation. For 22.5 hours a day, prisoners remain in their windowless cells with virtually no face-to-face contact with staff or other inmates. Under such stringent restrictions, prisoners at Pelican Bay do not work or have access to programs or recreation. All institutional orders and instructions are communicated to inmates via speaker systems. Originally designed to hold 2,080 prisoners, Pelican Bay's population soared to more than 3,200 (Austin and Irwin, 2001).

Whereas supermax prisons remain popular among many correctional administrators because they have come to represent well-ordered institutions, human rights organizations have questioned many of their tactics. In response to complaints by inmates at Marion who reported that they were routinely chained to their beds (mere concrete slabs) for periods lasting several days, Amnesty International criticized prison officials for violating the United Nation's Minimum Rules for the Treatment of Prisoners. Human rights groups have also turned a critical eye on the correctional practices at Pelican Bay, pejoratively referred to as Skeleton Bay and which a former corrections officer called the 'toilet of the corrections system' (Hentoff, 1993a: 21). The ACLU Prison Project and the Pelican Bay Information Project repeatedly criticized the institution for its inhumane conditions.

Prisoners are confined to their cells (8 foot by 10 foot cells) 22.5 hours per day, where the temperature registers a constant 85 to 90 degrees. The unrelenting heat produces headaches, nausea, and dehydration, and drains the inmates of their mental and bodily energy. According to one prisoner: 'The inside of your body always feels as though you have a fever and your skin is always moist with sweat, whether you move or not' (Hentoff, 1993a: 20; also see Dowker and Good, 2002; Haney, 1993).

A class-action suit filed by Pelican Bay's prisoners contained more than 2,500 individual grievances of excessive force, inadequate medical treatment, and pervasive sensory deprivation maintained through isolation (Hentoff, 1993b, 1993c). Human rights experts also criticize Pelican Bay officials for resorting to cell extraction as a tool for controlling unruly prisoners. When an inmate confined to his cell refuses an order from an officer, he is forcibly removed from the cell by a team of specially trained guards, sporting helmets and riot gear (e.g. shields, batons, and guns that fire gas pellets or rubber or wooden bullets). Officers restrain and hogtie the inmate, then carry him to an isolation cell. Though the guards are not supposed to harm the inmate, prisoners often are injured in the process of being tackled and restrained (Davis, 2001; Dowker and Good, 2002; Parenti, 1999; Weinstein and Cummins, 1996).

In their investigation, Human Rights Watch concluded that two Indiana supermax security prisons inflict a degree of cruel and inhumane treatment of inmates that constitutes torture under international human rights law. A central complaint in their report concerns the punishment of emotionally disturbed inmates who, for obvious reasons, have difficulty complying with rigid institutional rules. Rather than offering psychiatric treatment, mentally ill prisoners are disciplined for exhibiting bizarre and self-destructive behavior: 'Prisoners rub feces on themselves, stick pencils in their penises, stuff their eyelids with toilet paper, bite chunks of flesh from their bodies, slash themselves, hallucinate, rant and rave, or stare fixedly at the walls' (Human Rights Watch, 1997: 1–2). These psychotic symptoms are compounded by 'warehousing,' especially when prisoners are subjected to long-term isolation and sensory deprivation. Human Rights Watch also criticized those institutions for the procedures used to determine which inmates are remanded to the super maximum security prisons, charging that it is an unfair administrative decision that few inmates are allowed to appeal. Compounding matters, evaluations of classification schemes show that most prisoners confined to super maximum security prisons and units do not require that level of security (Isaacs and Lowen, 2007).

More recent research has examined the relationship between the degree of extended isolation inherent in supermax prisons and recidivism. In their study of the Florida Department of Corrections, Mears and Bales found 'evidence that supermax incarceration may increase violent recidivism' (2009: 1131; see Lovell *et al.,* 2007; Pizarro and Narag, 2008). In light of those findings, it is important to view supermax prisons with greater concern since the extended isolation of prisoners could very well undermine public safety once those convicts are released into the community (Liebling and Maruna, 2005; Travis, 2005; see also Carlton, 2007; Shalev, 2009).

Correctional overcrowding

Although overcrowding has always remained an institutional issue in corrections, the growing penal population greatly compounds the problem. Since 2000, state prisons were operating between full capacity and 15 percent beyond, while federal prisons were functioning at 31 percent beyond (Beck and Harrison, 2001). As will be discussed in greater depth in Chapter 15, correctional overcrowding has spawned the construction of numerous additional prisons and jails, at an enormous price to taxpayers, who must foot the bill for the rush to lock up more and more lawbreakers, many of whom are non-violent offenders. In Chapter 13, various efforts to implement alternatives to incarceration are surveyed. Still, those measures are tremendously underutilized and quite often the prevailing response to overcrowding is to build additional institutions while modifying many others. Given the decline in the rehabilitation philosophy, along with the emergence of the warehousing mentality, correctional administrators are retrofitting many of their buildings to make room for the influx of sentenced prisoners, transforming classrooms, gymnasiums, and recreation rooms into large dormitories.

As a result, prisoners face greater idleness, which contributes to tension and psychological stress, jeopardizing institutional safety. Moreover, even newly constructed facilities are built with only the bare necessities for warehousing prisoners and thus do not include space once designated for programs, education, and recreation. Regrettably, 'the bottom line is that crowding is now an accepted way of operating a prison system' (Austin and Irwin, 2001; Crouch *et al.,* 1999). Few prisoner lawsuits have succeeded in reducing prison overcrowding, and legislators are often unwilling to remedy the problem unless in the aftermath of a major disturbance. Then again, a typical response to overcrowding is to build more prisons – that, in turn, also become overcrowded, thus perpetuating the correctional treadmill fueled by the war on drugs and other tough-on-crime campaigns (Parenti, 1999; Welch, 1999a).

HOW ARE PRISONS ORGANIZED?

In terms of formal structure, prisons consist of three major organizational features: they are characterized as total institutions that are both paramilitary and bureaucratic. Although these organizational components overlap, it is important to understand their distinct qualities.

Prison as a total institution

In a classic sociological work, *Asylums: Essays on the Social Situations of Mental Patients and Other Inmates* (1961), Erving Goffman carefully examined the structure and process of total institutions. By definition, total institutions are 'place[s] of residence and work where a large number of like-situated individuals, cut off from the wider society for an appreciable period of time, together lead an enclosed, formally administered round of life' (Goffman, 1961: xiii). Total institutions are governed by a single authority situated within a strict hierarchy. They feature an inflexible chain of command, and communication channels flow only downward. Whether the residents are patients in a psychiatric hospital, recruits in the military, monks in a monastery, or inmates in a prison, their daily lives are organized according to a regimen and schedule determined by a single authority. In prisons, the single authority is the warden.

However, characterizing modern-day prisons as total institutions is somewhat inaccurate. Whereas prisons before the turn of the century certainly did operate as total institutions by remaining socially secluded, today prisons are more aligned with the community. Farrington (1992) challenged the popular notion that contemporary prisons are total institutions while carefully asserting that prisons today are somewhat less than total. Overall, today's prisons engage in 'a relatively stable and ongoing network of diverse transactions, exchanges and relationships' (1992: 6–7) which connect and bind together the prison, the immediate host community, and society at large.

Granted, being imprisoned is an isolating experience, and in no way should the adverse effects of seclusion be ignored. However, Farrington's contribution is an important one because he points out that convicts today have considerably more access to societal resources, especially attorneys and courts, than did inmates in past years. In effect, prisons and their inmates rarely exist totally outside society; rather, they remain as extensions of society.

Prison as a paramilitary organization

Much like their police counterparts, corrections officials have borrowed from the military model in structuring the prison organization. Although it is more accurate to refer to corrections as paramilitary, the distinct military influence on prisons is worth examining. The paramilitary influence in corrections can be traced to twelfth-century England, where jails (gaols) were administered by the sheriff (or shire-reeve) and his deputies. During that era, the paramilitary influence was used as a method of organizing and managing the staff. Not until centuries later did corrections officials attempt to formally impose the military model on inmates as a tool of discipline and reform, such as was done at New York's Elmira Reformatory in the 1870s (Smith, 1988). Although the military model has been recently resurrected as a strategy for prisoner reform (as in the case of prison boot camps), today the influence of the military model in corrections is used chiefly to organize and manage correctional staff.

To a greater or lesser degree, all correctional institutions conform to the military model. Indeed, the use of the term officer and the structure of rank (captain, lieutenant, sergeant, etc.) are clearly paramilitary. Still, the paramilitary features of corrections go beyond the use of titles and rank. There exists a strict hierarchy, an inflexible chain of command, and vertical communication lines, which are deliberately structured to enhance organizational performance. In the case of corrections, organizational performance means ensuring institutional security and maintaining internal order, and the paramilitary style of management is surmised as being capable of enhancing those directives. (See below: 'Working in Corrections: Tougher Prisons? A National Public Radio Interview.')

Prison as a bureaucracy

Because the major task of a correctional institution is to ensure security and maintain internal order, the question often asked is: what do bureaucracies have to do with corrections? Just as bureaucracies widely exist in the Internal Revenue Service (IRS), the Department of Motor Vehicles, and the financial-aid office of a university, so has a bureaucratic style of administration emerged in corrections.

A bureaucracy is 'an organization whose structure and operations are governed to a high degree by written rules' (Mann, 1984: 28). A bureaucracy rests on a hierarchical structure in which its employees occupy strictly defined roles. 'The logic behind bureaucratic structure is to produce entirely determinable, impartial, and impersonal operation' (Mann, 1984: 28; see also Weber, 1947).

Today, prisons are large and complex organizations, and the bureaucratic style of administration facilitates the day-to-day operation, which affects both staff and inmates. One of the prominent features of contemporary corrections is the excessive amount of paperwork. Correctional institutions are run by government agencies; therefore actions, commands, and requests are highly formalized through written documents and reports. Moreover, centralization shifts power from supervisors and wardens to high-level administrators. The recent legal developments in corrections have greatly contributed to this bureaucratic style; increasingly, corrections officials and staff are being held accountable for their policies and conduct. Inmates attempt to enforce this accountability by processing their complaints through the courts. Nevertheless, the bureaucratization of corrections does not imply that such a system is free of conflict and interference. Anyone who has had to deal with the IRS, the Department of Motor Vehicles, or a financial-aid office at a university can attest to the level of frustration caused by extensive red tape.

In sum, the evolution of American corrections shows that prisons are now less than total institutions. Social and legal developments have further shaped the prevailing paramilitary and bureaucratic style of administration.

WORKING IN CORRECTIONS

Tougher Prisons? A National Public Radio Interview

Host: The move to make prisons meaner is gaining all across the country and it has hit this area. Several New Jersey lawmakers have now signed on to a plan to impose tough new restrictions on New Jersey prison inmates, taking away amenities like weight rooms and TV sets. They are being joined by some law enforcement officials, anticrime activists and crime victims like Ryan St Michael, a Bergen County resident who says his sister was killed in a robbery 20 years ago.

Ryan: ... prisoners, a lot of prisoners, don't feel like prison is a bad place to be, and that was always the first point to punishment: to create an environment that people don't want to come back to. What we are doing is proposing a prison system for New Jersey that will be a no-amenities prison. A prison with no gym, no weight room, no law library, no air-conditioning, and no phone privileges. Just a day filled with menial work, teaching a work ethic to the violent and repeat offenders in this state.

Host: Politicians have made similar proposals to go back to the days of hard labor for years. But most have not been taken seriously until the last few years. Recently, states like Washington, Wisconsin, and Georgia have sharply cut back on the amenities in their prisons. Some have even begun forcing convicts to wear old-fashioned striped uniforms. Dr Michael Welch is a

Professor in the Criminal Justice Program at Rutgers University. He has also worked in prisons and taught college courses to inmates, the very kind of rehabilitation programs which anticrime advocates, like Ryan, want to eliminate. Welch says New Jersey lawmakers would be mistaken if they think that prisons are pleasant; he also says that proposals for tougher prisons don't address the root causes for crime.

Welch: Prisons and jails, in general, are not nice places to be. I worked for the Federal Bureau of Prisons a number of years ago, and I was a researcher in a minimum security unit in Fort Worth, Texas, where people like Roger Clinton were sentenced for drug dealing.

Host: You are talking about the President's brother?

Welch: Yes. And although it was a 'nice' place – a minimum-security unit with little violence – being in prison is not 'nice.' Inmates there would trade places with you in a New York minute. That is part of the philosophy of punishment in our society – to limit their liberty and take their freedom away, at least temporarily.

Host: There are a couple of images of prisons in this country which maybe are not really all that contradictory. And the one is of a real hell hole where if you are a relatively innocent person, if you are someone that is not a hardened criminal, you would never want to go and in fact you often hear of prisons that are almost riotous, that are out of control, you hear about guards misbehaving and so forth. At the same time, it is often suggested that very environment is not so hostile to someone who is a hardened criminal; that it is actually rather pleasant, and if you do add weight rooms, and decent prison food, and a place to stay, and a library, and television, and phone privileges and so forth it is sometimes suggested by the folks who want to take these amenities away, that prison isn't such a bad place to be if you are a hardened criminal.

Welch: In response, let me point out a recent study by criminologists Irwin and Austin who found that 20 percent of offenders in the prison system are indeed violent offenders. However, 80 percent of the inmate population is non-violent, including prisoners convicted of less serious offenses, especially drug violations. I suspect that most people – across the political spectrum – believe that violent offenders ought to be incarcerated. But for the most part the incarceration trend shows that the courts are increasingly sentencing a greater number of non-violent drug offenders to prison. According to the Sentencing Project, approximately 73 percent of incoming inmates in the federal prison system are non-violent drug offenders.

Host: You are suggesting then that this has less to do with how offenders are treated in prison, and even less to do with the current crime trend?

Welch: Certainly. Generally, violent crime has remained relatively constant since the 1960s. Now there is a little bit of fluctuation; also there is more attention to youthful offenders nowadays. But overall, violent crime has remained relatively constant, especially when you attend to population growth.

Host: Dr Welch, give me a sense here if there is any reason that we can give, if there is any good reason, that your average American can understand, why a criminal, whether a hardened criminal or merely someone who is a non-violent offender, really should have a library, for example, or a weight room or anything like that. How did those things get there to begin with? What is the justification?

Welch: Let's identify the origin of the debate. The debate is being fueled by politicians who want to exploit the views, attitudes, and prejudices of mainstream Americans in an effort to secure their elected posts. Yet, politicians underestimate the complexity of the opinions that citizens hold regarding punishment. Most people want punishment for offenders, but they also want inmates to be able to read, they want them to be rehabilitated, especially in the realm of substance abuse. We need to acknowledge the intersection of punishment and rehabilitation. A lot of these 'get-tough' proposals are merely symbolic. A recent *New York Times* article pointed out that in Louisiana, for instance, the state assembly passed legislation that bans martial arts programs for prisoners as well as the use of air-conditioners in housing units. It is interesting that they would include banning martial arts and air-conditioners as part of their legislation when in fact those prisons never have had martial arts programs and for the most part inmates do not have air-conditioners.

Host: So we are banning things they don't have anyway?

Welch: Absolutely. It is also crucial to acknowledge that prison staff have the task of managing inmates – often this involves a simple understanding of rewards and penalties. Michael Quinlan, former Director of the Federal Bureau of Prisons, aptly states that if inmates aren't kept busy, when you take away all of those activities they will find something to do with their time, and it probably won't be in the best interest of the staff trying to monitor their activities. At the very least, programs are necessary in prison because they serve as important management tools.

Host: You can understand though why some people may feel frustrated that we have this person who has committed some kind of a crime against society, and we have actually managed to catch him and get him through the legal system and go to all the expense of that, and go to all the expense of actually putting him in prison. And you are saying that we still have to appease the guy, we still have to give him something that he wants to do in order to keep him from becoming violent and causing more damage.

Welch: We also have to recognize the final destination of these inmates. They will return to our communities, and it is foolish to think they will commit crimes simply because they lifted weights in prison. They will be more likely to commit future crimes if they are unemployed, have ongoing problems with substance abuse – illegal drugs or alcohol – with family, or other psychological problems. If these problems aren't addressed while in prison, certainly we are setting them up for failure.

Host: Dr Michael Welch is a Professor in the Criminal Justice Program at Rutgers University in New Brunswick. He spoke to us from his home in Hoboken, New Jersey.

Carrissa Griffing transcribed the interview.

Contributions of Gresham Sykes

A discussion of power in prisons would not be complete without including Gresham Sykes's classic work, *Society of Captives* (1958; see also Sykes, 1956). Although some penologists overlook the immediate relevance of Sykes's contribution to present-day prisons because his research took place in the 1950s, many prison experts today continue to test his conclusions.

A central thesis in *Society of Captives* is that the authority exercised by corrections officers (COs) is vulnerable to corruption due to the relationships between the guards and the inmates. The key sources of this corruption of authority are friendships, reciprocity, and default. In his chapter 'The Defects of Total Power,' Sykes also draws on Weber's notions concerning bureaucracies, and points out that in addition to their formal relationships, COs also inevitably engage in informal relationships which reduce social distance. Indeed, to a greater or lesser degree, COs often form friendships with the convicts with whom they have close daily interaction. Similarly, in terms of reciprocity, 'the guard is evaluated in terms of the conduct of the men he controls' (Sykes, 1958: 56). COs are sometimes indebted to inmates whose cooperation leads to positive job evaluations from their supervisors; in other words, prisoners can make guards look good or bad.

Finally, default is referred to as 'the innocuous encroachment of the prisoner on the guard's duties' (Sykes, 1958: 57). Because prisons are complex organizations, inmates have minor roles (e.g. clerks, secretaries, program assistants) to facilitate the prisons' daily operations – a situation that offsets the balance of total power.

In the late 1970s to the mid-1980s, prison research both challenged (Lombardo, 1981) and confirmed (Hewitt *et al.*, 1984) Sykes's assertions about the corruption of staff authority. Because these researchers used different methodologies, their findings are difficult to compare. However, Glaser and Fry (1987: 31) provided additional support for Sykes's observation that 'guards are more likely to seek inmate cooperation with a carrot than with a stick.' That cooperation is achieved through both reciprocity and default. Glaser and Fry strongly emphasize that those sources of corruption of authority are not negative criticisms of prison staff; rather, 'staff–inmate reciprocity is probably a norm in the daily operation of any place of confinement' (1987: 38). In contrast to the total-power feature of a paramilitary bureaucracy is the reliance on inmate cooperation in modern prisons. Prisoners are rewarded for cooperation. The most common reward is the deliberate oversight of inmate violations. Glaser and Fry conclude 'that Sykes' corruption of authority perspective is still useful in understanding a confinement institution, and should be applied in further research focusing on the corruption processes' (1987: 38).

PAINS OF IMPRISONMENT

Life in prison is a punishing experience, and many advocates of retribution argue that it is supposed to be. Simply put, placing offenders behind bars is society's way of demonstrating its disapproval of crime. Moreover, the pains of imprisonment are intended to go beyond the body – indeed, a certain amount of emotional and psychological suffering is deliberately inflicted. Feelings of deprivation and frustration are key components of suffering in prison, and in his classic work, *Society of Captives* (1958), Gresham Sykes further delineates the following pains of imprisonment.

Deprivation of liberty

In American society, citizens are expected to cherish freedom and liberty. Therefore one way to punish offenders is to deprive them of their liberty. Clearly, that practice remains an important rationale for punishment, especially since imprisonment extends to offenders who are non-violent and do not pose a threat to society.

Restricting an individual's physical movement by way of seclusion and by eliminating routine contact with family and friends is one aspect of the deprivation of liberty. In fact, the physical conditions of a prison do not have to be harsh to achieve this objective. Even if someone is confined to one of the finest hotels and fed exquisite food while watching cable television, eventually that experience would become punishing if the person could not leave the room for days, weeks, months, or even years. Certainly, loneliness and boredom would set in, and most people would forfeit the posh accommodations, select meals, and cable television just to be able to return to the free world.

Deprivation of goods and services

By design, prisons deprive inmates of the goods and services that they are accustomed to obtaining in the free world. Although convicts do not ordinarily go hungry, and they are supposed to have a bed to sleep in, the basic elements of their material life are greatly minimized. Sykes argues that in our society, which values materialism and accumulation, material deprivation can be equated with personal inadequacy (1958: 70). Sykes's point may ring especially true for prisoners who engaged in crimes that were motivated by a desire for wealth or material goods.

Deprivation of heterosexual relationships

Few prisons allow inmates conjugal visits, and those that do, offer them very infrequently. Understandably, being deprived of heterosexual relationships is a punishing aspect of prisons; consequently, convicts pursue other means of sexual gratification. In prison masturbation is the most common method of sexual release while other inmates participate in voluntary homosexual relations (see Ross and Richards, 2002).

Deprivation of autonomy

In the course of a life span, an individual passes through childhood and the frustrating experience of being told what to do and when to do it. With maturity comes the autonomy to make personal decisions and to structure life according to personal preferences and needs. In prison, however, adults undergo additional punishment in that they are deprived of such autonomy. Inmates must eat, sleep, work, attend programs, and recreate according to a rigid institutional schedule. Obviously, it is frustrating to be denied simple explanations and justifications for rules and commands. Sykes adds that this invokes a 'profound threat to the prisoner's self-image because they reduce the prisoner to the weak, helpless, dependent status of childhood' (1958: 75).

Deprivation of security

Prisons, especially maximum security institutions, are dangerous places largely because they hold violent inmates. Surely, offenders often run the risk of exploitation or victimization within the walls. An inmate in the New Jersey State Prison told Sykes: 'The worst thing about prison is you have to live with other prisoners' (1958: 77).

In sum, each of the pains of imprisonment compounds the degree of punishment in prisons. In combination, they contribute to the pathology of the prison environment, insofar as such deprivations foster insecurity, which leads to intimidation, exploitation, harassment, assaults, sexual violence, and other predatory behaviors (see Irwin, 1980; Silberman, 1995).

PHENOMENOLOGY OF IMPRISONMENT AND SUFFERING

In keeping with the critical theme of this book, it is fitting to introduce phenomenology as a valuable framework for exploring corrections. Phenomenology is 'the study of the various forms and varieties of consciousness and the ways in which people can apprehend the world in which they live' (Mann, 1984: 286). That perspective is influenced by the work of philosophers Edmund Husserl and Alfred Schutz, and sociologist Peter Berger. Numerous social science methods borrow directly or indirectly from phenomenology insofar as researchers try to capture the world of convicts and guards. Investigations of their world are usually achieved through in-depth interviews and ethnographies.

Some applications of phenomenology in corrections have returned to phenomenology's formal concepts and principles. Meisenhelder (1985) and Welch (1991d) delineate the temporal component of suffering in prisons by focusing on the role that time plays in defining punishment. Traditionally, the concept of time has been used to quantify punishment in terms of the number of months or years that one is incarcerated. The logic is simple – the longer the sentence, the harsher the punishment.

The concept of time can also be used to explore the experience of punishment because time is experienced differently in the prison world than it is in the free world. That shift in the temporal field marks a qualitative difference that determines the degree of suffering. For example, in the free world, time is experienced as a resource, whereas in prison it is a burden. In the free world, people have time to be used as they see fit, even if they choose to 'waste' time. However, in prison, inmates are forced to 'do' time, and are faced with how slowly time seems to pass when one is bored and lonely. Meisenhelder asserts that looking toward the future gives meaning to life, and that 'without a definite sense of attainable future, time is likely to be experienced as meaningless, empty and boring' (1985: 45). Similarly, Farber (1944) points out that a key source of suffering is the perception that one's future is uncertain.

The phenomenological approach facilitates understanding of the link between the concept of time and suffering, insofar as prisoners understand that incarceration destroys or takes away their time. Certainly, proponents of retribution argue that the loss of time is the purpose of punishment and suffering (see Vuolo and Kruttshnitt, 2008).

INMATE SOCIAL SYSTEM AND SUBCULTURE

In view of the suffering, deprivations, and pains of imprisonment, Sykes and Messinger (1960) expound on Sykes's earlier work (1958) by constructing a theory explaining the underpinnings of the inmate social system. In their work, Sykes and Messinger hypothesize that inmates organize a social system (or society) and subculture as a reflection and accommodation of their suffering, deprivations, and pains.

At this point in the discussion, clarification of terms is necessary. The distinct features of a social system (or society) and of a culture should not be blurred, even though they are closely related. The terms social system and society refer to a social structure with interconnected units, and social roles emanate from the way society is arranged. The term culture, on the other hand, refers to shared or common ideas, beliefs, dogma, ideology, values, customs, mores, and language. Since the inmate social system exists as a 'mini-society,' the inmate culture is more accurately termed a subculture.

Officially designated as social outcasts, convicts undergo a formal degradation ceremony in prison from the beginning of their incarceration, such as having their heads shaved and being required to wear uniforms (even though one or both of these practices have been abandoned in some prisons, prisons remain places of persistent degradation). Those elements of degradation are reminders of convicts' moral unworthiness. While under strict control, inmates feel the stress associated with pervasive surveillance. Moreover, as their self-esteem becomes increasingly threatened, they search for ways to alleviate this torment. One way is to adapt to the situation by participating in the inmate social structure, replete with an inmate code (or system of values), specific roles (or typology), and the inmate special language (known as an argot).

A dominant theme in the inmate social system is solidarity, and that theme is reflected in the inmate code. Through solidarity, prisoners can partially alleviate the pains of imprisonment (e.g. isolation, loneliness, and boredom) and partially neutralize imprisonment's degrading features. Solidarity among convicts provides them with a meaningful social group, which may serve to restore inmates' self-respect and sense of independence. Other sociologists have explored that area of institutionalization. For example, Goffman (1961) referred to the unofficial organization and subculture as the underlife, adding that prison conditions shape that form of inmate collective behavior (also see Cloward, 1960; Schrag, 1961; Selke, 1993).

Inmate code

A closer look at the prisoner social system studied by Sykes and Messinger (1960) calls for elaborating on the inmate code. As is the case in the free world, the convict world is guided by rules and enforced by sanctions. The following are

Figure 5.2 Inmates performing pop icon Michael Jackson's dance routine during a press preview at Cebu City provincial jail on March 4, 2010. Dressed in tangerine jump suits, the roughly 1,500 convicted murderers, rapists and other inmates perform a series of Michael Jackson-inspired dances that have helped boost their morale while also making them Internet sensations.

Photo credit: Ted Aljibe/ AFP/Getty Images.

the five major categories of the inmate code discovered by Sykes and Messinger more than 50 years ago:

1 Don't interfere with inmate interests:
   – Never rat on a con.
   – Don't be nosey.
   – Be loyal to your class – the cons.
2 Don't lose your head:
   – Play it cool and do your own time.
3 Don't exploit inmates:
   – Don't break your word.
   – Don't steal from the cons.
   – Don't sell favors.
   – Don't be a racketeer.
   – Don't welsh on debts.
4 Don't weaken:
   – Don't whine.
   – Don't cop out (or cry guilty).
   – Don't suck around.
   – Be tough; be a man.
5 Don't be a sucker:
   – Don't accept the guards' view of the world.
   – Be sharp.

The more compliance to the inmate code, the higher the degree of convict solidarity. The code promotes strong normative imperatives, and noncompliance is met with sanctions ranging from ostracism to physical violence. Nevertheless, violations of the inmate code are commonplace in prison – understandably, those who disobey society's rules cannot always be expected to comply with inmate rules. Prisoners are known to breach the inmate code in several ways, and those patterns of rule-breaking further advance what Sykes and Messinger (1960) call a convict typology. As described briefly in the next section, it is important to note that much like the inmate code, the convict typology rests heavily on exaggerated images of masculinity by encouraging 'macho' behavior while condemning perceived weakness, including homosexuality (see Kruttschnitt, 1981).

Convict typology

Sykes (1958) and Sykes and Messinger (1960) point out that there is no compelling reason to believe that convicts embrace the inmate code with equal intensity. With that distinction in mind, several types of convicts are identified.

- *The right guy*. Also known as the 'real con' or the 'real man,' the right guy exemplifies the convict who enthusiastically celebrates the inmate code. He remains loyal to fellow prisoners and never lets others get down, no matter how rough things get. The right guy is dependable and always keeps his promises.

- *The rat or squealer.* The rat (also known as the snitch) provides inside information about other convicts to the staff and, because of his snitching, is vehemently despised by fellow inmates. The rat is often the victim of brutal attacks of revenge by other prisoners.
- *The tough.* The tough is a highly volatile and aggressive inmate who is always willing to fight, even over minor issues of dispute and sometimes without a reason.
- *The gorilla.* The gorilla is more predatory than the tough, and sets out to exploit other inmates by force.
- *The merchant or peddler.* The merchant violates the inmate code by engaging in rackets to sell goods that are in short supply. He also frequently engages in trickery and scams.
- *The weakling or weak sister.* The weakling is characterized by not having the capacity to be tough and withstand the pressures of incarceration.
- *The wolf, fag, and punk.* This category draws distinctions between certain forms of homosexuality. First, the wolf seeks homosexual relations as a result of his inability to cope with the deprivation of heterosexual relations. The fag plays the passive role in a homosexual relationship because he 'likes' it, or 'wants' to, and the punk is coerced or bribed into a passive role.
- *The rapo or the innocent.* Convicts who are always claiming their innocence or professing that they got a 'bum rap' fall into this category. Such complaints grow tiresome among other inmates, who simply do not want to hear relentlessly exaggerated complaints.
- *The square john.* The square john embraces free-world values, not inmate values, and aligns himself closely with the staff and administration.

Inmate slang

Slang, lingo, or argot is an important feature of the convict subculture. That unique way of speaking reflects prison dogma and ideology, thereby attaching a deeper meaning to the prison experience. The following is a list of 'prison lingo' assembled by John Stanley, a former career criminal who served lengthy sentences in state and federal prisons (see also Ross and Richards, 2002, 2003).

Slang term	*Meaning*
Hack	Correctional officer
Snitch, rat	Inmate who supplies information to prison staff (tattletale)
Hooch	Prison-made liquor
Hooter	Marijuana cigarette
Mota, smoke, reefer	Marijuana
Chiva	Heroin

The hole	Segregation unit located on the prison compound
Punk, hole, bitch	Male homosexual
Home, homey, holmes	Friend or companion
Homeboys	Inmates from the same hometown
Old thang	Inmate who has been incarcerated for many years
Short-timer	Inmate with only a short time of his sentence remaining
Down	Length of time served ('I have been down for 20 months')
Shank, shiv	Sharp prison-made weapon
Pipe	Unauthorized object to be used as a weapon
Leg rider; riding the leg, or 'get off his leg'	Inmate who goes out of his way to do special favors for staff; similar to a dog's 'hunching' his master's leg
Trembler	Inmate who is afraid of the prison environment
Cellee	Cellmate
Fall partners	Inmates who are convicted on the same case; codefendants
Cop out	Inmate's written request to the staff
In chain	Traveling with cuffs and leg irons
Diesel therapy	Traveling on the Federal Bureau of Prisons bus
Shot	Incident report for a violation of prison rules

PRISONIZATION

Sykes and Messinger (1960) contributed to the understanding of how the inmate social structure is arranged and the purposes it serves. What is missing in their description, however, is the social process by which incarcerated individuals become prisoners. Similar to the ways in which recruits become officers, a gradual socialization process transforms those behind bars into prisoners. In an equally important contribution, Clemmer (1958) popularized the term prisonization. Clemmer refers to the term assimilation, which is used to demonstrate how immigrants undergo the process of acculturation and gradually take on the sentiments and traditions of their new land. Accordingly, prisonization is 'the taking on in greater or less degree the folkways, mores, and customs, and general culture of the penitentiary' (Clemmer, 1958: 299; also see Welch, 1996e).

The process of prisonization begins with a transformation of the convicts' status. For example, identification numbers replace their names, and they may be required to wear institutional uniforms, both of which are reminders that they occupy the bottom rung of the institutional hierarchy. Another aspect of prisonization is the convict language, and even an inmate who does not use this slang certainly learns its meanings. Clemmer argued that prisonization reinforces the inmates' criminal status, further deepening their commitment to the convict ideology – or way of life.

While all inmates are exposed to prisonization, not every convict completes the full process. A number of factors determine the extent to which inmates are prisonized. Prisonization depends on the inmate's personality, relationships with people outside prison, affiliation with prison primary or semi-primary groups, placement on a work gang, and acceptance of the dogma or codes of the prison culture. Furthermore, age, criminality, nationality, race, and regional conditioning remain important determinants.

In light of these factors, Clemmer (1958) constructed the following schemata of prisonization, which may lead inmates into completing the prisonization process.

1 A sentence of many years, thus a long subjection to the universal factors of prisonization.
2 A somewhat unstable personality made more unstable by an inadequacy of 'socialized' relations before commitment, but possessing, nonetheless, a capacity for strong convictions and a particular kind of loyalty.
3 A dearth of positive relations with persons outside the walls.
4 A readiness and a capacity for integration into a prison primary group.
5 A blind, or almost blind, acceptance of the dogmas and mores of the primary group and the general penal population.
6 A chance placement with other persons of a similar orientation.
7 A readiness to participate in gambling and abnormal sex behavior.

Two major models shape the debate on prisonization: the deprivation model and the importation model. The deprivation model acknowledges the pains of imprisonment presented by Gresham Sykes in *Society of Captives* (1958), including the deprivations of liberty, goods and services, heterosexual relationships, autonomy, and security. By its very nature, prison deprives convicts of basic needs, which in turn creates frustration, pressure, and strain. Hence, prisonization serves to alleviate feelings of deprivation and the pains of imprisonment.

According to the importation model, however, the pressure created in prison has less to do with deprivations and more to do with the characteristics of inmates. Prisoners import their ideas, attitudes, and behaviors from their outside lives as street criminals into the prison. Although the debate as to whether prisonization can be attributed to deprivation or importation sometimes polarizes, the most reasonable position is to borrow from both models. Certainly, convicts experience deprivation, and they also tend to import their own characteristics into prison. Prisonization may generate some positive effects, such as inmate solidarity. At the same time, however, it also produces negative effects by reinforcing convict attitudes, beliefs, and values. As a consequence of these negative effects, Clemmer (1958) equated prisonization with criminalization. Moreover, because prisonization leads to the rejection of conventional values, Clemmer argued that it also impedes reform and rehabilitation.

The concept of prisonization, albeit a popular one, has been subject to extensive scrutiny by penologists. The critique of prisonization stems from three critical approaches (Hawkins, 1976). The first line of criticism addresses Clemmer's assumption that the degree of prisonization is determined by the length of confinement; hence, the longer the sentence, the higher the degree of prisonization. The most significant finding that challenged this linear proposition was revealed by Stanton Wheeler (1961), who suggested a curvilinear, or U-shaped, pattern. That is, convicts experienced a cyclical fluctuation during their incarceration, from holding conformist attitudes to holding antisocial attitudes, and then returning to conformist attitudes upon nearing completion of their sentence. Since inmates are prisonized and deprisonized, the overall impact of the inmate subculture was found to be relatively short. These findings were supported by subsequent research by Garabedian (1963) and Glaser (1964).

The prisonization thesis also is criticized for failing to take into account that informal groups vary within the larger institution with respect to their characteristics, behavior, and functions. Moreover, the orientation of the institution itself contributes to these patterns of behavior. Treatment-oriented institutions tend to promote cooperation between informal leaders and prison staff, which in turn facilitates rehabilitation (Grusky, 1959). Conversely, custodial prisons increase deprivation for inmates, thereby contributing to hostile, antisocial attitudes toward the prison staff (Berk, 1996).

The final criticism of prisonization returns to the debate between deprivation and importation theories. It has been argued that what is understood as prisonization resulting from deprivation is actually a form of antisocial behavior that is deeply rooted in the convicts' criminal history. John Irwin and Donald Cressey (1964) note that what is often called inmate culture stems from beliefs, attitudes, and lifestyles imported from the free world. James Jacobs (1974) supported this position by illuminating the process by which street gangs import their organizational roles and ideologies from the free world into the penitentiary. It should be noted, however, that the prison environment serves to strengthen the subcultural identity among inmates. In sum, it is difficult to assume that the mere process of incarceration leads to what Clemmer described as prisonization because prisons vary according to orientation, size, and security level. Perhaps what best resembles prisonization in the classic sense is the assimilation that occurs in repressive maximum-security penitentiaries (Welch, 1996e). (See 'Comparative Corrections: Inmate Subculture in an Israeli Prison', below).

Implications for policy and programming

Policy and programming continue to be influenced by ideas concerning prisonization, as well as by formal and informal mechanisms of control. Although corrections administrators recognize the negative aspects of gang activities (e.g. violence, weapons, drugs, and other forms of contraband), they also acknowledge the positive aspects of gangs. Prison staff at times co-opt gang leaders in an effort to maintain internal order. For instance, officers sometimes encourage gang leaders to control unruly inmates in exchange for favors and privileges, producing a paradox that bolsters the power of gang leaders to the detriment of all. Subsequently, if gang leaders become too powerful and use their influence to challenge the prison staff, administrators often transfer them to another institution where they will yield considerably less power.

In terms of programming, a criticism expressed by corrections administrators is that gang members do not 'program.' That is, they do not enroll and participate in counseling and rehabilitation programs. The reason for that prohibition among gang members is that counseling is regarded as an individual activity, while the purpose of a gang is to convert imprisonment into a group experience. One exception, though, are programs that offer educational objectives – many gangs value self-improvement activities, such as reading and earning high school-equivalency diplomas. To that end, some gang leaders often encourage members to assist each other with studying and other academic tasks.

Policy also extends to other aspects of programming, most notably attempts to prepare convicts to enter the community upon their release. Work release, educational release, furlough, and other programs take into consideration the negative effects of incarceration. Those programs are based on the assumption that every inmate undergoes at least some negative transformation, even though the term prisonization is not always used to describe the process (see Peat and Winfree, 1992; Yablonsky, 1989).

In sum, Clemmer's contribution to penology clearly has had a lasting impact on the field. The concept of prisonization has become widely accepted by many prison experts. Despite its criticisms, numerous studies focusing on the effects of incarceration and institutional adjustment continue to rely on the notion of prisonization – whether the concept is stated or merely implied. Other components of prisonization and socialization, such as inmate codes, argot, and social roles, also remain vital subjects in penology (Welch, 1996e).

COMPARATIVE CORRECTIONS

Inmate Subculture in an Israeli Prison

As discussed throughout much of this chapter, the social world of convicts is shaped significantly by its subculture, providing prisoners with informal means to garner power and neutralize their rejection from the free world. It has been argued that such prison dynamics are universal and present in virtually all types of institutions and in all societies. With that understanding, criminologists Tomer Einat and Haim Einat set out to explore the formation of the inmate subculture in an Israeli prison. Specifically, Einat and Einat concentrated on inmate argot (or slang) with the assumption that language facilitates coping with the prison environment. While the Israeli Prison Service declares that its institutions are rehabilitation oriented, in practice the Israeli prison regime is first and foremost concerned with security and custody, enforcing 'industrial silence.' Consequently, relations among prisoners are based on power and are predominantly aggressive. Not surprisingly, inmate argot reflects the conflicts prisoners experience with each other and the custodial staff.

In their interviews with Hebrew-speaking inmates serving terms of at least ten years, Einat and Einat (2000) discovered key territories of language, including prisoner status, drugs, sexual relations, and nicknames for prison staff. In reference to prisoner status, argot expressions mirrored the importance of loyalty and warnings against snitching.

> A prisoner who sings, becomes a snitch and a maniac has to know that he will be treated as a maniac ... He will be ambushed, knifed, his face will be cut ... so everybody will know who he is, and that they should never act like him. (Einat and Einat, 2000: 315)

Israeli prisoners, much like their international counterparts, gain satisfaction from resisting the prison authorities. By doing so, those prisoners improve their status among fellow inmates, earning nicknames such as ustazim (leaders), rais (arbitrator), and asli baldum (what a man!).

Drugs provide an escape from the pains of imprisonment, and so remain central to the inmate subculture. In the Israeli prison studied by Einat and Einat, inmates had their own terms for withdrawal syndrome (*kriz*) and insanity caused by drug use (*atraf* and *chocho*). Sexual contact in prison also alleviates the stress and strain of a prison environment marked by the deprivation of heterosexual relationships. Israeli prisoners use the term sandwich to refer to homosexual intercourse, scuba diver to describe oral sex, and muffler to mean the male sex organ. Prison argot pertaining to sex also reflects the power dynamics between the strong and the weak. 'Prisoners who cooperate with the authorities during investigations are known as whores and prisoners who submit to other inmates without a fight are termed cocksinelles (transvestites)' (Einat and Einat, 2000: 316).

Penologists have determined that, given the structure of the prison social world, inmates hold ambivalent attitudes toward their keepers. On the one hand, prisoners distrust and despise corrections officers and on the other they show certain forms of deference and subordination, especially because the staff have the power to control prisoners during their stay.

> Believe me, they [corrections officers] are all maniacs ... worse than our maniacs. First because they file complaints about us about everything, they think they have power and they are full of poses. Second, they are all contaminated. Some of them have traded drugs with us. Some of them have been fixed up with prostitutes by us. Some have accepted financial bribes from us in exchange for knives, pistols, and other things. (Einat and Einat, 2000: 318–19)

Then, when a corrections officer enters the room during the interview, the prisoner changes his tone dramatically.

How are things my brother? What's up? Believe me, they [corrections officers] are poor things and have a hard job. They're also stuck with us in the prison, and living with all the brara [criminals] is definitely not easy. (Einat and Einat, 2000: 319)

In sum, this research offers support for the idea that prisoners do not feel any obligation to conform to the norms imposed on them by prison authorities. Along with that resistance inmates develop their own subculture, shaped by a common language. Like prisoners in other nations, 'Israeli's prison community masters argot and uses it proudly' (Einat and Einat, 2000: 320).

ADJUSTMENT AND STRATEGIES OF COPING

In addition to the various forms of deprivation, inmates endure multiple sources of stress. For instance, convicts must cope with frustrations caused by guards, the administration, and fellow prisoners alongside threats of violence – all of which are exacerbated by overcrowding. Compounding worries, of course, are concerns about appeals, parole, and post-release – including employment, family, and general survival in the free world (see Bergner, 1998; Harvey, 2007; Walens, 1997).

In response to those institutional stressors, inmates choose strategies of coping that meet their particular emotional and personal needs. Prisoners rarely rely on a single method of coping, resorting to strategies aimed at the long and short term. Litigation and exercising grievance mechanisms are long-range strategies given that they are labor-intensive and require lengthy turnaround periods. Similarly, some convicts withdraw into a 'niche,' or place of refuge, becoming deeply involved in a project or work assignment or affiliated with a clique or gang. Indeed, rebellion is sometimes interpreted as a strategy for coping: for example, participating in labor strikes against the administration by refusing to report to their job assignments or even committing individual or collective acts of violence. Still many experts view such aggression and 'acting out' as signs of lack of coping (see Crouch et al., 1999; Ross and Richards, 2002, 2003; Sabo, et al., 2001; Terry, 1997).

CONTRABAND AND THE UNDERGROUND ECONOMY

Throughout much of this book, we have explored the role that economic forces play in shaping corrections – especially those dynamics external to the prison. In this section, attention is turned to the internal economics shaping the institution as well as the convict social world. It is important to bear in mind that the economy inside 'the joint' unfolds both formally and informally. Formal systems remain the economic base of prisons; for example, inmates are employed by staff to work in the kitchen, the laundry, or other prison industries. Those prisoners are paid modest wages that vary from job to job and from institution to institution: generally, hourly compensation often ranges between 15 cents and a few dollars. The formal system also includes the prison commissary, where inmates purchase such items as cigarettes and junk food. The method of exchange often involves a system of 'book credits' that enables the administration to monitor spending and supervise inmate accounts.

The informal economic system is often called the underground or *sub rosa* economy and features the unofficial exchange of contraband (prohibited goods), such as weapons, drugs, alcohol, free-world money, cell phones, and other items that might facilitate an escape or be used to bribe convicts or staff. As mentioned, the deprivation of goods and services remains a deliberate form of suffering and the imposition of poverty is often referred to as a 'fringe punishment' (see Gleason, 1978, 1985; Kalinich, 1986; Kalinich and Stojkovic, 1985, 1987; Williams and Fish, 1974, 1985).

Although the convict code prohibits engaging in business rackets and exploiting fellow inmates, the underground economy thrives because it conforms to a set of business ethics and morality. Thus many economic activities persist in part because they allow prisoners to 'wheel and deal' without being viewed negatively as 'merchants.' That subcultural aspect of the informal economy fosters a sense of cooperation and fairness among the convicts. Moreover, the underground economy is not a mere metaphor: it is a recognizable system replete with principles of supply and demand, consumerism, profit, division of labor, and monetary currency. The flourishing nature of such economic systems among inmates demonstrates the pervasive element of materialism inside prisons – not unlike the free world.

The accumulation of commodities is greatly curtailed by limits on storage and risk of confiscation. Therefore the informal economic system is primarily a service economy involving, for example, prostitution and various other 'favors.' Since free-world dollars (a.k.a., greenbacks) are banned inside prisons and jails, the currency most often used are items that are not considered contraband, such as coffee, candy, junk food, and toilet articles – all of which are available at the commissary. Indeed, that form of exchange makes the purchase of services possible without detection by the staff. The most popular underground currency in many prisons is cigarettes, featuring denominations: singles, packs of 20, and cartons of 10 packs.

In addition to illegal drugs, such as marijuana, cocaine, and heroin, convict-made alcohol (a.k.a. prison hooch) is a leading commodity in the underground economy. Obviously, inmates are attracted to 'hooch' for its intoxicating effects that offer a temporary 'escape' from the stress of prison. There are, however, many disadvantages facing the alcohol enterprise. The production process requires the gathering of raw materials along with manufacturing, warehousing, distribution, and eventually consumption. Each of those aspects is logistically difficult and prone to detection. Nevertheless, convicts are known to be ingenious in such ventures, as the following example shows:

> An improved technology is being used in Alabama State Prisons. Inmates obtain small, flexible containers – a prophylactic or a plastic bag is suitable. The ingredients – some water, sugar, fruit, and yeast – are sealed in a bag. A man sleeps with the bag between his legs and his body heat hastens the fermentation. This simplified process is faster and involves less risk of discovery.
>
> (Williams and Fish, 1985: 169)

As one might imagine, convict-made alcohol rarely tastes good, and many inmates who do drink 'hooch' usually get sick and vomit.

Another alcohol-related story that circulated in the Federal Bureau of Prisons originated from one of the system's minimum-security institutions. In that case, a small group of white-collar criminals, who were accustomed to partaking in cocktail hours in the free world, persuaded a fellow inmate to climb the fence and visit the neighborhood liquor store. When he returned with the essentials for making martinis, one inmate questioned the absence of olives. The inmate returned to the liquor store for the olives, only to be caught climbing the fence on his way back to the prison.

Prisoners in Leavenworth penitentiary describe the smuggling procedure involving visiting girlfriends:

> The heroin was delivered inside a balloon, no different from those used at children's birthdays parties. She was supposed to hide it in her vagina, like a tampon. Once inside the prison visiting room, she would step into the women's bathroom, remove the balloon, and conceal it in her mouth. Visitors were allowed to kiss an inmate once when a visit began and once when it ended. The balloon would be exchanged during the first kiss. Hutchinson [the inmate] would swallow it and either regurgitate it later when he was alone in his cell or reclaim it after it passed through his system.
>
> (Earley, 1992: 11)

Underscoring the notion of symbiotic relationships within the prison social world is the realization that some officers themselves participate in the underground economy. Sometimes 'dirty' guards, in a genuine attempt to be friendly, bring to inmates items believed to be harmless, such as junk food. But on occasion, staff import illegal drugs for personal profit or to lure inmates into sexual favors. The most prevalent form of participation in the *sub rosa* economy involves officers who 'turn a blind eye' and refuse to report violations involving contraband. In doing so, guards create another form of leverage which can be used as bargaining power to informally control prisoners (Kalinich, 1986; Kalinich and Stojkovic, 1985, 1987; McCarthy, 1995; Ross and Richards, 2002, 2003).

GANGS IN PRISON

As discussed previously, the convict social world is shaped in large part by the personal traits that inmates import into prison (see Clemmer, 1958; Schrag, 1960; Irwin and Cressey, 1964; Schwartz, 1971). Such importation also applies to the emergence of street gangs in prisons. One of the classic examinations of gangs behind bars was completed by Jacobs (1974, 1985). In his study of Stateville (Illinois), Jacobs concentrated on the structure and workings of four major gangs based in Chicago. Two of those gangs are the Black P Stone Nation and the Disciples, both characterized by high-level, syndicate-like criminal activities. The Vice Lords, the third gang in Jacobs's study, is an older and more conservative gang, boasting street activities ranging from benevolent community organization to small business ventures. Finally, the Latin Kings at that time were a relatively small group inside Stateville but known as one of the largest gangs on the streets of Chicago.

Behind bars, these gangs are organized by a list of written rules resembling the inmate code. Gangs are formally structured, and this degree of organization is reflected by the many services provided by their members. Physical security and psychological support are two of the major functions of these gangs. For instance, to offset the deprivations of goods, gang members contribute cigarettes (as well as contraband) to a 'poor box' which needy members may draw from. Clearly, there exists firm belief in sharing with others.

Gangs are constantly trying to improve their communication networks to their neighborhood contacts as well as family members, keeping them apprised of any problems behind bars while staying in touch with what is happening on the street. Inside the prison, gangs extend to members a sense of family and brotherhood along with an array of psychological benefits: personal and group identification, a feeling of belonging, and an air of importance. As one inmate reported to Jacobs: 'It's just like a religion. Once a Lord, always a Lord' (1974, 1985: 194). That religious-like devotion is further expressed in gang symbols, colors, insignia, salutes, and titles, as well as the gang's own oral history of legendary events and heroes.

Like other formal organizations, gangs have clearly defined roles and levels of status. At the so-called entry-level position, members occupy the role of Indians or soldiers. Those recruits have the task of proving themselves by carrying out low-level tasks, such as running messages for the higher-ups. Other duties of the rank and file vary from gang to gang. For instance, the Vice Lords discourage their members from using senseless violence and would rather reward their soldiers for helping other members with such personal difficulties as learning to read (Jacobs, 1974, 1985).

Understandably, the leaders or chiefs remain the core group of the gang. Policies, activities, and directives emanate from those positions of power that are imported from the street. In his research at Stateville, Jacobs pursues that element of importation theory by demonstrating that when a high-ranking gang official is incarcerated, he maintains his status as a leader on the inside.

Contrary to popular belief, gangs in Stateville at the time of Jacobs's study were not engaged in warfare with their rivals. Rather, gangs value a peaceful coexistence, noting that 'international war' must be avoided at all costs. Moreover, gang leaders do not appear to have any overarching objectives or goals while in prison, as a clinical counselor explained to Jacobs:

> What the gang leaders want is a moderately comfortable existence for their people within the prison and an opportunity to maintain their ties with the gang on the street as well as to promote their gang identity within the prison.
>
> (Jacobs, 1974, 1985: 198)

In view of that situation, gang leaders sometimes overtly support prison policies and often serve as intermediaries between the administration and their soldiers. The following example illustrates that dynamic in a case involving a Disciple who locked himself in his own cell and refused to be moved to an isolation cell (or the hole):

> The chief guard called the Disciple leader to his office and discussed the potentially explosive consequences of the situation. Subsequently the leader went to the cell of the irate soldier and talked to him about the pros and cons of provoking a violent confrontation with staff. The next morning the gang member went peaceably to isolation.
>
> (Jacobs, 1974, 1985: 200)

There are, of course, risks in allowing such prisoner intervention. Having a gang leader mediate such incidents undermines the authority of frontline officers. Consequently, correctional staff tend to experience alienation in ways that exacerbate tensions and morale problems within their own ranks.

Other activities behind bars support the contention that gangs remain an integral part of their outside communities. Jacobs found that, on occasion, gang leaders have met with their rivals and agreed on treaties affecting gang activities on the streets. In a very real sense, the process of importation can be viewed as a two-way street.

Finally, it is useful to touch on another unique component of the gang subculture in prison. Among the complaints expressed by administrators is that gang members do not 'program,' meaning that they do not enroll in counseling and treatment programs. As mentioned previously, the reason for that prohibition is that counseling is viewed as an individual activity, and the purpose of a gang is to convert imprisonment into a group experience. Programs that offer educational objectives are an exception – the gangs in Stateville do value self-improvement activities such as reading and earning high school-equivalency diplomas.

Several investigations have focused on gang activities in other prison systems. In Texas, for instance, two gangs in particular continue to grow. The Texas Syndicate was formed in 1975 by a group of inmates who had served sentences in the California system. The Mexican Mafia (or MEXIKANEMI or Soldiers of

Azthan), the largest gang in the Texas system, formed in the late 1980s. Both of these gangs have a reputation of being involved in the trafficking of illegal drugs.

Like many correctional systems across the nation, the jail complex at Rikers Island (New York) has had to deal with rising gang membership. Since 1992, corrections officials have become increasingly concerned with the rise of the Latin Kings (all Hispanics) and the Netas (mostly Hispanics but including other racial and ethnic groups). The Netas derive their name from a term used in an Indian ritual in Puerto Rico. Rikers Island administrators report that gang members compound institutional tension by engaging in violence against other inmates as well as staff; these threats are taken seriously given the proliferation of razors and shanks (prisoner-made knives) among the convict population. In planning and executing their attacks, gang members communicate with hand signals that allow them to act en masse and defy guards' orders.

In prisons elsewhere, concern is also extended to convicts belonging to white supremacist gangs, such as the Ku Klux Klan, the Aryan Nation, WAR (White Aryan Resistance), Posse Comitatus, and other neo-Nazi and racist skinhead groups. Some of these gang members also derive inspiration from the Order, a right-wing racist group that carried out the assassination of Alan Berg, a Denver radio shock jock (the story was depicted in the movie *Talk Radio* with Eric Bogosian). The ideology of white supremacists is drawn from their belief that white Northern European people are superior to other races. Researchers have delved into the problem of white supremacist gangs operating behind bars; among their findings are key expressions of power embodied in tattoos (Mason and Becker, 1994: 61–5):

White Power. The belief that reflects commitment to the 'natural' domination of members of the white race (descendants of Northern European immigrants) over 'degenerate' peoples.

ZOG (Zionist Occupation Government). Rallying cry of the white-supremacist movement, promoting a belief that the government of the United States, and of the world in general, is under the control of the Jews.

Blood in the Face. The belief that only peoples of Northern European descent can blush; this idea is understood to be one of the markers of whether or not an individual is human or animal.

Swastika (Hakenkreuz, Broken Cross). Marked on the top of the head under the hair or elsewhere on the body. The tattoo on top of the head is often associated with members of the Aryan Brotherhood.

Shamrock (clover). Mark meant to symbolize the white race.

Band. Worn around the lower leg, arm, or biceps, with the repeated words white power in the form of a torque.

Knuckles. Tattooed with 'skin' on the right hand and 'head' on the left hand.

Small dots. Appear on the web between thumb and forefinger; each dot is supposed to indicate a murder committed for the cause.

Skull, demon, serpent. Marks that represent the alienation of the individual from the common social values of society.

Since the classic work of Jacobs on prison gangs dating back to the 1970s, other investigations have continued to explore the reach of street gangs into the prison and jail populations (ACA, 1994; Camp and Camp, 1985, 1987; Earley, 1992; Pelz, 1996; Silberman, 1995).

Although it is sometimes difficult to determine the relative scholarly value of works listed on the Internet, the following websites offer an overview of gangs in prison. In particular, they focus on the six major prison gangs that boast a nationwide membership: Neta, Aryan Brotherhood, Black Guerrilla Family, Mexican Mafia, La Nuestra Familia, Texas Syndicate.

- The original prison gangs: http://www.gangsorus.com/prisongangs.html
- Major prison gangs: http://www.dc.state.fl.us/pub/gangs/prison.html
- The gangs behind bars: http://findarticles.com/p/articles/mi_m1571/is_n36_v14/ai_21161641/
- The influence of prison gang affiliation on violence and other prison misconduct: http://www.bop.gov/news/research_projects/published_reports/cond_envir/oreprcrim_2br.pdf

In Chapter 9, we shall return to the subject of prison, especially with respect to riots, disorder, and violence.

JIHAD-BASED RADICALIZATION IN POST-9/11 AMERICA

Since the attacks of September 11th (2001), security experts have expressed concern that American prisons could become 'breeding grounds' for homegrown terrorists, especially given the large number of prisoners practicing the Islamic faith. Consider the testimony of Michael Waller before the US Senate who said that radical Islamic groups 'dominate Muslim prison recruitment in the U.S. and seek to create a radicalized cadre of felons who will support their anti-American efforts. Estimates place the number of Muslim prison recruits at between 15–20 percent of the prison population' (2003: 13). Similarly, a 17-member blue-ribbon task force issued a report stating: 'Prisons have long been places where extremist ideology and calls to violence could find a willing ear, and conditions are often conducive to radicalization' (Cilluffo and Saathoff, 2006: i). Despite that heightened concern, some researchers have concluded that while gangs behind bars continue to be involved in street crime, there is no evidence that jihad-based radical groups were making any gains (Klein, 2007).

In their study, Useem and Clayton (2009) went further to determine whether such radicalization was taking place in American prisons. Their findings indicate that the probability of terrorist plots being hatched from behind bars is relatively low, citing the following reasons: (1) order and stability in American prisons have been achieved; (2) prison administrators have implemented strategies to counter the 'importation' of radicalism; (3) correctional leadership infused antiradicalization into their agencies; (4) prisoners' low levels of education mean they lack the sophistication needed to carry out terrorism. While recognizing that most Muslim inmates in US prisons are converts, Useem and Clayton learned further that convicts in general are not politically engaged in ways that prompt them to take a strong interest in international affairs. Rather, prisoners tend to focus on their own fate in the criminal justice system. As one convict revealed about fellow inmates: 'They don't follow politics much. They want to play checkers, dominoes, run around the yard. They don't care as long as they get fed.' Likewise, another prisoner opined: 'We don't discuss Iraq ... Inmates are focused on prison life. Everyone wants to go home' (Useem and Clayton, 2009: 565; see Austin, 2009; Blazak, 2009; Hamm, 2009; Marquart, 2007).

OUTCASTS IN PRISON

An exploration of the prison social world would not be complete without acknowledging the presence of certain outcasts behind bars. Prisoners tend to compare themselves with other inmates on the basis of their crimes, thereby forming opinions of their own moral standing. Many of those convicted of run-of-the mill street offenses (e.g. drug violations, burglary) feel morally superior to inmates who have committed crimes of senseless violence, and especially sexual assault. Not surprisingly, those serving sentences for rape and child molestation tend to occupy the lowest position in the prison hierarchy, becoming outcasts in a social world of convicts. Likewise, snitches (a.k.a. rats, informants, stool pigeons, stoolies) are also viewed as outcasts by other inmates. Both of these groups of outcasts have been the subject of interest by those writing about life in the convict social world.

Given the predatory nature of their offense, sex offenders are widely condemned and stigmatized by their other inmates. Even so, prisoners convicted of raping women have a higher status (or less stigma) than those who molest children, commonly referred to as pedophiles, baby rapers, diddlers, or short-eyes. The mistreatment of sex offenders behind bars frequently goes beyond mere harassment; indeed, these particular convicts also are subject to serious threats of physical harm. Due to such intimidation, convicted sex offenders often choose to serve their sentence in isolation (or protective custody) where they do not have contact with the general inmate population.

Whereas some attacks on sex offenders are limited to minor injuries, other cases have involved brutal torture. The following incident took place during the New Mexico State Prison riot in 1980:

> The worst nightmare in the cellblock, however, was the execution of thirty-four year old James Perrin. The death squad saved him for last. Perrin was serving a life sentence for raping and murdering two little girls and their mother. In every prison in the nation, baby rapers ('short eyes') are despised, the one criminal in the jungle worse than all the others, someone even the most deranged convict can look down on. Everyone, after all, especially when insecure and oppressed, needs someone they can feel better than.

There would be no caring for Jimmy Perrin in this life. After blowtorching his door open, four executioners, including the one who'd originally taunted him, dragged James out of his cell, tied him spread-eagle to the bars and cooked him slowly with the roaring flame of the acetylene torch, melting his three hundred pounds of flesh to bone. They worked on him for half an hour, first burning his genitals, then his face, moving the torch up and down his body, bringing him around with smelting salts when he drifted into the comfort of unconsciousness until nothing could bring him back anymore. Maybe this was enough penance to save Jimmy Perrin from any future hells.

(Stone, 1982: 127, 129)

The case of Jimmy Perrin, obviously, is both extreme and rare. Nevertheless, it does point to the level of fear that many sex offenders experience while incarcerated.

In a classic study of the tactics and rationales for harassing outcasts, Akerstrom (1986, 1988, 1989) compared the victimization patterns of sex offenders with those of snitches. Although Akerstrom's study took place in nine Swedish correctional institutions, the findings are useful to understanding victimization in American prisons and elsewhere. Akerstrom discovered that sex offenders (both rapists and child molesters) were viewed by other prisoners as being irrational, bizarre, and 'sick.' Correspondingly, inmates tended to distance themselves from sex offenders who, in turn, were also excluded from many prisoner activities (e.g. socializing). Interestingly, Akerstrom found that sex offenders were not routinely assaulted by other inmates due in large part to that social distance. However, when attacks did occur, the prevailing rationale for the beating was to seal the status boundary. In other words, sex offenders were assaulted by other prisoners as an expression of the perpetrator's perceived superiority over the outcast.

By contrast, snitches are generally not viewed as irrational or bizarre by fellow prisoners. Rather, snitches – or 'rats' – are seen as being exceedingly rational and calculating: simply put, they furnish information to the staff in order to advance their own interests, such as gaining favors or improving their chances for parole. Akerstrom found that snitches were attacked with more enthusiasm by other prisoners due to the perception that they had violated the convict code that prohibits informing. Accordingly, the assaults symbolized a sealing of the normative boundary. Whereas sex offenders were sometimes assaulted as a means of recreation (some inmates simply derive a sense of satisfaction from victimizing others), snitches were beaten out of a profound sense of duty.

Research on the subject of snitching in American prisons is scant (Johnson, 1961; Wilmer, 1965). A key exception is an investigation carried out by Marquart and Roebuck (1991). Their work is unique insofar as the snitches they studied were not deemed outcasts. On the contrary, those convicts who routinely provided information to the staff seemed to function as surrogate guards, thereby occupying higher-status positions in the prison hierarchy. As elite prisoners, snitches wielded enormous power over other inmates. That unusual dynamic, however, is not representative of most American prisons where snitches are almost universally viewed as outcasts. The reason snitches serve as surrogate COs, as noted in the Marquart and Roebuck research, is attributed to the way in which the Texas Department of Corrections (TDC) structured the convict social world. At the time of that study, the TDC implemented a system of inmate social control that relied on building tenders (BTs, or trustees). Building tenders were elite convicts who served as an additional layer of management; their duty was to supervise and manage the rank-and-file inmates. Instead of being stigmatized as outcasts, those elite prisoners enjoyed considerable power, earning rewards and favors from the prison staff.

In the case of the TDC, the building tenders were co-opted by prison authorities. In addition to solving internal problems and preventing violence among inmates in their units, building tenders functioned as snitches so as to relay information about prisoner misconduct to the administrators (see Kessler and Roebuck, 1996; Stojkovic, 1996a). The building-tender system is now defunct, as a result of the impact of a class-action civil suit filed against the TDC: in that case, *Ruiz* v. *Estelle* (1980), a federal judge ruled that such a system was corrupt and unconstitutional. Chapter 12 discusses that landmark case and further outlines the intricate components of the building-tender system. In sum, the Marquart and Roebuck study greatly advances the understanding of the symbiotic relationship between COs and prisoners managing the convict social world.

CULTURAL PENOLOGY

In Prison Playing Just to Kill Time ... or Maybe to Help Solve a Murder

Through the lens of cultural penology, we are drawn into the world of crime and punishment. Very often that attraction blends entertainment with real cases of violence. In a curious development in South Carolina, the Department of Corrections sells to prisoners decks of playing cards that feature victims of unsolved crimes. 'The cards ask: Do you know who killed me? And they ask: Do you know where I am? And they ask: Do you know something? Anything?' (Barry, 2009: EV1).

The seven of hearts spins to a stop, and gazing up is Victoria Duncan, last seen driving off with two men in 1998, later found beaten to death in York County. She disappears under the king of spades, Christi Hanks, a prostitute from the Anderson area, found dead in a field in 2006.

Here comes the 10 of spades, Tracy Ann Johnson, beaten to death in her home in Greer in 2000, only to be covered by the four of hearts, Richard Martin. He left Nancy's Lounge in Anderson one night in 1995 and was found an hour later, dying from a blunt trauma to the head in the middle of Welcome Road.

> Hands are won and lost as the inmates shuffle and toss the cards on top of one another. Their discards form kaleidoscopic arrangements in which the dead and the missing peer up together, as though from a deep, shared hole.
>
> (Barry, 2009: EV2)

The decks of cards are available in the prison canteens for $1.72. Since 2008, prisoners have bought more than 10,000 packs. Even more intriguing is the lure of snitching whereby some convicts are led to believe they might actually gain favors from the South Carolina criminal justice system by reporting information on unsolved cases. 'Each card asks that you please call 888-CRIME-SC if you have any information about a case; each card also whispers, "Call *49," an anonymous prison hot line' (Barry, 2009: EV2).

While prosecutors still hope that the cards might somehow produce important leads in solving cases, thus far there is no real evidence that prisoners are fully participating in the game of snitching. 'The "unsolved" decks, long since stripped of any reverence, are now part of the everyday prison culture.' Inmates complain that the cards are too expensive, that the cards are not as sturdy as those they replaced, and 'sometimes a card is just a card' (Barry, 2009: EV5). Nonetheless, those developments offer another opportunity to appreciate the range and depth of cultural penology as it extends from the free world to convicts behind bars (see Natapoff, 2009).

CLASSIFICATION OF PRISONERS AND ITS PROBLEMS

To manage inmates and reduce risks of rule infractions, violence, and escape, correctional administrators implement classification schemes in sorting prisoners to their proper level of security. Still, the classification process is complex and ongoing thoughout much of the convicts' stay during incarceration. When prisoners are first admitted to a correctional system, they are subject to an initial classification by which they are matched to a facility with an appropriate security level and housing assignments. Additionally, consideration is given to prisoners' needs regarding medical, mental health, vocational, and educational services and programs. Following the initial assessment, classification committees then periodically review prisoners' classification. Under reclassification, adjustments to the inmates' classification are made while taking into account rule infractions or any other development that may signal a need for a change in security, custody, or programs (Flynn, 1996).

Although classification dates back to the emergence of the penitentiary, over time the process became increasingly informed. In 1982, the National Institute of Corrections issued 14 principles for classification, including recommendations that prisons develop detailed written procedures and policies governing classification and that measurement and testing instruments used

Figure 5.3 View of the courtyard and buildings in the prison of Ensisheim, eastern France, on December 12, 2009 during a visit by a French official.

Photo credit Johanna Leguerre/AFP/Getty Images.

in the decision-making process be valid, reliable, and objective. Moreover, the classification procedures must be consistent with constitutional requisites, and there must be an opportunity for administration and line staff to be heard when undertaking development of a classification system.

Every jurisdiction determines its own classification scheme, and commonly there is considerable variation from system to system. There are three approaches to classification, namely consensus, equity, and prediction. Under the consensus model, correctional personnel are surveyed to determine which factors are important to include in classification. The equity model sets out to restrict factors in the classification decision to legally relevant behavioral characteristics, most notably criminal history. The predictive model relies on legal, social, psychological, and medical factors to predict institutional behavior, such as rule infractions, escapes, and violence. To improve prediction, classification committees consult psychological tests and profiles that are administered to prisoners during the initial screening. As a practical matter, most jurisdictions tend to blend each of those approaches in an effort to maximize the classification process (Craddock, 1996; Seiter, 2002).

Since classification models endeavor to predict institutional conduct, their ability to do so is often questioned. Accurately predicting human behavior is quite difficult. A common problem facing classification schemes is overclassification from which prisoners are designated to higher security institutions and assigned greater supervision than is warranted. The result is twofold. First, overclassification produces greater expenditures because higher security costs more than lower security. Second, those prisoners are subjected to conditions of confinement that are typically harsher and more restrictive than is necessary to secure them.

Classification and administrative segregation

In any given correctional facility, the vast majority of prisoners are placed in the so-called general population where they are allowed to 'program,' meaning they are permitted to work and participate in various activities such as educational programs. By contrast, a relatively small proportion of convicts are classified as so dangerous and disruptive that they are assigned to a special control unit referred to as administrative segregation, also known as 'ad seg,' 'the hole,' or 'lockup.' Whereas super maximum security prisons operate entirely under tight security, control units are special housing quarters located within an institution where most inmates are classified into the general population (see the section on super maximum security prisons). Two other features of special housing are worth noting. Disciplinary segregation is reserved for prisoners who have been found guilty of a serious rule infraction and are placed in a segregation unit for a specific length of time (typically no more than 14 days). Some prisoners are housed in protective custody (PC) for their own wellbeing because they feel threatened in the general population, perhaps due to being accused of snitching. Those in PC will remain there until they decide they wish to re-enter the general population, or they may elect to stay there until they are released from prison. PC units are designed to be less punitive than administrative segregation or disciplinary segregation units, allowing those prisoners to participate in some programs and work assignments (Austin and Irwin, 2001; Belbot, 1996).

Conversely, administrative segregation and disciplinary segregation are designed to be punitive. Often those prisoners are confined to their cells for 22 to 23 hours per day with minimal access to programs and recreation. It is important to emphasize that prisoners are assigned to administrative segregation by corrections administrators and not sentenced there by the courts. Commonly those prisoners are assigned to administrative segregation on the basis of their perceived status, such as being an ongoing threat to prison stability, staff, and other prisoners, even though they have not been charged with any specific rule infractions. Although there are administrative procedures regulating the transfer of prisoners to ad seg units, critics insist that these guidelines are often ignored; as a result, decisions are made according to subjective criteria with minimal due process. Austin and Irwin (2001) point out that administrators can exercise virtually unreviewable discretion in assigning prisoners to a lockup unit.

As mentioned previously, a very small percentage (approximately 5 percent) of prisoners are held in lockup units; still, the use of administrative segregation is gaining popularity among corrections officials. Recently, a team of researchers examined the use of lockup units in Texas, one of the two largest prison systems in the world (California being the biggest). In 1998 when the study began, Texas had nearly 130,000 prisoners in its system. Due to a wave of prisoner violence in the early 1980s, the Texas Department of Corrections implemented a policy in which a convict who was determined to be associated with a known security threat group (STG) was transferred to ad seg for an indefinite period of time. According to Texas prison guidelines, a prisoner is designated as a member of an STG if it can be confirmed that he or she is affiliated with one of ten gangs the administration regard as security threats. Administrative segregation consists of two groups. Group A includes assaultive prisoners, while those in Group B are classified as nonassaultive. Moreover, many of those in Group B have had no major (or even minor) disciplinary infractions, for several months or years; still, because they are viewed as being affiliated with an STG, they could remain in lockup indefinitely (Austin *et al.,* 1998).

Between 1994 and 1998, the ad seg population grew at a faster rate (65 percent) than the general population (46 percent). Equally important, the average length of time to the inmates' earliest release date is 13 years. Unless returned to the general population, those in administrative segregation could remain in lockup, in what amounts to total solitary confinement, for 13 years. Based on the findings of their investigation, researchers recommended that the Texas Department of Corrections reverse its policy of housing prisoners in lockup for such lengthy periods of time based simply on their association with gang members. Their report concluded that at least one-third of those in ad seg could be released to the general population without jeopardizing institutional security. Adding to the controversy over ad seg is the practice of releasing those prisoners directly to the community upon completion of their sentences. 'An estimated 450 inmates are released in such a manner each year. In other words, they go directly from lockup to the community with no parole supervision requirements, as they have "maxed out" of their prison terms' (Austin *et al.,* 1998).

While debate over the extensive use of ad seg continues, focus has been turned to the debilitating effects of lockup, especially for those prisoners who are confined to control units for protracted periods of time. First, the lockup experience has the potential to produce a self-fulfilling prophecy in which prisoners tend to develop those characteristics they are perceived as having; as a result, they may become violent and disruptive due to the harsh conditions of confinement. Second, long-term incarceration in solitary confinement contributes tremendously to psychological impairment, including an array of psychiatric disorders such as severe depression, anxiety, and paranoia. Finally, those problems are carried with them when they eventually re-enter the community. Many ex-cons, especially those who were housed in lockup, become prisonized to the extent that they fail to adjust to life in the free world, thus resorting to crime and returning to prison (Austin and Irwin, 2001; Welch, 1996e).

DOES CRIME PAY? TIME SERVED BY THOSE SENTENCED IN THE SAVINGS AND LOAN SCANDAL

In furthering a critical look at the role of social class in the distribution of punishment, it is instructive to examine the length of sentences of those convicted for major white-collar offenses. Consider the Savings and Loan (S&L) scandal of the 1980s that produced losses estimated at $250 billion, and possibly reaching a total of one trillion dollars when factoring in the interest payments over the next several decades. To understand the toll that the S&L scandal has had on individuals, the bailout costs each US taxpayer approximately $15,000

(Friedrichs, 1996; Rosoff *et al.*, 2002). Clearly, those lessons loom large as Americans sort out the financial meltdown since 2008 and the enormous bailout of the financial industry (see Tillman, 2009).

In their book *Big Money Crime: Fraud and Politics in the Savings and Loan Crisis* (1997), Kitty Calavita, Henry Pontell, and Robert Tillman compare the prison sentences of the major players in the S&L scandal (those who stole more than $100,000 or more) with other types of theft and drug offenses. Those convicted of S&L theft served an average of 36.4 months in prison. By comparison, persons convicted of burglary served 55.6 months, those convicted of motor vehicle theft served 38.0 months, and non-violent, first-time drug offenders served an average of 64.9 months in prison.

It is not surprising that such disparities in sentencing breed cynical views of incarceration, undermining the legitimacy of the criminal justice system. 'Suite thugs don't go to jail because street thugs have to ... The double standard makes no sense whatsoever when you consider the damage done by the offense' (Leaf, 2002: 76). The overall losses from all bank robberies in the United States in 1992 totaled $35 million, a figure that is approximately 1 percent of the cost of Charles Keating's fraud at Lincoln Savings & Loan (Calavita *et al.*, 1997; Leaf; 2002; see also Mackenzie and Green, 2008).

CONCLUSION

This chapter explores the social world of imprisonment by relying on three levels of analysis: the macro, the meso, and the micro. A macro perspective views corrections in its broadest context by attending to the various social forces. The macro approach is particularly relevant in view of the growing incarceration enterprise. The meso and micro levels of analysis encourage a deeper look into corrections as a system, an organization, a social world, as well as a subculture. Such analysis carefully distinguishes between the formal and informal structures that shape relationships between the administrators, COs, and convicts. In many instances, those alliances are symbiotic in ways that merge staff and the convict social worlds at various junctures, including but not limited to subcultures, prison gangs, and the underground economy.

SUMMARY

In the first part of this chapter, the social world of imprisonment is characterized as an incarceration enterprise that is growing in both scope and scale. The chapter examines the system-related aspects of corrections by addressing such issues as the types of correctional systems and overcrowding. Furthermore, the contemporary prison has become a less-than-total institution and increasingly more bureaucratic, though still retaining its paramilitary tradition. The final section describes what it is like to be imprisoned. The social world of convicts is shaped by the pains of imprisonment alongside various deprivations. The inmate social system and subculture are also explored, with a review of the inmate typology, slang, prisonization, strategies of coping, gangs, and outcasts.

REVIEW QUESTIONS

1 How do the current trends in incarceration affect the future of corrections?
2 Discuss the prison as a total institution, a paramilitary organization, and a bureaucracy.
3 What is it like to be incarcerated, and how does the prison environment affect the inmate subculture?
4 How is the inmate subculture shaped by political and economic forces?

RECOMMENDED READINGS

Abbott, J.H. (1981). *In the Belly of the Beast: Letters from Prison*. New York: Vintage.

Austin, J. and Irwin, J. (2001) *It's About Time: America's Imprisonment Binge*. Belmont, CA: Wadsworth.

McShane, M.D. and Williams, F.P. (1996) *Encyclopedia of American Prisons*. New York: Garland.

Ross, J.I. and Richards, S. (2003) *Convict Criminology*. Belmont, CA: Thomson/ Wadsworth.

Sabo, D., Kupers, T.A. and London, W. (2001) *Prison Masculinities*. Philadelphia: Temple University Press.

CHAPTER 6

Women in Corrections

The history of women's institutions reflects the history of women. Because women have long been thought to hold a special place in society, deviant women have been treated differently not only from their more law-abiding sisters but also from their male counterparts.
(Joycelyn M. Pollock-Byrne)

LEARNING OBJECTIVES

After studying this chapter, you should be able to answer the following questions:

1 How has the history of punishing women offenders shaped contemporary correctional practices?
2 What are the past and present theories of female criminality?
3 How has feminist criminology influenced modern criminal justice and corrections?
4 What are the program needs of women prisoners?
5 What are the principal characteristics of women behind bars, and how do women's prisons differ from men's prisons?

The condition of the women prisoners is most deplorable. They are usually in the oldest part of the prison structure. They are almost always in the direct charge of men guards. They are treated and disciplined as men are. In some of the prisons children are born in prison – either from male prisoners or just 'others.' In one institution the women are living in a fire-trap with the doors locked on the outside and the key in the hands of a young man.

One of the most reliable women officials in the South told me that in her state at the state farm for women the dining room contains a sweatbox for the women who are punished by being locked up in a narrow place with insufficient room to sit down, and near enough to the table so as to be able to smell the food.

Over the table there is an iron bar to which women are handcuffed when they are strapped, and on the wall there is the sign, 'Christ died to save sinners.'

The mode of punishment is flogging with a split hose containing holes so that each lash raises and at the same time breaks the blister ... Last week ... a woman was flogged 35 lashes.

(Tannenbaum, 1924: 104–6)

INTRODUCTION

Corrections in America remains a male-dominated enterprise for two basic reasons. First, 93 percent of the inmate population is male. Second, men occupy the positions of power that determine the course of punishment in society. Men dominate government, the judiciary, and the legal profession, as well as criminal justice administration and personnel. Therefore, from every conceivable angle, the policies and strategies of corrections emerge from male perspectives on crime and punishment.

As the roles of women undergo transition in society, long-held traditional views about women face numerous challenges within criminal justice and prisons. Today, the presence of women in corrections continues to expand. Women now represent the fastest-growing segment of the correctional population, and now more than ever, they serve as various rank-and-file staff and administrators (Grana, 2002; Muraskin, 2000). However, resistance to change persists in corrections – a reflection of the larger struggles that women face in society. Like other social arenas, corrections has a conservative bias that often resists efforts to reduce inequality. For centuries, men have governed the penal apparatus; therefore traditional views regarding crime, punishment, and gender symbolize that form of domination, or hegemony. Understandably, bringing about major changes in corrections requires a rethinking about the role of women in society as well as in criminal justice (see Bosworth, 1999).

This chapter examines the nature of women in prison while attending to major political and economic developments. In doing so, the discussion sets out to explain key transformations within corrections that parallel enduring social problems, namely inequality, sexism, and discrimination against women. So as to advance a critical understanding of punishment, the chapter begins with a history of corrections for women.

A HISTORY OF PUNISHMENT AND CORRECTIONS FOR WOMEN

Chapters 2 and 3 point out that the punishment of women offenders has differed somewhat from that of male convicts. This section offers a closer examination of those variations so as to sort out the unique tactics and rationales for sanctioning women, particularly as they have changed over time.

Diverging from the male system of confinement

A prominent theme in the history of women and punishment is the persistent concern over female morality. Compared with their male counterparts, women engaging in deviant or criminal behavior are viewed as more depraved and morally corrupt – a view that generates more intense forms of social control for women. Fidelity, obedience, and other aspects of morality were closely monitored by earlier European as well as colonial American societies. For instance, women accused of adultery, as well as those openly criticizing men (or spreading gossip), were subjected to punishments specifically designed for women. As described previously, those women were often subject to the brank and the ducking stool. Moreover, in colonial America, men could be punished for not keeping their wives in check; consider the 'cuckold's court,' a ritual that forced men to ride backward on a donkey. That embarrassing spectacle reinforced the notion that the social order required men to dominate and control women (Burford and Schulman, 1992; Dobash *et al.*, 1986).

In the early 1800s, women prisoners in England and America were not segregated from male convicts. As expected, women suffered horrific physical and sexual abuse; even when women were confined to separate wings of male institutions, male warders often exploited them. These atrocities fueled the crusade of early reformers, including Elizabeth Fry, who dedicated herself to the improvement of prison conditions for women in England (Dobash *et al.*, 1986). As cited in *Observations on the Sitting, Superintendence and Government of Female*

Figure 6.1 A lock and chain around a female with bare feet.

Stock photo.

Prisoners (1825), Fry advocated reforms similar to those of John Howard, such as work, training, religion, and routine. Moreover, her recommendations also reinforced traditional views of femininity by teaching women inmates proper manners and etiquette. Fry argued in favor of women warders, rather than male guards, because women staff could serve as role models for 'true womanhood.' Additionally, women warders could protect women prisoners from sexual abuse and lend a sympathetic ear to their personal problems (Freedman, 1974).

Similar reforms were carried out in the 1820s in the United States. Dorothea Dix, Abby Hopper Gibbons, Mary Wistar, and Sarah Doremus led several campaigns to improve the conditions of confinement for women: most notable was their insistence that female inmates be supervised solely by female warders. The New York Prison Association provided additional support for such reforms, and in 1845, Gibbons and Doremus established the Ladies Association within that organization (Freedman, 1974; also see Barnes and Teeters, 1946). Due to widespread complaints about publicly operated institutions, a privatization movement expanded to several parts of the nation between the 1820s and the 1890s. For example, in New York City, the House of Refuge opened in 1825 and the Magdalen Home opened in 1833. Later, the House of Shelter was established in 1869 in Indiana. These homes assisted wayward women, providing religious instruction, discipline, and education, and promoting such skills as sewing, cooking, etc. (Freedman, 1981; see also Barnes and Teeters, 1946).

Nonetheless, the overriding objective of these programs was to instill the traditional value of femininity. Elizabeth Farnham, who was appointed as the matron of Mt Pleasant (New York) in 1844, advocated the development of 'softer' institutional environments by including such feminine features as decorations, curtains, and flowers. Aspects of her program resembled those of a finishing school – a piano was placed in a common area, and educational and reading classes were offered. Opponents charged that Farnham was too lenient with the residents and that she failed to follow a religious regimen. Consequently, Farnham served as matron for only two years before being forced to resign (Feinman, 1984; Freedman, 1981).

An important distinction needs to be made between the women reformers and the political activists and suffragists during that era. Those campaigning to improve women's institutions set out to promote female morality, virtue, and purity by mentoring their 'fallen sisters' – implying that those women had 'fallen from grace.' Unlike the suffragists, who fought for equal rights (and the right to vote), prison reformers did not advocate a political agenda per se. Curiously, many of the prison reformers deliberately distanced themselves from politics, adhering to the social norm that 'proper ladies' ought not to be involved in politics.

The reformatory movement

For wayward, deviant or criminal women, intensive strategies of social control emerged during the American reformatory era of the late 1800s and early 1900s.

Once again, the purpose of incarceration was to promote a sense of femininity and to encourage 'ladylike' attitude and behavior. Although women's prisons during the reformatory movement often relied on harsh punishment, they did mark some improvement over earlier penal practices when women were not segregated from male convicts. Moreover, reformers succeeded in staffing those institutions with women, constituting a major victory in the campaign to protect female inmates from abuse and exploitation.

The later stages of the reformatory movement also incorporated other shifts in correctional programs. Although emphasis on female morality and femininity remained central to the reform of women, an application of the medical model soon emerged. The medical model was gaining popularity among administrators of institutions for men and juveniles, and so it was fitting that women be presented with similar classification procedures and individualized treatment. That trend was met by a change in correctional personnel. Women began pursuing careers in institutions, and unlike reformers of the previous generation, these new professionals did not possess a religious zeal. The new generation of women prison specialists had training in law, medicine, and social work (Rafter, 1985). Nevertheless, an important objective of the imprisonment of women persisted – namely, the reinforcement of female sex roles. The duties assigned to women in prison, such as cooking, cleaning, sewing, and spinning, continued to reflect traditional sex-role stereotypes. Due in part to a prevailing conservative bias in corrections today, it is not surprising that women inmates are still assigned similar domestic tasks while in prison.

Another important development in the history of women's prisons was the emergence of two types of facilities: the reformatory and the custodial institution. Although these types of prisons shared numerous characteristics, it was believed that reformatories were less harsh and promoted more optimism toward reform since they generally housed less serious offenders. Whereas reformatories were concerned largely with the problem of female immorality, custodial institutions focused more on female criminality. Eventually, socioeconomic and racial issues produced a two-tiered system for women inmates. Women sent to reformatories generally were young, unhardened, guilty of misdemeanors, and, more significantly, white. African-Americans, by contrast, were excluded from reformatories and sent to custodial institutions where inmates were older and convicted of more serious crimes. Generally, reformatories were located in the North while custodial institutions dominated the correctional landscape in the Southern states, thereby further reinforcing a racial divide (Lekkerkerker, 1931; Rafter, 2001).

By the 1930s, the reformatory movement had been virtually exhausted. Several factors explain its demise. Prostitution, which had previously been a target of moral crusaders, failed to fuel widespread law enforcement campaigns against women, due in large part to the decline of influential religious zealots. Perhaps more important factors were economic woes and the effects of the Great Depression. During the post-reformatory era, several state custodial institutions closed because of financial hardship. State inmates were transferred to private reformatories, thereby disrupting the experiment of the reformatory. From that time on, institutions for women took on a modified reformatory approach (Rafter, 1985; see Hayman, 2006; Hannah-Moffat, 2001).

Positivism, discipline and gender: early corrections in Argentina

As discussed in Chapter 4, Michel Foucault (1977) views punishment from the perspective of power, especially as it relates to discipline. According to Foucault, efforts to discipline men have focused on transforming convicts into law-abiding workers. Although these aims extend to the disciplining of women, the emphasis was less on industrial labor and more on domestic chores, thereby reinforcing traditional sex roles (Howe, 1990; Newman, 1978). Interestingly, in England and Scotland, discipline in early women's prisons overshadowed rehabilitation, despite the rhetoric of correctional therapy. Petty rules and prohibitions were enforced even when the behaviors involved were not considered to be unusual in the free world, such as smoking cigarettes or using profanity, both still considered to be 'unladylike' (Dobash *et al.*, 1986).

Those forms of discipline indeed crossed gender lines in other societies as well. Consider the case of Argentina where the early positivism shaped the correctional apparatus system so as to improve its capacity to deliver discipline (Salvatore, 2007, 1996, 1992; see also Botsman, 2005). Between 1890 and 1940, Argentine positivists used their scientific appeal to medicalize the conception of crime and similar social problems; by doing so, they soon annexed the criminal justice apparatus where they would experiment with certain populations, policies, and institutions. At the forefront of the movement was José Ingenieros, who modified Lombrosian criminology, making it more suitable to a rapidly changing Argentine society. Nonetheless, positivism in Argentine criminology remained very much a clinical project, relying on classification, diagnostic exams, anthropometric measurements, family histories, and psychological tests. Positivism influenced a generation of physicians, lawyers, and professors to advocate key innovations for prisons: indeterminate sentences, segregation of convicts according to dangerousness, individualized treatment, and labor therapy (Rodriguez, 2006). Positivists were not only guiding policies for criminal justice but also branching out into other spheres of social policy. By widening the definition of antisocial conduct, positivists 'legitimized a new power to supervise, control, and punish behavior that, in classical penology, would not have qualified as "crime" (e.g., alcoholism, mental illness, prostitution)' (Salvatore, 2007: 259; see Cohen 1985; Foucault, 2003; Sozzo, 1998, 2006). Cloaked as science, positivism also carried into policy implications for both class and gender.

Elitist visions of a modern Argentina contained clear gender biases that prevented positivists from visualizing the incorporation of women into industry since the prevailing concern was focused largely on immigrant men (Salvatore, 1996). The gender divide was reinforced by tensions between the local Catholic Church and the state, paving the way for divergent forms of penal discipline. While male offenders were sentenced to state-of-the-art correctional institutions modeled after positivism, their female counterparts were sent to different facilities under the firm control of a religious order that dissociated itself from the new criminological science. Indeed, the stunning continuity of the religious approach in the penal reform of female lawbreakers is evident in the influence of the nuns of the Good Shepherd (El Buen Pastor) who formally gained control of prisons for women from 1890 until as recently as the 1970s. Given the rise of the modern Argentine state committed to secularization and positivism, it seems out of step for the government to abdicate a significant part of its correctional apparatus to a religious organization. Deciphering that apparent contradiction involves more than an analysis of science versus religion; indeed, attending to the role of certain social groups in the shaping of public policy seems to offer a more coherent explanation. Historian Lila Caimari reminds us that practical considerations were important as the state leaned toward permitting the Good Shepherd to assume authority over female rehabilitation.

> Everyone agreed on the moral danger involved in leaving it to male administration. This prison needed a female staff that was trained and willing to live with the inmates. Such a staff did not exist in the state bureaucracy or in other religious orders, and it would take a long time to train one. Because they lived in convents – where they were often secluded in cells and used to severe regulations and all kinds of privations – nuns were perceived as naturally adapted to a penitentiary regime. Furthermore, their investiture gave them an aura of authority, vis-à-vis both inmates and secular members of the staff.
>
> (1997: 189–90)

Financial matters also figured in the state's decision to transfer the female prison population to the Good Shepherd since the nuns requested a minimal budget to care for a relatively small number of incarcerated women. Still, once the deal was set, the Good Shepherd succeeded in keeping the state out of the operations of reforming women inmates. Apart from those practical considerations, theoretical assumptions about female criminality weighed heavily. Lombrosian criminology distinguished women from men, postulating that females succumb to crime due to moral weakness, irrationality, and low intelligence (Lombroso and Ferrero, 2004). Moreover, since many of them had engaged in prostitution (which was not even a criminal offense), a religious solution seemed more fitting than criminal science (Guy, 1990, 2001; Rodriguez, 2006).

Lombroso himself advocated the use of convents over prisons in reforming female criminals. 'Nuns can train them to replace sexual love – the most frequent cause of female crime – with religiosity. Honesty and religious fanaticism will become substitutes for criminal tendencies. I have witnessed this process myself, even in a cellular prison where nuns were not trained to reform inmates' (Lombroso, 2006b: 344). In their recent translation of Lombroso's *Criminal Man*, Gibson and Rafter comment: 'The Italian state, like many Catholic countries, handed over the administration of women's prisons to orders of nuns in the nineteenth and early twentieth centuries. As a non-religious Jew and a socialist, Lombroso generally opposed the interference of the Catholic Church in public affairs. It is a measure of his low regard for women that Lombroso recommends religiosity, as opposed to rational science, as best suited to mold their weak and immoral minds' (2006b: 399; see Barton, 2005).

Traditional sex-role stereotypes involving labor work also influenced patterns of penal discipline. Compared to male prisoners who were subjected to job training to meet the industrial demands of an emerging modern economy, women inmates were expected to find work as domestic servants – an occupation in high demand in early twentieth-century Buenos Aires. Therefore acquiring such skills as sewing, cooking, washing, and ironing could be easily transferred to that area of the labor market (Caimari, 1997). Perhaps adding to long-term reform, working as a domestic servant for a middle-income or wealthy employer meant those women would be exposed to the virtues of family life on a daily basis. Recall that compared to Italian positivists, the Argentines paid closer attention to environmental forces in curbing criminality.

To reiterate, the enduring control over the care of women prisoners by the Good Shepherd was much more than the appeal of religion over science, especially given that Lombrosian criminologists also explained female crime along lines of immorality. The power of certain social groups in formulating state policies is paramount when considering how the Good Shepherd maintained its authority over women's penality until the 1970s. The poor conditions of confinement at the Correctional House for Women (Asilo Correccional de Mujeres) became a concern of law professors and students at the University of Buenos Aires. Inspired by positivist criminology, these activists formed a group called the Patronado de Recluidas y Liberadas (PRL) in 1933: it campaigned fervently to extend legal protection and improved care for female prisoners. The work of the PRL was hamstrung from the beginning since the Mother Superior never allowed the group into the correctional institution. Therefore, instead of introducing to female offenders the advances in modern criminology such as individualized treatment, those women were 'subjected to endless, useless religious speeches that forced them to see their crimes in terms of sin and forgiveness, completely dissociated from the reality around them' (Caimari, 1997: 205; see Ruggiero, 1992, 2004).

Despite compelling complaints of prisoner neglect at the Correctional House for Women, the state did not alter its arrangement with the Good Shepherd, giving the religious order full reign over the reform of female prisoners for decades to follow. As Caimari summarizes: 'Limited material resources, combined with dominant conceptions about gender, crime, and work seem to have conspired against applying the new criminological approach to the question of female crime' (1997: 208). Furthermore, Caimari concludes that the creation of a well-invested penal apparatus for women did not interest government leaders because that population did not pose a significant threat to the project of a modern Argentine state. However, by the 1970s, hundreds of young women accused of being subversive activists were rounded up and sent to the prisons of the Good Shepherd, and soon most female correctional facilities were reassigned to state control (Caimari, 1997, 2001; see Feitlowitz, 1998; Rodriguez, 2006: Welch and Macuare, 2011). (See 'Comparative Corrections: Adultery, Stoning, and Gender Persecution', below.)

COMPARATIVE CORRECTIONS

Adultery, Stoning and Gender Persecution

Adultery, the voluntary sexual intercourse by a married person with someone other than one's spouse, is a transgression that has been shaped historically by cultural, religious, and criminal justice forces. Dating back to ancient Israel, adultery reflected the imperatives of a staunchly patriarchal society, and violators customarily were stoned to death. Still, punishments for adultery were reserved for women more so than men, largely because wives were considered the property of their husbands. Indeed, adultery of the married woman was likened to sexual theft from the husband's estate. Other legal disparities demonstrate further the double standard of adultery, including an 1857 divorce law in Britain that permitted a husband to divorce his wife for adultery alone, but demanded that the wife prove additional grounds. Similarly in the United States, a former Texas law (informally known as a 'Texas Divorce') permitted a man who caught his spouse in an act of adultery to murder her with impunity; however, the wife was not granted the corresponding right (Lampe, 1985; Lawson, 1988; Welch, 2000b, 1997a).

Recently, international human rights groups have expressed concern over incidents in Pakistan and Nigeria, where authorities have sentenced to death by stoning women found guilty of adultery. In one case, Zafran Bibi was convicted of adultery after she had accused her brother-in-law of rape. Under strict Islamic law, known as hudood, rape itself is a crime but it is so difficult to prove that men are rarely convicted; paradoxically, women who report rape are usually charged with adultery. 'With the men, they apply the principle that you are innocent until guilty,' said Asma Jahangir, an official of the independent Human Rights Commission of Pakistan. 'With the women, they apply the principle that you are guilty until proven innocent' (Mydans, 2002: A3). Zafran, in accusing her brother-in-law of rape, admitted that she had had sexual contact outside of marriage – a violation of the law, which forbids all forms of adultery. Following the letter of the law, the judge sentenced Zafran to death, despite her having recently given birth to a child who was conceived as a result of the rape. The accused man was set free without charges. Under the law, four male witnesses, all Muslims and all citizens of upright character, must testify to having seen the rape occur. The testimony of women and non-Muslims is not admissible.

It is estimated that 80 percent of the women confined to Pakistani prisons have been convicted of adultery, typically serving sentences of 10 to 15 years. Human rights advocates report that abuse of women in Pakistan is endemic. Often, wives are locked inside their homes by husbands, who subject them to various forms of punishment, including beatings, acid attacks, burning, and rape. Hundreds of women each year are victims of 'honor killings' – murdered for perceived breaches of modesty, frequently with the support of traditional communities. Not only are women at risk, but young girls as well. A man can deflect rape charges by claiming that his victim consented. Girls who have reached puberty are treated as adults and subject to prosecution. Many girls, some as young as 12, have been convicted of adultery and punished with imprisonment and public whippings (Mydans, 2002).

In a similar case in Nigeria, Safiya Hussaini was sentenced to be buried up to the shoulders and then stoned to death for adultery and giving birth out of wedlock, a violation of Shariah, or Islamic law. The judge ordered the sentence to be carried out as soon as her child was weaned. Hussaini, a 35-year-old mother of five, had been divorced by her husband, which is permitted under Islamic law on the grounds that he could not support her. Later, Hussaini was raped by a 60-year-old man, and when her pregnancy was apparent police arrested and interrogated her, prompting a confession. Attorney General Aliya Abubakar Sanyinna defended the state's actions, insisting that adultery is the second most serious crime under Islamic law, the first being insulting Allah. 'Adultery is more serious than murder. Society is injured by her act. The danger is that it will teach other people to do the same thing,' said Sanyinna, adding that he 'would be happy to cast the first stone' (Dowden, 2002). In the face of mounting public pressure, however, the regional tribal government grudgingly relented, sparing the life of Hussaini. Human rights advocates celebrated the ruling, including US Representative Betty McCollum (Dem., Minn.) who had submitted to Congress a resolution calling for Nigeria's national government to intervene. McCollum characterized such punishments for adultery as 'gender persecution' (*New York Times*, 2002b: 45; *Village Voice*, 2002).

BIASED THEORIES OF FEMALE CRIMINALITY

Just as the practice of punishment is dominated by men, so too is the study of crime. Consequently, it should not be surprising to learn that ideas and concepts driving criminology are generally 'constructed by men, about men' (Leonard, 1982: xi). Those male-dominated forms of knowledge tend to neglect the social forces behind female criminality; moreover, they are patriarchal insofar as they cast women – and female offenders – as passive and submissive to men. Among the pitfalls of patriarchal knowledge is that it fails to explore in accurate terms women within a social structure. In view of that problem, traditional criminology 'is simply not up to the analytical task of explaining women in crime' (Leonard, 1982: xi; also see Howe, 1990). Such criticism stems further from the observation that prevailing theories of crime are androcentric. That is, widely accepted notions of crime and justice are based on male experiences as well as a male view of the world. Men construct the world according to their perspective, and in doing so they exercise their power to place women into subordinate positions within the social scheme (Daly and Chesney-Lind, 1988; MacKinnon, 1982).

Criminology has long set out to explain male as well as female criminality, particularly by way of the scientific investigation of crime known as positivism (see Chapter 4). Curiously though, even after its demise in the understanding of male criminality, the biological and psychological orientation of positivism continued to influence the study of female criminality. In extreme forms, positivist theories reflect misogyny (the contempt, distrust, or hatred of women) insofar as female offenders were viewed as more defective or immoral than their male counterparts.

Perceptions of women as the weaker – and inferior – sex have persisted for centuries. In the late 1800s, scientists began to incorporate this bias into the study of female criminality. Although according to today's standards those theories appear far-fetched, they represented state-of-the-art research more than 100 years ago. Correspondingly, the conclusions were often widely praised within the scientific community. Van de Warker (1875–76) proposed that women enter crime to secure the attention of men. 'This drive was so strong the female would commit serious crime to achieve it. For instance, infanticide was explained by the social stigma and poor future an illegitimate birth would bring; the woman would kill the baby to improve her chances of getting a husband' (Pollock-Byrne, 1990: 10).

Cesare Lombroso's positivistic research of female criminality was bolstered by the ambition of Guglielmo Ferrero, together leading to their influential book *Criminal Woman, the Prostitute, and the Normal Woman* published originally in 1893 (see 2004). The methods used in studying female offenders, however, were those also used to examine male inmates, such as measuring cranial and facial characteristics. Soon, body types supplemented assumptions about moral deficiencies in explaining some forms of female criminality, such as prostitution. Lombroso and Ferrero borrowed heavily from Darwinian evolution theory, asserting that prostitutes were primitive throwbacks. Several other interpretations of female criminality emulated Darwinian thought. For instance, Lombroso and Ferrero applied Darwin's principle of natural selection when they proposed that criminal women do not reproduce because their unattractive physical traits prevent men from pursuing them sexually.

As noted previously, positivistic explanations for female criminality remained popular long after their demise in mainstream criminology, due in large part to sexist attitudes within society as well as in the research community. A key element of sexism is the confusion between sex and gender. Lombroso and other criminologists repeatedly failed to distinguish between traits that are biological and inherent in the sex and those traits that are socially induced (i.e. gender differences). For example, the claim that women are biologically determined to be submissive while neglecting to recognize that women are socialized to remain passive illustrates the confusion between sex and gender (see Welch, 1997a).

In the early 1900s, criminologists began to follow one of two theoretical models of female criminality. The first theory was social determinism that advocated sterilization and lengthy periods of confinement for female offenders so that they would not breed future criminals. The second theory pointed to the negative influence that 'bad' men have on 'weak' women. In other words, 'weak' women were viewed sympathetically as being unable to take control over their own lives, leaving them vulnerable to the manipulation of 'bad' men. Treatment specialists accordingly emphasized the improvement of moral and social habits that would enable women to attract 'good' men. Despite the differences between these competing theories, both were firmly rooted in sexist stereotypes that depict women in condescending and patronizing terms (Freedman, 1981).

The next trend in criminological thought concerning women followed a deeper sociological approach. In the late 1940s, female liberation theory emerged: its early advocate was Pollak (1950), who argued that female criminality is linked to changes in society. For instance, as women gained more freedom and equality, they would also have more opportunity to commit crime. This train of thought drew considerable attention in the 1960s and 1970s when criminologists began interpreting crime within a larger social and cultural context, especially in the light of the women's movement. Most notable are the books by Freda Adler, *Sisters in Crime* (1975), and Rita Simon, *Women and Crime* (1975).

Present-day criminological research, which remains a predominantly male-dominated enterprise, often fails to address adequately female criminality (see Ajzenstadt, 2009; Hannah-Moffat and O'Malley, 2007; van Mastrigt and Farrington, 2009). Still, the two prevailing explanations of female criminality involve notions of opportunity and socialization. Hoffman-Bustamante (1982) cites five major factors that integrate opportunity and socialization:

1 Differential role expectations for men and women.
2 Sex differences in socialization patterns and the application of social control.
3 Structurally determined differences in opportunity to commit particular offenses.
4 Differential access or pressure toward criminally oriented subcultures and careers.
5 Sex differences built into crime categories.

Other examinations of female criminality focus increasingly on social and economic developments, specifically the impact that poverty has on crime (see Chapter 4). Although poverty affects both male and criminality, poverty has become more prevalent among women (and their children), thereby supporting the concept of 'the feminization of poverty.'

> In the United States, the fastest-growing type of family structure is that of female-headed households and, because of the high rate of poverty among those households, their increase is mirrored in the growing numbers of women and children who are poor; almost half of the poor in the U.S. today live in families headed by women.
>
> (Gimenez, 1990: 43; also see Mink, 1994)

It has been said that the women's movement is a phenomenon that generally benefits females who are white, educated, middle-income, and suburban, leaving behind impoverished women of color who have yet to gain from the fight for equality. Contrary to earlier notions that women engage in crime due to having more opportunities, today many women who resort to crime do so not out of a sense of liberation but rather as an attempt to deal with economic hardship (see Barak *et al.*, 2001; Bosworth and Flavin, 2007; Muraskin, 2001).

PORTIA AND PERSEPHONE IN JUSTICE

In her insightful writings on jurisprudence and gender, Robin West (1988) tackles the distinctions between radical feminism and cultural feminism. For instance, radical feminists view gender in the context of power whereby women are akin to the worker in a Marxist analysis of society (see Chapter 4). Departing from a strict economic stance, cultural feminists explore women with respect to child-rearing, personal needs, and morality. The study of cultural feminism benefits also from the work of Carol Gilligan (1982), who contends that compared to men, women have a different morality and set of ethics. In very basic terms, men value rule-making, objectivity, and justice in the Western legal tradition while women tend to place greater emphasis on intimacy and relationships. Although radical feminists might argue in equalization of rights for women, cultural feminists are more cautious since establishing the same rights as men would not meet the different needs of women.

In an exercise useful to decipher gender differences in perceptions of justice, Frances Heidensohn (1986) and Kathleen Daly (1989) consider the dichotomy of Portia and Persephone. The Portia model is considered to be a 'male' version of justice, emphasizing fairness, equal treatment, and rationality. By contrast, the Persephone model, or the 'female' version of justice, draws largely on Gilligan (1982) by placing importance on personal needs, motives, and relationships. Clearly, criminal justice is predominantly a male phenomenon since men commit most crimes. Upon detection and arrest, those men are processed by other men who dominate the fields of policing, prosecution, and the courts.

Adhering to the Portia model of justice, punishment is delivered in ways that strive toward fairness and equal treatment of convicts regardless of gender. However, as Heidensohn points out, equal treatment may not always be fair due to the social reality that women may have different economic needs, may have been victimized, and in other ways may be in a different social position compared to their male counterparts. Equal rights are only relevant when the individuals involved are equal in other ways.

The Persephone model of justice proposes an alternative to the Portia paradigm by replacing the equalization with an approach that takes into account the special situation of women in society. Borrowing further from Gilligan's work, Heidensohn asks what a justice model would look like based on the feminine 'caring' perspective. She points out that the juvenile justice system purports to be such a model. Similarly, Daly (1989) favors the Persephone model because it attends to individual offenders, their personal relationships, and responsibilities such as parenting. By doing so, the Persephone model upholds the ethics of care in the context of justice.

FEMINIST CRIMINOLOGY

Over the past few decades, critical criminology has been expanded to other realms of inquiry, most notably feminist thought. Feminism 'is best understood as both a world view and a social movement that encompasses assumptions and beliefs about the origins and consequences of gendered social organization as well as strategic directions and actions for social change' (Simpson, 1989: 606). Indeed, men as well as women can be feminists. According to Alleman, 'feminism is a way of seeing the world; it is not strictly a sexual orientation. To be a feminist is to combine a female mental perspective with a sensitivity for those social issues which primarily influence women' (1993: 4; Flavin, 2001). Still, to those who ardently defend the traditional, male-dominated social order, feminism is often distorted and at times vehemently attacked. Pat Robertson (former Republican presidential hopeful) represents an extreme reaction against feminism. According to Robertson, feminism 'encourages women to leave their husbands, kill their children, practice witchcraft, destroy capitalism and become lesbians' (Ivins, 1992: 248).

Feminist criminology is a theoretical framework whereby feminist assumptions are applied to the nature of female crimes; additionally, it sets out to explain how female offenders are treated within the criminal justice system. Two basic critiques continue to guide feminist examination of crime: (1) current criminology continues only marginally to address women in crime; and (2) when theories about female criminality do emerge, women are characterized in stereotypical and distorted terms (Heidensohn, 1986). Having said that, Simpson (1989) insists that feminist criminology is not a single theory, but rather a paradigm offering diverse perspectives and agendas. To be somewhat schematic, feminist criminology is represented by four major perspectives: liberal feminism, Marxist feminism, socialist feminism, and radical feminism. Although each perspective has its distinct features, there is considerable overlap among their interpretations of feminism (see Daly, 1994a; Flavin, 2001; Howe, 1993; Messerschmidt, 1993, 1988, 1986).

Liberal feminism

Liberal feminists view discrimination and inequality as problems that can be corrected without fundamentally changing society. That version of feminism adheres to liberalism and its commitment to democratic government. Liberal feminists believe that women's oppression is caused by inequity in civil rights and in educational and employment opportunities. At the heart of the problem is discrimination stemming from gender inequality; moreover, that imbalance in power is perpetuated by socialization patterns from which females are taught to embrace gender-role stereotypes.

Nonetheless, liberal feminists believe that society is not inherently unequal. By shifting political influence, equality for women can be achieved through affirmative action, the passage of the equal rights amendment, and other equal-opportunity laws. Applying these notions to criminal justice, many liberal feminists condemn the criminalization of deviance against females, such as vice crimes (i.e. prostitution) alongside growing enthusiasm to prosecute women on the margins of drug trafficking (i.e. drug couriers).

Marxist and socialist feminism

Both Marxist and socialist feminism are rooted in conflict theory and in particular critical criminology that points to the structure of capitalism as it oppresses women (see Chapter 4). Although both Marxist feminists and socialist feminists are guided by the principles of radical social thought, especially in the context of power, significant differences exist between the two. Marxist feminists view the oppression of women as an extension of the control of the working class by the ruling class. Marxist feminists tend to identify themselves as Marxists first, and then as feminists. Conversely, socialist feminists see themselves as feminists first, and socialists second. Socialist feminists are influenced by Marxist critiques of capitalism, but argue that women are oppressed not only because they occupy a subordinate economic class but also because they are women. Indeed, their sex is, in itself, a class (Alleman, 1993; Jurik, 1999).

Other distinctions between Marxist feminists and their socialist counterparts are worth discussing. Again, Marxist feminists identify capitalism and class relations as the origins of women's oppression. In greater detail, women are assigned a subordinate economic position that is perpetuated by gender formation. Whereas under feudalism the basic economic relation was master and slave, under capitalism that form of oppression is applied to the relation of husband and wife. The oppression of women is reinforced by patriarchy and the division of labor (e.g. women's work in the home and responsibilities for raising the family).

Marxist feminists propose bringing women fully into economic production and improving the rewards of work; additionally, they believe that childcare ought to be socialized in the public sphere so as to reduce the financial burden of parenting (e.g. state funded childcare programs). Marxist feminists also endorse the elimination of the male-dominated inheritance system that has historically perpetuated economic inequality. As discussed in Chapter 4, the criminal justice system in a capitalist society serves as a mechanism to control the lower-income classes. Marxist feminists apply that notion of control to female offenders, pointing to the harsh penalties given to them even for non-violent crimes, including prostitution and drug violations (see Huling, 1995; Chapter 16).

Going a step beyond Marxism, socialist feminists argue that patriarchy (male dominance) is just as oppressive as capitalism. In other words, women are exploited not only economically but sexually as well. Socialist feminists purport that gender oppression is an inherent feature of capitalist societies. From this perspective, 'socialist-feminists describe a synthesis between two systems of domination, class and patriarchy (male supremacy)' (Simpson, 1989: 607). Socialist feminists propose a transformation of the social order in which equality is based on gender as well as class.

Radical feminism

Similarly for radical feminists, inequality stems from patriarchy and the subordination of women maintained by male aggression and control of women's sexuality. Such domination is rooted deeply in society and goes beyond social class and economic forces. The gender inequality is caused by man's biological need to harness and exploit women. That gender formation is rooted in power relations stemming from male heterosexuality (Alleman, 1993).

Some radical feminists favor agendas that call for separatism: socially separating women from men rather than striving toward equality. They propose to establish women-centered and all-women social institutions that are void of power relations. Criminal justice initiatives recommended by radical feminists include proposals to reduce rape and other forms of violence against women. Additionally, radical feminists challenge the pornography and sex industries that are based on economic exploitation for male pleasure (see Firestone, 1970; Simpson, 1989)

Postmodern feminism

As an emerging school of thought, postmodern feminism has caught the imagination of a new generation of criminologists, particularly those interested in delving further into critical analysis. Proponents of the perspective suggest that social justice can be better understood by converging postmodernism with feminism. Borrowing from postmodern theorists Derrida (1976) and Baudrillard (1983), criticism is aimed at the role of language in constructing realities of women. By deconstructing language, signs, symbols, and text, postmodern feminists demonstrate how narratives, or stories, are used to perpetuate gender inequality. Nancy Wonders (1999, 1996) presents the fundamentals of the perspective by turning attention to four points of convergence linking postmodernism and feminism: a critique of objectivity, a focus on process, the centrality of identity and difference, and a new conception of power.

Postmodernists and feminists question the general notion of an objective reality or truth, insisting that social reality is subject to interpretation. For example, 'the truth that some women are witches and deserving of punishment and incapacitation seemed like a fact at one point in time, but it was determined to be a story at a later point time' (Wonders, 1999: 116). Similarly, slavery remained an integral part of America's early experience due in large part to the so-called 'truth' that slaves were not fully human: a version of reality that was inscribed in law designed to undermine their emancipation. By attending to the subjective nature of social reality, it becomes evident that the 'truth' – the stories or narratives – are inherently political, privileging some perspectives over others.

The 'truth' also serves to produce notions of identity from which certain people are excluded from participating in the construction of reality because they are viewed as being different. Social identity is predicated on race, class, and gender, and those considerations are used as the basis of difference, thus perpetuating inequality. Postmodern feminism traces inequality to the ways in which meaning is attached to certain behaviors, reinforcing notions of difference. 'If the state claims that young people who used drugs are criminal (rather than "ill" as is done in many other industrialized countries), then the state has played an active role in shaping the identity of teenagers and others who used drugs – it has changed who they are' (Wonders, 1999: 118).

Attending to process also refines our understanding of the construction of social reality. By focusing on interpretative strategies, postmodern feminists reveal the process by which social reality is created day to day. In studying the criminal system, an interpretative approach yields crucial information about how criminal identities and notions of justice are shaped. Any person who has visited a courtroom or a prison realizes that judges, prosecutors, defendants, convicts, and corrections officers are conforming to a shared reality about who plays the role of the controller and who plays the role of the controlled. Unquestionably, those roles are patterned by structures of power that exist in hierarchies. Postmodern feminists remind us of the importance of language – particularly sexist vocabularies – that reproduces gender inequality by linguistically conveying meaning, positionality, identity and difference (e.g. 'whore,' 'crack whore,' 'assistant crack whore') (see Arrigo, 1995; West and Fenstermaker, 1995).

At the current stage of theory construction, feminist criminology, much like mainstream criminology, lacks a unified approach. While contemporary researchers fault dominant theories for not adequately addressing female criminality, feminist criminologists also have not developed a comprehensive theoretical model from which to interpret female criminality. At best, there remain consistent themes in feminist analyses of crime, such as inequality, sexism, and discrimination (see Bosworth and Flavin, 2007).

Feminists have begun to evaluate their own progress. Correspondingly, some activists are uneasy with the predominantly white, middle-income, suburban agenda that often neglects the needs of the poor and women of color (Tong, 1989). 'This failure has made feminism appear unattractive to, if not useless to, large numbers of women, and has produced a theory bereft of the intellectual base essential for undertaking a critique of the fundamental social practices it seeks to correct' (Arp et al., 1990: 24). Feminist criminologists have set out to correct this bias by concentrating on women of color, especially those who see 'the women's liberation movement as hopelessly white and middle-class, immune to their concerns' (Simpson, 1989: 608; see Barak et al., 2001; Johnson, 2003). The recent contributions of feminist criminology with regard to race are discussed further in Chapter 8. (See 'Cultural Penology: PMS and Biological Theories of Female Criminality', below.)

CULTURAL PENOLOGY

PMS and Biological Theories of Criminality

Sexist notions about women and crime do not die easily. In female biology as it affects women psychologically, there has been interest in premenstrual syndrome (PMS) and its correlation with female criminality. Some observers assume that women are prone to violent 'acting-out' behavior and other forms of deviance during critical stages of their menstrual cycle. While the debate over the relationship between PMS and crime remains controversial, Rittenhouse (1991) offers reasons why biological theories about female criminality persist.

Cultural context and dramatic events, according to Rittenhouse, serve as important foundations from which PMS can emerge as a seemingly plausible theory. A prevailing cultural context tends to promote the notion that women are vulnerable to losing control over their behavior as a result of the effects of PMS. That idea was advanced by some dramatic events involving British trials in which two women charged with manslaughter used PMS as a defense. In the early 1980s, the British 'courts reduced to manslaughter the sentences of two women charged with murder on the grounds that severe PMS reduced their capacity to control their behavior' (Rittenhouse, 1991: 413).

Many experts dispute the validity of the PMS theory of crime, specifying methodological problems such as questionable self-reports (Morris, 1987). Nevertheless, it is important to examine the cultural context that facilitates such scientific reasoning. Strong social resistance against women's search for equality still persists, and one of the primary mechanisms used to offset the upward mobility of women in society is to question their competence. Therefore the belief that women experience diminished responsibility while suffering from PMS serves to marginalize women. Furthermore, sexist humor about PMS reflects deep-seated anxieties about women in positions of political power. Sexist jokes about vice-presidential nominee Geraldine Ferraro (in 1984) and more recently presidential hopeful Hillary Clinton (in 2008) suggest that voters think twice about electing a woman. For instance, a woman President might launch nuclear weapons while suffering from PMS (see Schneider, 2000; Welch, 1997a).

WOMEN IN PRISON

By 2008, more than 105,250 women were in prison: comprising 7 percent of the US penal population (see Table 6.1). The female prison population expanded 3 percent nationwide between the years 2000 and 2007 with the highest regional increase in the West (3.5 percent). The percentage of female prisoners grew slightly nationwide (0.3) from 2007 to 2008 with the largest regional increase occurring in the Northeast (1.5 percent). Against that trend, the West reported

Table 6.1 Number of prisoners under state and federal jurisdiction, by sentence length, race, Hispanic origin, and gender, 2008

	Total	Male	Female
Prisoners by sentence length			
Total under jurisdiction	1,610,446	1,495,594	114,852
Sentenced to more than 1 year	1,540,036	1,434,784	105,252
Estimated prisoners by race[a]			
White[b]	591,900	562,800	29,100
Black[b]	528,200	477,500	50,700
Hispanic	313,100	295,800	17,300

[a]Based on prisoners sentenced to more than 1 year. Excludes American Indians, Alaska Natives, Asians, Native Hawaiians, other Pacific Islanders, and persons identifying two or more races.
[b]Excludes persons of Hispanic or Latino origin.

Source: Sabol *et al.* (2009: 2).

an overall decrease in the percentage of women behind bars (0.4) (see Table 6.2). Women aged 35 to 39 made up the largest percentage (19.8 percent) of sentenced female prisoners; correspondingly, that age group had the highest rate of imprisonment (201 per 100,000 women in the US resident population), followed by women aged 30 to 34 (190 per 100,000) (Sabol *et al.*, 2009). It is important to note that these figures apply only to women in prison and do not include the large number of women in jail and detention or those on probation and parole (see Chapters 11, 13).

CRITICAL ANALYSIS OF DATA

Referring to Table 6.2 (page 180), identify in each region the states that have the most and the fewest female prisoners for the year 2008.

Types of offense

Among the many differences between women prisoners and their male counterparts are the offenses for which they are sentenced to prison. Whereas more than 50 percent of male prisoners held in state prisons have been convicted of violent crimes, just over 32 percent of women inmates have been sentenced for similar offenses. For murder, the percentages are comparable: male prisoners (11 percent) and female prisoners (9.5 percent). Still, the sheer numbers capture the vast difference between male and female murderers. State prisons hold more than 638,000 men convicted of homicide compared to nearly 30,000 women. The majority of women in prison are serving time for property crimes (nearly 30 percent), in particular for fraud (10 percent) and larceny (nearly 9 percent).

The other roughly one-third of all women inmates have been convicted of drug violations: that 28 percent translates to more than 25,000 females in state prison for a nonviolent drug offense (Sabol *et al.*, 2009; see Tables 6.3 and 6.4). These vexing problems perpetuated by the war on drugs are explored in greater detail in Chapters 13 and 16.

CRITICAL ANALYSIS OF DATA

Referring to Table 6.3 (page 182), which property offense was committed least by Hispanic prisoners?

For Table 6.4 (page 183), which offense was committed least by female prisoners?

Characteristics of women behind bars

While about two-thirds of women under probation supervision are white, nearly two-thirds of those confined to correctional facilities are minority: black, Hispanic, and other races. It is important to note that Hispanics account for about one in seven women in state prisons but nearly one in three female prisoners in federal custody (see Chapter 8).

In terms of age, women in prison are older than their counterparts in local jails or under probation supervision (Chapter 11). While about one in five women on probation or in local jails are under the age of 25, one in eight state prisoners and one in eleven federal prisoners are of that age. Nearly a quarter of federal prison inmates are at least 45 years old, a characteristic that has growing implications for health-care delivery to elderly prisoners (see Chapter 16). With respect to marital status, adult women under correctional care, custody, or control are substantially more likely than those in the general population to have never been married. Nearly half of women in both state prisons and local jails have never been married; as we shall examine further in Chapter 13, seven out of ten women under correctional sanction have children under the age of 18 (Greenfeld and Snell, 2000).

Social class

As an indication of social class, government statistics show that the majority of women involved with the criminal justice system are at least high-school graduates. An estimated 60 percent of those on probation, 55 percent of those in local jails, 56 percent of those in state prisons, and 73 percent of those in federal prison have completed high school, and 30 to 40 percent of high-school graduates have attended some college or more. In a more direct examination of socioeconomic circumstances, women prisoners struggled more than male inmates prior to entering prison. About four in ten women in state prison reported that they had been employed full-time prior to their arrest. By contrast, nearly six in

Table 6.2 Female prisoners under the jurisdiction of state or federal correctional authorities, by jurisdiction, December 31, 2000, 2007, and 2008

Region and jurisdiction	Number of female prisoners			Average change, 2000–2007	Percent change, 2007–2008
	12/31/2000	12/31/2007	12/31/2008		
U.S. total	93,234	114,505	114,852	3.0%	0.3%
Federal	10,245	13,338	13,273	3.8	-0.5
State	82,989	101,167	101,579	2.9	0.4
Northeast	9,082	9,694	9,844	0.9%	1.5%
Connecticut[a]	1,406	1,496	1,502	0.9	0.4
Maine	66	139	156	11.2	12.2
Massachusetts	663	790	751	2.5	-4.9
New Hampshire	120	202	234	7.7	15.8
New Jersey	1,650	1,410	1,299	-2.2	-7.9
New York	3,280	2,754	2,587	-2.5	-6.1
Pennsylvania	1,579	2,463	2,954	6.6	19.9
Rhode Island[a]	238	282	243	2.5	-13.8
Vermont[a]	80	158	118	10.2	-25.3
Midwest	14,598	17,929	17,741	3.0%	-1.0%
Illinois	2,849	2,824	2,721	-0.1	-3.6
Indiana	1,452	2,295	2,493	6.8	8.6
Iowa[b]	592	717	749	2.8	4.5
Kansas	504	625	569	3.1	-9.0
Michigan	2,131	2,080	1,957	-0.3	-5.9
Minnesota	368	602	628	7.3	4.3
Missouri	1,993	2,522	2,449	3.4	-2.9
Nebraska	266	399	390	6.0	-2.3
North Dakota	68	147	160	11.6	8.8
Ohio	2,808	3,822	3,913	4.5	2.4
South Dakota	200	369	355	9.1	-3.8
Wisconsin	1,367	1,527	1,357	1.6	-11.1
South	39,652	48,503	49,050	2.9%	1.1%
Alabama	1,826	2,158	2,231	2.4	3.4
Arkansas	772	1,066	1,060	4.7	-0.6
Delaware[a]	597	577	557	-0.5	-3.5
District of Columbia	356		–		–
Florida	4,105	6,854	7,151	7.6	4.3

Region and jurisdiction	Number of female prisoners 12/31/2000	12/31/2007	12/31/2008	Average change, 2000–2007	Percent change, 2007–2008
Georgia[b]	2,758	3,545	3,692	3.7	4.1
Kentucky	1,061	2,441	2,270	12.6	-7.0
Louisiana	2,219	2,458	2,516	1.5	2.4
Maryland	1,219	1,184	1,060	-0.4	-10.5
Mississippi	1,669	1,962	1,981	2.3	1.0
North Carolina	1,903	2,626	2,778	4.7	5.8
Oklahoma	2,394	2,607	2,524	1.2	-3.2
South Carolina	1,420	1,604	1,633	1.8	1.8
Tennessee	1,369	1,923	2,129	5.0	10.7
Texas	13,622	13,931	13,853	0.3	-0.6
Virginia	2,059	2,933	2,967	5.2	1.2
West Virginia	303	634	648	11.1	2.2
West	19,657	25,041	24,944	3.5%	-0.4%
Alaska[a]	284	564	503	10.3	-10.8
Arizona[b]	1,964	3,460	3,766	8.4	8.8
California	11,161	11,628	11,620	0.6	-0.1
Colorado	1,333	2,335	2,294	8.3	-1.8
Hawaii[b]	561	746	728	4.2	-2.4
Idaho	493	800	758	7.2	-5.3
Montana	306	301	363	-0.2	20.6
Nevada[c]	846	1,179	982	:	:
New Mexico	511	576	569	1.7	-1.2
Oregon	596	1,060	1,109	8.6	4.6
Utah	381	632	640	7.5	1.3
Washington	1,065	1,514	1,404	5.2	-7.3
Wyoming	156	246	208	6.7	-15.4

— Not applicable. After 2001, responsibility for sentenced felons from the District of Columbia was transferred to the Federal Bureau of Prisons.
: Not calculated.
[a]Prisons and jails form one integrated system. Data include total jail and prison populations.
[b]Prison population based on custody counts.
[c]Includes estimates for Nevada for December 31, 2007.

Source: Sabol *et al.* (2009: 21–2).

Table 6.3   Estimated number of sentenced prisoners under state jurisdiction, by offense, gender, race, and Hispanic origin, year end 2006

Offense	All inmates	Male	Female	White[a]	Black[a]	Hispanic
Total	1,331,100	1,238,900	92,200	474,200	508,700	248,900
Violent	667,900	638,100	29,800	217,100	256,400	145,300
Murder[b]	144,500	135,700	8,800	34,700	61,400	36,800
Manslaughter	16,700	14,900	1,800	6,900	6,100	2,400
Rape	54,800	54,400	400	26,600	16,900	7,400
Other sexual assault	105,500	104,100	1,400	56,800	20,600	23,900
Robbery	179,500	172,400	7,100	37,500	91,500	33,900
Assault	136,600	128,800	7,900	42,800	49,800	34,700
Other violent	30,300	27,800	2,400	11,800	10,100	6,100
Property	277,900	251,200	26,700	135,300	96,000	25,000
Burglary	138,000	132,300	5,700	68,700	53,600	2,800
Larceny	51,600	43,800	7,800	23,300	17,600	7,200
Motor vehicle theft	27,100	25,500	1,600	10,900	7,100	7,900
Fraud	34,400	25,000	9,400	19,200	10,000	2,900
Other property	26,800	24,700	2,100	13,300	7,600	4,200
Drug offenses	265,800	240,500	25,400	72,100	117,600	55,700
Public-order offenses[c]	112,300	106,100	6,200	48,200	35,400	21,000
Other/unspecified[d]	7,200	2,900	4,300	1,400	3,300	1,900

Note: Totals based on prisoners with a sentence of more than 1 year. Detail may not add to total due to rounding. See *Methodology* for estimation method.
[a]Excludes Hispanics and persons identifying two or more races.
[b]Includes negligent manslaughter.
[c]Includes weapons, drunk driving, court offenses, commercialized vice, morals and decency offenses, liquor law violations, and other public-order offenses.
[d]Includes juvenile offenses and other unspecified offense categories.

Source: Sabol *et al.* (2009: 37).

ten male inmates had been working full-time prior to arrest. Approximately 37 percent of women and 28 percent of men had incomes of less than $600 per month prior to arrest. While just under 8 percent of male inmates had been receiving welfare assistance prior to arrest, nearly 30 percent of female inmates reported receiving welfare assistance at the time just before the arrest that brought them to prison (Greenfeld and Snell, 2000; see Barak *et al.*, 2001).

Alcohol and drug use

Approximately half of women offenders confined in state prisons had been using alcohol, drugs, or both at the time of the offense for which they had been incarcerated. Among those female prisoners, drug use at the time of the crime was reported more often than alcohol use, a different pattern from that found among men in state prisons. On every measure of drug use (ever used, using regularly, using in the month before the offense, and using at the time of the offense), women in state prisons reported higher usage. Forty percent of female inmates, compared to 32 percent of male convicts, had been under

Table 6.4 Estimated percent of sentenced prisoners under state jurisdiction, by offense, gender, race, and Hispanic origin, year end 2006

Offense	All inmates	Male	Female	White[a]	Black[a]	Hispanic
Total	100%	100%	100%	100%	100%	100%
Violent	50.2%	51.5%	32.3%	45.8%	50.4%	58.4%
Murder[b]	10.9	11.0	9.5	7.3	12.1	14.8
Manslaughter	1.3	1.2	2.0	1.5	1.2	1.0
Rape	4.1	4.4	0.5	5.6	3.3	3.0
Other sexual assault	7.9	8.4	1.5	12.0	4.1	9.6
Robbery	13.5	13.9	7.7	7.9	18.0	13.6
Assault	10.3	10.4	8.5	9.0	9.8	13.9
Other violent	2.3	2.2	2.6	2.5	2.0	2.5
Property	20.9%	20.3%	28.9%	28.5%	18.9%	10.9%
Burglary	10.4	10.7	6.2	14.5	10.5	1.1
Larceny	3.9	3.5	8.5	4.9	3.5	2.9
Motor vehicle theft	2.0	2.1	1.8	2.3	1.4	3.2
Fraud	2.6	2.0	10.2	4.0	2.0	1.2
Other property	2.0	2.0	2.3	2.8	1.5	1.7
Drug offenses	20.0%	19.4%	27.5%	15.2%	23.1%	22.4%
Public-order offenses[c]	8.4%	8.6%	6.7%	10.2%	7.0%	8.4%
Other/unspecified[d]	0.5%	0.2%	4.6%	0.3%	0.6%	0.8%

Note: Totals based on prisoners with a sentence of more than 1 year. Detail may not add to total due to rounding. See *Methodology* for estimation method.
[a]Excludes Hispanics and persons identifying two or more races.
[b]Includes negligent manslaughter.
[c]Includes weapons, drunk driving, court offenses, commercialized vice, morals and decency offenses, liquor law violations, and other public-order offenses.
[d]Includes juvenile offenses and other unspecified offense categories.

Source: Sabol *et al.* (2009: 37).

the influence of drugs when the offense occurred. By contrast, every measure of alcohol use was higher for male inmates than for their female counterparts. About 25 percent of women on probation, 29 percent of women in local jails, 29 percent of women in state prisons, and 15 percent of women in federal prisons had been consuming alcohol at the time of the crime (Greenfeld and Snell, 2000; Chapter 16).

Just over half of women confined in state prisons reported drinking alcohol in the year before the current offense, compared to two-thirds of male offenders in state prisons. Daily drinkers accounted for about 25 percent of female inmates and 29 percent of male convicts. At the time of the offense, 29 percent of women offenders and 38 percent of male inmates had been under the influence of alcohol. About six in ten women in state prison described themselves as using drugs in the month before the offense, five in ten described themselves as a daily drug user, and four in ten were under the influence of drugs at the time of the offense.

Nearly one in three women serving time in state prisons said they had committed the offense that brought them to prison in order to obtain money to support their drug habit. Substance-abusing women inmates were more likely than drug/alcohol-involved male inmates to report having received treatment. Nearly 56 percent of women substance abusers in state prisons, compared to 41 percent of males, had ever been in substance abuse treatment; 20 percent of women and 14 percent of men had received such treatment since prison admission. Nearly a third of both men and women inmates with substance abuse problems indicated that they had participated in some other type of voluntary program, such as Alcoholics Anonymous or Narcotics Anonymous, since entering prison (Greenfeld and Snell, 2001; Kelley, 2003).

In terms of drug use, it is important to acknowledge the persistent problem of AIDS and HIV. An estimated 2,200 women serving time in state prisons were HIV-positive, constituting 3.5 percent of the female inmate population. By comparison, an estimated 20,200 male inmates – 2.2 percent of the male prison population – was HIV-positive (Greenfeld and Snell, 2000; see Chapter 16).

Problems with alcohol and drugs overlap considerably with various forms of abuse. Research on the subject indicates that 90 percent of women in prison have experienced one or more types of abuse: emotional, physical, sexual, and psychological (Browne *et al.*, 1999; Girshick, 1999; Marcus-Mendoza and Wright, 2003; Owen, 1998; United States General Accounting Office, 1999).

Criminal history

The vast majority of women in prison have a criminal history, though typically not as extensive as their male counterparts. Approximately 65 percent of women confined in state prisons had prior convictions, compared to 77 percent of male prisoners. Similarly, male inmates were twice as likely as female convicts to have had a juvenile history (38 percent versus 19 percent). Male inmates had also accumulated more convictions than women. While about a third of women prisoners had three or more prior convictions, about 43 percent of male inmates had records containing at least three prior convictions. Still, women prisoners were substantially more likely than male inmates to have had a correctional status at the time of the offense that resulted in incarceration; specifically, about one in three women inmates had been on probation when their offense occurred compared to one in five male inmates. It should also be noted that 40 percent of female first-timers, compared to 65 percent of male first-timers, serving a prison sentence had been convicted of a violent offense. In all, about 20 percent of all women prisoners and 8 percent of all male convicts were incarcerated in state prisons nationwide as offenders serving their first sentence after conviction for a non-violent crime (Greenfeld and Snell, 2001).

IS THERE A CHIVALRY FACTOR?

A persistent controversy in criminal justice is the notion of a chivalry factor. This concept suggests the male-dominated criminal justice system treats women offenders differently from their men counterparts. In particular, the chivalry perspective assumes the criminal justice system protects and sometimes excuses women for their crimes, resulting in fewer women being formally processed into the system, as well as being sentenced more leniently. Whether that form of preferential treatment actually exists has been debated for decades and continues to draw considerable attention (Daly and Tonry, 1997; Goodstein, 2000; Herzog and Oreg, 2008; McCoy, 2000).

Gender-based research in the area of sentencing is quite complex due to the multitude of variables that may affect sentencing (e.g. race, age, employment status, dependants). Still, numerous investigations have attempted to identify the influence that sex has on sentencing. Wilbanks found that the sex of the defendant was not a powerful predictor of outcome; however, 'it also appears that females are treated less favorably at some points (the front end of the system) and more favorably at others (the back end of the system)' (1986: 528). Wilbanks concedes that his findings do not benefit from controlling additional variables (that is, without all things being equal because of the nature of his data set). Nevertheless, he charges that his results dispute the 'view that the criminal justice system operates uniformly in favor of females' (Wilbanks, 1986: 528; see Bickle and Peterson, 1991; Goontz, 2000).

Likewise, Crew's study revealed little support for the hypothesis that female offenders receive more lenient sentences. Moreover, 'there is no consistent evidence of an "evil women" effect whereby women are penalized more harshly than men' (1991: 77). Crew identifies the type and seriousness of the offense as being important in determining the length of a sentence but admits a bias in the sample selection that may conceal actual differences between men and women offenders. Crew goes on to note that 'preferential treatment for women tends to occur at the in/out decision rather than in determining the length of sentence' (1991: 78; see Demuth and Steffensmeier, 2004; Nagel and Hagan, 1982).

In their comparison of gender and imprisonment decisions, Steffensmeier et al. (1993) acknowledge that judges are influenced by two major concerns, blameworthiness (e.g. as indicated by prior record, type of involvement, remorse) and practicality (e.g. as indicated by childcare responsibility, pregnancy, emotional or physical problems, availability of adequate jail space). Steffensmeier et al. conclude in their study of Pennsylvania courts that 'when men and women appear in (contemporary) criminal court in similar circumstances and are charged with similar offenses, they receive similar treatment' (1993: 411; see Silby and Wilson, 2004).

Returning to Crew's research (1991), it has been discovered that patriarchal values tend to emerge in sentencing. For instance, economic roles are an important consideration for the legal processing of men; accordingly, judges attend to the traditional role of women in the family. 'The most parsimonious explanation of the complex relationship between gender and sentencing is that the legal system is more concerned with maintaining families and protecting children than with discriminating on the basis of sex' (Crew, 1991: 80). Therefore legal officials are agents of a patriarchal state and exercise their power in ways that maintain the family unit (see Daly, 1994a; Farr, 2000; Glick and Fiske, 2000).

Studies suggesting that women are treated more leniently than men in the criminal justice system often are confounded by a number of other factors. Research that produces some evidence that the chivalry factor exists concede that the degree of preferential treatment is slight (Steffensmeier, 1988; Tjaden and Tjaden, 1981). More importantly, many scholars look beyond gender and find other variables that affect sentencing decisions, such as perceived dangerousness, criminal history, and likelihood of future criminal conduct (Steffensmeier *et al.*, 1993). When such factors are taken into account, women are more likely to be sentenced to probation because they, unlike men, are evaluated favorably on each of the factors (see Steffensmeier, 1988; Tjaden and Tjaden, 1981). Other relevant variables also affect judicial decisions regarding women, especially economic dependency and single parenthood (Steffensmeier *et al.*, 1993). Including additional variables in the study of differential sentencing patterns helps clarify the connection between gender and punishment (see Crawford, 2000a; Wood and Grasmick, 1999).

In light of research on the chivalry factor, it is crucial to maintain a critical perspective. While it is important to detect and document disparities in sentencing, there remain larger questions pertaining to gender inequality in criminal justice. So as not to lose sight of the big picture, one should continue to explore the sources and causes of female criminality, especially non-violent offenses motivated by distinctive forms of economic survival contoured along lines of gender. To be discussed in greater detail, the nature of drug violations and their assigned penalties indeed lends itself to gender alongside race, ethnicity, and social class (see Kempf-Leonard and Sample, 2000; Spohn 1999; Chapters 8 and 16).

PROGRAMS IN WOMEN'S PRISONS

In women's prisons, programs generally fall into five major categories. The first set of programs are those relating to education, most of which are remedial in nature; however, some advanced students in prison classrooms earn college credits. In the second category are programs that facilitate the maintenance of the institution. Inmates are commonly given such work assignments as clerical work, food service, general cleaning, and ground maintenance. Vocational programs constitute the third category. Still, these training programs remain somewhat sex-role stereotyped (e.g. training in office skills and cosmetology). The fourth area of programs includes those considered treatment-oriented, such as individual and group counseling as well as those aimed at reducing chemical dependency. Finally, there are programs based on medical and health care (Sharp, 2003b).

As noted previously, many women inmates lack even a basic educational background. Correspondingly, remedial education is strongly recommended, especially in areas of reading, writing, and mathematics. Not surprisingly, illiteracy affects many inmates – both male and female. Given that deficiency, the goals of education must be reasonable in order to be achieved. Many illiterate prisoners set their sights on earning the General Equivalency Diploma (GED). Educational programs are regarded as being so valuable that administrators are willing to pay inmates to enroll in those programs. Although compensation is generally low, it can nevertheless be used to purchase commissary items such as cigarettes, snack food, or, in women's prisons, brand-name soaps and shampoos.

Work assignments for female convicts parallel the chores in male prisons. While offsetting some of the costs to operate the institution, menial jobs serve to keep the inmates busy; moreover, boring tasks may also be assigned to convicts – of both sexes – as a form of in-house punishment. For instance, the practice of scrubbing and rescrubbing floors several times during the day, even when it is evident that the floors do not need cleaning, speaks to the historical pattern of disciplining prisoners. Like their male counterparts, women convicts are paid for their work. Wages are usually set between 10 cents and a few dollars per hour. What little money is earned is usually spent in the commissary. Sometimes the prisoners' earnings are placed into a restitution fund (i.e. a fund for victim compensation) as ordered by a judge.

Vocational programs are not without their biases, limitations, and weaknesses. Many of the vocational programs for women inmates emphasize skills that are essentially sex-role-oriented. Several reasons explain why such stereotyped programs persist. First, even though women sometimes administer female prisons, the concept of imprisonment is largely a male construction. Therefore programs reflect the traditional ways in which women are expected to behave by society. Compounding matters, few women convicts view themselves as politically progressive or liberated. Their conservative self-identity is probably attributable to their relatively low educational background that reinforces their willingness to accept traditional sex roles. The second reason involves logistics. That is, even if there were a large demand among women for other vocational programs, most institutions lack the resources to offer advanced programs such as computer science and mechanics. Although there is nothing inherently wrong with domestic and clerical service or cosmetology, some programs are self-defeating. For instance, some states require a license to work in cosmetology, and such licensing is denied to ex-cons. Moreover, cosmetology and clerical work are 'pink-collar' jobs, which are generally low-paying and often considered dead-end employment. By contrast, computer science and mechanic training usually lead to better-paying jobs (Ehrenreich, 2003).

Whereas the objective of educational and vocational programs is to develop social and work skills, treatment-oriented programs aspire to promote coping skills. Most prisons offer an array of such programs, including alcohol and drug rehabilitation, as well as mental health services. Due to the relatively small inmate populations of women's prisons, individual therapy is more available than in male institutions. Programs designed to help women improve their parenting skills are in great demand. During the mothers' incarceration, most children are cared for by their maternal grandmothers, and upon release women convicts usually return to their parenting duties. Such programs not only prepare mothers to resume caring for their children, but also assist them in utilizing their prison visitation time with their children. Most women's prisons offer weekend visits with children, as well as furloughs that allow women to return home for several days. Such programs are vital in the strengthening and maintenance of families, and could offset some of the strain that occurs when a mother is incarcerated (Flavin, 2001; see Chapter 13).

Women generally require more medical attention than men; consequently, female prisons respond to a greater demand for healthcare. Prison administrators are expected to deal with a range of medical services, including gynecological and prenatal care alongside an array of medications. Because women's prisons are relatively small institutions, policy-makers believe that installing extensive medical services in the prison cannot be justified financially. Therefore women inmates requiring greater medical attention than the prison provides must be transported to hospitals. Compounding matters, many prisons are located in rural areas, therefore transporting inmates to urban medical centers can be problematic. In addition to the security risks inherent in transportation, there are other medical issues that need to be addressed such as patient-doctor confidentiality. Many medical concerns become the subject of litigation. But even when the courts uphold the inmates' petition for better medical attention, some prison administrators react slowly to court orders (Muraskin, 2000; see Chapter 12).

THE SOCIAL WORLD OF WOMEN'S PRISONS

Just as Chapter 5 explores the social world of men's prisons, it is fitting here to continue looking into the cultural and organizational aspects of women's institutions. In particular, this section examines the inmate social world, the convict code, inmate roles, the pseudofamily, the 'guard' social world, and the issues surrounding male correctional officers working in female prisons.

Inmate social world

The convict social world in female prisons resembles that of their male counterparts insofar as women inmates also form close bonds with each other. But while men's institutions are characterized as harsh, coercive, and punitive environments, prisons for women tend to be less oppressive and, most significantly, less violent. Nevertheless, women – like men – also feel the major effects of incarceration, including a loss of freedom, and the lack of emotional support. Moreover, women are likely to suffer more from being separated from their children, thereby compounding their sense of guilt, depression, and low self-esteem while imprisoned (Gartner and Kruttschnitt, 2003; Owen, 2003).

Because prisons for women are generally less violent and have fewer gang networks, female convicts tend to adhere to a different subculture. Whereas male prisoners are drawn to gangs and their subcultures out of a sense of protection, women seek group affiliation for emotional support. A popular topic among those writing about women's prisons is the extent of homosexuality. While one ought to be cautious not to overgeneralize, it is suggested that homosexual relations in female institutions tend to be more consenting and less coercive than in men's prisons where such contact often takes the form of assault or prostitution.

In prison women tend to bond more closely to one another emotionally, and homosexuality often represents their need for involvement. Still, researchers have focused more on homosexuality among female convicts than among their male counterparts, thereby raising an important observation. Such an unbalanced look at homosexuality appears to reflect the historical interest in women's morality as well as their sexuality (see Farr, 2000).

Convict code

As discussed in Chapter 5, the convict code provides a set of rules that govern institutional life. Still, men and women prisoners generally do not follow those principles with the same degree of commitment. Men tend to 'stay cool' and 'do their own time,' compared to women who frequently become involved in the problems of their peers. Although sharing personal concerns with fellow women inmates might ease emotional difficulty, there are several adverse effects of having one's problems known to others. In women's prisons, convicts spread gossip and rumors so as to control or humiliate each other, therefore women prisoners risk exacerbating their personal problems by disclosing them (see Mahan, 1984).

Figure 6.2 Mexico City, Mexico – December 17, 2009: Paola Durante poses for a photograph during a Christmas celebration with prisoners at the Feminine Prison of Santa Marta Acatitla.

Photo by Juan Villa/Jam Media/LatinContent/ Getty Images.

Another difference concerning the inmate code involves contact with the staff. In men's prisons, prisoners tend to avoid a lot of friendly communication with the officers. Convicts generally distrust officers and view those who talk regularly with staff as potential snitches. Conversely, women inmates often engage in casual conversations with staff, and at times even seek their assistance in sorting out personal problems. Still, it is suggested that many female convicts uphold the tenets of the inmate code that prohibit snitching. Whereas the inmate code serves as a relevant construct in studying men in prison, its usefulness is limited in women's prisons because their social world is organized differently (Mahan, 1984; Owen, 2003).

Inmate roles

As noted previously, inmates tend to occupy roles in the convict social world that reflect their personal place in the subculture. In men's prisons, those roles include the merchant, the gorilla, punk, the real man, etc. Women's institutions feature similar roles. In her classic study, Heffernan (1972) developed a typology of women prisoners: the square, the cool, and the life. Interestingly, these roles resemble the square, the thief, and the con described by Irwin and Cressey (1964) in their study of male prisons.

As Heffernan writes, the square is a female prisoner who does not possess a criminal orientation; moreover, she resists the effects of prisonization by identifying more with the staff. The cool straddles the line between prisonization and convention but generally attempts to keep her stay behind bars as comfortable as possible without getting into trouble. As a hardened criminal, the life is overly attached to the prison subculture by making it a way of life; she has a strong criminal orientation and frequently violates institutional rules. Women inmates may also assume the role of the politician (one who works well with the staff) or the outlaw (one who relies on violence to get her way). Among the other roles played by female convicts are those of the snitch, the inmate cop, the jive bitch, and the booster (Giallombardo, 1966, 1974; Simmons, 1975).

Social organization and the pseudofamily

Prominent features of the inmate social world for women are the pseudofamily along with a complex network of friendships and homosexual liaisons. While men tend to join gangs while in prison, women convicts gravitate to relationships that resemble families, cliques, or dyads. A pseudofamily is best characterized as a set of roles that include father and mother figures that care for their daughters. In some cases, an extended family may emerge in which women assume the role of grandparents, aunts, and uncles. Stereotypes tend to pattern the pseudofamily from which key roles are enthusiastically embraced. The mother functions as a warm, caring, and nurturing family figure. Often the father will take on masculine characteristics in terms of sporting a short hairstyle, wearing men's clothing, and acting authoritatively. Still, some pseudofamilies do not have a father figure; instead, they are structured around two women who live as partners. Perhaps even more common are women who serve as mother figures to several mostly younger prisoners without an elaborate family structure or rigid role-playing (Van Wormer and Bartollas, 2000).

Institutional staff tend to recognize those pseudofamilies, and internal order is sometimes established by rewarding the mother figures for controlling problem inmates. At the request of a corrections officer, for instance, a mother figure may calm down an unruly daughter (Fox, 1984). Nonetheless, the degree of control or influence depends on the level of commitment of a particular convict to the pseudofamily. It is suggested that inmates who have recently entered the prison are often highly committed to the pseudofamily (MacKenzie *et al.*, 1989). Similarly, prisoners with few family contacts outside of prison and those serving lengthy sentences are more likely to turn to the pseudofamily for emotional support. As inmates near the end of their sentences, they often rely less on the pseudofamily for support. The degree of commitment to a pseudofamily is further determined by the quality of family life the convict had prior to incarceration. Prisoners who experienced an abusive family life sometimes will seek a better family in the form of a pseudofamily (Van Wormer and Bartollas, 2000). As women's prisons began to introduce more family programs, visitations, and furloughs in the late 1970s and 1980s, the need for pseudofamilies was dramatically reduced (Fox, 1984). Today many women's prisons encourage inmates to maintain strong family ties outside the institution; consequently, their emotional needs are often met through those external ties (Owen, 2003, 1998).

Two final observations on the convict social world draw attention to matters of racial segregation and violence. Male and female prisons differ significantly along lines of race relations. While behind bars, men tend to segregate themselves into particular racial and ethnic groups. Women convicts, however, observe fewer such boundaries and often engage with fellow prisoners of different racial and ethnic backgrounds (see Chapter 8). Whereas exploitation and intimidation are common in women's prisons, extreme acts of violence are rare. When such aggression does take place, it is usually in response to theft, a dispute over personal relationships, or snitching. Generally, expressions of dominance in women's prisons parallel those in men's institutions. Women convicts, like their male counterparts, tend to target weaker inmates as a way to gain favors or contraband (e.g. drugs), though the presence of a black market in women's prisons is rather limited (Kruttschnitt and Krmpotich, 1990; see Chapter 9).

The 'guard' social world

Compared to male institutions, the 'guard' social world in women's prisons is different most notably because there is less social distance between the keepers and the kept. That phenomenon has historical precedence. As noted previously, early campaigns to reform female prisons attracted professional women who were less interested in the paramilitary model and devoted more to a social work orientation. A shift toward the social work model allows staff members to relax the social boundaries, allowing them greater interaction with the convicts. Moreover, that commitment to service rather than mere custody is facilitated by other factors, most notably the character of the prison population that has a low security level due to the non-violent background of women convicts.

Despite the less volatile environment found in women's prisons, many correctional officers (of both sexes) report that it is sometimes easier to work in male institutions. Male convicts, they say, often are more respectful and less demanding than their female counterparts. Consider the experience of Sarah Lehane, a corrections officer with considerable experience supervising male as well as female inmates. After a violent incident in the male institution, Lehane considered transferring to the state female correctional facility, fully realizing that women's prisons present a different kind of challenge. Lehane reflected:

> The thing with females is they're more emotional. You actually have to be even more people-oriented. They question everything. They cry – omigod, not more crying! You think of their crimes, and you think, Now she's crying because I told her to clean her room? If a man hasn't seen his son, they keep it inside, but then get in a fistfight every couple months. Whereas the female will cry for 20 years … It's hard working with people. My next job will be with machinery, something that doesn't talk back.
>
> (Conover, 2001: 156; see Jenne and Kersting, 2002; Lawrence and Mahan, 2002; Richards *et al.*, 2002)

Still, some female officers would rather work with women convicts because they enjoy discussing mutual interests, thereby presenting an opportunity to take on the role of the counselor.

The question of 'guard' subcultures in women's institutions has been raised. It is suggested that because those facilities are less threatening than those of men, 'guard' subcultures are less likely to emerge. An additional factor is that the female officer population is much less homogeneous than the male officer population. However, Pollock-Byrne (1990) notes that it is possible that there is a 'guard' subculture in women's prisons, but it might be so different from male subcultures as to be unrecognizable.

WORKING IN CORRECTIONS

Male COs in Female Prisons

In early penal institutions, women inmates were not only confined along with male prisoners but were also guarded by men. By the late eighteenth century, women prisoners were segregated from male convicts but still supervised by men. Serious problems remained. Women inmates were often raped and forced into prostitution by their male custodians. In response to these atrocities, separate institutions for women were established in the early nineteenth century, staffed and administered entirely by female warders. Separate institutions for women set out to accomplish the following goals. First, prisons for women would prevent sexual abuse and exploitation by male guards. Second, female staff would serve as role models of 'true womanhood' for women offenders viewed as deviant and wayward. Third, women inmates would benefit from sympathetic counseling (Freedman, 1981, 1974; Young, 1932; Zupan, 1992).

Due to a shortage of qualified women to work in female prisons, along with a general lack of faith in the administrative skills of women wardens, correctional institutions for women have returned to male-dominated leadership and correctional officers (COs). Traditionally, male officers were assigned to perimeter security positions where they had little or no contact with female inmates. Today, male officers routinely supervise women inmates – even in living units. Such staff assignments raise issues of privacy for female prisoners, leading to several structural and policy changes. For instance, privacy doors and glazed windows in shower and toilet areas have been installed. Additionally, male COs announce their entry into shower and toilet areas, and in some facilities female personnel must accompany them. Restrictions on pat searches in many institutions require that male officers use the back of their hand during frisks and often such frisks must be done in the presence of other officers (Zupan, 1992).

In her research inside women's prisons staffed by men, Linda Zupan (1992) explored the reactions that female inmates have toward male COs. In general, women prisoners disclosed favorable evaluations of male officers, often saying that they were treated more fairly, more respectfully, and with more honesty than by female COs. Many female inmates viewed male officers as being less likely to become argumentative. Moreover, it was found that male officers rarely responded to minor rule infractions and usually did not exhibit favoritism. Zupan offers the following excerpts from her interviews with female inmates:

The ladies obey the male. Women [correction officers] are jealous of inmates.

Men are dominant and women are used to being told what to do by men and they do it.

Women [officers] tell them what to do and inmates buck it.

Lady officers take out frustrations on women and they go off on women. Men don't have attitude problems. They listen more. Women are 'alley cats.' Female inmates argue with female officers. A man gives [an] order or [a] look and women [inmates] obey.

> Since they [male officers] arrived, fights between inmates have declined. Male officers are more respectful than females. Inmates are more likely to obey male officers ... [inmates] will cuss women officers.
>
> Men don't play favorites like women do. They treat everyone the same.
>
> Male officers break up fights. They are not scared ... Women officers are scared of fights. Male officers don't need backup.
>
> Men talk to us like real people. Ladies treat us bad. Ladies talk down to you.
>
> (1992: 305)

Although female inmates voice numerous complaints about women officers, they still are drawn to them to discuss personal problems. Women convicts would also rather undergo pat searches by female than male COs; likewise, they prefer that solely women supervise shower and toilet areas. In her study, Zupan also learned that sexual advances and harassment by male officers were not common occurrences. In fact, 'several inmates indicated that female officers were more likely to make sexual advances and sexually harass inmates than were male officers' (Zupan, 1992: 306). Finally, it was believed that male officers were more easily conned by female inmates.

Despite the drawback of having male officers in women's prisons, generally there is little inmate resistance. Indeed, there are some positive effects of having male staff in female institutions. For example, administrators report that the appearance and grooming of some female inmates improved, and sometimes they became more obedient to the commands of male officers (Zimmer, 1986). Such findings raise important questions about the presence of male officers in women's prisons. 'Does this preference actually reflect differential treatment female inmates receive from male and female officers, or does it reflect instead the traditional and stereotypical attitudes held by female inmates?' (Zupan, 1992: 308). In other words, one might wonder whether the authority of female officers is undermined by the sexist view that women cannot competently manage correctional institutions.

In the previous section on postmodern feminism, it was noted that social identity is predicated on race, class, and gender, and these considerations are used as the basis of difference from which inequality is perpetuated. Recent scholarship on women prisoners has taken cues from postmodern feminism and contested the sexist stereotypes prevalent in mainstream penology. By attending closely to various forms of resistance, Bosworth (1999, 1998, 1996; Bosworth and Carrabine, 2001) reveals that power relations between inmates and staff are rarely fixed; rather they are continuously negotiated. Moreover, the fluctuation between domination and subordination is greatly influenced by gender (as well as race), allowing female convicts to assume positions of power contrary to female stereotypes. Instead of behaving either passively or immaturely, Bosworth found that in the face of adversity, many women prisoners resort to acts of defiance that realign the balance of power between the keepers and the kept. Such resistance 'is a practical accomplishment that can challenge or maintain prevailing power relations, providing the possibility that prisons may be altered from the inside out by those very individuals who are subject to its control' (Bosworth and Carrabine, 2001: 513; see also Carlen, 1983; Shaw, 1992).

CO-CORRECTIONS

An innovative program designed to help reform women and men inmates was co-corrections. These prisons were unique minimum-security facilities that housed both female and male convicts in the same institution. Opening in 1971, the Federal Correctional Institution (FCI) at Fort Worth, Texas, featured a prison environment that was relatively 'softer' than most other facilities. Like other federal minimum-security units, FCI Fort Worth housed inmates classified as low-risk and non-violent: most were white-collar offenders or drug violators.

At FCI Fort Worth, women and men inmates were placed in separate living units, but during the day they worked, attended programs, and recreated together. Physical contact between the coed prisoners was limited to hand-holding. Inmates risked being transferred to a higher-security (same-sex) institution if they were caught engaging in sexual contact. Many men and women inmates often formed close friendships and nonphysical romances. Nevertheless, an inherent irony existed; as one convict put it: 'It seems that the primary objective is to put men and women together and keep them apart' (Mahan, 1986: 137). Although many inmates preferred serving sentences in coed prisons, due in large part to the less threatening atmosphere, there was a small number of prisoners who would have preferred to be sentenced to a same-sex institution. Some convicts complained that in co-correctional prisons there are too many petty rules and the daily supervision by staff seems heavier. Moreover, the families of inmates sometimes expressed suspicions and jealousies of life in a coed prison (Mahan, 1984; Smykla, 1978).

The rationale of the co-correctional experiment was to facilitate the inmates' return to the community. A more humane environment featuring the presence of the opposite sex was believed to achieve that goal since the 'prison world' thus resembled the 'free world' in obvious ways. Observers of FCI Fort Worth tended to focus on its co-correctional status, overlooking its other programs. The administrators at the institution took pride in being one of the most programmed facilities in the nation. Convicts assigned to FCI Fort Worth were encouraged to take advantage of the numerous programs offered, particularly those specializing in chemical dependency. Many women inmates enthusiastically enrolled in family-oriented programs in which visitations from spouses and children were strongly recommended. In the eyes of conservative politicians, however, minimum-security facilities were depicted as coed 'country clubs.' Those critics often fail to acknowledge the significant pains of imprisonment, such as the loss of liberty and separation from one's family.

In the late 1980s, the Federal Bureau of Prisons re-evaluated its stand on co-corrections. In view of the tough-on-crime campaigns and President George Bush's initiative to eliminate furlough and other unpopular policies, the US Department of Justice worried that co-corrections did not uphold the 'tough' image of prison life that the White House had been fiercely promoting. Consequently, in 1988 the co-correctional program at FCI Fort Worth was discontinued and the institution was converted to an all-male facility. The co-correctional program at FCI Pleasanton, California, was terminated in 1990: that facility became an all-female institution now known as FCI Dublin. By 1999, there were no co-correctional facilities on record (Mahan, 2000).

ABUSE OF WOMEN BEHIND BARS

Over the past decade, greater attention has been directed to women who have been victims of abuse by custodial staff. In 1992, a major case involving physical and sexual assault surfaced in the Georgia women's prison at Hardwick. In what is described as 'one of the worst episodes of its kind in the history of the nation's women's prisons,' 14 former correctional employees (including a former deputy warden) were convicted of widespread physical and sexual abuse (Applebome, 1992: A-1). More than 119 female prisoners reported incidents of rape, sodomy, and forced abortions. The investigation also revealed an incident in which a mentally disturbed woman was stripped and hog-tied on a concrete floor.

Figure 6.3 Inmates in Parmasola's prison, in Santa Cruz, Bolivia on November 27, 2009. In Parmasola there are some 1,500 prisoners, men and women, who coexist together in the jail's district. Children can remain with their parents until they are six years old.

Photo by Desiree Martin/AFP/Getty Images.

In 1993, numerous reports surfaced in three Washington, DC, correctional facilities where women prisoners were awakened at two or three in the morning for a 'medical visit' or a 'legal visit' only to be escorted to the kitchen, the clinic, or the visiting hall to have sex with male staff members, including corrections officers, administrators, deputy wardens, chaplains, contractors, and food-service workers. Many of the inmates were enticed to deliver sexual favors in exchange for privileges such as extra phone calls, cigarettes, drugs, or better work assignments. The National Women's Law Center filed a class action suit on behalf of the prisoners, and in 1994 a judge determined that there was a 'pattern and practice of misconduct so severe that it violated the Eighth Amendment protection against cruel and unusual punishment' (Siegal, 2002a: 135). In a similar case in 1998, three women prisoners at the federal facility FCI Dublin (California) were sold as sex slaves to male convicts in an adjoining unit. To resolve a civil suit, the Federal Bureau of Prisons paid a settlement of $500,000.

Human rights organizations have joined the cause to protect female prisoners from abuse. In 1996, the Women's Rights Project at Human Rights Watch issued an extensive report detailing the abuse of women inmates in California, Georgia, Michigan, New York, and Washington, DC. 'We found that in the course of committing such gross misconduct, male officers have not only used actual or threatened physical force, but have also used their near total authority to provide or deny goods and privileges to female prisoners to compel them to have sex or, in other cases, to reward them for having done so' (Human Rights Watch, 1996: 1). In 1999, Amnesty International released a similar report entitled 'Not Part of My Sentence': Violations of Human Rights of Women in Custody. The title of the report quotes a woman prisoner who said that being forced to perform oral sex on a corrections officer was not part of the judge's sentence. Amnesty International documented serious problems of sexual abuse in women's institutions in Illinois, Massachusetts, New Hampshire, Texas, West Virginia, and Wyoming.

Human rights groups express frustration in dealing with the abuse of women prisoners in part because unions that legally represent accused corrections officers do not take seriously the harm committed. According to Christine Doyle of Amnesty International: 'Guards look at this as a workplace violation, as something fun to do on the job. They don't look at these women as human beings. The message that these are human beings they are exploiting isn't getting through' (Siegal 2002a: 137). Amnesty International recommends that the role of male staff in female institutions be restricted in accordance with the United Nations' Standard Minimum Rules for the Treatment of Prisoners, stating that women prisoners should be attended and supervised only by women officers.

The abuse of women in custody goes beyond traditional jails and prisons. Tragically, such abuse also occurs against undocumented immigrants and asylum seekers held by the immigration authorities. In 2000, 90 female detainees held at INS Detention Center at Krome (Florida) were transferred to a county-operated jail – a move intended to protect them – as federal agents continued their investigation of sexual abuse at the facility (Chardy, 2000). Authorities had already charged corrections officer Lemar Smith with sexually assaulting a male-to-female transsexual detainee. The victim, an asylum seeker from Mexico, said she was raped in an isolation cell a second time after she reported the initial assault to three staff supervisors. At least a dozen detention officers were removed from duty at Krome or reassigned to jobs amid a widening sex and bribery scandal (Sullivan, 2000). Indeed, the problems at Krome highlight the struggle to protect its immigration detainees not just at local jails but at the facilities the immigration service operates directly or indirectly through contracts with private corporations.

Human rights advocates applauded the move to protect the women, but also expressed concern about transferring the detainees to a county jail. Attorneys for the detainees recommended that the women be released into the community or be supervised at shelters. However, Robert A. Wallis (then INS District Director) decided that the agency would transfer the women 'to a full-service, state-of-the-art facility that would ensure those detainees the most safe, secure and humane detention conditions possible' (Tulsky, 2000: EV2). Cheryl Little, an immigrants' rights lawyer, expressed concern over the transfer: 'No question about it: It's a jail. It would be highly inappropriate to move the women to local county jails. None of the women at Krome are serving criminal sentences' (Chardy, 2000: EV2). Others also commented on the controversy. Wendy Young of the Women's Commission for Refugee Women and Children, which issued a blistering report on the conditions of women at the immigration detention center, added: 'County prisons and hotels are not acceptable alternatives to Krome. Conditions are harsh and very punitive. INS detainees are second-class citizens at county jails because they don't get their constitutional rights like the other inmates' (Chardy, 2000: EV3; Women's Commission for Refugee Women and Children, 2000, 1998). Acknowledging the ironies of immigration control inherent in detention policy, Young remarked: 'Where else in the United States do you jail the people who were sexually abused rather than the people who committed the abuse?' (Tulsky, 2000: EV1). Cheryl Little agreed: 'Clearly, we didn't want females at Krome exposed to abusive officers. But in trying to solve one problem, they created another. They are, in some ways, punishing the victims' (Tulsky, 2000: EV2).

Regrettably, the government's plan to protect the detainees by transferring them to a county jail failed. Two days after being admitted to a Miami-Dade County jail, a number of the women allegedly were 'flashed' by a male inmate, and in a separate incident that same day, another female inmate was allegedly the victim of a sexual attack by a male prisoner, triggering an internal investigation at the facility. Critics of detention practices were infuriated, noting that the women were supposed to be segregated from male inmates and supervised only by female officers. 'The irony is not lost on these women. The women were supposedly transferred for their own protection, and they're telling me they're every bit as vulnerable as they were at Krome. The women are being unduly punished and victimized,' said Cheryl Little (Chardy, 2000; Ross, 2001: EV1; see Egelko, 2000; Grossman, 2000; Human Rights Watch, 1998; Welch, 2002b;

Women's Commission for Refugee Women and Children, 2000, 1998; Chapter 11).

CONCLUSION

From the outset, the chapter has examined various differences between female offenders and their male counterparts, taking into account the historical, cultural, and socioeconomic forces shaping popular views of women prisoners alongside strategies to deal with them. While drawing on feminist criminology to provide a sharper interpretation of female criminality, the discussion explores the characteristics of women convicts and their special needs. In addition to taking into consideration forms of suffering unique to female inmates, it is vital that prison practices remain committed to providing adequate healthcare and medical services (Baunach, 2002; Chesney-Lind, 2002; Grana, 2002). As the war on drugs continues to add to a growing penal population, policy-makers should remain mindful that drug and alcohol addictions produce serious problems, including complications to pregnancy. With that concern in mind, medical specialists recommend that access to services such as prenatal care should be greatly improved inside women's prisons (Chapter 16).

Still, given that most female convicts are non-violent and pose few flight risks, it is crucial to develop news ways of dispensing punishment while not imposing more security than is necessary. That objective can be achieved through strategies that go beyond the use of prison – even minimum-security facilities. The tough on crime stance that has produced mass incarceration ought to be tempered with sensible alternatives to incarceration. As noted throughout the chapter, progressives remind us of the value of programs involving community corrections that serve to keep families together (see Fishman, 1990; Padilla and Santiago, 1993; Chapter 13).

SUMMARY

This chapter explores pressing issues inherent to women in prisons, especially those stemming from structural inequality. As a history of punishment reveals, correctional strategies for females were designed to make women more obedient, moral, and ladylike. These objectives have been furthered by a male-dominated criminology that perpetuates androcentric notions of female criminality since they reinforce sex-role stereotypes. Feminist criminologists propose a rethinking of the concepts of female crime, thereby offering alternative interpretations of women, criminal justice, and social control. Whereas the discussion herein focused on the convict social world as it unfolds in female institutions, one should be mindful of broader sociological insights that attend to women in society.

REVIEW QUESTIONS

1 How has the history of corrections shaped the punishment of female offenders? In what ways have women's prisons changed over the years, and how have they remained the same?
2 What is meant by androcentrism in criminology and corrections?
3 What are the different perspectives in feminism and how does each address women in crime and corrections?
4 What are the current patterns of female crime?
5 Is there a chivalry factor in criminal justice? What additional variables need to be addressed in measuring sentencing disparities?
6 How do women's prisons differ from those of men?

RECOMMENDED READINGS

Bosworth, M. and Flavin, J. (2007) *Race, Gender, and Punishment: From Colonialism to the War on Terror.* New Brunswick, NJ and London: Rutgers University Press.

Cook, S. and Davies, S. (2000) *Harsh Punishment: International Experiences of Women's Imprisonment.* Boston: Northeastern University Press.

Daly, K. (1994) *Gender, Crime, and Punishment.* New Haven, CT: Yale University Press.

Girshick, L. B. (1999). *No Safe Haven: Stories of Women in Prison.* Boston: Northeastern University Press.

Owen, B. (1998) *'In the Mix': Struggle and Survival in a Women's Prison.* Albany, NY: State University of New York Press.

Rafter, N. (1985) *Partial Justice: State Prisons and Their Inmates, 1800–1935.* Boston: Northeastern University Press.

CHAPTER 7

Juveniles in Corrections

Juvenile delinquency is one of the most complex and intractable social problems facing America today. Because it is complex, and because there are multiple paths by which any kid can become delinquent, it follows logically that there can be no easy or simple solutions to it. But that doesn't keep us from trying.
(James O. Finckenauer, author of *Scared Straight! and the Panacea Phenomenon*)

LEARNING OBJECTIVES

After studying this chapter, you should be able to answer the following questions:

1 What is the cycle of juvenile justice and in which phase of the cycle are we today?
2 What are the major historical developments in juvenile justice?
3 How have the landmark legal decisions shaped the juvenile justice system?
4 What are the current patterns and trends in juvenile offenses?
5 What is the nature of juvenile institutions and what impact do corrections and juvenile programs have on delinquency?

When Shahid was strutting around Newark with an automatic pistol jammed into his waistband, stealing cars, selling drugs and mugging people, he would sometimes hear older boys talking about the prison where New Jersey sends its most incorrigible teenagers. But Shahid, who stole cars for money and excitement and said he felt no pangs of conscience over shooting someone that he thought 'deserved it' didn't imagine the prison here as some kind of hellhole to be avoided at all costs. It seemed more like a testing ground, where he could see how he measured up against the worst of the worst. 'It was like an adventure to me,' he said. 'Something I wanted to find out about, a little quest, a little Indiana Jones.' For two years, Shahid, an 18-year-old who was arrested for car theft, was locked up in central New Jersey, behind the steel doors and barbed-wire of the state's toughest institution for teenagers, the Juvenile Medium Security Facility.

(Treaster, 1994: A12)

INTRODUCTION

Because criminal justice policies are subject to a diversity of opinion, they often remain controversial. The ongoing debate over juvenile justice is no exception: should juvenile offenders be punished, rehabilitated, or both? Still, even in the face of a growing penal populism, many citizens expect the criminal justice system to treat juveniles more leniently than adult criminals. Ideas of differential treatment for juveniles continue to undergo considerable discussion, taking into account numerous practical considerations alongside a vast body of scholarly research on why certain youths turn to crime. The study of juvenile justice covers a good deal of theoretical analysis, encompassing such theories as labeling, social strain, social conflict, juvenile subcultures, gangs, and so on. Although a genuine appreciation of theories of delinquency is crucial to understanding the overall field of juvenile justice, this chapter focuses more narrowly on juveniles in corrections. It explores the historical and legal developments of juvenile justice; current statistics, patterns, and trends regarding youthful offenders; as well as special programs and interventions designed specifically for juveniles.

While taking into account each of these areas of interest, a vexing question persists: what role should corrections play in society's campaign against youthful offenders? Attempts to answer that question draw on the critical theme of this book. As this chapter further indicates, a well-informed critique of juvenile justice benefits from taking a hard look at a host of social problems as well as the socioeconomic forces that influence patterns of juvenile offenses. Correspondingly, those forces combined with traditional notions of morality also shape the prevailing responses to crimes committed by youths. As we shall see, some interventions aimed at juvenile offenders seem benevolent and well intentioned while others follow a more punitive path toward harsh treatment and social control.

Figure 7.1   Troubled teen boy in close-up behind fence.
© iStockphoto.com

HISTORICAL DEVELOPMENTS IN JUVENILE JUSTICE

Juvenile justice is a term that refers to the formal system designed to deal with juvenile delinquents (those charged with less serious crimes such as drug violations) as well as youthful offenders (those charged with more serious crimes such as assault). An understanding of how the current system is intended to operate requires knowledge of the key developments in the history of juvenile justice. Certainly, it is by looking at the past that we can comprehend the present as well as anticipate the future. Chapters 2 and 3 examined how crime was reconceptualized, thus leading to the invention of more innovative methods of punishment and correction. This section explores a similar process of re-evaluating the nature of juvenile justice and its impact on a system aimed at dealing with problem youths.

The cycle of juvenile justice

In taking a critical approach to the history of juvenile justice, Bernard (1992) argues that the same sequence of policies has been repeated during the last 200 years. Bernard depicts the cycle of juvenile justice as having four distinct stages. First, there emerges a societal perception that juvenile crime is exceptionally high, thereby leading to a call for the harsh punishment of offenders. However, due to an absence of lenient or intermediate penalties, authorities are forced either to mete out harsh punishments or refrain from taking action. Therefore many less serious offenders who are believed to become worse if punished harshly are let off virtually scot-free.

In the second phase of the cycle, authorities recognize that both imposing harsh punishments and doing nothing at all contribute equally to the proliferation of juvenile crime. That realization sets the stage for the third stage whereby the introduction of lenient treatments serves as a middle ground or intermediate set of punishments. That approach leads to a sense of optimism that juvenile crime will soon decline.

Finally, authorities and the general public soon begin to sense that juvenile crime is mounting, and both accuse the system of being 'too soft' for issuing lenient penalties. Consequently, there is a renewed emphasis on harsh punishments as authorities boast a tough-on-crime stance and eliminate lenient treatments. Thus the cycle starts over again, returning to the point where authorities must choose between harsh punishments and doing nothing at all.

Bernard's insights parallel other critiques of the criminal justice system, in particular, those of Morris and Tonry (1990), who assert that currently the system is both too harsh and too lenient (see Ferdinand, 1989). Nevertheless, Bernard proposes a deeper understanding of the evolution of juvenile corrections. By doing so, he points to three prevailing myths that further drive the cycle of juvenile justice.

1 Delinquency in the past was much more serious than it is today – the myth of progress.

2 Delinquency in the past was about the same as it is today – the myth that nothing changes.

3 Delinquency in the past was much less serious than it is today – the myth of the good old days.

(1992: 12)

Clearly, each of these myths is based on a rather simplistic view of the juvenile justice system. Bernard argues that most people do not believe in the first myth (the myth of progress), even though, he asserts, there is considerable truth to it. Generally, according to Bernard, delinquency is less of a problem than it was 20 years ago.

Bernard writes that more people believe in the second myth (that nothing changes) despite the fact that delinquency has changed over time. He also notes that popular belief in the second myth is grounded in convenience. That is, it is simply convenient to believe that nothing changes – an attitude that cuts to the root of conservativism. Because the conservative perspective is concerned with maintaining the status quo, its proponents find it convenient to ignore the very social problems that contribute to delinquency: poverty, inequality, unemployment, racial discrimination, urban slums, under-funded schools. 'This means, in order to solve the problem of delinquency, we do not have to solve those social problems with programs that would be difficult and expensive (i.e., inconvenient)' (Bernard, 1992: 13).

More people believe the third myth than the two other myths combined. Bernard claims that the myth of the 'good old days' is true in some respects and false in others. Yet it remains a myth because, in many instances, people refer to the past as the good old days regardless of whether those days were actually better or not.

A critical approach to juvenile corrections has the task of determining exactly what has changed and what has remained the same. Acceptance of the aforementioned myths further perpetuates the cycle of juvenile justice because they each fail to learn the lessons of history. As noted previously, philosopher George Santayana stressed the importance of understanding history: 'Those who do not know history are condemned to repeat it' (1905: 284). Perhaps key to breaking the cycle of juvenile justice is a willingness to learn the lessons of the past.

Unchanging aspects of juvenile delinquency and juvenile justice

According to Bernard, there are five aspects of juvenile delinquency and juvenile justice that have stayed the same for at least 200 years (and in some cases since the beginning of civilization) (1992: 21):

1 Juveniles, especially young males, commit more crime than other groups.

2 There are several laws that only juveniles are required to obey.

3 Juveniles are punished less severely than adults who commit the same offenses.

4 Many people believe that the current group of juveniles commit more frequent and serious crimes than juveniles in the past – that is, there is a 'juvenile crime wave' at the present time.

5 Many people blame juvenile justice policies for the supposed juvenile crime wave, arguing that they are too lenient (serious offenders laugh at 'kiddie court') or that they are too harsh (minor offenders are embittered and channeled into a life of crime).

A history of juvenile delinquency and juvenile justice provides evidence that those developments have yet to change in more than 200 years.

Modernization of juvenile delinquency

The term juvenile delinquency can be traced to a London report published in 1816. From there it traveled to New York then soon spread to other major urban centers in America (Pierce, 1969; Sanders, 1970). Before juvenile delinquency became a popular catchall term, numerous other categories were used to identify society's troubled youth: 'black-guard children,' 'stubborn children,' 'poor vagrant children,' or 'young criminals' (Bernard, 1992). As the term juvenile delinquency took hold, social policy was formulated to deal with troubled youths in a more systematic fashion. Similar to practices emerging during the Jacksonian era, institutionalization became a leading solution to a 'growing' problem of delinquency. In 1825, America's first juvenile institution opened in New York City, serving as a model for other facilities in cities across the nation.

The terms juvenile delinquency and juvenile institutions emerged at a point in American history when the country was undergoing significant transformation. In addition to its struggles as a new republic, the nation was becoming less rural and agricultural, turning more urban and industrialized. In a word, America was becoming modern. While modernity advances a society in many ways, it also brings about widespread social anxiety about societal stability and safety. It is in that social context that juvenile delinquency needs to be understood critically. As cities such as Philadelphia, New York, and Boston expanded into huge urban centers, social life was transformed in ways that precipitated fear and feelings of insecurity (Rothman, 1971; Shelley, 1981).

Modernization comprises three major factors, each of which contributes to a sharper interpretation of the emergence of juvenile delinquency in America: (1) the breakdown of traditional mechanisms of social control, (2) industrialization, and (3) urbanization (Bernard, 1992). During colonial times, parents were required by law to serve as the traditional mechanism for controlling their children. When parents failed to achieve this task, children were sent to other families where they often worked as servants. In cases involving severe offenses, children (much like their adult counterparts) were transported or publicly subjected to corporal and capital punishments. Toward the end of the 1700s, however, those harsh punishments were eliminated, and youthful offenders were then imprisoned in adult prisons. Eventually, juries became reluctant to convict children because they saw the injustice of confining children in adult institutions (Barnes and Teeters, 1946; Mennel, 1973).

A major consequence of industrialization, the second factor in modernization, is that additional goods are manufactured through mass production. Indeed, the proliferation of such goods, which are movable and thus subject to theft, directly affects the level of property crimes. In preindustrial societies, theft was less common because there were simply fewer items that could be stolen. During that period, most of what constituted property and wealth was land (Michalowski, 1985). Historically, juveniles have committed a larger proportion of property crime than adults, so it stands to reason that as property crime increases, so does the involvement of youthful offenders.

Another consequence of modernization is urbanization. As factories emerged in cities, they attracted workers from the countryside as well as immigrants in search of employment; however, not everyone seeking employment was able to secure a job. Nonetheless, urban areas underwent a population boom, consisting of the employed as well as the unemployed, some of whom resorted to street crime as their means of survival (see Chapter 4). Compounding problems, dense population placed further strains on families, undermining their ability to supervise and control their children.

The first juvenile institution

Due to industrialization, urbanization, and immigration, the size and character of American cities were changing dramatically, leading to the perception that social life was becoming increasingly chaotic. Consequently, civic and business leaders, who were generally Protestant gentlemen born before the American Revolution into wealthy families residing in small towns, believed that the new republic was being threatened by growing social disorder. In particular, juvenile delinquency was viewed as evidence of social breakdown. It was theorized that further deterioration of the moral fabric of society could be avoided by initiating a social movement known as child-saving. For many concerned citizens, that campaign seemed like a benevolent form of social control since elitist leaders proposed that young, poor immigrants could be transformed into productive workers. It should be noted that many of those immigrant children were Irish Catholics who remained the object of scorn by those in power, namely those of English Protestant heritage.

Following the publication of several reports on juvenile delinquency and pauperism, the Society for the Reformation of Juvenile Delinquents (formerly the Society for the Prevention of Pauperism) opened the New York House of Refuge. At that time, the institution was located beyond the edge of the city surrounded by open fields and cultivated farms (Pierce, 1969). Critics argued that the New York House of Refuge functioned more as a poorhouse and less as a penitentiary. By the end of its first year, the institution confined 73 children who could hardly be considered criminal; many were charged with such minor offenses as vagrancy, stealing, or running away from the poorhouse (Fox, 1970).

Furthermore, what appeared to be a driving force in their incarceration was their low socioeconomic standing. Historians suggest that the institution's true mission was to prevent these youths from becoming paupers; such assertions were supported by the institution's heavy emphasis on work, as well as on the moral benefits of financial security (Krisberg and Austin, 1993; Rendleman, 1971).

Public officials became concerned that, after spending several years in the House of Refuge, juveniles were released back to the city streets where they would resume their troubled lives. In 1828, an additional policy took effect, featuring the placing-out (or farming-out) system. Upon their reform as productive workers, juveniles were often sent West to the newly settled states, such as Ohio, Illinois, and Indiana, where they would become indentured farm workers until the age of 21. More than 50,000 children were transported from New York City, and their parents were never notified of their whereabouts. Most of these youths were never heard from again (Trattner, 1974). The campaign to send children elsewhere can be traced to Britain where in the early seventeenth century, child migrants were shipped across the Atlantic to the Virginia colony. The scheme expanded in the nineteenth and twentieth centuries, with a total of perhaps 150,000 children sent to Australia, New Zealand, Canada, and Rhodesia. Much like their American counterparts, those children not only lost contact with their parents but were also committed to brutal and often sexually abusive orphanages (Burns, 2009).

The practice of institutionalizing juvenile delinquents was rarely challenged, and institutions similar to the New York House of Refuge were established in Boston (the House of Reformation, in 1826) and Philadelphia (the House of Refuge, in 1828). In addition to their emphasis on the moral value of labor, these institutions enforced discipline and education by way of corporal punishment (Schlossman, 1977). Moreover, the influence of religious forces on juvenile institutions should not be overlooked. Daily routine for these juveniles included religious instruction whereby Catholic immigrants were subjected to Protestant teachings. The implication was that Catholic immigrants were lazy and unproductive, and that those character flaws could be corrected by adopting a Protestant, or morally superior, worldview. Furthermore, when the Catholic Church attempted to gain access to these institutions, government officials and institutional administrators actively resisted (Pisciotta, 1982).

During the emergence of the juvenile justice system, there was no clear distinction between the problems of poverty, child welfare, and crime. 'In general, young America used the coercive power and punitive sanctions of criminal law to handle many problems that were clearly noncriminal' (Lerman, 1990: 7). In short, the reformatory embodied the mission of a juvenile almshouse, a workhouse, and a house of correction.

Rothman (1980) contributes to a critique of the emergence of the juvenile justice system in the context of the progressive era (1900–20). During that period, social reformers eventually acknowledged and responded to adverse social conditions, especially as they affected members of the lower classes confined to many types of institutions (i.e. prisons, reformatories, and insane asylums). The question raised by Rothman is whether social reforms were based on conscience or convenience. Did such reforms reflect a genuine sense of humanitarianism, or did they reflect a convenient attempt to control and manage the lower class (i.e. minorities and immigrants)? Rothman concludes that the progressive reform of the juvenile reformatories was actually couched in false promises. Genuine reforms rarely took place and what began as an attempt to ease the conscience of the liberal reformers soon became a convenient mechanism for managing the youths of the lower class. 'In the end, when conscience and convenience met, convenience won' (Rothman, 1980: 10).

LEGAL DEVELOPMENTS IN JUVENILE JUSTICE

The juvenile justice system was modified over the years in response to key legal developments, including several landmark court rulings. Beginning with some of those legal challenges, this section surveys the emergence of the first juvenile court as well as more recent changes affecting the rights of juveniles.

Early legal challenges to juvenile institutions

A full appreciation of the complex evolution of the juvenile justice system calls for an understanding of the legal challenges to juvenile institutions. The first landmark case stems from the commitment of Mary Ann Crouse to the Philadelphia House of Refuge. Mary Ann, like many other children committed to such institutions, had not been charged with a crime. Rather, her mother had her committed because she felt the institution could prevent her from becoming a pauper. Mary Ann's father objected to her commitment and filed a *writ of habeas corpus*, thereby requiring the state to explain its reasons for such a commitment. Since Mary Ann had not been charged with a criminal offense, it was argued that the state could not legally impose punishment and should release her. The Pennsylvania Supreme Court ruled on that case (*Ex parte Crouse*) in 1838, denying the father's petition.

The decision was as complicated as it was controversial. First, by arguing that the House of Refuge was not a prison but rather a charitable school, the court said that Mary Ann was being helped, not punished. Second, the court pointed to the good intentions of those who managed the institution. It was generally believed that those managing these institutions possessed benevolent motives. Third, the court relied on the legal concept *parens patriae* ('parent of the country'), a term that emerged in England in the fourteenth century to protect children whose parents died. However, the *Crouse* case marked the first time the concept had been applied to a child whose parents were alive. In other words, it was argued that state custody, not parental custody, was in the best interest of the child. *Parens patriae* later become a major legal principle in the further development of the juvenile justice system. Finally, in response to Mr Crouse's argument that Mary Ann was denied formal due process, the court maintained that Mary Ann did not require the same legal protections granted to defendants in a criminal trial because she was not undergoing punishment. Again, the court maintained that she was being helped (Mennel, 1973; Rendleman, 1971).

An equally important case involved Daniel O'Connell who was committed to the Chicago House of Refuge in 1870. Daniel, like Mary Ann Crouse, had not been charged with a criminal offense, but was committed for the purpose of averting a future of pauperism. Daniel's parents contested by filing a *writ of habeas corpus*, and in contrast to the ruling in the *Crouse* case, Daniel was ordered to be released by the Illinois Supreme Court. Unlike the *Crouse* decision, the court ruled that Daniel was being punished, not helped. Curiously, the court rejected the *parens patriae* doctrine and recognized the need to extend formal due process to juveniles. The impact of the *O'Connell* case would be felt three decades later in 1899 when the first juvenile court was established in Chicago (Mennel, 1973; Rendelman, 1971).

The emergence of the first juvenile court

The idea that children could be taken away from their parents and institutionalized because the state believed that the child risked becoming a criminal or pauper was dismantled in Illinois as a result of the *O'Connell* case. As a consequence of those legally challenged procedures, the first juvenile court was founded in 1899 under the Illinois Juvenile Court Act. However, the newly formed juvenile court was not a junior criminal court; rather, it stood as an extension of the social welfare system, where children of diverse needs and problems could be attended to. In contrast to voluntary agencies, the juvenile court exercised coercive powers that forced parents to comply with court orders. Responding to the fallout of the *O'Connell* decision, the first juvenile justice system was formed by influential and powerful leaders who proposed that the state should somehow establish legal mechanisms to control the delinquent and neglected population (Bernard, 1992).

At the time, many advocates of the new system saw themselves as humanitarians, simply upholding the practice of protecting children. However, present-day critics such as Anthony Platt (1977 [1969]) argue that the social movement that led to the first juvenile court was shaped more by political forces than by purely benevolent motives. According to Platt, the new system actually resurrected earlier notions of social control concerning the delinquent population (and their parents) by returning to the concept of *parens patriae*. Those updated measures of control emerged as another round of child-saving campaigns driven by the paternalistic views of the powerful, turning legally binding mechanisms to exert coercion over the lower class. That form of coercion was achieved by promoting correctional programs featuring labor, paramilitary discipline, and religious instruction, all of which were designed to inculcate middle-class values and lower-class skills.

During that era, the new system was regarded as the best model to deal with children who were either delinquent or neglected. By 1917, juvenile courts had been established in all but three states. One of the lasting effects of the emergence of the first juvenile court was that it reinforced the legal concept of juvenile delinquency. Furthermore, the Illinois act distinguished between children who were dependent and neglected (also known as predelinquent) and those who were delinquent (those under 16 years of age and charged with legal violations). The coercive components of the juvenile court remained, such as assigning delinquents to juvenile probation or committing them to institutions or reform programs.

The current juvenile court

Much like its earlier version, the current juvenile court is based on paternalistic attitudes on the part of judges who have the administrative tasks of preventing juvenile crime and rehabilitating the offender. Generally, the juvenile justice system assumed an individualistic approach by setting out to dispense personalized justice. During the 1960s, another wave of legislation prompted changes in the juvenile justice system. In New York, for instance, legislation was passed that created a family court system. The family court was designed to expand the scope of the legal system to include all matters involving the family, including children regarded as delinquent, dependent, and neglected. The family court also dealt with issues relating to paternity, adoption, and family support. Emerging from that legislation was the broader classification known as 'person in need of supervision' (PINS), encompassing youths involved in noncriminal behavior such as running away, truancy, and incorrigibility. The mission of the modern-day court is to minimize the authoritative features and maximize the relationship with social service agencies.

Further activity in the Supreme Court during the 1960s and 1970s also shaped the contemporary juvenile justice system. In particular, several landmark decisions were made in the following cases: *Kent* v. *United States*, *In re Gault*, *In re Winship*, and *McKeiver* v. *Pennsylvania*. Due to their important contributions to the juvenile justice system, these cases are described further in the following sections.

Kent v. *United States* (1966)

In 1961, 16-year-old Morris A. Kent, Jr, was arrested in the District of Columbia for housebreaking, robbery, and rape after his fingerprints were found to match those at the crime scene. (Kent's fingerprints were on file since he had had earlier juvenile court contact.) Kent remained in police custody for two days of interrogation, eventually confessing to the crimes.

Kent's mother contacted an attorney who consulted with the social service director of the juvenile court. The lawyer learned that the juvenile court was considering waiving jurisdiction and transferring the case to the district court for trial. Kent's attorney stated that he would oppose the waiver, arguing that the case ought to remain in juvenile court. Though detained, Kent was never arraigned nor granted a hearing by a judicial officer to determine whether there was probable cause for his arrest. Kent's lawyer continued to fight the waiver by arranging a psychiatric examination that certified that Kent suffered from severe psychopathology. The lawyer also filed a motion requesting access to Kent's social service file from the juvenile court. The judge eventually waived jurisdiction in the Kent case, thereby permitting it to go to trial in the US District Court for the District of Columbia. The judge did so, however, without ruling on the motions filed by Kent's attorney – nor did the judge hold a hearing or confer with Kent, his mother, or his lawyer.

In the district court, Kent was convicted of housebreaking and robbery, but on the rape charge he was found not guilty by reason of insanity. Kent was sentenced to 30 to 90 years in prison. On appeal, Kent's lawyer challenged the conviction on the grounds that his client's detention, fingerprinting, and interrogation were unlawful. Additionally, the waiver was challenged because there were no hearings and no findings on the part of the judge, and because Kent's attorney was denied access to the social service file.

The Supreme Court, in a 5-4 decision, nullified the juvenile court's waiver of jurisdiction, citing the lack of due process and fair treatment guaranteed by the Fourteenth Amendment. In response to *Kent*, the Supreme Court issued several safeguards for juveniles. First, juveniles are entitled to a hearing (along with legal counsel) when a waiver is being considered. Second, attorneys must have access to the juveniles' social service files. Finally, juveniles are entitled to a statement of reasons in the event that a case is waived.

In re Gault (1967)

As another landmark case resulting in the extension of basic constitutional rights to juveniles, *In re Gault* demonstrates the importance of due process. In 1964, 15-year-old Gerald Francis Gault and his friend Ronald Lewis were taken into custody by the Gila County (Arizona) sheriff. Their arrest was initiated by a complaint by their neighbor Mrs Cook, who reported receiving an obscene phone call. The arresting officer took Gault from his home without advising his parents (both of whom were at work) that their son was being taken into custody.

Gault's mother learned of his arrest from the Lewis family. When she arrived at the detention home, she was informed that a hearing at juvenile court was scheduled for the next day. At the hearing, the proceedings were neither recorded nor transcribed – further, the record of the substance of the proceedings was never made available. Moreover, the complainant, Mrs Cook, did not appear at the hearing. As far as the facts were concerned, discrepancies existed in what the juveniles had told the officers. At one point, Gault admitted to making one of the lewd phone calls; he later claimed that he merely dialed Mrs Cook's number and handed the phone to Lewis. Nevertheless, Gault remained in detention for almost a week. At the next hearing, discrepancies surrounding the incident remained. And once again Mrs Cook did not appear, even though Mrs Gault requested that she be present at the hearing.

The judge concluded that Gault had made lewd phone calls and committed him to the state industrial school until the age of 21 – in effect, a six-year-term. (Incidentally, if an adult had been convicted of the same offense, the conviction would have resulted only in a fine of $50.) Under Arizona law, appeals in juvenile cases were not allowed. With a *writ of habeas corpus*, an appeal was initiated only to be dismissed by higher local and state courts. Eventually, the US Supreme Court in 1967 reviewed the case and ruled that Gault had been denied fundamental constitutional rights, including notice of charges, right to counsel, right to confront and cross-examine witnesses, and privilege against self-incrimination. The Court ruled that juveniles also have the right to a transcript of the proceedings as well as a right to appeal.

Other significant legal developments

Another landmark ruling by the US Supreme Court that further shaped the juvenile justice system is found in *In re Winship* (1970). Supporters of *Winship* advocated making certain aspects of juvenile courts comparable to adult criminal courts. In 1970, the Supreme Court decided in *Winship* that juveniles be judged according to the same standard of proof as is afforded adult defendants, that is 'beyond a reasonable doubt' instead of a 'preponderance of the evidence.'

Two other influential cases are worth noting. In *McKeiver* v. *Pennsylvania* (1971), the US Supreme Court ruled that due process of law does not require a jury in juvenile court hearings (though in some situations the judge is permitted to use an advisory jury). Advocates of the ruling proposed that some informality of the juvenile court be preserved. Similarly, the public's right of access should also be limited in juvenile court hearings; however, in many states, hearings involving serious offenses commonly are open to the public. Finally, *Breed* v. *Jones* (1975) affirmed that Fifth Amendment protections against double jeopardy also extend to juveniles (see Dunkel and Van Zyl Smit, 2007).

VIOLENT JUVENILE OFFENDERS

As noted in Chapter 1, crime remains at a near 30-year low. That major trend has prompted much scholarly attention, especially given the implications to violent crime. 'An American's chances of being the victim of a violent crime are still lower than at any point since the 1970s. According to surveys conducted by the U.S. Department of Justice, the odds of being a violent-crime victim dropped nearly 60 percent since 1994, and those odds have not increased in recent years' (Butts and Snyder, 2006: 1; see Blumstein and Wallman, 2006).

Similarly, the nation witnessed dropping rates of youth violence, due in part to youth crime policies and programs, including detention reform, family treatment, and substance abuse interventions. Some observers, however, are worried that the trend of declining youth crime might be over. Between 2004 and 2005, arrests among juveniles (youth under the age of 18) for violent crime spiked: juvenile arrests for murder grew 20 percent and robbery arrests involving juveniles rose 11 percent. Still, Butts and Snyder (2006) point out that the overall increase in the violent crime arrest rate for juveniles amounted to a mere 1 percent (or 283 arrests per 100,000). 'The increase of 12 arrests per 100,000 was about one-twentieth the amount it would take for the arrest rate to return to the level of 1994. In other words, arrests would have to grow at the same pace for 19 more years before the juvenile violent crime arrest rate would be as high as it was in 1994' (2006: 3-4).

Despite these trends, violent juvenile crime remains a serious problem. Turning from arrest data to victimization surveys, concern is well founded. Relying on the most recent available data at the time of their analysis, McCurley and Snyder (2004) found that between 1997 and 1998, 19 percent of the victims of nonfatal violent crimes were victimized by a juvenile offender. Similarly, approximately two-thirds (62 percent) of the victims of nonfatal violence committed by juvenile offenders were themselves younger than 18, and about one-third (38 percent) were adults. McCurley and Snyder (2004: 1) report other important findings:

- Most (95 percent) of the victims of sexual assaults committed by juveniles were younger than 18, as were 43 percent of victims of robberies by juveniles, 53 percent of aggravated assaults, and 61 percent of simple assaults.
- Almost half (48 percent) of the victims of nonfatal violent crimes committed by juveniles were other juveniles who were acquaintances of the offender.
- Most (74 percent) of the victims who reported violent crimes by juveniles said the offender was a male.
- Among victims of simple assault by juveniles, more than half (52 per cent) of those older than 30 were the offender's parent or step-parent.
- Among all victims of violent crimes involving juvenile offenders, 17 percent faced multiple juveniles acting together and 15 percent faced juveniles and adults acting together. Among victims of robberies involving juveniles, 61 percent faced multiple offenders.
- About one in two juvenile victims of violent crime (51 percent) faced a juvenile offender.
- About one in ten adult victims of violent crime (9 percent) faced a juvenile offender.

The patterns of violent youth crime are clear: most victims of juvenile violence were juveniles and nearly all victims of juvenile crime knew their offender (McCurley and Snyder, 2004; Snyder and Sickmund, 1999).

In their efforts to reduce juvenile violence, organizations such as the National Council on Crime and Delinquency and the Office of Juvenile Justice and Delinquency Prevention continue their efforts to study chronic violent juvenile offenders. While keeping a critical eye on the roles of social and economic inequality in juvenile violence, researchers attend to other factors, including:

- *Family.* Violent juveniles are less attached to and monitored by their parents.
- *School.* Violent juveniles have less commitment to school and attachment to teachers.
- *Peers.* Violent juveniles' peers are more likely to be delinquent, and they themselves are more like to be gang members.
- *Neighborhood.* Violent juveniles are more likely to reside in poor areas with high crime rates.

Researchers have also identified three pathways to chronic delinquency. First, aggression escalates to fighting, then more extreme violence. Second, minor covert behavior becomes property damage, then serious delinquency. Third, stubborn behavior moves toward defiance, then authority avoidance (Snyder and Sickmund, 1999; see Barry, 2005; Bouhours and Daly, 2007; Loughran *et al.*, 2009).

Juveniles in adult jails and prisons

Among the ongoing controversies in corrections is whether juveniles should be incarcerated in adult prisons or even held in adult jails. As of 2000, the most recent census available shows that more than 7,600 youth younger than 18 were held in adult jails nationwide in the year 2000. Those under-18 inmates accounted for 1.2 percent of the total jail population and have been less than 2 percent of the jail population since 1994. Eighty percent of jail inmates younger than 18 were convicted or awaiting trial as adult criminal offenders. They were held as adults because they were transferred to criminal court or because they were in states where all 17-year-olds (or all 16- and 17-year-olds) are considered adults and eligible for criminal prosecution (Sickmund, 2004).

Turning attention to youth in adult prisons, recent surveys have found that most are 17-year-olds, males, minorities, and person offenders, accounting for 2 percent of new court commitments to state adult prisons. Another key finding shows that youth younger than 18 constituted 6 percent of all new court commitments to state prisons for robbery and 4 percent for homicide. For most other offense categories the under-18 proportion of admissions was below 3 percent. Still, overall six in ten youth newly admitted to state prisons had committed a person offense (Sickmund, 2004).

Compared with young adult inmates aged 18 through 24 at admission, Sickmund (2004) reports that new commitments involving youth younger than 18 had a substantially greater proportion of person offenses (i.e. robbery and assault) and a smaller proportion of drug offenses (i.e. drug trafficking). Males accounted for 96 percent of new court commitments to prison involving youth younger than 18. Females younger than 18 sent to adult prisons primarily involved charges of robbery, assault, murder, burglary, and drugs.

Sickmund (2004) also finds the growth in under-18 prison admissions was greater for black males than for white males.

- From 1985 to 1999, prison admissions increased 38 percent for white males younger than 18 and 68 percent for black males in the same age group. Since 1995, however, the number of admissions in this age group has generally declined for both white and black males. During the period when the number of prison admissions for youth younger than 18 was on the rise, increases were greater for black males and recent declines have been greater for white males.

- Robbery and aggravated assault accounted for a large proportion of the increase in prison admissions for both white and black males younger than 18. Unlike their white counterparts, however, black males also saw a large increase in drug admissions (from 30 to 490). In comparison, admissions of white males younger than 18 for drug offenses increased from 20 to 60.

(p. 21).

Attention to race and victimization also reveals that person offenses accounted for the majority of new admissions for both white and black males younger than 18. For whites, 56 percent of admissions were for person offenses (i.e. robbery, 22 percent, and aggravated assault, 16 percent). For blacks, the proportion of admissions involving person offenses was higher (66 percent), showing a greater proportion of robbery admissions (38 percent) (Sickmund, 2004; see Chapter 8).

Whereas tough-talking politicians boast that juveniles who have committed serious and violent crimes should be treated as adults and as a result be incarcerated in adult prisons, critics point out that in doing so, youth are at risk of victimization, including assault, rape, and suicide. Compounding these problems, researchers find that juveniles who have become victims in adult prisons are more likely to suffer long-term damage from the incarceration experience, making them even more antisocial (Henderson, 2002: Reddington and Sapp, 2002; Ziedenberg and Schiraldi, 2002). According to Mark Soler of the Youth Law Center in Washington, 'The state legislatures are all moving to try juveniles in adult court, which is really a move to lock up more kids in big institutions ... But those institutions are incredibly expensive, and they're also schools for crime. The kids come out as very tough, hardened criminals' (Treaster, 1994: A-12). Soler asserts that juveniles do better in small community-based programs. Youth advocates recognize that preventative programs are important in dealing with violent juveniles. Those interventions concentrate on the various aspects of juvenile crime by setting out to strengthen the family, support core social institutions (e.g. schools, churches, community programs), intervene immediately when delinquency behavior occurs, and identify and control violent and habitual delinquents. Despite those policy recommendations, juvenile justice is moving toward more punitive directions, driven in part by popular stereotypes of juvenile superpredators.

Moral panic over juvenile superpredators

As a conceptual framework, moral panic has improved our understanding of the social construction of crime, particularly those forms of lawlessness perceived as being *new*: for example, mugging (Hall *et al.*, 1978), crack babies (Humphries, 1999), crank (i.e. methamphetamine or 'speed') (Jenkins, 1994b), and freeway violence (Best, 1999). According to Stanley Cohen, moral panic has occurred when:

> A condition, episode, person or group of persons emerges to become defined as a threat to societal values and interest; its nature is presented in a stylized and stereotypical fashion by the mass media; the moral barricades are manned by editors, bishops, politicians, and other right-thinking people.
>
> (Cohen, 1972: 9)

Cohen (1972) encountered moral panic while studying societal reaction to unconventional youths in England. In his groundbreaking book, *Folk Devils and Moral Panics*, Cohen explored the roles of the media, politicians, and criminal justice officials in fueling anxiety over British youth culture in 1964 when Mods and Rockers were depicted as new threats to public safety. Together, the media and members of the political establishment publicized exaggerated claims of dangers posed by rebellious youth; in turn, inflammatory rhetoric was used to justify enhanced police powers and greater investment in the traditional criminal justice apparatus.

Over the past decade, there has been renewed anxiety over youth crime. However, rather than exploring the problem objectively, politicians, law enforcement officials, and even some professors have engaged in moral panic: a turbulent, excited, or exaggerated response to a social problem (Welch *et al.*, 1998, 1997). Consider the following alarmist and sensationalistic statements about youth crime, all of which point to an emerging moral panic over youth violence.

> These are not the Cleaver kids soaping up some windows. These are middle school kids conspiring to hurt their teacher, teenagers shooting people and committing rapes, young thugs running gangs and terrorizing neighborhoods and showing no remorse when they get caught.
>
> (Zell Miller, Georgia Governor, *New York Times*, January 24, 1994: A12)

> And there is a growing uneasiness among city officials about the number of youths carrying weapons to school and walking the corridors with guns and knives.
>
> (Clyde A. Isley, Mount Vernon Police Commissioner, *New York Times*, January 30, 1994: 1)

> Our streets are being stained with the blood of our children, and it's going to stop. Damn it. It has got to stop.
>
> (Pete Wilson, California Governor, *New York Times*, January 24, 1994: A14)

The ominous increase in juvenile crime coupled with the population trends portend future crime and violence at nearly unprecedented levels.

(Louis Freeh, FBI Director, *Chicago Tribune*, November 19, 1995: 3)

This (drop in crime) is also the lull before the storm.

(John J. DiIulio, Professor of Politics and Public Affairs at Princeton University, *New York Times*, November 19, 1995: 18)

Unless we act now, while our children are still young and impressionable, we may indeed have a bloodbath of teen violence by the year 2005.

(James Alan Fox, Dean of the College of Criminal Justice at Northeastern University in Boston, *New York Times*, May 23, 1995: A14)

I describe it as a boa constrictor phenomenon ... noting that the number of Americans under the age of 18, now 60 million, will increase to more than 70 million by the turn of the century. We can see that bulge of youth population coming.

(William J. Bratton, New York City Police Commissioner, *New York Times*, November 13, 1994: A14)

Perhaps the most memorable example of moral panic over youth violence was the claim by Professor John J. DiIulio of Princeton University that American society was facing a new breed of superpredators. The notion of superpredators fueled the media's distortion of youth crime while enabling law-and-order enthusiasts to further their commitment to more penalties, police, and prisons. DiIulio's remark even made its way into legislation. In 1996, Congress introduced the Violent Youth Predator Act. Although the bill was later renamed, Congressional hearings on the subject were riddled with DiIulio's claim of superpredators. James Wooten, President of the Safe Streets Coalition, testified to lawmakers:

They live in an aimless and violent present, have no sense of the past and no hope for the future; and act, often ruthlessly, to gratify whatever urges or desires drive them at the moment. They commit unspeakable brutal crimes against other people, and their lack of remorse is shocking. They are what Professor DiIulio and others call urban 'superpredators.' They are the ultimate nightmare, and their numbers are growing.

(Federal Document Clearing House, 1997; also see Schiraldi and Keppelhoff, 1997)

In classic moral panic fashion, the term 'superpredator' took on a life of its own. Not only were superpredators believed to be the new menace of society, but their numbers were also perceived as growing. According to DiIulio, the 'swelling legion of Godless, fatherless, valueless kids' will result in an additional 270,000 superpredators roaming the streets by the year 2010. Without offering data to support his claim, DiIulio stated that 6 percent of all newly born children would become superpredators. Professor Franklin Zimring weighed into the controversy. 'Congress and professors and others can make catastrophic errors in statistical projections. Not little ones. Whoppers' (cited in Mills, 1999: 3). 'If Dilulio were correct in his estimation, we would already have 1.9 million of these superpredators on the streets, enough to make the whole country look like one of Quentin Tarantino's nightmares. We do not' (Kappeler *et al.*, 2000: 184; see Bernard, 1999; Glassner, 1999).

Alarmist reactions to crime offered by politicians, law enforcement officials, and professors contribute substantially to moral panic because their messages are delivered by seemingly credible authorities who add a heightened sense of anxiety and urgency. In turn, moral panic over youth crime creates a demand for greater expenditure in the criminal justice apparatus aimed at street crime. Unquestionably, youth crime is indeed a social problem, producing social and personal harms. The concept of moral panic does not necessarily mean that 'there's nothing there,' but rather that the state-sponsored strategies designed to deal with such problems are 'fundamentally inappropriate' (Cohen, 1972: 204). Whereas the following statements clearly address the problem of serious juvenile offenses, they also endorse a state-sponsored intervention that many criminologists would find inappropriate.

> The laws were written when kids were committing juvenile crimes, but now they're committing adult crimes like rape and murder. The laws are anachronistic and need to be changed.
> (Andrew J. Stein, Chairman of the New York City Commission on Juvenile Offenders, *New York Times*, June 25, 1994: 27)

> Punishment has to be swift and certain. When children commit adult crimes, they should be prosecuted as adults. We can't coddle criminals because they are young. We're not just talking about gang members. What we are seeing is total disregard for pain and human life among the young. It's scary, and I predict it will only get worse.
> (Jeanine Ferris Pirro, Westchester (NY), County District Attorney, *New York Times*, January 30, 1994: 15)

Critics of harsher penalties for youthful offenders insist that moral panics contribute to the escalating vocabulary of punitive motives. Moreover, that tough way of talking about juveniles serves to justify inappropriate strategies of dealing with delinquency. In doing so, a vocabulary of punitive motives ignores the root causes of crime and violence, including social, political, and economic inequality (Melossi, 1985; Welch *et al.*, 1998, 1997).

CULTURAL PENOLOGY

A Critique of Gangsta Rap and Youth Violence

Over the past two decades, a growing number of critical criminologists have continued to investigate the role of culture in the social construction of juvenile delinquency, thereby advancing further cultural criminology. According to Ferrell and Sanders (1995: 3), cultural criminology 'explores the common ground between cultural and criminal practices in contemporary social life – that is, between collective behavior organized around imagery, style, and symbolic meaning, and that categorized by legal and political authorities as criminal.' Moreover, cultural criminology, in the words of Presdee, 'is interested in the larger movements at work in contemporary society. That is, the social context in which crime comes into being and is played out: in short, the criminalizing process' (2000: 16; also see Ferrell and Websdale, 1999; Welch *et al.*, 2002). Cultural criminology offers a unique perspective of delinquency, especially in light of the tendency to blame youth culture for youth violence. Indeed, rap music – with its distinctive rebellious edge – too often is accused of inciting antisocial behavior among teens, especially blacks and Latinos.

Blaming youth culture and its music for allegedly having an adverse influence on teenagers is anything but new. That was certainly the case when jazz, blues, R&B, and rock n' roll hit critical mass, attracting the attention of large numbers of teens, from all racial and ethnic backgrounds. Because those forms of music had their origins in African-American culture, they were viewed has posing a more insidious threat to white youth and a white society. For generations, black-inspired music has taken on many forms of expression but the popular response tends to be the same, namely condemnation. Nowadays, rap music – particularly, gangsta rap – has caught the ire of politicians and self-appointed criminal justice experts who claim that such music is harmful not only to youth but to society at large, producing delinquency along with an array of antisocial behaviors.

Moral crusaders who condemn rap music commonly call for censorship and under some circumstances criminalization. As in the case of 2 Live Crew's album *As Nasty As They Wanna Be*, rap is the only music genre to be declared as 'criminally obscene' by a federal judge. Similarly, Ice-T's song *Cop Killer* prompted a boycott by five fraternal law enforcement associations whose memberships included more than 500,000 police officers. Adding to the frenzy were NWA's *Fuck the Police* and Tupac Shakur's *Outlaw*. In 1994, lawmakers were so alarmed over the perceived negative effects of rap that Congress held a special hearing to explore the matter (Ballard and Coates, 1995; Dyson, 1996). It is important not to overlook the underpinning racial considerations. 'In short, the attacks on black and white youth's cultural expressions differ in important ways. Unlike heavy metal music, the ideology surrounding the harmfulness of rap music results in the criminalization of both black youths and their music' (Tatum, 1999: 330; hooks, 1994).

Despite all the condemnation there has been surprisingly little scholarly investigation into the effects of rap on adolescents. Tatum (1999) reviewed the literature to find only nine empirical studies. After examining the extant research, Tatum states: 'We cannot conclude with any degree of certainty that violent and sexually explicit rap lyrics lead impressionable youths to antisocial, criminal, and delinquent behavior. Unfortunately, it appears that present arguments regarding the harmfulness of rap music are based on factors other than scholarly analysis' (1999: 351). Nevertheless, there is persistent condemnation of rap music, especially by moral guardians who, in an effort to *sanitize* popular culture, refer to rebellious lyrical expression as *moral pollution* (see Douglas, 1984; Dubin, 1992). In taking a critical look at youth culture and the notion that rap incites youth violence, it is useful to keep in mind a basic tenet of cultural criminology: 'The criminalization process then is that cultural process whereby those in power come to define and shape dominant forms of social life and give them specific meanings' (Presdee, 2000: 17; Welch *et al.*, 2002).

PROCESSING DELINQUENCY CASES

The juvenile justice system is an expansive enterprise with numerous critical decision points. Police arrest more than 1 million juveniles each year for violent and serious crimes as well as status offenses. However, not all arrests lead to formal processing in the juvenile justice system. Approximately a third of the offenses are not processed at all – the youths are released with no more than a reprimand. This section describes the juvenile justice system in terms of how it processes delinquency cases, beginning with law enforcement and then continuing with petition and intake, detention, and finally adjudication and disposition.

Law enforcement

As noted previously, the police release about a third of status offenders or juveniles involved in delinquency with no more than a warning. In many instances, the police sit the youths in the patrol car, lecture them about crime, and otherwise frighten them about being processed into the juvenile justice system. Also, the police commonly bring juveniles to the station and have their parents pick them up – another tactic intended to deter them from future delinquency.

Law enforcement officers wield enormous discretion, and in dealing with juveniles they take into account several considerations. For example, the police assess the attitude of the victim; the juvenile's prior record; the seriousness of the offense; and the age, sex, race, and demeanor of the offender. Moreover, the police often anticipate how the case will be handled by the court in determining whether to release the juvenile. In cases involving serious crimes, the police certainly opt to arrest the juvenile (or *take him or her into custody* – a term used in many jurisdictions). In such cases, the police may still refer the juvenile to a diversion or delinquency program. If the offense is serious enough, the police are likely to refer the case to the juvenile court.

Petition and intake

At the petition and intake stage of the juvenile justice system, the offender is referred to the court by the police, a victim, parents, school officials, or a social worker. Upon reporting the alleged offense (in the form of a petition), the case is then formally processed. A petition is a document that requests the court to assume jurisdiction over the juvenile.

The next phase involves an intake hearing (or screening) in which a preliminary assessment of the facts is conducted by a referee on behalf of the court. The referee (or hearing officer) is a social worker, a lawyer, a probation officer, or another person assigned to the case by the court. Typically, the intake hearing sets out to protect the interests of the youth, but legal judgements are also made concerning the probable cause of the petition.

In serious cases, the referee may recommend further judicial processing. Very often, however, the hearing officer exercises his or her discretion and either dismisses the case or makes a referral to a social service agency. In sum, the decision to recommend further processing is determined by the sufficiency of the evidence and the seriousness of the offense, as well as whether the court's scarce resources could be used effectively in resolving the case.

Detention

The next stage in juvenile court proceedings involves a detention hearing in which a decision is made to release the juvenile to a parent or guardian or to retain him or her in custody. During the detention hearing, it is determined whether the juvenile requires protection and whether the juvenile poses a threat to society. Moreover, the likelihood of the juvenile's being further processed into judicial proceedings is also considered (see the section on 'Juveniles in Custody' below).

Adjudication and disposition

An adjudication inquiry marks the next phase of the juvenile justice process. During the adjudication inquiry, a judge decides whether the facts of the case merit a formal court hearing. In many ways, the adjudication inquiry resembles the intake hearing; however, at this stage a magistrate administers the hearing. The options of the magistrate include dismissing the case, ordering a referral to a social service agency, or recommending a formal adjudication hearing (see Kupchik, 2006).

At the adjudication hearing, a judge presiding on behalf of the juvenile determines whether the juvenile actually committed the alleged offense. (Given the unique status of juvenile justice processing, such processing is treated as civil not criminal proceedings.) If the judge determines that the juvenile committed the offense and that further adjudication is necessary, a disposition hearing is scheduled.

The purpose of a disposition hearing is to resolve a juvenile case by relying on the discretion of a juvenile court judge. The judge has numerous alternatives at his or her disposal. For instance, the judge has the authority to dismiss the case, issue a reprimand, impose a fine, require restitution or community service, refer the juvenile to a social service agency, order probation, place the juvenile into a foster home (as a means of protecting the child), or mandate commitment to a juvenile institution.

JUVENILES IN CUSTODY

Steady increases in the delinquency caseload handled by juvenile courts have driven the growth in the number of youths in the detention system. That larger trend began to pick up momentum during the 1990s while continuing to the present. By 1998, the juvenile courts handled 1.8 million delinquency cases, a 44 percent jump from the 1.2 million cases in 1989. The greater influx of delinquency cases entering the system produced a 25 percent increase in the number of cases involving detention at some point between referral and case disposition. In 1998, there were 66,100 more detentions than in 1989, creating a significant demand for juvenile detention bed space that has increased nationwide. Surveys reveal that the character of the nation's detention population shifted dramatically during that period, with a greater proportion of youth charged with person and drug offenses. In 1998, there was an 88 percent increase in the number of person offenses (i.e. assault, rape, homicide), creating a 63 percent increase in the number of detentions. During that time frame, juveniles entering the system on drug charges leaped 148 percent, producing a 55 percent increase in the number of detentions (Harms, 2002; Sickmund, 2004; Snyder and Sickmund, 1999).

According to the most recent census conducted by the US Bureau of the Census for the Office of Juvenile Justice and Delinquency Prevention that surveys both public and private juvenile residential placement facilities in every state, there were 134,011 youth held in 2,939 facilities (as of 1999; see Sickmund, 2004).

The vast majority of residents in juvenile residential placement facilities on October 27, 1999, were juvenile offenders (81 percent). Juvenile offenders held for delinquency offenses accounted for 78 percent of all residents. Delinquency offenses are behaviors that would be criminal law violations for adults. Status offenders accounted for a small proportion of all residents (4 percent). Status offenses are behaviors that are not law violations for adults, such as running away, truancy, and incorrigibility.

(Sickmund, 2004: 3)

Figure 7.2 Young criminals working at Iksha labour colony for juvenile offenders, in Moscow, Russian Federation, February 2, 2007. Russian deputy prosecutor general Sergey Fridinsky noted the previous year that criminality among juvenile offenders had grown by 10 percent over the last three years. Furthermore, according to reports, major offences among juvenile delinquents had also grown.

Photo by Oleg Nikishin/ Epsilon/Getty Images.

Sickmund (2004) reports that juvenile facilities had more juvenile delinquents in placement in 1999 than at any time since 1991: a 43 percent increase in the number of juvenile offenders held and a 50 percent increase in the number of delinquents held.

State custody rates in 1999 indicate a broad range – from 96 (Hawaii, Vermont) to 632 (South Dakota) per 100,000 juveniles. Twenty states had declining or stable rates while the rest of the nation reported increases (see Tables 7.1 and 7.2).

CRITICAL ANALYSIS OF DATA

With reference to Table 7.1, how many states report a double-digit (percentage) drop in custody rate?

CRITICAL ANALYSIS OF DATA

With reference to Table 7.2, how many more (or fewer) juvenile offenders are in residential placement in your state compared to New Jersey? And for New Jersey students, compare your state's number with that of Hawaii (and given the chance would you move there?).

It was also reported that person offenders constituted 35 percent of juvenile offenders in custody nationwide while drug offenders constituted 9 percent (see Table 7.3). As will be discussed in detail in Chapter 8, race figures prominently. 'On any given day in 1999, nearly two-thirds (65 percent) of juvenile offenders in placement in public facilities were minority youth. In private facilities the

Table 7.1 Percent change in custody rate between 1997 and 1999 by state

Rhode Island	−30	Ohio, Oregon, South Carolina, Virginia	4
Tennessee	−28	Dist. of Columbia, Indiana, Massachusetts, Mississippi	6
Nevada	−18	Colorado, Delaware	8
Maine	−25	Florida, New Hampshire	9
Missouri, Montana	−17	New Mexico	11
North Dakota	−11	Illinois, Kentucky, Minnesota, North Carolina, Texas	13
Hawaii, Washington	−8	Michigan	14
Arizona, California	−6	South Dakota	16
Pennsylvania, Wisconsin	−5	Arkansas	18
Wyoming	−4	Utah	31
Alabama, Iowa, Nebraska	−3	Vermont	36
Georgia	−1	Oklahoma	40
Kansas, Maryland	0	Idaho	52
Alaska, Connecticut	1		
Louisiana, West Virginia	2		
New Jersey, New York	3		

Source: Sickmund (2004: 7).

proportion of minority youth was just over half (55 percent)' (Sickumnd, 2004: 9; see Chapter 15). That pattern of racial proportion was consistent across nearly all states; moreover, the nationwide census shows that Blacks have the highest custody rates.

CRITICAL ANALYSIS OF DATA

With reference to Table 7.3, identify the state where you live and those states bordering it. Among those states, which one has the highest violent index percentage and which has the lowest public order percentage? (Those students living in Alaska, Hawaii, and the District of Columbia are exempt from this exercise. You may enjoy a relaxing moment before returning to the book.)

As noted throughout the chapter, the juvenile justice system and the custody population are dominated by male offenders. 'In 1999, males represented half of the juvenile population and were involved in approximately three-quarters of juvenile arrests and delinquency cases processed in juvenile courts, but they represented 87% of juveniles in residential placement' (Sickmund, 2004: 14). By comparison, females accounted for 13 percent of youth in residential placement. Furthermore, the proportion of female juveniles in residential placement was greater for private facilities (16 percent) than for public facilities (12 percent); similarly, it was greater for detained juveniles (18 percent) than committed juveniles (12 percent). It should be mentioned that the female proportion among those admitted to placement under a diversion agreement was large (40 percent) (Sickmund, 2004).

Table 7.2 Nationwide in 1999, 371 offenders were held in juvenile facilities per 100,000 juveniles in the population

State of offense	Juvenile offenders in residential placement on October 27, 1999		State of offense	Juvenile offenders in residential placement on October 27, 1999	
	Number	Rate		Number	Rate
U.S. total	108,931	371	**Upper age 17 (continued)**		
Upper age 17			Oklahoma	1,123	273
Alabama	1,589	333	Oregon	1,549	404
Alaska	382	419	Pennsylvania	3,819	285
Arizona	1,901	334	Rhode Island	310	284
Arkansas	705	234	South Dakota	603	632
California	19,072	514	Tennessee	1,534	256
Colorado	1,979	407	Utah	985	320
Delaware	347	431	Vermont	67	96
Dist. of Columbia	259	704	Virginia	3,085	415
Florida	6,813	427	Washington	2,094	307
Hawaii	118	96	West Virginia	388	202
Idaho	360	220	Wyoming	310	488
Indiana	2,650	384	**Upper age 16**		
Iowa	1,017	296	Georgia	3,729	475
Kansas	1,254	383	Illinois	3,885	322
Kentucky	1,188	270	Louisiana	2,745	580
Maine	242	167	Massachusetts	1,188	206
Maryland	1,579	269	Michigan	4,324	417
Minnesota	1,760	290	Missouri	1,161	205
Mississippi	784	229	New Hampshire	216	167
Montana	246	220	South Carolina	1,650	441
Nebraska	720	342	Texas	7,954	370
Nevada	789	378	Wisconsin	1,924	338
New Jersey	2,386	273	**Upper age 15**		
New Mexico	855	378	Connecticut	1,466	513
North Dakota	235	297	New York	4,813	334
Ohio	4,531	345	North Carolina	1,429	221

Note: The rate is the number of juvenile offenders in residential placement per 100,000 juveniles age 10 through the upper age of original juvenile court jurisdiction in each state. U.S. total includes 2,645 juvenile offenders in private facilities for whom state of offense was not reported and 174 juvenile offenders in tribal facilities.

Source: Sickmund (2004: 7)

A disturbing trend is that juveniles charged with offenses of low severity are being detained for longer periods of time. Thus the net continues to widen as youths with minimal offense histories are also being detained. Most of these youths could be safely referred to noninstitutional programs. A return to the notion of the cycle of juvenile justice sheds light on the trend toward detention. The popular view that juvenile crime is undergoing another resurgence when it has actually declined nationally over the past decade has led to several policy changes. According to the National Council on Crime and Delinquency:

Table 7.3 The offense profile for most states had a greater proportion of juveniles held for person crimes than for property crimes

State of offense	Most serious offense						State of offense	Most serious offense					
	Violent Index	Other person	Property	Drug	Public order	Status		Violent Index	Other person	Property	Drug	Public order	Status
U.S. total	25%	10%	29%	9%	23%	4%	Missouri	22%	7%	35%	7%	14%	16%
Alabama	9	13	27	7	32	11	Montana	20	12	41	5	20	2
Alaska	20	8	35	3	32	2	Nebraska	14	5	52	5	18	5
Arizona	9	14	32	17	26	3	Nevada	13	11	25	17	32	2
Arkansas	16	14	32	5	29	4	New Hampshire	15	40	25	1	11	7
California	34	7	28	7	23	1	New Jersey	24	5	20	22	21	9
Colorado	25	18	27	6	21	3	New Mexico	15	5	32	16	31	0
Connecticut	13	12	17	21	34	3	New York	32	7	26	11	10	14
Delaware	18	15	32	11	22	2	North Carolina	19	18	40	8	13	2
Dist. of Columbia	14	15	27	25	19	0	North Dakota	8	22	27	6	10	27
Florida	22	13	34	10	20	1	Ohio	27	8	31	8	22	4
Georgia	20	11	30	8	29	2	Oklahoma	33	6	37	6	13	5
Hawaii	23	13	36	3	23	3	Oregon	52	7	31	2	8	0
Idaho	21	15	28	3	31	3	Pennsylvania	18	13	20	12	31	5
Illinois	30	5	22	12	29	1	Rhode Island	29	11	21	17	20	1
Indiana	9	18	30	8	26	10	South Carolina	16	7	26	6	41	3
Iowa	16	19	35	8	17	5	South Dakota	11	10	33	5	35	6
Kansas	25	14	34	6	20	1	Tennessee	18	6	23	8	27	18
Kentucky	16	14	26	9	19	16	Texas	29	11	30	8	20	1
Louisiana	27	6	39	12	10	6	Utah	27	6	29	11	20	7
Maine	16	21	50	1	10	2	Vermont	27	18	31	0	9	13
Maryland	16	11	30	24	19	1	Virginia	21	11	26	7	30	4
Massachusetts	35	10	29	8	16	2	Washington	36	7	34	6	16	1
Michigan	27	9	30	5	18	12	West Virginia	19	10	29	8	20	14
Minnesota	21	12	28	5	26	8	Wisconsin	24	15	34	7	16	4
Mississippi	6	7	25	5	57	0	Wyoming	6	9	34	13	22	16

Percent of juveniles held for Violent Crime Index offenses

Wyoming 6 9 34 13 22 16

Percent of juveniles held for Violent Crime Index

District of Columbia

0%D
15%P

tribal

- Nationally, 29% of juveniles in residential placement were being held for property crimes. In comparison, 35% were held for person offenses (Violent Index plus other person offenses).
- States with the highest proportions of Violent Crime Index offenders were Oregon (52%), Washington (36%), Massachusetts (35%), California (34%), and Oklahoma (33%). North Dakota (8%), Mississippi (6%), and Wyoming (6%) had the lowest proportions.
- The proportion of juveniles held for drug offenses ranged from 25% in the District of Columbia to 1% in Maine and New Hampshire and 0% in Vermont.

Note: U.S. total includes 2,645 juvenile offenders in private facilities for whom state of offense was not reported and 174 juvenile offenders in tribal facilities.

Source: Sickmund (2004: 8).

'The common perception that juvenile crime is out of control has caused policy makers to erode provisions of the juvenile court law and to impose more punitive sanctions for juvenile offenders. This has resulted in higher national youth incarceration rates, especially for minority youths' (1991: 4; see Chapter 8).

It is equally important to address the socioeconomic status of youths in custody. Youths processed by the juvenile justice system have historically represented the lower social class. Moreover, low socioeconomic youths are also more likely to be processed by the system when other factors are present: poor academic performance, family disruption, and association with other delinquents. Certainly, those factors serve as a foundation for the labeling process (see De Jong and Jackson, 1998; Feld, 1999). Many policy experts agree that juvenile detention is the gateway into the juvenile justice system and the foundation upon which the apparatus is built. For many troubled teens, being incarcerated in a detention facility is a robust predictor of continuing incarceration in the juvenile and adult justice systems (Wordes *et al.*, 2001; see Applegate *et al.*, 2000; Fader *et al.*, 2001). In California, like other jurisdictions, juvenile detention construction continues to boom – in large part due to yesterday's news, when juvenile arrests were at their peak. The number of detention beds planned for construction with legislative funding, ironically, has doubled even though the rate of juvenile felony arrests has declined by 45 percent in California over the past ten years. Wordes *et al.* (2001) emphasize that detention is costly not only in terms of additional construction but also for ongoing operational costs (e.g. staff, healthcare, programs). Especially amid the economic downturn at the turn of the century, investing public funds into detention facilities is unwise, particularly given that such spending detracts from social services that have enormous potential to reduce delinquency.

Events shaping juvenile institutions

Juvenile institutions should not be viewed apart from their history since much of what is done in terms of organization and management is rooted in the past. For example, the paramilitary influence in juvenile institutions can be traced to the reformatory era, especially to the Elmira Reformatory in the 1870s (Smith, 1988). Juvenile institutions during the 1920s also borrowed from military influences due to the social impact of World War I. In addition to required uniforms, living units became known as barracks; cottage groups, companies; housefathers, captains: and superintendents, majors or colonels (National Conference of Superintendents of Training Schools and Reformatories, 1962).

During the 1930s, juvenile programs took to the outdoors in the form of forestry camps, ranches, and various educational and vocational schools. Those programs were modeled after the camps operated by the Civilian Conservation Corps (CCC). The rationale was to rehabilitate troubled youth by removing them from the city and instilling a sense of independence through work and education. Both the paramilitary and the camp influences exist today as basic features in the organization and management of juvenile institutions and programs. To a greater or lesser degree, today's institutions and programs may adopt a paramilitary approach toward discipline or a camp-style regimen to foster self-confidence and esteem.

Another development that shaped current juvenile corrections is the decarceration movement. During the 1970s, a campaign sought to remove status offenders from institutions housing juvenile delinquents (as well as eliminating any contact with adults in jails). The goal was to assign youths to the least restrictive alternative by emphasizing community-based programs over institutional care (Lerman, 1984).

A benchmark event in decarceration is the deinstitutionalization experiment in Massachusetts. In 1969, Jerome Miller, a psychiatric social worker at Ohio State University, was hired to supervise the Department of Youth Services (DYS). Miller was distressed by the degree of corruption and abuse evident within the training schools. Miller (1991) recalls such incidents as teenagers' being stripped naked and held for days in dark concrete cells, forced to drink from toilets, and ordered to kneel for hours on a stone floor with pencils under their knees. Other sadistic incidents include the punishment of a boy who was strapped to a bed frame and beaten on the bare soles of his feet with wooden paddles.

In two short years, Miller revolutionized the practice of juvenile justice. He reoriented the style of training schools toward the adoption of a treatment and rehabilitation model. In an attempt to force the community to take responsibility for troubled youths rather than simply warehousing them, Miller closed virtually all the state's large reform schools. By 1972, the youth population in DYS training schools fell from more than 2,000 to less than 200. Most juveniles had been reassigned to group homes, foster care, and private treatment facilities, or even returned to their families for community supervision. Miller's tactics, however, also produced considerable political fallout in the community as well as among the staff.

Despite the political bureaucratic resistance, resulting in Miller's resignation, the deinstitutionalization experiment in Massachusetts had important long-term effects. Even though Massachusetts still uses some training schools, the reliance on such institutions has changed dramatically. Moreover, the improvements in Massachusetts did not go unnoticed by other state juvenile justice systems, and many other agencies made similar modifications in their own systems. Still, Miller was unsuccessful in engineering comparable degrees of reform in other states.

Sexual victimization in juvenile facilities

Decades following the courageous work of Jerome Miller, advocates remain concerned over the plight of juveniles in custody, especially in light of ongoing problems with overcrowding, harsh conditions of confinement, neglect, and physical abuse (Rayman, 2009a, 2009b, 2009c; Snyder and Sickmund, 1999; see Chapter 9). Critical attention also needs to be directed at sexual victimization in juvenile facilities. Since 2003, the Prison Rape Elimination Act (PREA) requires the Bureau of Justice Statistics (BJS) to carry out an annual review and analysis of the incidents and effects of prison rape.

In 2010, the BJS released findings in the most recent review, focusing specifically on juveniles in custody. Immediately, child advocates and human rights workers expressed deep concern as the BJS revealed: 'An estimated 12% of youth in state juvenile facilities and large non-state facilities (representing 3,220 youth nationwide) reported experiencing one or more incidents of sexual victimization by another youth or facility staff in the past 12 months or since admission, if less than 12 months' (Beck *et al.*, 2010: 1). Furthermore, approximately 2.6 percent of youth (700 nationwide) reported an incident involving another youth while another 10.3 percent (2,730) reported an incident involving facility staff. Of those reported having sex or other sexual contact with facility staff, 4.3 percent of youth (1,150) did so as a result of some type of force while another 6.4 percent of youth (1,710) engaged in sexual contact without any force, threat, or other explicit form of coercion. It should also be noted that 95 percent of all youth reporting staff sexual misconduct said female staff had victimized them: in 2008, 42 percent of staff in state juvenile facilities were female. Rates of reported sexual victimization varied among youth:

- 10.8 percent of males and 4.7 percent of females reported sexual activity with facility staff.
- 9.1 percent of females and 2.0 percent of males reported unwanted sexual activity with other youth.
- Youth with a sexual orientation other than heterosexual reported significantly higher rates of sexual victimization by another youth (12.5 percent) compared to heterosexual youth (1.3 percent).
- Youth who had experienced any prior sexual assault were more than twice as likely to report sexual victimization in the current facility (24.1 percent), compared to those with no sexual assault history (10.1 percent).

(Beck *et al.*, 2010: 1)

Compounding problems, among those youths victimized by another youth, 20 percent said they had been physically injured; 5 percent reported they had sought medical attention for their injuries. Among those victimized by staff, 5 percent reported a physical injury; fewer than 1 percent of them had sought medical attention (Beck *et al.*, 2010: 1).

Human rights advocates weighed into the controversy. 'The widespread sexual abuse of children in juvenile facilities shows that public officials either aren't paying attention or can't be bothered to do the right thing,' said Jamie Fellner, senior counsel for the US Program at Human Rights Watch. Fellner added: 'The high rates of victimization are powerful testimony to the failure of governments to safeguard the boys and girls in their care' (Human Rights Watch, 2010: 1). Child protection experts press the government to develop enforceable standards to prevent sexual abuse in juvenile facilities, including: greater supervision; screening for vulnerability to abuse; medical and mental health services; reporting mechanisms; investigations; staff training; administrative sanctions; internal monitoring; and external audits.

THE SOCIAL WORLD OF JUVENILE INSTITUTIONS

Much like their adult counterparts, incarcerated juveniles tend to organize their institutional lives in ways that capture collective experiences. Accordingly, the social world of juvenile institutions resembles that of adult prisons. As we shall explore further, juveniles also follow social patterns that are often gender-specific (see Chesney-Lind and Irwin, 2008; Harvey, 2007; Payne, 2009).

Institutionalized boys

The effects of prisonization are evident among boys confined to juvenile institutions. One aspect, in particular, is the construction of an inmate value system similar to the convict code among adults. Bartollas *et al.* (1976) identified the following principles in a high-security juvenile institution in Ohio. These principles have also surfaced in numerous other juvenile facilities across the nation.

- Exploit whomever you can.
- Don't play up to the staff.
- Don't rat on your peers.
- Don't give in to others.
- Be cool.
- Don't get involved in others' affairs.
- Don't steal squares (cigarettes).
- Don't buy the treatment games of the staff.

Researchers found that African-Americans compared to white youths uphold many principles differently. Whereas the African-American youths appeared to have more solidarity ('defend your brother'), whites were more likely to be independent ('don't trust anybody' and 'everybody for himself'). Moreover, the prevalence of the inmate code is determined by the level of security of the institution as well as the criminal history of the youths. Juveniles most likely to adopt the inmate code are those with extensive criminal histories and those confined in higher-security facilities, especially institutions considered to be more custodial than treatment-oriented (Elrod and Brooks, 2003; Phillips, 2008; Polsky, 1962; Sieverdes and Bartollas, 1986). (See 'Working in Corrections: Juvenile Detention: Boys Are Not Men', below.)

Institutionalized girls

Overall, females accounted for 13 percent of juveniles in residential placement. More than 35 percent of those females in residential placement were held in private facilities. In comparison, private facilities held 28 percent of males in residential placement.

The proportion of females placed in private facilities varied substantially by offense category: 66% of all females held for a status offense were in private facilities, as were 42% held for simple assault, 25% held for aggravated assault, and 15% held for robbery. In general for both males and females, the less serious the offense category, the greater the likelihood the resident was in a private facility.

(Sickmund, 2004: 14)

It is important to note that females in residential placement tended to be younger than their male counterparts: 30 percent of females were younger than 15 compared with 21 percent of males. Also for girls in placement, the peak ages were 15 and 16, each accounting for approximately one-quarter of all females in placement facilities; for males, the peak ages were 16 and 17 (Sickmund, 2004).

Obviously, the younger the juvenile population, the more staff have to attend to the emotional and psychological needs of those in custody (girls as well as boys), departing significantly from the prevailing practice in adult corrections where social and psychological services are a low priority. Unfortunately, facilities for juvenile girls tend to be more restrictive and offer fewer programs than boys' detention centers.

Whereas the existence of preferential treatment toward adult females continues to be debated, research suggests that female juveniles are treated more harshly by the criminal justice system than male juveniles. Meda Chesney-Lind (1982) found that female juveniles are more likely to be institutionalized than male juveniles. That finding may be explained, in part, by widespread assumptions regarding girls who enter the criminal justice system. For example, it is often assumed that female delinquents are more psychologically disturbed than male delinquents and that their home lives are more disrupted.

As discussed in Chapter 6, the morality of women is often the target of intervention within the criminal justice system whether or not their offenses are sexual (e.g. prostitution). Not surprisingly then, the tendency for a male-dominated system to punish and regulate female morality and sexuality extends to girls as well (see Bittle, 2002; Terry and Dank, 2010; Williams, 2010). Chesney-Lind makes the following observation:

Indeed, physical examinations of young women often conducted in search of venereal disease, pregnancy or other substances are routine in many jurisdictions regardless of the nature of the charge against them. It is clear that these examinations are not only degrading but also serve to remind all women that any form of deviance will be defined as evidence of sexual laxity.

(1982: 93)

Compared to boys, girls are more likely to serve longer sentences, during which time they are subjected to programs that instill traditional roles for females. That approach to domestic work reaches back to 1856 when the first state-operated institution opened, the Massachusetts State Industrial School for Girls.

The social world of incarcerated female delinquents often resembles that of adult females in prison. The formation of 'make-believe families' or surrogate unions is relatively common in institutions for girls. Such relationships provide affection and support, especially for those girls who have intermittent family contact (Foster, 1975). Like their adult counterparts, some of those pseudo-families, courtships, or kinships involve sexuality; however, lesbianism is not always an aspect of the relationship. Although some institutions currently do not enforce rules against sexual contact among girls, in the past some facilities pontificated against the evils and dangers of lesbianism. To reiterate, the emphasis on moral 'correctness' is deeply engrained in the criminal justice as well as the juvenile justice system for girls (Chesney-Lind and Shelden, 2004; Giallombardo, 1974; Zahn, 2009).

WORKING IN CORRECTIONS

Juvenile Detention: 'Boys Are Not Men'

As noted in previous chapters, working in corrections does not always mean serving as a corrections officer. There are many other types of role that allow those working in corrections to view inmates from a noncustodial point of perspective. That is particularly the case in juvenile corrections. Following years of experience working as a counselor in the Massachusetts Department of Youth Service, Jackson Katz reflects: 'A staff-secure detention center is not a prison, and boys are not men' (2001: 215). The term 'staff-secure detention' refers to a facility that has alarms on the doors but no locks, and it is the responsibility of each staff member to account for the whereabouts of each child at all times. Since the facility relies on counselors rather than corrections officers, staff members form relations with the teens that are commonly characterized as gentle but firm guidance. Katz reminds us that juvenile facilities hold a diverse group of youngsters: some are likeable, others ornery, some cocky and aggressive, and others shy and withdrawn. Still, 'these were not, by and large, innocent kids caught up in a Dickensian life of orphanages and cold and uncaring adult institutions' (Katz, 2001: 207–8). Some of them had committed offenses that were truly serious, at times leaving behind injured victims.

Despite the seriousness of their crimes, they are still boys who needed help, much like other kids who make mistakes but are fortunate enough not to wind up in juvenile detention. That realization remains with Katz and others who have worked in juvenile corrections. Those held behind bars are rarely white, middle-class kids but rather low-income minorities whom the criminal justice system targets in its enforcement campaigns. Speaking as a white male who as a teenager himself tested society's limits, Katz writes: 'Can we honestly say that, if we hadn't been shielded by our class and race privileges, we wouldn't have been harassed more frequently by the police and prosecuted more vigorously?' (2001: 208). Adding: 'Can we honestly say that, if we had been born into poverty, we never would have acted out in ways that might have brought the attention of the police and other agents of state authority?' (2001: 208). In the movie *Good Will Hunting*, the main character is a troubled white teen who exhibits violent tendencies. After a series of arrests for fighting, the judge sentences Will not to juvenile detention but to therapy at a local college. Had Will been black perhaps he would have been criminalized by the system, thus becoming a likely candidate for detention.

While taking into account the class and race divide in the criminal justice apparatus, Katz also explores the significance of gender in an effort to understand why so many boys act out in criminal ways and how cultural constructs of masculinity contribute to that behavior. Frequently, boys are locked up for exhibiting behaviors that are expected of them in their immediate peer cultures. Such compulsive masculinity offers an image of toughness that generally compensates for feelings of shame, powerlessness, and frustration. Most boys, regardless of race, ethnicity, and social class, experience these feelings of inadequacy. But all too often white boys – like Will Hunting – are sentenced to counseling, while their black and Latino counterparts are funneled further into the criminal justice machinery (Majors and Billson, 1992; Messerschmidt, 1993).

Counselors in juvenile detention centers spend a great deal of time sitting around and talking with the kids, getting to know them while shooting pool and playing cards. Adding to their observations, counselors supervise them in their living units (known as dorms) where each youth is assigned a cube, a personal space with a bed and their belongings. Counselors are not expected to know all the circumstances under which adolescents are confined but, by being observant, counselors gain a glimpse into the troubled lives of those in detention. Katz recalls one particularly revealing moment from his days as a counselor. One night, Darryl, one of the boys for whom Katz was responsible, was on the phone in the shift area talking to his mother, about a half-hour after lights out. Katz kept an eye on Darryl without trying to eavesdrop too noticeably on one of the few semiprivate conversations he was allowed to have. Then, abruptly, he slammed the phone down and darted into his cube, where he sobbed into his thin pillow. At the time Katz did not know much about Darryl other than that he was an African-American kid from the inner city. Katz consulted another counselor who had more information about Darryl's home life. It turned out that while Darryl was speaking to his mother on the phone, her boyfriend started yelling and beating her. Darryl had to listen to the violence, utterly powerless to help his mother. Katz wonders how many boys resort to delinquency after witnessing their mothers being physically abused.

I wonder how I would have felt as a child in a situation similar to Darryl's. What if I were powerless to stop a man from assaulting my mother? I knew Darryl was feeling guilty – if not outright responsible – for his mother's suffering. He blamed himself because he loved her but could not protect her. He was the one who had screwed up and gotten himself locked up. (Katz, 2001: 212–13).

A week later, Darryl bolted from the detention center. Katz and the other counselors were not surprised.

Katz regrets that many of those who wind up in juvenile detention are on their way to a lifetime of being in and out of prison. They are immature, troubled teens whose adverse family and social environments are merely compounded by cultural processes that demand that they measure up to impossible gender codes, particularly an image of masculinity that sets them up for an array of criminal behavior.

Critical criminologists have begun to borrow from feminist scholarship that examines the relationship between gender identity construction and adolescent male criminality. Drawing from gender research, it is suggested that those working in juvenile corrections remain mindful of the emotional and psychological development of those in custody alongside the sociological insights into the gendered nature of various delinquencies. In stressing his point that boys are not men, Katz further recommends that criminal justice majors in college be introduced to the importance of gender in studying crime and the correctional system's self-defeating tendency to treat youthful offenders as adults. 'As feminists in the field have known for years, sometimes the greatest challenge is getting men in positions of influence and authority to see and acknowledge the obvious' (Katz, 2001: 215-16; see also Keller, 1992; Mitchell *et al.*, 2000).

CORRECTIONAL TREATMENT AND ALTERNATIVE PROGRAMS

As noted throughout this chapter, the debate over what should be done to juveniles entering the criminal justice system remains among the most controversial issue in corrections. Should criminal justice officials simply punish juveniles, or should attempts be made to treat and reform them? Even if the latter is the preferred option, questions persist over the strategy of treatment or reform. Should juveniles undergo intensive remedial education as well as be enrolled in psychological and therapeutic programs? Taken further, should innovative programs be designed that might scare or shock the juvenile into a law-abiding life?

In attempting to answer these questions, careful consideration should be given to the theoretical underpinnings of crime and delinquency, especially before embarking on any correctional intervention. Unfortunately, in the field of juvenile justice there has been little effort to attach a theoretical framework to correctional strategies. Finckenauer and Gavin (1999) discovered that a major limitation of juvenile correctional programs is that they are simply too eclectic. By borrowing from multiple theoretical assumptions, these interventions stray

Figure 7.3 Youth prisoners accused of the genocide in Rwanda in 1994 working in a field in Gitagata, Rwanda, April 20, 1995. About one million people were killed in about a hundred days, making it one of the worst genocides in modern history.

© Per-Anders Pettersson/Contributor/ Getty.

from important conceptual guideposts. Finckenauer and Gavin call for an approach to juvenile interventions that is both theory-based and theory-testing; from that foundation, programs become properly developed, administered, and evaluated.

In their examination of numerous programs for juvenile offenders, Finckenauer and Gavin (1999) identify two major orientations. The first orientation is the individual factor approach in which the juvenile remains the primary focus of the intervention. The second orientation is the social factor approach, in which consideration is also turned to the family, peer group, and community as well as society. The individual factor approach generally relies on psychologically based intervention such as behavior modification. Delinquent or violent behavior is modified to shape the juvenile into a law-abiding person. Techniques such as modeling and instituting a token economy are commonly used to reward positive behavior changes. Such a strategy is used at the Achievement Place, a community-based, family-style home for juvenile delinquents in Lawrence, Kansas. Six to eight boys (12 to 16 years old) are assigned to a home with two professional teaching parents. The program sets out to correct behavioral deficiencies by promoting conduct that improves the youths' abilities to interact with others (Levitt *et al.*, 1981).

The program is based on modern behavior therapy insofar as it assumes that behavior problems stem from skill deficiencies. In brief, juveniles are taught skills through the use of a token economy and through contracting, strategies that issue rewards for positive behavior as well as impose punishments for negative behavior. The goal is to reinforce positive behavior. Through a token economy, juveniles earn points for completing chores and homework. Points are exchanged for privileges, including snacks, television programs, and home visits on the weekend. Accordingly, points are taken away for poor performance in school and neglecting household responsibilities, as well as for misconduct and rule infractions.

The Achievement Place complements its program with individual counseling, child advocacy, and self-government run by peers. In that particular modeling and reward approach, juveniles are subjected to forms of criticism that are nonemotional and nonpunitive. Although the Achievement Place reports success in reducing incidents of recidivism and returning its clients to high school, a major limitation of the program is that it relies heavily on exceptional staff. Overall, many individual-oriented programs are likely to show some degree of effectiveness provided that they are equipped with highly skilled and motivated personnel. Unfortunately, most programs are not funded well enough to attract and retain such highly qualified staff. Indeed, ongoing budget cuts by state governments undermine effective treatment programs for juveniles.

Social factor programs are designed to focus more on the juveniles' social network because they assume that behavior is greatly influenced by family members, friends, and peers. An innovative program is wilderness training in which juveniles are enrolled in a group-based experience that removes them from the city and places them in unfamiliar surroundings. The purpose is to force streetwise youths to readjust their city-based survival skills that are generally marked by self-sufficiency and detachment. In a wilderness environment with other youths, juveniles must become more willing to cooperate and rely on each other, hence promoting prosocial skills and attitudes. In their attempt to offset the adverse effects of urban life on juveniles, wilderness programs are reminiscent of the farming-out strategies proposed by the progressives a century ago.

As is the case with most other juvenile programs, rigorous evaluations of wilderness programs are rare, thus their effectiveness remains questionable. Moreover, those programs claiming a certain degree of success must be subjected to careful scrutiny, especially with regard to their selection of participants. Many programs set out to improve their success rates by selecting low-risk juveniles while excluding high-risk or hardcore offenders. Wilderness programs also face the problems of lack of funding and the frequent staff turnover that results from the demanding work schedules.

Other programs with the objective of promoting prosocial behavior – without the logistical difficulties of wilderness programs – can be found in secure and nonsecure facilities. Programs based on the positive aspects of peer interaction have remained popular. Such interventions place a high premium on developing trust, honesty, and group support while downplaying the traditional concepts of obedience and conformity. One example is Guided Group Interaction (GGI), using group dynamics in a free-discussion format designed to foster a supportive atmosphere. In essence, juveniles are re-educated to accept the rules of society and to find personal satisfaction within social boundaries. The group of eight to 12 juveniles meets five times each week for 90-minute sessions with a facilitator – typically a counselor. During the course of the program, the group takes on different formations. The purpose of the interaction is to confront the dynamics of cliques, deviant social roles, and negative self-conceptions. Over time, individual defenses are broken down and members must examine their own conduct and be willing to accept the support of the group. Moreover, members are encouraged to look beyond their own difficulties and lend assistance to others (Finckenauer and Gavin, 1999).

A clear advantage that social factor programs have over individual factor programs is the simple economic benefit. Treating youths collectively rather than individually is more cost-effective, which may very well explain why those programs have grown in popularity. Nonetheless, both individual-oriented and social-oriented programs are products of liberal and positivistic notions about delinquency. That is, those interventions assume that a combination of psychological makeup and social influences determines delinquency. Conversely, classical theorists prefer juvenile interventions that focus more on the individual's lack of obedience and disregard for both self and others in society.

Restitution

Restitution is a correctional practice that often has the support of politicians and citizens across the political spectrum. The idea of restitution is simple: require juveniles to compensate their victims. By participating in such programs as community service, they symbolically engage in a form of restorative justice (see Chapter 13). Even though restitution generally is viewed favorably in its own right, recently there has been interest in determining whether sanctioned compensation actually reduces recidivism among juveniles. In one of the few studies of its kind, Butts and Snyder (1992) evaluated a juvenile restitution program in Utah and its impact on recidivism. They found that for cases involving robbery, assault, burglary, theft, auto theft, and vandalism, 'recidivism is lower when juveniles agree or are ordered to pay restitution to their victims directly or through earnings derived from community service' (Butts and Snyder, 1992: 1). Certainly, additional research in different jurisdictions is needed to determine the overall impact of restitution on recidivism. Nevertheless, restitution has gathered support because of its philosophical position that offenders must be held accountable for their actions, and that victims deserve compensation (see Arrigo and Schehr, 1998).

Youth gang intervention programs

An important source of juvenile delinquency is involvement in youth gangs, and although an in-depth analysis of gangs is beyond the scope of this chapter, some brief mention of intervention programs is worthwhile. Prompted by the concern that youth gangs have grown more violent, Spergel *et al.* (1990) surveyed 254 experts from 45 cities and six special program sites. Their study identified five common strategies for dealing with youth gangs.

- *Suppression*: tactics such as prevention, arrest, imprisonment, supervision, and surveillance.
- *Social intervention*: crisis intervention, treatment for youths and their families, outreach, and referral to social services.

- *Social opportunities*: provision of basic or remedial education, training, work incentives, and jobs.
- *Community mobilization*: improved communication and joint policy and program development among justice, community-based, and grassroots organizations.
- *Organizational development or change*: special police units, vertical prosecution, vertical probation case management, and special youth agency crisis programs.

The survey also revealed the most frequently employed strategies: suppression, the most frequently employed strategy (44 percent), was followed by social intervention (31.5 percent), organizational development (10.9 percent), community mobilization (8.8 percent), and social opportunities (4.8 percent). Conservative thinkers might generally agree that suppression should remain the most frequently employed strategy. However, progressive liberal and critical criminologists would argue that more emphasis needs to be placed on social opportunities, especially since youth gang activity is concentrated in inner cities among minorities of low socioeconomic status (see Curry and Spergel, 1993; Pitts, 2008).

Preserving families to prevent delinquency

Whereas many programs are designed to deal with juveniles after they have already entered the criminal justice system, some interventions set out to establish preventive measures. Currently, there are several programs recommended by the US Department of Justice, Office of Juvenile Justice and Delinquency Prevention (OJJDP, 1992c). The first program is known as *Targeted Outreach*: a delinquency intervention program operated by the Boys and Girls Clubs of America. Next is a program operated by *Court Appointed Special Advocates* (CASA): it is aimed at ensuring that the courts become familiar with the needs of any neglected or abused child. Finally, the *Permanent Families for Abused and Neglected Children* program serves as a training and technical assistance project of the National Council of Juvenile and Family Court Judges (NCJFCJ).

In sum, correctional treatment and alternative programs for juveniles cover the gamut from individual factor approaches to those geared toward social factors (Finckenauer and Gavin, 1999). In maintaining a critical view of these interventions, it is important to remain skeptical of programs that boast high rates of effectiveness without offering compelling supportive evidence. Likewise, it is imperative to look critically at the media, especially when it hypes tough-on-crime programs. Just as some conservative observers call for tougher penalties for youthful offenders, others go further by advocating such innovations as scared-straight programs and military-style boot camps (also known as shock incarceration – see Chapter 13).

SCARED-STRAIGHT PROGRAMS

So-called scared-straight programs subject juveniles to intensive confrontation with adult prisoners who go to great lengths to intimidate and humiliate the youths. The aim is to 'scare' them into living a 'straight' life. Those programs emerged in the 1980s when the social and political mood was shifting increasingly toward punitive sanctions for juvenile offenders. Within that law-and-order framework, enormous publicity was given to confrontation-style programs that appeared to be tough on juveniles. Especially due to the way the media seemed to promote scared-straight programs, the public appeared willing to endorse such rough and tumble approaches to juvenile justice. The media alongside tough-on-crime politicians went to great lengths to link scared-straight to deterrence and the prevention of delinquency.

The original scared-straight program started at Rahway State Prison in New Jersey in 1976 when a group of inmates serving lengthy sentences initiated a Juvenile Awareness Program. These convicts, known as lifers, set out to counsel juveniles who were at risk of becoming delinquent. Their technique of counseling was unique. The lifers invited groups of juveniles to their prison where they exposed them to the harsh realities of prison life. Complete with no-holds-barred profanity, insults, and physical and sexual threats, the lifers were determined to scare those juveniles into leading a straight life. The publicity around the program generated enormous public interest, especially in light of a documentary entitled *Scared Straight* that aired first locally in Los Angeles and then nationally in 1979. That Oscar- and Emmy Award-winning film was so intense and seemed so convincing that soon 38 states developed similar confrontation-style programs for juveniles (Cavender, 1981; Finckenauer and Gavin, 1999; Lundman, 1993).

Rahway's scared-straight program boasted clear effectiveness, reporting that 90 percent of the 10,000 juveniles went straight. Law-and-order politicians and their constituents alike quickly embraced that widely cited figure. Such an unusually high success rate, however, prompted researchers to look more carefully at the program. Among the most extensive evaluations of Rahway's scared-straight program was that conducted by Finckenauer and Gavin (1999). They revealed that the lifers did not keep systematic records. Therefore it was difficult to determine exactly how they arrived at the conclusion that their program was 90 percent effective, especially when there was no follow-up. There were also questions about what constituted the hardcore juvenile delinquents that the program claimed to be so effective in deterring from crime. It is also important to consider that the initial notoriety of Rahway's prison program was brought to the public by way of the film. Moreover, the movie director himself conceded that he had asked the youths to be cocky going into the prison and pensive coming out – thereby creating the impression that they had undergone some transformation.

Finckenauer and Gavin also learned that the scared-straight program at Rahway prison was made available to high-school classes in the form of a field trip; thus many of the youths exposed to the confrontation of inmates were already straight. Despite the popularity of scared-straight programs, largely a result of the sharp images of tough reform, such interventions are based on questionable theoretical assumptions. That is, the notion that juveniles can be scared into a law-abiding life fails to convince most experts. Although the convicts were well intentioned, the scared-straight program was hardly a carefully planned intervention; it lacked a clear strategy, theory, data, and follow-up procedures (Vito and Wilson, 1985).

The Rahway scared-straight program also had its share of institutional problems. The enormous publicity seemed to disrupt the internal order of the institution since some inmates were obsessed with a 'showtime mentality.' Eventually, the program was downscaled to a prison tour and a relatively low-key discussion. Nonetheless, the popularity of confrontation-style interventions continued to grow. Similar scared-straight programs were established at San Quentin (California), Southern Michigan, Virginia, Idaho, and Hawaii. Still, those programs also failed to produce convincing evidence that the intervention was effective. In an evaluation of the project in Hawaii, researchers concluded that it is unrealistic to expect that any single experience, no matter how profound, would have a significant impact on a problem so complicated and intractable as juvenile delinquency (Buckner and Chesney-Lind, 1983: 245). The publicity surrounding scared-straight programs points to the importance of recognizing that as programs become 'media-generated phenomena' they have a 'bandwagon' effect. Consequently, impressionable politicians and citizens want to believe claims of effectiveness, even though such findings are rife with methodological problems (Cavender, 1981). (See 'Comparative Corrections: Punishing Teenagers with Gang-Rape in Pakistan,' below.)

COMPARATIVE CORRECTIONS

Punishing Teenagers with Gang-Rape in Pakistan

The notion of administering sexual violence as a means of punishing females seems beyond belief but that is precisely what occurred in the village of Meerwala, Pakistan where, in 2002, an 18-year-old was gang-raped by four men. A panchayat, or tribal jury, ordered the penalty on the grounds that her brother had been involved in an illicit affair with a woman from a higher tribe. The panchayat had threatened that all the women in the man's family would be raped unless the 18-year-old submitted herself to the brutal punishment. The victim said that she and her father and uncle begged for mercy as four men dragged her to a room and raped her. Fearing that armed enforcers would shoot on sight anyone who dared to intervene, hundreds of bystanders stood motionless. 'They raped me for one hour and afterward I was unable to move,' said the victim in a television interview (*New York Times*, July 6, 2002: A6). Adding to the spectacle, the victim was ordered to return home naked before a thousand onlookers (*New York Times*, July 2, 2002: A4).

The incident serves to reinforce the power of a traditional patriarchal council that relies on violence and intimidation to control its villagers. Beyond that immediate community, however, the ordeal provoked enormous outrage among the Pakistani people, criminal justice officials, and human rights organizations. Authorities encouraged villagers to cooperate with their investigation. Police reported that they had arrested one of the four rapists and were continuing their search for the others. The Pakistani government reached out to assist the victim and compensated her with a check for more than $8,000. 'I would have committed suicide if the government had not come to my help,' the victim told Pakistan's women's development minister (*New York Times*, July 6, 2002: A6).

PUNISHING SCHOOLS AND PREPARING FOR PRISON

As the nation became increasingly conservative during the Reagan revolution of the 1980s, many citizens expressed approval of police tactics for schools, particularly those located in the inner city. Correspondingly, Principal Joe Clark emerged as a celebrity for his tough methods at the Eastside High School in Paterson, New Jersey, where he patrolled the halls with a baseball bat and bullhorn. As the widely popular movie *Lean On Me* celebrated Clark's no-nonsense form of discipline, critics recognized racist overtones. The image of a principal – even a black one – wielding a weapon and barking orders at inner-city students reinforces the racist stereotype that black and Latino youths must be manhandled in order to be kept under control. Racist stereotypes were politically potent in the 1980s: for instance, President Reagan often dropped the term 'welfare queen' in an effort to gain support for his plan to reduce public assistance. Similarly, while campaigning for the presidency in 1988, Vice President George Bush exploited the case of Willie Horton, a black prisoner who had raped a white woman while temporarily released from a Massachusetts furlough program (see Newburn and Jones, 2005). It is in that political and social context that we ought to interpret the rise of Joe Clark.

Clark resigned as principal shortly after the movie *Lean On Me* was released but he and his tough tactics were once again in demand. In 1995, Clark was appointed Director of the Essex County Juvenile Detention Center which houses 270 youths under the age of 18 waiting court appearances or transfers to prison. Maintaining his reputation as a tough disciplinarian, Clark resumed carrying his signature bullhorn but soon a clear pattern of abuse emerged. During his first year on the job, the Juvenile Justice Commission criticized Clark for shackling and cuffing some juvenile detainees for two days. In 1997, the Division of Youth and Family Services rebuked Clark for excessive use of restraints on juveniles. The Juvenile Justice Commission in 1999 cited Clark for numerous violations of the Manual of Standards and in 2001 the Commission issued a report condemning Clark's use of straitjackets and other restraints as 'egregious violations of professional standards' (*New York Times*, 2001, December 5: D5).

The Commission's report further noted that juvenile detainees were placed in handcuffs (euphemistically called 'restraint mittens') attached to belts around their waists for periods ranging from two to eleven days. Clark was also cited for violating professional standards after he ordered eight juveniles to be locked in their cells for 37 consecutive days. According to state detention regulations, the center's social service staff must monitor juveniles placed in solitary confinement, so that they can assess the situation and improve it. But investigators found that many of the lockdowns were ordered for disobeying rules such as disrespectful conduct toward the staff and other nonviolent behavior. In the face of controversy, Clark stood his ground:

> I would not subject the doctors, the medical staff, my teachers, my social workers, my administrative staff, and innocent inmates and detainees to this type of pathological deviants, little miscreants who are wreaking uncontrolled havoc. I am the administrator here, and I will not give into those liberalized attempts by a bureaucracy to condone and encourage terrorism in this detention facility and consequently in the community.
>
> (Newman, 2001: NJ4)

In 2002, five weeks after the Juvenile Justice Commission released its report criticizing Clark's performance at the Essex County Juvenile Detention Center, Clark announced that he would resign, saying that the state's operating rules were too lenient (Hanley, 2002). While the most recent chapter in Clark's career closed, the notion of getting tough on juvenile detainees persists, a popular view reinforced by stereotypes that low-income minorities are especially menacing (see Welch *et al.*, 2002, 2004).

More recently, scholars have taken a keen interest in the policing – and prison – tactics as they continue to transpire in schools. This trend is not merely restricted to inner-city schools but has expanded to suburban educational settings as well. In their influential work, *Punishing Schools*, Lyons and Drew throw critical light on a growing popularity of imposing on students management regimes borrowed from maximum-security prisons. Consider the scenario: jack-booted police officers in paratrooper pants with German shepherds conducting a random drug search as students stand silently – motionless – at attention. In a revealing passage in their book, a teacher expresses concern that the police officers have crossed the line in pursuit of contraband: 'Holy shit, dogs are not allowed near the kids! ... the dogs are trained to go nuts as they pick up a certain smell ... My God, what if somebody stuck something in their jeans pockets ... and what if the dog made a mistake!' (2006: 33; see Liptak, 2009).

Lyons and Drew's critique of the punitive school goes further by recognizing the remnants of 'managerial criminology' whereby zero-tolerance initiatives are 'goal-free' – meaning that nobody really believes such tactics actually work (Feeley and Simon, 1992). Most drug searches do not discover contraband, and students know how to hide their 'shit' or even get high before attending school. To be clear, the 'goal-free' logic does not serve any rationally formulated policy; still, it persists as ritual, and a potent one at that. The ritual is a disciplinary exercise to show students that the authorities are in charge. Taken further, it produces an Alice-in-Wonderland mindset insofar as searches are viewed as successful by some educational administrators who conclude: 'I consider it a success if we find something in a lockdown ... and I consider it a success if we *don't* find something. If we don't, that's a day in suburbia there weren't any drugs here' (Lyons and Drew, 2006: 44; see Bazemore *et al.*, 2004).

In his insightful research on the subject of punishing schools, Paul Hirschfield (2008) looks deeper into the criminalization of school discipline. By doing so, he takes into account a host of social problems, such as a troubled domestic economy alongside mass unemployment and the incarceration of disadvantaged minorities. All together these problems exacerbate the fiscal crisis facing urban public education. In response, Hirschfield discovers a shift in 'school disciplinary policies and practices and staff perceptions of poor students of color in a manner that promotes greater punishment and exclusion of students perceived to be on a criminal justice "track"' (2008: 79; see Sweeten *et al.*, 2009). It seems that the heavy-handed use of discipline serves to identify troubled youths who it is presumed will fail in today's economy, resorting to a life of street crime and eventually prison. As labeling theory informs us, these punitive attitudes targeting young black or Latino youths often produces a self-fulfilling prophecy, thereby contributing to a mass imprisonment of young minorities (see Atrum, 2003; Foucault, 1977; Kupchik, 2009; Kupchik and Monahan, 2006; Chapters 5 and 8).

CONCLUSION

Since the 1960s, juvenile corrections have undergone considerable transformation. Finckenauer (1984) best summarizes these changes by referring to them as the 'Big Ds' – diversion, decriminalization, deinstitutionalization, and due process. Current correctional reformers became influential in diverting youths away from the criminal justice system. They also succeeded in decriminalizing several status offenses that were traditionally used exclusively to control youths. Deinstitutionalization stands as another benchmark campaign that forced communities to deal with delinquency rather than simply warehousing troubled youths. Finally, the transformation in juvenile corrections was further made possible by decisions handed down by the United States Supreme Court. Such decisions ensured that youths were guaranteed certain rights of due process (see Krisberg and Austin, 1993; Jacobs, 1990).

These changes notwithstanding, criminal justice policy targeting juveniles today remains influenced by the conservative tough-on-crime movement of the 1980s. In particular, harsh penalties have returned to the exclusion of more lenient treatments. Unfortunately, that trend brings us full circle in the cycle of juvenile justice. As Bernard describes stage one of the cycle: 'Juvenile crime is thought to be unusually high. There are many harsh punishments and few lenient treatments. Officials often are forced to choose between harshly punishing juvenile offenders and doing nothing at all' (1992: 4).

A major criticism of the widespread use of harsh penalties is that they fail to address any of the social problems that are closely related to the causes of delinquency. Many of those social problems are interrelated, such as poverty, unemployment, family disorganization, and substance abuse. Furthermore, the realization that delinquency is greatly concentrated in the inner city among minorities requires acknowledgement of discrimination and calls attention to the federal government's abandonment of the nation's large cities. Although conservative commentators indeed have a point when they argue that families are instrumental in controlling delinquency, their family-values rhetoric stops short of formally recognizing the relationship between economic opportunity and delinquency (see Currie, 1998; Sabates, 2008; Weenink, 2009).

Equally important in the discussion of juveniles in corrections are the limitations of many liberal approaches to crime and delinquency, especially those that endorse the welfare approach (i.e. social rehabilitation). Duffee (1980) insists that many liberal approaches to crime and delinquency fail to address the broad range of social, political, and economic processes. He goes on to suggest that crime and delinquency must be controlled at the level of root causes as well as at the behavioral level (see Lerman, 1982, 1970).

Many progressive liberal and critical criminologists agree on the basic relationship between economic forces and crime and delinquency; together they challenge policies that attempt to combat social problems by simply throwing money at them. Clearly, serious investments need to be made to further social programs intended for juveniles, but such budgetary allocation ought not be made in lieu of promoting genuine economic justice.

Finally, it is fitting to conclude this chapter with the Juvenile Justice Policy Statement of the National Council on Crime and Delinquency (1991) for it combines concern for current correctional practices with larger social issues.

Position 1
Restrict adult court jurisdiction over juveniles to those aged 16 or older who are accused of serious and violent crimes, and, prior to any transfer of jurisdiction, require a hearing in which the prosecutor must demonstrate convincingly that the minor is not amenable to rehabilitation in the juvenile justice system.

Position 2
Prohibit the incarceration of minors in adult jails, lockups or correctional facilities.

Position 3
Remove jurisdiction over status offenders – runaways, truants and other noncriminal youth – from a justice system that cannot meet their needs, and restore an emphasis on the delivery of support services for these troubled teenagers, including family preservation services.

Position 4
Dedicate a meaningful share of resources to assessment of the needs of arrested youth and to the delivery of treatment to these youth, with particular attention to the treatment needs of institutionalized youth.

Position 5
Apply modern risk-screening methods upon arrest and in the juvenile court to determine which arrested youth require pretrial detention, to determine which youth need secure confinement after trial and to determine the length of secure confinement.

Position 6
Reduce the high rate of minority youth incarceration by allocating an adequate share of state and federal resources to programs and services for these youth.

Position 7
Prohibit the application of the death penalty to any individual whose offense was committed before the age of 18.

Position 8
Support delinquency prevention research and successful delinquency prevention programs with an adequate share of state and federal funds.

SUMMARY

The chapter began with an in-depth look at the historical developments in the juvenile justice system with particular attention paid to the rise of early institutions and the legal challenges to incarceration. The examination of contemporary corrections for juveniles relies on the work of Thomas Bernard (1992), who demonstrated that policy is trapped within a cycle of juvenile justice that precludes the formation of meaningful changes that would better address problems associated with delinquency. This chapter also emphasizes the impact of legal developments in juvenile justice, including how due process rights now apply to juveniles. It is also noted that violent crimes by juveniles have increased and that most of these cases are transferred to the adult courts. In addition to exploring the social world of juvenile institutions, this chapter reviews numerous programs and interventions. While recognizing the many limitations of such programs, there is caution against accepting panaceas.

REVIEW QUESTIONS

1 What ought to be done to break the cycle of juvenile justice?
2 What are the significant legal developments in juvenile justice and which landmark decisions have had the most impact on juvenile justice today?

3   To what extent do violent juvenile offenders burden the juvenile justice system, and how prevalent are transfers to adult courts?

4   How are juvenile cases processed and how does the juvenile justice system differ from the adult system?

5   How do juvenile institutions compare with adult institutions?

6   With regard to the numerous programs, what ought to be done to reduce juvenile delinquency?

RECOMMENDED READINGS

Bernard, T. J. (1992) *The Cycle of Juvenile Justice*. New York: Oxford University Press.

Feld, B. (1999) *Bad Kids: Race and the Transformation of the Juvenile Court*. New York: Oxford University Press.

Finckenauer, J. O. and Gavin, P. (1999) *Scared Straight! and the Panacea Phenomenon*. Englewood Cliffs, NJ: Prentice-Hall.

McCorkle, R. and Miethe, T. D. (2000) *Panic: The Social Construction of the Street Gang Problem*. Upper Saddle River, NJ: Prentice-Hall.

Rothman, D. J. (1980) *Conscience and Convenience: The Asylum and Its Alternatives in Progressive America*. Boston: Little, Brown.

CHAPTER 8

Minorities in Corrections

I'm doing time all my life, man. Don't make much difference if I do it here or out there. It's still time. (The words of an African American inmate, as told to penologist Leo Carroll, on whether life in prison is so terribly different from life in the ghetto)

LEARNING OBJECTIVES

After studying this chapter, you should be able to answer the following questions:

1 Is the criminal justice system racist?
2 What constitutes individual and institutional racism in the criminal justice system?
3 How has racial discrimination emerged at various stages of the criminal justice process?
4 How is the prison experience different for African American, Hispanic, and white inmates?
5 What developments have taken place in the hiring of minorities in corrections?

[When] I first arrived ... we were told ... to keep all eyes forward, no talking, no 'reckless eyeballing,' and ... to stay behind the man ... in front of you. It was then that I noticed that the white boys ... all of 'em over six-foot or better, ... set up [beat] a guy ... about 5–9 or 5–11, being jacked up off the ground and literally whupped, with black jacks ... [He] still had on a set of ... dog-cuffs, them cuffs that you put on your wrists and they hold you between your legs with a chain. The chains is directly up under the nutsack, and one yank of this heavy chain, man, and you just look at this and say, 'Hey, man, these some cooool folks, man,' and it's really a heavy experience. It was right then and there I made up my mind ... hey, there's 'no-win' under these conditions, refusing against the administration by brute force. You couldn't win. When you walked into the building you sense it, these big ol' hillbillies standing here, all around you, all you see is white folks, and you hardly ever see black. – An African American prisoner describes the culture shock he experienced upon entering the institution.

(Thomas, 1991: 133)

INTRODUCTION

In light of the huge volume of minority offenders processed through the criminal justice system, many students and professors alike might be astonished to learn that until very recently most corrections textbooks did not offer a separate chapter on people of color in prisons. Certainly, many such books discussed racial biases as they exist within the penal apparatus. But without an entire chapter on the topic, the significance of race and ethnicity appears secondary. Since minorities are disproportionately represented in the American correctional population, it is only fitting to examine more carefully how racism and discrimination emerge at various stages of the criminal justice system. This chapter sets out to foster a critical understanding of the structural and procedural biases against minorities, especially since such forms of prejudice violate the very ideals of justice (Keen and Jacobs, 2009; Mann *et al.*, 2007; Miller, 2008; Tonry, 1995).

In addition to discussing specific minority groups, such as African Americans, Hispanics (or Latinos) and American Indians (or Native Americans), the chapter demonstrates the problem in isolating racism from classism. Maintaining a critical approach to race in criminal justice, it is crucial that social class also be considered; indeed, a person's socioeconomic standing (i.e. employment, income, level of education) often determines the way one is treated in the criminal justice system. Still, there are methodological obstacles in studying racism since many criminologists tend to treat race as a crude measure of social class, and on average whites have higher socioeconomic status than non-whites. Compounding matters, criminal justice bureaucracies generally collect data on race but not always on class. 'As a practical matter, then, it is much simpler to contrast people of different races than people of different classes, but many differences among racial groups are really class differences, caused by differences in access to money, rather than differences in skin color' (Best, 2001: 118; see Kovandzic *et al.*, 1998; Rose and Clear, 1998; Welch, 1995c; Welch *et al.*, 1998). With that concern in mind, the chapter attends closely to the complex interplay between social class, race and ethnicity – as well as gender.

Figure 8.1   An African American male with hands hanging out prison bars.

© iStockphoto.com

RACISM AND INSTITUTIONAL RACISM

What is racism, and how does it differ from institutional racism? 'Racism is the ideology contending that actual or alleged differences between different racial groups assert the superiority of one racial group' (Doob, 1993: 5). As an ideology, racism exists as a deep-seated attitude or belief. When an individual or group expresses racism, it is often referred to as individual racism. However, as racism emerges in discriminatory policies and practices within systems (e.g. political, economic, educational, and criminal justice systems), it is termed institutional racism. Although specific incidents of individual racism are somewhat easy to detect, institutional racism is not. Institutional racism contributes to systemwide norms that lead to discrimination; still, it is difficult to pinpoint because it lacks the visible offensiveness of individual racism. In sum, racism 'serves the interest of the group endorsing it – in this case the majority group – which becomes the chief beneficiary of political, economic, and social discrimination' (Doob, 1993: 5–6).

THE MYTH OF A RACIST CRIMINAL JUSTICE SYSTEM?

Whether the criminal justice system is racist continues to be fiercely debated. Many criminal justice experts often rely on conventional wisdom that the system is racist, while others argue that such characterizations are a myth. At the forefront of that dialogue is William Wilbanks and his controversial book *The Myth of a Racist Criminal Justice System* (1987). His thesis is straightforward: 'I take the position that the perception of the criminal justice system as racist is a myth' (Wilbanks, 1987: 5). However, Wilbanks does distinguish between individual and institutional racism; moreover, he believes that incidents of individual racism do occur (among individual police officers, attorneys, judges, etc.). Still, Wilbanks does 'not believe that the system is characterized by racial prejudice or discrimination against blacks; that is, prejudice and discrimination are not "systematic"' (Wilbanks, 1975: 5–6). Wilbanks confines his argument to the current criminal justice system, conceding that racial prejudice and discrimination have occurred in the past.

In his book, Wilbanks relies heavily on numerous studies to support his claims, and scholars agree that his research is thorough and comprehensive in scope. Nonetheless, Wilbanks does not conclusively determine that the criminal justice system is as fair to minorities as it is to Whites. Rather, he states that: 'there is insufficient evidence to support the charge that the system is racist today' (1987: 8). Given that conclusion, supporters of the view that the criminal justice system is not racist might very well find Wilbanks's work disappointing.

Perhaps the most important contribution made by Wilbanks is his systematic critique of the methodologies used to investigate racial discrimination in the criminal justice system. In a summary of his research, Wilbanks states: '[I have] attempted to point out the difficulties in proving or disproving the existence of racial discrimination to the point of sentencing by illustrating how different research methods and interpretations lead to different conclusions about a race effect' (1991: 158). Despite these limitations, Wilbanks asserts that the following findings are generally valid across the literature (1991: 158–9):

1 Racial discrimination in sentencing has declined over time.
2 Race of the defendant does not have consistent impact across crimes and jurisdictions.
3 Race of the victim may be a better predictor of sentence than race of the defendant.
4 Extralegal variables (e.g. race, sex, age, socioeconomic status of the defendant) are not as predictive of sentence as legal variables (e.g. type of crime, strength of evidence).
5 The Black/White variations in sentences are generally reduced to near zero when several legal variables are introduced as controls.

Criticism surrounding Wilbanks's book encompasses several issues. For example, much of the research used to test hypotheses about racial discrimination in the criminal justice system involves studies on sentencing. Critics charge that racial discrimination often occurs during earlier stages of the criminal justice process (e.g. arrest, prosecution, and conviction) as well as during later stages (e.g. parole).

Another problem that confounds studies on racial discrimination is the simplistic use of dichotomous racial categories: black and white. Also important is the examination of discrimination against other minorities, such as Native American and Hispanic defendants. Moreover, large databases often fail to acknowledge that many Hispanics are categorized as white. The inclusion of Hispanics in the white group conceals evidence of discrimination against them; moreover, it confounds efforts to make simple comparisons to other minority groups (e.g. African American).

Finally, Wilbanks does not dispute the argument that racial discrimination in the criminal justice system is a function of class discrimination. Many scholars insist that racism and classism should not be examined independently since racism is a form of economic (and social) control, and a potent one at that (Reiman, 2000; Welch, 2005a). Acknowledging the link between racism and classism, Bob Bohm summarizes his reaction to Wilbanks's book: '[He] is probably correct that the criminal justice system is not racist in a "systematic" sense. What appears as racism is really class discrimination because a disproportionate number of minority-group members are poor' (1987: 641).

HISTORICAL CONSIDERATIONS

As is discussed in Chapters 2 and 3, the criminal justice system historically has engaged in processing disproportionate numbers of minorities and recent immigrants, most of whom represent the lower socioeconomic strata. Correspondingly, it is the notion of a criminal class that perpetuates those biases. As the US experienced several waves of immigration, the elites (or Nativists) issued testimonies claiming that the Irish, German, and Scandinavian immigrants were less intelligent than 'real' Americans. Moreover, when it was realized that immigrant groups had high rates of unemployment, that finding was attributed to their 'innate sense of laziness' rather than discrimination. Early Americans often did not hide their animosity toward certain ethnic groups. In the mid-1800s, it was not uncommon to see postings for work that stipulated 'No Irish Need Apply.' When some of those young, impoverished, unemployed immigrants turned to street crime, perhaps in an attempt to survive harsh economic conditions, the entire ethnic group was depicted as a distinct class of criminals. Over the course of several generations, the Irish assimilated into American culture and were able to move upward economically. Still, the pattern of blaming social problems on the most recent immigrant groups continued. Soon other recent immigrant groups – Italians and Eastern Europeans and later Hispanics – became viewed as the criminal class and as threats to American society (Bailey, 1991; Brotherton and Kretsedemas, 2008; Carlson, 1975; Welch, 2002b; see Chapter 4).

Unlike immigrant groups, African Americans have not been afforded similar paths of social mobility. As descendants of slaves, African Americans are generally described as the nation's 'internal aliens.' Historically, being African American has meant having fewer legitimate economic opportunities in society and more contact with the criminal justice apparatus compared to other racial and ethnic groups. In 1833, de Beaumont and de Tocqueville reported: 'in those states in which there exists one negro to thirty whites, the prisons contain one negro to four white persons' (1833: 61). Following the Civil War, first- and second-generation immigrants from Europe were over-represented in the prison population in the Northern states while prisons in the South were overwhelmingly African American (Sellin, 1976). Today, African Americans are disproportionately represented in prison systems in all states (Tonry, 1995;

Wacquant, 2000). As this chapter shall continue to point out, individual as well as institutional racism against African Americans tends to run much deeper than prejudice directed toward other groups. Consider, for instance, the landmark case involving the Scottsboro Boys.

Long before the mainstream civil rights movement of the 1960s, the cases of nine young men known as the Scottsboro Boys became symbols of the fight against racism. In 1931, two women accused the nine African American youths of gang rape while aboard a freight train in Alabama. The incident took several turns before accusations of rape surfaced. A brawl erupted between white and African American drifters aboard a Memphis-bound train. The whites were beaten and tossed off the slow-moving train. One of the whites reported the fight to the sheriff in Jackson County, Alabama. A posse was deputized and ordered to round up every Negro on the train and bring them to Scottsboro. The nine teenagers, aged 13 to 19, were arrested on assault charges and hauled back to the county jail in Scottsboro.

In a separate incident, two white women, Victoria Price (age 19) and Ruby Bates (age 17) were approached by the authorities as they were seen running alongside the railroad tracks. Frightened that they might be arrested for vagrancy, the women told the posse that the nine African Americans while aboard the train raped them. The charges erupted into a racial inferno. An angry crowd quickly gathered at the jailhouse chanting, 'Give 'em to us' and 'Let those niggers out.' The National Guard had to be called to protect the defendants from the vigilante mob (Goodman, 1994).

The trial took place less than two weeks after the arrests. Rumors about the alleged rapes added to the hostility surrounding the trial. One version of the episode included details of Ruby Bate's having her breast chewed off by the attackers. The testimony of the accusers became so graphic that the judge would not allow any women or men under 21 into the courtroom. Not surprisingly, eight of the nine defendants were found guilty and sentenced to death. During the appeals, however, the cases received greater scrutiny. Prominent attorney Samuel S. Liebowitz (dubbed the 'New York Jew nigger lover' by his detractors) successfully argued that the defendants had been denied adequate counsel: a violation of the due process clause of the Fourteenth Amendment. Later, Liebowitz moved that the exclusion of blacks from the grand jury also was unconstitutional. In 1932, the Supreme Court concurred, setting the stage for having the convictions reversed. After being imprisoned for several years, eventually each of the defendants regained his freedom (Goodman, 1994). Despite the suffering and anguish endured by the nine youths, the Scottsboro cases emerged as celebrated victories in the fight for civil rights and equality in the criminal justice system (see Myrdal, 1944).

MINORITIES IN PRISON

As discussed in previous chapters, racial and ethnic minorities are overrepresented in the American criminal justice system. By 2008, the imprisonment rate for

Table 8.1 Imprisonment rate per 100,000 persons in the US resident population, by race, Hispanic origin, and gender, 2008

	Male	Female
Total[a]	952	62
White[b]	487	50
Black[b]	3,161	149
Hispanic	1,200	75

Note: Imprisonment rates are the number of prisoners under state or federal jurisdiction sentenced to more than 1 year per 100,000 persons in the U.S. resident population in the referenced population group.

[a]Total includes American Indians, Alaska Natives, Asians, Native Hawaiians, other Pacific Islanders, and persons identifying two or more races.
[b]Excludes persons of Hispanic or Latino origin.

Source: Sabol *et al.* (2009: 2).

black males reached 3,161 (per 100,000 residents) followed by Hispanic males (1,200) and white males (487). Black females were incarcerated at a rate of 149 followed by Hispanic females (75) and white females (50) (see Table 8.1). It is important to note the recent trends in incarceration rates with respect to race, Hispanic origin, and gender, since the year 2000.

From 2000 to 2008 the imprisonment rate for black men decreased from 3,457 per 100,000 in the US resident population to 3,161, and the imprisonment rate for black women declined from 205 per 100,000 in the US resident population to 149. During that timeline, the incarceration rate for Hispanic men remained relatively steady at about 1,200 per 100,000 in the US resident population. For white men the imprisonment rate increased from 449 per 100,000 in the US resident population in 2000 to 487 per 100,000 in 2008 (see Table 8.2). Despite a drop in the imprisonment rate for black men since 2000, by 2008 they were still incarcerated at a rate six and half times higher than white males (Sabol *et al.*, 2009; see Beck and Harrison, 2001).

CRITICAL ANALYSIS OF DATA

Look at Table 8.2 and carry out the following task. With respect to gender, race, and Hispanic origin, identify the year in which each group reported its highest estimated rates of sentenced prisoners.

Turning attention to Table 8.3, we can see the change in the number of sentenced prisoners in state prisons by race and Hispanic origin as well as by offense from 2000 to 2006. The total number of sentenced offenders in state prisons increased by 124,700 to reach 1,331,100 state prisoners. The number of sentenced blacks fell to 508,700 in 2006, declining by 53,300 prisoners since 2000. More than

Table 8.2 Estimated rate of sentenced prisoners under state or federal jurisdiction, per 100,000 US residents, by gender, race, and Hispanic origin, December 31, 2000–8

Year	Males				Females			
	Total[a]	White[b]	Black[b]	Hispanic	Total[a]	White[b]	Black[b]	Hispanic
2000	904	449	3,457	1,220	59	34	205	60
2001	896	462	3,535	1,177	58	36	199	61
2002	912	450	3,437	1,176	61	35	191	80
2003	915	465	3,405	1,231	62	38	185	84
2004	926	463	3,218	1,220	64	42	170	75
2005	929	471	3,145	1,244	65	45	156	76
2006	943	487	3,042	1,261	68	48	148	81
2007	955	481	3,138	1,259	69	50	150	79
2008	952	487	3,161	1,200	68	50	149	75

Note: Totals based on prisoners sentenced to more than 1 year. Imprisonment rates are per 100,000 U.S. residents in each reference population group.

[a]Includes American Indians, Alaska Natives, Asians, Native Hawaiians, other Pacific Islanders, and persons identifying two or more races.
[b]Excludes persons of Hispanic or Latino origin.

Source: Sabol *et al.* (2009: 5).

half of that drop (56 percent) was made up of 29,600 fewer blacks imprisoned for drug offenses. Looking more closely at those changes along lines of race and drug violations, we find that the number of sentenced white and Hispanic prisoners convicted of a drug offense increased from 2000 to 2006. Those trends offset the decline in the number of imprisoned black drug offenders. Specifically, incarcerated white drug offenders increased by 13,800 prisoners and the number of Hispanic drug offenders increased by 10,800; overall, the number of sentenced drug offenders in state prison increased by 14,700 prisoners (Sabol *et al.*, 2009: 6).

CRITICAL ANALYSIS OF DATA

Table 8.3 reveals important data on race and Hispanic origin and offense. Examine the number of prisoners (in 2006) for each group and identify the offense that is most represented.

A critical understanding of incarceration rates broken down by race also prompts us to narrow our focus to consider age. Table 8.4 clearly shows that the impact of penal sanctions is greatest on men of color; in particular, black men aged 30–34 have the highest imprisonment rate, registering at 8,032 per 100,000 US residents. That group is followed by black men aged 35–39 and black men aged 25–29 (7,392 and 7,130 respectively) (Sabol *et al.*, 2009: 36). As to be discussed in Chapter 13, these age groups for both male and female prisoners also account

Table 8.3 Change in number of sentenced prisoners in state prisons, 2000 to 2006, by race and Hispanic origin and offense

Race and Hispanic origin	Number of prisoners in 2006	Change since 2000	Percent of total change
Total offenses	1,331,100	124,700	100.0 %
Violent	667,900	78,800	63.2
Property	277,900	39,400	31.6
Drugs	265,800	14,700	11.8
Other[b]	119,500	−8,200	−6.6
White[a]	474,200	37,500	100 %
Violent	227,500	15,100	40.3
Property	126,200	17,600	46.9
Drugs	72,000	13,800	36.8
Other[b]	48,500	−9,000	−24.0
Black[a]	508,700	−53,300	100 %
Violent	267,900	−5,500	10.3
Property	89,700	−7,100	13.3
Drugs	115,700	−29,600	55.5
Other[b]	35,400	−11,100	20.8
Hispanic or Latino	248,900	70,400	100 %
Violent	141,600	54,500	77.4
Property	32,800	4,400	6.3
Drugs	54,100	10,800	15.3
Other[b]	20,400	700	1.0

Note: Data are for inmates sentenced to more than 1 year under the jurisdiction of state correctional authorities. The estimates for gender were based on jurisdiction counts at year end (NPS 1B). The estimates by race and Hispanic origin were based on data from the 2004 Survey of Inmates in State Correctional Facilities and updated by year end jurisdiction counts; estimates within offense categories were based on offense distributions from the National Corrections Reporting Program, 2006, updated by year end jurisdiction counts. All estimates were rounded to the nearest 100. Detail may not add to total due to rounding.

[a]Excludes persons of Hispanic or Latino origin.
[b]Includes public order and other unspecified offenses.

Source: Sabol *et al.* (2009: 6).

for a large proportion of parents behind bars, thereby posing greater problems for their children who are cared for by other relatives.

CRITICAL ANALYSIS OF DATA

Refer to Table 8.4. For each category (i.e. gender, race, and Hispanic origin), identify the age group with the highest estimated rates of sentenced prisoners.

From a critical standpoint, racial and ethnic disparities in the correctional system point to serious flaws in a democratic society. In terms of advancing social reform and improving criminal justice policy, it is important to consider the following concerns: (1) impact on the life prospects for African American males;

Table 8.4 Estimated rate of sentenced prisoners under state or federal jurisdiction per 100,000 US residents, by gender, race, Hispanic origin, and age, December 31, 2008

Age	Males				Females			
	Total[a]	White[b]	Black[b]	Hispanic	Total[a]	White[b]	Black[b]	Hispanic
Total[c]	1,434,800	477,500	562,800	295,800	105,300	50,700	29,100	17,300
18–19	23,800	6,500	10,400	4,900	1,000	400	300	200
20–24	208,400	59,400	85,000	48,400	11,500	5,400	3,000	2,300
25–29	246,400	66,000	102,800	60,000	16,000	7,300	4,400	3,100
30–34	238,100	70,700	96,800	54,400	18,500	8,900	5,000	3,200
35–39	226,700	75,200	90,500	45,900	20,800	9,900	5,900	3,200
40–44	202,500	75,500	77,400	35,600	17,900	8,700	5,100	2,600
45–49	136,300	53,100	51,300	22,600	10,700	5,200	3,100	1,500
50–54	75,800	31,600	27,000	12,300	5,000	2,500	1,400	700
55–59	39,100	19,000	11,900	6,200	2,100	1,300	500	300
60–64	19,200	10,700	4,700	3,000	1,000	600	200	200
65 or older	15,800	9,300	3,700	2,200	600	400	100	100

Note: Totals based on prisoners with a sentence of more than 1 year.

[a]Includes American Indians, Alaska Natives, Asians, Native Hawaiians, other Pacific Islanders, and persons identifying two or more races.

[b]Excludes persons of Hispanic or Latino origin.

[c]Includes persons under age 18.

Source: Sabol *et al.* (2009: 36).

(2) impact on the African American community; (3) failure of the 'get tough' approach to crime control; (4) implications for the war on drugs; (5) strategies for more effective criminal justice policies and programs; and (6) the need for a broad approach to crime and crime control (Mauer, 1999, 1990; Sentencing Project, 1997). (Each of these areas of social policy will be discussed in the conclusion of this chapter.) Before returning to the issue of minorities behind bars, it is important that we also explore other interrelated areas of the criminal justice system. The following sections briefly examine patterns of racial profiling, detention, sentencing, and incarceration as they affect minorities adversely.

RACIAL PROFILING AND 'DRIVING WHILE BLACK (OR BROWN)'

Among the more controversial issues in contemporary criminal justice is racial profiling, 'the use of race as a key factor in police decisions to stop and interrogate citizens' (Weitzer and Tuch, 2002: 435). Contrary to the view that racial profiling is harmless, many incidents are humiliating and traumatic. On their 40th wedding anniversary, Etta and James Carter were returning to their home in Philadelphia after attending their daughter's wedding in Florida. The couple were pulled over by police for 'wobbly driving.' The canine corps was called in to assist police searching for drugs. Every item from the vehicle was removed and placed on the side of the highway, where the Carters were ordered to sit. When Mrs Carter requested to use a portable toilet located in their SUV, the police refused and threatened to handcuff her if she did not remain quiet. Eventually, Mrs Carter soiled herself. After the three-hour ordeal, the Carters were allowed to repack their vehicle and resume traveling. The police did not find drugs or other contraband. The Carters were deeply offended by their mistreatment by police, whom the couple believed harassed them simply for 'driving while black' (American Civil Liberties Union, 1999: 1).

Racially discriminatory police stops, known as pretextual stops or 'driving while black or brown' (DWB), affect minorities at all levels of socioeconomic status. Such stops are not confined to the nation's highways; they occur on city streets and in suburban neighborhoods as well. Moreover, pretextual stops are not limited to motorists but are also used against pedestrians. Three types of pretextual stops persist. First, 'out of place' or 'border patrol' pretextual stops occur in predominantly white areas where 'being black or brown' is viewed as being suspicious. Second, 'urban control' pretextual stops are aimed at young minorities whom police have profiled as drug traffickers despite any evidence other than their race. Finally, pretextual Terry stops target minority pedestrians, usually young African Americans and Latinos. In 1968, the US Supreme Court, in *Terry* v. *Ohio*, ruled that police did not need a warrant to stop and frisk a person if a 'reasonable prudent [officer] in the circumstances [is] warranted in the belief that his safety or that of others is in danger.' Police often take advantage of their wide discretion under Terry to frisk young minorities who are doing nothing more than walking in their own communities. New York City police records showed 45,000 such stops over two years, 35,000 of which were innocent people. Only 5,000 arrests were substantiated by physical evidence (e.g. drugs) (ACLU, 1999; also see Crawford, 2000a, 2000b; Russell, 2002, 1998).

While racial profiling is well documented, the fact that it does not benefit law enforcement is commonly overlooked. Professor David Cole (2001) examined the so-called hit rates and found that racial profiling yields no significant increases in arrests. 'If blacks are carrying drugs more often than whites, police should find drugs on the blacks they stop more often than on the whites they stop. But they do not' (Cole and Lamberth, 2001: 13WK). In New Jersey, for instance, where police have eventually admitted to racial profiling, searches conducted with the subject's consent in 2000 produced contraband (mostly drugs) on 25 percent of whites, 13 percent of blacks, and only 5 percent of Latinos (Cole, 2001; Cole and Lamberth, 2001; Engel *et al.*, 2002).

By relying on racial profiling, law enforcement agencies widen their net in an effort to apprehend more lawbreakers. Not only has that strategy failed but since large numbers of innocent persons are stopped and frisked, police inadvertently erode their own legitimacy. Simply put, citizens who have been subjected to (or have witnessed) racial profiling tend to view the criminal justice system as unfair and racist (Harcourt, 2007a, 2007b; Taylor, 2000; Weitzer and Tuch, 2002; Welch, 1999a).

Over the past two decades, the media, politicians, and civil rights advocates have weighed into the controversy. In 1999, President Clinton condemned the practice and ordered federal agencies to collect information on the race of persons stopped and questioned by the police. Several states have passed or are considering legislation requiring law enforcement agencies to collect demographic data on persons they stop. Still, many police organizations resist such requirements, claiming that racial profiling rarely occurs and data collection would place an unnecessary burden on officers (MacDonald, 2002; see Stewart *et al*, 2009). (See 'Comparative Corrections: Racializing Violence in Britain', below.)

DETENTION, RACE AND CLASS

Police sweeps considered racially motivated cross socioeconomic boundaries, adversely affecting lower- as well as middle-income minorities. By contrast, bail procedures generally constitute more of a problem involving social class. Suspects are more likely to be detained if the bail is sufficiently higher than they can afford, regardless of their race or ethnicity. The Correctional Association of New York (1991) notes that at Rikers Island, two-thirds of the pretrial detainee population remain in jail because they are simply too poor to meet their bail, even though sometimes their bail may be as low as a few hundred dollars. Certainly, race and social class intersect since, at Rikers Island, whites represent only 5 percent of the pretrial detainee population (Wynn, 2001).

As discussed in greater detail in Chapter 11, jail detention raises several issues. Most notably, defendants who are unable to post bail are more likely to be convicted than those who can, 'because they cannot aid in their own defense (e.g., by locating witnesses who may only be known to the defendant by an alias or street name), raise funds for their defense, and enter the courtroom in the company of a bailiff, which may influence the judge's or jury's opinion concerning the defendant's guilt' (Patterson and Lynch, 1991: 40; Walker *et al.*, 2002, 1996).

Most jurisdictions have guidelines that determine bail decisions, and discrimination is often assumed to exist in the form of bail's being set in excess of those limits. However, Patterson and Lynch showed more precisely how discrimination emerges by taking into account both racial and gender differences.

> These data indicate that racial/gender differences among suspects do not influence decisions to set bail in excess of guideline limits. However, these data do indicate that white females are significantly more likely than others to receive bail amounts below schedule guidelines. Further, relative to whites, nonwhite suspects are less likely to receive bail below schedule amounts.
>
> (1991: 50–1)

What is learned from the Patterson and Lynch (1991) study is that discrimination does not always emerge in the form of harsher treatment of a particular group, but rather as favoritism for another (see Beck and Karberg, 2001; Tartaro and Sedelmaier, 2009; Williams, 2003).

SENTENCING, RACE, ETHNICITY, AND CLASS

Central to a critical understanding of minorities in corrections is sentencing, particularly disparities in race, ethnicity, and class, as well as gender. Whereas criminologists have long been interested in studying inequities in sentencing, until recently various methodologies produced conflicting results. The most current empirical analyses of sentencing, however, demonstrate clear relationships among key demographic variables. Steffensmeier *et al.* (1998: 763) documented the 'punishment cost of being young, black, and male' by revealing that, compared to any other group, they are sentenced to the harshest prison terms.

Steffensmeier *et al.* interpret their findings according to a 'focal concerns' theory of sentencing in which judges' sentencing decisions reflect their evaluation of blameworthiness of the offender, their desire to safeguard the community by incapacitating dangerous criminals, and the social costs of their sentencing decision. Still, judges rarely have enough information to assess accurately the offender's blameworthiness or dangerousness; consequently, they resort to a form of 'perceptual shorthand' that rests on negative stereotypes of young, black males.

As a follow-up study, Spohn and Holleran (2000) replicated the Steffensmeier *et al.* research, finding comparable results. 'Young black and Hispanic males face greater odds of incarceration than middle-aged white males, and unemployed

Figure 8.2 An unidentified Texas department of corrections officer watching over prisoners working outside the prison at Ellis Unit in Huntsville, Texas USA on April 17, 1997. Texas has about 450 prisoners on death row. The state leads all records in executing people around the US. The prisoners are executed by lethal injection.

© Per-Anders Pettersson/Contributor/Getty.

black and Hispanic males are substantially more likely to be sentenced to prison than employed white males' (p. 281). Confirming the Steffensmeier *et al.* notion of 'perceptual shorthand,' Spohn and Holleran conclude that their study provides evidence that there exists the perception that certain types of offenders are regarded as being more problematic than others, thus requiring greater formal social control (see Provine, 2007; Shute *et al.*, 2005; Western, 2006).

The interpretation of biases in sentencing also reaches into other theoretical critiques, including those exploring social control. Consider the classic work by Steven Spitzer (1975), who introduced the notion of social dynamite. That concept is used to describe popular perceptions that a certain segment of the population, namely young minority males, is particularly menacing (see the section on 'Cultural Penology: Moral Panic Over Wilding', below). It is important to note that Spitzer and many of the aforementioned studies attend closely to economic forces as they shape social control. In particular, unemployment remains a key consideration in sentencing. Young minority males who are out of work at the time of sentencing often face prison terms in part because being jobless is perceived by the authorities as a potential threat to public safety. In the absence of gainful employment, according to that explanation, the courts presume that young men of color will eventually resort to street crime if returned to the community (see Covington 1997, 1995; Crawford *et al.*, 1998; Everett and Nienstedt, 1999; Nobling *et al.*, 1998; Steffensmeier and Demuth, 2001).

COMPARATIVE CORRECTIONS

Racializing Violence in Britain

Society's tendency to racialize crime exhibits further the usefulness of social constructionism, particularly as we turn critical attention to racism elsewhere. The United Kingdom and the United States not only share a common racial and ethnic heritage but both nations also struggle with contemporary racial tensions that permeate criminal justice. Like their North American counterparts, British criminologists continue to reveal that race and class are significant forces shaping popular images of lawlessness. The racialization of violence in England is traced to the turn of the century. During that era, port cities relied heavily on the work of black (African and Afro-Caribbean) seamen. In 1919, race riots broke out in these locales, leaving in their wake political and ideological notions that blacks were a problem population that ultimately would have to be contained by greater investment in criminal justice (Cashmore and McLaughlin, 1991).

In the post-1945 period, race continued to emerge as a potent symbol of social disorder, most significantly during the 1970s when British authorities ambitiously campaigned against mugging. In their classic book, *Policing the Crisis*, Hall *et al.* (1978) examined critically the process by which moral panic over mugging produced greater anxiety over black males and their perceived tendencies toward violence. Due to heightened political and media attention, blacks were criminalized and depicted as incompatible with British culture and society. Enoch Powell, a British Member of Parliament, fueled the controversy, labeling mugging a 'black crime' (Solomos, 1993). 'This construction of racial meanings around violence which gathered pace in the 1970s mugging phenomenon became a strategy to justify repressive crime control measures geared towards addressing the public order threat supposedly posed by inner-city black communities' (Kalunta-Crumpton, 2002: 42; see Gilroy, 1987, 1982; Keith, 1996).

Negative stereotypes of blacks continued to resonate into the 1980s when police clashed with black youths protesting the overpolicing of their communities compounded by police brutality. Following the 1981 Brixton riot, Sir Kenneth Newman (then Metropolitan Police Commissioner) issued a crass biological interpretation: 'In the Jamaicans, you have people who are constitutionally disorderly. It's simply in their make-up. They are constitutionally disposed to anti-authority' (Clare, 1984: 52). Again, an emerging moral panic contributed to a sense that British society was endangered by racial outsiders who resort to uncivilized acts of crime and violence (Benyon, 1984; Benyon and Solomos, 1987; Phillips, 2008; see Welch, 2003d).

In the 1990s, the media and politicians echoed the perceived threat posed by Jamaican 'Yardies,' depicted as dangerous drug traffickers who resort to violence as a means to expand their economic territories. Police Commissioner Sir Paul Condon announced that black males commit a significant proportion of violent street crimes even though official statistics showed the contrary (Home Office, 1999, 1994). As British criminologists continue to document, the racialization of crime is a phenomenon that is not unique to the United States; indeed, their research typifies the far-reaching implications of studying crime from the perspective of social constructionism and moral panic (see Cohen, 1972; Matthews and Young, 1986).

RACE, ETHNICITY AND PRISON LIFE

As discussed throughout, minorities – especially young African American men – are disproportionately represented in the correctional population. As prison systems nationwide expand in scope, the proportion of people of color continues to mount. From that standpoint, Scott Christianson observes 'not only has the prison system gotten bigger, but it also has gotten blacker' (1991: 62-3; see Keen and Jacobs, 2009). Regrettably, much of the classic works on prison life often neglected the relevance of race relations behind bars (Clemmer, 1940, 1958; Sykes, 1958). In an effort to bring issues of race to the forefront, Leo Carroll set out to explore that very important dimension to institutional life. Like other sociologists, Carroll recognized that prisons are microcosms of society at large. Carroll goes on to write that prisons greatly resemble society, but only its worst aspects, that is the slum:

Over half of the residents of the contemporary prison are drawn from racial and ethnic minority groups, and most were residents of ghettos prior to their incarceration. Many slum dwellers have been characterized as untrustworthy and perhaps dangerous in the eyes of others; this is true of all prison inmates.

(1990: 511)

Like much of the free world, prison society tends to be segregated by race and ethnicity (Goodman, 2008; Simon, 2000; Spencer *et al.*, 2009). Still, that form of segregation is usually self-imposed as convicts gravitate to their own racial and ethnic groups; moreover, many of those friendships are affiliated with common neighborhoods as prisoners seek out fellow 'home-boys' for support and a sense of belonging. In his work on the subject, Carroll (1990) takes a close look at how such segregation in prison defines the prison experience and shapes adaptation to its pain (see Massoglia, 2008; Steiner and Wooldredge, 2009; Wacquant, 2002). The sections which follow turn critical attention to different racial and ethnic groups within the sphere of imprisonment.

African American prisoners

Given historical antecedents, African Americans have long struggled against both formal (i.e. slavery) and informal (i.e. prejudice and discrimination) oppression. For lower-income blacks in particular, the harsh treatment meted out by the criminal justice system is emblematic of those forms of control. According to the words of convict-author George Jackson, prison 'simply looms as the next phase in a sequence of humiliations' (Jackson, 1970: 9). In prison, convicts (of all races) refer to the warden as 'the man,' a term intended to make a linguistic link to the master of slaves. That slang is borrowed from the free world where African Americans also view members of the establishment as 'the man,' whether they are bosses in the workplace or cops on the beat. The term expresses the suspiciousness and skepticism that minorities have toward powerful people in business as well as government. Similarly, prisoners refer to correctional officers as cops since their duties are virtually another form of policing – but behind bars.

Dynamics between convicts and guards are very much shaped along lines of race given that most officers are white and most inmates are black. Carroll found that African American inmates are often justified in feeling discriminated against by white correctional officers. He reports that white staff members perceive black convicts as being more dangerous than white inmates and, consequently, impose stricter surveillance on them. That pattern was especially evident in remote institutions where white rural correctional officers guarded black urban inmates. Although white officers watch African American inmates more carefully, they also intimidate them.

It's a frightening effect. Here you are all alone by ten or fifteen blacks and it's your problem, you know. Good luck! What are they gonna do to me? Are they gonna drive me into the ground? Or is one gonna come at me with a razor blade and slash my throat? Or are they gonna beat the shit outta me? Believe me, all this is possible ... Well whenever possible, I don't book 'em. 'Course that's not always possible. I mean there are some things you can't let go.

(1988: 136)

African American inmates are unjustly subjected to more cell searches and are likely to be denied passes that permit them to move more freely within the institution. To be black in prison means to experience added forms of debasement and humiliation at the hands of the staff and the administration (Thomas, 1991).

To counter the effects of long-term humiliation in prison, African American inmates in the late 1960s and early 1970s established formal organizations that would become a source of support and pride. At that time, the civil rights movement was making its way into correctional institutions. Black nationalism, as a political campaign against racism and oppression, appealed immensely to African American prisoners. Afro-American Societies emerged in many prisons, and their political ideology served to add cohesion among African American 'brothers.'

Precisely the manner by which inmates cope with the stress of prison life has been the interest of a long line of researchers. Studies have found that African American convicts appear to deal with the pressure of institutionalization better than whites; moreover, black prisoners have reported higher levels of self-esteem than their white counterparts (Harris, 1975, 1976). Compared to white convicts, blacks report less psychological stress and claim to feel relatively safe behind bars. One explanation for these findings is that harsh prison life bears a closer resemblance to the inner-city where minority inmates grew up (Jones, 1976). If so, then once again we are reminded of the writings of convict-author George Jackson, who placed prisons on the continuum of humiliations for African Americans.

Soledad Brother

The life and literary work of George Jackson loom large in cultural penology, especially given the notoriety of his legendary book *Soledad Brother* (1970). Jackson emerged as a significant figure in the black militant and prisoners' rights movement in the late 1960s. His story gained national – even international – attention due to a series of incidents at Soledad prison (California). In 1969, corrections officers in Soledad singled out eight white and seven African American inmates to be searched for weapons. Accordingly, they were ordered outdoors to the exercise yard. Soon a fight broke out between the groups of convicts. Although controversy continues to obscure the sequence of events, prisoners said that a tower guard – without warning – fired pinpoint strikes at the African Americans, killing three of them. Inmates accused the officers of contributing to the death of one of the fatally injured prisoners who lay bleeding to death since he was not allowed to be moved for more than 20 minutes, thereby delaying crucial medical attention.

Days following the shooting, a grand jury in Monterey County ruled that the officers' use of force was justifiable. The news from the court fueled anger among convicts at Soledad. Later that day, inmates beat to death a white guard. Following days of investigation, the authorities charged three African American prisoners with murder: Fleeta Drumgo, John Clutchette, and George Jackson. They and their fellow convicts fiercely denied any involvement in the killing of the guard, arguing that the prison authorities handpicked those particular prisoners due to their militant black activism. The case against Drumgo, Clutchette, and Jackson, known as the Soledad Brothers, became widely publicized. Several key political activists, including Angela Davis and other members of the Black Panther Party, waged a campaign of support for the defendants. After a long and very complicated series of events, the charges against Drumgo, Clutchette, and Jackson were eventually dismissed.

George Jackson, a staunch resister of racism, continued his political activism from behind bars. In his critically acclaimed book, *Soledad Brother*, Jackson shared his experience as a black man in American society. When Jackson was 18, he was sentenced to one year to life for stealing $70 from a gas station. He went on to spend more than 12 years in prison, 7½ years in solitary confinement. The letters in his book took on great significance in the context of the militant black movement. His words are characterized as half-poem, half-essay – speaking to more than those to whom he writes.

he did not steal he pointed a gun @ the clerk... which is violent strong-arm Robbery

If I leave here alive, I'll leave nothing behind. They'll never count me among the broken men, but I can't say that I'm normal either. I've been hungry for too long, I've gotten angry too often. I've been lied to and insulted too many times. They've pushed me over the line from which there can be no retreat. I know that they will not be satisfied until they've pushed me out of this existence altogether. I've been the victim of so many racist attacks that I could never relax again ...

I can still smile now, after ten years of blocking knife thrusts, and the pick handles of faceless sadistic pigs, of anticipating and reacting for ten years, seven of them in solitary. I can still smile sometimes, but by the time this thing is over I may not be a nice person. And I just lit my seventy-seventh cigarette of this twenty-one hour day. I'm going to lay down for two or three hours, perhaps I'll sleep ... From Dachau, with love, George.

(Jackson, 1970: 162)

In 1971, a prison guard who said he was trying to escape killed Jackson. Many skeptics question that version of the event, suggesting that he was murdered in retaliation for his prison activism. Jackson's struggle remains an important chapter in a long story of African Americans behind bars.

Hispanics and punishment

The changing ethnic landscape of America reflects continued growth of the Hispanic (or Latino) population, particularly in major cities. Overall, the number of Hispanic Americans has increased 55 percent since 1980, currently constituting 10 percent of the US population. By 2010, Hispanics are expected to represent the largest 'minority' group in the United States, surpassing the number of African Americans. It is important not to lump Hispanics into a single ethnic group given the degree of diversity often found in various geographic regions: Mexican Americans in the Southwest, Cuban Americans in Florida, and Puerto Rican Americans in the Northeast, along with immigrants from Colombia, the Dominican Republic, El Salvador, Nicaragua and Venezuela – just to name a few. Mirroring previous experiences of immigrants, Hispanics face discrimination, most notably in criminal justice. But until recently, few criminologists focused specifically on problems facing Hispanics, opting to sort them conveniently into the minority category with African Americans (Aguirre and Baker, 2000a, 2000b; Marshall, 1997; Sampson and Lauritsen, 1997).

Breaking new ground, Steffensmeier and Demuth (2001) set out to discern the degree of prejudice and hostility toward Hispanics in the form of harsh sentencing, particularly in the war on drugs. Based on Pennsylvania sentencing data, Steffensmeier and Demuth discovered that 'besides the overall more lenient treatment of white defendants, our main finding is that Hispanic defendants are the defendant subgroup most at risk to receive the harshest penalty' (2001: 145; see also De Jesus-Torrez, 2000; Diaz-Cotto, 2000, 1998; Muñoz, 2000).

While addressing the significance of the previously mentioned 'focal concerns' theory, Steffensmeier and Demuth (2001) expand their interpretation to include problems of cultural assimilation. In some respects, Steffensmeier and Demuth conclude that Hispanics may be even more disadvantaged than their black counterparts. First, Hispanics, much like urban African Americans, struggle against the effects of poverty, unemployment, poor education, and single-parent families (Healey, 1995; Tarver *et al.*, 2002). Second, Hispanics commonly are stereotyped as lazy, irresponsible, and prone to crime and gang activity (Alvarez, 2000; Rodriguez, 2002).

Third, due to such negative stereotyping, Hispanics are targets in ambitious law-enforcement campaigns, namely the war on drugs (Meeker *et al.*, 2000; Portillos, 2002). Fourth, the expanding Hispanic population has been met with resistance by dominant white groups who perceive them as a social threat – competing for jobs, challenging the primacy of the English language, and straining the welfare system (Mata and Herrerias, 2002; Perry, 2000; Welch, 2002b). Together, those factors contribute to an understanding of the social threat hypothesis, in which relatively large increases in the Hispanic population over a relatively short period of time produce social and economic conflict with dominant (white) groups who are influential in intensifying greater social control such as tougher criminal justice sanctions (Bontrager *et al.*, 2005; Crawford *et al.*, 1998; Keen and Jacobs, 2009).

As noted previously, there were a total of 313,100 Hispanics prisoners nationwide by year end 2008. The imprisonment rate for Hispanic males (1,200) is dramatically lower than for black males (3,161) but more than double that of white males (487). Similarly, Hispanic women were incarcerated at a rate of 75, compared to black females (149) and white females (50) (see Table 8.1). Whereas the rate of imprisonment for Hispanic males has stayed relatively constant since year 2000, it has increased for Hispanic women (see Table 8.2). Also since 2000, the number of Hispanic prisoners sentenced for violent offenses increased 77 percent, followed by drug violations (15 percent) and property crimes (6 percent) (see Table 8.3; Sabol *et al.*, 2008; see Nielsen *et al.*, 2005; Martinez and Valenzuela, 2006).

White convicts

Although whites dominate the staff and administration of prisons, they represent the numerical minority among inmates. Whites are often outnumbered by the combined groupings of African Americans and Hispanics (Sabol *et al.*, 2009). An illustration of how being a 'numerical minority' adversely affecting white inmates has been reported at Rikers Island in New York City. In some instances, white inmates are not allowed to use telephones that are designated by African American as 'black' phones. For some white inmates, they must 'get in good' with the Hispanic prisoners in order to be able to use their phones. Not surprisingly, many white inmates resent being hassled by African American inmates. In the following passage, a white prisoner explains both his frustration and respect for African American inmates:

They think they're so superior and they push you around all the time. Like in the dining hall. If I was late and tryin' to catch up with a buddy and cut in front of one of them, I'd probably get piped. But they cut in front of white men all the time and nothin happens ... It's the same in the wings. The tier I'm on used to be all white. Now it's 50-50 and it ain't safe for a white to walk along it. If he does he better walk quick and keep his eyes open ... In here I got to hate 'em even more than I did ... You gotta respect 'em as men, though. They stand up for what they think is right and they won't back down. They can't be bullied. They ain't afraid to be counted. I hate 'em but I respect 'em, ya know? ... The only way I can see to make it better is to have two joints, one for them and one for us.

(Carroll, 1988: 147)

White convicts occasionally are placed in situations in which the guards maliciously fuel racial tensions, Jack Abbott, in his book *In the Belly of the Beast*, shares his experiences in prison. 'At Leavenworth and Atlanta, I was always thrown into all-black cells ... The idea was to get me to be attacked by blacks. The idea was to get me to hate blacks. I personally have never had any problems with them ... This is because I am known among them. But my case is exceptional, and as a rule whites are turned into active racists by this method' (Abbott, 1981: 182).

It has been reported that imprisonment may be more painful for whites than minorities, as noted by measures of psychological distress and suicide attempts (see Chapter 9). These findings suggest that white prisoners tend to internalize their pain and suffering by turning their frustration toward themselves rather than at the system (Carroll, 1990; Johnson, 1976). 'The stress for whites does not seem to be related to any single focal concern. Like Hispanics, white inmates show great concern for their separation from significant others, and like blacks, a goodly number see themselves as victims of unjust treatment' (Carroll, 1990: 518). As is the case in the free world, 'whiteness' among white prisoners lacks a clear consciousness or political ideology. Due to the lack of widespread discrimination against whites in society, there does not seem to be a white 'experience' in the same way that minorities have a 'black' or 'Hispanic' experience (see Allen, 1997; Garner, 2007; Webster, 2009).

In prison, white inmates certainly form cliques but they are generally not as cohesive as African American or Hispanic groups, due in part to the lack of cultural bonding usually found among minorities (see Jacobs, 1977). One exception to the observation that whites do not bond in ways that minorities do has been the emergence of white counter-organizations. In reaction to a sense of victimization by minority inmates, or simply a result of a sense of racial superiority – or both – groups like the White Aryan Nation (or Aryan Brotherhood), the Ku Klux Klan, and the American Nazi Party have emerged in some prisons, particularly in California, Illinois, and Texas (see Chapter 9).

By the year 2008, there were a total of 591,900 white prisoners nationwide. The incarceration rates for white males (487) and for white females (50) are the lowest of all categories of race and gender (see Table 8.1). Since 2000, those rates have steadily increased: for white males from 449 to 487 and for white females from 34 to 50 (see Table 8.2). The number of white prisoners sentenced for property offenses since 2000 increased 47 percent, followed by violent offenses (40 percent), and drug offenses (37 percent) (see Table 8.3; Sabol *et al.*, 2008)

WORKING IN CORRECTIONS

Correctional Officers of Color

Recognizing that correctional work has traditionally been the occupational domain of white males, minority prison officers often face various forms of racism and discrimination. In his early research on the topic, Ben Crouch (1991) explains that as minorities sought employment in corrections in the late 1960s, the CO force became increasingly fragmented. During this transition from a predominantly white custodial staff to a more racially mixed one, white officers became suspicious of African American officers. Similarly, John Irwin (1977) found that black COs were viewed by white staff as 'pro-prisoner' and therefore less trustworthy. Adding to an already tense work atmosphere, white officers have expressed hostility toward African American officers while white prison administrators rarely promote blacks into supervisory positions, subjecting them to both individual and institutional racism.

Minorities working in corrections have challenged institutional racism. For example, in the New York Department of Corrections, African American correctional officers filed a suit in 1972 against the administration for discrimination in the promotional process. Consequently, a quota system was established – only to be challenged by white officers claiming reverse discrimination. The courts then dismantled the quota system, but faulted the Department of Corrections for the lack of upward mobility for black officers (Jacobs and Zimmer, 1983).

Later, in 2001, a corrections officer at Rikers Island Jail Complex in New York City, Billy M. Jones, filed a $7.5 million lawsuit against the Department of Corrections (DOC) claiming that it had discriminated against him by subjecting him to a hostile work environment. In reviewing the case, a Manhattan federal court judge found that Jones's suit did indeed have merit and recommended that it go to trial. Jones described in detail numerous incidents, including virulent racial slurs and comments by fellow corrections officers. In one particular incident, a dead fish was left on the desk of an African American officer who had complained about racist graffiti written in the officers' log book and a message, 'I hate niggers,' scrawled on the wall of the officers' restroom (Noel, 2001: 52). In another incident, other officers shot at windows of cars belonging to African American officers with BBs, allegedly. In light of those humiliating and physically threatening incidents, Jones 'described an environment that a reasonable person would find hostile or abusive' (Noel, 2001: 52). The judge concluded that the DOC 'itself should shoulder the blame because the agency repeatedly ignored Jones' complaints about "hostile incidents" by his colleagues' (Noel, 2001: 52).

Racism against corrections employees goes beyond the frontline staff; it also surfaces at the higher levels of administration. A case in point is Robert Matthews. In addition to being the youngest administrator (at age 33) to be appointed warden in the history of the Federal Bureau of Prisons, he is also the first African American to be put in charge of Leavenworth Penitentiary. Despite his ambition and achievements in the Federal Bureau of Prisons, Matthews still faced racial hostility, especially from many of the white officers who reported to him. In a local bar near the penitentiary where guards spent their free time, racial slurs remained a common feature of conversation. 'A white guard would later recall a conversation that took place before Matthews reported to work. "There is nothing wrong with niggers," one guard said. "In fact, I think everyone should own a few of them!" When the laughing ended, he added, "But work for a nigger warden? Holy shit, what's the bureau coming to?"' (Earley, 1992: 46).

In response to individual and institutional racism, some correctional systems have improved their efforts to recruit and promote minority officers. 'The primary needs are for a racially and ethnically integrated staff to serve as a model of effective cooperation, to promote a climate that encourages interracial understanding, and to ensure that all prisoners are defined and treated as equals' (Carroll, 1990: 523; see also Camp *et al.*, 2001; Chaires and Lentz, 2001; McShane, 2000).

MINORITY WOMEN IN CORRECTIONS

As discussed in Chapter 6, women of color in the criminal justice system, as well as in society, must contend with the adverse effects of both racism and sexism. Moreover, since minority women are also more likely to live in poverty, they must contend with the harsh realities of classism as well.

> Class-oppressed men, whether they are white or black, have privileges afforded them as men in a sexist society. Similarly, class-oppressed whites, whether they are men or women, have privileges afforded them as whites in a racist society … Those who are poor, black, and female have all the forces of classism, racism, and sexism bearing down on them.
>
> (Mantsios, 1988: 66–7, quoted in Simpson, 1991: 115)

Still, the plight of minority women often is overlooked. Even mainstream feminists have neglected concerns of minority women largely because the women's movement has traditionally focused on a predominantly white, middle-class, and suburban agenda. As noted previously, 'many women of color see the women's liberation movement as hopelessly white and middle class, immune to their concerns' (Simpson, 1989: 608). In an effort to remedy that neglect, alternative approaches to feminism set out to enhance awareness and sensitivity toward minority women, revealing further the complex interplay of gender, class, and race oppression (Bosworth and Flavin, 2007; Collins, 1986; Davis, 1989, 1981).

So as to deepen our understanding of race, gender, and class, some criminologists have turned critical attention to women minorities in the criminal justice system. Hill and Crawford, for instance, explored racial differences among female offenders and found that 'the unique position of black women in the structure of power relations in society has profound effects not shared by their white counterparts' (1990: 621). Consequently, their research suggests that due to an array of socioeconomic factors (e.g. poor education, unemployment, and low income), African American women are more likely than white females to turn to street crime out of a sense of survival (e.g. drug trafficking and prostitution) (see Johnson, 2003; Handler and Hasenfeld, 2007).

In terms of punishment, a familiar scenario surrounding race and sentencing emerges. In the 1980s as the national economy was polarizing, Rosenbaum compared the juvenile and adult criminal histories between African American and white female offenders in California. She found 'significant differences did emerge in the sentences received as adults. Black women received more severe sentences as adults than did the white, Asian, or Latino women' (1988: 125). Rosenbaum concludes that her study identified 'clear-cut discrimination' against African American women. Not only were those women more likely to be incarcerated, but they were also sentenced to more time both in jail and/or prison and on probation' (1988: 135). As discussed previously, it is difficult to isolate such variables as race and social class since they overlap considerably. Sentencing generally reflects discrimination against the poor as well as against minorities (Barak *et al.*, 2001; see Mann, 1989, 1993; Mann and Zatz, 2002).

MINORITIES IN JUVENILE JUSTICE

Research on minorities in juvenile justice has consistently confirmed patterns that whites are treated more leniently than African Americans. Studies dating back to the 1970s found that minority (and lower-income) youths were more likely to be committed to state institutions than were whites, regardless of their offense (Chiricos *et al.*, 1972; Jankovic, 1977). This form of discrimination against minority youth is considered typical throughout the criminal justice system. Even with control of additional variables, race has emerged as a powerful predictor of arrest, incarceration, and release among minority youths (Crutchfield *et al.*, 1994). Other investigations also have found that African American youths were more likely to be recommended for formal processing, referred to court, adjudicated delinquent, and given harsher dispositions than comparable white offenders (Bishop and Frazier, 1988; Rosenbaum, 1988; Tollet and Close, 1991).

As noted in Chapter 7, minority youth, especially African Americans, are overrepresented at all stages of the juvenile justice system, including all juvenile arrests, juvenile arrests for violent crime, delinquency cases involving detention, and cases judicially waived to criminal court. As Sickmund (2004) reveals, more than six in ten juvenile offenders in residential placement were minority youth. Nearly two-thirds (65 percent) of juvenile offenders in placement in public facilities were minority youth and in private facilities the proportion of minority youth was just over half (55 percent). Nationally, custody rates were highest for blacks (see Table 8.5).

CRITICAL ANALYSIS OF DATA

With regard to Table 8.5, which five states reported the highest figures for American Indian juveniles? Is there a regional pattern?

Critical attention needs to be turned to the various decision points in the juvenile justice system so as to pinpoint where minority overrepresentation exists. In 2002, the Juvenile Justice and Delinquency Prevention (JJDP) Act 'broadened the concept of disproportionate minority confinement to encompass disproportionate minority contact at all stages of the system' (Sickmund, 2004: 12). According to the JJDP Act, each state had to determine the extent of the problem and demonstrate measures to reduce it where it exists. As Figure 8.3 indicates, black juveniles are overrepresented at all stages of the juvenile justice

Table 8.5 For every 100,000 non-Hispanic black juveniles living in the US, 1,004 were in a residential placement facility on October 27, 1999 – the rate was 485 for Hispanics and 212 for non-Hispanic whites

State of offense	Custody rate (per 100,000)					State of offense	Custody rate (per 100,000)				
	White	Black	Hispanic	American Indian	Asian		White	Black	Hispanic	American Indian	Asian
U.S. total	212	1,004	485	632	182	Missouri	146	554	161	265	145
Alabama	208	588	249	314	93	Montana	148	1,463	614	652	704
Alaska	281	612	421	799	290	Nebraska	220	1,552	744	1,648	290
Arizona	234	957	473	293	125	Nevada	305	1,019	312	511	249
Arkansas	139	575	137	0	256	New Hampshire	150	1,278	578	0	0
California	269	1,666	623	612	238	New Jersey	70	1,108	327	0	6
Colorado	257	1,436	719	789	223	New Mexico	211	1,011	520	257	111
Connecticut	160	2,143	1,243	518	196	New York	169	1,119	143	466	34
Delaware	203	1,143	304	0	0	North Carolina	123	466	152	238	123
Dist. of Columbia	173	855	369	0	0	North Dakota	204	1,136	544	1,187	847
Florida	306	964	200	202	87	Ohio	221	1,038	430	112	75
Georgia	273	878	163	861	72	Oklahoma	194	821	297	343	56
Hawaii	39	87	90	0	121	Oregon	353	1,689	478	1,074	270
Idaho	203	871	344	278	173	Pennsylvania	123	1,230	902	154	249
Illinois	152	1,005	271	590	37	Rhode Island	155	1,363	680	0	474
Indiana	280	1,260	370	168	46	South Carolina	244	772	50	293	421
Iowa	240	1,726	545	1,231	465	South Dakota	436	2,908	1,091	1,653	1,235
Kansas	239	1,691	642	612	295	Tennessee	170	576	132	0	91
Kentucky	192	1,030	133	0	182	Texas	204	965	391	140	96
Louisiana	223	1,127	290	249	139	Utah	267	1,043	692	946	366
Maine	166	390	272	332	0	Vermont	93	698	0	0	0
Maryland	136	575	131	0	12	Virginia	225	1,024	323	166	104
Massachusetts	93	648	806	0	232	Washington	232	1,507	323	827	249
Michigan	243	1,058	1,112	428	215	West Virginia	166	1,060	251	0	292
Minnesota	183	1,504	630	1,783	459	Wisconsin	164	1,965	725	845	398
Mississippi	118	300	3,454	0	113	Wyoming	396	2,752	847	939	482

- In half of the states, the ratio of the minority custody rate to the nonminority white custody rate exceeded 3.3 to 1. In four states (Connecticut, New Jersey, Pennsylvania, and Wisconsin), the ratio of minority to nonminority rates exceeded 8 to 1.

- In Florida, Idaho, Maine, Nevada, Oregon, and Vermont, the ratio of minority to nonminority rates was less than 2 to 1.

Note: The custody rate is the number of juvenile offenders in residential placement on October 27, 1999, per 100,000 juveniles age 10 through the upper age of original juvenile court jurisdiction in each state. U.S. total includes 2,645 juvenile offenders in private facilities for whom state of offense was not reported and 174 juvenile offenders in tribal facilities. Minorities include blacks, Hispanics, American Indians, Asians/Pacific Islanders, and those identified as 'other race.'

Source: Sickmund (2004).

Ratio of minority custody rate to non-minoritywhite custody rate

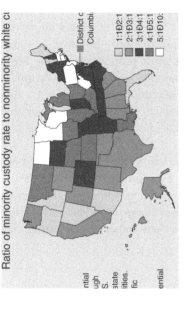

Ratio of minority custody rate to nonminority white cu

District c
Columbi

1:1–2:1
2:1–3:1
3:1–4:1
4:1–5:1
5:1–10:

system compared with their proportion in the population. 'Research also suggests that differences in the offending rates of white and minority youth cannot explain the minority overrepresentation in arrest, conviction, and incarceration counts' (Snyder and Sickmund, 1999: 191).

Racial and ethnic effects can be found at any stage of processing within the juvenile justice system. Across numerous jurisdictions, however, a substantial volume of research suggests that disparity is most pronounced at the beginning stages. The greatest disparity between majority and minority youth court processing outcomes occurs at intake and detention decision points. Research also suggests that when racial/ethnic differences are identified, they tend to accumulate as youth are processed through the justice system (Feld, 1999; Snyder and Sickmund, 1999).

Long-term research reveals substantial variation across rural, suburban, and urban areas. Introducing the concept 'justice by geography,' Feld (1999) offers evidence of significant differences in outcome depending on the jurisdiction in which the youth is processed. For instance, cases in urban jurisdictions are more likely to receive severe outcomes at various stages of processing than are

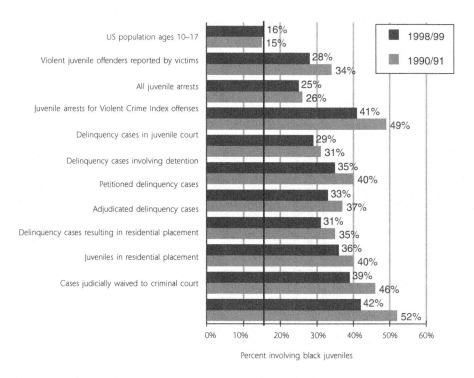

■ Nationally, for all stages of juvenile justice system processing, the black proportion was smaller in 1998/99 than in 1990/91.

Figure 8.3   Black juveniles are overrepresented at all stages of the juvenile justice system compared with their proportion in the populace.

Source: Sickmund (2004: 12).

cases in non-urban areas. Since minority populations are concentrated in urban areas, that effect may work to the disadvantage of minority youth and result in greater overrepresentation (Sickmund, 2004; Snyder and Sickmund, 1999). More importantly, the type of neighborhood in which the juvenile resides has a greater impact on the likelihood of delinquency than do racial characteristics. 'African-Americans living in nondisadvantaged areas do not have higher rates of delinquency than whites living in nondisadvantaged areas' (OJJDP, 1994: 21).

In their work, Tollet and Close (1991) cite two reasons to explain why a disproportionate increase in minorities in the juvenile justice system should concern us. First, extensive involvement in the system can have enduring effects on youths. Second, those difficulties can further undermine their chances of completing school, getting good jobs, and developing into successful, law-abiding citizens. 'Given the paucity of opportunities already faced by many minority youth due to social, economic, and political circumstances, they can ill afford the additional stigma associated with criminal justice intervention' (p. 86; see Weenink, 2009).

CULTURAL PENOLOGY

Moral Panic Over Wilding: Manufacture of Menace in the Media

As discussed in the previous chapter, the concept of moral panic – a turbulent reaction to a social problem – has helped criminologists interpret the social construction of certain forms of crimes. Indeed, the media, in an effort to discover new types of menace, tend to publicize exaggerated claims of dangers posed by adolescents. Likewise, government and criminal justice officials further contribute to moral panic by relying on inflammatory rhetoric used to justify enhanced police powers and greater investment in the traditional criminal justice apparatus. With that phenomenon in mind, researchers set out to examine the moral panic emerging in New York City in 1989 after a young woman, while jogging in Central Park, was attacked and raped – reportedly by seven youths. The tragic event popularly became known as wilding, a stylized term describing sexual violence committed by a group of urban teenagers. As a newly discovered menace to public safety, wilding consumed the media and also captured the attention of politicians and members of the local criminal justice establishment who campaigned for tougher measures in dealing with youth violence (Welch et al., 2002a, 2002b).

Whereas a common view of moral panic suggests that pseudo-disasters quickly burst into formation then dissipate, Welch et al. (2002, 2004) stress its lingering effects. Moral panic over wilding reinforces racial biases prevalent in criminal stereotypes, particularly the popular perception that young black (and Latino) males constitute a dangerous class. Compounded by sensationalistic news coverage on wilding, along with carjacking, gang banging, and other stylized forms of lawlessness associated with urban teens, minority youth remain a lightning rod for public fear, anger, and anxiety over impending social disorder, all of which contribute to more law-and-order campaigns. It is important to note that moral panic often touches on bona fide social ills. Still, rather than enlightening the public toward an informed understanding of the problem – in this case, youth violence – the media and politicians pander to popular fear, resulting in renewed hostility toward black and Latino males.

As is typically the case in moral panic, the source of immediate threat is discovered by the media in its search for an original twist to a news story. Customarily, the media convey the newness of a breaking story in the form of an expression, word, or phrase; indeed, wilding captured the public's imagination about crime, producing an amplified fear of sexual violence. Three days after the April 19, 1989, attack on the Central Park jogger, the *New York Times* reported:

> The youths who raped and savagely beat a young investment banker in Central Park on Wednesday night were part of a loosely organized gang of 32 schoolboys whose random, motiveless assaults terrorized at least eight other people over nearly two hours, senior police investigators said yesterday.
>
> Chief of Detectives Robert Colangelo, who said the attacks appeared unrelated to money, race, drugs or alcohol, said that some of the 20 youths brought into questioning had told investigators that the crime spree was the product of a pastime called 'wilding.'
>
> (Pitt, 1989: 1)

As if details of the brutal attack were not sufficient to drive the story, the media relied on the word wilding for purposes of news sensationalism; conveniently, legal terminology (i.e. rape, assault, and attempted murder) was replaced by inflammatory language imbued with moral panic. Conforming to the classic genesis of moral panic, law enforcement officials also participated in the initial reification of the term. The chief of detectives not only described wilding as a 'pastime' for the suspects but contributed to its invention by suggesting that the activity was a new form of menace: '"It's not a term that we in the police had heard before," the chief said, noting that the police were unaware of any similar incidents in the park recently' (Pitt, 1989: 1).

As a storytelling institution, the media relied on the dramatic style of infotainment in its coverage of the Central Park jogger attack. Moreover, the story's repetition reinforced popular notions of violence, victimization, and criminal stereotypes, all of which fueled moral panic. Consider the following features of the criminal event. The attack occurred in New York City's Central Park, a city and a public space that has been mythologized with a notorious reputation for predatory violence. The victim was a white female whose physical attributes, social status, and personal biography were injected into virtually every media account. She was described as young, beautiful, and educated as well as a Manhattan investment banker (Barth, 1989: 8). Perhaps adding to the story's enduring level of interest, the victim remained anonymous.

Seven youths were charged as adults with rape, assault, and attempted murder. Eventually, charges against one suspect were dropped. Another youth turned state witness as part of a plea bargain and pled guilty to one count of robbery (for an earlier incident, not in connection to the rape incident); all other charges against him were dropped (Wolff, 1989). Although being acquitted of attempted murder, three youths were convicted of first-degree rape and first-degree assault and sentenced to maximum juvenile prison terms of five to ten years (Sachar, 1990). A sixth youth was convicted of attempted murder and rape; although 14 years old at the time of the crime, he was sentenced to a maximum five- to ten-year prison term as a juvenile. Finally, the seventh defendant was acquitted of attempted murder and rape but convicted of assault, riot, and sexual abuse and sentenced to 8½ to 26 years in prison (Phillips *et al.*, 1990).

The trial may have put to rest the legal concerns of the crime, but in the public consciousness, a new form of menace had been discovered. Wilding had been added to a growing roster of crimes associated with urban culture, along with mugging, looting, gang banging, drive-by shootings, and carjacking. Curiously though, the term wilding has its roots in contemporary music and urban culture, specifically Tone-Loc's rap remake of the 1960s, pop tune *Wild Thing*. It is widely believed that wilding is an abbreviated pronunciation of 'wild thing.' Still, music critic Dave Marsh doubts the suspects ever used the term to describe the attack on the Central Park jogger: 'In fact, it's a fantasy, dreamed up in a reporter's shack or a precinct house. Nobody has ever heard kids use anything like that phrase; you can be sure you won't hear it in any of the taped confessions in the trial' (Marsh, 1990: 50). Marsh contends that the term wilding was invented as a reaction to anti-hip-hop hysteria. '"Wilding" retains its forceful currency because here in New York, cradle of rap and hip hop though it is, the powers-that-be don't approve of that culture' (Marsh, 1990: 50). Marsh joins many social commentators who condemn the use of the word wilding to describe the attack on the Central Park jogger because it trivializes the brutal nature of the offense and contributes to racial tension (Gates, 1990).

The popular use of buzzwords such as wilding, mugging, looting, gang banging, drive-by shootings, and carjacking generally are racially biased because they are used to describe black (and Latino) lawbreakers more so than white offenders. Although initially introduced by the media to stylize its infotainment, the term wilding made a greater impact on society and culture by becoming another synonym for youth violence, contributing to fear of crime and moral panic. Not only does youth violence have a new name, wilding, it also has a face, typically that of young black (and Latino) males residing in urban centers. As a complex phenomenon, the invention of wilding feeds moral panic by drawing on racial criminal stereotypes. Whereas much of the pioneering work on moral panic emphasized its implications to the political economy, nowadays that facet of the paradigm tends to be neglected in contemporary scholarship. Returning to that earlier theme, Welch *et al.* (2002a, 2002b) demonstrate that moral panic over youth violence symbolizes not only a threat to society at large but also to a prevailing political economy that thrives on racial and economic inequality.

In 2002, 13 years after the trial, a Manhattan judge threw out the convictions of the five young men sentenced to prison for the attack on the Central Park jogger. Following an unusual sequence of events, Judge Charles T. Tejada granted recent motions made by defense attorneys and the Manhattan district attorney to vacate all convictions in light of new evidence identifying another man, Matias Reyes, as the lone attacker. Reyes, a convicted murderer and rapist serving time for another offense, stepped forward in January 2002 claiming that he, and he alone, violently raped the Central Park jogger. Matching DNA evidence corroborated Reyes's testimony. The decision to vacate the convictions of the young men, who had completed their prison terms and were then in their mid-twenties, raises grave questions about their confessions and police interrogation tactics (Saulny, 2002b; see Chancer, 2005a, 2005b; Cole, 2009).

NATIVE AMERICANS IN CRIMINAL JUSTICE

Compared to a growing criminological literature on race and ethnicity, few studies have explored the Native Americans (American Indians) in the context of the criminal justice system. Some researchers suspect that such neglect is due to the unique legal status of Native Americans and their relationship with the federal government (Zatz *et al.*, 1991). Indeed, Native Americans' involvement in the criminal justice system is complicated by jurisdictional and cultural considerations (Archambeault, 2003; Nielsen, 2000; Nielsen and Silverman, 1996).

Three levels of government may process tribe members who are involved in criminal cases: the tribe, the state, and the federal government. Several factors determine the jurisdiction, including the type of crime, whether it occurred on or off a reservation, and whether Indians or non-Indians were involved (Deloria and Lytle, 1983). A major difference exists between the tribal and governmental legal systems; perhaps most importantly, tribal proceedings are often informal whereas the government legal system follows highly formal procedures. Not surprisingly, problems arise when American Indians are subject to both systems, since rules and courtroom norms differ in each legal setting. Compounding matters, differences also exist among tribes that favor their own system of justice and conflict resolution (Nielsen, 2000; Melton, 2002).

Currently, the federal government recognizes more than 300 tribes, each relying on different court processing and sentencing. In addition, tribes possess limited sovereignty and the federal government restricts penalties imposed in

Figure 8.4   Former AIM activist Leonard Peltier, a Chippewa-Lakota Indian serving a life sentence for the murder of two FBI agents he maintains he didn't commit, writing a letter as he sits on his bunk next to the sink and toilet in his cell at Leavenworth Penitentiary, KS.

Photo by Taro Yamasaki/Time Life Pictures/Getty Images.

tribal courts to one year in jail and/or a $5,000 fine. Numerous other differences exist between tribal courts and government courts. Whereas government courts attempt to determine whether the defendant is guilty, tribal courts often mediate cases to restore harmonious relations within the tribe. For Native Americans, incarceration is not a common method of punishment. Many tribes often assign penalties in the form of restitution and compensation, as well as social and religious sanctions (Melton, 2002).

Generally, American Indians hold negative attitudes toward local police and government courts due in large part to perceived (and actual) injustices against tribal members processed through the government's system. Lujan (1990) found such views to be especially pronounced among the Navajo and Pueblo, who refer to government courts as foreign. In light of cultural differences, American Indians often experience confusion when appearing in government courts; for instance, it is not uncommon for some Indian defendants to plead guilty to a charge without adequate legal counsel. Zatz *et al.* (1991: 104) reveal other considerations that affect American Indians in government courts:

- unfamiliarity and uncomfortableness with the court and its ambience, including its physical structure and the formality of its rituals;
- lack of confidence in receiving a fair trial, particularly given the extreme unlikelihood of having a jury of peers (i.e. other Indians);
- uncertainty of their ability to communicate what they see as the relevant aspects of their case, especially to non-Indian defense attorneys;
- desire to get the process over with as soon as possible.

In terms of their treatment in the criminal justice system, American Indians are subject to harsher penalties than non-Indians. The bias against Indians is particularly apparent in arrest decisions, types of sentences, and parole decisions (Melton, 2002). Many overlapping social issues shape further the experiences of Indians in the criminal justice system. In addition to living under poverty-stricken conditions, many Indians also suffer from alcoholism. Local police therefore often rely on arrest to socially control public drunkenness.

The Native American general crime rate stands at about 25 percent higher than that of whites, but much lower than that of African Americans. In terms of violent offenses, Native Americans stood below the rates for the total US population, and for property crimes they ranked above the white population but below African Americans. More significantly, Native Americans were overrepresented in alcohol-related offenses (e.g. public intoxication, driving under the influence) but underrepresented in drug violations. Biases against Native Americans have also been found in sentencing. Native Americans were more likely to serve prison sentences than non-Indians who were convicted of the same offenses. Indians also tend to serve longer sentences prior to release on parole than non-Indians (Nielsen, 2000). Similar patterns exist for Native American women and juveniles. Overall, they are overrepresented in prison and jails where they are commonly denied access to spiritual counseling, ceremonies, and culturally sensitive substance abuse treatment programs (Nielsen and Silverman, 1996; Silverman, 1996).

Zatz et al (1991) identify several explanations for the harsh treatment of American Indians in the criminal justice system. First, Native Americans are subjected to racist stereotypes and labeling. For example, they may be viewed by non-Native Americans as 'drunken Indians' or 'uncivilized savages' (Lujan, 2002; Riding In, 2002). Second, some criminal justice officials actually believe that they are doing Indian defendants a favor by jailing them since the living conditions on the reservations are so adverse. That form of paternalism is especially pronounced in incidents whereby intoxicated Indians are removed from the street 'for their own good' because it gives them a chance to sober up. A third consideration involves language and cultural factors in government courts that rely on formal and, at times, confusing legal terms and procedures.

Finally, efforts to end discrimination against Native Americans must address a host of social problems that contribute to the plight of Indians in American society, such as poverty, unemployment, alcoholism, and drug abuse (Tarver et al., 2002). Additionally, 'it also must be recognized that the paternalism on the part of the Federal government towards the American Indian population has led to a loss of cultural identity, including religion, lifestyle, and governance' (Zatz et al., 1991; see also Blagg, 2008; Bracken et al., 2009).

Modern-day banishment of Native Americans

Adrian Guthrie and Simon Roberts, both 17 years old, were convicted of robbing and beating a pizza deliveryman in Alaska. Since the youths were American Indians – members of the Tlingit tribe – the state court, after lengthy considerations, conferred the case to a tribal panel, marking the first time a state court has conferred a criminal case to a tribal court (*New York Times*, 1994a). Although Guthrie and Roberts were first-time offenders, they still faced prison terms of three to five years because of the gravity of their offenses. The youths severely beat their victim, Tim Whittlesey, with a baseball bat, resulting in permanent damage to his hearing and eyesight.

In an unusual turn of events, the tribal panel decided not to incarcerate Guthrie and Roberts; instead, the two youths were sentenced to banishment. It was said that banishment was a traditional form of punishment, though rarely used in modern times. For 18 months, the youths would be banished to separate uninhabited islands in a southeast Alaskan archipelago. There they would be denied modern conveniences and would be forced to cut and notch logs which would be sent to the mainland to be used as construction materials.

As their banishment drew national attention and mainstream support, an array of opponents challenged the punishment. State officials argued that banishment would violate child welfare laws. Forestry officials said the youths could not cut trees without tribal and federal permits. Even more interesting was the assertion by members of the Tlingit tribe that there was no such thing as banishment in their culture.

CONCLUSION

This chapter explores issues concerning minorities in criminal justice and corrections. Although racism and discrimination remain at the center of the discussion, other problems such as classism are also examined. A major objective of the chapter is to reveal the harsh reality of institutional racism as it persists in American society. The corrosive effects of racism, together with those of classism, offer important implications for criminal justice and social policy.

Over the past few decades, Marc Mauer of the Sentencing Project has studied young African American men and their involvement in the criminal justice system. Here his findings are summarized alongside several related issues.

- *Impact on the life prospects for African American males.* Because the effects of criminal justice involvement include potentially lifelong forms of stigma, the likelihood persists that the future life prospects of young African American males are seriously hampered. Thus 'we risk the possibility of writing off an entire generation of black men from having the opportunity to lead productive lives in our society' (Mauer, 1990: 4, 1999).
- *Impact on the African American community.* At a time when young adults are beginning families, learning constructive life skills, and forming careers, the African American community becomes more debilitated because one-fourth of its young male adults are under the control of the criminal justice system. Given that more young African Americans are in the criminal justice system than in college, the long-lasting impact on the African American community is evident.

- *Failure of the get-tough approach to crime control.* Mauer asserts that the get-tough-on-crime campaign has been an experiment, and a failed one at that. 'Yet even with a tripling of the prison population since 1973, at tremendous financial cost, victimization rates since that time have declined less than 5 percent' (Mauer, 1990, 1999).

- *Implications for the war on drugs.* Not only does the war on drugs represent a law enforcement attempt to control a much larger social problem, but it also targets disproportionately minorities and the poor, resulting in higher incarceration rates for African Americans and Hispanics than for whites. Mauer also points to the current imbalance of law enforcement versus treatment, and notes: 'A continued emphasis on law enforcement at the expense of prevention and treatment has little hope for long-term results' (1990: 5, 1999).

- *Strategies for more effective criminal justice policies and programs.* Mauer proposes diversion programs that offset the negative effects of being processed in the criminal justice system while at the same time dispensing punishment and reducing recidivism. Accordingly, the use of jails and prisons should be reserved as sanctions of last resort.

- *The need for a broad approach to crime and crime control.* 'The problem of crime is one that cannot be solved entirely by the criminal justice system. Even with the most resourceful police, prosecutors, judges, and corrections officials, the criminal justice system is designed to be only a reactive system, not one of prevention' (Mauer, 1990: 6, 1999). A broad approach to crime and crime control addresses those social factors, which directly and indirectly affect crime, such as unemployment, poverty, and substance abuse.

As scholarly work on minorities in the criminal justice system continues, it is recommended that further critiques on race and ethnicity be situated in the context of social class (Markowitz and Jones-Brown, 2001; Miller, 2008; Onwudiwe and Lynch, 2000; Welch, 1995c, 1999a). Moreover, other racial and ethnic groups, namely Asians and Pacific Islanders, also deserve the attention of criminologists (Johnson and Betsinger, 2009; Mann *et al.*, 2007; Perry, 2000; Tarver *et al.*, 2002).

SUMMARY

In this chapter, various issues related to minorities in criminal justice and corrections are discussed in detail. Both individual and institutional racism are addressed as they emerge at the various stages of the criminal justice system: arrest, detention, sentencing, incarceration, and parole. In addition to acknowledging several historical considerations of minorities in corrections, the chapter also presents the contemporary debate over race and the criminal justice system. Although experts on both sides of the argument offer diverse views as to the form and degree of racial discrimination in the criminal justice system, more research is needed to clarify the relationship between race and punishment alongside social class. Discussion also explores the prison life of minorities, noting that African American and Hispanic inmates tend to place their racial and ethnic identities at the forefront of the prison experience. The chapter also brings to light the unique problems facing minority women, juveniles, and Native Americans while incarcerated.

REVIEW QUESTIONS

1 What are the main points in the debate over whether the criminal justice system is racist?
2 What have researchers found in studying racial discrimination at each stage of the criminal justice system?
3 How have political forces, especially the civil rights movement, shaped the prison experience for African American inmates?
4 How is the involvement of Native Americans in the criminal justice system complicated by jurisdictional and cultural considerations?
5 What are the recommendations of Marc Mauer for social and criminal justice policies as they affect young African American men?

RECOMMENDED READINGS

Barak, G., Flavin, J. M. and Leighton, P. S. (2001) *Class, Race, Gender, and Crime: Social Realities of Justice in America*. Los Angeles: Roxbury.

Mann, C. R., Zatz, M. and Rodriguez, N. (2007) *Images of Color, Images of Crime*. New York: Oxford University Press.

Markowitz, M. and Jones-Brown, D. D. (2001) *The System in Black and White: Exploring the Connections between Race, Crime, and Justice*. Westport, CT: Praeger.

Miller, L. (2008) *The Perils of Federalism: Race, Poverty, and the Politics of Crime Control*. New York: Oxford University Press.

Russell, K. (1998) *The Color of Crime: Racial Hoaxes, White Fear, Black Protectionism, Police Aggression, and Other Microaggressions*. New York: New York University Press.

PART III PENAL VIOLENCE

CHAPTER 9

Assaults and Riots

It is ironic that the most violent individuals in society, once apprehended and convicted, are isolated within settings where violence is especially commonplace
(Frank J. Porporino)

Prison seems to either produce or reinforce the very behavior it is supposed to correct
(John Lowman and Brian MacLean)

LEARNING OBJECTIVES

After studying this chapter, you should be able to answer the following questions:

1 What are the goals and motives of prison violence?
2 What are the various theories of prison riots?
3 What are the main developments in the riots at Attica and New Mexico?
4 What are the key elements of the various forms of institutional violence?
5 What strategies are offered to reduce institutional violence?

At 9:46 A.M., Monday, September 13, 1971, New York State Police launched tear gas onto the Attica Penitentiary's D yard while helicopters broadcasted surrender announcements to inmates. Moments later, the gunfire began. Fifteen minutes later, the shooting subsided and 10 hostages and 29 inmates lay dead or dying while more than 80 other inmates suffered gunshot wounds.

'One out of every ten persons in D yard that morning was struck by gunfire and more than a quarter of the hostages died of bullet wounds' (*Attica: The Official Report*, 1972: 332).

INTRODUCTION

Since prisons nationwide hold hundreds of thousands of violent offenders, it stands to reason that those institutions can be the most dangerous places in society. Criminal histories of felons contribute significantly to the degree of violence in prisons; still, a multitude of other factors also warrant careful consideration. For instance, harsh institutional conditions fuel anger, frustration, and fear – emotions that dominate the experience of imprisonment.

Institutional violence is as old as prisons themselves. In America, the first major prison riot occurred in 1774 at the Simsbury prison – a primitive institution constructed over an abandoned copper mine in Connecticut. Between 1900 and 1985, more than 300 riots erupted in American prisons and jails (Dillingham and Montgomery, 1985; see Welch, 1999b). Although not all those disturbances resulted in fatalities and major destruction of the institution, some riots are remembered as devastating events – in particular, the uprisings in the state penitentiaries at Attica (New York) in 1971 and New Mexico in 1980 (see Braswell *et al.*, 1994; Montgomery and Crews, 1998).

This chapter examines two levels of institutional violence – individual and collective. Special emphasis also is placed on the various forms of prison violence: inmate versus inmate, inmate versus staff, and staff versus inmate violence, as well as self-inflicted injuries. In an attempt to explain the nature of collective violence, the riots at Attica and New Mexico are systematically analyzed. Overall, the discussion promotes a critical approach to institutional violence and offers numerous recommendations for reducing violence.

MOTIVES AND GOALS OF PRISON VIOLENCE

Recognizing various types of prison violence must begin with an understanding of why and how violence emerges in the prison setting. Just as there are different forms of violence, there also exist various motives or goals. Generally, the motives and goals of prison violence are characterized as either instrumental or expressive (Bowker, 1985; Welch, 1996h, 2002c). Instrumental violence stems from incentive-motivated aggression, whereas expressive violence is rooted in annoyance-motivated aggression (Porporino and Marton, 1983; Zillman, 1978). 'Aggressive behavior can be regarded as functional (i.e., useful for the individual) in two ways; it can be used to attain various rewards or incentives, or it can be used to deal with annoyance (e.g. frustration, mistreatment, provocation)' (Porporino and Marton, 1983: 9). As explained in the following sections, the former is known as incentive-motivated aggression while the latter is annoyance-motivated aggression.

Instrumental violence and incentive-motivated aggression

Instrumental violence is rational or calculative because it sets out to achieve a particular goal (Bowker, 1985). Additionally, because it is often planned, instrumental violence typically emerges from incentive-motivated aggression (Porporino and Marton, 1983). Instrumental violence includes incidents in which convicts threaten or physically or sexually assault other prisoners for the purpose of garnering power, enhancing status, or promoting a particular self-image within the prison society. In efforts to dominate fellow inmates, prisoners may employ violence (or the threat of violence) to obtain what they want, for example, a more desirable living situation, sexual contact, commodities (e.g. cigarettes, junk food, sneakers), contraband (e.g. drugs, weapons), and various services (e.g. laundry tasks and paperwork for legal matters) (Bowker, 1985; Ellis *et al.*, 1974; Porporino and Marton, 1983; Toch, 1977). Instrumental violence is not restricted to individual violence; it also is evident in collective disturbances (i.e. riots, hostage-takings), especially when goals are set and demands are formally pronounced.

Figure 9.1   Armed prison officials guarding the maximum security prison Fraijanes II, 36 km west of Guatemala City, where inmates rioted April 23, 2010. Two guards of the prison system were held hostage by prisoners demanding better care. In the detention center are held Mexican cartel members of the 'Los Zetas' gang and the Mara 18.

Photo by Johan Ordonez/AFP/Getty Images.

Expressive violence and annoyance-motivated aggression

Expressive violence is not necessarily rational insofar as goals are not consciously pursued. Rather, violence of this type tends to be impulsive and expressive in the emotional sense, characterized by a spontaneous release of tension (Bowker, 1985). Expressive violence stems from annoyance-motivated aggression that is 'engaged in to escape, to reduce, or terminate acute or chronic annoyance' (Porporino and Marton, 1983: 10). Given that correctional environments feature numerous annoyances, such as overcrowding, lack of privacy, idleness, and incessant noise, even seemingly minor irritations can precipitate violence. Expressive violence is apparent in both individual outbursts of violence and in collective disturbances, as depicted by a mob mentality. In either case, expressive violence requires a psychological state of readiness coupled with a volatile situation or precipitating event.

Instrumental and expressive violence are not mutually exclusive; many violent incidents involve a combination of the two dynamics. For instance, sometimes prisoners consciously engage in assaults so that others will perceive them as being savagely violent. Brutal displays of expressive violence are instrumental because they bolster the reputations of certain convicts, thereby enhancing their power and status among their peers. Riots and disturbances commonly feature both expressive and instrumental violence. Although riots may be instrumental and goal-oriented, they also serve as opportunities for inmates to vent pent-up rage over inhumane conditions and unjust prison practices.

Distinguishing between incentive-motivated aggression (instrumental violence) and annoyance-motivated aggression (expressive violence) is crucial to institutional management. 'Misreading the type of violence which is occurring could actually serve to aggravate the situation' (Porporino and Marton, 1983: 11). Given the impulsive nature of annoyance-motivated aggression, punitive measures are ineffective and may even exacerbate the situation. As corrections officials detect an increase in annoyance-motivated aggression among inmates, they should attempt to reduce the sources of irritation (e.g. crowding, idleness) and develop programs or activities designed to reduce tension (Wooldredge, 1998; Wooldredge *et al.*, 2001).

SOURCES OF PRISON VIOLENCE

Although there are multiple causes of prison violence, this section concentrates on three of the most common: the violent prisoner, the social climate of violence, and overcrowding (Crews and Montgomery, 2002; see 'Working in Corrections: Violence Escalates in Federal Prisons' below).

The violent prisoner

Simply put, prisons are violent institutions because they house violent offenders (see Hebenton and Seddon, 2009; Simon, 1998). That line of reasoning is especially true of maximum-security penitentiaries that hold the most dangerous criminals. Therefore, violence in prison stems from the aggressive methods sometimes used to eliminate annoyances, settle disputes, or gain goods or services. Although prison violence frequently occurs in maximum-security prisons, similar incidents also occur in medium- and occasionally in minimum-security facilities, prompting research into other sources of violence. For years, penologists have examined the social climate of violence and overcrowding (Butler, 2008; Montgomery and Crews, 2002).

The social climate of violence

To reiterate, some incidents of violence tend to be consciously motivated (i.e. instrumental violence), whereas others are more accurately depicted as outbursts (i.e. expressive violence). Often inmates resort to violence due to contextual features of their environment. Hans Toch examined the social climate of violence in prisons and concluded that the situational context is not the sole producer of violence, but may enhance or reduce the likelihood of occurrence (1985; see Wooldredge, 1998). Toch identifies a number of motives and contextual features that contribute to prison violence.

- *Payoffs.* Acting violently in prison has rewards, such as peer admiration or the creation of fear (which may be instrumental by serving as a form of protection).
- *Immunity or protection.* Violence in prison is perpetuated because victims generally adhere to a code of silence by not 'ratting' on the aggressors.
- *Opportunities.* The institutional routine and internal architecture provide numerous opportunities for assaults. Violence often takes place when the risk of being observed by staff is minimal and in places which conceal the attack.
- *Temptations, challenges, and provocations.* The climate of violence is replete with temptations, challenges, and provocations to engage in violence against inmates who are regarded as deserving an assault.
- *Justificatory premise.* Since especially inmates themselves view prisons as violent places, violence is justified because the norms permit it.

WORKING IN CORRECTIONS

Violence Escalates in Federal Prison

Compared with state prisons, federal prisons for years were viewed as institutions with relatively less violence. However, that reputation has begun to change, and federal correctional officers are taking note. In its efforts to expand the war on crime, Congress has passed legislation that broadens the category of federal offenses. Consequently, violent street criminals who would otherwise be sent to state penitentiaries are winding up in federal correctional institutions. According to Fred Stock, warden of the Atlanta Federal Penitentiary: 'They're young and they have less respect for the rights of people and property and, even after they are incarcerated, they don't have respect for themselves' (Holmes, 1995: A14).

Important structural changes also have contributed to the increase in violence. Due to stricter sentencing and parole requirements also passed by Congress in the 1980s, inmates are serving longer prison terms with less incentive to earn 'good time.' Federal prisoners are currently required to serve 85 percent of their sentences before being eligible for parole. Traditionally, the use of parole was an important method of controlling inmates since they did not want to forfeit their 'good time' by violating institutional rules. But now, correctional officers, who have the daily task of prison management and inmate control, have fewer devices at their disposal.

The federal prison system is still reeling from a rash of violent attacks. Most notable was the murder of guard D'Antonio Washington by convicts in the penitentiary at Atlanta. In the attack, a prisoner crushed Washington's skull by striking him repeatedly with a hammer. Warden Stock commented further: 'There are a lot of dangerous people here. After all, that's why they're in prison' (Holmes, 1995: A14).

Overcrowding

As correctional populations grow, institutional resources, programs, and services predictably fail to keep pace with demand. As a result, prison overcrowding places enormous strain on the institution as a whole, as well as on its prisoners. Moreover, overcrowding serves as an interactive variable, insofar as it exacerbates existing institutional problems and makes prison life even more irritating for inmates. One particular institutional task strained by overcrowding is the normal institutional placement procedure; as a result, offenders are often mismatched with facilities and programs.

Erratic inter-institutional movement caused by the influx of new prisoners taxes the management of violence-prone inmates further. 'Rather than crowded prison conditions, per se, the resulting destabilization of inmate social networks may be the principal factor leading to increased violence' (Porporino, 1986: 213). Research suggests that inter-institutional movement, as a form of transiency, limits the social control process that ordinarily functions to suppress violence. A stable prison environment is characterized by networks of ties and inmate relationships, but high degrees of transience (the continual influx of relative strangers) place enormous strain on the prison society (increasing the number of abrasive interactions, through the breakdown of the *sub rosa* prison economy). The effect is destabilization, leading to aggression and violence (Clements, 1979; Ellis, 1984; Porporino, 1986).

Despite some advances in the understanding of the relationship between inmate movement and violence, the overall relationship between overcrowding and violence remains to be clearly delineated. As noted, overcrowding serves as an interactive variable, meaning that other variables must also be taken into account. Still, even when other variables (e.g. age) are carefully controlled, contradictory results are common. Consequently, '[I]t is difficult to derive any clear policy or program implications from this set of contradictory findings' (Porporino, 1986: 230; also see Montgomery and Crews, 2002; Porporino and Dudley, 1984; Porporino and Marton, 1983).

A report by the Bureau of Justice Statistics (1989a) found little evidence that prison (not jail) population density is *directly* associated with inmate–inmate assaults and other disturbances. Nevertheless, most forms of aggression are *indirectly* fueled and exacerbated by overcrowding. The Bureau of Justice Statistics emphasizes that violence occurs more frequently in maximum-security facilities, irrespective of their population densities. However, other studies have found that overcrowding is an important factor affecting institutional violence (Farrington and Nutall, 1985; Gaes and McGuire, 1985). Clearly, additional research is needed to assess more precisely the impact that overcrowding has on prison violence. Moreover, that knowledge ought to be taken into account to formulate preventive measures (McCorkle *et al.*, 1995; Reisig, 1998; Wooldredge *et al.*, 2001).

EXPLAINING PRISON RIOTS

By definition, prison riots are 'incidents that involve the seizure of control over part or all of the prison through violence or force, the destruction of property, and the presentation of demands by a group of inmates' (Martin and Zimmerman, 1990a: 714; see Crews and Montgomery, 2002). In addition to the violent inmates, the social climate of violence, and the overcrowding, numerous other factors are associated with prison riots. Therefore various theories attempting to explain prison riots rely on different aspects of the prison organization. In an effort to improve the understanding of these diverse theoretical approaches, Martin and Zimmerman (1990a) introduced a typology of prison riots (see Fleisher, 1989: Silberman, 1995; Useem and Reisig, 1999). The typology consists of six conceptual models: environmental conditions, spontaneity, conflict, collective behavior/social control, power vacuum, and rising expectations.

Environmental conditions model

In this particular model, the focus is on the preconditions of the prison with regard to environmental components of the institution, such as poor, insufficient, and/or contaminated food; a lack of professional leadership; brutality; inadequacy or absence of treatment programs; idleness and monotony; political interference; and groups of refractory, hard-core convicts (Barak-Glantz, 1985). Accordingly, the American Correctional Association (1981) offers four categories of causes:

institutional environment; characteristics of the inmate population; administrative practices; and noninstitutional causes (see Wooldredge *et al.*, 2001). These preconditions are present in most prisons. Nonetheless, large-scale riots are rare occurrences. Hence, such institutional problems are necessary conditions, but not sufficient causes, for prison riots.

Spontaneity model

Proponents of this model assert that riots (and disturbances) are unplanned, spontaneous events. 'Riots occur when some incident sets off a chain of events that becomes a collective violent disturbance aimed at taking control of a prison or some portion of a prison' (Martin and Zimmerman, 1990: 718). This model explains the coupling of the preconditions (the time bomb waiting to explode) with the detonator (a spontaneous event, such as an officer assaulting an inmate). The spontaneous event should not be interpreted as the cause of the violence, but rather as the spark.

Conflict model

The consequences of official repression in prison are at the center of the conflict perspective. The first consequence of official repression is the engendering of subcultural (value) conflicts. Second, official repression limits the strategies

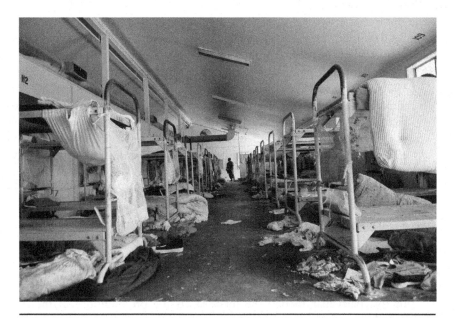

Figure 9.2   The aftermath of a prison riot inside the California Institution for Men in Chino, California, August 19, 2009. After touring the prison where the riot took place on August 8, California Governor Arnold Schwarzenegger said that the prison system is collapsing and needs to be reformed.

Photo by Michal Czerwonka/Getty Images.

needed to resolve conflicts. When inmates are prevented from resolving conflict (with other inmates or staff/administration) by way of bargaining or mediating, they resort to combat. In view of that conflict, riots are not viewed as abnormal but rather as expected (albeit desperate and destructive) reactions to repressive conditions (McCorkle *et al.*, 1995; Useem and Reisig, 1999).

Collective behavior/social control model

Although prisons are generally viewed as coercive institutions, the daily maintenance of order is not achieved by force. Rather, prisons rely on a combination of formal (or official) and informal (or unofficial) control mechanisms that promote a sense of cooperation, participation, and compliance. Prison stability, however, is sometimes delicate, and any major failure of formal or informal control mechanisms can lead to a disturbance or riot (Useem and Reisig, 1999).

Power vacuum model

Prisoners are sensitive to fluctuations in administrative personnel because inmates rely on staff leadership to establish routines and clarify rules. When frequent administrative or staff turnover occurs, inmates experience tension due to the perception that the institution lacks competent management. Moreover, an administration that is in constant flux often fails to address legitimate prisoner concerns and needs. Riots and disturbances are more likely to take place when inmates perceive a power vacuum, and such inmate action is a symbolic attempt to establish stability (see Welch, 1999b, 1995b).

Rising expectations model

This model contends that disturbances and riots are more likely to occur when progress decelerates following a period of improvement. Institutional reform promotes the expectation that all problems will be resolved. Consequently, violence erupts when reform fails to live up to its expectations.

In sum, the typology just described ought to be met with some caution. Since considerable overlap exists among the conceptual models, they should not be interpreted as independent of one another. An advancement of the understanding of prison riots must take into account the unique contributions from various studies. Certainly, these models supplement rather than supplant each other (see Carrabine 2004, 2000; Montgomery and Crews, 2002; Useem and Reisig, 1999; Wooldredge *et al.*, 2001).

THE RIOT AT ATTICA

Perhaps no other prison riot has received as much notoriety as the uprising at Attica (New York). From the onset, Attica became a metaphor for an array of social problems, including racism, oppression, and injustice. Metaphors aside, in-depth investigations of Attica have concluded that racism, oppression, and injustice were salient features before, during, and after the riot (*Attica: The Official Report*, 1972; Mahan, 1994: Useem, 1985; Useem and Kimball, 1987; Wicker, 1975; see also Oswald, 1972, and the 1991 commemorative issue of *Social Justice* devoted to the Attica riot).

Between September 9 and 13, 1971, 43 persons died at the upstate New York maximum-security prison. Most alarmingly, 39 were killed and more than 80 others were wounded by gunfire during the 15 minutes it took the state police to retake the institution. 'With the exception of Indian massacres in the late 19th century, the State Police assault which ended the four-day prison uprising was the bloodiest one-day encounter between Americans since the Civil War' (*Attica: The Official Report*, 1972: 130).

Attica was not unlike most overcrowded maximum-security prisons in the nation in the early 1970s. At the time of the riot, the institution held more than 2,200 inmates. Compounding matters, the prisoners were simply warehoused, since few meaningful programs of education and rehabilitation were offered. Like that of many other large prisons in the nation, the inmate population was becoming increasingly urban and minority (54 percent African American, 37 percent white, and 8.7 percent Spanish-speaking, with almost 80 percent from urban ghettos) (*Attica: The Official Report*, 1972: 3). By contrast, prison officials and staff were predominantly white and rural. Racism between the officers and the inmates was mutual. Rural white officers were suspicious of convicts from the ghettos, and minority prisoners did not trust the staff, viewing them as hicks, cowboys, or good ol' boys. Each of their perspectives, or worldviews, was shaped ideologically. The white rural officers held traditional, conservative, and status quo views of law and order. Conversely, minority inmates were influenced by the radical social and religious manifestos promoted by the Black Panther party and the Black Muslims.

Those polarized worldviews widened the social distance between the keepers and the kept. It became convenient for staff and administration to blame the radical and revolutionary convicts for the riot because doing so deflected attention away from the administration's egregious flaws in prison management. According to the Official Report of the New York State Special Commission on Attica: 'Contrary to [these] popular views, the Attica uprising was neither a long-planned revolutionary plot, nor a proletarian revolution against the capitalist system' (*Attica: The Official Report*, 1972: 105). Rather, the riot began as a spontaneous burst of violence. Prison officials, who did not have a riot-control plan and relied on an antiquated communications system, were unable to quell the disturbance. Following a period of chaos, inmate leaders (who were not involved in the initial violence) representing the Muslims, Black Panthers, and Young Lords, organized prisoners and took control of the situation.

The chronology of events began the day before the riot when a misunderstanding between COS (correctional officers) and prisoners led to an officer being assaulted by a convict. That night, two inmates were removed from their cells and placed in administration detention. Other inmates vowed revenge, and the next morning the CO who was at the center of the controversy was attacked. The violence spread as angry inmates broke through a defective weld in the gate located in the 'Times Square' section of the prison. At that moment, prisoners attacked officers, took hostages, and destroyed property. By 10:30 a.m., prisoners had seized control of four cell blocks and all the yards and tunnels. Soon 1,281 inmates and over 40 hostages gathered in the D yard. Shortly thereafter, fellow inmates killed three convicts: one was accused of being an informant, the second was a vocal white racist, and the third was mentally unstable and dangerous (*Attica: The Official Report*, 1972: 109–10).

Negotiations

The stage was then set for negotiations that were not planned but simply unfolded over time. Inmate leaders were readily prepared to offer their demands (better food, improved healthcare, religious freedom, etc.) since they had already sent the administration a list of recommendations for institutional reform in July. Throughout the negotiations, convicts remained frustrated over the administration's unwillingness to take concrete steps toward prison reform. Commissioner Oswald and the observers negotiated a settlement based on 28 points of reform but rejected the inmates' demand for criminal amnesty (stating that prisoners would not be charged with crimes taking place during the uprising and would be transported to a non-imperialist country). At that moment, a peaceful settlement was unlikely.

The commission investigating the riot tried to ascertain why a peaceful negotiation failed and cited several contributing factors. First, the poor negotiating conditions did not facilitate effective communication between the parties; indeed, the entire process was marred by mistrust. The negotiation was further knocked off track when Oswald refused to return to the yard where the negotiations were held because an inmate proposed holding him hostage. Consequently, the observers' committee (consisting of several high-profile persons, such as journalist Tom Wicker and radical lawyer William Kunstler), which was not created to serve as intermediaries, was left to mediate with the inmate leaders. Competing views among the observers precluded effective resolution. The climate surrounding the negotiation was tense. Making matters worse, prison officials knowingly reported false rumors to the media, such as the announcement that hostages had died of slit throats.

Storming of the prison

Commissioner Oswald urged the inmates to accept a revised set of demands, and when the prisoners rejected the proposal, Oswald issued an ultimatum. In turn, inmates snubbed the ultimatum. Then Oswald ordered the state police to storm the prison. At 9:46 a.m., Monday, September 13, state police launched tear gas onto the D yard while helicopters broadcast surrender announcements to convicts. Soon the gunfire began. Fifteen minutes later, the shooting subsided and ten hostages and 29 inmates lay dead or dying while more than 80 other inmates suffered gunshot wounds. 'One out of every ten persons in D yard that morning was struck by gunfire and more than a quarter of the hostages died of bullet wounds' (*Attica: The Official Report*, 1972: 332).

Aftermath

The storming of the prison did not end the violence; for many inmates, it was just the beginning. Hundreds of prisoners were subsequently stripped naked and beaten by COs, troopers, and sheriffs' deputies. The agony was prolonged because prison officials withheld immediate medical care for those suffering from gunshot wounds and injuries stemming from the widespread reprisals. In fact, when the shooting stopped, there were only ten medical personnel available to treat more than 120 seriously wounded inmates and hostages, and only two of them were physicians. Doctors at local hospitals who could have assisted the wounded were not dispatched by prison officials until four hours later. In the aftermath, reprisals by officers against inmates were manifested as brutal displays of humiliation:

> Injured prisoners, some on stretchers, were struck, prodded or beaten with sticks, belts, bats, or other weapons. Others were forced to strip and run naked through gauntlets of guards armed with clubs which they used to strike inmates as they passed. Some were dragged on the ground, some marked with an 'X' on their backs, some spat upon or burned with matches, others poked in the genitals or arms with sticks.

> (From *Inmates of Attica* v. *Rockefeller*, 1971, quoted in Deutsch *et al.*, 1991: 22)

Prisoners' class-action suit

On February 27, 1991, the United States Court of Appeals for the Second Circuit removed a final obstacle, permitting a class-action civil rights suit to proceed. The suit, *Al-Jundi* v. *Mancusi* (1991) was filed on behalf of the 1,200 prisoners who were killed, wounded, denied medical care (following the storming of the prison), and beaten by officers. Following years of legal resistance, the case went to trial on September 30, 1991, in Buffalo, New York. The suit sought to hold liable four top supervisory officials: Russell Oswald (Commissioner of Corrections), Major John Monahan (commander of the assault force), Vincent Mancusi (Attica's prison warden), and Karl Pfeil (deputy warden).

The jury found Deputy Warden Pfeil liable for violent reprisals following the riot and for permitting police and COs to beat and torture inmates. The jury deadlocked on the liability of the three other state officials (Oswald and Monahan are deceased). Additional litigation surfaced in the aftermath of the uprising. In 1989, seven former Attica prisoners and their families were awarded nearly $1.3 million for injuries suffered during the storming of the prison. In 1992, a federal jury found that the prisoners' constitutional rights were violated and that Karl Pfeil was liable for having overseen brutal reprisals after the rebellion. Five years later, a federal court ordered Pfeil to pay a $4 million award to Frank B. B. Smith, one of the prisoners beaten by guards. But in 1999, a federal appeals court overturned that ruling saying that the 1992 liability finding against Pfeil was invalid. Then in 2000, a federal judge, determined to conclude one of the darkest chapters in prison history, announced that the inmates who were beaten and tortured during the 1971 riot would receive an $8 million settlement from New York State (Chen, 2000). Such legal action demonstrates that state prison officials are not above the law even under such war-like conditions as large-scale riots (see Haberman, 2000; Welch, 2009c; Wicker, 2001).

THE NEW MEXICO STATE PRISON RIOT

Whereas the riot at Attica symbolizes the political struggles that often occur between prisoners and staff (and administration), the uprising at the New Mexico State Prison stands as an example of sheer brutality among convicts. As an apt description, Mahan (1985) refers to the New Mexico riot as a 'killing ground.' After midnight, on Saturday, February 2, 1980, violence erupted when a seasoned officer approached two rowdy convicts who had become intoxicated by drinking prison hooch (prison-made alcohol). An altercation soon followed, and the inmates overpowered the veteran officer and his two backups. The incident would have remained isolated, but the convicts snatched the prison keys and began moving into other sections of the prison. Meanwhile, three officers were taken hostage, raped, and beaten into unconsciousness (Morris, 1983; Rolland, 2002, 1997).

As was the case in the riot at Attica, the officials at New Mexico were not prepared to deal with a large-scale riot. The institution was inexcusably understaffed; at the time of the riot, there were only 22 COs supervising 1,157 inmates in a prison built to hold 800. The riot might have been prevented from spreading but other officers were unable to produce a complete set of prison keys. Perhaps the worst institutional flaw of all, though, was the failure of 'shatterproof' glass installed at the control center – the prison's lifeline. When the inmates broke the protective glass and seized the control center, they had full access to the facility. There they pushed buttons that electronically opened all interior gates. The violence quickly spread and the degree of brutality that awaited other prisoners was simply horrific.

Small cliques of convicts sought revenge against snitches and other prison outcasts, including child molesters, known as diddlers or short-eyes. The string of violent encounters that erupted was preceded by several preparatory events. First, prisoners stormed the institution's pharmacy where they consumed massive amounts of drugs such as amphetamines (i.e., speed). The drug-induced euphoria of those prisoners generated 36 hours of frantic and savage destruction. Others preferred alternative sources of mood alteration; for example, some inmates broke into the shoe shop where they sniffed the intoxicating fumes of glue (Morris, 1983; Rolland, 2002, 1997).

To further prepare themselves for the impending acts of revenge, inmates confiscated prison records identifying informers and those convicted of sex offenses, the two most despised criminal types in the prison society. Finally, inmates added to their arsenal of shanks (prison-made weapons) by equipping themselves with tools and blowtorches stolen from the prison maintenance supply room. Now they were ready to create a nightmare that would shock even the most jaded prison expert. The impending rampage would exceed the typical forms of beatings characteristic of prisons. For the next several hours, inmates unleashed their rage by raping, burning, decapitating, castrating, and eviscerating fellow prisoners. As noted in Chapter 5, the execution-style burning of Jimmy Perrin, known by fellow convicts as 'the baby raper', was particularly shocking. Still, other prisoners faced similar acts of torture. As inmate W. G. Stone writes in his book *The Hate Factory: The Story of the New Mexico Penitentiary Riot*:

> They were in their heyday, working off months and years of pent-up rage, gouging out eyes, pounding on bloated bodies. When a group of them found Paulina Paul's decapitated head, they stuck it on top of a broomstick and paraded around the prison in a primitive rite of victory.
>
> (1982: 126)

Unlike the riot at Attica, the New Mexico riot had no identified course of action; it was simply a series of independent acts of revenge. There was no carnival atmosphere, no leadership, no lists of grievances, no organization – only unspeakable brutality (Mahan, 1994).

> They would have struck more fear in the officials' hearts if they'd brought out the charred remains of the two men tortured to death with the pressured flames of the acetylene torches. One, an informant, was held down by four of the executioners while a fifth turned the torch straight into his eyes, burning them until the back of his head exploded from the pressure and heat. Those who found his body later could still see the terror on what was left of his face.
>
> (Stone, 1982: 127)

Four other inmates were burned so extensively that their race could not be determined when their corpses were recovered. It is important to note that not all the inmates participated in the riot; African American inmates (9 percent of the inmate population) organized and protected themselves by avoiding the disturbance (Office of the Attorney General of the State of New Mexico, 1980). By the second day of the riot, more than two-thirds of the white and

Chicano prisoners fled the institution and surrendered to authorities (Useem and Kimball, 1987). In large part, the violence was the direct work of small cliques of prisoners, mostly Chicano (58 percent of the inmate population), who took full advantage of the uprising to settle their differences with rival Chicano inmates (Colvin, 1992, 1982). Additional acts of brutality consisted of the following: a snitch had a steel rod driven through one ear and out the other; another was stomped to death and a perpetrator carved 'rat' into his abdomen; seven inmates were found slashed to death in their cells; a rope was tied to the neck of a convict who was nearly decapitated when his body was thrown off the tier; and a prisoner whose eyes were nearly gouged out was beheaded with a shovel (*Newsweek*, 1980).

Although most of the aggression was directed at other inmates, seven of the 12 COs who were taken hostage were beaten and raped, at times with blunt instruments such as ax handles. Incidents of brutality against COs were confined to those whom convicts despised. Some COs were more fortunate, as one inmate explains: 'I think it was the record of the individual guards. Take for instance an old man named [name]. He was really liked by inmates. He kept his clothes, was fed, wasn't abused, [and] he wasn't beaten on' (Useem and Kimball, 1987: 90). Some officers escaped the prison with the aid of inmates.

In 36 hours, $36 million of damage was incurred. All the more tragic though, 33 inmates were killed at the hands of other prisoners. Still, the lives of 12 hostages were spared, and three reasons are cited for their survival. First, inmates feared an armed assault upon the killing of a hostage. Second, hostages provided some leverage (or bargaining chips) in negotiating with authorities for such exchanges as media access and supplies. Finally, prisoners wanted some of the guards to simply suffer; 'A dead man does not suffer and they [the inmates] wanted to fuck them [the guards] up' (Useem and Kimball, 1987: 89).

Explanations for the riot

Numerous sociological explanations for the riot at New Mexico have been issued (see Mahan, 1994; Saenz, 1986; Useem, 1985; Useem and Kimball, 1989, 1987). Generally, these studies focused on prison conditions, correctional philosophy, and institutional management. In his analysis Colvin (1992, 1982) compares the structure of control and inmate social structure during two important time frames: 1970 through 1975 and 1976 through 1980. During the earlier period, the control of the penitentiary was based on the philosophy of rehabilitation. Institutional programs not only benefited individual convicts but also served institutional functions as well. Programs provided inmates with a constructive outlet for their tension by diverting and redirecting their attention and energies to positive activities. Consequently, internal order was maintained and the prison generally became safer.

Another significant aspect of the earlier period (1970–5) was the presence of a contraband and drug economy. It had been reported that staff and officials turned a blind eye to the underground economy, taking action only when violence surfaced. That particular feature of prison life also served an institutional function. That is, prisoners controlled one another non-violently because they did not want the staff to crackdown on the flow of contraband. In some ways, the *sub rosa* economy contributed to institutional stability since during that period assaults and escape attempts were relatively infrequent occurrences.

During the next time frame (1976–80), the administration abruptly shifted its correctional philosophy from rehabilitation to pure custody (or 'warehousing'). The introduction of the custodial philosophy resulted in the elimination of programs, leaving prisoners with few institutional opportunities. As expected, the new administrative regime also cracked down on the underground economy, especially the drug trade. Outlets that had once served to release inmate tension had been removed. In years to come, institutional pressure would build to the point where even an altercation between a prisoner and an officer might precipitate a major riot.

It should be understood that 'prison warehousing' does not solely lead to prison riots. But in the case of New Mexico, the custodial philosophy combined with other factors added to growing institutional pressures. For example, during the period leading up to the riot, officers initiated a system of snitching that involved involuntary informing. Such a system of involuntary snitching forced prisoners into a classic double bind. COs told inmates that they had no choice other than to snitch on fellow prisoners; if they did not cooperate, the COs would falsely tell other convicts that they had informed. Obviously, inmates were placed in a no-win situation.

One of the consequences of the involuntary snitch system was that it forced prisoners to become increasingly suspicious of their fellow inmates. Mistrust among prisoners eventually fragmented the inmate society into small cliques. In effect, the staff had divided and conquered the inmate society by turning prisoners against one another. During that time, many inmates set out to promote a violent reputation for the purpose of protecting themselves from snitches. As violence became more frequent, members of the administration convinced themselves that they were dealing with a 'new breed' of inmate who could be controlled only through punitive and coercive measures.

Both predisposing and precipitating factors contributed to the riot. In the first instance, predisposing factors are chronic problems that contribute indirectly to prison violence: overcrowding, inadequate food and medical services, and security lapses. Precipitating factors are conditions or events that lead directly to heightened tension in the prison. In the case of New Mexico, frequent turnovers in the administration added to an already tense atmosphere; in addition, the warden had deliberately ignored court-ordered reforms. Compounding matters, transfers to a lower-security facility were terminated, thereby reducing the formal incentive for inmates to exhibit good behavior. Finally, a mass escape of 11 inmates created a backlash against all prisoners who were subjected to even greater coercive control within the institution. So, at the time of the fight between the drunken inmates and the officer on Saturday, February 2, the penitentiary was already a powder keg requiring only a spark to ignite the savage uprising (see Moore, 2009; see also 'Comparative Corrections: Prison Violence in Brazil' below).

COMPARATIVE CORRECTIONS

Prison Violence in Brazil

The prison riot at Attica offers numerous lessons on the volatile conditions of large maximum-security penitentiaries and flawed measures used to regain control amid a major riot. Such problems are not solely an American concern; indeed, around the world corrections officials contend with the dangers of prison violence. Our attention now turns to the Brazilian penitentiary, Carandiru, the largest prison in Latin America, holding more than 7,400 inmates. Carandiru is well known not only for its size but also for its squalid conditions that have contributed greatly to inmate protests and disturbances. In 1992, human rights organizations condemned government officials for their handling of a prison riot, especially the use of excessive force with which police massacred 111 inmates.

Such a show of force against prisoners did little to improve the safety of Carandiru. In 2001, other large-scale disturbance broke out. Similar to the pattern of violence found at the New Mexico prison riot, cliques of inmates vented their frustration against other prisoners as well as staff, taking nearly 3,000 people hostage. That tragic event proved too much for government leaders, who closed the prison permanently. In his book, *Carandiru Station*, Dr Drauzio Varella, a physician who worked in the prison infirmary, chronicles the problems at the penitentiary, particularly its abysmal conditions, overcrowding, violence, and rebellion. Much like the aftermath of the riot of Attica, *Carandiru Station* has sparked public debate over prison reform. Since 1999, the book has emerged a national and international bestseller; in 2002, the BBC broadcast a radio play of *Carandiru Station* and later that year a movie entitled *Carandiru* was released worldwide (Rohter, 2002). Prison reformers hope that the book and movie will prompt deeper public and political consciousness of the harsh realities of prison life. (See also the classic books and movies *Papillon* by Henri Charrière (1970) and *Accomplices to Crime: The Arkansas Prison Scandal* by Thomas Murton and Joe Hyams (1969), depicted in the film *Brubaker.*)

INMATE–INMATE VIOLENCE

Physical assaults between inmates constitute a daily problem in most prisons and jails. Moreover, such violence is exacerbated by several limitations of the prison organization. First and foremost, officers attribute violence to lack of adequate supervision. As overcrowding outpaces the hiring of COs, violence becomes increasingly imminent. Assaults are more likely to occur in facilities that do not have adequate supervision, especially where interior architecture limits supervision (Zupan, 1991). The proliferation of weapons in an institution also is the result of security lapses, and when officers feel that they do not have the ability to control inmates, they often permit prisoners to protect themselves by any means necessary (see Associated Press, 2009; Colvin, 1982).

In his book *Warehousing Violence* (1989), Mark Fleisher describes the significance of prison-made weapons – shanks – that convicts use to protect themselves or to attack fellow inmates. The most common weapons are strap-on shanks or short sticking devices made 'by embedding a galvanized nail into a melted plastic handle (dining hall utensils are plastic)' (Fleisher, 1989: 199). Such attacks are known as stickings or shankings, and victims are not stabbed, but are stuck or shanked. According to prisoners, short shanks aren't intended to kill their victims, but are used to 'teach loud-mouth motherfuckers some manners' (Fleisher, 1989: 200; see Conover, 2002).

Prisoners often strap on a shank with cloth handles that wrap firmly around the aggressor's wrist – a practice commonly known as strapping down with a shank. The purpose of securing the shank to the hand is to keep the weapon from being taken away during the attack, thus avoiding the possibility of having the shank used against the aggressor. Some convicts will strap the shanks to their hands with masking tape or heavy electrical tape. Thick cloth handles wrapped around the shank could also permit the inmate to conceal the weapon from the prison's metal detector (Conover, 2002; Fleisher, 1989).

Figure 9.3 The National Civil Police and the prison guards of Pavoncito regaining control of the maximum security prison in the department of Fraijanes, 40 km east of Guatemala City, on March 27, 2007. At least five inmates were injured during the riot between members of the gang Mara Salvartucha (MS), who were transferred from the El Infierno prison after riots there, and the 'Paisas' – common prisoners who are not involved in gangs. The members of MS were first transferred from El Boquerón prison to El Infierno, a day after the murder of four policemen apparently involved in the assassination of three Salvadoran lawmakers and their driver on February 19.

Photo by Orlando Sierra/AFP/Getty Images.

In some instances, corrections officers instigate 'cockfights' by pitting together prisoners who have deep personal conflicts with each other and allowing them to 'duke it out' without interference from the staff. In another type of arranged violence, COs may organize gladiator matches whereby prisoners are ordered to fight an opponent for sport and wagering. In a widely publicized incident, one inmate – due to his size and strength – was repeatedly coerced by officers to engage in gladiator games at a California state prison. During one such brutal contest that occurred in the exercise yard, that prisoner was shot without warning from a CO in the watchtower. The bullet lodged in his spine, permanently paralyzing him below the waist (Nieves, 1998; see Rayman, 2009a, 2009b, 2009c; Welch, 1999b; Chapter 12 this volume).

SEXUAL ASSAULT IN PRISON

The nature of sexual assault in prisons is often poorly understood. Although sexual attacks do take place, rape in correctional institutions is not a common occurrence. In fact, early research found that the frequency of sexual assault in correctional institutions is overstated (Lockwood, 1980, 1982, 1985; Nacci, 1982; Nacci and Kane, 1984). More recently, however, it has been suggested that reported estimates of rape may under-represent the incidence of rape in prison because correctional officers may inhibit reporting by treating victims insensitively or by ignoring the assault altogether (Eigenberg, 1994: 145; see Gaes and Goldberg, 2004).

In a classic study of rape in prison, Lockwood (1980, 1982) systematically examined sexual assault in correctional institutions and found that sexual violence falls into two groups. In the first category, sexual violence is a form of domination that is used to coerce the victim. 'The primary causes of violence are subcultural values upholding men's rights to use force to gain sexual access' (Lockwood, 1982: 257). The other category includes cases in which the target reacts violently to propositions perceived as threatening; as a result, sexual assault emerges as a form of self-protection (see Donaldson, 2001; Kupers, 2001).

The overarching fear – real and imagined – of sexual assault reveals the consequences of non-enforcement because it contributes to a predatory atmosphere of mistrust that can lead to violence (Bowker, 1980; Chonco, 1989; Jones and Schmid, 1989; Nacci, 1982; Tewksbury, 1989). According to Robertson (1995: 339):

> Incarceration exposes male inmates to a 'world of violence' where staff cannot or will not protect them from rape, assault, and other forms of victimization. To make matters worse, retreating in the face of danger is neither normative nor feasible; in prison your back is always against the wall. Most inmates have but two options: to fight in self-defense or become passive victims of a predatory subculture.

Facing such threats, vulnerable prisoners are left to their own devices, and in prison parlance, they must either 'fuck or fight' (Eigenberg, 1994: 159). Under those conditions, there are four possible configurations of violence: (1) the aggressor sexually assaults his victim; (2) during the attack, the victim wards off the aggressor with violence; (3) the potential victim reacts with a pre-emptive strike against the aggressor as a measure of self protection; (4) the victim later retaliates against the aggressor. Paradoxically, such diagrams of violence tend to blur the line between aggressor and victim (Robertson, 2000c, 1999, 1995; see also Abbott, 1981). Consider the following testimony:

> Well, the first time [a potential sexual aggressor] says something to you or looks wrong at you, have a piece of pipe or a good heavy piece of two-by-four. Don't say a damn thing to him, just get that heavy wasting material and walk right up to him and bash his face in and keep bashing him till he's down and out, and yell loud and clear for all the other cons to hear you, Motherfucker, I'm a man. I came in here a mother fucking man and I'm going out a mother fucking man. Next time I'll kill you.
>
> (Thomas, 1967: 256; quoted in Robertson, 1995: 340)

It is the frequency of sexual *harassment* (insults and offensive propositions) that may lead some observers to believe that rape is rampant in prisons, a conclusion that is largely attributable to the level of fear generated. Nacci's (1982) pioneering study of sexual assault in the federal prison system found that only two out of 330 inmates surveyed had been compelled to perform undesired sex acts, but 29 percent had been propositioned by other inmates. Similarly, Lockwood's (1980) examination of sexual assault in the New York State prison system found that 28 percent of the inmates surveyed had been aggressively approached by inmates seeking sexual favors. Lockwood concluded that: 'the problems caused by sexual propositions in prison affect far more men than those suffering the devastating consequences of sexual assault' (1985: 90). Problems stemming from sexual assault include fights, social isolation, racism, and fear (Lockwood, 1991; Tewksbury, 1989).

Although homosexual rape might be infrequent in correctional institutions, its sociological implications should not be neglected. Most forms of violence (with the exception of genuine acts of self-defense) are expressions of dominance, hence the central feature of sexual assault is the struggle for power and status. Obviously, sexual assault ought to be distinguished from physical attacks (e.g. punching and stabbing) due to its sexual nature. Aside from the sexual gratification that may occur, homosexual rape in prison is an expression of dominance rooted in exaggerated images of masculinity and status. That is, the aggressor attempts to establish his masculinity (or machismo) by reducing the status of his victims and declaring them 'girls' or 'women.' In doing so, the aggressor demonstrates his own sexist view of the world by assuming that females occupy a lower social status. The phenomenon of institutional sexual assault is also reinforced by the prison society, which perpetuates the belief that 'real men' do not get raped. In the essay 'The Sexual Jungle,' convict-journalist Wilbert Rideau writes:

Rape in prison is rarely a sexual act, but one of violence, politics, and an acting out of power roles. 'Most of your homosexual rape is a macho thing,' says Colonel Walter Pence, the chief of security at the Louisiana State Penitentiary at Angola. 'It's basically one guy saying to another "I'm a better man than you and I'm gonna turn you out to prove it." ... It's definitely a macho/power thing among the inmates. And it's basically the insecure prisoners who do it.'

(1992: 75: see Abbott, 1981)

As is the case with heterosexual rape in society, the inherent political nature of sexual assault in prison must not be overlooked since power and status are the driving forces behind such incidents (Gilligan, 2002; Paczensky, 2001). Given the importance of reducing sexual victimization – in and outside of prison – more research is needed to unveil the form and frequency of assaults, thereby improving measures for prevention (Chonco, 1989; Jones and Schmid, 1989; Tewksbury, 1989).

INMATE-STAFF VIOLENCE

As will be discussed further in Chapter 14, employment as a correctional officer is characterized by hazardous duty, and many officers are routinely reminded of the dangers of working in a tense atmosphere. Officers must supervise inmates who have the potential to direct and vent their anger at the staff. For safety purposes, most COs prefer to work alongside a fellow officer. Due to overcrowding and budgetary constraints, however, such staffing arrangements are difficult to maintain. Today officers are guarding increasingly greater numbers of convicts, thereby raising the potential for violence.

In their classic study, Camp and Camp (1993) found that assaults on staff by inmates are relatively common. In the 45 jails they surveyed, they found an annual average of nearly 50 assaults per institution. Still, it is widely acknowledged that such incidents are greatly under-reported. Failure to report such assaults is due to the CO subculture that tends to downplay assaults by inmates on staff in order to maintain the COs' macho image (Jefferis, 1994). In his research, Fleisher also detected that aspect of the 'guard' subculture: 'In several cases of inmate unarmed assault on line staff, staffers' black eyes, bloody noses, and contusions weren't "injuries," by staffers' definitions, but simply obvious (and proud) signs of "not taking any bullshit from convicts" ' (Fleisher, 1989: 199).

In their attempt to uncover the hidden incidents of assault on staff by inmates, Parsonage and Miller (1991) similarly learned that actual violence against officers does indeed exceed official reports. The researchers found that among the 112 officers in a Pennsylvania county prison, 21 percent had been physically assaulted in the line of duty during the previous year, and 72 percent had been threatened with physical violence. Over the course of their careers as COs, 56 percent had been physically assaulted and 89 percent had been threatened with physical assault (see Jefferis, 1994).

Research offers two categories that distinguish between fundamentally different types of assaults on officers. First, assaults may occur during volatile situations. For example, an officer might be assaulted when intervening between fighting inmates or during an incident in which prisoners – in the heat of the moment – lose their temper and assault staff members. Secondly, some assaults are premeditated in which convicts carefully plan their attacks on officers, catching officers off guard (Bowker, 1980). In his extensive work, Kevin Light investigated patterns of assaults on officers and found numerous interactional themes that help explain the motives of violence. One interactional theme encompasses assaults ensuing from an officer's command that the inmate objects to. The following case illustrates this type of assault: 'Inmate was standing on stairs leading to the gym and correctional officer told him to move. Inmate refused and correctional officer repeated his order. Inmate punched correctional officer on side of face' (Light, 1991: 251, 1990a, 1990b). Inmates may also lash out against staff to express their protest against being unjustly treated. Similarly, prisoners may react violently to an officer's attempt to search the inmate's person, cell, or property. Light recorded the following incident from staff records: 'CO was pursuing inmate who had fled from [the] area to avoid being frisked before entering the mess hall, when inmate turned around and punched CO in the mouth' (1991: 253). Officers also run the risk of assault when approaching emotionally unstable prisoners. 'An inmate was entering mess hall, he broke from line and struck correction officer with his fists. As he was being subdued by CO, inmate slashed him with a razor blade on left arm and side of face (Report cites "apparent psychotic episode" as cause, and refers to inmate's "catatonic state")' (Light, 1991: 256–7).

Other assaults are categorized according to the following interactional themes: inmate fighting, movement, restraint, contraband, sexual assault, and a category termed 'other.' The following is an example of an incident included in the 'other' category: 'While checking that inmate's cell door was locked on rounds, correctional officer received urine thrown in his face by inmate. Inmate then attempted to hit CO with broom and glass jar' (Light, 1991: 249). Although officers cannot expect to work in prisons that are completely free of violence, they can exercise caution in dealing with convicts. Training helps officers deal effectively with violent inmates and identify volatile situations (or 'hot spots'), thereby reducing the risk of assault. Just as important, prison administration also has the responsibility to improve those institutional conditions that engender violence (see Crew and Montgomery, 2002; Fleisher, 1989; Silberman, 1995; Useem and Reisig, 1999).

STAFF VERSUS INMATES

The nature of violence directed at prisoners by members of the custodial staff is complex. Still, there are two basic permutations of such aggression: official and unofficial force. Let us explore further.

Official force

While addressing the problems of staff assaulting prisoners, it is important to distinguish between incidents that are official (formal) acts of force and those that are unofficial (informal). Since some convicts do become violent on occasion, it is understandable that in response staff members resort to force in subduing such prisoners. Official force is used in situations when life or property is threatened. Most prisons employ a team of officers to restrain violent or disorderly inmates. In the federal prison system, administrators in each institution have developed Special Operations Response Teams (SORTs) to control violent inmates and avert larger disturbances. In the course of being tackled and restrained, inmates sometimes suffer minor or major injuries. Still, prison officials warn against viewing those incidents as assaults because the goal is to restrain – not injure – inmates. Since administrators specifically order and supervise the use of official force, it clearly constitutes a measure of formal control. Most institutions videotape the intervention, thereby verifying the officers' appropriate use of force. Documenting through the use of videotape is an important procedure because the use of force is always subject to becoming excessive, subsequently leading to charges of excessive force. Whereas official force is used to protect life or property, excessive force constitutes a form of punishment or reprisal.

For many reasons, the use of force in corrections remains controversial. Some administrators contend that liberal use of force is necessary to maintain institutional control whereas others find that a more limited use of force is more effective. In view of well-publicized incidents in which COs have been charged with excessive force, correctional managers have instituted formal procedures clarifying which situations warrant the use of force. For example, following the 1986 riot at Rikers Island (New York) in which numerous reports of excessive force were filed, the Department of Correction formed the Special Committee on the Use of Force. *The Final Report of the Special Committee on the Use of Force* (1988) outlines several recommendations to reduce inmate and staff violence by addressing the following key areas: the jail environment, supervision, use of force policy, investigation and adjudication, inmate programs, the regulation of inmate behavior, and the department's management information system (see also New York State Commission of Correction, 1987a).

Today most institutions have stated policies and procedures regulating the use of official force. However, such documents do not preclude the misuse of force. At Rikers Island, two years after the *Final Report* was published, another riot took place, and once again, numerous claims of excessive force inflicted on inmates were cited. After the riot, a physician reported treating 24 inmates with stick marks and serious head, back, and shoulder injuries that were consistent with being struck by wooden batons. Legal Aid Society lawyers said that many inmates were forced to remove much of their clothing and pass through a hallway where the officers beat them (New York State Commission of Correction, 1991; Welch, 1991c). In the final analysis, there always exists a fine line between the use of appropriate and excessive force in correctional institutions (see Adams, 1998; Hamm *et al.*, 1994).

Unofficial force

The use of unofficial force as a measure of informal control is best illustrated when a staff member assaults a prisoner. Such incidents may involve an individual CO striking an inmate, or even more reprehensible, a group of officers known as a 'goon squad.' While there are relatively few studies on the subject of official force, there is even less research on unofficial force. Among the rare examinations of unofficial force is a classic study by James Marquart who conducted participant observation at the Texas Department of Corrections (TDC) in the 1980s. Marquart worked as a CO for 19 months, during which time only the warden and a few administrators were informed that his task was to collect data on the use of unofficial force.

Marquart identified varying degrees of severity in the use of unofficial force. The least severe were forms of verbal intimidation (racial and ethnic slurs) aimed at threatening, degrading, and lowering a convict's self-esteem. Next were minor incidents of physical abuse reserved for inmates who resisted an officer's authority or had violated institutional rules. Such minor assaults were known as *tune-ups*, *attitude adjustment*, or *counseling*. Marquart, as an example of a tune-up taking place, reports the following incident after disciplinary court:

> The first inmate was tried for refusing to work. The tape recorder was shut off and a supervisor said, 'You're going to work from now on, you understand?' After this, the supervisor slapped him on the head, kicked him in the ass, and literally threw him out the door. The next inmate came in and was tried and found guilty of self-mutilation. He ingested numerous razor blades. One supervisor yelled at him. 'It's hard enough for me to keep the rest of these inmates in razor blades to shave with around here, let alone having you eat them all the time.' The inmate stuttered and a supervisor slapped him twice across the face.
>
> (Marquart, 1986: 352)

The next degree of unofficial force was referred to as an *ass whipping*. Convicts were subjected to an *ass whipping* upon committing more serious violations, such as threatening an officer or fighting back during a tune-up. That type of assault generally featured the use of weapons, namely batons and aluminum-cased flashlights. Additionally, some officers inflicted the *tap dance* in which the prisoner was restrained on the floor while an officer stepped on the inmate's head. Although *ass whippings* and *tap dances* were violent, the recipient usually did not require hospitalization. *Severe beatings*, on the other hand, constituted the most brutal type of unofficial force. Consequently, injured prisoners required hospitalization. Inmates who attacked staff members, incited work strikes (or riots), or attempted to escape typically faced a *severe beating*.

Marquart (1986) learned that unofficial force, as a mechanism of social control, serves various functions or purposes. First, coercion maintains control and order, insofar as those who challenge authority are subjected to informal punishment. Secondly, unofficial force maintains status and deference by instilling a sense of fear and subordination among inmates toward the prison staff. In the context of the 'guard' subculture, Marquart found that unofficial force was also used as a strategy to move upward in the prison organization. That is, in pursuit of upward mobility, young officers occasionally inflicted injury on inmates to exhibit their worthiness. By showing that they had 'snap,' or 'balls,' those officers earned respect from senior COs, thereby priming themselves for promotion within the guard hierarchy. Often younger officers were socialized by senior COs who taught them the techniques of unofficial force. Finally, coercion builds solidarity among officers who exhibited high morale and formed close bonds with one another (in and outside the prison). Sharing 'war stories' of assaulting inmates, while adhering to secrecy, also added to a sense of camaraderie among staff members. In sum, the main finding of Marquart's research should be underscored; that is, not all officers used unofficial force at TDC. In fact, only a small, but significant, group of guards relied on those types of assaults. Specifically, young (aged 18 to 24, with only a few years of experience), white officers who sought upward mobility were those most likely to use unofficial force. The fearless use of violence served as one of their means for promotion within the system (see Lurigio, 2009; Marquart, 2007; Souryal, 2009; Zimbardo, 2007).

Obviously, assaults on inmates by officers remain a serious issue. In a Supreme Court case involving Angola penitentiary (Louisiana) inmate Keith Hudson, *Hudson* v. *McMillian* (1992), the prisoner argued that beatings inflicted by officers constituted a form of cruel and unusual punishment. The High Court concurred that when officers maliciously and sadistically assault inmates, contemporary standards of decency are violated. More importantly, assaults do not have to be as severe as broken bones or concussions to be unconstitutional. Even assaults involving injuries as minor as a split lip or a broken dental plate, as claimed in the Hudson incident, are unconstitutional. A case in point: two correctional officers at the Great Meadow state prison in Comstock, New York, were dismissed after a videotape recorded them beating an inmate in 1993. In the film, the officers are shown striking a handcuffed prisoner as he groaned in pain. Two other officers were suspended for filing a false report about the incident. Investigators called the assault disgusting when it was revealed that the prisoner was struck in the head with batons, 'sounding like a crack of the bat.' A prison monitor concluded: 'The inmate didn't do anything to deserve it. The force was unnecessary and excessive' (Fisher, 1993: B1). More recently, in 2000, a corrections officer at the Nassau County Jail (New York) pleaded guilty to acting as a lookout while two other officers entered a cell and severely beat an inmate who died in custody days later. The victim, Thomas Pizzuto, was serving a 90-day sentence for driving while intoxicated and other traffic violations. Pizzuto, a recovering heroin addict, is believed to have angered the corrections officers by clamoring for his methadone treatment (Cooper, 2000).

CULTURAL PENOLOGY

Symbols of Violence in Prison

In his book *A World of Violence: Corrections in America* (1995), Matthew Silberman draws critical attention to the symbols of violence in prison. Indeed, the penal environment – inside and out – is replete with signs that serve as constant reminders of impending violence. On the exterior one can recognize traditional Gothic prison architecture, featuring monumental walls, high fences, razor wire, and gun towers. The interior boasts metal bars (or grilles), electronic gates, metal detectors, and surveillance cameras. Since COs do not carry guns inside the institution, they must rely on body alarms and walkie-talkies to alert fellow officers of an attack or disturbance. A prominent symbol of violence in some institutions is called deuces – a code for officers to dial 2-2-2 – for backup. COs intuitively know the urgency conveyed by the deuces code; still, efforts to rescue a victim of violence – staff or prisoner – often come too late because attacks are typically very brief encounters. Perpetrators often use quick assaults to maximize the element of surprise, and in the time it takes to react injuries have already been inflicted.

Silberman considers the significance of the symbols of violence and their impact on the prison psyche. Subtle symbols, though just as compelling, are 'war stories.' Rookie guards and fish (newly admitted inmates) are subjected to institutional folktales – all of which underscore the dangers and horrors of prison life. Although war stories are either greatly exaggerated or altogether false, their symbolism resonates. Fleisher repeats the following folktale told by a CO at the federal penitentiary at Lompoc (California):

> I remember back about 1981 or '82. I had just come to work on the evening watch, when there was triple deuce. We went running out to industries. There was [convict Brown], who had taken a pipe about two feet long and hit [convict Terry] unconscious. Brown, he took a sissy shank and cut off Terry's head, damn near. His head was hanging on by a little piece of flesh. There was blood everywhere. The PA [physician assistant] was there. He tried to save him. They got him on a gurney and the PA held his head on, while they carried him in. The work corridor and the main corridor were covered in blood. What a mess!
>
> (1989: 223–4)

COs and convicts alike enjoy repeating stories of institutional folklore. Indeed, all prisons have their own unique inventory of 'war stories' that serve as symbols of violence (see Brown, 2009; May, 2000; Page, 2002).

SELF-INFLICTED VIOLENCE

A final permutation of violence in prisons is perhaps the most perplexing. Suicide, self-inflicted injury, and mutilation raise serious questions about the extent to which the prison experience affects certain inmates. As discussed in greater depth in Chapter 16, suicide ought to be distinguished from other acts of self-inflicted violence, such as mutilation. Whereas suicide (either accidental or deliberate) signals the clearest form of desperation and deep emotional pain, mutilation appears to be more of a strategy to manipulate prison officials. For example, in the Texas Department of Corrections, inmates known as 'cutters' routinely lacerate themselves with razor blades: the intent is to be remanded to a medical unit. While in the infirmary, those convicts benefit from individual attention from medical staff, and during the time it takes for their injuries to heal, work and other harsh realities of prison life are temporarily suspended (see Welch and Gunther, 1997a, 1997b).

STRATEGIES TO REDUCE VIOLENCE

It is unreasonable to presume that all incidents of prison and jail violence can be prevented. However, policy-makers and administrators can employ measures to make correctional institutions safer places for officers and inmates. It is necessary to acknowledge that all levels and forms of prison and jail violence are associated with institutional conditions. Overcrowding has been cited as one factor; still, there are multiple sources of stress and frustration (poor food services, inadequate healthcare, lack of meaningful programs, etc.) that, when left unchecked, may lead to violence (Welch, 1996h, 1995c; Wooldredge et al., 2001).

Administrators need to focus on staff training that addresses both individual and collective violence. At the individual level, officers must learn skills (i.e. conflict resolution) that permit them to effectively deal with frustrated and angry inmates whose behavior might escalate into violence. At the collective level, officers must be prepared to prevent and control large-scale disturbances. Explicit policies and procedures, ranging from strategies for containing the disturbance to the appropriate use of force, are necessary components of institutional control (Vaughn, 1995).

Other preventive measures focus on the following: better screening of inmates to determine who is more likely to resort to aggression; the introduction of ombudsmen, formal procedures for filing grievances, and dispute resolutions that are taken seriously by inmates, staff, and administration; neutralization of the impact of gangs by denying them the recognition they need to generate power; architectural designs that improve supervision; and development of strategies to counter public indifference.

Fleisher (1989) offers another reportedly successful strategy for managing long-term prisoners who are prone to violence. That is, assign them to a high-security institution where they are subjected to greater supervision. Moreover, high-security institutions must provide well-implemented prison industry programs that offer relatively decent hourly wages for inmates who comply with institutional rules. In essence, such programs operate on the principle of positive reinforcement by rewarding pro-social behavior.

Correctional philosophies that dictate the course of daily operations also are important in preventing violence. Colvin (1992) argues that rehabilitative ideologies coupled with meaningful programs are more effective and efficient in maintaining order and safety than is the custodial philosophy. Since maintaining stability in prison requires the cooperation of convicts, administrators can encourage their participation to help create a less violent environment. It should be noted, however, that strict coercive and punitive controls oriented toward incapacitation often undermine long-term institutional stability (Crews and Montgomery, 2002).

Clearly, violence takes place when existing controls are strained or break down. DiIulio (1987) contends that despite overcrowding, budget limitations, and racial polarization, disruption can be reduced by establishing what he calls good government. He proposes that a prison can operate as a constitutional government that holds convicts, staff, and administrators to the same standards of the law. Through the introduction and maintenance of constitutional government, prisons can promote civility and justice (also see Colvin, 1981; Gill, 1996; Martin and Ekland-Olson, 1987; Useem and Kimball, 1989).

Architecture and the New Generation philosophy

Since the future of corrections entails the construction of additional institutions, it is imperative that more attention be given to architecture. Zupan (1991) emphasizes the importance of prison architecture by pointing out that better-designed correctional facilities can lead to safer and more humane environments. The traditional architecture of correctional institutions features the linear/intermittent-surveillance design that has serious limitations. For example, the linear/intermittent design limits supervision, thereby contributing to violence and misconduct because it provides more opportunities for such acts with less fear of detection (Welch, 1991b). Zupan proposes greater use of new-generation jails to reduce violence. 'Underlying the New Generation philosophy is the assumption that inmates engage in violent and destructive behavior in order to control and manipulate a physical environment and organizational operations which fail to provide for their critical human needs' (Zupan, 1991: 5).

The new generation philosophy is driven by widely accepted assertions regarding human (not necessarily criminal) behavior. Individuals tend to engage in violence and misconduct when their critical needs are not met (e.g. safety, privacy, personal space, activity, familial contact, social relations, and dignity). In an effort to meet those critical needs in the new generation jail, prisoners are divided into manageable groups (between 16 and 46) and housed in modules in which the custodial staff have maximum observation, supervision, and interaction with inmates (Zupan, 1991; Welch, 1991b).

Critics, however, argue that new-generation jails are effective because they control only 'softer prisoners,' and not hard-core violent offenders. The new generation approach has not yet been systematically tested with a high-security convict population. Instead, current and future trends suggest that more attention is being given to technological advances to improve supervision (e.g. monitors and videotaping) as well as traditional methods of fortifying the institution –

including more nuts and bolts and bricks and mortar (see Sparks *et al.*, 1996; Useem and Goldstone, 2002).

Prison build-up and disorder?

As discussed in Chapter 1, the enormous build-up in American corrections has given scholars and policy-makers good reason to be concerned about the long- and short-term consequences of greater reliance on incarceration. Among those concerns are warnings of more violence, riots, and escapes due to an expanding penal apparatus that cannot keep pace with a seemingly endless influx of convicts. Simply put, institutions are expected to become unstable as daily operations give way to 'prison riots, hostage taking, gang warfare, and inmate to inmate, inmate to staff, and staff to inmate violence' (Blomberg and Lucken, 2000: 132; see also Hagan, 1995; Wacquant, 2001).

It has been suggested that due to instability, prisons would lose their authority over the mounting convict population that would exert its power over staff and administration. As an analogue, unstable prisons would resemble 'failed states' in which central governments can no longer effectively manage and control the population (Goldstone and Useem, 1999; Useem and Goldstone, 2002). Scholars interested in determining whether such a scenario has actually unfolded have visited the notion of a lawless prison. Bert Useem and Anne Piehl (2006), for instance, have taken a close look at prison build-up and found that the huge expansion in corrections has not produced disorder. Rather than discovering increases in chaos behind bars, they report that prison riots have become less common; moreover, those prisons also boast a lower homicide rate and fewer escapes.

With that evidence, Useem and Piehl conclude that the trend of order rather than disorder stems from political and correctional leadership that has made prisons more effective in dealing with a booming inmate population. Certainly, the correctional build-up has created negative consequences (e.g. perpetuating the racial and economic divide in criminal justice) but diminished prison order is not among them (see Irwin, 2005). Still, they caution 'prisons are not inherently unstable institutions, but neither are they inherently stable. Prisons can change from order to disorder, and the reverse, rather rapidly' (2006: 89; 2008; see Liebling, 2004; Sparks *et al.*, 1996; Steiner and Wooldredge, 2009).

JACK HENRY ABBOTT: A LEGACY OF VIOLENCE

Jack Henry Abbott is remembered as a complex and controversial figure in modern penology, especially considering his literary accomplishments marred by his conviction of manslaughter shortly after his release on parole. While in prison in 1978, Abbott initiated a lengthy correspondence with the author Norman Mailer, who was at the time was writing *The Executioner's Song* (1979), a fictionalized biography of executed murderer Gary Gilmore. Abbott and Gilmore served time together in the Utah state penitentiary, thus Mailer was not only eager to learn more about Gilmore but also took an interest in Abbott's own writings. Mailer was tremendously impressed by Abbott's ability to convey the stark reality of prison life, and was instrumental in having Abbott's letters published in the prestigious *New York Review of Books*. Abbott's collection of writings culminated in *In the Belly of the Beast* (1982). The book, featuring an introduction by Mailer, was not only commercially successful but highly acclaimed by critics. In *The New York Times Book Review*, critic Terrence Des Pres called *In the Belly of the Beast*, 'awesome, brilliant, perversely ingenuous; its impact is indelible, and as an articulation of penal nightmare it is completely compelling' (Worth, 2002b: B2). When Abbott was being considered for parole, Mailer wrote a supportive letter on his behalf: 'Mr. Abbott has the makings of a powerful and important writer' (Worth, 2002b: B1). Mailer pleaded for Abbott's release, guaranteeing him gainful employment; subsequently, Abbott was transferred to a New York halfway house in early June 1981, where he worked as a researcher earning $150 a week. Abbott was quickly embraced as a curious celebrity, appearing on nationally televised news programs and attending dinners with New York's literary elite.

Just six weeks after his release, Abbott's fame turned tragic when, during a confrontation outside a restaurant, he stabbed a man to death. His victim was 22-year-old Richard Adan, an aspiring actor working nights as a waiter. The murder brought intense criticism of Mailer, who was ridiculed for having romanticized Abbott for his literary talent while failing to recognize the ex-con's capacity for violence. Mailer said he 'felt a large responsibility' for the death of Adan, insisting that he 'never thought Abbott was close to killing and that's why I have to sit in judgment on myself. I just was not sensitive to the fact' (Worth, 2002: B1).

After the deadly incident, Abbott eluded police and fled New York City; following a month-long manhunt, he was apprehended in Louisiana and extradited to New York, where he was convicted of first-degree manslaughter and sentenced to 15 years to life. In 1990, Abbott was sued in civil court by Adan's widow, who was awarded $7.57 million in damages. The award included Abbott's future earnings as well as the $100,000 he had already earned from *In the Belly of the Beast* and $15,000 he had earned from the rights to a film about the murder and another book he had written titled *My Return* (1987). Abbott had already been barred from using any of the proceeds of *My Return* under New York State's so-called Son of Sam law that prevents offenders from profiting from their crimes.

In his book *In the Belly of the Beast*, Abbott chronicles his life as a state-raised convict. He spent the better part of his first 12 years being shuttled among foster homes before being sent to the Utah state reformatory. At age 18, Abbott was released and only six months later, he was sent to the Utah penitentiary to serve time for writing bad checks. Three years later, he stabbed one convict to death and injured another in a prison brawl, adding more time to his sentence. In 1971, at the age of 25, he escaped briefly and robbed a bank, an offense that added a 19-year federal sentence on top of state time. Self-educated, Abbott delved into the revolutionary philosophies of Mao and Stalin and wrote critically about violence and racism in America and in its prisons.

In 2002, corrections officers at the Wende Correctional Facility (New York) found Abbott, aged 58, hanging from a bed sheet – an apparent suicide. After learning of Abbott's death, Mailer lamented: 'His life was tragic from beginning to end. I never knew a man who had a worse life. What made it doubly awful is that he brought a deadly tragedy down on one young man full of promise and left a bomb crater of lost possibilities for many, including most especially himself' (Worth, 2002: B1).

CONCLUSION

As stated earlier, violence – in society as well as in correctional institutions – remains a serious social problem. Just as many of the sources of violence in the *free world* are diverse (e.g. harsh living conditions, the drug trade, proliferation of weapons, alcohol abuse, etc.), so too is the case of the *convict world* (e.g. overcrowding, harsh conditions of confinement, the underground economy, and the prevalence of violent convicts). Jeffrey Reiman, in his thoughtful book The *Rich Get Richer and the Poor Get Prison*, raises several concerns about the role of prisons in society as well as deplorable institutional conditions that pave the way for violence. As a remedy, Reiman proposes that prisons should be both civilized and civilizing. Obviously, violent prisons can hardly be considered civilized. Moreover, if prisoners do not become more civilized during their incarceration, then public safety is compromised when aggressive convicts are released into the community. Whereas single incidents of victimization rarely transform non-violent offenders into dangerous predators, the impact that persistent assaults have on prisoners should not be dismissed. Even for inmates who have not been assaulted in prison, the experience of incarceration is profound. For prisoners who have endured repeated violence, those negative effects of institutionalization are all the more dramatic. It is no exaggeration to say that those inmates suffer a level of punishment exceeding the sentence imposed by the judge (Amnesty International, 1999; Blazak, 2009; Earley, 1992; Welch, 2002c).

SUMMARY

This chapter examines the problem of violence in correctional facilities. In doing so, it presents the two basic levels of institutional violence – collective and individual. Incidents of collective violence, such as riots and large-scale disturbances, have become relatively infrequent occurrences. Although individual acts of lethal violence (i.e. homicide) are also in decline, the threat of such aggression remains a routine problem in many prisons and jails. Discussion considers key permutations of violence: inmate–inmate, inmate–staff, and staff–inmate. So as to understand the theoretical explanations of those forms of aggression, the chapter turns critical attention to the various motives, goals, and sources of penal violence. Each of those components of violence is explored in two in-depth analyses – the riots at Attica and New Mexico. The chapter concludes by offering strategies to reduce institutional violence.

REVIEW QUESTIONS

1   What are the differences between instrumental and expressive violence?
2   Explain the key assertions of the various theoretical models of prison riots.
3   What were the political forces shaping the riot at Attica?
4   How did the violence in the New Mexico prison riot differ from the violence at Attica?
5   What is the difference between official and unofficial force in prisons? Give some examples of each.

RECOMMENDED READINGS

Attica: The Official Report of the New York State Commission (1972) New York: Bantam Books.

Fleisher, M. (1989) *Warehousing Violence*. Newbury Park, CA: Sage.

Silberman, M. (1995) *A World of Violence: Corrections in America*. Belmont, CA: Wadsworth.

Stone, W. G. (1982) *The Hate Factory: The Story of the New Mexico Penitentiary Riot*. Agoura, CA: Dell.

Wicker, T. (1975) *A Time to Die*. New York: Quadrangle.

CHAPTER 10

The Death Penalty

I never felt the death penalty was a deterrent, and I don't care if it costs more, I don't care as long as the guy pays with his life. (New York Assemblyman Anthony Seminerio)

Capital punishment is for those who have no capital. (An old prison adage)

If there were a death penalty, more people would be alive. (Nancy Reagan)

LEARNING OBJECTIVES

After studying this chapter, you should be able to answer the following questions:

1 What is the history of the death penalty and how have past forms of execution shaped contemporary death sentences?

2 What are the key issues in the debate over the death penalty?
3 What are the current patterns of death sentences and executions?
4 What are the landmark decisions affecting the death penalty?
5 How is the execution process actually carried out?

On August 9, 1969, four members of Charles Manson's bizarre cult snuck into the California estate of film director Roman Polanski. Though Polanski was fortunate enough to be away at the time, his wife, actress Sharon Tate, who was eight months pregnant, and her guests were not so lucky. In one of this century's most ghastly mass murders, Charles 'Tex' Watson, Susan Atkins, Leslie Van Houten, and Patricia Krenwinkle viciously slaughtered Tate, Abigail Folger (heiress to the Folger coffee empire), Voyteck Frykowski (a Polish writer and producer), Jay Sebring (famous hair stylist), and 18-year-old Steven Parent. To no avail, Tate pleaded with the intruders to spare her unborn child. 'Look, bitch, I have no mercy for you,' replied one of the killers. Watson and the other Manson fanatics mercilessly shot, stabbed, and clubbed their victims to death – leaving their bodies in pools of blood. The killers used the blood of Tate and the others to scrawl messages on the wall, including 'PIG' and 'WAR.' The next evening, those four killers struck again. This time the nightmare was repeated in the home of grocery store magnate Leno and Rosemary La Bianca, both of whom also were stabbed to death by the sadistic Manson family members. Borrowing from the Beatles' song, the killers left behind the phrase 'HELTER SKELTER' written with the blood of the La Biancas. Proponents of the death penalty argue that if ever there were a case that merits execution, it's the Manson murders. Indeed, Watson, Atkins, Van Houten, Krenwinkle, as well as Manson were convicted and sentenced to death. In 1972, however, their sentences were commuted to life imprisonment as a result of the Supreme Court's banning of executions. (Bugliosi and Gentry, 1974: 38–9).

INTRODUCTION

Undoubtedly, the death penalty is among the most polarizing topics in American criminal justice since most citizens either strongly favor or strongly oppose executions. And while advocates and opponents alike resort to intellectual arguments in explaining their views over capital punishment, they often back their positions with emotionally charged opinions (see Borg, 1998). Still, the debate unfolds several practical concerns involving deterrence, costs, and overall fairness in death sentencing. In taking a critical approach to capital punishment, this chapter examines those issues but also takes aim at some of the myths shaping the discourse over the use of executions.

The discussion begins with a brief history, followed by the rationales for executions, a current look at death sentences, and landmark US Supreme Court decisions. So as to open some space for further critique, the chapter also explores some key theoretical debates, namely deterrence and brutalization. Remaining mindful of social and racial inequality in the use of the death penalty, attention also is turned to other controversies: the execution of juvenile offenders, the mentally retarded, and the mentally disturbed, as well as miscarriages of justice in which the innocent are wrongfully convicted and sentenced to death. Finally, the chapter features a graphic look at the execution process along with a review of alternatives to the death penalty.

A BRIEF HISTORY OF EXECUTIONS

A particularly revealing dimension of the death penalty is the degree of ingenuity and planning devoted to executions. Historically, societies have introduced elaborate execution procedures, reflecting meticulous preoccupation with eliminating certain social outcasts. An ancient method of execution in Asia involved the exposure of the condemned to a gradual death from insect bites. Consider the following procedure:

> He was encased in a coffin-like box, from which his head, hands, and feet protruded, through holes made for that purpose; he was fed with milk and honey, which he was forced to take, and his face was smeared with the same mixture; he was exposed to the sun, and in this state he remained for seventeen days, until he had been devoured alive by insects and vermin, which swarmed about him and bred within him.
>
> (Frederick Wines, 1895: 70, quoted in
> Barnes and Teeters, 1946: 414)

Other barbaric methods of execution have emerged throughout history, such as beheading, burning, stoning, drowning, flaying and impaling, skinning alive and hanging on sharp stakes. Throwing the condemned to the lions or wild beasts remained popular in ancient Rome, and in early Asian societies criminals were sometimes sewn inside a sack with poisonous reptiles. In medieval Europe, some lawbreakers – and accused heretics – were hung upside down and sawed in half vertically (Barnes, 1972; Barnes and Teeters, 1946).

As discussed in Chapters 2 and 3, the death penalty is driven by various rationales. Besides the obvious goal of inflicting immense pain and suffering on the condemned, some death penalties were based on simple revenge and retribution. Still other executions were intent to offer greater symbolic meaning; for instance, in pre-Christian times beheadings were a sacrificial act to placate as well as ward off evil. During later periods in European history, beheading became viewed as an honorable death. While executions were thought to provide permanent banishment, they also were aimed at producing a cleansing effect by ridding the community of evil (Newman, 1978).

Early forms of execution sometimes involved villagers who in an attempt to vent their collective rage over certain criminals willfully participated in public stonings. Public executions during the late Middle Ages continued to take place in the marketplace or village square; however, the unbridled rage of past executions was blunted by formal ceremony orchestrated by the monarchy. Under those circumstances, executions were ritualized as brutal displays of 'justice' for a larger audience of citizens, thereby reinforcing royal power while issuing seemingly potent messages of deterrence (Abbott, 1991; Foucault, 1977; Johnson, 1998).

Eventually, executions were brought behind the closed doors of prisons. Although contemporary scholars continue to debate explanations for the decline of the public spectacle, it has been suggested that over time the executions placed the monarchy in an unfavorable light since such brutality became viewed as excessive. Paradoxically, these displays of 'justice' undermined rather than maintained the legitimacy of rulers. Similarly, it is theorized that by moving punishment to the prison, offenders would be kept from receiving public sympathy. Since penitentiaries were shut off to the public, punishment also became mystified: exactly what type of horrific punishments was inflicted on prisoners remained a mystery to those in the community. While playing on the public imagination, such mystification furthered notions of deterrence, allowing the monarchy – or state – to regain its legitimacy and right to punish society's wrongdoers (see Bentham, 1995; Foucault, 1977; Smith, 2008).

Although executions are driven by political gains aimed at reinforcing the government's legitimate right to punish serious offenders, religious forces have also figured prominently. Along with the use of torture and the execution of accused heretics during the Inquisition, other forms of capital punishment have been motivated and justified with religious fervor aimed at punishing sinners. In Colonial America, each colony created its own list of acts considered capital crimes, including death sentences for religious transgressions such as idolatry, witchcraft, blasphemy, bestiality, adultery, and an array of sexual violations (see Chapters 2 and 3). Then during America's early nationhood, capital punishment became increasingly restricted to secular crimes. Also economic forces soon influenced the prosecution of certain capital crimes, particularly in the effort to maintain a slave economy. Death sentences in the South were extended to such crimes as concealing and stealing slaves along with acts intent on inciting slaves to rebel (Bedau, 1982; Bowers *et al.*, 1984).

The guillotine and the emergence of modern execution

Even a brief history of execution warrants critical attention directed at the guillotine, especially given its deep implications for technology, science, and politics. As Philip Smith (2008, 2006, 2003) reminds us, the French Revolution was accompanied by a serious commitment to law and justice, through which the monarchy and its use of arbitrary power were replaced. Although early versions of the guillotine had been around for at least two centuries, the invention was greatly improved by Dr Joseph Ignace Guillotin (1738–1814). Along with his colleague Dr Louis, Guillotin lobbied to have the device adopted as the quintessential form of French execution since it combined state-of-the-art technology with modern politics and its quest for equality.

The *ancien régime* perpetuated class biases – even the application of death. Nobles were beheaded with a sword while commoners were hanged. Under the new laws of the French Republic each citizen would die in exactly the same, egalitarian way. The French Minister of Justice officially authorized the guillotine in 1792, and the method of beheading was consequently adopted in Article 3. It was reasoned that the guillotine would provide the swiftest and least painful mode of death.

> The new technology of death proposed by Dr Ignace Guillotin to the Assemblée Nationale embodied revolutionary and Enlightenment ideals of humanism, science and efficiency – qualities we have already suggested revolutionaries viewed with an almost religious awe (Hunt, 1984). Viewed from a distance the device has a certain aesthetic appeal. The frame in which the blade runs is rectangular, the angled blade (couperet) appears triangular and the head collar (la lunette républicaine) makes a circle. This geometrical combination of rectangle, circle and triangle can be read as embodying an abstract, remote and mathematical beauty that is consistent with Enlightenment ideals of reason and universality (Arasse, 1987). Aside from this Euclidean symbolism, the guillotine was supported by empiricist scientific discourses and procedures. These mobilized the knowledge-bases of anatomy and natural science to attest to and justify the need for a machine-like functionality in rational design. Experimental testing had been used to establish its efficiency.
>
> (Smith, 2003: 34)

Like many scholars before him, Foucault offers a critical interpretation of the guillotine. He notes that the device matches a new juridical ethic while embracing the ideals of modern society: simply put, the guillotine emerged as a 'machine for the production of rapid and discrete deaths' (1977: 15). Chief among the technological benefits of the device was its capacity for processing up to 20 victims per hour (see Barnes and Teeters, 1946).

Interpretations of the guillotine by both Foucault and Smith further our understanding of executions being propelled by scientific projects involving physics, anatomy, and medicine. In a lecture to the French Assemblée Nationale in 1790 Guillotin boasted the 'humane' quality of modern execution:

> The blade hisses, the head falls, blood spurts, the man exists no more. With my machine I'll cut off your head in the blink of an eye and you will feel nothing but a slight coolness on the back of the neck.
>
> (quoted in Smith, 2003: 35)

While Dr Guillotin relied on medical discourse to promote the device as humane and therefore consistent with the ideals of the French Republic, other experts used a competing set of scientific knowledge to refute those claims. In 1795, Professor Soemmering challenged the scientific foundation of the guillotine,

Figure 10.1   A picture from the Criminal Museum in Rome dated January 12, 2006 showing a guillotine used by the Papal State. After 1798 the Roman Republic was proclaimed to be under Napoleonic rule and Pius VI was deported to France. The French introduced the guillotine in the former Papal State. The first condemned prisoner to be put to death with the new instrument was Tommaso Tintori, beheaded on February 28, 1810. The executioner went on to use the guillotine at least six times from 1810 to 1813.

Photo credit Alberto Pizzoli/AFP/Getty Images.

insisting that the device issued a 'horrible mode of death. In the head, separated from the body of the victim, sentiment, and personality remain alive for some time, and feel the after-pain afflicting the neck' (quoted in Smith, 2003: 38). Soemmering went on to argue that the head was primary as a seat of pain. Some witnesses of executions said they observed the decapitated head grinding its teeth. Citing the phenomenon of phantom limbs, Soemmering suggested that the intense pain could persist for up to a quarter of an hour. The debate continued as other physicians and scientists proposed that the guillotine did not produce acute pain; rather, by severing the spinal column, the device delivered instant death (see Smith, 2008). The guillotine would remain the primary form of execution in France for nearly two centuries. It was last used in 1971 and in 1981 the device along with the death penalty were abolished in France.

More recently, executions are facilitated by other technological mechanisms, such as the electric chair and lethal injection. Much like the debate over the guillotine, proponents tend to rely on scientific claims that these devices make the execution more humane. Turning to other medical evidence, critics insist that electrocution as well as lethal injection fail to deliver a quick and painless death. Opponents also contend that technology primarily serves to streamline the death sentence, thereby making the task easier for the state and the executioner. As we shall discuss further, technology creates social and psychological distance between the condemned and the executioner. In doing so, modern innovations prevent the executioner from soiling his hands and minimizes a sense of guilt associated with taking the life of another person. Similarly, the application of science produces a sanitizing effect by making executions appear painless and efficient, thereby allowing the government to avert accusations of brutality.

DEBATE OVER THE DEATH PENALTY

Perhaps given the serious nature of capital punishment, it is not surprising that the debate over its use is not only convoluted but emotionally charged as well. Still, the debate is far from being resolved. In this section, the major arguments put forth by the proponents and opponents of the death penalty are discussed.

Arguments favoring the death penalty

Tradition

Simply put, proponents of the death penalty sometimes argue that since execution has remained a powerful form of punishment throughout much of history, its tradition should continue (see Chapters 2 and 3).

Retribution

Many proponents of capital punishment strongly believe that individuals who commit heinous crimes (e.g. first-degree homicide) ought to be punished by equally harsh sanctions, including death. The retribution argument is firmly rooted in revenge, upholding the principle of *lex talionis* or 'an eye for an eye.' In landmark cases, the U.S. Supreme Court offers a diversity of opinion on whether retribution should remain a valid argument for executions (see *Furman* v. *Georgia*, 1972).

Community solidarity

Sociologists observe that executions have the capacity to promote community solidarity and cohesion in part because when laws and penalties are collectively enforced, a sense of justice is maintained. In more extreme expressions of solidarity, some contemporary executions have galvanized public outrage while also prompting festive celebration. Consider the 1989 electrocution of serial killer Ted Bundy in

Florida where large rallies formed outside prison fences; certainly, that gathering harked back to the enthusiastic crowds attending public hangings in earlier times (see Kennedy, 2000; Smith, 2008, 2006, 2003; Chapter 4 this volume).

Community protection

Proponents also suggest that executions serve as the ultimate incapacitation, thereby protecting society from violent offenders. It is often argued that without executions, convicted murderers might escape from prison or be paroled by the authorities. In either case, the safety of the community would he jeopardized. Critics point out, however, that paroled murderers have extremely low rates of recidivism and rarely commit murder after serving lengthy prison terms (see Bohm, 1999; Dow and Dow, 2002).

Deterrence

Many advocates of the death penalty contend that executions send such a powerful message to members of society that other acts of homicides are deterred (Rubin, 2009). That argument, however, is challenged by numerous empirical studies (Donohue and Wolfers, 2005; Fagan et al., 2006). An upcoming section fully discusses the issue of deterrence, noting, among other things, the absence of conclusive evidence. Moreover, recent research suggests that executions may actually precipitate future violence (Cochran and Chamlin, 2000; Cochran et al., 2004).

Financial costs

Some supporters assert that those convicted of first-degree murder ought to be executed so as to avoid the high cost of their life-long incarceration. That belief is another widely accepted myth given that executions are exceedingly expensive. Court and legal costs stemming from complex trials and lengthy appeals (which are in place to ensure against the execution of an innocent person) are paid for by tax dollars (Garey, 1985). In his research, Raymond Paternoster (1991: 118) cites three specific aspects of capital punishment contributing to its high cost:

1 Capital trials are far more expensive for the state to prosecute and for the defendant to defend than non-capital trials due to the numerous and complex legal issues that must be resolved before the sentence of death can be imposed.
2 Capital trials are really two separate trials: a guilt and a penalty phase. Each stage requires far more preparation and additional resources than non-capital cases.

3   The appeals process in capital cases is also complex and lengthy, demanding large financial expenditures necessary to bring such cases to a final legal determination.

Costs vary from state to state and case to case, but generally, executions are three to four times more expensive than life imprisonment. Estimates for Ted Bundy's execution in 1989, for instance, range from $6 to $10 million (Bohm, 1999).

Public opinion

Since public opinion polls have shown steady support for the death penalty, some proponents argue that legislation on capital punishment ought to reflect public sentiment (see Bohm, 1999).

Prevention of vigilante-style justice

Some proponents of the death penalty suggest that without capital punishment, members of the community might take justice into their own hands. Therefore it is reasoned that capital punishment should be carried out by the state to prevent vigilante-style justice against those convicted of heinous crimes. Recall that in the 1930s the National Guard was called in to protect the Scottsboro Boys, who were being threatened by an angry mob outside the jailhouse (see Chapter 8). In administering death sentences, the state also preserves the image of official justice while maintaining law and order (see Brown, 2009).

Arguments opposing the death penalty

Violation of contemporary standards of decency

In a constitutional democracy, standards of decency continuously evolve, and such changes are represented in its laws. Simply put, continuous legal reforms are emblematic of a civilized society. Opponents of the death penalty insist that executions are a form of social vengeance that impedes society's moral progress (Ogletree and Sarat, 2009, 2006).

Cruel and unusual punishment

Regardless of landmark Supreme Court decisions upholding the death penalty, many critics charge that executions constitute a form of cruel and unusual punishment that violates the Eighth Amendment of the US Constitution (Bohm, 1999; Dow and Dow, 2002). Given the complexity of such legal concerns, we shall return to these issues in a later section.

Error, finality, and irreversibility

Although legal appeals are commonly exhausted to ensure against the execution of an innocent person, the criminal justice system is not fully equipped to prevent all errors. Despite existing safeguards, innocent persons have been executed, and due to the finality of the punishment, errors cannot be rectified (Baumgartner *et al.*, 2008; Naughton, 2007). The problem of wrongful executions also is examined in a later section.

Arbitrariness, discrimination, and the discretionary bias

Another criticism of the death penalty is that it lacks uniformity, thereby making it an arbitrary and capricious form of punishment. Simply because a person has been convicted of first-degree homicide does not mean that execution is inevitable. In fact, the majority of those convicted of first-degree homicide are *not* executed. An inherent discretionary bias exists within the criminal justice system that determines the administering of the death sentence. Prosecutors possess the unreviewable power to charge – or not charge – defendants with a capital offense. Clemency in the form of an executive pardon via the governor to cease an execution is also entirely discretionary. Opponents claim the discretionary and arbitrary nature of capital punishment perpetuates discrimination and racism (Jackson and Jackson, 2001; Waldo and Paternoster, 2003).

A CURRENT LOOK AT THE DEATH PENALTY

So as to understand the patterns and trends in the use of capital punishment in the United States, we turn to recent data provided by the Bureau of Justice Statistics (BJS).

- In 2008, 37 inmates were executed: 18 in Texas; 4 in Virginia; 3 each in Georgia and South Carolina; 2 each in Florida, Mississippi, Ohio, and Oklahoma; and 1 in Kentucky.
- Thirty-six executions were by lethal injection; 1 by electrocution.
- Of persons executed in 2008, 20 were white and 17 were black. All 37 inmates executed were men.
- Thirty-seven states and the federal government had capital statutes at year end 2008.
- Between 1977 and 2008, 7,658 people have been under sentence of death. Of these, 15 percent were executed, 5 percent died from causes other than execution, and 38 percent received other dispositions.
- A total of 111 inmates were received under sentence of death during 2008, representing the smallest number of admissions since 1973.
- A total of 119 inmates were removed from under sentence of death – 37 were executed and 82 were removed by other methods, including sentences

or convictions overturned, commutations of sentence, and deaths by means other than execution.

- In 2009, 48 executions had been carried out (as of November 30), 12 more than the number executed as of the same date in 2008.

(Snell, 2009: 1).

The BJS report for 2008 also includes other details on the death penalty. The most common method of execution is lethal injection followed by electrocution, lethal gas, and hanging and the firing squad (Snell, 2009: 5; Table 10.1).

Table 10.1 Method of execution, by state, 2008

Lethal injection	Electrocution	Lethal gas	Hanging	Firing squad
Alabama[a]	Alabama[a]	Arizona[a,b]	Delaware[a,c]	Idaho[a]
Arizona[a,b]	Arkansas[a,d]	California[a]	New Hampshire[a,e]	Oklahoma[f]
Arkansas[a,d]	Florida[a]	Missouri[a]	Washington[a]	Utah[g]
California[a]	Illinois[a,h]	Wyoming[i]		
Colorado	Kentucky[a,j]			
Connecticut	Oklahoma[f]			
Delaware[a,c]	South Carolina[a]			
Florida[a]	Tennessee[a,k]			
Georgia	Virginia[a]			
Idaho[a]				
Illinois[a]				
Indiana				
Kansas				
Kentucky[a,j]				
Louisiana				
Maryland				
Mississippi				
Missouri[a]				
Montana				
Nevada				
New Hampshire[a]				
New Mexico				
New York				
North Carolina				
Ohio				
Oklahoma[a]				
Oregon				
Pennsylvania				
South Carolina[a]				
South Dakota				
Tennessee[a,k]				
Texas				
Utah[a]				
Virginia[a]				
Washington[a]				
Wyoming[a]				

Table 10.1 continues overleaf

Table 10.1 continued

Note: The method of execution of federal prisoners is lethal injection, pursuant to 28 CFR, Part 26. For offenses under the Violent Crime Control and Law Enforcement Act of 1994, the execution method is that of the state in which the conviction took place (18 U.S.C. 3596). In February 2008, the Nebraska Supreme Court ruled that electrocution violated the state's constitution. As of 12/31/2008, Nebraska had no authorized method of execution.

[a]Authorizes two methods of execution.

[b]Authorizes lethal injection for persons sentenced after November 15, 1992; inmates sentenced before that date may select lethal injection or gas.

[c]Authorizes lethal injection for those whose capital offense occurred after June 13, 1986; those who committed the offense before that date may select lethal injection or hanging.

[d]Authorizes lethal injection for those whose offense occurred on or after July 4, 1983; inmates whose offense occurred before that date may select lethal injection or electrocution.

[e]Authorizes hanging only if lethal injection cannot be given.

[f]Authorizes electrocution if lethal injection is held to be unconstitutional, and firing squad if both lethal injection and electrocution are held to be unconstitutional.

[g]Authorizes firing squad if lethal injection is held unconstitutional. Inmates who selected execution by firing squad prior to May 3, 2004, may still be entitled to execution by that method.

[h]Authorizes electrocution only if lethal injection is held illegal or unconstitutional.

[i]Authorizes lethal gas if lethal injection is held to be unconstitutional.

[j]Authorizes lethal injection for persons sentenced on or after March 31, 1998; inmates sentenced before that date may select lethal injection or electrocution.

[k]Authorizes lethal injection for those whose capital offense occurred after December 31, 1998; those who committed the offense before that date may select electrocution by written waiver.

Source: Snell (2009: 5).

Taking into account matters of race within the four major regions, there are a disproportionate number of blacks on death row. For year 2008, of the 234 prisoners under sentence of death in the Northeast, 140 are black (compared to 85 whites). In the Midwest, of the 270 prisoners under sentence of death, 124 are black (compared to 143 whites). In the South and West, a similar pattern exists: 750 blacks (out of 1,706) and 297 (out of 946), respectively (Snell, 2009: 7; see Table 10.2).

CRITICAL ANALYSIS OF DATA

Locate your state of residence (or one of the states nearest to you) in Table 10.2 and compare the number of black prisoners under sentence of death (year 2008) with the figures for the federal jurisdiction. Which is greater?

In addition to the disproportionate number of blacks on death row nationwide (nearly 42 percent overall), there are other key findings in the BJS report. In the absence of clear income indicators that might point to socioeconomic status, we turn to available data on education. About 41 percent of prisoners under sentence of death have an education at the high school level (or its equivalent) and 37 percent have an education ranging between the 9th and 11th grade. Nearly 14 percent have at least an 8th grade or less (Snell, 2009: 8; see Table 10.3). A current look at capital punishment in the US also prompts us to consider other demographic characteristics, such as the age of those arrested for a capital offense. The most common age group includes offenders between the ages of 20 and 24 at the time of arrest (27 percent) followed by those between 25 and 29 years (23 percent) (see Table 10.4).

CRITICAL ANALYSIS OF DATA

With respect to the data for prisoners under sentence of death and specifically the age at the time of arrest (Table 10.4), complete the following task. Create two major age groups: 39 and younger and 40 and older. Then add the numbers in each group and calculate the percentages. Which is greater?

Moving from the BJS data on prisoners under sentence of death, Table 10.5 lists the numbers of persons executed per state since 1930 and since 1977 (the post-*Gregg* era – see p. 337). Overall, 4,995 prisoners have been put to death since 1930 and more recently, 1,136 since 1977. In the post-*Gregg* era, the leading states for execution are Texas (423), Virginia (102), and Oklahoma (88).

CRITICAL ANALYSIS OF DATA

Turn your attention to Table 10.5. Which states have not carried out at least one execution since 1930?

LANDMARK US SUPREME COURT DECISIONS

The death penalty reached its peak in the 1930s when 1,520 people were put to death in the United States. By the next decade, the death penalty began to decline – 1,174 executed in the 1940s, 682 during the 1950s, and 191 in the 1960s (Paternoster, 1991). Although the framers of the US Constitution did not appear to be concerned over the use of capital punishment, lawyers and civil rights activists during the 1950s and 1960s initiated a movement to legally dismantle the death penalty. Opponents of capital punishment then and now argue that executions violate the Eight Amendment (banning cruel and unusual punishment) as well as infringe upon the Fourteenth Amendment (guaranteeing due process).

The abolition movement in the 1960s was propelled by the report of the President's Commission on Law Enforcement and Administration of Justice, declaring that the death penalty 'is most frequently imposed and carried out on the poor, the Negro, and the members of unpopular groups' (1967: 28). Those words supported ongoing efforts by the National Association for the Advancement of Colored People (NAACP) Legal Defense and Education Fund and the American Civil Liberties Union (ACLU), groups challenging the constitutionality of capital punishment due to its discriminatory nature. By 1968, an unofficial moratorium on executions was established; more than 500 scheduled executions

Table 10.2 Prisoners under sentence of death, by region, jurisdiction, and race, 2007 and 2008

Region and jurisdiction	Prisoners under sentence of death, 12/31/07			Received under sentence of death, 2008			Removed from death row (excluding executions), 2008[a]			Executed, 2008			Prisoners under sentence of death, 12/31/08		
	Total[b]	White[c]	Black[c]	Total[b]	White[c]	Black[c]	Total[b]	White[c]	Black[c]	Total[b]	White[c]	Black[c]	Total[b]	White[c]	Black[c]
US total	3,215	1,806	1,338	111	65	44	82	53	27	37	20	17	3,207	1,798	1,338
Federal[d]	48	21	26	3	2	1	0	0	0	0	0	0	51	23	27
State	3,167	1,785	1,312	108	63	43	82	53	27	37	20	17	3,156	1,775	1,311
Northeast	233	84	139	7	4	3	6	3	2	0	0	0	234	85	140
Connecticut	9	4	5	1	0	1	0	0	0	0	0	0	10	4	6
New Hampshire	0	0	0	1	0	1	0	0	0	0	0	0	1	0	1
New York	0	0	0	0	0	0	0	0	0	0	0	0	0	0	0
Pennsylvania	224	80	134	5	4	1	6	3	2	0	0	0	223	81	133
Midwest	272	144	125	14	8	6	14	8	6	2	1	1	270	143	124
Illinois	13	8	5	3	3	0	1	1	0	0	0	0	15	10	5
Indiana	14	11	3	0	0	0	1	1	0	0	0	0	13	10	3
Kansas	7	3	4	2	2	0	1	1	0	0	0	0	8	4	4
Missouri	45	25	20	6	3	3	1	0	1	0	0	0	50	28	22
Nebraska	9	8	1	0	0	0	0	0	0	0	0	0	9	8	1
Ohio	181	86	92	3	0	3	10	5	5	2	1	1	172	80	89
South Dakota	3	3	0	0	0	0	0	0	0	0	0	0	3	3	0
South	1,732	952	757	58	33	25	49	32	16	35	19	16	1,706	934	750
Alabama	199	106	93	9	3	6	3	2	1	0	0	0	205	107	98
Arkansas	38	14	24	3	2	1	0	0	0	0	0	0	41	16	25
Delaware	19	10	9	1	0	1	0	0	0	0	0	0	20	10	10
Florida	388	255	133	16	11	5	12	10	2	2	1	1	390	255	135
Georgia	106	59	46	3	1	2	1	1	0	3	2	1	105	57	47
Kentucky	38	31	7	0	0	0	1	0	1	1	1	0	36	30	6
Louisiana	85	31	53	3	1	2	4	4	0	0	0	0	84	28	55
Maryland	5	1	4	0	0	0	0	0	0	0	0	0	5	1	4
Mississippi	65	32	32	0	0	0	3	2	1	2	2	0	60	28	31
North Carolina	166	69	88	1	0	1	6	3	3	0	0	0	161	66	86
Oklahoma	80	43	33	9	4	5	2	0	2	2	2	0	85	45	36
South Carolina	59	23	36	4	4	0	2	1	1	3	1	2	58	25	33

Tennessee	96	56	38	0	0	0	9	7	2	0	0	0	87	49	36
Texas	367	214	148	9	7	2	4	2	1	18	9	9	354	210	140
Virginia	21	8	13	0	0	0	2	0	2	4	1	3	15	7	8
West	930	605	291	29	18	9	13	10	3	0	0	0	946	613	297
Arizona	117	100	14	6	5	0	4	3	1	0	0	0	119	102	13
California	655	389	238	20	12	7	6	4	2	0	0	0	669	397	243
Colorado	1	0	1	1	0	1	0	0	0	0	0	0	2	0	2
Idaho	17	17	0	0	0	0	0	0	0	0	0	0	17	17	0
Montana	2	2	0	0	0	0	0	0	0	0	0	0	2	2	0
Nevada	82	50	31	1	0	1	2	2	0	0	0	0	81	48	32
New Mexico	2	2	0	0	0	0	2	2	0	0	0	0	2	2	0
Oregon	35	31	3	0	0	0	0	0	0	0	0	0	35	31	3
Utah	9	7	1	1	1	0	0	0	0	0	0	0	10	8	1
Washington	8	5	3	0	0	0	0	0	0	0	0	0	8	5	3
Wyoming	2	2	0	0	0	0	1	1	0	0	0	0	1	1	0

Note: Some figures shown for year end 2007 are revised from those reported in *Capital Punishment, 2007 – Statistical Tables*, NCJ 224528. The revised figures include 6 inmates who were either reported late to the National Prisoner Statistics program or were not in custody of State correctional authorities on 12/31/07 (3 in Pennsylvania and 1 each in Georgia, Virginia, and Arizona). The revised figures also exclude 11 inmates who were relieved of a death sentence before 12/31/07 (5 in Texas and 1 each in Ohio, Florida, Kentucky, Louisiana, North Carolina, and Nevada).

[a]Includes 16 deaths from natural causes (3 each in Pennsylvania, Florida, and North Carolina; 2 each in Alabama and California; and 1 each in Ohio, Tennessee, and Nevada) and 7 deaths from suicide (2 each in Texas and California; and 1 each in Pennsylvania, Illinois, and Florida).

[b]Includes American Indians, Alaska Natives, Asians, Native Hawaiians, and other Pacific Islanders.

[c]Counts of white and black inmates include persons of Hispanic/Latino origin.

[d]Excludes persons held under Armed Forces jurisdiction with a military death sentence for murder.

Source: Snell (2009:7).

Table 10.3 Demographic characteristics of prisoners under sentence of death, 2008

Characteristic	Prisoners under sentence of death, 2008		
	Year end	Admissions	Removals
Total inmates	3,207	111	119
Gender			
Male	98.2%	97.3 %	99.2 %
Female	1.8	2.7	0.8
Race[a]			
White	56.1%	58.6 %	61.3 %
Black	41.7	39.6	37.0
All other races[b]	2.2	1.8	1.7
Hispanic origin			
Hispanic	13.2%	19.8 %	8.1 %
Non-Hispanic	86.8	80.2	91.9
Number unknown	384	5	8
Education			
8th grade or less	13.5%	17.1 %	19.2 %
9th–11th grade	36.5	31.7	36.4
High school graduate/GED	40.8	41.5	35.4
Any college	9.2	9.8	9.1
Median	12th	12th	11th
Number unknown	528	29	20
Marital status			
Married	22.2%	18.3 %	20.2 %
Divorced/separated	20.1	19.5	27.9
Widowed	2.9	4.9	1.9
Never married	54.7	57.3	50.0
Number unknown	371	29	15

Note: Calculations are based on those cases for which data were reported. Detail may not add to total due to rounding.

[a]Includes persons of Hispanic/Latino origin.
[b]At year end 2008, inmates in 'all other races' consisted of 27 American Indians, 35 Asians, and 9 self-identified Hispanics. During 2008, 1 American Indian and 1 Asian were admitted; and 1 Asian and 1 self-identified Hispanic were removed.

Source: Snell (2009: 8).

were placed on hold while the courts decided the fate of the death penalty. That same year, the US Supreme Court ruled on *Witherspoon* v. *Illinois* in which it determined that 'death-qualified juries' were unconstitutional. That is, in capital cases, states could no longer impanel only those jurors who supported the death penalty while excluding jurors who opposed executions. Also in 1968, the High Court struck down a key provision in capital punishment, namely the federal kidnapping act (the Lindburgh Act) in *United States* v. *Jackson*. It seemed that the abolition movement was gradually gaining momentum in the courts (see Ogletree and Sarat, 2009).

| Age | Prisoners under sentence of death | | | |
| | At time of arrest | | On December 31, 2008 | |
	Number*	Percent	Number	Percent
Total number under sentence of death on 12/31/08	2,957	100 %	3,207	100 %
19 or younger	311	10.5	0	
20–24	811	27.4	44	1.4
25–29	682	23.1	222	6.9
30–34	507	17.1	388	12.1
35–39	317	10.7	564	17.6
40–44	172	5.8	543	16.9
45–49	93	3.1	575	17.9
50–54	36	1.2	394	12.3
55–59	21	0.7	245	7.6
60–64	5	0.2	161	5.0
65 or older	2	0.1	71	2.2
Mean age	29 yrs		43 yrs	
Median age	27 yrs		43 yrs	

Note: The youngest person under sentence of death was a black male in Texas, born in June 1988 and sentenced to death in June 2007. The oldest person under sentence of death was a white male in Arizona, born in September 1915 and sentenced to death in June 1983.

*Excludes 250 inmates for whom the date of arrest for capital offense was not available.

Source: Snell (2009: 10).

Furman v. *Georgia*

In 1972, the moratorium became official when the US Supreme Court ruled to invalidate the death penalty. In that landmark case, *Furman* v. *Georgia*, the Court found that the capital punishment violated the Eighth Amendment of the U.S. Constitution. Specifically, the Court concluded that state statutes that leave arbitrary and discriminatory discretion to juries in imposing death sentences are unconstitutional. In other words, the arbitrary and capricious manner of assigning death sentences by juries was 'cruel and unusual.' However, the decision was based, in part, on narrow considerations. In particular, state statutes were unconstitutional because they did not offer judges and juries any guidelines or standards to determine death sentences. The death penalty was officially banned throughout the nation, and the more than 600 prisoners on death row had their sentences commuted to life imprisonment.

It is important to emphasize that in the *Furman* decision, the US Supreme Court did not necessarily rule against execution as a form of punishment; rather, it faulted the legal procedure (i.e. arbitrariness or randomness as a result of

Table 10.5   Number of persons executed, by jurisdiction, 1930–2008

| | Number executed | |
Jurisdiction	Since 1930	Since 1977
US total	4,995	1,136
Texas	720	423
Georgia	409	43
New York	329	0
North Carolina	306	43
California	305	13
Florida	236	66
South Carolina	202	40
Ohio	200	28
Virginia	194	102
Alabama	173	38
Mississippi	164	10
Louisiana	160	27
Pennsylvania	155	3
Oklahoma	148	88
Arkansas	145	27
Missouri	128	66
Kentucky	106	3
Illinois	102	12
Tennessee	97	4
New Jersey	74	0
Maryland	73	5
Arizona	61	23
Indiana	60	19
Washington	51	4
Colorado	48	1
Nevada	41	12
District of Columbia	40	0
West Virginia	40	0
Federal system	36	3
Massachusetts	27	0
Delaware	26	14
Connecticut	22	1
Oregon	21	2
Utah	19	6
Iowa	18	0
Kansas	15	0
Montana	9	3
New Mexico	9	1
Wyoming	8	1
Nebraska	7	3
Idaho	4	1
Vermont	4	0
South Dakota	2	1
New Hampshire	1	0

Source: Snell (2009: 12).

the absence of standards and guidelines). Accordingly, the Court permitted states to rewrite capital punishment statutes that would attempt to safeguard against constitutional violations. That safeguard could be achieved by one of two methods. States could adopt a two-stage trial procedure in which the culpability of the defendant would first be established and then the sentence would be determined in a separate trial. Another approach permitted states to draft mandatory death sentences for certain crimes (i.e. capital offenses), thereby eliminating the discretion from the jury (see Palmer, 2010).

Gregg v. Georgia

As expected, several states responded to the task of rectifying the problem of arbitrariness in order to reintroduce capital punishment statutes. In 1976, the US Supreme Court ruled on *Gregg* v. *Georgia*, a landmark case in that it decided that capital punishment is not, in itself, cruel and unusual punishment. The cornerstone of *Gregg* was that the conditions and procedures of death sentences be clearly established. The High Court upheld Georgia's newly written 'bifurcated trial structure,' thereby permitting the reinstatement of the death penalty (see Palmer, 2010).

That same year, the US Supreme Court issued opinions on four other cases. Consistent with *Gregg*, the Court also approved similar procedures introduced in Texas (*Jurek* v. *Texas*) and in Florida (*Proffitt* v. *Florida*). Against the tide of those rulings, the Court reversed cases in North Carolina (*Woodson* v. *North Carolina*)

Figure 10.2 January 17, 1977: Gary Gilmore executed in Utah State Prison for the murder of two students, the first person to be executed in the United States for over ten years.

Photo by Keystone/Getty Images.

and Louisiana (*Roberts* v. *Louisiana*) because those states attempted to completely eliminate all capital discretion. Other key decisions by the U.S. Supreme Court imposed further limits on the capital punishment. In *Coker* v. *Georgia* (1977) the death sentence for rape was struck down because it was deemed an excessive and disproportionate penalty, violating the Eighth Amendment. In *Enmund* v. *Florida* (1982), the Court refused to permit the death penalty to be imposed on a 'non-triggerman' in a felony-murder conviction.

Ring v. Arizona

In a more recent landmark decision, the US Supreme Court in 2002 ruled in *Ring* v. *Arizona* that juries rather than judges must make the factual determination that subjects a convicted murderer to the death penalty. The 7-to-2 decision invalidated capital punishment laws in five states (Arizona, Colorado, Idaho, Montana, and Nebraska) and cast doubt on those in four others (Alabama, Delaware, Florida, and Indiana). In those nine states, there are nearly 800 death row prisoners. While inmates whose appeals have been exhausted will have difficulty benefiting from the ruling, others will be entitled to resentencing. For those states affected by the decision, legislatures will have to redraft their capital punishment statutes. The decision also requires that the federal death penalty statute be revised in accordance to *Ring v. Arizona* (see Greenhouse, L., 2002c).

As a result of *Ring* v. *Arizona*, fewer prisoners may be executed. James S. Liebman, professor of law at Columbia University, notes: 'There is quite general agreement that over time and over geography, the likelihood of getting a death sentence is greater from a judge than from a jury' (Liptak, 2002a: A21). Still, skeptics remain cautious in their optimism in curbing executions. '*Ring* will probably save lives but does not overtly question the underlying principles and practice of capital justice' (Shapiro, 2002: 16). Others agree. For the vast majority of those on death row, the ruling simply 'clarified – with a nip and tuck – the nation's commitment to capital punishment' (Zeller, 2002: 16; see also the *New York Times*, June 25, 2002). While nine states must reconfigure their capital punishment laws, *Ring v. Arizona* confirms the validity of the death penalty in 29 states (see Palmer, 2010).

Legal scholarship and empirical research

Adding further to the complexity of capital punishment, the ongoing debate tends to draw on two bodies of knowledge: legal scholarship or empirical research. Activity in the courts usually follows the tradition of legal scholarship by relying on interpretations of the US Constitution and legal precedent. The other body of expertise consists of empirical researchers who set out to examine systematically the relationship between, for example, executions and homicide rates. With regard to the death penalty, recent questions have been raised about the role that social science plays in the formulation of legal decisions.

In his work, James Acker (1991) explored such questions by examining the citation of evidence based on social science research in US Supreme Court death penalty cases. He found that the High Court has made extensive use of evidence based on social science research. However, the preponderance of such citations appears in *dissenting* opinions, meaning that the overall impact of social science research in death penalty rulings is often neutralized. Still, Acker points out that social science research has influenced the way the Supreme Court views capital punishment by encouraging legal authorities to consider factual evidence. Acker characterizes that development as a significant trend. 'Social science findings may serve as a check, and perhaps ultimately as a corrective mechanism, to assure the continued legitimacy of the Court's death penalty decisions' (Acker, 1991: 439; see Lachance, 2009; Palmer, 2010).

DO EXECUTIONS SERVE AS A DETERRENT?

A particularly influential belief shaping public opinion on capital punishment is the notion of deterrence. It is widely believed that executions serve to significantly inhibit other acts of homicide. Critics, however, insist that such a belief is among the more prevalent myths in the debate over the death penalty. Samuel Walker (2001) characterizes the myth of deterrence and the death penalty as a *crime-control theology* since it rests on faith rather than facts; indeed, numerous empirical studies fail to support the hypothesized relationship between deterrence and capital punishment (Blumstein *et al.*, 1978; Bohm, 1999; Donohue and Wolfers, 2005; Peterson and Bailey, 1991; Sellin, 1967).

An informed discussion of executions as a deterrent must first clarify the parameters of the analysis. The issue is not whether the death penalty deters more than no penalty; rather, the question is whether the death penalty deters more than other harsh penalties, such as life imprisonment without parole. The current debate over deterrence and the death penalty began in earnest with the 1975 article by Isaac Ehrlich, an economist who claimed that each execution prevented eight murders. As has been noted in previous chapters, the nation took a dramatic shift toward a conservative law-and-order approach to crime during the 1970s. Understandably, supporters of the death penalty celebrated Ehrlich's research; in fact, the study was cited in the *Gregg* decision (also see Yunker, 1976). Ehrlich had given deterrence theory a much-needed boost following Zimring and Hawkins's (1973) thorough critique of deterrence propositions. Despite the popularity of Ehrlich's research, its high-level statistical analysis was not immune from methodological problems. Social scientists soon attempted to test his findings by way of replication: the research procedure by which data are re-analyzed to determine whether previous findings are supported. Ehrlich's research did not pass the test of replication. Several re-examinations of his data also failed to produce what Ehrlich claimed was a deterrent effect (Bowers and Pierce, 1975; Forst, 1983; Passell, 1975; see also Bowers *et al.*, 1984; Klein *et al.*, 1978).

Not surprisingly, given the popularity of deterrence theory among mainstream economists and criminologists, another round of research has returned to the matter of executions (Cloninger and Marchesini, 2001; Dezhbakhsh *et al.*, 2003; Ehrlich and Liu, 1999; Mocan and Gittings, 2003). More recently, Land *et al.* have asked the question: 'Does the death penalty save lives?' (2009: 1009). In re-examining claims that many lives are saved through reductions in subsequent homicide rates after executions, Land *et al.* conclude that those 'findings are not robust enough to model even small changes in specifications that yield dramatically different results' (p. 1009). Similarly, Donohue and Wolfers report the following:

> Our key insight is that the death penalty – at least as it has been implemented in the United States since *Gregg* ended the moratorium on executions – is applied so rarely that the number of homicides it can plausibly have caused or deterred cannot be reliably disentangled from the large year-to-year changes in the homicide rate caused by other factors.
>
> (2005: 794; see Berk, 2005; Fagan *et al.*, 2006)

So, is the dispute over deterrence and capital punishment resolved? Hardly. Advocates and opponents of the death penalty continue their debate not only with respect to deterrence but other considerations as well (Berk, 2009; Donohue, 2009; Kovandzic *et al.*, 2009; Rubin, 2009). Moreover, from that debate there is growing concern that executions may actually promote violence rather than suppress it.

DO EXECUTIONS PROMOTE VIOLENCE?

Proponents of deterrence theory argue that publicizing executions is a necessary component of capital punishment. It is through such widespread exposure that the tough law-and-order message of death sentences is conveyed. Recently, however, another theory has emerged in the context of publicized executions. *Brutalization theory* suggests that publicized executions do not deter violence; instead, they promote violence. So as to understand the scope of brutalization theory, we move to unpack the main elements of *deterrence theory*.

Deterrence theory rests on the major assumption that potential killers are restrained from committing murder because they identify with the person being executed. That is, potential killers are expected to realize that if they commit murder, they, too, will suffer a similar fate. Publicized executions are thought to reinforce that central idea, thereby curbing future homicides. Similarly, brutalization theory also assumes that members of society identify with executions. Rather than identifying with the condemned, however, it is proposed that some killers identify with the executioner. Consider a primary message inherent in capital punishment: certain persons *deserve* to die. Indeed, executions are sometimes viewed as a 'public service' by some of its supporters, suggesting that society is better off without convicted murderers (see Katz, 1988).

According to brutalization theory, publicized executions create an *alternative identification process* that promotes imitation, not deterrence. Considering that dynamic, is it possible that following a publicized execution, murder rates might increase? Measuring that phenomenon has been the task of brutalization theorists. In their pioneering work, Bowers and Pierce (1980b) hypothesized that some murderers view their victims as being similar to executed offenders. Correspondingly, they found an increase in homicides soon after well-publicized executions, a trend that is reported as evidence of a *brutalization*, not a deterrent, effect (see also Forst, 1983; King, 1978; Philips, 1980; Stack, 1987). Bowers and Pierce specify that the brutalization effect has an impact on individuals who are prone to violence, not those who are generally non-violent. For those prone to violence, the publicized execution reinforces the belief that vengeance is justified.

Given its significance in the understanding of capital punishment, the brutalization effect has been subject to additional research. Cochran *et al.* (1994: 306) studied the return of capital punishment in Oklahoma and found evidence of a predicted brutalization effect. Cochran and his colleagues took into account various types of murder and discovered that brutalization was more prevalent in *stranger homicides* in which social ties (or social controls) are much weaker for persons not known to one another. Cochran *et al.* contend that, in general, if inhibitions against the use of lethal violence to resolve problems created by 'unworthy' others are reduced by executions, 'such a brutalization effect is most likely to occur in "situated transactions" … where inhibitions against the use of violence are already absent or considerably relaxed' (1994: 110). In a widely cited replication, Bailey (1998) confirmed Cochran *et al.*'s findings. Moreover, that analysis on the different types of murder indicates that the impact of capital punishment in Oklahoma was much more extensive than previously suggested. Bailey emphasized that 'detailed combinations of homicide circumstances and victim offender relationships must be considered, as well as the possibility that the deterrent/brutalization impact of capital punishment may differ for different dimensions of capital punishment' (1994: 731–2; see Cochran and Chamlin, 2000).

Considerable debate also persists on the issue of whether executions should be televised. Proponents of the death penalty favor televised executions because they maintain that the publicity will have a deterrent effect. Opponents of capital punishment, however, are more diverse in their opinions. Some death penalty abolitionists oppose televised executions because they believe that a brutalization effect might occur. Other opponents of death sentences favor televised executions so that viewers may actually witness the gruesome realities of the death penalty. Accordingly, such exposure might alter their opinion of executions toward abolition (Leighton, 1999; Smith, 2008, 2003)

IS THE DEATH PENALTY NEEDED TO PROTECT THE POLICE?

As a related issue, proponents of the death penalty argue that capital punishment is necessary to protect police from becoming victims of homicide during the performance of their duties (van den Haag and Conrad, 1983). Again, such reasoning is rooted in deterrence theory. Currently, 38 states permit capital punishment in cases involving the killing of a law enforcement official in the line of duty (Snell, 2009).

Although there is no shortage of research on the death penalty, few investigations have examined incidents of cop killings as they pertain to capital punishment. Bailey and Peterson (1987) set out to rectify that deficit in research. Specifically, they responded to the research question: 'Does the death penalty provide an added measure of protection for the police in the performance of their duties?' Bailey and Peterson found 'no support to the view that the death penalty provides a more effective deterrent to police homicides than alternative sanctions' (1987: 22). They concluded that 'the safety of police officers from lethal violence is an important problem, but its resolution does not lie in capital punishment' (Bailey and Peterson, 1987: 22). Those researchers agree with Creamer and Robin (1970), who emphasize the importance of training. Police officers can reduce the risk of lethal violence by relying on their training. Improved training in dealing with potentially violent encounters serves as better protection against murder in the line of duty than does the existence of death penalty statutes.

IS CAPITAL PUNISHMENT RACIST?

Current examinations of racism and the death penalty must not ignore the historical considerations involving formal and informal (i.e. lynchings) executions of African Americans. Following the Civil War, Black Codes were formally established to perpetuate the economic subordination of former slaves. Such codes instituted harsher penalties for crimes committed by African Americans, leading to racial disparities in the use of executions. As a type of informal – and illegal – sanction, lynchings of African American men also were carried out by vigilante mobs. Bowers *et al.* (1984) report that in the 1890s there were more lynchings (1,540) than legal executions (1,098). Although lynchings gradually declined, hundreds of such illegal executions characterized each decade: between 1900 and 1909 there were 885 reported lynchings; between 1910 and 1919, 621 lynchings; and between 1920 and 1929, 315 lynchings (see also Brundage, 1993; Dray, 2002; Jackson and Jackson, 2001; Tolnay and Beck, 1994, 1992).

A long-standing criticism of capital punishment is that it is administered in ways that are arbitrary and capricious, even though some safeguards have been introduced in compliance with landmark decisions (*Gregg* v. *Georgia*, 1976). Moreover, research indicates that such arbitrariness and capriciousness produce racially discriminatory applications of capital punishment (Bowers *et al.*, 1984; Keil and Vito, 1989; Paternoster, 1991).

Some observers assume that the death penalty is racially discriminatory in large part because the criminal justice system treats African American murderers harsher than their white counterparts. That assumption is too simplistic. To clarify the extent of apparent racism in the death penalty, one must take into account the race of the *victim* alongside the race of the offender. Indeed, various studies have set out to identify such patterns of racial disparity involving the death penalty. Paternoster (1983) revealed that African Americans who kill whites have a 4.5 times greater chance of facing the death penalty than do African Americans who kill African Americans. When the race of the victim is ignored, the chance of African Americans and whites receiving a death sentence is almost equal (also see Paternoster, 1984). Numerous other studies have also found that African Americans charged with murdering whites were more likely to be sentenced to death than were other combinations of race of the offender and race of the victim (Bowers, 1983; Bowers and Pierce, 1980a; Foley and Powell, 1982; Lewis, 1978: Radelet and Pierce, 1985; Riedel, 1976; Zimring *et al.*, 1976). In their research, Keil and Vito found that in Kentucky, 'prosecutors were more likely to seek the death penalty in cases in which blacks killed whites and that juries were more likely to sentence to death blacks who killed whites' (1989: 511).

A major report published by the federal government's General Accounting Office (GAO) and presented to the Senate and House Judiciary Committees further supports the charge that the death penalty is racially biased:

> Our synthesis of the 28 studies shows a pattern of evidence indicating racial disparities in the charging, sentencing, and imposition of the death penalty … In 82 percent of the studies, race of the victim was found to influence the likelihood of being charged with capital murder or receiving the death penalty. i.e., those who murdered whites were more likely to be sentenced to death than those who murdered blacks. This finding was remarkably consistent across data sets, states, data collection methods and analytical techniques.
>
> (1992: 2)

More recent research continues to verify further a racial bias in the administration of capital punishment. Sorensen and Wallace (1999: 559) 'found that homicide cases involving black defendants and white victims fared worse than other racial combinations in all of the pretrial decisions made.' Specifically, Sorensen and Wallace revealed that those cases were more likely to result in first-degree charges, to be served notice of aggravating circumstances, and to proceed to capital trial. In a similar study, Brock *et al.* (1999) discovered disparities based on race of the offender and victims resulting from decisions made by both prosecutors and juries. 'Blacks who killed whites fared worst in these decisions' (Brock *et al.*, 1999: 159; see also Baldus *et al.* 1994, 1990: Bright, 2002: Liptak, 2003; *McCleskey* v. *Kemp* 1987).

CULTURAL PENOLOGY

Deathwork: An Ethnography of Execution

Despite the vast number of studies on the death penalty, the image of an actual execution remains somewhat abstract. Few capital punishment experts have first-hand knowledge about the grim task of putting someone to death. Although witnessing and studying the execution process can be personally distressing, it is crucially important that social scientists not avoid such research. Robert Johnson's classic study *Deathwork: A Study of the Modern Execution Process* offers the rare opportunity to examine the procedure of executions.

Johnson uses a method of social science research known as ethnography: a qualitative procedure that sets out to reveal the experiential facets of social life, usually through close observation and in-depth interviews. Johnson's ethnography provides a better understanding of the psychological and emotional aspects of living on death row. Being confined to death row is psychologically tormenting, thereby facilitating the execution process. Johnson contends that after years of being warehoused to death row in a tomblike cell (5 × 7 feet), the prisoner is reduced simply to a hollow body void of emotion, passively accepting its fate. Observers agree that the prisoner is emotionally dead weeks before the execution. Thus the task of the prison is to keep the body alive until the execution, a task essentially of human storage (also see Abu-Jamal, 1995; Rideau and Wikberg, 1992). Unlike earlier public executions that unfolded as gaudy pageants celebrating violence, the modern execution process has become increasingly bureaucratic. 'We have replaced meaningful ritual with mechanical ritualism. The result is a bureaucratic execution procedure that abrogates our humanity under the guise of justice' (Johnson, 1998: 29).

A key focus of Johnson's observation of the execution process is the deathwatch: a period of 24 to 48 hours before the execution in which the prisoner is continuously supervised while undergoing the final preparation for death. During that time, the inmate eats his last meal and boxes his personal belongings. The prisoner's head and right leg are shaved to improve conductivity and minimize singeing and burning. Still shaving serves other functions; it often inflicts a final blow to the prisoner's already depleted will to live. A member of the execution team explains the process to Johnson:

When you get to the point of shaving the man's head, that usually will take just about all the strength a man has out of him. It's not long before he actually becomes a walking dead man. Because he knows that there is no more hope after that point. I've done six executions, and it's the same way for all of them. I have seen no change in it. Like when Delilah cut Samson's hair, that was it. It took all of his strength. There was nothing left.

(1998: 92)

Figure 10.3 'Old Sparky', the decommissioned electric chair in which 361 prisoners were executed between 1924 and 1964, pictured November 5, 2007 at the Texas Prison Museum in Huntsville, Texas. From the chaplain who shares the condemned prisoner's final hours to the guard who attaches the needles and the prison director who orders the fatal injection: the relentless march of Texas executions is taking a heavy toll.

Photo by Fanny Carrier/AFP/Getty Images.

Next, the prisoner takes his final shower and puts on a fresh jumpsuit that features Velcro instead of buttons and zippers (to keep the body from burning during the electrocution). He is weighed and photographed (his picture will join a display of other executed inmates). Then the prisoner is 'stored' in the empty death cell where the death warrant is read. Soon he takes the last walk to the death chamber.

The warden handpicks nine correctional officers to serve as the prison's execution team. They supervise the shaving and the final preparation, and escort the prisoner to the electric chair. There they securely fasten him to the chair with straps and electrodes. Given the bureaucratic nature of modern-day executions, those tasks are broken down to simple chores that proceed with surgical precision. One member of the execution team may be responsible for fastening the right leg strap, another secures the headpiece, and so on until the prisoner is fastened in the chair (Abramson and Isay, 2002).

Although restraining shackles and cuffs are available, they are not expected to be used. Struggles are not likely to occur because the prisoner's spirit has been broken. 'Modern execution etiquette does not permit a bound prisoner to be taken to his death. The condemned prisoner must be under the social, not physical, control of his keepers' (Johnson, 1998: 84). Again pointing to the bureaucratic procedure, Johnson adds: 'The official's goal, and in the end perhaps the prisoner's as well, is a smooth, orderly and ostensibly voluntary execution, one that looks humane and dignified and is not sullied in any way by obvious violence' (1998: 84).

The execution proceeds as 2,500 volts of electricity jolt the prisoner 'starting at the head, passing through the body, then to the heart and other internal organs, some of which explode, before the current comes to ground through the ankle' (Johnson, 1998: 111). Recalling a particular execution, Johnson writes: 'His body stiffened spasmodically, though only briefly. A thin swirl of smoke trailed away from his head, then dissipated quickly. (People outside the witness room could hear crackling and burning: a faint smell of burned flesh lingered in the air, mildly nauseating some people)' (1998: 111). The execution team waits until the corpse cools off before they remove it from the chair.

Executions are not always the clean, machine-like procedures that people are led to expect. Numerous executions have featured mishaps, which have turned 'humane executions' into horrific torture. One of the most terrifying moments in modern-day executions involved 17-year-old Willie Francis, who was strapped into the electric chair in Louisiana in 1946. 'The youth became the first known person to walk away from his own execution. Witnesses described how his "lips puffed out and he groaned and jumped so that the chair came off the floor." He yelled, "Take it off. Let me breathe." When the application of several jolts did not kill him ... [he was] granted a reprieve' (Wikberg, 1992: 289). Francis was returned to death row where he recuperated from the ordeal. A year later, he was executed again; that time, he did not walk away from the chair.

Over the years, experts have noted that electrocution often involves mutilation and excessive burning. Numerous other problems with electric chairs have been reported. For example, in 1990, Jessie Tafero was burned to death instead of electrocuted when his botched execution produced flames, smoke, and sparks shooting six inches above his head (Wikberg, 1992). Even when an electrocution appears to go smoothly, experts assert that such a procedure is inherently painful. Dr Harold Hillman, an English physiologist and director of the Unity Laboratory in Applied Neurology at the University of Surrey, concluded that 'execution by electrocution is intensely painful since the prisoner retains consciousness; moreover, death is not instantaneous' (Wikberg, 1992: 284). Due to the problems encountered with the electric chair, several states have replaced electrocution with lethal injection.

THE EMERGENCE OF LETHAL INJECTION

Technological forces continue to shape the death penalty; most recently, such applications of science have given rise to lethal injection. Most states in which death sentences are permitted rely on lethal injection as the means of execution (Snell, 2009). In their book *The Rope, the Chair and the Needle*, Marquart *et al.*

offer a chronology of the evolution of technology of executions in Texas – from hanging, to electrocution, and finally, to lethal injection.

The rituals surrounding lethal injection are strikingly similar to those leading to electrocution as well as hanging. The death row prisoner is granted a last meal of his choice. Then the inmate showers and puts on a clean set of 'prison whites.' In the case of lethal injection, however, the convict also meets with a prison physician who inspects the prisoner's arm in search of a good vein, one that will sustain injection (Trombley, 1992).

The procedure for lethal injection places the prisoner in the execution chamber while the executioner is situated in an adjoining room. An opening in the wall permits the tubes of lethal dosages of sodium pentathol, Pavulon, and potassium chloride to be strung from the adjoining room to the execution chamber. The prisoner is restrained to a gurney (a movable hospital bed) while a medical technician inserts the needle. A physician stands nearby, supervising the procedure. The executioner releases the lethal drugs through the tubes (Marquart *et al.*, 1994).

The execution may take place relatively swiftly, in approximately 12 minutes, or it can go on for almost an hour. The length of time it takes for the condemned to expire depends on the individual's biochemistry and its ability to ward off lethal doses of drugs. The outward effect of the drugs commonly suggests that the condemned has 'fallen asleep' while yielding to a 'quick and painless' death (Marquart *et al.*, 1994: 147). Although the technological features of lethal injection create the appearance of a more humane and efficient form of execution, not all lethal injections occur without a hitch. In some cases, the drugs invoke violent choking, gasping, and writhing – forcing the condemned to squirm grotesquely under the leather straps of the gurney. Marquart *et al.* report that in some instances, veins that would accommodate the needle are difficult to locate. In the case of Raymond Landry, 'two minutes after the solution was flowing, the syringe popped out, spraying the mixture of drugs across the room toward the witness window' (1994: 147).

Anticipating that lethal injection might be declared unconstitutional as a form of execution, most states stipulate an alternative. Having passed constitutional muster, electrocution, lethal gas, hanging, and firing squad remain on the books of several states should lethal injection ever be struck down by the US Supreme Court (Halperin, 2001–2). Recently critical attention has been directed at pancuronium bromide, the chemical used in lethal injections. Medical experts insist that pancuronium bromide, marketed under the trade name Pavulon, 'paralyzes the skeletal muscles but does not affect the brain or nerves. A person injected with it remains conscious but cannot move or speak' (Liptak, 2003: A18). Simply put, the paralysis masks intense distress, leaving a wide-awake prisoner unable to speak or cry out for help while slowly suffocating. In 2001, veterinarians in Tennessee banned the use of pancuronium bromide to euthanize pets (Liptak, 2003). In the years to follow, more controversy ensued.

In 2009, Ohio prison officials executed Kenneth Biros with a one-drug intravenous lethal injection, a method never before used on a human. Biros was convicted of sexually assaulting and killing Tami Engstrom in 1991 after offering to drive her home from a bar. Biros stabbed Engstrom more than 90 times then scattered her body parts in Ohio and Pennsylvania. Biros admitted to the killing but said it was done during a drunken rage.

The new method of lethal injection involved a large dose of anesthetic, similar to how animals are euthanized. Although some experts have hailed the method as painless and an improvement over the three-drug cocktail used in most states, it is unlikely to resolve the debate over capital punishment. While approving the shift to a single drug, death penalty opponents argue that the new method has yet to be properly vetted by legal and medical experts. Moreover, since it has never been tried out on humans before, it is the equivalent of human experimentation (Urbina, 2009).

WORKING IN CORRECTIONS

Sam Jones, Modern Executioner

A discussion of the execution process would not be complete without addressing the relatively obscure existence of the modern executioner. Few writings have revealed the thoughts and feelings of those contemporary *deathworkers*, perhaps because most of them prefer to remain anonymous. In a rare glimpse into the perspective of the executioner, Wikberg and Rideau (1991) reveal an insightful interview with Sam Jones (an alias). Jones reports earning $400 per execution; thus far he has pushed the button unleashing the electrical current in 19 executions. The following excerpt is borrowed from a dialogue with Jones conducted by criminal defense attorney Clive Stafford Smith.

Smith: Let me ask you this then. Say someone stabs somebody 71 times, could you be prepared to go in there and stab the person 71 times?
Jones: If it were required, I could do it, yes.
Smith: You could? For four hundred bucks?
Jones: Well, the money don't have anything to do with it.
Smith: What is the most gruesome thing you would be prepared to do for the four hundred dollars?
Jones: Whatever.
Smith: You'd take a candle and sort of drop hot wax on them, pull their nails out and then kill them, or something like that?
Jones: If that's what they wanted. If that's what the state tells me to do.
(Wikberg and Rideau, 1992: 4–5)

Jones goes on to say that he is never bothered by what he does. In fact, he boasted that he would even execute a family member if that person were convicted of a capital offense. 'There is nothing to it. It's no different to me executing somebody and goin' to the refrigerator and getting a beer out of it' (Wikberg and Rideau, 1992: 5).

Whether Jones's attitude toward capital punishment is typical of the attitudes of other executioners is difficult to know since there are so few investigations of executioners and how they view the procedure of *deathwork* (see Cabana, 1996; Dow, 2002; Johnson, 2002).

SHOULD JUVENILE OFFENDERS BE EXECUTED?

Several recent cases demonstrate that juveniles are as capable of brutal acts of murder as are adults. Wayne Thompson was 15 when he and his half-brother, then 27, and two other men in their twenties savagely shot and stabbed his former brother-in-law, later tossing the body into Oklahoma's Washita River. All the defendants, including Thompson, were sentenced to the death penalty for premeditated (first-degree) murder. In another case, two 13-year-old St Charles, Missouri, boys were charged with sexually assaulting and strangling with shoelaces two children (an 8- and an 11-year-old). Finally, in Fresno, California, four boys (aged 14, 15, 16, and 17) equipped with three shotguns, a rifle, a handgun, and a bag of crack cocaine went on a shooting spree, killing one person and injuring nine others. In view of such incidents, the question persists over whether juveniles who have been convicted of heinous acts of murder should be executed (see Lachance, 2009).

The execution of juvenile offenders is not a new phenomenon. The history of juvenile executions in America is traced to the Plymouth Colony where, in 1642, the first execution of a juvenile took place following a conviction of bestiality. Executions continued through the next several centuries, but racial patterns in executions soon became apparent as African American youths were executed in disproportionate numbers.

Of the more than 8,000 executions that have been administered in the United States, about 2.5 percent have involved juveniles (Snell, 2001). Opponents issue well-articulated criticisms against the execution of juveniles. Victor Streib (1991, 1987) points out that the American legal system formally recognizes that children occupy a unique position in society and that laws ought to reflect that position. Moreover, the US Supreme Court has traditionally handed down decisions that distinguish between juvenile and adult offenders, especially in view of clear differences of maturity. Streib further argues that executing juveniles violates contemporary standards of decency and conflicts with established practices of juvenile justice. Those criticisms of juvenile executions likewise are supported by the American Law Institute, the National Commission on Reform of Criminal Law, and the American Bar Association (see Nelson, 2001). At the heart of Streib's campaign to abolish the juvenile death penalty is the concept of 'a measurable contribution to goals of punishment,' that encompasses retribution, deterrence, and incapacitation. Streib contends: 'A careful analysis of the death penalty for juveniles reveals that it make no such measurable contribution to these goals for these offenders' (1991: 332).

The US Supreme Court has faced deep concerns over the constitutionality of the death penalty for juveniles. In the Wayne Thompson case (*Thompson* v.

Oklahoma, 1988), the High Court ruled that the execution of a person under the age of 16 at the time of his or her offense constitutes cruel and unusual punishment as prohibited by the Eighth Amendment and made applicable to the states by the Fourteenth Amendment. The following year, however, in *Stanford* v. *Kentucky* (1989), the US Supreme Court supported the death penalty for persons who were 16 or 17 at the time of their offense. The majority noted that the death penalty did not violate the 'evolving standards of decency'; therefore, executions were not considered cruel and unusual punishment.

By 2000, seven jurisdictions had not specified a minimum age for which the death penalty could be imposed. In some states, the minimum age had been set forth in the statutory provisions that determined the age at which a juvenile could be transferred to adult court for trial as an adult. Fourteen states and the federal system had required a minimum age of 18, and 17 states had set an age of eligibility between 14 and 17 (Snell, 2001).

In 2002, Toronto M. Patterson, who was 17 years old when he killed his cousin in 1995, was put to death in Texas. The US Supreme Court declined to stay the execution, but three justices issued an unusual dissent, urging the Court to reconsider allowing juveniles to be sentenced to death. Justice John Paul Stevens, who dissented when the court last reviewed the issue in 1989, said he remained convinced that it is unconstitutional to execute people for crimes committed when they are younger than 18. 'I think it would be appropriate to revisit the issue at the earliest opportunity,' added Stevens (Liptak, 2002: A1). Many experts agreed that the controversy would become the focus of the Court's next major death penalty case. 'This is the next frontier,' noted Elisabeth Semel, the director of the death penalty clinic of the Boalt School of Law at the University of California at Berkeley (Liptak, 2002: A1; see *New York Times*, 2002).

That 'next frontier' was finally visited in 2005 when the US Supreme Court forbid the imposition of the death penalty on offenders who were under the age of 18 when their crimes were committed. In that case, *Roper* v. *Simmons* (2005), the Court cited the Eighth and Fourteenth Amendments (see Palmer, 2010).

SHOULD EMOTIONALLY DISTURBED AND MENTALLY RETARDED OFFENDERS BE EXECUTED?

An ongoing area of concern is determining under which circumstances the death penalty is suitable. For instance, is the death penalty appropriate punishment for emotionally disturbed and mentally retarded persons who have been convicted of murder? Recall the unusual case of Alvin Ford (*Ford* v. *Wainright* (1986); see Chapter 4). The death sentence of Ford was challenged because while confined to death row, he was diagnosed as emotionally disturbed. Ford's paranoid schizophrenic condition was characterized by delusions in which he referred to himself as Pope John Paul III, and he believed that '135 of his friends and family were being held hostage in the prison and that he was their only salvation'

(Paternoster, 1991: 92). His delusions also involved a belief that he would not be executed since he 'owned the prisons and controlled the governor of Florida through mental telepathy … [eventually] Ford became almost completely incomprehensible, speaking only in a bizarre, code-like language' (Paternoster, 1991: 92–3: see also Miller and Radelet, 1993). Ford was removed from death row and placed in a medical unit until it was determined that he was no longer emotionally disturbed. Ford was later returned to death row, where he died of natural causes.

In 2002, the US Supreme Court granted a last-minute reprieve to James Blake Colburn, a death row prisoner in Texas who suffers from severe mental illness. By intervening, the High Court halted the execution one minute before Colburn was to be led to the death chamber. Colburn's lawyers petitioned the Court on the grounds that Colburn was incompetent to be executed and had been denied his constitutional rights during proceedings in state court. Colburn confessed to the 1994 stabbing and strangulation of Peggy Murphy, but his case was complicated by his long psychiatric history. At age 14, Colburn was diagnosed as having paranoid schizophrenia. At 17, he was raped and soon began hearing voices and suffering from delusions. Colburn told his mother that he saw a devil slither out of his stomach. He frequently heard voices instructing him to commit suicide. Records show that Colburn attempted suicide at least 15 times and had often tried to be admitted into public mental health units only to be discharged with a bottle of pills. Once Colburn was voted out of a support group for disclosing that he had suicide ideation (Yardley, 2002a).

Colburn's stay of execution came seven months after the trial of another mentally ill defendant in Texas. The case of Andrea Yates generated immense concern from mental health advocates who argued that emotionally ill defendants should not be executed. Yates, who had been convicted of drowning her five children, was given a life sentence rather than the death penalty (Yardley, 2002a). In Colburn's case, attorneys pointed out that he had been so heavily medicated with antipsychotic drugs that he dozed through much of his trial. Therefore, his lawyers argued, Colburn's proceedings were unconstitutional because his condition rendered him incompetent to stand trial. At the trial, prosecutors showed a videotaped confession in which Colburn, void of emotion, chewed a sandwich while recounting the grisly details of the killing. Prosecutors argued that Colburn was simply *mean* rather than mentally ill. More recently, at least two jurors have expressed doubts over the death sentence. One juror now says that she would not have voted for the death penalty had she realized that Colburn's demeanor was caused by chronic schizophrenia (Yardley, 2002a).

The US Supreme Court until recently did not extend such prohibitions to the mentally retarded (those scoring below 70 on a standardized intelligence test). It has been speculated that in the past, numerous mildly retarded offenders have been executed, but the courts never knew their level of intelligence because such tests were not administered. Today, however, defendants are commonly administered intelligence tests, meaning that the courts are generally aware of the defendant's level of intelligence. The High Court ruled in *Penry* v. *Lynaugh* (1989) that states have the right to execute mentally retarded people convicted of capital murder. Critics insist that the execution of mentally retarded offenders (even those who are only mildly retarded) raises grave moral and ethical issues (Reed, 1993).

In 2002, the US Supreme Court barred the execution of mentally retarded offenders. The landmark decision, *Atkins* v. *Virginia*, was based on the Court's view that a national consensus rejects such executions as excessive and inappropriate. Of the 38 states that have reinstated the death penalty, 18 prohibit executing the retarded, up from two states when the Court last considered the question in 1989. The case involves Daryl R. Atkins, who was convicted of committing a murder and robbery at the age of 18 and is known to have an IQ of 59. The ruling could move 200 or more mentally retarded prisoners from death row. It is estimated that as many as 10 percent of those convicted of capital murder are mentally retarded (see Human Rights Watch, 2001). One study contends that at least 44 mentally retarded inmates have been executed since 1976 (Keyes *et al.*, 2002).

Demonstrating the global significance of *Atkins* v. *Virginia*, the 15 countries of the European Union filed a brief on behalf of Atkins, as did a group of senior American diplomats who told the court that 'the practice of executing retarded offenders was out of step with much of the world and was a source of friction between the United States and other countries' (Greenhouse, L., 2002d: A14). Amnesty International reported that since 1995, only three countries were known to have executed mentally retarded people: Kyrgyzstan, Japan, and the United States. Whereas *Atkins* v. *Virginia* dramatically alters the landscape of capital punishment, the Court offered the states virtually no guidance on who must be considered retarded and who gets to make that determination. The ruling will produce complicated legal activity on two fronts. In the judiciary, defendants accused or convicted of capital crimes will argue that they are mentally retarded. Similarly, legislatures will have to establish procedures to determine who is, in fact, retarded (Liptak and Rimer, 2002).

In 2009, Bobby Wayne Woods was put to death in Texas after his attorneys lost a battle to convince the courts that he was too mentally impaired to qualify for execution. Woods was convicted of raping and killing his former girlfriend's 11-year-old daughter. Exams administered to Woods over the years placed his IQ between 68 and 86, prompting a bitter debate between his lawyers and the state over whether he was too impaired to face execution. The state and federal courts repeatedly sided with prosecutors.

The debate reflects the gray area left by the US Supreme Court when it ruled in *Atkins* v. *Virginia* (2002) that the mentally impaired were not eligible for the death penalty but left it up to state courts to determine which prisoners qualified as impaired. Law professor Maurie Levin, who represented Woods, said in a pleading 'his I.Q. hovers around 70, the magical cutoff point for determining whether someone is mentally retarded. He's transparently childlike and simple,' she said before the execution. 'It's a travesty' (McKinley, 2009: EV2). State courts have applied the standard established in *Atkins* unevenly. In

Alabama, Mississippi, and Texas the courts have held that inmates with scores as low as 66 are not impaired, while a prisoner in California with a score of 84 was declared mentally retarded (McKinley, 2009).

HAVE INNOCENT PEOPLE BEEN EXECUTED?

Among the more distressing problems of the death penalty is the risk of executing an innocent person. Indeed, such a miscarriage of justice stands as an egregious error of the worst kind. For decades, there has been speculation that many innocent people have been executed; however, most reports were anecdotal and investigations were less than systematic. Then, in 1987, Hugo Bedau and Michael Radelet revealed a systematic examination of 350 defendants believed to have been wrongly convicted in capital (or potential capital) cases between the years 1900 and 1985. In their research, Bedau and Radelet did not include simply any case that appeared suspect. Rather, they employed strict standards of miscarriages of justice and accepted cases only on the basis of overwhelming evidence that an innocent person had been falsely convicted.

In an expanded volume of the work, Radelet *et al.* released *In Spite of Innocence: Erroneous Convictions in Capital Cases*, a book cataloging the cases of 416 defendants falsely convicted of crimes punishable by death. Of those 416 cases (between 1900 and 1991), approximately one-third were sentenced to death, and the authors persuasively document 23 cases in which the defendant was executed, Most of the remaining defendants, although trapped in the machinery of justice, fortunately escaped execution. Radelet *et al.* refer to them as the lucky ones. Nevertheless, they still experienced years of incarceration and the agony of uncertainty; consequently, their lives were virtually ruined.

In at least two dozen cases, not only were the defendants lucky, but they benefited from timely events as well. For example, in 1939, Isidore Zimmerman was within two hours of electrocution before his stay of execution was ordered. What is remarkable about his case, and numerous others, is that he was later exonerated, but not without spending 24 of his 66 years in prison. In a similar case spanning the mid-1950s through the early 1960s, Lloyd Miller escaped execution seven times, once when he was seven hours from execution. Later, Miller was completely vindicated. Radelet *et al.* contend that these cases are neither isolated nor unique; they cataloged 25 additional cases, including the following:

- In 1932 in North Carolina, Gus Langley had his head shaved ready for electrocution when a technical error in his death sentence was discovered that stayed the execution. Later new evidence proved that his alibi was legitimate.
- In 1942 in North Carolina, William Wellman was seated in the electric chair when the governor, having just learned that another man had confessed, issued a reprieve.
- In 1957 in Ohio, Harry Bundy was only three days from execution when a witness to the crime chanced to read about the case, notified the authorities and secured a stay of execution.

- As the Columbus, Ohio, newspaper observed, 'It was sheer luck that saved [Harry] Bundy from execution.'

(1992: 275–6)

One might argue that those cases are simply old and out of date, and that similar miscarriages of justice do not occur in today's advanced and sophisticated criminal justice system. Unfortunately, that argument is false. In 1983 Joseph Brown was within 13 hours of execution before a stay of execution was ordered. Three years later, his conviction was overturned when the court of appeals learned that the prosecutors relied on perjured testimony. Similarly, in 1983, William Jent and Earnest Brown came within 16 hours of electrocution when a stay of execution was granted. Their convictions were vacated because the prosecution had suppressed evidence. In 1993, Walter McMillan was released after being held for six years on death row in Florida. McMillan was convicted on perjured testimony, and evidence had been withheld from his attorneys. As in similar cases, the state is suspected of a racially motivated prosecution (Radelet *et al.*, 1992; see Cole, 2009, 2001; Leo, 2008).

The Thin Blue Line

Among the most publicized cases is that of Randall Dale Adams, featured in the documentary *The Thin Blue Line* (1988). In that film, producer director Errol Morris presents a series of interviews in which it becomes clear that Adams was not guilty of killing a Dallas cop in 1976. What is all the more unusual about this case is that perjured testimony was provided by the real culprit himself, David Harris. At the time of the murder, Harris was 16 years old – too young to be given the death penalty. So it is believed that Adams became the target of the prosecution because he was old enough to be executed. And, given the serious nature of cop killing, an execution was imminent. Adams was within several days of execution when closer scrutiny of his case led to his being taken off death row. Subsequently, his sentence was commuted to life imprisonment. Soon thereafter, the documentary *The Thin Blue Line* shed crucial light on his wrongful conviction. Following a series of legal maneuvers, Adams was freed in 1989. It was later revealed that the prosecution was guilty of suppressing evidence and knowingly using perjured testimony to convict Adams so that it could convict a suspect who was old enough to be executed. During the period when Adams was confined to death row, Harris was free to commit further incidents of violence. Indeed, Harris killed again: in Beaumont in 1985. He is currently on death row at the Texas Department of Corrections in Huntsville. The Adams case reveals in detail how a misguided prosecutor, in pursuit of execution, failed to protect the community by allowing the real killer to remain at large.

The case of Jesse Jacobs

Shortly after midnight on January 4, 1995, Jesse DeWayne Jacobs was put to death by lethal injection in Texas. Because 87 other prisoners have been executed in Texas since the state reinstated the death penalty in 1976, Jacobs's execution looked relatively routine. However, Jacobs's case is plagued by serious problems – most notably, his innocence.

Certainly, many convicts fight to the finish, proclaiming their innocence, especially when facing the death penalty. However, Jacobs's innocence was widely acknowledged, even by the prosecutor who convicted him. As Jacobs was being prepped for lethal injection, he optimistically believed that the courts would intervene at the last moment. Just before Jacobs was put to death, he replied: 'I have news for all of you, there is not going to be an execution. This is premeditated murder by the state of Texas, I am not guilty of this crime' (Hentoff, 1995: 22).

Here is how Jacobs's story unfolds. In 1986, Jacobs and his sister Bobbie Jean Hogan were arrested for the fatal shooting of Etta Ann Urdiales. At the time, Hogan was intimately involved with Urdiales's estranged husband. Separate trials were ordered, and Jacobs confessed that he had abducted Urdiales at his sister's request so that these women could have a meeting to sort out their differences. Hogan had hoped to persuade Urdiales to cease contact with her ex-husband and to give up custody of her children. In addition to confessing that he abducted Urdiales, Jacobs initially claimed responsibility for shooting her as well. Although his sister shot Urdiales, Jacobs took the rap because he was already facing life imprisonment for the kidnapping. Moreover, Jacobs had a previous conviction for murder, and at the time of the incident, he was out on parole.

Later, Jacobs reconsidered his confession and decided not to take the rap for his sister. He then told the truth: Jacobs abducted Urdiales and took her to an abandoned farmhouse so that his sister could meet with her. Jacobs left the house to sit on the porch when he heard gunfire. Quickly returning, Jacobs saw his sister with a gun, and on the floor was a fatally wounded Urdiales. Jacobs explained to the jury that he '"did not know [the murder] was going to take place" and that he "would not have had anything to do with it if he would have known his sister was armed"' (Hentoff, 1995: 22). Nevertheless, the prosecutor insisted that Jacobs, a previously convicted murderer, shot Urdiales to death. The jury concurred, and Jacobs was convicted and sentenced to death.

Seven months later, during the Hogan trial, Peter Speers, the same prosecutor who secured the conviction against Jacobs, presented to the jury a different version of the killing. Curiously, the new version of the incident accurately placed Hogan in the role of the shooter, thereby removing Jacobs as the assailant. Referring to the previous trial, Speers said he 'changed his mind "about what really happened. And I'm convinced ... that Bobbie Hogan pulled that trigger"' (Hentoff, 1995: 22). In the Hogan trial, Speers even went so far as to declare Jacobs innocent. The prosecutor stressed: 'Jacobs was telling the truth when he testified that he did not in any way anticipate that the victim would be shot' (Hentoff, 1995:

22). Moreover, since Jacobs was not aware of his sister's intention to shoot Urdiales, he was free from accomplice liability under state law.

Hogan was convicted of involuntary manslaughter and was sentenced to a ten-year prison term. Hogan's conviction and the prosecutor's admission that her brother was falsely imprisoned changed nothing for Jacobs. The state of Texas refused to vacate Jacobs's conviction, nor did he receive legal relief from the court of appeals. Eventually, Jacobs's case reached the US Supreme Court, but it, too, refused to keep him from being executed. In his five-page dissent opinion, Supreme Court Justice John Paul Stevens argued it was 'fundamentally unfair for the state of Texas' to put Jacobs to death (Hentoff, 1995: 22; also see Verhovek, 1995). The *Jacobs* case resembles that of *Herrera* v. *Collins* (1993) in which the US Supreme Court also ruled that 'actual innocence' is not enough to avert execution. In *Herrera*, Justice Harry Blackmun retorted: 'Nothing could be more shocking than to execute a person who is actually innocent,' and charged the High Court with coming 'perilously close to murder' (Hoffman, 1993: 817; see Sarat, 2008, 2005, 2001).

According to Jacobs, 'I have committed a lot of sins in my life ... Maybe I do deserve this. But I am not guilty of this crime' (Verhovek, 1995: E6). Not all observers, however, view Jacobs's execution as tragic. Laurin A. Wollan, Jr, an associate professor of criminology at Florida State University, who advocates the death penalty, concedes that the criminal justice system makes mistakes. Still, 'the value of the death penalty is its rightness vis-à-vis the wrongness of the crime, and that is so valuable that the possibility of the conviction of the innocent, though rare, has to be accepted' (Verhovek, 1995: E6).

CAUSES OF WRONGFUL CONVICTION

Nowadays, questions concerning the effectiveness of capital punishment have reached critical mass in light of numerous cases involving innocent people being released from death row. Since DNA has confirmed many of those exonerations, it is difficult to retain a high level of confidence in the criminal justice system's ability to convict only the guilty. In 2002, then Illinois Governor George Ryan, a conservative Republican committed to law and order, suspended all executions in his state after DNA had cleared 13 death row inmates. A year later, in 2003, Ryan stunned the political establishment by commuting all Illinois death sentences to prison terms of life or less. In one sweep, the mass commutation of 167 prisoners became the largest emptying of death row in US history. 'The facts that I have seen in reviewing each and every one of these cases raised questions not only about the innocence of people on death row, but about the fairness of the death penalty system as a whole,' announced Ryan (Wilgoren, 2003: 1).

C. Ronald Huff, in his presidential address to the American Society of Criminology, discussed his research on wrongful convictions and its implications for public policy (2002; Huff *et al.*, 1996). Borrowing from Borchard's (1932) seminal work, Huff chronicled the causes of wrongful conviction, including:

eyewitness error; overzealous police and prosecutors who engage in misconduct; ineffective defense counsel; forensic science errors, incompetence, and fraud (see Liebman *et al.*, 2000). As these factors are examined in greater detail below, it is important to bear in mind that usually more than one cause contributes to a wrongful conviction.

Eyewitness error

Contrary to popular opinion, eyewitness identification is frequently marred by error, albeit unintentional. In their groundbreaking book, *Actual Innocence*, Scheck *et al.* (2000) found that 84 percent of the DNA exonerations that they evaluated were based, at least in part, on eyewitness misidentification. Similarly, experts have written extensively on how police line-ups are subject to error and should be banned in fairness to suspects (Wells *et al.*, 1998).

Overzealous and unethical police and prosecutors

Regrettably, some police and prosecutors are influenced by the ultra-suppression-oriented organizational subcultures that lead to unprofessional, unethical, and, at times, criminal behavior. Compounding matters, by arresting and convicting the wrong person, the real offender remains free to victimize members of the community. Scheck *et al.* (2000) reported that 63 percent of the DNA exonerations that they examined had involved police and/or prosecutorial misconduct. Curiously, in 381 murder convictions that had been reversed due to misconduct, not once was a prosecutor disbarred and most of the time they were not even disciplined (see Lenza *et al.*, 2005)

False and coerced confessions

A common question among observers of the criminal justice system is: why would anyone confess to a crime that he or she did not commit, especially when it is punishable by death? With that concern in mind, it is important to scrutinize the interrogation process, in which police investigators rely on coercive tactics in extracting confessions, regardless of their veracity (Dixon and Travis, 2007; Leo, 2008, 2001). Scheck *et al.* (2000) reported that 15 of the first 62 post-conviction DNA exonerations in their data set (or about one in four) involved false confessions.

Inappropriate use of informants

When it serves their interest, police and prosecutors resort to informants, commonly known as jailhouse snitches. Paradoxically, authorities rely on the testimony of informants even though they realize that snitches are generally untrustworthy simply because they are convicted felons who are willing to say anything to cut a deal (Natapoff, 2009). Twenty-one percent of the DNA exonerations studied by Scheck *et al.* (2000) contained evidence of testimony fabricated by informants.

Ineffective defense counsel

Inadequate defense counsel is widely recognized in the criminal justice system as a problem that disproportionately affects indigent defendants, many of whom are people of color. Making matters worse, the adversarial system of justice is compromised by 'guilty plea wholesalers,' essentially unethical lawyers who hustle their clients by pleading them guilty without investigating their cases (Huff *et al.*, 1996; see McKie, 2002; Welch, 1999a).

Forensic errors, incompetence, and fraud

Whereas technology has the potential to be used constructively, such as detecting wrongful convictions via DNA testing, it also can be used destructively. Huff (2002) reminds us that forensic evidence is still an emerging field and must develop a better system of quality control and guard against the unethical use of technology in which 'junk scientists' have contributed to wrongful convictions (see Cole, 2001; Lynch *et al.*, 2008; McCartney, 2006). A case in point is Fred Zain, who while serving as director of the West Virginia State Police Crime Lab produced fraudulent lab reports. During his 16-year tenure, Zain knowingly facilitated numerous wrongful convictions (Castelle and Loftus, 2001).

Problems facing the death penalty should prompt further consideration of its utility as a public policy. Huff (2002) issued eight policy recommendations that carry the potential to instill fairness and caution:

1   Persons who are wrongfully convicted should be entitled to fair compensation. Moreover, states should assemble strategies designed to reintegrate these persons into the community, attending to their employment and counseling needs.
2   Capital punishment should be abolished and replaced with prison terms of 20 to 30 years, or life imprisonment. In doing so, there remains an opportunity to review cases that become suspect in light of new evidence, an option that is eliminated should the prisoner be executed.
3   In cases involving biological evidence, testing should be available for those defendants, as recommended by the National Commission on the Future of DNA Evidence.
4   For defendants' facing eyewitness testimony, the court should issue precise cautionary instructions to juries, apprising them of the possibility of misidentification.

5   Legal counsel for the suspect should be present during all identification procedures.

6   All interrogations of suspects should be recorded in full, thereby eliminating problems caused by edited versions of police questioning.

7   Police, prosecutors, and criminalists who engage in unethical, unprofessional, or illegal conduct contributing to wrongful conviction should be removed from their positions of public trust and subject to criminal and civil penalties.

8   Review commissions charged with examining cases with apparent problems should be established at the state and national levels. Additionally, the development of private organizations aimed at investigating wrongful convictions is encouraged, such as Scheck and Neufeld's Innocence Project and Jim McCloskey's Centurion Ministries.

(McCloskey, 2001)

Policy considerations such as these not only contribute to restoring public confidence in the criminal justice system but also further preserve the principles of justice on which democracy rests (see Burnett, 2002: Sherrill, 2001; Westervelt and Humphrey, 2001).

AN ALTERNATIVE TO THE DEATH PENALTY

One of the conclusions drawn by Johnson (1998) in his book *Deathwork* is that the execution process constitutes a form of torture. Indeed he borrows from novelist Albert Camus, who insists that capital punishment amounts to death *with* torture. The death penalty is equated with torture because the wait on death row is emotionally excruciating and psychologically debilitating. Johnson criticizes prison authorities for relying on the deliberate dehumanization of death row inmates to facilitate the execution process. As previously mentioned, by the final stage of the execution process, the condemned person is already dead, killed by the torturous confinement. 'On death rows, as in the death camps [in Nazi Germany], killing is made easier by the dehumanization of the victims' (Halperin, 2001–2; Johnson, 1998: 136).

Opponents of capital punishment charge that executions along with the conditions of death row are cruel and unusual; in turn, they propose a viable alternative to death sentences. Given what is known about the death penalty (e.g. a lack of compelling deterrence, high financial cost, pattern of unfair sentencing, and the risk of executing an innocent person), critics argue that those who are convicted of truly heinous murders ought to be sentenced to life imprisonment without parole. Moreover, the convicted should provide restitution for the surviving family of the victim.

Critics of life imprisonment without parole, however, argue that unless the offender is executed, he or she always has the chance – albeit slim – to be paroled. Their detractors for being 'soft' on crime often ridicule politicians who support life imprisonment without parole rather than capital punishment.

Interestingly, some government leaders, while refusing to yield to the pressures of changing their positions in favor of the death penalty, have created their own political rhetoric. For instance, while Mario Cuomo served as governor of New York, he continuously opposed capital punishment. In support of his stand on life imprisonment without parole, Cuomo coined his alternative to capital punishment as 'death by imprisonment.' Opponents of capital punishment continue to insist that retribution for serious violent crimes can be met by life imprisonment without parole, thereby dispensing justice without resorting to death sentences (see Appleton and Grover, 2007; Prejean, 1993; van Zyl Smit, 2002, 2001) (See 'Comparative Corrections: Iranian Professor Sentenced to Death', below)

COMPARATIVE CORRECTIONS:

Iranian Professor Sentenced to Death

As religious and secular values occasionally collide in a modern world, it is important to remain mindful of their effects on criminal justice. In 2002, Hashem Aghajari, a university professor in Tehran, Iran, was sentenced to death in a closed-door trial for apostasy in which he was accused of insulting the Prophet Muhammad. Aghajari was charged after he delivered a speech in which he proclaimed that people are not 'monkeys' and therefore should not follow religious leaders blindly. The death sentence was met with enormous public outcry, particularly by thousands of students engaging in massive demonstrations. While denouncing the sentence, students chanted demands for the resignation of Mahmoud Hashemi Sharoudi, a hard-liner in the Iranian judiciary. Protestors also called for the resignation of then President Mohammad Khatami, the leader of Iran's reform movement, in a sign of frustration with numerous liberal setbacks. In a statement, activists declared that the death sentence was an affront to the university students and professors and demanded that the judiciary overturn the penalty. 'The death sentence for Mr. Aghajari is punishing him for his opinion, which is against the Constitution and human rights' (Fathi, 2002a: A6). Several professors and the director of the humanities department at Modaress Training University resigned in protest. The speaker of the Parliament expressed 'hatred and disgust over the verdict' (p. A6) and two members of Parliament from the city where the sentence was issued also resigned in protest.

To restore order, hard-line government officials directed security forces to crack down on students, spraying tear gas and arresting hundreds of protestors. Conservative leaders underestimated the reaction from students who represent Iran's overwhelmingly young population: 70 percent of the 65 million Iranians are younger than 30. Many students are well read and share Western democratic ideals; moreover, professors who studied in Europe and the US teach them. Adding to their global views, students enjoy access to the Internet and satellite television. 'This is a force that the government counted on for support, but now the establishment is faced with its high expectations and demands,' said Qassem Sholeh-Saadi, a professor of law and political science at Tehran University (Fathi, 2002b: 22). The students have recognized that by challenging the death sentence of Aghajari they can expand their platform for social reform. One student explained, 'Students would not burst into such protests if they had basic freedoms such as wearing what they wish, listening to music or if men and women could freely mingle. But because there are bans on such simple freedoms, the students have to express their demands in political terms' (p. 22; see Hood, 2000; Johnson, 2008; Welch, 2000a).

CONCLUSION

While taking a critical approach, this chapter attends to key social forces shaping the emergence and maintenance of capital punishment. The discussion considers the power of religious forces in condemning wrongdoers to death. As modern society moved away from institutional religion and toward secularism, technology (the application of science) figured prominently in the administration of executions (e.g. the guillotine, the electric chair, and lethal injection).

Political forces have also determined the course of executions since the state (the body of political leaders) carries out executions for crimes that are legislatively approved. Even though political forces also shape the appeals process, the defendant is often at an enormous disadvantage since the momentum of the criminal justice machinery moves stridently toward execution. Finally, economic forces facilitate the use of the death penalty insofar as many defendants facing death sentences are of low socioeconomic status. Among the many consequences of being poor and facing serious criminal charges is not having access to the resources necessary for an adequate defense. Indigent defendants rely on public defenders, who are often overburdened and sometimes ill-prepared to defend their clients against prosecutors who have vast legal resources at their disposal.

SUMMARY

This chapter presents a critical examination of the death penalty. In doing so, it examines the history of executions by attending to the various political, economic, religious, and technological forces that shape capital punishment. This chapter also discusses the various issues contained in the continuing death penalty debate. Proponents of capital punishment refer to tradition, retribution, community solidarity and protection, deterrence, costs, public opinion, and the prevention of vigilante-style justice to justify their position. Conversely, critics of the death penalty point to several problems plaguing the use of executions, including violations of contemporary standards of decency as well as the Eighth and Fourteenth Amendments; error, finality, and irreversibility;

arbitrariness, discrimination, and discretionary bias; and considerations of the nature of homicide. The chapter carefully confronts myths associated with capital punishment, especially false beliefs that executions offer a compelling deterrent effect and that they cost less than life imprisonment. Other major developments discussed in this chapter include landmark Supreme Court decisions, public opinion, and the brutalization effect of executions. Attention is also turned to the executions of minorities, juveniles, offenders who are emotionally disturbed or mentally retarded, and those who are actually innocent. Finally the chapter takes an in-depth look at the execution process, especially electrocution and lethal injection.

REVIEW QUESTIONS

1 How do modern executions resemble those of the past, and how are executions today different from those of earlier times?
2 Which arguments offered by proponents of the death penalty are most convincing?
3 Which arguments offered by opponents of the death penalty are most convincing?
4 Should offenders who are juveniles, emotionally disturbed, or mentally retarded be executed? Why, or why not?
5 Which cases demonstrate that innocent people have been falsely convicted of murder, and falsely executed?

RECOMMENDED READINGS

Bohm, R. M. (1999) *Deathquest: An Introduction to the Theory and Practice of Capital Punishment in the United States*. Cincinnati, OH: Anderson.

Dow, D. R. and Dow, M. (2002) *Machinery of Death: The Reality of America's Death Penalty Regime*. New York: Routledge.

Johnson, R. (1998) *Deathwatch: A Study of the Modern Execution Process*. Belmont: CA: West/Wadsworth.

Leo, R. A. (2008) *Police Interrogation and American Justice*. Cambridge, MA: Harvard University Press.

Scheck, B., Neufeld, P. and Dwyer, J. (2000) *Actual Innocence*. New York: Doubleday.

PART IV PENAL PROCESS

CHAPTER 11

Jails and Detention

Communities should explore alternatives to incarceration. Many jail detainees are not threats to society and should not occupy scarce and expensive cell space ... jails cannot – should not – continue to be society's dumping ground. (Joel A. Thompson and G. Larry Mays)

LEARNING OBJECTIVES

After studying this chapter, you should be able to answer the following questions:

1 What roles do jails play in the criminal justice system as well as in society in general?
2 Who goes to jail?
3 What are current jail conditions like?
4 What is the nature of jail litigation? What other problems are facing jail management?
5 What are the various aspects of jail reform and the alternatives to detention?

In 2000, Garibaldy Mejia, a 54-year-old grandfather and livery cab driver, was stopped by immigration agents in a New York airport upon returning from the Dominican Republic where he had attended his father's funeral. Mejia's green card and passport were confiscated and he was placed in detention because in 1985 he had been arrested with a small amount of cocaine, a misdemeanor. Given the minor nature of that particular offense, Mejia had pleaded guilty, paid a $100 fine, and agreed to serve two years' probation. Under new immigration laws, however, nearly all drug offenses, regardless of the magnitude, are grounds for deportation. Even though Mejia had established himself as a productive member of his community since his drug violation, he was transported to the Federal Correctional Institution in Oakdale, Louisiana (a facility specifically designed to hold criminal aliens), as the government prepared its case to deport him (Hedges, 2000).

INTRODUCTION

It is often said that jails are among the most ignored institutions in the criminal justice system – widely ignored by the public, by policymakers, and, surprisingly, even by penologists. Although correctional experts have produced volumes of research on prisons, the importance of studying jails has, until recently, been overlooked. As a result of that long-term neglect, major misconceptions about jails have emerged. Most notably, jails are sometimes falsely characterized as 'small prisons,' or merely as a subset of the prison system, rather than the unique institutions they are (Burns, 2002; Kerle, 1998; Welch, 1992a).

Although jails and prisons differ in numerous ways, the main distinction between them is commonly drawn along the lines of the legal status of their inmates. Whereas prisons house convicted felons (those serving sentences of one year or more), jails hold pre-trial detainees, convicted misdemeanants (those serving sentences of less than one or two years, depending on the state), as well as convicted felons awaiting transfer to their assigned prisons. In addition to city, county, and federal jails there are detention centers supervised by the US Department of Homeland Security (DHS) and Immigration and Customs Enforcement (ICE), formerly known as the Immigration and Naturalization Service (INS). As we shall see, these facilities play a key role in the government's campaign against unauthorized immigration along with its war on terror (Welch, 2006, 2002b).

Observers of criminal justice find that jails are often misused. For example, jails often serve as drunk tanks, truant halls, and shelters for the homeless mentally ill (Adler, 1986; Thompson and Mays, 1991; Zupan, 2002). As discussed in herein, jails are complex institutions dealing with multiple demands placed upon them. Because jails process those whom other social and criminal justice agencies refuse, they are often referred to as the 'dumping grounds' (Moynahan and Stewart, 1980: 104). Jails, like prisons, are institutions that deal with persons most drastically affected by society's most pressing problems (poverty, unemployment, inadequate education, inaccessible healthcare, substance abuse, racism, discrimination, etc.). Still, jails receive significantly more of them than do prisons. This chapter examines how jails differ from prisons, especially in view of the role that jails play both in the criminal justice system as well as in larger society. As we shall see, key social forces – politics and economics – shape the use and misuse of jails in American cities. Compounding matters, jails often are given the lowest priority within the criminal justice system, perpetuating such problems as inadequate funding and lack of reform.

Although the courts do not formally regard detention as a form of punishment, it is very much a punitive experience. The loss of liberty and various humiliations contained in detention often are reserved for those who cannot financially secure their release by meeting the required bail. Even at the early stages of determining guilt or innocence, the criminal justice system treats people differently on the basis of their social class. Whereas upper- and middle-income defendants tend to await trial while in the community, their lower-income counterparts face months of detention in jail (Irwin, 1985, 2004; Welch, 1994; Wynn, 2001).

Slowly but surely, research on detention is gaining ground; currently, the jail literature can be divided into five general groupings:

1   Sociological studies of jails which examine the role of jails within society
2   The deplorable conditions characteristic of most jails
3   Inmate litigation
4   Additional problems in jail management
5   Jail reform and alternatives.

Before embarking on each of those major sections, we should address two basic questions: what are the patterns of detention and who goes to jail?

PATTERNS, TRENDS, AND INMATE CHARACTERISTICS

In its most recent report available, the Bureau of Justice Statistics provides a glimpse of jail patterns and trends. By 2008, the average daily population of inmates confined in local jails stood at 776,573, a figure that translates into an incarceration rate of 258 (per 100,000 US residents). That percentage has increased since 2000 when 618,319 inmates were confined in local jails, an incarceration rate of 226 (Minton and Sabol, 2009; see Table 11.1).

Figure 11.1   Aerial view of Rikers Island, New York City, February 13, 2002.

Photo by Todd Maisel/ NY Daily News Archive via Getty Images.

Table 11.1 Inmates confined in local jails at mid-year, average jail population, and incarceration rate, 2000–8

Year	Inmates confined at midyear		Average daily population[a]		Incarceration rate[b]
	Number	Percent	Number	Percent	
2000	621,149	2.5%	618,319	1.7%	226
2001	631,240	1.6	625,966	1.2	222
2002	665,475	5.4	652,082	4.2	231
2003	691,301	3.9	680,760	4.4	238
2004	713,990	3.3	706,242	3.7	243
2005	747,529	4.7	733,442	3.9	252
2006[c]	765,819	2.4	755,320	3.0	256
2007[d]	780,174	1.9	773,138	2.4	259
2008	785,556	0.7	776,573	0.4	258
Average annual increase					
2000–2007		3.3%		3.2%	
2007–2008		0.7		0.4	

[a]Average daily population is the sum of the number of inmates in jail each day for a year, divided by the number of days in the year.
[b]Number of inmates confined at midyear per 100,000 U.S. residents.
[c]Based on revised data from selected jail jurisdictions for the number of inmates confined at midyear 2006.
[d]Based on revised data from selected jail jurisdictions for the number of inmates confined at midyear 2007 and the average daily population in 2007.

Source: Minton and Sabol (2009: 2).

CRITICAL ANALYSIS OF DATA

Table 11.1 shows a steady annual increase in the incarceration rate, except for which year?

Not surprisingly, the largest local jails are located in the nation's largest urban areas. As Table 11.2 indicates, the jail with the largest average daily population is located in Los Angeles County (California), followed by New York City, Harris County (Texas), Cook County (Illinois), Maricopa County (Arizona), and Philadelphia City (Pennsylvania). Indeed, as these figures show, most of these jails are well above their capacity, meaning that overcrowding is a key feature of large urban jails (Minton and Sabol, 2009).

CRITICAL ANALYSIS OF DATA

Turning attention to Table 11.2, identify the three jail jurisdictions closest to your residence. Which has the highest average daily population and which has the lowest?

Tracking the characteristics of inmates is important to understand
to jail. As Table 11.3 demonstrates, in 2008, the vast majority of inmates
male (87 percent). In terms of race and ethnicity, nearly 43 percent of inmates
held in local jails were white, followed by blacks (39 percent) and Hispanics
(16 percent). Clearly, these statistics indicate that blacks are overrepresented in
the jail population. Attention should also be turned to the conviction status of
inmates. Table 11.3 shows that nearly 63 percent of inmates held in local jails
are unconvicted, meaning that their cases have yet to reach trial. Those inmates
are commonly referred to as 'pre-trial detainees' (Minton and Sabol, 2009; see
Beck et al., 2002).

Furthering the trend of incarcerating more non-violent offenders who suffer
from an array of drug and emotional problems, figures from the Bureau of
Justice Statistics (2002) show that 27 percent of jail inmates were held for a
property offense, 24 percent for a public order offense, and 22 percent for a
drug offense. By comparison, about 26 percent of the jail inmates were being
held for a violent offense. (More than half of all inmates had previously served
time in jail or prison, and nearly two-thirds had been on probation.) Over
the years, increasingly more jail inmates were experiencing greater drug use.
Compared to jail inmates in 1989, inmates in 1996 reported a higher percentage
of use of every type of drug except cocaine. Among convicted inmates who said
they used drugs in the month before the offense, 17 percent had participated
in a treatment or self-help program since admission. Self-help groups included
12-step programs like Narcotics/Alcoholics Anonymous. The Bureau of Justice
Statistics also indicates that a quarter of the jail inmates said they had been
treated at some time for a mental or emotional problem, and nearly half of
the jailed women reported having been physically or sexually abused prior to
admission (27 percent had been raped) (Harlow, 1998).

It ought to be emphasized that jail detention is not a required feature of the
criminal justice process. Still, one pattern is clear. Jail cells are reserved more
for lower-income persons charged with criminal offenses than for middle or
high socioeconomic status. The Bureau of Justice Statistics finds that a lower
percentage of jail inmates than the general population were employed: 64
percent of jail inmates, compared to 74 percent of those aged 18 to 64 in the
general population. Nearly half reported incomes of less than $600 a month (at
most $7,200 annually) before their most recent arrest. A third of jail inmates
reported incomes of $1,000 or more (at least $12,000 a year). In an effort to
make ends meet, about 22 percent of the inmates reported one or more kinds
of financial support from government agencies. Approximately 14 percent said
they received money from welfare, including Aid to Families with Dependent
Children (AFDC), food stamps, and the Special Supplemental Nutrition Program
for Women, Infants, and Children (WIC); 7 percent from Social Security or
Supplemental Security Income; and 3 percent from unemployment insurance,
workers' compensation, or veterans' compensation. As further evidence of their
relatively low socioeconomic status, 47 percent of jail inmates did not graduate
from high school (Harlow, 1998).

Table 11.2 The 50 largest local jail jurisdictions: number of inmates held, average daily population, and rated capacity

	Number of inmates[a]			Average daily population[b]			Rated capacity[c]			Percent of capacity occupied[d]		
	2006	2007	2008	2006	2007	2008	2006	2007	2008	2006 %	2007 %	2008 %
Total	224,706	227,121	229,680	224,355	226,208	227,667	235,424	238,766	242,524	95 %	95 %	95 %
Los Angeles County, CA	19,062	19,175	19,533	19,287	19,266	19,836	22,411	21,364	22,349	85	90	87
New York City, NY	13,641	14,120	13,804	13,494	14,004	13,849	19,674	19,686	19,554	69	72	71
Harris County, TX	9,464	9,900	10,063	9,091	9,430	10,000	9,241	9,391	9,391	102	105	107
Cook County, IL	9,505	9,410	9,984	9,345	9,496	9,900	10,114	10,158	10,158	94	93	98
Maricopa County, AZ	9,243	9,466	9,536	9,733	8,941	9,265	7,270	7,270	9,395	127	130	102
Philadelphia City, PA	8,725	8,607	8,824	8,772	8,448	8,811	7,269	8,685	8,685	120	99	102
Miami-Dade County, FL[e]	6,502	6,835	7,082	6,765	6,844	7,050	6,005	6,005	5,845	108	114	121
Dallas County, TX	7,354	6,261	6,252	7,140	6,389	6,385	7,145	7,145	7,665	103	88	82
Orange County, CA	6,455	6,841	6,216	6,513	6,571	6,000	7,019	7,019	7,019	92	97	89
Shelby County, TN	5,413	5,741	5,925	5,300	5,570	5,765	6,839	6,811	6,675	79	84	89
San Bernardino County, CA[e]	5,603	5,639	5,596	5,628	5,596	5,593	5,914	5,914	5,970	95	95	94
Broward County, FL	6,121	5,782	5,509	5,949	6,051	5,500	6,254	6,452	5,722	98	90	96
San Diego County, CA	5,117	5,133	5,435	5,333	5,172	5,363	4,768	4,778	4,972	107	107	109
Santa Clara County, CA	4,421	4,748	4,664	4,750	4,852	4,660	4,169	4,169	3,825	106	114	122
Sacramento County, CA	4,197	4,361	4,592	4,049	4,592	4,563	4,991	4,775	5,075	84	91	90
Alameda County, CA	3,993	3,978	4,345	3,982	4,282	4,371	4,469	4,505	4,243	89	88	102
Orange County, FL	4,051	4,180	4,665	3,835	4,146	4,294	4,352	4,721	4,721	93	89	99
Bexar County, TX	4,084	4,088	4,279	4,015	4,067	4,062	4,294	4,294	4,598	95	95	93
Baltimore City, MD[e]	4,038	4,182	4,265	4,156	4,126	4,010	3,683	3,683	3,683	110	114	116
Hillsborough County, FL[e]	3,929	3,913	3,857	4,384	3,949	3,985	4,190	4,190	4,190	94	93	92
Jacksonville City, FL	3,613	3,581	3,799	3,493	3,725	3,606	3,137	3,137	3,137	115	114	121
Pinellas County, FL	3,695	3,510	3,463	3,502	3,644	3,559	3,363	3,353	4,155	110	105	83
Riverside County, CA	3,264	3,492	3,597	3,258	3,433	3,530	2,884	3,129	3,132	113	112	115
Davidson County, TN	3,450	3,641	3,934	3,202	3,445	3,528	3,679	3,679	3,679	94	99	107
Tarrant County, TX	3,475	3,341	3,574	3,500	3,500	3,500	4,564	4,564	4,379	76	73	82
Gwinnett County, GA	2,998	3,142	3,415	2,716	3,033	3,311	2,076	3,538	3,419	144	89	100
Allegheny County, PA	3,026	3,113	3,219	3,370	3,076	3,246	3,342	3,341	3,371	91	93	95
Clark County, NV[e,f]	3,354	3,237	3,121	3,136	3,274	3,115	2,859	2,859	2,957	117	113	106
Fresno County, CA	3,467	3,294	3,047	3,538	3,094	3,049	3,778	3,778	3,778	92	87	81
Milwaukee County, WI	2,917	3,139	3,025	2,892	2,905	3,037	3,000	3,000	3,000	97	105	101

Jurisdiction											
District of Columbia[a,g]	3,214	3,103	3,046	3,584	3,325	3,012	3,825	3,522	3,522	84	88	86
DeKalb County, GA	2,779	2,772	3,365	3,117	2,619	2,906	3,636	3,636	3,636	76	76	93
Palm Beach County, FL	2,766	2,854	2,987	2,630	2,882	2,900	3,365	3,345	3,359	82	85	89
Fulton County, GA	2,816	2,899	2,821	2,970	2,936	2,789	3,115	3,115	3,115	90	93	91
Travis County, TX	2,548	2,954	2,533	2,595	2,813	2,662	3,056	3,176	3,137	83	93	81
King County, WA	2,499	2,638	2,517	2,560	2,715	2,657	3,154	3,154	3,154	79	84	80
Orleans Parish, LA	1,898	2,526	2,370	1,569	2,722	2,613	1,845	2,721	2,633	103	93	90
Mecklenburg County, NC	2,466	2,778	2,647	2,335	2,647	2,610	2,668	2,668	2,668	92	104	99
Bernalillo County, NM	2,410	2,635	2,589	2,292	2,497	2,607	2,048	2,236	2,236	118	118	116
Cobb County, GA	2,540	2,591	2,467	2,510	2,561	2,579	2,559	2,559	2,559	99	101	96
Franklin County, OH	2,553	2,408	2,544	2,561	2,592	2,457	2,531	2,541	2,541	101	95	100
Polk County, FL	2,565	2,454	2,369	2,605	2,464	2,456	1,808	1,808	1,808	142	136	131
Suffolk County, MA	2,531	2,407	2,494	2,387	2,426	2,445	2,932	2,858	2,990	86	84	83
Denver County, CO	2,429	2,371	2,299	2,469	2,417	2,380	1,710	1,710	1,792	142	139	128
Kern County, CA	2,279	2,279	2,368	2,279	2,338	2,372	2,698	2,698	2,698	84	84	88
Marion County, IN	3,114	2,501	2,336	3,064	2,425	2,344	2,463	2,412	2,656	126	104	88
Wayne County, MI[c]	2,641	2,400	2,363	2,646	2,538	2,336	2,725	2,721	2,721	97	88	87
Lee County, FL[e]	2,024	2,321	2,205	1,861	2,039	2,313	1,683	1,683	1,683	120	138	131
Essex County, NJ	2,154	2,056	2,389	2,051	2,056	2,260	2,410	2,370	2,434	89	87	98
El Paso County, TX	2,303	2,324	2,351	2,142	2,275	2,226	2,440	2,440	2,440	94	95	96

Note: Jurisdictions are ordered by their average daily population in 2008.

[a]Number of inmates held in jail facilities on the last weekday in June.

[b]Based on the average daily population for the year ending June 30. Average daily population is the sum of the number of inmates in jail each day for a year, divided by the number of days in the year.

[c]Number of beds or inmates assigned by a rating official to facilities within each jurisdiction.

[d]Number of inmates at midyear divided by the rated capacity multiplied by 100.

[e]Based on revised data.

[f]Confined population total for Clark County, NV, excludes inmates held in contract facilities.

[g]Includes the Central Detention Facility (D.C. Jail), Correctional Treatment Facility (Contract Adult Detention Center), and contractual bed space at four halfway houses.

Source: Minton and Sabol (2009: 7).

Table 11.3 Characteristics of inmates in local jails at midyear, 2000 and 2005–8

Characteristic	Percent of inmates				
	2000	2005	2006	2007	2008
Gender					
Male	8.6 %	87.3 %	87.1%	87.1%	87.3 %
Female	11.4	12.7	12.9	12.9	12.7
Adults	98.8 %	99.1 %	99.2%	99.1%	99.0 %
Male	87.4	86.5	86.3	86.3	86.4
Female	11.3	12.6	12.9	12.8	12.6
Juveniles[a]	1.2	0.9	0.8	0.9	1.0
Held as adults[b]	1.0	0.8	0.6	0.7	0.8
Held as juveniles	0.2	0.1	0.2	0.2	0.2
Race/Hispanic origin[c]					
White[d]	41.9 %	44.3 %	43.9%	43.3%	42.5 %
Black/African American[d]	41.3	38.9	38.6	38.7	39.2
Hispanic/Latino	15.2	15.0	15.6	16.1	16.4
Other[d,e]	1.6	1.7	1.8	1.8	1.8
Two or more races[d]	...	0.1	0.1	0.1	0.2
Conviction status[b]					
Convicted	44.0 %	38.0 %	37.9%	38.0%	37.1 %
Male	39.0	33.2	32.8	32.9	32.3
Female	5.0	4.9	5.0	5.2	4.8
Unconvicted	56.0	62.0	62.1	62.0	62.9
Male	50.0	54.2	54.3	54.3	55.2
Female	6.0	7.7	7.8	7.7	7.8

Note: Detail may not sum to total due to rounding.

... Not collected.

[a]Persons under age 18 at midyear.

[b]Includes juveniles who were tried or awaiting trial as adults.

[c]Estimates based on reported data and adjusted for nonresponses.

[d]Excludes persons of Hispanic or Latino origin.

[e]Includes American Indians, Alaska Natives, Asians, Native Hawaiians, and other Pacific Islanders.

Source: Minton and Sabol (2009: 7).

Finally, middle-aged inmates constituted a growing part of the jail population. In 1996, 24 percent of jail inmates were between the ages of 35 and 44, compared to 17 percent in 1989 and 12 percent in 1983. By comparison, the percentage between the ages of 18 and 24 dropped from 40 percent in 1983 to 29 percent in 1996 (Harlow, 1998). As discussed in Chapter 16, an aging correctional population is taking its toll on the cost of providing medical and healthcare.

SOCIOLOGICAL STUDIES OF JAILS

Sociological studies of jails, though relatively few in number, reach beyond the jail's immediate role in the criminal justice system to focus on its larger function within society. Among the most recurrent themes to emerge in the literature is the perspective that detention patterns are determined less by crime rates and more by economic forces.

Due to an expanding post-industrial society, workers struggle to find viable employment. That problem is most evident in large urban areas where some of those persons come into contact with the criminal justice system, creating another social phenomenon known as 'warehousing.' Simply put, 'warehousing' is the practice of detaining massive numbers of inmates in city jails where the only institutional goal is to secure custody. Human storage, not rehabilitation or reform, is the primary objective in 'warehousing,' and it is members of the urban underclass who are most likely to be subjected to that form of social control. This section explores that phenomenon by addressing the critical observation that jails are used to manage the underclass (Irwin, 1985; Welch, 1994, 1999a).

Managing the underclass in American society

The aforementioned BJS figures on the profile of jail inmates provide ample evidence that jail populations are disproportionately poor, African American or Hispanic, uneducated, and unemployed. Additionally, jail populations consist of disproportionate numbers of people who have drug-abuse problems and who reside in the inner sections of our nation's major cities. Those socioeconomic characteristics make the issue of social class too important to ignore. Generally, those in jail occupy one of two segments of the so-called lower class: the working poor or the underclass. Although the jail experience adversely affects both groups, those who are considered to be among the working poor appear to be less disrupted since, at the very least, they possess some skills and an opportunity to survive economically upon their release. By contrast, the underclass, by its very definition, are those who have far more limited means to survive; they are uneducated, possess virtually no job skills, and have little or no work experience. For the underclass, the jail experience reinforces their inability to lead a productive and economically independent life (see Gibbs, 1982; Klofas, 1990; Weisheit and Klofas, 1989; Welch, 1991c, 1989b; Wilson, 1987).

John Irwin contributed significantly to the discourse of the social function of jails and the underclass in his book *The Jail: Managing the Underclass in American Society* (1985). Simply put, Irwin contends that jails are used in American society to manage the underclass. In his analysis of jails, Irwin identifies an economically subordinate social group that he classifies as the 'rabble.' The rabble are socially detached insofar as they do not belong to any conventional social network; compounding matters, they are disorganized, disorderly, and viewed by the conventional world as offensive to its middle-class sensibilities. Irwin found that the 'rabble' are detained for minor offenses and do not fit the stereotype of a dangerous and threatening criminal (see Beck *et al.*, 2002; Harlow, 1998).

Although it is commonly assumed that jail inmates are detained for the purpose of protecting society while they await trial, Irwin learned that many of them represent no such threat. Rather, these detainees – known as 'disreputables' (e.g. petty hustlers, derelicts, and junkies) – are generally held for non-violent and minor offenses (e.g. drug possession), and are simply too poor to meet their bail. By the very nature of their economic standing, the rabble are unable to adequately defend themselves in the legal sense. Therefore, from the moment of arrest, they are at the mercy of the police, jail staff, their court-appointed attorneys, as well as the courts (see Wynn, 2001).

Since the issue of social class is vital in determining who goes to jail, Irwin places his findings within a larger social context. He concludes that jails function as an extension of the welfare state and become a means by which society manages and controls the underclass. Similar arguments have been developed by Piven and Cloward, who in their book, *Regulating the Poor: The Functions of Public Welfare* (1971), found that throughout contemporary history, welfare has been used to reduce social unrest and reinforce the poor's social position in a class-based society (also see Klofas, 1990; Spitzer, 1975; Welch, 1994).

According to Irwin, the criminal justice system is likely to continue placing disproportionate emphasis on managing the underclass rather than pursuing more serious offenders. Such strategies of policing serve as a 'political diversion,' drawing attention from the apparent lack of success in dealing with the 'hard-core' criminals (Irwin, 1985: 112). Although critics argue that Irwin overstates his case, 'claiming that jailed persons are less involved in serious criminality than is the case,' there is agreement with him 'regarding the broader issues of public policy toward members of the rabble class who get caught up in law-breaking, and in many cases, who get sent to jails' (Backstand *et al.*, 1992: 228).

The jail experience

In taking a closer look at the jail experience, Irwin discovered that the rabble undergo a distinct form of socialization by which they are stigmatized and kept constrained within the underclass. Inspired by the work of Erving Goffman in *Asylums* (1961), Irwin outlined various passages of the jail experience, comprising four stages: disintegration, disorientation, degradation, and preparation (see also Gibbs, 1987, 1982).

Disintegration

Unlike employed, middle-class persons, who are perceived as being reputable and thus generally released on their own recognizance or who are able to meet bail, disreputable individuals (the rabble) are detained. Detention marks the outset of the disintegration state because it tends to destroy the few social ties the rabble might have. Simply being denied convenient access to telephones makes it difficult to contact family, friends, and court-appointed attorneys. Moreover, being detained prevents these people from taking care of such personal affairs as calling their employers, paying rent and bills, etc.

Although having convenient access to a telephone while in jail is often rare, sometimes circumstances may make the problem worse. For example, in New York City's Rikers Island jail complex, there are complaints that African American inmates monopolize one telephone while Hispanic inmates dominate the other, leaving white detainees (who represent only 5 percent of the pre-trial detainee population) without regular access to telephones (see Wynn, 2001). Obviously, without regular contact with family, friends, and lawyers, jail inmates undergo considerable disintegration. Upon release, former detainees have the stressful task of picking up the pieces. Irwin observes:

> Unlike released convicts and mental patients, they [jail inmates] have received no official preparation for their release. And when they do get out, city, county, and private agencies rarely offer them any help in coping with the problems of re-entering society. In trying to pick up the pieces of their shattered lives, most of them will be working alone, with virtually no resources and many handicaps.
>
> (1985; 52; see also Weisheit and Klofas, 1989)

Disorientation

Among the psychological effects of being arrested and detained is a profound sense of internal disorganization and demoralization. After months of detention, released inmates understandably re-enter society in a state of confusion. The degree of disorientation is compounded by the fact that while they are detained, detainees must replace their personal routines with the routine of the institution. Inmates eat according to a schedule organized by the staff and, assuming they can actually do so, sleep according to a routine dictated by the institution. Eventually, their sense of independence is replaced by feelings of powerlessness. As Irwin notes, while in jail, detainees eat, urinate, defecate, wash, change clothes, and bathe without privacy while also being continuously subjected to stares, comments, insults, and threats.

'Persons who are arrested and thrown in jail experience a sudden blow that hurls them outside society. It not only unravels their social ties; it stuns them and reduces their capacity and their resolve to make the journey back into society' (Irwin, 1985: 66). Irwin concedes that being detained once or twice does not lead to permanent social isolation. However, since many inmates are rabble who are detained somewhat frequently, their ability to bounce back is significantly strained. Overall, 'the jail is not the only expelling process, of course; economic misfortune and drug abuse are others' (1985: 66).

Degradation

As might be expected, the jail experience also involves relentless humiliation, as inmates are stripped of their dignity. They are met with hostility from police officers and jail staff as well as other detainees. Under routine surveillance by the staff, detainees are subjected to frisks, strip searches, and body-cavity examinations. Irwin provides us with a glimpse of the humiliation of a 'keister search,' as told by a deputy:

> Now bend over and spread your cheeks, I ordered. The kid bent over and grabbed his buttocks, pulling them apart. The plastic bag [of narcotics] inserted into his rectum had broken. The red pills had partially melted from his body heat, and his anus was a flaming scarlet color. The intestinal pressure had forced some of the pills out through his sphincter where they remained matted in his anal hair. We began to laugh with black humor at the grotesque sight. When the cops became bored with the game, the kid was ordered to dig the narcotics out of his rectum.
>
> (1985: 77)

In some jails, inmates are required to wear orange jumpsuits instead of their own clothes, contributing to a loss of personal identity. Detainees also endure a barrage of insults: they are often called 'slime balls,' 'dirt balls,' 'pukes,' 'scum,' 'kronks,' and, the most popular reference, 'assholes' (see Saulny, 2002a). Following months of lock-up, their outward appearances are likely to change. Since shaving is not always easy, many inmates grow beards and their hair becomes long and straggly. A slovenly appearance not only adds to the degradation but also adversely affects their court appearances. In court, inmates are judged not solely or even primarily in terms of their crimes but rather for their character that is generally assessed by their physical appearance (Irwin, 1985).

Preparation

Irwin points out that a great majority of those arrested and those detained are not sentenced to serve a jail or prison term. Considering the humiliation and degradation experienced at the hands of the criminal justice system, however, all those arrested are subjected to some form of punishment, even those whose charges are dismissed. One way to view that pattern of social disgrace is to recognize it as a process that is meant to be punitive (Feeley, 1979).

Whereas reputable people are likely to pick up the pieces and move forward with their lives upon release, the rabble are less able to do so. With limited means to survive and few resources and economic opportunities at their disposal, the rabble often fall victim to the self-fulfilling prophecy constructed by the criminal justice system. For many, accepting the label of 'loser' or 'asshole' and dropping out of society become the inevitable options: hence, the rabble become even more defeated, socially disintegrated, and marginalized. In sum, 'the jail experience prepares them for an acceptance of the rabble life' (Irwin 1985: 84; see Feuer, 2002).

CULTURAL PENOLOGY

Jailing as Social Sanitation

A sharper understanding of the social – and cultural – function of jails invites exploration into both its *stated* and *unstated* purposes. Generally speaking, the *stated* purpose of the jail is to hold those who have been charged with offenses but cannot meet their bail. Since the process of release is based on a financial arrangement, those who are too poor to meet their bail are likely to be detained. However, to say that poor people are detained only because they cannot meet their bail is too simplistic (Welch, 1994, 1999). Poor people charged with offenses often are detained because police, victims, and witnesses also view them as disreputable. A person's disrepute is not interpreted as a single quality, 'but as a configuration of attributes that constitutes a "type" of person' (Irwin, 1985: 25). Still, not all poor people are viewed as disreputable. Indeed, poor people charged with a crime who are also viewed as being reputable are usually given desk appearance tickets or released on their own recognizance. Considering those distinctions, the *unstated* purpose of the jail is to detain the rabble – those who are poor, disreputable, and socially detached (Irwin, 1985, 2004; Welch, 2005a).

So why is the jail in the business of locking up poor and disreputable people? What larger social – cultural – purpose is served by 'warehousing' the rabble, especially when it is clear that those individuals are not dangerous and do not pose an imminent threat to the community? In attempting to answer that question, we turn to the notion of *social sanitation*, a process by which the police remove socially offensive (disreputable) people from specific urban zones and detain them in local jails, thereby creating the illusion that certain sections of a city are reputable (see Beckett and Herbert, 2008; Body-Gendrot, 2000; Cohen, 1979; Harcourt, 2001; Parr, 2009).

From a cultural standpoint, every medium to large city has a 'desirable' section as well as one considered 'seedy.' Among the many duties expected of city police is to keep the 'desirable' section free of the 'riffraff,' or disreputable people, particularly those who offend the middle-class sensibilities of the conventional world (e.g. street-walking prostitutes, the homeless, bums, junkies, drug peddlers) (see LeDuff, 2002; Oxenhandler, 2002; Steinhauer, 2002). It is important to emphasize that the 'rabble' are not regarded by the police as dangerous but rather as 'offensive' to society at large. While the truly dangerous felons go to prison, the merely 'rabble' are sent to jail for a temporary stay (Irwin, 1985; Klofas, 1990, 1987; McCarthy, 1990; Spitzer, 1975). From a cultural perspective social sanitation operates as a form of *social control* insofar as it attempts to purify certain urban zones from persons regarded as 'pollution' (Douglas, 1984; Smith, 2001; Welch,

2006a, 2004). Certainly, the social-sanitation role of the jail has historical precedence. As feudalism was unraveling and more vagabonds, beggars, prostitutes, 'gonophs' (petty thieves), and peasants drifted into the urban centers, additional jails (or gaols) were constructed for the purposes of social sanitation (Chesney, 1972; Fishman, 1923).

Jails in Indian country

Whereas jails are unique institutions – especially compared to their prison counterparts – jails in Indian country are even more distinctive. Such facilities are operated either by tribal authorities or the Bureau of Indian Affairs (BIA). Still, it is important to note that tribes retain jurisdiction over many crimes by American Indians in Indian country (including Alaska Natives): currently, 33 states contain approximately 300 Indian land areas, commonly known as reservations. Generally, the local governing authority on Indian lands is a tribal government or council. Jurisdiction over crimes in Indian country depends on several factors, including the identity of the victim and the offender, the severity of the crime, and where the crime occurred. Tribal authority to sentence offenders is limited to one year of imprisonment and a $5,000 fine or both (Minton, 2002).

Survey research conducted by the Bureau of Justice Statistics (BJS) offers a glimpse at the use of jails in Indian country. In 2007, 83 jails in Indian country held an estimated 2,163 inmates. These numbers are up from 1,745 inmates held in 68 facilities in 2004, marking a 24 percent increase. According to the BJS, an estimated four in ten inmates in Indian country jails were confined for a violent offense. Specifically, domestic violence (20 percent) accounted for the largest group of violent offenders, followed by simple or aggravated assault (13 percent) and rape or sexual assault (2 percent). The percentage of Indian country jail inmates held for drug offenses remained constant from 2004 to 2007 (7 percent) while DWI/DUI offenses decreased, from 14 percent in 2004 to 8 percent in 2007.

Given that most of these inmates were charged with non-violent offenses, it is not surprising to find that the average stay in jail was relatively short (4.5 days). The average length of stay for inmates was the highest (9.4 days) in facilities rated to hold 50 or more persons while those held in jails rated to hold 10 to 24 persons reported the shortest average length of stay (2.1 days).

In terms of healthcare, 78 out of 83 facilities responded to a survey addendum that shows 91 percent of inmates were covered by medical services. The majority (69) provided medical services offsite through the Indian Health Service, US Department of Health and Human Services. Most facilities reported they had policies to test for infectious diseases: HIV, hepatitis B, hepatitis C, and tuberculosis. Similarly, 72 Indian country jails provided mental health services to inmates, including 41 jails that screened inmates for mental health disorders at intake. Most facilities said they have at least one suicide prevention policy, and routinely perform risk assessment at intake.

Specialized programs or training were also extended to inmates held in Indian country jails: 59 facilities provided drug or alcohol dependency counseling or awareness programs, 38 offered domestic violence counseling, 9 provided sex offender treatment, 56 offered religious and spiritual counseling, 12 offered vocational training, and 14 provided job-seeking and interviewing skills training. Forty-one jails in Indian country offered inmates GED classes, 28 offered basic and high-school education classes, and 48 offered inmate work assignments which included facility support services, public work assignments, farming and agriculture work, and correctional industries (Minton, 2008).

Let us return to the 'rabble' hypothesis by Irwin (1985), who postulated that jails are used less to combat serious crimes and more to manage society's so-called 'riffraff,' that is those charged with minor offenses and who have a history of drug and alcohol dependency (see Welch, 1994). As reported by the BJS, recent data appear to offer support for the 'rabble' hypothesis considering that six out of ten jail inmates in Indian country are held for non-violent offenses (Minton, 2008). To understand critically the role of jails in Indian country, it is important to acknowledge the significance of poor socioeconomic conditions as they prompt social control tactics aimed at minor offenses, including drug and alcohol abuse. Moreover, attention to cultural – and historical – forces is vital to distinguish between criminal justice practices by the federal (and state) government with those of tribal authorities (see Lujan, 2002; Riding In, 2002; Zatz *et al.*, 1991; see also Chapters 8, 13, and 16).

THE DEPLORABLE CONDITIONS OF JAILS

Since 1166, when Henry II instructed each English shire (county) to establish a jail for detaining the accused, deplorable and inhumane conditions have been protested by advocates of jail reform (Moynahan and Stewart, 1980). Indeed, the history of the jail cannot be separated from its history as a horrific hellhole, especially when 'unscalable pits, dungeons, suspended cages and sturdy trees to which prisoners were chained pending trial are some of the predecessors of the jail' (Mattick, 1974: 782–3). Despite considerable progress, modern-day jails are often characterized as the 'ultimate ghetto,' the 'cloacal region' of the criminal justice system, 'storage bins for humans,' as well as social 'garbage cans' used to discard society's 'rabble' (Glaser, 1979; Goldfarb, 1975; Irwin, 1985; Mattick and Aikman, 1969; Welch, 1991a). As noted previously, much like the people detained there, jails remain the most neglected institutions within the criminal justice system. Throughout history, the poor have disproportionately occupied jails; today, those facilities continue to live up to their reputation as being the 'poorhouse' of the modern age (Flynn, 1973; Welch, 2002a).

Jail overcrowding

Overcrowding is considered the most pressing problem facing jails. Whereas the war on drugs has contributed to booming populations in both prisons and jails, the unique role of the jail within the criminal justice system compounds the problem of having to admit more inmates than there is space for (see Klofas *et al.*, 1992; Welsh *et al.*, 1991; Zupan, 2002). One of the major sources of jail overcrowding is prison overcrowding, insofar as inmates known as state-ready felons are held in local jails until space becomes available in the state prison. Unlike prisons, which hold relatively stable populations in terms of admissions and releases, jails operate more like people-processing stations, distinguished by a constant flow of traffic with around-the-clock activity. As a result, jails have significantly more contact with the general population than do prisons.

Not only is overcrowding itself a problem, but it becomes a source for other institutional problems as well. Overcrowding places enormous strain on classification, sorting, housing assignments, food services, medical services (especially with regard to inmates with HIV/AIDS and tuberculosis), security, and various programs (such as substance-abuse counseling). Overcrowding also disrupts the daily routine of the facility and places additional pressure on budgetary allowances. Still, the consequences of overcrowding reach beyond institutional operations to affect both inmates and staff. The social-psychological effects of overcrowding can be traced primarily to the stress it creates, resulting in anger, hostility, violence, anxiety, and depression. By their very nature, jails are stressful environments, and overcrowding – the result of 'warehousing' too many people in too little space – merely exacerbates preexisting problems (Klofas *et al.*, 1992).

Studies have documented the specific effects of overcrowding on staff in terms of increased sick call and disciplinary violation rates, as well as higher mortality rates (Werner and Keys, 1988; see also Leger, 1988; Paulus *et al.*, 1975). Overcrowding places additional stress not only on the staff and inmates, but also on the jail as an institution. Due to overcrowding, the jail's ability to respond to the requirements of healthcare, security, and maintenance of internal order is significantly strained (see Welch, 1998a).

The degree of disruption caused by overcrowding is far greater in jail than in prisons because they are designed for short-term confinement; indeed, little emphasis is placed on long-range routines for detainees. Consequently, there are few programs and services available that can occupy and pacify the inmates. Many violent incidents can be traced directly to inmates resorting to fistfights to relieve the boredom caused by idleness. Relatively short stays in jails also make it difficult for staff to sort out the troublemakers who are responsible for aggravating the already volatile conditions. Moreover, corrections officers have the ominous task of ensuring that fistfights do not escalate to large-scale disturbances and riots.

Whereas many jails have made great strides in reforming dangerous and inhumane conditions others still suffer from various institutional problems. As mentioned earlier, jail inmates may be forced to sleep on the floor, eat cold institutional food, and rely on unsanitary showers and toilets. They may be denied a sense of privacy and may endure threats of sexual and physical violence (Kerle, 1998; Welch, 1993a; Zupan, 2002).

Lockups

A review of deplorable conditions would not be complete without mention of the problems facing lockups, also known as holding pens, bullpens, or tanks. These facilities serve as detention centers for shorter periods of time than those of jails and are more numerous than local jails. The purpose of lockups is to hold pre-trial detainees who have recently entered the system. Some await their bond to be posted to secure their release; others are in the process of being arraigned (having charges formally filed against them). In either case, the length of detention is usually no more than 48 hours.

Unlike jails, which are generally county facilities, lockups are facilities commonly located in basements of city courthouses, police departments, or other municipal buildings. Lockups vary in size. Small-town lockups may have only a few cells or one large detention room, often called a bullpen or a tank, whereas large urban lockups may be divided into several bullpens and hold more than 100 detainees. Because lockups have a lower priority than jails, the deplorable conditions in lockups are more likely to go undetected by jail monitors, known as 'watchdogs.'

IMMIGRATION DETENTION

Since the 1990s as Congress bowed to mounting political pressure, no other federal agency has grown more rapidly and become more controversial than the Immigration and Naturalization Service (INS). With its new and expansive powers aimed at controlling illegal immigration, the INS could enforce laws that no longer permit judicial review, producing a record number of detentions and deportations. Proponents of tough law-and-order tactics praised the INS for its commitment to rid the nation of criminal aliens; however, immigration advocates argue that the laws unfairly target immigrants who have had minor brushes with the law. Under the 1996 Illegal Immigration Reform and Immigrant Responsibility Act, numerous crimes were reclassified as aggravated felonies requiring detention and possibly deportation, including minor misdemeanors such as shoplifting and low-level drug violations (also see the Antiterrorism and Effective Death Penalty Act). Ordinarily, persons convicted of these crimes rarely served jail terms and were placed on probation. Compounding the harshness of the revised statutes, enforcement was retroactive – meaning that persons who had been convicted before 1996 also were subject to detention and deportation; furthermore, judges have little or no discretion in determining under which conditions the law applies (Welch, 2002b, 2002c).

With unprecedented power in dealing with immigrants, the INS has stepped up its reliance on detention and deportation, policies that are fraught with contradictions and injustice. With that concern in mind, Welch (2002b) examines critically the 1996 immigration statute and its impact on the INS detention. That project discovered profound inconsistencies in the new law that demonstrate the ironies of social control whereby immigrants are subject to self-defeating – and inhumane – government strategies. Not only have recent changes in the statute failed to accomplish their stated objectives, but given their emphasis on confinement, those violating revised immigration laws are unnecessarily detained for protracted periods of time in facilities known for their harsh conditions. The punitive nature of the INS detention policy and its tendency to simply warehouse detainees are particularly distressing.

Traditionally, penologists have described jails and prisons as *total institutions* because they force prisoners to lose contact with the outside world, especially families who serve as a vital source of support (Goffman, 1961). Nowadays, though, contemporary correctional facilities have departed from their past, becoming *less than total* institutions allowing inmates to have a touch more contact with the free world (Farrington, 1992). The exception to that trend is INS detention, in which detainees remain exceedingly isolated from their families, their lawyers, and the courts (Welch, 1998b, 1997d, 1996g). Locked behind bars in criminal jails, limited in their English language ability, and fearing possible deportation, immigration detainees are both physically and emotionally isolated. A key element in overcoming this isolation is communication with friends and family in the outside world. Outside sources not only provide critical emotional support, they also offer the only financial and logistical resources available to help the detainee obtain legal counsel (Human Rights Watch, 1998: 65).

It should be understood that increased reliance on immigration detention mirrors policy shifts in the traditional criminal justice apparatus. Over the past two decades, crime control initiatives have increasingly adopted hard-line measures predicated on the three Ps: penalties, police, and prisons. Regrettably, the immigration authorities have taken cues from the prevailing criminal justice agenda by channeling more resources into enforcement and detention while neglecting its responsibility to provide services that help immigrants assimilate (Welch, 2002a).

Critical attention should also be turned to the role of immigration detention centers within the larger *corrections-industrial complex*, a controversial phenomenon in which upswings in incarceration are driven in part by profit motives (Welch, 2002b, 2000c; see also Chapter 15). The corrections-industrial complex portends tragic consequences for modern penology given that prisoners are treated as raw materials that produce economic gain for local and private jails. Since the 1990s, immigration authorities joined the so-called *corrections-industrial complex*, creating the need for a larger number of detainees to fill an expanding volume of expensive jail space. More recently, those developments have intersected the war on terror. In the wake of the attacks on 9/11, the INS was reorganized into an agency now known as Immigration and Customs Enforcement (ICE), an agency housed in the newly established US Department of Homeland Security. In 2008, the number of ICE detainees reached 9,957, a 2.4 percent increase from the previous year (Sabol *et al.*, 2009; see Dow, 2004; Chapter 16).

SEPTEMBER 11 AND GREATER SHIFTS TOWARD DETENTION

The terrorist attacks on the World Trade Center and the Pentagon have given the debate over immigration control a new resonance. On October 26, 2001, President George W. Bush signed into law the USA Patriot Act (Uniting and Strengthening America by Providing Appropriate Tools Required to Intercept and Obstruct Terrorism). The following are some of the statute's key provisions:

- Make it a crime to knowingly harbor a terrorist.
- Let the US Attorney General hold foreigners considered suspected terrorists for up to seven days before charging them with a crime or beginning deportation proceedings. The administration had initially sought to be able to hold them indefinitely, but Congress refused and limited such detention to seven days.
- Permit federal authorities to obtain court orders for 'roving wiretaps,' which would allow them to tap any phone a suspected foreign terrorist might use rather than a single phone.
- Make it easier for US criminal investigators and intelligence officers to share grand jury, wiretap, and other information.
- Give the US Treasury Department new powers to target foreign countries and banks deemed money-laundering threats.
- Authorize funds to triple the number of border patrol agents along the US northern border and to triple the number of Immigration and Naturalization Service inspectors at each port of entry along the northern border.
- Allow law enforcement to obtain a subpoena to get from Internet providers records about the e-mail transmissions of suspected terrorists.
- Increase the statute of limitations as well as the punishment for many terrorist crimes.

(Reuters, 2001: EV1)

Although the Patriot Act received overwhelming bipartisan support, civil liberties and immigrants' rights organizations have found that the new law has had unfair consequences not only for immigrants but also for US citizens (Hentoff, 2001; Shapiro, 2001). Chief among these concerns are racial profiling, mass detention, and government secrecy (Welch, 2006a).

Racial profiling

As the US Justice Department vastly widens the scope of its investigations, civil libertarians accuse the government of engaging in wanton racial profiling that may scare away people who might be able to help (Butterfield, 2001a). In response to the government's plan to interrogate thousands of men who it believes might have information about the terrorist attacks, James Zogby, executive director of the Arab American Institute, said: 'The kind of broad net-casting

Figure 11.2   Detainees wait to be processed inside Homeland Security's Willacy Detention Center, a facility with ten giant tents that can house up to 2,000 detained illegal immigrants, 10 May 2007, in Raymondville, Texas. The US$65 million facility was constructed as part of the Secure Border Initiative the previous July and is now where many of the former 'catch and release' illegals are detained for processing.

Photo by Paul J. Richards/AFP/Getty Images.

that was done right after September 11 may have been excusable, but at this point there has to be a better way of conducting this investigation' (Farragher and Cullen, 2001: EV1). The Justice Department has targeted for questioning men, aged 18 to 33, who have entered the US legally on non-immigrant visas after January 1, 2000, from a list of countries from which known operatives of Osama bin Laden have entered the United States. Hussein Ibish, spokesman for the American-Arab Anti-Discrimination Committee in Washington, was critical of the investigation: 'This notion that all people of this category are red flags for scrutiny just stigmatizes young Arab men. It suggests that we're starting to rely increasingly on a crude type of stereotyping in our police work. And it encourages the public to find people of this description suspicious' (Farragher and Cullen, 2001: EV2). Attorney General John Ashcroft defended his tactics, insisting that the unconventional warfare triggered by the terrorist attacks calls for unconventional law enforcement methods (see Harcourt, 2007).

Terrorism experts flatly disagreed. Professor Edith Flynn of Northeastern University described the tactic as 'a fishing expedition' that suggested how little hard evidence the authorities have to proceed with in their attempts to prevent another terrorist attack. Flynn also questioned whether it will work, 'unless you have well-schooled questioners who could detect untruthfulness. Because of the inherent cultural differences, I really wonder how effective it will be' (Farragher and Cullen, 2001: EV3). Although immigration rights groups favor thorough investigations, they are concerned that the Justice Department's net is so broad it will inevitably ensnare men who are afraid to refuse to speak to federal officials out of fear of legal consequences. 'It is inherently intimidating for an individual, especially one who has just arrived in this country, to be questioned by the FBI,' said Lucas Guttentag of the American Civil Liberties Union. 'It is not at all clear what the consequences of not talking to them would be, and whether the next knock on the door would come from the immigration service' (Farragher and Cullen, 2001: EV3).

Mass detention

In less than two months following the September 11 attacks, the government had rounded up and detained more than 1,200 immigrants of Middle Eastern descent. Although the Patriot Act expanded the powers of the Department of Justice and the INS, it limited the length of detention to seven days before the government must charge the detainee of a crime. Once charged under the new law, however, detainees found to be engaged in terrorist activities can be held for six months. Without hesitation, the Justice Department forged ahead with its broad powers, including the government's new rule to listen in on conversations between inmates and their lawyers. Robert Hirshon, president of the American Bar Association, said his group was 'deeply troubled' by the rule because it ran 'squarely afoul' of the US Constitution and impinged on the right to counsel (Reuters, 2001: EV1). Even members of Congress were distressed by the new rule. Senator Patrick Leahy (D-Vt), chairman of the Senate Judiciary Committee, stated in a letter to Ashcroft that the new policy raised grave concerns: 'I am deeply troubled at what appears to be an executive effort to exercise new powers without judicial scrutiny or statutory authorization' (Reuters, 2001: EV2). These new rules further empower an agency that already enjoys considerable authority.

Weeks after September 11, evidence surfaced of abuse and mistreatment against those detained, prompting tremendous concern among human rights advocates.

- In Mississippi, a 20-year-old student from Pakistan reported that he was stripped and beaten in his cell by other inmates while jail guards failed to intervene and denied him proper medical care.
- In New York, prosecutors are investigating an Egyptian detainee's courtroom allegations of abuse by a guard, and the Israeli Consulate is concerned about five Israeli men who say they were blindfolded, handcuffed in their cells, and forced to take lie detector tests.
- In three Midwestern states, US immigration officials cut off all visits and phone calls for detainees for a full week after the attacks, a directive that officials now say was mishandled.

- And in Texas, a man from Saudi Arabia initially was denied an attorney and was deprived of a mattress, a blanket, a drinking cup, and a clock to tell him when to recite his Muslim prayers, his lawyer said.

(Serrano, 2001: EV1)

Such mistreatment amounts to scapegoating, as it appears unlikely that any of those detainees played a direct role in the attacks on the World Trade Center or the Pentagon; none of them was held as a material witness, and two had been released (Welch, 2006a). In the two years following the attacks, the government's dragnet failed to link the vast majority of those detained to the terrorism investigation. Most of those who were swept up were charged on immigration violations, most notably overstaying their visas (Serrano, 2001).

Government secrecy

Compounding the controversy over mass detention, the government has maintained a policy of secrecy. For a year following the investigation into the attacks on the World Trade Center and the Pentagon, Attorney General Ashcroft repeatedly denied access to basic information about many of those in detention, including their names and current location. Such secrecy has been denounced by human rights and civil liberties advocates as well as by news organizations and even some political leaders, who have complained that the Attorney General has failed to explain adequately the need for such drastic measures. Kate Martin, Director of the Center for National Security Studies, said: 'The rounding up of hundreds of people secretly, arresting them and putting them in jail where their families don't know where they are and not telling the public is unprecedented and extraordinary in this country' (Donahue, 2001a: EV1). Martin added: 'This is frighteningly close to the practice of "disappearing" people in Latin America' [where secret detentions were carried out by totalitarian regimes] (Williams, 2001: 11).

Reports that detainees have been subjected to solitary confinement without being criminally charged as well as being denied access to telephones and attorneys raise questions about whether they are deprived of due process. Moreover, those deprivations clearly contradict assurances by the Justice Department that everyone arrested since September 11 has had access to counsel. Eventually, key members of Congress began to challenge the sweeps of aliens in search of terrorists. Seven Democrats, most notably a co-author of Ashcroft's anti-terror legislation, Senate Judiciary Committee Chairman Patrick Leahy (Vt), and the only senator to vote against it, Russ Feingold (Wis), requested from the Attorney General detailed information on the more than 1,200 people detained since the terror attacks. Specifically, the lawmakers asked for the identity of all those detained, the charges against them, the basis for holding those cleared of connection to terrorism, and a list of all government requests to seal legal proceedings, along with the rationale for doing so. The lawmakers stated that while the officials 'should aggressively investigate and prevent further attacks,' they stressed the

Justice Department's 'responsibility to release sufficient information ... to allow Congress and the American people to decide whether the department has acted appropriately and consistent with the Constitution' (Cohen, 2001: EV1).

Unlike people charged criminally, INS detainees are not entitled to government-appointed counsel, thus many are not represented. Some civil-rights advocates complain that law enforcement officials are charging people with immigration violations, holding them in solitary confinement, and then interrogating them before they can consult attorneys who might advise them not to talk at all (Cohen, 2001). In an effort to abolish the Justice Department's secrecy on detentions, a coalition of 21 news and civil liberties organizations filed a request under the Freedom of Information Act to release information about the people detained. In 2002, a federal appeals court declared that the Bush administration acted unlawfully in holding hundreds of deportation hearings in secret. The court issued stinging language criticizing the government's failure to recognize fundamental civil liberties. 'Democracies die behind closed doors. When the government begins closing doors, it selectively controls information rightfully belonging to the people. Selective information is misinformation,' wrote Judge Damon Keith (Liptak, 2002c: A1). Months following the court's ruling, however, the Justice Department still refused to comply with the court order and continued its commitment to government secrecy.

Understandably, the tragic events of September 11 have had a tremendous impact on American society, and as political leaders strive to balance national security with civil liberties, immigrants' rights will likely remain in flux for the foreseeable future. Unfortunately, the Justice Department's initial response to the threat of terrorism has pushed the envelope of civil liberties, especially in light of racial profiling and mass detentions shrouded in secrecy (Welch, 2006a). (See 'Comparative Corrections: The Global War on Terror and Detention' below.)

COMPARATIVE CORRECTIONS

The Global War on Terror and Detention

Much like the United States, nations around the globe have responded to the recent threat of terrorism by enacting legislation that provides government with greater powers. In the name of national security, those governments have taken controversial steps that human rights advocates say undermine individual freedom, liberties, and human rights. 'In the post-9/11 world, infringements of core rights – rights that may not be violated, even during a public emergency – are not being called into question' (Jilani, 2002: 2). Among the measures that have drawn considerable concern is the arbitrary and prolonged use of detention to hold those suspected of terrorist activity, broadly defined in some instances to include peaceful protest of governmental policies (Welch, 2006a). The following list contains some recent antiterrorism legislation with new provisions for detention.

China. Since the attacks of September 11, Beijing has intensified its crackdown on Uighur opponents of Chinese rule in Xinjiang, claiming that they are connected to 'international terrorism.' Officials have detained thousands and placed new restrictions on the religious rights of Muslims.

India. The newly passed Prevention of Terrorism Act allows the police to hold suspects for three months without charge and for three additional months with approval from a special court. The law also criminalizes journalists and other professionals for meeting with any member of a 'terrorist organization,' whatever the purpose.

Malaysia. Since September 11, the government has increased its enforcement of the 1960 International Security Act, which allows detention without trial. Recently, 40 Malaysians accused of links to 'international terrorism' have been detained under the Act.

Nepal. After the Maoist Communist Party of Nepal broke off peace talks with the government and attacked police and army posts in November 2001, the government issued a state of emergency and promulgated the Terrorism and Disruptive Activities Ordinance. Dozens of people, including lawyers, students, teachers, and journalists, have been arrested under the statute. The Ordinance allows preventative detention for up to 90 days, 180 days with Home Ministry approval.

Philippines. Human rights organizations report indiscriminate mass arrests and torture of suspected members of and sympathizers with the Abu Sayyaf Group, which allegedly has links to Al Qaeda. Currently, foreign 'terrorist' suspects are detained indefinitely under old immigration law.

Singapore. Thirteen suspected Islamic militants received two-year detention orders under the Internal Security Act, which allows detention without charge or trial.

South Africa. The draft antiterrorism bill could criminalize strikes and attempts by non-violent demonstrations to deliver a petition to a foreign embassy. The bill also provides for detention without trial and for wider police powers to search vehicles.

Thailand. In March 2002, Thai police detained 25 foreigners at the request of US agencies. A senior police officer said the United States had requested more arrests as part of a joint operation against 'international terrorism.' Initial investigations showed the 25 detainees had no connection to 'terrorist networks.'

United Kingdom. The Antiterrorism, Crime and Security Act of 2001 allows indefinite detention of non-UK nationals without charge or trial if the Home Secretary reasonably believes and suspects they are a national security risk and an 'international terrorist.' The belief and suspicion may be based on secret evidence (Jilani, 2002; see also Schuster, 2003; Yi, 2008).

INMATE LITIGATION

As noted in *Cook* v. *City of New York* (1984), inmates do not forfeit all their constitutional rights when they are incarcerated (see Chapter 12 for a more comprehensive discussion of inmates' rights). Although the facility may limit some inmate rights in order to meet reasonable institutional needs (*United States* v. *Lewis*, 1975), 'there is no iron curtain drawn between the Constitution and the prisons of this country' (*Wolff* v. *McDonnell*, 1974; see Branham, 2002; del Carmen *et al.*, 2002). Although there is now considerable litigation pending against jails, such litigation is a relatively new phenomenon. Until the 1970s, courts maintained a hands-off policy, rarely intervening on behalf of inmates. Since then, jail litigation has certainly increased, especially in efforts to reduce overcrowding and reform other conditions of confinement, such as inadequate recreation and medical facilities, services, and staffing (see Palmer, 2010).

The landmark case *Bell* v. *Wolfish* (1979) marks a significant development in jail management because the US Supreme Court ruled in favor of administrators, signaling a return to a hands-off approach (Klofas, 1990). In that case, detainees challenged the double-bunking practices of the Metropolitan Correctional Center (also known as the MCC, which serves as a federal jail) in New York City. The double-bunking policy was initiated when the pre-trial detainee population dramatically increased, thus inducing the Federal Bureau of Prisons to assign sentenced and unsentenced inmates to single-occupancy accommodations. The class-action suit alleged violations of constitutional rights (such as undue length of confinement, improper searches, and inadequate employment, recreational, and education opportunities). The High Court rejected the allegations that these conditions violated inmates' constitutional rights since nearly all pre-trial detainees were released within 60 days (see del Carmen *et al.*, 2002; Skinns, 2009).

Today jail managers remain alert to problematic conditions of confinement, often taking measures to avert litigation. Even in cases in which the courts rule in favor of jail administrators, the time and effort involved in litigation are a major distraction to daily jail management. Still, in cases of egregious violations of constitutional protections, jail officials often blame deplorable conditions on restricted budgets. Critics insist that financial constraints are not an excuse for operating a jail or lockup in which conditions are inhumane and unconstitutional. In an effort to avoid litigation, Embert (1986) suggests that jail administrators attend to the following potential problem areas:

1 Cruel and unusual punishment
2 Personal safety (suicide potential, fire and safety hazards)
3 Adequate medical and mental health care
4 Sanitation
5 Overcrowding
6 Abuse of force by correctional staff
7 Assault by other inmates
8 Due process in disciplinary actions

9 Right to mail, phone calls, and visitations
10 Freedom of religion.

As noted, deplorable jail conditions should be the concern of staff as well as inmates. Overcrowded and unsanitary jails are inherently dangerous places not only for those who are confined to them but also for those who work in them (see Palmer, 2010).

ADDITIONAL PROBLEMS IN JAIL MANAGEMENT

Litigation is merely one issue in the multiplicity of jail management problems. Therefore it is important to consider other related concerns, such as those affecting personnel and health and safety. In doing so, jail management is understood in the context of both political and economic forces among which there is an ongoing struggle for administrative power, resources, and budgetary allocations.

The political and organizational context of jails

Mays and Thompson (1991) neatly unveil the political and organizational context of jails, pointing to the unique role that jails play in the criminal justice system. In a rather geometric way of thinking, Mays and Thompson situate jails within three concentric circles:

- The innermost circle represents the jail and the actors directly involved in its day-to-day operations (inmates, custodial personnel, and administration).
- The middle circle is composed of those actors and institutions having close and continuing, although not daily, interaction with jail inmates and personnel (law enforcement agencies, courts, and watchdog groups).
- The outmost circle includes those individuals and groups that may affect both the jail and its immediate environment, but usually in indirect or unintentional ways (legislatures, the news media, and the public).

Each of these concentric circles exists within a larger sociopolitical context from which the outcomes of various issues are determined, including (1) local politics and limits on funding; (2) changes in law enforcement policies; (3) jail standards and inspections; (4) state corrections department policies; and (5) jail reform litigation. Mays and Thompson focus on how the concentric circles are influenced by fluctuations in the sociopolitical environment. For instance, jails rely on other political bodies and agencies for funding and resources. The public, which typically knows and cares very little about jails, influences local government in terms of how tax revenues are appropriated. Jails must compete for funding and scarce resources at two levels. First, jails must compete with schools, hospitals, libraries, parks, and the like. Second, jails must compete with other services within the criminal justice system, such as law enforcement patrol, crime prevention, and drug interdiction – all of which are more popular with the public than are jails. Primarily due to the lack of adequate funding, jails continuously struggle to deal with other management issues, namely work, personnel, and health and safety.

WORKING IN CORRECTIONS

A Job in a Jail

A number of important differences exist between correctional officers employed in prisons and those working in local and county jails. Compared with prison officers, jailers generally are less educated and receive less on-the-job training. But perhaps the most frustrating aspect of being a jailer is being paid substantially less than a prison CO – even though many consider jail work to be more difficult and hazardous. Unlike that of prisons, the detainee population that jailers must manage is diverse, undiagnosed, and mobile. Moreover, staff shortages are more common in jails than in prisons. Finally, jailers also differ from prison officers in that they believe that their profession has lower status and that there are fewer opportunities for advancement (see Byrd *et al.*, 2000; Metz, 2002; Welch, 1989a).

These organizational aspects of jail work become obstacles in jail management because they interfere with professional opportunity. Effective management, in or outside corrections, is contingent upon promoting professional growth that affects employee morale. Many jail officers have difficulty maintaining high morale and often experience each of the five types of alienation: powerlessness, normlessness, meaninglessness, social isolation, and self-estrangement. The following excerpts from interviews with jail officers capture these feelings of alienation (Regoli *et al.*, 1986):

The administration does not back officers in the decisions they make concerning reports they write about inmate misbehavior. I feel that when an officer is on a particular post, and that post changes or any post rules and regulations change, officers should be included for their input. I am the officer that works forty or fifty hours a week on the floor. But the administration seldom includes us in any policy-making. They should ask us for our opinions on what needs to be changed.

(43)

At times I actually feel I'm almost an inmate. I really feel that the lieutenants on up and some of the sergeants subconsciously view us as inmates with the tactics they use in relating to us.

(43)

A lot people think that it is dangerous for police to work the streets, but they do not stop and think what types of situations officers find themselves in, in the jail. I have had people come in here with knives and guns. Had it happen to me one night when I was out on the grill in the booking area with a female officer I was helping. They did not search a woman prisoner the city police brought in. I guess, because she was female the two male cops did not want to pat her down. It was winter and the prisoner had on a pair of gloves. She took her gloves off and sticks a gun in my chest, and says, 'Here, take this.' She was handing the gun to me, but it was pointed right at me. She could very well have shot it off right there.

(48)

I do not think it is enjoying the job that keeps officers here. It actually is a shit job.

(47)

Naturally, if officers feel that their work is unimportant, their conduct will reflect that attitude, and consequently, the operation of the facility will suffer (Byrd *et al.*, 2002; Metz, 2002). Problems that relate to an unprofessional staff are security lapses, assaults, use of excessive force, burnout, and high turnover. When these personnel problems are combined with other institutional problems (such as overcrowding), major disruptions and disturbances are imminent.

As a means of promoting occupational growth among jail officers, many administrators point to the classic Brodsky (1967) bill of rights for correctional officers:

1 Allow officers to participate in the management of the institution and be part of the decision-making process.
2 Ensure that the officers have clearly defined roles and loyalties.
3 Construct educational and training programs to further career development.
4 Make job assignments based on the officers' skills, abilities, and preferences.
5 Train officers to effectively manage people.
6 Further the level of professionalism.

Problems with special populations

Jails have the responsibility of securing relatively safe housing within an inherently unsafe environment, while providing inmates with necessary medical and mental health services. It is estimated that as many as a quarter of the jail population may be suffering from psychological disorders. Additionally, detainees often have other health ailments that require medical attention (e.g. HIV/AIDS and tuberculosis), and many inmates pose the ever-present risk of suicide (Harlow, 1998: Thompson and Mays, 1991; Vaughn and Smith, 1999; Welch, 2005a).

Three interrelated developments contribute to the pressure exerted on jails. First, the campaign to enforce drunk-driving laws has contributed to an increase in the jail population. Due to the emotional problems that many drunk drivers exhibit (alcohol and drug abuse, depression, and anxiety), those detained in jails remain high-risk suicide candidates (Welch and Gunther, 1997a, 1997b). An often-cited jail suicide profile is that of a 22-year-old single white male who has been arrested for an alcohol-related offense. Such suicides generally take place within 24 hours of arrest (Hayes, 1983: 467–70).

A second factor encompasses the mental health decarceration movement in which tens of thousands of mental patients were released or denied admission to state mental hospitals, beginning in the late 1970s (Price and Smith, 1985; Scull, 1981, 1984). Many of them became homeless while others drifted into contact with the criminal justice system, becoming detained in local jails (Belcher, 1988; Jerrell and Komisaruk, 1991; Kalinich *et al.*, 1991; Winfree and Wooldredge, 1991).

A third development further complicating jail management is the outbreak of contagious and infectious diseases, notably HIV/AIDS and tuberculosis. Jail administrators face the expensive task of providing basic medical attention to those special populations (Welch, 1999a, 1992b, 1991c, 1989b). Finally, two other important groupings within special populations that create additional problems for jail management are women and juveniles due to their special needs (i.e. medical services, youth counseling).

JAIL REFORM AND ALTERNATIVES

Due to the enormous influx of jail admissions, jail systems have adopted two key strategies to deal with overcrowding. One strategy is to expand capacity; the other is to reduce the number of admissions by implementing alternatives. This section addresses institutional reform by examining ways in which capacity is expanded, especially some of the innovative proposals such as the use of makeshift jails and architectural designs such as the new-generation jail. The discussion goes beyond institutional reform toward alternatives and community-based programs intended to reduce the number of inmates detained in jails while continuing to meet the needs of the criminal justice system (e.g. ensuring court appearances and participation in restitution and substance-abuse programs, without jeopardizing public safety).

Institutional reforms

The New-Generation jail

Jail reform ought not be viewed merely as a process involving attorneys filing class-action suits on behalf of detainees. Rather, reform should be seen as a common goal of both inmates and staff since they share common interests, especially with regard to health and safety. The keepers as well as the kept have to deal with the constant reminder that their safety is always at risk. A major factor contributing to staff and inmate fear and anxiety about potential violence is the architecture of the jail structure itself. Traditional jails are known for their linear intermittent surveillance style. Such a design contributes to inmate violence because its obstructed view of the cells provides more opportunities for misconduct with less concern about detection.

In a revealing study on new-generation jails, Zupan (1991) finds that these facilities provide safer and more humane environments for detainees and staff. By improving their physical features, new-generation jails offer direct inmate supervision. The new-generation philosophy is driven by widely accepted assertions regarding human (but not necessarily criminal) behavior. Individuals tend to engage in violence and misconduct when their critical needs are not met (e.g. safety, privacy, personal space, activity, familial contact, social relations, and dignity). In an effort to meet these critical needs, the new-generation jail separates detainees into manageable groups (between 16 and 46) and houses them in modules in which the correctional staff have maximum observation, supervision, and interaction with inmates (Zupan, 2002, 1991; see also Stohr *et al.*, 1994; Stohr *et al.*, 1992; Welch, 1991d; Zupan and Menke, 1991).

The new-generation philosophy is based on a sophisticated rationale that incorporates architectural design with correctional management. Under such a design, management becomes much more hands-on because the staff has more interpersonal contact with detainees. Consequently, officers must develop communication skills and rely on articulate ways to resolve problems and conflict, as well as to discipline unruly inmates. New-generation jails expect more from the staff, therefore careful attention must be paid to hiring only those officers who are able to deal with inmates under such a design. Although the research on new-generation jails should be expanded, Zupan concludes that inmates in such facilities 'experience significantly less psychological anxiety, physical health symptoms of stress, and physical anxiety than do inmates in traditional jails' (1991: 130). Moreover, these detainees were also more positive in their

Figure 11.3 An inmate inside Maricopa County Sheriff Joe Arpaio's tent city jail walking away from the bulletin board area (left) of the communal air-conditioned area inside the complex, May 3, 2010, in Phoenix, Arizona. This area of the tent city houses misdemeanor offenders.

Photo by Paul J. Richards/AFP/Getty Images.

evaluations of the staff and the facility, all of which adds to the effectiveness of humane jail management.

It is important to realize that new-generation jails will not immediately revolutionize jail practices. Quite simply, jails are a product of their past, and jail reform is often impeded by a lack of funding, overcrowding, mismanagement, and public and political apathy (Kerle, 1998; Welch, 1991d).

Institutional programs: substance abuse and shock-incarceration

While scrambling for available beds in overcrowded jails, many systems have developed institutional programs designed to release detainees sooner. Due to the prevalence of drug and alcohol dependence among jail inmates, many jail systems emphasize substance-abuse programs (Kerle, 1998; Zupan, 2002). Another institutional program adopted by jails is the shock-incarceration program, featuring a quasi-military boot camp regimen for young first-time offenders. A primary institutional benefit of the shock-incarceration program is that it imposes a shorter – albeit more intense – sentence, thereby making more beds available sooner. (For a more in-depth discussion of substance abuse and so-called boot camp programs see Chapters 13 and 16.)

Bail and pre-trial release

A sound discussion on alternatives should include issues surrounding bail and pre-trial release. The subject of bail is crucial to understanding pre-trial detention because it stands as one of the initial obstacles that keep many detainees in jail while awaiting trial. Bail is the securing of a specific amount of money as a condition for release from jail. A judge, who sets the bail high enough to ensure the appearance of the accused in court, usually determines the amount. The accused may turn to personal or family assets or to bondsmen, who charge as much as 10 percent of the total bail. Failure to appear in court results in forfeiting the bail.

The traditional approach to ensuring that the accused would appear in court involved a surety in which a relative or friend would promise to see that the defendant did appear. The current monetary bail system emerged in the late 1800s, and a major criticism is that it has an inherent class bias. Even today, many pre-trial detainees await trial in jail merely because they are too poor to meet their bail. In view of the socioeconomic bias against the poor, many legal observers criticize the monetary bail system for placing personal or family assets at a higher premium than liberty, considering that those people are technically innocent until proven guilty. At times such a procedure can violate the Eighth Amendment's prohibition of excessive bail.

Alternatives to detention

To offset overcrowding, the prevailing correctional policy beginning in the 1980s was to construct additional jails and prisons. In doing so, a valuable lesson was painfully learned – namely, that the construction of additional facilities did not keep pace with the incarceration rate. Simply put, policy-makers placed themselves on a 'correctional treadmill,' that proved to be expensive and self-defeating. That trend was particularly stressful for local jails forced to process a huge pre-trial detainee and misdemeanant population. As a result, most large city jail systems are renewing their interest in alternatives to incarceration. Jail officials have come to realize that most pre-trial detainees can await trial while in the community, and most misdemeanants can serve their sentences under community supervision without jeopardizing public safety. Indeed, while nearly 800,000 persons are held in jail, another 73,000 are supervised in the community, involving such programs as electronic monitoring and community service (Minton and Sabol, 2009; see Welch, 1994).

Alternatives to jail are not recent developments; most jail systems have had such programs for decades. Although many alternative programs are generally underutilized, jail officials are once again recognizing the value of implementing alternatives because they reduce both overcrowding and institutional spending. Policy-makers, realizing the futility of constructing additional jails, have enrolled increasing numbers of pre-trial detainees and misdemeanants in one of various alternative programs. While Chapter 13 describes these programs in detail, the following list offers a glimpse of the range of alternatives:

- Release on one's own recognizance
- Administrative mandatory furlough
- Probation alternative work service
- Restitution
- Fines
- Community service
- Work release
- Non-residential substance-abuse treatment programs
- Educational and job-training programs
- Weekend commitment to local jails
- House incarceration and electronic monitoring.

In sum, jails are complex social and political institutions. 'Thus while we may long for simple solutions we should be skeptical of those who offer them. Individuals and groups committed to jail reform should be prepared to stay for the long haul and to rejoice in even small victories' (Mays and Thompson, 1991: 19; and see Kerle, 1998).

CONCLUSION

Jail policy tends to swim against the tide of larger social problems, such as poverty, unemployment, homelessness, substance dependency, inadequate education, and inaccessible health care, each of which directly or indirectly contributes to the difficulties plaguing jails (Burns, 2002). The interconnection between jail practices and social forces makes it important to expand the awareness of social problems facing communities and to demand more ambitious social and economic policies. Given that drug arrests account for the latest surge in jail populations, treating drug dependency as a public health problem rather than a criminal justice problem makes good sense (see Chapter 16).

Other areas of social policy requiring continued development are employment and educational programs, especially considering that such investment has the potential to serve as a crime-control strategy (Kalinich and Embert, 1995; Welch, 1998a, 1994). John Irwin reminds us that social reforms must be addressed before jail reform 'because no progress at all can be made on reforming the jail until we begin to reform our fundamental societal arrangements. Until we do, the policy will continue to sweep the streets of the rabble and dump them in the jails' (1985: 118; 2004).

SUMMARY

This chapter examines how jails differ from prisons by attending to five major areas of inquiry: (1) sociological studies of jails; (2) the deplorable conditions of jails; (3) inmate litigation; (4) additional problems in jail management; and (5) jail reform and alternatives. Studies reveal that those most likely to be held in jails are minorities who are poor, uneducated, and unemployed – also known as the urban underclass or the 'rabble.' In discussing the jail experience, various phases of institutionalization are described, namely disintegration, disorientation, degradation, and preparation. Generally, deplorable conditions and overcrowding are commonly worse in jails than in prisons. Indeed these problems have prompted inmate litigation, as indicated by the large number of jails under court order. Finally, the chapter addresses other problems of jail management and jail reform, emphasizing that jails are unique institutions and ought not to be viewed as 'little prisons.'

REVIEW QUESTIONS

1 How do the prevailing political and economic forces determine who goes to jail?
2 What is the significance of the various phases of the jail experience and how do these phases contribute to a self-fulfilling prophecy?
3 What is meant by the concept of social sanitation and how does it improve our understanding of the use of jails in society?

4   What are the current problems relating to jail conditions and how have the courts addressed them?

5   Describe attempts at jail reform. What are the various alternatives to detention?

RECOMMENDED READINGS

Goldfarb, R. (1975) *Jails: The Ultimate Ghetto*. Garden City, NY: Anchor Press/ Doubleday.

Irwin, J. (1985) *The Jail: Managing the Underclass in American Society*. Berkeley, CA: University of California Press.

Kerle, K. E. (1998) *American Jails: Looking to the Future*. Boston: Butterworth-Heinemann.

Thompson, J. A. and Mays, G. L. (1991) *American Jails: Public Policy Issues*. Chicago: Nelson-Hall.

Welch, M. (2002) *Detained: Immigration Laws and the Expanding INS Jail Complex*. Philadelphia: Temple University Press.

Wynn, J. (2001) *Inside Rikers: Stories from the World's Largest Penal Colony*. New York: St. Martin's Press.

CHAPTER 12

Prisoners' Rights

A right is not what someone gives you; it's what no one can take from you (Ramsey Clark, former US Attorney General)

LEARNING OBJECTIVES

After studying this chapter, you should be able to answer the following questions:

1 What are the major developments in the history of prisoners' rights and what is the importance of the writ of habeas corpus?
2 What are jailhouse lawyers and what are their roles in inmate litigation?
3 How were the Texas and Arkansas prison systems reformed and what was the role of the courts?
4 What are the major constitutional rights exercised by prisoners?
5 What has been the impact of the prisoners' rights movement?

Dee Farmer was sentenced to federal prison upon conviction of credit-card fraud. At the time, Farmer, 18 years old, was undergoing medical treatment for Sex Reassignment Surgery (SRS). As a preoperative transsexual, Farmer exhibited feminine traits. Still, the Federal Bureau of Prisons classified Farmer as a biological male and assigned the prisoner to the federal correctional institution at Oxford (Wisconsin). Farmer was confined to protective custody during much of the time at Oxford. Upon a disciplinary infraction, Farmer was transferred to a higher-security institution within the system – the United

States penitentiary in Terre Haute (Indiana). There, Farmer resumed serving a sentence in administrative segregation, but was later transferred to the general population. Approximately a week later, Farmer was raped and physically beaten after spurning the sexual advances of another prisoner.

Farmer filed action against corrections officials, complaining that 'placing a known transsexual with feminine traits in the general population within a male prison with a history of violent inmate-against-inmate assaults' amounted to 'deliberate indifference.' In the suit, Farmer contended that such action violated the Eighth Amendment's ban on cruel and unusual punishment. The US District Court for the Western District of Wisconsin ruled that prison officials did not demonstrate deliberate indifference by failing to prevent the assault. On appeal, the US Court of Appeals for the Seventh Circuit affirmed without comment. However, the US Supreme Court agreed to hear the case in order to resolve a dispute among the circuits regarding the definition of deliberate indifference in cases of assault between inmates. In a 9–0 ruling, the High Court ruled in *Farmer* v. *Brennan* (1994) that prison officials can be found liable for failing to protect a prisoner from attacks from other inmates if administrators did not act when they knew of a 'substantial risk of serious harm.' Justice Souter, writing for a unanimous Court, ruled that because imprisonment deprives inmates of the means to protect themselves, prison officials cannot 'let the state of nature take its course.'

(see Greenhouse, 1994: A1; Vaughn, 1995, 1997)

INTRODUCTION

Citizens who are 'mad as hell' about crime are often perplexed about prisoners' rights and inmate litigation. They often ask: why should those who have been convicted of crimes be allowed to exercise legal rights from behind bars? Although it is important to acknowledge anger as an understandable reaction to crime, citizens should also be reminded that the United States is a nation of laws. Therefore legal rights extend to *all* citizens, including convicts – even those convicted of the most heinous crimes. The courts have declared that inmates do not check their rights at the front gate of the prison. Advocates of prisoners' rights turn to *Wolff* v. *McDonnell* (1974), where it is set forth that no iron curtain stands between the Constitution and the nation's prisons.

This chapter carefully examines the emergence of the prisoners' rights movement and inmate litigation. In exploring the complex terrain of prison law, legal issues should be discussed in their proper social context. To that end, this chapter takes into account key social forces influencing legal developments, particularly politics and economics. At its most fundamental level, law is a formal mechanism designed to resolve disputes and maintain societal stability. Ideally, these goals are pursued with a sense of fairness and justice. Moreover, corrections officials are not above the law; they, too, must comply with rules and regulations. When corrections officials violate laws, prisoners have the right to legal recourse.

An important moment in prisoner litigation occurred in the aftermath of the Attica prison riot (see Chapter 9). Deputy Warden Pfeil was found liable for violent reprisals that followed in the wake of the riot, and for permitting police and guards to beat and torture inmates (*Al-Jundi* v. *Mancusi*, 1991). Also mentioned in Chapter 9 is *Hudson* v. *McMillian* (1992), in which a prisoner was beaten by correctional officers while a supervisor watched and quipped, 'Don't be having too much fun, boys' (Elvin, 1992: 6). In response to *Hudson*, the US Supreme Court ruled that when staff maliciously and sadistically assault inmates, contemporary standards of decency are violated.

These cases demonstrate the need for legal recourse to protect prisoners from acts of brutality, as well as from other constitutional violations. Whereas the *Hudson* and Attica cases point to particular incidents, in some institutions cruel and unusual punishments are more pervasive and systemic. At the Arkansas state penitentiary, for instance, a particularly barbaric feature of inmate punishment was the use of the 'Tucker telephone.' Until 1968, staff punished inmates by restraining them to a treatment bed in the Tucker hospital and attaching electrical wires to their big toe and penis. As an officer turned the crank of the generator (taken from an old crank-style telephone), an electrical current flooded the prisoner's body, often causing fainting and sometimes irreversible damage to the testicles (Murton and Hyams, 1969). Eventually, an inmate class-action suit, *Holt* v. *Sarver* (1970), brought the Arkansas prison system to federal court. In addition to exploring the details of the Arkansas case, the chapter considers other issues central to inmates' rights: the historical development of prisoners' rights; legal services in prison, prisoner litigation, and jailhouse lawyers; constitutional rights; and human rights violations and political imprisonment.

HISTORICAL DEVELOPMENT OF PRISONERS' RIGHTS

Dating back to ancient Rome, a common form of punishment was to strip convicted criminals of their citizenship and formally pronounce them slaves. By virtue of losing their liberty, the offenders were then subject to spend their lives in penal slavery. In legal terms, that punishment was known as civil death. Consequently, the felon's property was confiscated and his wife was declared a widow, becoming eligible to remarry. As previously mentioned, slavery represents the intersection of politics with economics. Slaves do not have legal rights, nor are they allowed to benefit financially from their labor. The parallel between slavery and punishment in America persisted decades after the Emancipation Proclamation.

In one of the first landmark decisions addressing prisoners, *Ruffin* v. *Commonwealth* (1871), the court ruled that convicted felons not only had forfeited their liberty, but for the length of their sentences also were slaves of the state. Ruffin 'as a consequence of his crime, not only forfeited his liberty, but all his personal rights, except those which the law in its humanity accords to him.' In the decision, the court ruled that Ruffin 'is *civiliter mortuus*; and his estate, if he has any, is administered like that of a dead man.' The court went on to state that the Bill of Rights applies only to freemen, not convicted felons and men civilly dead who have forfeited their constitutional protection (see Wallace, 2001).

The impact of that decision was felt for the next 90 years, during which time the courts were unwilling to consider the complaints of inmates, including those concerning the general conditions of incarceration, constitutional deprivations, and the abuse of institutional authority. In sum, the *Ruffin* case served as the legal justification for courts to maintain a hands-off doctrine. As a result, corrections officials were permitted to operate prisons and jails free from constraints, even if physical abuse of inmates was employed to instill discipline and horrific living conditions persisted in the prison (see Pollock, 2002).

In the 1960s, however, the courts began to retreat from the hands-off doctrine, a change precipitated by the civil rights movement. Indeed, many veteran civil rights lawyers were instrumental in shaping the prisoners' rights movement. As a result of the cooperation of a few sympathetic judges, several successful legal challenges against correctional systems were made. Still, the prisoners' rights movement did not produce results overnight. Actually, several years passed before inmates benefited from any of the key legal decisions. For example, *Monroe* v. *Pape* (1961) resurrected the Civil Rights Act of 1871 and allowed lawyers to file an action in the federal court against state abuses of an individual's rights without first exhausting state judicial remedies. Three years later, the US Supreme Court handed down a landmark decision in *Cooper* v. *Pate* (1964) that applied directly to prisoners. In fact, the importance of *Cooper* is that it overturned *Ruffin*, thereby formally recognizing the constitutional rights of prisoners. Specifically, prisoners in state and local institutions were now entitled to the protection of the Civil Rights Act of 1871.

Parallels between the civil rights movement and the prisoners' rights movement were more than symbolic. As correctional populations became increasingly African American and Hispanic in the 1960s and 1970s, the prisoners' rights movement was viewed as a civil rights movement behind bars. Prisoners' rights cases were based on the constitutional safeguards pertaining to due process; cruel and unusual punishment; censorship, free communication, and access to the courts; and religious and racial discrimination (Jacobs, 2001; Palmer, 2010; Welch, 2002a).

Writ of habeas corpus

The most fundamental legal relief available to all persons confined to federal or state correctional institutions is the writ of habeas corpus (from the Latin 'you should have the body'). Guaranteed by Article 1, section 9 of the United States Constitution, the writ of habeas corpus allows individuals to seek relief by challenging the lawfulness of their confinement. Originally, the rationale behind the writ of habeas corpus was to permit individuals to contest the *legality* of their confinement, but in 1944, in *Coffin* v. *Reichard*, the Sixth Circuit US Court of Appeals ruled that prisoners could challenge the *conditions* of their confinement by way of the writ of habeas corpus. In the *Coffin* case, the conditions of confinement extended to the physical abuse of prisoners (see Palmer, 2010; Palmer and Palmer, 1999).

LEGAL SERVICES IN PRISON

Although the *Coffin* decision allowed prisoners to seek relief from federal courts, having complete and unobstructed access to courts (as guaranteed by the Fourteenth Amendment) was often easier said than done. Many state correctional institutions imposed regulations that required inmates to submit all legal documents to correctional administrators before they were to be filed with the court. The rationale behind that regulation was to enable correctional officials to censor a prisoner's documents, thereby interfering with the inmate's access to the courts. That problem was partially addressed in *Ex parte Hull* (1941) in which the Supreme Court stated that a prisoner's right to apply to a federal court for a writ of habeas corpus may not be impaired by the state or its officers. It was the business of the courts, not correctional officials, to determine the merit of the petition.

Despite the *Hull* rule, inmates continued to struggle with their right to have unobstructed access to the courts. Prisoners who filed suits often faced formal (official) and informal (unofficial) punishments. In many instances, prisoners were subjected to disciplinary action for filing suits, and COs often hassled litigious inmates, stealing documents from their cells and otherwise interfering with their legal activities. Eventually, the courts acknowledged that corrections officials often interfered with an inmate's access to the courts, either by deliberately sabotaging the prisoner's legal attempts or by denying the prisoner the basic materials and resources required to complete legal documents, such as a law library.

It should be noted that some correctional systems forbade the practice of jailhouse lawyering whereby knowledgeable inmates assisted others in the preparation of writs of habeas corpus and other forms of legal relief. In Tennessee, jailhouse lawyering was banned, whether or not a fee was involved. A prisoner there named Johnson, who had spent nearly one year in solitary confinement for repeated violations of the ban on jailhouse lawyering, filed suit against the state. In *Johnson* v. *Avery* (1969), the US Supreme Court ruled that because many inmates are indigent or illiterate, or lack knowledge about their constitutional rights, they may rely on the assistance of others, unless the institution offers a better alternative for legal assistance. Subsequently, other key decisions addressed the problem of prisoners not having adequate access to the courts. Correctional institutions are now required to establish an adequate law library (*Younger* v. *Gilmore*, 1971) or legal services program (*Bounds* v. *Smith*, 1977) and to permit inmates to rely on jailhouse lawyers in filing civil rights actions against prison staff and administrators.

Just as citizens turn to the courts to settle their disputes, so do prisoners. For convicts, however, the opportunity to have the courts hear their grievances is still a relatively recent phenomenon. Over the past 40 years, prisoners have been able to seek relief in the courts primarily because the judiciary has become willing to process such cases. During the past five decades, the onslaught of suits has been tremendous. Although the heavy volume of inmate suits might seem to indicate a victory for the rights of prisoners, the exceedingly high dismissal rate must also be considered. Prisoner lawsuits have the worst success rate of any type of civil suit filed in federal court (Burnett, 1998; Dunn, 1994).

Inmate litigation often incites indignant reactions among citizens who believe that convicts should have only limited access to the courts. That viewpoint has generated several misconceptions concerning prisoner litigation. A false perception exists that inmates habitually abuse their constitutionally guaranteed right of access to the courts. Due to that misconception, the wave of inmate suits beginning in the 1960s was erroneously interpreted as legal pollution and a national disease (Manning, 1977). Legal scholars also caution that characterizing prisoner litigation as an unfair bombardment of the legal system is misleading (Thomas *et al.*, 1986). Before 1960, there were virtually no prisoner cases processed by the courts, so as the hands-off doctrine was dismantled it appeared as if there was a deluge or explosion of inmate suits.

Another misconception suggests that inmates only file frivolous suits, lacking legal or substantive merit. Some prisoners have filed frivolous cases. For example, in one case, a convict complained about the commissary deodorant, and in another a prisoner filed a petition citing cold toilet seats and the need for television antennas (Possley, 1980; Locin, 1981). In 1992 a prisoner filed a civil rights suit demanding $1 million for cruel and unusual punishment suffered when a CO refused to refrigerate his ice cream snack, leaving it to melt (Dunn, 1994). In another case, a prisoner filed an injunction to stay prison officials from reading his thoughts (Thomas *et al.*, 1986). These cases, like all other frivolous suits, were dismissed.

Critics of inmate litigation insist that even frivolous suits take their toll on the courts since the suits still must be filed and reviewed. Advocates of prisoner litigation, however, argue that the burden caused by inmate suits is exaggerated and that the system need not be modified (Burnett, 1998; Dunn, 1994). Indeed, the courts have formally addressed the problem of frivolous cases filed by inmates. In the case *In re Green* (1981), the courts cited a prisoner who, in the 1970s, had filed as many as 700 suits on behalf of himself and fellow inmates. The courts characterized Green's suits as frivolous, irresponsible, and lacking legal merit. Still, such frivolous cases are atypical of prisoner litigation. But when frivolous cases do surface, very often they are subjected to intense media scrutiny, dramatization, and sensationalism. As a result, prisoner litigation is often mocked or inaccurately portrayed as imposing an unfair burden on the legal system. As is demonstrated throughout this chapter, the vast majority of inmate cases are based on serious and blatant violations of constitutional rights, including petitions citing barbaric living conditions, physical abuse, and assaults.

WORKING IN CORRECTIONS

The Jailhouse Lawyer

Over the past 30 years, scholars have focus
engage in extensive litigation, those who assur
Jailhouse lawyers are not simply prisoners wh
inmates at some point file a writ of habeas corpus while many other
alternative forms of legal relief during incarceration. Rather, jailhouse lawyers
are prisoners who 'make a prison career out of law' (Milovanovic and Thomas,
1989: 50; also see Milovanovic, 1988; Thomas, 1988). Jailhouse lawyers go
beyond using the law to resolve their own grievances; they also help 'other
prisoners shape and translate their personal troubles and problems of prison life
into legal issues and claims' (Milovanovic and Thomas, 1989: 50). Milovanovic
and Thomas (1989) also note that jailhouse lawyers serve as gatekeepers,
weeding out suits that lack legal merit. 'The most talented JHLs [jailhouse
lawyers] attempt to link a particular issue that affects only a single inmate
to one that may ultimately affect broader prison policies' (Milovanovic and
Thomas, 1989: 50). JHLs are permitted to help prisoners file legal documents
when no other legal assistance is available; thus, in institutions with limited
availability of legal assistance, the presence of JHLs is magnified.

Prison Litigation Reform Act

Among the major recent developments in inmate litigation is the enactment
of the Prison Litigation Reform Act in 1996. That legislation was driven in
large part by public and political perceptions that inmate litigation was out of
control and that frivolous lawsuits were clogging the courts. Moreover, the PLRA
represented a shift toward victims' rights, a social movement that purported
that prisoners had more rights than victims. The PLRA set out to reduce the
number of civil rights suits (Section 1983) by limiting what the courts can do
in prison cases and imposing sanctions for filing frivolous cases. That statute
was further bolstered by Title I of the Antiterrorism and Effective Death Penalty
Act (AEDPA), also passed in 1996. The AEDPA sought to regulate the filing of
habeas corpus petitions, especially in death penalty cases (see del Carmen *et al.*,
2002). Despite its popularity, some lawmakers were concerned that the PLRA
had been rushed into law without carefully considering that it may undermine
prisoners' rights. Senator Edward Kennedy complained that the 'PLRA was
the subject of a single hearing in the Judiciary Committee, hardly the type of
thorough review that a measure of this scope deserves' (*Congressional Record*,
S2296: 142, March 19, 1996). Critics argue that at a time when lawmakers
were looking for ways to make prisons tougher, the PLRA served to keep poor
conditions and other grievances from public scrutiny (Robertson, 2002, 2000a).

'Essentially, the PLRA makes it far more difficult to use litigation as a means of correcting deficient prison conditions. In effect, the courts have moved from "hands off" to active intervention in the management of prisons' (Austin and Irwin, 2001: 95).

LANDMARK REFORM CASES: TEXAS AND ARKANSAS

The cases involving Texas and Arkansas are explored in this section to further emphasize the importance of prisoner litigation, especially as it relates to institutional reform. The in-depth analyses provide a critical understanding of the issues involved in prison reform, as well as the complexity of such suits.

Reforming the Texas Department of Corrections

For more than a generation, the Texas Department of Corrections (TDC) has been one of the most meticulously studied prison systems in America. Such attention is due, in large part, to the depth and extent of legal intervention that has forced administrators to reform institutional conditions and restructure management practices. Often referred to as America's toughest prison system, the TDC was noted for its use of building tenders (BTs) to supervise and manage the inmate population (Press, 1986). BTs were hardened convicts 'deputized' by the administration as elite prisoners, serving as inmate-guards or trusties. 'They were the inmates who really ran the asylum: the meanest characters the administration could co-opt into doing the state's bidding' (Press, 1986: 46).

Although Texas law forbids prisoners from serving in supervisory and administrative roles, the TDC ignored the prohibition. Moreover, some BTs were supplied with weapons to bolster their control of other inmates. Often with the tacit approval of the staff, BTs armed with homemade clubs would severely beat stubborn or aggressive inmates, a process called 'counseling' or 'whipping him off the tank.' The following passage describes the role and duties of BTs:

> When new inmates arrived at a living area, BTs informed them of the 'rules,' which meant 'keep the noise down, go to work when you are supposed to, mind your own business, and tell us [the BTs] when you have a problem.' In addition to these tasks, the BTs broke up fights, gave orders to other inmates, and protected the officers in charge of the cell blocks from attacks by the inmates.
>
> (Marquart and Crouch, 1985: 563)

The BT system was elaborate, featuring its own hierarchy of high-, medium-, and low-level convict 'guards.' It existed as a structure of control that pitted inmates against inmates, cultivating an atmosphere of fear and distrust among the inmate population (Marquart and Crouch, 1985).

In the 1970s and 1980s, the TDC was also known for its numerous problems: extensive overcrowding (230 percent capacity), lengthy sentences (a result of mandatory sentence laws), poor chances for parole, and excessive violence. During a seven-day stretch in 1981, 11 inmates were killed by fellow prisoners, and 70 prisoners and COs were severely injured (*New York Times*, 1981). Although some administrators believed that BTs helped reduce aggression in their prisons, critics argued that BTs served to escalate the degree of violence at the TDC.

In response to overcrowding, inadequate inmate security, and various problems regarding institutional services, an inmate class-action suit, *Ruiz* v. *Estelle*, was filed in 1972. Six years later, the case reached trial, with federal Judge William Wayne Justice presiding. Following years of litigation, Judge Justice declared unconstitutional the conditions and operations at the TDC. Several key aspects of prison reform were ordered:

- the construction of new facilities to reduce overcrowding;
- the placement of the new facilities near urban settings;
- the abolition of the building tender system;
- the hiring of additional correctional officers and staff;
- the adherence of due process rights in disciplinary hearings guaranteed by *Wolff*;
- the improvement of the following services: medical, mental health, educational, and occupational.

Unfortunately, litigation rarely leads to immediate or smooth changes in correctional institutions. In the case of the TDC years passed before any noticeable reforms occurred. Meanwhile, overcrowding, physical abuse, poor services, corruption, graft, mismanagement, and, especially, violence persisted. In one of a series of scholarly examinations of the TDC, Marquart and Crouch (1985) set out to study the impact of court-ordered structural reforms. The goal of their research was to analyze the staff's control of prisoners before, during, and after the court's intervention. In brief, Marquart and Crouch discovered that after court-ordered reforms, violence among inmates and between inmates and COs escalated.

Although advocates of prison reform applaud court-ordered intervention, they recognize that as traditional control structures (order based on coercion) are dismantled, violence (related to gang activity) often occurs during the period of disorganization before new control structures (order based on bureaucratic-legal initiatives) can be established (Irwin, 1980; Jacobs, 1977). That phenomenon has become known as the paradox of reform (Engel and Rothman, 1983). Crouch and Marquart (2001) tested the paradox-of-reform hypothesis at the TDC and found that the period of disorganization, typically characterized by an upswing in violence, was short term. Moreover, Crouch and Marquart challenged the view that inmates felt safer in the 'old days' (see DiIulio, 1987). Given the punitive and coercive nature of inmate control, few prisoners felt safe in the old days, especially those who felt the most threatened, namely African American inmates. 'Our data make it apparent that perceptions of risk and actual rates of violence in a prison do not co-vary; low rates of violence before reforms do not mean that prisoners felt safe' (Crouch and Marquart, 2001: 250). A reduction of the likelihood of violence and disorder during reforms requires greater intervention to neutralize gang activity. Marquart and Crouch recommend that reforms be phased in gradually rather than established by rigid timetables.

In sum, several scholarly examinations of the TDC have contributed much needed knowledge about the effects of litigation on prison reform. In particular, several works illustrate how the TDC evolved from a repressive institutional order to one that was legalistic, to one that is currently bureaucratic (see Crouch and Marquart, 1989; DiIulio, 1990, 1987; Martin and Ekland-Olson, 1987). Not since Jacobs's *Stateville* (1977) has so much attention been focused on the impact of litigation on prison reform. (See Chapter 5 for a complete discussion of Stateville.)

Reforming the Arkansas prison system

At the outset of this chapter, reference was made to the Arkansas prison system's use of the Tucker telephone. The prison scandal at Arkansas, though, extended beyond correctional methods of inhumane punishment. Indeed, it was the degree of corruption that eventually became the center of controversy. In 1967, newly elected governor Winthrop Rockefeller made a bold move to reform the state prisons by appointing Thomas O. Murton as chief of the prison system. Murton's tenure was an intriguing one, inspiring the movie *Brubaker* (featuring Robert Redford as the reform warden). In his book, written with Joe Hyams, *Accomplices to Crime: The Arkansas Prison Scandal* (1969), Murton describes the extent of brutality inflicted by COs against inmates. Starvation and beatings were routine. Prisoners also were subjected to having needles rammed under their fingernails and being whipped with leather straps five feet long.

Much like other prison systems at the time, such as the TDC, the Arkansas system used convict 'guards,' known as trusties. These elite inmates ruled the institution and were generally rewarded for controlling the inmate population. Trusties had better living arrangements, clothing, and food, and numerous other privileges that permitted them to gamble, to obtain alcohol and drugs, and even to live in shacks outside the institution where they enjoyed visits from girlfriends.

Historically, prison administrators found that using trusties rather than additional COs was cost-effective. Their interest in running a cost-effective prison did not stop with the use of trusties. To avoid spending funds on institutional services, administrators deprived inmates of adequate diets, housing, clothing, medical attention, and so on. As a flagship of efficient incarceration practices, the Arkansas prison system had not received state funding for nearly 50 years. The prison system relied on the exploitation of inmate labor to provide what little money was needed to operate the institutions; in that sense, the Arkansas prison system resembled the plantation prisons of earlier years. Local economic and political forces contributed to the operation of the prison. Convicts were 'loaned' out to local farmers and businesses that paid prison officials for the use

of cheap labor. Such an arrangement was reminiscent of the contra[...]
popular after the Civil War in the South (Paulson, 2002).

Among the many facets of the prison scandal were allegations that inmate[...]
the Cummins prison farm were murdered and buried in a neighboring pasture.
It was reported that over the course of several years, more than 100 prisoners
were killed while serving sentences at the Cummins prison farm (*Newsweek*,
1968). In view of these allegations, national attention turned to the Arkansas
prison scandal and Murton was removed from his job in an effort to keep him
from generating further publicity (see Murton, 1976).

Eventually, the inmates had their day in court to protest the inhumane
conditions and physical abuse at the hands of the staff. In *Holt* v. *Sarver* (1970),
a federal judge ruled that the Arkansas prison system was in violation of the
Eighth Amendment's ban on cruel and unusual punishment. The case also
cited issues pertaining to racial segregation and the Fourteenth Amendment's
equal-protection clause and violations of the Thirteenth Amendment that
protects inmates from being subjected to forced, uncompensated labor.

In sum, a critical understanding of the complexity of prisoner litigation and
prison reform should not dismiss the importance of the prevailing political and
economic forces (see Carroll, 1998b). In the aforementioned cases, political forces
surfaced in the form of resistance between federal judges and state officials. Such
antagonism is exacerbated further by the fact that state government is mandated
to allocate financial funds from its budget for prison reform. Paradoxically,
citizens generally contest proposals that use tax dollars for improving institutional
conditions and correctional services, even though they often favor the building
of more prisons (Welch, 2005a).

MAJOR DEVELOPMENTS IN INMATE LITIGATION

Although few institutional reform cases are as sweeping as those in Texas and
Arkansas, hundreds of correctional facilities across the nation are under court
order for various reasons. By the late 1990s, 35 states along with the District
of Columbia, Puerto Rico, and the Virgin Islands were under court order or
consent decree to either limit correctional crowding or improve conditions of
confinement (Criminal Justice Institute, 1998).

Regardless of the volume of suits, not all cases filed by prisoners result in
institutional changes. Very often the courts side with the administration of the
facility regarding certain policies and practices. As discussed in Chapter 11, a
significant class-action suit, *Bell* v. *Wolfish* (1979), addressed the rights of pre-
trial detainees. In particular, inmates challenged the practice of double-bunking
at the overcrowded Metropolitan Correctional Center (a federal jail) in New
York City. The suit also alleged violations of constitutional rights (such as
undue length of confinement, improper searches, and inadequate employment,
recreational, and educational opportunities). The US Supreme Court rejected
the argument that such conditions violated inmates' constitutional rights. More
importantly, because nearly all pre-trial detainees were released within 60 days,

inking was not regarded as unconstitutional. It has been suggested that
olfish signaled a return to a hands-off approach by the courts.

ears later, in *Rhodes* v. *Chapman* (1981), the US Supreme Court upheld
ble-bunking practice in the Southern Ohio Correctional Facility in
e. Citing the 'totality of conditions' test, the High Court ruled that
bunking, in and of itself, is neither cruel nor unusual punishment. That
also cautioned federal district courts to stop acting as administrators
ana give corrections officials the broad discretion they need to operate their
institutions (also see *Block* v. *Rutherford*, 1984).

Also in the 1980s, additional restrictions were placed on the constitutional
rights of prisoners. For instance, in *Hudson* v. *Palmer* (1984), Russel Palmer
argued that correctional officers unreasonably searched his cell. In that case, the
US Supreme Court ruled that Palmer, as a prisoner, was not entitled to the same
degree of Fourth Amendment protection (i.e. privacy and protection against
unreasonable search) as citizens in the community. The Court went on to explain
that incarceration requires that the rights of inmates be restricted to ensure the
safety and security of the institution. It is under the restriction of those rights
that the institution must continue its enforcement against contraband (i.e. drugs
and weapons).

Prisoners in the 1990s have found it difficult to fight against conditions
considered cruel and unusual because the US Supreme Court decided in *Wilson*
v. *Seiter* (1991) that inmates have to prove that prison officials acted with
'deliberate indifference' to basic human needs. That ruling significantly curtails
Eighth Amendment protections for prisoners because proving that prison officials
acted with deliberate indifference to basic human rights is often difficult. (See
Palmer, 2010, and del Carmen *et al.*, 2002, for a review of other leading cases
in corrections.)

Three-strikes laws and their constitutionality

Sentencing laws designed to control habitual offenders have been in existence
since the 1920s. More recently, their popularity reemerged in the 1990s under
the rubric 'Three Strikes and You're Out' requiring judges to sentence 'repeat
offenders' with three convictions to longer prison terms. The rationale of
three-strikes laws rests on the basic assumptions of deterrence. 'If the cost of a
behavior greatly exceeds its benefits, the behavior is less likely to be chosen. If
the behavior continues in spite of the cost the cost must be increased' (Mentor,
2002: 813). Half the states in the United States have a version of three-strikes
laws but it is the 1994 California statute that has become controversial, in large
part because it imposes a penalty of 25 years to life. Compounding matters,
California's three-strikes law is the only one of its kind to treat a misdemeanor as
the third strike. Conversely, the typical three-strikes law applies only to felonies,
and in some cases only violent felonies. Opponents of California's three-strikes
law argue that treating a misdemeanor as a felony violates the principle of penal
proportionality. In other words, the punishment does not fit the crime. The

California statute is so disproportionate, legal scholars argue, that such sentencing violates the Eighth Amendment's ban on cruel and unusual punishment (Zeigler and del Carmen, 2001; Zimring *et al.*, 2001).

Eventually, the US Supreme Court decided to review whether sentences of 25 years-to-life in prison imposed under California's three-strikes law are unconstitutionally cruel when the third strike is a minor property offense. Specifically, the High Court examined two cases. One defendant, Gary A. Ewing, who had previous convictions for robbery and burglary, received a 25-years-to-life sentence for the theft of three golf clubs. In the other case, Leandro Andrade, who had earlier convictions for burglary, received 50 years to life for shoplifting videotapes valued at $153.54 from two Kmarts; the two violations earned him consecutive 25-years-to-life sentences. The US Court of Appeals for the Ninth Circuit ruled that the sentence was so disproportionate to the crime as to violate the Eighth Amendment's prohibition against cruel and unusual punishment. In 2003, the U.S., Supreme Court upheld California's 'three-strikes' law, rejecting constitutional challenges to the sentences of Ewing and Andrade. Justice Sandra Day O'Connor added that any criticism of the law 'is appropriately directed at the Legislature' (Greenhouse, L. 2002a: A16; see *Ewing* v. *California*, No. 01-6978; *Lockyer* v. *Andrade*, No. 01-1127). The third strike for more than half of the 7,000 prisoners sentenced under the California law was a non-violent offense. Of those, 340 were sentenced for a crime of petty theft with a prior (Greenhouse, L. 2002a).

It is important to keep in mind that three-strikes laws are fraught with contradictions. Such legislation marks a profound shift in the politicization of crime, whereby politicians issue unsubstantiated claims that judges are soft on crime. Moreover, three-strikes laws were passed by legislatures at a time when

Figure 12.1 Three Strikes law crusader Mike Reynolds, the angry dad of murder victim Kimber Reynolds, going through bundles of mail and petitions on his desk while working to pass law to jail repeat offenders to prevent them from committing more crimes ('Three Strikes and You're Out'), at home.

Photo by John Storey/Time Life Pictures/Getty Images.

there was a general impression that violent crime was increasing, even though the overall crime rate was dropping. Three-strikes laws also were formulated according to the notion that rehabilitation was no longer a viable option in controlling crime. Still, key events in California mobilized the three-strikes movement – in particular, the murders of Kimber Reynolds and Polly Klaas, whose parents embarked on a widely publicized campaign to pass Proposition 184. In 1994, California voters approved the three-strikes law by a 72 to 28 percent margin. Even as the legislation was being written, a study indicated that although there would be a reduction in crime, the new law would lead to a 120 percent increase in California's prison budget due to the enormous growth in its correctional population (see Welch, 2005a).

Other evaluations of three-strikes laws demonstrate that such measures have not reduced violent crime (Schichor and Sechrest, 1996). Recently, Kovandzic *et al.*, (2002) found that jurisdictions with three-strikes laws experienced short-term and long-term increases in homicide (see also Marvell and Moody, 2001). Similarly, the National Institute of Justice (NIJ) found that even though three-strikes laws were intended to target serious offenders, more than 70 percent of defendants charged under such statutes were non-violent offenders. That NIJ report also revealed that three-strikes laws significantly reduced plea bargaining from 90 percent of criminal cases to 14 percent, leading to greater jail overcrowding (Flynn, 1995). Finally, three-strikes laws have contributed to racial disparities in the prison population since minorities have been disproportionately prosecuted and sentenced under those laws (Austin, 1999; Austin and Irwin, 2001). As discussed in Chapter 16, three-strikes laws, especially in California, will eventually have an enormous impact on a growing elderly prison population that is more costly to house due to the rising cost of medical and healthcare (Auerhahn, 2002; Mauer, 2002).

Racial segregation in correctional facilities

Until the 1960s, correctional facilities traditionally segregated inmates by race. Often the rationale for segregation was to reduce the risk of racial conflict among prisoners. However, segregation policies did not promote equal living conditions. Due to institutional racism, housing quarters were somewhat better for white inmates than for African Americans. Moreover, white inmates were assigned more desirable work assignments (e.g. office and clerical duties), whereas African American inmates were assigned manual labor and menial chores (e.g. janitorial duties).

The first case to succeed in challenging racial segregation in prisons was *Washington* v. *Lee* (1966). In that case, Judge Frank Johnson disagreed with prison officials who cited security reasons for their segregation policies. The judge emphasized that segregation could not be justified, regardless of concerns that prison administrators had about institutional security. When the Alabama prison system, as well as other state prison systems, desegregated, few racial incidents occurred. Still, the Supreme Court does permit correctional institutions to segregate inmates temporarily, provided that racially motivated violence is imminent (*United States* v. *Wyandotte County Kansas*, 1973). Arguments that favor racially segregated prisoners on the basis that inmates prefer such segregation have been rejected by the courts (*Jones* v. *Diamond*, 1981; see Henderson *et al.*, 2000).

CONSTITUTIONAL RIGHTS

Following a period of considerable progress toward inmates' rights, the courts have struck a balance between prisoners' rights and the need for correctional institutions to maintain internal safety and order. Although the judicial trend over the past several decades might be viewed as favoring prison officials, the courts sometimes have not only recognized prisoners' rights but fervently defended them as well. In this section, the landmark decisions affecting inmates' rights – specifically, those pertaining to constitutional rights – are presented. Generally, prisoner litigation involving constitutional rights often focuses on the First, Fourth, Eighth, and Fourteenth Amendments to the US Constitution (see Branham, 2002; del Carmen *et al.*, 2002; Palmer, 2010).

The First Amendment to the Constitution

> Congress shall make no law respecting an establishment of religion, or prohibiting the free exercise thereof; or abridging the freedom of speech, or of the press; or the right of the people peaceable to assemble, and to petition the Government for a redress of grievances.

Cases filed by inmates to challenge institutional policies and practices related to First Amendment rights typically fall into four areas: religious freedom, freedom of speech, censorship of personal correspondence, and the right to assemble

Religious freedom

In view of the religious forces that shaped the emergence of corrections, the practice of Christian religions has traditionally been encouraged in American prisons and jails. The obvious rationale for promoting organized religion in correctional institutions stems from the notions of personal reform and rehabilitation inherent in religious doctrines. However, during the 1960s and 1970s, increasingly larger numbers of African American inmates began practicing the Muslim faith, often to the confusion and dismay of white prison officials who held traditional Christian beliefs. At one point, prison officials expressed doubt as to whether the Muslim faith constituted a religion. That doubt, however, was put to rest by the US Supreme Court in *Fulwood* v. *Clemmer* (1962) that formally recognized the Muslim faith, thereby asserting for its followers constitutional protection.

Despite that ruling, considerable resistance toward the black muslim inmates on the part of prison officials continued. Prison officials viewed black Muslims as revolutionary and believed that their assemblages posed a 'clear and present danger' to security. Although the US Supreme Court recognized the right to religious freedom for black Muslims, prison officials were permitted to place restrictions on religious observance when they determined that 'legitimate penological interests' were at stake (*O'Lone* v. *Estate of Shabazz*, 1987: also see *Jones* v. *Willingham*, 1965: *Cooke* v. *Tramburg*, 1964). Given the nature of those decisions, black Muslim inmates continue to argue that prison officials often prevent them from freely exercising their faith, further citing racism on the part of their keepers.

Federal judges concur that religious freedoms guaranteed by the Constitution extend to prisoners, even those who practice non-Western religions (such as Muslims and Buddhists; see *Cruz* v. *Beto*, 1972). Consequently, the courts have ruled that followers of such faiths be permitted to practice their religion and be allowed to possess relevant reading materials, including the Koran. The courts specified that prison officials must make 'reasonable provisions' for the dietary and other needs of Muslims and other orthodox prisoners of other religions. Moreover, inmates are allowed to wear religious symbols, such as medals and head covers, and to wear their hair in conformity with religious beliefs and practices.

Controversies surrounding religious freedoms continue to surface, especially with newly established religions. As a result, the courts have been forced to determine whether there exists a sincere devotion to a particular religion, and to place restrictions on newly established religions that are patently void of religious sincerity. For example, in *Thiriault* v. *Silber* (1978), the court ruled that the Church of the New Song (CONS) was not a genuine religious faith and did not constitute a religion protected by the First Amendment. As a result, Harry Thiriault and other members of the Church of the New Song were denied unreasonable dietary requirements, such as porterhouse steaks and sherry. Further, the US Supreme Court has ruled that institutional prohibitions on the practice of Satanism do not violate inmates' First Amendments rights (*Childs* v. *Duckworth*, 1983).

Freedom of speech

Restrictions on prisoners' freedom of expression have been upheld by the courts, as long as those restrictions are related to the safety and security of the institution. Prison officials may prohibit speech that is disruptive, as in the case of *Roberts* v. *Papersack* (1966) that involved a prisoner who distributed writings provoking an inmate protest against the administration staff.

Censorship of personal correspondence

Two landmark cases, both in California, confronted the issue of censorship of personal correspondence of prisoners. In *Procunier* v. *Martinez* (1974), the US Supreme Court strongly took into consideration First Amendment freedoms.

But what is unique about that case is that the High Court based its decision on the First Amendment rights of citizens corresponding with inmates. Censoring the personal correspondence of prisoners would restrict the right to freedom of speech of citizens. On that issue, the Court set out to strike a balance between the rights of prisoners and the interests of the institution by permitting prison officials to impose censorship when institutional interests are jeopardized (i.e. security, order, and rehabilitation). However, the Court declared that the degree of censorship may not be any greater than is absolutely necessary. Furthermore, prison officials could not censor the correspondence of an inmate because of unflattering remarks expressed in correspondence, including unwelcome opinions or factually incorrect statements.

The other landmark case addressing censorship was *Pell* v. *Procunier* (1974) in which prisoners challenged the institutional ban on interviews with the press. The US Supreme Court supported a prisoner's right to correspond with the press, but only when such correspondence did not undermine security, order, and rehabilitation.

In a later case, the US Supreme Court has supported prison policies that place additional restrictions on mail correspondence. In *Thornburgh* v. *Abbott* (1989), the Court upheld the Federal Bureau of Prison's policy to restrict prisoners' receipt of incoming publications as long as the restriction was reasonably related to institutional interests. Such a ruling made it easier for prison officials in the Federal Bureau of Prisons to censor incoming mail since a 'reasonableness' standard is both broad and vague. By resorting to such a loose standard as reasonableness, the courts have granted greater discretion to prison administrators.

The right to assemble

The First Amendment guarantees citizens the right to assemble. Whether that right extends to prisoners, however, has been argued before the US Supreme Court. In *Goodwin* v. *Oswald* (1972), the High Court ruled that inmates had the right to organize unions, noting that there are no federal or state laws prohibiting such activity. Prisoner unions resemble labor unions insofar as they are concerned with work issues, such as improving safety and working conditions, increasing inmate-worker participation in management decisions, ending contract labor, increasing compensation, and so on.

Five years later, however, the US Supreme Court decided that prison officials could prohibit inmates from soliciting others to join a union, and that barring union meetings did not violate the First Amendment (*Jones* v. *North Carolina Prisoner Union*, 1977). Prison officials could bar meetings and other union activities for reasons of security, safety, and rehabilitation. In sum, prison officials have broad discretion to prohibit prisoner unionization by claiming that it threatens security overall, and their claims generally go unchecked.

The Fourth Amendment to the Constitution

The right of the people to be secure in their persons, houses, papers, and effects, against unreasonable searches and seizures, shall not be violated, and no Warrants shall issue, but upon probable cause, supported by Oath or affirmation, and particularly describing the place to be searched, and the persons or things to be seized.

Since prisons and jails place security and safety as their highest priority, the courts have consistently ruled that prisoners are not guaranteed the same protection against unreasonable searches that extend to other citizens. Indeed, such searches are necessary to confiscate weapons and other contraband. In *Moore* v. *People* (1970), the US Supreme Court upheld the practice of random searches, shakedowns, and seizures in prison: noting, however, that such searches were not to be used to harass or humiliate the inmate. Later cases – *Bell* v. *Wolfish* (1979) and *Hudson* v. *Palmer* (1984) – further supported the practice of searches by asserting that the Fourth Amendment has no applicability to a prison cell.

Fourth Amendment cases nonetheless become more controversial when searches involve visitors and staff. Visitors are often subjected to pat-downs upon entering the prison in an effort to detect contraband (drugs, weapons, etc.). Subjecting visitors to strip searches (or 'bend or spreads') invites questions concerning Fourth Amendment protections. Prison officials are generally permitted to conduct a strip search on a visitor as long as they have reasonable suspicion; still, what constitutes reasonable suspicion is not always clear. Since the courts have resorted to the loose standard of reasonable suspicion, the prison administrators are granted greater discretion.

In *Smothers* v. *Gibson* (1985), a 68-year-old mother of an inmate was subjected to a strip search on the suspicion that she was smuggling drugs. Citing two specific reasons, the court found that such a strip search was unreasonable. First, the search was conducted one hour after the visit began. Second, in the eight years that she had been visiting her son (on a weekly basis), she was strip-searched seven times – each time without incident. Although not all strip searches (which are truly degrading and humiliating) are unreasonable, in some situations the intent is to harass the prisoner and/or a visitor.

When staff members are suspected of smuggling contraband, prison officials are required to meet a higher standard to properly conduct a search. *In Security and Law Enforcement Employees District Council #82* v. *Carey* (1984), the court upheld a correctional officer's claim that his strip search (and body-cavity inspection) was unconstitutional. The court further noted that body-cavity searches of prison personnel could be conducted only upon the issue of a search warrant supported by probable cause.

The Eighth Amendment to the Constitution

Excessive bail shall not be required, nor excessive fines imposed, nor cruel and unusual punishments inflicted.

Recall the importance of *Ruiz* v. *Estelle* (1980) (Texas) and *Holt* v. *Sarver* (1970) (Arkansas) discussed earlier in the chapter. In both cases, the US Supreme Court ruled that the conditions of confinement were so barbaric that they violated the Eighth Amendment's ban on cruel and unusual punishment. In fact, the Court went so far as to declare the Texas and Arkansas prison systems unconstitutional so that the mere sentencing of an offender to these institutions constituted cruel and unusual punishment.

In Chapter 10, the Eighth Amendment's relevance to the death penalty is discussed in depth. Still the Eighth Amendment's ban on cruel and unusual punishment reaches beyond capital punishment to include other penalties imposed in correctional institutions. In this section, several issues are presented in the context of cruel and unusual punishment: physical abuse, deadly force, solitary confinement, and medical treatment and services, including the right to treatment and the right to refuse treatment.

Physical abuse

Since prisoners are wards of the state, it is incumbent upon prison officials to protect inmates from physical and sexual abuse, whether staff members or other prisoners inflict injuries. With regard to physical abuse in the form of whippings (or flogging), it was not until 1968 that the US Supreme Court ruled that the use of leather straps constituted a cruel and unusual form of punishment. In *Jackson* v. *Bishop* (1968), inmates in the Arkansas prison system successfully

Figure 12.2 Female jail inmates chained together as they bury cadavers at Maricopa County's paupers' graveyard in Phoenix, Arizona, May 17, 2000. Maricopa County Sheriff Joe Arpaio began the first female chain gang. With a reputation of being the nation's toughest law enforcement officer, Sheriff Arpaio said he does not believe in discrimination. As a result, the women in Arpaio's jail are treated exactly like the men.

Photo by Joe Raedle/Liaison.

challenged the use of the strap that was traditionally used as a penalty for the following infractions: insubordination, weapons possession, rioting, refusal to work, and homosexuality (see Baro, 1995; Rayman, 2009a, 2009b, 2009c).

Deadly force

If a prisoner attempts to inflict severe bodily injury on a staff member or another inmate, prison officials, with the consent of the courts, may impose deadly force (*Beard* v. *Stephens*, 1967; *Whitley* v. *Albers*, 1986). In some cases, deadly force may be used to prevent an escape. Yet, whatever the circumstances, the courts emphatically declare that all reasonable means must be exhausted before the imposition of deadly force. It should be noted that the death of inmates by the official use of deadly force is a rare – albeit tragic – occurrence.

Solitary confinement

Solitary confinement is known by several euphemisms – administrative detention, segregation, or isolation – and by such nicknames as the hole, the bing, or the strip cell. In solitary confinement, the prisoner is placed in a cell that is often smaller than a standard cell. While there, the inmate is restricted to a modest diet and subjected to around-the-clock surveillance. Generally, solitary confinement means being locked up 23 hours a day, with one hour of exercise, sometimes scheduled in the early hours of the morning, such as 3:00 a.m., so as to avoid contact with the general population.

Solitary confinement is expected to be reserved for inmates who have been accused of serious infractions: assault (physical and sexual), an escape attempt, or excessive disruption. The use of solitary confinement as a form of punishment has been upheld by the US Supreme Court (*Sostre* v. *McGinnis*, 1971) noting the need for prison officials to protect inmates and staff from troublesome convicts and to prevent escapes. However, prison officials must comply with restrictions on the use of solitary confinement. For example, the duration of an inmate's stay in solitary confinement should not be excessive, and the physical and hygienic conditions of the cell must be maintained. Prison officials are required to document which violations are punishable by solitary confinement. In practice, though, these restrictions are deliberately vague, thereby allowing prison officials enormous discretion in imposing solitary confinement. Nevertheless, prison officials realize that when inmates are subjected to barbaric or debasing procedures, such as denuding prisoners, exposing them to winter chills, or denying them soap and toilet paper, the inmates' petitions are more likely to precipitate judicial action.

Medical treatment and services

For prisoners, the right to adequate and proper medical services is protected by several legal actions, ranging from state statutes to the Civil Rights Act of 1964, as well as the due process clauses of the Fifth and Fourteenth Amendments. Moreover, the Eighth Amendment also protects the right to medical care, since denying an inmate adequate and proper medical attention constitutes a form of cruel and unusual punishment. That argument was upheld in the landmark case *Estelle* v. *Gamble* (1976), in which the US Supreme Court ruled that physicians who do not adequately respond to the medical needs of prisoners and staff who deliberately delay or interfere with the delivery of medical services inflict an unnecessary and wanton degree of pain. In 1992, for instance, New York State officials were ordered to pay a female prisoner $304,000 for refusing to provide her with a blanket when she was cold (instead, staff suggested that she sleep in her coat) and for not treating an infection that left her deaf in one ear (*New York Times*, 1992b). In general, however, the courts refuse to specify what constitutes adequate and proper medical care, and although inmates are entitled to medical attention, they are not guaranteed impeccable services (*Priest* v. *Cupp*, 1976). Chapter 16 offers greater attention to healthcare and its implications to constitutional law.

The Fourteenth Amendment to the Constitution (Section 1)

> All persons born or naturalized in the United States, and subject to the jurisdiction thereof, are citizens of the United States and of the State wherein they reside. No State shall make or enforce any law that shall abridge the privileges or immunities of citizens of the United States; nor shall any State deprive any person of life, liberty, or property, without due process of law; nor deny to any person within its jurisdiction the equal protection of the laws.

The significance of the Fourteenth Amendment as it applies to prisoners is that it imposes due process and the Bill of Rights on the states (hence, the notion of 'equal protection'). Further, the Fourteenth Amendment pertains to prisoners' rights by encompassing both legal services to inmates and due process rights in disciplinary hearings. Since an earlier section addressed legal services in prison, this segment deals with issues related to procedural due process.

In the landmark case outlining the due process rights of prisoners, *Wolff* v. *McDonnell* (1974), the US Supreme Court found that the state of Nebraska had proceeded improperly in revoking an inmate's good time (a reward for good behavior that reduces a prisoner's sentence). The High Court upheld the prisoner's claim that his good time was revoked unfairly because his due process rights were violated in the disciplinary hearings. Although the Court concurred that an inmate facing disciplinary charges is not entitled to the same due process as defendants in a trial, the Court did establish minimum requirements for disciplinary proceedings. For example, a prisoner must receive advance written notice of the alleged violation, and he or she must have sufficient time to prepare a defense.

For prisoners, the *Wolff* ruling provided a greater contribution to the protection of due process rights than an earlier decision relating to disciplinary hearings. In

Landman v. *Peyton* (1966), a federal appeals judge argued that inmates needed to be protected from disciplinary hearings conducted with capricious and arbitrary actions. Although *Landman* was an important case for prisoners, *Wolff* added to the protection of due process rights by specifying certain safeguards.

More recently, though, prison officials have gained some leverage in disciplining inmates by being required to present only 'some evidence' to support the committee's conclusion. As expected, the controversy lies in the realization that such evidence does not have to be proved beyond a reasonable doubt. Moreover, the evidence does not have to be clear and convincing or substantial, nor is a preponderance of evidence required (*Superintendent, Massachusetts Correctional Institute at Walpole* v. *Hill*, 1985).

CULTURAL PENOLOGY

Dungeons & Dragons Prison Ban Upheld

Cultural penology prompts us to turn critical attention to the role of punishment not only in society at large but also in the sphere of entertainment where it has the capacity to conjure up images of danger (see Brown, 2009; Rafter, 2006; Smith, 2008). Recently, the popularity of the game 'Dungeons & Dragons' has caught the eye of prison officials – as well as the judiciary. In 2010, US Court of Appeals for the Seventh Circuit rejected the claims in a lawsuit brought by prisoner Kevin T. Singer, who challenged a ban on the game by the Waupun Correctional Institution in Wisconsin. Singer argued that his First Amendment and Fourteenth Amendment rights were violated by the prison's decision to ban the game and confiscate his books and other materials, including a 96-page handwritten manuscript he had created for the game.

Singer, who was sentenced to life in prison for bludgeoning and stabbing his sister's boyfriend to death, has been 'a D&D enthusiast since childhood,' according to the court's opinion. Prison officials banned the game at the recommendation of the institution's specialist on gangs, who said it could lead to gang behavior and fantasies about escape. 'Dungeons & Dragons' could 'foster an inmate's obsession with escaping from the real-life correctional environment, fostering hostility, violence and escape behavior,' prison officials said in court. 'That could make it more difficult to rehabilitate prisoners and could endanger public safety,' they said (Schwartz, 2010: EV1).

'We are pleased with the ruling,' said John Dipko, a spokesman for the Wisconsin Department of Corrections, who added that the prison rules 'enable us to continue our mission of keeping our state safe' (Schwartz, 2010: EV2). Some scholars took notice. Ilya Somin, an associate professor of law at George Mason University, asked, 'Should prisons ban *The Count of Monte Cristo* on the grounds that it might encourage escape attempts?'(Schwartz, 2010: EV2). Somin went on to say the prison's action was reminiscent of a media frenzy in the 1980s surrounding the supposedly pernicious effects of gaming. 'Ideally, you should really have more evidence that there is a genuine harm before you restrict something' (Schwartz, 2010: EV2).

IMPACT OF THE PRISONERS' RIGHTS MOVEMENT

Among the more systematic examinations of the prisoners' rights movement is that delivered by sociologist James Jacobs (2001). In his assessment, the prisoners' rights movement over the past several decades has had a significant impact on correctional administration and management. That is, correctional institutions have been forced to rely less on coercive mechanisms to control inmates and to resort to more bureaucratic measures instead. Prisoner litigation has increased operational standards for correctional institutions, thereby prompting them to function more bureaucratically than in the past. Today prison officials must formally respond to grievances and lawsuits by producing their own reports concerning the alleged violations. Additionally, prisons and jails have become increasingly bureaucratic, owing to the establishment of due process safeguards, which enhance the formality of disciplinary hearings and other procedures. Understandably, some correctional officers feel alienated due to their perception that the courts are on the side of convicts. In response, correctional officers have formed unions, thereby generating an adversarial relationship with correctional administrators.

Another consequence of the prisoners' rights movement has been the emergence of a 'new breed' of prison administrator (commissioners, directors, wardens, superintendents, etc.). Given the current emphasis on the legal framework of the correctional system, administrators are now expected to be proficient in law; indeed, many highly recruited administrators are attorneys. It is understood that a good administrator can spot legally problematic issues quickly and resolve them before they surface as lawsuits. According to Bud Kerr, president of the American Jail Association: 'Corrections is a highly specialized field and the decision you make in your relationships with inmates, whether good or bad, will probably be reflected in the numbers of lawsuits against your agency' (1994: 4).

The prisoners' rights movement also affects inmates themselves; they have become acutely aware of their constitutional rights and other legal safeguards. That movement has promoted a higher level of political and legal consciousness among prisoners. Jacobs (1980, 2001) further explains that the prisoners' rights movement has attracted increasing attention from the press and media. Consequently, inmate cases and court-ordered reforms (such as those in Arkansas, in Texas, and at Attica) have come under great public scrutiny, often to the chagrin of prison officials (see Welch, 2010a).

Additional efforts to develop national standards are being made by corrections officials themselves, and many of the items of concern (increased correctional resources, improved conditions, better training) were supported by the American Correctional Association and included in the accreditation process. Perhaps the greatest impact of the prisoners' rights movement has been that prison and jail officials have taken the initiative to resolve questionable policies. In some instances, prison officials have set out to improve conditions before they become embroiled in expensive and protracted litigation (see Pollock, 2002; Smith, 2000).

ALTERNATIVES TO INMATE LITIGATION

Generally, prison reformers understand that relying on prisoner litigation to resolve disputes should be a last resort. Litigation is extremely time-consuming, labor-intensive, and, more importantly, painstakingly slow. Furthermore, suits that are eventually adjudicated may take years to be processed, with few changes being made in the interim. For prisoners who wish to attract immediate attention to their grievances, there are alternative channels at their disposal. Most correctional institutions have grievance boards installed to hear inmate complaints. Since grievance boards are internal mechanisms, staffed by institutional employees (and at times an outside observer), the turnaround time is significantly shorter than that involving court cases. Some institutions have established inmate grievance procedures that involve fellow prisoners who, along with staff, determine the merit of complaints and seek resolutions.

The introduction of an ombudsman has also proved to be a useful alternative to litigation in several correctional systems. An ombudsman is an outside public official who possesses considerable expertise in correctional matters and dispute resolution. The duties of an ombudsman include investigating the complaint and rendering a recommendation. The ombudsman's report, complete with an exhaustive examination of the grievance, is submitted to both the warden and the director of the department of correction. In some correctional systems, mediators are contracted to provide a more hands-on negotiation between the inmate(s) and the administration.

COMPARATIVE CORRECTIONS:

Foucault and the Groupe d'Information sur les Prisons

Prior to 1975 when *Discipline and Punish* was first published, Michel Foucault had been extensively involved in a campaign for prisoners' rights, a role apparently so earnest that he delayed publication of the book for two years so as to keep from being accused of using his activism to advance a set of theoretical ideas on penality (Foucault, 2001). At the beginning, it was not so much 'common law' criminals but rather political prisoners that brought Foucault into the orbit of the penal apparatus. In the early 1970s, the French government was still reeling from the tumultuous May '68 demonstrations. The state resorted to using legislation and confinement to gain an upper hand; specifically, it passed the *loi anti-casseurs* ('anti-wreckers' law) which held liable organizers of protests for any disturbances. The imprisonment of those political activists was compounded by the government's order to ban the Gauche Proletarienne (GP), a Maoist group that had emerged amid the social unrest of 1968. The targeting and arrest of ex-GP would add tremendously to the state's reliance on punitive social control, underscoring the political thrust of the prison regime (Artières *et al.*, 2003; Cicchini and Porret, 2007).

Inside French prisons the conditions of confinement worsened, prompting strong resistance. Hunger strikes among the political prisoners not only exacerbated tension within the prison system but attracted unwanted attention from the outside. Enter Foucault and Daniel Defert, who joined ranks with historian Pierre Vidal-Naquet and Jean-Marie Domenach. Together they established an ambitious collective called the Groupe d'Information sur les Prisons (GIP). Although the group announced that it was not geared toward reforms, per se, it was clear that their activist agenda was rooted in resistance that would ultimately lead to significant change inside prisons. The GIP's overarching objective was to gather information about French prisons so as to build 'a case for a de facto trial of the prison service' (Brich, 2008: 28).

The GIP became official in 1971, announcing that it would create a network of journalists, magistrates, lawyers, physicians, and psychologists who in turn would reach out to prisoners, former prisoners, and their families. Ideally, the GIP would use the voices of prisoners to expose the harsh conditions of confinement in France, but it would be the convicts themselves who would determine the course of action – not the GIP. The campaign, nonetheless, was very much a community project whereby the GIP would collect prisoner testimonies, issue press conferences, and publish various articles, reports, and pamphlets: all aimed at alerting 'public opinion to the insalubrious nature of prisons, and to the unjust and inhumane treatment endured by countless inmates' (Brich, 2008: 26).

The GIP was more than just a campaign to publicly condemn what it charged as the horrific nature of prisons marked by unsafe and unhealthy conditions; indeed, the group was firmly committed to abolishing the unjust penal apparatus. In the early days of the GIP, Foucault spoke at a press conference: his words reflected a growing concern over a carceral continuum that would continue to envelop larger segments of society. 'They tell us that the prisons are overpopulated. But what if it were the population that were being overimprisoned?' Foucault went on to say that there is scant information about prisons – 'the hidden region of our social system' (Macey, 1993: 258). With deep suspicion of official statistics generated by the state, the GIP would embark on a project of gathering first-hand accounts of a prison system that had become intolerable. In the blunt words of Foucault: 'Prisoners are being treated like dogs' (Macey, 1993: 261). So as to be sure that 'real changes take place,' Foucault proposed that a survey be prepared 'to gain concrete knowledge about prisoners' real situation (and not simply what the administration tells us about it)' (Macey 1993: 258; see Artières *et al.*, 2003).

Curiously, as Foucault looked back on his involvement with the GIP, he felt personally disappointed with a 'lack of success' in the prisoners' rights movements, saying at one point we 'achieved nothing' (Eribon, 1991: 234). To the contrary, others cite clear breakthroughs and credit Foucault as being instrumental to the cause. By turning unwanted attention on the intolerable conditions of incarceration, for instance, prisoners earned the right to read the daily press. Moreover, the GIP set in motion a chain of resistance that would continue in other organizations, namely the Comité d'Action des Prisonniers (CAP) and the Association pour la Défense des Droits des Détenus (ADDD).

Largely as a result of the work of the GIP, the prison issue had been placed on the public and political agenda, much more than in either Britain or the USA, where no comparable group ever succeeded in organizing large-scale actions outside the walls of prisons. In their different ways, the ADDD and the CAP continued its work, but as *Le Monde* was to note, Foucault's leadership was sorely missed.

(Macey 1993: 289; see Chantraine, 2010; Welch, 2010a)

HUMAN RIGHTS VIOLATIONS AND POLITICAL IMPRISONMENT

Ordinarily, when human rights violations and political imprisonment are mentioned, one generally thinks of nations possessing deplorable records of human rights, including China, El Salvador, Iraq, North Korea, Northern Ireland, and Russia, to name just a few. Still, it is important that we recognize that human rights violations and political imprisonment also occur within US borders (see Cohen, 2001). Amnesty International is a leading organization monitoring cases involving human rights violations and political imprisonment. The group works impartially to free prisoners of conscience (i.e. individuals jailed solely for their beliefs, sex, or ethnic origin who have not used or advocated violence), to ensure fair trials for all political prisoners, and to abolish torture and executions worldwide. Human Rights Watch, another group, began in 1978 with the founding of Helsinki Watch. Like Amnesty International, Human Rights Watch is an independent, non-governmental organization (NGO), supported by contributions from private citizens (see Coyle, 2002; Murphy and Whitty, 2007; Welch, 2005b). As mentioned in Chapter 5, Amnesty International and Human Rights Watch have investigated human rights violations in super-maximum security units, particularly the US Penitentiary at Marion (Illinois) and California's Pelican Bay prison. In this section, controversial penal practices are examined, including the currently banned use of prisoners as human guinea pigs and the re-emergence of chain gangs. Additionally, the cases of Elmer (Geronimo, ji Jaga) Pratt and Wen Ho Lee are discussed in the context of the political forces that had driven their prosecutions. To begin, a critical look is taken at the internment of Japanese Americans during World War II.

Internment of Japanese Americans during World War II

The bombing of Pearl Harbor in 1941 dramatically altered the way the US government treated people of Japanese ancestry, even those born and living as citizens in America. As a result of wartime hysteria and racism, 120,000 Japanese Americans (including children) were officially labeled enemies of the state and quickly rounded up to be detained in what amounted to concentration camps located predominantly in America's western states. For decades to follow, that 'dirty little secret' was rarely discussed in the public forum and certainly not taught in US schools (Robinson, 2001).

From 1942 to 1945, under the direction of the War Relocation Authority (WRA), Japanese Americans were *interned* to a system of 10 military-style barracks scattered across the nation in such remote areas as the Sierra Nevada Mountains in California, Arizona, Arkansas, Mississippi, Montana, Oklahoma, and Utah. The camps were fortressed with barbed wire fences and watchtowers, and were supervised by armed soldiers; at night, military searchlights reminded the internees that they were prisoners of war – even in their own country. Those men, women, and children were never accused nor convicted of any crime. Their constitutional rights were trampled: their homes, property, businesses, and belongings were confiscated and never recovered. Two-thirds of the internees were US citizens, while many of their sons (33,000) served in the US armed forces, and when interned boys reached military age, they too were drafted into American military service (Holmes, 2000; Wiener, 1995).

Although the evacuation was reportedly organized around concerns for national security, critics insist that racism played a defining role in the detention of Americans of Japanese descent. Novelist John Steinbeck corresponded directly with President Roosevelt, reminding him that Japanese Americans were loyal citizens who condemned the attack on Pearl Harbor (Lewis, 1995). Lieut. General John DeWitt, who oversaw the internment operation, publicly expressed sentiments construed as racist: 'A Jap is a Jap … it makes no difference whether he's an American or not.' In his military reports, DeWitt characterized people of Japanese descent as 'subversive' members of an 'enemy race' whose 'racial strains are undiluted' (Raskin, 1991: 117). The US Supreme Court supported DeWitt's evacuation plan under the umbrella of war powers. In *Korematsu* v. *United States* (1944), a case involving a Japanese American who defied the resettlement orders, the High Court insisted that Korematsu's constitutional rights were not violated. Conversely, critics argue the Court erroneously validated racial discrimination (Raskin, 1991; Wiener, 1995).

In 1988, Congress finally offered the internees a formal apology for that shameful violation of civil and human rights. Under the Civil Liberties Act, the federal government pledged restitution to 60,000 Americans of Japanese descent who were incarcerated during the war. According to William Yoshimo, national director of the Japanese American Citizens League, 'the $20,000 payment [per former internee] has more symbolic meaning than financial value: How do you put a price tag on years of confinement, denial of freedom and disgrace?' (Abrams, 1991: 57). That human rights violation has left deep emotional scars on the psyches of Japanese Americans. Historian Jon Wiener (1995: 694) laments: 'It's especially depressing because a new anti-immigration movement is now on the rise … the existing barracks are not just relics, they are a frightening reminder of what could come next.' In the 1980s, the federal government reactivated one of its internment camps in Arizona so that the Immigration and Naturalization Service (INS) could detain hundreds of Central American refugees who crossed the border to escape a war financed by the US government (Deutsch and Susler, 1990; Kahn, 1996).

More recently, the Japanese American interments have been once again publicly discussed, particularly in light of the US government's war on terror. In the months following the attacks of September 11, the US Department of Justice rounded up and detained more than 1,200 Arab immigrants and foreign nationals. Compounding matters, that form of mass detention has taken place behind a thick wall of secrecy since the US Justice Department has refused to divulge information concerning the identity of those being held (Welch, 2006a, 2002b). Many concerned citizens took notice, most notably those who previously suffered similar forms of detention. Janice Mirikitani, San Francisco's poet laureate, said that when she read that the government is seeking the power to detain immigrants considered suspect and saw polls showing that Americans support racial profiling she felt a horrible sense of déjà vu. 'Oh, no. Not again. For me, and other Japanese Americans, what we immediately felt was great concern about what could happen to Afghan Americans or Arab Americans. It made us want to speak out and say, "Never again" ' (Nieves, 2001: EV1). Mirikitani, age 59, was an infant when she was imprisoned by the federal government. Her entire family – both sets of grandparents, eight aunts, and her parents, all American citizens – were rounded up after the Japanese attack on Pearl Harbor, herded into freight trains and dumped in remote camps ringed with barbed wire where they spent three and a half years during World War II (Nieves, 2001: EVI; see Chapter 11 for more discussion on immigration detention).

Re-emergence of Chain Gangs

From its inception, the rationale of chaining inmates expanded beyond the utilitarian notion of security; indeed, there is enormous symbolic value in the act. Because chain gangs are spectacles of punishment, being chained – especially in public – is degrading, dehumanizing, and reduces prisoners to beasts of burden (Adams, 1998). In America, chain gangs took on additional symbolism, signifying racism and slavery. Following the Civil War, the Reconstruction required manual labor to rebuild the South's economy and infrastructure. While inmates in the North worked in prison factory shops, their Southern counterparts – disproportionately black – labored outside prison walls on the plantations and public works projects (Lichtenstein, 1993). Prisoners were chained together in crews of five to seven, and the grueling ordeal was heightened by nature's worst elements, most notably the debilitating heat (Ayers, 1984; Barnes and Teeters, 1946; Ives, 1970).

Eventually, the brutality of chain gangs was criticized publicly. In the 1930s, the story of Robert E. Burns shocked the common conscience. In his book *I am a Fugitive from a Georgia Chain Gang*, and later the movie, Burns brought attention to inhumane chain gangs in the South (see also John Spivak's *Georgia*

Nigger, 1932). Burns's exposé was credited with playing a pivotal role in the campaign to abolish chain gangs. While a fugitive in New Jersey, Burns – armed with the courtroom tenacity of Clarence Darrow – successfully fought extradition to Georgia. Burns's hearing precipitated and amplified public outrage concerning chain gangs, prompting state officials across the South to discontinue the practice. Georgia, the last holdout, finally abolished its chain gangs in 1945 (Sifakis, 1992).

The prohibition of chain gangs would eventually give way to a 'tough-on-crime' campaign that resurfaced in the 1990s. A particularly punitive feature of the recent 'law-and-order' movement is the demand for retribution. As public outcry over crime escalates, there has been renewed interest in returning to earlier penal practices, such as requiring prisoners to wear prison stripes and stripping them of amenities (e.g. television, weightlifting equipment, and cigarettes). Most anachronistic is the revival of chain gangs. The year 1995 became a watershed when state and county corrections departments in Alabama, Arizona, Florida, Indiana, Iowa, Maryland, Oklahoma, and Wisconsin reinstated chain gangs (see Welch, 2003a).

In Alabama, prisoners who are shackled at the ankle in three-pound leg irons and bound together by eight-foot lengths of chain are forced to work the fields with shovels and swing blades for 12 hours a day (American Correctional Association, 1995). Other chain gangs spend their days breaking rocks into pea-sized pellets, a demeaning chore imbued with pure punishment since the state has no use for crushed rock (*New York Times*, 1996). Ron Jones, Prison Commissioner of Alabama, refers to the public spectacle in offering a rationale for recent chain gangs: 'Deterrence … the sight of chains would leave a lasting impression on young people' (Bragg, 1995:16). Jones even proposed that women inmates also be shackled to chain gangs; the measure, however, was rejected by the Governor (*New York Times*, 1996). Tough-talking Jones further boasts that COs armed with shotguns loaded with double-aught buckshot supervise the chain gang, obligated by law to shoot if a prisoner attempts to escape. Smugly, Jones remarks: 'People say it's not humane, but I don't get much flak in Alabama' (Bragg, 1995: 16). Human rights advocates, however, take exception to Alabama's chain gangs: 'People lose touch with humanity when you put them in chains. You are telling him he is an animal' (Alvin J. Bronstein, executive director of the National Prison Project of the American Civil Liberties Union, quoted in Bragg, 1995: 16). In 1995, the Southern Poverty Law Center filed suit in the Federal District Court arguing that chain gangs are barbaric and inhumane.

The issue of race is of major significance to the chain gang controversy in Alabama, where observers point out that blacks are overrepresented in these gangs. Congressman Alvin Holmes insists: 'The only reason they're doing it is because an overwhelming majority of the prisoners are black. If the majority were white, they wouldn't have the chain gang' (Jackson, 1995: 12). 'I think it's a reminder of the way it used to be, putting the African American male in chains,' adds Representative John Hilliard (Jackson 1995: 12). Serving two years for receiving stolen property, one inmate who spends his days on the chain gang breaking rocks said, 'they're treating us like ... slaves' (Jackson, 1995: 16). Holmes remembers that as a child in Alabama he never saw a white man on a chain gang: 'The only people you ever saw were black. The whole purpose of having the chain gang is racist to the core. There are certain whites in key positions who want things back the way they used to be' (Jackson, 1995: 14).

In Queen Anne's County (Maryland), the antebellum notion of chain gangs has taken a futuristic twist. Corrections officials have proposed the use of 'chainless' chain gangs by attaching stun belts to prisoners assigned outdoor work detail, leaving convicts writhing in the dirt if they attempt to escape or engage in violence. Supporters claim that stun belts reduce the costs of supervision and purport 'there is no long-term physical damage to a prisoner who is stunned' (Kilborn, 1997: 11). Amnesty International has challenged the practice, arguing that stun belts are cruel, inhumane, degrading, and can be used to torture prisoners.

In reinstating chain gangs, corrections officials insist that they have the overwhelming support of citizens. However, many people question the logic, utility, and overall fairness of chain gangs. 'If these guys are so dangerous, they shouldn't be out on those crews. And if they're not dangerous, why put them in chains?' asks Mary Chambers, a Maryland resident. Furthermore, Chambers notes: 'You have people in there for drunk driving. Maybe they have a problem. But do you put them in chains?' (Kilborn, 1997: A18).

The controversy over chaining extends beyond chain gangs to include inhumane restraining practices employed not as security measures but for disciplinary purposes. In Alabama, inmates filed a class-action suit challenging the use of the hitching post at the Fountain Correctional Center, where those who refuse to (or are late for) work were handcuffed to a triangular rail about 4½ feet off the ground. Prisoners were hitched as long as five hours at a stretch, exposed to the blazing sun, and often went for as long as seven hours without water, food, and access to a toilet. That practice was monitored by the American Civil Liberties Union Prison Project, asserting that there are alternative, humane ways to discipline balky inmates (i.e. isolation cells and/or loss of privileges). Furthermore, there are claims of racism insofar as the hitching post appeared to be reserved solely for black inmates. In 1997, a federal magistrate ruled that the Alabama corrections officials should not be allowed to hitch inmates to posts, commenting: 'Short of death by electrocution, the hitching post may be the most painful and tortuous punishment administered by the Alabama prison system.' State corrections officials appealed the magistrate's opinion but a federal appeals court found that the practice of the hitching post did violate the Eighth Amendment's prohibition against cruel and unusual punishment (ACLU, 2002; Greenhouse, 2002b; Smith, 2008).

Prisoners as human guinea pigs

Journalist Jessica Mitford rocked the corrections establishment when she critically examined prisons in her controversial book *Kind and Usual Punishment: The*

Prison Business. Among her attacks on American corrections was the unethical use of prisoners as human guinea pigs in drug-testing experiments. Although the World Medical Association in 1961 had recommended that inmates not be used as subjects of experiments, the proposal was never formally adopted, in part because American physicians and drug researchers opposed it. An advocate of the use of prisoners as subjects quipped: 'Criminals in our penitentiaries are fine experimental material – and much cheaper than chimpanzees' (Mitford, 1971: 152–3).

Since the Food and Drug Administration (FDA) requires that all new drugs be tested on humans before being approved and marketed, pharmaceutical companies set out to persuade prisoners to participate in clinical trials. During the 1960s, state and federal inmates nationwide were accepting financial compensation (and in some cases, a reduction in their sentences) in return for their involvement in drug experiments. Moreover, correctional institutions themselves were generously compensated by drug companies for allowing access to prisoners.

Prisoners in Ohio and Illinois, for instance, were injected with live cancer cells and blood from leukemia patients; researchers were interested in learning whether cancer could be contracted from other patients. According to Walter Rugaber of *The New York Times* (1969), in the 1960s, hundreds of inmates involved in various experiments were stricken with serious diseases, and an undetermined number of the victims died (see Mitford, 1971).

An inmate at Vacaville prison (California) discussed his participation in a drug-testing experiment:

> Yeah, I was on research, but I couldn't keep my chow down. Like I lost about 35 pounds my first year in the joint, so I started getting scared. I hated to give it up because it was a good pay test. Hey man, I'm making $30 a month on the DMSO thing (chronic topical application of dimethylsulfoxide).
>
> (Mitford, 1971: 158).

The use of inmates as human guinea pigs in drug experiments raises serious ethical issues, and in many instances constitutes a violation of human rights. Although some of the experiments were innocuous, others were extremely painful and potentially dangerous. During the late 1960s, efforts succeeded in curbing and eventually eliminating the use of prisoners in drug research.

Although the use of prisoners in drug experiment was uncovered during the 1960s, reports of a similar scandal broke in 1993 when the Department of Energy (DOE) declassified thousands of documents verifying the use of human guinea pigs in radiation experiments. From 1944 to 1973, the DOE conducted thousands of radiation tests on the elderly, terminally ill patients, mentally retarded children, and prisoners – as well as people in good health (Hilts, 1995, 1994; *New York Times*, 1993c).

In 1963 the DOE continued its efforts to study the effects of radiation on 131 inmates at two prisons in Oregon and Washington State. Each volunteer was paid $200 and signed a consent form stating that 'I hereby agree to submit to X-ray radiation of my scrotum and testes' (*Newsweek*, 1993: 15). After the experiments, the prisoners were given vasectomies – 'to avoid the possibility of contaminating the general population with irradiation-induced mutants,' according to the chief researcher (*Newsweek*, 1993: 15). In 1976, Oregon prisoners filed a class-action suit against the state. Subsequently, the state legislature granted medical attention to several inmates and awarded a lump sum of $2,215 to be divided among nine prisoners (*Newsweek*, 1993; Ridgeway, 1994). Although prisoners are no longer used as human guinea pigs, past experiments illuminate human rights violations against people deemed unpopular and expendable (see Hornblum, 1998).

Controversy over cell extraction

Human rights advocates criticize Pelican Bay corrections officials for over-relying on the practice of cell extraction in controlling unruly prisoners. When an inmate confined to his cell refuses an order from an officer, the prisoner is subject to cell extraction. A team of specially trained COs (sporting helmets and riot gear, and equipped with shields, batons, and guns that fire gas pellets or rubber or wooden bullets) forcibly remove the convict from his cell. Officers restrain and hog-tie the inmate, and then carry him to an isolation cell. Although the COs are not supposed to harm the inmate, at times prisoners are injured in the process of being tackled and restrained. At Pelican Bay, there are reports of serious errors committed in the use of cell extraction. The case of Lolofora Contreras draws attention to such problems:

> During the middle of the night, guards come by the cells and order the prisoners to 'show skin.' (To make sure the prisoner is where he's supposed to be.) Lolofora Contreras is deaf. When a guard, late at night, banged on Contreras' cell door and shouted for him to show skin, the prisoner was sleeping. He kept sleeping because he couldn't hear the order. It was known that Contreras is deaf. It's not possible to have a prisoner who can't hear without the prison officials knowing about it. So those guards could have shined a flashlight in his eyes to awaken him. Instead, in the violent tradition of cell extraction, they rushed into the cell, beat Contreras, and tied him up. The same thing happened to Contreras another time.
>
> (Hentoff, 1993a: 20)

Although the Contreras incidents reveal poor judgment on the part of the staff, corrections management experts defend the use of cell extraction. Officials insist that it is an effective way of controlling unruly inmates. They emphasize that the implementation of a team of officers (who wear padded equipment) reduces the risk of injury – for inmates as well as staff. Balky prisoners often play out the ritual of cell extraction and view the confrontations as challenges. In an effort to reduce the risk of injury, some institutions have introduced the use of pepper mace to extricate recalcitrant inmates.

Political activists, the FBI, and COINTELPRO

Elmer (Geronimo, ji Jaga) Pratt was convicted of murder in a California court in 1972. Many years later, in 1997, Pratt was released when the volume of evidence proving his innocence and demonstrating government misconduct was too great for the judiciary to ignore. Pratt was a leader in the Black Panther Party, a militant African American organization striving for self-determination in the 1960s when the FBI's Counter Intelligence Program (COINTELPRO) monitored him and other black activists (e.g. Martin Luther King, Malcolm X). During that time COINTELPRO relied on tactics of questionable legality, implementing more than 285 counterintelligence actions against leftists campaigning for civil rights and an end to the war in Vietnam. The purpose of COINTELPRO was to infiltrate, disrupt, and otherwise 'neutralize' the entire leftist movement in the United States (Davis, 1997). Under the guise of national security, COINTELPRO's surveillance operation carried out a methodical campaign, targeting thousands of Panthers and framing them for various crimes. In 1969 alone, 33 members of the Black Panther Party were shot and killed by police (Burnham, 1990).

Pratt serves as a reminder of the lengths to which the FBI and COINTELPRO would go to frame – 'neutralize' – black activists. Not only was Pratt convicted of a murder that he did not commit but the government had evidence in its possession proving his innocence. The FBI withheld surveillance documents that established Pratt being 350 miles from the scene of the crime at the time of the murder. During his trial, the victim's wife identified another man as the assailant but was coerced by the prosecution to accuse Pratt. Compounding matters, the prosecution relied on the testimony of witness Julius Butler, who, unbeknownst to the jury, was a paid FBI informant. Prosecutors knew Butler was a police informant even though during the trial he testified that he was not. In overturning Pratt's conviction, Orange County Superior Court Judge Everett Dickey stated: 'jurors might have seen the case differently if the prosecution had not suppressed evidence bearing on Mr. Pratt' (*New York Times*, 1998: 22; Kasindorf, 1997).

While serving time in more than five California prisons, Pratt was confined to solitary confinement for eight years without reading material, a bed, or basic toilet facilities. He was denied parole 16 times. Less than 1 percent of convicted murderers in California serve as long as Pratt did (Kasindorf, 1997). After nearly 30 years behind bars, Pratt was released from prison when a judge reversed his conviction, noting that the prosecution had suppressed key evidence that would likely have exonerated him (Terry, D., 1997). Eventually, Pratt was victorious in a legal battle over his false imprisonment and civil rights violations. In 2000, the City of Los Angeles and the federal government settled a lawsuit granting Pratt an undisclosed sum; persons close to the case estimate the settlement at $4.5 million. According to Pratt's lawyer, Stuart Hanlon, 'It doesn't prove that justice works. To me, if it takes 27 years and this kind of legal "struggle" to get someone out, it doesn't prove anything about justice' (Purdum, 2000: A8). Pratt's lawyers believe the settlement was agreed to by government officials who

Figure 12.3   October 1970: assistant professor of philosophy at the University of California Angela Davis arrested in New York for her membership of the Black Panther Party.

Photo by Keystone/Getty Images.

did not want a trial that would focus not only on the prosecution of Pratt but also on what they called 'a broader pattern of harassment of Black Panthers in the 1960s and 1970s and subsequent cover-ups that they said would implicate officials still serving in law enforcement' (Purdum, 2000: A8).

Other Black Panthers remain in prison on convictions that legal experts seriously question, including Dhoruba al-Mujahid Bin Wahad, who was also targeted by COINTELPRO and is currently serving a term of 25 years to life. Bin Wahad and his supporters contend that he was falsely accused of attempted murder of a New York City policeman, and the FBI withheld crucial documents exposing witness tampering by government agents (Deutsch and Susler, 1990). Bin Wahad continues his fight to reopen his case.

In the 1960s and 1970s, the FBI and COINTELPRO expanded their investigative scope considerably, encompassing individuals and groups associated with the American Indian Movement (AIM). Among the most controversial prosecutions of American Indians is that of Leonard Peltier, who has been incarcerated for more than 25 years, convicted of killing FBI agents. Observers note that Peltier's trial was fraught with manufactured evidence and perjured FBI testimony. Furthermore, the FBI conceded that it could not prove who shot the agents, and Peltier's co-defendant was acquitted on the basis of self-defense (Churchill and Vander Wal, 2002a, 2002b; Deutsch and Susler, 1990).

As the growing number of civil and constitutional violations mounted – threatening the FBI's good-guy image – the agency announced that it would dismantle COINTELPRO. Still, the FBI continued, and in some ways accelerated, illegal monitoring of US citizens and domestic groups, especially those with leftist agendas, In the 1980s, the FBI deployed unauthorized wiretaps, physical surveillance, and informers to spy on hundreds of organizations opposed to President Reagan's policies in Central America, including Amnesty International, the American Federation of Teachers, the National Council of Churches, the Maryknoll Sisters, the Sanctuary Movement, and the Plowshare protestors (Barrenador, 1996; Bennett, 1996; Rosoff *et al.*, 2002).

Also during the 1980s, the US Department of Justice acquired several key tools to be used against political defendants, such as the Bail Reform Act of 1984 that permits the government to detain suspects indefinitely without bail if officials determine them to be a danger to the community or at risk of flight. The Justice Department also reactivated a seldom-used criminal statute of seditious conspiracy against political dissenters and enjoyed the broad powers afforded by the newly created Racketeer Influenced Corrupt Organization Act (RICO) 1970. Although RICO was originally designed as a legal utensil in the battle against organized crime, US attorneys quickly learned that it could also be used to prosecute political activists. Contributing to the growing arsenal of prosecutorial weapons are the expansive antiterrorist guidelines that grant law enforcement agents and prosecutors additional methods for investigation and law enforcement: anonymous petit jury, courtroom security, motions *in limine*, and *ex parte* submissions (Deutsch, 1984; Deutsch and Susler, 1990; Welch, 2006a, 2002a)

Espionage, racial profiling, and politics

In a case that blends espionage, racial profiling, and politics, the FBI's investigation of scientist Wen Ho Lee provides a potent statement on how quickly a committed civil servant can become scapegoated for perceived lapses in national security. In the mid-1990s, the US Department of Energy (DOE) became convinced that China had stolen the design for the W-88, the nuclear warhead deployed aboard the Trident submarines. The W-88 is believed to be the most potent weapon in the world. In response, the director of intelligence and counterintelligence of the DOE embarked on a mission to find the culprit. His suspicions swiftly led him to Lee, a naturalized American born in Taiwan who had worked at the agency for 17 years.

The first red flag, according to the DOE, was that Lee had many contacts with Chinese nuclear scientists both in China and at Los Alamos (New Mexico). Still, it is a common practice for scientists across borders to discuss their findings in an effort to improve research. Moreover, in that case the US government felt that sharing scientific information would create the leverage necessary to pressure Beijing into joining international arms control agreements (Stober and Hoffman, 2002). Given the volume of exchanges between DOE scientists with those in China, leaks of top-secret information could have come from hundreds of sources. Still, the investigation moved forward with Lee as its only suspect. Caucasian Americans employed by the DOE with just as much contact with the Chinese were never probed. Lee, however, did little to divert scrutiny. He had compiled a private archive of some 1,600 electronic files containing classified documents. Lee claimed that he created the file to keep from losing data that would otherwise be wiped out by a computer crash, a problem that had occurred previously.

In 1999, the DOE eventually turned the investigation over to the FBI officials, who charged Lee with espionage. Over the course of three years, agents failed to link him to the stolen plans, and some suspected that the W-88 design was never actually divulged to the Chinese. The role of the media in the Lee case became particularly evident when the story broke in *The New York Times*. But critics charged *The New York Times* with overstepping its journalistic boundaries by taking a prosecutorial stance against Lee, thereby escalating the government's case (Stober and Hoffman, 2002).

Next enter the role of campaign politics. Former Congressman Bill Richardson (D-NM) had become the new secretary for the DOE and was rumored to be on Al Gore's shortlist as a vice-presidential running mate. Having a scientist accused of passing secrets to China would severely damage Richardson's image as a defender of national security; considering that, he fired Lee. Subsequently, the DOE became a tense work environment imbued with a modern version of McCarthyism as officials continued their investigations. Any criticism of the case against Lee would surely raise suspicion, and scientists feared losing their security clearances as well as their jobs.

Lee was indicted on 59 counts, mostly related to espionage and treason. Upon his arrest, Lee was denied bail and kept under particularly harsh conditions of confinement: he was shackled (each time he was escorted from his cell) and denied access to radio, television, books, and newspapers. Accusations of racial profiling soon spread, especially considering that other – non-Chinese – scientists at Los Alamos were never investigated. The view that Lee was racially profiled appeared to help his defense, attracting attorneys skilled at poking holes in the seemingly shaky case. For all its prosecutorial efforts, the government settled for a guilty plea to a single count and Lee was sentenced to time served. Despite his ordeal, Lee believes that he was fortunate that the prosecution took place in the Unites States. 'If I had been accused of such a thing in China or Russia, I would probably be dead. I would have been shot if this happened in Taiwan under the Kuomintang' (Lee, quoted in Persico, 2002: 10; see also Lee, 2002).

The controversy over Lee offers a critical look at national security since the attacks of September 11, 2001. 'If anyone wonders about the shocking failure of intelligence that preceded Sept. 11, the Lee case gives fair warning' (Persico, 2002: 9). The misdeeds of the DOE, the FBI, the CIA, and the Justice Department in handling the Lee investigation 'echoes our failure to put together what we should have known about the terrorists' who attacked the World Trade Center and the Pentagon (Persico, 2002: 9–10).

CONCLUSION

The purpose of this chapter is not only to describe prisoners' rights and correctional law but also to call attention to the importance of inmate litigation. As emphasized throughout the chapter, seeking legal relief is often a necessary means of protecting prisoners from inhumane conditions, physical abuse, and other constitutional violations. The prisoners' rights movement revolutionized the way correctional institutions are operated and managed. Moreover, the prisoners' rights movement has had an impact on how society views corrections and the mistreatment of inmates. Today when egregious violations against inmates occur, such incidents are subject to greater scrutiny by both the press and mainstream citizens. At times, such scrutiny occurs whether or not legal action has been taken.

At the Texas Department of Corrections, for instance, there had been little criticism of the long-standing practice of asking inmates to volunteer (but also to earn good time) for an exercise to train dogs to track escapees. The inmates would serve as prey in what was nicknamed by senior prison officials 'the ultimate hunt.' Texas is one of the few states that still use prisoners known as dog boys; most other state correctional systems use professional dog trainers or civilian volunteers. Several inmates have been injured – two seriously. The state prison system compensated two inmates $14,000 for injuries sustained during these exercises. One prisoner was bitten 120 times and another inmate 56 times. Critics have called that practice a slave sport, and a state representative said he would introduce legislation to abolish the practice (Belkin, 1990). Although 'the ultimate hunt' has yet to generate a lawsuit, it does expose some of the degrading and inhumane features of prison life.

In this chapter, prisoners' rights and inmate litigation are presented in the context of social forces, in particular politics and economics. The discussion of the evolution of the prisoners' rights movement over the course of American history notes that major social events, such as the civil rights movement, precipitated changes in corrections. However, after decades of court ruling benefiting inmates, few court decisions have yielded any monumental victories for prisoners. Indeed, the courts have upheld controversial prison practices that have placed further restrictions on inmates' constitutional rights. Perhaps the struggle now for prisoners' rights advocates is to keep from losing the ground that was gained during the pinnacle of the prisoners' rights movement (see Jones, 2006).

SUMMARY

In an attempt to outline the complex field of prisoners' rights and inmate litigation, this chapter turns first to the early history of correctional law and then gradually moves to more recent developments: the judicial retreat from the hands-off doctrine and the landmark institutional reform cases in Texas and Arkansas. In those cases the judiciary declared the entire prison system unconstitutional, meaning that the mere sentencing of offenders to them constituted cruel and unusual punishment. Among other court-ordered reforms, these institutions were required to dismantle the system of building tenders and discontinue the use of trusties.

The basis for much prisoner litigation has been violations of constitutional rights. Most inmate suits revolve around the First, Fourth, Eighth, and Fourteenth

Amendments to the US Constitution. Suits claiming First Amendment violations include infringements of religion, speech and assembly, and censorship of personal correspondence. Under the Fourth Amendment, landmark decisions have addressed the issue of searches, often supporting the administration's need to maintain security.

Petitions alleging cruel and unusual punishment, including claims of physical abuse, deadly force, solitary confinement, and the right to receive or to refuse medical treatment, are classified as Eighth Amendment cases. Finally, the US Supreme Court has set requirements of due process in disciplinary hearings, an issue raised by the Fourteenth Amendment. The chapter concludes by presenting cases that encompass human rights violations and political imprisonment.

REVIEW QUESTIONS

1 How did political and economic forces affect the historical development of prisoners' rights?
2 What roles did building tenders (BTs) have in the Texas Department of Corrections, and why did the courts decide to dismantle the building tender system?
3 What were the main points of contention in the case against the Arkansas prison system?
4 What are some modern-day instances of human rights violations in American corrections?
5 How do the Geronimo Pratt and Wen Ho Lee cases illuminate the role of racial politics?

RECOMMENDED READINGS

del Carmen, R., Ritter, S. and Witt, B. A. (2002) *Briefs of Leading Cases in Corrections*, 3rd edn. Cincinnati, OH: Anderson.

Martin, S.J. and Ekland-Olson, S. (1987) *Texas Prisons: The Walls Came Tumbling Down*. Austin, TX: Texas Monthly Press.

Murton, T. O. and Hyams, J. (1969) *Accomplices to Crime: The Arkansas Prison Scandal*. New York: Grove.

Palmer, J. (2010) *Constitutional Rights of Prisoners*, 9th edn. New Providence, NJ: LexisNexis.

Thomas, J. (1988) *Prisoner Litigation: The Paradox of the Jailhouse Lawyer*. Totowa, NJ: Rowman & Littlefield.

CHAPTER 13

Alternatives to Incarceration

The question is: What is the purpose of these establishments that are proposed as alternatives to the old prison? It seems to me that they are not so much alternatives as quite simply attempts to ensure through different kinds of mechanisms and set-ups the functions that up to then have been those of prisons themselves. (Michel Foucault)

LEARNING OBJECTIVES

After studying this chapter, you should be able to answer the following questions:

1 How did probation and parole emerge and how are they administered today?
2 What are the most viable alternatives to incarceration?
3 How are prison boot camps administered and what is their impact on corrections?
4 What is the significance of restorative justice?
5 Taking a critical approach to alternatives to incarceration, what are the implications for social control?

In 1976, Michel Foucault was invited to the University of Montreal to address a number of questions posed by the organizers of a conference on the rights of prison inmates. He began his talk as follows:

You have asked me to speak about an alternative to the prison in the context of a conference on the 'failure of the prison'. I must say I find this an awkward topic to address because of this problem of an alternative and, additionally, the problem of failure. The question of an alternative to prison typically brings to mind the scenario of a choice between different kinds of punishment, for example, when asking a child to choose between being caned or being deprived of dessert as punishment. It is a false or at least a loaded question since it in effect asks people to take for granted the existence of a penal regime that grants to particular individuals the right to punish people for particular things, and to consequently think about which system of punishment should operate: imprisonment or some other form of punishment?

(2009: 13)

In the lecture, Foucault went on to discuss how shifts in the economy and in the mechanisms for regulating populations mean that the carceral functions of the prison are today being disseminated at the level of the social body in ways that now operate beyond the space of prison. Indeed, those functions are disseminated through multiple forms of control, surveillance, normalization, and re-socialization.

INTRODUCTION

As noted throughout this book, the scale and scope of American corrections is vast. In 2008, over 7.3 million persons were in prison or jail or on probation or parole, amounting to 3.2 percent of all US adult residents or 1 in every 31 adults. Approximately, 70 percent of the persons under correctional supervision were supervised in the community, either on probation or parole. Probationers (4,270,917) represented the majority (84 percent) of the community supervision population while parolees (828,169) accounted for a smaller share (16 percent). The probation (0.9 percent) and parole (0.9 percent) populations grew at the same rate. Overall, 5.1 million adults were under community supervision: the equivalent of about 1 in every 45 adults in the US (Glaze and Bonczar, 2009).

Whereas *institutional corrections* refers to the confinement of offenders to facilities such as prisons and jails, *community corrections*, a catch-all term, refers to

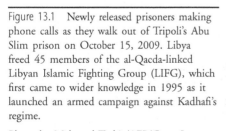

Figure 13.1 Newly released prisoners making phone calls as they walk out of Tripoli's Abu Slim prison on October 15, 2009. Libya freed 45 members of the al-Qaeda-linked Libyan Islamic Fighting Group (LIFG), which first came to wider knowledge in 1995 as it launched an armed campaign against Kadhafi's regime.

Photo by Mahmud Turkia/AFP/Getty Images.

alternative programs designed to punish, supervise, or treat offenders within the community. The most common forms of community corrections are probation and parole, but over the years numerous other programs have been created, such as community service, intensive supervision programs (ISPs), electronic monitoring, and day-fine programs, to name just a few. The reason for the emergence of so many different interventions is the existence of so many different correctional goals and philosophies (Clear and Terry, 2000; Rex, 2005).

Previous chapters have discussed at length the various goals and philosophies in institutional corrections, such as deterrence, incapacitation, and rehabilitation. The same goals and philosophies are applicable to community corrections, and very often a particular sanction may meet several objectives (Wodahl and Garland, 2009). For example, an offender may be sentenced to probation, which includes intensive supervision, community service, a fine, and drug or alcohol treatment. Community corrections sanctions facilitate systemwide goals insofar as they generally reduce costs and alleviate overcrowding at prisons and jails. The forthcoming sections carefully examine the various forms of community corrections and analyze their objectives, their overall effectiveness, and other pertinent issues. In keeping with the theme of this book, alternatives to incarceration are presented in the context of the social forces that shape them – in particular, economics and politics alongside technology. As we shall see, the discussion throws critical light on those developments, especially with respect to social control.

PROBATION

Probation is the imposition of a sentence whereby the offender is permitted to remain in the community but is subjected to supervision and other conditions specified by the court. The term *probation* derives from the Latin *probatio*, which means 'test on approval' (Barnes and Teeters, 1946: 374).

Emergence of probation

At its earliest stage of development, probation stemmed from the practice of suspending an offender's sentence. Its legal roots can be traced to judicial reprieve, a practice in the English courts whereby a defendant was awarded a suspended sentence and provided with an opportunity to appeal to the crown for a pardon (Barnes and Teeters, 1946; Grinnel, 1941). Early American courts benefited from legislation based on the notions of judicial reprieve that granted judges the right to suspend sentences for offenders. Judges began suspending sentences for offenders convicted of non-violent and minor crimes with the strict stipulation that the offenders exhibit good behavior. Eventually, conditions of suspended sentences were established along with certain forms of supervision.

The pioneer of probation was John Augustus, a Massachusetts shoemaker who took a keen interest in the court system in general and defendants in particular. Truly a savior to many poor men, women, and children, Augustus personally intervened in the lives of those who could not meet their bail or pay their fines. By 1858 Augustus had bailed out 1,152 men and 794 women and girls (National Probation Association, 1939). Once Augustus had the defendant released, he would help that person secure employment and begin a reformed lifestyle. When the defendant later returned to court for sentencing, Augustus would report to the judge that the defendant had made personal improvements, rendering incarceration unnecessary. Typically, the judge concurred and levied a fine of only 1 cent (National Probation Association, 1939).

Over the years that type of advocacy evolved into a more formalized process, leading to the first probation law passed in 1878 in Massachusetts. Still, probation was not widely adopted. By 1900 only six states had enacted probation statutes. However, with the emergence of the juvenile court in Chicago in 1899, the need for probation for adults as well as juveniles was recognized. Consequently, by 1940, 42 states (along with the District of Columbia, Alaska, Hawaii, Puerto Rico, and the federal Congress) had approved legislation pertaining to probation (Barnes and Teeters, 1946). By 1956 probation was available in every state (President's Commission on Law Enforcement and Administration of Justice, 1967).

In the 1940s, the courts further defined probation and its mission. In *Roberts v. United States* (1943), the US Supreme Court declared that probation is to be used to 'provide an individualized program offering a young or unhardened offender an opportunity to rehabilitate himself without institutional confinement under the tutelage of a probation officer.' The ideals of rehabilitation expressed in *Roberts* can be traced to the progressive era of corrections in the 1870s.

Chapter 3 explores the principles of corrections offered by progressives; likewise their contributions to the field of probation also are significant. In contrast to the Jacksonians who, in the 1820s and 1830s, advocated the use of institutionalization for many criminals, progressives believed that not all offenders required imprisonment. Borrowing from modern medicine and its emphasis on diagnosis and individual treatment, progressives endorsed a case-by-case approach to crime and delinquency. For progressives, the 'task was to understand the life history of each offender or patient and then to devise a remedy that was specific to the individual' (Rothman, 1980: 5). Although progressives understood that many serious offenders ought to be institutionalized, they believed that many others could be treated in the community. Indeed, probation would serve to structure such treatment.

How probation is administered

Approximately four times as many offenders are sentenced to probation as are sent to prison. However, determining which offenders are permitted to serve their sentences in the community involves a complex process. Today, there are more than 2,000 adult and juvenile probation agencies administered by municipal, county, state, or federal government. Depending on the jurisdiction, probation services are managed by either the judicial or the executive branch of government (BJS, 2001). Administering probation is extremely task-oriented, involving the following: preparing the pre-sentence investigation report, granting the probation, establishing the conditions, determining the length of supervision, and clarifying the violations (see Gelsthorpe and Morgan, 2007; Mair, 2004).

Pre-sentence investigation (PSI) report

The pre-sentence investigation is crucial to the overall enterprise of probation because it helps the court determine which offenders are suitable candidates to serve their sentences in the community. The PSI report facilitates this process by disclosing a complete history of the offender, including prior criminal activity, substance abuse, employment record, educational background, and so on. After the offender's conviction, and before sentencing, the judge may request that a PSI report is prepared. It is the responsibility of the probation agency in the jurisdiction to complete such a report. The nature of the PSI report is to document the facts about the crime and the offender, not to determine guilt or innocence.

The PSI report serves several purposes. First, it provides the court with additional background information about the offender so that an appropriate sentencing decision can be made. Second, the PSI report facilitates the supervision and treatment of the offender because the report addresses problem areas such as substance abuse, emotional instability, family discord, unemployment, and deficiencies in education. Knowledge of such problems allows the probation officer to provide assistance and intervention. Third, the PSI report assists correctional staff in the event that the offender is sentenced to prison or jail. Correctional administrators commonly rely on the PSI report to help determine appropriate treatment or programs for the offender. Finally, the PSI report facilitates parole decisions, including the establishment of the conditions of parole (see Abadinsky, 2003).

In some jurisdictions, the PSI report includes a victim impact statement (VIS). The VIS appraises the harm experienced by the victim, such as physical, psychological, social, and financial problems. The purpose of including a VIS with the PSI report is to clarify the consequences of the offender's crime. Moreover, the VIS facilitates restitution to the victim (to be discussed in a later section of this chapter.)

The PSI report is a multifaceted document that relies on several sources of information. First, the probation officer conducts an in-depth interview with the defendant and often contacts the arresting officer, the victim, relatives, friends, employers, and others for additional information. The probation officer also must review official records and reports, beginning with the defendant's arrest record, commonly referred to as a rap sheet. Subsequently, the probation officer checks court records to determine the outcome of any arrest; the scope of the investigation is widened when out-of-state agencies must be contacted. Another aspect of the report is a summary of psychiatric or psychological evaluations (if available) because the status of the defendant's mental health is often pertinent to the case.

The courts may request one of two types of pre-sentence investigations, either a long or a short report. A long report is usually ordered for serious offenses and for defendants who have an extensive criminal history. A short report is usually requested for minor offenses (i.e. misdemeanors) and for defendants who do not have a lengthy criminal history. Moreover, judges in some states have the discretion to omit a pre-sentence investigation altogether. In jurisdictions where sentencing guidelines are relied upon, the role of the PSI report is reduced or completely obviated. The trend toward reducing reliance on the PSI is also found in jurisdictions where there is an extended use of plea bargaining, whereby a defendant enters a plea of guilty in exchange for a lenient sentence. In such situations, a pre-trial plea investigation, similar to a short PSI report, is prepared.

PSI reports, both long and short, must be succinct and readable, containing only pertinent information. Whether the contents of the report remain confidential is determined by each state. Many states permit full disclosure of the report so that the defendant may contest information that may be false or considered unfair; full disclosure is particularly important considering that some report information is based on hearsay, rumors, or suspicions. Other states protect the confidentiality of the report, citing, among other reasons, that sources of information must be concealed. Otherwise, sources might be reluctant to share information with the probation officer.

PSI reports are the target of much criticism. For instance, research reveals that in many cases, the probation officer's recommendations in the PSI report have a significant impact on sentencing because some judges rely heavily on the report to the exclusion of other information. As a result, the weight of the report is inappropriately enhanced, thereby diminishing judicial discretion (Drass and Spencer, 1987; Kittrie et al., 2002; Rosencrance, 1988). Additional studies have found that some probation officers prepare PSI reports in ways that advance their personal careers and promote their individual perspectives about defendants (Rosencrance, 1992). Another problem is that PSI reports may reflect inadequate investigation and preparation due to probation officers' enormous workloads.

Granting probation

Although the PSI report may affect sentencing decisions, the granting of probation often is determined by additional circumstances. In some jurisdictions, statutory restrictions specify which crimes must be punishable by a prison sentence (e.g. murder, kidnapping, rape, or a second or third felony conviction). In jurisdictions where the judge has the discretion to grant probation, he or she may seek further recommendations from the prosecutor or local police.

Judges also usually respond to the individual characteristics of the offender, such as criminal history, age, employment status, family ties, and bonds to the community (Abadinsky, 2003).

Systemwide influences affect sentencing. For instance, a judge might be more likely to grant probation when the prisons or jails are beyond capacity, especially if those facilities are under court order to reduce overcrowding. As financial costs become more of an issue, probation might be granted in some cases on the grounds that it is cheaper than imprisonment, especially if the offender is non-violent and low-risk. In such a case, the judge feels confident that granting probation does not jeopardize the safety of the community.

Conditions of probation

Probationers are required to meet several conditions of probation, perhaps the most crucial one being that they lead a law-abiding life. Other conditions often include maintaining employment, meeting family responsibilities, pursuing educational or vocational training, undergoing substance-abuse treatment, or receiving medical and psychiatric attention. Probationers also are expected to refrain from consorting with convicted felons and to make payments to a restitution fund. Moreover, probationers must receive permission from their probation officers to travel outside the jurisdiction. The PSI report may indicate additional problems to be addressed in the conditions of probation. For instance, if the probationer has a history of child molestation, he or she would be ordered to avoid places frequented by children.

Conditions of probations may be categorized into three general types: punitive, risk, and management (O'Leary and Clear, 1982; Pierson *et al.*, 2002). Punitive conditions are required activities that the probationer must perform, such as restitution and community service. The rationale behind punitive conditions reflects societal condemnation of the offender's crime. Risk conditions address problem areas of the probationer's life – for example, substance abuse – that are assumed to be related to the probationer's offense. Dealing with such problems (through formal intervention, such as substance-abuse counseling) is an attempt to reduce the risk of recidivism. Finally, management conditions facilitate the supervision process; probationers are required to report changes in address, employment, and the like so that records can be updated.

Length of supervision

Each state determines the length of probation. Typically, misdemeanor convictions are assigned a period of two years of probation, and felony convictions a period of five years. In some states, probationers are discharged from supervision if exemplary conduct warrants such action. At times, probation is terminated solely as a result of the need to reduce the caseloads of probation officers.

Violation of probation

Probationers who violate the conditions of probation risk having their probation revoked. There are two types of violations: new offenses and technical violations. Committing a new offense violates the condition of leading a law-abiding life, and the probationer is subject to having his or her probation revoked. Technical violations include failures to meet other conditions of probation; such violations may include not securing employment, failing to attend substance-abuse programs, or leaving the jurisdiction without the permission of the probation officer. The probation officer has the discretion to revoke probation for any offender who violates the conditions of probation. However, the gravity of the violation usually determines whether revocation actually takes place.

For minor infractions (e.g. leaving the jurisdiction without authorization), probation officers often resort to warning the probationer. Repeated violations, as well as major violations (e.g. committing a serious felony), may result in the revocation of probation. The probation officer must first file a notice with the court; subsequently, the case is scheduled on the court calendar. Meanwhile, the probationer is provided with a copy of the alleged violations and is required to appear for a preliminary, or probable-cause, hearing. Depending on the jurisdiction, either a judge or a court official presides over the hearing. If the probationer denies the charges, the judge (or court official) decides whether there is sufficient cause to believe that the violation occurred, and if there is, a revocation hearing is scheduled.

Probationers are permitted to have attorneys present at revocation hearings and are allowed to testify and to introduce witnesses. Unlike criminal trials, in which guilt must be proved 'beyond a reasonable doubt,' revocation hearings require only a 'preponderance of the evidence' to find a probationer guilty. If the judge determines that the probationer violated the conditions of probation, then the probationer can either be reprimanded and returned to supervision or have his or her probation revoked. In cases of revocation, the offender is ordered to serve a jail or prison term. The judge has the discretion to determine the length of time to be served in prison or jail. In some states, the courts are permitted to include 'street time' (time served under supervision) in determining the length of the sentence (Kittrie *et al.*, 2002).

Effectiveness of probation

Like so many criminal sanctions, the effectiveness of probation is commonly measured according to rates of recidivism, meaning whether or not the probationer returns to criminal behavior. However, comparing recidivism rates is difficult since evaluations tend to rely on one of four methods: violation of the conditions of probation, arrest for a new offense, conviction for a new offense, and revocation of probation. Compounding matters, probation officers have tremendous discretion in dealing with probationers, at times overlooking conduct that violates a condition of probation (Clear and Dammer, 2002, 2000).

In a comprehensive examination, Geerken and Hennessey (1993) reviewed the findings of 17 follow-up studies of adult probationers and found that recidivism rates varied enormously, ranging from 12 to 65 percent (also see Petersilia, 1997).

More recently, attention has turned to drug treatment and its effectiveness among probationers. Benedict *et al.* (1998) examined whether participation in court-ordered drug treatment programs reduces recidivism among property offenders who have a history of drug use. Overall, their research supports the contention that drug treatment does reduce further criminal behavior. 'Given these results, court service personnel should strive to provide drug treatment programs for male felony property offenders with a history of drug abuse, and supervisors should closely monitor probationers' success in treatment to assure lower rates of recidivism' (Benedict *et al.*, 1998: 183; see also Weatherburn and Bartels, 2008).

Despite the degrees of effectiveness of probation as measured by varying recidivism rates, conventional wisdom suggests that probation seems to work for some probationers better than others, depending further on the level of supervision and competence of probation officers. Moreover, compared to the costs of incarceration, such alternatives clearly are worth implementing, especially for non-violent offenders who do not pose a high risk to public safety.

Mission of probation

Clearly, probation continues to be plagued by several key problems. In addition to budgetary restraints and enormous caseloads, conditions that undermine the effectiveness of probation, most probation agencies also fail to offer a clearly defined mission. Numerous experts have pointed to the lack of direction in probation services and strongly recommend that agencies formulate an explicitly stated mission (Petersilia, 1997). In response to this recommendation, probation agencies have introduced several proposals, most of which can be grouped into three broad categories: (1) service orientation; (2) differential supervision; and (3) intensive supervision (Pierson *et al.*, 2002; Rosencrance, 1986).

The service-orientation approach stresses the importance of providing assistance to the probationer. Downplaying the law enforcement role, the service-oriented probation officer provides guidance and counseling, and makes referrals to social service agencies. Such an approach encompasses the basic notions of rehabilitation.

The differential supervision approach is considered a centrist approach between assistance and control. A key aspect of differential supervision is the use of risk and need assessment. Probationers are classified according to their risk potential (for committing further law violations) and their individual needs (such as substance-abuse counseling). Recognizing the importance of both rehabilitating the probationer and protecting the community, the probation officer manages his or her cases by balancing these two objectives.

The intensive-supervision approach, regarded as the most punitive of the three missions, employs strict surveillance. Intensive supervision often includes curfews, several face-to-face contacts with the probation team, weekly verification of employment, etc. (Erwin and Bennett, 2002; MacKenzie and Brame, 2001; Petersilia, 1997).

In an analysis of the three prevailing missions of probation, Rosencrance (1986) offered a critical report on each of them. In sum, Rosencrance calls for the elimination of probation supervision as it currently exists and proposes a new probation mission. Although Rosencrance does not espouse the complete abolition of probation, he recommends that probation services be restricted to supervising probationers. Further, through the use of computers, monitoring would become a clerical task of the court. Computers can monitor adherence to the conditions of probation, such as attendance at treatment programs, employment, community service, and so on. In his proposal for the reorganization of probation, Rosencrance argues that an unambiguous mission be established limiting probation services to court investigation tasks and thereby creating greater opportunities for social service agencies to meet the individual needs of the probationer.

PAROLE

Parole, from the French *parole*, meaning 'word of honor,' is the conditional release of a prisoner after serving a portion of his or her sentence in a correctional institution. The three primary theoretical perspectives on parole are grace theory, custody theory, and contract theory. Advocates of the grace theory view parole as a privilege, which can be revoked if offenders violate the conditions of early release. Custody theory assumes that parolees will remain in the custody of the parole board. Although they are permitted to serve their sentences in the community, offenders face legal restrictions that abridge their freedom. Finally, parole can be viewed from the perspective of contract theory, whereby offenders agree to the terms and conditions of their release; violations of such conditions may result in the revocation of parole.

Emergence of parole

A history of parole includes several key developments. First, in colonial America around the year 1655, a method of supervision was established to monitor felons who had been transported from England. Upon completing their sentences, many felons became indentured servants, a practice that subjected the offenders to supervision, ensuring that they would remain a source of free labor (Abadinsky, 2003). The second development in parole took place in 1840, when Alexander Maconochie became the superintendent of the British penal colony on Norfolk Island, situated off the coast of Australia. Captain Maconochie created the mark system by which prisoners could earn credit for good behavior, thereby reducing the length of their sentences (Barnes and Teeters, 1946). The third development involves the work of Sir Walter Crofton, who, influenced by Maconochie's mark system, introduced the Irish system in 1854 while serving as director of the Irish prison system.

Alexander Maconochie: indeterminate sentencing and the mark system

During his tenure as superintendent at Norfolk Island, Maconochie had serious reservations about determinate sentences (flat sentences). Under determinate sentences, prisoners served the entire sentence without hope for early release – even if they remained model inmates. Therefore prisoners had no incentives to exhibit good conduct while incarcerated. Realizing the limitations of determinate sentencing, Maconochie set out to develop indeterminate sentencing that would be based on a mark system. Under the mark system, inmates would be rewarded for good behavior by having their sentence reduced. That approach not only improved inmate management but also prepared prisoners to return to the community. The mark system consisted of five basic principles:

1   Release was based on the completion of a determined and specific amount of labor.
2   The amount of labor a prisoner had to perform was expressed in the number of marks that the prisoner had to earn by improvement of conduct, frugality of living, and habits of industry.
3   While in prison, inmates had to earn all privileges and services. All sustenance and indulgences were added to their debt of marks.
4   When qualified by good conduct, prisoners would work with six to seven other inmates. As a whole, the group would be answerable for the conduct and labor of each member.
5   In the final stage, prisoners, while still obliged to earn their daily marks, were given a proprietary interest in their own labor and were subject to less rigorous discipline to prepare for release into society.

Although various forms of early release had existed before the mark system, Maconochie, sometimes referred to as the father of parole, was the first to formalize indeterminate sentencing. Maconochie suggested that when prisoners keep the keys to their own prisons, they soon learn how to fit them to the lock (Barnes and Teeters, 1946). Maconochie's humanitarian contributions to corrections also included the elimination of corporal punishment. His tenure as administrator ended after four years amid accusations that he coddled inmates. Soon thereafter Norfolk Island regressed to the practice of harsh treatment of prisoners.

Sir Walter Crofton: the Irish system

Another correctional innovation, the Irish system, was developed during the mid-1800s by Sir Walter Crofton. As warden of the penal system in Ireland, Crofton was inspired by Maconochie's principles in indeterminate sentencing. Crofton designed a system of progressive stages in which inmates were rewarded for good behavior, thereby allowing them to earn their freedom gradually.

The Irish system consisted of four stages. In the first stage, prisoners were subjected to solitary confinement. In the second stage, prisoners remained incarcerated and, together with other inmates, were given work assignments. During the second stage, prisoners were provided the opportunity to earn marks that would promote them to the next phase. The third stage awarded prisoners greater liberty; they were transferred to an open institution where, upon further progress, they could earn a ticket of leave. Finally, in stage four, prisoners earned the ticket of leave granting them conditional release into the community where police supervised them. The conditions of release consisted of maintaining employment and leading a crime-free life; felons who violated those conditions were returned to prison (Barnes and Teeters, 1946).

The development of parole in the United States

During the progressive era, American penologists were eventually convinced of the viability of parole. Zebulon Brockway, the superintendent of the Elmira reformatory, combined parole with indeterminate sentences for young offenders, thereby initiating America's first parole system in 1876. Other states, including Illinois, Massachusetts, Michigan, and Pennsylvania, followed Elmira's example. By 1944, every state had passed parole legislation (Cahalan, 1986; Wines, 1975).

Evolution of parole in America

In the United States, the responsibility for obtaining early release was traditionally in the hands of the prisoner; that is, the inmate's behavior record was an important consideration in the parole decision. Eventually though, the authority of administrators who made decisions on parole became more influential than the inmate's record of good behavior. Jonathan Simon, in his book *Poor Discipline: Parole and the Social Control of the Underclass, 1890–1990* (1993), discusses the evolution of parole in the context of the prevailing political, economic, and technological forces. Simon notes that a crucial component of parole when it emerged in the late nineteenth century was employment. Offenders were required to maintain employment as a condition of their release. After World War II the number of unskilled industrial jobs – the type of work parolees needed to survive in the community – began to decline. Due to the reduction in employment opportunities for parolees, parole officers began conducting their duties in ways that were characterized as clinical. That is, parole authorities renewed their emphasis on rehabilitation. Subsequently, treatment – instead of employment – became the cornerstone of modern parole.

During the 1970s, when rehabilitation was being dismantled, strategies of parole shifted to management and surveillance. Unable to rely on the positive effects of rehabilitation and employment to keep parolees from returning to crime, parole officers eventually resorted to technologically advanced mechanisms of supervision and social control (e.g. computerized databases that track parolees). Today parole agencies rely on revised measures of prediction and classification, drug testing, and electronic monitoring (Simon, 1993). (The technologies of community corrections are addressed in upcoming sections.)

How parole is administered

The passage of determinate-sentencing legislation has had a great impact on the parole process. In particular, determinate sentencing eliminated parole boards' discretion that was a controversial aspect of the parole process. According to determinate-sentencing procedures, prisoners are released after they have served the sentence ordered by the judge, minus good time. More than half of the jurisdictions in the US follow such procedures. Fifteen states depart from the procedure set by determinate sentencing and instruct the parole board to follow specified guidelines. Such guidelines, which take into consideration characteristics of the crime and of the offender, provide a standard for all applications for release. Presently, California, Minnesota, and Pennsylvania combine determinate sentencing with parole guidelines.

There are three types of parole release: mandatory, expiration, and discretionary. In mandatory release, a prisoner who has served a certain length of his or her sentence (minus good time) as specified by determinate-sentencing laws (or parole guidelines) is paroled. Community supervision is a condition of mandatory release. When a prisoner has served the full length of his or her sentence (minus good time), expiration release is ordered, and community supervision is not required. Finally, discretionary release refers to an approach in which the offender is paroled at the discretion of the parole board, thereby permitting the offender to serve the remainder of his or her sentence in the community with supervision.

Parole boards and procedures

Most state parole boards consist of members appointed by different bodies of government. In an effort to strike a balance of power, the legislative (the state assembly) and executive (the governor's office) branches of government each select candidates to serve on the parole board. Very often the appointments are staggered, meaning that the selections are made at different times. In Alabama, the Board of Pardons and Paroles consists of three members serving six-year

Figure 13.2   The first meeting of the Parole Board set up under the Criminal Justice Act 1967 to advise the Home Secretary on the release of prisoners on license, November 7, 1967. Among those meeting at the Home Office are (*left to right*) chairman Lord Hunt, the Honourable Sir Arthur James (1916–76, Judge of the High Court of Justice, Queen's Bench Division), criminology lecturer Roy King and the Honourable Mr Justice Roskill (1911–96). In the background is Bill Pearce, then Chief Probation Officer for Inner London.

Photo by Wesley/Keystone/Getty Images.

terms. The New York State Board of Parole has 15 members serving six-year terms.

Given the political nature of the appointments, members of parole boards are often selected not necessarily due to their expertise in criminal justice, but rather because they can be expected to make conservative, low-risk decisions. Naturally, government officials want to avoid embarrassing or unpopular decisions by the parole board. Compounding matters, political patronage can influence – and corrupt – the parole process.

Parole hearings are held at the correctional institution where the parole board is provided with the necessary materials such as the inmate's folder (or jacket) complete with the pre-sentence investigation report as well as institutional reports documenting the prisoner's behavior in prison. The prisoner's progress in educational, vocational, treatment, and other programs is reported, as are institutional misconduct and rule violations. Psychological and physical examinations are also available. Interviews with the inmate by the members of the parole board generally are part of the protocol. However, such interviews are exceedingly brief, typically lasting less than 10 minutes. In some states, neither hearings nor interviews are conducted; under such procedures, the parole board relies solely on written reports.

The parole board considers a number of key factors in reaching parole decisions: the nature and severity of the crime, criminal history, institutional conduct, the prisoner's age, substance-abuse history, and the length of time served. More than half of the state correctional systems permit victims and family members to meet with the parole board, and often a recommendation is solicited from the prosecutor. In the final analysis, if the parole board determines that the prisoner is suitable for release, a release date is scheduled.

Risk and needs assessment

In the late 1970s and early 1980s, parole (and probation) authorities began formalizing their classification schemes. Wisconsin emerged as a frontrunner in the campaign to establish clear-cut procedures for assessing a parolee's risk (of recidivism) and needs (for assistance and services). By assessing parolees' risks and needs, parole agencies can anticipate the problems that parolees might experience in the community. Consequently, authorities can impose an appropriate level of supervision: intensive, maximum, moderate, or minimum. With the help of the National Institute of Corrections, Wisconsin's risk and needs assessment was adopted by numerous jurisdictions nationwide (Abadinsky, 2003).

Although the use of such instruments to compile valuable information about the parolee formalizes the parole process, their predictive value remains questionable. Even when parole decisions are based on comprehensive assessments, predicting which parolees will succeed and which will fail is still difficult (see Harcourt, 2007).

Nevertheless, assessments can be useful instruments because they quantify items of risk (including histories of criminal activity, violence, substance abuse, etc.) and needs (including family, financial, emotional, health, and drug or alcohol difficulties) for parole officers. Given the information provided by the assessment, officers can adjust their caseloads (numbers of clients to be supervised) as well as their workloads (amount of time needed for their cases).

Conditions of parole

Parolees, like probationers, are required to meet the conditions of their release. First and foremost, the parolee is expected to lead a crime-free life. Both standard and special conditions are specified prior to release. Standard conditions generally apply to all parolees and include restrictions on travel, prohibitions on associating with other offenders, and requirements for securing employment. Special conditions, such as being required to undergo treatment for substance abuse, address the special needs or risks of an offender.

The duration of parole is based on both the length of the sentence and state law governing the parole system. Typically, parolees are subject to supervision for more than one year. In California, for example, supervision of a non-life parolee can be terminated after one year of satisfactory performance, and that of a lifer after three years.

Revocation of parole

As is the case with probation, parole can be revoked for technical violations and new offenses. Technical violations are transgressions related to the conditions of parole – for instance, failing to attend substance-abuse counseling. Additionally, a parolee who commits a new offense is in violation of the requirement to lead a crime-free life. Repeated technical violations and serious new crimes are grounds for revocation of parole.

Crucial legal developments in the area of parole revocation warrant attention. In a landmark decision, the US Supreme Court ruled in *Morrissey* v. *Brewer* (1972) that some (not all) due process safeguards (under the Fourteenth Amendment) apply to parolees (and probationers) facing revocation. The purpose of applying some due process safeguards to parole revocation is to ensure that the facts reported in alleged parole violations are verified by the authorities. The Court established procedural safeguards by requiring a two-stage process featuring a preliminary hearing and revocation hearing for parole revocation. Although the Court added procedural safeguards to parole revocation, it stopped short of ruling on whether parolees were entitled to counsel during the hearings.

In general, a parolee has the right to waive a preliminary hearing. However, the preliminary hearing is necessary if the parolee is to be detained on a warrant pending a revocation hearing. At the preliminary hearing, the parolee is permitted to contest the alleged violations and has a limited right to question witnesses and the parole officer, and to introduce evidence. Although the state is not constitutionally bound to provide counsel, an attorney can represent the parolee. If probable cause to believe that the parolee has committed the alleged violations is determined by the hearing officer, the parolee is detained until the revocation hearing is completed; if probable cause is not found, the parolee is returned to supervision.

At the revocation hearing, the hearing officer or members of the parole board determine whether the parolee is guilty of the alleged violations and whether such violations are serious enough to revoke parole and return the offender to prison (Abadinsky, 2003). If the offender is returned to prison, state laws governing parole determine the length of confinement. Customarily, technical violations result in a penalty of one year in prison. In certain cases, the length of confinement is offset by the time spent under supervision in the community (known as street time). Nevertheless, it is not uncommon for parole violators to serve up to two years in prison.

Effectiveness of parole

During the 1980s, a campaign to abolish parole emerged. It was argued that parole was another example that the criminal justice system was 'soft,' because those offenders who were released early were not getting their just deserts. Critics also pointed out that parole was defeating a primary purpose of the criminal justice system – community protection. In sum, the overall effectiveness and fairness of parole were seriously questioned. Consequently, in the 1980s, 29 states (and the federal system) either abolished parole, substantially modified its use through the establishment of specific guidelines, or substituted discretionary release with mandatory release and determinate sentences.

Much like its probation counterpart, determining the effectiveness of parole remains difficult due to competing definitions of recidivism along with contrasting research methods (see Geerken and Hennessey, 1993). As a result, the evaluation literature is riddled with contradictory findings. According to Abadinsky, 'the methodology of some research efforts is simply unsound; however, even methodologically sound research has not conclusively determined whether parole is successful' (2002: 1130). Still, policy-makers have the task of improving parole practices so that they better serve the parolee and safeguard the community.

Several factors influence the lack of overall effectiveness of parole. First, high failure rates must be viewed in the light of the lack of sufficient resources allocated to parole agencies. As caseloads increase and sufficient resources (in the form of personnel and related expenses) decrease, supervision becomes lax. Moreover, the lack of resources affects parolees who need services and programs related to unemployment and substance abuse, as well as to other social and personal difficulties. Prison overcrowding further compounds the high failure rate of parole. As available prison cells become increasingly scarce, more inmates are released early to accommodate new admissions. Thus more high-risk offenders are likely to be released into the community (Davey, 2010).

Numerous other explanations for the lack of effectiveness have been proposed. A classic study concluded that parole is administered too late for many offenders. That is, the longer prisoners are kept behind bars, the less likely they are to succeed on parole (Gottfredson *et al.*, 1973; see also Austin and Irwin, 2001). That finding continues to be relevant today, especially in view of the lack of prison programs and rehabilitation services. Traditionally, parole was used as a reward for personal reform or rehabilitation; without such institutional programs, however, inmates are less prepared to succeed when they re-enter the community (see Christian, 2010; Hipp and Yates, 2009; Turnbull and Hannah-Moffat, 2009).

Surviving after release

Considering the adverse social and economic situations of the vast majority of parolees, Austin and Irwin (2001) are surprised at the number of offenders who actually succeed while on parole (see Welch, 1995d), Parolees face various obstacles, most notably unemployment and substance abuse. Following years of institutional routine that structures their daily lives, prisoners are ejected into a fast-moving, complex society where they face the enormous task of survival. Indeed, Austin and Irwin (2001) report that one of the many obstacles to 'making it' after release is the shock of re-entry. Although release from prison is tremendously exhilarating, the prospects of survival are frightening for parolees (see Hirschfield and Piquero, 2010; Maruna, 2001; Maruna and Immarigeon, 2004; Nellis, 2009).

Even for most adults who are college-educated, possess marketable job skills, and are otherwise employable, the task of securing viable work remains a challenge. For those who have a substandard education, possess few job skills, and bear the stigma of being an ex-con, the prospects of employment are exceedingly bleak. As Austin and Irwin (2001) note, for the uneducated and unemployable who must face a rapidly changing and increasingly competitive and unforgiving society, the odds are almost insurmountable. The following narrative illustrates the frustrations experienced by parolees in the search for employment:

> *R.C., a 22-year-old black man.* I've been looking for work for two weeks. I'm staying with friends, cause my mother can't help me. I've been staying away from my old neighborhood and friends, cause I don't want to get back into that life. I've been pretty nervous cause I don't know how to live like this. If I was going back to selling drugs, I wouldn't be nervous, cause I would know what I was gonna do. But I made up my mind I wasn't gonna sell no drugs.
>
> I go to different places, fill out applications. I've been to San Leandro, Hayward, Oakland, Berkeley. I'm in the process of getting my California ID. I have to have that. Now every day I am going to different places and trying to get a job. I got a friend who got a job at the Oakland Airport. He says something might come up there. If I don't get a job through some agency or friends, I'm gonna do something I thought I would never do – work for McDonalds.
>
> (Austin and Irwin, 2001: 148)

Without viable employment, parolees must depend on family and friends for support, housing, and meals – a dependence that is both frustrating and stressful. The degree of frustration and stress caused by both unemployment and the shock of re-entry can make returning to crime (e.g. burglary or using and selling drugs) an increasingly tempting alternative (Vennard and Hedderman, 2009).

Additionally, parolees must face other sources of stress, such as dealing with parole officers. Parole officers, especially those who are less human service-oriented and more law enforcement-oriented, can compound parolees' stress by hassling them and threatening revocation. In view of the many obstacles, it is not surprising that so many offenders fail to meet the conditions of parole (Richards, 1995; Richards and Jones, 1997; Ross and Richards, 2009; see 'Working in Corrections: The Meaning of Tropes' below). In light of those problems, aftercare is gaining serious attention by some policy-makers who have realized that without improved assistance and supervision, parolees are greatly disadvantaged after release. In their evaluation of parole in the California Youth Authority, Josi and Sechrest (1999) found high-quality aftercare – as embodied in a re-entry program entitled 'Lifeskills95' – was key in reducing recidivism. By rethinking the role of aftercare in parole, Josi and Sechrest state that the long-term goal of that program is 'to substantially alter the traditional way in which juvenile offender aftercare and community reintegration have been designed and managed in this country' (1999: 51; see also Dailey, 2001; Girshick, 2003; O'Brien, 2001).

WORKING IN CORRECTIONS

The Meaning of Tropes

As the war on crime began to escalate during the early 1970s, criminal justice agencies underwent considerable transformation to accommodate the 'tough-on-crime' stance. Whereas probation and parole departments previously had been viewed as part of the rehabilitative mission of criminal justice, the war on crime reshaped those agencies, producing three broad areas of change. First, probation and parole departments gravitated toward crime control and surveillance and away from service and assistance. Second, probation and parole officers were expected to conform to rising expectations of professional responsibility so that they could uphold the rule of law. Third, their work environment became increasingly rational and bureaucratic (Feeley and Simon, 1992; Fogel, 1984; Simon, 1993).

In his research, influenced by semiotics (the study of language and its meaning), criminologist John Crank set out to explore these basic territories of change and how they emerged in the parlance of probation and parole officers. Much of the early professional training of officers begins in the classroom of academies where instructors, who are tremendously experienced in the field, share their views of probation and parole work. It is in that learning environment that Crank studied how experiences are transmitted to recruits and how so-called 'war stories,' or tropes, are introduced to help rookies understand the complexities of their job (see Shearing and Ericson, 1991). In examining 'war stories' Crank discovered that linguistic devices such as tropes are instrumental in maintaining organizational culture faced with structural changes. Mirroring the areas of occupational change in probation and parole work, Crank reveals tropes in three domains: crime fighting, the morality of personal responsibility, and bureaucracy.

Crime Fighting

In the first domain, crime fighting, recruits learn quickly that probation and parole officers are members of the larger law enforcement fraternity committed to controlling criminals. As stated numerous times in the academy classes, the figurative term offender replaced the terms probationer and parolee. 'Keep in mind: we do not service clients. We supervise offenders,' stressed one instructor (Crank, 1996: 276). So that recruits understood fully that they faced hazardous duty, 'war stories' highlighted the dangerousness of some offenders. The following example illustrates how a chilling 'war story' can be used to emphasize the importance of thorough body search, including the groin area.

> This is a place where people hide all kinds of stuff. There was a case in California where a guy was up for parole. He went before the board, and they turned him down. He bent over and pulled a stabbing tool out of his anal cavity. He jumped over the desk and stabbed a parole board member that he didn't like in the shoulder a couple of times.
>
> (Crank, 1996: 277)

Indeed, such 'war stories' remind recruits that as probation and parole officers they would be on the front lines of the war on crime.

The Morality of Personal Responsibility

Due to organizational shifts in probation and parole work over the past few decades, officers are expected to be accountable for their actions. Above all, officers must conduct themselves with utmost professionalism in all spheres of the job, including making house calls, interacting with other sectors of the criminal justice system, and appearing in court. During a lecture on courtroom procedure, the instructor shared the following trope to stress personal responsibility and demeanor.

> Don't read a (news) paper [in court]. I was in reviewing a case, leafing through the pages [of a newspaper], and the judge stopped, pointed at me, pointed to the bailiff, and the bailiff made a big circle around the courtroom, a big show, and came up to me and said 'Please don't rustle your paper.'
>
> (Crank, 1996: 279)

Although tropes were introduced as concrete examples of proper professionalism, they also served to remind recruits that they must control their emotions. Classroom instructors emphasized how crucial it was that officers contain their anger, particularly given the frustrating nature of their work. Consider the following 'war story.'

> A PR24 (baton) is a deadly weapon. A few years ago an LASD officer saw a fellow he knew standing on a corner, a guy he knew was a burglar. He told him to leave. He drove around the block and when he came back the guy was still there. He executed a power takeout with a PR24 and hit the guy across the skull, and literally knocked his brains out the side of his head. So be careful. You may be tempted to strike someone, but you'll end up in the trick bag.
>
> (Crank, 1996: 279)

To reiterate his point, the training officer spelled out the importance of maintaining personal responsibility along with emotional integrity.

Bureaucracy

In light of the growing bureaucratic nature of probation and parole work, instructors discussed not only ways to conform to new and complex organizational procedures but also ways to resist them. By doing so, recruits learned how to offset some of the dehumanizing – and absurd – aspects of their professional duties. Tropes concerning the bureaucracy stressed the importance of using one's common sense, a significant cultural guidepost found in many criminal justice agencies. Very often officers must balance the bureaucratic excess against the offender's special needs. The following trope demonstrates how an officer can sympathize with a parolee who is trying to meet the conditions of parole but is faced with difficult personal and financial circumstances.

> We have a bad situation in our country. A lot of times it is impossible to find work for an unemployed mother. There's no way minimum wage can provide the support [she can get] from unemployment and ADC. However, a condition of parole is employment. You may have to talk to your supervisor. A low-skill offender with three children, her children will literally starve if she has to take a minimum-wage job. They can't afford child care. You can write it up so that they have to work, but you can write it up so that they can take care of their children at home.
>
> (Crank, 1996: 283)

Efforts to resist the dehumanizing and contradictory facets of the bureaucracy may also serve as a 'success stories,' another type of trope found in the training of probation and parole officers. In a class on case supervision, the instructor proudly disclosed his experience with a 'successful' probationer who overcame personal obstacles.

> The judge ordered a high school completion (a needs form) for a woman with an IQ of 70. What I did was put my woman into Rancho High School classes. She wrote a book report she was exceptionally proud of. I sent a report to the judge telling him what she had accomplished. The judge liked it.
>
> (Crank, 1996: 283)

In sum, the three domains identified in Crank's research (i.e., crime fighting, the morality of personal responsibility, and bureaucracy) represent ways in which probation and parole officers use their own common sense to navigate the often difficult organizational terrain within the agency. By studying tropes, or 'war stories,' we discover how experienced supervisors socialize officers so that they may adapt to changing organizational imperatives while adhering to the work culture of probation and parole (also see Bayens *et al.*, 1998; Pierson *et al.*, 2002).

GOAL CONFLICT IN PROBATION AND PAROLE

The work of probation and parole officers combines elements of two sometimes conflicting professions: law enforcement and social work. On the one hand, probation and parole officers parallel police officers because their duties involve law enforcement and surveillance. On the other hand, probation and parole officers resemble social workers because they are expected to provide assistance, services, and guidance toward rehabilitation. Over the past few decades, researchers and practitioners have argued that the goals of law enforcement and rehabilitation generally conflict with each other. At the root of the conflict is the assertion that the parole officer's police role undermines the client's willingness to share personal and sensitive information with the officer (Allen *et al.*, 1985; Glaser, 1969; Klockars, 1972; Lipsky, 1980; McCleary, 1978; Ohlin *et al.*, 1956; Sigler and Bezanson, 1970; von Hirsch and Hanrahan, 1979).

Proposals to reduce goal conflict in the probation and parole systems suggest that agencies should adopt one goal over the other. Von Hirsch and Hanrahan (1979) and Stanley (1976) argue that rehabilitation should become the dominant goal of probation. Conversely, Rosencrance (1986) and Duffee (1984) recommend that law enforcement remain the prevailing objective of probation, leaving rehabilitation to those who are truly treatment experts (i.e. substance-abuse specialists and therapists). An additional component of goal conflict stems from the fact that most probation and parole agencies suffer from goal ambiguity because they fail to offer an explicit, well-defined mission. Hence, the primary mandate of many agencies lacks clarity (Petersilia, 1985a).

Studies have explored whether probation staff, supervisors, and administrators prefer a specific orientation. Contrary to the polarized views of many criminal justice scholars, who argue in favor of one perspective over the other, are the views of practitioners who recognize the existence of and prefer a dual-goal system. Indeed, many probation personnel cite the importance of both law enforcement and rehabilitation (Ellsworth, 1990).

Some studies conclude that probation officers are becoming more law enforcement-oriented and less client assistance-oriented. In their study, Harris *et al.* (1989) found that probation officers embraced authority over assistance because they found authority to be a more meaningful concept in supervision than treatment or assistance. Although the shift toward a law enforcement-oriented approach among probation officers is consistent with the nation's renewed emphasis on law and order, there are other possible influences, including the

Figure 13.3   Paris Hilton leaving court after being sentenced to 45 days in jail for violating probation.

Photo by Jean Baptiste Lacroix/WireImage.

reduction of resources allocated to probation agencies. Generally, it is more expensive (although perhaps more cost-effective) and more labor-intensive (requiring more effort on the part of the officer) to administer rehabilitation than simply to provide simple supervision (see Pierson *et al.*, 2002).

OTHER ALTERNATIVES TO INCARCERATION

Focusing on the criminal justice system in terms of either those incarcerated or those on probation, however, creates a polarized view of the system. That is, 'at each end of the continuum, the system tends to overuse both prison (as an indicator of severity) and probation (as an indicator of leniency)' (Welch, 1991b). As a result, an enormous gap exists where intermediate punishments – intensive probation, substantial fines, community service orders, residential controls, and treatment orders – are both underdeveloped and underutilized. In a classic work, *Between Prison and Probation: Intermediate Punishments in a Rational Sentencing System*, Norval Morris and Michael Tonry cite that uneven distribution as evidence that the criminal justice system is 'both too lenient and too severe: too lenient with many on probation who should be subject to tighter controls in the community, and too severe with many in prison and jail who would present no serious threat to community safety if they were under control in the community' (1990: 3).

Interchangeability of punishments

Morris and Tonry present the principle of interchangeability of punishments in the context of intermediate sentences by addressing a common sentencing dilemma: 'Can a sentencing system fairly and justly impose a prison sentence on one offender and a community-based sentence on his in-all-respects like situated brother?' (1990: 82). The following hypothetical, though not atypical, case helps illustrate Morris and Tonry's principle of interchangeability of punishments:

Two young offenders are convicted of robbery; both have a record of drug addiction. Posit equal severity of crime and criminal record. The sentencing guidelines, expressed or customary, in the jurisdiction of their crime suggest a prison term of one year. Criminal A, aged 19, is black, has been unemployed for the past six years, reads at a fifth-grade level, and lives in a crowded apartment with his unmarried mother who has two other children on welfare.

Criminal B, also 19, is white, has steady employment which need not be terminated if he is not sent to prison, graduated from high school, is now involved in trade training, and lives with his parents in a middle-class neighborhood.

Are the following sentences justified?

For Criminal A, one year's imprisonment with a recommendation to the correctional authorities that he be given the opportunity to participate in a drug treatment program while in prison and a release procedure that may assist him to avoid his present drug dependency.

For Criminal B, two years' intensive supervision probation with the following conditions: an appropriate period in a residential drug treatment facility, thereafter at least weekly outpatient contact with that facility with regular urine testing to ensure that he is free of drugs, and an obligation of at least weekly contacts with the probation officer. Restitution and a fine may also be appropriate; he must certainly work and contribute from his current earnings to the cost of his probation supervision and his drug treatment. If he lacks funds and cannot find work, add or extend an obligation of community service.

This is not an unreal hypothesis. The fact of a responsible home and a job and an education makes a dramatic difference to the possibilities of imposing a more socially protective punishment on B than on A ...

To insist on equal suffering by Criminal B because of the adverse social conditions of Criminal A is to purchase an illusory equality at too high a price. It is a leveling down and benefits neither Criminal A nor the community. The criminal law cannot rectify social inequalities; those inequalities will inexorably infect rational punishment policies. But this hypothetical situation leaves an uneasy sense of moral imbalance and forces us to the consideration of how deserved punishments can operate fairly in a world of social inequality.

It may be that evenhandedness in punishment should not be measured only in terms of rough equivalence of suffering, whether of pain or of degrees of loss of autonomy, but also in the functions to be fulfilled by a sentencing system.

(1990: 102–4)

A review of Morris and Tonry's book and, in particular, the aforementioned case study, commends the authors for courageously taking on such a difficult case. However, their justifications appear somewhat problematic (Welch, 1991b). Whereas most observers of that case study probably would not recommend that both offenders be imprisoned, the proposed comprehensive sentencing system (which is supposed to be equipped with various intermediate punishments) appears to be unable or unwilling to construct an appropriate intermediate punishment for criminal A (the African American offender) that would prevent him from occupying expensive and scarce prison space. It is difficult to believe that such a comprehensive sentencing system could devise an elaborate intermediate punishment for criminal B (the white offender) and simply incarcerate criminal A (the African American offender). Although Morris and Tonry may have a point when they suggest that criminal law cannot rectify social inequalities, they fail to acknowledge that criminal law and sentencing themselves tend to reflect social inequalities (Welch, 1991b).

Morris and Tonry concede that the existing sentencing system tends to resist intermediate sentencing proposals, citing such issues as constitutional, legal, political, organizational, bureaucratic, ideological, and financial complexities. Still, Morris and Tonry seem to understate the significance of social class as another crucial impediment to sentencing reforms. It appears that intermediate punishments are generally available to middle- and upper-income offenders but are somehow difficult to administer to their lower-income counterparts (Welch, 1991b; see also Wood and Grasmick, 1999).

Pre-trial diversion

At the heart of intermediate sanctions is diversion. In the criminal justice system, diversion refers to a procedure in which defendants are diverted either from prosecution or from incarceration. In the first scenario, a young offender who has been charged with a minor offense, and who possesses a scant criminal history or no criminal record at all, is spared prosecution through assignment to community corrections. Diversion also applies to non-violent offenders who pose few risks to the community.

Pre-trial diversion programs, common in many jurisdictions, are designed to weed out cases involving young first-time defendants who are charged with minor crimes. Many pre-trial diversion initiatives require the defendant to complete a form of community service or attend a counseling program in exchange for having the charges dropped by the authorities. If the defendant fails to comply with the conditions of the diversion program, prosecution resumes. Diversion has become increasingly popular. In many jurisdictions, the courts continue to administer such programs. Moreover, given the large numbers of staff and resources needed to operate pre-trial diversion, it is not uncommon for private foundations to be contracted by the courts to administer the programs.

Pre-trial release

Chapter 11 discusses the importance of pretrial release for defendants who otherwise would be detained in jail. If defendants are non-violent and pose few risks to the community, releasing them into the community pending trial makes sense. Pre-trial release benefits the criminal justice system because it is less costly than detention and it alleviates jail overcrowding. Additionally, pre-trial release greatly benefits defendants because they can continue (or pursue) employment, and maintain family and community ties. Moreover, pre-trial release grants defendants a greater opportunity to prepare for trial, thereby preserving the principle of presumption of innocence. Pre-trial release can take place under three different conditions. First, defendants can be required to post bail to secure their release. Second, defendants can be released on their own recognizance (ROR). Third, they can be released under supervision (RUS).

COMPARATIVE CORRECTIONS

Alternatives to Incarceration in Sub-Saharan Africa

Unlike the United States and Europe, sub-Saharan African criminal justice proceedings generally are less formalized and conform to cultural traditions in several key ways. First, most African societies view the individual as a member of a social group; therefore, crimes are interpreted as conflicts that should be resolved by groups representing the offender and the victim. Second, the goal of the intervention is to restore social harmony between the groups. Finally, the process by which the conflict is to be resolved invites a wide range of public participation under the direction of an arbitrator who is a community leader. Penalties often take the form of compensation or restitution and commonly are enforced by social pressure. Customarily, the conflict is put to rest by an integrative ritual, such as an event in which the groups share a banquet (Stephens, 2000; Stern, 2002).

Despite the importance of traditional customs prevalent in sub-Saharan African criminal justice proceedings, over time ruling governments have adopted incarceration practices inherited from former colonial powers. Versions of British, Dutch, French, and Portuguese laws have become the official base from which criminal justice is administered, producing a clash of cultures. According to the European model, sub-Saharan African nations have become more reliant on the use of incarceration, even though under traditional customs imprisonment does not contribute to a restoration of social harmony. Other problems have emerged. Law enforcement suffers from corruption; pre-trial and sentenced offenders are pushed into overcrowded prisons where food is inadequate, water can be scarce, and diseases are rampant. Compounding matters, human rights organizations object to the practice of housing children along with adults, including some who prey on vulnerable youth (Stern, 2002, 1999, 1998).

In the 1990s, responding to political pressure from international human rights groups, several sub-Saharan African countries undertook initiatives designed to reform their criminal justice systems. In 1996, a Special Rapporteur on Prisons and Conditions of Detention in Africa was appointed to oversee the reforms. Bolstering the campaign to improve correctional and judicial systems, the Kampala Declaration was ratified, establishing a broad agenda for reform. A key component of the Declaration was the plan to develop greater alternatives to prison while adhering to larger human rights considerations. By doing so, criminal justice proceedings would once again encourage local community participation.

Many sub-Saharan African countries have legislation allowing for alternatives to incarceration. Benin, Chad, the Ivory Coast, Niger, Senegal, and Togo all have statutes permitting suspended sentences. Namibia has a law allowing community service to replace sentences of up to five years. Kenya, Lesotho, Malawi, and Swaziland also have measures that transform short prison sentences into public work carried out in the community. Although such provisions have the backing of legislators, they have rarely been exercised due to the lack of resources and funds.

To correct that problem, reformers have set out to implement alternatives to imprisonment that would alleviate overcrowding while reducing unnecessary incarcerations. Recent reforms in Zimbabwe offer a compelling example of the viability of community sanctions. Reformers found that the vast majority of prisoners were minor offenders (including fine defaulters); in fact, two-thirds of those in prison were serving sentences of three months or less. Given the nature of that correctional population, alternatives to incarceration could be introduced without exacting a high risk to public safety. Correspondingly, community service orders were given to those sentenced to prison terms of one year or less. Evaluations of the program were impressive. Of the 17,000 persons sanctioned by community service orders, 90 percent satisfactorily completed the conditions of probation and parole. Moreover, the prison population dropped from 22,000 to 18,000 (Stern, 1999, 1998). Reforms in Zimbabwe also capitalized on community involvement by recruiting professionals outside the criminal justice system. Social workers, teachers, and healthcare providers aided the success of the program while contributing to the reintegration of offenders into the community (see also Koichi, 1995; Stephens, 2000).

Dispute resolution and restitution

Since many crimes take place between persons who are related to or acquainted with each other, court systems can reduce their dockets by diverting such cases to dispute resolution (or mediation or conciliation) programs. These programs are particularly relevant because many criminal cases are dismissed because of complainant non-cooperation. Generally, dispute resolution involves a third-party mediator who examines the complaint and brings the parties together to resolve the dispute peacefully. For example, a teenager who is charged with vandalizing a neighbor's home may agree to restitution in the form of lawn care for several months to avoid a criminal prosecution.

Dispute resolution is equally appropriate when victims do not know the offender. With greater concern being ascribed to victims' rights, many states have created victim-offender reconciliation programs (VORPs). VORPs use the dispute-resolution format to guide the parties toward agreement on ways in which offenders can provide restitution to their victims. Restitution can take the form of services or financial reimbursement. VORPs not only humanize the criminal justice process, but also place emphasis on holding offenders accountable for their crimes without relying on imprisonment (Harris, 1992; Lawrence, 2002; Umbreit, 2002).

Community service

Community service allows us to understand the connection between economic forces and punishment. That is, ordering the offender to serve the community through unpaid labor imposes punishment. Unpaid labor as a form of punishment existed in ancient Babylonian, Greek, and Roman societies (Schafer, 1970). Today, community service programs have emerged as popular sanctions because they achieve several objectives simultaneously. While subjecting the offender to punishment, such service has the capacity to benefit the community. Through community service, the offender might also develop a sense of affiliation with the community rather than feel further alienated (Greene, 2002).

Community service sanctions have gained much attention over the past 20 years, especially as a result of the publicity surrounding celebrity offenders who have been ordered to provide unpaid labor. For example, Oliver North, Michael Milken, Zsa Zsa Gabor, Leona Helmsley, and Tonya Harding have had community service appended to their sentences. It should be noted that community service as a sanction did not emerge as a way to punish celebrities; rather, it was initially aimed at low-income offenders who would have difficulty paying fines. The labor is not intended to be humiliating; however, it is certainly burdensome. Some examples of community service projects are painting senior citizens' centers and nursing homes, clearing neighborhood lots, and preparing dilapidated buildings for renovation (Martin, 2002).

While advocates correctly argue that community service is a sensible alternative to incarceration and other more serious sanctions such as probation, it is misleading to assume that it can be used to generate revenue since there are many costs attached to administering such programs. More recently, criminologist Douglas McDonald reminds us of the problem of net-widening: 'In theory community service saves the city money by avoiding jail costs. But it is hard to be sure, since many of those who are sentenced would have been let off with no punishment in an earlier era' (quoted in Worth, 2002a: B2; McDonald, 1992).

Day fines and probation fees

Although the use of monetary fines as a form of punishment has always played a role in the American criminal justice system, its implementation has traditionally departed from the practices of European and South American nations (see O'Malley, 2009, 2010). In the US, the amount of the fine is fixed according to the crime committed. In other nations, however, the amount of the fine is based on the offender's ability to pay. In response to recommendations that the American criminal justice system replace fixed fines with day fines (which are based on the offender's ability to pay as well as the severity of the offense), the National Institute of Justice (NIJ) and the Vera Institute of Justice set out to develop such an experiment (Winterfield and Hillsman, 1993). The general concept is simple: determining the amount of punishment to be administered to an offender is separated from a consideration of how much money that offender must pay. Judges determine how much punishment an offender deserves; this is then denominated in some unit other than money. Those *punishment units* are translated into monetary terms based on how much money the offender makes per day.

Practically speaking, the day-fine approach consists of a simple, two-step process. First, the court uses a 'unit scale' or 'benchmark' to sentence the offender to a certain number of day-fine units (for example, 15, 60, or 120 units) according to the gravity of the offense and without regard to income. To guide the court's choices, benchmarks or unit scales are typically developed by a planning group of judges, prosecuting attorneys, and defense counselors familiar with disposition patterns in a court. The value of each unit is then set at a percentage of the offender's daily income, and the total fine amount is determined by simple multiplication.

More than half the states permit local authorities to require probationers to pay at least some of the cost of their supervision. Criminal justice officials have suggested that it is not unreasonable to expect probationers who are employed to help offset the expenses of community corrections, especially when the monthly fee is modest – between $20 and $40. However, probation fees are controversial. Critics charge that probation fees are not an efficient method of generating revenue because most probationers are indigent. Moreover, some opponents argue that it is unethical and perhaps illegal to require probationers to pay for services they are entitled to receive (Marciniak, 2000; Parent, 1996).

Work release

As an alternative to total incarceration, work-release programs permit eligible (minimum-security, low-risk, non-violent) inmates to maintain employment in the community but to return to the institution after completing the workday. As early as 1913, Wisconsin initiated work release under the state's Huber law that included the release of jailed misdemeanants (Johnson and Kotch, 1973). However, work-release programs nationwide were slow to develop until the 1970s. Today most states have some form of work release but the extent to which these programs are utilized varies. Still, work release is consistent with other types of correctional intervention that feature labor as a form of rehabilitation, ostensibly promoting a work ethic and a positive self-image, as well as practical employment skills. Moreover, offenders' earnings can be allocated toward victim restitution.

Among the criticisms of work-release programs is the argument that if inmates can be trusted enough to leave the institution for work, then why not permit them to remain in the community? Rather than requiring those inmates to return to an expensive prison cell, why not assign them to less restrictive and less expensive housing – for instance, a halfway house or even their own home? (Some jurisdictions have responded to that problem by housing work-release inmates in less restrictive facilities.) Another complaint stems from the perception that work-release prisoners take jobs away from law-abiding citizens; understandably, that criticism becomes more intense during recessionary periods when unskilled workers find it difficult to secure employment.

Nevertheless, work release continues to endure as a correctional program because it provides an opportunity for the inmate to be gradually reintroduced into the community and serves as a testing period. Inmates who succeed at work release are generally considered good candidates for parole. Many states have also developed similar programs known as study release, whereby inmates attend educational or vocational training programs in the community (Turner, 2002).

Halfway houses

Halfway houses provide correctional supervision midway between incarceration and the community. Traditionally, halfway houses serve as an intermediate step in an inmate's progression from prison to the community. Halfway houses have a long history in the US, dating back to 1817 in Massachusetts where temporary shelter was established for discharged and mostly destitute convicts. The halfway house provided offenders with housing, meals, and an opportunity to develop a trade (Meehan, 2002).

Halfway houses conform to the correctional principle that offenders should be placed in those correctional settings that provide the fewest restrictions without jeopardizing public safety. Ideally, halfway houses provide various programs and services designed to facilitate the offender's return to the community. Such vital programs and services include employment assistance, educational and vocational training, alcohol- and substance-abuse counseling, and individual and group counseling. Although often challenged by residential groups who oppose the placement of convicted felons in their neighborhoods, halfway houses offer a less expensive and perhaps more methodical and comprehensive way of returning inmates to the community.

Intensive supervision programs

Intensive supervision programs (ISPs), as the name implies, involve more frequent contact between offenders and their supervising officers as well as a greater number of restrictions than typically characterize regular probation (Richardson, 2002). Generally, ISPs target felons who have committed serious crimes and thus pose high risks to the community. By being required to maintain frequent contact with supervising officers and by being subjected to many restrictions (e.g. curfews, home detention, drug-abuse treatment, urinalysis and breathalyzer tests, and unannounced searches), ISP probationers are expected to resist involvement in further criminal activity. Moreover, intensive and frequent contact with the criminal justice system is presumed to lead to better detection of unlawful conduct. Among the driving forces behind ISPs is the need to alleviate prison and jail overcrowding. Still, corrections officials realize that their reliance on community supervision must not engender the perception that offenders are being turned loose into the community without strict supervision.

As is the case with other programs expected to reduce recidivism, the question of the effectiveness of ISPs should be addressed. Thus far, ISPs are subject to mixed reviews. Compounding matters, various evaluation studies rely on contrasting research methods that make generalizations difficult (Bayens *et al.*, 1998; Erwin and Bennett, 2002; MacKenzie and Brame, 2001). According to Richardson (2002: 912), 'Although intensive probation programs appear to have good "face validity," in that they look good on the surface, research shows that they have not been effective in reducing correctional costs or preventing crime.'

Despite the lack of achievement of the stated goals of ISPs, Tonry (1990) reports that there is enthusiastic support for them from probation officers and departments. The support for ISPs is often driven by their ability to generate positive images for parole authorities. ISPs suggest that some parolees are being subjected to greater supervision, a belief that supports the goal of getting tough with offenders. However, critics insist that although ISPs promise intensive supervision, they often do not deliver high-frequency contact between officers and clients. Additional attention needs to be focused on the evaluation process, insofar as shoddy research methods restrict the understanding of program effectiveness. Until improvements are made in evaluation research, it should not be assumed that more control is always better control (see Caputo, 2004).

Electronic monitoring

Throughout this book, reference has been made to the technological forces that shape punishment and corrections. A clear example of technology in corrections is the introduction of electronic monitoring (EM). Attaching an electronic monitor to the ankle of a probationer to track his or her whereabouts certainly appears futuristic. It brings to mind the notion of Big Brother, the personification of state power in George Orwell's futuristic novel *1984*, in which citizens are subjected to governmental surveillance and control by way of cameras and other technologies. For all practical purposes, however, the future is now. EM is an example of how what used to be considered futuristic technology can be applied to modern-day problems. Interestingly, the inception of EM is traced to a judge in New Mexico, who was inspired by Spider-Man comics (Corbett and Marx, 1992). Thirty years ago EM was used in only a few jurisdictions. Today EM programs operate in all 50 states; moreover, it is likely that the EM boom will continue well into the future (Courtright, 2002). The EM movement is driven, in large part, by prison and jail overcrowding, but 'it is, in concept, politically palatable; and it breathes new life into beleaguered correctional professionals' (Baumer and Mendelsohn, 1992: 55).

Unlike incarceration, which totally eliminates offenders' freedom, EM restricts freedom while permitting offenders to remain in the community. While wearing electronic monitors, EM probationers are permitted to work and attend school. If probationers leave the area to which they are restricted, the monitor transmits an electronic message to the probation department, notifying the officers of a violation. EM probationers are also subjected to curfews that require them to stay at home while not working or attending school. During the curfew period, EM probationers are still obligated to wear the monitors and are subject to random phone calls from their probation officers. Although home confinement is commonly a condition of EM, very often the reverse situation is the case; that is, EM is a condition of home confinement.

Overall, conclusions concerning EM programs' effectiveness remain tentative because the evaluation process is hampered by numerous methodological problems. For instance, limitations exist in sampling procedures because participants are often volunteers; therefore, they are not representative of the offender population. Moreover, few studies employ rigorous research methods, and most programs are not evaluated with the use of random assignment of subjects to experimental and control groups. Thus EM offenders are not compared with other offenders who share similar characteristics and criminal histories (Courtright, 2002).

Another major point of contention surrounding EM programs is the 'cream puff factor' (Petersilia, 1988. 1987). That is, offenders believed to be most suitable for EM are generally misdemeanants regarded as low-risk and cooperative. Rarely are felons admitted to EM programs, particularly those who are violent and prison-bound. To ensure that EM programs yield favorable reviews, officials tend to stack the deck with offenders who are least likely to recidivate, with or without EM. Such offenders are, in no uncertain terms, the best of the worst. In view of the tendency to admit only the 'best' offenders to EM programs, serious questions remain about the overall effectiveness and the evaluations of such programs. Rogers and Jolin pose this question: 'So what have we really proven if we report that, to date, most of the electronic monitoring programs have had low recidivism rates?' (1992: 319). Although some correctional officials hope that EM will become a technological panacea, scholars agree that most favorable reviews of EM are overstated. 'To those who have seen other new and promising innovations, it comes as no surprise that there is no magic bullet' (Baumer and Mendelsohn, 1992: 66; Finn and Muirhead-Steves, 2002; Stanz and Tewksbury, 2000).

Finally, Corbett and Marx (1992) address EM in broader social terms by noting that it reflects other forms of surveillance in society, including drug testing, audio and video recording, night-vision technology, and so on (see Marx, 1988). It is argued that techniques of surveillance common in maximum-security prisons are diffusing into society at large. 'We appear to be moving toward, rather than away from, becoming a "maximum-security society"' (Corbett and Marx, 1992: 86; see also Cohen, 1985, 1979; Foucault, 1977).

Additionally, both economic and technological forces have an impact on EM. Corbett and Marx explain that surveillance has become capital-intensive rather than labor-intensive; technology makes surveillance cheaper than traditional forms of supervision because fewer officers are capable of monitoring many more offenders.

CULTURAL PENOLOGY

Correctional Boot Camps

Among the most newsworthy forms of penal innovation, correctional boot camp (or shock-incarceration) programs require young, non-violent offenders to serve short terms in a quasi-military regimen inspired by images of the grueling lifestyle of a military boot camp or basic training. It is believed that these offenders might benefit more from an intensive correctional experience than from a standard prison sentence. Although the application of the military model in corrections is not entirely new, it has re-emerged as a popular method of inflicting harsh punishment and discipline on young offenders.

Imagine boarding an old, beat-up school bus and being driven 60 miles south of Atlanta. While the scorching heat is virtually unbearable, you're oblivious to the sweat rolling off your brow because you are preoccupied with your arrival at Georgia's Shock Incarceration program, where you will spend the next 90 days. Nervously, you run your fingers through your hair and suddenly realize that soon your head will be shaved. But having your head shaved and wearing a prison uniform is not going to be the worst part of this experience. For the next three months, your day will begin at 5 a.m., you will be told what to do, and how to do it, by COs who enthusiastically embrace their role as 'drill sergeants.'

Throughout each day, COs will relentlessly scream at you in face-to-face encounters that will make you wince. You will be ordered to march in formation everywhere you go, even to the mess hall where you will eat in silence. In fact, silence is observed all day, except for one hour when you will be allowed to talk with the other prisoners in your platoon. Also during that hour of free time you can watch television, but only public television or the news. Each day you will be subjected to inspections and forced to squeeze out one push-up after another on a stretch of blistering asphalt known as 'Hell's Half-Acre.' Let us not overlook the hard labor. Most of your day will be devoted to working on a chain-gang digging sewer lines, cutting grass, and painting buildings. During the course of all this, you will feel humiliated, intimidated, pissed-off, upset, and depressed. And like many other prisoners, you might choose to quit the Shock Incarceration program (commonly known as a correctional boot camp), opting to serve a longer but less intense prison sentence.

(Welch, 1997c: 184)

Correctional boot camps have expanded enormously since their inception in 1983 in Georgia. Nowadays, boot camp programs can be found in local, state, and federal correctional systems. Although they were originally designed as an alternative sanction for young males bound for prison, boot camps are increasingly popular for juvenile and even female offenders (Gover and MacKenzie, 2002). In 1993, Congress began preparing to spend hundreds of millions of dollars to open more military-style boot camps for young offenders (Nossiter, 1993; Veneziano *et al.*, 2000).

Although these programs enroll offenders who are highly screened volunteers, there is considerable attrition. Many inmates either voluntarily withdraw from the program or are dismissed for various infractions or other reasons. In some instances, the attrition rate is as high as 50 percent (MacKenzie and Shaw, 1990). Inmates who do not complete the program must serve their sentences in prison or return to the court for resentencing (MacKenzie, 1993). In many states, graduates of boot camps are placed on intensive supervision in the community.

Although the popularity of boot camps in the public mind is fueled by images of intense punishment, the primary driving force behind such programs is essentially administrative – the need to reduce prison overcrowding. In theory, prison boot camps emanate from fundamentally different, although not mutually exclusive, correctional philosophies. Most programs are based on the concepts of deterrence and rehabilitation. Furthermore, borrowing from the military model, prison boot camps attempt to instill in inmates a sense of discipline and respect for authority.

Despite their popularity, boot camps have been subjected to much criticism. Morash and Rucker (1990) emphasize the history of military approaches to corrections and explore popular images of masculinity inherent in them. They argue that the development of a correctional program that tends to dehumanize its participants, especially recruits who are disproportionately minorities and members of low-income groups, is perplexing and troubling (see Lutze and Murphy, 1999). One of the questions raised by Morash and Rucker reveals an interesting paradox: 'Why would a method that has been developed to prepare people to go into war, and as a tool to manage legal violence, be considered as having such potential in deterring or rehabilitating offenders?' (1990: 206). Morash and Rucker point out that the obvious aspects of the military approach should be recognized as being incompatible with the goals of rehabilitation. For example, boot camps endeavor to instill unquestioned obedience to authority and to promote aggression, both of which are inconsistent with prosocial behavior.

Introducing the military model into corrections is not a new or novel idea. In 1821 John Cray applied a military correctional plan to Auburn prison that was intended to maintain order in the overcrowded institution (McKelvey, 1977: 14). The military model was later practiced at the Elmira reformatory during the progressive era, but Zebulon Brockway eliminated lockstep marching and compulsory silence because they were regarded as humiliating. Elmira's military approach gradually incorporated other aspects of reform, such as academic and vocational training, as well as attempts to improve self-esteem. Eventually, Elmira's plan to combine rehabilitation with punishment failed as a result of renewed abuse against prisoners (Johnson, 1987: 41; Pisciotta, 1983: 620–1; Smith, 1988).

Ironically, the US military has officially abandoned the traditional style of boot camps that was known for its intimidating and humiliating forms of discipline. Reasons cited by a military task force for restructuring basic training include inconsistent philosophies, policies, and procedures; unreasonable leadership; dysfunctional stress; and the arbitrary use of authority, leading to stress and anger (Faris, 1975; Marlowe *et al.*, 1988; Raupp, 1978). The negative aspects of the traditional boot camp lead to an important question: how could such an approach encourage prosocial behavior? A critical look at boot camps reveals that, in actuality, they probably do not promote prosocial conduct; moreover, there is potential to increase aggression, leading to antisocial behavior.

Both studies by Morash and Rucker (1990) and Lutze and Murphy (1999) explore an area of boot camps that has been virtually unexplored by other experts, namely the conventional and popular stereotypes associated with masculinity. By focusing on issues of gender, they illuminate the unstated importance of defining masculinity in terms of aggression and forcefulness. It appears that boot camps set out to cultivate an exaggerated version of masculinity while undermining any so-called feminine qualities, such as empathy, sensitivity, and cooperation. That approach should come as no surprise considering that the military is a male-dominated institution known for promoting an exaggerated form of masculinity characterized by aggression, force, and physical strength. Indeed, in the military, the masculinity of its recruits is relentlessly challenged, and such terms as *little girl, woman, wife,* and *girly man* are used to denigrate those who fail tests of physical strength and endurance (see Eisenhart, 1975: Steihem, 1981).

In response to the criticism that correctional boot camps draw too much from the military model and not enough from the treatment model, most programs now feature a more pronounced rehabilitation orientation. For example, the New York State shock-incarceration program is described in its brochure as a highly structured and regimented routine, including extensive discipline, physical labor, exercise, and intensive drug rehabilitation. The program also boasts its emphasis on education, work ethics, and job skills (*Fourth Annual Report to the Legislature on Shock Incarceration – Shock Parole Supervision New York State*, 1992; see Lutze and Murphy, 1998).

Over the past three decades, researchers have set out to examine the effectiveness of correctional boot camps. Although such programs remain popular among 'tough-on-crime' politicians as well as the public, 'research to date has not found any significant difference between re-offending rates of those who serve time in boot camps and those in traditional facilities' (Gover and MacKenzie, 2002: 124). Moreover, there is evidence that correctional boot camps have few lasting effects once offenders return to the community. Still, policy-makers point to the benefit of cost-effectiveness: that is, correctional boot camps are cheaper than traditional prisons because the sentences are much shorter (Gover *et al.*, 2002; see Carlson and Garrett, 1999).

Several conceptual problems also contribute to doubts over prison boot camps. First, the uncritical acceptance of such programs without examination of the unstated or implied assumptions that underlie them remains an important drawback. Governor of Georgia Zell Miller strenuously defended Georgia's correctional boot camps against questions of their overall effectiveness: 'Nobody can tell me from some ivory tower that you take a kid, you kick him in the rear end, and it doesn't do any good. And I don't give a damn what they say, we're going to continue to do it in Georgia' (Nossiter, 1993: 9). Second, no evidence has been found to support the idea that young offenders can be scared into adopting prosocial behavior (see scared-straight programs in Chapter 7). Third, the reliance on an outmoded military model emphasizing exaggerated versions of masculinity appears to promote aggression and undermine the rehabilitative ideal of prosocial behavior.

Correctional boot camps suffer from key contradictions: among them is the practice of subjecting young offenders to intensive training and discipline only to eject them back into an economy that will not absorb them. 'Even if the typical 90-day regime of training envisioned by proponents of boot camps is effective in reorienting its subjects, at best it can only produce soldiers without a company to join' (Feeley and Simon, 1992: 464). From a critical perspective, it is important to note that while boot camps appeal to conservatives and liberals alike, they represent another form of social control aimed at modifying the individual while ignoring social conditions (Turner, 2010; Simon, 1995; Welch, 1999a).

RESTORATIVE JUSTICE

Although politicians have pushed for greater tough-on-crime measures – including 'three strikes' laws, the death penalty, and chain gangs – in an effort to assuage an angry and fearful public, they often do so without fully realizing that citizens hold complex views on punishment and rehabilitation. Surveys show that citizens support early intervention programs over prisons (Cullen *et al*, 1998), favor alternatives to incarceration (Turner *et al.*, 1997), and continue to share a rehabilitative philosophy toward lawbreakers (Applegate *et al.*, 1997; see also Maruna and King, 2009). With these considerations in mind, restorative justice has emerged as a firm but humane approach to criminal sanctions. Restorative justice acknowledges the harm that crime has not only on people but also their communities; accordingly, it proposes remedies aimed at repairing those social relationships (Crawford and Newburn, 2003; Center for Restorative Justice and Mediation, 1996; Wilmerding, 1997).

While holding offenders accountable, restorative justice seeks reintegration as well as empowering victims, thus restoring communities marred by crime. Such proposals have reached critical mass in some states, such as Maryland where restorative justice resonates in its 1997 Juvenile Causes Act. Under that law, the justice system offers programs that address the needs of the victims and the community as well as the offender. Similarly, Vermont's correctional system has been redesigned to provide intensive treatment and supervision to high-risk offenders, along with a restorative program for low-risk offenders who are required to make reparation to the victim and community (Walther and Perry, 1997), Both conservatives and liberals tend to support restorative justice as a humane and balanced approach to crime because it holds offenders accountable while addressing the needs of the victim and community (Clear, 1994; Daly, 2006).

As promising as restorative justice appears, several potential problems could undermine its effectiveness. Although restorative justice embraces progressive ideals in confronting crime, it does so by relying on coercion to ensure that offenders cooperate with the conditions of the program and mediation. Should offenders fail to fulfill the growing requirements of the program, they face harsher penalties. Critics charge that such coercion contradicts the progressive nature of restorative justice by shifting power back to the criminal justice system and away from the community (Levrant *et al.*, 1999). Likewise, net-widening remains a concern insofar as reparation programs extend to minor crimes and low-risk offenders. Should these offenders fail to comply with the conditions of the program, they too risk being penalized by greater sanctions (Walther and Perry, 1997). Paradoxically, restorative justice tends to expand the number of program (and technical) requirements, thus increasing the likelihood of non-compliance. Compounding matters, that degree of non-compliance – coupled with heightened public scrutiny and a demand for offender accountability – produces a greater number of revocations. Ultimately, the courts could resentence to prison minor, low-risk offenders who probably never would have been formally processed by the criminal justice system if it were not for the existence of a restorative justice program (Cullen *et al.*, 2001; Pavlich, 2005; Ward and Langlands, 2008).

In sum, although restorative justice policies propose to remedy crime by introducing seemingly benevolent and progressive ideals, they inadvertently could enhance the punitive tendency of the system in several ways:

- Offenders may lose certain rights and privileges that they are granted through the current adversarial process.
- Offenders may be coerced into participating in restorative justice programs because of formal pressures from practitioners within the criminal justice system.
- Restorative justice may widen the net of social control by targeting low-risk offenders.
- Offenders may be subjected to greater levels of supervision.
- Offenders may have a greater likelihood of incarceration for technical violations because of the increased probation conditions and scrutiny they face.
- Restorative justice programs may not achieve their goal of offender reintegration and therefore fail to restore fully the harmed relationships that result from the crime.

(Levrant *et al.*, 1999: 9–10)

Consequently, the truly progressive intent of restorative justice is jeopardized by the propensity for adopting 'get tough' measures as a means of enforcing reparation programs (see Aertsen *et al.*, 2006; Walgrave, 2008).

CONCLUSION

Even though alternatives are less costly than imprisonment, scholars and practitioners caution against the tendency to oversell, oversimplify, or over-accept the financial angle of community corrections (Davey, 2010; Kittrie *et al.*, 2002; McSparron, 1992). Still, the fact remains that all forms of criminal justice intervention are costly. With that concern in mind, the success of community corrections is contingent upon the proper allocation of funds. Often community corrections fail due to financial neglect by legislatures and other government bodies.

Incarceration is costly in other ways, including the toll it takes on the community (Rose and Clear, 1998; Thompson, 2008). Indeed, many persons are adversely affected when a defendant is sentenced to serve time in prison rather than in the community: mothers, fathers, spouses, and most notably children (Comfort, 2008; Lanier, 2003). The Bureau of Justice Statistics found: 'Parents held in the nation's prisons – 52% of state inmates and 63% of federal inmates – reported having an estimated 1,706,600 minor children, accounting for 2.3% of the U.S. resident population under age 18.' Moreover, between 1991 and 2007, parents held in state and federal prisons increased by 79 percent (357,300 parents) while the children of incarcerated parents increased by 80 percent (Glaze and Maruschak, 2008: 1). In a society that boasts family values, one might wonder why the criminal justice system does not better utilize alternatives to incarceration in ways that keep parents and their children together (Foster and Hagan 2007; Rodriguez *et al.*, 2009).

As Foucault (2009) observed, alternatives to incarceration do not eliminate the social control; instead, they serve to extend it into the community by imposing varying degrees of supervision on offenders. Consequently, sociologists and criminologists worry over the net-widening problem inherent in community corrections (Cohen, 1979, 1985; Welch, 2005a). Discussed previously in Chapter 4, the creation of more alternatives expands the net of criminal justice, drawing into the system less serious offenders who otherwise would not have been formally processed. Policy analysts point out that community corrections programs run the risk of encompassing a larger – and perhaps different – population than originally expected (Austin and Irwin, 2001). In a sense, such programs serve as additives, not alternatives, to incarceration. Morris and Tonry summarize the problem of net-widening:

> Many alternative punishments, including the community service order, are supported by the argument that they will be imposed on those who otherwise would receive a jail or prison term. This claim proves exceedingly difficult to measure, and there is a considerable record of the pool of offenders sentenced to the 'alternative' being drawn not from those who otherwise would have gone to jail or prison but from those who otherwise would have been sentenced to a less restrictive punishment – to probation or to a suspended sentence.
>
> (1990: 157–8)

The problem of net-widening leads to questions about the overall usefulness of programs that include offenders who should be diverted from the system. Moreover, financial questions concerning these programs persist; indeed, it has been suggested that net-widening results in cost-widening (Bottoms *et al.*, 2004; Morris and Tonry, 1990; Welch, 1999a).

SUMMARY

This chapter explores the many strategies and programs related to alternatives to incarceration. The first section examines probation and parole in their historical and present-day contexts by citing the influence of politics, economics, and technology. Discussion also extends to the technical procedures, showing how cases proceed through the system. In the second portion of the chapter, an array of community corrections are presented, in particular, pre-trial diversion, pre-trial release, dispute resolution and restitution, community service, day fines and probation fees, work release, halfway houses, and intensive supervision programs (ISPs). The chapter also evaluates electronic monitoring and correctional boot camps while remaining mindful of their implications to social control and net widening.

REVIEW QUESTIONS

1 What is the difference between inclusionary and exclusionary measures of social control? Give some examples of each.
2 Why is it difficult to assess the effectiveness of probation and parole?
3 How have political, economic, and technological forces shaped community corrections?
4 What are the criticisms of correctional boot camps?
5 What are the limitations of community corrections?

RECOMMENDED READINGS

Clear, T. and Dammer, H. (2000) *The Offender in the Community.* Belmont, CA: West/Wadsworth.

Maruna, S. (2001) *Making Good: How Ex-convicts Reform and Rebuild Their Lives.* Washington, DC: American Psychological Association.

Petersilia, J. (1997) *Community Corrections: Probation, Parole, and Intermediate Sanctions.* New York: Oxford University Press.

Rothman, D. J. (1980) *Conscience and Convenience: The Asylum and Its Alternatives in Progressive America.* Boston: Little, Brown.

Simon, J. (1993) *Poor Discipline: Parole and the Social Control of the Underclass, 1890–1990.* Chicago: University of Chicago Press.

CHAPTER 14

Working in Prison

It's hard working with people. My next job will be with machinery, something that doesn't talk back (Sarah Lehane, corrections officer)

LEARNING OBJECTIVES

After studying this chapter, you should be able to answer the following questions:

1 What are the various forms of power that corrections officers rely on in controlling prisoners?
2 What are the dominant features of the social world of corrections officers?
3 What is it like to work inside a prison?
4 What is it like for women corrections officers to work in a male prison?
5 How do corrections officers strive to regain control over their workplace?

In a revealing interview, Dr Peter Carlson, a former federal warden, discussed his experience working in prison. When asked about the prevalence of myths and misconceptions perpetuated by the media, he responded:

> I have made a concerted effort to avoid watching movies and television shows that are focused on corrections unless a friend specifically tells me it is worthwhile. The entertainment media typically portrays a correctional worker as stupid or corrupt, or stupid *and* corrupt. While each trait may occasionally appear within the profession, these qualities are found in all walks of life.

It is to our credit as a society that we particularly shun these characteristics when we find them in any of our law enforcement agencies. It may be *de rigueur* to expect integrity issues from a businessperson or a politician, but our culture will not tolerate unethical behavior from those who are expected to enforce the law.

Recognizing that movies or shows that are about corrections cannot hold an audience's attention by showing the mundane aspects of working 'inside,' popular entertainment shows tend to focus on the extreme and the unusual. For example, the HBO series *'OZ'* crams more serious incidents (e.g. rape, abuse, violence, theft, and general corruption) in one 30-minute segment than a typical correctional worker will see in a full career of correctional work. This media portrayal of corrections does a huge disservice to the profession. Many people have formed such an image of corrections that they would not want to accept employment in such a wicked and evil environment. Once employed in a correctional facility, one comes to the understanding that most inmates behave reasonably well while confined and do not present a significant threat to the correctional work force.

In fairness I want to mention one prison-related movie that I did find to fairly represent the good and bad of corrections: *The Green Mile.* I really loved the movie and, science fiction elements aside, I thought the film truly presented the fact that correctional workers are basically good folks doing a tough job.

(Personal interview, September 26, 2003)

INTRODUCTION

Over the past several decades, American corrections has emerged as a wide and sprawling apparatus of social control, adversely affecting the lives of increasingly more citizens. Due to greater legislation espousing tough-on-crime measures, the courts have continued a trend of locking up large volumes of offenders, including those convicted of non-violent drug violations. In response, prisons and jails have increased personnel so as to deal with their booming populations. Other chapters consider various penal work issues, such as juvenile corrections (Chapter 7), minority correctional workers (Chapter 8), death row (Chapter 10), detention (Chapter 11), probation, parole, and boot camps (Chapter 13), and healthcare workers in corrections (Chapter 16). This chapter explores in depth the corrections profession while focusing on the forms of power that officers use to manage and control inmates. In doing so, the social world of officers is given a critical look, in particular the so-called 'guard' subculture alongside key facets of prison work. Similarly, attention is turned to the socialization of correctional staff as well as concerns over female officers assigned to male prisons. Discussion concludes with a glimpse of how custodial personnel members strive to gain control over the prison work environment.

Figure 14.1 Old prison jail cells with the doors closed at a historic Idaho prison.
© iStockphoto.com

THE SOCIAL WORLD OF COs

For decades, researchers have examined correctional officers (COs) by way of participant observation, interviews, and surveys. Early explorations included descriptions that ridiculed prison workers. For instance, one observer remarked that some guards were 'less than quick-witted, less than the highest level of intelligence' and referred to a few of them as 'sadists' (Davidson, 1974: 30). More recent studies, however, tend to portray COs in a more sympathetic light, often as 'regular guys' who in the context of a stressful and hazardous environment simply do the best job they can. Still, the literature covers an array of work issues and problems. Philliber notes: 'A review of current research yields the distinct impression that COs [correctional officers] are alienated, cynical, burned out, stressed but unable to admit it, suffering from role conflict of every kind, and frustrated beyond imagining' (1987: 9; Herberts, 1998; Kauffman, 1988; Stojkovic, 2003). So as to offer a fuller account of prison work, this section considers the prevailing themes and findings of research on correctional officers (See 'Comparative Corrections: An Australian Squarehead Working in Prison' below.)

Correctional work in transition

In his pioneering research, Ben Crouch (1991) attends to the transition of guard work over the past few decades in view of a changing social context. The most consequential developments have been the following: the debate over rehabilitation, changes in the size and composition of inmate populations, and judicial intervention. As a result of the re-emergence of rehabilitation in the late 1950s, it was presumed that COs were struggling with role conflict insofar as they felt torn between controlling inmates and rehabilitating them. However, despite a wealth of research citing role conflict among officers, Toch and Klofas found 'no evidence of "role conflict" among officers, of unendurable strain, cognitive dissonance or experienced pressure of conflicting goals' (1982: 43–4; see Jacobs and Retsky, 1975; Pogrebin, 1978, 1980; Pogrebin and Atkins, 1983). It is now generally understood that a major problem in role-conflict research is that many of the investigators are actually studying different things. Therefore understanding the extent of role conflict requires better clarification and measurement of the concept itself (Philliber, 1987).

During the earliest stages of the prison population boom, COs were forced to adjust their work styles because they found themselves processing and supervising a greater influx of convicts. Naturally, as inmates increasingly outnumbered officers, they felt overwhelmed, stressed out, and spread too thin. In periods of increased demands, correctional staff members are expected to work harder and participate in tasks and duties that might be outside their areas of expertise. If these additional demands are ill-defined, then COs are likely to experience role ambiguity whereby they lack a clear understanding of what is expected of them. Overcrowding also exerts pressure on officers in large part because the inmates they deal with are more frustrated, upset, and angry.

Finally, as noted earlier in previous chapters, the emergence of judicial intervention to protect the civil rights of inmates forced additional changes and pressures on prison management. The judiciary has reversed its hands-off policy in dealing with prisoners' complaints, thereby upsetting the traditional power relationships between COs and inmates (see Alpert *et al.*, 1983; Crouch and Marquart, 1989; Haas, 1977, 1981).

In addition to role conflict and role ambiguity, Crouch (1991) points to other problems affecting the worklife of a CO: danger on the job, loss of control, stress, and deviant behavior.

Danger on the job

As mentioned, prisons are inherently hazardous and dangerous work settings. Until the 1960s, inmate assaults against COs were relatively infrequent. However, as the power base in prisons underwent changes, prisoners became more willing to confront the administration legally and even challenge guards physically (Freeman, 2000). Officers rarely hide their concerns about their physical safety on the job; indeed, many of them identify danger as the major drawback in working in prisons (Jacobs, 1981; Lombardo, 1981; Chapter 9).

Loss of control

As discussed in the case study of Stateville penitentiary, later in the chapter, authoritarian dominance over inmates is a thing of the past. That restructuring of power in prisons is perceived by COs in two ways. First they view the restructuring of power as a loss of control over inmates. Second, they subsequently experience a sense of abandonment by the administration, which is perceived as siding with convicts. Yet the question remains: how have officers reacted to that perceived loss of control and abandonment? Research points to several ways in which COs may respond to the loss of control and abandonment. Alienation stands as a common reaction among officers because they feel that they no longer have control over their work environment. Some officers may also become punitive to the extent that they assault inmates or misuse disciplinary action against them. Finally, officers may develop cynical attitudes in the workplace. Such cynicism leads some to retreat within the organization by avoiding responsibility and by putting forth only minimal effort (Poole and Regoli, 1981, 1980a, 1980b; Toch and Klofas, 1982; Webb and Morris, 2002).

Stress

Stress remains the key characteristic of COs' lives because it stems from so many different sources, and it greatly affects them not only at work but also while off duty. For years, researchers have devoted considerable time analyzing stress among officers (Cheek and Miller, 1983; Cullen *et al.*, 1985; Guenther and Guenther, 1974; Stalgaitis *et al.*, 1982; Stinchcomb, 1986). The following are identified as key sources of such stress:

- role conflict and role ambiguity;
- lack of communication with superiors and contradictory goals;
- lack of standard policies;
- little input into decisions;
- little training;
- the characteristics of corrections work itself, such as danger and lack of predictability;
- factors external to the system, such as being trapped in the job and earning a low salary.

Further research has located key factors contributing to high stress among officers: working in a maximum security prison; being female; having more years of corrections work experience; and lacking supervisory, peer, and family support. Many officers often fail to openly acknowledge their stress, adhering to the imperatives of a subculture of 'macho male guards.' Perhaps as result they suffer from a higher-than-average number of stress-related illnesses while reporting high rates of divorce (Cheek and Miller, 1983; Slate, 1996; Cullen *et al.*, 1985; Lancefield *et al.*, 1997; Wright and Sweeney, 1996).

Racial and gender integration of the CO forces

As the field of corrections is becoming less of a 'good ol' white boy' network and includes more female and minority COs, the workforce is undergoing dramatic changes (see Chapters 6, 8). Although experts agree that these changes are for the better, such developments have immediate consequences insofar as the guard force has a tendency to become more fragmented. While addressing matters of race and gender, correctional institutions continue to move toward work environments that are better integrated in ways that also improve inmate management (Bowling and Phillips, 2002; Britton, 2003; Edgar and Martin, 2004; Spencer *et al.*, 2009).

Deviant behavior

Officer deviance involves the drifting from established rules and policies. Serious violations and crimes committed by officers include the following: introduction of trafficking and contraband, grand theft, warehouse sabotage, sexual relations with inmates, bartering with convicts, inappropriate use of force, horseplay leading to injury of prisoners, assisting in escape, and theft of weapons. Understandably, those forms of misconduct disrupt institutional security and management while adding to the financial costs of operation (Crawley, 2004a; Crouch, 1991; Souryal, 2009).

COMPARATIVE CORRECTIONS

An Australian Squarehead Working in Prison

Quite often when people in the free world meet someone who is employed in a prison, they assume that person to be a member of the security staff, namely a corrections officer. Although corrections officers constitute the bulk of the workforce in a prison, there are many other types of correctional workers – administrators, program directors, healthcare providers, and educators, to name just a few. Not only corrections officers but also convicts commonly view these workers as being different due in large part to their higher socioeconomic status. Unlike many of the officers and inmates, these workers come to be employed in corrections after years of higher education and experience in other fields. This class divide is not unique to the United States; indeed, prisons in other nations also employ various professionals with middle-class backgrounds.

In Australia, those persons are called *squareheads*. Raised in a middle-class neighborhood and benefiting from all that privilege has to offer, David Denborough chose to work in a prison, teaching welfare/sociology to long-termers in a maximum security prison. In an effort to explore the class divide, Denborough naively asked the prisoners what they would have called him if they had met as children. Flatly, one inmate replied, 'a squarehead.' 'When I asked him what that word meant, he elaborated with a grin: "A stuck-up poof who can't fuck" ' (Denborough, 2001:75).

Being middle-class and well educated did not keep Denborough from exploring the implications of social class. Inspired by feminist writings and his father's anti-nuclear protest, Denborough set out to challenge the status quo by exploring the consequences of imprisonment. 'In many ways, choosing to work in a men's maximum-security prison was the result of wanting to know more about the most masculine institution in our culture. My first crucial learning was that men like me – white, middle class men – are generally not found in the prison system' (p. 73). Moreover, Denborough notes, to be middle class means that one's culture is rarely the 'object' of analysis. Being a 'professional' allows the middle class to maintain an invisible privilege.

While working in prisons, 'professionals' often deny the impact of class relations by mystifying the correctional enterprise, referring to prisons as 'correctional facilities' knowing full well that the inmates are not undergoing rehabilitation.

> Becoming aware of these issues of class has similarly altered my views on crime. Where once my perception of crime involved stereotypical views of working-class men committing property offenses or street crimes, now the first image to flash into my mind is the crime that is prison. I think of the crime that the middle-class commit in allowing those who live in poverty to be criminalized and brutalized. I realize now that the use of prisons does not reduce violence; instead it both creates and moves it around so that it occurs behind prison walls, among working-class people. It was a further shock to my squarehead consciousness to discover that many people who commit armed robberies understand their actions through sophisticated analyses of capitalism and that some are knowledgeable about whole histories of which I am completely unaware, histories of worker or prison movements.
>
> (Denborough, 2001: 76)

Denborough's critical examination of the role of socioeconomics in corrections reminds us that the class divide is a defining element in criminal justice, not only in countries known for their repressive incarceration practices but also in more democratized societies such as Australia, Western Europe, Canada, and the United States. It is not surprising that many so-called 'squareheads' who have worked in prisons eventually make their way into academia, where they share with students their liberal, and at times radical, views on corrections. In the words of Denborough, 'Working in prisons means that I now witness injustice that once I did not see. It is a part of privilege to have the option to be cocooned from the results of injustice including poverty and incarceration. Being a witness brings further responsibilities to reach out to my own kind, my people' (p. 79).

THE 'GUARD' SUBCULTURE

A popular topic among penologists has been the 'guard' subculture. Sociologists and anthropologists define a subculture as a 'more or less coherent assembly of beliefs and perspectives which borrows its form and content from a wider culture in which it is embedded' (Mann, 1984: 382). In this sense, a subculture features exaggerated ideas that are promoted and shared by its members. Crouch and Marquart (1990b) found that the guard subculture is vital to the occupational socialization of the recruit. Rookies listen to, observe, and imitate ranking officers. Moreover, the presence of the guard subculture teaches rookies the following: how to perceive convicts, how to anticipate trouble, and how to manage inmates.

Perceiving inmates

Experienced officers introduce rookies to the 'proper' perspective toward inmates, which means perceiving them as lazy and adverse to hard work, as well as assuming that they turned to crime as the easy way out. Similarly, officers portray some convicts as being particularly menacing. The recounting of atrocities or 'war stories' reinforces these perceptions.

> An example of an atrocity story shared at Midwest [prison] involves an inmate who tried to procure sexual favors from his cellmate. Despite his cellmate's pleas the aggressor tortured him by sticking a pencil under his fingernails. Still refusing to give in, or even cry out, the attacker poked both his eyes out with the pencil. The tortured inmate still refused to submit. In desperation, the aggressor placed the pencil in his victim's nose, ramming it into his brain and killing him. Once his victim was dead, the torturer sodomized the body.
>
> (Crouch and Marquart, 1990b: 277)

Certainly, the veracity of such stories should be questioned, since many of these anecdotes persist as folk tales and legends. Nevertheless, such stories are an important part of the subculture since they serve the function of shaping and affirming the perception that some prisoners are especially dangerous. Another activity that shapes perceptions is the *sorting* of inmates, which goes beyond the formal classifications. Experienced officers point out to rookies that they need to differentiate between the troublemakers and the 'model' prisoners. Such sorting transcends observed inmate behaviors and frequently is based on racial and ethnic slurs (Crouch and Marquart, 1990b: 280; Farkas and Manning, 1997; Riley, 2000; Stojkovic, 1996b).

Anticipating trouble

Also by way of the guard subculture, rookies learn how to anticipate trouble, such as escapes, hostage situations, riots, collective vendettas, the possession of weapons, and consumption of homemade intoxicants known as 'hooch' (Crouch and Marquart, 1990b).

Managing inmates

Rookies are reminded that they must control prisoners by their words and actions. This form of prisoner management style is largely informal. By keeping a social distance, officers are expected to keep convicts off balance as a pre-emptive move against inmate games. In the days before widespread professionalization, some officers routinely used profanity when instructing inmates: 'Listen, motherfucker, get over there and (mop the floor) or I'm going to do somethin' bad to you' god damn ass' (Crouch and Marquart, 1990b: 282). Similarly, some officers would 'act crazy' in an effort to 'mess' with the minds of convicts. 'Acting crazy means the guard responds to the inmate in ways quite unrelated to the inmate's question or problem; in this way, the inmate is put off and becomes uncertain of himself.' For instance, in the following case, a prisoner approaches an officer to request a visit to the infirmary (Crouch and Marquart, 1990b: 283):

Officer: What the hell do you want?
Inmate: Boss, I got a terrible headache. Can I go to the hospital?
Officer: (Loudly) How the hell do I know you've got a headache?
Inmate: Well … (Inmate returns to his cell.)

It should be noted that among researchers there is debate over whether a guard subculture actually exists. Early on Duffee (1975) proposed that his findings supported the presence of a guard subculture while Klofas (1984) argued that the observed differences between officers, administrators, and inmates were not sufficient to constitute a guard subculture. For instance, merely socializing after work does not in itself constitute a subculture (see Esselstyn, 1966). Nevertheless, Philliber (1987) concedes that superior officers do teach and reward lower-ranking guards for various control tactics used against inmates, which might be interpreted as evidence of a subculture (Marquart, 1986). However, scholars point out that many studies do not adequately define or measure the presence of a guard subculture, suggesting once again that researchers are studying different things (see Conover, 2000; Hepburn, 1985; Lombardo, 1981; Poole and Regoli, 1981).

THE STANFORD UNIVERSITY MOCK PRISON EXPERIMENT

Research suggests that the ways in which the prison world is arranged have an enormous impact on both inmate and staff behavior. One of the most startling investigations was the mock prison experiment conducted at Stanford University (Haney *et al.*, 1973; Zimbardo, 1972, 1983). In that study, two dozen men responded to a newspaper advertisement to volunteer for a simulated prison project. Zimbardo and his associates note that these men were mature, emotionally stable, normal, intelligent college students (without criminal records) from middle-class homes throughout the US and Canada. At the flip of a coin, these subjects were randomly assigned to the inmate group or the guard group. Subjects were expected to assume their roles in ways they felt were appropriate.

After being oriented to the prison, the guards were permitted to formally construct the rules and their enforcement. Soon the prisoners were processed and incarcerated, and the events which took place quickly went beyond the expectations of the researchers:

> At the end of only six days we had to close down our mock prison because what we saw was frightening.
>
> In less than a week the experience of imprisonment undid (temporarily) a lifetime of learning; human values were suspended, self-concepts were challenged and the ugliest, most base, pathological side of human nature surfaced. We were horrified because we saw some boys (guards) treat others as if they were despicable animals, taking pleasure in cruelty, while other boys (prisoners) became servile, dehumanized robots who thought only of escape, of their individual survival and of the mounting hatred for the guards.

The Stanford University mock prison experiment generated much interest, but it also remains controversial due in part to its methodology. That is, the experiment encouraged subjects to uncritically embrace their stereotypical perceptions of guards. Unlike the case with standard hiring procedures, the prospective officers were not screened nor formally trained. Instead, the experiment randomly assigned subjects to the guard group then issued uniforms, silver reflective sunglasses, night sticks, and 'blanket authority to run the prison as they saw fit' (Johnson, 1987: 121). (In real life, correctional officers working directly with inmates do not carry weapons.)

Despite its flaws, the study points to the importance of socialization and the adoption of a role, whether that is the role of the inmate or that of a guard. In each case, there are role expectations and behaviors that are determined by the structural arrangements of prison. Zimbardo adds: 'Individual behavior is largely under the control of social forces and environmental contingencies rather than on personality traits, character, will power or other empirically unvalidated constructs' (1983: 101; 1972, 2007; see Cheliotis, 2006; Lurigio, 2009).

THE SOCIALIZATION OF COs

Although questions remain about the existence of a *guard* subculture, it is clear that correctional officers undergo a distinct form of occupational socialization. Every occupation has its unique patterns of organizational orientation, maintenance, and ritual, and the corrections profession is no exception. One becomes a CO via occupational socialization, and that process teaches them not only the *formal* procedures of penal work but also, just as importantly, the *informal* ones. As mentioned, formal procedures involve a long list of official rules and policies created in the context of a bureaucratic prison; by contrast, the informal procedures pertain to the unofficial ways in which officers deal with convicts. Both formal and informal procedures are determined, first and foremost, by the ways in which prison is socially arranged (Bennett *et al.*, 2008; Gray and Salole, 2006).

Becoming a prison CO

The specific socialization of real COs, not subjects in an experiment, is treated in the work of Crouch and Marquart (1990b), who draw on their own research and experiences as COs, as well as the contributions of other investigators. Perhaps the question most often asked of a corrections officer is: why did you become a prison officer? That question is understandable from the view that few children dream of growing up to work as COs. Those who have conducted interviews have found that officers themselves did not have these ambitions early in life. In fact, they report being at the crossroads of life (seeking better employment) at the time of their entry into the field of corrections. Referring to these situations as turning points, Crouch and Marquart note that many of the COs were unemployed or dissatisfied with their current jobs at the time they pursued correctional work.

Still the question remains as to why they would pursue this particular line of work. Several reasons persist. Many of the men had military experience and found that criminal justice agencies, with their emphasis on a paramilitary organization, were particularly interested in hiring them. Two additional considerations were proximity and social relationships. Many applied to work in a prison because they lived in close proximity to the institution, and many reported having friends or relatives who introduced them to prison work. Some applicants are drawn to corrections from a social-work orientation (those wanting to help inmates) while others are perversely fascinated by the idea of having power over convicts. Still, most recruits enter the world of prisons due to some key features of prison work – a steady paycheck and a secure job. Moreover, recruits find that few technical skills are needed at the hiring stage (see Conover, 2000; Kifer *et al.*, 2003).

Formal training

Upon being hired, recruits are formally oriented to the institution. At that stage, they undergo classroom training featuring lectures that address the mechanics of the facility. Recruits learn the operation of locks and keys and two-way radios, as well as counting procedures. Supervisors reinforce a consistent theme at that stage of the training: that is, recruits are always reminded not to trust inmates and to avoid doing them favors or associating with them (Gordon, 2006; Josi, 1996; Lambert *et al.*, 2009).

Informal training: entering the prison world

Although the formal training certainly has its place in occupational socialization, the real introduction to the job takes place informally as the new recruits become immersed in the prison environment. At that phase, rookies begin to learn the ropes, and they find the prison world to be dramatically different from the free world.

> The ghetto-like atmosphere of a maximum-security prison is quite overpowering to the uninitiated. Perhaps as many as 2,000 men live, eat, work, urinate, sleep, and recreate in a very limited concrete steel building. This concentration of life presents the new guard with an unfamiliar and at the very least distracting sensory experience as simultaneously he hears doors clanging, inmates talking or shouting, radios and televisions playing, and food trays banging; he smells an institutional blend of food, urine, paint, disinfectant, and sweat. And what he sees is a vast array of inmate personalities portrayed by evident behavior styles.
>
> (Crouch and Marquart, 1990b: 273)

Rookies must adapt to other salient features of the prison world – especially the sexual behavior apparent among convicts. Officers are accustomed to witnessing such behaviors as masturbation (the most common sexual activity) as well as voluntary homosexual relations. Some of those relations involve prison 'queens,' whose overt homosexuality and transvestite tendencies are characterized by the altering of their physical appearances to those of women. So-called 'queens' tend to pluck their eyebrows, shave their body hair, and wear feminine clothing (Eigenberg, 2000; Hensley *et al.*, 2002; Hensley, 2003).

Rookies also undergo occasional ridicule from convicts who look at them as prison cops. Further, their uniforms, like those of the police in the free world, are symbols that they are agents of social control. That viewpoint is expressed in the argot of inmates in which officers are called an array of nicknames: 'the Man,' 'screws,' 'the heat,' 'bulls,' 'hacks,' 'Pecker neck,' 'Squeaky,' 'Tomato Face,' and 'Pussy Foot' (Crouch and Marquart, 1990b: 274; Farkas and Manning, 1997; Riley, 2000). To determine if they have the 'guts' to be an officer prisoners commonly test rookies. Inmates draw from a host of tactics intended to startle, fool, and embarrass rookies. For example, 'as doors clang shut, the rookie may hear an inmate scream in mock pain and terror. "My hand! You got my hand!" If the officer rapidly reopens the doors in fear, he will have been played a fool' (Crouch and Marquart, 1990b: 275).

As mentioned, Crouch and Marquart (1990b) found that for recruits, the guard subculture facilitates the learning process. In addition to the aforementioned facets of socialization, recruits eventually internalize three fundamental tenets of prison work:

1 Security and control are paramount.
2 Maintain social distance from inmates.
3 Be tough, be knowledgeable, and be able to handle inmates.

Outcomes of CO socialization

After rookies complete the rites of passage, questions still remain about their future success as COs. Crouch and Marquart (1990b) present four basic outcomes among COs: (1) the abject and limited failures, (2) the ritualists, (3) the successful officers, (4) the insiders.

The abject and limited failures

Abject failures are those COs who quit during the early stages of their career, and they do so for various reasons, ranging from fear to racial discrimination (Jacobs and Grear, 1977). Limited failures are officers who continue to show up for work but simply cannot project the proper 'guard' image. Sometimes this failure is due to their size (whether too small or overweight), which elicits constant ridicule from inmates. Limited failures are often assigned to posts where they have minimal contact with inmates.

The ritualist

Some COs tend to retreat from taking their jobs seriously and show up simply to earn a paycheck. Ritualists, then, keep a low profile and go through the motions but actually avoid responsibilities.

The successful officers

Successful officers are those who are worthy of respect by both peers and convicts. This categorization is not meant to imply that they are liked by others, but that they represent the CO role in every facet. That is, they demonstrate excellent skills in exercising the fundamental tenets of prison work. Generally, successful officers are viewed as being fair-minded and mature.

The insiders

Insiders are successful COs who achieve additional mobility in the prison hierarchy. Still, many officers believe that promotions have less to do with merit and more with politics. COs call it having 'pull,' 'juice,' or 'connections' (Jacobs, 1977; Welch, 1984, 1989a). It is not surprising that the ambition of those on the 'fast track' is recognized and rewarded by superiors (Conover, 2000; Crouch and Marquart, 1990b).

BASE OF POWER IN CONTEMPORARY PRISONS

As we shall discuss in detail, James B. Jacobs's *Stateville* greatly contributes to the understanding of the various shifts of power in corrections. Still, a key question persists: 'If the power of prison COs has been altered and reduced by recent social, legal and bureaucratic intrusions in American prisons, as has been reported by many observers, then what is the base of power by which guards currently exert control over prisoners?' (Hepburn, 1985: 145; see Lancefield *et al.*, 1997; Liebling and Price, 1999, 2001).

In his research, John Hepburn set out to identify the ways in which COs gain prisoner compliance. Although correctional institutions function as bureaucracies, they are also distinctly coercive organizations, in that officers must preserve institutional security and internal order. In doing so, COs may rely on one or more bases of power. In this context, Hepburn borrows from sociologist Max Weber, who defines power as 'the probability that one actor within a social relationship will be in a position to carry out his own will despite resistance, regardless of the basis on which this probability rests' (1968: 53). Hepburn then adds: "The basis of one's power is a resource to be mobilized, and one can have multiple bases of power, or resources" (1985: 146). The following are the bases of power from which COs may choose.

• *Legitimate power.* Legitimate power derives from a formal authority to command. That is, 'the prison guard has the right to exercise control over prisoners by virtue of the structural relationship between the position of the guard and position of the prisoner' (Hepburn, 1985: 146).

Figure 14.2   Sergeant D. Turner watching inmates as they walk down the long hallway on their way out to the recreation yard, September 4, 2009. Due to the jail overcrowding the inmates get only four hours of recreation a week at the Deuel Vocational Institution near Tracy, California.

Photo by Tony Avelar/The Christian Science Monitor/Getty Images.

- *Coercive power.* Since prisons are inherently coercive organizations, it is understandable that coercive power emerges as a prominent method of control. Hepburn points out that coercive power emanates from the convict's perception that COs have the ability and willingness to punish disobedience.
- *Reward power.* COs may also rely on the distribution of rewards to control inmates. Indeed officers can be influential in granting inmate privileges, housing and work assignments, the accumulation of 'good time,' and release on furloughs or parole. In addition to these formal rewards, officers may also dispense informal rewards such as promoting special favors and overlooking minor infractions.
- *Expert power.* If COs exhibit special skills, knowledge, or expertise, inmates may interpret such competence as a form of expert power. Officers may be viewed, especially in treatment-oriented institutions, as part of the treatment staff, thus possessing counseling and conflict-resolution skills.
- *Referent power.* Inmate compliance may also be based on the COs' ability to earn the respect and admiration of prisoners through leadership and persuasive diplomacy. COs who are fair-minded and evenhanded often gain the respect of inmates.

Following his survey of COs in five prisons, Hepburn found that of 'the five bases of power evaluated, legitimate and expert power are thought by guards to be the most important reasons why prisoners comply. Referent power ranked third, followed by coercive and reward power, respectively' (1985: 159). Do those sources of power run counter to the bureaucratization of prisons? No. Hepburn believes that reliance on legitimate and expert power conforms to a bureaucracy's emphasis on position and expertise. Moreover, it is suggested that the use of these types of power may contribute to more harmonious and humane relationships between officers and convicts (Britton, 2003; Jones, 2006a; Vuolo and Kruttshnitt, 2008; Welch, 1987). (See 'Working in Corrections: A Warden's View of Correctional Work' below.)

STATEVILLE PENITENTIARY: FROM PATRIARCHAL TO BUREAUCRATIC CORRECTIONS

In his classic book, *Stateville: The Penitentiary in Mass Society* (1977), James B. Jacobs makes a systematic examination of the prison by studying the administrative methods used to control inmates. Attending to several distinct time periods, Jacobs's analysis was guided by key theoretical insights of Max Weber insofar as the authority exercised by the administration was influenced by shifts in political dominance, correctional reform, and changes in the convict population. The important phases in the history of Stateville are as follows.

Search for a stable equilibrium, 1925–36

Modeled after Jeremy Bentham's panopticon, Stateville opened in 1925, with a mission to provide Illinois with a humane alternative to Joliet that was built in

1860 and criticized for its brutal and inhumane conditions (see Chapters 2 and 4). Soon, administrative problems also surfaced at Stateville as officials criticized the warden and his staff of political patronage. Due to the void in a strong administrative leadership, inmate gangs emerged as the basis of institutional power. In sum, Jacobs recognized that external political forces could disrupt efforts to achieve internal order: 'The influence on the prison of the partisan political system had to be reduced before a stable social order could be achieved' (1977: 27).

Emergence of personal dominance, 1936–61

In 1936, Joseph F. Ragen was appointed warden with hopes that he would become the 'reform' warden; indeed, Ragen lived up to this expectation as he personally dominated Stateville. Ragen became known as 'Mr Prison,' and his ability to achieve total internal order by way of constructing an authoritarian system was contingent upon his 'gaining a large measure of economic, political, and moral autonomy' (Jacobs, 1977: 28). His skills and leadership galvanized Ragen's control of Stateville. Among the politicians and elite staff members, Ragen earned respect and intense loyalty. However, many of the rank-and-file officers feared Ragen and resented his authoritarian style. Ragen worked as a hands-on warden, personally inspecting staff and convicts daily. He ruled both officers and prisoners with an iron hand. Inmates were subjected to harsh punishment and strict discipline while co-opting convict leaders with legitimate and illegitimate opportunities. Few dared to challenge Ragen's authority, thereby further transforming his administration into a patriarchal organization.

Challenge to institutional authority, 1961–70

The Ragen administration officially came to an end in 1961 when he retired as warden to become director of public safety of Illinois. Yet his presence was still felt at Stateville until he retired from his position as director of that post in 1965. The new warden, Frank Pate, could not instill his own style of leadership, and many administrative directives continued to emanate from Ragen's office in the state capital.

Soon social forces outside the institution began to seriously challenge Stateville's administration. 'Staff reaction to the loss of institutional autonomy, the emergence of racial consciousness, and the penetration of juridical norms, was a consistent strategy of resistance' (Jacobs, 1977: 52). These challenges were extensions of social changes in the larger society, most notably the civil rights movement. During that time, black Muslim inmates earned support from the courts in challenging the warden's policies that curbed prisoners' rights. Eventually those external forces forced a major shift in administrative authority. Stateville's reliance on a charismatic authority was replaced by rational authority in the form of a bureaucracy. The warden was now viewed less as an individual (as was Ragen) and more as an 'office' occupied by a high-level bureaucrat. Due to his inability to adopt a more flexible administrative regime in the light of these new developments, Warden Pate resigned in 1970.

Emergence of a professional administration, 1970–75

The transformation from a patriarchal organization driven by charismatic authority to a bureaucratic organization based on rational-legal authority was further established in 1970 when the Department of Corrections was created. The director, located in the state capital, usurped the autonomy once enjoyed by the warden. The system became further bureaucratized by certain initiatives. Top administration positions were filled by highly educated experts who supervised the development of rehabilitation programs, thereby bringing more specialists into the system. Furthermore, the department sought the advice of the American Correctional Association and a number of academic consultants.

A major consequence of those progressive changes was staff resistance from those who had worked under Ragen and Pate. That backlash was fueled by staff perceptions that the new administrators were permissive, favoring convicts over staff. Compounding matters, the inmate composition began changing. Soon four Chicago-based street gangs became conspicuously present in Stateville: the Blackstone Rangers (later renamed the Black P Stone Nation), the Devil's Disciple Nation (also known as the Black Gangster Disciple Nation), the Conservative Vice Lords, and the Latin Kings. These gangs posed an additional challenge to the staff and administration. COs could no longer intimidate prisoners into conforming to institutional rules; accordingly, as violence began to escalate, staff retreated. The solution to widespread violence was to isolate and segregate inmates. In sum, this period was characterized as a 'crisis in control,' and the newly installed human relations model failed to offset institutional tensions.

Restoration, 1975 and beyond

During this period, David Brierton took over the administrative reins at Stateville. He rejected the rehabilitation ideal and human relations model of management. In their place, Brierton further bureaucratized the institution by adopting a 'corporate' model that was rational, problem-solving, task-oriented, professional, cost-conscious, and detached. Under that new regime, Brierton believed that the system could effectively respond to institutional and inmate needs.

The lesson to be learned from Stateville, as developed by Jacobs, is that external social forces help shape the ways by which prisons graduate from an autocratic style of administration to a bureaucratized version of corrections. Again, in view of the social changes that took place in the 1960s and 1970s, present-day prisons are likely to remain somewhat less-than-total institutions (Farrington, 1992).

WORKING IN CORRECTIONS

A Warden's View of Correctional Work

As this chapter demonstrates, much of the focus on prison work is directed at corrections officers. Still, scholars should recognize other key correctional professionals, including those who hold administrative positions (Jacobs, 1977). In an effort to learn more about the administrative side of contemporary corrections, Dr Peter Carlson, a former federal warden, agreed to be interviewed.

To begin with, Dr. Carlson, would you please describe your professional career in corrections? How did you become interested in correctional work, and will you elaborate on each phase of your career?

I literally fell into corrections as a career. Following graduation with a BA in psychology from Willamette University in 1968, I took a job at the Oregon State Penitentiary, a job that I intended to limit to summer employment before I went to graduate school. In those days, a little-known federal agency known as LEAA (Law Enforcement Assistance Administration) would pay for undergraduate or graduate school if you agreed to work in the field of law enforcement or corrections. I loved working at the state prison and decided to take advantage of the federal funding and earn my master's degree while working. In those days there was no criminal justice degree so I pursued my MS in education, with an emphasis on 'disadvantaged populations.'

Two years later, my supervisor sat down with me and suggested that I had a future in the business but said he was not going to die or retire any time soon. He recommended I look at the federal system, where there were many more promotional opportunities. So I soon found myself heading to the US Penitentiary on McNeil Island, Washington. I was fascinated by the change in venue. I liked the camaraderie among the staff and have always appreciated that we all look out for one another's back. In the Federal Bureau of Prisons, staff always used the term 'Bureau Family' and it was true. I've been retired now for several years and I really miss the great people that I had the honor to work with over a span of 30 years.

I also liked the change in clientele. New types of inmates with crimes that were much more interesting: counterfeiters, spies, organized crime chiefs, and run-of-the-mill bank robbers. I enjoyed working with inmates. Our crooks always felt it was in their position description to try to snooker whatever they could from the staff, and I liked the give-and-take between us. Even during my assignments to high-security penitentiaries, I found that I enjoyed my time around our 'thugs.' Many people tend to portray correctional work as days of tension and high drama; while there were certainly tough moments, the majority of my time inside was very enjoyable and rewarding.

The federal system believed in transferring you when they promoted you, so as my career progressed, my wife, daughter, and I enjoyed various areas of the country. Over time we lived in many corners of the east, west, north, and south. As time passed and my experience grew, I eventually served as an associate warden, warden, and finally as the assistant director/regional director of the agency.

As a federal retiree today, I absolutely believe that I could not have picked a more rewarding career. I believe I had a positive impact on many inmates, helped develop and promote many exceptional staff members, and had the opportunity to serve our country as a federal law enforcement officer. Who could ask for more?

Looking back on your career, what are you most satisfied with in terms of your achievements? Conversely, what is most disappointing?

The highlight of my career was the exceptional colleagues with whom I worked. Many outstanding supervisors had a hand in shaping me as a young staff member, and I hope that I was able to give others similar assistance. If I was successful in developing others, I am a proud retiree. All of us need to remember that we are only as good as those around us, and we are dependent upon our co-workers for support, friendship, and our professional reputations.

What was disappointing? As a senior agency leader I had to make some hard decisions when dealing with personnel situations such as integrity issues and lapses of good judgment in the personal and professional lives of staff members. I believe all correctional and law enforcement officials are occasionally disappointed by some life decisions made by individual staff members that reflect poorly on one's agency.

By and large, I have been very pleased and proud of correctional workers as a group and believe they are public servants in the finest sense of the word.

From your point of view, what are the most serious problems and challenges facing corrections?

The challenges of correctional management, both inside a penal facility and outside in the community, are numerous. Serious issues include overcrowding, tight budgets, zealous interest in institutional oversight by politicians, prison gang management and daily security concerns, and staff issues are significant items of weight for all institutional leaders.

In my mind, the trend toward harsher sentencing practices and longer sentences represents one of the most worrisome problems in criminal justice today. Federal and state sentencing practices have become draconian and the result is more prisons and jails being built and substantial overcrowding for existing facilities. While I support this for violent offenders, I do not believe we benefit from longer terms of imprisonment for other categories of criminals.

Improving professionalism is an ongoing objective among criminal justice officials. In the realm of corrections, what areas of professionalism do you believe need the most improvement?

First let me hasten to say that the overwhelming majority of correctional workers today are outstanding citizens and true public servants. Correctional work is challenging and certainly not for everyone. Staff in the business must be self-confident, able to work well with others, and focused on doing their work efficiently and effectively. Correctional staff must have a high sense of integrity, as inmates and the community watch law enforcement personnel day-in and day-out and each one of us must be clear that we are role models in everything we do.

How can we improve professionalism? Improved recruitment practices are the most critical and swift means of improving the overall level of professionalism within the field. If we hire good people and train them well, the organization can't help but move into the future with a solid, professional workforce.

Give a correctional career serious consideration. The pay and career promotion opportunities are exceptional. As the recruitment slogan for the Federal Bureau of Prisons indicates, 'Do your career Justice!'

Describe your transition into academic life and discuss your plans for research and writing.

I've been a part of academia since my retirement in 1999 and serve as an associate professor at Christopher Newport University, a Virginia state university. I've prepared for this for many years by teaching as an adjunct professor and by completing my doctorate in public administration. I love my new profession and enjoy working with my new 'inmates' ... college students. I particularly like channeling some bright young students into corrections for their career.

I've co-edited one college text entitled *Prison and Jail Administration: Practice and Theory* and written numerous articles in professional journals. My research interests are varied; I am currently engaged in a study of new FBI agents that have left local law enforcement for federal employment. I will soon expand this study to include federal correctional workers.

For further reading on this topic see: Bryans, 2007; Cullen *et al.*, 2001; Murphy and Whitty, 2007.)

WOMEN COs IN MEN'S PRISONS

Guarding in men's prisons traditionally has been the occupational domain of white males. Recently, however, more women and minorities have joined the forces of correctional officers, despite resistance to their inclusion. As the CO force becomes more heterogeneous, it also becomes more fragmented. While Chapter 8 addresses concerns facing minority officers, this section focuses on women officers in men's prisons.

Most women working in the correctional system are not employed as COs; more often they serve as members of the clerical or food services staffs. In view of the resistance against women officers by male administrators as well as by the rank-and-file male staff, it is not surprising that most women occupy the lowest ranks of the CO hierarchy. Indeed, women have had more difficulty breaking through organizational barriers than have male minorities (Crouch, 1991). Early on, women applicants resorted to litigation so as to challenge the claim that being male is a bona fide occupational qualification for employment in men's prisons (Alpert, 1984).

Against allegations that females do not possess the ability to supervise and control inmates, women COs have proved otherwise. Early research found that women officers are not any more likely to be conned or manipulated than their male counterparts (Peterson, 1982). Although women officers are sometimes criticized for not being able to physically subdue aggressive convicts, they are credited with being able to prevent violence by effectively calming angry and upset inmates. Women officers also have to deal with concerns over inmate privacy, especially while male inmates shower or use the restroom; still, research suggests that male inmates are not particularly sensitive about such privacy issues (Kissel and Katasampes, 1980).

Due to various forms of resistance against women officers, it is important to realize that since women officers enter a profession and subculture dominated by males, it is not surprising that they are often subjected to sexist attitudes, remarks, and conduct. The prevalence of sexual harassment in the workplace in general leads to the assumption that men's prisons will likely not be dramatically transformed into less sexist environments for women anytime soon. Still, different types of discrimination need to be addressed, particularly as they affect promotion. Since women are attracted to correctional work for reasons similar to those of men (namely job security and salary), it is understandable that women will experience anger and frustration when overlooked for promotions. As mentioned, most women officers occupy the lowest ranks in men's prisons, and subsequently, are less likely to be promoted into supervisory positions largely due to institutional sexism and discrimination (see Britton, 2003; Jurik, 1985).

Much of the literature on women officers in men's prisons focuses on the negative aspects of their work (Jurik, 1985, 1988; Owen, 1988; Zimmer, 1986). However, Wright and Saylor surveyed women officers employed in federal institutions for men, and found those women 'regard working in male prisons as a positive experience. Job satisfaction is high, female prison workers have positive opinions about their supervisors, and they believe that they are personally effective in working with male inmates' (1991: 523). Clearly, as women officers continue to enter such non-traditional occupations as corrections, it is necessary to examine the positive as well as the negative features of their work (Britton, 1997; Martin and Jurik, 1996; Walters, 1993). (See 'Cultural Penology: Guarding Male Prisoners: A Woman's Perspective.' below.)

REGAINING CONTROL

The corrections profession is still undergoing considerable transition (see Liebling and Arnold, 2004; Ross *et al.*, 2008). In the process, COs collectively have set out to regain some of the control lost over the past few decades. In addition to the evolving bureaucratization of corrections, COs use two other means of restructuring prison relations: unionization and professionalization.

Unionization

A key trend in the corrections profession, similar to that of other criminal justice professions, is to unionize. This organizational development stems from COs feeling abandoned by both administrators and the courts which have handed down decisions in favor of prisoners' rights. Some of the areas of occupational concern for which officers rely on union leadership are increased wages, improved working conditions, and limiting of the power of administrators. In their attempt to gain more control over their work lives, however, COs find that unions cannot remedy other institutional problems, such as loss of control, loss of status, and racial tension (Jacobs, 1983). Moreover, because unions function on the principle of seniority, many low-ranking officers may find that unionization impedes promotions (Wynne, 1978). In the final analysis, unions may have only limited impact on the overall scheme of staff–management relations, especially when the bureaucratic and paramilitary aspects of the prison are taken into consideration. However, unionization does mark an important occupational development. COs are now reconceptualizing themselves as workers exercising their employee rights (Haghighi, 1996).

Professionalization

An issue commonly agreed upon by conservative, liberal, and radical penologists is that COs need and deserve continuing professionalization. Whereas unionization emerges from a horizontal alignment among officers, professionalization emanates from administrative initiatives. 'Professionalization connotes, among other things, the hiring of better-educated people, more sophisticated and protracted training, and the enlargement of or diversification of the guard role' (Crouch, 1991: 178). The objective of professionalization is to upgrade the staff in ways that promote more humane and professional management of inmates. In turn, the prison environment becomes less hostile and safer. However, numerous obstacles block such improvements. For example, professionalization is a strategy requiring firm financial investment. Moreover, additional resources are needed for both sophisticated training and salaries high enough not only to attract better-educated applicants but also to retain them. Understandably, political forces greatly interfere with additional appropriation of government funds for prison personnel (Jurik and Musheno, 1986; see Chapter 15).

Another problem, 'beyond informal resistance from "custody-oriented" staff and administrators, is the fact that the formal, paramilitary organization of prison security is structurally incompatible with professional autonomy' (Crouch, 1991: 178). Traditionally, prisons have relied on a strict adherence to hierarchical structures that are not conducive to processing input from the rank-and-file officers. In such structures, orders from the top filter down to the ranks, to the bottom. Finally, since correctional officers believe that they will experience more autonomy through professionalization, it is pointed out that legal developments actually limit correctional officer autonomy because their actions must comply with court directives. In sum, both unionization and professionalization potentially risk raising the expectations of correctional officers, only to lead to disappointment, dissatisfaction, and low morale (Crouch and Marquart, 1989).

CULTURAL PENOLOGY

A Woman's Perspective on Guarding Male Convicts

Souza-Baranowski, a large, maximum-security prison in Massachusetts, is named to memorialize a corrections officer and an industrial-arts instructor who were killed by an inmate in 1972 at Norfolk state penitentiary. Fittingly, tension between prisoners and staff continues at Souza-Baranowski, where 42-year-old Sarah Lehane works as a corrections officer. In 2001, as Lehane and her fellow officers supervised the mess hall during evening chow, an irate prisoner smashed an officer in the face with a tray. As the officer crumpled to the floor other inmates joined in the skirmish, kicking the injured officer. With more than 200 prisoners in the mess hall, corrections officers had the daunting task of rescuing the injured officer and subduing the aggressors while keeping the other prisoners at bay. Indeed, officers know full well that an incident such as that could quickly escalate into a major riot. At the center of the episode was Lehane, who instinctively came to the aid of the injured officer, hurling her body into the violent scrum or what she called 'the pig pile.' In less than three minutes, the melee produced injuries to nine officers, including a twisted knee and bruised shoulder for Lehane. Still, she felt lucky that day; another officer suffered a fractured skull and swelling of the brain (Conover, 2001).

Rather than celebrating a sense of victory against the prisoners, Lehane, who is closing in on 20 years' correctional experience, reflected on the risk of violence in her particular workplace, conceding that the incident rattled her. 'You tell yourself you're safe, and you wouldn't walk in the door if you didn't think so, but deep down – logically – you know it's not true, that if you've got guys doing triple life, nobody's safe in there" (Conover, 2001: 156).

Captain Tom Lehane, Sarah's husband, shared her feelings, having watched the violence on a video monitor from another location in the prison. Tom re-evaluated whether he thought it was good idea for his wife to work at Souza-Baranowski; eventually he suggested that she transfer to Framingham, the state prison for women where she had spent most of her career. 'The incident really put a strain on our marriage,' confessed Sarah. Still, Sarah was determined to stay at Souza-Baranowski, realizing that even as a woman in a male prison, she benefited from her years of experience. 'Seniority is everything and inmates respect officers who've put in time – they'll pull stuff on a rookie that they wouldn't with me.' Sarah notes that with experience, one learns to deal with tense situations that otherwise could explode into uncontrollable disturbances. Moreover, the ability to deal with volatile prisoners has little to do with the size and sex of the officer. Even if she had been male, 23 years old, and weighed 300 pounds, Lehane says, it wouldn't have helped her in the mini-riot: 'When there's 12 inmates on you, it's not a strength issue. You lose because of the numbers' (Conover, 2001: 154, 156; see Britton 1997; Martin and Jurik, 1996).

CONCLUSION

Working in prison, especially as a corrections officer, offers experiences rarely encountered by persons in other fields, even within criminal justice. Most officers' workdays involve virtually constant interaction with prisoners, many of whom are frustrated – and at times, volatile – due largely to the pains of imprisonment. It is the daily chore of officers to keep order in the institution while also maintaining the cooperation of convicts; in doing so, staff members must resort to various forms of power (e.g. legitimate power, reward power, expert power).

More so than any other component of criminal justice, corrections officers spend their work hours within a social world detached from the relative safety of the free world. Among the most notable features of the corrections officers' social

Figure 14.3 A prisoner working in a workshop in the San Sebastian Prison in San Jose, on August 27, 2009. The prison, which houses 653 prisoners, including 150 foreigners, has installed workshops for computing, carpentry, crafts, and literacy, to complement high school or college careers for many Costa Rican prisoners who are preparing for a life of freedom and, above all, to help endure captivity.

Photo by Yuri Cortez/AFP/Getty Images.

world are the dangers of the job that, along with various conflicts with inmates and administrators, produce tremendous stress. Penologists have long taken an interest in the work life of corrections officers, attending closely to the 'guard' subculture shaping their perceptions of convicts. Indeed, those perceptions, in turn, affect the ways they manage and control the prison population. Like members of other professions, corrections officers respond to occupational socialization – both formal and informal training – from which they construct shared meanings about the nature of their work. Relatedly, socialization for corrections officers, coupled with their various experiences on the job, produces distinctive outcomes (e.g., ritualists, successful officers). For both the keepers and the kept, the prison social world is contoured significantly by socioeconomic, racial, and gender considerations.

SUMMARY

This chapter focused on the corrections profession, and more specifically the social world of officers. In doing so, the discussion set out to depict what it is like to work in prison, addressing the various forms of power along with the many sources of job-related stress. While exploring the 'guard' subculture, key consideration was given to the socialization of officers that creates somewhat diverse careers in corrections. Finally, the chapter acknowledged that the corrections profession remains in transition as officers strive to regain control over their workplace; consequently, unionization and professionalization continue to transform the field of corrections.

REVIEW QUESTIONS

1 What are the most effective forms of power used to manage prisoners?
2 Describe the Stanford University mock prison experiment and elaborate on its flaws. What does that experiment teach us about the social psychology of the prison environment and what doesn't it teach us?
3 How did Stateville Penitentiary evolve over time, particularly in terms of its organizational structure?
4 What is a 'squarehead,' and what is meant by the term 'class divide'?
5 What was Sarah Lehane's experience working as a corrections officer in a male prison, and how does her approach to correctional work compare to stereotypes of women employed in criminal justice?

RECOMMENDED READINGS

Britton, D. (2003) *At Work at the Iron Cage: The Prison as Gendered Organization.* New York: University of New York Press.

Conover, T. (2000) *New Jack: Guarding at Sing Sing.* New York: Random House.

Earley, P. (1992) *The Hot House: Life Inside Leavenworth Prison.* New York: Bantam Books.

Jacobs, J. B. (1977) *Stateville: The Penitentiary in Mass Society.* Chicago: University of Chicago Press.

Martin, S. E. and Jurik, N. J. (1996) *Doing Justice, Doing Gender: Women in Law and Criminal Justice Occupations.* Thousand Oaks, CA: Sage.

CHAPTER 15

The Corrections Industry

Did you know that it costs forty thousand dollars a year to house each prisoner? Jeez, for forty thousand bucks a piece I'll take a few prisoners into my house. I live in Los Angeles – I already have bars on the windows. (Andy Rooney, on prisons)

LEARNING OBJECTIVES

After studying this chapter, you should be able to answer the following questions:

1 How does a capitalist society produce prisoners for a corrections industry and what role does the criminalization of drugs play?
2 What is the corrections-industrial complex?
3 What are the major issues shaping the debate over the privatization of corrections?
4 What is the role of the immigration service in the detention industry?
5 What are the current developments in the use of convict labor?

Located in the western plains of Oklahoma, Sayre, population 4,114, is like a lot of impoverished small towns fighting for its existence. So city officials scoured the financial landscape in an effort to identify businesses that would survive economic downturns. After considerable thought, municipal officials agreed that a private prison holding 1,440 inmates and employing 270 employees would offer their community considerable staying power. 'In my mind, there's no more recession-proof form of economic development,' said Jack McKennon, the city manager who persuaded the Corrections Corporation of America (CCA) to build a prison in Sayre, adding, 'nothing's going to stop crime.' Due to its successful prison in Sayre, CCA is the largest taxpayer in the county. Prisoners themselves also contribute to the tax base, paying the city's 3.5 percent sales tax for snacks and sodas they buy in the commissary. They also pay 35 to 45 percent tax for telephone calls, approximately 100 per day, all collect, all long distance, mostly to Wisconsin from where the prisoners are shipped.

The CCA prisoners also help the town recover from hard economic times by cleaning bricks brought in from the torn-down high school. At no cost to the city, inmates prepare the bricks to be returned to the town square, where a new city hall is being built. According to economics professor Thomas Pogue, opening private prisons is becoming a popular option for down-and-out towns: 'It's a more stable industry for a town than a manufacturing plant.' Pogue adds, however, that there is a wage problem since private prisons do not pay as well as state prisons, 'but these prisons are being located where people don't have a choice.' The mayor insists, 'the prison is a super positive for us. But it's a life raft, an inner tube. We're still on the ocean. We're not going down, but we're not going up either.' (Kilborn, 2001: A1, A12)

INTRODUCTION

The private prison experience at Sayre represents an expanding phenomenon in corrections. Since the early 1980s, when the race to incarcerate quickly outpaced available prison space, state and federal prison systems responded by constructing additional facilities. Criminal justice scholars agree: 'the growth in demand for prison space was one of the most steady, dependable sociopolitical facts in the country. No aspect of government service matched this pattern of growth in demand, not welfare, education, health care, or infrastructure' (Clear and Frost, 2002: 425; Welch, 2003e). Despite massive investment in prisons, corrections officials still had to turn to the private sector to house the overflow of the booming inmate population. Private prison companies, recognizing that corrections is indeed an industry, welcome the opportunity by building facilities in small towns where residents embrace the new business, even though wages would be meager. In the 1990s, 245 prisons were erected in 212 of the nation's 2,290 rural counties. During that time, an average of 25 new rural prisons opened annually, up from 16 in the 1980s and four in the 1970s (Kilborn, 2001; see Hallett, 2007; Selman and Leighton, 2010).

In this chapter, the corrections industry is examined critically, taking into account the ways in which economic forces shape incarceration within both the public and private sectors. In the first section, particular attention is paid to the production of prisoners and the emergence of corrections in a market economy. Next, the privatization of corrections is explored in depth, giving careful consideration to the corrections-industrial complex and other related issues. The chapter also features a hard look at the detention industry prompted by the immigration authorities, including recent controversies in the war on terror. The discussion concludes with a critique of convict labor.

CORRECTIONS AS INDUSTRY

As discussed in Chapter 4, various research studies show that trends in imprisonment are driven more by economic forces than crime rates (Dunaway *et al.*, 2000; Lynch *et al.*, 2000; White, 1999). With that realization in mind, it is crucial to consider two prominent features of the economic-punishment nexus: the tendency in a capitalist system to reduce labor alongside the commercial features of the political economy. Together those economic and market forces propel the corrections industry.

Under normal conditions of capitalism, the surplus population swells as opportunities for labor are diminished, resulting in unemployment and marginalization. Subsequently, a proportion of the surplus population inevitably becomes snared in the ever widening net of the criminal justice apparatus where they serve as raw materials for the corrections industry, an enterprise responding to the forces of a free market economy. These mutually reinforcing activities contribute significantly to the economic-punishment nexus, thereby maintaining coercive mechanisms of social control. Moreover, the continued reliance on incarceration presents grave threats to democracy and social equality. According to Nils Christie: 'The major dangers of crime in modern societies are not the crimes, but that the fight against them may lead societies towards totalitarian developments' (1994:16). In this section, we examine the prison business in light of market forces escalating incarceration that, in turn, produces significant harms to people and to a democratic society. Setting the stage for this critical inquiry is an overview of the production of prisoners in a capitalist society, followed by a close analysis of the corrections industry and its adverse effects.

Production of prisoners

Among the contradictions of capitalism is the economic marginalization of a large segment of society, thus creating a surplus population from which deviance

Figure 15.1 Corrections Corp. showing crime pays as states turn jails private – signage outside La Palma Correctional Center in Eloy, Arizona, May 11, 2010. La Palma, which houses about 2,900 convicts from California, is one of 65 facilities operated by Corrections Corp. of America, the largest private-prison operator in the US.

Photo by Joshua Lott/Bloomberg via Getty Images.

and crime are produced. Because those marginalized are significant in both sheer numbers and their perceived threat to the social order, the state invests heavily in mechanisms of social control (De Giorgi, 2006; Lynch, 2007; Shelden, 2001). Law enforcement and corrections constitute some of the more coercive measures of social control designed to deal with the portion of the surplus population considered a problem. Within the political economy, the criminal justice system functions traditionally as a social control apparatus by protecting capitalist relations of production. Given the emergence of the corrections enterprise, it is clear that such operations of social control themselves are engaged in the accumulation of capital. Before identifying the character and composition of the corrections industry, it is fitting that we acknowledge key dimensions of the political economy that contribute to lawlessness, an activity that produces the raw materials necessary for the corrections industry, namely prisoners.

Because large-scale economic marginalization restricts opportunities for legitimate financial survival in a market economy, unlawful economic enterprises emerge. Perhaps the most widespread underground economy is the illicit drug industry, a form of financial activity (and mood-altering escape from the harsh conditions of poverty) created by the structural inequality of capitalism. Curiously, the selling and consumption of illegal drugs has become increasingly criminalized to the extent that vast resources of the state are allocated to control these behaviors. Added measures aimed at prohibiting the drug industry (i.e. harsher penalties and mandatory minimum sentences) contribute significantly to the ironies of social control (Welch, 2005a).

For instance, although the drug trade is an outlaw industry, its underground economy conforms to free world, free market, and capitalist principles insofar as costs attached to illegal drugs are contingent upon demand and scarcity. Therefore reducing the supply merely drives up the price of drugs. This increase in value makes trafficking more profitable, hence attracting more individuals and groups willing to venture such risks. Wilkins (1991) similarly points out that the cost of illegal drugs reflects the risk, not the type or quality of the product. Drug peddlers are not so much selling drugs but – like insurance companies – they are trading in risk.

In sum, the criminalization of drugs, paradoxically, escalates rather than deters the drug trade. Higher penalties increase the risk of selling drugs, making the activity more lucrative, and in the end recruiting an endless supply of peddlers who already have been marginalized economically. As drug peddlers are apprehended, convicted, and incarcerated they subsequently serve as raw materials for the corrections industry, an economic enterprise considered to be legitimate by many proponents of a free market (Shelden and Brown, 2000; *Social Justice*, 2000; Welch, 1999a).

Corrections in a market economy

Over the past two decades, imprisonment has become big business, and the bitter 'not-in-my-backyard' attacks on prisons have been replaced with welcome mats, such as the one in Canon City (CO) reading 'Corrections Capital of the World.' The mayor of Canon City proudly boasts: 'We have a nice, nonpolluting, recession-proof industry here' (Brooke, 1997: 20). In Leavenworth (KS), another community that added a private prison to its already well-stocked corrections arsenal – featuring a federal penitentiary, a state prison, and a military stockade – a billboard reads 'How about doin' some TIME in Leavenworth?' Bud Parmer, site acquisition administrator for Florida Department of Corrections, concedes: 'There's a new attitude … small counties want a shot in the arm economically. A prison is a quick way to do it' (Glamser, 1996: 3A; Yeoman, 2000). Economically strapped towns induce jail and prison construction by offering land, cash incentives, and cut-rate deals on utilities: in return for these accommodations, locales receive jobs and spur other businesses such as department stores, fast-food chains, and motels, all of which contribute to the tax base (Kilborn, 2001; Martin, 2000; Thies, 2001).

Prisons are courted not only on Main Street but also on Wall Street where industrial corrections has created a bull market – further evidence that crime does indeed pay. Tremendous growth in the prison population coupled with astonishing increases in expenditures has generated a lucrative market economy with seemingly unlimited opportunities for an array of financial players: entrepreneurs, lenders, investors, contractors, vendors, and service providers. The American Jail Association promoted its conference with advertisements reeking of crass commercialism: 'Tap into the Sixty-Five Billion Dollar Local Jails Market' (Donziger, 1996b), The World Research Group organized a convention in Dallas billed 'Private Correctional Facilities: Private Prisons, Maximize Investment Returns in this Exploding Industry.' Without much hesitation, corporate America has caught the scent of new public money. The Dallas meeting included representatives from AT&T, Merrill Lynch, Price Waterhouse, and other golden-logo companies (Teephen, 1996). The prison industry also has attracted other capitalist heavyweights, including the investment houses of Goldman Sachs and Salomon Smith Barney, who compete to underwrite corrections construction with tax-exempt bonds that do not require voter approval. Defense industry titans Westinghouse Electric, Alliant Techsystems, Inc., and GDE Systems, Inc. (a division of the old General Dynamics) have also entered the financial sphere of criminal justice, not to mention manufacturers of name-brand products currently cashing in on the spending frenzy in corrections. While attending the American Correctional Association's annual meeting, Rod Ryan, representing Dial Corporation, delightedly replied: 'I already sell $100,000 a year of Dial soap to the New York City jails. Just think what a state like Texas would be worth' (Elvin, 1994/5: 4; Bates, 1999).

A critical look into the financial infrastructure reveals that the private prison industry rests on important forms of investment and stockholdings. Moreover, private correctional companies receive significant capital support from larger corporations and financial institutions. Indeed, that economic backing can be easily traced to institutional stockholders and their volume of shares. For example, Corrections Corporation of America (CCA) lists 114 institutional stockholders that together amount to 28,736,071 shares of stock. RS Investments

Wesley Capital MGMT holds the largest number of shares of CCA stock, and 36 institutional stockholders with a total of 9,587,496 shares support Capital Research & MGMT. The GEO Group has 82 institutional stockholders accounting for 9,583,019 shares. Wells Fargo (and Northwest Corporation) holds the most GEO Group stock, followed by Fidelity Management and Research and Wells Capital MGMT (Welch and Turner, 2008).

It ought to be noted that that even before private prison companies demonstrate much of a track record in the realm of financial performance, they are able to generate substantial sums of money in both the equity and debt markets with the assistance of major national and regional underwriters and lenders. CCA has also developed a way to extract even more investment capital from the stock market to pay for its ambitious expansion plans. The solution resides in REITs (Real Estate Investment Trusts). REITs are publicly traded entities that own and manage real estate but do not pay corporate income taxes. However, they must distribute 95 percent of their operating income as dividends to shareholders. These characteristics are intended to boost the price of REIT shares and thereby help raise even more capital (Dyer, 2000; Good Jobs First, 2003; see Hall, 2004a, 2004b, 2004c).

The corrections industry operates according to a unique set of economic dynamics in that the supply–demand principle operates in reverse. 'More supply brings increased demand. Industry insiders know that there are more than enough inmates to go around' (Adams, 1996: 463). This point is particularly significant considering the ongoing production of prisoners in American capitalist society exacerbated by the war on drugs and other tough-on-crime initiatives. Thus investors are betting that the corrections industry will continue to proliferate because its raw materials – prisoners – are relatively cheap and in constant supply. As we shall discuss in greater detail, a corrections industry that behaves according to market forces produces serious problems and injustices for a democratic society.

PRIVATIZATION OF CORRECTIONS

Among the current trends in corrections likely to continue into the near, and perhaps distant, future is privatization. Still, the practice of transferring governmental dollars to private contractors has generated intense debate (Logan, 1990; Shefer and Liebling, 2008). Much of the debate centers on political ideology, particularly between conservatives who invite free market principles into corrections and progressive liberals (and radicals) who complain that the pursuit of profit has no place in criminal justice. Paradoxically, the government contributes to the increase in the correctional population by not exercising more alternatives to incarceration, thereby prompting the state to consider the private sector for available prison cells (Ogle, 1999; Chapter 13).

Enthusiasts of privatization contend that government has failed miserably in its operation of corrections, and that private correctional companies can do a better job by reducing costs, increasing efficiency, and improving the quality of programs and services. Critics, however, point out that claims of cost-effectiveness are incomplete and misleading; moreover, they stress that the state ought not sidestep its moral and ethical obligation to administer justice. Since privatization is driven by a profit motive, critics argue that managers tend to respond to the fiscal incentive to reduce costs at the expense of prisoners by downscaling programs and services. At the same time, privatization contributes to excessive use of incarceration since profits are generated through increased volume – that is, a steady expansion of the correctional population. In addition to allegations of inmate abuse, opponents also raise questions about legal liability. In this section, various issues surrounding privatization are given careful thought. But first a few observations on the history of privatization in corrections.

A brief history of the privatization of corrections

During the early Reagan years, the prevailing political and economic philosophy encouraged government officials to turn to the private sector to administer public services, such as sanitation, healthcare, security, fire protection, and education. By introducing free market principles into the administration of public services, it was argued that private companies would compete against each other to provide the best service at the lowest cost. At the time, it seemed that the privatization of corrections appeared to be a new and novel approach to some old problems (i.e. overcrowding and mounting costs) (Nathan, 2004, 2003a, 2003b).

In that context, the privatization of prisons was introduced as a new and novel approach to some old correctional problems, most notably overcrowding and mounting costs. Judith Greene, a policy analyst, summarizes the phenomenon:

> The private prison industry emerged in the U.S. amid a rising tide of neo-liberal free market economic ideas and neo-conservative zeal for moralistic discipline that propelled the country's criminal justice through a series of campaigns to 'get tough on crime.' Reagan administration officials' ardor for mandatory prison sentences and zero-tolerance approaches to crime control and drug enforcement launched a national crusade to 'take back' criminal justice policies and practices from the hands of the supposedly liberal elite of criminologists and a defense-oriented legal establishment. The rapid embrace of their ideas by the public sent prison populations levels shooting through the roof.
>
> (2003: 56; see also Greene, 2002; Sinden, 2003)

Nonetheless, the privatization of punishment and corrections has a long history steeped in politics and economics (Spitzer and Scull, 1977a, 1977b).

As noted in previous chapters, many correctional strategies throughout history were administered by the private sector. The transportation of prisoners to penal colonies where they worked as indentured servants was an operation carried out by independent businessmen who had contractual agreements with the state. Similarly, the construction of early correctional institutions was facilitated by the private sector insofar as funds were raised through non-state subscriptions. In 1634 in Massachusetts, a fort was constructed on Castle Island that served military purposes but also held incorrigible prisoners who were too troublesome for Boston's common prison (Powers, 1966). In Maryland in 1666, an independent businessman agreed to build a prison for the colony in exchange for a thousand pounds of tobacco and a lifetime appointment as its superintendent. Likewise, many of the colonial and Jacksonian institutions were closely affiliated with the private sector, including the Walnut Street Jail, Newgate of New York, Auburn, and Sing Sing (Semmes, 1938).

The business relationship between government and the private sector was straightforward: contracts permitted independent businessmen to use prisoners to manufacture goods to be sold on the open market, and a portion of the profits were returned to the prison to offset the expenses of institutional operation. Similar business arrangements were customary in Southern plantation prisons whereby economic forces became powerful determinants in shaping corrections. Ideally, such prisons were designed to become financially self-sufficient institutions that would not have to depend on heavy tax expenditures (see Murton and Hyams, 1969).

Eventually, the presence of the private sector was challenged by both labor and business. Labor officials protested against the unfair practice of using cheap convict labor to manufacture goods that led to a loss of jobs among law-abiding citizens. Fellow businessmen also challenged privatization on the grounds that the bidding system was rigged, creating unfair competition. As early as the 1840s in New York, legislation was passed that curbed privately operated prison industries. Prison shops were managed by state officials and the products sold in a closed market of state agencies (Shichor, 2002).

Privatization today

Beginning in the early 1980s, the modern privatization movement spread swiftly nationwide and, by 2000, 31 states, the District of Columbia, and the federal prison system reported that more than 87,000 of their prisoners were being held in private facilities. These private correctional facilities held 5.8 percent of all state prisoners and 10.7 percent of federal inmates (Beck and Harrison, 2001). By 2008, the portion of the prison population held in private facilities increased more than 5 percent overall (to 128,524 inmates). For federal prisoners the percentage jumped nearly 11 percent (to 33,162 inmates) (Sabol *et al.*, 2009).

Currently, the scope of privatization is ever widening, reaching beyond correctional institutions that are owned and operated by private companies. Most prisons and jails use some form of privatization in such areas as medical and mental health services, substance abuse counseling, educational programs, food services, and the management of prison industries. Nonetheless, it is the ownership and management of correctional institutions that generates the most controversy.

The corrections-industrial complex

Among the most significant developments stemming from the current wave of privatization is the corrections-industrial complex, a term reminiscent of the phrase, 'military-industrial complex,' developed by sociologist C. Wright Mills and later memorialized by President Dwight D. Eisenhower. In his critically acclaimed work, *The Power Elite* (1956), Mills presented evidence of an integrated collective of politicians, business leaders (i.e. defense contractors), and military officials who together determine the course of state policy. Eisenhower heeded the warning of misplaced power in his 1961 farewell address, advising that government 'must guard against acquisition of unwarranted influence' by the military-industrial complex (Eisenhower, 1985: 748).

Nowadays, critical criminologists apply similar concepts to the growing reliance on prisons, noting the emergence of a corrections-industrial complex comprising politicians, business leaders, and criminal justice officials (Adams, 1996; Christie, 1994; Shelden and Brown, 2000; Sudbury, 2005). The corrections-industrial complex is an incarnation of the 'iron triangle' of criminal justice whereby a form of subgovernment control has taken hold (Thomas, 1994b). Operating well below the radar of public visibility, key players in the corrections subgovernment influence the course of policy and spending, including (1) private corporations eager to profit from incarceration (e.g. Corrections Corporation of America, Cornell Companies, and GEO Group), (2) government agencies anxious to secure their existence (e.g. Bureau of Justice Assistance, National Institute of Justice), and (3) professional organizations (e.g. the American Bar Association, the American Correctional Association) (Lilly and Deflem, 1996; Lilly and Knepper, 1993). The 'iron triangle' of criminal justice siphons power from each of these sectors, creating a formidable pocket of displaced influence over government (see Donziger, 1996a; Nuzum, 1998; *Social Justice*, 2000).

The corrections-industrial complex replicates the subgovernmental model in four ways:

1 Each of the participants in the corrections subgovernment shares a close working relationship supported by the flow of information, influence, and money.
2 There is a distinct overlap between the interests of for-profit companies and professional organizations and the interests of the federal agencies maintained by the flow of influence and personnel.
3 The corrections-industrial complex operates without public scrutiny and exercises enormous influence over correctional policy.
4 The corrections-industrial complex shows signs of becoming a fixture within the national policy area of punishing lawbreakers as the participants define their activities in the public interest.

(Lilly and Knepper, 1993: 157–61)

It should be emphasized that the vast majority of economic activity in the corrections-industrial complex is restricted to purchasing goods and services

(Lilly and Deflem, 1996). Only a relatively small percentage of prisoners are confined to privately owned and operated correctional facilities (Sabol *et al.*, 2009). 'States pretty much have a monopoly in the prison industry ... Although private companies, backed by venture capital firms, have been trying to cash in on the prison boom, so far they have only made progress through niche marketing" (Adams, 1996: 462–3). Still, there is considerable speculation that state (and federal) officials will eventually transfer a proportion of their inmates to private corrections. Growth expectations of privatized corrections have already have materialized on Wall Street where correctional corporations, investors, and shareholders are enjoying healthy returns, compounding capital for an expanding industry of social control (Dyer, 2000; Welch and Turner, 2008).

WORKING IN CORRECTIONS

Job Satisfaction among Staff in Private and Public Prisons

Private and public prisons have been compared on such issues as cost-effectiveness, quality of services, and various institutional problems including drug misconduct, escapes, and violence. What the literature on the subject appears to lack is information on personnel, particularly their levels of job satisfaction. Addressing that gap in knowledge, Sparkman *et al.* (2002) set out to measure job satisfaction among correctional staff in private and public prisons. Job satisfaction is a crucial element of organizational effectiveness, especially considering that when correctional workers are dissatisfied with their jobs, they tend to leave those jobs for other employment. Moreover, high job turnover in corrections undermines organizational effectiveness since new recruits being hired to replace experienced staff require more training and greater levels of supervision (see Lambert *et al.*, 1999; Welch, 1989a).

Sparkman and his colleagues found several key discrepancies in comparing correctional staff in private and public prisons. Employees in public prisons:

1 had higher salaries;
2 were more likely to hold non-security jobs, such as administrator or caseworker;
3 were older;
4 had more job experience – both at their present facilities and in the field of corrections overall.

Clearly, many of these findings are interrelated given that 'most persons who hold nonsecurity jobs in prison earn more money than security staff, and they also tend to be older, more experienced staff who, in some cases, have advanced to their present positions from the security ranks' (Sparkman *et al.*, 2002: 237). The study found both groups were quite dissatisfied with pay; however, higher pay was associated with higher job satisfaction among private staff.

Higher-paid private employees were significantly more satisfied with pay, promotion, opportunities, coworkers, and with their jobs in general. However, this trend did not hold true for state prison staff. Higher-paid state prison staff exhibited greater satisfaction with being paid more, but they were no more satisfied on any other job satisfaction measure than public staff members who were paid less.

(Sparkman *et al.*, 2002: 237)

In their research Sparkman *et al.* discovered that public employees expressed dissatisfaction with promotion opportunities while those working in private prisons were significantly more positive about their prospects for promotion. Two interpretations of this finding are presented. First, private prisons, like other private businesses, are continuously pursuing new ventures that create new job opportunities for their employees. Therefore private employees view new business contracts as opportunities for advancement. Secondly, the promotion process in both private and public prisons is viewed as highly bureaucratic and political. However, employees in private prisons believe that they can overcome those obstacles by their job performance, especially since private correctional firms aiming at expanding are interested in identifying and promoting the best workers. With those considerations in mind, it is important that further research be conducted on the work experiences of private prison employees (Crawley, 2004b; McElligott, 2008; Shefer and Liebling, 2008).

MAJOR ISSUES IN THE PRIVATIZING OF CORRECTIONS

Privatization in corrections remains controversial in large part due to an array of complicated political, economic, and moral considerations. This section reviews

Figure 15.2 Prison ships may ease overcrowding in jails – a general view of HMP *Weare* on October 24, 2006 in Portland, near Weymouth, England. The floating prison, now closed, was the only one in the UK when it opened in 1997. The then Home Secretary John Reid called on private companies to open and run similar types of vessels to alleviate the overcrowding crisis in UK prisons.

Photo by Matt Cardy/Getty Images.

some of the major issues shaping the debate, including the right to punish, profit motives in corrections, legal liability, cost savings, quality of services, and institutional violence. (See 'Cultural Penology: Penal Excess in a Consumer Society' below).

The right to punish

Critics of privatization insist that the right and power to punish are exclusively limited to the state. The American Civil Liberties Union challenges privatization on the grounds that the government should not retreat from its responsibility of safely securing the incarceration of those sentenced to prison or jail. Abdicating that authority to the lowest bidder runs counter to the fundamental principles of the administration of justice, since criminal punishment is a public not a private matter. Conversely, defenders of privatization contend: 'Law and tradition both make quite clear that privatization has been, and continues to be, an acceptable alternative to conventional governmental discharge of public responsibilities' (Durham, 1994: 274: Gowdy, 2001; Paterson, 2008).

Profit motives in corrections

Proponents of privatization correctly point out that government has generally failed at establishing a correctional system that meets even its most basic objectives, producing overcrowded institutions that are do not deliver adequate programs and services. Those advocates go on to claim that privatization has been shown to be an effective way to administer other public services (e.g. healthcare, sanitation). Therefore they propose that with adequate monitoring privatization can succeed in corrections. Opponents of privatization insist, however, that profiting from corrections is different fundamentally from other forms of privatization because it reduces the administration of justice to the accumulation of capital at the expense of programmatic and humanitarian ideals (Shichor, 2002, 1999; Lanza-Kaduce *et al.*, 1999).

Legal liability

Questions remain whether states are legally liable for the actions of private correctional companies, especially when managers fail to comply with safety codes – or perhaps even more dramatically, in cases resulting in the death or serious injury of prisoners. In *Medina* v. *O'Neill* (1984), the court found both the government and the private company liable for damages in the death of one inmate and the serious injury of another. Even more significantly, the US Supreme Court, in *Richardson* v. *McKnight* (1997), ruled that employees of private correctional firms under contract with a state or local government are not entitled to the immunity from prisoner lawsuits that protects COs who are on the public payroll. The case stems from a CCA (Corrections Corporation of America) facility where an inmate sued two COs for injuries caused by keeping him in unduly tight physical restraints. In his dissenting opinion, however, Justice Antonin Scalia echoed the chorus of privatization advocates claiming that the decision would make private corrections more expensive for taxpayers. Revealing cynicism and contempt for those behind bars, Scalia added that this case would also lead to windfalls for prisoners who bring suits and lawyers who represent them (see Greenhouse, 1997; Verhovek, 1997).

Cost savings

While many public correctional systems turn to private corrections as a way to reduce costs, there remains an ongoing debate over whether the private sector is capable of lowering correctional expenses. Several studies question the overall claim that private prisons save costs (Austin and Coventry, 2001; General Accounting Office, 1996; McDonald et al., 1998; Pratt and Maahs, 1999). Still, in cases in which a savings was documented, the cost reduction was produced by lower labor costs; in effect, private correctional companies hired staff at considerably lower wages, with fewer job benefits (Nelson, 1998). As a result of hiring personnel at lower wages, private prisons assembled correctional staff that had less experience and training than their public counterparts. As will be discussed in greater detail, staff inexperience and poor training leave the facility vulnerable to many problems, including turnover, drug misconduct, escapes, and violence.

It should be mentioned that one of the keys to lowering costs is promoting competition. Private companies will try to outbid each other by keeping their costs to a minimum; however, if there are fewer private companies in the correctional marketplace, it is less likely that costs will be controlled. As noted previously, CCA, Cornell, and the GEO Group are the dominant players in private corrections (Welch and Turner, 2008). What is good news for those companies in terms of greater market share and increased profits is bad news for government in terms of fewer choices among competitors and increased costs.

In sum, the General Accounting Office (1996) concluded that private corrections did not fulfill the claim that their services would generate substantial savings; moreover, there is evidence that privatization of corrections invites political corruption, produces poor-quality services, and exacerbates the conditions that lead to abuse and violence. While the financial figures for CCA, Cornell, and the GEO Group confirm high dividends, these windfalls remain in the private sector without passing a saving on to taxpayers, even though the raw materials (i.e. prisoners) belong legally to the public sector (as wards of the state). Upon closer scrutiny we see that privatizing corrections has less to do with saving tax dollars and more to do with shifting funds from the public to the private sector (Dickenson, 2008; Gran and Henry, 2008; Nathan, 2010).

Quality of services

Since the private sector has long argued that it can provide a higher quality of correctional service, researchers have remained interested in gathering evidence that would test that claim. Contradicting the claim of higher-quality service, Camp and Gaes (2002) found that private facilities experienced significant problems with staff turnover, escapes, and drug use. Data for staff turnover at the 84 private prisons studied showed that nearly half of all private prisons had turnover rates that exceeded 50 percent. These figures are significantly higher than government operated prisons, specifically the federal prison system that had a turnover rate of 4.4 percent (see Gaes *et al.*, 2004).

Escapes from prisons are relatively rare. Still, when escapes do occur, they point to a major problem in security. Researchers have found that such security problems are more common in private prisons than those operated by the government. Among the problems associated with escapes are inadequate numbers of staff, inexperienced staff, insufficiently trained staff, and physical plant deficiencies, all of which are more common in private facilities (Austin *et al.*, 2000; Camp and Gaes, 2002; Clark, 1998; Crane, 2000).

Drug misconduct serves as another important indication of both quality of correctional service and institutional security since substance abuse by inmates while behind bars reflects poorly on the staff's ability to detect and control the problem. Based on data drawn from random drug testing of prisoners, Camp and Gaes (2002) discovered that drug misconduct was a greater problem in private prisons than in facilities operated by the government. Contraband drugs probably signal the occurrence of several failures, including an inability to monitor visiting rooms, inmates on gate passes, and inmate mail, or an inability to collect intelligence information.

Camp and Gaes (2002) conclude that private prisons appear to have systemic problems in maintaining secure facilities, particularly in light of problems associated with escapes and drug misconduct. 'The failures that produce escapes or illegal drug use can result from problems in policy and procedures, in technology, and in staff capabilities ... and we suggest that the "greener" the workforce, the more likely there will be lapses in fundamental security procedures' (Camp and Gaes, 2002: 445). Furthermore, the 'greenness' (or inexperience) of personnel is not limited to line staff but extends to mid-level supervisory staff. That problem is significant because those managers have the responsibility of supervising line staff, monitoring procedures, setting policy, and providing training (Harding, 2001; Shichor, 2002, 1999; Skinns, 2009).

Institutional violence

Opponents of privatization also contend that the safety of inmates hangs in the balance when private correctional companies assume custody. Austin and Coventry (2001) reported that both prisoner-on-staff and prisoner-on-prisoner assaults were more common in private prisons. Much like escapes and drug misconduct, institutional violence is strongly associated with staff inexperience, poor training, and questionable hiring practices. At a private prison in Texas, COs were videotaped assaulting prisoners with stun guns; compounding matters, the officers were hired despite records they had abused prisoners while working in state institutions. CCA had employed at least two wardens in Texas who were disciplined for beating inmates while working for the state department of corrections. Even company president David Myers supervised an assault on inmates who took a guard hostage while Myers was serving as warden of a Texas prison 1984; in that incident, 14 guards were found to have used excessive force, beating subdued and handcuffed prisoners with riot batons. In a CCA facility for juveniles in South Carolina, child advocates were horrified to learn that children were abused by staff, including instances in which some boys were hogtied and shackled together (Bates, 1998a). Allegations of rape and assault at a privately run juvenile facility in Colorado prompted state officials to concede that it does not guarantee the safety of children at private jails (see Mobley, 2002).

In Tullulah, Louisiana, an economically depressed town of 10,000, James R. Brown set out to build a private corrections facility for juveniles, a venture that soon became the community's largest employer and taxpayer. Brown, a local businessman with no experience in corrections, is the son of an influential former state senator. Not surprisingly, Brown secured a no-bid contract for Trans-American, a company that he had formed with two close friends of Governor Edwin W. Edwards. In 1997, Brown and his associates were pulling in $24,448 for each of its 620 boys and young men aged 11 to 20; however, that operation had become 'so rife with brutality, cronyism and neglect that many legal experts say it is the worst in the nation' (Butterfield, 1998b: A1).

Abuse ran rampantly through that crowded institution holding the state's poorest and most vulnerable minority youths: 82 percent were black, and many were mentally retarded or emotionally disturbed. Injuries such as black eyes, broken noses or jaws, and perforated eardrums stemmed from fights between the detainees as well as beatings by the inadequately trained, poorly paid COs earning $5.77 an hour; not surprisingly, staff turnover reached 100 percent. Staff members used pepper spray on the boys and occasionally pitted them against each other for sport. Amid the stifling heat and poor ventilation, many youths deliberately violated rules in order to be sent to solitary confinement where the cells were air-conditioned. Meals were meager and clothes were in short supply, precipitating scuffles over shirts and shoes. For years, there were no books. Nearly all the teachers were uncertified and instruction was limited to an hour a day. Medical and psychiatric services were commonly inaccessible and inadequate; the infirmary was often closed because there were not enough staff for supervision.

The appalling conditions at Tullulah were symptomatic of larger contradictions produced by shifting resources from social services to criminal justice, then again to privatized corrections. The incarceration of adolescents (including the retarded or mentally ill) is escalated by politicians who rush to build new prisons while neglecting education and psychiatric services; as in the case of Tullulah, the problem is compounded by the state's handing the responsibility for juvenile offenders to private interests (Butterfield, 1998b; Wideman, 1995). During a wave of negative publicity over the private juvenile facility in Tullulah, the state of Louisiana took over temporary management when the warden resigned following a lawsuit, critical reports by federal investigators, and several disturbances by inmates (Butterfield, 1998c; also see Butterfield, 2000).

CULTURAL PENOLOGY

Penal Excess in a Consumer Society

Criminologists have indeed taken a cultural turn in their analysis of punishment and the growing reliance on incarceration (Brown, 2009; Garland, 2006; Smith, 2008). Moreover, that line of inquiry has also extended not only into politics but also into the sphere of economics. By attending to market forces we are mindful of how citizens and government officials participate in a consumer culture, continuously in search of products (e.g. car alarms) and services (e.g. private security guards) aimed at making people feel safer in an otherwise risky – and dangerous – world (Lynch, 2007; Vaughn, 2002). As Ian Loader (2009, 1999) observes, a culture based on market principles is driven by 'appetites' that must be fed through endless consumption. Among the corrosive consequences of such consumption in the realm of criminal justice is *penal excess*, leading to record-breaking rates of imprisonment (Hallsworth, 2000; Pratt, 2007; Young, 2007).

As mentioned previously, the profit motive in the privatization movement may also result in the encouragement of excessive use of incarceration simply because it is good for business. That financial concern is particularly relevant because if correctional companies are keeping costs down to bid competitively, then presumably they will set out to generate profits by increasing their volume. An increase of volume, simply put, means a continuous expansion of the correctional population. A Corrections Corp. co-founder said of the move to privatize corrections, 'You just sell it like you were selling cars or real estate, or hamburgers' (Bates, 1998a: 12). That perspective on profit-making reveals the extent to which prisoners are commodified in a free market, and the likelihood of long-term growth explains why many privatization enthusiasts are attracted to the corrections industry in the first place. According to one CCA warden: 'I don't think we have to worry about running out of product' (Bates, 1998a: 18; see Burton-Rose, 1998).

Not surprisingly, self-serving interests driving privatization from outside its institutions now have seeped inside. Staff in CCA facilities have the option to purchase their company's stock, thereby placing corrections officers in a privileged position where they can manipulate the length of sentences. As stockholders, COs have a vested interest in maintaining high occupancy for protracted periods of time; consequently, they may be inclined to ensure that inmates maximize their stay behind bars. Disciplining prisoners for rule infractions can result in the loss of 'good time,' that extends the duration of time served – thus increasing profits. The New Mexico Corrections Department found that inmates at the CCA facility lost 'good time' eight times more frequently than prisoners in a state institution. With the financial incentive to revoke 'good time,' not only do private corrections companies unjustly treat prisoners, but also the taxpayers who foot the bill for extra time served. In Tennessee, CCA guards said privately that they are encouraged to send balky inmates to administrative segregation; by placing prisoners in the 'hole,' the company earns an extra $1,000 because 30 days are added to the sentence (Bates, 1998a, 1999; see Urbina and Hamill, 2009).

Given the influence of capital over politics, critics are also concerned over the emergence of a private 'prison lobby' in which a fully-fledged corporate public relations campaign sets out to whip up crime hysteria in order to generate profits. Sentencing guidelines, parole rules, corrections budgets, and new criminal legislation are areas in which private prison operators have a vested interest and could influence policy decisions. The 'prison lobby' has the capacity not only to pressure lawmakers to rely more heavily on incarceration, but the public relations arm of the campaign can manipulate public fear of crime through the media (Welch *et al.*, 1998, 1997; Welch *et al.*, 2000).

In the public sector, corrections officers unions already have stormed the political arena to lobby for their financial interests. For instance, the California Correctional Peace Officers Association (CCPOA) has emerged as a fierce and effective lobby, spending hefty amounts of its $8 million annual membership dues to defeat political candidates it deems soft on crime and persuade lawmakers to pass prison-friendly legislation (e.g., 'three strikes' laws). Recently, 38 of the last 44 CCPOA-sponsored bills became law. During the 1990s, California's spending on corrections has pushed salaries for guards higher than those of California public school teachers as well as tenured associate professors at most state universities. Similar corrections union activity has surfaced in other states, most notably in New York (Macallair, 1997; Sullivan, 1998; see also Davey, 1998). (See 'Working in Corrections: Job Satisfaction Among Staff in Private and Public Prisons', p. 514.)

PRIVATE JAILS FOR IMMIGRATION DETAINEES

As discussed in Chapter 11, the federal agency Immigration and Customs Enforcement (ICE) detains thousands of undocumented immigrants and asylum seekers who are either waiting to have a hearing or waiting to be deported. Due to its limited jail capacity, the agency rents cells from other correctional facilities, including county jails and private correctional facilities. In doing so, the ICE has become a key player in the corrections industry (Welch, 2003c, 2002b, 2002c). Despite criticism from human rights groups, the business of detaining undocumented immigrants and asylum seekers has produced a vast network of more than 900 jails nationwide, all eager to cash in on lucrative government contracts that usually pay twice the cost of housing inmates charged with criminal offenses (Casimir, 2001).

With huge budget increases in the aftermath of 9/11, ICE has spent even more funds on detention. The agency uses more than a third of its detention budget to rent cells, mostly in remote rural counties where the costs are low and there are beds to spare. Immigration detainees are the fastest-growing segment of the nation's correctional population. The agency policy shift toward detention and away from parole has not occurred in a vacuum. For the past two decades, immigration authorities have been responding to key ideological and market forces driving the uncritical acceptance that greater law enforcement activities coupled with fewer social services not only is rational and legitimate but lucrative as well (Burke, 2001; Hedges, 2001; INS, 2001; Welch, 2000c, 1996g).

Strapped for housing space, ICE creates significant financial opportunities for local jails and private corrections companies where most of the agency's detainees are confined. At an average cost of $60 per day per detainee, the ICE spends more half a million dollars each day to house its detainees in local jails. This arrangement provides a valuable source of income for local governments; in some cases, county debts have been paid and taxes reduced due to revenue from the immigration detention. While 'not in my backyard' used to be a popular reaction by local residents protesting new jails and prisons, nowadays communities welcome such institutions, especially in regions hit hard by economic downturns. As noted, more than 900 local jails have joined the vast network of facilities eager to house immigration detainees. Like those of many communities, the Wicomico County jail (MD) has come to rely heavily on the financial windfall brought to them by the agency. The warden continues to lobby county administrators in an effort to bring even more immigration detainees to Wicomico, boasting: 'Renting beds is a lucrative business. If I built 500 beds, I could rent them all tomorrow morning' (Montgomery, 2000: EV3; see Casimir, 2001; Firestone, 1999; PRNewswire, 2001; Ross, 2000).

On the business side of detention and incarceration, there is considerable speculation that privatization will continue to expand. The economic formula is simple. Investors in private corrections are anticipating more prisoners to be incarcerated for longer periods of time. Evidence of current – and future – financial gain in private corrections is another blunt reminder of the economic forces driving correctional policy. Although many corporations and their investors benefit financially from the privatization of corrections, there exists a downside with tragic consequences, including the unjust detention of undocumented immigrants and asylum seekers who, in effect, become raw materials for the corrections business (Bates, 1998a; Parenti, 1999; Welch and Turner, 2008).

Since the events of September 11, 2001, there has been another round of debate over the role of ICE in privatization (Talvi, 2003). Human rights organizations are not only concerned with civil liberties issues but also worry that the corrections industry will continue its profiteering from the housing of immigration detainees. In the months following the attacks, the US government rounded up more than 1,000 foreign nationals (holding valid US visas). In response to signals that additional jail space would be needed, stocks of private companies that build and operate prisons for governments zoomed as high as 300 percent. James MacDonald, prisons-security analyst at First Analysts Securities, noted: 'Unfortunately, these are becoming good investments' (Tharp, 2001: EV1). Due to the detention prospects contained in the war on terror, several publicly traded prison companies received good financial news from the Federal Bureau of Prisons when it announced plans to expand its correctional capacity for ICE detainees. Financial analysts noted that many security companies received huge and immediate profits from supplying COs and new security in the aftermath of the terror attack. In a third-quarter conference call, Steve Logan, the CEO of Cornell Companies – the third largest private prison firm – notes:

> I think it's clear that since September 11 there's a heightened focus on detention … more people are gonna get caught. So I would say that's positive … The other thing that you're seeing that to be honest with you I have no idea how this is going to impact us but it's not bad it can only be good is with the focus on people that are illegal and also from Middle Eastern descent in the United States there are over 900,000 undocumented individuals from Middle Eastern descent. That's, keep in mind, that's half of our entire prison population. That's a huge number, and that is a population, for lots of reasons that is being targeted. So I would say the events of 9/11 let me back up – the federal business is the best business for us. It's the most consistent business for us and the events of September 11 are increasing that level of business.
>
> (Not With Our Money, 2002)

While challenging the apparent racist rhetoric used to describe Arabs and Muslims as 'dangerous,' civil liberties groups criticize the detention of persons accused of non-criminal immigration violations, especially in jails built to house criminals. The ongoing trend in detention further threatens to infuse the immigration system with a potent element of profiteering. 'This is a really bizarre thing where our growth industry is our prison system. It is something that we have to be very concerned about,' said James Haggerty of the Catholic Legal Immigration Network (Donohue, 2001b: EV2). Following 9/11 as the US officially entered a recession, the corrections industry began to prosper once again. James MacDonald observed: 'Crime always goes up in a bad economy. Where there are good times and jobs are plentiful, people who get out of prison can usually find work and don't have to go back to their old ways. When the economy fails, so do the former inmates' (Tharp, 2001: EV2; see James, 2002; Welch, 2002b). (See 'Comparative Corrections: Refugee Detention on Christmas Island' below.)

COMPARATIVE CORRECTIONS

Refugee Detention on Christmas Island

As noted in Chapter 11, the detention of undocumented immigrants and asylum seekers is drawing considerable criticism from human rights and civil liberties organizations, including the American Civil Liberties Union, Amnesty International, and Human Rights Watch. The controversy, however, is not confined to the United States. Currently, many European nations as well as Australia are grappling with issues of illegal immigration; among the responses is a greater reliance on detention. Many of those detention practices, however, strain international standards ensuring the fair treatment of refugees and asylum seekers (Schuster, 2003; Welch, 2004; Welch and Schuster, 2005a, 2005b).

Compounding matters in Australia, immigration authorities have privatized their entire detention apparatus. The Department of Immigration and Citizenship (DIAC) recently announced that Serco Australia Pty Ltd is now the preferred tenderer for the new contract for the provision of a range of immigration detention services at immigration residential housing and immigration transit accommodation around Australia. That form of privatization has been criticized by human rights advocates who insist that the state – not a corporation – should carry out the public duty of operating detention facilities (see Grewcock, 2008; Pickering, 2008; Weber, 2006). Still, some Australians welcome not only privatization but also the expansion of detention, since for their communities it has brought an economic boom.

> 'The good times are back on Christmas Island,' said Trish O'Donnell, this island's sole real estate agent. Three-quarters of Australians probably didn't know Christmas Island belonged to Australia, but now it's a speculators' market. All thanks to the I.D.C. That's short for the Immigration Detention Center.
>
> (Onishi, 2009a: EV1)

In 2008, the Australian government opened a $370 millon facility to detain the increasing number of asylum seekers coming by boat to Christmas Island, a small chunk of land that rests on the tip of an extinct volcano sticking out of the Indian Ocean. Christmas Island is more than 200 miles south of Indonesia and almost 1,000 miles away from mainland Australia. The island was uninhabited until the discovery of phosphate drew the British there a century ago, then followed indentured workers from China and Malaysia.

When Christmas Island became Australian territory 50 years ago, Australian managers who were paid Australian wages supervised Asian laborers paid Asian wages. Managers resided in a well-kept neighborhood called Silver City that was off limits to Asians. In 1980, the colonial-like system was dismantled due to reforms pushed through by a new union. Ethnic Chinese account for

60 percent of the population, and ethnic Malay 20 percent, while whites make up the other 20 percent. 'At work, there was a European mess and an Asian mess," said Foo Kee Heng, an ethnic Chinese man who used to work in mining and is now deputy president of the Christmas Island shire (Onishi, 2009a: EV2).

As the phosphate industry began to unravel in the 1980s, the local people worried over economic instability. The opening of an immigration detention center has not gone unnoticed. Tucked away in the jungle at the other end of the island, the IDC has brought the whiff of quick, new money.

> The math was simple enough. Since the start of the year, the number of asylum-seekers has grown steadily, so that it now tops the population of local residents, around 1,100. As immigration officials, guards, interpreters and others now fly in from mainland Australia for stretches of days or weeks, the island's limited facilities are enjoying a boom. Hotels are booked weeks in advance. Rents have doubled. Lucky Ho's and a handful of other restaurants turn away patrons without reservations.
>
> (Onishi, 2009a: EV1)

Despite the apparent good economic news brought by the IDC, immigrant rights advocates complain that detention is not the answer (Gaylord, 2001; Grewcock, 2007; Pickering, 2008). In Australia, where there is growing hostility toward illegal immigrants, the government is required to enforce mandatory detention, in which all persons who arrive without proper travel documents and request asylum are forced into a detention camp. Nearly 2,000 so called 'boat people' – refugees from Afghanistan and Sri Lanka – have been sent to the detention center at Christmas Island. The facility is fortified by an electrified, 13-foot razor-wire fence. Critics, including the government's own human rights commission, have urged the authorities to close the IDC and move the detainees to the mainland where they would have access to the refugee review system. Opponents compare the IDC 'to Guantanamo Bay or describe it as a reincarnation of the many notorious prisons in Australia's convict history' (Onishi, 2009b: A5).

In Australia as well as in America, the detention of immigrants raises numerous ethical concerns. According to the United Nations High Commissioner for Refugees, refugees and asylum seekers are to be confined only as a last resort and only for brief periods of time. The problem is greatly compounded by contracting with private correctional companies known for neglecting the needs of detainees and for resisting attempts to be monitored by human rights organizations (Grewcock, 2008; Welch, 2002b).

THE NEW GEO-ECONOMY FOR CONVICT TRANSPORTATION

As European nations ventured into their own colonial campaigns, they instituted transportation as a means of transferring labor while serving to banish certain lawbreakers to distant lands. As discussed in Chapter 2, such punishment was particularly brutal. In Russia, the 850,000 convicts exiled to Siberia between 1807 and 1899 were forced to march between 4,700 and 6,700 miles while being chained together. The journey often lasted two to three years, producing steep death rates (Sellin, 1976). At the infamous Devil's Island in French Guiana – depicted in the movie *Papillon* – approximately 68,000 of the 70,000 prisoners died before completing their sentence (Tappan, 1960). Other European countries also resorted to transportation, in particular Spain (Hispaniola), Portugal (North Africa, Brazil and Cape Verde), Italy (Sicily), Denmark (Greenland), and Holland (Dutch East Indies) (Barnes and Teeters, 1946).

Aside from those important geo-penal developments, American and Australian criminologists tend to direct their studies to the British version of transportation, noting that England began transporting rogues, vagabonds, and sturdy beggars to colonial land in 1598 in an attempt to rid itself of a growing underclass and ease overcrowding in prisons and gaols (jails). In the Australian and American colonies, penal slaves would serve lengthy sentences in forced labor, and a century later, the use of transportation expanded considerably. The Transportation Act of 1718 stated specifically that the purpose of transportation was to deter criminals as well as to supply the colonies with labor. In 1787, England expanded the policy by declaring that offenders sentenced to three or more years of imprisonment were eligible for transportation; furthermore, the penalty for an unauthorized return was execution. Still, the practice extended beyond its penal and economic functions to fulfill other government initiatives, namely social sanitation whereby vagrants and other social (and political and religious) undesirables also were transported in an effort to purify certain urban zones (Welch, 1994; see Chapter 11). Also in the realm of expressive punishment, transportation lent itself to humiliating public spectacle; in London, men and women alike were placed in heavy chains and drawn in open carts through the local crowds, who jeered and terrorized them (Johnson, 1988).

The practice of transportation was not solely a state operation; essentially it was privatized through contracts, under which felons became the property of the ships' captains. Perhaps due to that contractual arrangement, convicts were subjected to horrible conditions aboard these vessels (known as 'floating hells'), and many died en route to the penal colony. Convicts who survived the voyage were subsequently sold at a high price to American colonists, usually becoming indentured servants. Upon completion of their term, lasting from seven to 14 years, the banished felons were allowed to remain in the colony as free citizens, some even being granted land by their owners (Barnes, 1968; Rusche and Kirchheimer, 1968). Overall, an estimated quarter of a million prisoners had been sent to the American colonies when, at beginning of the Revolutionary War, the King terminated the practice, not wanting banished felons to be recruited as soldiers against their British monarchy (Barnes and Teeters, 1946; Shaw, 1966). In Australia, Britain continued to rely on transportation, sending approximately 134,000 there between 1786 and 1867 (Sutherland *et al.*, 1992; see Hughes, 1986). In the American colonies, however, the demise of transportation merely contributed to the rise of slavery, putting into motion an enduring character

of the new Republic in which racism, plantation labor, and punishment wou
become tightly wound (Rusche, 1982; Smith, 1965).

Recently scholars have returned to the significance of historical developments
in an effort to decipher contemporary penal practices, especially those with
linkages to the private sector (Bozovic, 1995a; Feeley, 2002). Additionally, critical
attention has turned to the importance of race in formulating penal measures
that remained very much rooted in the practice of slavery: most notably, the
convict lease system that flourished in the South from 1865 to the 1920s
(Perkinson, 2009). 'Caught between the legal restrictions of abolition and a
paramount need for cheap labor, convict leasing emerged as a uniquely Southern
solution to the postbellum labor shortage and facilitated a continuation of the
ideology of white supremacy' (Hallett, 2004: 51; see Shelden, 2001). Furthering
a deeper understanding of contemporary privatization as it intersects with the
continued plight of African Americans, Hallett (2007, 2002) presents an analysis
of commerce with prisoners in a new colonialism. He connects his findings
on the commodification of prisoners to the legacy of the convict lease system
whereby convicts – predominantly racial minorities – serve as raw materials for
penal privatization (see Weiss, 2001, 1989, 1987; Western and Beckett, 1999).

With those historical trends in full view, it is useful to consider recent
developments in the transportation of convicts. Even though prisoners are
frequently transferred to correctional facilities within their own state, the practice
of transferring them across state lines is a phenomenon that has been generally
neglected in the critical scholarship on prison privatization. Looking into the
modern version of transportation we find that prisoners are being shipped across
state lines for the sole purpose of occupying cells in private prisons and detention
facilities. Unlike earlier forms of transportation in which prisoners were ferried
to a colonial land to perform labor, the value of prisoners under the current
scheme is to exploit their capacity to serve their sentences in private prison cells
at government and taxpayer expense (Welch and Turner, 2008).

For decades, the federal government, particularly the immigration service, has
been sending its prisoners and detainees to private correctional facilities located
in various jurisdictions. Still, there is something inherently significant for state
correctional systems to do so. Moreover, the distances that some prisoners travel
are comparable to those transported in earlier eras. The Corrections Corporation
of America (CCA) owns and operates correctional and detention facilities across
the country and many receive prisoners from considerable distances. Its Florence
Correctional Center in Arizona houses prisoners from as far away as Hawaii
(and Alaska), as do the Otter Creek Correctional Facility in Wheelwright,
Kentucky and the Diamond Back Correctional Facility in Watonga, Oklahoma.
West Tennessee Detention Facility in Mason, Tennessee imports prisoners from
Vermont. The GEO Group (Global Expertise in Outsourcing) also trades in
the transportation of prisoners; its Bill Clayton Detention Center in Littlefield,
Texas includes in its correctional population inmates from Wyoming.

Furthering a penal-economic analysis informed by historical practices is the
very idea that transporting prisoners can be used to generate profit. So often
we view contemporary incarceration as a static phenomenon in which convicts

nain relatively stationary during their imprisonment. Modern transportation, ich like its ancestral counterpart, demonstrates that dynamic incarceration dering commodified prisoners mobile is good for business. What is good business, however, is not always good for prisoners. Modern transportation, particularly to states located far from the inmates' home states, deepens the incarceration experience and leads to further isolation. Not only is long-distance telephone contact expensive but so too is travel for families and friends of prisoners. Over time, one could expect even less contact for inmates serving lengthy sentences, imposing further hardship on those confined and their loved ones.

Aside from the adverse effects that modern transportation creates for prisoners and their families, there is a political and economic impact on their communities. In understanding critically the emergence of the census, it is important to remember that the first US Constitution acknowledged that slaves could not vote but nevertheless counted each slave as three-fifths of a person so as to allocate political representation in Congress. Consequently, the power of slaveholders was sharply inflated, giving them distinct advantages in influencing legislative matters. Nowadays the movement of prisoners within a given state also creates an unwarranted advantage in districts where the felons are confined at the expense of their home neighborhoods.

> The culprit is a provision in the census that counts prison inmates as 'residents' of the institution where they are held, often for relatively short periods of time. Denied the right to vote in all but 2 of the 50 states, the inmates are nonetheless treated as voters when the State Legislators draw up legislative districts. This practice mattered little 30 years ago when the prison population was tiny. But with about 1.4 million people in prison today, it can be used to shift political power from one part of the state to another.
>
> (*New York Times*, 2005b: A22; see also *New York Times*, 2006)

The total number of felons held behind bars is the equivalent of two congressional districts. Moreover, the number of prisoners serving time outside their home district exceeds one million (*Marin Independent Journal*, 2006). Peter Wagner of the Prison Policy Initiative studied the problem in New York State and found that seven upstate Senate districts met the population requirements only because they included prisoners in their count. Wagner also discovered similar findings in 21 other counties nationwide where at least 21 percent of the so-called residents lived under lock and key (Wagner, 2006, 2004). Gatesville, Texas, a city of 15,600, has half of its population housed in six state prisons. In California, Marin County with a population of 247,000 is a prime beneficiary of the practice of counting prisoners as residents since it includes in its census 6,000 'residents' inside San Quentin prison. That form of district formation violates the principle of one person one vote while penalizing the prisoners' home district. Since prisoners are technically unemployed, the district is capable of artificially lowering its per capita incomes in ways that unfairly increase their share of federal dollars allocated for the poor. A case in point is New York City that loses 36,000 residents who are shipped to upstate prisons. Congressman Jose Serrano from the Bronx insists it is an issue of fairness: 'Because federal dollars are based on population, prisoners should be counted in their last known permanent residences where they are likely to return to upon release' (*Marin Independent Journal*, 2006: 1). Indeed, these forms of social and political inequality are perpetuated by the penal-economic nexus (see Alexander, 2010; Behan and O'Donnell, 2008; Clegg, 2010; McCoy, 2010; Uggen and Inderbitzin, 2010).

CONVICT LABOR

Blending notions of restitution with rehabilitation, correctional facilities strive to put prisoners to work. Many of those jobs directly benefit the institution, such as washing dishes, mopping floors, painting walls, and other tasks that defray the cost of operating a prison. Additionally, there is work that benefits the state, including picking up litter alongside highways, manufacturing license plates, and fielding telephone calls for state agencies. For their work, prisoners earn a meager wage (ranging from $1.40 to $8.00 per day) that is usually spent at the commissary on snacks and cigarettes, though equally importantly, they also accumulate 'good time' that reduces their stay in prison (Chesler, 2001). As popular as prison labor is, it becomes controversial when it is used to generate private profit. Currently, 33 states have passed laws that allow the contracting of prison labor to private companies, ranging from telemarketing to light manufacturing (Burton-Rose, 1998). Labor organizations are taking a strong stance against the use of convict labor because it is viewed as unfair competition to paid labor. Other opponents insist that many recent forms of contracting prison labor violate legislation passed during the Great Depression intended to restrict products made by prisoners to a closed market comprising government agencies (Hawes-Cooper Act 1929; Ashurst-Sumners Act 1935; see Chapter 3).

Recently, scholars have turned their critical attention to the growing use of convict labor and its implications for the classic penal theory of Rusche and

Figure 15.3 Inmates work in a sewing workshop at a prison in Chongqing Municipality, China on March 7, 2008. There are nearly 5,000 inmates in the prison. China is working to improve education in prisons and help prisoners return to society as law-abiding citizens, with measures to better protect the legitimate rights and interests of inmates.

Photo by China Photos/Stringer/ Getty Images.

Kirchheimer, who proposed: 'Every system of production tends to discover punishments which correspond to its productive relationships' (1968: 3). According to Robert Weiss: 'The move toward employing prison labor to satisfy a shortage of low-wage labor, and the political resistance to the increased competition, are a manifestation of a long and close correspondence between punishment and developments in the political economy' (2001: 254). Weiss furthers his analysis by acknowledging that the 'same social forces that funneled millions of young men of color into U.S. prisons and jails are now increasing their utility as prison labor for capital accumulation' (2001: 255; Meredith, 2000; Tatge, 2000; Western and Beckett, 1999).

Christian Parenti, author of *Lockdown America* (1999), weighs into the controversy, arguing that the use of convict labor for private production is not likely to expand significantly. Parenti points out that prison labor is not keeping pace with booming incarceration rates; thus it does not appear to be a driving force behind the lockup binge. In his assessment, Parenti finds that prison labor is not a great source of profit in the state sector; most prison industries eventually cost the government money or at best break even. Compounding matters, government officials who purchase goods from UNICOR, the federal prison industry, have complained that prison-made products are 'inferior, cost more and take longer to procure' (Parenti, 1999: 232). Similar criticisms have been leveled at other state prison industries in California, Texas, and Virginia.

Whereas the initial prospect of employing cheap prison labor is strong enough to attract private firms, the profits are not lucrative enough to keep those companies from returning to the free world. Upon closer examination, there are several key reasons why private companies have reconsidered their plans to use convict labor. First is the lack of space inside correctional facilities that is necessary for the manufacturing and assembly of goods. As discussed, prison officials are constantly scrambling to locate available cells due to overcrowding caused by the influx of sentenced felons. Secondly, private companies are sensitive to their public image and many consumers view products made by convicts as morally tainted. Therefore large and commercially successful companies are unwilling to risk additional profits for bad publicity. Even small startups and subcontractors that have ventured into convict labor have learned the stinging lessons of the marketplace. For example, an apparel company, 'Inkarcerated,' attempted to market prison-made sportswear crassly bearing the slogan 'Fitness is a life sentence.' Due to the stigma of prison labor, few retailers were interested in being associated with 'Inkarcerated' and the company joined the ranks of poorly conceived ventures that failed to recognize the harsh reality of commerce (Parenti, 1999: see Burton-Rose, 1998).

Parenti reveals a third obstacle in the use of convict labor for private manufacturers: the opposition of correctional unions that demand full authority over production inside their facilities. In their efforts to compete in the open market, private firms require flexibility, mobility, and efficiency, all of which run counter to the maintenance of prisons. Corrections officers, for obvious reasons, place a greater priority on institutional safety than private profits, especially considering the risks involved in introducing into the inmate population materials that can he transformed into weapons. 'We want to defray the costs and keep inmates busy, but it's our backs that get stuck with the homemade knives when things get out of control,' reasoned one officer union representative (Parenti, 1999: 234). To minimize the threat of weapons and disorder, corrections officers dictate the course of production by adhering to thorough searches, counts, and occasional lockdowns – activities that are time-consuming and disruptive to manufacturing. In California, the corrections officers union prohibits the use of long tractor-trailers to ship products or materials inside the prison compound, forcing companies to rely on smaller delivery trucks that, in turn, drive up production costs. Transporting goods from prisons located in rural areas also adds to the cost of doing business behind bars. Even the weather can interfere with manufacturing in prisons, since many institutions halt all production when it rains hard because the noise drowns out sound; occasionally, the workday is discontinued when fog rolls in, thus obscuring the visibility necessary to patrol prison grounds.

Fourth, the overall quality of prison goods has been judged inferior, particularly in light of the resistance of some inmates who enjoy 'sticking to the man' by slowing production and in some instances sabotaging the assembly of goods. With those considerations in mind, Parenti wonders why private firms would continue their quest for convict labor: 'There is too much cheap, militarily disciplined labor on the outside to make the hassles and irrationalities of doing business in prison worthwhile. With wages as low as 40 cents an hour in Honduras, and generous tax breaks to boot, why open a sweatshop inside some bureaucratic hellhole where you have to pay minimum wage?' (Parenti, 1999: 235; also see Matthews, 1999; Taylor, 1999).

CONCLUSION

Contrary to popular and political beliefs, a vast criminal justice system boasting a booming prison population ought not be hailed as a social achievement. When we consider that a large segment of those behind bars are non-violent offenders and are disproportionately poor, black, and Latino, the prevailing system of justice is revealed to be not only flawed but also symptomatic of a society – and state – that has failed to come to grips with social, economic, and racial inequality (Becket and Sasson, 2000; Currie, 1998). Still, the corrections industry continues to generate ideological and financial windfalls for politicians, corporations, and a growing cast of opportunists who perpetuate the myth that more prisons means greater public safety. Donziger reveals the overarching fallacy in mythologizing the relationship between imprisonment and crime: 'If more prisons paid off in less crime, the results would be obvious by now' (1996b: 24).

This chapter offers a critical interpretation of the corrections industry by turning attention from the popular notion of a crime-punishment nexus to the market forces shaping the contours of social control. To reiterate, the duality of economies and punishment rests on two central observations. First, under its normal operations, capitalism tends to reduce labor, and in doing so, it swells the surplus population – a proportion of which is then subject to the state's mechanisms of coercive control. Second, the commercial features of the market economy enable private interests to commodify prisoners as raw materials for a corrections industry, creating a high-volume, profit-driven system of punishment. Moreover, the prevailing reliance on incarceration, either for purposes of social control, generating profits, or both, threatens democracy by shifting even greater power to the state and the corporate class.

A keen observer recognized a paradox in the penal-economic nexus: 'The tremendous profits accruing to the prison-industrial complex demonstrate that the free market works best when people aren't free' (Pranis, 1998: 3; see also Pranis, 2003; Downes, 2001). In its wake, citizens – especially the impoverished and racial minorities – are left vulnerable to an overzealous, over-financed criminal justice machine. 'This may prove to be the most lasting impact of the movement to translate societal problems into profit-making opportunities,' laments Marc Mauer of The Sentencing Project (1999: 2; see Blomberg and Lucken, 2000).

SUMMARY

In this chapter, the corrections industry is examined so as to shed critical light on the economic forces shaping an emerging market for corrections. By doing so, careful consideration is given to the production of prisoners in a capitalist society, providing financial opportunities for both the public and private sectors. As corrections officials consider strategies to deal with prison and jail overcrowding, they must contend with the numerous and complex issues involved in privatization, including the right to punish, the profit motive, legal liability, cost savings, quality of services, institutional violence, and the encouragement of excessive use of incarceration. Furthermore, as the US continues to grapple with problems associated with illegal immigration and the war on terror, government leaders face the daunting task of maintaining national security while protecting civil liberties, particularly with respect to controversial detention practices.

REVIEW QUESTIONS

1 What is meant by the production of prisoners in a capitalist society?
2 What are major components of the corrections-industrial complex?
3 According to critics of privatization, how do efforts to reduce costs undermine the management of correctional facilities?
4 What are the human rights and civil liberties implications of detaining undocumented immigrants in private prisons?
5 Why are some critics skeptical about the expansion of convict labor in the private sector?

RECOMMENDED READINGS

Burton-Rose, D. (1998) *The Celling of America: An Inside Look at the U.S. Prison Industry.* Boston: Common Courage.

Hallett, M. (2007) *Private Prisons in America: A Critical Race Perspective.* Urbana, IL: University of Illinois Press.

Parenti, C. (1999) *Lockdown America: Police and Prisons in the Age of Crisis.* New York: Verso.

Selman, D. and Leighton, P. (2010) *Punishment for Sale: Private Prisons, Big Business, and the Incarceration Binge.* Lanham, MD: Rowman & Littlefield.

Social Justice (2000) Special Issue on Critical Resistance to the Prison-Industrial Complex, 27 (3).

CHAPTER 16

The War on Drugs

As President of the United States, within my first 45 days at the White House, I will work with my Secretary of Defense and the Joint Chiefs of Staff to seek further ways to use our military power – particularly technological capabilities – to fight the war on drugs. We will come up with a plan that focuses on the appropriate military means to augment our Federal and state drug enforcement agencies. (Senator Bob Dole, Republican Presidential Candidate)

LEARNING OBJECTIVES

After studying this chapter, you should be able to answer the following questions:

1 What is the nature of the war on drugs in the American society?
2 What are the three schools of thought on drug-control policy?
3 What are the various healthcare issues in corrections, and what measures are being taken to deal with HIV/AIDS, TB, aging prisoners, etc.?
4 What are the fundamental differences between the criminalization and medicalization approaches to drug control?

Terrence Stevens, an African-American with no previous drug convictions, symbolizes the punitive reality of the war on drugs. He was busted for possessing five ounces of cocaine, a violation punishable by 15 years to life under New York's so-called Rockefeller drug law. Stevens' prison sentence is the equivalent for more serious offenses, including murder and kidnapping and longer than the minimum terms for armed robbery, manslaughter, and rape. The case of Stevens invited greater media scrutiny due to his medical condition. As a kid growing up in a housing project in East Harlem, he developed muscular dystrophy. At the time of his arrest, Stevens was confined to a wheelchair and while in prison, he relies on fellow convicts to bathe, dress, and lift him onto and off the toilet. Correctional officers appear to ignore his disability. During a routine strip search, he told the guards that he was unable to remove his pants. For not complying with the order, he was sent to solitary confinement for 40 days. Upon appeal, the disciplinary charge was dropped, but only after he had served the punishment. Incidentally, the person who was arrested along with Stevens was not sentenced to prison; rather, he drew probation for testifying against Stevens (Purdy, 2000; see also Peters, 2009).

INTRODUCTION

Michael Tonry, author of *Malign Neglect: Race, Crime, and Punishment in America*, points out that drug offense sentences are the single most important cause for the enormous growth of the prison population in the United States since 1980. Correctional population figures support that claim. The percentage of state prisoners incarcerated for a drug violation nearly quadrupled from 1980 (6 percent) to 1996 (23 percent). Likewise, the percentage of drug offenders among federal prisoners jumped to 60 percent in 1996 from 25 percent in 1980. The increase in drug violators accounted for nearly three-quarters of the total increase in federal inmates and one-third of the total increase in state inmates during that 16-year span (BJS, 1998; Menhard *et al.*, 2001; Spohn and Holleran, 2002). Since then, the trend has continued. In 2006, an additional 265,800 drug violators were sentenced to state prisons, a 12 percent increase since 2000. Moreover, racial disparities persist. For Latinos, the growth was 15 percent, and for whites it was 37 percent. Even more dramatically, for blacks the increase reached more than 55 percent (Sabol *et al.*, 2009).

The continued rise in the number of drug offenders sentenced to prison, coupled with legislation demanding tougher penalties for drug violations, demonstrates the failure of deterrence theory in the war on drugs. The idea that incarcerating more drug offenders for long periods of time would lead to diminished drug crimes has not materialized. According to Jacqueline Cohen and her associates, 'Observers of the criminal justice system who in general agree on little else have joined in arguing that increased penalties for drug use and distribution at best have had a modest impact on the operation of illicit drug markets, on the price and availability of illicit drugs, and on consumption of illicit drugs' (1998: 1260). Even more recently, criminologists have tested the deterrence hypothesis underpinning the war on drugs. Spohn and Holleran (2002) compared recidivism rates for offenders sentenced to prison with those offenders on probation.

We find no evidence that imprisonment reduces the likelihood of recidivism. Instead, we find compelling evidence that offenders who are sentenced to prison have higher rates of recidivism and recidivate more quickly than do offenders placed on probation. We also find persuasive evidence that imprisonment has a more pronounced criminogenic effect on drugs offenders than on other types of offenders.

(p. 329; see also Dwyer and Moore, 2010)

In the United States, substance abuse – especially among minorities – is conceptualized more as a criminal justice problem than a public health issue. Although officials give lip service to treatment programs, the bulk of expenditure in the war on drugs is devoted to enforcement and punishment (Office of the National Drug Control Policy, 2010a, 2010b; Staley, 2000; see O'Mahony, 2008; UNODC, 2009). The analysis contained in this chapter carefully attends to key assumptions driving the war on drugs, and by doing so it recognizes the consequences for corrections. In particular, lengthy discussion sets out to explain how the prevailing campaign to control drugs tends to produce problems for jails and prisons. As we shall see, criminalization of drug use is intertwined with major healthcare issues pertaining to substance-abuse treatment, HIV/AIDS, tuberculosis (TB), and aging prisoners. To begin, we turn to the ongoing debate over drug control policy.

DEBATE OVER DRUG-CONTROL POLICY

Competing perspectives on the war on drugs have indeed complicated the debate over drug control. Curiously, conventional views on drug-control policy may not always match traditional ideologies in criminal justice. At times, conservatives and liberals alike hold positions that are the opposite of what would be expected. For instance, many conservatives support legalization or at least decriminalization while many liberals continue to endorse the prevailing criminalization approach to drug control. Because both conservatives and liberals tend to stray from their traditional points of view in forming opinions about drug control, Zimring and Hawkins (1991b) devised new terminology to identify three schools of thought on drug-control policy: public health generalism, legalism, and cost-benefit specificism.

Public health generalism finds that the consumption of psychoactive substances (including alcohol) leads to such problems as increasing costs for health treatment, excessive time taken off from work, family problems, and shortened life spans. Therefore this perspective places emphasis on the harmfulness of substances rather than on their legality, turning attention to crucial substance abuse as a disease or illness. Legalism, on the other hand, focuses not on the personal harm suffered by the individual, but on the social harm inflicted on society. Accordingly, the consumption of legally prohibited substances should be subject to criminal sanctions because such illegal behavior strains normative boundaries. Cost-benefit specificism supports the idea that 'the formulation of drug policy

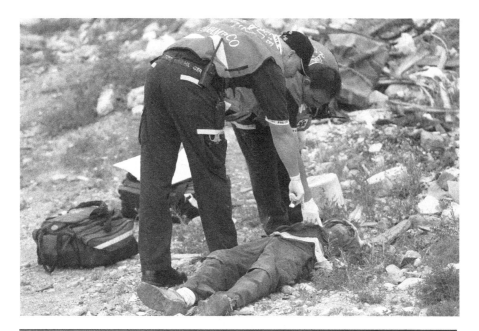

Figure 16.1   Mexican drug war fuels violence: medical personnel inspect a bullet-riddled body on March 23, 2010 in Juárez, Mexico. Secretary of State Hillary Rodham Clinton, Defense Secretary Robert Gates, and Homeland Security Secretary Janet Napolitano all visited Mexico that day for discussions centered on Mexico's endemic drug-related violence. The border city of Juárez, Mexico has been racked by violent drug-related crime recently and has quickly become one of the most dangerous cities in the world in which to live. As drug cartels have been fighting over ever-lucrative drug corridors along the United States border, the murder rate in Juárez has risen to 173 slayings for every 100,000 residents. President Felipe Calderón's strategy of sending 7,000 troops to Juárez has not mitigated the situation. Out of a population of 1.3 million, 2,600 people died in drug-related violence last year and 500 so far this year, including two Americans recently who worked for the US Consulate and were killed as they returned from a child's party.

Photo by Spencer Platt/Getty Images.

involves balancing both the costs of abuse and the likelihood of reducing them by legal prohibition against the manifold costs of enforcing prohibitive laws' (Zimring and Hawkins, 1991b: 109). Four components of drug-control strategy – supply reduction, treatment, prevention/education, and decriminalization – are central to the debate on the war on drugs. As discussed here, each of those schools of thought adheres to a different set of policy recommendations (see Lindesmith, 2007; Nadelmann, 2007).

Supply reduction

The legalistic perspective, adopted by federal officials in the *National Drug Control Strategy* (Office of the National Drug Control Policy, 2010a, 2010b; see also Office of the National Drug Control Policy, 2002), proposes continued expenditures on law enforcement and interdiction to reduce the supply of illegal drugs. In turn, it is assumed that the consumption of illegal drugs will decline. Public health generalists disagree with efforts to limit the supply of illegal drugs because they contend that non-prohibited drugs (e.g. alcohol) are just as harmful. Unlike public health generalists, however, cost-benefit specifists do not believe that all substances are equally harmful; moreover, they argue that cocaine (i.e. crack), for example, is more harmful than alcohol. Accordingly, cost-benefit specifists support initiatives to limit those drugs perceived as being more harmful. Critics of that perspective, however, acknowledge the fact that since alcohol abuse is more widespread than cocaine abuse, it constitutes a greater social problem (Welch, 1997a; see Caulkins and Macoun, 2003; Kerr et al., 2005).

Treatment

In general, treatment within the criminal justice system is often disrupted since the goal of punishment tends to supersede rehabilitation (see Chapter 4). The problem of goal conflict is particularly troubling for substance-abuse programs within the criminal justice system, especially given the coercive nature of mandatory treatment. Despite the problem of goal conflict, legalists endorse compulsory treatment programs whereby drug violators are intimidated into participating into treatment to ensure compliance. Moreover, upon completion of such programs, participants are intimidated into abstinence. Critics, however, contend that by coercively imposing treatment, the government undermines the genuine potential for individual rehabilitation.

With the aim of improving overall effectiveness, cost-benefit specifists advocate treatment as long as high-risk, active users are the target of such programs. Furthermore, treatment will have a greater impact when the focus of intervention is heavy drug users also involved in other crimes (e.g. burglary). Simply put, treatment would be producing 'more bang for the buck.' Given the widespread use of drugs – legal and illegal – public health generalists endorse campaigns to expand the availability of treatment programs (Granfield and Cloud, 2007; National Institute of Drug Abuse, 2007; Surratt, 2007).

Prevention and education

Although proponents of each of the schools of thought endorse substance-abuse prevention campaigns, they differ with regard to the content of preventive/educational messages. Legalists support anti-drug propaganda and oppose the dissemination of factual, informative messages. With a greater emphasis on morality, 'the legalist drug message to children is that illegal drugs are a bad thing and that drug takers are bad people' (Zimring and Hawkins, 1991b: 112; Cintron and Roth, 2001).

Public health generalists believe that revealing pure information about drugs, including both the desirable effects (e.g. euphoria) as well as the undesirable effects (e.g. withdrawal, physiological damage), promotes an honest representation of substances. It is their belief that an individual who is well educated about both legal and illegal drugs is more likely to avoid substance abuse than someone who has been deliberately misinformed by the government.

Cost-benefit specifists believe that preventive/educational messages can help draw distinctions between extremely harmful drugs (i.e. crack cocaine and injectable heroin, with particular cautions against needle sharing) and less harmful drugs (i.e. marijuana). As expected, legalists fear that such messages may appear to condone substance abuse and fall short of chastising those 'bad persons' who have used drugs. 'From the legalist perspective, this [the casual use of less harmful drugs] undermines the gospel of absolute abstention from illicit drugs and tends to demoralize the faithful never-users who are the most important target audience of the legalist appeal' (Zimring and Hawkins, 1991b: 113; see Cintron and Roth, 2001; Rosenbaum, 2007).

Decriminalization and legalization

Public health generalists favor decriminalization because it reconceptualizes substance abuse from a criminal justice issue to one of public health. Moreover, the campaign to decriminalize (some) drugs permits more open discussion of the harm caused by legal drugs (i.e. alcohol and prescription medication) vis-à-vis illegal drugs. In making those distinctions, cost-benefit specifists endorse decriminalization, but only for less harmful drugs.

The legalistic perspective tends to resist reframing the drug problem into a public health issue, maintaining a hard line in prohibiting substances that are currently prohibited. Zimring and Hawkins capture the vehement tone of many legalists: 'Proposals to decriminalize are characterized as "stupid," "irrational," and their purveyors are portrayed as "naive," with the same sinister undertones to the adjective that used to be aimed at those who were accused of communist sympathies' (1991b: 113).

Proposals for decriminalization tend to invite angry criticism by legalists, some of whom resort to distorting the facts at hand. For example, some legalists deliberately undermine the dispassionate notions of decriminalization by equating it with legalization. That ploy often works because the term *legalization* conjures up images of American society turning into a drug free-for-all. Early on, the Office of the National Drug Control Policy announced that the decriminalization of any drug 'would be an unqualified national disaster' (1989: 7). Moreover, staunch supporters of the war on drugs take the metaphor of war seriously and view decriminalization as admitting defeat or as surrendering to the enemy.

At this point, it is worth distinguishing between legalization and decriminalization. Proposals to legalize drugs emulate the current regulation of legal drugs, such as alcohol and tranquilizers. Decriminalization is considered less drastic, insofar as some drug violations (e.g. marijuana possession) would not be subjected to existing punitive sanctions but instead would be treated as minor offenses, similar to traffic violations. Consequently, the violator would be granted a summons and be expected to appear in court and to pay a fine. Although advocates of legalization and supporters of decriminalization do not agree on all aspects of drug-control policy, they do agree on three basic assumptions (Nadelmann, 1991, 1989, 2007):

1 Under legalization, drug use and abuse would not rise beyond current rates.
2 Some illegal drugs are not as harmful as widely believed; indeed, some are less harmful than some legal drugs.
3 The criminalization of drugs produces more problems than benefits.

These assumptions deserve some brief clarification. First, both decriminalization and legalization advocates do not accept the assumption that non-drug users would begin taking illegal substances if they were legalized. Most individuals are aware of the health hazards of various substances (e.g. alcohol, cigarettes, amphetamines); accordingly, many choose not to consume those substances. 'The image the legalizers have of the so-called average man and woman is that they are reasonable, rational, temperate, measured, and genteel. Large numbers of people are not going to do that which seriously endangers their lives' (Goode, 1993: 359). Second, evidence shows that certain illegal drugs, such as marijuana, are less harmful than is widely believed. In fact, since marijuana is not a physically addictive substance, it is less harmful than either alcohol and tobacco, substances known to produce physical addiction in some users (see Erickson *et al.*, 2010; Husak, 2002, 2000).

Finally, the continued criminalization of drugs has proven to be self-defeating and counterproductive. Chief among the problems generated by the prevailing prohibition of drugs is the high volume of street – and violent – crime owing to the profit motive. Advocates of decriminalization and legalization propose to eliminate the financial incentive from the drug trade, thereby reducing the violence common among drug dealers. Moreover, tax dollars currently being allocated for the armament of the war on drugs (i.e. police and prisons) could be better spent on education, housing, healthcare, and so on (Welch, 2005a; see Office of the National Drug Control Policy, 2010b).

RACE, CLASS, AND THE WAR ON DRUGS

Throughout, this book focuses attention on the economic forces that contribute to an expanding underclass – that is, those who have few meaningful economic opportunities available to them and few resources for survival. Inner-city minorities constitute the fastest-growing segment of the underclass. Moreover, it is in such low-income neighborhoods that local, state, and federal efforts have stepped up the war on drugs.

Drug use and abuse arise as attempts to escape the harsh living conditions inherent to inner cities. The proliferation of drugs in these areas can also be attributed to feelings of alienation that emerge from a sense of not having a future, from loss of hope, and from defeat. According to Rosenbaum, 'The drug abuse of the underclass is a *symptom* of a much deeper problem faced by tens of millions of individuals with blocked opportunities and severely limited life options' (1989: 18; see Sandberg and Pedersen, 2009)

For some members of the urban underclass, trafficking drugs represents one of the desperate ways to offset harsh living conditions. The illegal drug market offers not only tangible rewards (e.g. fast cash) but also cultural objects greatly valued in a consumer society (e.g. flashy clothes, jewelry, luxury cars) (see Loader, 2009; Maher and Daly, 2007; Spitzer, 1975).

Curiously though, the war on drugs is waged less against the so-called kingpins and more against low-level drug violators, namely impoverished minorities who often cannot adequately defend themselves against the ambitious law enforcement campaigns. Moreover, many of those drug peddlers are merely exercising one of the few economic options available to them, and their risky behavior stems from the perception that they have nothing to lose. By contrast, middle-income persons with meaningful jobs, intact families, and other social ties are less likely to take on the risk of arrest and incarceration.

War on drugs enthusiasts tend to hail their campaigns as a success, pointing to high arrest and conviction rates, as well as a booming correctional population. Still, the prohibition of drugs does nothing to address the economic forces that contribute to drug-related problems among the growing underclass. As noted, the prime targets of the war on drugs are racial minorities in impoverished neighborhoods where drug peddling is more visible and it is easier to make arrests (Surratt, 2007; Reinarman, 2007; Walker, 2001).

THE CRACK CONTROVERSY

Among the institutional disparities apparent in the American criminal justice system disproportionately affecting people of color and the poor is the assignment of disparate penalties for similar drug offenses. A particularly blatant bias is the discrepancy between penalties for crack versus powdered cocaine. Current federal legislation delivers a disproportionate impact on impoverished African American offenders, especially compared to their white, middle-class counterparts. That is clearly evident since crack (a cheaper form of cocaine) is more prevalent among inner-city African American drug users whereas powdered cocaine is more prevalent in the middle-class suburbs and its users are more evenly divided racially (US Sentencing Commission, 1991). Many experts conclude that the pharmacological differences between crack and powdered cocaine are negligible (Hatsukami and Fischman, 1996). Despite such scientific evidence many legislators support tougher sanctions for crack, arguing that the nature of trafficking invites greater violence and gang activity. Still, critics disagree, insisting that the policy is unfair, impractical, and perhaps in the end profoundly racist (Gray, 2001; Welch *et al.*, 1999; Welch *et al.*, 1998).

Congress legislated against the recommendations of the United States Sentencing Commission that had proposed that violations of crack and powdered cocaine be subject to equal penalties. Under then federal law, a conviction of possession or distribution of five grams of crack cocaine would draw a mandatory five-year sentence with no parole. By contrast, someone would have to possess or distribute 500 grams of the more expensive powdered cocaine to get the same sentence, thereby establishing a 100-to-1 ratio. The convictions quickly accumulated; in 1995, 14,000 of the 90,000 federal prisoners were serving sentences under those laws for crack cocaine offenses (US Sentencing Commission, 1995).

The Bureau of Justice Statistics reported that although half of crack users are white, the sale of the substance often is concentrated in impoverished inner-city neighborhoods where minority peddlers are overrepresented. Moreover, the agency also found that in 1994, 90 percent of those convicted of federal crack offenses were African American and 3.5 percent were white. By contrast, 25.9 percent of those convicted on federal powdered cocaine violations were white, 29.7 percent were African American, and 42.8 percent were Hispanic (Bureau of Justice Statistics, 1997).

Such biases have been challenged in court, albeit unsuccessfully. The US Supreme Court refused to address a racial bias evident in the Los Angeles criminal justice system. Twenty-four black defendants, all charged under federal law with crack offenses, cited compelling statistical evidence of racial prejudice and discrimination. Between 1990 and 1992, state authorities prosecuted over 200 white crack dealers while federal authorities prosecuted none, and federal penalties for crack offenses are far more severe than state penalties. Interestingly, when the trial court ordered the government to reveal its criteria for deciding whether to prosecute under state or federal law, the government refused. On appeal, the US Supreme Court declined to order the government to disclose its criteria, thus blocking the defendants' effort to document racial discrimination (ACLU, 1996; *US* v. *Armstrong*, 1996). Adding to the growing body of evidence of racial disparities in drug control, the US Sentencing Commission (1995) reported that only minorities were prosecuted under federal law for crack in 17 states and many cities. Scott Wallace of the National Legal Aid and Defender Association responded: 'Part of what amazes a lot of us is that Congress and the President are rejecting the recommendation of a body that was set up precisely to remove politics and snap judgments from the sentencing process so there isn't discrimination' (Smothers, 1995: A18).

By 2002, the US Department of Justice remained steadfastly opposed to changing the law to reduce prison terms for crack offenses, arguing that the disparities were not as large as generally believed. When faced with the evidence that showed that drug sentences unfairly punish blacks, Deputy Attorney General Larry D. Thompson stated: 'The current federal policy and guidelines for sentencing crack cocaine are appropriate' (Lewis, 2002: A24). Thompson added that if there are to be any changes, the sentences for powdered cocaine offenses should be increased. The Justice Department analyzed 46,413 cases convicted and sentenced under federal guidelines from 1996 and 2000. The study found that the average sentence for possession of five grams of crack cocaine with intent to distribute was 71 months, compared to 13 months for those involving five grams of powder. Thompson insisted that some disparity was justified because 'higher penalties for crack offenses appropriately reflected the greater harm posed by crack cocaine' (Lewis, 2002: A24).

Critics flatly disagree. Federal Judge Terry Hatter, Jr, a fierce opponent of the sentencing guidelines: said, 'If there is any disparity, it should be the reverse. There should be higher penalties for powder. I mean, you can't make the crack form without having the powder form first, and the powder form comes from outside [the country]' (Lewis, 2002: A24). Hatter elaborated on his position, saying that the government was associating crack with crime because it was sold in impoverished neighborhoods where crime was already rampant. Opponents of current drug sentencing guidelines have received support from conservative lawmakers. Republican Senators Orrin Hatch and Jeff Sessions proposed that the law be changed by raising the amount of crack mandating a five-year sentence while reducing the amount of powdered cocaine for the same sentence (see Kautt and Spohn, 2002).

In 2010, the US Senate Judiciary Committee unanimously passed a bill that would reduce the sentencing disparity between federal crack and powdered cocaine offenses. Lawmakers recognized that disparate sentencing policies enacted for federal crack cocaine offenses in 1986 have had a negative impact on the nation's criminal justice system. The bill would reduce the ratio between crack and powdered cocaine from 100:1 to 20:1 and authorize the US Sentencing Commission to enhance penalties for aggravating factors like violence or bribery of a law enforcement officer. Moreover, the proposal would also eliminate the mandatory minimum sentence for simple possession of crack (see US Sentencing Commission, 2010).

'This is an exciting vote, but also disappointing. We hoped the Committee would go further in making crack penalties the same as powder. There was no scientific basis for the 100:1 disparity between crack and powder cocaine created 24 years ago, and there is no scientific basis for today's vote of 20:1,' said FAMM (Families Against Mandatory Minimums) President Julie Stewart. 'However, if this imperfect bill becomes law, it will provide some long-overdue relief to thousands of defendants sentenced each year' (Guard, 2010: 1). The 20:1 ratio could affect nearly 3,100 cases annually, dropping sentences by an average of about 30 months. However, the bill would not reduce sentences for those currently incarcerated for crack offenses (US Sentencing Commission, 2010).

DRUG PENALTIES: LOSS OF COLLEGE AID AND WELFARE BENEFITS

In 1999, Russell Selkirk was found guilty of smoking marijuana. For that offense, a judge issued Selkirk a $250 fine, suspension of his driver's license, 20 hours of community service, and a year of probation. Then one month later, when Selkirk applied for financial aid for the forthcoming academic year, he learned of a second penalty – loss of eligibility for low-interest federal education loans and grants. Selkirk said with amazement, 'It's like two penalties for the same crime' (Schemo, 2001: A12). Whereas the law had been in effect since

1998, it was not fully enforced until President George W. Bush took office. Specifically, students become ineligible for federal financial aid and loans for one year after a possession conviction, or for two years after a conviction for selling drugs, unless they undergo a rehabilitation program that requires two random urine tests. Repeat offenders face permanent loss of federal aid to attend college. Republican Gary Johnson, then Governor of New Mexico, points out that no other law carries such a provision. Johnson, who has sponsored state legislation to decriminalize possession of small amounts of marijuana, said: 'You can rob a bank, you commit murder, just about any other crime and not be denied student aid, but a drug charge would deny you student aid' (Schemo, 2001: A12).

The penalty disproportionately affects the poor, who rely on financial aid, and racial minorities, who make up a large percentage of those arrested for drug offenses. David Borden, executive director of the Drug Reform Coordination Network, stated: 'There is every reason to believe that there will be some racial disparity in the way this law operates. It's a second punishment that only affects those who qualify for financial aid' (Schemo, 2001: A12). Indeed, students from wealthier families who are convicted on drug charges are not adversely affected since they do not rely heavily on financial aid. Of the more than 10 million students who applied for federal financial aid in 2000, more than 9,000 were found to be ineligible due to drug convictions. Shawn Heller, who founded Students for a Sensible Drug Policy, reminds us that during the 2000 presidential campaign, Vice-President Al Gore acknowledged smoking marijuana while in college. George W. Bush declined to answer questions about whether he had used cocaine and other drugs, saying, 'When I was young and irresponsible, I was young and irresponsible.' To that statement, Heller responded: 'If you're president of the United States of America, you don't have to answer these questions, but if you're coming from a poor family and trying to get an education, you do' (Schemo, 2001: A12). Making matters worse, the Department of Education began applying the law retroactively to any aid applicant with a drug conviction in the last couple of years.

Drug penalties that strip students of financial aid also extend to those receiving other forms of public assistance. While the Clinton administration hailed its victory to end 'welfare as we know it,' few observers realized that the Welfare Reform Act of 1996 included a provision that denies welfare benefits to more than 92,000 women convicted of drug violations, as well as their 135,000 children. Oddly, ex-cons who served time for murder or other violent offenses are fully eligible for welfare benefits. The law targets primarily the poor, especially women of color, considering that more than 48 percent of those affected by the statute are African American or Latino (Ridgeway, 2002). States can opt out of the lifetime ban, but 42 still enforce it. In many instances, the person is only a minor or first-time offender who is a single parent in need of treatment rather than punishment (Schwartz, 2002). Marc Mauer of the Sentencing Project, an organization that has studied the impact of the law, said that the lifetime ban on welfare benefits 'places children and their families at a much higher risk for failure and ensures ever growing societal costs to repair the damage' (Thompson, 2002: 31; see Sentencing Project, 2002; Tourigny, 2001).

CULTURAL PENOLOGY

The Myth of Crack Babies

The war on drugs has proved to be an all-encompassing campaign that shapes the way people distinguish between good and evil in today's society. Since that campaign is presented as a moral form of law enforcement, it tends to define drug offenders as being morally bad. Perhaps the most dramatic targets of the war-on-drugs crusaders are pregnant women who use illegal drugs. These women have been characterized as *evil mothers*, who are willing to endanger the health of their unborn children in pursuit of self-indulgent drug-induced highs. Harming innocent children, especially through the use of illegal drugs, arouses intense anger among most citizens – as it should. Thus the prevalence of drug use has resulted in the construction of yet another social problem, that of the so-called crack babies (Humphries, 1999; Welch, 1997b).

In the late 1980s, medical reports claimed that babies born to crack-addicted mothers had significantly lower birth weights and smaller heads, were more likely to suffer from seizures, and exhibited more behavioral aberrations than babies born to drug-free women. Without waiting for additional research to validate the claims that the mother's use of crack was the *sole* reason for these complications, the mass media generated countless stories about crack babies. Those messages conveniently supported the war-on-drugs campaign, and government officials cited crack babies as another reason to step up anti-drug efforts (see Reinarman, 2007).

However, most statements by government officials, newspaper editors, and other influential figures concerning crack babies were more than simply exaggerated – they were false. For example, the then federal 'drug czar,' William Bennett, declared that each year in the late 1980s, more than 375,000 crack babies were born in the United States. A careful examination of that figure revealed that crack babies would have accounted for 1 out of every 10 births in the nation; put that way, it seems very unlikely that crack babies could have accounted for that huge proportion of births. Bennett's false claim did not bring an end to the story over crack babies. Rather, the story gained momentum as key members in the media repeated the falsehood, most notably columnist Jack Anderson and the *New York Times* editor A. M. Rosenthal (Gieringer, 1990; Goode, 1993).

Had government officials and other interested parties waited for further studies to determine the precise impact that crack has on pregnancy, they would have learned that previous research (e.g. Chasnoff *et al.*, 1989) lacked crucial methodological safeguards, most importantly, controls. As Erich Goode (1993) points out, many of those women also consumed alcohol, and those who drank heavily were at high risk of giving birth to infants suffering from fetal alcohol syndrome and fetal alcoholic effects. Also significant is that the nutritional condition of these women was poor, and many of them smoked cigarettes that contain nicotine, a carcinogen linked to low birth weights.

Moreover, those women had received virtually no prenatal care, and many had also contracted sexually transmitted diseases. Goode goes on to note: 'Factors that vary with cocaine use are known to determine poorer infant outcomes; mothers who smoke crack and use powdered cocaine are more likely to engage in *other* behaviors that correlate with poor infant health' (1993: 56). Therefore it is difficult to determine exactly what effect crack has on the fetus when evidence of other toxins (alcohol, nicotine, etc.) and risky behaviors are also present.

In the debate over the issue of crack babies, no one is saying that crack does not adversely affect the health of the mother and the infant. However, to imply that crack is the sole cause of poor infant health, without mentioning the influence of other contributing factors, is irresponsible and manipulative. Goode critically summarizes the phenomenon of crack babies: 'Even from the beginning, some experts challenged the veracity of the crack-baby syndrome. But it was not until the early 1990s that enough medical evidence was assembled to indicate that the syndrome is, in all likelihood, mythical in nature' (1993: 56; also see Coles, 1991, 1992; Day *et al.*, 1992; Neuspiel *et al.*, 1991; Richardson and Day, 1991; Richardson, 1992). While the early hype surrounding crack babies was headline news, later developments in that area of research were not as well publicized and the media seemed to move onto other stories.

Regardless of developments in research on crack babies, support for the arrest and prosecution of pregnant women who use illegal drugs continued to mount. Indeed, advocates of the criminalization strategy justified their position by making reference to crack babies and other infants born to drug-addicted mothers. One such advocate, attorney Paul Logli (1991), endorsed legal intervention to protect defenseless babies from the alleged health hazards posed by their drug-addicted mothers. Despite myriad legal and constitutional difficulties that complicate the formulation of laws against pregnant drug users, Logli asserts the 'local prosecutors have a legitimate role in responding to the increasing problem of drug-abusing pregnant women and their drug-affected children' (1991: 299).

Critics of such legal intervention charge that such prosecutions suggest an intersection between the war on drugs and the pro-life movement as both campaigns strive to broaden social control over women. Furthermore, that particular law enforcement campaign is widely viewed as discriminatory because it targets poverty-stricken teenagers who do not have the legal resources to defend themselves. As Mariner *et al.* note: 'Singling out pregnant women highlights the fact that they are being punished not for any act harming the fetus but because they are pregnant and use drugs' (1991: 292–3).

Opponents of the criminalization approach, citing the absence of both adequate prenatal care and accessible substance-abuse treatment as a contributing factor in the birth of at-risk babies, argue that coercive and punitive measures simply do not work. Mariner *et al.* (1991) and Maher

(1990) contend that criminalization is self-defeating. It drives pregnant women away from sources of assistance (e.g. prenatal care and substance-abuse treatment), even when those sources are available, because they fear that if they seek help, they will lose custody of their babies after birth. Women's rights advocates do not morally defend acts of irresponsibility and negligence on the part of pregnant addicts. However, they charge that 'injecting the criminal law can only deepen the tragedy ... Drug use during pregnancy is a real problem that can only be compounded by treating it as a crime' (Mariner *et al.*, 1991: 293; see also Logan, 1999; Murphy and Rosenbaum, 1999; Murphy and Sales, 2001).

FROM THE WAR ON DRUGS TO INTERVENTION

Due to the enormous impact that the war on drugs and its mandatory minimum sentences are having on prisons and jails, corrections officials must contend with the daunting task of administering healthcare to a larger and aging inmate population. In the following sections, medical and healthcare issues are carefully considered, including HIV/AIDS, tuberculosis, and suicidal inmates. Each of these areas of medical intervention remains compounded by conflicting views over the proper role of healthcare in correctional facilities. So that we do not lose sight of the importance of contextualizing drug control policy within the realm of public heath, the discussion begins with an overview of substance-abuse treatment in corrections.

Substance-abuse treatment

While advocating for greater investment in substance-abuse programs in correctional facilities, experts remind us of the importance of three components necessary for sound policy (Austin and Irwin, 2001; Inciardi, 2002). For substance-abuse treatment to be an effective part of reducing crime, it is first assumed that most prisoners are drug abusers and that they commit large numbers of crimes due to their drug use. In a widely cited study, *Behind Bars: Substance Abuse and America's Prison Population*, the National Center on Addiction and Substance Abuse (CASA, 1998) estimated 70 to 80 percent of all inmates have committed a crime while under the influence of drugs (and/or alcohol), committed a drug crime, or used a drug on a regular basis. It stands to good reason that enrolling those inmates in drug treatments while behind bars serves to reduce the chances of them returning to drugs as well as crime.

According to its analysis, CASA reports that drug addicts commit an average 100 crimes per year; therefore, a state government could gain $36,700 dollars in avoided criminal justice and healthcare expenditures for every inmate who completes a treatment program at a cost of $6,500. The cost-benefit analysis rests on the assumption that each successfully treated offender would likely be employed at a salary of $21,400, producing $32,100 in overall economic benefits. According to that formula, CASA concludes that only 10 percent of the prisoners entering drug treatment must succeed for the intervention to be financially justified.

The second component assumes that in order to become effective, treatment programs would have to he expanded considerably inside correctional facilities. Regrettably, the number of inmates who are enrolled in well-staffed and well-funded treatment programs is rather small. In many institutions, treatment programs are either non-existent or restricted to a select few due to the lack of resources and personnel. Another important reason for expanding the pool of those in treatment is to offset the problem of attrition. Because all programs suffer from a certain drop-out rate, it is crucial that the number of those enrolled remain high so that the overall effectiveness of the program is not hampered (Austin and Irwin, 2001).

Finally, it is assumed that the intervention will have a significant effect on those participating, thus reducing their chances of resorting to drugs and crime. The body of evaluation literature continues to examine the effectiveness of treatment programs (see Gray, 2001; Inciardi, 2002; National Institute of Drug Abuse, 2007; Walker, 2001). In a comprehensive assessment of seven model drug treatment programs for prison and jail inmates, Lipton (1995) issues favorable findings with respect to their capacity to reduce drug use and recidivism. Participants who successfully completed all phases of treatment had lower rates of continued drug use and recidivism.

Despite the potential for drug treatment programs, there remain obstacles that undermine their overall effectiveness. Since it is assumed that participants who are likely to succeed in the community do so because they have secured gainful employment, it is crucial that treatment programs also offer job training and placement. Moreover, those programs must also play a significant role in assisting ex-cons in locating employers willing to hire them. That concern sheds light on the importance of after-care, in which those who are released from prison have ongoing contact and support with treatment programs in the community, helping them achieve their goals of staying clean and having steady work (see Nadelmann, 2007; Surratt, 2007).

California's Proposition 36

In a move suggesting that citizens are growing weary of merely 'warehousing' drug offenders, California residents backed Proposition 36 with 61 percent of the vote. Under the new law that took effect in 2001, first-time and second-time drug violators are subject to treatment rather than imprisonment, becoming the nation's most ambitious experiment in drug rehabilitation. California locks up more drug offenders per capita than any other state, including huge numbers of non-violent first-time and second-time drug offenders. Under Proposition 36, those who want to avoid going to jail and receive help from one of the 300 private treatment services (in Los Angeles) must enter a conditional guilty plea;

then, they will be supervised during treatment by one of 26 special judges. Upon successfully completing the program, offenders' records are cleared. To further enforce the law, participants are subject to compulsory drug testing.

The initiative is aimed at reducing the cost of incarceration, and each of California's 58 counties have their own plan to meet the requirements of the new law. But while the state has allocated $120 million a year to the program, local government officials worry that they will not have sufficient funds to carry out the statewide mandate. In Los Angeles county (the state's largest), supervisors say their program could be financially overwhelmed in its effort to handle about one-third of the state's expected eligible offenders. Moreover, Proposition 36 did not set aside funds for drug testing, fueling the debate over whether the measure will ever achieve its objectives (*New York Times*, 2001b, July 3).

Among the challenges facing Proposition 36 is the realization that many of those who have sought treatment are considered far more serious addicts than policy-makers expected, a problem compounded by mental illness, homelessness, and unemployment. Judge Stephen Marcus of Los Angeles County noted: 'One of the lessons we are learning is that we are getting a lot of people who are so addicted they just aren't ready for treatment,' adding, 'their addiction is so powerful it controls everything in their lives' (Butterfield, 2001: A6). To their surprise, government officials have discovered that the majority of those entering programs are hard-core addicts requiring maximum treatment.

Despite these complications, advocates continue their support for the initiative. Bill Zimmerman, executive director of the Campaign for New Drug Policies, a group that backed the referendum, said: 'The key thing is people who formerly were being incarcerated are now getting treatment' (Butterfield, 2001: A6). Zimmerman remains optimistic that the social movement toward rehabilitation will persist, and his organization is lobbying other states considering similar laws, including Florida, Michigan, Missouri, and Ohio. In those states and elsewhere, officials are rethinking their commitment to spending on corrections as a central component to drug control, alternatively turning attention to the promise of cost-effective drug treatment programs.

A critique of drug intervention

In proposing an alternative to the war on drugs, it should be noted that the medical model – much like its criminalization counterpart – suffers from key institutional biases. Most notably, the medicalization of drug abuse tends to remain directed at individuals rather than social structures. Scholars and researchers contend that widespread dependencies on drugs (legal as well as illegal) will not be contained by relying solely on rehabilitation initiatives (Lindesmith, 2007; Pepinsky, 2010). A drug control strategy exclusively based on treatment not only would divert attention from its fundamental causes (e.g. alienation rooted in social and economic inequality) but also would transfer authority from law enforcement agencies to a medical establishment (Chapter 4).

Although the medicalization of drug abuse is widely supported as a humane alternative to criminalization, there remains a dark side of rehabilitation as a form of public policy. That is, the medical model empowers a class of experts and professionals acting as agents of social control, but under the guise of humane intervention (Foucault, 1965, 1973; Lesieur and Welch, 2000). The medical model is further confounded by socioeconomic realities since its experts and professionals derive their financial wellbeing and status from the same economic system as those who carry out state mandates. Consequently, medical's personnel may not be any less inclined to use their authority to manage and regulate those upon whom the system casts as needing intervention. The medical establishment also reduces the competency of people to provide for and take care of themselves, thereby leaving them further dependent on a class of professionals as well as the state. According to Dennis Sullivan, 'the rehabilitative mask of love' was no more effective than the fist of the prison (1980: 54; see Pepinsky, 2010).

That view should not imply that critical criminologists oppose substance-abuse treatment; on the contrary, many of them fully endorse rehabilitation on the condition that it is voluntary and not coerced by the state or by a class of professional experts and technicians (see Welch, 2005a; 1997b). Still, on the larger social scale the goal is to eradicate dependency on drugs, and such an objective will not be achieved by adopting solely a medical and individualistic approach. Attention must be directed at injustices produced by social hierarchies and political-economic infrastructures that obstruct the fulfillment of inherent human needs. The contradictions in the social structure foster the need for people to consume drugs while simultaneously becoming addicted to state control. In reconceptualizing the drug problem from this critical perspective, it is understood that social, political, and economic reforms are necessary to correct the problems reproduced by inequality, exploitation, and repression (Gill, 1996; Welch *et al.*, 1999; Welch *et al.*, 1998).

Figure 16.2 A man is arrested as Rio's police occupy the Morro do Borel slum to install a peacemaker police unit to help in the control of drug traffic in Rio de Janeiro, Brazil, April 28, 2010.

Photo by Guilherme Pinto/ Globo via Getty Images.

PENAL HARM VERSUS MEDICAL CARE

As noted in previous chapters, many prisons and jails have been undergoing a deliberate shift toward making confinement harsher. By eliminating programs and various so-called 'amenities' (i.e. recreational opportunities), correctional institutions have yielded to the *penal harm movement*. That campaign rests on two (faulty) assumptions. First, prisons are described as being comfortable environments, providing 'three hots and a cot.' Second, these comfortable prison conditions contribute to recidivism and higher crime rates (Clear, 1994; Cullen, 1995).

Recently, critics have become concerned that the penal harm movement is having an adverse effect on prison healthcare, especially since from that perspective medical attention behind bars is too considered to be an 'amenity' or even a 'luxury.' The issue is subject to intense debate. On the one side, there are healthcare professionals who advocate the 'principle of equivalence' as an extension of the Hippocratic Oath. From their perspective, physicians pledge themselves to use medical treatment to help the sick, regardless of their social status, hence drawing no differences between patients in the free world and those under lock and key (Anno *et al.*, 1996; Harding, 1987). On the other side of the debate are proponents of the 'principle of less eligibility,' who contend that conditions of confinement should remain below the minimum standard of living of working people or people on welfare in the free world (see Melossi, 1985; Rusche and Kirchheimer, 1938). Similarly, it is suggested that those in or near the center of social life should have more privileges than those further out on society's margin. According to that theory, prisoners would receive fewer benefits in terms of medical care as well as legal protection than persons fully integrated in the free world. The penal harm movement clearly embraces retribution. Its opponents, however, insist that denying medical treatment to prisoners as a means of inflicting pain and suffering violates the Hippocratic Oath, raising serious ethical issues in the delivery of correctional healthcare (Delgado and Humm-Delgado, 2008).

In 1976, the US Supreme Court ruled in *Estelle* v. *Gamble* that prisoners are constitutionally entitled to adequate medical care; still, that right does not mean that inmates will have unqualified access to healthcare. Since that decision, lower courts have weighed into the debate. In *Anderson* v. *Romero* (1995: 524) and *Forbes* v. *Edgar* (1997: 267), the courts held that under the US Constitution prisoners are not entitled to the 'best' medical attention. Going even further, the courts have ruled that medical care afforded to inmates is not required to be 'perfect, the best obtainable, or even very good' (*Brown* v. *Beck*, 1980: 726; *Hawley v. Evans*, 1989: 603). In comparing court holdings between prison and free-world healthcare, Vaughn and Carroll (1998) found evidence that the courts have embraced the principle of less eligibility, thereby adding leverage to the penal harm movement.

Unlike free-world patients, inmates are denied access to medical specialists, timely delivery of medical services, technologically advanced diagnostic techniques, the latest medication and drug therapies, and up-to-date surgical procedures. Moreover, inmates routinely are denied second opinions and the right to choose from alternative medical therapies, whereas free-world patients enjoy these luxuries. In addition, liability frequently attaches in the free world, but not in prison medical care cases.

(Vaughn and Carroll, 1998: 32)

Compared to citizens in the free world, prisoners – due to their lower social rank – have fewer legal remedies for claims of inadequate medical care. Compounding matters, the 1996 Prison Litigation Reform Act has further restricted inmates' access to the courts (*Carson* v. *Johnson*, 1997; *McGore* v. *Wrigglesworth*, 1997).

Concerned that the penal harm movement is pulling the US away from international standards governing the treatment of prisoners, Vaughn and Smith (1999) remind us of the significance of the 'deprivation of liberty' view of punishment. The sole purpose of incarceration, according to that perspective, is to restrict the freedoms of those sentenced to prison, hence lawbreakers are sent to prison *as* punishment not *for* punishment (Council of Europe, 1987). Espousing the belief that prisons should resocialize criminal offenders, Penal Reform International states that prison managers must be 'concerned with ensuring prisoners' personal dignity, their physical and mental well-being, education and recreational facilities, religious provisions, and standards of hygiene and medical and psychiatric care' (1990: 5). The penal harm movement has contributed to greater role conflict among healthcare providers in corrections insofar as its workplace culture is divided into two irreconcilable camps: those committed to the tenets of penal harm and those adhering to the deprivation of liberty perspective.

In their research Vaughn and Smith unveiled evidence that some correctional health providers identified with the custodial subculture and its aim of inflicting pain and suffering on prisoners (see Hornblum, 1997; Murton, 1971). Specifically, six methods of ill treatment were discovered. In the first method, medical care was used to humiliate prisoners. For instance, a sergeant and a detention deputy escorted a psychiatric prisoner to the jail barber, who used a razor to sculpt the word 'fuckhead' on the back of the prisoner's head. He was then paraded around the institution to further degrade him. The second tactic involved withholding medical care from HIV-positive prisoners and those with AIDS. In one case, a prisoner urged jail medical officials to distribute his AIDS medication but was told that it was too much trouble, adding '[Y]ou are in jail not a hotel: if you don't like it bond out' (Vaughn and Smith, 1998: 202). Third, medical staff also withheld medical care from other prisoners, including an incident in which a detainee was diagnosed with a fractured neck vertebra. The physician at the jail prescribed aspirin. Weeks later, the detainee complained that aspirin was insufficient to reduce the pain; medical staff retaliated by denying him all treatment, including aspirin (see Abramsky, 2002).

In the fourth method of ill treatment, prisoners were subjected to extreme temperatures and sleep deprivation. At the Pelican Bay State Prison in California, naked prisoners were locked in telephone booth-sized cages and exposed to 'cold therapy.' A federal court found that such ill treatment failed to 'serve any legitimate penological purpose' and that it exhibited a 'callous and malicious intent to inflict gratuitous humiliation and punishment' (*Madrid* v. *Gomez*, 1995: 1172). Fifth, medical staff used dental care as a means of ill treatment (and torture). For example, prisoners were forced to wait weeks or months for dental care for abscessed teeth, and when care was finally available the correctional dentist pulled the wrong teeth (Walens, 1997: 86). Finally, medical staff falsified prisoners' medical records in an effort to conceal acts of negligence and other forms of ill treatment. Research on penal harm medicine attempts to demonstrate that the larger movement toward retribution has permeated correctional healthcare (see Dabney and Vaughn, 2000; Vaughn, 1999a). Still, it is important to acknowledge that incidents of ill treatment are confined to a few select healthcare providers who have identified with the custodial subculture. 'Many correctional health workers are dedicated professionals performing a difficult job in a less-than-ideal environment' (Vaughn and Smith, 1999: 219; see also Kerle *et al.*, 1999). (See 'Comparative Corrections: Penal Harm Medicine in North Korea' below.)

COMPARATIVE CORRECTIONS

Penal Harm Medicine in North Korea

Whereas penal harm medicine remains controversial in American prisons, overseas the problem has taken on much greater significance. In North Korea, for instance, recent allegations charge prison officials with forced abortions and baby killings. For several years, thousands of North Koreans have fled to China in an effort to escape political and economic repression. Compounding problems for those refugees, China has recently stepped up its efforts to track down and deport them. From March to May 2000, more than 8,000 defectors – mostly women – were deported to North Korea, where they were labeled as traitors and summarily imprisoned in a host of penitentiaries and concentration camps. Overall, the North Korean prison system holds more than 200,000 people in conditions so brutal that an estimated 400,000 people have died in custody since 1972, according to the US Committee for Human Rights in North Korea, a private group based in Washington, DC.

Allegations that North Korean prison officials have ordered forced abortions and baby killings are not only numerous but come from an array of witnesses, including prisoners and staff. Song Myung Hak, a former prisoner, said that she watched as a squad of male guards herded new women prisoners together and one by one asked if they were pregnant. Those who admitted to being pregnant were escorted to a medical unit where they were forcibly injected with abortion shots. The practice of forced abortions is driven by strong nationalistic overtones, since many of the women became pregnant in China before being deported to North Korea. 'The guards would scream at us: "You are carrying Chinese sperm from foreign countries. We Koreans are one people, how dare you bring this foreign sperm here,"' said one former prisoner. If babies were born alive, prisoners would be forced to kill them, often by smothering them with plastic sheets.

Willy Fautre, director of Human Rights Without Borders, a group based in Brussels, reports that in 2001 several hundred babies were killed in North Korean prisons. 'This is a systematic procedure carried out by guards and the people in charge of the prisons – these are not isolated cases,' insisted Fautre. Lee Soon Ok, who was employed as an accountant for six years at the Kaechon political prison, recalled in an interview that she twice saw prison doctors kill newborn babies, sometimes by stepping on their necks. Lee, who testified on human rights abuses at a hearing of the US House of Representatives International Relations Committee, added that with virtually no medical care for prisoners, surgical abortion was not an option: 'Giving birth in prison is 100 percent prohibited. That is why they kill those babies' (Brooke, 2002: A1).

North Korea's official news agency announced that the charges by Human Rights Without Borders that 'unborn and newly born babies are being killed in concentration camps' were 'nothing but a plot deliberately hatched by it to hurl mud' at North Korea. However, Selig S. Harrison, director of the national security program at the Center for International Policy in Washington, DC, finds the allegations consistent with other human rights atrocities in North Korea, noting that it 'is a repressive, repugnant, totalitarian state, and it certainly uses repugnant methods in its prison system and in its concentration camps.'

Source: Brooke (2002: A1, A6)

CRITICAL ANALYSIS

In previous chapters the exercises entitled 'Critical Analysis of Data' have focused on numerical data. Still, critical analysis extends to other forms of evidence. Looking again at the aforementioned story on North Korea, apply your own critical analysis by returning to the boxed insert 'Cultural Penology: The Myth of Crack Babies.' Do you see any parallels with respect to threats to children? Using your on-line skills, visit the web and search for similar news stories on the controversy over forced abortions and baby killings in North Korean prison camps. Which organizations are cited in those stories? Do you detect any particular political agendas?

HIV/AIDS IN CORRECTIONS

The problem of intravenous (IV) drug use cannot be separated from its related illnesses, especially acquired immunodeficiency syndrome (AIDS) and human immunodeficiency virus (HIV, the infection that leads to AIDS). Since the late 1980s, HIV/AIDS has become a disease less associated with gay, white middle-class men and more with minority lower-income intravenous drug users of both sexes. The most prevalent methods of HIV/AIDS transmission among that population are sharing contaminated hypodermic needles and having unprotected sexual contact with an infected person.

The prevalence of HIV/AIDS alongside drug infractions and related street crime among lower-income minority groups tends to attract the attention of the criminal justice apparatus. As police and courts process those violators into the system, many of them eventually make their way to places of confinement. Indeed, on a daily basis jails and prisons must contend with the various problems associated with HIV/AIDS. Moreover, because correctional administrators do not have the discretion to select which violators are to be sent to penal facilities, they are forced to deal with the ideological, political, legal, and ethical consequences of policy- and decision-making (Welch, 1999a, 1989b).

Scope of the problem

So as to recognize the extent of the problem of HIV/AIDS facing corrections, it is important to map out some key figures. According to a recent report published by the Bureau of Justice Statistics:

- In 2008, a reported 21,987 inmates held in state or federal prisons were HIV positive or had confirmed AIDS, accounting for 1.5 percent of the total custody population. That figure remained stable between 2007 and 2008.
- That year, 1.5 percent (20,075) of male inmates and 1.9 percent (1,912) of female inmates held in state or federal prisons were HIV positive or had confirmed AIDS.
- Florida (3,626), New York (3,500), and Texas (2,450) reported the largest number of prisoners who were HIV positive or had confirmed AIDS. These three states account for 24 percent of the total state custody population, but 46 percent of the state custody population who were HIV positive or had confirmed AIDS.
- New York reported the largest decreases (down 450 from 2007 to 2008) in the number of prisoners who were HIV positive or had confirmed AIDS. Between 2007 and 2008, California (up 246) and Florida (up 166) reported the largest increases in the number of prisoners who were HIV positive or had confirmed AIDS.
- In 2007, the most recent year for which general population data are available, the overall rate of estimated confirmed AIDS among the state and federal prison population (0.41 percent) was more than twice the rate in the general population (0.17 percent).
- In 2008 an estimated 5,733 state and federal prisoners had confirmed AIDS, and during 2007, 130 state and federal prisoners died from AIDS-related causes.

(Maruschak, 2009; see also Maruschak 2001).

As we turn attention to how HIV/AIDS poses challenges for corrections, it is crucial to note that the illness is more prevalent among black and Latino inmates (of low socioeconomic status) than their white counterparts (Maruschak, 2009; see Flavin, 2002; Inciardi, 2002). Before examining these institutional issues, the discussion considers some of the wider myths and misconceptions about HIV/AIDS.

Myths and misconceptions about HIV/AIDS

An understandable reaction to HIV/AIDS is fear and anxiety. In response, concerned individuals turn to the scientific community not only with hope that medical researchers will eventually develop a cure, but also for help in understanding the nature of the illness and in learning how to protect themselves from infection. Early on, however, some members of the medical establishment acted irresponsibly by perpetuating myths and misconceptions rather than dispensing sound knowledge on HIV/AIDS. The famous sex researchers Masters and Johnson, along with Robert Kolodny, for instance, published a popular book about HIV/AIDS in 1988. In *Crisis: Heterosexual Behavior in the Age of AIDS*, the authors made statements about the transmission of HIV/AIDS that ran counter to what was known about the disease at the time. Masters, Johnson, and Kolodny asserted that HIV/AIDS had clearly broken out among heterosexuals, and that illness could be contracted from saliva and hard substances such as toilet seats. When confronted by the Presidential Commission on AIDS about such claims, Masters and his associates conceded that 'they had no independent data to support their conclusions' (Sirica, 1991: 14). Critics charged that Masters, Johnson, and Kolodny knowingly disseminated false information about HIV/AIDS in an effort to capitalize commercially from book profits. In stoking public anxiety, the authors perpetuated myths about the disease (Welch, 1989b).

It is important to realize that 'there is not a general epidemic of HIV infection in the United States. Instead, there is really a series of smaller, overlapping epidemics – for example, homosexual men, IV drug users, and sexual partners of IV drug users' (Hammett, 1989: 16). Still, there has been a misconception that correctional workers have an exceedingly high risk of contracting HIV/AIDS while carrying out their job duties. Even though correctional officers supervise and interact daily with numerous inmates who are HIV-positive (and with those who are known to have AIDS) no job-related cases of HIV infection or AIDS have been documented among correctional staff (Hammett *et al.*, 2007).

Another misconception suggests that HIV/AIDS is spreading rapidly within the correctional population. That concern is driven by the stories of homosexual rape and IV drug abuse among inmates, as well as by general misunderstanding of how HIV/AIDS is transmitted. As Chapter 9 notes, the prevalence of homosexual rape in correctional facilities is greatly exaggerated. To be clear, no evidence thus far supports the claim that there is widespread transmission of HIV among inmates (Hammett *et al.*, 1999, Hammett, 2006).

It is crucial to properly confront myths and misconceptions about HIV/AIDS since misinformation and confusion lead to unnecessary fear among staff members (and inmates) who are in close proximity to prisoners with HIV/AIDS. Health experts recommend that accurate information about the illness be disseminated within correctional facilities so that administrators can avert overzealous or misguided management decisions (see Delgado and Humm-Delgado, 2008).

Correctional policy on HIV/AIDS

In the development of sound correctional policy on HIV/AIDS, several key issues should be taken into account so that inmate management decisions have a sound and reasonable basis. The following sections address many concerns, chief among them: mass screening, education and training, medical care, support services, housing and programming policies, precautionary and preventative measures, and legal issues, along with relevant sociological and psychological considerations (see Hammett, 2006; Hammett *et al.*, 2007).

Mass screening

Among the most controversial management issues in dealing with HIV/AIDS in corrections is mass screening: the mandatory testing of all inmates, or all releases in the absence of clinical indicates (Hammett *et al.*, 1999). Critics of that policy contend that mass screening tends to rely on the misconception that rates of transmission are higher in correctional institutions than in the larger society; thus it is believed that mass screening is necessary to identify all infected inmates. Critics of mass screening further point out that there is no evidence of higher transmission rates in prisons and jails than in the general population. Therefore it is proposed that educational programs be offered to all inmates (and staff) without identifying infected prisoners. Hammett *et al.* (1999) also caution that mass screening can lead to the problem of stratifying the prison population into a stigmatized class and so-called 'safe' class.

Mass screening also raises issues of confidentiality and reliability. Opponents insist that confidentiality of test results is difficult to protect, and patient information (or rumors) can lead to victimization during incarceration and discrimination upon release (e.g. in obtaining health insurance, housing, and employment). The reliability of testing also has been questioned, and the cost of repeat tests to confirm cases is prohibitive, especially in large institutions.

Legal issues pertaining to mass screening also should be addressed. Opponents point out that mass screening (that involves involuntary testing) can be challenged on the basis of existing laws requiring the person's informed consent. In view of that issue, voluntary testing (or on-request testing if clinical symptoms are present) for early detection and therapeutic intervention has become the trend. Arrangements for voluntary testing are made with local public health departments or other agencies; additionally, such testing is available to inmates and staff in response to possible transmission incidents. In sum, mass screening tends to generate more institutional – and budgetary – strains (Hammett *et al.*, 1999).

In light of those policy concerns, screening for HIV is a common practice. As of 2008, a total of 24 states reported testing all inmates for HIV at admission or sometime during custody. Among those 24 states, 23 tested prisoners at admission, five tested while in custody, and six tested upon release. In addition to the federal prison system, all 50 states tested inmates if they had clinical indication of HIV infection or if they requested an HIV test. The federal system along with 42 states tested inmates following an incident in which an inmate was exposed to a possible HIV transmission. Eighteen states (and the federal system) tested inmates who belonged to specific 'high-risk' groups (Maruschak, 2009; see Arriola *et al.*, 2001; Desai *et al.*, 2002; Hammett *et al.*, 2007).

Education and training

It is recommended that HIV/AIDS education and training should be granted high priority so that both inmates and staff possess informed knowledge about the nature of the disease and its transmission. Indeed many correctional institutions have taken education and training seriously, to the extent that such programs are required for staff as well as for inmates. Educating inmates about HIV/AIDS strives to reduce risky behavior (i.e. needle sharing and unprotected sexual contact). Moreover, education allays fears about contracting HIV/AIDS through casual contact. Hammett *et al.* (1999) recommend that education and training be repeated periodically so that advances in research can be shared in a timely fashion. The use of peer trainers in cooperation with professionals is also suggested since it adds further credibility to HIV/AIDS education (see Hammett, 2006; Hammett *et al.*, 2007).

Medical care and medication

Administrators eager to provide adequate health care for prisoners with HIV/ AIDS often face the issue of funding. As is the case outside prison, health care in general is expensive. Such costs are even higher for correctional populations, especially for inmates with HIV/AIDS. Although it may be tempting to compromise medical services for prisoners due to budgetary limitations, many administrators overcome such problems by lobbying state officials for greater funding. In some instances, the courts support efforts to increase spending on medical services in corrections. Regardless of those efforts, budgetary constraints have a negative impact on healthcare for inmates with HIV/AIDS, particularly those in need of medication. Some medications (e.g. AZT) are shown to delay the progression of the disease in some patients. Still, due to the high cost of these drugs, some correctional systems do not dispense the medication in ways that promote effectiveness; in many cases, dosages are limited or the entire distribution is curtailed. Recently, Hammett *et al.* (2007) found that most state and federal prison systems provide antiretroviral treatment for HIV; however, many of those systems have more aggressive criteria for initiating treatment than these in national treatment guidelines. Most prison systems employ either 'pill lines' or keep-on-person methods for administration of HIV medications.

Support services

Given the emotional and psychological stress related to HIV/AIDS, correctional administrators are advised to recognize the importance of providing counseling and support to infected inmates. Many of those programs are administered by outside professionals and advocacy groups; in some institutions, prisoners conduct their own support and counseling sessions. Counseling is intended not only to benefit inmates who must cope with the disease during their incarceration, but also to prepare them to return to the community. Upon their release, ex-cons are encouraged to notify their sexual partners and to avoid behaviors that may transmit HIV to others. Furthermore, ex-cons will have to deal with insurance companies or apply for Medicaid, and seek psychological services within the community. Prison health advocates, however, are dismayed to find that between 1996–7 and 2005, the proportion of correctional systems offering support groups for inmates with HIV declined to about one-third. Still, almost all correctional systems continue to provide some discharge planning for inmates with HIV. The most prevalent methods of linking soon-to-be-released inmates to community-based services are the use of referral lists or specific appointments for HIV medical treatment (Hammett *et al.*, 2007; see Welch, 2000d).

Housing and programming policies

A prevailing practice for institutional housing is the mainstreaming of infected prisoners into the general correctional population rather than segregating them. Still, many institutions administer mainstreaming on a case-by-case basis. Clearly, those suffering from advanced stages of AIDS might need to remain in a medical unit, but those who are asymptomatic would certainly be good candidates to remain in the general population. Since 1985, the number of states that segregate inmates with HIV/AIDS from the rest of the prison population has declined from 38 to three. In Alabama and Mississippi, all inmates testing positive for HIV are segregated both residentially and programmatically. Prisoners with HIV/AIDS in California live in separate quarters but join the population for work assignments and educational and vocational programs. Perhaps fueling the myth that HIV can be transmitted through food, some correctional systems exclude prisoners with HIV from food service assignments (Hammett *et al.*, 1999). More recently, the trend has been for greater mainstreaming of both prisoners with HIV and those with AIDS into the general population with no restrictions (Hammett *et al.*, 2007; see also Courtenay and Sabo, 2001; Flavin, 2002, 1998).

Precautionary and preventive measures

Although precautionary and preventive measures are necessary, they should be taken without inflaming fears. A commonly accepted practice of infection control is taking universal precautions; that is, training staff to approach all inmates as if they are infected. The use of protective gear, such as gloves, masks, and infectious waste receptacles, is strongly encouraged to reduce the risk of contacting blood and body fluids. Given the current controversy over condom distribution that practice has been adopted in only a few correctional institutions. Hammett *et al.* (2007) report that only four correctional systems make condoms available to inmates for use within their facilities. Those facilities tend to provide condoms on a 'targeted' basis (e.g. to 'vulnerable populations' only), or through a sick call request process (see Hammett *et al.*, 1990).

Legal issues

Since the mid-1980s, numerous lawsuits have been filed which address HIV/AIDS-related issues: unnecessary segregation, inadequate medical care, inadequate HIV/AIDS education, challenges to mass screening, and breaches of confidentiality. In *Harris* v. *Thigpen* (1990) in Alabama a prisoner contested the policy of mass screening, as well as segregation of HIV and AIDS inmates, and charged that medical care was inadequate. Inmates were later disappointed when, in 1990, the court ruled in favor of the Alabama correctional system. The court stated that the system's policies represented reasonable measures in dealing with infected inmates. Nevertheless, similar cases filed by inmates challenging HIV/AIDS policies and charging that the institution neglects the medical needs of HIV/AIDS inmates continue to reach the courts (Vaughn and Smith, 1999).

Sociological and psychological considerations

It is commonly understood that persons infected with HIV/AIDS who are detained in jail or incarcerated in prison generally suffer more than infected persons outside prison. Most of them who are in prison and jail are low-income, minority, IV drug users from the inner city; hence they most likely have faced a lifetime of racism and classism. Against that background they also endure a serious disease that carries profound stigma, a mark of social disgrace, separating the condemned or so-called 'defected' persons from those regarded as 'morally superior' (Goffman, 1963). Indeed, persons known to be HIV-positive sometimes are viewed by society as evil or morally corrupt, and the disease is sometimes interpreted as deserved punishment for homosexuality or use of illegal drugs (Sontag, 1988; Welch, 1989b, 2000d).

Inside correctional institutions, fellow inmates as well as staff often shun persons with HIV/AIDS. Even worse, some of them are subject to harassment and physical assault. For instance, after an incident in which an HIV-positive inmate bit a corrections officer, nine officers severely beat the inmate in retaliation. Later, the prisoner attempted suicide and bled to death while chained to a bed in the psychiatric unit (Dougherty, 1998; see Siegal, 2002b; Vaughn and Smith, 1999).

As noted previously, prisoners with HIV/AIDS comprise a unique group that has special medical and psychological needs; indeed, their form of suffering is compounded by the social aspects of prison life (see Massoglia, 2008; Schnittker and John, 2007). While having to face the prospect of dying from AIDS poses psychological and emotional challenges, being incarcerated exacerbates such aspects of suffering as depression, hopelessness, helplessness, isolation, low self-esteem, worthlessness, and grief. Likewise, anger is a common emotion, usually directed at the disease, inadequate medical care, discrimination, and rejection (Welch, 1991d, 1999a, 2000). Persons with AIDS also are prone to neurological deficits such as encephalopathy, surfacing as dementia in the late stages of the disease. Other symptoms include withdrawal, psychomotor retardation, confusion, disorientation, and seizures (CDC, 1996).

In view of the heightened form of suffering among prisoners with HIV/AIDS in corrections, government officials have begun to support legislation, known as compassionate release or medical parole, that leads to the early release of certain prisoners who suffer from HIV/AIDS and other terminal diseases (New York State Commission of Correction, 1987b). Additional policy recommendations have been made by the National Commission on AIDS that advances efforts to medicalize, not criminalize, the problems associated with drugs and HIV/AIDS. Among the recommendations are the following:

1 The federal government should devise a single plan for the nation to combat HIV/AIDS.
2 Treatment for drug abuse should be made available to all who need it.
3 Laws and regulations preventing drug users from getting clean needles and bleach for cleaning them should be abolished.
4 Medical coverage should be provided for all citizens, and the cost of prescription drugs should be covered.

These suggestions have the potential to add much needed reforms to the criminal justice system by relieving the system of unnecessary responsibilities and inappropriate demands, such as those related to drug control and treatment of prisoners with HIV/AIDS (see Hammett, 2006).

TUBERCULOSIS IN CORRECTIONS

Another serious health care issue facing correctional facilities is tuberculosis (TB), a highly contagious disease caused by bacteria that become airborne when an infected person coughs or sneezes. The disease is spread when others breathe in the bacteria in the air and, consequently, become infected. TB commonly affects the respiratory system and may sometimes lead to death. Jails and prisons are particularly vulnerable to the spread of TB due to overcrowded conditions and poorly ventilated cells and dormitories.

The makeup of confined populations also helps explain why such institutions are at high risk for TB outbreaks. TB is associated with IV drug use and HIV/AIDS as well as other medical and social factors prevalent in correctional institutions. In addition to IV drug users and those with HIV/AIDs, inmates at the greatest risk of being infected with TB are those who are born in foreign countries, blacks, Hispanics, alcoholics, and those with other serious medical problems (Hammett *et al.*, 1999). Correctional administrators are advised to recognize TB as an extremely serious health hazard in jails and prisons. Moreover, concern over TB is heightened in cases involving what is known as 'drug-resistant TB' that is difficult to treat with traditional medications. This strain of TB is often linked to haphazard drug taking (i.e. not taking medications as directed by a physician).

Inside correctional facilities, a key factor contributing to the spread of TB is the absence of comprehensive control programs for the disease. Prison and jail administrators are advised to consult TB experts to establish medical interventions, such as preventative therapy, treatment, and improved screening procedures. The computerization of screening is suggested to prevent inmates from getting lost in the system before their TB tests are examined. Direct and indirect strategies are equally important in combating TB in corrections. Direct strategies involve detection, isolation, and treatment. The Centers for Disease Control (CDC) recommend isolation for TB-infected patients and modification of the airflow in isolation rooms to keep TB germs from spreading into hallways. Indirect strategies involve preventative education for inmates and staff so that they understand the disease and the ways in which it is spread.

Experts report that most state and federal prison systems are following CDC recommendations regarding the screening of inmates and staff and the isolation and treatment of persons with TB disease. However, substantial improvement is needed in city and county jail systems. 'Continuing problems with adherence to regimens for the treatment of TB disease following release to the community may be amenable to improvement by better education, discharge planning, linkages with health departments and community-based providers, incentives to appear for follow-up appointments (e.g., food coupons and bus tokens), and shorter courses of therapy' (Hammett *et al.*, 1999: 90; see also Tulsky *et al.*, 1998).

Recently, the judiciary has empowered correctional facilities to take aggressive measures in detecting and controlling TB, including the mandatory screening of inmates. Moreover, courts have held correctional systems liable for neglecting to implement such measures, thereby placing inmates at risk of acquiring TB (Gostin, 1995; Hammett *et al.*, 1999). Despite improvements in controlling TB, such health-related problems persist, especially in jails that hold immigration detainees. At the Sarasota County jail (Florida), a female immigration detainee with TB was not seen by a doctor after urinating blood for 24 hours despite multiple requests (Saewitz, 2002).

AGING PRISONERS

Although the war on drugs, mandatory minimum sentences, three-strikes laws, and other tough-on-crime measures have remained politically popular, experts have been reminding us that locking up more offenders for longer periods means that increasingly large numbers of prisoners are aging behind bars (Flanagan, 1995; Welch, 2005a). Moreover, it is crucial to note that prisoners are disproportionately drawn from groups that have the poorest health status in free society (e.g. low income, urban dwellers, and minorities). Many of those convicts also tend to have lengthy histories involving drug and alcohol use, along with smoking tobacco. While incarcerated, prisoners are subjected to institutional conditions that further undermine their health and present opportunities for the spread of infectious disease (Massoglia, 2008; Pettit and Western, 2004).

Researchers continue to track the causes of death in prisons. The Bureau of Justice Statistics reports that nearly nine out of ten deaths in state prisons were attributed to medical conditions.

- Half were the result of heart diseases and cancer.
- Two-thirds involved inmates age 45 or older.
- Two-thirds were the result of medical problems which were present at the time of admission.

The study also found that male state prisoners had a death rate 72 percent higher than their female counterparts (Mumola, 2007: 1).

Healthcare costs typically exceed 25 percent of prison operating costs and are the fastest-growing item of corrections budgets, due in large part to an aging prison population requiring greater and more expensive medical attention (Lamb-Mechanick and Nelson, 2000; McDonald, 1999). Many states spend in excess of $70,000 per year to house and care for their most elderly and infirm prisoners in facilities that function as both penitentiaries and nursing homes (Leone, 2002; Morton, 2001). In 1999, US prisons housed more than 43,000 prisoners over the age of 55, a 50 percent increase since 1996. Overall, approximately 12 percent of male prisoners and 14 percent of female prisoners report a chronic physical impairment, while 25 percent of all inmates aged 45 or older report a physical impairment. Nearly 40 percent of state prisoners aged 45 and older report more inclusive medical problems and have surgery rates that are twice that of the general inmate population (Maruschak and Beck, 2001). Ten years later, those trends continue while at the same time healthcare costs have rocketed (Taxman and Ressler, 2010; Schnittker and John, 2007).

Expenses stemming from medical services for aging inmates extends beyond the exorbitant costs of medication and routine laboratory work; administrators also have to alter the physical features of the institution to make them accessible for wheelchairs and less mobile inmates. Indeed, the aging prison population has dumbfounded many administrators: 'We've not been in the geriatric business,' said Gary Hilton of New Jersey's Department of Corrections. 'I know how to run prisons, not old-age homes' (Malcolm, 1988: A1, 6; see Drummond, 1999).

Program needs also change as the prison population ages. Older inmates are less interested in GED classes and other educational programs and more interested in learning how to secure Social Security benefits upon their release. Preparing them to return to the community might be the most pressing problem facing the correctional system. Having grown old in prison, these prisoners must return to a society that often does not meet the needs of the lower-income elderly. Like their lower-income aging peers, elderly ex-cons have few family members to support them and are likely to have difficulty surviving on benefits available from an overburdened social service system. In sum, aging prisoners will continue to place a huge financial burden on correctional systems while presenting little public safety threat (Auerhahn, 2002; Mauer, 2002; Nieves, 2002).

SUICIDAL INMATES

Suicide in correctional facilities remains a serious problem, especially in jails where for years it had been the leading cause of death. According to the Bureau of Justice Statistics, jail suicide rates declined steadily from 129 per 100,000 inmates in 1983 to 47 per 100,000 in 2002.

> In 1983 suicide accounted for the majority of jail deaths (56%), but by 2002, the most common cause of jail deaths was natural causes (including AIDS) (52%), well ahead of suicides (32%). Suicide rates in State prison fell from 34 per 100,000 in 1980 to 16 per 100,000 in 1990, and have since stabilized.
>
> (Mumola, 2005: 1; see also Mumola, 2007)

Despite a reduction in the suicide rate in jails and prisons, that cause of death remains a significant problem, especially as mental health experts point out that most suicides in penal facilities are foreseeable and preventable. Indeed, there is considerable knowledge about the nature of institutional suicide and how to prevent it. Jail suicide is partially precipitated by the intense emotional toll brought on by being abruptly thrust into the throes of the criminal justice system and consequently being separated from family and other sources of emotional support. During the first several hours and days – when suicides are most likely to occur – a jail inmate suffers from the humiliation of incarceration, fear of the unknown, and loss of control over his or her life – all within harsh and degrading condition of confinement (Irwin, 1985; Welch, 1994).

Due to the availability of key information on jail suicide, coupled with the need to establish preventative measures, there is a tendency for some jails to rely on profiles constructed for the purpose of identifying the 'typical' suicidal inmate. Such profiles, based on condensed or composite data, can be useful but ought not be uncritically accepted (Rowan and Hayes, 1995; see Haycock, 1992). Several profiles have been generated by different researchers and competing methodologies; taken together, these profiles tend to be more postdictive than predictive (Kennedy and Homant, 1988). Due to the differences among various jail environments and inmate populations, it is difficult to establish a reliable jail suicide profile that can be generalized from one facility to the next. Rather than rely solely on inmate characteristics – especially in the form of a profile – it is recommended that jails administer institutional reforms, including correcting architectural flaws and developing staff training and procedures to prevent jail suicide.

In sum, different types of factors contribute to jail suicide. Some factors relate to individuals or 'persons at risk' (as purported by importation theory), including persons who are intoxicated, have a history of depression and suicide, and have been charged with murder or manslaughter (DuRand *et al.*, 1995). Other factors stem from the environment of the jail or 'risky places' (in reference to deprivation theory), particularly facilities that suffer from various architectural flaws, such as those that have an obstructed view of the inmate population (Haycock, 1992). Similarly, because jails are 'people-processing stations' operating 'around the clock,' Winfree and Wooldredge (1991) remind us that the sheer volume of admissions and releases creates ample opportunities for jail suicide. Experts agree that in addition to architectural reforms, a key to suicide prevention is hiring a capable and properly trained staff that can identify risky inmates and remain vigilant while carrying out a 'suicide watch' (Rowan and Hayes, 1995; see Liebling, 1999).

In an effort to learn more about the causes of jail suicide, Welch and Gunther (1997a, 1997b) examined the litigation, specifically lawsuits that concentrated on several areas of institutional policy and practice: (1) inadequate training and supervision; (2) a lack of policies and procedures for screening and monitoring; (3) deficient jail conditions; (4) insufficient staff; and (5) overcrowding.

Inadequate training and supervision

The majority of cases studied specifically cited inadequate training and supervision as the cause of jail suicide. Several cases suggest that many jails and their staff failed to learn from the past mistakes at other facilities. In *Simmons* v. *City of Philadelphia* (1990) the jury found that the evidence was sufficient to support the claim that the city violated that detainee's civil rights by being deliberately indifferent to the serious medical needs of the decedent. The evidence demonstrated that the intoxicated inmate was at a high risk of committing suicide. In addition to the suicide being foreseeable and preventable, the attending officer had no training in suicide prevention.

In *Buffington* v. *Baltimore County* (1990), a suicidal detainee was placed in an isolation cell even as arresting officers were completing paperwork for emergency commitment to a psychiatric hospital. Within one hour, the decedent hanged himself by his pants. The plaintiff's suit against officers and police administrators alleged deliberate indifference to the obvious suicide risk of the decedent. In particular, the suit claimed that the officers failed to monitor adequately suicidal inmates and were inadequately trained to identify and assist inmates at risk of suicide. Two officers were found liable, and the appeals court concluded that the suicide could have been averted if the police were offered better suicide prevention training, closer adherence to national standards on jail suicide prevention, and written regulation.

Lack of policies and procedures for screening and monitoring

Another area of institutional policy and practice that remains problematic is the absence of clear procedures for screening and monitoring potentially suicidal inmates. In *Layton* v. *Quinn* (1982), the decedent had threatened and attempted suicide while in custody, and was subsequently transferred to a disciplinary cell located farthest from the guard station where he committed suicide. Initially, the county defendants were granted governmental immunity but the appeals court reversed the ruling, citing the prior court orders that explicitly required county officials to establish policies and procedures for the admission, custody, care, and treatment of jail inmates.

In a case encompassing the need to intervene, the plaintiffs in *Heflin* v. *Stewart County, Tenn.* (1992) prevailed in presenting compelling evidence that the jailers acted with deliberate indifference after discovering the decedent hanging in his cell. In fact, the deputy and his staff left the decedent hanging as they checked for a pulse and signs of respiration. Because the deputy did not detect a pulse or respiration, he left the decedent hanging even though he reported that the body was warm and the feet were touching the floor. The body was not removed from the hanging position until photographs were taken, approximately 20 minutes after the hanging was discovered. The appeals court affirmed the award of damages to the plaintiffs, concluding that the deputy and his staff demonstrated unlawfulness by doing nothing to attempt to save the decedent.

Deficient jail conditions

In many of the cases studied, deficient jail conditions were specifically cited in the suit. In *Soto* v. *City of Sacramento* (1983), city and county officials were held liable for improperly placing the suicidal detainee in an isolation cell; additionally, the cell in which the decedent was confined had a history of jail suicide. Similarly in *Partridge* v. *Two Unknown Police Officers at Houston* (1985), the plaintiffs succeeded in their Section 1983 suit against the city for the suicide of their son. When arrested, the decedent was violent and agitated but was later composed when brought to the city jail. Information about his aggressive behavior was not passed on to the booking officer from the arresting officers. Furthermore, the booking officer did not consult the decedent's record that included a notation about a prior suicide attempt. The decedent's father also warned the officers that his son (who was wearing medical alert bracelets) was unstable. The decedent committed suicide a few hours after being confined to an isolation cell. The city was found liable for being deliberately indifferent to the serious medical (psychological and psychiatric) needs of a detainee.

In another case involving a suicide in solitary confinement, *Lewis* v. *Parish of Terrbonne* (1990), the decedent had been treated for a suicide attempt (drug overdose) in a local hospital and transported to the local jail. The transport deputy was given a report from the hospital's psychiatrist (indicating that the patient was suicidal and that special precautions be taken) for the warden. Although the warden did not read the report from the psychiatrist, he was aware of the decedent's suicide risk. Following an incident in which the decedent assaulted an officer, the warden assigned him to an isolation cell where the suicide occurred. The appeals court upheld the jury verdict of deliberate indifference and failing to carry out the constitutional duty of protecting inmates prone to suicide.

Insufficient staff

Many cases cite insufficient staff in their suits. In *Cabrales* v. *County of Los Angeles* (1989), for example, the decedent was examined by the institution's psychiatrists following a suicide attempt. The psychiatrists, however, concluded that the suicide attempt was merely a 'gesture' to manipulate the staff. The decedent, no longer ruled a suicide risk, was returned to the general population where he committed suicide several days later. The plaintiff alleged that the institution deprived that decedent of adequate mental health services and supervision. The jury found the jail commander and county liable because medical understaffing prevented psychiatrists from providing adequate assessments. Similarly, the plaintiffs in *Layton* also prevailed in their wrongful death suit partially on the basis that the county was negligent in failing to comply with court orders to hire sufficient staff personnel.

Overcrowding

Clearly, overcrowding remains a contributing factor in jail suicide since it compounds understaffing and inadequate supervision. Likewise, overcrowding can adversely affect medical services and treatment, leaving at-risk inmates even more vulnerable (see *Cabrales*). Although jail overcrowding can exacerbate the stress of incarceration that, in turn, might contribute to suicidal ideation, it is suggested that overcrowding could have a preventative effect. In overcrowded jails 'the wonder is not that jail inmates contemplate suicide, but rather that they find any space to attempt it' (Haycock, 1991: 428). It is when suicidal inmates are improperly placed in isolation cells that the risk of suicide mounts, inadvertently furnishing them with the space and opportunity to commit suicide. With that line of reasoning, it has been recommended that fellow inmates be paid to serve as monitors to supervise suicidal prisoners, even though issues of liability remain.

Regardless of how their corresponding suits fared in court, one can reasonably argue that many of those suicides were both foreseeable and preventable.

Indeed, the tragedy of jail suicide is compounded by institutional problems that can be (and should have been) corrected: inadequate training and supervision; a lack of policies and procedures for screening and monitoring; deficient jail conditions; insufficient staff. Jail suicides are even more tragic when several behavioral and psychological indicators are ignored (e.g. intoxication due to alcohol and/or drugs, severe depression, self-destructive behavior, delusional ideation, and hesitation cuts on wrists) (Welch and Gunther, 1997a, 1997b).

Although considerable knowledge has been generated about custodial suicide, jails do not always effectively screen or take extra precaution in dealing with suicidal inmates. Since jail suicides are admittedly relatively rare events, it is sometimes understandable why some jail personnel fail to detect accurately a suicide risk or fail to treat a suicide risk seriously. At times, staff inaction stems from their perception that some inmates are simply gesturing and not seriously contemplating suicide. Some staff members view these inmates as manipulative, and their gestures as attempts to attract sympathy and attention from the staff. That is particularly true in cases involving self-injury and mutilation; indeed, some inmates exhibit extremely bizarre behaviors, including cutting their bodies with sharp objects.

The case of John McCoy (a pseudonym) illustrates an inmate who had a history of self-inflicted injuries and suicidal behavior (*Jail Suicide Update*, 1992). While being detained, McCoy began eating light bulbs, leading to discharge of blood from his rectum. McCoy refused treatment and eventually resumed ingesting light bulbs that left shards of glass in his throat. Following a series of interventions by psychiatric staff, McCoy was returned to jail and placed in protective custody; staff were instructed to observe him at 15-minute intervals. Hours later, McCoy was found hanging by a sheet from the bars in his cell. The injuries sustained led to severe brain damage.

Even in the face of extremely bizarre or annoying gesturing behavior, experts stress that manipulative inmates require intervention because sometimes their actions to lead to death or serious injuries (Haycock, 1992; also see *Cabrales*, 1989). 'Current research on suicidal gestures and attempts within the correctional setting is replete with evidence to view *all* threats and acts of self-injury as potentially suicidal behavior' (*Jail Suicide Update*, 1992: 1; see Koziak, 2001; Maris *et al.*, 2000; Tartaro and Lester, 2009).

MENTAL HEALTH SERVICES

Mental health services in prisons and jails run the gamut from substance-abuse treatment to suicide intervention, and may include individual therapy, group therapy, behavior modification, and social therapy. By virtue of their similar objectives, most of those programs overlap considerably. While mental health services (e.g. individual counseling) are intended to focus on the needs of the individual inmate, such intervention strategies serve institutional needs as well. Prisons and jails are better managed, are more stable, and experience less disruption (and violence) when mental health services effectively reach the inmate population. Mental health services are designed to assess predisposing problems that prisoners bring into the institution; at the same time, a well-implemented mental health protocol also will address psychological and emotional stressors caused by the incarceration experience (Massoglia, 2008; Schnittker and John, 2007).

Many correctional experts endorse the humane features of mental health services, in part because they offer enormous practical value (Delgado and Humm-Delgado, 2008; Jones, 2006). Such support is especially true regarding treatment for mentally ill inmates because changes in mental hospital systems (e.g. decarceration) have forced prisons and jails to deal with those emotionally disturbed prisoners. While managing the mentally ill in corrections, mental health professionals often work in tandem with the medical staff due to vital psychiatric and medication need. Mental health professionals also are expected to assist inmates who are mentally retarded. Mental retardation affects more of the inmate population than is often acknowledged, generally because many mentally retarded inmates are only mildly retarded; therefore, their low intelligence sometimes goes undetected. Additionally, many mentally retarded inmates have learned to conceal their low IQs by acting in ways that do not reveal their deficiencies. Along with education experts, mental health staff members play a vital role in meeting the special needs of those inmates (Petersilia, 1997). (See 'Working in Corrections: Developing Support Groups for Men in Prison' below.)

Figure 16.3   A mentally ill inmate remains at Tacumbú jail in Asunción, April 16, 2010. Tacumbú is one of the most overpopulated prisons of the world, which was built originally for 800 inmates and now houses 3,147, of which only 701 have been sentenced.

Photo by Norberto Duarte/AFP/Getty Images.

WORKING IN CORRECTIONS

Developing Support Groups for Men in Prison

As mentioned in previous chapters, the field of corrections offers professionals many opportunities existing outside the traditional custodial orientation of the prison. Indeed, many free-world workers have rewarding careers behind bars, including physicians, nurses, substance-abuse specialists, teachers, and therapists. A case in point is Dr Harris Brieman, founder of the Prison Council Project. Brieman reminds us 'the prison experience is one of isolation and emptiness, fear and mistrust, violence and chaos – an assault on the soul' (2001: 218). Rather than delving into one's personal misery, Brieman challenges prisoners by asking them: 'What can you do while incarcerated to keep your sanity, to develop your creativity, to not only survive but also realize your human potential and prepare for your return to society?' In an effort to assist prisoners with their own transformation, Brieman introduced a rehabilitation fellowship program at the Shawangunk Correctional Facility in New York. Convicts call their fellowship the 'King of Hearts' to symbolize their commitment to providing service and positive leadership and to serve as just and compassionate role models for other men.

The fellowship program serves as a forum that addresses universal issues and concerns: the desire to heal personal wounds and overcome emotional trauma; the struggle to build communities where a sense of meaning and purpose can be shared; and the need to create a world where peace and justice reign. Moreover, the program focuses on masculine development, accountability, and responsibility. 'Incarcerated men often experience heightened tendencies common to all men in our culture: tendencies to become frozen into macho armor, to experience emotional isolation and numbness, to participate in cut-throat competition, and to make desperate attempts at domination' (Brieman, 2001: 219). Compounding those cultural and gender circumstances, many prisoners were raised in a broken home in urban 'war zones' known for violence, drugs, racism, and poverty. The program acknowledges that the prison social structure – emphasizing retribution and warehousing – merely perpetuates the cycle of aggression by neglecting the sources of violence and victimization. If prisoners are to return to the community as law-abiding persons, they must have the opportunity while incarcerated to improve themselves both emotionally and spiritually. In doing so, participants in the program strive to reduce their aggression and become positive role models.

Many members of the program serve as mentors for other inmates, helping them with therapeutic, educational, and vocational initiatives. According to Brieman, 'we believe it is a sign of a mature man to have the emotional depth, the intellectual discipline, and the physical control to let such conflicts be creatively experienced, contained, and transformed, rather than destructively or violently expressed' (2001: 220). The issues raised in the program are diverse and vary from session to session; for instance, participants have examined:

- the meaning of masculinity by exploring the basic archetypal structures that exist in every man's psychology – the King, the Warrior, the Magician, and the Lover;
- the spiritual journey as a foundation for sanity;
- the necessity of ongoing education;
- the importance of the power of family;
- the inner work involved preparing for parole and release;
- the economics and politics of racism and social injustice;
- the importance of mentoring and community service.

The ultimate goal of the program is to break the cycle of violence and give something back to the community. The 'Fellowship of the King of Hearts' encourages prison administrators and inmates at other institutions to develop similar programs aimed at healing and justice. (For more information contact OASIS, the Prison Council Project, PO Box 31, Woodstock, NY, 12498; (914) 679-7441.)

CONCLUSION

Admittedly, this chapter covers a good deal of territory in an effort to shed critical light on the war on drugs. Beginning with an overview of drug-control policy, discussion then turns to the competing viewpoints on supply reduction, treatment, prevention and education. In a similar vein, attention is turned to key proposals for decriminalization and legalization. Still, the thrust of the chapter is aimed at understanding the consequences that the war on drugs is having on prisons and jails. So as to outline some of the major developments in corrections, several health care issues are examined: substance-abuse treatment, HIV/AIDS, TB, aging prisoners, and mental health programs.

From a critical perspective, the war on drugs is fraught with problems concerning socioeconomics and race since the poor and minorities are the prime targets of drug enforcement. While there is merit to charges that the crackdown on those particular drug users stems from institutional racism and classism, it is important not to overlook the wider reach of America's drug problem (Welch *et al.*, 1999; Welch *et al.*, 1998). For more than 50 years, researchers have confirmed that endemic drug abuse is strongly associated with mass deprivation, economic marginality, and cultural and community breakdown (Lindesmith, 2007; Nadelmann, 2007).

According to Elliott Currie (1998, 1993) the quality of life for many Americans continues in a downward spiral; just as significant, that decline has transpired without offering any indication that economic opportunities will improve. As prospects for many lower-income persons become bleaker, the rewards of consuming and selling drugs seem more tempting. Therefore any realistic policy geared toward reducing drug use in general and drug trafficking in particular should be informed of key political and socioeconomic forces that drive those interrelated problems. Central to the debate over the war on drugs are concerns over the limitations of both criminalization and medicalization, prompting policy-makers to envision broader social reforms that address deep economic disparities in American society (see Friesendorf, 2007).

SUMMARY

This chapter describes the war on drugs from the standpoint of policy and practice. By doing so, it considers three perspectives offered by public health generalists, legalists, and cost-benefit specialists; together, they outline the prospects and challenges of drug-control policy. Keeping attention on the war on drugs as it impacts corrections, the discussion delves into an array of healthcare matters, including substance-abuse treatment, HIV/AIDS, TB, aging prisoners, mental health services, and suicidal inmates. Throughout the chapter, readers are reminded of the signficance of social class and race. Indeed, the vast majority of those swept up in the war on drugs and put behind bars are low-income minorities, many of whom are convicted of non-violent drug violations.

REVIEW QUESTIONS

1 What are the political and economic forces driving the war on drugs and what are the implications for race and social class?
2 What are the stated and unstated assumptions of each school of thought on drug-control policy?
3 What is the controversy surrounding the myth of crack babies?
4 What are the myths and misconceptions about HIV/AIDS and how do such myths apply to corrections?
5 How has the war on drugs contributed to an aging inmate population and what are the implications for prison medical care?

RECOMMENDED READINGS

Delgado, M. and Humm-Delgado, D. (2008) *Health and Health Care in the Nation's Prisons*. Lanham, MD: Rowman & Littlefield.
Gray, J. P. (2001) *Why Our Drug Laws Have Failed and What We Can Do About It*. Philadelphia: Temple University Press.
Humphries, D. (1999) *Crack Mothers: Pregnancy, Drugs, and the Media*. Columbus, OH: Ohio State University.
Husak, D. (2002) *Legalize This! The Case for Decriminalizing Drugs*. New York: Verso.
Inciardi, J. and McElrath, K. (2007) *The American Drug Scene*. New York: Oxford University Press.

CHAPTER 17

The War on Terror

If you don't violate someone's human rights some of the time, you probably aren't doing your job. I don't think we want to be promoting a view of zero tolerance on this. That was the whole problem for a long time with the CIA. (Government agent speaking anonymously).

LEARNING OBJECTIVES

After studying this chapter, you should be able to answer the following questions:

1 What is meant by the term 'state crime' and how does it apply to the war on terror?
2 What is the unlawful enemy combatant designation and how does it reflect militarized power?
3 How does the detention center at Guantánamo Bay compare and contrast with maximum-security prisons?
4 How has torture re-emerged in the war on terror and what specific laws and treaties does it violate?

For years, the legal battles over how the Bush administration defined and applied the unlawful enemy combatant designation continued to unfold in the US courts. In late 2004, federal judge Joyce Hens Green was still interested in scanning the limits of presidential power to detain enemy combatants and whether the White House satisfied the requirement laid out in the June (2004) US Supreme Court decision to provide a justification for their detention acceptable to federal courts. In court, Green introduced a hypothetical case to Brian Boyle, a Justice Department lawyer: Could the President of the United States imprison 'a little old lady from Switzerland' as an enemy combatant if she donated to a charity not knowing that her money was eventually used to finance the activities of Al Qaeda terrorists? After a long pause, Boyle responded: 'Possibly.' Boyle then went on to explain that the enemy combatant definition 'is not limited to someone who carries a weapon.' Especially given the global reach of the enemy combatant definition, Green pressed Boyle about the temporal scope of the war on terror and the application of the powers under the enemy combatant order: 'When will they end?' To which Boyle conceded: 'I wish I could give you an answer'.

(Lewis, 2004: A36)

INTRODUCTION

As this book demonstrates, a growing number of critical criminologists are committed to throwing light on illegal and unethical actions carried out by state, corporate, and organizational elites. Crimes by the powerful are particularly significant due in large part to their immense reach and consequence. Michalowski and Kramer remind us that great power and great crime are inseparable:

> It is only those with great political and economic power who can, with the stroke of a pen, the utterance of an order, or even a knowing nod of the head send thousands to their deaths or consign millions to lives of unrelenting want and misery. When economic and political powers pursue common interests, the potential for harm is magnified further (2006b: 1)

While there are varied definitions of state crimes alluding to governmental crime, political crime, and state-organized crime, it is generally agreed that such violations constitute 'illegal, socially injurious [harmful], or unjust acts which are committed for the benefit of a state or its agencies, and not for the personal gain of some individual agent of the state' (Kauzlarich *et al.* 2001: 175; see also Chambliss, 1989; Friedrichs, 1998; Ross, 2000). That perspective on state crime similarly lends itself to an array of unlawful acts and human rights atrocities in the American war on terror (see Kramer *et al.*, 2005; Welch, 2003f). In this chapter, three instances of state crime occurring in the name of US national security are examined: the unlawful enemy combatant designation, the use of Guantánamo Bay, and torture. As we proceed, it is important to remain mindful of key socio-legal transformations that serve to reconfigure state power, especially as it reproduces impunity (Agamben, 2005; Butler, 2004; Ericson, 2007). Certainly, what distinguishes state crimes from the run-of-the-mill street-level offenses is their apparent immunity, adding to speculation that such crimes have no bounds (Chomsky, 2003; Welch, 2009a, 2007, 2006a).

UNLAWFUL ENEMY COMBATANTS

The decision by George W. Bush to process terror suspects by way of military tribunals rather than by criminal courts is notable because it reveals how the President opted to interpret and exercise the particular powers of the office. As the record demonstrates, Bush issued a military order rather than an executive one. As a result, the war on terror became militarized in ways that go beyond popular metaphor, becoming a carefully planned strategy housed in the Department of Defense. The military order mandated the establishment of military tribunals according to rules and regulations dictated by the Pentagon's civilian general counsel, William J. Haynes, II, and submitted to Secretary of Defense Donald Rumsfeld for departmental promulgation. Among other things, those military tribunals depart from past practices since they targeted non-US citizens: previous tribunals never distinguished between citizens and foreign nationals (Katyal and Tribe, 2002; Welch, 2008a).

By initiating a military strategy, Bush's choice of options is especially significant. 'For the first time in American history, the characterization of terrorism as a criminal act to be dealt with by the civilian courts would be superseded by its characterization as an act of war' (Pious, 2006: 225). So as to appear that his military order was not unilateral, Bush claimed that Congress provided its support in the joint resolution authorizing the President 'to use all necessary and appropriate force against those nations, organizations, or persons he determines planned, authorized, committed, or aided the terrorist attacks that occurred on September 11, 2001' (P.L. 107–40 Sec. 2(a), September 18, 2001). These events set the stage for a series of crucial political and military decisions that reconfigured power in the war on terror. As we shall see, the Bush administration put into motion several unusual strategies to detain and prosecute terror suspects, tactics that continue to raise serious questions over their constitutionality and legality under international law (Jinks and Sloss, 2004; Kacprowski, 2004; Margulies, 2004).

Precisely how the Bush administration exercised the unlawful enemy combatant designation has been subjected to legal scrutiny. In 2006, the US Supreme Court in *Hamdi* v. *Rumsfeld* (2004; see *Rasul* v. *Bush and United States* 2004) invalidated the system of military commissions Bush had set up for trying terrorism suspects saying that the tribunals required Congressional authorization. The court also required that suspects be treated in accordance with a provision of the Geneva Conventions, Common Article 3, which prohibits cruel and inhumane treatment, including 'outrages upon personal dignity.' In response to that ruling, Congress set out to assemble a tribunal system believed to be congruent with the decision of the High Court. After months of relatively narrow debate, Congress passed the Military Commissions Act (MCA) of 2006, a measure that Bush swiftly signed into law. Under the revised proceedings, the government – specifically, the executive branch and the military – enjoys numerous built-in advantages in determining whether a suspect fits the classification of unlawful enemy combatant.

The MCA reconfigured and recentralized power in the war on terror in ways that gut due process and meaningful judicial oversight; in fact, the MCA created few differences from its predecessor that Bush ordered into effect on November 1, 2001. Likewise, the new law poses serious threats to international human rights by preventing suspects from filing suit via the writ of habeas corpus to challenge the legality of their detention or to raise claims of torture and other abuses (Swanson, 2004). Human rights advocates complain that the MCA tribunal system does not meet the fair trial provisions required by the Geneva

Conventions and human rights law (Cole, 2003; Kacprowski, 2004; Paust, 2005). Scholars studying conceptions of power have taken a keen interest in the unlawful enemy combatant designation, particularly as it points to a newly configured form of power. Butler's remarks on the subject are instructive:

> In the current war prison, officials of governmentality wield sovereign power, understood here as a lawless and unaccountable operation of power, once legal rule is effectively suspended and military codes take its place. Once again, a lost or injured sovereign becomes reanimated through rules that allocate final decisions about life and death to the executive branch or to officials with no elected status and bound by no constitutional constraints.
>
> (2004: XV)

Butler's observations on the lawless nature by which persons are designated as unlawful enemy combatants further the notion of impunity since it points to the absence of accountability (Welch, 2009a, 2007). Indeed indefinite detention, as a form of state crime, not only contradicts principles of due process contained in the rule of law but also vaporizes basic ideals of justice. Agamben (2005, 1998) also weighs into the controversy, arguing that persons denied legal rights, including unlawful enemy combatants, are stripped completely of protection, rendering them vulnerable to the whims of the state, including acts of crime. Agamben enriches his analysis by invoking the concept of homo sacer (sacred man) that has its origin in Roman law. Homo sacer refers to those who could not be sacrificed according to ritual because they were outside the zone of divine law, thus their lives had no value to the gods. Nevertheless, they could still be killed with impunity because they also remained out of the reach of juridical law, which meant their lives had no value to their contemporaries. The notion of homo sacer has profound ontological implications pertaining to unlawful enemy combatants as they intersect with impunity. In essence, those who are refused their rights are also denied a sense of belonging to any community. Moreover, the sovereign (one who decides the exception) who orders the exclusion possesses an unreviewable power, and is therefore totally unaccountable (see Amnesty International, 2005; Human Rights Watch, 2007; Welch, 2007).

GITMO: GUANTANAMO BAY (CUBA)

GITMO is part of a larger naval installation (Guantánamo Bay Naval Base, Cuba) located on a 45 square-mile strip of land on the southeast tip of Cuba which the US has leased in perpetuity since 1903, following the Spanish-American War (Golden, 2006a). For decades, the naval base enjoyed a relatively quiet existence until the events of September 11 when the US Department of Defense put into motion plans to utilize sectors of the base for the expressed purpose of detaining and interrogating terrorist suspects. There the US military has held upwards of 600 detainees (320 in 2008 and about 120 in 2010), many of whom were captured in Afghanistan in the early phases of the war on terror following the attacks on the World Trade Center and the Pentagon. The US government insists the detainees are terrorists affiliated with the Taliban or al-Qaeda (i.e. unlawful enemy combatants) and pose an imminent threat to national security. On these grounds, the Bush White House argued that it had the authority to detain them indefinitely; some selected detainees would be eligible for military tribunals but not civilian criminal courts (Lewis, 2004). Aside from the legal controversies that surround GITMO addressed in this chapter, there exist important institutional dimensions of the detention camp that deserve mentioning so as to provide a visual outline of the penal setting.

GITMO is a joint military prison and interrogation camp under the leadership of the Joint Task Force of Guantánamo (JF-GTMO). In January 2002 when the first contingent of detainees arrived, GITMO was still a work in progress, literally. At the time, marines had just completed a makeshift prison, Camp X-Ray, consisting of dozens of rows of steel-mesh cages, ringed by a perimeter of razor-wire fence, and exposed to the harsh elements of the Caribbean (Rose, 2004). Eventually, detainees were transferred to newly constructed cellblocks, leaving Camp X-Ray to be slowly swallowed by the jungle. At present, GITMO comprises three detention sectors: Camp Delta (with detention camps 1 through 6), Camp Echo (a 612-unit detention center which stands as part of Camp Delta), and Camp Iguana (a smaller, low-security compound located about a half-mile from the main detention area). More recent renovations are evident in Camp

Figure 17.1 Guantánamo prison remains open over a year after Obama vowed to close it. Detainees jog inside a recreation yard at Camp 6 in the Guantánamo Bay detention center in Guantánamo Bay, Cuba, March 30, 2010. US President Barack Obama pledged to close the prison by early 2010 but has struggled to transfer, try or release the remaining detainees from the facility, located on the US Naval Base.

Photo by John Moore/Getty Images.

6, a new 30 million dollar medium-security facility modeled after a county jail in southern Michigan. Altogether the detention complex is commonly referred to by the military as GITMO (and at times called by its former name, Camp X-Ray). The security force consists mostly of US Army military police and US Navy Master-at Arms (Pious, 2006). Visiting journalists have been granted tours of some of the detention units accompanied by explanations that some parts of the camp are easier to manage than others. For example, Tim Golden (2006a: E16) describes Camp 4 as: a newer wing where Level 1, or 'highly compliant,' prisoners were allowed to live in communal barracks, serving their own food and moving freely in and out of small recreation yards. Some detainees are held in Camp 1, for Level 2, or 'compliant,' detainees, while a handful are held in Camp 5, the maximum-security area (see Levy, 2007; Vogel, 2002).

Institutional control

Institutional control by its very nature refers to complete order as determined by the rigid rules geared toward a smooth operation of the prison, dealing with disruptions in a swift and firm manner. Indeed, this form of control often implies a heavy-handed approach to custodial management. A mere mentioning of the name GITMO brings to mind images of a harsh – even brutal – show of force and tight control. Moreover, this extreme degree of control is notable for its militaristic thrust; for all their strong-armed tactics, other supermax prisons are still paramilitary in their organization (Welch, 2009b). In the early days (January 2002) of GITMO, unlawful enemy combatants were transported from the worldwide 'battlefield' of the war on terror via military aircraft to a makeshift prison built by marines called Camp X-Ray:

> A dozen rows of steel-mesh cages open to the elements, ringed by a razor-wire fence. On arriving, the detainees had been led into a compound and photographed as they waited to be processed. Shackled hand and foot, dressed in orange jumpsuits, still wearing the black-lens goggles, surgical masks, headphones, and taped-on gloves which they had been forced to don at the start of their twenty-seven hour flight, the detainees knelt in the Gitmo dust, as crew-cut servicemen loomed in threatening poses over them. Within a few days, the US Defense Secretary, Donald Rumsfeld, would regret allowing these pictures to be released: to have done so, he said, was 'probably unfortunate'. The front-page headline used with the photos in Britain's conservative *Daily Mail* typified responses outside the United States. It consisted of a single word: 'TORTURE!'
>
> (Rose, 2004: 2)

Formal military tactics deployed for purposes of control are backed up with claims by US politicians that these prisoners were the 'worst of the worst,' a common trope echoing of 'superpredators' described by conservatives supporting the need for supermax prisons (Bennett and DiIulio, 1996). Even so, widely circulated quotes from military leaders add a heightened alert over the particular 'dangerousness' of detainees at GITMO. In the words of General Richard E. Myers, chairman of the Joints Chiefs of Staff, those prisoners, given half the chance, 'would gnaw through hydraulic lines in the back of a C-17 to bring it down' (Rose, 2004: 2).

The cages of Camp X-Ray were eventually replaced by a permanent structure called Camp Delta but like other supermax prisons, the conditions of confinement are Spartan at best. The cells consist of prefabricated metal boxes painted a faded green, somewhat larger than a king-size bed (56 square feet). Institutional control benefits from the physical environment of each cell that has in it a hard steel wall-mounted bed, two-and-a-half feet wide. There is an Asian-style toilet, a hole in the floor that faces an open grill in the door where guards are expected to pass by every 30 seconds. A single water tap is situated so close to the floor that the prisoner must kneel down. The Pentagon reports that the spout is located low so as 'to accommodate Muslim foot-washing needs.' However, critics contend that the physical environment is designed to humiliate detainees (Rose, 2004: 60; see Amnesty International, 2005). Institutional control also extends to cultural reminders of the significance of GITMO in a post-9/11 world. Hanging in the makeshift office where guards are permitted to send e-mail is a poster of the Twin Towers captioned 'Are you in a New York state of mind? Don't leak information our enemy can use to kill US troops or more innocent people' (Rose, 2004: 58).

Institutional control at GITMO is facilitated by means of authoritarianism, a form of detainee management that is 'based on militaristic lines of regulation' (Carrabine, 2004: 40; 2000). GITMO, like other supermax prisons, frequently relies on coercive tactics to control the population, especially prisoners who try to buck the system. In such instances, GITMO's punishment squad – the Extreme Reaction Force (ERF) – is activated for purposes of 'cell extraction,' a no-nonsense control tactic also used in civilian prisons for removing a recalcitrant prisoner from his cell to be placed in solitary confinement. At GITMO, solitary confinement is known as 'Romeo block' where detainees remain naked (or half-naked) for days or even more than a week. Former detainees report that those 'ERF-ing' had become so common that it found a place in the GITMO jargon. Detainees who had been 'ERF-ed' for even minor rule infractions (e.g. having an extra drinking cup in their cell) claim that they were subjected to having their Koran mishandled, and their private parts grabbed and pepper-sprayed by a team of guards in riot gear; in the process, prisoners' eyes have been poked and their heads flushed in their toilet, and they have been forcibly kneeled on, kicked, and punched prior to being dragged out of their cell in chains then having their beard, head, and eyebrows shaved. Whereas civilian prisons are required to have disciplinary hearings to determine whether solitary confinement is warranted, such proceedings do not exist in GITMO (Amann, 2004; Conover, 2003; Rose, 2004).

Micro-economy of perpetual penalty

Recall in Chapter 4 on theoretical penology that Michel Foucault described the ideal purpose of prisons as being to transform convicts into becoming docile, obedient, and useful. That form of discipline, however, tends to minimize its reliance on blunt force while maximizing techniques that are economical and subtle. For example, discipline is achieved through incremental rewards (and deprivations) contained in a token economy and behavior modification schemes, or what Foucault describes as a 'micro-economy of perpetual penalty' (1977: 181).

Whereas GITMO does not spare its use of physical force against detainees, it is understood that such authoritarian control tends to undermine the detainee compliance needed to generate 'intel.' Moving toward other forms of institutional control, detainees are subject to a clear set of rules governing their conduct. Revealing the significance of the micro-economy of perpetual penalty at GITMO, a former detainee noted: 'There is only one rule that matters. You have to obey whatever the US government personnel tell you to do' (Rose, 2004: 69). With the threat of strict punishment looming overhead, detainees at GITMO are required to adhere to the Detainee Standards of Conduct that contains a list of 13 rules, including the following:

- Detainees WILL NOT be disrespectful to any US Security Forces personnel or other detainees.
- Detainees WILL follow the orders of US Security Forces at ALL times.
- Detainee units can and WILL be searched at any time.
- Detainees WILL NOT harass, annoy, harm or otherwise interfere with the safety or operation of the detention facility.

Foucault (1977) recognizes the role of spatialization and the arrangement of objects in the disciplinary process. These features are evident at GITMO where even the most minute detail is placed under close inspection. Consider Rule 9 of the Standards of Conduct:

- Detainees WILL at all times display their comfort items in the front of their unit in the following order:

  a. Soap
  b. Shower shoes
  c. Toothpaste
  d. Toothbrush
  e. Small towel
  f. Water bottle

In his later work, Foucault returns to the significance of rules especially as they pertain to a more defined conception of power that emphasizes the role of political actors and agencies in exercising control. That idea is important considering rules since such 'prohibitions' simply do not spring out of thin air; rather, they are constructed by and enforced by specific persons and groups. As Foucault notes: 'Power acts by laying down the rule' (1978: 83), adding: 'All modes of domination, submission, and subjugation are ultimately reduced to an effect of obedience' (p. 85). At GITMO, as is the case in all prisons, rules and their enforcement lend organizational structure to the institution while maintaining control over its population.

Interrogation

Military personnel claim to have expertise in dealing with its special population staff GITMO. Even more to the point, the interrogation program (and some say the entire prison) is run by so-called experts who claim to possess special – even 'scientific' – knowledge on extracting intelligence, or 'intel,' needed to protect national security (Welch, 2009c). The GITMO Joint Task Force has two main divisions: the Joint Detention Group and the Joint Interrogation Group. The Detention Group has responsibility over all aspects of incarceration while the Interrogation Group handles the interrogation process. Still, the Groups work in tandem, as Major-General Geoffrey Miller said, 'to set the conditions' for interrogation, by 'softening-up' the detainees (Rose, 2004: 87; Human Rights Watch, 2004, 2005).

The Bush team situated GITMO deep inside the war on terror, providing a unique venue where intelligence is gathered through 'expert' interrogation methods. According to Major-General Miller: 'Harvesting intelligence through prisoner interrogations has become Guantanamo's principle raison d'etre.' Miller's description of GITMO further suggests a clinical project when he said: 'I think of Guantanamo as the interrogation battle lab in the war against terror' (Rose, 2004: 80–1). Under Miller's tutelage beginning in January 2003, interrogation become more frequent and intense, a departure from General Baccus's reign when interrogations were relatively infrequent and low-key. Former detainees Asif Iqbal and Shafiq Rasul said they were interrogated five times in 2002 and none in the last half of that year; then, after Miller took charge, they were interrogated more than 200 times over a 15-month stretch (Rose, 2004; Human Rights Watch, 2004).

To aid interrogations that would sometimes last up to 20 continuous hours, a long list of techniques were routinely deployed: dietary manipulation, sleep deprivation (or 'adjustment' to refer to reversing the sleep cycle from night to day), isolation (up to 30 days), shackling in uncomfortable positions ('stress and duress'), exposure to extreme heat and cold as well as to loud noise/music, strobe lights, and unpleasant smells. Interrogators also relied on an array of physical, psychological, and cultural tactics intended to heighten fear and anxiety among Muslim males, such as death threats aimed at them and their families, nudity, sexual humiliation, and the use of dogs. Another cultural technique involved depriving Muslim detainees of their Koran or, in a widely reported incident, of flushing it down a toilet (Amnesty International, 2005; see Harbury, 2005; Hersh,

2004). Much attention has also been focused on the more extreme techniques that human rights lawyers characterize as torture, for example 'waterboarding' that induces suffocation and the sensation of drowning. All along, guards and interrogators would be led to believe that they were immunized from being prosecuted for torture or war crimes since their actions were supposedly authorized by the President of the United States as Commander-in-Chief (Danner 2004; Greenberg and Dratel, 2005; Stout, 2008).

As noted previously, with the use of a micro-economy of perpetual penalty, interrogations do not solely rely on blunt force to extract 'intel' from detainees at GITMO. Expanding their repertoire, interrogators adopt tactics they believe are 'scientific,' drawing on 'the psychology of interrogation' (Leo, 2008; Welch, 2009c). Upon visiting GITMO in 2003, the International Committee of the Red Cross noted that medical files detailing the mental health of detainees were shared with interrogators so that they could develop 'interrogation plans,' a violation of medical ethics ensuring patient–doctor confidentiality (Physicians for Human Rights, 2009; see Mayer, 2009).

Despite the application of so-called 'scientific' techniques, many detainees at GITMO refused to cooperate with interrogators. Moreover, they embarked on broader forms of resistance aimed at confronting the injustice of being held indefinitely without charge. Such resistance was met with greater forms of authoritarian control. For a while GITMO guards thought that their renewed toughness was contributing to the overall control of the institution. However, in their desperation, several detainees launched a series of hunger strikes. GITMO officers responded by ordering forced-feeding. Then as medical staff realized that hunger strikers were able to manipulate the feeding tubes by reversing the flow of nutrients, the military personnel resorted to even harsher tactics.

Participating in a hunger strike was to be treated as a 'disciplinary' matter, and like all rule infractions, it would be met with force, namely restraint chairs in which detainees would be strapped down for a painful feeding protocol. Human rights lawyers condemned the use of restraint chairs but officials at GITMO insisted that they were necessary and produced firm results, gaining the upper hand in detainee control. But that control did not last long as some detainees attempted mass suicide attempts by ingesting hoarded medication. When guards swiftly searched the housing units for medication and other contraband, detainees rioted, prompting guards to fire rounds of rubber bullets and pepper spray. Once again, some detainees took desperate measures: on July 9 (2005), three committed suicide by hanging themselves in the back corners of their cells. Although each of the deceased had been involved in hunger strikes, their medical files revealed no signs of depression or psychological problems (Golden 2006a; Risen and Golden, 2006; see Risen, 2006).

GITMO in a post-9/11 world

Because the threat of terrorism is very real and continues to reverberate in American society, the idea of a detention center located safely on the other end of a foreign island is often welcomed by the general public as it searches for ways to reduce anxiety in a post-9/11 world (Ericson 2007; Welch 2006b). For many in the mainstream, GITMO offers emotional security by providing a seemingly pragmatic solution not unlike other punitive sentiments (e.g. 'lock-em up and throw away the key'). Furthermore, GITMO serves potent symbolic purposes, offering 'evidence' that the US government is 'doing something' in the war on terror as well as 'getting tough' with terrorists.

A close reading of the chronology of GITMO, however, reveals that many of those held are not the 'worst of the worst' as the Bush administration proclaimed. There is considerable evidence of innocent persons being arrested elsewhere and transported to the prison. Indeed, some were apprehended at the hands of those hoping to cash in on the lucrative bounties offered by the US government (Amnesty International, 2005; Human Rights Watch, 2004, 2005; Rose, 2004). The fact that many detainees have been released appears to indicate that they were wrongly placed at GITMO in the first place.

The problem of 'mistaken identity' is a serious ethical matter with strong implications for human rights (see Butler, 2004; Gregory, 2006). Among other things, wrongful detention points to the importance of international law that entitles all arrested persons to a fair trial along with a host of due process guarantees. Clearly those fundamental procedures would reduce the number of errors in the pursuit of terrorists. Such mistakes, it should be noted, also threaten national security since it means the government is wasting its time and energy on the wrong persons; clearly, those resources could be better used in worthwhile investigations (Welch, 2009a).

WORKING IN CORRECTIONS

A Warden at GITMO

In 2004, the US Supreme Court struck down the government's policy of denying GITMO detainees access to federal courts (*Hamdi* v. *Rumsfeld*; *Rasul* v. *Bush*). However, that ruling said little about how detainees would be treated within the institution, giving the military administrators at GITMO a free hand in how they chose to deal with the population. To be clear, GITMO, even in its short history, has undergone a series of changes with respect to how it is managed. One particular warden was criticized for 'coddling' detainees (Brigadier-General Rick Baccus) while another is accused of brutality (Major-General Geoffrey Miller) (Harbury 2005; Hersh 2004). As we shall discuss here, warden Colonel Mike Bumgarner has been characterized in the media as a reform-minded administrator committed to upholding the Geneva Conventions and the humane treatment of detainees, a plan that has met with considerable controversy (Golden, 2006a).

As noted, resistance at GITMO takes many forms, including collective rebellion, hunger strikes, and mass suicides. Eventually, new incoming wardens have to deal with the problems created by coercive techniques and the harsh conditions of confinement, and the fact that many of detainees would probably be held indefinitely. Consider the tour of duty of Colonel Mike Bumgarner, who took over as the warden of Guantánamo Bay in April 2005. He received his marching orders from the overall commander of the military's joint task force at Guantánamo, Major-General Jay W. Hood, who provided some simple instructions: keep the detainees and his guards safe and prevent escapes. Furthermore, Hood suggested that Bumgarner 'study the Third Geneva Convention, on the treatment of prisoners of war, and begin thinking about how to move Guantánamo more into line with its rules.' Though he knew the conventions well, Baumgarner thought to himself: 'How do you deal with an individual whom the President of the United States and the Secretary of Defense have called the worst of the worst?' (Golden, 2006a: EV1). Still, he did not have much time to ponder international law since he was focused on the 530 prisoners, most of who were classified as 'non-compliant,' including some who had assaulted guards.

> In older parts of the camp, the detainees would sometimes bang for hours on the steel mesh of their cells, smashing out a beat that rattled up over the razor wire into the thick, tropical air. Occasionally they would swipe at the guards with metal foot pads ripped from their squat-style toilets, declassified military reports say. The detainees rarely tried to fashion the sort of shanks or knives made by violent prisoners in the United States. But they did manage to unnerve and incite the young guards, often by splattering them with mixtures of bodily excretions known on the blocks as 'cocktails.' (Golden, 2006a: EV2)

Despite those frequent disruptions, Bumgarner had been aware that many of the detainees were not the hardened terrorists the Pentagon officials had claimed, although he did believe that many of them were dangerous. Soon he began to engage some of the more influential detainees as a means gaining greater control of the prison in the face of growing resistance. In his initial message to the detainees, he said: 'Look, I'm willing to give you things, to make life better for ya, if y'all will reciprocate.' What he asked in return was 'Just do not attack my guards' (Golden, 2006a: EV3).

While reaching out to the prisoners, he also began to make other modifications of the penal environment, including installing clocks on the cellblock walls so that prisoners could anticipate their prayer sessions. Due to complaints about the tap water, bottled water was distributed at mealtimes, even going so far as to remove the stars-and-stripes labels along with the brand names Patriot's Choice and Freedom Springs. These nominal though seemingly genuine acts of respect did not go far given the overall repressive nature of GITMO. Within two months, some prisoners went on a hunger strike, demanding better living conditions, proper treatment of the Koran by guards, and an end to having the 'The Star-Spangled Banner' played over distant loudspeakers during or right after the evening call to prayer. But more importantly, they insisted on fair trials or freedom. The unusually large number of prisoners then on hunger strike worried the medical staff.

As resistance began to take hold, Bumgarner retained his personal style of management, focusing on a particularly influential detainee, Shaker Aamer (a.k.a. The Professor) who was initiating several disobedience campaigns. 'You're either gonna start complying with the rules,' Bumgarner recalls warning him, 'or life's gonna get really rough.' The warden did not mean to threaten physical force, only to emphasize strongly 'Aamer's few privileges – like, say, his use of a toothbrush – hung in the balance.' In his discussions with Aamer, he found common ground on how to make GITMO a more 'peaceful place.' That is: bring the institution in line with the Geneva Conventions and encourage staff to treat the detainees with respect, citing an annoying practice of referring to prisoners in transit as 'packages.' 'We are not "packages," a detainee told the warden, "We are human beings" (Golden, 2006a: EV4, EV6).

THE ABU GHRAIB SCANDAL, IRAQ

In late 2002, the *Washington Post* published detailed accounts of American intelligence officers who had resorted to abuse and torture of detainees held at Bagram Air Base in Afghanistan (Priest and Gellman, 2002; see 'Comparative Corrections: Detainee Abuse in Afghanistan', below). Even though the story appeared front page, it generated little public or political interest. Then some 15 months later, the horrors of Abu Ghraib were exposed. A significant difference between the two otherwise similar reports of abuse and torture was the availability of explicit photographs. Within days of the breaking story, graphic visual evidence circulated around the globe. Pictures of nude Iraqi prisoners taunted by dogs, simulating sex acts, and stacked in human pyramids confirmed suspicions that the US military was operating outside the orbit of international law, relying on abuse and torture to extract information or merely as a means of punishment and humiliation (Hersh, 2004). Writer Susan Sontag examined the incidents at Abu Ghraib within a broader historical context.

> Rape and pain inflicted on the genitals are among the most common forms of torture. Not just in Nazi concentration camps and in Abu Ghraib when Saddam Hussein ran it. Americans, too, have done and do them when they are told or made to feel, that those over whom they have absolute power deserve to be humiliated, tormented. They do them when they are led to believe that the people they are torturing belong to an inferior race or religion.
>
> (2004: 28)

Images at Abu Ghraib are remarkably similar to pictures snapped at public lynchings in the American South during the 1880s through the 1930s, typically featuring a naked mutilated body of a black man dangling from a tree. In the foreground of those pictures are townspeople milling about, or like the MPs at Abu Ghraib, grinning and pointing. Again the dynamic of scapegoating is clearly evident. 'The lynching photographs were souvenirs of a collective action

Figure 17.2   Visitors passing by a 285.5 kg patinated bronze sculpture by British artist Marc Quinn entitled Mirage and inspired by a picture taken at Abu Ghraib prison during the preview day of Art Basel, the world's premier modern and contemporary art fair which took place from June 10 to 14, 2009, in Basel. The international art show featured 290 leading art galleries from all continents. Twentieth- and twenty-first-century art works by over 2,500 artists were on display. More than 60,000 art collectors, art dealers, artists, curators and art lovers were expected to attend the annual meeting place of the art community.

Photo by Fabrice Coffrini/AFP/Getty Images.

whose participants felt perfectly justified in what they had done' (Sontag, 2004: 27). Indeed, the Abu Ghraib photographs were not taken to conceal the events but to document and share them, becoming trophies or, as author Luc Sante (2004) observed, in the age of accessible technology 'Here's-me-at-war. jpeg.' It is that casualness in the face of abuse and torture that is disconcerting. Sontag compares American soldiers in Iraq to tourists, or as Defense Secretary Donald Rumsfeld put it: 'running around with digital cameras and taking these unbelievable photographs and passing them off, against the law, to the media, to our surprise' (Sontag, 2004: 42).

The photographs not only verify torture and abuse but also shame the US government, its military, and Americans themselves. Perhaps that is the reason why there was so much concern to control the spin of the scandal. The government and military quickly unleashed the standard 'bad apples' explanation to counter the realization that the extensive use of abuse and torture was systemic (*New York Times*, 2004c). Adding to the long-term controversy over Abu Ghraib is the realization that those human rights abuses would be blamed solely on a handful of reservists featured in the photographs and not on high-level military officers.

In light of that particular trajectory of blaming, there is reason to believe that the Pentagon along with the Bush White House perpetuated a culture of impunity in which ranking military leadership and key policy-makers are immune from accountability and punishment (see the forthcoming section 'Obama's War on Terror').

> Under Commander in Chief, George W. Bush, the notion of command accountability has been discarded. In Mr. Bush's world of war, it's the grunts who take the heat. Punishment is reserved for the people at the bottom. The people who foul up at the top get promoted. There was no wholesale crackdown on criminal behavior.
>
> (Herbert, 2005a: A25)

The 'few bad apples' explanation of Abu Ghraib has retained steady currency even as the scandal made its way through a series of commissions, none of which has been independent of the Defense Department. For example, the Church report based on an investigation by Vice Admiral Albert Church III concludes that only the lowest-ranking soldiers are to be held accountable, not their commanders or civilian overseers. Critics, however, note that it selectively ignores Bush's declaration that the Geneva Conventions did not cover terrorists and that Iraq is part of the war against terror. The Church commission also ignores Rumsfeld's approval of interrogation techniques for Guantánamo Bay that violate the Geneva Conventions and it glosses over the way military attorneys were ordered to ignore their own legal opinions and instead adhere to Justice Department memos on how to make torture appear legal (Greenberg and Dratel, 2005; Danner, 2004).

The Church report said:

> None of the pictured abuses at Abu Ghraib bear any resemblance to approved policies at any level, in any theatre. Admiral Church and his investigators must have missed the pictures of prisoners in hoods, forced into stress positions and threatened by dogs. All of those techniques were approved at one time or another by military officials, including Mr. Rumsfeld.
>
> (*New York Times*, 2005e: A22)

Curiously though, another investigation by former Defense Secretary, James Schlesinger, reported 'both institutional and personal responsibility at higher levels' for Abu Ghraib. But the panel declined to name names. 'Who will? Not the Pentagon, clearly' (*New York Times*, 2005e: A22). The Senate Armed Services Committee plans additional hearings, but that's inadequate. Human rights advocates insist that Congress should open a serious investigation, but to date lawmakers have shown little interest (see Harbury, 2005; Smeulers and van Niekerk, 2009).

In a more recent acknowledgement of the degree of detainee abuse occurring in Iraq before and even during the Abu Ghraib investigation, three former members of the Army's elite 82nd Airborne Division say soldiers in their battalion at

Camp Mercury near Falluja routinely beat and abused prisoners to help gather intelligence on the insurgency and to amuse themselves. One of the sources is Captain Ian Fishback, who presented some of his allegations in letters to top aides of two senior Republicans. Fishback approached the Senators' offices only after he tried to report the allegations to his superiors for 17 months (Human Rights Watch, 2005; Schmitt, 2005). One sergeant said he was a guard and acknowledged abusing some prisoners at the direction of military intelligence personnel. Detainees were also stacked in human pyramids (fully clothed) and forced to hold five-gallon water jugs with outstretched arms or do jumping jacks until they lost consciousness.

> 'We would give them blows to the head, chest, legs and stomach, and pull them down, kick dirt on them. This happened every day.' The sergeant continued: 'Some days we would just get bored, so we would have everyone sit in a corner and then make them get in a pyramid. This was before Abu Ghraib but just like it. We did it for amusement.'
>
> (Schmitt, 2005: A1, A6)

The sergeant stated that he had acted under orders from military intelligence personnel to 'soften up' detainees, whom the unit called PUCs (Persons Under Control) to make them more cooperative during formal interviews. 'They wanted intel. As long as no PUCs came up dead, it happened.' He added, 'We kept it to broken arms and legs and shit.' In one disclosure a sergeant said he had seen a soldier break open a chemical light stick and beat the detainees with it. 'That made them glow in the dark, which was real funny, but it burned their eyes, and their skin was irritated real bad' (Human Rights Watch, 2005: 2).

> Soldiers referred to abusive techniques as 'smoking' or 'fucking' detainees, who are known as 'PUCs,' or Persons Under Control. 'Smoking a PUC' referred to exhausting detainees with physical exercises (sometimes to the point of unconsciousness) or forcing detainees to hold painful positions. 'Fucking a PUC' detainees referred to beating or torturing them severely. The soldiers said that Military Intelligence personnel regularly instructed soldiers to 'smoke' detainees before interrogations.
>
> One sergeant told Human Rights Watch: 'Everyone in camp knew if you wanted to work out your frustration you show up at the PUC tent. In a way it was sport ... One day [a sergeant] shows up and tells a PUC to grab a pole. He told him to bend over and broke the guy's leg with a mini Louisville Slugger, a metal bat.'
>
> (Human Rights Watch, 2005: 2)

Even after the Abu Ghraib scandal became public, 'We still did it, but we were careful' (Schmitt, 2005: A6). Human Rights Watch (2005) pointed out that those accounts show that abuses resulted from civilian and military failures of leadership and confusion about interrogation standards and the application of the Geneva Conventions. Moreover, they contradict claims by the Bush team that detainee abuses by US military abroad have been infrequent, exceptional, and unrelated to policy (Mayer, 2009; Sands, 2008; Welch, 2006a).

COMPARATIVE CORRECTIONS

Detainee Abuse in Afghanistan

The Pentagon persistently claims that detainee abuse is not systemic or widespread but rather confined to a rowdy weekend at Abu Ghraib. Mounting evidence, however, demonstrates a very different reality. Reports from the war in Afghanistan indicate that some forms of maltreatment are more of a result of formal – and informal – policy in the war on terror (Human Rights Watch, 2004; Priest and Gellman, 2002; Rohde, 2004). Consider the following incident:

> Even as the young Afghan man was dying before them, his American jailers continued to torment him. The prisoner, a slight, 22-year-old taxi driver known only as Dilawar, was hauled from his cell at the detention center in Bagram, Afghanistan, at around 2 a.m. to answer questions about a rocket attack on an American base. When he arrived in the interrogation room, an interpreter who was present said his legs were bouncing uncontrollably in the plastic chair and his hands were numb. He had been chained by the wrists to the top of his cell for much of the previous four days.
>
> (Golden, 2005a: A12)

Military coroners determined that Dilawar had died from 'blunt force trauma' to the legs. Soon after, soldiers and others at Bagram told the investigators that military guards had repeatedly struck him in the thighs while he was shackled (Golden, 2005a: A12). Even in the face of autopsy findings of homicide and statements by soldiers that Dilawar (and another prisoner) died after being struck by guards, military investigators initially recommended closing the case without bringing any criminal charges.

Even in the face of autopsy findings of homicide and statements by soldiers that two prisoners died after being struck by guards, military investigators initially recommended closing the case without bringing any criminal charges. The Army's Criminal Investigation Command reported to their superiors that they could not determine precisely who was responsible for the detainees' injuries and military lawyers concurred. 'I could never see any criminal intent on the part of the M.P.s to cause the detainee to die,' one of the lawyers, Major Jeff A. Bovarnick, told investigators, referring to one of the deaths. 'We believed the M.P.'s story, that this was the most combative detainee ever' (Golden, 2005b: A18). The decision to close the case was among a series of apparent missteps in an Army inquiry that ultimately took nearly two years to complete but eventually resulted in criminal charges against seven soldiers. Documents indicate that crucial witnesses were not interviewed, reports and memos disappeared, and key pieces of evidence were mishandled. As the case was made public, in large part due to tireless investigative journalism, the *New York Times* commented:

President Bush said the other day that the world should see his administration's handling of the abuses at Abu Ghraib prison as a model of transparency and accountability. He said those responsible were being systematically punished, regardless of rank. It made for a nice Oval Office photo-op on a Friday morning. Unfortunately, none of it is true.

(*New York Times,* 2005b: A18)

The horrific story of the deaths at Bagram confirms that what happened at Abu Ghraib was no aberration, but rather is part of a prevailing pattern. It shows the deep impact of the initial decision by Bush administrators that they were not going to observe the Geneva Conventions, or even US law, for detainees captured in antiterrorist operations. As the investigative file on Bagram reveals, mistreatment of detainees was routine: 'shackling them to the ceilings of their cells, depriving them of sleep, kicking and hitting them, sexually humiliating them and threatening them with guard dogs – the very same behavior later repeated in Iraq' (*New York Times,* 2005b: A18). As further evidence of systematic abusive tactics is the use of the 'common peroneal strike,' referring to a blow to the side of the leg just above the knee that can cause severe damage. The taxi driver, Dilawar, died after 'blunt force injuries to the lower extremities' stopped his heart, according to the autopsy report (*New York Times,* 2005b: A18; see Davey, 2005; Weisman, 2005; Welch, 20006a).

TORTURE IN THE WAR ON TERROR

As a stark example of state crime, US operatives have participated in torture in Southeast Asia during the 1960s and 1970s as well as in Latin America in the 1980s (Harbury, 2005; McCoy, 2006; Welch, 2009c). What is new about torture's re-emergence in the war on terror is the attempt by government officials to justify it in legal terms. Its advocates argue that given the state of emergency in a post-9/11 society, the US is engaged in fourth-generation warfare involving non-state actors (Cheney, 2005). Such torture tactics have a basic policy goal: to correct the information deficit on al-Qaeda since the US government has relatively little formalized intelligence on that network of terrorists (Clarke, 2004). In efforts to meet that objective the Bush White House once again entered the domain of impunity. By deliberately rewriting the prohibitions on torture, authors and architects along with those who order and carry out torture would be immune from punishment, even in cases in which there exists credible evidence of war crimes (Danner, 2004; Welch, 2006a).

Keeping the focus on impunity, there is compelling documentation on precisely how the executive branch of the US government set out to remove itself from the rule of law in planning a policy of torture. In *The Torture Papers: The Road to Abu Ghraib*, Greenberg and Dratel (2005) reveal in glaring detail the Bush administration's playbook by which it would concoct a legal defense for the use of torture in the war on terror (see Hersh, 2004; Sands, 2008). The legal narrative contained in official memos exhibits three aims that would facilitate the unilateral and unfettered detention, interrogation, abuse, judgment, and punishment of prisoners:

- the desire to place the detainees beyond the reach of any court or law;
- the desire to abrogate the Geneva Convention with respect to the treatment of persons seized in the context of armed hostilities; and
- the desire to absolve those implementing the policies of any liability for war crimes under US and international law.

(Dratel, 2005: xxi)

In December 2002, nearly a year and a half before the Abu Ghraib prison scandal broke in the media, Dana Priest and Barton Gellman for the *Washington Post* unveiled a front-page story involving questionable interrogation tactics used on terrorism suspects held by American authorities in secret overseas facilities. The story offers evidence that stress and duress techniques have become part and parcel of the war on terror. Journalists describe clandestine detention units located in US-occupied Bagram Air Base in Afghanistan where metal shipping containers hold those believed to be high-level al Qaeda operatives and Taliban commanders. Detainees who refuse to cooperate with CIA interrogators are sometimes kept standing or kneeling for hours in black hoods or spray-painted goggles. Often detainees are forced into awkward, painful positions and deprived of sleep with a 24-hour bombardment of lights.

> Those who cooperate are rewarded with creature comforts, interrogators whose methods include feigned friendship, respect, cultural sensitivity and, in some cases, money. Some who do not cooperate are turned over – 'rendered,' in official parlance – to foreign intelligence services whose practice of torture has been documented by the US government and human rights organizations.
>
> (Priest and Gellman, 2002: A1)

Although the American government publicly denounces the use of torture, each of the current national security officials interviewed by the *Washington Post* defended the use of violence against captives as just and necessary. Moreover, they expressed confidence that the American public would back them. According to one official who has supervised the capture and transfer of accused terrorists: 'If you don't violate someone's human rights some of the time, you probably aren't doing your job. I don't think we want to be promoting a view of zero tolerance on this. That was the whole problem for a long time with the CIA' (Priest and Gellman, 2002: A1). Apparently, there seems to be considerable public support for torture. A CNN poll revealed that 45 percent of those surveyed would not object to having someone tortured if it would provide information about terrorism (Williams, 2001).

Nevertheless, when the *Washington Post* story broke, human rights organizations wasted little time in confronting the government. Ken Roth, executive director of Human Rights Watch, responded to torture allegations by sending a firmly worded letter to the White House, insisting that the Bush administration must promptly investigate and address allegations of torture of suspected al-Qaeda detainees or risk criminal prosecution. Roth continued, saying that he was 'deeply concerned' by allegations made in the *Washington Post* that detainees had been subjected to torture or other forms of mistreatment while in US custody in Afghanistan or while held by US allies. 'Torture is always prohibited under any circumstances,' said Roth. 'US officials who take part in torture, authorize it, or even close their eyes to it, can be prosecuted by courts anywhere in the world' (Roth, 2002: 1).

Not only is torture known to be an unreliable method of extracting information from detainees, in the long run it also undermines legitimacy for a government (Leo, 2008; Welch, 2009c). 'As a tool for collecting information, moreover, torture is notoriously ineffective (since people in pain have the unfortunate habit of lying to make it stop) and has done little to solve long-term security threats' (Press, 2003: 16). Adding to the controversy is recent debate over the precise definition of torture. At the international level, the widely accepted definition is clearly laid out in Article 1 of the Convention Against Torture and Other Cruel, Inhuman or Degrading Treatment or Punishment (1984):

> [T]he term 'torture' means any act by which severe pain or suffering, whether physical or mental, is intentionally inflicted on a person for such purposes of obtaining from him or a third person information or a confession, punishing him for an act he or a third person has committed or is suspected of having committed, or intimidating or coercing him or a third person, or for any reason based on discrimination of any kind, when such pain or suffering is inflicted by or at the instigation of or with the consent or acquiescence of a public official or other person acting in an official capacity. It does not include pain or suffering arising only from, inherent in or incidental to lawful sanctions.

After 9/11, however, the Bush White House developed its own interpretation of the Convention Against Torture, raising grave concerns that political appointees deliberately weakened the document that the US ratified in 1994. A memorandum by Jay S. Bybee, then Assistant Attorney General, for Alberto R. Gonzales (then Attorney General) attempted to change the standard contained in the Convention Against Torture by arguing: 'Physical pain amounting to torture must be equivalent in intensity to the pain accompanying serious injury, such as organ failure, impairment of bodily function, or even death' (Greenberg and Dratel, 2005: 172–214; see Danner, 2004). As a paper trail of legal arguments favoring torture and as a tainted historical record fixed squarely onto the Bush presidency, 'The Torture Papers' are nothing less than remarkable. As Dratel notes: 'Rarely, if ever, has such a guilty governmental conscience been so starkly illuminated in advance' (2005, xxi; see Cohen 2006, 2001; Welch, 2011).

Compounding matters, several government officials have publicly revealed that they endorse interrogation tactics that squarely fit into the ambit of torture. While being questioned by the Senate, CIA Director Porter J. Goss was confronted by Senator John McCain (who spent five years as a prisoner of war in Vietnam). When McCain asked Goss about the CIA's reported use of 'waterboarding,' in which a prisoner is made to believe that he will drown, Goss replied only that the approach fell into 'an area of what I will call professional interrogation techniques' (Jehl, 2005: A11; see Herbert, 2005b).

Numerous incidents of torture have been officially documented. In 2003, two army officers were handed career-ending punishments for staging mock executions of Iraqi prisoners. Mock executions, in which a prisoner is made to believe that his death is imminent, are clearly prohibited by the Army as a form of torture. In one of those cases, a US captain 'took an Iraqi welder out to the desert and had him dig his own grave before staging an attempt to shoot him.' The captain – who had been cited in a similar act of mock execution – was court-martialed, convicted of aggravated assault and battery and sentenced to 45 days' confinement and loss of 12,000 dollars in pay (*New York Times*, 2005c: A10). With the exception of a mere handful of cases in which US soldiers have been prosecuted for violating rules banning torture, there remain questions as to the extent of such cruelties and how involved are officials connected to the Bush White House and the Pentagon. In particular, there are concerns over the American practice of extraordinary rendition in which detainees are outsourced to a third party for purposes of torture (e.g. Egypt, Jordan, Morocco, and Syria) so as to skip over legal prohibitions contained in the Convention Against Torture (Grey, 2006; Mayer, 2009). In 1998, Congress passed legislation declaring that it is 'the policy of the United States not to expel, extradite, or otherwise effect the involuntary return of any person to a country in which there are substantial grounds for believing the person would be in danger of being subjected to torture, regardless of whether that person is physically in the United States' (Mayer, 2005: EV2).

It should also be noted that the employment of privatized 'interrogators' who are not bound by legal or military codes provides another avenue for impunity. Commenting on the lack of accountability, P. W. Singer said: 'Legally speaking [military contractors] fall into the same grey zone as the unlawful combatants detained at Guantanamo Bay' (Singer, 2005: 121). True, the *Hamdan* ruling raised questions over the legality of the Bush administration's secret CIA detention program while 'making clear that the abusive interrogation techniques used by the CIA violated the United States' obligations under international law and that CIA operatives could be held criminally liable for such abuses' (Human Rights Watch, 2006: 1). However, given that the CIA exists within the sovereignty of presidential power, it remains conveniently insulated due to it being a covert agency shrouded in secrecy and because there is lacking any political will to prosecute its personnel for state crimes involving torture (see Cohen, 2001; Sands, 2008; Welch, 2011).

CULTURAL PENOLOGY

Neocolonial Detention in Iraq

Theorists and historians observe that it is through colonialism that a distant power attempts to modernize societies and people it considers primitive. Moreover, by way of a complex cultural process, a colonial power also creates a colonial other as a way to reproduce and privilege itself. 'This is not to say that other cultures are supine creations of the modern, but it is to acknowledge the extraordinary power and performative force of colonial modernity' (Gregory, 2006: 4). That performative force is evident in the ways in which stories – or narratives – are constructed. Derek Gregory elaborates that modern colonialism produces two potent narratives: the first are stories that 'the West' tells itself about itself, and the second are stories about the colonial other, an alterity that gives back 'the West' an image of itself (see Dussel 1995; Said 1978). Because the reciprocated image of 'the West' is conveyed as a benevolent one which takes credit for spreading its 'glorious creativity' to primitive lands, the momentum of empire mediates its own destruction, apologetically known as a 'white man's burden' or what Niall Ferguson calls a 'savage war of peace' in reference to America's post-9/11 militarism (2001: 35, 2005; see Kagan, 2006; Rhodes, 2003; Wheatcroft, 2006).

Drawing further on Gregory's view that colonial powers tend to create narratives that 'the West' tells itself about itself (as well as to others) we turn to Operation Iraqi Freedom: Official Website of the Multi-National Force—Iraq as a source of knowledge or 'savoir' underpinning the occupation (http://www.mnf-iraq.com). Given that the website serves as a public relations tool endorsing the occupation, it is not surprising to find daily articles, press briefings, transcribed press conferences, videos, and various 'puff pieces' that deliver a decidedly positive spin on the heavy US military presence in Iraq. Stories describing the occupation frequently inject such upbeat words as progress, prosperity, productivity, and partnership, thereby underscoring its central neo-liberal message, freedom. Upon entering the website, visitors are shown portals to the following: 'News' (with 'Freedom Journal Iraq' and 'Iraqi Freedom Minute'), 'The New Face of Iraq,' 'Inside the Force,' 'Fight for Freedom' (with 'Freedom Facts'), and 'For the Troops' (with 'Operation Tribute to Freedom') (Welch, 2008b).

The Official Website of the Multi-National Force also dispenses a good deal of text recounting the stated purpose of detaining Iraqi civilians. As one might expect, the benevolent depiction of the US occupation of Iraq spills over into the website's characterization of the detention centers. So as to gain further insight into a phenomenon that could be described as neocolonial discipline, Welch (2010a) has developed a critique of US military assertions concerning detention (see Adler and Longhurst 1994; Carrabine 2000, 2004). Key to the way in which American power is expressed through detention practices in Iraq is an elaborate system involving reintegration programs, review boards, and release. Turning attention to the overall scope of American authority in the realm of Detention Operations, we take a look at the tightly constructed stories about what the US military tells itself about itself (as well as to others) and what it says about the Iraqis it detains.

Imperative Security Threats

According to Operation Iraqi Freedom: Official Website of the Multi-National Force — Iraq, Detainee Operations are described as carrying out the duty to provide custody and care for 'individuals who pose a threat to the security of Iraq' (MNF, 2008a: 1). As of September 2008, approximately 19,000 Iraqi civilians were in detention centers controlled by the US military, and that number is down from a peak of 26,000 during the summer of 2007 (and another 37,000 in Iraqi custody). It should be emphasized that about 18,000 detainees were held at Camp Bucca (April 2008) and 3,000 at Camp Cropper (June 2008), together making them what the US military boasts as 'largest and the busiest detention centers in the world' (MNF, 2008a: 1). By September 2008, over 12,000 detainees had been released back into their communities compared with only 9,000 the previous year (MNF, 2008a: 1).

Throughout history, local people have resisted colonialism by refusing to cooperate and in many cases engaging in sabotage and guerrilla warfare. Iraqi opposition to American neocolonialism is no exception; still, the US military must deal with another modern form of resistance, namely the media. Iraqi journalists persistently question the legal legitimacy of detention, prompting US officials to resort to spin (see Cohen, 2001). During a press conference local reporters criticized the Americans for not following Iraqi law in detaining civilians. The US military countered by depicting itself in benevolent terms, claiming that it is providing safety to Iraqi citizens and their government. By doing so, the US military adopts much of the same language found in the larger war on terror, especially as it contends with risk, security, and dangerousness. Indeed, as the following item reveals, those in detention have not been charged with a criminal offense but rather simply viewed by the Americans as posing a threat (see Ericson, 2007; Simon, 2007).

> Those in coalition detention have been deemed an imperative threat to the citizens of Iraq, the Government of Iraq, and those security forces that are working to ensure peace and stability. Those captured who have been identified as having broken the law, are turned over to the Government of Iraq and processed according to Iraqi Law. Coalition Forces detain persons based on threat and the Government of Iraq imprisons based on Iraqi law. Basically, Coalition Forces hold detainees and the Government of Iraq holds prisoners and inmates.
>
> (MNF, 2008b: 2)

The detention of Iraqi civilians appears to be driven by virtually the same logic and vocabulary that the US military uses to describe its holding of unlawful enemy combatants at Guantánamo Bay. Agamben (2005) refers to these developments as a 'state of exception' whereby law is suspended due to a national emergency. When challenged by an Iraqi journalist over the US military's terminology concerning 'imperative security risks,' Major-General Douglas Stone, Commander, Multi-National Force — Iraq, responded:

> You used the term initially 'prison.' I don't use the term 'prison.' I use 'detention facility,' because a prisoner is somebody who has been incarcerated, arrested – our guys aren't – who have been taken on a specific charge with evidence before a court and then tried, found guilty and given a sentence for either rehabilitation or retribution in a prison. That process is not the process we run. Our process is a warfighting process where a judgment is made that an individual is an imperative security risk. That individual has been taken off the battlefield as a civilian internee, held until such time as the judgment is made that they're no longer an imperative security risk, and then released back into the population.
>
> (MNF, 2008c: 4)

In her critique of what she calls the 'new war prison' at Guantánamo Bay, Judith Butler points to significant socio-legal transformations in a post-9/11 world. She concludes that the war on terror is administered by recently created petty sovereigns who are mobilized by tactics of power they do not fully control. Moreover, they are granted the power to render unilateral decisions, 'accountable to no law and without any legitimate authority' (2004: 56). That form of power is lawless or, as Butler puts it, 'a "rogue" power par excellence' (p. 56). Arguably, a similar 'rogue' power that deems certain persons as unlawful enemy combatants at Guantánamo Bay appears to have surfaced in Iraq where some civilians are labeled imperative security risks – prompting the US military to take them off the 'battlefield.' Mirroring the perspective of Agamben (2005), Butler recognizes that these decisions take place within a state of emergency, thereby removing accountability from the field of operations. Consequently, pseudo-institutions are produced to serve the war on terror, most notably 'a law that is not a law, a court that is not a court, a process that is not a process' (Butler 2004: 62).

OBAMA'S WAR ON TERROR

The election of President Obama has prompted both optimism and concern over how he will handle the war on terror. Early in his presidential campaign, Obama sought advice from Richard Clarke, the former White House counterterrorism chief who had become one of Bush's harshest critics on national security. 'It is time to turn the page,' Obama declared in a speech in 2007. 'America is at war with terrorists who killed on our soil; we are not at war with Islam.' He criticized claims of 'unchecked presidential power' and promised to close the detention center at Guantánamo Bay. He rejected the Military Commissions Act and embraced the Geneva Conventions, adding 'no more illegal wiretapping of American citizens, no more national-security letters to spy on citizens who are not suspected of a crime' and 'no more ignoring the law when it is inconvenient' (Baker, 2010: 11).

As President, Obama decided to make one of his first acts a strike against the Bush legacy. He signed executive orders that banned harsh interrogation techniques such as waterboarding and ordered the prison at Guantánamo closed within one year. Still, skepticism lingered due to the number of Bush holdovers in the Obama administration (Baker, 2010). Adding to these worries, Obama left intact the surveillance program, embraced the Patriot Act, retained the authority to use renditions, and maintained some of Bush's claims to state secrets. He preserved the military commissions and national security letters he criticized during the campaign, albeit with more due-process safeguards. Obama plans to hold indefinitely dozens of suspected terrorists without charges. He expanded Bush's campaign of unmanned drone strikes against al-Qaeda in the tribal areas of Pakistan, vowing to strike terrorists there without permission of the local government. Living up to his campaign rhetoric, Obama has significantly shifted focus from Iraq to Afghanistan where troop levels are set to triple on his watch (Baker, 2010; Savage, 2010).

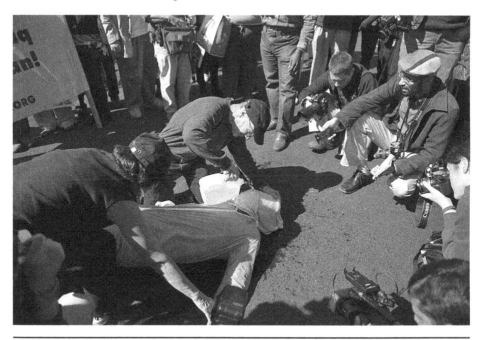

Figure 17.3 Anti-war activists demonstrating waterboarding torture during a demo in front of the White House in Washington, DC on October 5, 2009. The demonstrators are calling for an end to the war in Iraq.

Photo by Mandel Ngan/AFP/Getty Images.

Despite continuity in his use of military might in the war on terror, former Bush officials have criticized Obama, especially for investigating incidents of torture. In 2009, Attorney General Eric Holder decided to release legal memos describing specific interrogation techniques used by the CIA as well as to reinvestigate allegations of abuse by its officers. Nonetheless, the White House refused to release photographs of abused detainees. In another controversy, Holder has announced plans to try in civilian court Khalid Shaikh Mohammed (the self-declared mastermind of the 9/11 attacks), a move that prompted protests by Republicans as well as Democrats. Similarly, the decision to close the Guantánamo Bay prison sparked a revolt in Congress where members of both parties expressed fears about suspected terrorists being transferred to prisons in their states. Even efforts to empty Guantánamo have been derailed, including a proposal to release into the US 17 Chinese Uighurs deemed no threat to Americans (Shane, 2010; Welch, 2009c).

In an attempt to sort out some of the legal issues situated at the core of the war on terror, Obama met with civil liberties and human rights lawyers. Much of the discussion concerned the military commissions that Obama decided to keep. Also addressed was the dilemma of how to deal with the hardest cases at Guantánamo: namely, those who could not be prosecuted because of tainted evidence but still deemed too dangerous to release. 'He wasn't entirely comfortable with any of the options,' according to Tom Malinowski of Human Rights Watch (Baker, 2010: 24; see Sands, 2008; Savage, 2010).

Anthony Romero of the American Civil Liberties Union (ACLU) was relieved that Obama seems more open to rethinking Bush-era policies. Still, he views Obama as suffering from the 'hubris' of wanting to maintain much of the executive power he inherited from the previous administration. 'He believes he can do it better and smarter and more in keeping with constitutional principles than his predecessor did.' Romero went on to express reservations about Obama's handling of the war on terror. 'If he's shown himself willing to adhere to some of the Bush policies in the absence of an attack, one worries about what he'll do when an attack comes' (Baker, 2010: 24). In the first few months of his administration Obama seemed poised to hold terrorism suspects indefinitely without charges; he even considered legislation that would permanently authorize preventive detention. In response, the ACLU prepared a campaign against the proposed law. But the White House reversed course. Although the Obama administration would continue to hold indefinitely without charges 50 detainees left from the Bush era, it would not enshrine the power in law (Baker, 2010; Welch, 2008a).

The botched airplane bomb plot above Detroit airport on Christmas Day in 2009 raised new questions over whether Obama would be 'tough' enough to advance the war on terror, even though he has continued to track down and kill suspected extremists. Obama had authorized the CIA to greatly expand a program inherited from Bush using unmanned Predator and Reaper drones to launch missiles at suspected al-Qaeda hideouts along the Pakistan–Afghanistan border. Critics complain that such 'targeted assassinations' are morally suspect and endanger civilians. After some reflection on the matter, Obama said pointedly,

'The CIA gets what it needs' (Baker, 2010: 27). In his first year in office, the CIA launched 53 such strikes, more than during Bush's entire presidency. Obama has doubled the number of drones on the Pakistani border while increasing the presence over Yemen and Somalia (Baker, 2010; Savage, 2010).

In other developments in the war on terror, Obama has been criticized for upholding a controversial assassination policy. Dennis Blair, Director of National Intelligence, confirmed US forces are authorized to kill US citizens abroad. Speaking before the House Intelligence Committee, Blair acknowledged Obama is continuing a Bush-era policy authorizing the killing of US citizens if they're considered a terrorist threat to the US. Blair said, 'Being a US citizen will not spare an American from getting assassinated by military or intelligence operatives overseas if the individual is working with terrorists and planning to attack fellow Americans.' In response, Glenn Greenwald, a legal analyst, wrote that the assassination policy gives Obama 'the power to impose death sentences on his own citizens without any charges or trial' (Democracy Now, 2010).

Despite these apparent setbacks, human rights advocates praise the Obama administration for following through with efforts to investigate whether Bush's advisors violated federal law in the planning of harsh interrogation tactics. The findings, however, are mixed. Ethics lawyers in the Office of Professional Responsibility concluded that Justice Department lawyers involved in justifying waterboarding and other interrogation tactics had demonstrated 'professional misconduct.' Investigators concluded that Jay S. Bybee (currently a federal judge) and John Yoo (a law professor at the University of California, Berkeley) had ignored legal precedents and provided slipshod legal advice to the Bush team in possible violation of international and federal laws on torture (see Sands, 2008).

Conversely, a separate review by Obama's Justice Department announced that Bybee and Yoo had used flawed legal reasoning but were not guilty of professional misconduct. That report rejected harsher sanctions recommended by Justice Department ethics lawyers. David Margolis, a career lawyer at the Justice Department, said that the ethics lawyers, in condemning the actions by Bybee and Yoo, had given short shrift to the national climate of urgency after the 9/11 attacks. Members of Congress weighed into the issue. Representative John Conyers, who leads the House Judiciary Committee, said the ethics office made clear that the authors of the interrogation memorandums dishonored their office and the entire Justice Department. Likewise, Senator Richard Durbin noted: 'Mr. Bybee and Mr. Yoo may keep their law licenses, but they will not escape the verdict of history' (Lichtblau and Shane, 2010: 4).

As the war on terror mounts in Afghanistan, human rights advocates have doubled their efforts to challenge Obama's position that detainees held by the US military at Bagram Air Base can be kept in secret. After nearly a year of legal wrangling, the White House finally released the names of 645 detainees kept at the detention center at Bagram, giving up its long-held policy that such information could not be made public. The detainee list was produced by a Freedom of Information Act lawsuit filed by the ACLU. Those attorneys also demanded detailed information about conditions, rules, and regulations at the prison. 'Releasing the names of those held at Bagram is an important step toward transparency and accountability at the secretive Bagram prison, but it is just a first step,' said Melissa Goodman, a lawyer for the ACLU (Rubin and Rahimi, 2010: 1).

For human rights lawyers attempting to represent Bagram detainees, having names without other information is of limited value, according to Tina Foster, a lawyer for the International Justice Network. Former detainees have reported abusive treatment at Bagram, especially in the first two or three years it was in existence. As mentioned previously, in 2002 two detainees died after being beaten by US military personnel. Some former detainees described improved living conditions but have criticized the detention system for continuing to hold them indefinitely without charges or trial. Foster adds: 'While it's very important in terms of US government transparency, it means very little to the individuals named because the US government still maintains that everybody whose name appears on that list is not entitled to any human rights under US law' (Rubin and Rahimi, 2010: 2; Welch, 2011, 2007).

CONCLUSION

Critical criminology emerged as an alternative to mainstream criminology that fails to examine forms of wrongdoing among political, economic, and governmental elites. In an effort to illustrate that degree of scholarly neglect, Michalowski and Kramer (2006) reviewed the leading criminology journals and found that a mere 3 percent of published articles involved studies on crimes committed by the powerful. Specifically, they examined three top journals: *Criminology*, *Justice Quarterly*, and the *British Journal of Criminology*. Between 2000 and 2005, those journals together published 575 articles, of which 18 fell into the category of state, corporate, white collar, or political crimes (see Ruggiero and Welch, 2009).

It is with those concerns in mind that we seek to broaden our understanding of state crime contained in the war on terror and human rights. Green and Ward insist that criminology should not be neutral between human rights violators and their victims, and that state crime should be viewed as 'state organisational deviance involving the violation of human rights' (2004: 2). Green and Ward are not arguing that all deprivations of human freedom and wellbeing constitute crimes: 'That would be to equate "crime" with the much broader concept of "social harm", and would call for a kind of analysis that goes beyond criminology' (2004: 8). Moreover, it is important to be wary of how the language of human rights is being used to justify war: or what Chomsky (2003) refers to as the 'new military humanism' whereby political leaders of powerful nations claim that bombings and other military adventures are important tools to protect human rights (see Gearty, 2006; Welch, 2003f).

Bridging these matters, critical criminologists should continue to track the interplay between the political and economic elements of the social order, particularly since they also provide a foundation for state crime committed within an array of antiterrorism maneuvers. In reference to wider forms of domination, Green and Ward argue that the war on terror has 'become the key strategic device through which the United States is enforcing its hegemony through a series of military incursions in some of the world's most unstable regions' (2004, 191; see Ross, 2000).

SUMMARY

Taking a critical approach to state crime, this chapter delved into three instances of serious violations of human rights in the American war on terror: the unlawful enemy combatant designation, the use of Guantánamo Bay, and torture. In doing so, the discussion draws from an array of social theorists who insist that since the attacks of 9/11, executive power has become not only increasingly militarized but also reconfigured in ways that tend to override judicial and legislative oversight. The chapter closes with recent development in Obama's war on terror.

REVIEW QUESTIONS

1 Why is the Military Commissions Act so controversial?
2 How is institutional control established at Guantánamo Bay?
3 According to *The Torture Papers: The Road to Abu Ghraib* (Greenberg and Drakel, 2005), how did the Bush administration attempt to concoct a legal defense for the use of torture in the war on terror?
4 What is meant by neocolonial detention as carried by the US military in Iraq?

RECOMMENDED READINGS

McCoy, A. (2006) *A Question of Torture: CIA Interrogation, From the Cold War to the War on Terror*. New York: Metropolitan Books.

Mayer, J. (2009) *The Dark Side: The Inside Story of How the War on Terror Turned into a War on American Ideals*. New York: Anchor Books.

Sands, P. (2008) *Torture Team: Rumsfeld's Memo and the Betrayal of American Values*. New York: St. Martin's Press.

Weiner, T. (2007) *Legacy of Ashes: The History of the CIA*. New York: Doubleday.

Welch, M. (2006) *Scapegoats of September 11th: Hate Crimes and State Crimes in the War on Terror*. New Brunswick, NJ and London: Rutgers University Press.

Welch, M. (2009) *Crimes of Power and States of Impunity: The US Response to Terror*. New Brunswick, NJ and London: Rutgers University Press.

REFERENCES

Abadinsky, H. (1994) *Probation and Parole: Theory and Practice* (4th edn). Englewood Cliffs, NJ: Prentice-Hall.

Abadinsky, H. (2002) 'Parole,' in D. Levinson (ed.), *Encyclopedia of Crime and Punishment*. Thousand Oaks, CA: Sage.

Abadinsky, H. (2003) *Probation and Parole: Theory and Practice* (8th edn). Upper Saddle River, NJ: Prentice-Hall.

Abbott, G. (1991) *Lords of the Scaffold: A History of the Executioner*. New York: St. Martin's Press.

Abbott, J. H. (1981) *In the Belly of the Beast: Letters from Prison*. New York: Vintage Books.

Abbott, J. H., with Zack, N. (1987) *My Return*. Buffalo, NY: Prometheus Books.

Abram, K. M. (1990) 'The problem of co-occurring disorders among jail detainees: antisocial disorder, alcoholism, drug abuse, and depression,' *Law and Human Behavior*, 14 (4): 333–44.

Abrams, A. (1991) 'It seemed so unfair,' *New York Newsday*, June 19, Part II, pp. 49, 56–7.

Abramsky, S. (2002) 'The shame of prison health,' *The Nation*, July 1, pp. 28–34.

Abramson, S. and Isay, D. (2002) 'The stopping point: interview with a tie-down officer,' in D. Dow and M. Dow (eds), *Machinery of Death: The Reality of America's Death Penalty Regime*. New York: Routledge.

Abu-Jamal, M. (1995) *Live from Death Row*. New York: Addison-Wesley.

Acker, J. R. (1991) 'Social science in Supreme Court death penalty cases: citation practices and their implications,' *Justice Quarterly*, 8 (4): 421–46.

Acorn, L. R. (2002) 'Working in a boot camp,' in T. Gray (ed.), *Exploring Corrections*. Boston: Allyn & Bacon.

Adams, K. (1996) 'The bull market in corrections,' *Prison Journal*, 76 (4): 461–7.

Adams, R. (1998) *Abuses of Punishment*. New York: St. Martin's Press.

Adamson, C. R. (1983) 'Punishment after slavery: southern state penal systems,' *Social Problems*, 30 (5): 555–69.

Adamson, C. (1984) 'Toward a Marxian theory of penology: captive criminal populations as economic threats and resources,' *Social Problems*, 31 (4): 435–58.

Adler, F. (1975) *Sisters in Crime: The Rise of the New Female Criminal*. New York: McGraw-Hill.

Adler, F. (1981) *Incidence of Female Criminality in the Contemporary World*. New York: New York University Press.

Adler, F. (1986) 'Jails as a repository for former mental patients,' *International Journal of Offender Therapy and Comparative Criminology*, 30: 225–36.

Adler, M. and Longhurst, B. (1994) *Discourse, Power and Justice: Towards a New Sociology of Prisons*. London: Routledge.

Aertsen, I., Daems, T., and Robert, L. (2006) *Institutionalizing Restorative Justice*. Cullompton: Willan.

Agamben, G. (1998) *Homo Sacer: Sovereign Power and Bare Life*, trans. Daniel Heller-Roaxen. Stanford, CA: Stanford University Press.

Agamben, G. (2005) *State of Exception*, trans. Kevin Attell. Chicago: University of Chicago Press.

Aguirre, A. Jr and Baker, D. (2000a) 'Special issue on Latinos and the criminal justice system,' *Justice Professional*, 13 (1): 6–22.

Aguirre, A. Jr, and Baker, D. (2000b) 'Latinos and the United States criminal justice system: introduction,' *Justice Professional*, 13 (1): 3–6.

Aguirre, A. Jr, Davin, R. P., Baker, D. V., and Lee, K. (1999) 'Sentencing outcomes, race, and victim impact evidence in California: a pre- and post-Payne comparison,' *Justice Professional*, 11 (3): 297–310.

Ainlay, J. (1975) 'Book review: the new criminology and critical criminology,' *Telos*, 26: 213–25.

Ajzenstadt, M. (2009) 'The relative autonomy of women offenders' decision making,' *Theoretical Criminology*, 13 (2): 201–25.

Akers, R. L. (1979) 'Theory and ideology in Marxist criminology,' *Criminology*, 16 (February): 527–44.

Akers, R. L. (1990) 'Rational choice, deterrence, and social learning theory in criminology: the path not taken,' *Journal of Criminal Law and Criminology*, 81 (Fall): 653–76.

Akerstrom, M. (1986) 'Outcasts in prison: the cases of informers and sex offenders,' *Deviant Behavior*, 7: 1–12.

Akerstrom, M. (1988) 'The social construction of snitches,' *Deviant Behavior*, 9: 155–67.

Akerstrom, M. (1989) 'Snitches on snitching,' *Society*, 26 (2): 22–6.

Alexander, C. R. and Cohen, M. A. (1999) 'Why do corporations become criminals? Ownership, hidden actions, and crime as an agency cost,' *Journal of Corporate Finance*, 5: 1–34.

Alexander, M. (2010) *The New Jim Crow: Mass Incarceration in the Age of Colorblindness*. New York: New Press.

Alford, C. F. (2000) 'What would it matter if everything Foucault said about prisons was wrong?' *Theory and Society*, 29: 125–46.

Alleman, T. (1993) 'Varieties of feminist thought and their application to crime and criminal justice,' in R. Muraskin and T. Alleman (eds), *It's a Crime: Women and Justice*. Englewood Cliffs, NJ: Prentice-Hall.

Allen, H. F. and Abril, J. C. (1997) 'The new chain gang: corrections in the next century,' *American Journal of Criminal Justice*, 22: 1–12.

Allen, H., Eskridge, C., Latessa, E., and Vito, G. (1985) *Probation and Parole in America*. New York: Free Press.

Allen, T. (1997) 'The invention of the white race,' Volume Two: *The Origin of Racial Oppression in Anglo-America*. London: Verso.

Alpert, G. (1984) 'The needs of the judiciary and misapplication of social research: the case of the female guard in men's prisons,' *Criminology*, 22 (August): 441–56.

Alpert, G., Crouch, B., and Huff, C. (1983) 'Prison reform by decree: the unintended consequences of Ruiz v. Estelle,' *Justice System Journal*, 9 (Winter): 291–305.

Alvarez, A. (2000) 'Unwelcome citizens: Latinos and the criminal justice system,' in Criminal Justice Collective of Northern Arizona (ed.), *Investigating Differences: Human and Cultural Relations in Criminal Justice*. Boston: Allyn & Bacon.

Amann, D. (2004) 'Guantanamo Bay,' *Columbia Journal of Transnational Law*, 42: 263–348.

American Civil Liberties Union (1999) 'Driving while black or brown,' *Spotlight: National Members' Bulletin*, Issue 4.

American Civil Liberties Union (2002) *Hope Triumphs: Supreme Court Says Hitching Post for Alabama Prisoners is 'Cruel and Unusual.'* Press Release, July 27. Washington, DC: ACLU.

American Civil Liberties Union Immigrants' Rights Project (1993) *Justice Detained: Conditions at the Varick Street Immigration Detention Center, A Report by the ACLU Immigrants' Rights Project*. New York: American Civil Liberties Union.

American Correctional Association (1970) *Transactions of the National Congress on Prison and Reformatory Discipline, Albany 1871*. Reprinted by American Correctional Association, October, pp. 1–8.

American Correctional Association (1981) *Riots and Disturbances in Correctional Institutions*. College Park, MD: American Correctional Association.

American Correctional Association (1983) *The American Prison: From the Beginning … A Pictorial History*. College Park, MD: American Correctional Association.

American Correctional Association (1985) *Private Sector Operation of a Correctional Institution*. Washington, DC: US Department of Justice.

American Correctional Association (1993) *Female Offenders: Meeting the Needs of a Neglected Population*. Laurel, MD: American Correctional Association.

American Correctional Association (1994) *1994 Directory of Juvenile and Adult Correctional Institutions, Agencies and Paroling Authorities*. Laurel, MD: American Correctional Association.

American Correctional Association (1995) *Gangs in Correctional Institutions: A National Assessment*. Laurel, MD: American Correctional Association.

American Jail Association (1991) *Who's Who in Jail Management*. Hagerstown, MD: American Jail Association.

Amnesty International (1999) *'Not Part of My Sentence': Violations of Human Rights of Women in Custody*. New York: Amnesty International.

Amnesty International (2005) *Guantanamo and Beyond: The Continuing Pursuit of Unchecked Executive Power*. New York: Amnesty International.

Amo, B. J. (1991) *Prison Health Care: Guidelines for the Management of an Adequate Delivery System*. Washington DC: National Institute of Justice.

Anderson, P. (1977) 'The antinomies of Antonio Gramsci,' *New Left Review*, 100: 5–80.

Andrews, D. A., Zinger, I., Hoge, R. D., Bonta, J., Gendreau, P., and Cullen, F. T. (1990) 'Does correctional treatment work? A clinically relevant and psychologically informed meta-analysis,' *Criminology*, 28 (3): 369–404.

Anglin, D., Hser, Y., and McGlothin, W. (1987) 'Sex differences in addict careers,' *American Journal of Drug and Alcohol Abuse*, 13: 59–71.

Anno, B. J., Faiver, K. and Harness, J. (1996) 'A preliminary model for determining limits for correctional care services,' *Journal of Correctional Health Care*, 3: 67–84.

Applebome, P. (1992) '14 are charged with sex abuse in women's jail,' *New York Times*, November 14, pp. A1, A7.

Applegate, B., Cullen, F., and Fisher, B. (1997) 'Public support for correctional treatment: the continuing appeal of the rehabilitative ideal,' *Prison Journal*, 77: 237–58.

Applegate, B. K., Turner, M. G., Sanborn Jr, J. B., Latessa, E., and Moon, M. (2000) 'Individualization, criminalization, or problem resolution: a factorial survey of juvenile court judges' decisions to incarcerate youthful felony offenders,' *Justice Quarterly*, 17 (2): 309–32.

Appleton, C. and Grover, B. (2007) 'The pros and cons of life without parole,' *British Journal of Criminology*, 47: 597–615.

Arasse, D. (1987) *La Guillotine et l'imaginarie de la Terreur*. Paris: Flammarion.

Archambeault, W. (2003) 'Soar like an eagle, dive like a loon: human diversity and social justice in the Native American prison experience,' in J. I. Ross and S. Richards (eds), *Convict Criminology*. Belmont, CA: Wadsworth.

Archibold, R. (2010) 'California, in financial crisis, opens prison doors,' *New York Times*, March 23, pp. EV1-5.

Armour, J. D. (1997) *Negrophobia and Reasonable Racism: The Hidden Costs of Being Black in America*. New York: New York University Press.

Arnold, R. (1990) 'Processes of victimization and criminalization of black women,' *Social Justice*, 17 (3): 153–66.

Aronowitz, S. and DeFazio, W. (1994) *The Jobless Future: Sci-Tech and the Dogma of Work*. Minneapolis, MN: University of Minnesota Press.

Arp, W., Dantico, M. K., and Zatz, M. (1990) 'The Immigration Reform and Control Act of 1986: differential impacts on women?' *Social Justice*, 17 (2): 23–39.

Arrigo, B. A. (1995) 'The peripheral core of law and criminology: on postmodern social theory and conceptual integration,' *Justice Quarterly*, 12 (3): 447–72.

Arrigo, B. A. (1999) *Social Justice, Criminal Justice: The Maturation of Critical Theory in Law, Crime and Deviance*. Belmont, CA: West/Wadsworth.

Arrigo, B. A. and Schehr, R. C. (1998) 'Restoring justice for juveniles: a critical analysis of victim offender meditation,' *Justice Quarterly*, 15 (4): 629–66.

Arriola, K., R. Braithwaite, R., and Kennedy, S. (2001) 'A collaborative effort to enhance HIV/STI screening in five county jails,' *Public Health Report*, 116: 520–9.

Artières, P., Quero, L., and Zancarini-Fournel, M. (2003) *Le groupe d'information sur les prisons. Archives d'une lutte 1970–1972*. Paris: Éditions de l'IMEC.

Arvanites, T. M. and Asher, M. A. (1998) 'State and county incarceration rates: the direct and indirect of race and inequality,' *American Journal of Economics and Sociology*, 57: 207–22.

Ashford, J. B. and LeCroy, C. W. (1988) 'Predicting recidivism: an evaluation of the Wisconsin juvenile probation and aftercare risk instrument,' *Criminal Justice and Behavior*, 15 (June): 141–9.

Associated Press (2009) 'Gangs blamed as 19 inmates die in prison melee in Mexico,' August 15, p. EV1-2.

Atrum, R. (2003) *Judging School Discipline: The Crisis of Moral Authority*. Cambridge, MA: Harvard University Press.

Attica: The Official Report of the New York State Commission (1972) New York: Bantam Books.

Auerhahn, K. (1999) 'Selective incapacitation and the problem of prediction,' *Criminology*, 37 (4): 703–34.

Auerhahn, K. (2002) 'Selective incapacitation, three strikes, and the problem of aging prison populations: using simulation modeling to see the future,' *Criminology and Public Policy*, 1 (3): 353–88.

Auerhahn, K. (2003) *Selective Incapacitation and Public Policy: Evaluating California's Imprisonment Crisis*. Albany, NY: SUNY Press.

Auletta, K. (1982) *The Underclass*. New York: Random House.

Aulette, J. and Michalowski, R. (2006) 'The fire in Hamlet,' in R. Michalowski and R. Kramer (eds), *State-Corporate Crime: Wrongdoing at the Intersection of Business and Government*. New Brunswick, NJ and London: Rutgers University Press.

Austin, J. (1990) *America's Growing Correctional-Industrial Complex*. San Francisco: National Council on Crime and Delinquency.

Austin, J. (1999) 'The impact of three strikes and you're out,' *Punishment and Society*, 1: 131–62.

Austin, J. (2009) 'Prisons and fear of terrorism,' *Criminology and Public Policy*, 8 (3): 641–6.

Austin, J. and Coventry, G. (2001) *Emerging Issues on Privatized Prisons*. Washington, DC: Bureau of Justice Assistance.

Austin, J. and Irwin, J. (1990) *Who Goes to Prison?* San Francisco: National Council on Crime and Delinquency.

Austin, J. and Irwin, J. (2001) *It's About Time: America's Imprisonment Binge*. Belmont, CA: Wadsworth.

Austin, J. and Krisberg, B. (1981) 'Wider, stronger, and different nets: the dialectics of criminal justice reform,' *Journal of Research in Crime and Delinquency*, 18: 165–96.

Austin, J. and Krisberg, B. (1982) 'The unmet promise of alternatives to incarceration,' *Crime and Delinquency*, 28: 374–409.

Austin, J. and McVey, A. D. (1989) *The 1989 NCCD Prison Population Forecast: The Impact of the War on Drugs*. San Francisco: National Council on Crime and Delinquency.

Austin, J., Jones, M., and Bolyard, M. (1993) *The Growing Use of Jail Boot Camps: The Current State of the Art*, National Institute of Justice, Research in Brief, October.

Austin, J., Crane, R., Griego, B., O'Brien, J., and Vose, G. A. (2000) *The Consultants' Report on Prison Operations in New Mexico Correctional Institutions*. Middletown, CT: Criminal Justice Solutions, LLC.

Austin, J., Repko, S., Harris, R., McGinnis, K., and Plant, S. (1998) *Evaluation of the Texas Department of Criminal Justice Administrative Segregation Population*. Washington, DC: National Council on Crime and Delinquency.

Ayers, E. (1984) *Vengeance and Justice: Crime and Punishment in the 19th Century American South*. New York: Oxford University Press.

Aylward, A. and Thomas, J. (1984) 'Quiescence in women's prisons litigation: some exploratory issues,' *Justice Quarterly*, 1 (2): 253–76.

Backstand, J. A., Gibbons, D., and Jones, J. F. (1992) 'Who is in jail? an examination of the rabble hypothesis,' *Crime and Delinquency*, 38 (2): 219–29.

Bader, E. J. (1989) 'Prison control unit exposed in new documentary,' *Guardian*, December 27, p. 19.

Bailey, F. Y. (1991) 'Law, justice, and Americans: an historical overview,' in M. J. Lynch and E. B. Patterson (eds), *Race and Criminal Justice*. New York: Harrow & Heston.

Bailey, F. and Hale, D. (1998) *Popular Culture, Crime, and Justice*. Belmont, CA: West/Wadsworth.

Bailey, W. (1996) 'Correctional outcome: an examination of 100 reports,' *Journal of Criminal Law, Criminology, and Police Science*, 57: 153–60.

Bailey, W. C. (1998) 'Deterrence, brutalization, and the death penalty: another examination of Oklahoma's return to capital punishment,' *Criminology*, 36 (4): 711–34.

Bailey, W. C. and Peterson, R. D. (1987) 'Police killings and capital punishment: the post Furman period,' *Criminology*, 25 (1): 1–26.

Bailey, W. C. and Peterson, R. D. (1989) 'Murder and capital punishment: a monthly time series analysis of execution publicity,' *American Sociological Review*, 54 (5): 722–43.

Baker, P. (2010) 'Inside Obama's war on terrorism,' *New York Times Magazine*, January 4, pp. EV1-32.

Baldus, D. C., Woodworth, G., and Pulaski, C. (1990) *Equal Justice and the Death Penalty*. Boston: Northeastern University Press.

Baldus, D. C., Woodworth, G., and Pulaski, C. (1994) 'Reflections on the "inevitability" of racial discrimination in capital sentencing and the "impossibility" of its prevention, detection, and correction,' *Washington and Lee Law Review*, I (51): 359–430.

Ball, R. (1997) 'Prison conditions at the extreme: legal and political issues in the closing of West Virginia's prison for men and women,' *Journal of Contemporary Criminal Justice*, 13 (1): 55–72.

Ball, R. A., Huff, C. R., and Lilly, J. R. (1988) *House Arrest and Correctional Policy: Doing Time at Home*. Beverly Hills, CA: Sage.

Ballard, M. and Coates, S. (1995) 'The immediate effects of homicidal, suicidal, and nonviolent heavy metal and rap songs on the moods of college students,' *Youth and Society*, 23: 76–98.

Barak, G. L. (1982) 'Punishment and corrections,' *Crime and Social Justice*, 18: 108–17.

Barak, G. (1998) *Integrating Criminologies*. Boston: Allyn & Bacon.

Barak, G., Flavin, J. M., and Leighton, P. S. (2001) *Class, Race, Gender, and Crime: Social Realities of Justice in America*. Los Angeles: Roxbury.

Barak-Glantz, I. L. (1985) 'The anatomy of another prison riot,' in M. Braswell, S. Dillingham, and R. Montgomery (eds), *Prison Violence in America*. Cincinnati, OH: Anderson.

Barbanel, J. (1989) 'Lauder likes TV but at Rikers jail it's an "outrage,"' *New York Times*, June 15, p. B1.

Barkan, S. E. and Cohen, S. F. (1994) 'Racial prejudice and support for the death penalty by whites,' *Journal of Research in Crime and Delinquency*, 31 (2): 202–9.

Barker, V. (2006) 'The politics of punishing: building a state governance theory of American imprisonment,' *Punishment and Society*, 8 (1): 5–32.

Barnes, H. (1968 [1927]) *The Evolution of Penology in Pennsylvania*. Montclair, NJ: Patterson Smith.

Barnes, H. E. (1972) *The Story of Punishment: A Record of Man's Inhumanity to Man*. Montclair, NJ: Patterson Smith.

Barnes, H. and N. Teeters (1946) *New Horizons in Criminology* (3rd edn). New York: Prentice-Hall.

Baro, A. L. (1995) 'Tolerating illegal use of force against inmates,' in D. Close and N. Meier (eds), *Morality in Criminal Justice: An Introduction to Ethics*. Belmont, CA: Wadsworth.

Barrenador, G. (1996) 'On the political offense: comments on Bennett's "political trials,"' *Social Anarchism*, 22: 12–34.

Barry, D. (2009) 'In prison playing just to kill time and just maybe to help solve a murder,' *New York Times*, November 15, pp. EV1–5.

Barry, D. and Clear, T. (1984) *The Effects of Criminal Sanctions. Report to the National Institute of Justice*. Washington, DC: National Institute of Justice.

Barry, M. (2005) *Youth Offending in Transition: The Search for Social Recognition*. Abingdon, UK: Routledge.

Barth, I. (1989) '"Punch-out": brutal fun for Brownsville teens,' *New York Newsday*, Ideas section, April 30, p. 8.

Bartollas, C. (2002) 'Living in a juvenile prison,' in T. Gray (ed.), *Exploring Corrections*. Boston: Allyn & Bacon, pp. 88–95.

Bartollas, C., Miller, J., and Dinitz, S. (1976) *Juvenile Victimization: The Organizational Paradox*. Beverly Hills, CA: Sage.

Barton, A. (2005) *Fragile Moralities and Dangerous Sexualities: Two Centuries of Semi-Penal Institutionalization for Women*. Aldershot: Ashgate.

Bates, E. (1998a) 'Private prisons,' *The Nation*, January 5, pp. 11–18.

Bates, E. (1998b) 'Private prisons, cont,' *The Nation*, May 4, p. 5.

Bates, E. (1999) 'Prisons for profit,' in K. Hass and G. Alpert (eds), *The Dilemmas of Corrections*. Prospect Heights, IL: Waveland Press, pp. 592–604.

Batiuk, M. E., Moke, P., and Rountree, P. W. (1997) 'Crime and rehabilitation: correctional education as an agent of change,' *Justice Quarterly*, 14 (1): 167–80.

Baudrillard, J. (1983) *Simulations*. New York: Semiotext.

Bauman, Z. (2000) 'Social uses of law and order,' in D. Garland and R. Sparks (eds), *Criminology and Social Theory*. Oxford: Oxford University Press.

Baumer, T. L. and Mendelsohn, M. I. (1992) 'Electronically monitored home confinement: does it work?' in J. Byrne, A. Lurigio, and J. Petersilia (eds), *Smart Sentencing: The Emergence of Intermediate Sanctions*. Newbury Park, CA: Sage.

Baumer, T. L., Maxfield, M. G., and Mendelsohn, R. I. (1993) 'A comparative analysis of three electronically monitored home detention programs,' *Justice Quarterly*, 10 (1): 121–42.

Baumgartner, F., De Boef, S., and Boydstun, A. (2008) *The Decline of the Death Penalty and the Discovery of Innocence*. Cambridge: Cambridge University Press.

Baunach, P. J. (2002) 'Critical problems of women in prison,' in T. Gray (eds), *Exploring Corrections*. Boston: Allyn & Bacon, pp. 127–34.

Bayens, G. J., Manske, M. W., and Smykla, J. O. (1998) 'The attitudes of criminal justice work groups toward intensive supervised probation,' *American Journal of Criminal Justice*, 22 (2): 180–206.

Bazemore, G., Stinchcomb, J., and Leip, L. (2004) 'Scared smart or bored straight? Testing a deterrence logic in an evaluation of police-led truancy intervention,' *Justice Quarterly*, 21 (2): 269–98.

Beaumont, G. de and Tocqueville, A. de (1964 [1833]) *On the Penitentiary System in the United States*. Philadelphia: Carey, Lea, & Blanchard.

Beccaria, C. (1981 [1764]) *On Crimes and Punishments*, trans. Henry Paolucci. Indianapolis, IN: Bobbs-Merrill.

Beck, A. and Harrison, P. (2001) *Prisoners in 2000*. Washington, DC: US Department of Justice, Bureau of Justice Statistics.

Beck, A. and Karberg, J. (2001) *Prison and Jail Inmates at Midyear 2000*. Washington, DC: Bureau of Justice Statistics.

Beck, A., Harrison, P., and Guerino, P. (2010) *Sexual Victimization in Juvenile Facilities Reported by Youth, 2008–09*. Washington, DC: Bureau of Justice Statistics.

Becker, G. S. (1968) 'Crime and punishment: an econometric approach,' *Journal of Political Economy*, 76 (2): 169–217.

Becker, H. (1963) *Outsiders: Studies in the Sociology of Deviance*. New York: Free Press.

Becker, P. and Wetzell, R. (eds) (2007) *Criminals and Their Scientists*. New York: Cambridge University Press.

Beckett, K. (1999) *Making Crime Pay*. New York: Oxford University Press.

Beckett, K. and Herbert, S. (2008) 'Dealing with disorder: social control in the post-industrial city,' *Theoretical Criminology*, 12 (1): 5–30.

Beckett, K. and Sasson, T. (2000a) 'The war on crime as hegemonic strategy: a neo-Marxian theory of the New Punitiveness in U.S. Criminal Justice Policy,' in S. Simpson (ed.), *Of Crime and Criminality*. Thousand Oaks, CA: Pine Forge.

Beckett, K. and Sasson, T. (2000b) *The Politics of Injustice: Crime and Punishment in America*. Thousand Oaks, CA: Pine Forge Press.

Beckett, K. and Western, B. (2001) 'Governing social marginality: welfare, incarceration, and the transformation of state policy,' *Punishment and Society*, 3: 43–59.

Bedau, H. A. (1982) *The Death Penalty in America* (3rd edn). New York: Oxford University Press.

Bedau, H. A. and Radelet, M. L. (1987) 'Miscarriages of justice in potentially capital cases,' *Stanford Law Review*, 40 (November): 21–179.

Beha, J., Carlson, K., and Rosenblum, R. H. (1977) *Sentencing to Community Service*. Washington, DC: US Government Printing Office.

Behan, C. and O'Donnell, I. (2008) 'Prisoners, politics, and the polls,' *British Journal of Criminology*, 48: 319–36.

Belbot, B. (1996) 'Administrative segregation,' in M. D. McShane and F. P. Williams (eds), *Encyclopedia of American Prisons*. New York: Garland, pp. 8–11.

Belcher, J. R. (1988) 'Are jails replacing the mental health system for the homeless mentally ill?,' *Community Mental Health Journal*, 24 (3): 185–94.

Belkin, L. (1990) 'Inmates are prey in "ultimate hunt,"' *New York Times*, August 16, p. B10.

Bellin, E. (1993) 'Tuberculosis in jail,' *Journal of the American Medical Association*, May 10, pp. 20–9.

Benedict, W. R., Huff-Corzine, L., and Corzine, J. (1998) '"Clean up and go straight": the effects of drug treatment on recidivism among felony probationers,' *American Journal of Criminal Justice*, 22 (2): 169–88.

Bennett, J. R. (1996) 'Political trials and prisoners in the United States: a case for political defense,' *Social Anarchism*, 22: 5–11.

Bennett, J., Crewe, B., and Wahidin, A. (2008) *Understanding Prison Staff*. Cullompton: Willan.

Bennett, W. and DiIulio, J. (1996) *Body Count: Moral Poverty – And How to Win America's War Against Crime and Drugs*. New York: Simon & Schuster.

Bentham, J. (1789 [1982]) *An Introduction to the Principles of Morals and Legislation*, ed. J. Burns and H. L. A. Hart. London: Methuen.

Bentham, J. (1995) *The Panopticon Writings*, ed. and intro. M. Bozovic. London: Verso.

Benyon, J. (1984) *Scarman and After*. Oxford: Pergamon.

Benyon, J. and Solomos, J. (1987) *The Roots of Urban Unrest*. Oxford: Pergamon.

Bergner, D. (1998) *God of the Rodeo: The Search for Hope, Faith, and a Six-Second Ride in Louisiana's Angola Prison*. New York: Ballantine.

Berk, B. B. (1996) 'Organizational goals and inmate organization,' *American Journal of Sociology*, 71: 522–34.

Berk, R. (2005) 'New claims about executions and general deterrence: déjà vu all over again,' *Journal of Empirical Legal Studies*, 2: 303–30.

Berk, R. (2009) 'Can't tell: comments on "does the death penalty save lives?,"' *Criminology and Public Policy*, 8 (4): 845–52.

Bernard, T. (1981) 'The distinction between conflict and radical criminology,' *Journal of Criminal Law and Criminology*, 72 (1): 362–79.

Bernard, T. J. (1992) *The Cycle of Juvenile Justice*. New York: Oxford University Press.

Bernard, T. J. (1999) 'Juvenile crime and the transformation of juvenile justice: is there a juvenile crime wave?' *Justice Quarterly*, 16 (2): 337–56.

Bernard, T. J. and Engel, R. S. (2001) 'Conceptualizing criminal justice theory,' *Justice Quarterly*, 18 (1): 1–30.

Bernstein, N. (2005) *All Alone in the World: Children of the Incarcerated*. New York: New Press.

Berry, B. (2000) 'Exclusion, inclusion, and violence: immigrants and criminal justice,' in Criminal Justice Collective of Northern Arizona (ed.), *Investigating Differences: Human and Cultural Relations in Criminal Justice*. Boston: Allyn & Bacon, pp. 59–70.

Best, J. (1999) *Random Violence: How We Talk About New Crimes and New Victims*. Berkeley, CA: University of California Press.

Best, J. (2001) *Damned Lies and Statistics: Untangling Numbers from the Media, Politicians, and Activists*. Berkeley, CA: University of California Press.

Bickle, G. and Peterson, R. (1991) 'The impact of gender-based family roles on criminal sentencing,' *Social Problems*, 38: 372–94.

Bishop, D. M. and Frazier, C. (1988) 'The influence of race in juvenile justice processing,' *Journal of Research in Crime Delinquency*, 25: 242–63.

Bittle, S. (2002) 'When protection is punishment: neoliberalism and secure care approaches to youth prostitution,' *Canadian Journal of Criminology*, 44: 317–50.

Blagg, H. (2008) 'Colonial critique and critical criminology: issues in Aboriginal law and Aboriginal violence,' in T. Anthony and C. Cunneen (eds), *The Critical Criminology Companion*. Sydney: Hawkins Press.

Blair, R. B. and Black, C. M. (1984) *Significant Differences Between Local Jailers and State Prison Guards: Fact or Fantasy?* Paper presented at the Annual Meeting of the Academy of Criminal Justice Sciences, Chicago.

Blazak, R. (2009) 'The prison hate machine,' *Criminology and Public Policy*, 8 (3): 633–40.

Blomberg, T. and Cohen, S. (2003) *Punishment and Social Control* (2nd edn). New York: Aldine de Gruyter.

Blomberg, T. G. and Lucken, K. (2000) *American Penology: A History of Control*. Hawthorne, NY: Aldine de Gruyter.

Blumberg, M. (1990a) *AIDS: The Impact on the Criminal Justice System*. Columbus, OH: Merrill.

Blumberg, M. (1990b) 'The transmission of HIV: exploring some misconceptions related to criminal justice,' *Criminal Justice Policy Review*, 4 (4): 288–305.

Blumstein, A. and Wallman, J. (2006) *The Crime Drop in America*. New York: Cambridge University Press.

Blumstein, A., Cohen, J., and Nagin, D. (1978) *Deterrence and Incapacitation: Estimating the Effects of Criminal Sanctions on Crime Rates*. Washington, DC: National Academy of Sciences.

Body-Gendrot, S. (2000) *The Social Control of Cities: A Comparative Perspective*. Oxford: Blackwell.

Bohm, R. (1987) 'Myths about criminology and criminal justice: a review essay,' *Justice Quarterly*, 4 (4): 631–42.

Bohm, R. (1989) 'Humanism and the death penalty, with special emphasis on the post-Furman experience,' *Justice Quarterly*, 6 (2): 173–96.

Bohm, R. (1991a) 'American death penalty opinion, 1936–1986: a critical examination of the Gallup Polls,' in Robert Bohm (ed.), *The Death Penalty in America: Current Research*. Cincinnati, OH: Anderson.

Bohm, R. (1991b) 'Race and the death penalty,' in M. J. Lynch and E. B. Patterson (eds), *Race and Criminal Justice*. New York: Harrow & Heston.

Bohm, R. M. (1982) 'Radical criminology: an explication,' *Criminology*, 19 (4): 565–89.

Bohm, R. M. (1995) Personal communication, February 1.

Bohm, R. M. (1999) *Deathquest: An Introduction to the Theory and Practice of Capital Punishment in the United States*. Cincinnati, OH: Anderson.

Bohm, R., Clark, L. J., and Aveni, A. F. (1990) 'The influence of knowledge on reasons for death penalty opinions: an experimental test,' *Justice Quarterly*, 7 (1): 175–88.

Bohm, R., Clark, L. J., and Aveni, A. F. (1991) 'Knowledge and death penalty opinion: a test of the Marshall Hypothesis,' *Journal of Research in Crime and Delinquency*, 28 (3): 360–87.

Boland, B. (1990) *The Prosecution of Felony Arrests*. Washington, DC: US Department of Justice.

Bonapace, R. (1994) 'Can sex offenders really be "cured"?' *New York Times*, August 21, pp. 13–14, 15.

Bonger, W. A. (1916) *Criminality and Economic Conditions*. Boston: Little, Brown.

Bontrager, S., Bales, W., and Chiricos, T. (2005) 'Race, ethnicity, threat and the labeling of convicted felons,' *Criminology*, 43 (3): 598–622.

Boonin, D. (2008) *The Problem of Punishment*. New York: Cambridge University Press.

Borchard, E. (1932) *Convicting the Innocent: Sixty-Five Actual Errors of Criminal Justice*. Garden City, NY: Doubleday.

Borg, M. J. (1998) 'Vicarious homicide victimization and support for capital punishment: a test of Black's theory of law,' *Criminology*, 36 (3): 537–68.

Bosworth, M. (1996) 'Resistance and compliance in women's prisons: towards a critique of legitimacy,' *Critical Criminology*, 7 (2): 5–19.

Bosworth, M. (1998) 'The imprisoned subject: agency and identity in prison,' *Social Pathology*, 4 (1): 48–54.

Bosworth, M. (1999) *Engendering Resistance: Agency and Power in Women's Prisons*. Aldershot, UK: Dartmouth.

Bosworth, M. (2002) *The U.S. Federal Prison System*. Thousand Oaks, CA: Sage.

Bosworth, M. (2010) *Explaining U.S. Imprisonment*. Thousand Oaks, CA: Sage.

Bosworth, M. and Carrabine, E. (2001) 'Reassessing resistance: race, gender and sexuality in prison,' *Punishment and Society*, 3 (4): 501–15.

Bosworth, M. and Flavin, J. (2007) *Race, Gender, and Punishment: From Colonialism to the War on Terror*. New Brunswick, NJ and London: Rutgers University Press.

Botsman, D. (2005) *Punishment and Power in the Making of Modern Japan*. New York: Oxford University Press.

Bottoms, T., Rex, S., and Robinson, G. (2004) *Alternatives to Prisons: Options for an Insecure Society*. Cullompton: Willan.

Bouhours, B. and Daly, K. (2007) 'Youth sex offenders in court: an analysis of judicial sentencing remarks,' *Punishment and Society*, 9 (4): 371–94.

Bowers, W. J. (1983) 'The pervasiveness of arbitrariness and discrimination under post-Furman statutes,' *Journal of Criminal Law and Criminology*, 74: 1067–100.

Bowers, W. J. and Pierce, G. (1975) 'The illusion of deterrence in Isaac Ehrlich's research on capital punishment,' *Yale Law Journal*, 85: 187–208.

Bowers, W. J. and Pierce, G. (1980a) 'Arbitrariness and discrimination under post-Furman capital statutes,' *Crime and Delinquency*, 74: 1067–100.

Bowers, W. J. and Pierce, G. (1980b) 'Deterrence or brutalization: what is the effect of executions?,' *Crime and Delinquency*, 26: 453–84.

Bowers, W. J. with Pierce, G. and McDevitt, J. F. (1984) *Legal Homicide: Death as Punishment in America, 1864–1982*. Boston: Northeastern University Press.

Bowker, L. (1980) *Prison Victimization*. New York: Elsevier.

Bowker, L. (1985) 'An essay on prison violence,' in M. Braswell, S. Dillingham, and R. Montgomery (eds), *Prison Violence in America*. Cincinnati, OH: Anderson.

Bowling, B. and Phillips, C. (2002) *Racism, Crime and Justice*. London: Longman.

Box, S. and Hale, C. (1982) 'Economic crisis and the rising prisoner population in England and Wales,' *Crime and Social Justice*, 17: 20–35.

Box, S. and Hale, C. (1983) 'Liberation and female criminality in England and Wales,' *British Journal of Criminology*, 23 (1): 35.

Boyle, P. and Haggerty, K. (2009) 'Spectacular security: mega-events and the security complex,' *International Political Sociology*, 3: 257–74.

Bozovic, M. (1995a) 'Introduction' to *The Panopticon Writings by J. Bentham*, ed. and intro. M. Bozovic. London: Verso.

Bozovic, M. (1995b) *The Panopticon Writings by Jeremy Bentham*, trans. M. Bozovic. New York: Verso.

Bracken, D., Deane, L., and Morrisette, L. (2009) 'Desistance and social marginalization: the case of Canadian Aboriginal offenders,' *Theoretical Criminology*, 13 (1): 61–78.

Bragg, R. (1995) 'Chain gangs to return to roads of Alabama,' *New York Times*, March 26, p. 16.

Braithwaite, J. (1989) *Crime, Shame and Reintegration*. Cambridge: Cambridge University Press.

Branham, L. (2002) *The Law of Sentencing, Corrections, and Prisoners' Rights* (6th edn). St Paul, MN: West.

Braswell, M. C., Montgomery, R. H., and Lombardo, L. X. (eds) (1994) *Prison Violence in America*. Cincinnati, OH: Anderson.

Breed, A. and Krisberg, B. (1986) 'Is there a future?' *Corrections Today*, 48: 14–26.

Brewster, M. (2000) 'A review of *Crack Mothers: Pregnancy, Drugs, and the Media* by D. Humphries,' *Social Pathology*, 6 (2): 145–8.

Brich, C. (2008) 'The Groupe d'information sur les prisons: the voice of prisoners? or Foucault's?' *Foucault Studies*, 5: 26–47.

Bridges, G. S. and Beretta, G. (1994) 'Gender, race, and social control: toward an understanding of sex disparities in imprisonment,' in. G. Bridges and M. Myers (eds), *Inequality, Crime, and Social Control*. Boulder, CO: Westview.

Bridges, G. S. and Myers, M. A. (1994) *Inequality, Crime and Social Control*. Boulder, CO: Westview.

Bridges, G. S., Crutchfield, R. D., and Simpson, E. E. (1987) 'Crime, social structure and criminal punishment: white and nonwhite rates of imprisonment,' *Social Problems*, 34 (4): 345–62.

Brieman, H. (2001) 'Support groups for men in prison: the fellowship of the king of hearts,' in D. Sabo, T. Kupers, and W. London (eds), *Prison Masculinities*. Philadelphia: Temple University Press, pp. 218–21.

Bright, S. B. (2002) 'Discrimination, death, and denial: race and the death penalty,' in D. Dow and M. Dow (eds), *Machinery of Death: The Reality of America's Death Penalty of Regime*. New York: Routledge, pp. 45–78.

Britton, D. M. (1997) 'Perceptions of the work environment among correctional officers: do race and sex matter?' *Criminology*, 35 (1): 85–106.

Britton, D. (2003) *At Work at the Iron Cage: The Prison as Gendered Organization*. New York: University of New York Press.

Brock, D. E., Sorensen, J., and Marquart, J. W. (1999) 'Racial disparities after Penry,' *Justice Professional*, 12 (2): 159–72.

Brodsky, S. L. (1967) 'A bill of rights for the correctional officer,' *Federal Probation*, 38–40.

Bronstein, A. J. (1980) 'Offender rights litigation: historical and future developments,' in I. P. Robbins (eds), *Prisoners' Rights Sourcebook: Theory, Litigation, Practice*, Vol. II. New York: Clark, Boardman.

Brooke, J. (1997) 'Prisons: a growth industry for some; Colorado County is a grateful host to 7,000 involuntary guests,' *New York Times*, November 2, pp. EV1–2.

Brooke, J. (2002) 'North Koreans talk of baby killings: defectors say prison deaths and abortions are routine,' *New York Times*, June 6, pp. A1, A6.

Brotherton, D. and Kretsedemas, P. (2008) *Keeping Out the Other: A Critical Introduction to Immigration Policy Today*. New York: Columbia University Press.

Brown, M. (2009) *The Culture of Punishment: Prison, Society and Spectacle*. New York: New York University Press.

Browne, A., Miller, B., and Magin, E. (1999) 'Prevalence and severity of lifetime physical and sexual victimization among incarcerated women,' *International Journal of Law and Psychiatry*, 22 (3–4): 301–22.

Browning, S. L., Cullen, F. T., Cao, L., Kopache, R., and Stevenson, T. J. (1993) *Race and Getting Hassled by the Police: A Research Note*. Paper presented at the Annual Meeting of the Academy of Criminal Justice Sciences, Kansas City, MO.

Brownstein, H. (2000) *The Social Reality of Violence and Violent Crime*. Boston: Allyn & Bacon.

Brundage, W. F. (1993) *Lynching in the New South: Georgia and Virginia, 1880–1930*. Champaign, IL: University of Illinois Press.

Bryans, S. (2007) *Prison Governors: Managing Prisons in a Time of Change*. Cullompton: Willan.

Buckner, J. C. and Chesney-Lind, M. (1983) 'Dramatic cures for juvenile crime: an evaluation of a prisoner-run delinquency prevention program,' *Journal of Criminal Justice and Behavior*, 10: 227–47.

Bugliosi, V. and Gentry, C. (1974) *Helter Skelter: The True Story of the Manson Murders*. New York: W. W. Norton.

Bureau of Justice Statistics (1988) *Pretrial Release and Detention: The Bail Reform Act of 1984*. Washington, DC: US Department of Justice.

Bureau of Justice Statistics (1989a) *1989 Survey of Inmates on Local Jails*. Washington, DC: US Department of Justice.

Bureau of Justice Statistics (1989b) *Prison Rule Violators*. Washington, DC: US Department of Justice.

Bureau of Justice Statistics (1990a) *Black Victims*. Washington, DC: US Department of Justice.

Bureau of Justice Statistics (1990b) *Hispanic Victims*. Washington, DC: US Department of Justice.

Bureau of Justice Statistics (1992a) *National Update*. Washington, DC: US Department of Justice.

Bureau of Justice Statistics (1992b) *Prisons and Prisoners in the United States*. Washington, DC: US Department of Justice.

Bureau of Justice Statistics (1992c) *Profile of Jail Inmates, 1989*. Washington, DC: US Department of Justice, US Government Printing Office.

Bureau of Justice Statistics (1993a) *Correctional Populations in the United States, 1991*. Washington, DC: US Department of Justice.

Bureau of Justice Statistics (1993b) *Jail Inmates, 1992*. Washington, DC: US Department of Justice.

Bureau of Justice Statistics (1994) *National Corrections Reporting Program, 1992*. Washington, DC: US Department of Justice.

Bureau of Justice Statistics (1997) *Correctional Populations in the United States, 1997*. Washington, DC: US Department of Justice.

Bureau of Justice Statistics (1998) *Prisoners in 1997*. Washington, DC: US Department of Justice, Bureau of Justice Statistics.

Bureau of Justice Statistics (1999) *Sourcebook of Criminal Justice Statistics 1999 (at 116,339)*. Washington, DC: US Department of Justice, US Government Printing Office.

Bureau of Justice Statistics (2000) *Federal Drug Offenders, 1999 with Trends 1984–1999*. Washington, DC: US Department of Justice, US Government Printing Office.

Bureau of Justice Statistics (2001) 'National Correctional Population Reaches New High: Grows by 126,400 During 2000 to Total 6.5 Million Adults.' Press Release. Washington, DC: US Department of Justice.

Bureau of Justice Statistics (2002a) *Corrections Statistics*. Available at: http://www.ojp.usdoj.gov/bjs/correct.

Bureau of Justice Statistics (2002b) *Expenditure and Employment Statistics*. Available at: http://www.ojp.usdoj.gov/bjs/eande.htm#selected.

Bureau of Justice Statistics (2002c) *Demographic Trends in Correctional Populations*. Available at: http://www.ojp.usdoj.gov/bjs/gcorpop.htm#DemCorrPop.

Bureau of Justice Statistics (2007) *Survey of Inmates in State and Federal Correctional Facilities*. Washington, DC: Bureau of Justice Statistics.

Burford, E. J. and Schulman, S. (1992) *Of Bridles and Burning: The Punishment of Women*. New York: St. Martin's Press.

Burgess, A. (1962) *A Clockwork Orange*. New York: Ballantine Books.

Burke, H. (2001) 'INS setting new rules for detainees,' *Herald News* (NJ), January 3, pp. EV1–4.

Burnett, C. (1988) *Older Offenders: Current Trends*. Binghamton, NY: Haworth.

Burnett, C. (1998) '"Frivolous" claims by the Attorney General,' *Social Justice*, 25 (2): 184–204.

Burnett, C. (2002) *Justice Denied: Clemency Appeals in Death Penalty Cases*. Boston: Northeastern University Press.

Burnham, M. (1990) 'Human rights issue for the 90s in the United States,' *International Review of Contemporary Law*, 1: 21–30.

Burns, J. (2009) 'Apology opens wounds of British migrant program,' *New York Times*, November 22, pp. EV1–4.

Burns, R. E. (1932) *I Am a Fugitive From a Georgia Chain Gang*. New York: Vanguard.

Burns, R. (2002) 'Assessing jail coverage in introductory criminal justice textbooks,' *Journal of Criminal Justice Education*, 13 (1): 87–99.

Burton-Rose, D. (1998) *The Celling of America: An Inside Look at the US Prison Industry*. Boston: Common Courage.

Butler, J. (1990) *Gender Trouble: Feminism and the Subversion of Identity*. New York: Routledge.

Butler, J. (2004) *Precarious Life: The Powers of Mourning and Violence*. London: Verso.

Butler, M. (2008) 'What are you looking at? Prisoner confrontations and the search for respect,' *British Journal of Criminology*, 48: 856–73.

Butterfield, F. (1992) 'Are American jails becoming shelters from the storm?' *New York Times*, July 19, p. E4.

Butterfield, F. (1998a) '"Defying gravity," inmate population climbs,' *New York Times*, January 19, p. A10.

Butterfield, F. (1998b) 'Profits at a juvenile prison come with a chilling cost,' *New York Times*, July 15, pp. A1, A14.

Butterfield, F. (1998c) 'Jail for youths is taken over by Louisiana,' *New York Times*, July 24: A16.

Butterfield, F. (2000) 'Company to stop operating troubled prison,' *New York Times*, April 27, p. A21.

Butterfield, F. (2001a) 'Police are split on questioning of Mideastern men: some chiefs liken plan to racial profiling,' *New York Times*, November 22, pp. A1, B6.

Butterfield, F. (2001b) 'New drug-offender program draws unexpected clients,' *New York Times*, September 29, p. A6.

Butterfield, F. (2002a) 'Study finds steady increase at all levels of government in cost of criminal justice,' *New York Times*, February 11, p. A14.

Butterfield, F. (2002b) 'Study shows building prisons did not prevent repeat crimes,' *New York Times*, June 3, p. A11.

Butts, J. and Connors-Beatty, D. J. (1993) 'The juvenile court's response to violent offenders: 1985–1989,' in *OJJDP Update on Statistics*. Washington, DC: Office of Juvenile Justice and Delinquency Prevention.

Butts, J. and Snyder, H. N. (1992) *Restitution and Juvenile Recidivism*. Washington, DC: Office of Juvenile Justice and Delinquency Prevention.

Butts, J. and Snyder, H. N. (2006) *Too Soon to Tell: Deciphering Recent Trends in Youth Violence*. Chicago: Chapin Hall Center for Children at the University of Chicago.

Bynam, T. (1981) 'Parole decision making and Native Americans', in R. L. McNeely and C. E. Pope (eds), *Race, Crime, and Criminal Justice*. Beverly Hills, CA: Sage.

Bynam, T. and Paternoster, R. (1984) 'Discrimination revisited: an exploration of frontstage and backstage criminal justice decision making,' *Sociology and Social Research*, 69: 90–108.

Byrd, T. G., Cochran, J. K., Silverman, I. J., and Blount, W. R. (2000) 'Behind bars: an assessment of the effects of job satisfaction on jail employees' inclinations to quit,' *Journal of Crime and Justice*, XXIII (2): 69–94.

Byrne, J. W. (1992) 'The control controversy: a preliminary examination of intensive probation supervision programs in the United States,' in T. Ellsworth (ed.), *Contemporary Community Corrections*. Prospect Heights, IL: Waveland.

Cabana, D. (1996) *Death at Midnight: The Confession of an Executioner*. Boston: Northeastern University Press.

Cahalan, M. W. (1986) *Historical Corrections Statistics in the United States, 1850–1984*. Washington, DC: US Government Printing Office.

Caimari, L. (1997) 'Whose criminals are these? church, state and patronatos and the rehabilitation of female convicts (Buenos Aires, 1890–1940),' *The Americas*, 54 (2): 185–208.

Caimari, L. (2001) 'Remembering freedom: life as seen from the prison cell (Buenos Aires Province, 1930–1950),' in R. D. Salvatore, C. Aguirre, and G. Joseph (eds), *Crime and Punishment in Latin America*. Durham, NC: Duke University Press, pp. 391–414.

Calavita, K. (1992) *Inside the State: The Bracero Program, Immigration, and the INS*. New York: Routledge.

Calavita, K., Pontell, H., and Tillman, R. (1997) *Big Money Crime: Fraud and Politics in the Savings and Loan Crisis*. Berkeley, CA: University of California Press.

Camp, C. G. and Camp, G. M. (1984) *Private Sector Investment in Prison Services and Operations*. Washington, DC: US Department of Justice.

Camp, C. G. and Camp, G. M. (1997) *The Corrections Yearbook, 1997*. South Salem, NY: Criminal Justice Institute.

Camp, G. M. and Camp, C. G. (1985) *Prison Gangs: Their Extent, Nature and Impact on Prisons*. Washington, DC: US Department of Justice.

Camp, G. M. and Camp, C. M. (1993) *The Corrections Yearbook, 1993*. New York: Criminal Justice Institute.

Camp, S. D. and Gaes, G. (2002) 'Growth and quality of US private prisons: evidence from a national survey,' *Criminology and Public Policy*, 1 (3): 427–49.

Camp, S. D., Saylor, W. G., and Harer, M. D. (1997) 'Aggregating individual-level evaluations of the organizational social climate: a multilevel investigation of the work environment at the Federal Bureau of Prisons,' *Justice Quarterly*, 14 (4): 739–62.

Camp, S. D., Saylor, W. G., and Wright, K. N. (2001) 'Racial diversity of correctional workers and inmates: organizational commitment, teamwork, and workers' efficacy in prisons,' *Justice Quarterly*, 18 (2): 411–28.

Caputo, G. (2004) *Intermediate Sanctions in Corrections*. Denton, TX: University of North Texas Press.

Cardozo-Freeman, I. (1994) *Chief: The Life History of Eugene Delorme, Imprisoned Santee Sioux*. Lincoln, NE: University of Nebraska Press.

Carlen, P. (1983) *Women's Imprisonment: A Study in Social Control*. London: Routledge & Kegan Paul.

Carlen, P. (1994) 'Gender, class, racism, and criminal justice: against global and gender-centric theories, for post-structuralist perspectives,' in G. Bridges and M. Myers (eds), *Inequality, Crime, and Social Control*. Boulder, CO: Westview.

Carlson, P. M. and Garrett, J. S. (1999) *Prison and Jail Administration: Organization, Principles, and Practices*. Gaithersburg, MD: Aspen.

Carlson, R. A. (1975) *The Quest for Conformity: Americanization Through Education*. New York: Wiley.

Carlson, S. and Michalowski, R. J. (1997) 'Crime, unemployment, and social structures of accumulation: an inquiry into historical contingency,' *Justice Quarterly*, 14 (2): 209–42.

Carlton, B. (2007) *Imprisoning Resistance: Life and Death in an Australian Supermax*. Sydney: Institute of Criminology Press.

Carr, P. (2010) 'The problem with experimental criminology: a response to Sherman's "evidence and liberty,"' *Criminology and Criminal Justice*, 10: 3–10.

Carrabine, E. (2000) 'Discourse, governmentality and translation: towards a social theory of imprisonment,' *Theoretical Criminology*, 4 (3): 309–31.

Carrabine, E. (2004) *Power, Discourse and Resistance: A Genealogy of the Strangeways Prison Riot*. Dartmouth: Ashgate.

Carroll, L. (1990) 'Race, ethnicity, and the social order of the prison,' in D. Kelly (ed.), *Criminal Behavior* (2nd edn). New York: St. Martin's Press.

Carroll, L. (1992) 'AIDS and human rights in the prison: a comment on the ethics of screening and segregation,' in C. A. Hartjen and E. E. Rhine (eds), *Correctional Theory and Practice*. Chicago: Nelson-Hall.

Carroll, L. (1998a) *Hacks, Blacks, and Cons: Race Relations in a Maximum Security Prison*. Prospect Heights, IL: Waveland.

Carroll, L. (1998b) *Lawful Order: A Case Study of Correctional Crisis and Reform*. New York: Garland.

Cashmore, E. and McLaughlin, E. (1991) *Out of Order*. London: Routledge.

Casimir, L. (2001) 'Asylum seekers are treated like criminals in the U.S.,' *New York Daily News*, February 16, pp. EV1–4.

Castelle, G. and Loftus, E. (2001) 'Misinformation, and wrongful convictions,' in S. Westervelt and J. Humphrey (eds), *Wrongly Convicted: Perspectives on Failed Justice*. New Brunswick, NJ: Rutgers University Press.

Caulkins, J. and Macoun, R. (2003) 'Limited rationality and the limits of supply reduction,' *Journal of Drug Issues*, 33: 433–64.

Cavender, G. (1981) 'Scared straight: ideology and the media,' *Journal of Criminal Justice*, 9: 431–9.

Cavender, G. (1995) 'Alternative approaches: labeling and critical perspectives,' in J. Sheley (ed.), *Criminology: A Contemporary Handbook* (2nd edn). Belmont, CA: Wadsworth.

Center for Restorative Justice and Meditation (1996) *Restorative Justice: For Victims, Communities, and Offenders*. Minneapolis: University of Minnesota, Center for Restorative Justice and Mediation.

Centers for Disease Control (CDC) (1990) 'Screening for tuberculosis and tuberculosis infection in high risk populations: recommendations of the Advisory Committee for Elimination of Tuberculosis,' *Morbidity and Morality Weekly Report*, 39, RR-8, May 18.

Chaires, R. H. and Lentz, S. A. (2001) 'A divided land: probable impacts of current affirmative action and employment law trends on criminal justice staffing patterns in 2010,' *Justice Professional*, 14 (1): 43–66.

Chambliss, W. (1989) 'State-organized crime,' *Criminology*, 27 (2): 183–208.

Chambliss, W. (1999) *Power, Politics, and Crime*. Boulder, CO: Westview Press.

Chambliss, W. and Seidman, R. (1982) *Law, Order, and Power*. Reading, MA: Addison-Wesley.

Champion, D. J. (1991) 'Jail inmate litigation in the 1990s,' in J. A. Thompson and G. Larry Mays (eds), *American Jails: Public Policy Issues*. Chicago: Nelson-Hall.

Chancer, L. (2005a) 'Before and after the Central Park jogger: when legal cases become social causes,' *Contexts*, 4: 38–42.

Chancer, L. (2005b) *High-Profile Crimes: When Legal Cases Become Social Causes*. Chicago: University of Chicago Press.

Chantraine, G. (2008) 'The post-disciplinary prisons,' *Carceral Notebooks*, 4: 55–76.

Chantraine, G. (2010) 'French prisons of yesteryear and today: two conflicting modernities – a socio-historical view,' *Punishment and Society*, 12 (1): 27–46.

Chapman, J. (1980) *Economic Realities and Female Crime*. Lexington, MA: Lexington Books.

Chardy, A. (2000) 'Krome women to be moved,' *Miami Herald*, December 12, pp. EV1–3.

Charrière, H. (1970) *Papillon*. New York: William Morrow.

Chasnoff, I. J. *et al.* (1989) 'Temporary patterns of cocaine use in pregnancy,' *Journal of the American Medical Association*, 261 (March 24/31): 1741–4.

Cheek, F. E. and Miller, M. D. (1983) 'The experience of stress for correction officers: a double-bond theory of correctional stress,' *Journal of Criminal Justice*, 11 (2): 105–12.

Cheliotis, L. (2006) 'How iron is the iron cage of new penology? The role of human agency in the implementation of criminal justice policy,' *Punishment and Society*, 313–40.

Chen, D. W. (2000) '$8 million offered to end Attica inmates' suit,' *New York Times*, January 5, pp. A1, B5.

Cheney, R. (2005) 'The sleeper scenario: terrorism-support laws and the demands of prevention,' *Harvard Review of Legislation*, 42: 1–90.

Chermark, S. (1997) 'The presentation of crime in the news media: the news sources involved in the social construction of social problems,' *Justice Quarterly*, 14 (4): 687–718.

Chesler, C. (2001) 'Bank jobs lead to odd jobs: as inmates serve time, they also serve the state,' *New York Times*, July 15, p. NJ6.

Chesney, K. (1972) *The Victorian Underworld*. New York: Schocken Books.

Chesney-Lind, M. (1982) 'Guilty by reason of sex: young women and the juvenile justice system,' in B. Price and N. Sokoloff (eds), *The Criminal Justice System and Women*. New York: Clark Boardman.

Chesney-Lind, M. (1991) 'Patriarchy, prisons, and jails: a critical look at trends in women's incarceration,' *Prison Journal*, LXXI (1): 51–67.

Chesney-Lind, M. (1997) *The Female Offender: Girls, Women, and Crime*. Thousand Oaks, CA: Sage.

Chesney-Lind, M. (2002) 'The forgotten offender: women in prison, from partial justice to vengeful equity,' in T. Gray (ed.), *Exploring Corrections*. Boston: Allyn & Bacon, pp. 7–12.

Chesney-Lind, M. and Irwin, K. (2008) *Beyond Bad Girls: Gender, Violence, and Hype*. New York: Routledge.

Chesney-Lind, M. and Pollock, J. M. (1995) 'Women's prison's: equality with a vengeance,' in A. Merlo and J. M. Pollock (eds), *Women, Law, and Social Control*. Boston: Allyn & Bacon.

Chesney-Lind, M. and Shelden, R. G. (1992) *Girls: Delinquency and Juvenile Justice*. Pacific Grove, CA: Brooks/Cole.

Chesney-Lind, M. and Shelden, R. G. (2004) *Girls, Delinquency and Juvenile Justice*. Belmont, CA: Wadsworth.

Chilton, B. S. (2001) 'Criticizing postmodern criminal justice theory at its root: Nietzche's justice theory,' *Justice Professional*, 14 (1): 79–94.

Chiricos, T. G. and Bales, W. D. (1991) 'Unemployment and punishment: an empirical assessment,' *Criminology*, 29 (4): 701–24.

Chiricos, T. G., Jackson, P., and Waldo, S. (1972) 'Inequality in the imposition of a criminal label,' *Social Problems*, 19: 533–72.

Chomsky, N. (2003) *Hegemony or Survival: America's Quest for Global Dominance*. New York: Henry Holt.

Chonco, N. (1989) 'Sexual assaults among male inmates: a descriptive study,' *Prison Journal*, LXIX (1): 72–82.

Christian, J. (2010) 'The importance of family reunification in the prisoner reentry process,' in N. Frost, J. Freilich, and T. Clear (eds), *Contemporary Issues in Criminal Justice Policy*. Belmont, CA: Wadsworth.

Christianson, S. (1991) 'Our black prisons,' in K. C. Hass and G. P. Albert (eds), *Dilemmas of Corrections: Contemporary Readings* (2nd edn). Prospect Heights, IL: Waveland.

Christie, N. (1993) *Crime Control as Industry*. Oslo: Universiteflag.

Churchill, W. and Vander Wal, J. (2002a) *The COINTELPRO Papers: Documents from the FBI's Secret Wars Against Dissent in the United States*. Boston: South End Press.

Churchill, W. and Vander Wal, J. (2002b) *Agents of Repression: The FBI's Secret Wars Against the American Indian Movement and the Black Panther Party*. Boston: South End Press.

Cicchini, M. and Porret, M. (2007) *Les sphères du pénal. Avec Michel Foucault. Histoire et sociologie du droit de punir*. Lausanne: Editions Antipodes.

Cilluffo, F. and Saathoff, G. (2006) *Out of the Shadows: Getting Ahead of Prisoner Radicalization*. Report by George Washington University, Homeland Security Policy Institute, and the University of Virginia, Critical Incident Analysis Group. Available at: http://www.gwu.edu (accessed on June 15, 2008).

Cintron, M. and Roth, M. P. (2001) 'Drugs in the classroom: a historical approach to drug education,' *Journal of Criminal Justice Education*, 12 (1): 117–26.

Clare, J. (1984) 'Eyewitness in Brixton,' in J. Benyon (ed.), *Scarman and After*. Oxford: Pergamon.

Clark, J. (1998) *Report to the Attorney General: Inspection and Review of the Northeast Ohio Correctional Center*. Washington, DC: Office of the Corrections Trustee for the District of Columbia.

Clark, J. and Boudin, K. (1990) 'Community of women organize themselves to cope with the AIDS crisis: a case study from Bedford Hills Correctional Facility,' *Social Justice*, 17 (2): 90–109.

Clarke, R. (2004) *Against All Enemies: Inside America's War on Terror*. New York: Simon & Schuster.

Clear, T. R. (1993) 'Tougher is dumber,' *New York Times*, December 12, p. 21.

Clear, T. R. (1994) *Harm in American Penology: Offenders, Victims and Their Communities*. Albany, NY: State University of New York Press.

Clear, T. R. (1995) 'Correction beyond prison walls,' in J. Sheley (ed.), *Criminology: A Contemporary Handbook* (2nd edn). Belmont, CA: Wadsworth.

Clear, T. R. (2009) *Imprisoning Communities: How Mass Incarceration Makes Disadvantaged Neighborhoods Worse*. New York: Oxford University Press.

Clear, T. R. (2010) 'Policy and evidence: the challenge to the American Society of Criminology,' *Criminology*, 48: 1–26.

Clear, T. R. and Cole, G. F. (1990) *American Corrections* (2nd edn). Pacific Grove, CA: Brooks/Cole.

Clear, T. R. and Dammer, H. (2000) *The Offender in the Community*. Belmont, CA: West/Wadsworth.

Clear, T. R. and Dammer, H. (2002) 'Probation,' in D. Levinson (ed.), *Encyclopedia of Crime and Punishment*. Thousand Oaks, CA: Sage, pp. 1259–64.

Clear, T. R. and Gallagher, K. W. (1985) 'Probation and parole supervision: a review of current classification,' *Crime and Delinquency*, 31: 423–43.

Clear, T. R. and Frost, N. (2002) 'Private prisons,' *Criminology and Public Policy*, 1 (3): 425–6.

Clear, T. R. and Terry, K. (2000) 'Correction beyond prison walls,' in J. Sheley (ed.), *Criminology: A Contemporary Handbook* (3rd edn). Belmont, CA: Wadsworth, pp. 517–37.

Clear, T. R., Shapiro, C. A., Flynn, S., and Chayat, E. (1988) *Final Report of the Probation Development Project*. New Brunswick, NJ: Rutgers University Program Resources Center.

Clegg, R. (2010) 'Felons should not have an automatic right to vote,' in N. Frost, J. Freilich, and T. Clear (eds), *Contemporary Issues in Criminal Justice Policy*. Belmont, CA: Wadsworth.

Clements, C. B. (1979) 'Overcrowding prisons: a review of psychological and environmental effects,' *Law and Human Behavior*, 3 (3): 217–25.

Clements, C. B. (1982) 'The relationship of offender classification to the problem of prison overcrowding,' *Crime and Delinquency*, 28: 72–81.

Clemmer, D. (1958) *The Prison Community*. New York: Rinehart.

Clendenning, A. (2000) 'U.S. Supreme Court to take up detainee issue,' *Associate Press*, December 3, pp. EV1–3.

Clines, F. X. (1993) 'Some New Yorkers on probation will begin reporting to machines,' *New York Times*, May 24, pp. A1, B3.

Cloninger, D. and Marchesini, R. (2001) 'Executions and deterrence: a quasi-controlled group experiment,' *Applied Economics*, 35: 569–76.

Cloward, R. (1960) 'Social control in prisons,' in R. Cloward *et al.* (eds), *Theoretical Studies in Social Organization of the Prison*. New York: Social Science Research Council.

Cloward, R. (1969) 'Social control in prison,' in L. Hazelrigg (ed.), *Prison Within Society*. New York: Doubleday.

Cochran, J. and Chamlin, M. (2000) 'Deterrence and brutalization: the dual effects of executions,' *Justice Quarterly*, 17: 685–706.

Cochran, J. K., Chamlin, M. B., and Seth, M. (1994) 'Deterrence or brutalization? an impact assessment of Oklahoma's return to capital punishment,' *Criminology*, 32 (1): 107–34.

Cohen, A. K. (1976) 'Prison violence: a sociological perspective,' in A. K. Cohen, G. F. Cole, and R. G. Bailey (eds), *Prison Violence*. Lexington, MA: Lexington Books.

Cohen, F. (1992) 'Liability for custodial suicide: the information base requirements,' *Jail Suicide Update*, 4 (2): 5–7.

Cohen, J., Nagin, D., Wallstrom, G., and Wasserman, L. (1998) 'A hierarchical Bayesian analysis of arrest rates,' *Journal of the American Statistical Association*, 93: 1260–70.

Cohen, L. P. (2001) 'Denied access to attorneys some INS detainees are jailed without charges,' *Wall Street Journal*, November 1, p. EV1–3.

Cohen, S. (1972) *Folk Devils and Moral Panics: The Creation of Mods and Rockers*. Oxford: Blackwells.

Cohen, S. (1979) 'The punitive city: notes on the dispersal of social control,' *Contemporary Crises*, 3 (4): 339–57.

Cohen, S. (1985) *Visions of Social Control*. Cambridge: Polity.

Cohen, S. (2001) *States of Denial: Knowing About Atrocities and Suffering*. Cambridge: Polity.

Cohen, S. (2006) 'Neither honesty nor hypocrisy: the legal reconstruction of torture,' in T. Newburn and P. Rock (eds), *Politics of Crime Control: Essays in Honour of David Downes*. Oxford: Oxford University Press, pp. 297–317.

Cohen, S. and Young, J. (1981) *The Manufacture of News: Deviance, Social Problems and the Mass Media*. London: Constable.

Cole, D. (2001) *No Equal Justice: Race and Class in the American Criminal Justice System*. New York: New Press.

Cole, D. (2003) *Enemy Aliens: Double Standards and Constitutional Freedoms in the War on Terror*. New York: New Press.

Cole, D. and Lamberth, J. (2001) 'The fallacy of racial profiling,' *New York Times*, May 31, p. 13WK.

Cole, G. (1986) *The American System of Criminal Justice*. Monterey, CA: Brooks/Cole.

Cole, S. (2001) *Suspect Identities: A History of Fingerprinting and Criminal Identification*. Cambridge, MA: Harvard University Press.

Cole, S. (2009) 'Cultural consequences of miscarriages of justice,' *Behavioral Sciences and the Law*, 27: 431–49.

Coles, C. D. (1991) *Substance Abuse in Pregnancy: The Infant's Risk: How Great?* Paper presented at Symposium on Pregnant Drug Abusers: Clinical and Legal Controversy, American Psychiatric Association Annual Meeting, New Orleans, May 15.

Coles, C. D. (1992) 'Effects of cocaine and alcohol use in pregnancy on neonatal growth and neurobehavioral status,' *Neurotoxicology and Teratology*, 14 (January–February): 1–11.

Collins, J. J. and Schlenger, W. E. (1988) 'Acute and chronic effects of alcohol use on violence,' *Journal of Studies on Alcohol*, 49: 516–21.

Collins, P. H. (1986) 'Learning from the outsider within: the sociological significance of black feminist thought,' *Social Problems*, 33 (6): 514–32.

Colvin, M. (1981) 'The contradictions of control: prisons in class society,' *Insurgent Sociologist*, X (1): 33–45.

Colvin, M. (1982) 'The New Mexico prison riot,' *Social Problems*, 29 (5): 449–63.

Colvin, M. (1992) *The Penitentiary in Crisis: From Accommodation to Riot in New Mexico*. Albany: State University of New York Press.

Comfort, M. (2008) *Doing Time Together: Love and Family in the Shadow of the Prison*. Chicago: University of Chicago Press.

Common Sense for Drug Policy (2002) *Annual Causes of Death in the United States*. Available at: http://www.drugwarfacts.org/causes.

Conant, R. (1968) 'Rioting, insurrectional and civil disorderliness,' *American Scholar*, 37: 42–3.

Congressional Record (1996) Statement by Senator Edward Kennedy, S2296, p. 142, March 19. Washington, DC: US Government Printing Office.

Conley, D. J. (1994) 'Adding color to a black and white picture: using qualitative data to explain racial disproportionality in the juvenile justice system,' *Journal of Research in Crime and Delinquency*, 31 (2): 135–48.

Conover, T. (2000) *New Jack: Guarding at Sing Sing*. New York: Random House.

Conover, T. (2001) 'Hard time: behind bars with 1,000 male convicts,' *New York Times Magazine*, September 9, pp. 152–6.

Conover, T. (2002) 'The points that prisoners can make: on Rikers Island, manufacturing weapons from just about anything is an astonishing craft,' *New York Times Magazine*, July 21, pp. 18–19.

Conover, T. (2003) 'Land of Guantanamo,' *New York Times*, June 29, pp. A1, A17.

Conrad, J. P. (1984) 'The redefinition of probation: drastic proposals to solve an urgent problem,' in P. McAnany, D. Thomson, and D. Fogel (eds), *Probation and Justice: Reconsideration of Mission.* Cambridge, MA: Oelgeschlager, Gunn & Hain.

Conrad, P. and Schneider, W. (1992) *Deviance and Medicalization: From Badness to Sickness* (3rd edn). Columbus, OH: Merrill.

Contemporary Justice Review (2003) Symposium on Radical Criminology: 'Whatever Happened to It?'

Cook County Corrections (1990) *Long-Range Master Plan* (August). The Planning Collective, Ltd., in Association with National Council on Crime and Delinquency, Huskey and Associates.

Cook, D. and Hudson, B. (1993) *Racism and Criminology*. Thousand Oaks, CA: Sage.

Cook, P. (2009) 'Explaining the imprisonment epidemic,' *Criminology and Public Policy*, 8 (1): 25–7.

Cook, S. and Davies, S. (2000) *Harsh Punishment: International Experiences of Women's Imprisonment.* Boston: Northeastern University Press.

Cooper, M. (2000) 'Nassau guard admits role in jail beating: says he was lookout for 2 guards inside cell,' *New York Times*, January 5, pp. B1, B5.

Coorsh, R. (1995) 'Modern meat infection,' *Consumer's Research*, 78: 6.

Corbett, R. P. and Marx, G. T. (1992) 'Emerging technofallacies in the electronic monitoring movement,' in J. Bryne, A. Lurigio, and J. Petersilia (eds), *Smart Sentencing: The Emergence of Intermediate Sanctions.* Newbury Park, CA: Sage.

Cornish, D. and Clarke, R. (2006) 'The rational choice perspective,' in S. Henry and M. Lanier (eds), *The Essential Criminology Reader.* Boulder, CO: Westview Press.

Correctional Association of New York (1989) *Basic Prison and Jail Fact Sheet*. New York: Correctional Association of New York.

Correctional Association of New York (1991) Letter to CANY members, September 15.

Council of Europe (1987) *European Prison Rules*. Strasbourg: Council of Europe.

Countywide Criminal Justice Coordination Committee (1990) *1990 Programs Affecting Courts and Jails.* Subcommittee on Court Process. County of Los Angeles, CA.

Courtenay, W. and Sabo, D. (2001) 'Preventative health strategies for men in prison,' in D. Sabo, T. Kupers, and W. London (eds), *Prison Masculinities*. Philadelphia: Temple University Press, pp. 157–72.

Courtright, K. (2002) 'Electronic monitoring,' in D. Levinson (ed.), *Encyclopedia of Crime and Punishment.* Thousand Oaks, CA: Sage, pp. 610–13.

Covington, J. (1995) 'Racial classification in criminology: the reproduction of racialized crime,' *Sociological Forum*, 10 (4): 547–68.

Covington, J. (1997) 'The social construction of the minority drug problem,' *Social Justice*, 24 (4): 117–47.

Cox, V. C., Paulus, P. B., and McCain, G. (1984) 'Prison crowding research: the relevance for prison housing standards and a general approach regarding crowding phenomena,' *American Psychologist*, 39 (10): 1148–60.

Coyle, A. (2002) *A Human Rights Approach to Prison Management.* London: International Centre for Prison Studies.

Crane, R. (2000) 'Monitoring of Guadalupe and Lea County correctional facilities,' in   J. Austin, R. Crane, B. Griego, J. O'Brien, and F. Vose (eds), *The Consultants' Report on Prison Operations in New Mexico Correctional Institutions.* Middletown, CT: Criminal Justice Solutions.

Crank, J. P. (1996) 'The construction of meaning during training for probation and parole officers,' *Justice Quarterly*, 13: 265–90.

Crawford, A. and Newburn, T (2003) *Youth Offending and Restorative Justice.* Cullompton: Willan.

Crawford, C. (2000a) 'Gender, race, and habitual offender sentencing in Florida,' *Criminology*, 38 (1): 263–80.

Crawford, C. (2000b) 'Race and pretextual stops: noise enforcement in Midwest city,' *Social Pathology*, 6 (3): 213–27.

Crawford, C., Chiricos, C. T., and Kleck, G. (1998) 'Race, racial threat, and sentencing of habitual offenders,' *Criminology*, 36 (3): 481–512.

Crawford, J. (1988) *Tabulation of a Nation-wide Survey of Female Offenders*. College Park, MD: American Correctional Association.

Crawley, E. (2004a) 'Emotion and performance: prison officers and the presentation of self in prison,' *Punishment and Society*, 6 (4): 411–27.

Crawley, E. (2004b) *Doing Prison Work*. Cullompton: Willan.

Creamer, J. S. and Robin, G. D. (1970) 'Assaults on police,' in S. G. Chapman (ed.), *Police Patrol Readings* (2nd edn). Springfield, IL: Thomas.

Crew, B. K. (1991) 'Sex differences in criminal sentencing: chivalry or patriarchy?' *Justice Quarterly*, 8 (1): 59–83.

Crews, G. and Montgomery, R. (2002) 'Prison violence,' in D. Levinson (ed.), *Encyclopedia of Crime and Punishment*. Thousand Oaks, CA: Sage, pp. 1240–4.

Criminal Justice Collective of Northern Arizona University (2000) *Investigating Difference: Human and Cultural Relations in Criminal Justice*. Boston: Allyn & Bacon.

Criminal Justice Institute (1998) *Corrections Yearbook*. Middletown, CT: Criminal Justice Institute.

Crouch, B. (1980) *Keepers: Prison Guards and Contemporary Corrections*. Springfield, IL: Charles C. Thomas.

Crouch, B. (1991) 'Guard work in transition,' in K. C. Haas and G. P. Albert (eds), *The Dilemmas of Corrections: Contemporary Readings* (2nd edn). Prospect Heights, IL: Waveland.

Crouch, B. and Marquart, J. W. (1980) 'On becoming a prison guard,' in B. Crouch and J. Marquart (eds), *The Keepers*. Springfield, IL: C. C. Thomas; reprinted (1990) in S. Stojkovic, J. Klofas, and D. Kalinich (eds), *The Administration and Management of Criminal Justice Organizations*. Prospect Heights, IL: Waveland.

Crouch, B. M. and Marquart, J. W. (1989) *An Appeal to Justice: Litigated Reform of Texas Prisons*. Austin, TX: University of Texas Press.

Crouch, B. M. and Marquart, J. W. (1990a) 'Resolving the paradox of reform; litigation, prisoner violence, and perceptions of risk,' *Justice Quarterly*, 7 (1): 103–23.

Crouch, B. M. and Marquart, J. W. (1990b) 'On becoming a prison guard,' in S. Stojkovic, J. Klofas, and D. Kalinich (eds), *Administration and Management of Criminal Justice Organizations*. Prospect Heights, IL: Waveland.

Crouch, B. M. and Marquart, J. W. (2001) 'Resolving the paradox of reform: litigation, prisoner violence, and perceptions of risk,' in E. Latessa, A. Holsinger, J. Marquart, and J. Sorensen (eds), *Correctional Contexts: Contemporary and Classical Readings*. Los Angeles: Roxbury, pp. 229–38.

Crouch, B., Alpert, A., Marquart, J. W. and Haas, K. (1999) 'The American prison crisis: clashing philosophies of punishment and crowded cellblocks,' in K. Haas and G. Alpert (eds), *The Dilemmas of Corrections* (4th edn). Prospect Heights, IL: Waveland Press, pp. 84–100.

Crutchfield, R. D., Bridges, G. S., and Pitchford, S. R. (1994) 'Locking up youth: the impact of race on detention decisions,' *Journal of Research in Crime and Delinquency*, 31 (2): 166–82.

Culbertson, R. and Fortune, E. (1986) 'Incarcerated women: self-concept and argot roles,' *Journal of Offender Counseling, Services and Rehabilitation*, 10 (3): 25–49.

Culbertson, R. and Fortune, E. (1991) 'Women in crime and prison,' in K. C. Haas and G. P. Alpert (eds) *The Dilemmas of Corrections: Contemporary Readings* (2nd edn). Prospect Heights, IL: Waveland Press.

Cullen, F. T. (1995) 'Assessing the penal harm movement,' *Journal of Research in Crime and Delinquency*, 32: 338–58.

Cullen, F. T. and Agnew, R. (2006) *Criminological Theory: Past to Present*. New York: Oxford University Press.

Cullen, F. T. and Applegate, B. (1997) *Offender Rehabilitation: Effective Correctional Intervention*. Aldershot, England: Ashgate/Dartmouth.

Cullen, F. T. and Gendreau, P. (2000) 'Assessing correctional rehabilitation: policy, practice, and prospects,' in J. Horney (ed.), *Policies, Processes, and Decisions of the Criminal Justice System*. Washington, DC: National Institute of Justice.

Cullen, F. T. and Gendreau, P. (1989) 'The effectiveness of correctional rehabilitation: reconsidering the "nothing works" debate,' in L. Goodstein and D. L. MacKenzie (eds), *The American Prison: Issues in Research and Policy*. New York: Plenum.

Cullen, F. T. and Gilbert, K. (1982) *Reaffirming Rehabilitation*. Cincinnati, OH: Anderson.

Cullen, F. T. and Sundt, J. (2000) 'Imprisonment in the United States,' in J. F. Sheley (ed.), *Criminology: A Contemporary Handbook* (3rd edn). Belmont, CA: Wadsworth.

Cullen, F. T. and Wozniak, J. (1982) 'Fighting the appeal of repression,' *Crime and Social Justice*, 18: 23–33.

Cullen, F. T., Cullen, J. B., and Wozniak, J. F. (1988) 'Is rehabilitation dead? The myth of the punitive public,' *Journal of Criminal Justice*, 16: 303–17.

Cullen, F. T., Fisher, B., and Applegate, B. (2000) 'Public opinion about punishment and corrections,' *Crime and Justice: A Review of Research*, Vol. 27. Chicago: University of Chicago Press.

Cullen, F. T., Sundt, J. L., and Wozniak, J. F. (2001) 'The virtuous prison: toward a restorative rehabilitation,' in H. Pontell and D. Schichor (eds), *Contemporary Issues in Crime and Criminal Justice: Essays in Honor of Gilbert Geis*. Upper Saddle River, NJ: Prentice Hall, pp. 265–86.

Cullen, F. T., Link, B., Wolfe, N., and Frank, J. (1985) 'The social dimensions of correctional officer stress,' *Justice Quarterly*, 2 (4): 505–33.

Cullen, F. T., Latessa, E., Kopache, R., Lombardo, L., and Burton, V. (2001) 'Prison wardens' job satisfaction,' in E. Latessa, A. Holsinger, J. Marquart, and J. Sorensen (eds), *Correctional Contexts: Contemporary and Classical Readings*. Los Angeles: Roxbury, pp. 168–83.

Cullen, F. T., Wright, J., Brown, S., Moon, M., Blankenship, M., and Applegate, B. (1998) 'Public support for early intervention programs: implications for a progressive policy agenda,' *Crime and Delinquency*, 44: 187–204.

Currie, E. (1985) *Confronting Crime: An American Challenge*. New York: Pantheon.

Currie, E. (1993) *Reckoning: Drugs, the Cities, and the American Future*. New York: Hill & Wang.

Currie, E. (1998) *Crime and Punishment in America*. New York: Henry Holt.

Currie, E. (2002) 'Rehabilitation can work,' in T. Gray (ed.), *Exploring Corrections*. Boston: Allyn & Bacon, pp. 259–66.

Curry, G. D. and Spergel, L. A. (1993) 'Gang involvement and delinquency among Hispanic and African-American adolescent males,' *Journal of Research in Crime and Delinquency*, 29: 273–91.

Dabney, D. A. and Vaughn, M. S. (2000) 'Incompetent jail and prison doctors,' *Prison Journal*, 80 (2): 151–83.

Dailey, L. (2001) 'Reentry: prospects for postrelease success,' in D. Sabo, T. Kupers, and W. London (eds), *Prison Masculinities*. Philadelphia: Temple University Press, pp. 255–64.

Dallas Times Herald (1987) 'Rapist taken from town after protest,' May 27, p. A6.

Daly, K. (1987) 'Discrimination in the criminal courts: family, gender, and the problems of the equal treatment,' *Social Forces*, 66: 152–75.

Daly, K. (1989) 'Criminal justice ideologies and practices in different voices: some feminist questions about justice,' *International Journal of the Sociology of Law*, 17: 1–18.

Daly, K. (1994a) *Gender, Crime and Punishment*. New Haven, CT: Yale University Press.

Daly, K. (1994b) 'Gender and punishment disparity,' in G. Bridges and M. Myers (eds), *Inequality, Crime, and Social Control*. Boulder, CO: Westview.

Daly, K. (2006) 'Restorative justice and sexual assault: an archival study of court and conference cases,' *British Journal of Criminology*, 46 (2): 334–56.

Daly, K. and Chesney-Lind, M. (1988) 'Feminism and criminology,' *Justice Quarterly*, 5: 497–538.

Daly, K. and Tonry, M. (1997) 'Gender, race and sentencing,' in M. Tonry (ed.), *Crime and Justice: A Review of Research*, Vol. 22. Chicago: University of Chicago Press.

Dannefar, D. and Schutt, R. K. (1982) 'Race and juvenile justice processing in court and police agencies,' *American Journal of Sociology*, 87: 1113–32.

Danner, M. (2004) *Torture and Truth: America, Abu Ghraib, and the War on Terror*. London: Granta Books.

Danner, M., Michalowski, R., and Lynch, M. (1994) 'What does "critical" mean?', *Critical Criminologist*, 6 (2): 2.

Davey, J. D. (1998) *The Politics of Prison Expansion: Winning Elections by Waging War on Crime*. Westport, CT: Greenwood.

Davey, M. (2005) 'An Iraqi police officer's death, a soldier's varying accounts,' *New York Times*, May 23, pp. A1, A14.

Davey, M. (2010) 'Safety is issue as budget cuts free prisoners,' *New York Times*, March 4, p. EV1-4.

Davidson, R. T. (1974) *Chicago Prisoners: The Key to San Quentin*. New York: Holt, Rinehart & Winston.

Davies, J. C. (1972) 'Towards a theory of revolution,' in I. K. Feierabend, R. L. Feierabend, and T. R. Gurr (eds), *Prison Violence in America*. Englewood Cliffs, NJ: Prentice-Hall.

Davis, A. (1981) *Women, Race and Class*. New York: Random House.

Davis, A. (1989) *Women, Culture and Politics*. New York: Random House.

Davis, A. Y. (2001) 'Race, gender, and prison history: from the convict lease system to the supermax prison,' in D. Sabo, T. Kupers, and W. London (eds), *Prison Masculinities*. Philadelphia: Temple University Press, pp. 35–45.

Davis, J. K. (1997) *Assault on the Left: The FBI and the Sixties Antiwar Movement*. Westport, CT: Praeger.

Day, N. L., Richardson, G. A., and McGauhey, P. J. (1992) 'The effects of prenatal exposure to marijuana, cocaine, heroin, and methadone,' in H. L. Needleman (ed.), *Prenatal Exposure to Pollutants and Development of Infants*. Baltimore, MD: Johns Hopkins University Press.

de Beaumont, G. A. and de Tocqueville, A. (1833) *On the Penitentiary System in the United States and Its Application to France*. Philadelphia: Francis Lieber.

De Giorgi, A. (2006) *Re-Thinking the Political Economy of Punishment: Perspectives on Post-Fordism and Penal Politics*. Aldershot, UK: Ashgate.

De Jesus-Torres, M. (2000) 'Microaggressions in the criminal justice system at discretionary stages of its impact on Latino(a) hispanics,' *Justice Professional*, 13 (1): 69–90.

De Jong, C. and Jackson, K. C. (1998) 'Putting race into context: race, juvenile justice processing, and urbanization,' *Justice Quarterly*, 15 (3): 487–504.

de Koster, W., van der Waal, J., Achterberg, P., and Houtman, D. (2008) 'The rise of the penal state: neo-liberalism or new political culture?' *British Journal of Criminology*, 48: 720–34.

Debord, G. (1977) *Society of the Spectacle*. Cambridge, MA: Zone Books.

Deflem, M. (2008) *Sociology of Law: Visions of a Scholarly Tradition*. New York: Cambridge University Press.

del Carmen, R., Ritter, S. E., and Witt, B. A. (1993) *Briefs of Leading Cases in Corrections*. Cincinnati, OH: Anderson.

del Carmen, R., Ritter, S., and Witt, B. A. (2002) *Briefs of Leading Cases in Corrections* (3rd edn). Cincinnati, OH: Anderson.

Delgado, M. and Humm-Delgado, D. (2008) *Health and Healthcare in the Nation's Prisons*. Lanham, MD: Rowman & Littlefield.

Deloria, V. Jr and Lytle, C. M. (1983) *American Indians, American Justice*. Austin, TX: University of Texas Press.

Democracy Now (2010) *Intelligence Chief Confirms US Can Assassinate Americans Abroad*. Available at: http://www.democracynow.org/2010/2/5/headlines#2 (accessed on February 5, 2010).

Demuth, S. and Steffensmeier, D. (2004) 'The impact of gender and race-ethnicity in the pretrial release process,' *Social Problems*, 51: 222–42.

Denborough, D. (2001) 'Grappling with issues of privilege: a male prison worker's perspective,' in D. Sabo, T. Kupers, and W. London (eds), *Prison Masculinities*. Philadelphia: Temple University Press, pp. 73–7.

Derrida, J. (1976) *Of Grammatology*, trans. G. C. Spivak. Baltimore, MD: Johns Hopkins University Press.

Dershowitz, A. (2002) *Why Terrorism Works*. New Haven, CT: Yale University Press.

Des Roches, R. (1974) 'Patterns of prison riots,' *Canadian Journal of Criminology and Corrections*, 16: 332–51.

Desai, A., Latta, E., Spaulding, A., Rich, J., and Flanigan, T. (2002) 'The importance of routine HIV testing in the incarcerated population: the Rhode Island experience,' *AIDS Education and Prevention*, 14 (suppl. B): 45–52.

Deutsch, M. and Susler, J. (1990) 'Political prisoners in the United States: the hidden reality,' *International Review of Contemporary Law*, 1: 113–25.

Deutsch, M. and Susler, J. (1991) 'Political prisoners in the U.S.: the hidden reality,' *Social Justice*, 18 (3): 92–106.

Deutsch, M., Cunningham, D., and Fink, E. (1991) 'Twenty years later – Attica civil rights case finally cleared for trial,' *Social Justice*, 18 (3): 13–25.

Dezhbakhsh, H., Rubin, P., and Shepard, J. (2003) 'Does capital punishment have a deterrent effect? New evidence from postmoratorium panel data,' *American Law and Economics Review*, 5: 344–76.

Diaz-Cotto, J. (1998) *Gender, Ethnicity, and the State: Latina and Latino Prison Politics*. Albany, NY: State University of New York Press.

Diaz-Cotto, J. (2000) 'The criminal justice system and its impact on Latinas(os) in the United States,' *Justice Professional*, 13 (1): 49–68.

Dickenson, L. (2008) 'Public participation/private contract,' *Social Justice*, 34: 148–72.

Dickey, C. (1990) 'A new home for Noriega,' *Newsweek*, January 15, pp. 66–9.

DiIulio, J. J. (1987) *Governing Prisons: A Comparative Study of Correctional Management*. New York: Free Press.

DiIulio, J. J. (1990) *Courts, Corrections and the Constitution: The Impact of Judicial Intervention on Prisons and Jails*. New York: Oxford University Press.

DiIulio, J. J. (2002) 'Why more control is better when governing prisons,' in T. Gray (ed.), *Exploring Corrections*. Boston: Allyn & Bacon, pp. 156–69.

Dillingham, S. and Montgomery, R. (1985) 'Prison riots: a corrections nightmare since 1774,' in M. Braswell, S. Dillingham, and R. Montgomery (eds), *Prison Violence in America*. Cincinnati, OH: Anderson.

Dixon, D. and Travis, G. (2007) *Interrogating the Images*. Sydney: Sydney Institute of Criminology.

Dobash, R. E., Dobash, R., and Gutteridge, S. (1986) *The Imprisonment of Women*. New York: Basil Blackwell.

Dobash, R. P. (1983) 'Labour and discipline in Scottish and English prisons: moral correction, punishment and useful toil,' *Sociology*, 17 (1): 1–25.

Donahue, B. (2001a) 'Rights groups prodding feds for information on detainees,' *Star-Ledger* (NJ), October 30, pp. EV1–2.

Donahue, B. (2001b) 'Immigrants fill a drop in county jail populations,' *Star-Ledger* (NJ), November 2, pp. EV1–3.

Donahue, J. D. (1988) *Prisons for Profit: Public Justice, Private Interests*. Washington, DC: Economic Policy Institute.

Donaldson, S. D. (2001) 'A million jockers, punks, and queens,' in D. Sabo, T. Kupers, and W. London (eds), *Prison Masculinities*. Philadelphia: Temple University Press, pp. 118–26.

Donohue, J. (2009) 'The impact of the death penalty on murder,' *Criminology and Public Policy*, 8 (4): 795–802.

Donohue, J. and Wolfers, J. (2005) 'Uses and abuses of empirical evidence in the death penalty debate,' *Stanford Law Review*, 58: 791–845.

Donzinger, S. (1996a) *The Real War on Crime: The Report of the National Criminal Justice Commission*. New York: HarperPerennial.

Donzinger, S. (1996b) 'The prison-industrial complex: what's really driving the rush to lock 'em up', *Washington Post*, March 17, p. 24.

Doob, C. B. (1993) *Racism: An American Cauldron*. New York: Harper Collins.

Dougherty, L. (1998) '9 guards indicted in beating,' *St Petersburg Times*, July 11, p. 1.

Douglas, M. (1984) *Purity and Danger: An Analysis of the Concepts of Pollution and Taboo*. London: Ark Paperbacks.

Dow, D. R. and Dow, M. (2002) *Machinery of Death: The Reality of America's Death Penalty Regime*. New York: Routledge.

Dow, M. (2002) '"The line between us and them": interview with warden Donald Cabana,' in D. Dow and M. Dow (eds), *Machinery of Death: The Reality of America's Death Penalty Regime*. New York: Routledge, pp. 175–91.

Dow, M. (2004) *American Gulag: Inside U.S. Immigration Prisons*. Berkeley, CA: University of California Press.

Dowden, R. (2002) 'This woman has been sentenced to death by stoning,' *New York Times Magazine*, January 27, pp. 28–31.

Dowker, F. and Good, G. (2002) 'Control units as a control mechanism,' in T. Gray (ed.), *Exploring Corrections*. Boston: Allyn & Bacon, pp. 223–34.

Downes, D. (2001) 'The "macho" penal economy: mass incarceration in the United States – a European perspective,' *Punishment and Society*, 3 (1): 61–80.

Drass, K. A. and Spencer, J. W. (1987) 'Accounting for pre-sentencing recommendations: typologies and probation officer's theory of office,' *Social Problems*, 34: 277–93.

Dratel, J. (2005) 'The Legal Narrative,' in K. Greenberg and J. Dratel (eds) *The Torture papers: The Road to Abu Ghraib*. New York: Cambridge University Press.

Dray, P. (2002) *At the Hands of Persons Unknown: The Lynching of Black America*. New York: Random House.

Dreyfus, H. L. and P. Rabinow (1982) *Michel Foucault: Beyond Structuralism and Hermeneutics*. Chicago: University of Chicago Press.

Drummond, T. (1999) 'Cellblock seniors: they have grown old and frail in prison. Must they still be locked up?' *Time*, 151 (24): 60.

Dubin, S. (1992) *Arresting Images: Impolitic Art and Uncivil Actions*. New York: Routledge.

Duffee, D. (1975) 'The correctional officer subculture and organizational change,' *Journal of Research in Crime and Delinquency*, 12: 155–72.

Duffee, D. E. (1980) *Explaining Criminal Justice: Community Theory and Criminal Justice Reform*. Cambridge, MA: Oelgeschlager, Gunn & Hain.

Duffee, D. (1984) 'Models of probation supervision,' in P. McAnany, D. Thomson, and D. Fogel (eds), *Probation and Justice: Reconsideration of Mission*. Cambridge, MA: Oelgeschlager, Gunn & Hain.

Dunaway, R. G., Cullen, F. T., Burton Jr, V. S., and Evans, T. D. (2000) 'The myth of social class and crime revisted: an examination of class and adult criminality,' *Criminology*, 38 (2): 589–632.

Dunkel, F. and Van Zyl Smit, D. (2007) 'The implementation of youth imprisonment and constitutional law in Germany,' *Punishment and Society*, 9 (4): 347–89.

Dunn, A. (1994) 'Flood of prisoner rights suits brings effort to limit filings,' *New York Times*, March 21, pp. A1, B4.

DuRand, C., Burtka, G., Federman, E., Haycox, J., and Smith, J. (1995) 'A quarter century of suicide in a major urban jail: implications for community psychiatry,' *American Journal of Psychiatry*, 152 (7): 177–80.

Durham, A. M. (1989) 'Origins of interest in the privatization of punishment: the nineteenth century American experience,' *Criminology*, 27 (1): 107–39.

Durham, A. M. (1990) 'Social control and imprisonment during the American Revolution: Newgate of Connecticut,' *Justice Quarterly*, 7 (2): 293–323.

Durham, A. M. (1994) *Crisis and Reform: Current Issues in American Punishment*. Boston: Little, Brown.

Durkheim, E. (1958 [1895]) *The Rules of Sociological Method*, trans. S. A. Soloway and J. H. Mueller. Glencoe, IL: Free Press.

Dussel, E. (1995) *The Invention of the Americas: Eclipse of 'the Other' and the Myth of Modernity*. New York: Continuum.

Dwight, L. (1826) *First Annual Report*. Boston: Boston Prison Discipline Society.

Dwyer, R. and Moore, D. (2010) 'Understanding illicit drug markets in Australia: notes toward a critical reconceptualization,' *British Journal of Criminology*, 50: 82–101.

Dyer, J. (2000) *The Perpetual Prisoner Machine*. Boulder, CO: Westview Press.

Dyson, M. (1996) *Between God and Gangsta Rap: Bearing Witness to Black Culture*. New York: Oxford University Press.

Eales, H. P. (1992) 'Tuberculosis control: the new disaster plan for jails,' *American Jails: The Magazine of the American Jail Association*, May/June, pp. 12–14.

Earle, A. M. (1792) *Curious Punishments of Bygone Days*. Rutland, VA: Charles E. Tuttle.

Earley, P. (1992) *The Hot House: Life Inside Leavenworth Prison*. New York: Bantam Books.

Edgar, K. and Martin, C. (2004) *Perceptions of Race and Conflict: Perspectives of Minority Ethnic Prisoners and of Prison Officers*, Home Office Online Report 11/04. London: Home Office.

Egan, T. (2002) 'Utah colleges fight to keep weapons out,' *New York Times*, January 25, p. A12.

Egelko, B. (2000) 'INS settles two suits alleging mistreatment,' *San Francisco Chronicle*, November 21, pp. EV1–3.

Egler, D. (1986) 'Canton, Mt. Sterling win prison prize,' *Chicago Tribune*, June 5, p. 2.

Ehrenreich, B. (2001) *Nickel and Dimed: On (Not) Getting By in America*. New York: Metropolitan.

Ehrlich, I. (1975) 'The deterrent effect of capital punishment: a question of life and death,' *American Economic Review*, 65: 397–417.

Ehrlich, I. and Liu, Z. (1999) 'Sensitivity analysis of the deterrence hypothesis: let's keep the econ in econometrics,' *Journal of Law and Economics*, 41: 455–88.

Eigenberg, H. M. (1994) 'Rape in male prisons: examining the relationship between correctional officers' attitudes toward male rape and their willingness to respond to acts of rape,' in M. Braswell, R. Montgomery, and L. Lombardo (eds), *Prison Violence in America*. Cincinnati, OH: Anderson.

Eigenberg, H. (2000) 'Correctional officers and their perceptions of homosexuality, rape and prostitution in male prisons,' *Prison Journal*, 80: 415–33.

Einat, T. and Einat, H. (2000) 'Inmate argot as an expression of prison subculture: the Israeli case,' *Prison Journal*, 80 (3): 309–25.

Eisenhart, R. W. (1975) 'You can't hack it little girl: a discussion of the covert psychological agenda of modern combat training,' *Journal of Social Issues*, 31: 13–23.

Eisenhower, D. D. (1961) The farewell speech of USA President, Dwight Eisenhower, given on 17 January. Available online at: http://en.wikisource.org/wiki/Military-Industrial_Complex_Speech.

Ellis, D. (1984) 'Crowding and prison violence: integration of research and theory,' *Criminal Justice and Behavior*, 11: 277–308.

Ellis, D., Grasmick, H., and Gilman, B. (1974) 'Violence in prisons: a sociological analysis,' *American Journal of Sociology*, 80: 16–34.

Ellsworth, P. C. and Ross, L. (1983) 'Public opinion and capital punishment: a close examination of the views of abolitionists and retentionists,' *Crime and Delinquency*, 29: 116–69.

Ellsworth, T. (1990) 'The goal orientation of adult probation professionals: a study of probation systems,' *Journal of Crime and Justice*, 13 (2): 55–76.

Elrod, P. and Brooks, M. (2003) 'Kids in jail: "I mean you ain't really learning nothin [productive],"' in J. I. Ross and S. Richards (eds), *Convict Criminology*. Belmont, CA: Thomson Wadsworth.

Elvin, J. (1992) 'A rare win for man behind bars,' *Civil Liberties*, 376: 6.

Elvin, J. (1994/5) '"Corrections-industrial complex" expands in US,' *National Prison Project Journal*, 10 (1): 1–4.

Embert, P. S. (1986) 'Correctional law and jails,' in D. B. Kalinich and J. Klofas (eds), *Sneaking Inmates Down the Alley: Problems and Prospects in Jail Management*. Springfield, IL: Charles C. Thomas.

Engel, K. and Rothman, S. (1983) 'Prison violence and the paradox of reform,' *Public Interest*, Fall, pp. 91–105.

Engel, R. S., Calnon, J., and Bernard, T. (2002) 'Theory and racial profiling: shortcomings and future directions in research,' *Justice Quarterly*, 10 (2): 249–74.

Erez, E. (1990) 'Victim participation in sentencing: rhetoric and reality,' *Journal of Criminal Justice*, 18: 19–31.

Eribon, D. (1991) *Michel Foucault*. London: Faber & Faber.

Erickson, P., Hyshka, E., and Hathaway, A. (2010) 'Legal regulation of marijuana: the better way,' in N. Frost, J. Freilich, and T. Clear (eds), *Contemporary Issues in Criminal Justice*. Belmont, CA: Wadworth.

Ericson, R. V. (2007) *Crime in an Insecure World*. Cambridge: Polity Press.

Erikson, K. (1966) *Wayward Puritans*. New York: Wiley.

Erwin, B. S. and Bennett, L. A. (2002) 'Intensive probation supervision,' in T. Gray (ed.), *Exploring Corrections*. Boston: Allyn & Bacon, pp. 294–302.

Esselstyn, T. C. (1966) 'The social system of correctional workers,' *Crime and Delinquency*, 12 (2): 117–24.

Ethridge, P. and Marquart, J. W. (1993) 'Private prisons in Texas: the new penology for profit,' *Justice Quarterly*, 10 (1): 29–48.

Everett, R. S. and Nienstedt, B. C. (1999) 'Race, remorse, and sentencing reduction: is saying you're sorry enough?' *Justice Quarterly*, 16 (1): 99–122.

Fader, J. J., Harris, P., Jones, P., and Poulin, M. (2001) 'Factors involved in decisions on commitment to delinquency programs for first-time juvenile offenders,' *Justice Quarterly*, 18 (2): 323–42.

Fagan, J., Zimring, F., and Geller, A. (2006) 'Capital homicide and capital punishment: a market share theory of deterrence,' *Texas Law Review*, 84: 1803–67.

Farber, M. (1944) 'Suffering and time perspective in the prisoner,' in K. Lewin (ed.), *Studies in Authority and Frustration*. Iowa City: University of Iowa Press.

Faris, J. H. (1975) 'The impact of basic combat training: the role of the drill sergeant,' in E. Goldman and D. R. Segal (eds), *The Social Psychology of Military Service*. Beverly Hills, CA: Sage.

Farkas, M. A., and Manning, P. (1997) 'The occupational culture of corrections and police officers,' *Journal of Crime and Justice*, 20: 51–68.

Farnworth, M., Longmire, D. R., and West, V. M. (1998) 'College students' views on criminal justice,' *Journal of Criminal Justice Education*, 9 (1): 39–57.

Farnworth, M., Teske, R. H. C., and Thurman, G. (1991) 'Ethnic, racial, and minority disparity in felony court processing,' in M. J. Lynch and E. B. Patterson (eds), *Race and Criminal Justice*. New York: Harrow & Heston.

Farr, K. A. (2000) 'Defeminizing and dehumanizing female murderers: depictions of lesbians on death row,' *Women and Criminal Justice*, 11: 49–66.

Farragher, T. and Cullen, K. (2001) 'Plan to question 5000 raises issue of profiling,' *Boston Globe*, November 11, pp. EV1–4.

Farrington, D. and Morris, A. (1983) 'Sex, sentencing and reconvictions,' *British Journal of Criminology*, 23 (3): 229.

Farrington, D. and Nutall, C. (1985) 'Prison size, overcrowding, prison violence, and recidivism,' in M. Braswell, S. Dillingham, and R. Montgomery (eds), *Prison Violence in America*. Cincinnati, OH: Anderson.

Farrington, D. P. and Langan, P. A. (1992) 'Changes in crime and punishment in England and America in the 1980s,' *Justice Quarterly*, 9: 5–46.

Farrington, K. (1992) 'The modern prison as total institution? Public perception versus objective reality,' *Crime and Delinquency*, 38 (1): 6–26.

Fathi, N. (2002a) '3rd day of protests in Tehran over scholar's death sentence,' *New York Times*, November 12, p. A6.

Fathi, N. (2002b) 'Iran student movement finds new vitality,' *New York Times*, December 8, p. 22.

Federal Document Clearing House (April 16, 1997) *Remarks made by James Wooten before the Subcommittee on Youth Violence of the Senate Committee on the Judiciary*. Washington, DC: US Government Printing.

Federal Register (2009) *The 2009 Poverty Guidelines for the 48 Contiguous States and the District of Columbia*, 74 (14), January 23: 4199–4201. Online at: http://aspe.hhs.gov/poverty/09poverty.shtml.

Feeley, M. (1979) *The Process Is the Punishment: Handling Cases in a Lower Criminal Court*. New York: Russell Sage Foundation.

Feeley, M. (2002) 'Entrepreneurs of punishment: the legacy of privatization,' *Punishment and Society*, 4 (3): 321–44.

Feeley, M. M. and Simon, J. (1992) 'The new penology: notes on the emerging strategy of corrections and its implications,' *Criminology*, 30 (2): 449–74.

Feinman, C. (1984) 'An historical overview of the treatment of incarcerated women: myths and realities of rehabilitation,' *Prison Journal*, 63 (2): 12–26.

Feinman, C. (1994) *Women in the Criminal Justice System* (3rd edn). Westport, CT: Praeger.

Feitlowitz, M. (1998) *A Lexicon of Terror: Argentina and the Legacies of Torture*. New York: Oxford University Press.

Feld, B. C. (1987) 'The juvenile court meets the principle of the offense: legislative changes in juvenile waiver statues,' *Journal of Criminal Law and Criminology*, 78 (3): 471–533.

Feld, B. C. (1999) *Bad Kids: Race and the Transformation of the Juvenile Court*. New York: Oxford University Press.

Femia, J. (1981) *Gramsci's Political Thought*. Oxford: Clarendon Press.

Ferdinand, T. N. (1989) 'Juvenile delinquency or juvenile justice: which came first?' *Criminology*, 27 (1): 79–106.

Ferguson, N. (2001) 'Welcome to the new imperialism,' *Guardian*, October 31, p. 35.

Ferguson, N. (2005) *Colossus: The Rise and Fall of the American Empire*. New York: Penguin Books.

Ferrell, J. and Sanders, C. R. (1995) *Cultural Criminology*. Boston: Northeastern University.

Ferrell, J. and Websdale, N. (1999) *Making Trouble: Cultural Constructions of Crime, Deviance, and Control*. New York: Aldine de Gruyter.

Ferrell, J., Hayward, K., Morrison, W., and Presdee, M. (2004) *Cultural Criminology Unleashed*. London: Glasshouse Press.

Feuer, A. (2002) 'Out of jail, into temptation: a day in a life,' *New York Times*, February 28, pp. A1, B7.

Final Report of the Special Committee on the Use of Force (1988) Submitted to Commissioner Richard J. Koehler, New York City Department of Corrections.

Finckenauer, J. O. (1973) 'Guided group interaction: a rehabilitative approach,' in R. E. Hardy and J. G. Cullen (eds), *Climbing Ghetto Walls: Disadvantagement, Delinquency and Rehabilitation*. Springfield, IL: Charles C. Thomas.

Finckenauer, J. O. (1982) *Scared Straight! and the Panacea Phenomenon*. Englewood Cliffs, NJ: Prentice-Hall.

Finckenauer, J. O. (1984) *Juvenile Delinquency and Corrections: The Gap Between Theory and Practice*. New York: Academic Press.

Finckenauer, J. O. (1988) 'Public support for the death penalty: retribution as just deserts or retribution as revenge,' *Justice Quarterly*, 5 (1): 81–100.

Finckenauer, J. O. and Gavin, P. W. (1999) *Scared Straight: The Panacea Phenomenon Revisited*. Prospect Heights, IL: Waveland.

Finn, M. A. and Muirhead-Steves, S. (2002) 'The effectiveness of electronic monitoring with violent male parolees,' *Justice Quarterly*, 19 (2): 293–312.

Finn, P. and Parent, D. (1992) *Making the Offender Foot the Bill: A Texas Program*. Washington, DC: National Institute of Justice.

Firestone, D. (1999) 'Local jails deal with federal dilemma on deportation,' *New York Times*, December 17, p. A22.

Firestone, S. (1970) *The Dialectic of Sex: The Case for Feminist Revolution*. New York: Bantam.

Fisher, I. (1993) 'Filmed beating of inmate leads to dismissal of 2 prison guards,' *New York Times*, January 5, pp. B–1, B–4.

Fishman, J. F. (1923) *Crucibles of Crime: The Shocking Story of the American Jail*. Montclair, NJ: Patterson Smith.

Fishman, L. T. (1990) *Women at the Wall: A Study of Prisoners' Wives Doing Time on the Outside*. Albany, NY: State University of New York Press.

Flanagan, T. J. (1995) *Long-Term Imprisonment*. Thousand Oaks, CA: Sage.

Flavin, J. (1998) 'Police and HIV/AIDS: the risk, the reality, the response,' *American Journal of Criminal Justice*, 23 (1): 33–58.

Flavin, J. (2001) 'Feminism for the mainstream criminologist: an invitation,' *Journal of Criminal Justice Education*, 29 (4).

Flavin, J. (2002) 'HIV/AIDS and the criminal justice system,' in D. Levinson (ed.), *Encyclopedia of Crime and Punishment*. Thousand Oaks, CA: Sage, pp. 831–7.

Fleisher, M. (1989) *Warehousing Violence*. Newbury Park, CA: Sage.

Fleisher, M. and Rison, R. (1999) 'Gang management in corrections: an organizational strategy,' in P. Carlson and J. Simon (eds), *Prison and Jail Administration*. Gaithersburg, MD: Aspen.

Florida Department of Corrections (1981) *Response to the Findings and Recommendations of the Ad Hoc Subcommittee of the House Committee on Corrections, Probation, and Parole*. Tallahassee, FL: Florida Department of Corrections.

Flowers, R. B. (1990) *Minorities and Criminality*. Westport, CT: Praeger.

Flynn, E. E. (1973) 'Jails and criminal justice,' in L. E. Ohlin (ed.), *Prisoners in America*. Englewood Cliffs, NJ: Prentice-Hall.

Flynn, E. E. (1980) 'From conflict theory to conflict resolution: controlling collective violence in prisons,' *American Behavioral Scientist*, 23: 745–76.

Flynn, E. E. (1992) 'The graying of America's prison population,' *Prison Journal*, 72: 2.

Flynn, E. E. (1995) 'Three-strikes legislation: prevalence and definitions,' in *Critical Criminal Justice Issues*, National Institute of Justice (158837). Washington, DC: National Institute of Justice, pp. 122–33.

Flynn, E. E. (1996) 'Diagnostic and receptive centers,' in M. D. McShane and F. P. Williams (eds), *Encyclopedia of American Prisons*. New York: Garland, pp. 152–5.

Fogel, D. (1978) 'Foreword' to R. McCleary, *Dangerous Men: The Sociology of Parole*. Beverly Hills, CA: Sage.

Fogel, D. (1979) *We Are Living Proof: The Justice Model for Corrections* (2nd edn). Cincinnati, OH: Anderson.

Fogel, D. (1984) 'The emergence of probation as a profession of service of public safety: the next ten years,' in P. McAnany, D. Thompson, and D. Fogel (eds), *Probation and Justice: Reconsidering the Mission*. Cambridge, MA: Oelgeschlager, Gunn & Hain, pp. 65–99.

Foley, L. A. and Powell, R. S. (1982) 'The discretion of prosecutors, judges, and jurists in capital cases,' *Criminal Justice Review*, 7: 1–22.

Fong, R. S. (1990) 'The organizational structure of prison gangs: a Texas case study,' *Federal Probation*, March, p. 36–43.

Forero, J. (2002) 'Prisoners in Peru seek a way out: captives of the war demand new trials,' *New York Times*, November 19: A6.

Forst, B. (1983) 'Capital punishment and deterrence: conflicting evidence?' *Journal of Criminal Law and Criminology*, 74: 927–42.

Foster, H. and J. Hagan, J. (2007) 'Incarceration and intergenerational social exclusion,' *Social Problems*, 54 (4): 399–433.

Foster, T. (1975) 'Make-believe families: a response of women and girls to the deprivations of imprisonment,' *International Journal of Criminology and Penology*, 3: 71–8.

Foucault, M. (1965) *Madness and Civilization*. New York: Random House.

Foucault, M. (1972) *The Archaeology of Knowledge*. London: Tavistock.

Foucault, M. (1973) *The Birth of the Clinic*. London: Tavistock.

Foucault, M. (1977) *Discipline and Punish: The Birth of the Prison*. New York: Vintage.

Foucault, M. (1978) *The History of Sexuality, Vol.1: The Will to Knowledge*, trans. Robert Hurley. London: Penguin.

Foucault, M. (1988) 'The dangerous individual,' in M. Foucault, *Politics, Philosophy, Culture: Interviews and Other Writings, 1977–1984*, ed. L. D. Kritzman. London: Routledge.

Foucault, M. (1991a) 'Questions of method,' in G. Burchell, C. Gordon, and P. Miller (eds), *The Foucault Effect: Studies of Governmentality*. Chicago: University of Chicago Press.

Foucault, M. (1991b) 'Governmentality,' in G. Burchell, C. Gordon, and P. Miller (eds), *The Foucault Effect: Studies of Governmentality*. Chicago: University of Chicago Press.

Foucault, M. (1996) 'The eye of power,' in S. Lotringer (ed.), *Foucault Live: Collected Interviews, 1961–1984*. New York: Semiotext(e), pp. 226–40.

Foucault, M. (2001 [1994]) *Dit et Ecrit. Volume I: 1954–1975; Volume II: 1976–1988*. Paris: Quarto/Gallinard.

Foucault, M. (2003) *Society Must be Defended: Lectures at the College de France, 1975–76*, trans. D. Macey. New York: Palgrave Macmillan.

Foucault, M. (2009) 'Alternatives to the prison: dissemination or decline of social control,' *Theory, Culture, and Society*, 26 (6): 12–24.

Fourth Annual Report to the Legislature on Shock Incarceration – Shock Parole Supervision New York State (1992) Albany, NY: New York State Department of Correction.

Fox, J. (1984) 'Women's prison policy, political activism, and the impact of the contemporary feminist movement: a case study,' *Prison Journal*, 64 (1): 15–36.

Fox, S. (1970) 'Juvenile justice reform: an historical perspective,' *Stanford Law Review*, 22: 1187–92.

Fox, V. (1971) 'Prison riots in a democratic society,' *Police*, 26 (12): 35–41.

Fox, V. (1972) 'Why prisoners riot,' *Federal Probation*, 35 (1): 9–14.

Freedman, E. (1974) 'Their sister's keepers: a historical perspective of female correctional institutions in the US,' *Feminist Studies*, 2: 77–95.

Freedman, E. (1981) *Their Sister's Keepers: Women's Prison Reforms in America, 1830–1930*. Ann Arbor, MI: University of Michigan Press.

Freeman, R. M. (2000) 'Planning for correctional emergencies: the need for an emergency life cycle-based post-traumatic stress disorder management component,' *Justice Professional*, 12 (3): 277–89.

Friedrichs, D. O. (1989) 'Comment – humanism and the death penalty: an alternative perspective,' *Justice Quarterly*, 6 (2): 197–210.

Friedrichs, D. (1996) *Trusted Criminals: White Collar Crime in Contemporary Society*. Belmont, CA: Wadsworth.

Friedrichs, D. (1998) *State Crime: Volumes I and II*. Aldershot: Aldershot/Dartmouth.

Friel, C. M., Vaughn, J., and del Carmen, R. (1987) *Electronic Monitoring and Correctional Policy: The Technology and Its Application*. Washington, DC: National Institute of Justice.

Friesendorf, C. (2007) *US Foreign Policy and the War on Drugs*. Abingdon: Routledge.

Gabbidon, S. L. (1996) 'An argument for including W. E. B. DuBois in the criminology/criminal justice literature,' *Journal of Criminal Justice Education*, 7 (1): 99–112.

Gaes, G. and Goldberg, A. (2004) *Prison Rape: A Critical Review of the Literature*. Washington, DC: National Institute of Justice, US Department of Justice.

Gaes, G. and McGuire, W. (1985) 'Prison violence: the contribution of crowding and other determinants of prison assault rates,' *Journal of Research in Crime and Delinquency*, 22 (1): 41–65.

Gaes, G., Camp, S., Nelson, J., and Saylor, W. (2004) *Measuring Prison Performance: Government Privatization and Accountability*. Walnut Creek, CA: Altamira Press.

Gallup, G. Jr (1993) *The Gallup Poll Monthly*, No. 339 (December). Princeton, NJ: Gallup Poll.

Gangi, R. (1990) 'Clean up holding pens,' *New York Times*, April 19, p. A24.

Garabedian, P. G. (1963) 'Social roles and processes of socialization in the prison community,' *Social Problems*, 11: 136–52.

Garey, M. (1985) 'The costs of taking a life,' *University of California – Davis Law Review*, 18: 1221–70.

Garland, D. (1990) *Punishment and Modern Society: A Study in Social Theory*. Chicago: University of Chicago Press.

Garland, D. (2001) *The Culture of Control: Crime and Social Order in Late Modernity*. Chicago: University of Chicago Press.

Garland, D. (2006) 'Concepts of culture in the sociology of punishment,' *Theoretical Criminology*, 10 (4): 419–47.

Garland, D. (2009) 'A culturalist theory of punishment,' *Punishment and Society*, 11 (2): 259–68.

Garner, S. (2007) *Whiteness: An Introduction*. London: Routledge.

Garofalo, R. (1914) *Criminology*. Boston: Little, Brown.

Gartner, R. and Kruttschnitt, C. (2003) 'Women and imprisonment: a case study of two California prisons,' in T. Blomberg and S. Cohen (eds), *Punishment and Social Control* (2nd edn). New York: Aldine de Gruyter.

Gastil, R. D. (1971) 'Homicide and a regional culture of violence,' *American Sociological Review*, 36: 412–27.

Gates, H. L. (1990) 'The case of 2 live crew tells much about the American psyche,' *New York Times*, Section 4, July 15, p. 18.

Gatrell, V. A. C. (1994) *The Hanging Tree: Execution and the English People, 1770–1886*. Oxford: Oxford University Press.

Gavzer, B. (1993) 'Held without hope,' *Parade Magazine*, March 21, pp. 4–7.

Gaylord, B. (2001) 'Australia migrants, many children, land at troubled camp,' *New York Times*, December 2, p. A4.

Gearty, C. (2006) *Can Human Rights Survive?* Cambridge: Cambridge University Press.

Geerken, M. and H. Hennessey (1993) 'Probation and parole: public risk and the future of incarceration alternatives,' *Criminology*, 31 (4): 549–64.

Geis, G. (1960) 'Jeremy Bentham,' in H. Mannheim (ed.), *Pioneers of Criminology*. London: Stevens.

Gelsthorpe, L. and Morgan, R. (2007) *Handbook of Probation*. Cullompton: Willan.

Gendreau, P. (1981) 'Treatment of corrections: Martinson was wrong!' *Canadian Psychology*, 22: 332–8.

Gendreau, P. and Ross, R. R. (1979) 'Effective correctional treatment: bibliography for cynics,' *Crime and Delinquency*, 25: 463–89.

Gendreau, P. and Ross, R. R. (1981) 'Correctional potency: treatment and deterrence on trial,' in R. Roesch and R. R. Corrado (eds), *Evaluation in Criminal Justice Policy*. Beverly Hills, CA: Sage.

Gendreau, P. and Ross, R. R. (1987) 'Revivification of rehabilitation: evidence from the 1980s,' *Justice Quarterly*, 4: 349–408.

Gendreau, P., Little, T., and Goggin, C. (1996) 'A meta-analysis of the predictors of adult offender recidivism: what works!' *Criminology*, 34 (November): 575–607.

General Accounting Office (1991) *Private Prisons – Cost Savings and BOP's Authority Need to Be Resolved*. Washington, DC: General Accounting Office.

General Accounting Office (1992) *Racial Disparities in the Death Penalty*. Washington, DC: US Government Printing Office.

General Accounting Office (1996) *Private and Public Prisons: Comparing Operational Costs and/or Quality of Service*. Washington, DC: US Government Printing Office.

General Accounting Office (1998) *Illegal Aliens: Changes in the Process of Denying Aliens Entry Into the United States*. Washington, DC: US Government Printing Office.

Gentry, C. (1995) 'Crime control through drug control,' in J. Sheley (ed.), *Criminology: A Contemporary Handbook* (2nd edn). Belmont, CA: Wadsworth.

Giallombardo, R. (1966) *Society of Women: A Study of a Women's Prison*. New York: Wiley.

Giallombardo, R. (1974) *The Social World of Imprisoned Girls*. New York: Wiley.

Gibbs, J. J. (1982) 'The first cut is the deepest: psychological breakdown and survival in the detention setting,' in R. Johnson and H. Toch (eds), *The Pains of Imprisonment*. Prospect Heights, IL: Waveland.

Gibbs, J. J. (1987) 'Symptoms of the psychopathology among jail prisoners: the effects of exposure to the jail environment,' *Criminal Justice and Behavior*, 14: 288–310.

Gibbs, J. P. (1975) *Crime, Punishment, and Deterrence*. New York: Elsevier.

Gibson, M. (2007) 'Cesare Lombroso and Italian criminology: theory and politics,' in P. Becker and R. Wetzell (eds), *Criminals and Their Scientists*. New York: Cambridge University Press, pp. 137–58.

Gibson, M. and Rafter, N. H. (2004) 'Editor's introduction' and 'Glossary' in Lombroso, C., *Criminal Woman, the Prostitute, and the Normal Woman*, trans. M. Gibson and N. H. Rafter. Durham, NC. Duke University Press.

Giddens, A. (1982) *Profiles and Critiques in Social Theory*. Berkeley, CA: University of California Press.

Gieringer, D. (1990) 'How many crack babies?' *Drug Policy Letter*, II (March–April): 4–6.

Gill, D. (1996) 'Preventing violence in a structurally violent society: mission impossible,' *American Journal of Orthopsychiatry*, 66 (1): 77–84.

Gilligan, C. (1982) *In a Different Voice*. Cambridge, MA: Harvard University Press.

Gilligan, J. (2002) 'How to increase the rate of violence – and why,' in T. Gray (ed.), *Exploring Corrections*. Boston: Allyn & Bacon, pp. 200–15.

Gilmore, R. W. (2007) *Golden Gulag: Prisons, Surplus, Crisis and Opposition in Globalizing California*. Berkeley, CA: University of California Press.

Gilroy, P. (1982) 'The myth of black criminality,' in M. Eve and D. Musson (eds), *The Socialist Register*. London: Merlin.

Gilroy, P. (1987) *There Ain't No Black in the Union Jack*. London: Hutchison.

Gimenez, M. (1990) 'The feminization of poverty: myths or reality?' *Social Justice*, 17 (3): 43–69.

Girshick, L. B. (1996) *Soledad Women: Wives of Prisoners Speak Out*. Westport, CT: Praeger (reviewed in *Justice Quarterly*, 15 (1)).

Girshick, L. B. (1999) *No Safe Haven: Stories of Women in Prison*. Boston: Northeastern University Press.

Girshick, L. B. (2003) 'Leaving stronger: programming for release,' in S. Sharp (ed.), *The Incarcerated Woman: Rehabilitative Programming in Women's Prisoners*. Upper Saddle River, NJ: Prentice Hall, pp. 169–83.

Glamser, D. (1996) 'Towns now welcome prisons,' *USA Today*, March 13, p. 3A.

Glaser, D. (1964) *The Effectiveness of a Prison and Parole System*. Indianapolis, IN: Bobbs-Merrill.

Glaser, D. (1969) *The Effectiveness of a Prison and Parole System* (2nd edn). Indianapolis, IN: Bobbs-Merrill.

Glaser, D. (1979) 'Some notes on urban jails,' in D. Glaser (ed.), *Crime in the City*. New York: Harper & Row.

Glaser, D. (1985) 'Who gets probation and parole? Case study versus actuarial decision making,' *Crime and Delinquency*, 31: 367–87.

Glaser, D. and Fry, L. J. (1987) 'Corruption of prison staff in inmate discipline,' *Journal of Offender Counseling, Services and Rehabilitation*, 12 (1): 27–38.

Glassner, B. (1999) *The Culture of Fear: Why Americans Are Afraid of the Wrong Things*. New York: Basic Books.

Glaze, L. and Bonczar, T. (2009) *Probation and Parole in the United States, 2008*. Washington, DC: Bureau of Justice Statistics, US Department of Justice.

Glaze, L. and Maruschak, L. (2008) *Parents in Prison and Their Minor Children*. Washington, DC: Bureau of Justice Statistics, US Department of Justice.

Gleason, S. E. (1978) 'Hustling: the "inside" economy of a prison,' *Federal Probation*, 42 (June): 32–40; reprinted (1985) in R. M. Carter, D. Glaser, and L. T. Wilkins (eds), *Correctional Institutions* (3rd edn). New York: Harper & Row.

Glick, P. and Fiske, S. (2000) 'Beyond prejudice and simple antipathy: hostile and benevolent sexism across cultures,' *Journal of Personality and Social Psychology*, 79: 763–75.

Glyn, A. (1990) 'Contradictions of capitalism,' in J. Eatwell, M. Milgate, and P. Newman (eds), *The New Pelgrave: Marxian Economics*. New York: W. W. Norton.

Goffman, E. (1961) *Asylums: Essays on the Social Situation of Mental Patients and other Inmates*. Garden City, NY: Anchor.

Goffman, E. (1963) *Stigma: Notes on the Management of Spoiled Identity*. Englewood Cliffs, NJ: Prentice Hall.

Golden, T. (2005a) 'In U.S. report, brutal details of 2 Afghan inmates' deaths,' *New York Times*, May 20, pp. A1, A12.

Golden, T. (2005b) 'Army faltered in investigating detainee abuse,' *New York Times*, May 20, pp. A1, A18.

Golden, T. (2006a) 'The battle for Guantánamo,' *New York Times Magazine*, September 17, pp. EV1–17.

Golden, T. (2006b) 'Military taking a tougher line with detainees,' *New York Times*, December 16, pp. EV1–6.

Goldfarb, R. (1975) *Jails: The Ultimate Ghetto*. Garden City, NY: Anchor Press/Doubleday.

Goldstone, J. and Useem, B. (1999) 'Prison riots as microrevolutions: an extension of state-centered theories of revolution,' *American Journal of Sociology*, 67 (4): 985–1029.

Good Jobs First (2003) *Financing the Private Prison Industry—Private and Public Money*. Available at: http://www.goodjobsfirst.org/pdf/jbch2.pdf.

Goode, E. (1993) *Drugs in American Society* (4th edn). New York: McGraw-Hill.

Goode, E. and Ben-Yehuda, N. (1994) *Moral Panics: The Social Construction of Deviance*. Cambridge, MA: Blackwell.

Goodman, J. (1994) *Stories of Scottsboro*. New York: Pantheon Books.

Goodman, J. (2008) '"It's just black, white, or hispanic": an observational study of racializing moves in California's segregated prison reception centers,' *Law and Society Review*, 42 (4): 735–70.

Goodstein, L. (2000) 'Chivalry explanation of female crime rates,' in N. Rafter (ed.), *Encyclopedia of Women and Crime*. Phoenix, AZ: Orix Press, pp. 26–8.

Goodstein, L., and Wright, K. N. (1989) 'Inmate adjustment to prison,' in L. Goodstein and D. L. MacKenzie (eds), *The American Prison: Issues in Research and Policy*. New York: Plenum.

Goontz, P. (2000) 'Gender and judicial decisions: do female judges decide cases differently than male judges?' *Gender Issues*, 18: 59–73.

Gordon, D. (1991) *The Justice Juggernaut: Fighting Street Crime, Controlling Citizens*. New Brunswick, NJ: Rutgers University Press.

Gordon, M. (2006) 'Correctional officer control ideology: implications for understanding a system,' *Criminal Justice Studies*, 19: 225–39.

Gostin, L. O. (1995) 'The resurgent tuberculosis epidemic in the era of AIDS: reflections on public health, law, and society,' *Maryland Law Review*, 54: 1–131.

Gottfredson, D. M., Neithercutt, M. G., Nuffield, J., and O'Leary, V. (1973) *Four Thousand Lifetimes: A Study of Time Served and Parole Outcomes*. Davis, CA: National Council on Crime and Delinquency, Research Center.

Gottfredson, S. D. and Gottfredson, D. M. (1994) 'Behavioral prediction and the problem of incapacitation,' *Criminology*, 32 (3): 441–74.

Gottschalk, M. (2006) *The Prison and the Gallows: The Politics of Mass Incarceration in America*. Cambridge: Cambridge University Press.

Gould, R. (1974) 'The officer inmate relationship: its role in the Attica rebellion,' *Bulletin of the American Academy of Psychiatry and the Law*, 2 (1): 34–5.

Gover, A. R. and MacKenzie, D. L. (2002) 'Boot camps,' in D. Levinson (ed.), *Encyclopedia of Crime and Punishment*. Thousand Oaks, CA: Sage, pp. 122–5.

Gover, A. R., Styve, G. J. F., and MacKenzie, D. L. (2002) 'Evaluating correctional boot camp programs: issues and concerns,' in T. Gray (ed.), *Exploring Corrections*. Boston: Allyn & Bacon, pp. 271–8.

Gowdy, V. (2001) 'Should we privatize our prisons? The pros and cons,' in E. Latessa, A. Holsinger, J. Marquart, and J. Sorensen (eds), *Correctional Contexts: Contemporary and Classical Readings*. Los Angeles: Roxbury, pp. 198–207.

Gramsci, A. (2008) *Selections from the Prison Notebooks*, ed. and trans. Q. Hoare and G. Smith. New York: International Publishers.

Gran, B. and Henry, W. (2008) 'Holding private prisons accountable: a socio-legal analysis of "contracting out" prisons,' *Social Justice*, 34: 173–94.

Grana, S. J. (2002) *Women and (In)Justice: The Criminal and Civil Effects of the Common Law on Women's Lives*. Boston: Allyn & Bacon.

Granfield, R. and Cloud, W. (2007) 'The elephant that no one sees: natural recovery among middle-class addicts,' in J. Inciardi and K. McElrath (eds), *The American Drug Scene*. New York: Oxford University Press.

Grasmick, H. G. and Bursick Jr, R. J. (1990) 'Conscience, significant others, and rational choice: extending the deterrence model,' *Law and Society Review*, 24 (3): 837–61.

Gray, F. C. (1973 [1847]) *Prison Discipline in America*. Montclair, NJ: Patterson Smith.

Gray, G. and Salole, A. (2006) 'The local culture of punishment: an ethnography of criminal justice worker discourse,' *British Journal of Criminology*, 46: 661–79.

Gray, J. P. (2001) *Why Our Drug Laws Have Failed and What We Can Do About It*. Philadelphia: Temple University Press.

Gray, T. and Meyer, J. (2002) 'Why inmate participation is better when managing prisons,' in T. Gray, *Exploring Corrections*. Boston: Allyn & Bacon, pp. 147–55.

Green, P. and Ward, T. (2004) *State Crime: Governments, Violence and Corruption*. London: Pluto.

Greenberg, D. F. (1977) 'The dynamics of oscillatory punishment process,' *Journal of Criminal Law and Criminology*, 68: 643–51.

Greenberg, D. F. (1981) *Crime and Capitalism*. Palo Alto, CA: Mayfield.

Greenberg, D. F. (1990) 'The cost-benefit analysis of imprisonment,' *Social Justice*, 17 (4): 49–75.

Greenberg, D. F. (1999) 'Punishment, division of labor, and social solidarity,' in W. Laufer and F. Adler (eds), *The Criminology of Criminal Law: Advances in Criminological Theory*, Vol. 8. New Brunswick, NJ: Transaction.

Greenberg, D. F. and Humphries, D. (1980) 'The co-option of fixed sentencing reform,' *Crime and Delinquency*, 26: 206–25.

Greenberg, D. F. and West, V. (2001) 'State prison populations and their growth, 1971–1991,' *Criminology*, 39 (3): 615–54.

Greenberg, K. and Dratel, J. (2005) *The Torture Papers: The Road to Abu Ghraib*. Cambridge: Cambridge University Press.

Greene, D. (2002) 'Community service,' in D. Levinson (ed.), *Encyclopedia of Crime and Punishment*. Thousand Oaks, CA: Sage, pp. 278–81.

Greene, J. (1992) *The Day-Fine System: A Tool for Improving the Use of Economic Sanctions*. New York: Vera Institute of Justice.

Greene, J. (2002) 'Entrepreneurial corrections: incarceration as a business opportunity,' in M. Mauer and M. Chesney-Lind (eds), *Invisible Punishment: The Collateral Consequences of Mass Imprisonment*. New York: Free Press, pp. 95–114.

Greene, J. (2003) 'Lack of correctional services,' in A. Coyle, A. Campbell, and R. Neufeld (eds), *Capitalist Punishment: Prison Privatization and Human Rights*. Atlanta, GA: Clarity Press, pp. 39–47.

Greenfield, L. A. and Snell, T. L. (2000) *Women Offenders*. Bureau of Justice Statistics. Washington, DC: US Department of Justice.

Greenhouse, L. (1994) 'Prison officials can be found liable for inmate-against-inmate violence, court rules,' *New York Times*, June 7, p. A18.

Greenhouse, L. (1997) 'Immunity from suits is withheld for guards in privately run jails,' *New York Times*, June 24, p. B10.

Greenhouse, L. (2002a) 'Supreme Court taps cases to decide 3-strikes issue: heft given to third strike is central,' *New York Times*, April 2, p. A16.

Greenhouse, L. (2002b) 'U.S. joins inmate in prison discipline case: justices weigh liability for shackling convict to a post for 7 hours,' *New York Times*, April 18, p. A22.

Greenhouse, L. (2002c) 'Justices say death penalty is up to juries, not judges,' *New York Times*, June 25, pp. A1, A20.

Greenhouse, L. (2002d) 'Citing "national consensus," justices bar death penalty for retarded defendants,' *New York Times*, June 21, pp. A1, A14.

Greenhouse, S. (2002) 'Alabama coal giant is sued over 3 killings in Colombia,' *New York Times*, March 22, p. A14.

Greenwald, H. (1983) 'Capital punishment for minors: an Eighth Amendment analysis,' *Journal of Criminal Law and Criminology*, 74 (4): 1471–517.

Greenwood, P. W. (1982) *Selective Incapacitation*. Santa Monica, CA: Rand.

Greenwood, P. W. and Zimring, F. E. (1985) *One More Chance: The Pursuit of Promising Intervention Strategies for Chronic Juvenile Offenders*. Santa Monica, CA: Rand.

Gregory, D. (2006) *The Colonial Present: Afghanistan, Palestine, Iraq*. Oxford: Blackwell.

Grewcock, M. (2007) 'Shooting the passenger: Australia's war on illicit migrants,' in M. Lee (ed.), *Human Trafficking*. Cullompton: Willan.

Grewcock, M. (2008) *A System of Penal Abuse: Australia's Immigration Detention Experience*. Paper presented to Criminal Justice Research Network, University of New South Wales, 13 August.

Grey, S. (2006) *Ghost Plane: The True Story of the CIA Torture Program*. New York: St. Martin's Press.

Grinnel, F. W. (1941) 'The common law history of probation,' *Journal of Criminal Law and Criminology*, May–June, pp. 15–34.

Gross, B. (1982) 'Some anticrime proposals for progressives,' *Crime and Social Justice*, 17: 17–24.

Gross, H. (1979) *A Theory of Criminal Justice*. New York: Oxford University Press.

Grossman, P. (2000) 'Two jail guards charged in sex assaults,' *Union Leader* (New Hampshire), December 20, pp. EV1–3.

Groves, B. and Sampson, R. (1986) 'Critical theory and criminology,' *Social Problems*, 33: S58–S80.

Grusky, O. (1959) 'Organizational goals and the behavior of informal leaders,' *American Journal of Sociology*, 65: 59–67.

Guard, D. (2010) *Senate Judiciary Votes to Reform Federal Crack Law*, Press Release. Available at: http://stopthedrugwar.org/in_the_trenches/2010/mar/11/press_release_senate_judiciary_v (accessed March 11, 2010).

Guenther, A. and Guenther, M. (1974) 'Screws and thugs,' *Society*, 12 (July–August): 42–50.

Gurr, T. R. (1972) 'Psychological factors in civil violence,' in I. K. Feierabend, R. L. Feierabend, and T. R. Gurr (eds), *Anger, Violence, and Politics*. Englewood Cliffs, NJ: Prentice Hall.

Gusfield, J. (1963) *Symbolic Crusade*. Urbana, IL: University of Illinois Press.

Guy, D. (1990) *Sex and Danger in Buenos Aires: Prostitution, Family, and Nation in Argentina*. Lincoln, NE: University of Nebraska Press.

Guy, D. (2001) 'Girls in prison: the role of the Buenos Aires Casa Correccional de Mujeres as an institution for child rescue, 1880–1940,' in R. D. Salvatore, R. C. Aguirre, and G. Joseph (eds), *Crime and Punishment in Latin America*. Durham, NC: Duke University Press, pp. 3659–90.

Guyes, R. (1988) *Nation's Jail Managers Assess Their Problems*. Rockville, MD: National Institute of Justice.

Haas, K. C. (1977) 'Judicial politics and correctional reform: an analysis of the decline of the "hands-off" doctrine,' *Detroit College of Law Review*, Winter, pp. 795–831.

Haas, K. C. (1981) 'The "new federalism" and prisoners rights: state supreme courts in comparative perspective,' *Western Political Quarterly*, 34 (December): 552–71.

Hacker, A. (1992) *Two-Nations: Black and White, Separate, Hostile, Unequal.* New York: Ballantine Books.

Hagan, J. (1974) 'Extra-legal attributes and criminal sentencing: an assessment of a sociological viewpoint,' *Law and Society Review*, 8: 357–83.

Hagan, J. (1995) 'The imprisoned society: time turns a classic on its head,' *Sociological Forum*, 10: 520–4.

Haghighi, R. (1996) 'Unions correctional officers,' in M. D. McShane and F. P. Williams (eds), *Encyclopedia of American Prisons*. New York: Garland, pp. 465–6.

Hall, B. (1829) *Travels in North America in the Years 1827 and 1828*. Edinburgh.

Hall, E. L. and Simkus, A. A. (1975) 'Inequality in the types of sentences received by Native Americans and whites,' *Criminology*, 13: 199–222.

Hall, L. (2004a) 'Shackles and shareholders: developments in the business of detentions,' *Bender's Immigration Bulletin*, April 1, pp. 394–404.

Hall, L. (2004b) 'Update to shackles and shareholders: developments in the business of detentions,' *Bender's Immigration Bulletin*, May 1, pp. 565–70.

Hall, L. (2004c) 'Nomads under the tent of blue: migrants fuel the U.S. prison industry,' *Rutgers Race and the Law Review*, 6 (2): 265–363.

Hall, S., Critcher, C., Jefferson, T., Clarke, J., and Roberts, B. (1978) *Policing the Crisis: Mugging, the State and Law and Order*. New York: Holmes & Meiser.

Halleck, S. L. and Witte, A. D. (1977) 'Is rehabilitation dead?' *Crime and Delinquency*, 23: 372–82.

Hallett, M. (2002) 'Race, crime, and for-profit imprisonment: social disorganization as market opportunity,' *Punishment and Society*, 4: 369–93.

Hallett, M. (2004) 'Commerce with criminals: the new colonialism in criminal justice,' *Review of Policy Research*, 21 (1): 49–62.

Hallett, M. (2007) *Private Prisons in America: A Critical Race Perspective*. Urbana, IL: University of Illinois Press.

Hallsworth, S. (2000) 'Rethinking the punitive turn: economies of excess and the criminology of the other,' *Punishment and Society*, 2 (2): 145–60.

Halperin, R. (2001–2) 'Lethal injection first introduced by Nazis,' *Amnesty Now*, Winter, p. 16.

Hamm, M. S. (1991) 'The abandoned ones: a history of the Oakdale and Atlanta prison riots,' in G. Barak (ed.), *Crimes by the Capitalist State: An Introduction to State Criminality*. Albany, NY: State University of New York Press.

Hamm, M. S. (1994) *Hate Crime: International Perspectives on Causes and Control*. Cincinnati, OH: Anderson/ACGS.

Hamm, M. (1995) *The Abandoned Ones: The Imprisonment and Uprising of the Mariel Boat People*. Boston: Northeastern University Press.

Hamm, M. (2009) 'Prison Islam in the age of sacred terror,' *British Journal of Criminology*, 49: 667–85.

Hamm, M. S., Coupez, T., Hoze, F. E., and Weinstein, C. (1994) 'The myth of humane imprisonment: a critical analysis of severe discipline in U.S. maximum security prisons, 1945–1990,' in M. Braswell, R. Montgomery, and L. Lombardo (eds), *Prison Violence in America*. Cincinnati, OH: Anderson.

Hammett, T. (1989) *1988 Update: AIDS in Correctional Facilities*. Washington, DC: National Institute of Justice.

Hammett, T. (2006) 'HIV/AIDS and other infectious diseases among correctional inmates: transmission, burden, and an appropriate response,' *American Journal of Public Health*, 96: 974–8.

Hammett, T. and Harrold, L. (1994) *Tuberculosis in Correctional Facilities*. Washington, DC: National Institute of Justice.

Hammett, T. and Moini, S. (1990) *Update on AIDS in Prisons and Jails*. Washington, DC: National Institute of Justice.

Hammett, T., Harmon, P., and Maruschak, L. (1999) *1996–1997 Update: HIV/AIDS, STDs, and TB in Correctional Facilities*. Washington, DC: National Institute of Justice.

Hammett, T., Kennedy, S., and Kuck, S. (2007) *National Survey of Infectious Diseases in Correctional Facilities: HIV and Sexually Transmitted Diseases.* Washington, DC: US Department of Justice, National Institute of Justice.

Hammett, T., Harrold, L., Gross, M., and Epstein, J. (1994) *1992 Update: HIV/AIDS in Correctional Facilities.* Washington, DC: National Institute of Justice.

Handler, J. and Hasenfeld, Y. (2007) *Blame Welfare: Poverty and Inequality.* New York: Cambridge University Press.

Haney, C. (1993) 'Infamous punishment: the psychological consequences of isolation,' *Journal of the National Prison Project*, 410: 1–3.

Haney, C., Banks, C., and Zimbardo, P. (1973) 'Interpersonal dynamics in a simulated prison,' *International Journal of Criminology and Penology*, 1: 69–97.

Hankinson, R. J. (1993) 'No political actions against Quayle's accuser,' *New York Times*, September 27, p. A16.

Hanley, R. (2002) 'Disciplinarian for juveniles quits in wake of censure,' *New York Times*, January 5, p. B5.

Hannah-Moffat, K. (2001) *Punishment in Disguise: Penal Governance and Federal Imprisonment of Women in Canada.* Toronto: University of Toronto Press.

Hannah-Moffat, K. and O'Malley, P. (2007) *Gendered Risks.* London: Routledge Cavendish.

Harbury, J. (2005) *Truth, Torture, and the American Way: The History and Consequences of U.S. Involvement in Torture.* Boston: Beacon Press.

Harcourt, B. (2001) *Illusion of Order: The False Promise of Broken Windows Policing.* Cambridge, MA: Harvard University Press.

Harcourt, B. (2007a) *Against Prediction: Profiling, Policing, and Punishing in an Actuarial Age.* Chicago: University of Chicago Press.

Harcourt, B. (2007b) 'Post-modern meditations on punishment,' *Social Research*, 74 (2): 307–83.

Harding, R. (2001) 'Private prisons,' in M. Tonry (ed.), *Crime and Justice: A Review of Research.* Chicago: University of Chicago Press.

Harding, T. (1987) 'Health in prisons,' *Council of Europe Prison Information Bulletin*, 10: 9–11.

Harjo, S. S. (2002) 'Redskins, savages, and other Indian enemies: a historical overview of American media coverage of Native peoples,' in C. Mann and M. Zatz (eds), *Images of Color, Images of Crime.* Los Angeles: Roxbury, pp. 56–70.

Harlow, B. (1998) *Barred: Women, Writing and Political Detention.* Middletown, CT: Wesleyan University Press.

Harms, P. (2002) *Detention in Delinquency Cases, 1989–1998.* Washington, DC: US Department of Justice, Office of Juvenile Justice and Delinquency Prevention.

Harris, A. R. (1975) 'Imprisonment and the expected value of criminal choice: a specification and test of aspects of the labeling perspective,' *American Sociological Review*, 40: 71–87.

Harris, A. R. (1976) 'Race, commitment to deviance and spoiled identity,' *American Sociological Review*, 41: 432–41.

Harris, M. K. (1992) 'The goals of community sanctions,' in T. Ellsworth (ed.), *Contemporary Community Corrections.* Prospect Heights, IL: Waveland.

Harris, M. K. and Spiller, D. P. (1977) *After Decision: Implementation of Judicial Decrees in Correctional Settings.* Washington, DC: Law Enforcement Assistance Administration.

Harris, P. W. (1986) 'Over-simplification and error in public opinion surveys on capital punishment,' *Justice Quarterly*, 3 (4): 429–56.

Harris, P. M., Clear, T. R., and Baird, S. C. (1989) 'Have community supervision officers changed their attitudes toward their work?' *Justice Quarterly*, 6 (2): 233–46.

Harrison, R. (1985) *Bentham.* London: Routledge & Kegan Paul.

Hartung, F. and Floch, M. (1957) 'A social-psychological analysis of prison riots,' in R. Turner and L. Killian (eds), *Collective Behavior.* Englewood Cliffs, NJ: Prentice-Hall.

Harvey, J. (2007) *Young Men in Prison: Surviving and Adapting to Life Inside*. Cullompton: Willan.

Harwood, H. J., Hubbard, R., Collins, J. J., and Valley Rachal, J. (1988) 'The costs of crime and the benefits of drug abuse treatment: a cost-benefit analysis using TOPS data,' in C. G. Leukefeld and F. M. Tims (eds), *Compulsory Treatment of Drug Abuse: Research and Clinical Practice*, NIDA Research Monograph 86. Rockville, MD: NIDA.

Hassine, V. (2002) '"Chemical shackles" as a control mechanism,' in T. Gray (ed.), *Exploring Corrections*. Boston: Allyn & Bacon, pp. 215–19.

Hawkins, D. F. and Hardy, K. A. (1989) 'Black-white imprisonment rates: a state-by-state analysis,' *Social Justice*, 16 (4): 75–94.

Hawkins, G. (1976) *The Prison: Policy and Practice*. Chicago: University of Chicago Press.

Haycock, J. (1991) 'Capital crimes: suicides in jail,' *Death Studies*, 15: 417–33.

Haycock, J. (1992) 'Manipulation and suicide attempts in jails and prisons,' *Jail Suicide Update*, 4 (4): 2–6.

Hayes, L. M. (1983) 'And darkness closes in … a national study of jail suicides,' *Criminal Justice and Behavior*, 10: 461–84.

Hayes, L. M. (1988a) *National Study of Jail Suicides: Seven Years Later*. Alexandria, VA: National Center of Institutions and Alternatives.

Hayes, L. M. (1988b) 'Research and training in jail suicide prevention,' *American Jails*, Fall, pp. 58, 60, 61.

Hayes, L. M. and Rowan, J. R. (1988) *Training Curriculum on Suicide Detection and Prevention in Jails and Lockups*. Alexandria, VA: National Center of Institutions and Alternatives.

Hayman, S. (2006) *Imprisoning Our Sisters: The New Federal Women's Prisons in Canada*. Montreal: McGill-Queens University Press.

Hayward, K. and Young, J. (2004) 'Cultural criminology: some notes on the script,' *Theoretical Criminology*, 8 (3): 259–74.

Headly, B. (1989) 'Crime and powerless racial groups,' *Social Justice*, 16 (4): 1–9.

Healey, J. (1995) *Race, Ethnicity, Gender, and Class*. Thousand Oaks, CA: Pine Forge Press.

Healy, J. and Woodyard, C. (2000) 'More people die despite recall,' *USA Today*, September 11, p. 1B.

Hebenton, B. and Seddon, T. (2009) 'From dangerousness to precaution: managing sexual and violent offenders in an insecure and uncertain age,' *British Journal of Criminology*, 49: 343–62.

Hedges, C. (2000) 'Condemned again for old crimes: deportation law descends sternly, and often by surprise,' *New York Times*, October 30, pp. B1, B3.

Hedges, C. (2001) 'Suit details the beatings of detainees in Louisiana,' *New York Times*, January 2, p. EV1-3.

Heffernan, R. (1972) *Making It in Prison: The Square, the Cool and the Life*. New York: Wiley.

Heidensohn, F. (1986) 'Models of justice: Portia or Persephone? Some thoughts on equality, fairness and gender in the field of criminal justice,' *International Journal of the Sociology of Laws*, 14: 287–98.

Henderson, M. (2002) 'Maximum-security offenders' attitudes toward placing juveniles in adult prisons,' in L. Fiftal and P. Cromwell (eds), *Correctional Perspectives: Views from Academics, Practitioners, and Prisoners*. Los Angeles: Roxbury, pp. 262–7.

Henderson, M. L., Cullen, F. T., Carroll, L., and Feinberg, W. (2000) 'Race, rights, and order in prison: a national survey of wardens on the racial integration of prison cells,' *Prison Journal*, 80 (3): 295–308.

Henry, S. and Lanier, M. M. (1998) 'The prison of crime: the arguments for an integrated definition of crime,' *Justice Quarterly*, 15 (4): 609–28.

Hensley, C. (2002) *Prison Sex: Practice and Policy*. Boulder, CO: Lynne Reimer.

Hensley, C., Wright, J., Tewksbury, R., and Castle, R. (2003) 'The evolving nature of prison argot and sexual hierarchies,' *Prison Journal*, 83: 289–300.

Hentoff, N. (1993a) 'The bloody art of prison cell extraction,' *Village Voice*, July 6, pp. 20–1.

Hentoff, N. (1993b) 'Buried alive in Pelican Bay,' *Village Voice*, June 22, pp. 20–1.

Hentoff, N. (1993c) 'Charles Dickens' report to Janet Reno,' *Village Voice*, June 15, pp. 22–3.

Hentoff, N. (1995) 'The Supreme Court approves of a premeditated murder,' *Village Voice*, February 7, pp. 22–3.

Hentoff, N. (2001) 'Terrorizing the Bill of Rights,' *Village Voice*, November 20, p. 32.

Hepburn, J. (1978) 'Race and the decision to arrest: an analysis of warrants issued,' *Journal of Research in Crime and Delinquency*, 15 (1): 54–73.

Hepburn, J. (1985) 'The exercise of power in coercive organizations: a study of prison guards,' *Criminology*, 23 (1): 145–64.

Herbert, B. (1999) 'Breathing while black,' *New York Times*, November 4, p. A29.

Herbert, B. (2005a) 'Torture, American style,' *New York Times*, February 11, p. A25.

Herbert, B. (2005b) 'On Abu Ghraib, the big shots walk,' *New York Times*, April 28, p. A25.

Herberts, S. (1998) *The Correctional Officer Inside Prisons*. New York: Nova Science.

Herman, E. and Chomsky, N. (2002) *Manufacturing Consent: The Political Economy of the Mass Media*. New York: Pantheon Books.

Hersh, S. (2004) *Chain of Command: The Road from 9/11 to Abu Ghraib*. New York: HarperCollins.

Hershberger, G. L. (1979) 'The development of the federal prison system,' *Federal Probation*, 33: 13–23.

Herzog, S. and Oreg, S. (2008) 'Chivalry and the moderating effect of ambivalent sexism,' *Law and Society Review*, 42 (1): 45–74.

Hewitt, J. D., Poole, E., and Regoli, R. (1984) 'Self-reported and observed rule breaking in prison: a look at disciplinary response,' *Journal of Criminal Justice*, 12: 437–47.

Hickey, J. and Scharf, P. (1980) *Toward a Just Correctional System*. San Francisco: Jossey-Bass.

Hill, G. and Crawford, E. M. (1990) 'Women, race, and crime,' *Criminology*, 28 (4): 601–26.

Hillsman, S. (1990) 'Fines and dayfines,' in M. Tonry and N. Morris (eds), *Crime and Justice: A Review of Research*, Vol. 12. Chicago: University of Chicago Press.

Hilts, P. (1994) 'Thousands of human experiments,' *New York Times*, October 22, p. 10.

Hilts, P. (1995) 'Radiation tests used some healthy people,' *New York Times*, January 19, p. B10.

Hipp, J. and Yates, D. (2009) 'Do returning parolees affect neighborhood crime? A case study of Sacramento,' *Criminology*, 47 (3): 619–55.

Hirsch, A. J. (1992) *The Rise of the Penitentiary: Prisons and Punishment in Early America*. New Haven, CT: Yale University Press.

Hirschfield, P. (2008) 'Preparing for prison? The criminalization of school discipline in the USA,' *Theoretical Criminology*, 12 (1): 79–101.

Hirschfield, P. and Piquero, A. (2010) 'Normalization and legitimation: modeling stigmatizing attitudes toward ex-offenders,' *Criminology*, 48 (1): 27–56.

Hirst, P. Q. (1975) 'Radical deviancy theory and Marxism: a reply to Taylor and Walton,' in I. Taylor, P. Walton, and J. Young (eds), *Critical Criminology*. Boston: Routledge & Kegan Paul.

Hoene, P. M. (2000) 'Keeping the streets safe: truth in sentencing and public opinion in Idaho,' *Justice Professional*, 12 (3): 291–304.

Hoffman, J. (1993) 'Is innocence sufficient? An essay on the United States Supreme Court's continuing problems with federal habeas corpus and the death penalty,' *Indiana Law Journal*, 68: 817–39.

Hoffman-Bustamante, D. (1982) 'Females, recidivism and salient factor score: a research note,' *Criminal Justice and Behavior*, 9 (1): 121–5.

Holmes, S. (1994) 'The boom in jails is locking up lots of loot,' *New York Times*, November 6, p. E3.

Holmes, S. (1995) 'Inmate violence is on rise as federal prisons change,' *New York Times*, pp. A1, A14.

Holmes, S. (2000) 'Census Bureau aided removal of Japanese, report says,' *New York Times*, March 17, p. A14.

Home Office (1994) *The Ethnic Origins of Prisoners: Ethnic Composition of Prison Population 1985–1993*, Home Office Statistical Bulletin. London: Home Office.

Home Office (1999) *Statistics on Race and the Criminal Justice System*. London: Home Office.

Hood, R. (2000) *The Death Penalty: A Worldwide Perspective* (3rd edn). Oxford: Oxford University Press.

hooks, b. (1994) *Outlaw Culture: Resisting Representation*. New York: Routledge.

Hornblum, A. (1997) 'They were cheap and available: prisoners as research subjects in twentieth century America,' *British Medical Journal*, 315: 1437–41.

Hornblum, A. (1998) *Acres of Skin: Human Experiments at Holmesburg Prison, a True Story of Abuse and Exploitation in the Name of Medical Science*. New York: Routledge.

Horowitz, C. (1944) 'Is Rikers about to explode? The dirty secret of cellblock 6,' *New York Times Magazine*, October 10, pp. 30–7.

Houston, J., Gibbons, D. C., and Jones, J. F. (1988) 'Physical environment and jail social climate,' *Crime and Delinquency*, 34 (4): 449–66.

Howard, J. (1929 [1777]) *State of Prisons*; reprinted by E. P. Dutton, New York.

Howe, A. (1990) 'Prologue to a history of women's imprisonment: in search of a feminist perspective,' *Social Justice*, 17 (2): 5–33.

Howe, A. (1993) *Punish and Critique: Towards a Feminist Analysis of Penalty*. New York: Routledge.

Howell, J. C. (1992) 'Program implications for research on chronic juvenile delinquency,' *Juvenile Justice*, November, pp. 8–16.

Hoy, D. C. (1979) 'Taking history seriously: Foucault, Gadamer, Habermas,' *Union Seminary Quarterly Review*, 34 (2): 85–95.

Hudson, B. (2003) *Understanding Justice* (2nd edn). Maidenhead: Open University Press.

Huff, C. R. (2002) 'Wrongful conviction and public policy,' *Criminology*, 40 (1): 1–18.

Huff, C. R., Rattner, A., and Sagarin, E. (1996) *Convicted But Innocent: Wrongful Conviction and Public Policy*. Thousand Oaks, CA: Sage.

Hughes, R. (1986) *The Fatal Shore: The Epic of Australia's Founding*. New York: Vintage.

Huling, T. (1995) 'Women drug couriers,' *Criminal Justice*, 9 (4): 14–19, 58–62.

Human Rights Watch (1996) *All Too Familiar: Sexual Abuse of Women in U.S. Prisons*. New York: Human Rights Watch.

Human Rights Watch (1997) *Cold Storage: Super-Maximum Security Confinement in Indiana*. New York: Human Rights Watch.

Human Rights Watch (1998) *Locked Away: Immigration Detainees in Jails in the U.S.* New York: Human Rights Watch.

Human Rights Watch (2001) *Beyond Reason: The Death Penalty and Offenders with Mental Retardation*. New York: Human Rights Watch.

Human Rights Watch (2004) *Guantanamo: Detainee Accounts*. New York: Human Rights Watch.

Human Rights Watch (2005) *Guantanamo: Three Years of Lawlessness*. New York: Human Rights Watch.

Human Rights Watch (2006) *Human Rights Watch World Report 2006: U.S. Policy of Abuse Undermines Rights Worldwide*. New York: Human Rights Watch.

Human Rights Watch (2007) *US Mark Five Years of Guantanamo by Closing It: Congress Should Restore Detainees' Access to Courts*. Available at: http://www.hrw.org (accessed January 5, 2010).

Human Rights Watch (2010) *US: 1 in 10 Children in Juvenile Facilities Report Sexual Abuse by Staff: Justice Department Should Issue Prison Rape Standards*. Available at: http://www.humanrightswatch.org (accessed January 7, 2010).

Humphrey, J. A. and Fogerty, T. J. (1987) 'Race and plea bargained outcomes: a research note,' *Social Forces*, 66: 176–82.

Humphries, D. (1993) 'Mothers and children, drugs and crack: reactions to maternal drug dependency,' in R. Muraskin and T. Alleman (eds), *It's a Crime: Women and Justice*. Englewood Cliffs, NJ: Regents/ Prentice Hall.

Humphries, D. (1999) *Crack Mothers: Pregnancy, Drugs, and the Media*. Columbus, OH: Ohio State University.

Hunt, G., Reigel, S., Morales, T., and Waldorf. D. (2002) 'Changes in prison culture: prison gangs and the case of the "Pepsi generation,"' in T. Gray (ed.), *Exploring Corrections*. Boston: Allyn & Bacon, pp. 220–2.

Hunt, L. (1984) *Power, Politics and Class in the French Revolution*. Berkeley, CA: University of California Press.

Husak, D. (2000) 'Liberal neutrality, autonomy, and drug prohibitions,' *Philosophy and Public Affairs*, 29 (1): 43–80.

Husak, D. (2002) *Legalize This! The Case for Decriminalizing Drugs*. New York: Verso.

Hussey, F. A. and Duffee, D. E. (1980) *Probation, Parole and Community Field Services: Policy Structure and Practice*. New York: Harper & Row.

Ignatieff, M. (1978) *A Just Measure of Pain: The Penitentiary in the Industrial Revolution – 1750–1850*. New York: Columbia University Press.

Ignatieff, M. (2004) *The Lesser Evil: Political Ethics in an Age of Terror*. Princeton, NJ: Princeton University Press.

Immarigeon, R. and Chesney-Lind, M. (1993) 'Women's prisons: overcrowded and overused,' in R. Muraskin and T. Alleman (eds), *It's a Crime: Women and Justice*. Englewood Cliffs, NJ: Regents/Prentice Hall.

Immigration and Naturalization Service (1999) *Strengthening the Nation's Immigration System*, Fact Sheet. Washington, DC: Government Printing Office.

Immigration and Naturalization Service (2000) *This Is INS*. Available at: http://www.ins.usdoj.gov/graphics/aboutins/thisisins/overview.htm.

Immigration and Naturalization Service (2001) *This Is INS*. Available at: http://www.ins.usdoj.gov/graphics/aboutins/thisisins/overview.htm.

Immigration and Naturalization Service (2002) *This Is INS*. Available at: http://www.ins.usdoj.gov/graphics/aboutins/thisisins/overview.htm.

Inciardi, J. A. (1986) *The War on Drugs*. Palo Alto, CA: Mayfield.

Inciardi, J. A. (1992) *The War on Drugs II*. Mountain View, CA: Mayfield.

Inciardi, J. A. (2002) *The War on Drugs III: The Continuing Saga of the Mysteries and Miseries of Intoxication, Addiction, Crime, and Public Policy*. Boston: Allyn & Bacon.

Inciardi, J. and McElrath, K. (2007) *The American Drug Scene*. New York: Oxford University Press.

Inciardi, J., Surratt, H., and Kurtz, S. (2007) 'African-Americans, crack and the federal sentencing guidelines,' in J. Inciardi and K. McElrath (eds), *The American Drug Scene*. New York: Oxford University Press.

Indefinite Detention Project of the Catholic Legal Immigration Network Inc. (2000) *Quarterly Report for the Indefinite Detention Project: October – December*. Available at: http://www.cscd.org.

Innis, L. and Feagin, J. R. (1989) 'The black "underclass" ideology in race relations analysis,' *Social Justice*, 16 (4): 13–34.

Irwin, J. (1977) 'The changing social structure of the men's correctional prison,' in D. Greenberg (ed.), *Corrections and Punishment*. Beverly Hills, CA: Sage.

Irwin, J. (1980) *Prisons in Turmoil*. Boston: Little, Brown.

Irwin, J. (1985) *The Jail: Managing the Underclass in American Society*. Berkeley, CA: University of California Press.

Irwin, J. (2004) *The Warehouse Prison: Disposal of the New Dangerous Class*. New York: Oxford University Press.

Irwin, J. (2005) *The Warehouse Prison: Disposal of the New Dangerous Class*. Los Angeles, CA: Roxbury Press.

Irwin, J. and Austin, J. (1994) *It's About Time: America's Imprisonment Binge*. Belmont, CA: Wadsworth.

Irwin, J. and Austin, J. (1998) 'Fanning the flames of fear,' *Crime and Delinquency*, 44: 32–48.

Irwin, J. and Cressey, D. (1964) 'Thieves, convicts and the inmate culture,' in H. S. Becker (ed.), *The Other Side*. New York: Free Press.

Irwin, J., Schiraldi, V., and Ziedenberg, J. (2000) 'America's one million nonviolent prisoners,' *Social Justice*, 27 (2): 135–47.

Isaacs, C. and Lowen, M. (2007) *Buried Alive: Solitary Confinement in Arizona's Prisons and Jails*. Tuscon, AZ: American Friends Service Committee.

Ives, G. (1970 [1914]) *A History of Penal Methods*. Montclair, NJ: Patterson Smith.

Ivins, M. (1992) 'Bush's people: notes from another country,' *The Nation*, September 14, pp. 229, 248–9.

Jackson, B. (1995) 'Is the Alabama prison system's return to the chain gang unfair to blacks?' *Jet*, September 18, pp. 12–16.

Jackson, G. (1970) *Soledad Brother: The Prison Letters of George Jackson*. New York: Bantam Books.

Jackson, J. L. Sr and Jackson, J. L. Jr (2001) *Legal Lynching: The Death Penalty and America's Future*. New York: Free Press.

Jackson, P. (1988) 'The uses of jail confinement in three counties,' *Policy Studies Review*, 7 (3): 359–605.

Jackson, P. (1991) 'Competing ideologies of jail confinement,' in J. A. Thompson and G. L. Mays (eds), *American Jails: Public Policy Issues*. Chicago: Nelson-Hall.

Jacobs, J. B. (1974) 'Street gangs behind bars,' *Social Problems*, 21 (3): 395–409; reprinted in R. M. Carter, D. Glaser, and L. Wilkins (eds) (1985) *Correctional Institutions* (3rd edn). New York: Harper & Row.

Jacobs, J. B. (1977) *Stateville: The Penitentiary in Mass Society*. Chicago: University of Chicago Press.

Jacobs, J. B. (1980) 'The prisoner's rights movement and its impact, 1960–1980,' in N. Morris and M. Tonry (eds), *Crime and Justice: An Annual Review*. Chicago: University of Chicago Press.

Jacobs, J. B. (1981) 'What prison guards think: a profile of the prison force,' in R. Ross (ed.), *Prison Guard and Correctional Officer: The Use and Abuse of the Human Resources of Prisons*. Toronto: Butterworth.

Jacobs, J. B. (1983) *New Perspectives on Prisons and Imprisonment*. Ithaca, NY: Cornell University Press.

Jacobs, J. B. (2001) 'The prisoners' rights movement and its impacts,' in E. Latessa, A. Holsinger, J. Marquart, and J. Sorensen (eds), *Correctional Contexts: Contemporary and Classical Readings*. Los Angeles: Roxbury, pp. 211–28.

Jacobs, J. B. and Grear, M. (1977) 'Drop-outs and rejects: an analysis of the prison guard's revolving door,' *Criminal Justice Review*, 2: 57–70.

Jacobs, J. B. and Kraft, L. J. (1978) 'Integrating the keepers: a comparison of black and white prison guards in Illinois,' *Social Problems*, 25: 304–18.

Jacobs, J. B. and Retsky, H. G. (1975) 'Prison guard,' *Urban Life*, 4 (1): 5–29.

Jacobs, J. B. and Zimmer, L. (1983) 'Collective bargaining and labor unrest,' in J. Jacobs (ed.), *New Perspectives in Prisons and Imprisonment*. Ithaca, NY: Cornell University Press.

Jacobs, M. D. (1990) *Screwing the System and Making It Work: Juvenile Justice in the No-Fault Society*. Chicago: University of Chicago Press.

Jacobson, M. (2005) *Downsizing Prisons: How to Reduce Crime and End Mass Incarceration*. New York: New York University Press.

Jail Suicide Update (1992) 'Case suicide of a manipulative inmate,' Winter, 4 (4): 6–8.

James, S. (2002) *Private Prison Operators Upbeat on Results*, Reuters, May 2, pp. EV1–2.

Jankovic, I. (1977) 'Labor market and imprisonment,' *Crime and Social Justice*, 8: 17–31.

Jankovic, I. (1982) 'Labor market and imprisonment,' in A. Platt and P. Takagi (eds), *Punishment and Penal Discipline*. San Francisco: Crime and Justice Associates.

Janus, M. (1985) 'Selective incapacitation: have we tried it? Does it work?' *Journal of Criminal Justice*, 13: 117–29.

Jefferis, E. (1994) 'Violence in correctional institutions,' *American Jails*, September/October, pp. 25–6, 30–2.

Jehl, D. (2005) 'Questions left by C.I.A. chief on torture use: Goss vouches only for current practices,' *New York Times*, March 18, pp. A1, A11.

Jenkins, P. (1982) 'The radicals and the rehabilitative ideal, 1890–1930,' *Criminology*, 20 (3–4): 347–72.

Jenkins, P. (1994a) *Using Murder: The Social Construction of Serial Murder*. New York: Aldine de Gruyter.

Jenkins, P. (1994b) 'The "Ice Age": the social construction of a drug panic,' *Justice Quarterly*, 11 (1): 7–31.

Jenne, D. and Kersting, R. (2002) 'Working in a male-dominated world: aggression and women correctional officers,' in L. Alarid and P. Cromwell (eds), *Correctional Perspectives: Views From Academics, Practitioners, and Prisoners*. Los Angeles: Roxbury, pp. 197–206.

Jerrell, J. and Komisaruk, R. (1991) 'Public policy issues in the delivery of mental health services in a jail setting,' in J. A. Thompson and G. L. Mays (eds), *American Jails: Public Policy Issues*. Chicago: Nelson-Hall.

Jilani, H. (2002) 'Antiterrorism strategies and protecting human rights,' *Amnesty Now* (a publication of Amnesty International), 27 (2): 1, 16–17.

Jinks, D. and Sloss, D. (2004) 'Is the president bound by the Geneva Conventions?' *Cornell Law Review*, 90: 97–202.

Johnson Foundation (1993) *Substance Abuse: The Nation's No. 1 Health Problem*. Princeton, NJ: Johnson Foundation.

Johnson, B. and Betsinger, S. (2009) 'Punishing the "model minority": Asian-American criminal sentencing outcomes in federal district courts,' *Criminology*, 47 (4): 1045–89.

Johnson, B. R., Larson, D. B., and Pitts, T. C. (1997) 'Religious programs, institutional adjustment, and recidivism among former inmates in prison fellowship programs,' *Justice Quarterly*, 14 (1): 145–66.

Johnson, D. (1994) 'A farmer, 70, saw no choice: nor did the sentencing judge,' *New York Times*, July 20, pp. A1, A10.

Johnson, D. (2008) 'The death penalty in Asia: introduction to a special issue of *Punishment and Society*,' *Punishment and Society*, 10 (2): 99–102.

Johnson, E. H. (1961) 'Sociology of confinement: assimilation and the prison "rat,"' *Journal of Criminal Law, Criminology, and Police Science*, 51: 528–33.

Johnson, E. H. and Kotch, K. E. (1973) 'Two factors in development of work release: size and location of prisons,' *Journal of Criminal Justice*, 1 (March): 44–5.

Johnson, H. A. (1988) *History of Criminal Justice*. Cincinnati, OH: Anderson.

Johnson, M. (1993) 'Mandatory minimums revisited,' *New York Times*, February 22, p. A16.

Johnson, P.C. (2003) *Inner Lives: Voices of African-American Women in Prison*. New York: New York University Press.

Johnson, R. (1976) *Culture in Crisis in Confinement*. Lexington, MA: D. C. Heath.

Johnson, R. (1984) 'A life for a life?' *Justice Quarterly*, 1 (4): 569–80.

Johnson, R. (1987) *Hardtime: Understanding and Reforming the Prison*. Monterey, CA: Brooks/Cole.

Johnson, R. (1992) 'Crowding and the quality of prison life: a preliminary reform agenda,' in C. A. Hartjen and E. Rhine (eds), *Correctional Theory and Practice*. Chicago: Nelson-Hall.

Johnson, R. (1998) *Deathwatch: A Study of the Modern Execution Process*. Belmont, CA: West/Wadsworth.

Johnson, R. (2002a) 'Life in the belly of the beast,' in T. Gray (ed.), *Exploring Corrections*. Boston: Allyn & Bacon, pp. 96–102.

Johnson, R. (2002b) 'Living and working on death row,' in T. Gray (ed.), *Exploring Corrections*. Boston: Allyn & Bacon, pp. 108–201.

Johnston, N. (2009) 'Evolving function: early use of imprisonment as punishment,' *Prison Journal*, 89 (1): 10S–34S.

Johnston, R. (1973) *The Human Cage: A Brief History of Prison Architecture*. New York: Walker.

Jones, C. H. (1992) 'Recent trends in corrections and prisoners' rights law,' in C. A. Hartjen and E. E. Rhine (eds), *Correctional Theory and Practice*. Chicago: Nelson-Hall.

Jones, D. (2006) *Humane Prisons*. Oxford: Radcliffe.

Jones, D. A. (1976) *The Health Risks of Imprisonment*. Lexington, MA: D. C. Heath.

Jones, R. and Schmid, T. (1989) 'Inmates' conceptions of prison sexual assault,' *Prison Journal*, LXIX (1): 53–61.

Josi, D. (1996) 'Correctional officers: selection and training,' in M. D. McShane and F. P. Williams (eds), *Encyclopedia of American Prisons*. New York: Garland, pp. 118–22.

Josi, D. A. and Sechrest, D. K. (1999) 'A pragmatic approach to parole aftercare: evaluation of a community reintegration program for high-risk youthful offenders,' *Justice Quarterly*, 16 (1): 51–80.

Journal of Prison Discipline and Philanthropy (1857) Philadelphia, January, p. 40.

Jurik, N. (1983) 'The economics of female recidivism,' *Criminology*, 21 (4): 3–12.

Jurik, N. (1985) 'An officer and a lady: organizational barriers to women working as correctional officers in men's prisons,' *Social Problems*, 32: 375–88.

Jurik, N. (1988) 'Striking a balance: female correctional officers, gender role stereotypes, and prisons,' *Sociological Inquiry*, 58 (3): 291–305.

Jurik, N. (1999) 'Socialist feminism, criminology, and social justice,' in B. Arrigo (ed.), *Social Justice, Criminal Justice*. Belmont, CA: Wadsworth, pp. 31–50.

Jurik, N. and Musheno, M. (1986) 'The internal crisis of corrections: professionalization and the work environment,' *Justice Quarterly*, 3 (December): 457–80.

Kacprowski, N. (2004) '"Stacking the deck" against suspected terrorists,' *Seattle University Law Review*, 26: 651–97.

Kagan, R. (2006) *Dangerous Nation*. New York: Alfred A. Knopf.

Kahn, R. (1996) *Other People's Blood: U.S. Immigration Prisons in the Reagan Decade*. Boulder, CO: Westview Press.

Kalinich, D. B. (1980) *Power, Stability and Contraband: The Inmate Economy*. Prospect Heights, IL: Waveland.

Kalinich, D. (1986) 'Overcrowding and the jail budget: addressing dilemmas of population control,' in D. Kalinich and J. Klofas (eds), *Sneaking Inmates Down the Alley: Problems and Prospects in Jail Management*. Springfield, IL: Charles C. Thomas.

Kalinich, D. and Embert, P. (1995) 'Grim tales of the future: American jails in the year 2010,' in J. Klofas and S. Stojkovic (eds), *Crime and Justice in the Year 2010*. Belmont, CA: Wadsworth.

Kalinich, D. B. and Stojkovic, S. (1985) 'Contraband: the basis for legitimate power in a prison social system,' *Crime and Behavior: An International Journal*, 12 (4): 435–51.

Kalinich, D. B. and Stojkovic, S. (1987) 'Prison contraband systems: implications for prison management,' *Journal of Crime and Justice*, X (1): 1–21.

Kalinich, D., Embert, P., and Senese, J. (1991) 'Mental health services for jail inmates: imprecise standards, traditional philosophies, and the need for change,' in J. A. Thompson and G. Larry Mays (eds), *American Jails: Public Policy Issues*. Chicago: Nelson-Hall.

Kalunta-Crumpton, A. (2002) 'Black and white violence in Britain: the articulation of race in popular and criminal justice discourses,' *Justice Professional*, 15, 1: 37–55.

Kalven, H. Jr and Zeisel, H. (1966) *The American Jury*. Boston: Little, Brown.

Kappeler, V. E., Blumberg, M., and Potter, G. (2000) *The Mythology of Crime and Criminal Justice* (3rd edn). Prospect Heights, IL: Waveland.

Kappeler, V. E., Vaughn, M., and del Carmen, R. V. (1991) 'Death in detention: an analysis of police liability for negligent failure to prevent suicide,' *Journal of Criminal Justice*, 19: 381–93.

Karmen, A. (1990) *Crime Victims: An Introduction to Victimology* (2nd edn). Pacific Grove, CA: Brooks/Cole.

Kasindorf, M. (1997) 'Black Panther Pratt free after 27 years,' *USA Today*, June 11, pp. A1, A3.

Katyal, N. and Tribe, L. H. (2002) 'Waging war, deciding guilt: trying the military tribunals,' *Yale Law Journal*, 111: 1259–310.

Katz, J. (1988) *Seductions of Crime: Moral and Sensual Attraction in Doing Evil*. New York: Basic Books.

Katz, J. W. (1993) 'Fort Dix finds new growth industry: housing U.S. prisoners,' *New York Times*, August 8: 13–14.

Katz, J. (2001) 'Boys are not men: notes on working with adolescent males in juvenile detention,' in D. Sabo, T. Kupers, and W. London (eds), *Prison Masculinities*. Philadelphia: Temple University Press, pp. 207–17.

Katz, S. R. (1997) 'Presumed guilty: how schools criminalize Latino youth,' *Social Justice*, 24 (4): 77–117.

Kauffman, K. (1988) *Prison Officers and Their World*. Cambridge, MA: Harvard University Press.

Kautt, P. and Spohn, C. (2002) 'Crack-ing down on the black drug offenders? Testing for interactions among offenders' race, drug type, and sentencing in federal drug sentences,' *Justice Quarterly*, 19 (1): 1–35.

Kauzlarich, D., Matthews, R., and Miller, W. J. (2001) 'Toward a victimology of state crime,' *Critical Criminology*, 10: 173–94.

Kauzlarich, D., Mullins, C., and Matthews, R. (2003) 'A complicity continuum of state crime,' *Contemporary Justice Review*, 6 (3): 241–54.

Keen, B. and Jacobs, D. (2009) 'Racial threat, partisan politics, and racial disparities in prison admissions: a panel analysis,' *Criminology*, 47 (1): 209–38.

Keil, T. J. and Vito, G. F. (1989) 'Race, homicide severity, and application of the death penalty: a consideration of the Barnett scale,' *Criminology*, 27 (3): 511–36.

Keith, M. (1996) 'Criminalization and racialization,' in J. Muncie, E. McLaughlin, and M. Langan (eds), *Criminological Perspectives*. London: Sage.

Keller, R. (1992) 'From "con" to counselor: changes in gender identity in a prison juvenile awareness program,' *Men's Studies Review*, 9 (1): 18–22.

Kelley, M. S. (2003) 'The state-of-the-art in substance abuse programs for women in prison,' in S. Sharp (ed.), *The Incarcerated Woman: Rehabilitative Programming in Women's Prisons*. Upper Saddle River, NJ: Prentice Hall, pp. 119–48.

Kelly, K. J. (1992) 'Supreme Court knockout: one-two punch for political asylum,' *The Nation*, March 2, pp. 272–3.

Kempf-Leonard, K. and Sample, L. (2000) 'Disparity based on sex: is gender-specific treatment warranted?' *Justice Quarterly*, 7: 89–128.

Kennedy, D. B. and Homant, R. J. (1988) 'Predicting custodial suicides: problems with the use of profiles,' *Justice Quarterly*, 5 (3): 441–56.

Kennedy, J. E. (2000) 'Monstrous offenders and the search for solidarity through modern punishment,' *Hastings Law Review*, 51: 817–39.

Kerle, K. E. (1998) *American Jails: Looking to the Future*. Boston: Butterworth-Heinemann.

Kerle, K., Stojkovic, S., Kiekbusch, R., and Rowan, J. (1999) 'A rejoinder to Vaughn and Smith's "Practicing Penal Harm in Medicine in the United States: Prisoners' Voices from Jail," *Justice Quarterly*, 16 (4): 897–906.

Kerr, B. (1994) 'Career in corrections,' *American Jails*, November/December, p. 4.

Kerr, J. R. (1969) 'Constitutional rights, tribal justice, and the American Indian,' *Journal of Public Law*, 18: 311–38.

Kerr, T., Small, W., and Wood, E. (2005) 'The public health and social impacts of drug market enforcement: a review of the evidence,' *International Journal of Drug Policy*, 16: 210–20.

Kessler, R. and Roebuck, J. (1996) 'Snitch,' in M. D. McShane and F. P. Williams (eds), *Encyclopedia of American Prisons*. New York: Garland, pp. 449–51.

Keve, P. W. (1991) *Prisons and the American Conscience: A History of U.S. Federal Corrections*. Carbondale, IL: University of Southern Illinois University Press.

Keyes, D., Edwards, W. and Perske, R. (2002) 'People with mental retardation are dying–legally,' *Journal of Mental Retardation*, 3: 243–44.

Kifer, M., Hemmens, C., and Stohr, M. (2003) 'The goal of corrections: perspectives from the line,' *Criminal Justice Studies*, 28: 47–69.

Kifner, M. (1994) 'Gacy executed, officials comment,' *New York Times*, October 2, p. A19.

Kilborn, P. (1997) 'Revival of chain gangs takes a twist: stun belts emerge as the latest tool to keep inmates in line,' *New York Times*, March 11, p. A18.

Kilborn, P. (2001) 'Rural towns turn to prisons to reignite their economies,' *New York Times*, August 1, pp. A1, A12.

Kilborn, P. and Clemetson, L. (2002) 'Gains of 90's did not lift all, census shows,' *New York Times*, June 2, pp. A1, A24.

King, A. and Maruna, S. (2009) 'Is a conservative just a liberal who has been mugged? Exploring the origins of punitive views,' *Punishment and Society*, 11 (2): 147–69.

King, D. R. (1978) 'The brutalization effect: execution publicity and the incidence of homicide in South Carolina,' *Social Forces*, 57: 683–87.

King, R. (2005) 'The effects of supermax custody,' in A. Liebling and S. Maruna (eds), *The Effects of Imprisonment*. Cullompton: Willan.

Kinkade, P. T. and Leone, M. (1992) 'The privatization of prisons: the wardens' views,' *Federal Probation*, 56: 4.

Kissell, P. and Katasampes, P. (1980) 'Impact of women corrections officers on the functioning of institutions housing male inmates,' *Journal of Offender Counseling, Services and Rehabilitation*, 4 (Spring): 213–31.

Kittrie, N., Zenoff, E., and Eng, V. (2002) *Sentencing, Sanctions, and Corrections: Federal and State Law, Policy, and Practice* (2nd edn). New York: Foundation Press.

Klein, G. (2007) 'An investigation: have Islamic fundamentalists made contact with white supremacists in the United States?,' *Journal of Police Crisis Negotiation*, 7: 85–101.

Klein, L. R., Forst, B., and Filatov, V. (1978) 'The deterrent effect of capital punishment: an assessment of the estimates,' in A. Blumstein, J. Cohen, and D. Nagin (eds), *Deterrence and Incapacitation: Estimating the Effects of Criminal Sanctions on Crime Rates*. Washington, DC: National Academy of Sciences.

Klein, P. (1920) *Prison Methods in New York*. New York: Columbia University Press.

Klein, S., Petersilia, J., and Turner, S. (1990) 'Race and imprisonment decisions in California,' *Science*, 247: 812–912.

Klepper, S., Nagin, D. S., and Tierney, L. (1983) 'Discrimination in the criminal justice system: a critical appraisal of the literature,' in A. Blumstein, J. Cohen, S. E. Martin, and M. H. Tonry (eds), *Research on Sentencing: A Search for Reform*, Vol. 2. Washington, DC: National Academy Press, pp. 55–128.

Klockars, C. B. (1972) 'A theory of probation supervision,' *Journal of Criminal Law, Criminology, and Police Science*, 63: 550–60.

Klockars, C. B. (1979) 'The contemporary crisis of Marxist criminology,' *Criminology*, 16: 477–515.

Klofas, J. M. (1984) 'Reconsidering prison personnel: new views of the correctional officer subculture,' *International Journal of Offender Therapy and Comparative Criminology*, 28: 169–75.

Klofas, J. M. (1987) 'Patterns of jail use,' *Journal of Criminal Justice*, 15: 403–11.

Klofas, J. M. (1990) 'The jail and the community,' *Justice Quarterly*, 7 (1): 69–102.

Klofas, J. M. (1993) 'Drugs and justice: the impact of drugs on criminal justice in a metropolitan community,' *Crime and Delinquency*, 39 (2): 204–24.

Klofas, J. M., Stojkovic, S., and Kalinich, D. A. (1992) 'The meaning of correctional crowding: steps toward an index of severity,' *Crime and Delinquency*, 38 (2): 171–87.

Koichi, H. (1995) *Probation Around the World: A Comparative Study*. London: Routledge.

Kovandzic, T., Sloan, J., and Vieraitis, L. (2002) 'Unintended consequences of politically popular sentencing policy: the homicide promoting effects of "three strikes" in U.S. cities,' *Criminology and Public Policy*, 1 (3): 399–425.

Kovandzic, T., Vieraitis, L., and Boots, D. P. (2009) 'Does the death penalty save lives? new evidence from state panel data, 1977 to 2006,' *Criminology and Public Policy*, 8 (4): 803–44.

Kovandzic, T., Vieraitis, L. M., and Yeisley, M. R. (1998) 'The structural covariates of urban homicide: reassessing the impact of income inequality and poverty in the post-Reagan era,' *Criminology*, 36 (3): 569–600.

Kowalski, G. S. and Petee, T. A. (1991) 'Sunbelt effects on homicide rates,' *Sociology and Social Research*, 75: 73–9.

Koziak, D. (2001) 'The deliberate indifference standard as applied to the suicide of incarcerated persons,' *Justice Professional*, 14 (4): 311–22.

Kramer, R. and Michalowski, R. J. (2005) 'War, aggression and state crime: a criminological analysis of the invasion and occupation of Iraq,' *British Journal of Criminology*, 45: 446–69.

Kramer, R. and Michalowski, R. (2006) 'The original formulation,' in R. Michalowski and R. Kramer (eds), *State-Corporate Crime: Wrongdoing at the Intersection of Business and Government*. New Brunswick, NJ: Rutgers University Press.

Kramer, R., Michalowski, R., and Rothe, D. (2005) 'The supreme international crime: how the U.S. war in Iraq threatens the rule of law,' *Social Justice*, 32 (2): 52–81.

Kratcoski, P. C. (1994) *Correctional Counseling and Treatment* (3rd edn). Prospect Heights, IL: Waveland.

Kraus, C. (1994) 'No crystal ball needed on crime,' *New York Times*, November 13, Section 4, p. 4.

Krisberg, B. and Austin, J. F. (1993) *Reinventing Juvenile Justice*. Thousand Oaks, CA: Sage.

Krohn, M. (1995a) 'Control and deterrence theories of criminality,' in J. Sheley (ed.), *Criminology: A Contemporary Handbook* (2nd edn). Belmont, CA: Wadsworth.

Krohn, M. (1995b) 'Sources of criminality: control and deterrence theories,' in J. Sheley (ed.), *Criminology: A Contemporary Handbook* (3rd edn). Belmont, CA: Wadsworth.

Kruttschnitt, C. (1981) 'Prison codes, inmate solidarity, and women: a re-examination,' in M. Warren (ed.), *Comparing Female and Male Offenders*. Beverly Hills, CA: Sage.

Kruttschnitt, C. and Green, D. (1984) 'The sex sanctioning issue: is it history?' *American Sociology Review*, 49: 451–551.

Kruttschnitt, C. and Krmpotich, S. (1990) 'Aggressive behavior among female inmates: an exploratory study,' *Justice Quarterly*, 7 (2): 371–90.

Kupchik, A. (2006) *Judging Juveniles: Prosecuting Adolescents in Adult and Juvenile Courts*. New York: New York University Press.

Kupchik, A. (2009) 'Things are tough all over: race, ethnicity, class and school discipline,' *Punishment and Society*, 11 (3): 291–317.

Kupchik, A. and Monahan, T. (2006) 'The new American school: preparation for post-industrial discipline,' *British Journal of Sociology of Education*, 27 (5): 617–631.

Kupers, T. (2001) 'Rape and the prison code,' in D. Sabo, T. Kupers, and W. London (eds), *Prison Masculinities*. Philadelphia: Temple University Press, pp. 111–17.

Kurki, L. (1997) 'International crime survey: American rates about average,' *Overcrowded Times*, 8 (5): 4–7.

Lab, S. P. and Whitehead, J. T. (1990) 'From "nothing works" to "the appropriate": the latest stop on the search for the secular grail,' *Criminology*, 28 (3): 405–18.

Lacey, N. (2008) *The Prisoners' Dilemma: Political Economy and Punishment in Contemporary Democracies*. Cambridge: Cambridge University Press.

Lachance, D. (2009) 'Executing Charles Starkweather,' *Punishment and Society*, 11 (3): 337–58.

Lamb-Mechanick, D. and Nelson, J. (2000) *Prison Health Care Survey: An Analysis of Factors Influencing per Capita Costs*. Washington, DC: American Correctional Association.

Lambert, E., Barton, S., and Hogan, N. (1999) 'The missing link between job satisfaction and correctional staff behavior: the issue of organizational commitment,' *American Journal of Criminal Justice*, 24: 95–116.

Lambert, E., Hogan, N., Barton, S., and Elechi, O. (2009) 'The impact of job stress, job involvement, job satisfaction, and organizational commitment on correctional staff support for rehabilitation and punishment,' *Criminal Justice Studies*, 22 (2): 10922.

Lampe, P. (1985) 'Friendship and adultery,' *Sociological Inquiry*, 55: 310–24.

Lancefield, K. *et al.* (1997) 'Management style and its effect on prison officers' stress,' *International Journal of Stress Management*, 4: 205–19.

Land, K., Teske, R., and Zheng, H. (2009) 'The short-term effects of executions on homicides: deterrence, displacement, or both?' *Criminology*, 47 (4): 1009–43.

Langan, P. (1991) 'America's soaring prison population,' *Science*, 251 (March): 1568–73.

Langan, P. A. and Cunniff, M. A. (1992) *Recidivism of Felons on Probation, 1986–89*, Bureau of Justice Statistics Special Report. Washington, DC: US Department of Justice.

Langan, P. and Levin, D. (2002) *Recidivism of Prisoners Released in 1994*, Bureau of Justice Statistics. Washington, DC: US Department of Justice. Available at: http://www.ojp.usdoj.gov/bjs/pub/pdf/rpr94.pdf.

Langworthy, R. and McCarthy, B. (1988) *Older Offenders: Perspectives in Criminology and Criminal Justice*. Washington, DC: American Correctional Association.

Lanier, C. (2003) '"Who's doing the time here, me or my children?" Addressing the issues implicated by mounting numbers of fathers in prison,' in J. I. Ross and S. Richards (eds), *Convict Criminology*. Belmont, CA: Thomson Wadsworth.

Lanier, M. and Henry, S. (1998) *Essential Criminology*. Boulder, CO: Westview.

Lanza-Kaduce, L., Parker, K., and Thomas, C. (1999) 'A comparative recidivism analysis of releases from private and public prisons,' *Crime and Delinquency*, 45: 28–47.

Lawes, L. E. (1935) *Cell 202*. New York: Farrar & Rinehart.

Lawrence, J. E. (1989) 'Substance abusers in jail: health service breakdown in five New York jails,' *American Journal of Criminal Justice*, XIV (1): 122–34.

Lawrence, J. E. and Zwisohn, V. (1991) 'AIDS in jail,' in J. A. Thompson and G. Larry Mays (eds), *American Jails: Public Policy Issues*. Chicago: Nelson-Hall.

Lawrence, R. (2002) 'Restitution programs,' in T. Gray (ed.), *Exploring Corrections*. Boston: Allyn & Bacon, pp. 319–21.

Lawrence, R. and Mahan, S. (2002) 'Women corrections officers in men's prisons: acceptance and perceived job performance,' in L. Alarid and P. Cromwell (eds), *Correctional Perspectives: Views From Academics, Practitioners, and Prisoners*. Los Angeles: Roxbury, pp. 188–96.

Lawson, A. (1988) *Adultery: An Analysis of Love and Betrayal*. New York: Basic Books.

Lea, H. C. (1969 [1887]) *The Inquisition of the Middle Ages*. New York: Harper & Row; originally published as Vol. I, *A History of the Inquisition of the Middle Ages*.

Leaf, C. (2002) 'White-collar criminals: they lie, they cheat, they steal, and they've been getting away with it for too long,' *Fortune*, March 18, pp. 62–76.

LeDuff, C. (2002) 'Loitering behind the clean streets: in Salt Lake City, hardly any work for stranded homeless people,' *New York Times*, February 14, pp. D1, D5.

Lee, M. (2007) *Inventing Fear of Crime: Criminology and the Politics of Anxiety*. Cullompton: Willan.

Lee, W. H. (2002) *My Country Versus Me: The First-Hand Account by the Los Alamos Scientist Accused of Being a Spy*. New York: Hyperion.

Leger, R. (1988) 'Perceptions of crowding, racial antagonism, and aggression in a custodial prison,' *Journal of Criminal Justice*, 16: 167–81.

Leighton, P. S. (1999) 'Televising executions, primetime "live"?' *Justice Professional*, 12 (2): 91–108.

Lekkerkerker, E. (1931) *Reformatories for Women in the U.S.* Gronigen, Netherlands: J. B. Wolters.

Lenza, M., Keys, D., and Guess, T. (2005) 'The prevailing injustices in the application of the Missouri death penalty (1978 to 1996),' *Social Justice*, 32 (2): 151–66.

Leo, R. A. (2001) 'False confessions: causes, consequences, and solutions,' in S. Westervelt and J. Humphrey (eds), *Wrongly Convicted: Perspectives on Failed Justice*. New Brunswick, NJ: Rutgers University Press.

Leo, R. (2008) *Police Interrogation and American Justice*. Cambridge, MA: Harvard University Press.

Leonard, E. (1982) *Women, Crime and Society*. New York: Longman.

Leone, M. C. (2002) 'Prisoners, elderly,' in D. Levinson (ed.), *Encyclopedia of Crime and Punishment*. Thousand Oaks, CA: Sage, pp. 1250–61.

Lerman, P. (1970) *Delinquency and Social Policy*. New York: Praeger.

Lerman, P. (1982) *Deinstitutionalization and the Welfare State*. New Brunswick, NJ: Rutgers University Press.

Lerman, P. (1984) 'Child welfare, the private sector, and community-based corrections,' *Crime and Delinquency*, 30: 5–38.

Lerman, P. (1990) 'Delinquency and social policy: a historical perspective,' in R. A. Weisheit and R. G. Culbertson (eds), *Juvenile Delinquency: A Justice Perspective* (2nd edn). Prospect Heights, IL: Waveland.

Lesieur, H. and Welch, M. (1991) 'Vice, public disorder and social control,' in J. Sheley (ed.), *Criminology: A Contemporary Handbook*. Belmont, CA: Wadsworth.

Lesieur, H. and Welch, M. (1995) 'Vice crimes: individual choices and social controls,' in J. Sheley (ed.), *Criminology: A Contemporary Handbook* (2nd edn). Belmont, CA: Wadsworth.

Lesieur, H. and Welch, M. (2000) 'Vice crimes: personal autonomy versus societal dictates,' in J. F. Sheley (ed.), *Criminology: A Contemporary Handbook* (3rd edn). Belmont, CA: Wadsworth.

Levitt, J. L., Young, T. M., and Pappenfort, D. M. (1981) *Achievement Place: The Teaching-Family Treatment Model in a Group-Home Setting*. Washington, DC: US Government Printing Office.

Levrant, S., Cullen, F. T., Fulton, B., and Wozniak, J. F. (1999) 'Reconsidering restorative justice: the corruption of benevolence revisited?' *Crime and Delinquency*, 45 (1): 3–27.

Levy, J. (2007) *My Trip to Guantanamo Bay* (Frontpagemagazine.com). Available at: http://www.aina.org/news/2007040293614.htm.

Lewin, T. (2001) 'Inmate education is found to lower risk of new arrest,' *New York Times*, November 16, p. A22.

Lewis, A. (2005) 'Introduction,' in K. Greenberg and J. Dratel (eds), *The Torture Papers: The Road to Abu Ghraib*. New York: Cambridge University Press.

Lewis, C. (1995) 'John Steinbeck's alternative to internment camps: a policy for the President, December 15, 1941,' *Journal of the West*, 34: 55–61.

Lewis, N. A. (2002) 'Justice department opposes lower jail terms for crack: aides cite small disparity against powder,' *New York Times*, March 20, p. A24.

Lewis, N. A. (2004) 'Fate of Guantanamo Bay detainees is debated in federal court,' *New York Times*, December 2, p. A36.

Lewis, O. F. (1967 [1922]) *The Development of American Prison Customs, 1776–1845*. Montclair, NJ: Patterson Smith.

Lewis, P. B. (1978) 'Life on death row: a post-Furman profile of Florida's condemned,' in P. W. Lewis and K. D. Peoples (eds), *The Supreme Court and the Criminal Process – Cases and Comments*. Philadelphia: W. B. Saunders.

Lewis, W. D. (1965) *From Newgate to Dannemora: The Rise of the Penitentiary in New York, 1797–1848*. Ithaca, NY: Cornell University Press.

Lichenstein, A. (1993) 'Good roads and chain gangs in the progressive South: the negro convict is a slave,' *Journal of Southern History*, LIX (1): 85–110.

Lichtblau, E. and Shane, S. (2010) 'Report faults 2 authors of Bush terror memos,' *New York Times*, February 19, p. EV1-4.

Liebling, A. (1999) 'Prison suicide and prisoner coping,' in M. Tonry and J. Petersilia (eds), *Prisons*. Chicago: University of Chicago Press.

Liebling, A. and Arnold, H. (2004) *Prisons and Their Moral Performance: A Study of Values, Quality, and Prison Life*. Oxford: Oxford University Press.

Liebling, A. and Maruna, S. (2005) *The Effects of Imprisonment*. Cullompton: Willan.

Liebling, A. and Price, D. (1999) *An Exploration of Staff–Prisoners Relationships at HMP Whitemoor*, Prison Service Research Report No. 6. London: HM Prison Services.

Liebling, A. and Price, D. (2001) *The Prison Officer*. Leyhill, UK: Prison Service Journal.

Liebman, J., Fagan, J., West, V., and Lloyd, J. (2000) 'Capital attrition: error rates in capital cases, 1973–1999,' *Texas Law Review*, 78: 1839–65.

Lifton, R. J. (1988) *Nazi Doctors: Medical Killing and the Psychology of Genocide*. New York: Basic Books.

Light, K. C. (1990a) 'Measurement error in official statistics: prison infraction data,' *Federal Probation*, 52: 63–8.

Light, K. C. (1990b) 'The severity of assaults on prison officers: a contextual study,' *Social Science Quarterly*, 71: 267–84.

Light, K. C. (1991) 'Assaults on prison officers: interactional themes,' *Justice Quarterly*, 8 (2): 243–62.

Lilly, J. R. and Deflem, M. (1996) 'Profit and penalty: an analysis of the corrections-commercial complex,' *Crime and Delinquency*, 42, 1: 3–20.

Lilly, J. R. and Knepper, P. (1993) 'The corrections-commercial complex,' *Crime and Delinquency*, 39 (2): 150–66.

Lindesmith, A. (2007) 'A sociological theory of drug addiction,' in J. Inciardi and K. McElrath (eds), *The American Drug Scene*. New York: Oxford University Press.

Lindesmith, A. A. and Levin, Y. (1937) 'The Lombrosian myth in criminology,' *American Journal of Sociology*, 42: 653–71.

Lippke, R. (2007) *Rethinking Imprisonment*. New York: Oxford University Press.

Lipsky, M. (1980) *Street-Level Bureaucracy*. New York: Russell Sage.

Liptak, A. (2002a) 'Fewer death sentences likely if juries make ultimate decision, experts say,' *New York Times*, June 25, p. A21.

Liptak, A. (2002b) '3 justices call for reviewing death sentences for juveniles,' *New York Times*, August 30, pp. A1, A15.

Liptak, A. (2002c) 'A court backs open hearings on deportation,' *New York Times*, August 27, pp. A1, A12.

Liptak, A. (2003) 'Critics say execution drug may hide suffering,' *New York Times*, October 7, pp. A1, A18.

Liptak, A. (2009) 'Strip-search of girl tests limit of school policy,' *New York Times*, March 23, pp. EV1–9.

Liptak, A. and Rimer, S. (2002) 'With little guidance, states face hard debate on who is retarded,' *New York Times*, June 21, pp. A1, A14.

Lipton, D. (1995) *The Effectiveness of Treatment for Drug Abusers Under Criminal Justice Supervision*. Washington, DC: Department of Justice.

Lipton, D., Martinson, R. M., and Wilks, J. (1975) *The Effectiveness of Correctional Treatment*. New York: Praeger.

Litowitz, D. (2002) 'Shaming offenders,' in T. Gray (ed.), *Exploring Corrections*. Boston: Allyn & Bacon, pp. 303–10.

Loader, I. (1999) 'Consumer culture and the commodification of policing and security,' *Sociology*, 33 (2): 373–92.

Loader, I. (2009) 'Ice cream and incarceration: on appetites for security and punishment,' *Punishment and Society*, 11 (2): 241–57.

Locin, M. (1981) 'Prisoners filing away with suits,' *Chicago Tribune*, October 18, pp. 1–6.

Lockwood, D. (1980) *Prison Sexual Violence*. New York: Elsevier.

Lockwood, D. (1982) 'Contribution of sexual harassment to stress and coping in confinement,' in N. Parisi (ed.), *Coping with Imprisonment*. Beverly Hills, CA: Sage.

Lockwood, D. (1985) 'Issues in prison sexual violence,' in M. Braswell, S. Dillingham, and R. Montgomery (eds), *Prison Violence in America*. Cincinnati, OH: Anderson.

Lockwood, D. (1991) 'Target violence,' in K. C. Haas and G. P. Alpert (eds), *The Dilemmas of Corrections*. Prospect Heights, IL: Waveland.

Logan, C. (1972) 'Evaluation research in crime and delinquency: a reappraisal,' *Journal of Criminal Law, and Criminology, and Police Science*, 63: 378–87.

Logan, C. (1990) *Private Prisons: Cons and Pros*. Oxford: Oxford University Press.

Logan, C. (1993) 'Well-kept: comparing quality of confinement in private and public prisons,' *Journal of Criminal Law and Criminology*, February, pp. 15–24.

Logan, E. (1999) 'The wrong race, committing crime, doing drugs, and maladjusted for motherhood: the nation's fury over "crack babies,"' *Social Justice*, 26 (1): 115–38.

Logli, P. A. (1991) 'Drugs in the womb: the newest battlefield in the war on drugs,' in R. C. Monk (ed.), *Taking Sides: Clashing Views on Controversial Issues in Crime and Criminology*. Sluice Dock, Guilford, CT: Dushkin.

Lombardo, L. X. (1981) *Guards Imprisoned: Correctional Officers at Work*. New York: Elsevier.

Lombroso, C. (1876) *The Criminal Man*. Milan: Hoepli.

Lombroso, C. (2006) *Criminal Man*, trans. M. Gibson and N. H. Rafter. Durham, NC: Duke University Press.

Lombroso, C. and Ferrero, G. (2004) *Criminal Woman, the Prostitute, and the Normal Woman*, trans. N. H. Rafter and M. Gibson. Durham, NC: Duke University Press.

Lombroso, C. and Ferrero, W. (1920 [1894]) *The Female Offender*. New York: Appleton.

Loughran, T., Mulvey, E., Schubert, C., Fagan, J., Piquero, A., and Losoya, S. (2009) 'Estimating a dose-response relationship between length of stay and recidivism in serious juvenile offenders,' *Criminology*, 47 (3): 699–740.

Loveless, P. (1994) 'Home incarceration with electronic monitoring: myths and realities,' *American Jails*, January/February, pp. 35–40.

Lovell, D., Johnson, L., and Cain, K. (2007) 'Recidivism of supermax prisoners in Washington State,' *Crime and Delinquency*, 53: 633–56.

Lovell, J. S. (2001) 'Crime and popular culture in the classroom: approaches and resources for interrogating the obvious,' *Journal of Criminal Justice Education*, 12 (1): 229–44.

Lujan, C. C. (1990) *American Indian Women and the Law*. Paper presented at the International Sociological Association Meetings, Madrid, Spain.

Lujan, C. C. (2002) 'Perpetuating the stereotypes of American Indian nations and peoples,' in C. Mann and M. Zatz (eds), *Images of Color, Images of Crime*. Los Angeles: Roxbury, pp. 116–25.

Lundman, R. J. (1993) *Prevention and Control of Juvenile Delinquency* (2nd edn). New York: Oxford University Press.

Lundsgaarde, H. P. (1977) *Murder in Space City*. New York: Oxford University Press.

Lurigio, A. (2009) 'The rotten barrel spoils the apples: how situational factors contribute to detention officer abuse toward inmates,' *Prison Journal*, 89 (1): 70S–80S.

Lurigio, A. J. and Petersilia, J. (1992) 'The emergence of intensive probation supervision programs in the United States,' in J. Byrne, A. Lurigio, and J. Petersilia (eds), *Smart Sentencing: The Emergence of Intermediate Sanctions*. Newbury Park, CA: Sage.

Lusane, C. (1994) *Pipe Dream Blues: Racism and the War on Drugs*. Boston: South End Press.

Lutze, F. E. (1998) 'Are shock incarceration programs more rehabilitative than traditional prisons? A survey of inmates,' *Justice Quarterly*, 15 (3): 547–66.

Lutze, F. E. and Murphy, D. W. (1999) 'Ultramasculine prison environments and inmate adjustment: it's time to move beyond the "boys will be boys" paradigm,' *Justice Quarterly*, 16 (4): 709–35.

Luxenberg, J. and Guild, T. E. (1993) 'Women, AIDS, and the criminal justice system,' in R. Muraskin and T. Alleman (eds), *It's a Crime: Women and Justice*. Englewood Cliffs, NJ: Regents/Prentice Hall.

Lynch, M. J. (2000) 'The power of oppression: understanding the history of criminology as a science of oppression,' *Critical Criminology*, 9 (1–2): 144–52.

Lynch, M. J. (2007) *Big Prisons, Big Dreams: Crime and the Failure of America's Penal System*. New Brunswick, NJ and London: Rutgers University Press.

Lynch, M. J. and Groves, W. B. (1989a) *A Primer in Radical Criminology* (2nd edn). New York: Harrow & Heston.

Lynch, M. J. and Groves, W. B. (1989b) *Radical Criminology, Radical Policy?* Paper presented at the Annual Meeting of the Criminal Justice Sciences, Washington, DC.

Lynch, M. J. and Michalowski, R. (2006) *Primer in Radical Criminology* (4th edn). Monsey, NY: Criminal Justice Press.

Lynch, M. J. and Patterson, E. B. (eds) (1991) *Race and Criminal Justice*. New York: Harrow & Heston.

Lynch, M. J. and Patterson, E. B. (eds) (1995) *Race and Criminal Justice: A Further Examination*. New York: Harrow & Heston.

Lynch, M. J., Hogan, M., and Stretesky, P. (1999) 'A further look at long cycles and criminal justice legislation,' *Justice Quarterly*, 16 (2): 431–50.

Lynch, M., Michalowski, R., and Groves, W. B. (2000) *The New Primer in Radical Criminology: Critical Perspectives on Crime, Power, and Identity*. New York: Criminal Justice Press.

Lynch, M., Cole, S., McNally, R., and Jordan, K. (2008) *Truth Machine: The Contentious History of DNA Fingerprinting*. Chicago: University of Chicago Press.

Lyon, D. (1991) 'Bentham's panopticism: from moral architecture to electronic surveillance,' *Queens Quarterly*, 98 (3): 596–617.

Lyons, W. and Drew, J. (2006) *Punishing Schools: Fear and Citizenship in American Public Education*. Ann Arbor, MI: University of Michigan Press.

Macallair, D. (1997) 'Lock 'em up legislation means prisons gain clout: in California, guards form a potent lobby to protect their interests,' *Christian Science Monitor*, December 21, p. 22.

McArthur, J. C. (1987) 'Neurological manifestations of AIDS,' *Medicine*, 66: 407–37.

McCarthy, B. R. (1990) 'A micro-level analysis of social structure and social control: intrastate use of jail and prison confinement,' *Justice Quarterly*, 7 (2): 325–40.

McCarthy, B. (1995) 'Patterns in prison corruption,' in D. Close and Nicholas Meier (eds), *Morality in Criminal Justice: An Introduction to Ethics*. Belmont, CA: Wadsworth.

McCarthy, B. (2002) 'Keeping an eye on the keepers: prison corruption and its control,' in M. Braswell, B. McCarthy, and B. McCarthy (eds), *Justice, Crime, and Ethics*. Cincinnati, OH: Anderson, pp. 253–66.

McCartney, C. (2006) *Forensic Identification*. Cullompton: Willan.

McCleary, R. (1978) *Dangerous Men: The Sociology of Parole*. Beverly Hills, CA: Sage.

McCloskey, J. C. (1989) 'Convicting the innocent,' *Criminal Justice Ethics*, 8 (Winter/Spring): 1–9.

McClosky, J. C. (2001) 'One man's view,' in L. Nelson and B. Foster (eds), *Death Watch: A Death Penalty Anthology*. Upper Saddle River, NJ: Prentice Hall, pp. 261–75.

McCorkle, R. and Miethe, T. (1998) 'The political and organizational response to gangs: an examination of "moral panic" in Nevada,' *Justice Quarterly*, 15 (1): 41–64.

McCorkle, R. C., Miethe, T., and Drass, K. (1995) 'The roots of prison violence: a test of the deprivation, management, and "not-so-total" institution models,' *Crime and Delinquency*, 41: 317–31.

McCoy, A. (2006) *A Question of Torture: CIA Interrogation, From the Cold War to the War on Terror*. New York: Metropolitan Books.

McCoy, C. (2000) 'Chivalry explanation of court outcome,' in N. Rafter (ed.), *Encyclopedia of Women and Crime*. Phoenix, AZ: Orix Press, pp. 25–6.

McCoy, C. (2010) 'If it's disparity, sure,' in N. Frost, J. Freilich, and T. Clear (eds), *Contemporary Issues in Criminal Justice Policy*. Belmont, CA: Wadsworth.

McCoy, T., Salinas, P. R., and Johnson, W. W. (1999) 'The execution of Karla Faye Tucker: an examination of the attitudes and motivations of protestors, supporters, and curiosity-seekers,' *Justice Professional*, 12 (2): 209–22.

McCurley, C. and Snyder, H. (2004) *Victims of Juvenile Crime*. Washington, DC: US Department of Justice, Office of Juvenile Justice and Delinquency Prevention.

McDonald, D. C. (1986) *Punishment Without Walls: Community Service Sentences in New York City*. New Brunswick, NJ: Rutgers University Press.

McDonald, D. C. (1989) *Private Prisons and Public Interest*. New Brunswick, NJ: Rutgers University Press.

McDonald, D. C. (1992) 'Punishing labor: unpaid community service as a criminal sentence,' in J. M. Byrne, A. J. Lurigio, and J. Petersilia (eds), *Smart Sentencing: The Emergence of Intermediate Sentences*. Newbury Park, CA: Sage.

McDonald, D. C. (1999) 'Medical care in prisons,' in M. Tonry and J. Petersilia (eds), *Prisons, Crime and Justice: Annual Review of Research*. Chicago: University of Chicago Press.

McDonald, D., Fournier, E., Russell-Einhorn, M., and Crawford, S. (1998) *Private Prisons in the United States: An Assessment of Current Practice*. Boston: Abt. Associates Inc.

MacDonald, H. (2002) 'The myth of racial profiling,' *City Journal* (New York), 11: 1–13.

McElligott, G. (2008) 'Bearing the neoconservative burden? Frontline work in prisons,' *Social Justice*, 34: 78–97.

Macey, D. (1993) *The Lives of Michel Foucault*. New York: Vintage.

McGaha, J., Fichter, M., and Hirschburg, P. (1987) 'Felony probation: a re-examination of public risk,' *American Journal of Criminal Justice*, XI: 1–9.

McKelvey, B. (1977 [1936]) *American Prisons: A History of Good Intentions*. Montclair, NJ: Patterson Smith.

MacKenzie, D. L. (1993) 'Boot camp prisons in 1993,' *National Institute of Justice Journal*, November, pp. 21–8.

MacKenzie, D. L. and Brame, R. (2001) 'Community supervision, prosocial activities, and recidivism,' *Justice Quarterly*, 18 (2): 429–48.

MacKenzie, D. L. and Shaw, J. W. (1990) 'Inmate adjustment and change during shock incarceration: the impact of correctional boot camp programs,' *Justice Quarterly*, 7 (1): 125–47.

MacKenzie, D. L., Robinson, J. W., and Campbell, C. S. (1989) 'Long-term incarceration of female offenders: prison adjustment and coping,' *Criminal Justice and Behavior*, 16 (2): 223–38.

MacKenzie, D. L., Shaw, J. W., and Gowdy, V. B. (1993) *An Evaluation of Shock Incarceration in Louisiana*, National Institute of Justice, Research in Brief, June. Washington, DC: National Institute of Justice.

Mackenzie, S. and Green, P. (2008) 'Performative regulation: a case study of how powerful people avoid criminal labels,' *British Journal of Criminology*, 48: 138–53.

Mackey, D. A. and Courtright, K. (2000) 'Assessing punitiveness among college students: a comparison of criminal justice majors with other majors,' *Justice Professional*, 12 (4): 423–41.

McKie, K. (2002) 'Executions and apologies: the U.S., international law and right to consular notification,' *Critical Criminology*, 11: 199–215.

McKinley, J. (2009) 'Killer with low IQ executed in Texas,' *New York Times*, December 3, pp. EV1–3.

MacKinnon, C. (1982) 'Feminism, Marxism, method, and the state: an agenda for theory,' *Signs: Journal of Women in Culture and Society*, 7 (3): 515–44.

MacLean, B. D. and Milovanovic, D. (1997) *Thinking Critically About Crime*. Vancouver, BC: Collective Press.

McLennan, R. (2008) *The Crisis of Imprisonment: Protest, Politics, and the Making of the American Penal State, 1776–1941*. Cambridge: Cambridge University Press.

McManimon, P. F. (2000) 'The Impact of the "No Early Release Act" on Prison Violence and Misconduct: A Test of the Deprivation and Importation Theories.' Unpublished dissertation, Rutgers University, School of Criminal Justice, Newark, NJ.

McRobbie, A. and Thornton, S. (1995) 'Rethinking moral panics for multi-mediated social worlds,' *British Journal of Sociology*, 46 (4): 559–74.

McShane, M. (1996) 'Marion Penitentiary,' in M. D. McShane and F. P. Williams (eds), *Encyclopedia of American Prisons*. New York: Garland, pp. 317–18.

McShane, M. (2000) 'Widening the workforce: diversity in criminal justice employment,' in Criminal Justice Collective of Northern Arizona (ed.), *Investigating Differences: Human and Cultural Relations in Criminal Justice*. Boston: Allyn & Bacon, pp. 207–18.

McShane, M. D. and Williams, F. P. (1996) *Encyclopedia of American Prisons*. New York: Garland.

McSparron, J. (1992) 'Community correction and diversion: costs and benefits, subsidy modes, and start-up recommendations,' in T. Ellsworth (ed.), *Contemporary Community Corrections*. Prospect Heights, IL: Waveland.

Maestro, M. (1973) *Cesare Beccaria and the Origins of Penal Reform*. Philadelphia: Temple University Press.

Maguire, B. (1998) 'The applied dimension of radical criminology: a survey of prominent radical criminologists,' *Sociological Spectrum*, 8: 133–51.

Mahan, S. (1984) 'Imposition or despair: an ethnography of women in prison,' *Justice Quarterly*, 1 (3): 357–58; reprinted in *Journal of Crime and Justice*, 7: 101–29.

Mahan, S. (1986) 'Co-corrections: doing time together,' *Corrections Today*, August, pp. 136–40, 164–5.

Mahan, S. (1994) '"An orgy of brutality" at Attica and the "killing ground" at Santa Fe,' in M. Braswell, R. Montgomery, and L. Lombardo (eds), *Prison Violence in America*. Cincinnati, OH: Anderson.

Maher, L. (1990) 'Criminalizing pregnancy – the downside of kinder, gentler nation?' *Social Justice*, 17 (3): 111–35.

Maher, L. and Daly, K. (2007) 'Women in the street-level drug economy: continuity or change?' in J. Inciardi and K. McElrath (eds), *The American Drug Scene*. New York: Oxford University Press.

Mair, G. (2004) *What Matters in Probation*. Cullompton: Willan.

Majors, R. and Billson, J. (1992) *Cool Pose: The Dilemma of Black Manhood in America*. New York: Lexington Books.

Malcolm, A. H. (1988) 'Prisons seen facing surge of the elderly,' *New York Times*, December 24, p. A1.

Mann, M. (ed.) (1984) *The International Encyclopedia of Sociology*. New York: Continuum.

Mann, C. R. (1989) 'Minority and female: a criminal justice double bind,' *Social Justice*, 16 (4): 95–114.

Mann, C. R. (1993) *Unequal Justice: A Question of Color*. Bloomington, IN: Indiana University Press.

Mann, C. R. and Zatz, M. (2002) *Images of Color, Images of Crime*. Los Angeles: Roxbury.

Mann, C. R., Zatz, M., and Rodriguez, N. (2007) *Images of Color, Images of Crime*. New York: Oxford University Press.

Manning, B. (1977) 'Hyperlexis: our national disease,' *Northwestern University Law Review*, 71: 767–82.

Manning, P. (1998) 'Media loops,' in F. Bailey and D. Hale (eds), *Popular Culture, Crime, and Justice*. Belmont, CA: West/Wadsworth, pp. 25–39.

Manning, R. (1989) 'A suicide prevention program that really works,' *American Jails*, Spring (18): 20–2.

Mansnerus, L. (2002) 'Sexual predators, pariahs without equal,' *New York Times*, August 18, pp. A1, A6.

Mantsios, G. (1988) 'Class in America: myths and realities,' in P. S. Rothenberg (ed.), *Racism and Sexism: An Integrated Study*. New York: St. Martin's Press.

Marciniak, L. (2000) 'The addition of day reporting to intensive supervision probation: a comparison of recidivism rates,' *Federal Probation*, 64: 34–9.

Marcus-Mendoza, S. and Wright, E. (2003) 'Treating the woman prisoner: the impact of a history of violence,' in S. Sharp (ed.), *The Incarcerated Woman: Rehabilitative Programming in Women's Prisons*. Upper Saddle River, NJ: Prentice Hall, pp. 107–11.

Margolick, D. (1993) 'As Texas death row grows, fewer lawyers help inmates,' *New York Times*, December 3, p. A1.

Margulies, P. (2004) 'Judging terror in the "zone of twilight,"' *Boston University Law Review*, 84: 383–443.

Marin Independent Journal (2006) 'Omitting prison from country population might reduce grants,' February 1 p. EV1-2.

Mariner, W. K., Glantz, L. H., and Annas, G. J. (1991) 'Pregnancy, drugs, and the perils of prosecution,' in R. C. Monk (ed.), *Taking Sides: Clashing Views on Controversial Issues in Crime and Criminology*. Sluice Dock, Guilford, CT: Dushkin.

Maris, R., Berman, A., and Silverman, M. (2000) *Comprehensive Textbook of Suicidology*. New York: Guilford.

Markowitz, M. W. and Jones-Brown, D. D. (2001) *The System in Black and White: Exploring the Connections between Race, Crime, and Justice*. Westport, CT: Praeger.

Marlowe, D. H., Martin, J. A., Schneider, R. J., Ingraham, L., Vaitkus, M. A., and Bartone, P. (1988) *A Look at Army Training Centers: The Human Dimensions of Leadership and Training*. Washington, DC: Department of Military Psychiatry, Walter Reed Army Institute of Research.

Marquart, J. W. (1986) 'Prison guards and the use of physical coercion as a mechanism of prisoner control,' *Criminology*, 24 (2): 347–66.

Marquart, J. W. (1995) Personal communication, February 1.

Marquart, J. W. (2007) *The American Correctional Environment and Prison Officers*. Testimony before the Commission on Safety and Abuse in America's prisons. Available at: http://www.prisoncommission.org (accessed June 1, 2008).

Marquart, J. W. and Crouch, B. M. (1985) 'Judicial reform and prisoner control: the impact of *Ruiz* v. *Estelle* on a Texas penitentiary,' *Law and Society Review*, 19 (4): 557–86.

Marquart, J. W. and Roebuck, J. (1991) 'Prison guards and snitches: social control in a maximum security institution,' in K. C. Haas and G. P. Alpert (eds), *The Dilemmas of Corrections* (2nd edn). Prospect Heights, IL: Waveland.

Marquart, J. W., Ekland-Olson, S., and Sorensen, J. R. (1994) *The Rope, the Chair, and the Needle: Capital Punishment in Texas, 1923–1990*. Austin, TX: University of Texas Press.

Marsh, D. (June 19, 1990) 'New York forum: hip hop gets a bad rap,' *New York Newsday*, pp. 50, 52.

Marshall, I. H. (1997) *Minorities, Migrants, and Crime*. Thousand Oaks, CA: Sage.

Marteilhes, J. (1894) *Secrets of the Prison House*. London.

Martin, J. C. (2002) 'Community service for offenders,' in T. Gray (ed.), *Exploring Corrections*. Boston: Allyn & Bacon, pp. 311–18.

Martin, R. (2000) 'Community perceptions about prison construction: why not in my backyard?' *Prison Journal*, 80 (3): 265–94.

Martin, R. and Zimmerman, S. (1990a) 'A typology of the causes of prison riots and an analytical extension to the 1986 West Virginia riot,' *Justice Quarterly*, 7 (4): 711–37.

Martin, R. and Zimmerman, S. (1990b) 'Adopting precautions against HIV infection among male prisoners: a behavioral and policy analysis,' *Criminal Justice Policy Review*, 4 (4): 330–48.

Martin, S. and Ekland-Olson, S. (1987) *Texas Prisons: The Walls Came Tumbling Down*. Austin, TX: Texas Monthly Press.

Martin, S. E. and Jurik, N. J. (1996) *Doing Justice, Doing Gender: Women in Law and Criminal Justice Occupations*. Thousand Oaks, CA: Sage.

Martinez, R. (2001) *Latino Homicide: Immigration, Violence, and Community*. New York: Routledge.

Martinez, R. and Valenzuela, A. (2006) *Immigration and Crime: Race, Ethnicity and Violence*. New York: New York University Press.

Martinson, R. (1974) '"What works?" questions and answers about prison reform,' *Public Interest*, 35: 22–54.

Martinson, R. (1979) 'New findings, new views: a note of caution regarding sentencing and reform,' *Hofstra Law Review*, 7: 243–58.

Maruna, S. (2001) *Making Good: How Ex-Convicts Reform and Rebuild Their Lives*. Washington, DC: American Psychological Association.

Maruna, S. and Immarigeon, R. (2004) *After Crime and Punishment: Pathways to Offender Reintegration*. Cullompton: Willan.

Maruna, S. and King, A. (2009) 'Public opinion and community penalties,' in T. Bottoms, S. Rex, and G. Robinson (eds), *Alternatives to Prisons: Options for an Insecure Society*. Cullompton: Willan.

Maruschak, L. M. (2001) *HIV in Prisons and Jails, 1999*. Washington, DC: Bureau of Justice Statistics.

Maruschak, L. (2009) *HIV in Prisons, 2007–2008*. Washington, DC: US Department of Justice, Bureau of Justice Statistics.

Maruschak, L. and Beck, A. (2001) *Medical Problems of Inmates, 1997*. Washington, DC: Bureau of Justice Statistics.

Marvell, T. B. and Moody, C. E. (1998) 'The impact of out-of-state prison population on state homicide rates: displacement and free-rider effects,' *Criminology*, 36 (3): 513–36.

Marvell, T. and Moody, C. (2001) 'The lethal effects of three-strikes laws,' *Journal of Legal Studies*, 30: 89–97.

Marx, G. (1988) *Undercover: Police Surveillance in America*. Berkeley, CA: University of California Press.

Marx, K. (1906) *Capital*, Vol. 1. New York: International.

Marx, K. (1976) Preface and Introduction to *A Contribution to the Critique of the Political Economy*. Peking: Foreign Languages Press.

Mason, J. J. and Becker, P. J. (1994) 'White power: know your bigots. Identifying and supervising white supremacists in a correctional setting,' *American Jails*, September/October, pp. 61–5.

Massoglia, M. (2008) 'Incarceration, health, and racial disparities in health,' *Law and Society Review*, 42 (2): 275–306.

Masters, W., Johnson, V., and Kolodny, R. C. (1988) *Crisis: Heterosexual Behavior in the Age of AIDS*. New York: Grove.

Mata, A. and Herrerias, C. (2002) 'Immigrant bashing and nativist political movements,' in R. Mann and M. Zatz (eds), *Images of Color, Images of Crime*. Los Angeles: Roxbury, pp. 137–52.

Mathiesen, T. (1997) 'The viewer society: Michel Foucault's "panopticon" revisited,' *Theoretical Criminology*, 1 (2): 215–34.

Mathos, K. (1995) Personal communication, February 1. New York: Legal Defense Fund.

Matthews, R. (1989) *Privatizing Criminal Justice*. London: Sage.

Matthews, R. (1999) *Doing Time: An Introduction to the Sociology of Punishment*. Basingstoke: Macmillan Press.

Matthews, R. (2005) 'The myth of punitiveness,' *Theoretical Criminology*, 9: 175–201.

Matthews, R. A. (2006) 'Ordinary business in Nazi Germany,' in R. Michalowski and R. Kramer (eds), *State-Corporate Crime: Wrongdoing at the Intersection of Business and Government*. New Brunswick, NJ and London: Rutgers University Press.

Matthews, R. and Young, J. (1986) *Confronting Crime*. London: Sage.

Mattick, H. W. (1974) 'The contemporary jails of the United States: an unknown and neglected area of justice,' in D. Glasser (ed.), *Handbook of Criminology*. Chicago: Rand McNally.

Mattick, H. W. and Aikman, A. (1969) 'The cloacal region of American corrections,' *Annals of the American Academy of Political and Social Sciences*, 381: 109–18.

Mauer, M. (1990) *Young Black Men and the Criminal Justice System: A Growing National Problem*. Washington, DC: Sentencing Project.

Mauer, M. (1992) *Americans Behind Bars: One Year Later*. Washington, DC: Sentencing Project.

Mauer, M. (1999) *Race to Incarcerate*. New York: New Press.

Mauer, M. (2002) 'Analyzing and responding to the driving forces of prison population growth,' *Criminology and Public Policy*, 1 (3): 389–92.

Mauer, M. and Chesney-Lind, M. (2002) *Invisible Punishment: The Collateral Consequences of Mass Imprisonment*. New York: New Press.

May, J. P. (2000) *Building Violence: How America's Rush to Incarcerate Creates More Violence*. Thousand Oaks, CA: Sage.

Mayer, J. (2005) 'Outsourcing torture,' *New Yorker*, February 21, pp. EV1–14.

Mayer, J. (2009) *The Dark Side: The Inside Story of How the War on Terror Turned into a War on American Ideals*. New York: Anchor Books.

Mayfield, M. (1993) 'Jail suicides invisible issue: hearings today highlight the problem,' *USA Today*, March 17, pp. 1A, 2A.

Mays, G. L. and Bernat, F. P. (1988) 'Jail reform litigation: the issue of rights and remedies,' *American Journal of Criminal Justice*, 12: 254–73.

Mays, G. L. and Thompson, J. A. (1991) 'The political and organizational context of American jails,' in J. A. Thompson and G. L. Mays (eds), *American Jails: Public Policy Issues*. Chicago: Nelson-Hall.

Mears, D. (2008) 'An assessment of supermax prisons using an evaluation research framework,' *Prison Journal*, 88: 43–68.

Mears, D. and Bales, W. (2009) 'Supermax incarceration and recidivism,' *Criminology*, 47 (4): 1131–66.

Mears, D. and Reisig, M. (2006) 'The theory and practice of supermax prisons,' *Punishment and Society*, 8 (1): 33–57.

Meehan, K. (2002) 'Halfway house,' in D. Levinson (ed.), *Encyclopedia of Crime and Punishment*. Thousand Oaks, CA: Sage, pp. 816–18.

Meeker, J. W., Dombrink, J., and Mallet, L. K. (2000) 'Access to justice for the poor and moderate-income populations: issues for California latinos,' *Justice Professional*, 13 (1): 91–102.

Megill, A. (1979) 'Foucault, structuralism, and the ends of history,' *Journal of Modern History*, 51 (September): 451–503.

Meisenhelder, T. (1985) 'An essay on time and the phenomenology of imprisonment,' *Deviant Behavior*, 6: 39–56.

Meisenkothen, C. (1999) 'Chemical castration: breaking the cycle of paraphiliac recidivism,' *Social Justice*, 26 (1): 139–54.

Melossi, D. (1985) 'Punishment and social action: changing vocabularies of punitive motive within a political business cycle,' *Current Perspectives in Social Theory*, 6: 169–97.

Melossi, D. (1993) 'Gazette of morality and social whip: punishment, hegemony, and the case of the USA,' *Social and Legal Studies*, 2: 259–79.

Melossi, D. (2001) 'The cultural embeddedness of social control: reflections on the comparison of Italian and North-American cultures concerning punishment,' *Theoretical Criminology*, 5 (4): 403–24.

Melossi, D. (2008) *Controlling Crime, Controlling Society: Thinking About Crime in Europe and America*. Cambridge: Polity Press.

Melossi, D. and Pavarini, M. (1981) *The Prison and the Factory: Origins of the Penitentiary System*. Totowa, NJ: Barnes & Noble.

Melton, A. P. (2002) 'Traditional and contemporary tribal justice,' in C. Mann and M. Zatz (eds), *Images of Color, Images of Crime*. Los Angeles: Roxbury, pp. 164–76.

Menhard, S., Mihalic, S., and Huizinga, D. (2001) 'Drugs and crime revisited,' *Justice Quarterly*, 18 (2): 301–22.

Mennel, R. M. (1973) *Thorns and Thistles: Juvenile Delinquents in the United States, 1825–1940*. Hanover, NH: University Press of New England.

Mentor, K. (2002) 'Habitual felony laws,' in D. Levinson (ed.), *Encyclopedia of Crime and Punishment*. Thousand Oaks, CA: Sage, pp. 813–16.

Meredith, R. (2000) 'Road from prison to jobs gets smoother,' *New York Times*, April 3: A1.

Merlo, A. V. (1993) 'Pregnant substance abusers: the new female offender,' in R. Muraskin and T. Alleman (eds), *It's a Crime: Women and Justice*. Englewood Cliffs, NJ: Regents/Prentice Hall.

Merlo, A. V. (1995) 'Female criminality in the 1990s,' in A. Merlo and J. M. Pollock (eds), *Women, Law, and Social Control*. Boston: Allyn & Bacon.

Merlo, A. and Benekos, P. (2000) *What's Wrong with the Criminal Justice System: Ideology, Politics, and the Media*. Cincinnati, OH: Anderson.

Messerschmidt, J. W. (1988) 'From Marx to Bonger: socialist writings on women, gender, and crime,' *Sociological Inquiry*, 58 (4): 378–92.

Messerschmidt, J. W. (1986) *Capitalism, Patriarchy, and Crime: Toward a Socialist Feminist Criminology*. Totowa, NJ: Rowman & Littlefield.

Messerschmidt, J. W. (1993) *Masculinities and Crime: Critique and Reconceptualization of Theory*. Lanham, MD: Rowman & Littlefield.

Metz, A. (2002) 'Life on the inside: the jailers,' in T. Gray (ed.), *Exploring Corrections*. Boston: Allyn & Bacon, pp. 64–8.

Michalowski, R. J. (1985) *Order, Law, and Crime: An Introduction to Criminology*. New York: Random House.

Michalowski, R. J. and Carlson, S. (1999) 'Unemployment, imprisonment, and social structures of accumulation: historical contingency in the Rusche-Kirchheimer hypothesis,' *Criminology*, 37 (2): 217–50.

Michalowski, R. and Kramer, R. (2006a) *State-Corporate Crime: Wrongdoing at the Intersection of Business and Government*. New Brunswick, NJ and London: Rutgers University Press.

Michalowski, R. and Kramer, R. (2006b) 'The critique of power,' in R. Michalowski and R. Kramer (eds), *State-Corporate Crime: Wrongdoing at the Intersection of Business and Government*. New Brunswick, NJ and London: Rutgers University Press.

Miller, B. and Welte, J. W. (1986) 'Comparisons of incarcerated offenders according to use of alcohol and/or drugs prior to offense,' *Criminal Justice and Behavior*, 13: 336–92.

Miller, J. G. (1991) *Last One Over the Wall: The Massachusetts Experiment in Closing Reform Schools*. Columbus, OH: Ohio State University Press.

Miller, K. and Radelet, M. (1993) *Executing the Mentally Ill: The Criminal Justice System and the Case of Alvin Ford*. Newbury Park, CA: Sage.

Miller, L. (2008) *The Perils of Federalism: Race, Poverty, and the Politics of Crime Control*. Oxford: Oxford University Press.

Mills, C. W. (1956) *The Power Elite*. New York: Oxford University Press.

Mills, S. (1999) 'On the record: interview with Franklin Zimring,' *Chicago Tribune*, May 2, Section 2, p. 3.

Milovanovic, D. (1988) 'Jailhouse lawyers and jailhouse lawyering,' *International Journal of the Sociology of Law*, 16: 455–75.

Milovanovic, D. (1996) 'Postmodern criminology: mapping the terrain,' *Justice Quarterly*, 13 (4): 567–610.

Milovanovic, D. (1997) *Chaos, Criminology, and Social Justice: The New Orderly (Dis)Order*. Westport, CT: Praeger.

Milovanovic, D. (1998) 'Counter visions: orderly (dis)order in juridico-semiotic,' *Social Pathology*, 4 (1): 1–25.

Milovanovic, D. and Henry, S. (1996) *Constitutive Criminology: Beyond Postmodernism*. London: Sage.

Milovanovic, D. and Thomas, J. (1989) 'Overcoming the absurd: prisoner litigation as primitive rebellion,' *Social Problems*, 36 (1): 48–60.

Mink, G. (1994) Guest Editor of Special Issue on Women and Welfare Reform, *Social Justice*, 21: 1.

Minton, T. (2002) *Jails in Indian Country, 2001*. Washington, DC: Bureau of Justice Statistics, US Department of Justice.

Minton, T. (2008) *Jails in Indian Country, 2007*. Washington, DC: Bureau of Justice Statistics, US Department of Justice.

Minton, T. and Sabol, W. (2009) *Jail Inmates at Midyear 2008 – Statistical Tables*. Washington, DC: Bureau of Justice Statistics, US Department of Justice.

Mitchell, O., MacKenzie, D. L., Styve, G. J., and Gover, A. R. (2000) 'The impact of individual, organizational, and environmental attributes on voluntary turnover among juvenile correctional staff members,' *Justice Quarterly*, 17 (2): 333–57.

Mitford, J. (1971) *Kind and Usual Punishment: The Prison Business*. New York: Vintage Books.

Mobley, A. C. (2002) 'Six of one, half-dozen of the other: private prisons and the conditions of confinement debate,' in L. F. Alarid and P. Cromwell (eds), *Correctional Perspectives*. Los Angeles: Roxbury, pp. 240–6.

Mocan, H. and Gittings, R. (2003) 'Getting off death row: commuted sentences and the deterrent effect of capital punishment,' *Journal of Law and Economics*, 46: 453–78.

Mokhiber, R. (1999) 'The ten worst corporations of 1999,' *Multinational Monitor*, December, pp. 9–18, 23.

Mokhiber, R. and Weissman, R. (2001) 'Corporations behaving badly: the ten worst corporations of 2001,' *Multinational Monitor*, 22 (12): 1–22.

Monmaney, T. (1998) 'Tainted food has major impact,' *Houston Chronicle*, September 17, p. 14A.

Montgomery, L. (2000) 'Immigrants in small-town jails generate an infusion of cash for counties,' *Washington Post*, November 25, p. EV1–3.

Montgomery, R. and Crews, G. (1998) *A History of Correctional Violence: An Examination of Reported Causes of Riots and Disturbances*. Lanham, MD: American Correctional Association.

Montgomery, R. and Crews, G. (2002) 'Prison riots,' in D. Levinson (ed.), *Encyclopedia of Crime and Punishment*. Thousand Oaks, CA: Sage, pp. 1231–5.

Moore, J. W. (1978) *Homeboys, Gangs, Drugs, and Prison in the Barrios of Los Angeles*. Philadelphia: Temple University Press.

Moore, J. (2000) 'Latino gangs: a question of change,' *Justice Professional*, 13 (1): 8–18.

Moore, S. (2009a) 'California struggles with paroled sex offenders,' *New York Times*, September 26, pp. EV1–5.

Moore, S. (2009b) 'California prison rocked by riot has troubled past,' *New York Times*, August 10, pp. EV1–4.

Morash, M. and Rucker, L. (1990) 'A critical look at the idea of boot camp as a correctional reform,' *Crime and Delinquency*, 36 (2): 204–22.

Morris, A. (1987) *Women, Crime and Criminal Justice*. New York: Blackwell.

Morris, N. and Miller, M. (1985) 'On "dangerousness" in the judicial process,' in M. Tonry and N. Morris (eds), *Crime and Justice: An Annual Review of Research*, Vol. 6. Chicago: University of Chicago Press.

Morris, N. and Rothman, D. J. (1995) *Oxford History of the Prison: The Practice of Punishment in Western Society*. New York: Oxford University Press.

Morris, N. and Tonry, M. (1990) *Between Prison and Probation: Intermediate Punishments in a Rational Sentencing System*. New York: Oxford University Press.

Morris, R. (1983) *The Devil's Butcher Shop: The New Mexico Prison Uprising*. New York: Franklin Watts.

Morton, J. B. (2001) 'Implications for corrections of an aging prison population,' *Corrections Management Quarterly*, 5: 78–88.

Moyer, I. L. (1992) *The Changing Roles of Women in the Criminal Justice System* (2nd edn). Prospect Heights, IL: Waveland.

Moyer, I. L. (1993) 'Women's prisons: issues and controversies,' in R. Muraskin and T. Alleman (eds), *It's a Crime: Women and Justice*. Englewood Cliffs, NJ: Regents/Prentice Hall.

Moynahan, J. M. and Stewart, E. K. (1980) *The American Jail: Its Growth and Development*. Chicago: Nelson-Hall.

Mueller, R. R. (1992) 'Tuberculosis: the deadly disease strikes jail populations,' *American Jails: The Magazine of the American Jail Association*, May/June, pp. 23–8.

Mullins, C. (2006) 'Bridgestone-Firestone, Ford, and the NHTSA,' in R. Michalowski and R. Kramer (eds), *State-Corporate Crime: Wrongdoing at the Intersection of Business and Government*. New Brunswick, NJ and London: Rutgers University Press.

Multi-National Force (MNF) (2008a) *300th Military Police Brigade Transfers Authority to 11th MP Brigade, Heads Home*, September 14, p. 1. Available at: http://www.mnf-iraq.com/index.php?option=com_conten t&task=view&id=22362&Itemid=128.

Multi-National Force (MNF) (2008b) *Operational Update: Brig. Gen. Perkins, Maj. Gen. Atta*, September 24, p. 1. Available at: http://www.mnf-iraq.com/index.php?option=com_content&task=view&id=22584 &Itemid=128.

Multi-National Force (MNF) (2008c) *Coalition Detainee Operations Release Over 10,000 Men Recommitted to Rebuilding Iraq*, August 2, p. 1. Available at: http://www.mnf-iraq.com/index.php?option=com_conte nt&task=view&id=21583&Itemid=128.

Mulvaney, J. (1991) 'Dragnet for black at college assailed,' *Newsday*, September 12, p. 12.

Mumola, C. (2005) *Suicide and Homicide in State Prisons and Local Jails*. Washington, DC: Bureau of Justice Statistics, US Department of Justice.

Mumola, C. (2007) *Medical Causes of Death in State Prisons, 2001–2004*. Washington, DC: Bureau of Justice Statistics, US Department of Justice.

Muñoz, E. A. (2000) 'Latino sentencing dispositions, 1997–1991: an empirical assessment of "gringo" justice,' *Justice Professional*, 13 (1): 19–48.

Muraskin, R. (1993) 'Disparate treatment in correctional facilities,' in R. Muraskin and T. Alleman (eds), *It's a Crime: Women and Justice*. Englewood Cliffs, NJ: Regents/Prentice Hall.

Muraskin, R. (2001) *It's a Crime: Women and Justice*. Upper Saddle River, NJ: Prentice Hall.

Murphy, S. and Rosenbaum, M. (1999) *Pregnant Women on Drugs: Combining Stereotypes and Stigma*. New Brunswick, NJ: Rutgers University Press.

Murphy, S. and Sales, P. (2001) 'Pregnant drug users: scapegoats of Reagan/Bush and Clinton-era cconomics,' *Social Justice*, 28 (4): 72–95.

Murphy, T. and Whitty, N. (2007) 'Risk and human rights in UK prison governance,' *British Journal of Criminology*, 47: 798–816.

Murton, T. (1971) 'Prison doctors,' *Humanist*, 31 (3): 24–9.

Murton, T. O. (1976) *The Dilemma of Prison Reform*. New York: Holt, Rinehart & Winston.

Murton, T. O. and Hyams, J. (1969) *Accomplices to Crime: The Arkansas Prison Scandal*. New York: Grove.

Musto, D. F. (1988) *The American Disease: Origins of Narcotic Control* (2nd edn). New York: Oxford University Press.

Mydans, S. (2002) 'In Pakistan, rape victims are the "criminals,"' *New York Times*, May 17, p. A3.

Myers, L. (1995) 'Crime decrease flashes warning youth offenses signal dangers for the future,' *Chicago Tribune*, November 19, p. 3.

Myers, M. A. and Talarico, S. M. (1986) 'The social context of racial discrimination in sentencing,' *Social Problems*, 33: 236.

Myrdal, G. (1944) *An American Dilemma: The Negro Problem and Modern Democracy*. New York: Harper & Brothers.

Nacci, P. L. (1982) 'Sex and Sexual Aggression in Federal Prisons.' Unpublished manuscript, US Federal Prison System, Office of Research.

Nacci, P. L. and Kane, T. R. (1984) 'Sex and sexual aggression in federal prisons: inmate involvement and employee impact,' *Federal Probation*, 8 (March): 46–53.

Nadelmann, E. (1989) 'Drug prohibition in the United States: costs, consequences, and alternatives,' *Science*, 245 (1 September): 939–47.

Nadelmann, E. (1991) 'The case of legalization,' in J. A. Inciardi (ed.), *The Drug Legalization Debate*. Newbury Park, CA: Sage.

Nadelmann, E. (2007) 'Common sense drug policy,' in J. Inciardi and K. McElrath (eds), *The American Drug Scene*. New York: Oxford University Press.

Nagel, I. H. and Hagan, J. (1982) 'Gender and crime: offense patterns and criminal court sanctions,' in N. Morris and M. Tonry (eds), *Crime and Justice*, Vol. 4. Chicago: University of Chicago Press, pp. 91–144.

Nagin, D. (1998) 'Criminal deterrence research at the outset of the twenty-first century,' in M. Tonry (ed.), *Crime and Justice: A Review of Research*, Vol. 23. Chicago: University of Chicago Press.

Natapoff, A. (2009) *Snitching: Criminal Informants and the Erosion of American Justice*. New York: University of New York Press.

Nathan, S. (2003a) 'Private prisons: emerging and transformative economies,' in A. Coyle, A. Campbell, and R. Neufeld (eds), *Capitalist Punishment: Prison Privatization and Human Rights*. Atlanta, GA: Clarity Press, pp. 189–201.

Nathan, S. (2003b) 'Prison privatization in the United Kingdom,' in A. Coyle, A. Campbell, and R. Neufeld (eds), *Capitalist Punishment: Prison Privatization and Human Rights*. Atlanta, GA: Clarity Press, pp. 162–78.

Nathan, S. (2004) 'Globalization and private prisons,' *Howard League Magazine*, 22 (31): 7–8.

Nathan, S. (2010) *Prison Privatization Report International*. Available at: http://www.psiru.org/ppri.asp.

Nation (1994) 'The caning of Michael Fay,' June 15, p. 544.

National Center on Addiction and Substance Abuse (CASA) (1998) *Behind Bars: Substance Abuse and America's Prison Population*. New York: Columbia University.

National Commission on Acquired Immune Deficiency Syndrome (1991) *Report – HIV Disease in Correctional Facilities*. Washington, DC: National Commission on AIDS.

National Conference of Superintendents of Training Schools and Reformatories (1962) *Institutional Rehabilitation of Delinquent Youth: Manual for Training School Personnel*. Albany, NY: Delmar.

National Council on Crime and Delinquency (1988) *Facts About Violent Juvenile Crime*. San Francisco: National Council on Crime and Delinquency.

National Council on Crime and Delinquency (1989) *The Impact of the War on Drugs*. San Francisco: National Council on Crime and Delinquency.

National Council on Crime and Delinquency (1991) *Juvenile Justice Policy Statement*. San Francisco: National Council on Crime and Delinquency.

National Institute of Drug Abuse (2007) 'Advances in therapeutic communities,' in J. Inciardi and K. McElrath (eds), *The American Drug Scene*. New York: Oxford University Press.

National Minority Advisory Council on Criminal Justice (1982) *The Inequality of Justice: A Report on Crime and the Admission of Justice*. Washington, DC: US Government Printing Office.

National Probation Association (1939) *John Augustus, First Probation Officer*. Washington, DC: National Probation Association.

Naughton, M. (2007) *Re-Thinking Miscarriages of Justice*. Basingstoke: Palgrave Macmillan.

Navarro, M. (1994) 'The inmate gangs of Rikers Island,' *New York Times*, May 8, pp. L29, L36.

Nellis, M. (2009) 'The aesthetics of redemption: released prisoners in American film and literature,' *Theoretical Criminology*, 13 (1): 129–46.

Nelsen, C., Corzine, J., and Huff-Corzine, L. (1994) 'The violent West reexamined: a research note on regional homicide rates,' *Criminology*, 32 (1): 149–61.

Nelson, J. F. (1991) 'Disparity in the incarceration of minorities in New York State,' in M. J. Lynch and E. B. Patterson (eds), *Race and Criminal Justice*. New York: Harrow & Heston.

Nelson, J. F. (1994) 'A dollar a day: sentencing misdemeanants in New York State,' *Journal of Research in Crime and Delinquency*, 31 (2): 183–201.

Nelson, J. (1998) 'Comparing public and private prison costs,' in D. McDonald, E. Fournier, M. Russell-Einhorn, and S. Crawford (eds), *Private Prisons in the United States: An Assessment of Current Practice*. Boston: Abt. Associates Inc.

Nelson, L. (2001) 'Killing kids,' in L. Nelson and B. Foster (eds), *Death Watch: A Death Penalty Anthology*. Upper Saddle River, NJ: Prentice Hall, pp. 59–74.

Nelson, L. and Foster, B. (2001) *Death Watch: A Death Penalty Anthology*. Upper Saddle River, NJ: Prentice Hall.

Nelson, W.R. and O'Toole, M. (1983) *New Generation Jails*. Boulder, CO: Library Information Specialists.

Nelson, W. R., O'Toole, M., Krauth, B., and Whitman, C. G. (1984) *Direct Supervision Models*. Washington, DC: National Institute of Corrections.

Neuspiel, D. R. *et al.* (1991) 'Maternal cocaine use and infant behavior,' *Neurotoxicology and Teratology*, 13 (March–April): 229–33.

New York State Commission of Correction (1987a) *Inquiry into Disturbances on Rikers Island, October 1986*. Albany, NY: New York State Commission of Correction.

New York State Commission of Correction (1987b) *Acquired Immune Deficiency Syndrome: A Demographic Profile of New York State Inmate Moralities, 1981–1986*. Albany, NY: New York State Commission of Correction.

New York State Commission of Correction (1991) *Investigation of Disturbances at Otis Bantum Correctional Center, August 14, 1990*. Albany, NY: New York State Commission of Correction.

New York Times (1981) 'Violence at Texas department of corrections,' December 13, p. 44.

New York Times (1989a) 'Inmates and guards join in suit on state of crowded jail in Seattle,' March 16, p. 9.

New York Times (1989b) 'Plan will put Jersey inmates in tents,' August 16, p. 11.

New York Times (1989c) 'Who wants new prisons? In New York, all of upstate,' June 9, pp. B1, B2.

New York Times (1989d) 'Missouri fetus unlawfully jailed, suit says,' August 11, p. 20.

New York Times (1990) 'States' prisons continue to bulge, overwhelming efforts at reform,' May 20, pp. A1, A32.

New York Times (1991a) 'Study finds abuse in high security prisons,' November 15, p. A15.

New York Times (1991b) '4 prisoners trapped in their cells, are killed by smoke from fire at Missouri jail,' September 15, p. 18.

New York Times (1992a) 'College official who released list of black students is demoted,' September 18, p. B2.

New York Times (1992b) '$304,000 awarded to prisoner in lawsuit,' August 8, p. 27.

New York Times (1993a) 'Inmates fight "work or be shackled" policy,' September 5, p. 43.

New York Times (1993b) 'Jail's use of special restraints is condemned by rights groups,' April 27, p. B4.

New York Times (1993c) 'Nuclear guinea pigs,' January 5, p. A14.

New York Times (1993d) 'Suit saying Quayle bought marijuana is dismissed,' October 10, p. 23.

New York Times (1994a) 'Tribal panel in Alaska banishes 2 teenagers,' September 4, p. 20.

New York Times (1994b) '4 jail officers accused in beating death,' October 5, p. B8.

New York Times (1994c) (Editorial) 'Don't trample prisoners' rights,' March 27, p. E16.

New York Times (1994d) 'Federal inquiry on county jail focuses on inmate punishment,' April 8, p. B7.

New York Times (1994e) 'Residents of dying California town see future in a prison,' May 8, p. 28.

New York Times (1996) 'Chain gangs for women cause furor,' April 28, p. 30.

New York Times (1998) 'Appeals in ex-Panther's case,' February 1, p. 22.

New York Times (2000) 'Dispute rises in Peru's handling of Lori Berenson's terror trial,' July 18, p. A5.

New York Times (2001a) 'Police procedure investigated after search of 10 teenagers,' May 25, p. B7.

New York Times (2001b) 'California drug program begins, despite Los Angeles's skepticism,' July 3, p. A10.

New York Times (2002a) 'Panel criticizes restraints on young inmates,' December 5, p. D5.

New York Times (2002b) 'Nigerian woman condemned to death by stoning is acquitted,' March 26, p. A5.

New York Times (2002c) 'Pakistani woman recalls jury-ordered rape,' July 6, p. A6.

New York Times (2002d) 'Council in Pakistan orders gang rape,' July 6, p. A4.

New York Times (2002e) 'Another death row ruling,' June 25, p. A24.

New York Times (2002f) 'The disgrace of juvenile executions,' October 24, p. A34.

New York Times (2004) 'Abu Ghraib, whitewashed,' July 24, p. A12.

New York Times (2005a) 'Abu Ghraib, whitewashed again,' March 11, p. A22.

New York Times (2005b) 'Phantom voters, thanks to the census,' December 27, p. A22.

New York Times (2005c) 'Patterns of abuse,' May 23, p. A18.

New York Times (2005d) '2 officers punished in 2003 for mistreatment of detainees,' May 18, p. A10.

New York Times (2005e) 'Abu Ghraib, whitewashed again,' March 11, p. A22.

New York Times (2006) 'Counting noses in prisons,' April 18, p. A26.

New York Times (2008a) 'The FISA follies, redux,' January 26, pp. EV1–2.

New York Times (2008b) 'Costs of incarceration' (editorial), April 4, p. EV1.

Newburn, T. (2007) *Criminology*. Cullompton: Willan.

Newburn, T. and Jones, T. (2005) 'Symbolic politics and penal populism: the long shadow of Willie Horton,' *Crime, Media, Culture*, pp. 72–87.

Newburn, T. and Jones, T. (2007) 'Symbolising crime control: reflections of zero tolerance,' *Theoretical Criminology*, 11: 122–34.

Newman, D. J. (2002) 'Prisons don't work,' in T. Gray (ed.), *Exploring Corrections*. Boston: Allyn & Bacon, pp. 243–9.

Newman, G. (1978) *The Punishment Response*. New York: Lippincott.

Newman, G. and Marongui, P. (1990) 'Penological reform and the myth of Beccaria,' *Criminology*, 28 (2): 325–46.

Newman, M. (2001) '"Bloodied but unbowed": Joe Clark, with a reputation as tough taskmaster, finds himself accused of abuse at youth center,' *New York Times*, December 23, p. NJ4.

Newsweek (1968) 'Arkansas prison scandal,' February 12, pp. 42–3.

Newsweek (1980) 'The killing ground,' February 18, pp. 66–76.

Newsweek (1989) 'The Bundy carnival: a thirst for revenge provokes a raucous send-off,' February 6, p. 66.

Newsweek (1993) 'America's nuclear secrets,' December 27, pp. 14–17.

Nielsen, A., Lee, M., and Martinez, R. (2005) 'Integrating race, place and motive in social organization theory: lessons from a comparison of Black and Latino homicide types in two immigrant destination cities,' *Criminology*, 43 (3): 837–72.

Nielson, M. (2000) 'Stolen lands, stolen lives: Native Americans in criminal justice,' in Criminal Justice Collective of Northern Arizona University (ed.), *Investigating Differences: Human and Cultural Relations in Criminal Justice*. Boston: Allyn & Bacon, pp. 47–58.

Nielson, M. and Silverman, R. A. (1996) *Native Americans, Crime, and Justice*. Boulder, CO: Westview.

Nieves, E. (1998) 'California examines brutal, deadly prisons,' *New York Times*, November 7, p. A7.

Nieves, E. (2001) 'Recalling internment and saying "never again,"' *New York Times*, September 28, pp. EV1–2.

Nieves, E. (2002) 'Freed from jail despite his pleas, 92-year-old is found dead in river,' *New York Times*, July 12, p. A12.

Nobling, T., Spohn, C., and DeLone, M. (1998) 'A tale of two counties: unemployment and sentence severity,' *Justice Quarterly*, 15 (3): 459–85.

Noel, P. (2001) 'Jailhouse rocked,' *Village Voice*, September 18, p. 50.

Norris, R. L. (1985) 'Prison Reformers and Penitential Publicists in France, England, and the United States, 1774–1847.' Unpublished dissertation, American University, Washington, DC.

Nossiter, A. (1993) 'As boot camps for criminals multiply, skepticism grows,' *New York Times*, December 18, pp. A1, A9.

Not With Our Money (2002) *Students Stop Prisons-for-Profit*. New York: Not With Our Money.

Nuzum, M. (1998) 'The commercialization of justice: public good or private greed?' *Critical Criminologist*, 1: 5–8.

O'Brien, P. (2001) *Making It in the 'Free World'*. Albany, NY: State University of New York Press.

O'Carroll, P. W. and Mercy, J. A. (1989) 'Regional variation in homicide rates: why is the West so violent?' *Violence and Victims*, 4: 17–25.

O'Leary, V. (1985) 'Reshaping community corrections,' *Crime and Delinquency*, 31: 349–66.

O'Leary, V. and Clear, T. R. (1982) *Controlling the Offender in the Community*. Lexington, MA: Lexington Books.

O'Mahony, P. (2008) *The Irish War on Drugs: The Seductive Folly of Prohibition*. Manchester: Manchester University Press.

O'Malley, P. (1999) 'Volatile and contradictory punishment,' *Theoretical Criminology*, 3: 175–96.

O'Malley, P. (2009) 'Theorizing fines,' *Punishment and Society*, 11 (1): 67–83.

O'Malley, P. (2010) *The Currency of Justice: Fines and Damages in a Consumer Society*. London: Routledge Cavendish.

Office of Juvenile Justice and Delinquency Prevention (1990) *Growth in Minority Detentions Attributed to Drug Law Violators*. Washington, DC: US Government Printing Office.

Office of Juvenile Justice and Delinquency Prevention (1992a) *Arrests of Youth, 1990*. Washington, DC: US Government Printing Office.

Office of Juvenile Justice and Delinquency Prevention (1992b) *Preserving Families to Prevent Delinquency*. Washington, DC: US Government Printing Office.

Office of Juvenile Justice and Delinquency Prevention (1993a) 'Characteristics of chronic offenders,' *Juvenile Justice*, Spring/Summer, p. 29.

Office of Juvenile Justice and Delinquency Prevention (1993b) *Children in Custody, 1991: Private Facilities*. Washington, DC: US Government Printing Office.

Office of Juvenile Justice and Delinquency Prevention (1993c) *Children in Custody, 1991: Public Facilities*. Washington, DC: US Government Printing Office.

Office of Juvenile Justice and Delinquency Prevention (1994) 'Disproportionate minority representation,' *Juvenile Justice*, II (1): 21.

Office of the Attorney General of the State of New Mexico (1980) *Report of the Attorney General on the February 2 and 3, 1980, Riot at the Penitentiary of New Mexico*. Santa Fe, NM: Office of the Attorney General of the State of New Mexico.

Office of the National Drug Control Policy (1989) *National Drug Control Strategy*. Washington, DC: US Government Printing Office.

Office of the National Drug Control Policy (2000) *Drug Policy Information Clearinghouse: Fact Sheet, March 2000*. Washington, DC: US Department of Justice.

Office of the National Drug Control Policy (2010a) 'ONDCP Update,' *Newsletter of the Office of National Drug Control Policy*, Vol. 1, Issue 1, January. Washington, DC: Office of the National Drug Control Policy.

Office of the National Drug Control Policy (2010b) *National Drug Control Budget*. Washington, DC: Office of the National Drug Control Policy.

Ogawa, B. K. (1999) *Color of Justice*. Boston: Allyn & Bacon.

Ogden, C. K. (1932) *Bentham's Theory of Fictions*. London: Kegan Paul.

Ogle, R. S. (1999) 'Prison privatization: an environmental Catch 22,' *Justice Quarterly*, 16 (3): 579–600.

Ogletree, C. (2002) 'Black man's burden: race and the death penalty in America,' *Oregon Law Review*, 81: 15–38.

Ogletree, C. and Sarat, A. (2006) *From Lynch Mobs to the Killing State*. New York: New York University Press.

Ogletree, C. and Sarat, A. (2009) *The Road to Abolition? The Future of Capital Punishment in the United States*. New York: New York University Press.

Ohlin, L. H., Piven, and H., Pappenfort, D. (1956) 'Major dilemmas of the social worker in probation and parole,' *National Probation and Parole Association Journal*, 11: 211–25.

Olivero, J. M. (1990) 'The treatment of AIDS behind the walls of correctional facilities,' *Social Justice*, 17 (1): 113–25.

Olivero, J. M. (1992) 'AIDS in prisons: judicial and administrative dilemmas and strategies,' in P. J. Benekos and A. V. Merlo (eds), *Corrections: Dilemmas and Directions*. Cincinnati, OH: Anderson.

Olson, E. (2002) 'Fair penalties or torture? U.N. at odds with Saudis,' *New York Times*, May 19, p. A5.

Onishi, N. (2009a) 'A remote island seeks a boom without a bust,' *New York Times*, November 26, pp. EV1–3.

Onishi, N. (2009b) 'Australia puts its refugee problem on a remote island, behind razor wire,' *New York Times*, November 26, p. A5, A12.

Onwudiwe, I. D. and Lynch, M. J. (2000) 'Reopening the debate: a reexamination of the need for a black criminology,' *Social Pathology*, 6 (3): 182–98.

Ostrow, R. (1992) 'FBI director announces crackdown on carjacking,' *Los Angeles Times*, September 16, p. A9.

Oswald, R. B. (1972) *Attica: My Story*. New York: Doubleday.

Ottu, N. (2000) 'Let punishment and treatment fit the culture,' *Justice Professional*, 12 (3): 253–75.

Owen, B. (1988) *The Reproduction of Social Control: A Study of Prison Workers in San Quentin*. New York: Praeger.

Owen, B. (1998) *'In the Mix': Struggle and Survival in a Women's Prison*. Albany, NY: State University of New York Press.

Owen, B. (2003) 'Understanding women in prison,' in J. I. Ross and S. Richards (eds), *Convict Criminology*. Belmont, CA: Thomson Wadsworth.

Oxenhandler, N. (2002) 'Carted away: in San Francisco, the possessions of the homeless are swept out of sight,' *New York Times Magazine*, February 3, pp. 42–3.

Paczensky, S. (2001) 'The wall of silence: prison rape and feminist politics,' in D. Sabo, T. Kupers, and W. London (eds), *Prison Masculinities*. Philadelphia: Temple University Press, pp. 127–32.

Padilla, F. M. and Santiago, L. (1993) *Outside the Wall: A Puerto Rican Woman's Struggle*. New Brunswick, NJ: Rutgers University Press.

Page, J. (2002) 'Violence and incarceration: a personal observation,' in L. Fiftal and P. Cromwell (eds), *Correctional Perspectives: Views from Academics, Practitioners, and Prisoners*. Los Angeles: Roxbury, pp. 147–9.

Pakulski, J. and Waters, M. (1996) *The Death of Class*. London: Sage.

Palmer, J. W. (2010) *Constitutional Rights of Prisoners* (9th edn). New Providence, NJ: Lexis/Nexis.

Palmer, J. and Palmer, S. (1999) *Constitutional Rights of Prisoners*. Cincinnati, OH: Anderson.

Palmer, T. (1983) 'The "effectiveness" issue today: an overview,' *Federal Probation*, 46: 3–10.

Parent, D. (1990) *Correctional Costs Through Offender Fees*. Washington, DC: National Institute of Justice.

Parent, D. (1993) 'Conditions of confinement,' *Juvenile Justice*, Spring/Summer, pp. 2–7.

Parent, D. (1996) 'Day reporting centers: an evolving intermediate sanction,' *Federal Probation*, 60 (December): 51–4.

Parenti, C. (1999) *Lockdown America: Police and Prisons in the Age of Crisis*. New York: Verso.

Parisi, N. (1980) 'Combining incarceration and probation,' *Federal Probation*, 44: 3–10.

Parisi, N. (1982) 'The prisoners' pressures and responses,' in N. Parisi (ed.), *Coping with Imprisonment*. Beverly Hills, CA: Sage.

Parker, R. N. (1989) 'Poverty, subculture of violence, and type of homicide,' *Social Forces*, 67: 983–1007.

Parr, S. (2009) 'Confronting the reality of anti-social behaviour,' *Theoretical Criminology*, 13 (3): 363–81.

Parsonage, W. H. and Miller, J. A. (1991) 'Berks County Prison Worker Safety Study.' Unpublished manuscript, University Park, PA.

Passell, P. (1975) 'The deterrent effect of the death penalty: a statistical test,' *Stanford Law Review*, 28 (1): 61–80.

Paternoster, R. (1983) 'Race of the victim and location of crime: the decision to seek the death penalty in South Carolina,' *Journal of Criminal Law and Criminology*, 74: 754–85.

Paternoster, R. (1984) 'Prosecutorial discretion in requesting the death penalty: a case of victim-based racial discrimination,' *Law and Society Review*, 18: 437–78.

Paternoster, R. (1987) 'The deterrent effect of the perceived certainty and severity of punishment: a review of the evidence and issues,' *Justice Quarterly*, 4 (June): 173–217.

Paternoster, R. (1991) *Capital Punishment in America*. New York: Lexington Books.

Paterson, C. (2008) 'Commercial crime control and the electronic monitoring of offenders in England and Wales,' *Social Justice*, 34: 98–110.

Patterson, E. B. and Lynch, M. J. (1991) 'Bias in formalized bail procedures,' in M. J. Lynch and E. B. Patterson (eds), *Race and Criminal Justice*. New York: Harrow & Heston.

Paulson, L. D. (2002) 'Tucker state farm,' in D. Levinson (ed.), *Encyclopedia of Crime and Punishment*. Thousand Oaks, CA: Sage, pp. 1641–2.

Paulus, P. B., Cox, C. V., McCain, G., and Chandler, J. (1975) 'Some effects of crowding in a prison environment,' *Journal of Applied Social Psychology*, 1: 86–91.

Paust, J. (2005) 'Executive plans and authorizations to violate international law concerning the treatment and interrogation of detainees,' *Columbia Journal of Transnational Law*, 43: 811–63.

Pavlich, G. (2005) *Governing Paradoxes of Restorative Justice*. London: Glasshouse Press.

Payne, A. (2009) 'Girls, boys, and schools: gender differences in the relationship between school-related factors and student deviance,' *Criminology*, 47 (4): 1167–200.

Peak, K. and Spencer, J. (1987) 'Crime in Indian country: another "trail of tears,"' *Journal of Criminal Justice*, 15: 485–94.

Pearce, J. (2002) 'Racial profiling,' *New York Times*, June 30, p. NJ6.

Peat, B. J. and L. T. Winfree (1992) 'Reducing the intro-institutional effects of "prisonization": a study of a therapeutic community for drug-using inmates,' *Criminal Justice and Behavior*, 19 (2): 206–25.

Peck, H. T. (ed.) (1922) *Harper's Dictionary of Classical Literature and Antiquity*. New York: American Book Company.

Pelz, M. (1996) 'Gangs,' in M. D. McShane and F. P. Williams (eds), *Encyclopedia of American Prisons*. New York: Garland, pp. 213–18.

Penal Reform International (1990) *International Instruments on Imprisonment*, Briefing No. 1. London: Penal Reform International.

Pepinsky, H. (1978) 'Communist anarchism as an alternative to the rule of criminal law,' *Contemporary Crisis*, 2: 315–27.

Pepinsky, H. (1991) *The Geometry of Violence and Democracy*. Bloomington, IN: Indiana University Press.

Pepinsky, H. (2010) 'Radical drug control,' in N. Frost, J. Freilich, and T. Clear (eds), *Contemporary Issues in Criminal Justice*. Belmont, CA: Wadsworth.

Perkinson, R. (2009) '"Hell exploded": prisoner music and memoir and the fall of convict leasing in Texas,' *Prison Journal*, 89 (1): 54S–69S.

Perry, B. (2000) 'Perpetual outsiders: criminal justice and the Asian American experience,' in Criminal Justice Collective of Northern Arizona (ed.), *Investigating Differences: Human and Cultural Relations in Criminal Justice*. Boston: Allyn & Bacon, pp. 102–11.

Persico, J. E. (2002) 'Life under suspicion,' *New York Times Book Review*, February 17, pp. 9–10.

Peters, J. (2009) 'Albany reaches deal to repeal 70s drug laws,' *New York Times*, March 25, pp. EV1–5.

Peters, T. (2002) 'The missing "x-factor": trust,' in T. Gray (ed.), *Exploring Corrections*. Boston: Allyn & Bacon, pp. 175–80.

Petersilia, J. (1983) *Racial Disparities in the Criminal Justice System*. Santa Monica, CA: Rand Corporation.

Petersilia, J. (1985a) 'Community supervision: trends and critical issues,' *Crime and Delinquency*, 31: 339–47.

Petersilia, J. (1985b) 'Probation and felony offenders,' *National Institute of Justice, Research in Brief*. Washington, DC: National Institute of Justice.

Petersilia, J. (1985c) *Probation and Felony Offenders*. Washington, DC: National Institute of Justice.

Petersilia, J. (1986) *Prison versus Population in California: Implications for Crime and Offender Recidivism*. Santa Monica, CA: Rand Corporation.

Petersilia, J. (1987) *House Arrest*, Report No. NCJ 1045559. Washington, DC: National Institute of Justice.

Petersilia, J. (1988) *Expanding Options for Criminal Sentencing*, Report No. R-3544-EMC. Santa Monica, CA: Rand Corporation.

Petersilia, J. (1993) 'Measuring the performance of community corrections,' in *Performance Measures for the Criminal Justice System*. Washington, DC: US Department of Justice.

Petersilia, J. (1997) *Community Corrections: Probation, Parole, and Intermediate Sanctions*. New York: Oxford University Press.

Peterson, C. (1982) 'Doing time with the boys: an analysis of women correctional officers in all-male facilities,' in B. Price and N. Sokoloff (eds), *The Criminal Justice System and Women*. New York: Clark Boardman.

Peterson, D. and Friday, P. (1975) 'Early release from incarceration: race as a factor in the use of shock probation,' *Journal of Criminal Law and Criminology*, 66: 79–87.

Peterson, R. D. and Bailey, W. C. (1991) 'Felony murder and capital punishment: an examination of the deterrence question,' *Criminology*, 29 (3): 367–98.

Peterson, R., Krivo, L., and Hagan, J. (2006) *The Many Colors of Crime: Inequalities of Race, Ethnicity, and Crime in America*. New York: New York University Press.

Pettit, B. and Western, B. (2004) 'Mass imprisonment and the life course: race and class inequality in U.S. incarceration,' *American Sociological Review*, 69: 151–69.

Pfohl, S. (1985) *Images of Deviance and Social Control*. New York: McGraw-Hill.

Philliber, S. (1987) 'Thy brother's keeper: a review of the literature on correctional officers,' *Justice Quarterly*, 4 (1): 9–38.

Phillips, C. (2008) 'Negotiating identities: ethnicity and social relations in a young offenders' institution,' *Theoretical Criminology*, 12 (3): 313–31.

Phillips, D. D. (1980) 'The deterrent effect of capital punishment: evidence of an old controversy,' *American Journal of Sociology*, 86: 139–48.

Phillips, K. (1990) *Politics of the Rich and Poor: Wealth and the American Electorate in the Reagan Aftermath*. New York: Random House.

Phillips, K., Nolan, J., and Pearl, M. (1990) 'Jogger trial rage,' *New York Post*, December 12, pp. 9, 34.

Physicians for Human Rights (2009) *Aiding Torture*. Washington, DC: Physicians for Human Rights.

Pickering, S. (2008) 'The new criminals: refugees and asylum seekers,' in T. Anthony and C. Cuneen (eds), *The Critical Criminology Companion*. Annandale, Australia: Hawkins Press.

Pièces originales et procedures du process fait à Robert-François Damiens, III, 1757.

Pierce, B. K. (1969) *A Half Century of Delinquents*. Montclair, NJ: Patterson Smith.

Pierson, E. J., Densmore, T. L., Shevlin, J. M., Madruga, O., and Childers, T. D. (2002) 'Working as a federal probation officer,' in T. Gray (ed.), *Exploring Corrections*. Boston: Allyn & Bacon, pp. 282–93.

Pious, R. M. (2006) *The War on Terrorism and the Rule of Law*. Los Angeles: Roxbury.

Pisciotta, A. W. (1982) 'Saving the children: the promise and practices of Parens Patriae, 1838–1898,' *Crime and Delinquency*, 28: 410–25.

Pisciotta, A. W. (1983) 'Scientific reform: the "new penology" at Elmira, 1876–1900,' *Crime and Delinquency*, 29: 613–30.

Pitt, D. (1989) 'Jogger's attackers terrorized at least 9 in 2 hours,' *New York Times*, April 22, pp. 1, 30.

Pitts, J. (2008) *Reluctant Gangsters: The Changing Face of Youth Crime*. Cullompton: Willan.

Piven, F. F. and Cloward, R. A. (1971) *Regulating the Poor: The Functions of Public Welfare*. New York: Vintage Books.

Pizarro, J. and Narag, R. (2008) 'Supermax prisons: what we know, what we do not know, and where are we going,' *Prison Journal*, 88: 23–42.

Plant, R. (1986) *The Pink Triangle: The Nazi War on Homosexuals*. New York: Henry Holt.

Platt, T. (1977 [1969]) *The Child Savers*. Chicago: University of Chicago Press.

Platt, T. (1982) 'Crime and punishment in the United States: immediate and long-term reforms from a Marxist perspective,' *Crime and Social Justice*, 18: 38–45.

Platt, T. (1985) 'Criminology in the 1980s: progressive alternatives to "law and order,"' *Crime and Social Justice*, 21–2: 191–9.

Ploeger, M. (1997) 'Youth unemployment and delinquency: reconsidering a problematic relationship,' *Criminology*, 35 (4): 659–76.

Pogrebin, M. (1978) 'Role conflict among corrections officers in treatment oriented institutions,' *International Journal of Offender Therapy and Comparative Criminology*, 22 (2): 149–55.

Pogrebin, M. (1980) 'Challenge to authority for correctional officers: a conflicting organizational dilemma,' *Journal of Offender Counseling, Services and Rehabilitation*, 4 (4): 337–42.

Pogrebin, M. and Atkins, B. (1983) 'Organizational conflict in correctional institutions,' *Journal of Offender Counseling, Services and Rehabilitation*, 7 (1): 23–31.

Pollak, O. (1950) *The Criminality of Women*. Philadelphia: University of Pennsylvania Press.

Pollock, J. M. (2002) 'Prisoners' rights,' in D. Levinson (ed.), *Encyclopedia of Crime and Punishment*. Thousand Oaks, CA: Sage, pp. 1237–49.

Pollock-Byrne, J. M. (1990) *Women, Prison, and Crime*. Pacific Grove, CA: Brooks/Cole.

Polsky, H. (1962) *Cottage Six*. New York: Russell/Sage.

Poole, E. and Regoli, R. (1980a) 'Role stress, custody orientation and disciplinary actions: a study of prison guards,' *Criminology*, 18 (August): 215–26.

Poole, E. D. and Pogrebin, M. R. (1991) 'Changing jail organization and management: toward improved employee utilization,' in J. A. Thompson and G. L. Mays (eds), *American Jails: Public Policy Issues*. Chicago: Nelson-Hall.

Poole, E. and Regoli, R. (1980b) 'Work relations and cynicism among prison guards,' *Criminal Justice and Behavior*, 7 (September): 303–14.

Poole, E. and Regoli, R. (1981) 'Alienation in prison: an examination of work relations among prison guards,' *Criminology*, 19 (August): 251–70.

Porporino, F. J. (1986) 'Managing violent individuals in correctional settings,' *Journal of Interpersonal Violence*, 1 (2): 213–37.

Porporino, F. J. and Dudley, K. (1984) *An Analysis of the Effects of Overcrowding in Canadian Penitentiaries*. Ottawa: Correctional Service of Canada.

Porporino, F. J. and Marton, J. P. (1983) *Strategies to Reduce Prison Violence*. Ottawa: Correctional Service of Canada.

Portillos, E. (2002) 'Latinos, gangs, and drugs,' in R. Mann and M. Zatz (eds), *Images of Color, Images of Crime*. Los Angeles, Roxbury, pp. 192–200.

Possley, M. (1980) 'Inmates using an out – they sue,' *Chicago Sun Times*, October 15, p. 20.

Potler, C. (1988) *AIDS in Prison: A Crisis in New York State Corrections*. New York: Correctional Association of New York.

Potter, G. and Kappeler, V. (1998) *Constructing Crime: Perspectives on Making News and Social Problems*. Prospect Heights, IL: Waveland Press.

Poveda, T. G. (2001) 'Estimating wrongful convictions,' *Justice Quarterly*, 18 (3): 689–708.

Powers, E. (1966) *Crime and Punishment in Early Massachusetts*. Boston: Beacon.

Powers, G. (1826) *A Brief Account of the Construction, Management and Discipline of the New York State Prison at Auburn*. Auburn, NY: Henry Hall.

Pranis, K. (1998) 'Letter to the editor,' *Nation*, March 16, pp. 2–3.

Pranis, K. (2003) 'Campus activism defeats multinational's prison profiteering,' in T. Herivel and P. Wright (eds), *Prison Nation: The Warehousing of America's Poor*. New York: Routledge, pp. 156–63.

Pratt, J. (2006) 'The dark side of paradise: explaining New Zealand's history of high imprisonment,' *British Journal of Criminology*, 46: 541–60.

Pratt, J. (2007) *Penal Populism*. London: Routledge.

Pratt, J. (2008) 'Scandinavian exceptionalism in an era of penal excess,' *British Journal of Criminology*, 48: 275–92.

Pratt, J., Brown, D., Brown, M., Hallsworth, S., and Morrison, W. (2005) *The New Punitiveness: Trends, Theories, Perspectives*. Cullompton: Willan.

Pratt, T. and Maahs, J. (1999) 'Are private prisons more cost-effective than public prisons? A meta-analysis of evaluation research studies,' *Crime and Delinquency*, 45: 358–71.

Prejean, H. (1993) *Dead Man Walking: An Eyewitness Account of the Death Penalty in the United States*. New York: Random House.

Presdee, M. (2001) *Cultural Criminology and the Carnival of Crime*. New York: Routledge.

President's Commission on Law Enforcement and Administration of Justice (1967) *The Challenge of Crime in a Free Society*. Washington, DC: US Government Printing Office.

Press, A. (1986) 'Inside America's toughest prison,' *Newsweek*, October 6, pp. 46–61.

Press, E. (2003) 'Tortured logic: thumbscrewing international law,' *Amnesty Magazine*, online at: http://www.amnestyusa.org .

Price, B. (1994) 'The criminologist and the Indian,' *The Criminologist*, 19 (6): 1, 4–5, 24.

Price, R. H. and Smith, S. S. (1985) 'Two decades of reform in mental health system,' in E. Seidman (ed.), *Handbook of Social Intervention*. Beverly Hills, CA: Sage.

Priest, D. and Gellman, B. (2002) 'U.S. decries abuse but defends interrogations "stress and duress" tactics used on terrorism suspects held in secret overseas facilities,' *Washington Post*, December 26, p. A1.

PRNewswire (2001) 'Wackenhut corrections open Val Verde correctional facility,' January 19, pp. EV1–2.

Program Services Office (1983) *Probation Classification and Service Delivery Approach*. Los Angeles County Probation Department.

Provine, D. M. (2007) *Unequal Under Law: Race in the War on Drugs*. Chicago: University of Chicago Press.

Pung, O. B. (2002) 'A defense of prisons,' in T. Gray (ed.), *Exploring Corrections*. Boston: Allyn & Bacon, pp. 237–42.

Purdum, T. S. (2000) 'Ex-black panther wins long legal battle,' *New York Times*, April 27, p. A8.

Purdy, M. (2000) 'For paralyzed inmate, rigid drug laws are the crueler trap,' *New York Times*, April 16, p. 35.

Quinney, R. (1980) *Class, State, and Crime*. New York: Longman.

Raab, S. (1992) 'Charges filed in crackdown at corrections: altered inmate records prompt hearings for 21,' *New York Times*, May 16, pp. 25–6.

Radelet, M. L. and Pierce, G. L. (1985) 'Race and prosecutorial discretion in homicide cases,' *Law and Society Review*, 19: 587–621.

Radelet, M. L., Bedau, H. A., and Putnam, C. E. (1992) *In Spite of Innocence: Erroneous Convictions in Capital Cases*. Boston: Northeastern University Press.

Rafter, N. (1985) *Partial Justice: State Prisons and Their Inmates, 1800–1935*. Boston: Northeastern.

Rafter, N. (1997) *Creating Born Criminals*. Urbana, IL: Illinois University Press.

Rafter, N. (2000a) *Shots in the Mirror: Crime Films and Society*. New York: Oxford University Press.

Rafter, N. (2000b) *Encyclopedia of Women and Crime*. Phoenix, AZ: Orix Press.

Rafter, N. (2001) 'Partial justice: women, prisons, and social control,' in E. Latessa, A. Holsinger, J. Marquart, and J. Sorensen (eds), *Correctional Contexts: Contemporary and Classical Readings*. Los Angeles: Roxbury, pp. 35–48.

Rafter, N. (2006) *Shots in the Mirror: Crime Films and Society*. New York: New York University Press.

Ramirez, A. (1994) 'Privatizing America's prisons, slowly,' *New York Times*, August 14, pp. A3, A6.

Raskin, J. (1991) 'Remember Korematsu: a precedent for Arab-Americans?' *The Nation*, February 4, pp. 117–18.

Raupp, E. R. (1978) *Toward Positive Leadership for Initial Entry Training: A Report by the Task Force on Initial Entry Training Leadership*. Fort Monroe, VA: United States Army Training and Doctrine Command.

Rayman, G. (2009a) 'Rikers fight,' *Village Voice*, February 4–10, pp. 13–16.

Rayman, G. (2009b) 'Rikers fight club: jail guard indicted for pitting inmates against each other,' *Village Voice*, April 9–15, pp. 14, 16.

Rayman, G. (2009c) 'Knockout punch,' *Village Voice*, April 15–21, pp. 13–14.

Reddington, F. and Sapp, A. (2002) 'Juveniles in adult prisons: problems and prospects,' in L. Fiftal and P. Cromwell (eds), *Correctional Perspectives: Views from Academics, Practitioners, and Prisoners*. Los Angeles: Roxbury, pp. 255–61.

Reddington, F. P. and Sluder, R. D. (1993) *Suicide in Jails: Patterns by Gender*. Paper presented at the Annual Meeting of the Academy of Criminal Justice Sciences. Kansas City, MO.

Reed, E. F. (1993) *The Penry Penalty: Capital Punishment and Offenders with Mental Retardation*. Landam, MD: University Press of America.

Reed, S. O. (1993) 'The criminalization of pregnancy: drugs, alcohol, and AIDS,' in R. Muraskin and T. Alleman (eds), *It's a Crime: Women and Justice*. Englewood Cliffs, NJ: Regents/Prentice Hall.

Reed, W. L. (1984) *Racial Differentials in Juvenile Court Decision Making: Final Report*. Washington, DC: US Department of Justice, National Institute for Juvenile Justice and Delinquency Prevention.

Regoli, R., Poole, E. D., and Pogrebin, M. (1986) 'Working in jail: some observations on the work relations of jailers,' in D. B. Kalinich and J. Klofas (eds), *Sneaking Inmates Down the Alley: Problems and Prospects in Jail Management*. Springfield, IL: Charles C. Thomas.

Reiman, J. (2001) *The Rich Get Richer and the Poor Get Prison: Ideology, Class, and Criminal Justice* (6th edn). Boston: Allyn & Bacon.

Reiman, J. (2009) 'Should we reform punishment or discard it?' *Punishment and Society*, 11: 395–404.

Reimers, D. M. (1998) *Unwelcome Strangers: American Identity and the Turn Against Immigration*. New York: Columbia University Press.

Reinarman, C. (2007) 'The social impact of drugs and the war on drugs: the social construction of drug scares,' in J. Inciardi and K. McElrath (eds), *The American Drug Scene*. New York: Oxford University Press.

Reisig, M. (1998) 'Rates of disorder in higher-custody of state prisons: a comparative analysis of managerial practices,' *Crime and Delinquency*, 44: 229–44.

Rendleman, D. (1971) 'Parens Patriae: from Chancery to the juvenile court,' *South Carolina Law Review*, 23: 205–15.

Renzema, M. (1992) 'Home confinement programs: development, implementation, and impact,' in J. Byrne, A. Lurigio, and J. Petersilia (eds), *Smart Sentencing: The Emergence of Intermediate Sanctions*. Newbury Park, CA: Sage.

Reuters (2001) 'US to listen in on some inmate-lawyer talks,' November 13, pp. EV1–3.

Rex, S. (2005) *Reforming Community Penalties*. Cullompton: Willan.

Rhoden, E. (1994) 'Disproportionate minority representation: first steps to a solution,' *Juvenile Justice*, Spring/Summer, pp. 9–14.

Rhodes, E. (2003) 'The imperial logic of Bush's liberal agenda,' *Survival*, 45 (1): 131–54.

Richards, S. C. (1995) *The Structure of Prison Release*. New York: McGraw-Hill.

Richards, S. (2008) 'USP Marion: the first federal supermax,' *Prison Journal*, 88: 6–22.

Richards, S. C. and Jones, R. S. (1997) 'Perpetual incarceration machine: structural impediments to postprison success,' *Journal of Contemporary Criminal Justice*, 13 (1): 4–22.

Richards, S., Terry, C., Murphy, D. (2002) 'Lady hacks and gentleman convicts,' in L. Alarid and P. Cromwell (eds), *Correctional Perspectives: Views From Academics, Practitioners, and Prisoners*. Los Angeles: Roxbury, pp. 207–16.

Richardson, G. A. (1992) 'Prenatal Cocaine Exposure.' Unpublished paper, Western Psychiatric Institute and Clinic, Pittsburgh, PA.

Richardson, G. A. and Day, N. L. (1991) 'Maternal and neonatal effects of moderate cocaine use during pregnancy,' *Neurotoxicology and Teratology*, 13 (July–August): 455–60.

Richardson, L. (2002) 'Intensive probation supervision,' in D. Levinson (ed.), *Encyclopedia of Crime and Punishment*. Thousand Oaks, CA: Sage, pp. 908–12.

Rideau, W. (1992) 'The sexual jungle,' in W. Rideau and R. Wikberg (eds), *Life Sentences: Rage and Survival Behind Bars*. New York: Times Books.

Rideau, W. and Wikberg, R. (1992) *Life Sentences: Rage and Survival Behind Bars*. New York: Times Books.

Ridgeway, J. (1994) 'This is not only a test,' *Village Voice*, January 11, pp. 15–16.

Ridgeway, J. (2002) 'This is your prison on drugs,' *Village Voice*, April 9, p. 26.

Riding In, J. (2002) 'American Indians in popular culture: a Pawnee's experience and views,' in C. Mann and M. Zatz (eds), *Images of Color, Images of Crime*. Los Angeles: Roxbury, pp. 14–27.

Riedel, M. (1976) 'Discrimination in the imposition of the death penalty: a comparison of the characteristics of offenders, sentenced pre-Furman,' *Temple Law Quarterly*, 49: 261–83.

Riley, J. (2000) 'Sensemaking in prison: inmate identity as a working understanding,' *Justice Quarterly*, 17 (2): 359–76.

Risen, J. (2006) *State of War: The Secret History of the CIA and the Bush Administration*. New York: Free Press.

Risen, J. and Golden, T. (2006) '3 prisoners commit suicide at Guantánamo,' *New York Times*, June 11, pp. EV1–5.

Rittenhouse, A. (1991) 'The emergence of premenstrual syndrome as a social problem,' *Social Problems*, 38 (3): 412–25.

Roberts, J. (1994) *Escaping Prison Myths: Selected Topics in the History of Federal Corrections*. Washington, DC: American University Press.

Robertson, J. E. (1995) '"Fight or F…" and constitutional liberty: an inmate's right to self defense when targeted by aggressors,' *Indiana Law Review*, 29 (2): 339–63.

Robertson, J. E. (1999) 'Cruel and unusual punishment in United States prisons: sexual harassment among male inmates,' *American Criminal Law Review*, 36: 1–51.

Robertson, J. E. (2000a) 'Psychological injury and the prison litigation reform act: a "not exactly" equal protection analysis,' *Harvard Journal on Legislation*, 37 (1): 105–58.

Robertson, J. E. (2000b) 'The majority opinion as the social construction of reality: the Supreme Court and prison rules,' *Oklahoma Law Review*, 53 (2): 161–96.

Robertson, J. E. (2000c) 'Sexual harassment of male inmates: the case for new constitutional tort,' *Correctional Law Reporter*, 11 (6): 83–4, 96.

Robertson, J. E. (2001) 'The jurisprudence of the PLRA: inmates as "outsiders" and the countermajoritarian difficulty,' *Journal of Criminal Law and Criminology*, 92: 187–210.

Robinson, G. (2001) *By Order of the President: FDR and the Internment of Japanese Americans*. Cambridge, MA: Harvard University Press.

Rodriguez, J. (2006) *Civilizing Argentina: Science, Medicine, and the Modern State*. Chapel Hill, NC: University of North Carolina Press.

Rodriguez, L. (2002) 'The color of the skin is the color of the crime,' in R. Mann and M. Zatz (eds), *Images of Color, Images of Crime*. Los Angeles: Roxbury, pp. 33–6.

Rodriguez, N., Smith, H., and Zatz, M. (2009) 'Youth is enmeshed in a highly dysfunctional family: exploring the relationship among dysfunctional families, parental incarceration, and juvenile court decision making,' *Criminology*, 47 (1): 177–208.

Rogers, R. and Jolin, A. (1992) 'Electronic monitoring: a review of the empirical literature,' in T. Ellsworth (ed.), *Contemporary Community Corrections*. Prospect Heights, IL: Waveland.

Rohde, D. (2004) 'U.S. rebuked on Afghans in detention,' *New York Times*, March 8, p. A6.

Rohter, L. (1992) '"Processing" for Haitians is time in a rural prison,' *New York Times*, June 21, p. E18.

Rohter, L. (2002) 'A prison story that carries a personal meaning,' *New York Times*, August 4, pp. AR13, 22.

Rolland, M. (1997) *Descent Into Madness: An Inmate's Experience of the New Mexico State Prison Riot*. Cincinnati, OH: Anderson.

Rolland, M. (2002) 'Realities of fear,' in L. Fiftal and P. Cromwell (eds), *Correctional Perspectives: Views from Academics, Practitioners, and Prisoners*. Los Angeles: Roxbury, pp. 150–6.

Romano, J. (1993) 'Jobs at prisons go beyond license plates,' *New York Times* (New Jersey edition), October 10, pp. 1, 11, 13.

Rose, D. (2004) *Guantanamo: America's War on Human Rights*. London: Faber & Faber.

Rose, D. R. and Clear, T. R. (1998) 'Incarceration, social capital, and crime: implications for social disorganization theory,' *Criminology*, 36 (3): 441–80.

Rosenbaum, J. L. (1988) 'Age, race, and female offending,' *Journal of Contemporary Criminal Justice*, 4 (3): 125–38.

Rosenbaum, M. (1989) *Just Say What? An Alternative View on Solving America's Drug Problem*. San Francisco: National Council on Crime and Delinquency.

Rosenbaum, M. (2007) 'Safety first: a reality-based approach to teens, drugs, and drug education,' in J. Inciardi and K. McElrath (eds), *The American Drug Scene*. New York: Oxford University Press.

Rosenblum, R. and Whitcomb, D. (1978) *Montgomery County Work Release/Pre-Release Program*. Washington, DC: US Government Printing Office.

Rosencrance, J. (1986) 'Probation supervision: mission impossible,' *Federal Probation*, L (1): 25–31.

Rosencrance, J. (1988) 'Maintaining the myth of individual justice: probation pre-sentence reports,' *Justice Quarterly*, 5: 235–56.

Rosencrance, J. (1992) 'A typology of presentence probation investigators,' in T. Ellsworth (ed.), *Contemporary Community Corrections*. Prospect Heights, IL: Waveland.

Rosoff, S. M., Pontell, H. N., and Tillman, R. H. (2002) *Profit Without Honor: White-Collar Crime and the Looting of America*. Upper Saddle River, NJ: Prentice Hall.

Ross, J. (2000) *Varieties of State Crime and Its Control*. Monsey, NY: Criminal Justice Press.

Ross, J. G. and Heffernan, E. (1977) 'Women in a coed joint,' *Quarterly Journal of Corrections*, 1: 4.

Ross, J. I. (1998) *Cutting the Edge: Current Perspectives in Radical and Critical Criminology*. Westport, CT: Praeger.

Ross, J. I. and Richards, S. (2002) *Behind Bars: Surviving Prison*. New York: Alpha Books.

Ross, J. I. and Richards, S. (2003) *Convict Criminology*. Belmont, CA: Thomson/Wadsworth.

Ross, J. I. and Richards, S. (2009) *Beyond Bars: Rejoining Society After Prison*. New York: Alpha.

Ross, K. (2000) 'Residents bombard Wackenhut over prison site,' *Miami Herald*, November 2, pp. EV1–3.

Ross, K. (2001) 'Sexual abuse fears reach beyond Krome,' *Miami Herald*, January 7, pp. EV1–2.

Ross, M., Diamond, P., Liebling, A., and Saylor, W. (2008) 'Measurement of prison social climate,' *Punishment and Society*, 10 (4): 447–74.

Roth, K. (2002) *United States: Reports of Torture of Al-Qaeda Suspects, December 27*. New York: Human Rights Watch.

Rothman, D. J. (1971) *The Discovery of the Asylum: Social Order and Disorder in the New Republic*. Boston: Little, Brown.

Rothman, D. J. (1980) *Conscience and Convenience: The Asylum and Its Alternatives in Progressive America*. Boston: Little, Brown.

Rothman, D. J. (1990) *The Discovery of the Asylum: Social Order and Disorder in the New Republic* (2nd edn). Boston: Little, Brown.

Rothman, S. (1994) *Living in the Shadow of Death: Tuberculosis and the Social Experiment*. New York: Basic Books.

Rowan, J. R. and Hayes, L. M. (1995) *Training Curriculum on Suicide Detection and Prevention in Jails and Lockups* (2nd edn). Mansfield, MA: National Center on Institutions and Alternatives.

Rubin, A. and Rahimi, S. (2010) 'Detainees at Bagram are named by US,' *New York Times*, January 16, pp. EV1–5.

Rubin, P. (2009) 'Don't scrap the death penalty,' *Criminology and Public Policy*, 8 (4): 853–60.

Ruggiero, K. (1992) 'Honor, maternity, and the disciplining of women: infanticide in late nineteenth-century Buenos Aires,' *Hispanic American Historical Review* 72 (3): 353–73.

Ruggiero, K. (2004) *Modernity in the Flesh: Medicine, Law, and Society in Turn-of-the-Century Argentina*. Stanford, CA: Stanford University Press.

Ruggiero, V. and Welch, M. (2009) 'Power crime: special issue,' *Crime, Law and Social Change*, 51 (3/4).

Rusche, G. (1982 [1933]) 'Labor market and penal sanctions: thoughts on the sociology of criminal justice,' *Crime and Social Justice*, 10: 2–8.

Rusche, G. and Kirchheimer, O. (1968 [1939]) *Punishment and Social Structure*. New York: Russell & Russell.

Russell, K. (1998) *The Color of Crime: Racial Hoaxes, White Fear, Black Protectionism, Police Aggression, and Other Microaggressions*. New York: New York University Press.

Russell, K. (2002) '"Driving while black": corollary phenomena and collateral consequences,' in C. Reasons, D. Conley, and J. Debro (eds), *Race, Class, Gender, and Justice in the United States*. Boston: Allyn & Bacon, pp. 191–200.

Ryan, F. (1993) *The Forgotten Plague: How the Battle Against Tuberculosis Was Won – and Lost*. Boston: Little, Brown.

Sabates, R. (2008) 'Educational attainment and juvenile crime,' *British Journal of Criminology*, 48: 395–409.

Sabo, D., Kupers, T. A., and London, W. (2001) *Prison Masculinities*. Philadelphia: Temple University Press.

Sabol, W. J. (1989) 'Racially disproportionate prison populations in the United States,' *Contemporary Crisis*, 13: 405–32.

Sabol, W., West, H., and Cooper, M. (2009) *Prisoners in 2008*. Washington, DC: Bureau of Justice Statistics.

Sachar, E. (1990) 'Of rape and assault,' *New York Newsday*, August 19, pp. 3, 36.

Saenz, A. (1986) *Politics of a Riot*. Washington, DC: American Correctional Association.

Saewitz, M. (2002) 'An advocacy center alleges women's health needs are ignored and cells are overcrowded,' *Sarasota Herald Tribune* [Florida], October 17, pp. EV1–2.

Sagatun, I. J. (1993) 'Babies born with drug addiction: background and legal responses,' in R. Muraskin and T. Alleman (eds), *It's a Crime: Women and Justice*. Englewood Cliffs, NJ: Regents/Prentice Hall.

Sager, M. (1993) 'The State of Michigan vs. Gary Fannon: a tragic miscarriage of justice continues,' *Rolling Stone*, September, pp. 51–3, 70.

Said, E. (1978) *Orientalism*. New York: Pantheon.

Salvatore, R. D. (1992) 'Criminology, prison reform and the Buenos Aires working class, 1900–1920,' *Journal of Interdisciplinary History*, 23 (2): 279–99.

Salvatore, R. D. (1996) 'Penitentiaries, visions of class, and export economies: Brazil and Argentina compared,' in R. D. Salvatore and C. Aguirre (eds), *The Birth of the Penitentiary in Latin America*. Austin, TX: University of Texas Press, pp. 194–223.

Salvatore, R. D. (2007) 'Positivist criminology and state formation in modern Argentina, 1890–1940,' in P. Becker and R. Wetzell (eds), *Criminals and their Scientists*. New York: Cambridge University Press, pp. 253–80.

Sampson, R. and Lauritsen, J. (1997) 'Racial and ethnic disparities in crime and criminal justice in the United States,' in M. Tonry (ed.), *Ethnicity, Crime, and Immigration: Comparative and Cross-National Perspectives*, Vol. 21. Chicago: University of Chicago Press.

Sandberg, S. and Pedersen, W. (2009) *Street Capital: Black Cannabis Dealers in a White Welfare State*. Bristol: Policy Press.

Sanders, W. B. (1970) *Juvenile Offenders for a Thousand Years*. Chapel Hill, NC: University of North Carolina Press.

Sands, P. (2008) *Torture Team: Rumsfeld's Memo and the Betrayal of American Values*. New York: Palgrave Macmillan.

Santamour, M. B. (1989) *The Mentally Retarded Offender and Corrections*. Washington, DC: American Correctional Association.

Santayana, G. (1905) *The Life of Reason*. London: Constable.

Sante, L. (2004) 'The Abu Ghraib photos: here's-me-at-war.jpeg,' *International Herald Tribune*, May 12, p. 6.

Sarat, A. (2001) *When the State Kills: Capital Punishment and the American Condition*. Princeton, NJ: Princeton University Press.

Sarat, A. (2005) *Mercy on Trial: What It Means to Stop an Execution*. Princeton, NJ: Princeton University Press.

Sarat, A. (2008) 'Memorializing miscarriages of justice: clemency petitions in the killing state,' *Law and Society Review*, 42 (1): 183–224.

Sasson, T. (1995) *Crime Talk: How Citizens Construct a Social Problem*. New York: Aldine de Gruyter.

Saulny, S. (2002a) 'Lawsuit says city allows brutality by jail officers,' *New York Times*, September 7, p. B3.

Saulny, S. (2002b) 'Convictions and charges voided in '89 Central Park jogger attack,' *New York Times*, December 20, pp. A1, B5.

Savage, C. (2010) 'Obama team is divided on tactics against terrorism,' *New York Times*, March 28, pp. EV1–9.

Savelsberg, J. (2002) 'Cultures of control in modern societies,' *Law and Social Inquiry*, 27 (3): 685–710.

Schafer, S. (1970) *Compensation and Restitution to Victims of Crime* (2nd edn). Montclair, NJ: Patterson Smith.

Scheck, B., Neufeld, P., and Dwyer, J. (2000) *Actual Innocence*. New York: Doubleday.

Schemo, D. J. (2001) 'Students find drug law has big price: college aid, critics say '98 rule is biased against the poor,' *New York Times*, March 3, p. A12.

Schichor, D. and Sechrest, D. (1996) *Three Strikes and You're Out: Vengeance as Public Policy*. Thousand Oaks, CA: Sage.

Schiraldi, V. and Keppelhoff, M. (1997) 'As juvenile crime drops, experts back-pedal and public policy pays the price,' *Star Tribune*, June 5, p. 24A.

Schlossman, S. L. (1977) *Love and the American Delinquent*. Chicago: University of Chicago Press.

Schmidt, A. K. (1989) 'Electronic monitoring of offenders increases,' *NIJ Reports*, 212: 2–5.

Schmitt, E. (2005) '3 in 82nd Airborne say beating Iraqi prisoners was routine,' *New York Times*, September 24, pp. A1, A6.

Schneider, M. (2000) 'Moving past biological determinism in discussions of women and crime during the 1870s–1920s,' *Deviant Behavior*, 21: 407–27.

Schnittker, J. and John, A. (2007) 'Enduring stigma: the long-term effects of incarceration on health,' *Journal of Health and Social Behavior*, 48: 115–30.

Schrag, C. (1960) 'Leadership among prison inmates,' *American Sociological Review*, 3 (Fall): 11–16.

Schrag, C. (1961) 'Some foundations for theory of corrections,' in D. R. Cressey (ed.), *The Prison*. New York: Holt, Rinehart & Winston.

Schur, E. (1971) *Labelling Deviant Behavior*. New York: Harper & Row.

Schuster, L. (2003) *The Use and Abuse of Political Asylum in Britain and Germany*. London: Frank Cass.

Schwartz, B. (1971) 'Pre-institutional vs. situational influence in a correctional community,' *Journal of Criminal Law, Criminology and Police Science*, 61: 532–43.

Schwartz, H. (2002) 'Out of jail and out of food,' *New York Times*, March 31, p. A27.

Schwartz, J. (2010) 'Dungeons and dragons prison ban upheld,' *New York Times*, January 26, pp. EV1–3.

Schwartz, M. D. and Friedrichs, D. O. (1994) 'Postmodern thought and criminological discontent: new metaphors for understanding violence,' *Criminology*, 32 (2): 221–46.

Sciolino, E. (2002) 'Rehabilitation joins retribution in Saudi drug war,' *New York Times*, February 11, p. A2.

Scott, G. R. (1938) *The History of Corporal Punishment*. London: T. Werner Lawrie.

Scull, A. (1981) 'Deinstitutionalization and the rights of deviants,' *Journal of Social Issues*, 37: 6–20.

Scull, A. (1984) *Decarceration: Community Treatment and the Deviant: A Radical Approach*. Englewood Cliffs, NJ: Prentice Hall.

Sechrest, D. K. and Collins, W. C. (1989) *Jail Management and Liability Issues*. Miami, FL: Coral Gables.

Sechrest, L., White, S. O., and Brown, E. (1979) *The Rehabilitation of Criminal Offenders: Problems and Prospects*. Washington, DC: National Academy of Sciences.

Seis, M. C. and Elbe, K. L. (1991) 'The death penalty for juveniles: bridging the gap between an evolving standard of decency and legislative policy,' *Justice Quarterly*, 8 (4): 465–88.

Seiter, R. (2002) *Correctional Administration: Integrating Theory and Practice*. Upper Saddle River, NJ: Prentice Hall.

Selke, W. L. (1993) *Prisons in Crisis*. Bloomington, IN: Indiana University Press.

Sellin, T. (1926) 'Felippo Franci – a precursor of modern penology,' *Journal of Criminal Law and Criminology*, XXVII (May): 104–12.

Sellin, T. (1967) *Capital Punishment*. New York: Harper & Row.

Sellin, T. (1973) 'Enrico Ferri,' in H. Mannheim (ed.), *Pioneers in Criminology*. Montclair, NJ: Patterson Smith.

Sellin, T. (1976) *Slavery and the Penal System*. New York: Elsevier.

Selman, D. and Leighton, P. (2010) *Punishment for Sale: Private Prisons, Big Business, and the Incarceration Binge*. Lanham, MD: Rowman & Littlefield.

Semmes, R. (1938) *Crime and Punishment in Early Maryland*. Baltimore: Johns Hopkins University Press.

Sentencing Project (1997) *Intended and Unintended Consequences: State Racial Disparities in Imprisonment*. Washington, DC: Sentencing Project.

Sentencing Project (2002) *Life Sentences: Denying Welfare Benefits to Women Convicted of Drug Offenses*. Washington, DC: Sentencing Project.

Serrano, R. (2001) 'Ashcroft denies wide detainee abuse,' *Los Angeles Times*, October 17, pp. EV1–4.

Sever, B. and Reisner, R. L. (2001) 'Racial composition of municipal legislative governing bodies and spending on public assistance and police,' *Justice Professional*, 14 (1): 19–42.

Sewell, W. H. Jr (1999) 'The concept(s) of culture,' in V. E. Bonnell and L. Hunt (eds), *Beyond the Cultural Turn*. Berkeley, CA: University of California Press.

Sewell, W. H. Jr (2005) *The Logics of History*. Chicago: University of Chicago Press.

Shalev, S. (2009) *Supermax: Controlling Risk Through Solitary Confinement*. Cullompton: Willan.

Shane, S. (2010) 'Destroying CIA tapes wasn't opposed, memos say,' *New York Times*, February 22, pp. EV1–3.

Shapiro, B. (2001) 'All in the name of security: the administration is using September 11 to curtail our civil liberties,' *The Nation*, October 22, pp. 20–2.

Shapiro, B. (2002) 'Rethinking the death penalty,' *The Nation*, July 22–29, pp. 14–19.

Sharp, S. (2003a) 'Mothers in prison: issues in parent–child contact,' in S. Sharp (ed.), *The Incarcerated Woman: Rehabilitative Programming in Women's Prisons*. Upper Saddle River, NJ: Prentice Hall, pp. 151–65.

Sharp, S. (2003b) *The Incarcerated Woman: Rehabilitative Programming in Women's Prisons*. Upper Saddle River, NJ: Prentice Hall.

Shaw, A. (1966) *Convicts and the Colonies*. London: Faber & Faber.

Shaw, M. (1992) 'Issues of power and control: women in prison and their defenders,' *British Journal of Criminology*, 32 (4): 438–53.

Shearing, C. D. and Ericson, R. V. (1991) 'Culture as figurative action,' *British Journal of Sociology*, 42: 481–506.

Shefer, G. and Liebling, A. (2008) 'Prison privatization: in search of a business-like atmosphere,' *Criminology and Criminal Justice*, 8 (3): 261–78.

Shelden, R. (2001) *Controlling the Dangerous Classes: A Critical Introduction to the History of Criminal Justice*. Boston: Allyn & Bacon.

Shelden, R. G. and Brown, W. (2000) 'The crime control industry and the management of the surplus population,' *Critical Criminology*, 9 (1–2): 39–62.

Shelley, L. I. (1981) *Crime and Modernization*. Carbondale, IL: Southern Illinois University Press.

Shepherd, J. (2004) 'Murders of passion, execution delays, and the deterrence of capital punishment,' *Journal of Legal Studies*, 33: 283–321.

Sherill, R. (2001) 'Death trip: the American way of execution,' *The Nation*, January 8–15, pp. 13–34.

Shichor, D. (1995) *Punishment for Profit: Private Prisons/Public Concerns*. Thousand Oaks, CA: Sage.

Shichor, D. (1999) 'Privatizing correctional institutions: an organizing perspective,' *Prison Journal*, 79 (2): 226–49.

Shichor, D. (2002) 'Issues concerning private prisons,' in L. Fiftal and P. Cromwell (eds), *Correctional Perspectives: Views from Academics, Practitioners, and Prisoners*. Los Angeles; Roxbury, pp. 223–32.

Shinnar, S. and Shinnar, R. (1975) 'The effect of the criminal justice system on the control of crime: a quantitative approach,' *Law and Society Review*, 9: 581–611.

Shrage, L. (1994) *Moral Dilemmas of Feminism: Prostitution, Adultery and Abortion*. London: Routledge.

Shute, S., Hood, R., and Seemungal, F. (2005) *A Fair Hearing? Ethnic Minorities in the Criminal Courts*. Cullompton: Willan.

Sickmund, M. (2004) *Juveniles in Corrections*. Washington, DC: US Department of Justice, Office of Juvenile Justice and Delinquency Prevention.

Siegal, N. (2002a) 'Stopping abuse in prison,' in T. Gray (ed.), *Exploring Corrections*. Boston: Allyn & Bacon, pp. 134–40.

Siegal, N. (2002b) 'Lethal lottery,' in T. Gray (ed.), *Exploring Corrections*. Boston: Allyn & Bacon, pp. 122–6.

Sieverdes, C. M. and Bartollas, C. (1986) 'Security level and adjustment patterns in juvenile institutions,' *Journal of Criminal Justice*, 14 (1): 135–46.

Sifakis, C. (1992) *The Encyclopedia of American Crime*. New York: Smithmark.

Sigler, J. and Bezanson, T. (1970) 'Role perceptions among New Jersey probation officers,' *Rutgers Camden Law Journal*, 2: 256–60.

Silberman, M. (1995) *A World of Violence: Corrections in America*. Belmont, CA: Wadsworth.

Silby, C. and Wilson, M. (2004) 'Differentiating hostile and benevolent sexist attitudes toward positive and negative sexual female subtypes,' *Sex Roles*, 51: 687–96.

Silverman, R. A. (1996) 'Patterns of Native American crime,' in M. Nielson and R. Silverman (eds), *Native Americans, Crime, and Justice*. Boulder, CO: Westview, pp. 58–74.

Silverstein, K. (1998) 'America's private gulag,' in D. Burton-Rose (ed.), *The Celling of America: An Inside Look at the U.S. Prison Industry*. Boston: Common Courage, pp. 156–83.

Simmons, I. (1975) 'Interaction and Leadership Among Female Prisoners.' Unpublished dissertation, University of Missouri, Columbia.

Simmons, S. M. (1989) '*Thompson* v. *Oklahoma*: debating the constitutionality of juvenile executions,' *Pepperdine Law Review*, 16.

Simon, J. (1993) *Poor Discipline: Parole and the Social Control of the Underclass, 1890–1990*. Chicago: University of Chicago Press.

Simon, J. (1995) 'They died with their boots on: the boot camp and the limits of modern penality,' *Social Justice*, 22: 25–47.

Simon, J. (1998) 'Managing the monstrous: sex offenders and the new penology,' *Psychology, Public Policy and Law*, 4: 452–67.

Simon, J. (2000) '"The society of captives" in the era of hyper-incarceration,' *Theoretical Criminology*, 4: 285–308.

Simon, J. (2007) *Governing Through Crime: How the War on Crime Transformed American Democracy and Created a Culture of Fear*. New York: Oxford University Press.

Simon, L. M. J. (1993) 'Prison behavior and the victim-offender relationship among violent offenders,' *Justice Quarterly*, 10 (3): 489–506.

Simon, R. (1975) *Women and Crime*. Lexington, MA: Lexington Books.

Simon, R. and De Wall, C. (2009) *Prisons the World Over*. Lanham, MD: Rowman & Littlefield.

Simon, R. and Landis, J. (1991) *The Crimes Women Commit, the Punishment They Receive*. Lexington, MA: Lexington Books.

Simonsen, C. (1996) 'Federal Bureau of Prisons,' in M. McShane and F. Williams (eds), *Encyclopedia of American Prisons*. New York: Garland, pp. 203–7.

Simpson, S. (1989) 'Feminist theory, crime and justice,' *Criminology*, 27 (4): 605–32.

Simpson, S. S. (1991) 'Caste, class, and violent crime explaining differences in female offending,' *Criminology*, 29 (1): 115–35.

Sinden, J. (2003) 'The problem of prison privatization: the US experience,' in A. Coyle, A. Campbell, and R. Neufeld (eds), *Capitalist Punishment: Prison Privatization and Human Rights*. Atlanta, GA: Clarity Press, pp. 39–47.

Singer, P. W. (2005) 'Outsourcing war,' *Foreign Affairs*, March/April, pp. 119–33.

Sirica, J. (1991) 'Testimony on AIDS,' *New York Newsday*, May 19, p. 14.

Skinns, L. (2009) 'I'm a detainee: get me out of here: predictors of access to custodial advice in public and private police custody areas in England and Wales,' *British Journal of Criminology*, 49: 399–417.

Skovron, S. E., Scott, J. E., and Cullen, F. T. (1989) 'The death penalty for juveniles: an assessment of public support,' *Crime and Delinquency*, 35 (4): 546–61.

Slate, R. (1996) 'Correctional officers: stress,' in M. McShane and F. Williams (eds), *Encyclopedia of American Prisons*. New York: Garland, pp. 129–31.

Smart, C. (1995) *Law, Crime, and Sexuality: Essays in Feminism*. London: Sage.

Smelser, N. J. (1963) *Theory of Collective Behavior*. New York: Free Press.

Smeulers, A. and van Niekerk, S. (2009) 'Abu Ghraib and the war on terror – a case against Donald Rumsfeld,' *Crime, Law and Social Change*, 51: 327–49.

Smith, A. E. (1965) *Colonists in Bondage: White Servitude and Convict Labor in America, 1607–1776*. Chapel Hill, NC: University of North Carolina Press.

Smith, A. (1973) 'The conflict theory of riots,' in South Carolina Department of Corrections (Collective Violence Research Project), *Collective Violence in Correctional Institutions: A Search for Causes*. Columbia, SC: State Printing Company.

Smith, B. A. (1988) 'Military training in New York's Elmira Reformatory,' *Federal Probation*, March, pp. 33–40.

Smith, C. (2000) *Law and Contemporary Corrections*. Belmont, CA: West.

Smith, D. A., Visher, C. A., and Davidson, L. A. (1984) 'Equity and discretionary justice: the influence of race on police arrest decisions,' *Journal of Criminal Law and Criminology*, 75: 234–49.

Smith, D. E. (1988) 'Crowding and confinement,' in R. Johnson and H. Toch (eds), *The Pains of Imprisonment*. Prospect Heights, IL: Waveland.

Smith, N. (2001) 'Global social cleansing: postliberal revanchism and the export of zero tolerance,' *Social Justice*, 28 (3): 68–75.

Smith, P. (2003) 'Narrating the guillotine: punishment technology as myth and symbol,' *Theory, Culture and Society*, 20 (5): 27–51.

Smith, P. (2006) 'Executing executions: aesthetics, identity, and the problematic narratives of capital punishment ritual,' *Theory and Society*, 25: 235–61.

Smith, P. (2008) *Punishment and Culture*. Chicago: University of Chicago Press.

Smolowe, J. (1994) '… and throw away the key,' *Time*, February 7, pp. 55–9.

Smothers, M. (1995) 'Fairness and crack sentences,' *New York Times*, June 4, p. A18.

Smykla, J. O. (1978) *Co-Corrections: A Case Study of a Coed Federal Prison*. Washington, DC: University Press of America.

Snell, T. (2009) *Capital Punishment, 2008 – Statistical Tables*. Washington, DC: Bureau of Justice Statistics, US Department of Justice.

Snyder, H. (1994) *Arrests of Youth, 1991*, OJJDP Update on Statistics. Washington, DC: US Government Printing Office.

Snyder, H. and Sickmund, M. (1999) *Juvenile Offenders and Victims: 1999 National Report*. Washington, DC: US Department of Justice. National Center for Juvenile Justice.

Social Justice (1991a) 'Attica: 1971–1991,' Commemorative Issue, 18: 3.

Social Justice (1991b) 'The War on Drugs: Commentary and Critique,' Special Issue: 18 (4).

Social Justice (2000) 'Critical Resistance to the Prison-Industrial Complex,' Special Issue, 27: 3.

Solomos, J. (1993) *Race and Racism in Britain*. London: Macmillan.

Sontag, S. (1988) *AIDS and Its Metaphors*. New York: Farrar, Straus, & Giroux.

Sontag, S. (2004) 'The photographs are us,' *New York Times Magazine*, May 23, pp. 24–9, 42.

Sorenson, J. and Wallace, D. H. (1999) 'Prosecutorial discretion in seeking death: an analysis of racial disparity in the pretrial stages of case processing in a Midwestern County,' *Justice Quarterly*, 16 (3): 559–78.

Sorenson, J., Widmayer, A. G., and Scarpitti, F. R. (1994) 'Examining the criminal justice and criminological paradigms: an analysis of ACIS and ASC members,' *Journal of Criminal Justice Education*, 5 (2): 149–66.

Soss, J., Langbein, L., and Metelko, A. (2003a) 'Race, threat and social control,' *American Sociological Review*, 62: 388–412.

Soss, J., Langbein, L., and Metelko, A. (2003b) 'Why do white Americans support the death penalty?' *Journal of Politics*, 65: 397–421.

Souryal, S. (2009) 'Deterring corruption by prison personnel: a principle-based perspective,' *Prison Journal*, 89 (1): 21–45.

Sozzo, M. (1998) 'Control sociale e intersección Institutional Psiquiatria-Justicia Penal,' in E. Bodelon and T. P. Novales (eds), *Las Transformationes del Estado y del Derecho Contemporaneos*. Madrid: Alianza, pp. 47–76.

Sozzo, M. (2006) *Reconstruyendo Las Criminologias Críticas*. Buenos Aires: Editorial Ad-Hoc.

Sparkman, E. L., Minor, K., and Wells, J. (2002) 'A comparison of job satisfaction among private and public prison employees,' in L. Fiftal Alarid and P. Cromwell (eds), *Correctional Perspectives*. Los Angeles: Roxbury, pp. 233–9.

Sparks, R. F. (1980) 'A critique of Marxist criminology,' in N. Morris and M. Tonry (eds), *Crime and Justice: An Annual Review of Research*. Chicago: University of Chicago Press.

Sparks, R., Bottoms, A., and Hay, W. (1996) *Prison and the Problem of Order*. Oxford: Clarendon Press.

Spelman, W. (1994) *Criminal Incapacitation*. New York: Plenum.

Spencer, J., Haslewood-Pocsik, I., and Smith, E. (2009) '"Trying to get it right": what prison staff say about implementing race relations policy,' *Criminology and Criminal Justice*, 9 (2): 187–206.

Spergel, I. A., Chance, R., and Curry, G. D. (1990) *National Youth Gang Suppression and Intervention Program*. Washington, DC: Office of Juvenile Justice and Delinquency Prevention.

Spierenburg, P. (1984) *The Spectacle of Suffering: Executions and the Evolution of Repression*. New York: Cambridge University Press.

Spitzer, S. (1975) 'Toward a Marxian theory of deviance,' *Social Problems*, 22: 638–51.

Spitzer, S. and Scull, A. (1977a) 'Privatization and capital development: the case of privatization,' *Social Problems*, 25: 18–29.

Spitzer, S. and Scull, A. (1977b) 'Social control in historical perspective: from private to public responses to crime,' in D. Greenberg (ed.), *Corrections and Punishment*. Beverly Hills, CA: Sage, pp. 265–86.

Spivak, J. (1932) *Georgia Nigger*. New York: Harcourt, Brace.

Spohn, C. (1999) 'Gender and sentencing of drug offenders: is chivalry dead?' *Criminal Justice Policy Review*, 9: 365–99.

Spohn, C. and Cederblom, J. (1991) 'Race and disparities in sentencing: a test of the liberation hypothesis,' *Justice Quarterly*, 8 (3): 283–304.

Spohn, C. and Holleran, D. (2000) 'The imprisonment penalty paid by young, unemployed black and hispanic male offenders,' *Criminology*, 38 (1): 281–306.

Spohn, C. and Holleran, D. (2002) 'The effect of imprisonment on recidivism rates of felony offenders: a focus on drug offenders,' *Criminology*, 40 (2): 329–57.

Stack, S. (1987) 'Publicized executions and homicide, 1950–1980,' *American Sociological Review*, 52: 532–40.

Stacy, H. (1998) 'Postmodern feminist justice: identity and reform,' *Social Pathology*, 4 (1): 26–38.

Staley, S. R. (2000) 'Same old, same old: American drug policy in the 1990s,' in J. Sheley (ed.), *Criminology: A Contemporary Handbook* (3rd edn). Belmont, CA: Wadsworth, pp. 543–59.

Stalgaitis, S., Meyers, A., and Krisak, J. (1982) 'A social learning theory for reduction of correctional officer stress,' *Federal Probation*, 56 (3): 33–41.

Stanley, D. T. (1976) *Prisoners Among Us*. Washington, DC: Brookings.

Stanz, R. and Tewksbury, R. (2000) 'Predictors of success and recidivism in a home incarceration program,' *Prison Journal*, 80 (3): 326–44.

Staples, W. G. (1990) *Castles of Our Consciousness: Social Control and the American State, 1800–1985*. New Brunswick, NJ: Rutgers University Press.

Steffensmeier, D. (1988) 'Assessing the impact of the woman's movement on sex-based differences in the handling of adult criminal defendants,' *Crime and Delinquency*, 26: 344–57.

Steffensmeier, D. and Demuth, S. (2001) 'Ethnicity and judges' sentencing decisions: hispanic-black-white comparisons,' *Criminology*, 39 (1): 145–78.

Steffensmeier, D. and Harer, M. D. (1991) 'Did crime rise or fall during the Reagan presidency? The effects of an "aging" U.S. population on the nation's crime rate,' *Journal of Research in Crime and Delinquency*, 28 (August): 330–59.

Steffensmeier, D., Kramer, J., and Streifel, C. (1993) 'Gender and imprisonment decisions,' *Criminology*, 31 (3): 411–46.

Steffensmeier, D., Ulmer, J., and Kramer, J. (1998) 'The interaction of race, gender, and age in criminal sentencing: the punishment cost of being young, black, and male,' *Criminology*, 36 (4): 763–98.

Steihem, J. H. (1981) *Bring Me Men and Women: Mandated Change at the U.S. Air Force Academy*. Berkeley, CA: University of California Press.

Steiner, B. and Wooldredge, J. (2009) 'The relevance of inmate race/ethnicity versus population composition for understanding prison rule violations,' *Punishment and Society*, 11 (4): 459–89.

Steinhart, D. (1988) *Public Attitudes Toward Youth Crime*. San Francisco: National Council on Crime and Delinquency.

Steinhauer, J. (2002) 'Inner circle of Bloomberg aides put homeless shelter in jail,' *New York Times*, August 14, pp. B1, B3.

Stephens, J. (2000) *Traditional and Informal Justice Systems and Access to Justice in Sub-Saharan Africa*. London: Penal Reform International.

Stern, V. (1998) *A Sin Against the Future: Imprisonment in the World*. London: Penguin Books.

Stern, V. (1999) *Alternatives to Prison in Developing Countries*. London: International Centre for Prison Studies and Penal Reform International.

Stern, V. (2002) 'Alternative punishments in Sub-Saharan Africa,' in D. Levinson (ed.), *Encyclopedia of Crime and Punishment*. Thousands Oaks, CA: Sage, pp. 18–21.

Stewart, E., Baumer, E., Brunson, R., and Simons, R. (2009) 'Neighborhood racial context and perceptions of police-based racial discrimination among black youth,' *Criminology*, 47 (3): 847–86.

Stinchcomb, J. B. (1986) *Correctional Officer Stress: Looking at the Causes, You May Be the Cure*. Paper presented at the Annual Meetings of the Academy of Criminal Justice Sciences, Orlando, FL.

Stober, D. and Hoffman, I. (2002) *A Convenient Spy: Wen Ho Lee and the Politics of Nuclear Espionage*. New York: Simon & Schuster.

Stohr, M. K., Self, R. L., and Lovrich, N. P. (1992) 'Staff turnover in new generation jails: an investigation of its causes and prevention,' *Journal of Criminal Justice*, 20 (5): 455–78.

Stohr, M. K., Lovrich, N. P. Jr, Menke, B. A., and Zupan, L. L. (1994) 'Staff management in correctional institutions: comparing DiIulio's "control model" and "employee investment model" outcomes in five jails,' *Justice Quarterly*, 11 (3): 471–98.

Stojkovic, S. (1996a) 'Building tenders,' in M. McShane and F. Williams (eds), *Encyclopedia of American Prisons*. New York: Garland, pp. 66–9.

Stojkovic, S. (1996b) 'Correctional officers: subculture,' in M. McShane and F. Williams (eds), *Encyclopedia of American Prisons*. New York: Garland, pp. 126–8.

Stojkovic, S. (2003) 'Accounts of prison work: corrections officers' portrayals of their work worlds,' in M. Pogregin (ed.), *Qualitative Approaches to Criminal Justice*. London: Sage.

Stolzenberg, L. and D'Alessio, S. J. (1997) 'The impact on prison crowding on male and female imprisonment rates in Minnesota: a research note,' *Justice Quarterly*, 14 (4): 793–810.

Stone, L. (1983) 'An exchange with Michel Foucault,' *New York Review of Books*, March 31, pp. 42–4.

Stone, W. G. (1982) *The Hate Factory: The Story of the New Mexico Penitentiary Riot*. Agoura, CA: Deli.

Stotland, E. (1976) 'Self-esteem and violence by guards and state troopers at Attica,' *Criminal Justice and Behavior*, 3 (1): 85–96.

Stout, D. (2008) 'Mukasey demurs on waterboarding,' *New York Times*, January 30, pp. EV1–3.

Strange, C. and Kempa, M. (2003) 'Shades of dark tourism: Alcatraz and Robben Island,' *Annals of Tourism Research*, 30: 386–405.

Stratton, J. (1973) 'Cops and drunks: police attitudes and actions in dealing with Indian drunks,' *International Journal of Addictions*, 8: 613–21.

Streib, V. L. (1987) *Death Penalty for Juveniles*. Bloomington, IN: Indiana University Press.

Streib, V. L. (1991) 'Juveniles in law and society,' in R. C. Monk (ed.), *Taking Sides: Clashing Views on Controversial Issues in Crime and Criminology*. Sluice Dock, Guilford, CT: Dushkin.

Streifel, C. (1992) 'A review of R. Simon and J. Randis' *The Crimes Women Commit, the Punishment They Receive*,' *Contemporary Sociology: A Journal of Reviews*, 21 (1): 82–3.

Strom, F. (1942) *On the Sacred Origin of the Germanic Death Penalties*. Stockholm: Wahlstrom & Widstraud.

Sudbury, J. (2005) *Global Lockdown: Race, Gender, and the Prison-Industrial Complex*. New York: Routledge.

Sullivan, D. (1980) *The Mask of Love: Corrections in America, Toward a Mutual Aid Alternative*. Port Washington, NY: Kennikat Press.

Sullivan, D. (1998) 'Editor's welcome to this forum,' *Contemporary Justice Review*, 1 (1): 1–5.

Sullivan, J. F. (1994) 'Whitman approves stringent restrictions on sex criminals,' *New York Times*, November 1, pp. B1, B6.

Sullivan, J. (2000) 'Prison conditions severe even for jails,' *The Oregonian*, December 9, pp. EV1–10.

Sullivan, R. F. (1973) 'The economics of crime: an introduction to the literature,' *Crime and Delinquency*, 19 (2): 138–49.

Surette, R. (1998) *Media, Crime, and Criminal Justice: Images and Realities*. Belmont, CA: West/Wadsworth.

Surette, R. (1999) 'Media echoes: systemic effects of news coverage,' *Justice Quarterly*, 16 (3): 601–32.

Surratt, H. (2007) 'Gender-specific issues in the treatment of drug involved women,' in J. Inciardi and K. McElrath (eds), *The American Drug Scene*. New York: Oxford University Press.

Suskind, R. (2004) *The Price of Loyalty: George W. Bush, the White House, and the Education of Paul O'Neill*. New York: Simon & Schuster.

Susler, J. (1991) *Profiles of Courage: The Case of the Puerto Rican Women Political Prisoners/Prisoners of War*. Chicago: Peoples Law Office.

Sutherland, E. H., Cressey, D. R., and Luckenbill, D. F. (1992) *Principles of Criminology* (11th edn). Dix Hills, NY: General Hall.

Swanson, S. (2004) 'Enemy combatants and the writ of habeas corpus,' *Arizona State Law Journal*, 35: 939–1022.

Sweeten, G., Bushway, S., and Paternoster, R. (2009) 'Does dropping out of school mean dropping into delinquency?' *Criminology*, 47 (1): 47–92.

Sykes, G. (1956) 'The corruption of authority and rehabilitation,' *Social Forces*, 34 (March): 258–61.

Sykes, G. (1958) *Society of Captives*. Princeton, NJ: Princeton University Press.

Sykes, G. M. (1974) 'The rise of critical criminology,' *Journal of Criminal Law and Criminology*, 65 (June): 206–13.

Sykes, G. and Messinger, S. (1960) 'The inmate social system,' in *Theoretical Studies in the Social Organization of the Prison*. New York: Social Science Research Council.

Sykes, G., Vito, G., and McElrath, K. (1987) 'Jail populations and crime rates: an exploratory analysis of incapacitation,' *Journal of Police Science and Administration*, 15: 72–7.

Takagi, P. (1980) 'The Walnut Street Jail: a penal reform to centralize the powers of the state,' in T. Platt and P. Takagi (eds), *Punishment and Penal Discipline: Essays on the Prison and Prisoners' Movement*. San Francisco: Crime and Justice Associates.

Talvi, S. (2003) 'Round up: INS "special registration" ends in mass arrests,' *In These Times*, February 17, p. 3.

Tannenbaum, F. (1924) *The Darker Phases of the South: Describing Women's Prisons in the South at the Turn of the Century*. New York: Putnam.

Tappan, P. (1960) *Crime, Justice, and Correction*. New York: McGraw-Hill.

Tartaro, C. and Lester, D. (2009) *Suicide and Self-harm in Prisons and Jails*. Lanham, MD: Rowman & Littlefield.

Tartaro, C. and Sedelmaier, C. (2009) 'A tale of two cities: the impact of pretrial release, race, and ethnicity upon sentencing decisions,' *Criminal Justice Studies*, 22 (2): 203–21.

Tarver, M., Walker, S., and Wallace, P. H. (2002) *Multicultural Issues in the Criminal Justice System*. Boston: Allyn & Bacon.

Task Force Report: Corrections (1967) The President's Commission on Law Enforcement and Administration of Justice. Washington, DC: US Government Printing Office.

Tatge, M. (2000) 'With unemployment low, a new group is in demand: ex-cons,' *Wall Street Journal*, April 24, p. A1.

Tatum, B. T. (1999) 'The link between rap music and youth crime and violence: a review of the literature and issues for future research,' *Justice Professional*, 11 (3): 339–53.

Taxman, F. and Ressler, L. (2010) 'Public health is public safety: revamping the correctional mission,' in N. Frost, J. Freilich, and T. Clear (eds), *Contemporary Issues in Criminal Justice*. Belmont, CA: Wadworth.

Taylor, D. L. (2000) 'Cultural mistrust and racial divides,' *Social Pathology*, 6 (3): 199–212.

Taylor, I. (1999) *Crime in Context: A Critical Criminology of Market Societies*. New York: Westview.

Taylor, I., Walton, P., and Young, J. (1973) *The New Criminology: For a Social Theory of Deviance*. London: Routledge & Kegan Paul.

Teephen, T. (1996) 'Locking in the profits,' *Atlanta Constitution*, December 10, p. 21.

Terry, C. M. (1997) 'The function of humor for prison inmates,' *Journal of Contemporary Criminal Justice*, 13 (1): 23–40.

Terry, D. (1997) 'Los Angeles confronts bitter racial legacy,' *New York Times*, July 20, pp. A1, A14.

Terry, K. and Dank, M. (2010) 'The CSEC population in New York City: supporting the arugument to abolish prosecuting prostituted teens,' in N. Frost, J. Freilich, and T. Clear (eds), *Contemporary Issues in Criminal Justice Policy*. Belmont, CA: Wadsworth.

Tewksbury, R. (1989) 'Fear of sexual assault in prison inmates,' *Prison Journal*, LXIX (1): 62–71.

Tharp, N. (2001) 'Crime, prisons, and economy,' *New York Times*, 3 July, pp. EV1–2.

Thies, J. (2001) 'The "big house" in a small town: the economic and social impacts of a correctional facility on its host community,' *Justice Professional*, 14 (2): 221–37.

Thomas, J. (1988) *Prison Litigation: The Paradox of the Jailhouse Lawyer*. Totowa, NJ: Rowman & Littlefield.

Thomas, J. (1991) 'Racial codes in prison culture: snapshots in black and white,' in M. J. Lynch and E. B. Patterson (eds), *Race and Criminal Justice*. New York: Harrow & Heston.

Thomas, J. and O'Maolchatha, A. (1989) 'Reassessing the critical metaphor: an optimistic revisionist view,' *Justice Quarterly*, 6 (2): 143–72.

Thomas, J., Keeler, D., and Harris, K. (1986) 'Issues and misconceptions in prisoner litigation: a critical view,' *Criminology*, 24 (4): 775–98.

Thomas, P. (1994a) 'Rural regions look to prisons for prosperity,' *Wall Street Journal*, July 11, pp. B1, B8.

Thomas, P. (1994b) 'Making crime pay: triangle of interests creates infrastructure to fight lawlessness: cities see jobs, politicians sense a popular issue – and business cashes in,' *Wall Street Journal*, May 12, p. A1.

Thompson, A. C. (2008) *Releasing Prisoners, Redeeming Communities: Reentry, Race, and Politics*. New York: University of New York Press.

Thompson, C. (2002) 'Seeking a welfare rule's repeal,' *Washington Post*, March 1, p. 31.

Thompson, J. A. and Mays, G. L. (1991) 'Paying the piper but changing the tune: policy changes and initiatives for the American jail,' in J. A. Thompson and G. L. Mays (eds), *American Jails: Public Policy Issues*. Chicago: Nelson-Hall.

Tift, L. and Sullivan, D. (1980) *The Struggle to be Human: Crime, Criminology, and Anarchism*. Orkney: Cienfuegos.

Tillman, R. (2009) 'Reputation and corporate malfeasance: collusive networks in financial statement fraud,' *Crime, Law and Social Change*, 51 (3–4): 365–82.

Time (1989) '"I deserve punishment": killer Ted Bundy bargains and postures to the end,' February 6, p. 34.

Tjaden, P. and Tjaden, C. (1981) 'Differential treatment of the female felon: myth or reality?' in M. Warren (eds), *Comparing Male and Female Offenders*. Newbury Park, CA: Sage, pp. 73–89.

Toborg, M. A. (1981) *Pretrial Release: A National Evaluation of Practices and Outcomes*. Washington, DC: US Government Printing Office.

Toby, J. (1979) 'The new criminology is the old sentimentality,' *Criminology*, 16 (February): 516–26.

Toch, H. (1977) *Living in Prison*. New York: Free Press.

Toch, H. (1985) 'Social climate and prison violence,' in M. Braswell, S. Dillingham, and R. Montgomery (eds), *Prison Violence in America*. Cincinnati, OH: Anderson.

Toch, H. and Grant, J. D. (1989) 'Noncoping and maladaption in confinement,' in L. Goodstein and D. L. Mackenzie (eds), *The American Prison: Issues in Research and Policy*. New York: Plenum.

Toch, H. and Klofas, J. (1982) 'Alienation and desire for job enrichment among corrections officers,' *Federal Probation*, 46 (March): 35–44.

Tollet, T. and Close, B. R. (1991) 'The over-representation of blacks in Florida's juvenile justice system,' in M. J. Lynch and E. B. Patterson (eds), *Race and Criminal Justice*. New York: Harrow & Heston.

Tolnay, S. E. and Beck, E. M (1992) 'Toward a threat model of southern black lynchings,' in A. E. Liska (ed.), *Social Threat and Social Control*. Albany, NY: SUNY Press.

Tolnay, S. E. and Beck, E. M. (1994) 'Lethal social control in the South: lynchings and executions between 1880 and 1930,' in G. Bridges and M. Myers (eds), *Inequality, Crime, and Social Control*. Boulder, CO: Westview.

Tong, R. (1989) *Feminist Thought: A Comprehensive Introduction*. Boulder, CO: Westview.

Tonry, M. (1990) 'Stated and latent functions of ISP,' *Crime and Delinquency*, 36 (1): 174–91.

Tonry, M. (1995) *Malign Neglect – Race, Crime, and Punishment in America*. New York: Oxford University Press.

Tonry, M. (2001) 'Punishment policies and patterns in western countries,' in M. Tonry and R. Frase (eds), *Sentencing and Sanctions in Western Countries*. New York: Oxford University Press, pp. 3–28.

Tonry, M. (2004) *Thinking about Crime: Sense and Sensibility in American Penal Culture*. New York: Oxford University Press.

Tonry, M. (2009) 'Explanations of American punishment policies,' *Punishment and Society*, 11 (3): 377–94.

Tourigny, S. C. (2001) 'Some new killing trick: welfare reform and drug markets in a U.S. ghetto,' *Social Justice*, 28 (4): 49–71.

Trattner, W. I. (1974) *From Poor Law to Welfare State*. New York: Free Press.

Travis, J. (2005) *But They All Come Back: Facing the Challenges of Prisoner Reentry*. Washington, DC: Urban Institute Press.

Treaster, J. B. (1994) 'Hard time for hard youths: a battle producing few winners,' *New York Times*, December 28, p. A12.

Trombley, S. (1992) *The Execution Protocol: Inside America's Capital Punishment Industry*. New York: Crown.

Trouille, H. L. (2000) 'Holiday camp or boot camp? Where does France stand in the prison reform debate?' *Justice Professional*, 13 (4): 391–404.

Tulsky, F. (2000) 'Detained immigrants who allege sex abuse are transferred to jail,' *San Jose Mercury News*, December 13, pp. EV1–2.

Tulsky, J. P., White, M. C., Dawson, C., Hoynes, T. M., Goldenson, J., and Schechter, G. (1998) 'Screening for tuberculosis in jail and clinic followup after release,' *American Journal of Public Health*, 88: 223–6.

Turk, A. (1976) 'Law as a weapon in social conflict,' *Social Problems*, 23: 276–91.

Turk, A. (1979) 'Analyzing official deviance: for nonpartisan conflict analysis in criminology,' *Criminology*, 16: 459–76.

Turnbull, S. and Hannah-Moffat, K. (2009) 'Under these conditions: gender, parole, and the governance of reintegration,' *British Journal of Criminology*, 49: 532–51.

Turner, M., Cullen, F., Sundt, J., and Applegate, B. (1997) 'Public tolerance for community-based sanctions,' *Prison Journal*, 77: 6–26.

Turner, S. (2002) 'Work release,' in D. Levinson (ed.), *Encyclopedia of Crime and Punishment*. Thousand Oaks, CA: Sage, pp. 1735–8.

Turner, S. (2010) 'Boot camps redux,' *Criminology and Public Policy*, 9 (1): 85–7.

Uggen, C. and Inderbitzin, M. (2010) 'The price and the promise of citizenship: extending the vote to non-incarcerated felons,' in N. Frost, J. Freilich, and T. Clear (eds), *Contemporary Issues in Criminal Justice Policy*. Belmont, CA: Wadsworth.

Umbreit, M. S. (2002) 'Restorative justice and meditation,' in T. Gray (ed.), *Exploring Corrections*. Boston: Allyn & Bacon, pp. 322–32.

United Nations Office on Drugs and Crime (UNODC) (2009) *World Drug Report, 2009*. New York: United Nations.

United States Department of Labor (2009) *Compliance Assistance – Fair Labor Standards Act (FLSA)*. Available at: http://www.dol.gov/whd/flsa/index.htm.

United States General Accounting Office (1999) *Women in Prison: Issues and Challenges Confronting the U.S. Correctional Systems*. Washington, DC: General Accounting Office.

Unnever, J. (2008) 'Two worlds far apart: black-white differences in beliefs about why African American men are disproportionately imprisoned,' *Criminology*, 46: 511–38.

Unnever, J. and Cullen, F. (2010a) 'The social sources of Americans' punitiveness: a test of three competing models,' *Criminology*, 48 (1): 99–130.

Unnever, J. and Cullen, F. (2010b) 'Racial-ethnic intolerance and support for the death penalty: a cross-national comparison,' *Criminology*, in press.

Urbina, I. (2009) 'New execution method is used in Ohio,' *New York Times*, December 8, pp. EV1–5.

Urbina, I. and Hamill, S. (2009) 'Judges plead guilty in scheme to jail youths for profit,' *New York Times*, February 12, pp. EV1–3.

US Department of Health and Human Services, National Institute of Drug Abuse (1992) *Socioeconomics and Demographics Correlates of Drug and Alcohol Use*. Washington, DC: US Department of Health and Human Services.

US General Accounting Office (1987) *Criminal Bail: How Bail Reform Is Working in Selected District Courts*. Subcommittee on Courts, Civil Liberties, and the Administration of Justice, Committee on the Judiciary, US House of Representatives.

US Marshal's Report (1986) *First Year Implementation of the Comprehensive Crime Control Act of 1984*. Washington, DC: US Marshal Service.

US Sentencing Commission (1991) *Mandatory Minimum Penalties in the Federal Criminal Justice System*. Washington, DC: US Sentencing Commission.

US Sentencing Commission (2010) *Preliminary Crack Cocaine Retroactivity Data Report*. Washington, DC: US Sentencing Commission.

Useem, B. (1985) 'Disorganization and the New Mexico prison riot,' *American Sociological Review*, 50 (5): 677–88.

Useem, B. and Clayton, O. (2009) 'Radicalization of U.S. prisoners,' *Criminology and Public Policy*, 8 (3): 561–92.

Useem, B. and Goldstone, J. (2002) 'Forging social order and its breakdown: riot and reform in US prisons,' *American Sociological Review*, 67 (4): 499–525.

Useem, B. and Kimball, P. A. (1987) 'A theory of prison riots,' *Theory and Society*, 16: 87–122.

Useem, B. and Kimball, P. A. (1989) *States of Siege: U.S. Prison Riots 1971–1986*. New York: Oxford University Press.

Useem, B. and Piehl, A. (2006) 'Prison buildup and disorder,' *Punishment and Society*, 8 (1): 87–115.

Useem, B. and Piehl, A. (2008) *Prison State: The Challenge of Mass Incarceration*. Cambridge: Cambridge University Press.

Useem, B. and Reisig, M. D. (1999) 'Collective action in prisons: protests, disturbances, and riots,' *Criminology*, 37 (4): 734–60.

van Bemmelen, J. M. (1960) 'Willem Adriaan Bonger,' in H. Mannheim (ed.), *Pioneers in Criminology*. London: Stevens & Sons.

van de Warker, E. (1875–6) 'The relations of women to crime,' *Popular Science Monthly*, 8: 1–16.

van den Haag, E. (1982) 'Could successful rehabilitation reduce the crime rate?' *Journal of Criminal Law and Criminology*, 73 (3): 1022–35.

van den Haag, E. (1982) 'Could successful rehabilitation reduce the crime rate?' *Journal of Criminal Law and Criminology*, 73 (3): 1022–35.

van den Haag, E. and Conrad, J. P. (1983) *The Death Penalty: A Debate*. New York: Plenum Press.

Van der Slice, A. (1936–7) 'Elizabethan houses of correction,' *Journal of the American Institute of Criminal Law and Criminology*, XXVII: 44–67.

van Mastrigt, S. and Farrington, D. (2009) 'Co-offending, age, gender and crime type: implications for criminal justice policy,' *British Journal of Criminology*, 49: 552–73.

Van Voorhis, P. (1987) 'Correctional effectiveness: the high cost of ignoring success,' *Federal Probation*, 51: 56–62.

Van Wormer, K. S. and Bartollas, C. (2000) *Women and the Criminal Justice System*. Boston: Allyn & Bacon.

van Zyl Smit, D. (2001) 'Abolishing life imprisonment?' *Punishment and Society*, 3: 299–306.

van Zyl Smit, D. (2002) *Taking Life Imprisonment Seriously*. The Hague: Kluwer Law International.

Vandiver, M. and Giacopassi, D. (1997) 'One million and counting: students' estimates of the annual number of homicides in the U.S.,' *Journal of Criminal Justice Education*, 8 (2): 135–44.

Vaughn, B. (2002) 'The punitive consequences of consumer culture,' *Punishment and Society*, 4 (2): 195–211.

Vaughn, M. S. (1995) 'Civil liability against prison officials for inmate-on-inmate assault: where are we and where have we been?' *Prison Journal*, 75: 12–28.

Vaughn, M. S. (1997) 'Prison officials' liability for inmate-to-inmate assault: a review of case law,' *Journal of Offender Rehabilitation*, 25 (1/2): 1–30.

Vaughn, M. S. (1999a) 'Practicing penal harm in the United States: prisoners' voices from jail,' *Justice Quarterly*, 16 (1): 175–232.

Vaughn, M. S. (1999b) 'Penal harm medicine: state tort remedies for delaying and denying health care to prisoners,' *Crime, Law and Social Change*, 31: 273–302.

Vaughn, M. S. and Carroll, L. (1998) 'Separate and unequal: prison versus free-world medical care,' *Justice Quarterly*, 15 (1): 3–40.

Vaughn, M. S. and del Carmen, R. V. (1993a) 'Legal and policy issues from the Supreme Court's decision on smoking in prisons,' *Federal Probation*, September, 57 (3): 34–9.

Vaughn, M. S. and del Carmen, R. V. (1993b) 'Research note: smoking in prison – a national survey of correctional administrators in the United States,' *Crime and Delinquency*, 39 (2): 225–39.

Vaughn, M. S. and del Carmen, R. V. (1993c) 'Smoke-free prisons: policy dilemmas and constitutional issues,' *Journal of Criminal Justice*, 21: 151–71.

Vaughn, M. S. and Smith, L. G. (1999) 'Questioning authorized truth: resisting the pull of the policy audience and fostering critical scholarship in correctional medical research – a reply to Kerle *et al.*,' *Justice Quarterly*, 16 (4): 907–18.

Veneziano, C., Veneziano, L., Bourns, W., Fichter, M., and Summers, K. (2000) 'Differences in expectations and perceptions among criminal justice officials concerning boot camps,' *Justice Professional*, 13 (4): 377–90.

Vennard, J. and Hedderman, C. (2009) 'Helping offenders into employment,' *Criminology and Criminal Justice*, 9 (2): 225–45.

Verhovek, S. H. (1995) 'When justice shows its darker side,' *New York Times*, January 8, p. E6.

Verhovek, S. H. (1997) 'Operators are not worried by ruling,' *New York Times*, June 24, p. B10.

Viadro, C. I. and Earp, J. A. (1991) 'AIDS education and incarcerated women: a neglected opportunity,' *Women and Society*, 17 (2): 105–17.

Village Voice (2002) 'Hanging judges,' April 2, p. 29.

Visher, C. A. (1995) 'Career offenders and selective incapacitation,' in J. F. Sheley (ed.), *Criminology: A Contemporary Handbook* (2nd edn). Belmont, CA: Wadsworth.

Visher, C. (2000) 'Career criminals and crime control,' in J. Sheley (ed.), *Criminology: A Contemporary Handbook* (3rd edn). Belmont, CA: Wadsworth, pp. 600–19.

Vito, G. (1992) 'Felony probation and recidivism: replication and response,' in L. Travis, M. S. Schwartz, and T. Clear (eds), *Corrections: An Issue Approach* (3rd edn). Cincinnati, OH: Anderson.

Vito, G. F. and Wilson, D. G. (1985) *The American Juvenile Justice System*. Beverly Hills, CA: Sage.

Vogel, S. (2002) 'Afghan prisoners going to gray area: military unsure what follows transfer to U.S. Base in Cuba,' *Washington Post*, January 9, p. A1.

Vold, G. (1958) *Theoretical Criminology*. New York: Oxford University Press.

Vold, G. B. and Bernard, T. J. (1986) *Theoretical Criminology* (3rd edn). New York: Oxford University Press.

Vold, G., Bernard, T., and Snipes, J. (1998) *Theoretical Criminology* (4th edn). New York: Oxford University Press.

Vold, G., Bernard, T., and Snipes, J. (2002) *Theoretical Criminology* (5th edn). New York: Oxford University Press.

von Hirsch, A. (1976) *Doing Justice: The Choice of Punishments*. New York: Hill & Wang.

von Hirsch, A. (1985) *Past or Future Crimes: Deservedness and Dangerousness in the Sentencing of Criminals*. New Brunswick, NJ: Rutgers University Press.

von Hirsch, A. (1993) *Censure and Sanctions*. New York: Oxford University Press.

von Hirsch, A. and Hanrahan, K. J. (1979) *The Question of Parole: Retention, Reform or Abolition?* Cambridge, MA: Ballinger.

Vuolo, M. and Kruttshnitt, C. (2008) 'Prisoners' adjustment, correctional officers, and context: the foreground and background of punishment in late modernity,' *Law and Society Review*, 42 (2): 307–35.

Wacquant, L. (2000) 'The new peculiar institution: on the prison as surrogate ghetto,' *Theoretical Criminology*, 4: 377–89.

Wacquant, L. (2001) 'Deadly symbiosis: when ghetto and prison meet and merge,' *Punishment and Society*, 3(1): 95–133.

Wacquant, L. (2002) 'The curious eclipse of prison ethnography in the age of mass incarceration,' *Ethnography*, 3: 371–97.

Wacquant, L. (2009) *Punishing the Poor: The Neoliberal Government of Social Insecurity*. Durham, NC: Duke University Press.

Wagner, P. (2004) *Prisoners: The US Census and the Political Geography of Mass Incarceration*. Paper presented at the conference Prisons and Penal Policy: International Perspectives, City University, Islington, London, June 23–25.

Wagner, P. (2006) *Importing Consensus: Prisoners and Political Clout in New York*, Prison Policy Initiative. Available at: http://www.prisonpolicy.org. (accessed April 17, 2006).

Waldo, G. and Paternoster, R. (2003) 'Tinkering with the machinery of death: the failure of a social experiment,' in T. Blomberg and S. Cohen (eds), *Punishment and Social Control* (2nd edn). New York: Aldine de Gruyter.

Walens, S. (1997) *War Stories: An Oral History of Life Behind Bars*. Westport, CT: Praeger.

Walgrave, L. (2008) *Restorative Justice, Self-interest, and Responsible Citizenship*. Cullompton: Willan.

Walker, S. (1994) *Sense and Nonsense About Crime and Drugs: A Policy Guide* (3rd edn). Belmont, CA: Wadsworth.

Walker, S. (1998) *Popular Justice: A History of American Criminal Justice*. New York: Oxford University Press.

Walker, S. (2001) *Sense and Nonsense About Crime and Drugs: A Policy Guide* (5th edn). Belmont, CA: Wadsworth.

Walker, S., Spohn, C., and DeLone, M. (1996) *The Color of Justice: Race, Ethnicity, and Crime in America*. Belmont, CA: Wadsworth.

Walker, S., Spohn, C., and DeLone, M. (2002) 'Corrections: a picture in black and white,' in T. Gray (ed.), *Exploring Corrections*. Boston: Allyn & Bacon, pp. 13–24.

Wallace, D. H. (2001) 'Prisoners' rights: historical views,' in E. Latessa, A. Holsinger, J. Marquart, and J. Sorensen (eds), *Correctional Contexts: Contemporary and Classical Readings*. Los Angeles: Roxbury, pp. 229–38.

Waller, M. (2003) Testimony: United States Senate Committee on the Judiciary, 'Terrorist Recruitment and Infiltration in the United States: Prisons and Military as an Operational Base,' October 14. Online at http://www.globalsecurity.com.

Walmsley, R. (1999) *World Prison Population List*, Research Findings No. 88. London: Home Office Research, Development and Statistics Directorate.

Walmsley, R. (2008) *World Prison Population* (8th edn). London: King's College.

Walsh, A. (1985) 'The role of the probation officer in the sentencing process: independent professional or judicial hack?' *Criminal Justice and Behavior*, 12: 289–303.

Walsh, A. (1991) 'Race and discretionary sentencing: an analysis of "obvious" and "non-obvious" cases,' *International Journal of Offender Therapy and Comparative Criminology*, 35 (1): 7–20.

Walsh, A. and Beaver, K. (2008) *Introduction to Biosocial Criminology*. New York: Routledge.

Walters, S. (1993) 'Gender, job satisfaction, and correctional officers: a comparative analysis,' *Justice Professional*, 7 (2): 23–34.

Walther, L. and Perry, J. (1997) 'The Vermont reparative probation program,' *ICCA Journal of Community Corrections*, 8 (2): 26–34.

Ward, T. and Langlands, R. (2008) 'Restorative justice and the human rights of offenders,' *Aggression and Violent Behavior*, 13 (5): 355–72.

Weatherburn, D. and Bartels, L. (2008) 'The recidivism rate of offenders given suspended sentences in New South Wales, Australia,' *British Journal of Criminology*, 48: 667–83.

Webb, G. L. and Morris, D. G. (2002) 'Working as a prison guard,' in T. Gray (ed.), *Exploring Corrections*. Boston: Allyn & Bacon, pp. 69–83.

Weber, L. (2006) 'The shifting frontiers of migration control,' in S. Pickering and L. Weber (eds), *Borders, Mobility and Technologies of Control*. Dordrecht: Springer.

Weber, M. (1947) *The Theory of Social and Economic Organization*. New York: Free Press.

Weber, M. (1968) *Economy and Society*. New York: Bedminster Press.

Weber, S. R. (1982) 'Native Americans before the bench: the nature of contrast and conflict in Native-American law ways and western legal systems,' *Social Science Journal*, 19: 47–55.

Webster, B. A. and McEwen, J. T. (1992) *Assessing Criminal Justice Needs*, National Institute of Justice, Research in Brief, August. Washington, DC: US Department of Justice.

Webster, C. (2009) 'Marginalized white ethnicity, race and crime,' *Theoretical Criminology*, 12 (3): 293–312.

Weenink, D. (2009) 'Explaining ethnic inequality in the juvenile justice system,' *British Journal of Criminology*, 49: 220–42.

Weiner, T. (2007) *Legacy of Ashes: The History of the C.I.A.* New York: Doubleday.

Weinstein, C. and Cummins, E. (1996) 'The crime of punishment: Pelican Bay maximum security prison,' in E. Rosenblatt (ed.), *Criminal Justice: Confronting the Prison Crisis*. Boston: South End Press.

Weisheit, R. (1985) 'Trends in programs for female offenders: the use of private agencies as service providers,' *International Journal of Offender Therapy and Comparative Criminology*, 29 (1): 35–42.

Weisheit, R. (1992) 'Patterns of female crime,' in R. G. Culbertson and R. Weisheit (eds), *Order Under Law* (4th edn). Prospect Heights, IL: Waveland.

Weisheit, R. A. and Klofas, J. M. (1989) 'The impact of jail on collateral costs and affective response,' *Journal of Offender Counseling, Services and Rehabilitation*, 14 (1): 51–66.

Weisheit, R. and Mahan, S. (1988) *Women, Crime, and Criminal Justice*. Cincinnati, OH: Anderson.

Weisman, S. R. (2005) 'Jail term for soldier in abuse case,' *New York Times*, May 23, p. A10.

Weiss, R. (1987) 'Humanitarianism, labour exploitation, or social control? A critical survey of theory and research on the origin and development of prisons,' *Social History*, 12: 331–50.

Weiss, R. (1989) 'Private prisons and the state,' in R. Matthews (ed.), *Privatizing Criminal Justice*. London: Sage.

Weiss, R. P. (2001) '"Repatriating" low-wage work: the political economy of prison labor reprivatization in the postindustrial United States,' *Criminology*, 39 (2): 253–92.

Weiss, R. P. and South, N. (1998) *Comparing Prison Systems: Toward a Comparative and International Penology*. Amsterdam: Gordon & Breach.

Weitzer, R. and Tuch, S. A. (2002) 'Perceptions of racial profiling: race, class, and personal experience,' *Criminology*, 40 (2): 435–546.

Welch, M. (1984) 'The Relationship Between Job Satisfaction and Personality Type Among Jail Officers.' Unpublished master's thesis, Illinois State University, Normal, IL.

Welch, M. (1987) *The Prison as a Complex Organization: An Application of Etzioni's Typology of Compliance Relations.* Paper presented at the Annual Meetings of the American Society of Criminology, Montreal.

Welch, M. (1989a) 'Evaluating the sources of job satisfaction among jail officers: a qualitative and quantitative approach,' *Justice Professional*, 4 (1): 120–40.

Welch, M. (1989b) 'Social junk, social dynamite and the rabble: persons with AIDS in jail,' *American Journal of Criminal Justice*, XIV (1): 135–47.

Welch, M. (1990) 'The value systems of incarcerated embezzlers compared to other inmates and the general population,' *Journal of Offender Counseling, Services and Rehabilitation*, 15 (2): 155–76.

Welch, M. (1991a) 'A review of *Between Prison and Probation: Intermediate Punishments in a Rational Sentencing System* by Norval Morris and Michael Tonry,' *American Jails: The Magazine of the American Jail Association*, November/December, pp. 118–22.

Welch, M. (1991b) 'Book review of *Jails: Reform and the New Generation Philosophy* by Linda L. Zupan,' *American Jails: The Magazine of the American Jail Association*, March/April, pp. 132–5.

Welch, M. (1991c) 'The expansion of jail capacity: makeshift jails and public policy,' in J. A. Thompson and G. L. Mays (eds), *American Jails: Public Policy Issues*. Chicago: Nelson-Hall.

Welch, M. (1991d) 'Persons with AIDS in prison: a critical and phenomenological approach to suffering,' *Dialectical Anthropology*, 16 (1): 51–61.

Welch, M. (1992a) 'How are jails depicted by corrections textbooks? A content analysis provides a closer look,' *American Jails: The Magazine of the American Jail Association*, July/August, pp. 28–34.

Welch, M. (1992b) 'Social class, special populations, and other unpopular issues: setting the jail research agenda for the 1990s,' in G. L. Mays (ed.), *Setting the Jail Research Agenda for the 1990s*. Washington, DC: National Institute of Corrections.

Welch, M. (1993a) 'Distortions and myths surrounding jail conditions and detention,' *American Jails: The Magazine of the American Jail Association*, November/December, pp. 55–60.

Welch, M. (1993b) 'Jails and higher education: moving toward the front-end of the learning curve,' *American Jails: The Magazine of the American Jail Association*, January/February, pp. 33–4.

Welch, M. (1994) 'Jail overcrowding: social sanitation and the warehousing of the urban underclass,' in A. R. Roberts (ed.), *Critical Issues in Crime and Justice*. Thousand Oaks, CA: Sage.

Welch, M. (1995a) 'Rehabilitation: holding its ground in corrections,' *Federal Probation: A Journal of Correctional Philosophy and Practice*, 59 (4): 3–8.

Welch, M. (1995b) 'A sociopolitical approach to the reproduction of violence in Canadian prisons,' in J. I. Ross (ed.), *Violence in Canada: Sociopolitical Perspectives*. Toronto: Oxford University Press.

Welch, M. (1995c) 'Race and social class in the examination of punishment,' in M. Lynch and E. B. Patterson (eds), *Race and Criminal Justice: A Further Examination*. New York: Harrow & Heston.

Welch, M. (1996a) 'Anniversary essay: the impact of David J. Rothman's *The Discovery of the Asylum* 25 years later,' *Social Pathology*, 2 (1): 32–41.

Welch, M. (1996b) 'Special issue – corrections, punishment and social control,' *Social Pathology*, 2 (1).

Welch, M. (1996c) 'A review of *Punishment, Crime, and Market Forces* by L. T. Wilkins,' *Social Pathology*, 2 (1): 67–9.

Welch, M. (1996d) 'Critical criminology, social justice, and an alternative view of incarceration,' *Critical Criminology: An International Journal*, 7 (2): 43–58.

Welch, M. (1996e) 'Prisonization,' in M. D. McShane and F. P. Williams (eds), *Encyclopedia of American Prisons*. New York: Garland.

Welch, M. (1996f) 'Race and social class in the examination of punishment,' in M. J. Lynch and E. B. Patterson (eds), *Justice with Prejudice: Race and Criminal Justice in America*. New York: Harrow & Heston.

Welch, M. (1996g) 'Prison violence in America: past, present, and future,' in R. Muraskin and A. R. Roberts (eds), *Visions for Change: Crime and Justice in the Twenty-First Century*. Englewood Cliffs, NJ: Prentice Hall.

Welch, M. (1996h) 'The immigration crisis: detention as an emerging mechanism of social control,' *Social Justice: A Journal of Crime, Conflict and World Order*, 23 (3): 169–84.

Welch, M. (1997a) 'Regulating the reproduction and morality of women: the social control of body and soul,' *Women and Criminal Justice*, 9 (1): 17–38.

Welch, M. (1997b) 'Violence against women by professional football players: a gender analysis of hypermasculinity, positional status, narcissism, and entitlement,' *Journal of Sport and Social Issues*, 21 (4): 400–19.

Welch, M. (1997c) 'A critical interpretation of correctional bootcamps as normalizing institutions: discipline, punishment, and the military model,' *Journal of Contemporary Criminal Justice*, 13 (2): 184–205.

Welch, M. (1997d) 'Questioning the utility and fairness of INS detention: criticisms of poor institutional conditions and protracted periods of confinement for undocumented immigrants,' *Journal of Contemporary Criminal Justice*, 13 (1): 41–54.

Welch, M. (1997e) 'A feature review of *The Abandoned Ones: The Imprisonment and Uprising of the Mariel Boat People* by M. S. Hamm (1995) Boston: Northeastern University,' *Social Pathology*, 3 (3): 202–6.

Welch, M. (1997f) 'The war on drugs and its impact on corrections: exploring alternative strategies to America's drug crisis,' *Journal of Offender Rehabilitation*, 25 (1–2): 43–60.

Welch, M. (1998a) 'Critical criminology, social control, and an alternative view of corrections,' in J. I. Ross (ed.), *Cutting the Edge: Current Perspectives in Radical and Critical Criminology*. Westport, CT: Praeger.

Welch, M. (1998b) 'Problems facing Immigration and Naturalization Service (INS) centers: policies, procedures, and allegations of human rights violations,' in T. Alleman and R. L. Gido (eds), *Turnstile Justice: Issues in American Corrections*. Englewood Cliffs, NJ: Prentice Hall.

Welch, M. (1999a) *Punishment in America: Social Control and the Ironies of Imprisonment*. Thousand Oaks, CA: Sage.

Welch, M. (1999b) 'The reproduction of institutional violence in American prisons,' in R. Muraskin and A. R. Roberts (eds), *Visions for Change: Crime and Justice in the Twenty-First Century* (2nd edn). Englewood Cliffs, NJ: Prentice Hall.

Welch, M. (2000a) *Flag Burning: Moral Panic and the Criminalization of Protest*. New York: de Gruyter.

Welch, M. (2000b) 'Adultery,' in N. H. Rafter (ed.), *Encyclopedia of Women and Crime*. Phoenix, AZ: Oryx Press, p. 5.

Welch, M. (2000c) 'The role of the Immigration and Naturalization Service in the prison industrial complex,' *Social Justice: A Journal of Crime, Conflict and World Order*, 27 (3): 73–88.

Welch, M. (2000d) 'The correctional response to prisoners with HIV/AIDS: morality, metaphors, and myths,' *Social Pathology*, 6 (2): 121–42.

Welch, M. (2002a) 'Assembly line justice,' in D. Levinson (ed.), *Encyclopedia of Crime and Punishment*. Thousand Oaks, CA: Sage, pp. 77–80.

Welch, M. (2002b) *Detained: Immigration Laws and the Expanding INS Jail Complex*. Philadelphia: Temple University Press.

Welch, M. (2002c) 'Detention in INS jails: bureaucracy, brutality, and a booming business,' in R. L. Gido and T. Alleman (eds), *Turnstile Justice: Issues in American Corrections* (2nd edn). Englewood Cliffs, NJ: Prentice Hall.

Welch, M. (2002d) 'The reproduction of violence in U.S. Prisons,' in L. Fiftal and P. Cromwell (eds), *Correctional Perspectives: Views from Academics, Practitioners, and Prisoners*. Los Angeles: Roxbury.

Welch, M. (2003a) 'Chain gangs,' in M. Bosworth (ed.), *Encyclopedia of Prisons*. Thousand Oaks, CA: Sage.

Welch, M. (2003b) 'Jack Abbott,' in M. Bosworth (ed.), *Encyclopedia of Prisons*. Thousand Oaks, CA: Sage.

Welch, M. (2003c) 'Immigration and naturalization detention centers,' in M. Bosworth (ed.), *Encyclopedia of Prisons*. Thousand Oaks, CA: Sage.

Welch, M. (2003d) 'Ironies of social control and the criminalization of immigrants,' *Crime, Law and Social Change: An International Journal*, 39: 319–37.

Welch, M. (2003e) 'Force and fraud: a radically coherent criticism of corrections as industry,' *Contemporary Justice Review*, 6 (3): 227–40.

Welch, M. (2003f) 'Trampling of human rights in the war on terror: implications to the sociology of denial,' *Critical Criminology: An International Journal*, 12 (1): 1–20.

Welch, M. (2004) 'Quiet constructions in the war on terror: subjecting asylum seekers to unnecessary detention,' *Social Justice: A Journal of Crime, Conflict and World Order*, 31 (1–2): 113–29.

Welch, M. (2005a) *Ironies of Imprisonment*. Thousand Oaks, CA and London: Sage.

Welch, M. (2005b) 'Restoring prison systems in war torn nations: correctional vision, monitoring, and human rights,' in J. Albanese (ed.), *Current Issues in International Crime Prevention and Criminal Justice*, papers from the Ancillary Meetings held within the framework of the United Nations Eleventh Congress on Crime Prevention and Criminal Justice, Bangkok, Thailand, April 18–25. Milan: ISPAC (International Scientific and Professional Advisory Council of the United Nations Crime Prevention and Criminal Justice Programme), pp. 99–116.

Welch, M. (2006) *Scapegoats of September 11th: Hate Crimes and State Crimes in the War on Terror*. New Brunswick, NJ and London: Rutgers University Press.

Welch, M. (2007) 'Sovereign impunity in America's war on terror: examining reconfigured power and the absence of accountability,' *Crime, Law, and Social Change*, 47 (3): 135–50.

Welch, M. (2008a) 'Militarizing power in the war on terror: unlawful enemy combatants and the Military Commissions Act,' in R. Haveman and A. Smeulers (eds), *Towards a Criminology of International Crimes*. Antwerp: Intersentia.

Welch, M. (2008b) 'Ordering Iraq: reflections on power, discourse, and neocolonialism,' *Critical Criminology: An International Journal*, 16 (4): 257–69.

Welch, M. (2009a) *Crimes of Power and States of Impunity: The U.S. Response to Terror*. New Brunswick, NJ and London: Rutgers University Press.

Welch, M. (2009b) 'American pain-ology in the war on terror: a critique of "scientific" torture,' *Theoretical Criminology*, 13 (4): 451–74.

Welch, M. (2009c) 'Fragmented power and state-corporate killings: a critique of Blackwater in Iraq,' *Crime, Law, and Social Change*, 51: 351–64.

Welch, M. (2009d) 'Revolt at Attica prison' ('La rivolta di Attica'), *Lo Squaderno*, 14 (December): 10–18. Available at: http://www.losquaderno.net.

Welch, M. (2010a) 'Detained in occupied Iraq: deciphering the narratives for neocolonial internment,' *Punishment and Society: The International Journal of Penology*, 12 (2): 123–46.

Welch, M. (2010b) 'Pastoral power as penal resistance: Foucault and the Groupe d'Information sur les Prisons,' *Punishment and Society: The International Journal of Penology*, 12 (1): 47–63.

Welch, M. (2011) 'War on terror, human rights and critical criminology,' in W. DeKeseredy and M. Dragiewicz (eds), *The Handbook of Critical Criminology*. New York: Routledge.

Welch, M. and Gunther, D. (1997a) 'Jail suicide under legal scrutiny: an analysis of litigation and its implications to policy,' *Criminal Justice Policy Review*, 8 (1): 75–97.

Welch, M. and Gunther, D. (1997b) 'Jail suicide and crisis intervention: lessons from litigation,' *Crisis Intervention and Time-Limited Treatment*, 3 (3): 229–44.

Welch, M. and Macuare, M. (2011) 'Penal tourism in Argentina: bridging Foucauldian and neo-Durkheimian perspectives,' *Theoretical Criminology*, in press.

Welch, M. and Macuare, M. (forthcoming) 'Penal tourism: diffusing knowledge in an Argentine prison museum.'

Welch, M. and Schuster, L. (2005a) 'Detention of asylum seekers in the UK and US: deciphering noisy and quiet constructions,' *Punishment and Society: The International Journal of Penology*, 7 (4): 397–417.

Welch, M. and Schuster, L. (2005b) 'Detention of asylum seekers in the US, UK, France, Germany, and Italy: a critical view of the globalizing culture of control,' *Criminal Justice: The International Journal of Policy and Practice*, 5 (4): 331–55.

Welch, M. and Turner, F. (2008) 'Private corrections, financial infrastructure, and transportation: the new geo-economy of shipping prisoners,' in Special Issue 'Securing the Imperium: Criminal Justice Privatization and Neoliberal Globalization,' *Social Justice: A Journal of Crime, Conflict and World Order*, 34 (3–4): 56–77.

Welch, M., Bryan, N., and Wolff, R. (1999) 'Just war theory and drug control policy: militarization, morality, and the war on drugs,' *Contemporary Justice Review*, 2 (1): 49–76.

Welch, M., Fenwick, M., and Roberts, M. (1997) 'Primary definitions of crime and moral panic: a content analysis of experts' quotes in feature newspaper articles on crime,' *Journal of Research in Crime and Delinquency*, 34 (4): 474–94.

Welch, M., Fenwick, M., and Roberts, M. (1998) 'State managers, intellectuals, and the media: a content analysis of ideology in experts' quotes in featured newspaper articles on crime,' *Justice Quarterly*, 15 (2): 219–41.

Welch, M., Ford, T. E., and Mabli, J. (1988) *Inmates' Attitudes Toward Substance Abuse and the Limitations of Programs and Their Evaluation.* Paper presented at the Annual Meeting of the Society for the Study of Social Problems, Atlanta, GA.

Welch, M., Price, E., and Yankey, N. (2002) 'Moral panic over youth violence: wilding and the manufacture of menace in the media,' *Youth and Society*, 34 (1): 3–30.

Welch, M., Price, E., and Yankey, N. (2004) 'Youth violence and race in the media: the emergence of wilding as an invention of the press,' *Race, Gender and Class*, 11 (2): 36–48.

Welch, M., Sassi, J., and McDonough, A. (2002) 'Advances in critical cultural criminology: an analysis of reactions to avant-garde flag art,' *Critical Criminology: An International Journal*, 11: 1–20.

Welch, M., Weber, L., and Edwards, W. (2000) '"All the news that's fit to print": a content analysis of the correctional debate in the *New York Times*,' *Prison Journal*, 80 (3): 245–64.

Welch, M., Wolff, R., and Bryan, N. (1998) 'Decontextualizing the war on drugs: a content analysis of NIJ publications and their neglect of race and class,' *Justice Quarterly*, 15 (4): 719–42.

Wells, G., Small, M., Penrod, S., Malpass, R., Fulero, S., and Brimacombe, C. (1998) 'Eyewitness identification procedures: recommendations for lineups and photospreads,' *Law and Human Behavior*, 22: 603–47.

Welsh, W. (1995) *Counties in Court: Jail Overcrowding and Court-Ordered Reform.* Philadelphia: Temple.

Welsh, W., Leone, M. C., Kinkade, P. T., and Pontell, H. N. (1991) 'The politics of jail overcrowding: public attitudes and official policies,' in J. A. Thompson and G. L. Mays (eds), *American Jails: Public Policy Issues.* Chicago: Nelson-Hall.

Werner, R. E. and Keys, C. (1988) 'The effects of changes in jail population densities on crowding, sick call, and spatial behavior,' *Journal of Applied Social Psychology*, 18 (10): 852–66.

West, C. and Fenstermaker, S. (1995) 'Doing difference,' *Gender and Society*, 9: 8–37.

West, D. (1972) 'I was afraid to shut my eyes,' in D. M. Peterson and M. Truzzi (eds), *Criminal Life: Views from the Inside.* Englewood Cliffs, NJ: Prentice Hall.

West, H. and Sabol, W. (2008) *Prisoners in 2007.* Washington, DC: Bureau of Justice Statistics.

West, R. (1988) 'Jurisprudence and gender,' *University of Chicago Law Review*, 55 (1): 1–72.

Western, B. (2006) *Punishment and Inequality in America.* New York: Russell Sage Foundation.

Western, B. and Beckett, K. (1999) 'How unregulated is the US labor market? The penal system as a labor market institution,' *American Journal of Sociology*, 104: 1030–60.

Westervelt, S. and Humphrey, J. (2001) *Wrongly Convicted: Perspectives on Failed Justice.* New Brunswick, NJ: Rutgers University Press.

Wheatcroft, G. (2006) 'Manifest destinies,' *New York Times Book Review*, December 17, pp. EV1–4.

Wheeler, S. (1961) 'Socialization in correctional communities,' *American Sociological Review*, 26: 697–712.

White, G. (1999) 'Crime and the decline of manufacturing, 1970–1990,' *Justice Quarterly*, 16 (1): 81–98.

Whitehead, J. (2002) 'Ethics and prison: selected issues,' in M. C. Braswell, B. R. McCarthy, and B. J. McCarthy (eds), *Justice, Crime, and Ethics.* Cincinnati, OH: Anderson, pp. 267–83.

Whitman, J. Q. (2003) *Harsh Justice.* New York: Oxford University Press.

Whitman, S. (1988) 'The Marion penitentiary: it should be opened up, not locked down,' *Southern Illinoisan*, August 7, p. 25.

Wicker, T. (1975) *A Time to Die*. New York: Quadrangle.

Wicker, T. (2001) 'The undying lessons from a modern massacre,' *New York Times*, September 2, p. AR24.

Wideman, J. (1995) 'Doing time, marking race,' *The Nation*, 261 (14): 503–6.

Wiener, J. (1995) 'Japanese-Americans remember: hard times at Heart Mountain,' *The Nation*, March 15, p. 694.

Wikberg, R. (1992) 'The horror show,' in W. Rideau and R. Wikberg (eds), *Life Sentences*. New York: Times Books.

Wikberg, R. and Rideau, W. (1992) 'The deathmen,' in W. Rideau and R. Wikberg (eds), *Life Sentences*. New York: Times Books.

Wilbanks, W. (1986) 'Are female felons treated more leniently by the criminal justice system?' *Justice Quarterly*, 3 (4): 517–29.

Wilbanks, W. (1987) *The Myth of a Racist Criminal Justice System*. Monterey, CA: Brooks/Cole.

Wilbanks, W. (1991) 'The myth of a racist criminal justice system,' in R. Monk (ed.), *Taking Sides: Clashing Views on Controversial Issues in Crime and Criminology*. Guilford, CT: Dushkin.

Wilgoren, J. (2003) 'Citing issue of fairness, governor clears out death row in Illinois,' *New York Times*, January 12, pp. 1, 22.

Wilkins, L. T. (1991) *Punishment, Crime and Market Forces*. Brookfield, VT: Dartmouth.

Williams, L. (2010) 'Provide justice for prostituted teens: stop arresting and prosecuting girls,' in N. Frost, J. Freilich, and T. Clear (eds), *Contemporary Issues in Criminal Justice Policy*. Belmont, CA: Wadsworth.

Williams, M. (2003) 'The effect of pretrial release in imprisonment decisions,' *Criminal Justice Review*, 28 (2): 299–316.

Williams, P. J. (2001) 'By any means necessary,' *The Nation*, November 26, p. 11.

Williams, V. L. and Fish, M. (1974) *Convicts, Codes, and Contraband*. Cambridge, MA: Ballinger.

Williams, V. L. and Fish, M. (1985) 'Formal and informal economic systems,' in R. M. Carter, D. Glaser, and L. T. Wilkins (eds), *Correctional Institutions* (3rd edn). New York: Harper & Row.

Williams, W. (1983) 'Juvenile offenders and the electric chair: cruel and unusual punishment or firm discipline for the hopeless delinquent?' *University of Florida Law Review*, Spring, pp. 11–21.

Williamson, H. E. (2002) 'Correctional officers,' in D. Levinson (ed.), *Encyclopedia of Crime and Punishment*. Thousand Oaks, CA: Sage, pp. 323–9.

Wilmer, H. A. (1965) 'The role of a "rat" in prison,' *Federal Probation*, 29 (March): 44–9.

Wilmerding, J. (1997) 'Healing lives, mending society,' *Quaker Abolitionist*, 3 (2): 4–5.

Wilson, D. B. (2002) 'Sex offender treatment,' in D. Levinson (ed.), *Encyclopedia of Crime and Punishment*. Thousand Oaks, CA: Sage, pp. 1482–5.

Wilson, J. J. (1992) 'OJJDP's comprehensive system approach for serious, violent, and chronic juvenile offenders,' *Juvenile Justice*, November, pp. 2–6.

Wilson, J. Q. (1975) *Thinking About Crime*. New York: Basic Books.

Wilson, J. Q. (2002) 'Rehabilitation,' in T. Gray (ed.), *Exploring Corrections*. Boston: Allyn & Bacon, pp. 250–8.

Wilson, M. (1931) *The Crime of Punishment*. New York: Harcourt Brace.

Wilson, W. J. (1987) *The Truly Disadvantaged: The Inner City, the Underclass, and Public Policy*. Chicago: University of Chicago Press.

Wines, F. H. (1895) *Punishment and Reformation*. New York: Crowell.

Wines, F. H. (1971 [1895]) *An Historical Sketch of the Rise of the Penitentiary System*. New York: Benjamin Blom.

Wines, F. H. (1975) *Punishment and Reformation: A Study of the Penitentiary System*. New York: Crowell.

Winfree, L. T. Jr (1987) 'Toward understanding state-level jail morality: correlates of death by suicide and by natural causes, 1977 and 1982,' *Justice Quarterly*, 4 (1): 51–71.

Winfree, L. T. Jr (1988) 'Rethinking American jail death rates: a comparison of national morality and jail mortality, 1978, 1983,' *Policy Studies Review*, 7 (3): 641–39.

Winfree, L. T. and Wooldredge, J. D. (1991) 'Exploring suicides and deaths by natural causes in America's large jails: a panel study of institutional change,' in J. A. Thompson and G. L. Mays (eds), *American Jails: Public Policy Issues*. Chicago: Nelson-Hall.

Winfree, L. T. Jr, Mays, G. L., and Vigil-Backstrom, T. (1994) 'Youth gangs and incarcerated delinquents: exploring the ties between gang membership, delinquency, and social learning theory,' *Justice Quarterly*, 11 (2): 229–55.

Winterfield, L. A. and Hillsman, S. T. (1993) *The Staten Island Day-Fine Project*. Washington, DC: National Institute of Justice.

Wodahl, E. and Garland, B. (2009) 'The evolution of community corrections: the enduring influence of the prison,' *Prison Journal*, 89 (1): 81S–104S.

Wolff, C. (1989) 'Youth in Central Park rampage to aid prosecutors,' *New York Times*, October 6, p. 3.

Wolfgang, M. (1996) 'Preface,' to C. Beccaria, *Of Crimes and Punishments*. New York: Marilio Publishers.

Women's Commission for Refugee Women and Children (1998) *Forgotten Prisoners: A Follow-Up Report on Refugee Women Incarcerated in York County, Pennsylvania*. New York: Women's Commission for Refugee Women and Children.

Women's Commission for Refugee Women and Children (2000) *Behind Locked Doors – Abuse of Refugee Women at the Krome Detention Center*. New York: Women's Commission for Refugee Women and Children.

Wonders, N. A. (1996) 'Determinate sentencing: a feminist and postmodern story,' *Justice Quarterly*, 13 (4): 611–48.

Wonders, N. (1999) 'Postmodern feminism, criminology, and social justice,' in B. Arrigo (ed.), *Social Justice, Criminal Justice*. Belmont, CA: Wadsworth, pp. 111–28.

Wood, P. B. and Grasmick, H. G. (1999) 'Toward the development of punishment equivalencies: male and female inmates rate the severity of alternatives sanctions compared to prison,' *Justice Quarterly*, 16 (1): 19–50.

Wooden, W. S. (1995) *Renegade Kids, Suburban Outlaws: From Youth Culture to Delinquency*. Belmont, CA: Wadsworth.

Wooden, W. S. and Parker, J. (1982) *Men Behind Bars: Sexual Exploitation in Prison*. New York: Plenum.

Wooldredge, J. (1998) 'Inmate lifestyles and opportunities for victimization,' *Journal of Research in Crime and Delinquency*, 35: 480–502.

Wooldredge, J., Griffin, T., and Pratt, T. (2001) 'Considering hierarchical models for research on inmate behavior: predicting misconduct with multilevel data,' *Justice Quarterly*, 18 (1): 203–32.

Wordes, M., Krisberg, B., and Berry, G. (2001) *Facing the Future: Juvenile Detention in Alameda County*. Oakland, CA: National Council on Crime and Delinquency.

Wordes, M., T. Bynum, T. S., and Corley, C. J. (1994) 'Locking up youth: the impact of race on detention decisions,' *Journal of Research in Crime and Delinquency*, 31 (2): 149–65.

Worth, R. F. (2002a) 'Alternatives to jail can be hard labor or stroll in the park,' *New York Times*, July 6, pp. A1, B2.

Worth, R. F. (2002b) 'Jailhouse author helped by Mailer is found dead,' *New York Times*, February 11, pp. B1, B2.

Wozniak, J. F. (2000) 'The voices of peacemaking criminology: insights into a perspective with an eye toward teaching,' *Contemporary Justice Review*, 3 (3): 267–89.

Wright, J., Beaver, K., DeLisi, M., Vaughn, M., Boisvert, D., and Vaske, J. (2008) 'Lombroso's legacy: the miseducation of criminologists,' *Journal of Criminal Justice Education*, 19 (3): 325–38.

Wright, K. N. (1991) 'A study of individual, environmental, and interactive effects in explaining adjustments to prison,' *Justice Quarterly*, 8 (2): 217–42.

Wright, K. N. and Saylor, W. G. (1991) 'Male and female employees' perceptions of prison work: is there a difference?' *Justice Quarterly*, 8 (4): 505–24.

Wright, R. A. (2000) 'Left out? The coverage of critical perspectives in introductory criminology textbooks, 1990–1999,' *Critical Criminology*, 9 (1–2): 101–22.

Wright, R. A. and Friedrichs, D. O. (1998) 'The most-cited scholars and works in critical criminology,' *Journal of Criminal Justice Education*, 211–32.

Wright, R. A. and Schreck, C. J. (2000) 'Red-penciled: the neglect of critical perspectives in introductory criminal justice textbooks,' *Journal of Crime and Justice*, XXIII (2): 45–68.

Wright, T. and Sweeney, D. (1996) 'Correctional officers: turnover,' in M. D. McShane and F. P. Williams (eds), *Encyclopedia of American Prisons*. New York: Garland, pp. 131–3.

Wright, W. E. and Dixon, M. (1977) 'Community prevention and treatment of juvenile delinquency: a review of evaluation studies,' *Journal of Research in Crime and Delinquency*, 14: 35–67.

Wynn, J. (2001) *Inside Rikers: Stories from the World's Largest Penal Colony*. New York: St. Martin's Press.

Wynne, Jr, J. M. (1978) *Prison Employer Unionism: The Impact on Correctional Administration Programs*. Washington, DC: National Institute of Law Enforcement and Criminal Justice.

Yablonsky, I. (1989) *The Therapeutic Community*. New York: Garden Press.

Yackle, L. W. (1989) *Reform and Regret: The Story of Federal Judicial Involvement in the Alabama Prison System*. New York: Oxford University Press.

Yardley, J. (2002a) 'Court stays execution of mentally ill Texan,' *New York Times*, November 7, p. A24.

Yardley, J. (2002b) 'Amid doubts about competency, mentally ill man faces execution,' *New York Times*, November 4, pp. A1, A18.

Yeager, M. (1979) 'Unemployment and imprisonment,' *Journal of Criminal Law and Criminology*, 70 (4): 586–8.

Yeoman, B. (2000) 'Steel town: Corrections Corporation of America is trying to turn Youngstown, Ohio into the private-prison capital of the world,' *Mother Jones*, May/June, pp. 39–45.

Yi, Y. (2008) 'Arrest as punishment: the abuse of arrest in the People's Republic of China,' *Punishment and Society*, 10 (1): 9–24.

Young, C. (1932) *Women's Prisons Past and Present and Other New York State Prison History*. Elmira, NY: Summary Press.

Young, J. (2007) *The Vertigo of Late Modernity*. London: Sage.

Young, T. R. (1983) 'Social justice vs. criminal justice: an agenda for critical criminology,' *Red Feather Institute: Transforming Sociology*, Series Special Packet, p. 352.

Yunker, J. (1976) 'Is the death penalty a deterrent to homicide? Some time series evidence,' *Journal of Behavioral Economics*, 5 (1): 1–32.

Zahn, M. (2009) *The Delinquent Girl*. Philadelphia: Temple University Press.

Zatz, M. S. (1987) 'The changing forms of racial/ethnic biases in sentencing,' *Journal of Research in Crime and Delinquency*, 24: 69–92.

Zatz, M., Lujan, C. C., and Snyder-Joy, Z. K. (1991) 'American Indians and criminal justice: some conceptual and methodological considerations,' in M. J. Lynch and E. B. Patterson (eds), *Race and Criminal Justice*. New York: Harrow & Heston.

Zedlewski, E. W. (1987) *Making Confinement Decisions*. Washington, DC: US Department of Justice, National Institute of Justice.

Zeigler, F. A. and del Carmen, R. (2001) 'Constitutional issues arising from "three strikes and you're out" legislation,' in E. Latessa, A. Holsinger, J. Marquart, and J. Sorensen (eds), *Correctional Contexts: Contemporary and Classical Readings*. Los Angeles: Roxbury, pp. 253–66.

Zeller, T. (2002) 'Tweaking death row,' *New York Times*, June 30, p. 16.

Ziedenberg, J. and Schiraldi, V. (2002) 'The risks juveniles face in adult prisons,' in L. Fiftal and P. Cromwell (eds), *Correctional Perspectives: Views from Academics, Practitioners, and Prisoners*. Los Angeles: Roxbury, pp. 251–4.

Zillman, D. (1978) *Hostility and Aggression*. Hillsdale, NJ: Lawrence Erlbaum.

Zimbardo, P. (1972) 'Pathology of imprisonment,' *Society*, 9: 2; reprinted in L. F. Travis, M. D. Schwartz, and T. R. Clear (eds) (1983) *Corrections: An Issues Approach* (2nd edn). Cincinnati, OH: Anderson.

Zimbardo, P. (2007) *The Lucifer Effect: Understanding How Good People Turn Evil.* New York: Random House.

Zimmer, L. E. (1986) *Women Guarding Men.* Chicago: University of Chicago Press.

Zimmerman, P. (2004) 'State executions, deterrence, and the incidence of murder,' *Journal of Applied Economics*, 7: 163–93.

Zimmerman, S., Martin, R., and Vlahov, D. (1991) 'AIDS knowledge and risk perceptions among prisoners,' *Journal of Criminal Justice*, 19 (3): 239–56.

Zimring, F. (2007) *The Great American Crime Decline.* New York: Oxford University Press.

Zimring, F. E. and Hawkins, G. J. (1973) *Deterrence: The Legal Threat in Crime Control.* Chicago: University of Chicago Press.

Zimring, F. E. and Hawkins, G. (1986) *Capital Punishment and the American Agenda.* New York: Cambridge University Press.

Zimring, F. E. and Hawkins, G. (1988) 'The new mathematics of imprisonment,' *Crime and Delinquency*, 34: 425–36.

Zimring, F. E. and Hawkins, G. (1991a) *The Scale of Imprisonment.* Chicago: University of Chicago Press.

Zimring, F. E. and Hawkins, G. (1991b) 'What kind of drug war?' *Social Justice*, 18 (4): 104–21.

Zimring, F. E. and Hawkins, G. (1995) *Incapacitation: Penal Confinement and the Restraint of Crime.* New York: Oxford University Press.

Zimring, F. E., Eigen, J., and O'Malley, S. (1976) 'Punishing homicides in Philadelphia: perspectives on the death penalty,' *University of Chicago Law Review*, 43: 227–52.

Zimring, F., Hawkins, G., and Kamin, S. (2001) *Punishment and Democracy: Three Strikes and You're Out in California.* New York: Oxford University Press.

Zupan, L. L. (1991) *Jails: Reform and the New Generation Philosophy.* Cincinnati, OH: Anderson.

Zupan, L. L. (1992) 'Men guarding women: an analysis of the employment of male correction officers in prisons for women,' *Journal of Criminal Justice*, 20: 297–309.

Zupan, L. L. (2002) 'The persistent problems plaguing modern jails,' in T. Gray (ed.), *Exploring Corrections.* Boston: Allyn & Bacon, pp. 37–63.

Zupan, L. L. and Menke, B. A. (1991) 'The new generation jail: an overview,' in J. A. Thompson and G. L. Mays (eds), *American Jails: Public Policy Issues.* Chicago: Nelson-Hall.

INDEX